Praise for

Wilson

"Woodrow Wilson's remarkable rise, the swiftest in all of our history, was matched by his even more remarkable fall, all accomplished in one crowded decade. He arguably has no equal—not Washington, not Lincoln, not Kennedy—in the aspirations he let loose in the tiniest villages of Europe and across the globe . . . The whole of Wilson blares through these 818 pages."

—*The Boston Globe*

"Quietly, methodically, intuitively, the author examines almost every aspect of his subject's life, from the religious to the sexual and almost everything in between . . . Nuanced and revealing."

—*The Washington Times*

"Mr. Berg is a terrific researcher, and *Wilson* exhumes hundreds of fresh quotes and details . . . A very good work of history."

—*The Wall Street Journal*

"Penetrating . . . readers can walk away with a profound and unique perspective on the man, offered by one of our most gifted biographers."

—*Deseret News*

"It has taken nearly a century for someone with Berg's own, somewhat Wilsonian drive to take the full measure of this singular president whose soul echoes, fitfully, in the professorial aura and singularity of Barack Obama."

—*USA Today*

"Berg is a masterful biographer; his books on Charles Lindbergh, Samuel Goldwyn, and Max Perkins have received well-deserved plaudits and prizes. *Wilson* is a comparably rewarding reading experience . . . An absorbing look at a formative period in American history and a magnanimous appraisal of an uncommon leader whose controversial idealism resounds to this day."

—*The Miami Herald*

"No previous biographer has told [Wilson's] story so well." —*The Daily Beast*

"Exhaustively researched and wonderfully written, *Wilson* captures not just the life of a president, but also the essence of the Progressive Era that spanned the last years of the nineteenth century and the first two decades of the twentieth . . . Berg's writing is quality biography . . . This vivid portrait of Wilson and America has much to offer readers who understand that the world and our nation are still confronting many of the issues that Wilson faced in the White House a century ago."

—Bookreporter.com

continued . . .

"[Berg] renders Wilson with an astute, sensitive understanding of the man and his presidency. Berg's research is deep and thorough." —*Booklist* (starred review)

"Accomplished biographer Berg emphasizes the extraordinary talents of this unlikely president in an impressive, nearly hagiographic account . . . Readable, authoritative, and, most usefully, inspiring." —*Kirkus Reviews*

"A thorough, entertaining account of our twentieth president . . . [An] excellent biography." —*Library Journal* (starred review)

PRAISE FOR

Max Perkins: Editor of Genius

"A highly readable work of literary history." —*The New York Times Book Review*

"An extraordinarily fine and moving portrait of the man who assembled America's favorite literary gang." —Russell Baker

"Talented, intelligent, and marvelously researched . . . A work that does honor to the subject." —*Chicago Tribune*

"A. Scott Berg has . . . (perhaps just in the nick of time) rescued Perkins from permanent obscurity." —*The Atlantic*

"In the history of American publishing there is no more legendary—and elusive—figure than Maxwell Evarts Perkins . . . Now the mystery has been solved in Scott Berg's exhaustive, penetrating, and wholly satisfying biography . . . Scrupulous, thoughtful, touching, memorable, and eminently rewarding." —Jonathan Yardley, *The Miami Herald*

"Max Perkins was the best of the best. This book brings him back alive." —Erskine Caldwell

continued . . .

"Thoroughly gripping . . . An account that reads, at once, as a harrowing thriller and a sobering study in the unreckoned consequences of fame."
—*The New York Times*

"A superb biography."
—*Time*

"The most outstanding piece of nonfiction that I have read this year."
—*USA Today*

"Berg brings us about as close as I suspect we will ever get to the man himself."
—*The New York Times Book Review*

PRAISE FOR

Kate Remembered

"A true gift for anyone who loved and admired the late Katharine Hepburn."
—*Chicago Tribune*

"A graceful and affectionate portrait."
—*Los Angeles Times*

"Hepburn puts on a hell of a performance throughout."
—*The Boston Globe*

"[An] affectionate, engrossing tribute. Leave it to Hepburn to make a grand exit."
—*Newsday*

"Hepburn's observations about everyone from Louis B. Mayer to Howard Hughes and Sean Penn are sharp, funny, and poignant."
—Maureen Dowd, *The New York Times*

"Touching . . . [An] unusual and unusually fitting 'account' . . . of a life lived outside the usual in virtually all things."
—*Entertainment Weekly*

"Hepburn sounds off plenty in Berg's fond recollection of their close twenty-year friendship . . . A worthy look at a candid Kate."
—*People*

"Her last performance, and one of her most touching."
—*The Washington Post Book World*

ALSO BY A. SCOTT BERG

Max Perkins: Editor of Genius

Goldwyn: A Biography

Lindbergh

Kate Remembered

WILSON

A. Scott Berg

BERKLEY BOOKS

New York

THE BERKLEY PUBLISHING GROUP
Published by the Penguin Group
Penguin Group (USA) LLC
375 Hudson Street, New York, New York 10014

USA • Canada • UK • Ireland • Australia • New Zealand • India • South Africa • China

penguin.com

A Penguin Random House Company

Frontispiece photo courtesy of Everett Collection. Insert I:
images 2, 16, 21, and 22 courtesy of the Woodrow Wilson Presidential
Library, Staunton, Virginia. Insert II: image 1 courtesy of the Newark (N.J.)
Public Library; images 8, 9, 27, and 28 courtesy of Culver Pictures;
images 11 and 13 courtesy of Everett Collection; image 17 courtesy of Woodrow
Wilson House, a National Trust Historic Site, Washington, D.C.; image 34
courtesy of the Library of Congress. Insert III: images 2, 3, and 21 courtesy
of Everett Collection; images 4, 31, and 32 courtesy of the Library of Congress;
image 38 courtesy of Culver Pictures. All other images appear through the
generous courtesy of the Department of Rare Books and Special
Collections, Princeton University Library.

BERKLEY® is a registered trademark of Penguin Group (USA) LLC.
The "B" design is a trademark of Penguin Group (USA) LLC.

The Library of Congress has catalogued the G. P. Putnam's Sons hardcover edition as follows:

Berg, A. Scott, date.
Wilson / A. Scott Berg.
p.   cm.
ISBN 978-0-425-27006-6
1. Wilson, Woodrow, 1856–1924.   2. Presidents—United States—Biography.
3. United States—Politics and government—1913–1921.   I. Title.
E767.B47   2013
973.91' 3092—dc23   2013009339
[B]

PUBLISHING HISTORY
G. P. Putnam's Sons hardcover edition / September 2013
Berkley trade paperback edition / September 2014

PRINTED IN THE UNITED STATES OF AMERICA

10   9   8   7   6   5   4   3   2   1

Cover design by Stephen Brayda
Front cover photograph © Culver Pictures
Interior text design by Marysarah Quinn and Claire Naylor Vaccaro

The text of this book is set in Garamond 3 LT Std. and Adobe Garamond Pro.
The display is set in Chevalier Com Stripes Caps.

To

BARBARA BERG, PHYLLIS GRANN,

and KEVIN MCCORMICK

CONTENTS

WHO is the happy Warrior? Who is he
That every man in arms should wish to be?
—It is the generous Spirit, who, when brought
Among the tasks of real life, hath wrought
Upon the plan that pleased his boyish thought:

. . . .

Who, whether praise of him must walk the earth
For ever, and to noble deeds give birth,
Or he must fall, to sleep without his fame,
And leave a dead unprofitable name—
Finds comfort in himself and in his cause;
And, while the mortal mist is gathering, draws
His breath in confidence of Heaven's applause . . .

—WILLIAM WORDSWORTH,
"Character of the Happy Warrior"

PART ONE

1

ASCENSION

So then after the Lord had spoken vnto them, he was receiued vp into heauen, and sate on the right hand of God.

—MARK, XVI:19

Dawn broke that day on a new epoch, one that would carry the name of a man whose ideas and ideals would extend well into the next century.

Shortly after seven o'clock on Wednesday, December 4, 1918, the sun rose over Hoboken, just as the nine-car special train of the twenty-eighth President of the United States chugged its way through the New Jersey city that fronted the western piers of New York harbor. One thousand soldiers and a Marine Corps guard of honor joined the local police in restraining the hundreds who stood in the chilly first light in hopes of catching a glimpse of the illustrious passenger. They wanted nothing more, wrote one observer, than "to cheer the president and to wish him God-speed on his momentous voyage." At last, the flag-draped locomotive sputtered to a halt so that its central car—named "Ideal"—stopped before a red carpet leading to Pier 4. A battalion of the 13th United States Infantry surrounded the train.

The passengers remained on board until eight o'clock, at which time President Woodrow Wilson and his second wife, Edith, stepped off the train, prompting a rousing rendition of "The Star-Spangled Banner" from an Army band. Brigadier General G. H. Mc-Manus, commander of the Port of Embarkation, stepped forward to welcome his Commander in Chief. In the last eighteen months, McManus's port had witnessed the deployment of two million "doughboys" (as American soldiers were called) who had gone off to fight "the Hun" and win the first truly global war in history. General John J. Pershing, who had led the American Expeditionary Force, had rallied his armies from the outset with the vow that they would be in "Heaven, Hell or Hoboken" by Christmas of 1917.

A year later than Pershing had promised, President Wilson tipped his hat and greeted the surrounding soldiers and sailors before proceeding through a huge shed, which was lined with three hundred Army Transport Service girls in khaki and infantrymen bearing fixed bayonets. Hundreds of flags, those of the United States and the Allied nations—Great Britain, France, Belgium, and Italy most recognizable among them—hung from the ceiling of this vast hall. Wilson walked beneath the glorious array and onto his home for the next ten days, the United States steamship *George Washington*. On December 4, 1917, that same ship had transported her first five thousand troops to fight in the war "over there." Now the great vessel was about to convey President Wilson and his team of aides and experts on a voyage of peace to Europe—not only to conclude what had been the greatest conflagration in the history of man but also to create a document that might guarantee that they had just fought "the war to end all wars."

As the President and Mrs. Wilson ascended the gangplank, the naval band on board struck up "Hail to the Chief," after which it reprised the National Anthem. Then the Wilsons settled into their flower-filled accommodations. The President's suite consisted of a green-curtained bedroom and bath and a large office, with a mahogany desk on which sat a white telephone for shipboard calls; attached to a wall was a wireless telephone by which the President could communicate with Washington or the *Pennsylvania*, the lead escort ship. Mrs. Wilson's bedroom—decorated in ivory with a pink bedspread, curtains, and plump cushions—connected to a large bath, a dining room large enough to seat six comfortably, and a sitting room with a writing desk, chairs, and a table. It was all to her liking, except for the soldiers outside their staterooms and patrolling the decks.

Never in history had so much security surrounded an American president. In addition to the military presence, eight members of the Secret Service were aboard the *George Washington*, with two more doing advance work in France. The ship, recalled agent Edmund W. Starling, "had been checked from bow to stern and from keel to masthead, and members of the Secret Service all over the United States had been busy investigating members of the crew. . . . There was not a fireman or cabin boy whose family and background had not been thoroughly looked into." The hopes of the world were on board, and everything was being done to ensure the safety of the transport.

At 10:15 the twin-stacked ship—722 feet long and weighing twenty-five thousand tons—backed into the Hudson River. Once its stern was sighted heading northward, all the vessels in the waters around the New York islands responded with bells and sirens and horns and whistles. Passengers on every craft jockeyed for rail position in order to wish Woodrow Wilson bon voyage.

Wearing a bearskin coat, the President, with his wife, joined Captain Edward McCauley, Jr., on the bridge. Wilson waved his hands and raised his hat to the crowds again and again in appreciation of the most spectacular send-off in New York history. It was difficult to imagine in that moment of purely joyful noise, with thousands of flags and handkerchiefs waving in his honor, that he was one of the most polarizing Presidents in the nation's history. As one of his earliest supporters, Oklahoma Senator Thomas Pryor Gore, once said: "Wilson had no friends, only slaves and enemies."

British Parliamentarian Cecil Harmsworth would later observe that he did not know of "any historic personage . . . who so strangely attracts and repels" as Woodrow Wilson. This was possibly because—as another Wilson acquaintance observed—"probably in the history of the whole world there has been no great man, of whom so much has been written, but of whom personally so little has been correctly known." Yet another, who, as a college student, had first encountered him, never lost sight of the personal paradox that was the man: "Stern and impassive, yet emotional; calm and patient, yet quick-tempered and impulsive; forgetful of those who had served him, yet devoted to many who had rendered but minor service . . . precise and business-like, and yet, upon occasion, illogical without more reason than intuition itself."

Theodore Roosevelt, the greatest political personality of the day, took potshots at Wilson at every possible opportunity; and during the 1912 Presidential campaign—which he lost to Wilson—advisers urged Roosevelt to smear his opponent with the rumors of an extramarital affair with a mysterious woman known as "Mrs. Peck." TR refused, fearing that would only give Wilson some allure—as he looked like nothing more than "an apothecary's clerk." In this matter, however, TR's political assessment was mistaken. For all the dour photographs of the very proper President, society doyenne Evalyn Walsh McLean insisted that the women of America found him extremely attractive, which made him the subject of much giddy Washington gossip. For his part, Wilson admitted his susceptibility "to all feminine attractions," as "girls of all degrees of beauty and grace have a charm for me which almost amounts to a spell." He was, by his own admission, extremely sexual, always aware of "the riotous element in my blood." Beneath his stern ministerial appearance churned a turbulent emotional life.

In wooing his first wife, the ethereal Ellen Axson of Rome, Georgia, Wilson indulged in one of the most expansive love correspondences in history—thousands of letters so passionate she said they kept her "in an almost constant state of intoxication." Cultured, well-read, and a talented artist, she abandoned any professional aspirations in order to serve her husband and raise their three daughters. She enabled his ambitions—all the way to the White House, in which she got to live only fourteen months before dying there. Bereft beyond words, he contemplated resignation.

But the war had just broken out in Europe, and what duty could not arouse in him, a friend did, by introducing him to a buxom, well-to-do, young Washington widow named Edith Bolling Galt. The President fell in love at first sight. Despite the political and practical difficulties of courting from the White House, the President romanced her, again through sheaves of letters and private meetings. Less than eighteen months after burying the first Mrs. Wilson, he married the second. She worshipped him. And from that day forward—in health and unexpectedly grave sickness—she almost never left his side. Unwittingly, she would later enter into a conspiracy that ran the government and which would result in an amendment to the Constitution to prevent such an occurrence from happening again. Throughout their marriage, she monitored a twitch in his lower left eyelid and a throbbing in his cheek.

Despite numerous chronic ailments—and a bad cold as he boarded the ship—sixty-one-year-old Woodrow Wilson appeared remarkably fit. He stood five feet ten and one-half inches and weighed a lean 170 pounds. Except for some youthful experimentation with mustaches and sideburns, he had always been clean-shaven, with strong cheekbones and a prominent chin; he had a fine straight nose, and ears large enough to make some look twice. His hair had thinned, but he always retained enough to cut close and part neatly on the left. Although his vision was weak—one eye virtually useless—his deep gray eyes were as understanding as they could be piercing. A pince-nez, which emphasized his erudition, became his trademark. That and a J-shaped jaw were all a caricaturist needed to conjure the man. He had a well-defined mouth, with full lips; and though the public mostly saw a solemn face, he had a toothy smile and a deep laugh, one generally reserved for intimate occasions. He told corny jokes, could not resist a pun, and always had a limerick at the ready—the raciest of which was about "an old monk from Siberia" who "eloped with the Mother Superior." He loved to sing, showing off his silvery second tenor voice. One adviser wrote, "I never knew a man whose general appearance changed so much from hour to hour." His demeanor could change as well. "He seems to do his best to offend rather than to please, and yet when one gets access to him, there is no more charming man in all the world than Woodrow Wilson."

More than the elegant profile and courtly mien contributed to Wilson's authoritative stature. Diplomat and historian George F. Kennan—who closely observed public figures throughout most of his 101 years—noted, "No man in modern times, to my mind, ever better looked or acted the part of an American president."

Twenty-six men had preceded Woodrow Wilson to the White House. Each generally pursued one of three well-worn paths, and sometimes a combination thereof: the earliest presidents especially rose through the ranks of state legislatures until they leapt to the national level, either in Congress, the Cabinet, or the diplomatic corps; a handful earned their stripes on the battlefield, where their leadership and heroism transformed them into national figures; several graduated from statehouses to the White House. Woodrow Wilson, it is true, did serve as Governor of New Jersey—but so briefly that it barely distracts from his having blazed a trail to the Presidency that is utterly unique. Quite simply, he enjoyed the most meteoric rise in American history, one with a most unlikely origin—a college campus.

Woodrow Wilson loved his alma mater, Princeton, with religious zeal; and as a professor and then its president, he not only reformed a country club college into a top-tier university but also developed a pedagogical model that many of America's institutions of higher education would subsequently adopt. His efforts to alter Princeton's social structure, however, forced him to leave under a cloud and to consider a lesson he taught without fully grasping himself: "If you want to make enemies, try to change something."

A career intellectual, he was the only President of the United States to have spent the majority of his life cloistered in academia. Like most of his predecessors, he studied the law; and he became the first President to earn a doctorate degree as well. As one of the nation's leading historians and first political scientists, he had written a dozen books and numerous articles and delivered countless lectures and speeches—often on matters that reached into the realm of public affairs. While advocating educational reforms at Princeton, he had fought against the injustices of privilege wherever he could, championing meritocracy. Wilson distinguished himself as a public thinker.

But he had spent most of his life in private frustration, half-fulfilled, as he long harbored hidden aspirations he seldom voiced. His intellectual vigor masked a lifelong ambition to hold high political office—to make history more than teach it. With Princeton's trustees thwarting his educational revolution, the impeccable Wilson accepted an offer to run for Governor of New Jersey. In so doing, he disabled the "machine" of the most corrupt state in the Union, defying the very bosses who had selected him to be their puppet. Wilson would later say he left Princeton for government service in order to get out of politics.

No American statesman ever had a shorter second act. As late as October 1910, at age fifty-three and never having run for public office, Woodrow Wilson headed a small, all-male college in a quiet town in New Jersey; in November 1912, he was elected President of the United States. He swiftly went from near obscurity to global prominence, becoming the most powerful man on earth. He would contend that it had all been choreographed—not by himself, but by Himself.

"No man in supreme power in any nation's life," wrote the University

of Virginia's president Edwin A. Alderman, ". . . was so profoundly penetrated by the Christian faith. He was sturdily and mystically Christian."
Born in a church manse, the son and grandson of Presbyterian ministers,
Wilson did not often preach Christianity from his bully pulpit, but he
ardently practiced it, infusing all his decisions with a piety and morality
that were never lost on his constituents. His devotion was genuine. Twice
a day he genuflected in prayer, he said grace before each meal, and he read
a chapter of the Bible every night. He referred to Sunday as the Sabbath.
And he appointed the first Jew to the Supreme Court.

Beholden to nobody, he had risen to his position through brainpower.
Wedding the complexity of his intellect with the simplicity of his faith,
placing principles before politics, he followed his conscience, never first
checking public opinion. He spoke only for himself, and he found much
of the nation agreeing with what he had to say. Arguably the least experienced person to hold the highest political office in the land, he was the
Presidency's most accomplished student of American history and politics.
As such, he proved to be an unexpectedly evolved political animal, with a
tough hide and sharp claws. In 1912 he entered one of the most thrilling
races in the nation's history and beat two worthy adversaries—a Republican incumbent, William Howard Taft, and the even more popular third-
party candidate, Theodore Roosevelt, the Progressive from the Bull Moose
Party.

Ambrose Bierce had recently defined politics in his *Devil's Dictionary* as
"the conduct of public affairs for private advantage." But Wilson defied
such thinking. In the middle of a period of great economic inequality—
when the nation's richest 1 percent owned half its wealth—he unveiled his
Presidential program. His "New Freedom" worked honestly to protect the
less favored 99 percent of his countrymen. In order to actualize his slate of
progressive reforms, he brought a bold new approach to his office, one in
which the executive and legislative branches co-operated the government.
He literally walked the walk, violating a century-old tradition by appearing regularly before Congress—not just to deliver his State of the Union
messages but whenever he had an important measure he wanted passed.

"What I am interested in is having the government of the United
States more concerned about human rights than about property rights," he
insisted. Toward that end, he lost no time in creating the Federal Reserve
Board, reducing excessive tariffs, reforming taxation, strengthening

anti-trust laws, inaugurating the eight-hour workday, establishing the Federal Trade Commission, developing agricultural programs, improving rural life, and making corporate officers liable for the actions of their companies. He even offered the first government bailout of a private industry in distress—cotton. Without so much as a breath of scandal, his New Freedom served as the foundation for the New Deal and Fair Deal and New Frontier and Great Society to come. Future President Harry Truman said, "In many ways, Woodrow Wilson was the greatest of the greats."

Wilson's reelection in 1916 was an even more electrifying contest than his first, a legendary squeaker. He ran on his strong legislative record and the powerful message that "He kept us out of war." He became the first Democratic President elected to two consecutive terms since Andrew Jackson in 1832.

And within weeks of his second inauguration, Woodrow Wilson returned to Congress to announce the most consequential shift in the history of American foreign policy, before or since. On April 2, 1917, he addressed a joint session of the legislature, with the Supreme Court, the Cabinet, and the diplomatic corps present as witnesses, in what one prominent journalist called "the most dramatic event that the National Capitol had ever known." In speaking to an isolationist nation, one that had long adhered to a policy of avoiding foreign entanglements, Wilson summoned the American people less to a war than a crusade, declaring that the United States must help make the world "safe for democracy."

In urging his countrymen to join in a war being fought an ocean away, to fight pre-emptively for principles instead of retaliating for attacks against them, to wed idealism with interventionism, Woodrow Wilson initiated one of the most far-reaching precepts of American foreign policy. "Democracy" had long been America's watchword. Wilson now added such terms as "self-determination" and "collective security" to the battle cry.

A dynamic Commander in Chief, Wilson transformed an introverted country with minor defensive capabilities into a competitive military nation. "Perhaps the greatest foreign army that ever crossed a sea in the history of the world prior to the present war was the Persian army of a million men, which bridged and crossed the Hellespont," wrote the Secretary of War, Newton D. Baker. Wilson instituted a program of selective service that would provide the potential to raise an army many times the size of that of Xerxes and would send millions of men across an ocean.

Throughout the war, Wilson's mightiest weapon was his oratory. With a resonant voice and precise diction, honeyed with a drop of Southern gentility, he became one of the most celebrated speakers of his time. He could extemporize for an hour or longer without a pause or misplaced word. He thought in metaphors, spoke in perfect sentences, and composed entire paragraphs in his head, relying on a superior vocabulary. When speaking formally, he resorted to prepared texts and proved even more eloquent. Muckraker Ida Tarbell said, "I doubt if there is any man in America that can talk . . . with such precision and at the same time so like a human being." He was the last President to compose all his own speeches.

Wilson codified his war aims—his terms for peace—into "Fourteen Points." Walter Lippmann, who drafted some of them, said they "merely voiced the common aspiration of liberal men for a better world order. It was assumed that they would create an environment in which a decent and orderly settlement could be made." The empires of four great dynasties had just toppled—the Hohenzollerns in Germany, the Habsburgs in Austria, the Romanovs in Russia, and the Ottomans in Turkey: no longer did divine right rule in Europe or across most of the world. It now fell upon the American President to reconfigure the pieces of those fallen empires.

More than a crowning touch, Woodrow Wilson's fourteenth point became his raison d'être, what he believed would be his sacred legacy. It was a concept under which all countries of the world might congregate, to avert war by settling disputes through pre-emptive peace talks. Others before him had championed similar organizations, but Woodrow Wilson was the first to stake his life on the idea, forever affixing his name to that vision of a League of Nations.

Wilson was especially sensitive to all sides in the impending negotiations because he was the only President in the history of the United States to have been raised in a country that had suffered a defeat in war. Born in Virginia and raised during the Civil War and Reconstruction in the Confederacy, Wilson grasped the tragedy that overcame the South after the Civil War, in which the aftermath, at times, proved worse than the defeat. He comprehended the feelings of guilt, even shame, the lingering anger, and the contrition; he saw why Southern eloquence turned toward euphemism, especially when it came to talking about "the recent unpleasantness." He had seen how racism stained the region; and he spent a lifetime sorting out his own feelings on that subject. His administration instituted segregation—"Jim Crow" laws—in Washington, D.C.

In asking his countrymen to engage in this first World War, he had insisted that Americans were fighting for what he called a "peace without victory." Feeling as right as he was righteous, he hoped to show the world that foreign policy might have a moral component as well as political or economic objectives. "Never before in the history of mankind," Edwin Alderman noted, "has a statesman of the first order made the humble doctrine of service to humanity a cardinal and guiding principle of world politics." Nor had any President ever suppressed free speech to so great an extent in order to realize his principles.

The first sitting President to leave the territorial United States, "he enjoyed a prestige and moral influence throughout the world unequaled in history," said John Maynard Keynes, a young economist who was part of the British delegation to the peace talks. Indeed, concurred his colleague Harold Nicolson, Wilson came "armed with power such as no man in history had possessed: he had come fired with high ideals such as have inspired no autocrat of the past."

Nobody could predict the quality of his mercy. He had, after all, spoken of fairness and severity in the same sentence, as well as of penalties without being punitive. The world could but wonder whether those who sought *revanche* and retribution could sign the same document required of those who believed Wilson was the "one man who would see that Germany was not looted and destroyed; that she would get justice at his hands." To his longtime secretary, Wilson had confessed before embarking, "This trip will either be the greatest success or the supremest tragedy in all history; but I believe in a Divine Providence. . . . It is my faith that no body of men however they concert their power or their influence can defeat this great world enterprise, which after all is the enterprise of Divine mercy, peace and good will." In the end, Henry Kissinger has noted, "Wilson's principles"—properly applied or misappropriated—"have remained the bedrock of American foreign-policy thinking."

For all his towering intellect and abiding faith, Woodrow Wilson was superstitious—especially about the number thirteen, which he considered talismanic. His first and last names comprised thirteen letters. In his thirteenth year of service at Princeton, he became the college's thirteenth president. In 1913 he became President of the United States, whose thirteen original colonies received tribute everywhere in the symbols of the nation, from the number of stripes on its flag to the number of arrows in the eagle's sinister talon on its national seal. Those close to the President knew that he had selected the date of the *George Washington*'s departure so that it would dock in France on December 13.

Five destroyers of the Atlantic Torpedo Flotilla escorted the ship through New York harbor until it met the dreadnought *Pennsylvania*, her convoy across the mine-littered Atlantic. Once the *George Washington* was on its course, the President's flag was hoisted on its mainmast. The sight of it snapping in the breeze signaled a salute from the destroyers, and twenty-one gunshots rent the air. And then, two airplanes shot out overhead and performed aerial acrobatics to everybody's astonishment and delight.

Anybody in Manhattan with a river view could catch a glimpse of the farewell, and every shoreline window, doorway, and rooftop was filled with cheering citizens and a kaleidoscope of stars and stripes. Down in the Battery, ten thousand New Yorkers huddled along the seawall to pay their respects; at Governors Island, soldiers gathered on the western shore to shout their goodbyes; all of Staten Island seemed to have turned out as well. And there, the Presidential ship passed the *Minnehaha*, which was bringing home a boatload of soldiers who had fought "over there." The President was moved by this signal that the war was really over. Indeed, he had made it known that he already believed "the history of mankind will be put into two grand divisions only, that before, and that after, this great world conflict."

With the sun shining upon the torch-bearing statue in the middle of the harbor, one could not help feeling as the President's friend and physician Rear Admiral Cary T. Grayson did—that "no person could have wished for a more auspicious commencement of an eventful trip." Despite the capriciousness of his constituency, *The New York Times* said the American public admired Mr. Wilson and considered him an "ambassador going beyond the seas not only to conclude a peace, but to establish relations of amity that will endure through all the coming years." Nobody realized he would be away from home for six months.

One young diplomat, Raymond B. Fosdick, wrote that watching the nation's farewell to the President "almost made the tears come to my eyes to realize what a tremendous grip on the hopes and affections, not only of

America but of the world, this one man has." That very morning, on his way to the boat, Fosdick had observed hundreds of young men and women leaving the ferry, sweatshop workers commuting in the dark. A few minutes later, Fosdick asked one of the laborers how many hours a day he worked. Fourteen, the man replied; and then, pointing to the *George Washington*, he added, "But do you see that boat. . . . There's a man aboard her that is going to Europe to change all that." When Fosdick related the story to the President, Wilson suddenly looked strained under the burden of impossible expectations.

When the *George Washington* reached the open water, the Wilsons lunched in their private dining room, after which the President napped. "The long strain of war was lifting," remembered Edith Wilson. "For three hours he slept without stirring, and got up looking refreshed and renewed." Some afternoons, the weary leader slept four hours—"storing up energy for the trials ahead." After these siestas, the Wilsons took long walks around the deck.

By the third day at sea, the *George Washington* had entered the Gulf Stream, and the weather turned summery. The President spent his mornings addressing his paperwork and holding meetings with members of the American Peace Commission. Several journalists had been invited on the voyage, and he always found time to speak to them, having enjoyed a cordial relationship with the press corps since his earliest days in office, when he became the first President to schedule regular White House press conferences.

Most nights, after a small dinner in their suite, the Wilsons attended the movies. There were two theaters on board equipped with motion picture projectors—the "Old Salt" Theatre for the troops belowdecks and the Martha Washington Theatre for the officers and the Peace Commission on an upper deck. The President preferred to watch with the enlisted men, thoroughly enjoying the latest from Charlie Chaplin, Douglas Fairbanks, William S. Hart, and Fatty Arbuckle. While he normally would not have attended a motion picture on a Sunday night, noted the ship's newsletter, "in true democratic fashion he always fits his personal convenience to the circumstances of the occasion, and he enjoyed the motion picture as much as anybody." When it ended, the President held an impromptu reception, shaking hands with all the men present, who gave him three rousing cheers.

On the morning of Tuesday, December 10, the hilly green fields and whitewashed towns of the Azores came into view, signaling the end of Wilson's holiday. He came on deck for a few breaths of air and then buckled down to business. The night before, a young, hotheaded attaché to the Commission, William C. Bullitt, had taken a seat next to him in the "Old Salt" Theatre and boldly explained that the team of advisers on board "was in a thoroughly skeptical and cynical mood" and that "it would have a fatal effect" if they reached Paris and met their British and French counterparts without knowing the President's precise intentions. Indeed, even Wilson's chief information officer, George Creel, complained that he "did not know a Goddam thing about what the President was thinking." Bullitt's chat made Wilson realize it was time to gather his advisers, each with his own specialty. Most of them, in fact, had been working in private under a nascent government program called "the Inquiry." This secret council on foreign affairs had, as the times suddenly demanded, become the nation's first central intelligence agency.

The Azores behind them, the President summoned ten members of the Inquiry to his office that Tuesday. For an hour, he articulated his vision on such topics as indemnities, borders, colonies, and—above all—the League of Nations, which would be essential to resolving all the other problems. If the forthcoming peace was based on "anything but justice and the will of the people rather than that of their leaders," he said, the next "catastrophe would not be a war but a cataclysm."

"I have never seen the President in a franker or more engaging mood," Bullitt wrote in his diary. "He was overflowing with warmth and good nature." His charm revived everybody's morale for the work ahead. Before the group dispersed, he asked them to remember one story—that not five months prior, General Pershing's AEF had joined the French at Château-Thierry, where they were ordered to retreat with the French army. The American commander tore up the orders and commanded his divisions to advance instead, thereby saving Paris and gaining momentum to win the war. "It is not too much to say that at Château-Thierry we saved the world," Wilson told his advisers, "and I do not intend to let those Europeans forget it. They were beaten when we came in and they know it. . . . They all acknowledged that our men at Château-Thierry saved them. Now they are trying to forget it." Wilson spent most of his last day at sea in his quarters, quietly preparing for the Peace Conference. "He goes to face the lions, if ever a man did," noted Raymond Fosdick.

The Wilsons watched the final movie of their voyage in the Martha Washington Theatre that night. Before the lights came up, fifty sailors—known as bluejackets—quietly gathered in the corner of the hall and, to the accompaniment of the orchestra that had supplied music during the film, softly sang "God Be with You till We Meet Again." Everybody stood, and all eyes turned to the President, whose head was bowed, tears rolling down his cheeks. Then they all sang "Auld Lang Syne."

During the voyage, the President had made a point of acquainting himself with all parts of the ship and its personnel. He posed for pictures with everyone, from the enlisted apprentice boys to the "black gang" in the boiler rooms. For the first time, motion pictures documented the history of the nation as much as the words of any reporter, as the Signal Corps had captured on film as much of the last year's events as possible. Captain Victor Fleming, a twenty-eight-year-old Californian who had launched a promising career in Hollywood as a cameraman before he was drafted, chronicled every interesting moment of the crossing. After his military service, he would return to Hollywood, where he would direct the biggest film stars in the world in such classic features as *The Wizard of Oz* and *Gone With the Wind*. But no cast would ever come close to rivaling the one that was about to assemble in Paris.

December is the gloomiest month in Brittany, where it rains more days than not. It had poured in Brest for weeks. So the President's entourage buzzed that morning that his lucky number had paid off—that Friday the thirteenth burst with sunlight as the *George Washington* swung into her anchorage outside the breakwater in the harbor. The President and Mrs. Wilson went on deck at nine o'clock to witness the reception—a fleet of nine battleships and forty destroyers and cruisers. The gun salutes were deafening. Planes soared overhead, and a large dirigible scudded across the clear skies. After an early lunch, a tender pulled to the side of the ship, and five American Admirals boarded, followed by a delegation of French dignitaries who were accompanied by Wilson's daughter Margaret, a singer who had been in Europe entertaining the troops.

The tender carried the Presidential party to the pier, which had been elaborately decorated with flowers and flags. And for the first time in history, a President of the United States set foot on European soil, muddy at that. The acting Mayor of Brest stepped forward to pay tribute to the President, with gratitude from the people of France for seeing "fit to personally aid in restoring peace to the world." After the President's reply, the French Foreign Minister Stéphen Pichon thanked Wilson for coming over "to give us the right kind of peace." The President graciously corrected him: "I think you mean that we all will cooperate to bring about a just peace."

A procession of motorcars transported the guests through the medieval streets—festooned with laurel wreaths and banners—past the largest crowd ever amassed in the picturesque city. At the railroad station, a crimson carpet ran the entire length of the platform, leading the American dignitaries to the special train normally reserved for the French President. It was furnished with big easy chairs, footstools, and cushions, in rose brocade, all arranged to maximize the view outside the oversized windows. Beyond this parlor were sleeping cars for the entourage and the French President's private carriage, which had been given to the Wilsons. The train left Brest at four, and stopped at seven so that Wilson could enjoy a five-course meal in the dining car, followed by a walk in the French countryside before he and his wife retired at ten o'clock.

The train rolled through the night. During the entire length of the journey—even at three o'clock in the morning, when Admiral Grayson looked outside his drawing room window—men, women, and children gathered alongside the tracks, standing in the dark, cheering the train's passage. But nothing, not even those advance welcomes, could have prepared the President for what awaited him in Paris.

Under brilliant skies, the train arrived precisely at ten o'clock at the private station in the Bois de Boulogne, a terminal reserved for visiting dignitaries of royal blood. The building's walls and pillars were draped in red, white, and blue, and, high above, from a pair of staffs, waved a huge Star-Spangled Banner and a Tricolore. President Raymond Poincaré, Premier Georges Clemenceau, and all the leadership of the French government, along with members of the American Embassy, greeted the Wilsons as they stepped off the train onto a crimson carpet. Bands played as the dignitaries entered a magnificent reception room fragrant from profusions of roses and carnations. After a few speeches of welcome, the two presidents led the procession outside, where eight horse-drawn carriages, each attended by coachmen and footmen in national livery, awaited. On the roadway above the station and on nearby rooftops and windows, thousands of admirers cheered wildly as they entered the first open victoria. The

Presidents' wives and Margaret Wilson entered the second carriage, followed by Clemenceau and the rest of the party, in hierarchical order. The Garde Républicaine, on horseback and wearing shimmering brass helmets with long black horsetails down the back, led the cavalcade along a four-mile route to the Wilsons' Paris lodgings.

"The cheering had a note of welcome in it," observed Admiral Grayson, "and it required the best efforts of the troops to prevent some of the over-enthusiastic breaking through and overwhelming the Presidential party." Irwin Hood "Ike" Hoover, the chief usher of the White House, said that behind the soldiers from many countries who lined the streets, "as far as the eye could see was one writhing, milling mass of humanity. They did not applaud; they screamed, yelled, laughed, and even cried." Sixty-eight-year-old diplomat Henry White, the lone Republican member of the American negotiating committee, said he had witnessed every important coronation or official greeting in Europe for fifty years and had never seen anything like it. Reporters claimed the crowds were ten times those that had recently assembled for the visiting monarchs of England and Belgium.

Reaching the Étoile, Wilson received a historic honor: the chains encircling the Arc de Triomphe had been removed, thus granting him the passage that had not been allowed to anybody since the end of the Franco-Prussian War in 1871, and only to Napoleon before that. Down the broad Champs-Élysées they rode, the crowds thickening. As Edith Wilson observed, "Every inch was covered with cheering, shouting humanity. The sidewalks, the buildings, even the stately horse-chestnut trees were peopled with men and boys perched like sparrows in their very tops. Roofs were filled, windows overflowed until one grew giddy trying to greet the bursts of welcome that came like the surging of untamed waters. Flowers rained upon us until we were nearly buried." More than an expression of gratitude from one nation to another, the demonstration grew personal.

They crossed the Seine at the Alexandre III Bridge to the Quai d'Orsay and then recrossed to the Place de la Concorde, into which 100,000 people had jammed, hoping for a glimpse of "Meester Veelson." The noise grew deafening, as the carriages proceeded through the Rue Royale, and the crowd kept roaring the phrase posted overhead in electric lights on a sign that spanned the street—"VIVE WILSON." President Poincaré declared that the reception "stood alone among the welcome given any previous visitor to Paris."

The wartime population of central Paris was a little over one million citizens, and newspapers estimated that two million people filled just the handful of arrondissements along President Wilson's route. Forgetting neither Alexander nor Caesar, not even Napoleon, France offered that day the most massive display of acclamation and affection ever heaped upon a single human being—sheer numbers alone making it the greatest march of triumph the world had ever known. To those who had just endured an apocalypse, observed future President Herbert Hoover—then in Europe to supervise the feeding of the hungry—"no such man of moral and political power and no such an evangel of peace had appeared since Christ preached the Sermon on the Mount. Everywhere men believed that a new era had come to all mankind. It was the star of Bethlehem rising again." Wilson gloried in the reception.

At 28 Rue de Monceau—behind a wall with two gatehouses—stood the three-story, three-hundred-year-old Murat Palace. The prince who lived there had offered it to the French government for the President's stay. The Wilsons hardly had enough time in which to bathe and change clothes for a luncheon for 250 that the Poincarés were hosting at the Élysée Palace, the first of a staggering number of public functions that would consume the next two weeks. "An American can have anything he wants in Paris to-day," wrote Raymond Fosdick in his diary, "—he owns the city. . . . I wonder . . . what will be the greeting of the French when the Peace is finished and Wilson comes to go home. I wish it would be guaranteed that their affection for America and the Americans would be as real and as enthusiastic as it is to-day. Poor Wilson! A man with his responsibilities is to be pitied. The French think that with almost a magic touch he will bring about the day of political and industrial justice. Will he? Can he?"

While Edith took a drive through the city that afternoon, her husband got to work, conferring with his chief adviser, a singular figure in his life and that of the Presidency. Colonel Edward Mandell House was President Wilson's most trusted confidant. In access and influence, he outranked everybody in Wilson's Cabinet, including the Secretary of State; and he quietly headed the Inquiry, reporting only to the President. In matters of diplomacy, he had carte blanche to speak for Wilson, and he became America's first modern national security adviser. As representatives of virtually every population in the world gravitated to Paris, each seeking a private audience with the President, House came to consider himself indispensable. He quietly took pride in one Ambassador's having referred to him as the "Super-Secretary of State."

But the eyes of the world remained fixed on one man, examining his every gesture and analyzing every nuance. On his first Sunday in Paris, after attending services at the American Presbyterian Church, Wilson and his wife visited the tomb of Lafayette, where he left a wreath and his personal card, on the back of which he had written, "In memory of the great Lafayette, from a fellow-servant of liberty." After lunch that day, Wilson received his first diplomatic caller, Premier Clemenceau. Colonel House noted that he had "never seen an initial meeting a greater success." At a subsequent meeting days later, the Premier expressed his feeling that the League of Nations should be attempted, but he was not confident of its success. For Wilson, failure was not an option. The American Ambassador in Rome would report just that week that the Italians regarded Wilson as a "Messiah sent to save them from all the ills that the war has brought on the world."

Weeks of formalities preceded the peace talks. Wilson took advantage of this time to explain his mission whenever he could, in interviews and at festivities in his honor. The ceremony that resonated most for him occurred on Saturday, December 21, when the University of Paris—the Sorbonne—conferred its first honorary degree in seven centuries and referred to its recipient as "Wilson the Just." He told the four thousand academicians, all robed in red, "There is a great wind of moral force moving through the world, and every man who opposes himself to that wind will go down in disgrace."

The Great War had taken the lives of 16.5 million people, roughly a third of them civilians; and another 21 million soldiers suffered wounds. Compared with the European statistics, the United States—entering late and battling at distant barricades—escaped relatively unscathed. But 116,000 brave Americans would not see Hoboken, and another 200,000 would return to the United States wounded.

Twelve hundred doughboys lay in beds at the American Hospital in Neuilly-sur-Seine, which the President and Mrs. Wilson visited that day. For more than four hours, they walked the wards and shook hands. Mrs. Wilson could barely contain herself as a doctor led them into the "facial ward," filled as it was with "human forms with faces so distorted and mutilated that the place seemed an inferno." Later that day, they called upon the wounded at the castle-like Val de Grâce, the largest French military hospital. Wilson's presence alone stirred the patients, many of whom had gathered in a parlor for a Christmas celebration. A slender soldier with one leg sat at a cheap upright piano, while others with bandaged faces gathered around, including one comrade with empty sockets for eyes and a Croix de Guerre on his chest. The pianist banged out the "Marseillaise," and the blind soldier sang along. Decades later, Edith Wilson would recall the song as "one of the most dramatic moments of my life," for the rendition had "tears in it—tears which had dropped from those sockets where eyes should have been."

After spending Christmas Day at General Pershing's headquarters outside Chaumont, dining with several units of the American Expeditionary Force, the Wilsons reboarded their special train for Calais, which they reached at nine the next morning.

Sir Charles Cust, King George V's personal equerry, had been sent from England to accompany the President on the hospital ship *Brighton* as it crossed the Channel. A squadron of British airplanes in battle formation buzzed overhead while two French dirigibles and a half dozen French airplanes followed the boat. Midway, the French destroyers circled back toward home, dipping their flags in salute. A frosty mist enshrouded much of the crossing, but by noon, the fog had evanesced, revealing the legendary chalk cliffs. They glowed as the *Brighton* pulled into port, and the big guns in Dover Castle—the same that once welcomed Sir Francis Drake—boomed a Presidential salute.

The Duke of Connaught, King George's uncle, stood at the gangplank, as Wilson became the first President ever to visit Great Britain. His party passed into the railway station, as girls in white dresses with small American flags as aprons strewed flowers along their path to the King's private train. By 2:30, they had reached Charing Cross Station, where the King and Queen, Prime Minister David Lloyd George, and His Majesty's entire government stood at the far end of the palm-lined red carpet, and an unlikely December sun shone.

Forewarned of the English reserve, the Americans were prepared for nothing like the extreme enthusiasm of the French. But Londoners were not to be outdone. The soldiers who lined the entire route from the station to Buckingham Palace held back the hundreds of thousands who amassed along the streets, crowded the rooftops, and leaned out of windows. Around the great Victoria Memorial, wounded veterans—many limbless young men—joined in the welcome, paying respects on behalf of the nearly one million people who had journeyed "a long way" from Tipperary and did not live to return. Several times along the route, the crowd burst into chants of "We want Wilson!"

In Pall Mall they enjoyed the most striking sight of the day: an elderly woman in front of Marlborough House, wearing no hat, a shawl around her shoulders, standing on the sidewalk, holding her own amid the masses and waving an American flag. When Edith Wilson's carriage was about to pass, her fellow passenger, a startled Princess Mary, saw the old woman and uttered, "Why, it's Grandmama." In the first carriage, President Wilson stood and waved his hat to her—the Dowager Queen Alexandra, widow of Edward VII and mother of the King—and she threw kisses in return.

Shortly after the Wilsons arrived at the Palace and settled into their apartments, King George V and Queen Mary informed the guests that the crowd was calling for them. And so, they joined the Royal Family on the Palace balcony. "I never saw such a crowd," Edith Wilson wrote her family back in America. The rest of the day was spent visiting various royals and touring the Palace, and the Wilsons dined privately with the King and Queen that night. But diplomatic meetings and more accolades filled the next few days, including Buckingham Palace's first state dinner in four years, with the Archbishop of Canterbury, classicist Gilbert Murray, painter John Singer Sargent, and Rudyard Kipling in attendance. At the end of another day of adulation, the Wilsons left in the Royal Train on an unofficial excursion that promised to be the most emotional leg of his journey.

Carlisle, England, in the northwesternmost corner of the country, not ten miles from the Scottish border, was the birthplace of Woodrow Wilson's mother, Janet—the daughter of the Reverend Thomas Woodrow. After the surfeit of adoration, this "peacemaker" yearned for a quiet retreat, and he arranged for what the press called "a pilgrimage of the heart."

British authorities had agreed to help the President keep his visit as "democratic" as possible, with a minimum of pageantry; but even in remote Carlisle, people insisted upon honoring Wilson. He and his wife awoke while the Royal Train was on a siding on the outskirts of town, after a night of torrential rain; and when Edith looked out the window of her stateroom, she saw "a mass of dripping umbrellas manoeuvring for places nearer the train. The whole population had turned out, and a sturdy-looking lot they were."

The Lord Mayor of Carlisle and other local leaders greeted the President and Mrs. Wilson at the Citadel station and escorted them to the Crown and Mitre Hotel for a public reception. There Wilson met a nonagenarian, the only surviving student from the Reverend Woodrow's Sunday school class. The Wilsons pressed on through the steady rain, stopping at the modest but sturdy two-story house in the middle of a red-brick row in Cavendish Place, the home the reverend had built for his family. Although suffering from influenza, the current residents welcomed them into what had been Janet Woodrow's small bedroom. Without tarrying, the President and his wife proceeded to the Lowther Street Congregational Church, where his grandfather had preached.

After delivering his sermon, the minister called Wilson to the high pulpit. He expressed reluctance, as he said his grandfather would have disapproved of a layman such as himself addressing a congregation. But he did speak emotionally of the memories that had washed over him that day—"of the mother who was born here . . . and her quiet character, her sense of duty and dislike of ostentation." And just as "the worst war ever"—as George Kennan would call it—had drawn nations together in physical force, now he believed they should be joined in "a combination of moral force."

Upon concluding the service, the minister invited the Wilsons into the vestry to sign the guest book. After the constant din of the last month—the greatest ovations that "had ever come before to a mortal man," said Herbert Hoover—Edith cherished this moment of seclusion. She welcomed the opportunity it provided her husband to consider his heritage and to contemplate where this rise had begun. In that moment, she turned and watched as he inhaled the silence; and, she observed, "he was profoundly moved."

2

PROVIDENCE

And wee know that all things worke together for
good, to them that loue God, to them who are the
called according to his purpose.

—ROMANS, VIII:28

Everything about Woodrow Wilson is arguable, starting with the date of his birth.

All pertinent documents and statements from the man
himself declared December 28, 1856, as his birthday; but
the copy of the New Testament in which his family recorded its vital statistics distinctly states that he was born
three nights after Christmas at "12¾ o'clock"—almost an
hour into the next day, the twenty-ninth. He was named
Thomas Woodrow Wilson, arguably in honor of his mother's father, though four months passed before the Reverend
Thomas Woodrow even learned of his grandson.

The Reverend Woodrow was but one of the newborn's
numerous ancestors who were ministers—all followers of
Martin Luther, whose disputation of corrupt practices of the
Roman Catholic Church in 1517 convoked other likeminded
protestants who sought a purer worship of Jesus Christ. After his excommunication, Luther was urged to contradict
his conscience and recant. He refused—in words Woodrow
Wilson would later employ: "I cannot do otherwise."

French-born theologian John Calvin responded to Luther's call by moving to Switzerland, where his sharp-toned polemics helped create "the most perfect school of Christ that ever was on earth since the days of the Apostles." So postulated Scottish clergyman John Knox, who visited in 1554 and wrote his "Letter to the Commonalty of Scotland," a treatise that revived his countrymen and stimulated a branch of Protestantism as progressive as it was obstinate. He considered government God's plan for preserving order, and wrote, "He hath made all equal"—a declaration that would later cross the Atlantic and help define a new nation. Knox's deity left nothing to the dark miracle of chance: all men's fates were predetermined by Divine Providence. By placing every necessity before mankind, the Creator offered divine direction in sending each person on his life's path. He foresaw all that was to come, as could be proved by looking back and seeing all that He had provided.

Knox did not wish to rid his country of Catholicism or even Anglicanism, but merely to see that Presbyterianism—the Kirk, governed by local elders—would direct the spiritual life of Scotland. When Charles I succeeded to the British throne and imposed new religious policy with an Anglican bias, Scots rebelled. In 1638 thousands flocked to Edinburgh to endorse a National Covenant that would establish Presbyterianism as the national church of Scotland. Some Scots signed the document in blood; other Covenanters shed theirs. Embattled farmers stood their ground, confronting militias of redcoats. Centuries later, Woodrow Wilson would take pride in being a spiritual heir of Knox and boast of his Covenanter blood.

Because a tenet of the Reformation was the allowance of every individual to commune with God, each person was encouraged to become literate enough to read Scripture. Knox stipulated that there be a schoolmaster attached to every church and a college to every "notable town." Great cities warranted universities. Thus the disciplines of religion, politics, and education were all wed under the canopy of Presbyterianism; and the Scots fought braveheartedly for that trinity. The bells of Protestantism could not be unrung.

With its people reading beyond their Bibles, Scotland quickly became Europe's first modern literate society; and there, the eighteenth century steaming into the nineteenth saw a confluence of thought from some of the greatest minds in history—Adam Smith, David Hume, and Lord Kames; inventors Baron Kelvin and James Watt; writers James Boswell,

Robert Burns, and the master of the historical novel, Sir Walter Scott, who articulated much of the impetus behind what became known as the Scottish Enlightenment when he wrote, "I am a Scotsman, therefore I had to fight my way into the world."

Amid this renaissance, in 1793, the Reverend Thomas Wodrow was born, himself a direct descendant of several generations of Presbyterian preachers and scholars. He and his wife from the Highlands lived in Paisley until 1820, when he became the first of his family in five hundred years to leave Scotland. They moved to Carlisle, England, where he presided over a Congregationalist church and, in accordance with the local pronunciation, changed the spelling of his name to Woodrow. They had eight children and lived in the house Woodrow Wilson would visit in 1918. On November 10, 1835, Thomas Woodrow took his family to Liverpool, where they boarded a ship for New York, joining a massive exodus of his parishioners who could no longer endure their hardscrabble existence.

Gales prolonged what should have been a six-week trip into a horrific sixty-two days, beset with rationing and flooding. As the ship approached Newfoundland, a storm shredded its sails to rags. One day fair enough for the children to play topside, Janet Woodrow—age nine—was swinging on a rope when the ship suddenly lurched, nearly throwing her overboard. Only her grasp on that lifeline kept her from drowning.

Landing in subzero weather in January 1836, the Woodrows found lodging in the city; and within weeks, the reverend was invited to serve a Presbyterian congregation in Poughkeepsie, New York, eighty miles up the Hudson River. He had preached but two Sabbaths when he was summoned back to Manhattan, only to learn that his wife had died four days prior. "Little did I anticipate that my removal to this country would be effected at so great a sacrifice," the Reverend Woodrow wrote his father-in-law. He soon accepted "a generous and kind offer" to teach and raise a congregation in Brockville, Ontario, but after one brutally cold winter there, he moved his family to Chillicothe, a town in south-central Ohio in need of a pastor. Over the next twelve years, Woodrow's sermons failed to fill the pews of his church. In 1843, he married a young widow, Harriet Love Renick, who bore him six more children. Disengaging from his first family, he drifted from one remote parish to another.

His son Thomas—from that first marriage—became a prosperous dry-goods merchant in Chillicothe and took in his sisters Marion and Janet—the

girl who had clung to the rope after nearly falling overboard during the
rough crossing. Called both Jessie and Jeanie, she never fully recovered
from having watched their sickly mother succumb so suddenly, and she
lived with depression most of her life. Thomas underwrote her education
at a girls' academy in Steubenville, Ohio, 150 miles to the east. There Jessie Woodrow first saw Joseph Ruggles Wilson.

Although he had been born in America, all the bands in Wilson's family tartan were as Scottish and Presbyterian as those of the Woodrows,
with one distinct variation. His forebears were Ulster Scots. His family's
footprints can be traced only as far back as his father, but Scotsmen had
settled in Ulster, the northern province of Ireland, since 1610, when James
I offered parcels from half a million acres of the island to any man who
would sign the Oath of Supremacy, recognizing him as the head of the
English Church. The government imposed onerous restrictions upon those
who clung to their Presbyterianism, and they became fiercely clannish.
Instead of accepting England's high-handedness, these transplanted Scots
fled, steadily abandoning their homes for America.

By the time the Colonies went to war against the British, Scots-Irish
constituted more than a sixth of their population. They were Scottish in
their nature, and the only suggestion of Irish influence could be detected
in the occasional extravagance of personality. Woodrow Wilson would
later admit that he could not document a single drop of Irish blood in his
veins, but he insisted there was "something delightful in me that every
now and then takes the strain off my Scotch conscience and affords me
periods of most enjoyable irresponsibility when I do not care whether
school keeps or not, or whether anybody gets educated or not." That twinkle invariably leavened his inflexibility, and it put him in the company of
a dozen United States presidents of Scotch-Irish descent.

Joseph Wilson's father, James, had been born in County Tyrone, where
he worked as a printer's devil. In 1807, at the age of twenty, this young
man in a hurry became part of the great Scottish Diaspora and sailed for
the United States of America. His destination was Philadelphia, the most
popular port for the Scots-Irish. Within a year, Wilson had proposed to a
sixteen-year-old he had met aboard ship; and shortly after that, he was
running the *Aurora*, a radical newspaper that had helped elect Thomas
Jefferson to the Presidency. By 1815, Wilson's work had attracted the

attention of a civic leader in Ohio, who encouraged him to relocate to a town barely drawn on maps. The Wilsons moved to Steubenville, where James published the local newspaper, entered the Ohio legislature, and, without any legal training, became a local judge. He and his wife produced ten children.

Their ninth child, Joseph Ruggles Wilson, proved the most prodigious. As a boy, he printed his own small newspaper; and when he turned eighteen, in 1840, he joined the Presbyterian Church of Steubenville and enrolled at Jefferson College in Canonsburg, Pennsylvania, where he became the class valedictorian. He was articulate, dynamic, and ruggedly handsome—almost six feet tall with a sturdy build and a chinstrap beard, which accentuated his big brown eyes and long, straight nose. He taught briefly in Mercer, Pennsylvania, until his deep faith took hold of him. Yearning to preach, he studied for a year at the Western Theological Seminary in Pittsburgh and another year at the Princeton Theological Seminary in New Jersey. While still considering careers, he returned home, to teach at the Steubenville Male Academy. One fall day, while raking leaves in his father's garden, the twenty-five-year-old professor caught Jessie Woodrow's glance for the first time, and they fell in love.

Jessie exuded more character than beauty—intelligence, strong spirit, and doleful gray eyes. Her religious heritage was not lost on the aspiring preacher. On June 7, 1849, the Reverend Dr. Thomas Woodrow married his twenty-one-year-old daughter to twenty-seven-year-old Joseph Wilson in what appeared to be a match made in heaven. Two weeks later, the Ohio presbytery ordained Wilson; and after a teaching job had sent him to Hampden-Sydney, Virginia, he received the unusual offer of serving as both a pastor in a nearby town and the principal of the neighboring girls' school.

Staunton, Virginia—a town of four thousand nestled in the Shenandoah Valley between the Blue Ridge Mountains and the Alleghenies—sat midway along the Great Philadelphia Wagon Road. Presbyterian communities dotted this trail, which originated in Pennsylvania and terminated in Augusta, Georgia. In March 1855, Joseph and Jessie Wilson and their two daughters moved into the manse of the Staunton Presbyterian Church, which sat above most of the community. The brick house (two stories at the front with a third—the staff basement—at the rear) bespoke the town's respect for its new clergyman. The twelve-room residence was built for

$4,000 in the Greek Revival style—with high ceilings, center halls, and four chimneys. Behind the house sat a large garden and several outbuildings, including a stable. Joseph Wilson preferred to write his sermons on a back porch from which he could look upon his church, the Augusta Female Seminary, and the homes of most of his congregants. And—arguably—on December 29, 1856, in the ground-floor front bedroom, Jessie gave birth to Thomas Woodrow Wilson, who was almost certainly named for her favorite brother.

Four months later—after a blizzard had buried Staunton, cutting people off from the outside world for ten days—Jessie Wilson was able to write her father about her son. "Tommy"—as he would be known until adulthood—had become "a fine healthy fellow," she said. "He is much larger than either of the others were—and just as fat as he can be. Every one tells me, he is a *beautiful* boy. What is best of all, he is just as *good* as he can be—as little trouble as it is possible for a baby to be." She did much of the child-rearing on her own, as Joseph would often leave for a week at a time to preach in outlying areas. His church was "prospering in every respect," she reported. But like his father, Joseph Wilson had a restless nature: he always looked to supplement his income and trade up.

In early 1857, Jessie's brother James—a minister as well as a distinguished scholar of theology and science who championed Darwin's theory of evolution—asked his brother-in-law to officiate at his wedding in Milledgeville, Georgia, that summer. While Joseph Wilson was there, the First Presbyterian Church of Augusta called upon him to deliver a sermon to its congregation. After hearing him preach, the church invited him back on a permanent basis. In early 1859, the Wilsons moved into the parsonage there. As their one-year-old grew to manhood and developed his political consciousness, he never released what he considered his Virginia birthright—that which had sent seven Presidents to the White House, starting with Washington and Jefferson.

After Staunton, Augusta was downright bustling—a dusty but prosperous city of thirteen thousand inhabitants, half of whom were slaves. (The issue of slavery disconcerted Jessie Wilson, but her husband had no second thoughts, creating an ambivalence that would follow Tommy to the White House.) Situated on the south bank of the Savannah River, midway between the Great Smoky Mountains and the Atlantic Ocean 120 miles away, the city flourished on large surrounding plantations of corn and cotton. Augusta thrived on its mills and warehouses and supporting merchantry. The business district ran for several blocks parallel to the riverfront, growing increasingly residential as it moved inland. Wide boulevards, spacious lots, and generous foliage lent an air of grace to the town, which also boasted a large arsenal, an imposing medical school, and a bell tower that was being erected as a fire lookout station. Farther out, and at a higher elevation, rose the Sand Hills district—sometimes called Summerville, because it became the popular retreat for those who could afford to escape the midyear torpor with its periodic outbreaks of malaria.

When a dollar a day was an acceptable working wage and some professionals earned $2,000 a year, the Reverend Wilson received an annual salary of $2,500 in quarterly payments. He also carried the prestige of shepherding a flock that ranged from the gentry of Summerville to the most indigent "colored" residents of Augusta. In his first year alone, he attracted five dozen new members to his house of worship on Telfair Street, in a fashionable part of town. On a block of its own, the fifty-year-old brick-and-stucco church—with a three-tiered Georgian tower, topped by a spire and cross—set the tone for the stately houses of the neighborhood. Within two years, the trustees of the church authorized a $500 raise for Wilson and a new house, kitty-corner from the family's original home.

The two-and-a-half-story brick manse, complete with a stable and a servants' building (kitchen, wood room, laundry, and sleeping quarters), had just been constructed on McIntosh Street with such modern conveniences as gas lighting and copper indoor plumbing. The parish bought the house for $10,000. The ground floor offered a spacious parlor and a proper study, which absorbed the sweet redolence of Joseph Wilson's pipe tobacco. (His son never took up smoking, insisting, "My father did enough of it in his lifetime to answer for both of us.") The house featured such niceties as porcelain doorknobs, elegant sconces, and decorative plaster surrounding the gas lighting fixtures. The bedrooms were upstairs, Tommy's at the rear. A low iron fence separated the house from the street corner. Joseph Wilson would continue to accept offers to preach out of town, in order to enhance his income, as he and his wife furnished the home with dark, heavy wood furniture. They lived modestly, but never like church mice.

"My earliest recollection," Woodrow Wilson would say, "is of standing at my father's gateway in Augusta, Georgia, when I was four years old, and hearing some one pass and say that Mr. Lincoln was elected and there was to be war." Tommy Wilson was, in fact, weeks shy of four in November 1860, but he accurately recalled the importance of the moment. "Catching the intense tones of [the stranger's] excited voice," Wilson said, "I remember running in to ask my father what it meant."

Thirty-three years later, as a college professor, Woodrow Wilson would answer his own question, in his book *Division and Reunion*. "The South had avowedly staked everything, even her allegiance to the Union, upon this election," he wrote. "The triumph of Mr. Lincoln was, in her eyes, nothing less than the establishment in power of a party bent upon the destruction of the southern system and the defeat of southern interests, even to the point of countenancing and assisting servile insurrection." As Southerners looked back, they saw twenty years of the North passing "personal liberty" laws, all meant to change the way half the country had successfully and legally operated for centuries. "Southern pride, too," Wilson wrote, "was stung to the quick by the position in which the South found itself. . . . The whole course of the South had been described as one of systematic iniquity; southern society had been represented as built upon a willful sin; the southern people had been held up to the world as those who deliberately despised the most righteous command of religion. They knew that they did not deserve such reprobation. They knew that their lives were honorable, their relations with their slaves human, their responsibility for the existence of slavery among them remote." In a powder keg of a decision, the Supreme Court had recently ruled in *Dred Scott v. Sandford* that slaves were property, not citizens, and as such had no legal standing. Any preacher worth his salt had plenty to say those days on the subject of this "peculiar institution," as Scripture offered plenty of fodder.

On the morning of January 6, 1861, a Sabbath Day, the Reverend Joseph Wilson preached on the "Mutual Relation of Masters and Slaves As Taught in the Bible." His mission that Sunday was to "show how completely the Bible brings human slavery underneath the sanction of divine authority." One of his leading arguments lay in Scripture's failure to denounce it, that man could not forbid what God did not—for "the Bible *could not* wink at prevailing error, much less at prevailing crime, least of all at prevailing ungodliness, through any fear of arousing angry opposition against Christianity on the part of such as might hold the civil power, or of such as might direct the sneer of hatred." Slavery, he contended, existed throughout the Roman Empire, and it was often referred to in the New Testament and never once condemned. Wilson exhorted his predominantly white congregation to be good masters.

That very week, on the Day of the National Fast at Plymouth Church in Brooklyn, New York, the most powerful religious voice of the day addressed the same topic but offered a different view. The renowned Reverend Henry Ward Beecher declared slavery "the most alarming and most fertile cause of national sin." He told his congregation that the South had borrowed its principles of slavery from the Roman law, and not from the old Hebrew, in which "the slave was a man, and not a chattel." Beecher concluded, "Why, that minister who preaches slavery out of the Bible is the father of every infidel in the community!"

The South's expressed reason for secession was bigger than slavery. It was, historian Woodrow Wilson explained later, that "power had been given to a geographical, a sectional, party, ruthlessly hostile to her interests." These Confederate states had long abided by the rules; they lived, as their grandfathers had, according to the Constitution. Their understanding of that document had just been interpreted by the highest court in the land, and now the North wanted to change those rules.

Because Dr. Wilson believed in educating all God's children, he taught a Sunday school class for Augusta's black youth. He welcomed Negro membership to his sermons, so long as they stayed in their place in the balcony. Considering segregation a policy that fostered harmonious race relations by preventing discord, he stood among the more liberal-minded preachers within the Southern synods. Far more typical of this new branch of the Presbyterian Church was pastor Robert Lewis Dabney of Virginia, who said, "The black race is an alien one on our soil; and nothing except . . . his subordination to ours, can prevent the rise of that instinctive antipathy of race, which, history shows, always arises between opposite races in proximity."

A schism in the Presbyterian Church paralleled the chasm along the Mason and Dixon Line. Two weeks after Joseph Wilson's discourse on slavery, Georgia became the fifth state to secede from the Union and to join the Confederate States of America under the leadership of Jefferson Davis. Two more states would immediately follow, and another four after the outbreak of war in April 1861, when Confederate forces attacked a United States military outpost at Fort Sumter, South Carolina. The next month, the General Assembly of the Presbyterian Church denounced secession as treasonous and required pastors to swear political allegiance to the federal government of the United States. Pastors of the 1,275 Presbyterian churches in the South acted instead on behalf of their 100,000 communicants, organizing the Presbyterian Church in the Confederate States of America. Dr. Wilson offered to host its first general assembly in Augusta. Once the organization had drafted its constitution, the other ministers elected him Permanent Clerk, a position he maintained for the next thirty-seven years. Even though two of his brothers would become Generals in the Union army, Joseph Wilson became an ardent spokesman for the Southern cause.

Over the next four years, Augusta escaped most of the horrors that ravaged the South, where the numbers worked against the Rebels from the start. The Union had twice as many soldiers as the Confederacy; it had superior transportation abilities, almost three times the railroad miles and four times the shipyards; and the North produced 97 percent of the nation's firearms. The Confederacy's chief advantage lay in the fervency of its beliefs, a defense of the way its people had lived for 250 years.

At the outset, the local militia appropriated the United States arsenal in Summerville for its own cause. Because the Medical College of Georgia stood just a block from the Presbyterian Church, Augusta became an important health center during the war. After the bloody Battle of Chickamauga, Dr. Wilson removed the pews from his church and converted it into an auxiliary hospital; a stockade to keep prisoners was built in the churchyard. He left town for several months in the middle of the fighting to serve as a chaplain to Southern troops in North Carolina.

By 1864 Union General William Tecumseh Sherman had captured Atlanta. Believing the most efficacious way of ending the war was to obliterate his enemy, he commenced his Savannah Campaign, burning everything in his three-hundred-mile path to the sea. As Sherman approached Augusta, the population took its cotton from the warehouses and piled it high in the main street, hoping the offering might satisfy the bloodthirsty General and spare the town. Inexplicably, Sherman did leave Augusta standing—with its cotton—later explaining that destroying the Augusta Powder Works offered no great military advantage. For years rumor held that the town escaped destruction because of a former local love from Sherman's early days in training, Cecilia Stovall, whose family was close to the Wilsons.

During the war, Tommy grew into a hypersensitive child. Small and frail, he developed an irritable digestive system that cursed him all his life. Becoming farsighted, he looked inward—turning shy and deeply emotional. The church organist could not help noticing how some of the hymns—especially the line "'Twas on that dark and doleful day"—would literally reduce the boy to tears.

Surprisingly, he did not become a bookworm. There was no mandatory schooling in Augusta at the time, and had there been, it would have been suspended because of the war. And so Tommy was still learning his letters at age nine and would not learn to read on his own until he was eleven. But he loved listening when his father read aloud. With his family gathered around him, Dr. Wilson delivered dramatic renditions of narrative poems and travel books along with Dickens and Sir Walter Scott. He turned regularly, of course, to the Good Book. Tommy delighted in fairy tales and those occasions when one of the household servants would read Joel Chandler Harris stories, the affectionately told tales in the Negro dialect of Uncle Remus.

Dr. Wilson let Tommy embrace language on his own, never pushing him or humiliating him for being so slow in learning to read. Tommy would later call himself "lazy"; but because of his faulty vision, ambidexterity, and ensuing problems with spelling and calculating, doctors a century later would suggest that he suffered from developmental dyslexia. He learned to compensate, and in his own time, he picked up Parson Mason L. Weems's mythic biography of George Washington, which was among the first books he read on his own.

Joseph Wilson had no desire to rush his son into a schoolroom. He put no faith in dogmatic education, believing that information had to permeate in order to penetrate. And so, the core of Tommy's early education came in accompanying his father on his ministerial rounds. On any given day, they might visit a munitions plant or a foundry, a mill or a cotton gin. Afterward, his father would drill him on what they had seen and challenge the way he expressed himself. "What do you mean by that?" Joseph Wilson would ask his son when he spoke in incomplete sentences. After the boy explained, his father would reply, "Then why don't you say so?" Thus, by the time Tommy Wilson had learned to transliterate words from sounds to letters, he had developed a strong ear for language, especially for the rolling cadences his father emitted from the pulpit.

For all his love, a powerful ego ruled Joseph Wilson, and he treated his family as subjects. He controlled all discussion at home. As Tommy matured and committed more of his thoughts to paper, his father came down harder in his demands for perfection. "When you frame a sentence," he would say, "don't do it as if you were loading a shotgun, but as if you were loading a rifle. Don't fire in such a way and with such a load that while you hit the thing you aim at you will hit a lot of things in the neighbourhood besides; but shoot with a single bullet and hit that one thing alone." He sent the boy to the dictionary time and again. Above all, Dr. Wilson wanted his son not just to absorb but to analyze. The mind, he would tell Tommy, "is not a prolix gut to be stuffed. . . . It is not a vessel made to contain something; it is a vessel made to transmute something. The process of digestion is of the essence, and the only part of the food that is of any consequence is the part that is turned into blood and fructifies the whole frame." To limber up for his own writing, Dr. Wilson would parse the speeches of Massachusetts statesman Daniel Webster—more for what Tommy would later call the "magic" in his rhetoric than for the Yankee politics—"to see if he could substitute other words to strengthen the speech." But never in the elder Wilson's experience, his son noted, could he find one word that might "improve the meaning of the address."

Like his father, Tommy had a lighter side. Dr. Wilson loved to engage in horseplay and never withheld displays of affection. Father and son kissed each other upon greeting for the rest of their lives. They played games together—chess and billiards, though never cards, which smacked of the devil. But the reverend's humor often turned mordant. One relative remembered that "Uncle Joseph was a cruel tease, with a caustic wit and a sharp tongue, and I remember hearing my own family tell indignantly of how Cousin Woodrow suffered under his teasing." In 1867, a younger brother, named for his father, was born into the family—eleven years Tommy's junior.

Tommy's "incomparable" father dominated his existence. He was "one of the most inspiring fathers that ever a lad was blessed with," Woodrow Wilson would later remark. And if he had his father's "face and figure," he would add, "it wouldn't make any difference what I had said." Although Joseph Wilson imposed few academic demands on his son, he had great expectations. And as Tommy got older, the most instructive moments of his youth came when his father relaxed on Sunday afternoons, after his sermon. With Tommy sitting on the rug beside him, they would have "wonderful talks." Wilson remembered one conversation in particular, in which his father talked to him of the old casuists—"students of con-science"—who had "resolved all sins into the one great sin of egotism, because that consists in putting oneself before God." Tommy realized, "If you make yourself the center of the universe, all your perspective is skewed. There is only one moral center of the universe, and that is God. If you get into right relations with Him, then you have your right perspective and your right relation and your right size." Nothing impressed Tommy more than sitting with his family in the fourth-row pew of the Presbyterian Church, looking up to the man in the pulpit whose booming basso made the Gospel thunder within the church walls.

By her constant example, Jessie Wilson taught her son a different but equally important lesson—humility. She was homely in every way—not just in her unadorned appearance but also her devotion to all household matters. "Aunt Jessie was a typical gentlewoman, delicate, refined, quiet, and dignified in manner, but with a firm Scotch character and will," one of her nieces recalled. "She was very domestic, loved her home and family, and always had beautiful flowers." Although she generally deferred to her forceful husband, she was not without opinions; and Tommy could always find comfort in her quiet devotion. "I remember how I clung to her (a laughed-at 'mamma's boy') till I was a great big fellow," he would later write his first wife, "but love of the best womanhood came to me and en-tered my heart through those apron-strings."

"She was so reserved," Wilson would remember toward the end of his life, "that only those of her own household can have known how lovable she was, though every friend knew how loyal and steadfast she was. I seem to feel still the touch of her hand, and the sweet steadying influence of her wonderful character." But she remained the more passive and often joyless parent, from whom Tommy inherited severity and aloofness. As an adult he would admit, "When I feel badly, sour and gloomy and everything seems wrong, then I know that my mother's character is uppermost in me. But when life seems gay and fine and splendid, then I know that the part of my father which is in me is in the ascendance." As an adult, he gravi-tated toward women who could both nurse and nurture.

Cosseted though he was, Tommy Wilson was indelibly scarred by the Civil War. For four years the fighting destabilized daily life. More than 600,000 soldiers died during that time, the greatest loss of human life in

American military history; and even the most sheltered child heard constant talk of death and disease. Tommy saw suffering firsthand—the wounded and the imprisoned; and while his family escaped actual desolation, he tasted deprivation, eating his mother's soup made of cowpeas, night after night. Wilson would later recall the end of the war—standing with the rest of Augusta, watching in humbled silence as Jefferson Davis, the President of the Confederate States himself, was marched through the streets, surrounded by federal guards.

Although only eight years old, he knew that there had been "deep color and the ardor of blood in that contest." And though the field was "lurid with the light of passion," he also recognized that in its midst stood a noble figure, Robert E. Lee—a great soldier, a modest man of duty, a gentleman. Wilson never forgot that day in 1870 when General Lee paraded through Augusta on a valedictory tour. Tommy was close enough to the General's side to look into his face and know forever that he had been "in the presence of consuming force."

Indeed, Wilson would note in his middle years, "It is all very well to talk of detachment of view, and of the effort to be national in spirit and in purpose, but a boy never gets over his boyhood, and never can change those subtle influences which have become a part of him, that were bred in him when he was a child." Woodrow Wilson was not, in truth, a dyed-in-the-wool Southerner, what with immigrant grandparents and an Ohio-born father. But he would repeatedly remind people "that the only place in the country, the only place in the world, where nothing has to be explained to me is the South."

The war over, Tommy ventured for the first time outside the family sphere. Joseph T. Derry, a twenty-four-year-old veteran of what he called the "War of Southern Independence," returned to his hometown of Augusta, where he opened a "select school for boys" in a cotton warehouse a few blocks from the Wilson home on Bay Street, near the riverbank. Professor Derry provided a classical education, opening each day with the reading of a psalm and the students' recitation of the Lord's Prayer. Courses in history and Latin followed, and then a colleague taught writing and bookkeeping. A remarkable class of teenagers would emerge from that warehouse—including Joseph Rucker Lamar, Tommy's next-door neighbor and closest friend, who became a Supreme Court Justice; a dean of Columbia Law School; a Congressman; a Consul to Beirut; and Pleasant

Stovall, a future newspaper owner whom Wilson would appoint as the American Ambassador to Switzerland. Tommy lagged markedly behind the others in his studies—"not because he was not bright enough," recalled Derry, "but because he was apparently not interested." What Wilson remembered most was the day the circus came to town, when he and some friends played hooky, following the elephant for hours—even though it meant a whipping upon their return to the classroom, for which they padded their pant seats with cotton.

Summer days and weekends were often spent on horseback, sometimes riding with Pleasant Stovall to the home of another friend, who lived on a plantation in the country. Other times he would visit relatives—the Boneses—in Summerville, who had a daughter, Jessie Woodrow Bones, a fearless tomboy. They both became enamored of James Fenimore Cooper's novels, especially the tales of Native Americans. In feathers and war paint, they spent hours playing with Indian weaponry—sometimes chasing local Negro children living in the woods just beyond town, sometimes attacking each other. It was all harmless fun, until the day Jessie pretended to be a squirrel up a tree and, carried away with the moment, Tommy shot at her with his bow and arrow. She fell to the ground, and Tommy carried her inside, confessing, "I am a murderer. It wasn't an accident. I killed her." She was merely stunned; but it marked an end to thoughtless games.

Tommy organized many of the neighborhood boys into what he called the "Light Foot Base Ball Club." The sons of a local merchant had been studying in New Jersey and had brought home this new game—which was just gaining popularity across the country. Tommy's frailty would never allow him to excel on the playing field, but he loved the sport and showed an increasing interest in being among other boys. It became further evident that his interest in social activities accorded with his ability to run them. With Tommy Wilson's growing proclivity for neatness and order, his Lightfoots almost certainly became the first baseball team in the United States with its own constitution, written by the second baseman himself.

Up a wooden ladder, in the hayloft of the stables behind the house, he conducted the Monday and Thursday meetings—all according to Robert's Rules of Order. There was a schedule for fines: a nickel for swearing, two and a half cents for lesser vulgarities; and absences cost a dime. "We knew how to make motions and second them," he recounted forty-five years later; "we knew that a motion could not have more than two amendments offered at the same time, and we knew the order in which the amendments had to be put, the second amendment before the first." Wilson granted that nothing important happened at these gatherings; but, he recalled, "I remember distinctly that my delight and interest was in the meetings, not in what they were for—just the sense of belonging to an organization and doing something with the organization, it did not matter what." Tommy Wilson realized that he was, by nature, a leader of boys.

Just as he was finding a place for himself in Augusta, his father itched to move on. Like his father before him, Joseph Wilson had a transient nature and a restive soul. Tommy observed the joy his father found in riding from church to church through growing communities in the South, ministering "to the most vital interests of the part of the country in which he lived." Among his travels in the last few years, he had regularly visited Columbia, South Carolina, home of the Columbia Theological Seminary, the premier academy of the Southern Presbyterian Church, on whose board he sat. In May 1870, the school invited Joseph to accept its professorship of Pastoral and Evangelistic Theology and Sacred Rhetoric. To teach the future preachers of Presbyterianism in the New South carried both honor and responsibility, but with them came a cut in pay and no free housing. But the school did offer $1,500 a year to serve as "Stated Supply" at the First Presbyterian Church, which meant delivering the Sunday sermon. Mid-July—"after much prayer and many misgivings"—he answered the call and re-moved his family.

Columbia, South Carolina, on the Congaree River, had been the first planned city in the state, a two-by-two-mile grid with the Capitol at its center. A new statehouse was approaching completion when the war had begun. In February 1865, Union forces overtook the city, raising the Stars and Stripes atop the old capitol and the rising new edifice. Ever since the seventeenth of that month, debate has raged as to what happened exactly— whether General Sherman had ordered the city's destruction, whether Union soldiers had drunkenly taken it upon themselves to set the city aflame, or, as has been suggested, whether evacuating Confederate soldiers had torched it themselves. Whatever the case, one-third of the city burned, including its government and commercial buildings and many of its fabled white mansions, leaving stumps of blackened pillars. Tar-paper shanties blotched the landscape, the seedlings of a new city. By the time the

Wilsons arrived in the fall of 1870, Columbia was in the middle of Reconstruction, which many considered worse than the fighting. "And so the war ended, with the complete prostration and exhaustion of the South," Woodrow Wilson wrote in *Division and Reunion*, his evenhanded history of the nineteenth-century United States. "The South had thrown her life into the scales and lost it; the North had strained her great resources to the utmost." The federal government, he tabulated, had spent close to $800 million and accumulated an additional debt of nearly $3 billion. Columbia became one gigantic fire sale, with businesses and properties available for any price.

As part of Reconstruction, the Republican Congress had divided the Southern states into military districts under the command of Army Generals; it also temporarily deprived fifteen thousand Confederate officials and senior officers from voting for delegates who were to compose state constitutional conventions. All this came at a moment when newly freed slaves were becoming enfranchised. As Wilson later wrote sympathetically, "Unscrupulous adventurers appeared, to act as the leaders of the inexperienced blacks in taking possession, first of the conventions, and afterwards of the state governments; and in the States where the negroes were most numerous, or their leaders most shrewd and unprincipled, an extraordinary carnival of public crime set in under the forms of law. . . . Negroes constituted the legislative majorities and submitted to the unrestrained authority of small and masterful groups of white men whom the instincts of plunder had drawn from the North."

In fact, the entire country encountered massive taxes, debt, fraud, and bribery. Industrialization and capitalistic expansion stimulated unbounded corruption in the North; and the South faced something worse. America's most pungent commentator, H. L. Mencken, would observe a half century later that the Confederates had gone into battle free but came out "with their freedom subject to the supervision and veto of the rest of the country—and for nearly twenty years that veto was so effective that they enjoyed scarcely more liberty, in the political sense, than so many convicts in the penitentiary."

Although slavery had been illegalized by 1870, fundamental prejudice could not be legislated away. Embittered whites felt they had been given good reason to scapegoat blacks. Granting full rights of citizenship to ex-slaves did not come easily, as the South Carolina constitution continued to limit suffrage to whites and adopted what was known as "Black Codes," which consigned blacks to the same menial positions they held before the war. These laws, the legislators claimed, were for the Negroes' protection. Into this society that one real estate broker described as "polite, refined, intelligent and sociable," the Wilsons arrived, amid its congenial but unsettling segregation.

A large number of local whites took advantage of the reigning confusion. And while many decent Union veterans migrated to the South simply to start new lives for themselves, the impressionable teenaged son of Columbia's new Presbyterian minister recalled only the unethical "carpetbaggers," swarming "out of the North to cozen, beguile, and use" the Negro.

Tommy Wilson could not but admire his father's new offices: the seminary was the most prestigious in the South, if not the country; and the First Presbyterian Church, built in 1853, was the tallest structure in town—a veritable Gothic cathedral with a 180-foot spire, surrounded by dozens of ornamental pinnacles rising from a crenellated roof. The interior was unadorned but grand—with high vaulted ceilings, lancet arches, and a white, horseshoe-shaped gallery encircling most of the vast sanctuary. It sat in the corner of a large, wooded churchyard and burying ground. They lived for a short while in a house opposite the seminary. Then Jessie Wilson came into a small inheritance from her brother William, a bachelor who had speculated in land and died young.

For $1,850, the Wilsons purchased one acre on Hampton Street, a block from the seminary and not much more than that from the church. For several thousand dollars more, they built a two-story wooden house in the Tuscan Villa style, white with green shutters. A three-sided bay window greeted visitors to the left of the front-door portico, and a verandah sat to the right. As in Augusta, a parlor, a dining room, and Dr. Wilson's study filled most of the ground floor; the upstairs contained four large bedrooms, a sitting room, a sewing room, and a bath. Each floor had a back porch. Magnolia trees shaded the yard and house, which sat behind a white picket fence.

Columbia had boasted a state university, a female college, and several private academies before the war, all of which were just rebounding. Tommy came under the tutelage of a neighbor, Charles H. Barnwell, whose family had distinguished itself in education. For seven dollars a month, he offered a classical course of study—to as many as four dozen boys—in a barn in the back of his house. Tommy remained less than a remarkable student.

Turning sixteen, he came under the sway of a young seminarian in his twenties named Francis J. Brooke. Preparing for the ministry, Brooke held services in his room, which Tommy attended, casually at first. A spellbinder, Brooke developed a local following; and, in time, he moved his prayer meetings to the seminary chapel. Within months—on July 5, 1873—young Wilson applied for membership in the First Presbyterian Church, and his admission became a turning point in his life.

Years later Woodrow Wilson would write an essay called "When a Man Comes to Himself," a treatise on finding oneself and one's place in the world. While he could not have articulated the thoughts at age sixteen, the essay recounted that first moment "when he has left off being wholly preoccupied with his own powers and interests and with every petty plan that centers in himself; when he has cleared his eyes to see the world as it is, and his own true place and function in it." For Tommy Wilson, embracing religion was his first step toward self-realization. "Christianity gave us, in the fullness of time, the perfect image of right living, the secret of social and of individual well-being; for the two are not separable, and the man who receives and verifies that secret in his own living has discovered not only the best and only way to serve the world, but also the one happy way to satisfy himself," he wrote. "Then, indeed, has he come to himself."

With the Grant Administration in Washington mired in scandal, Tommy's interest turned to Great Britain. He obsessed over the Prime Minister, William Gladstone. This great Liberal politician and orator in an age of parliamentary giants was born in Liverpool to Scottish parents. Like Wilson, he had Presbyterian roots, as one could divine from the high moral purpose that infused his speeches. Elementary education and individual liberties were the cornerstones of his policies, and he was said to be an avid reader of Sir Walter Scott. Tommy Wilson read everything by and about him that he could obtain. He found a portrait of Gladstone as well, which he hung over his desk. One day Jessie Woodrow Bones asked who it was. "That is Gladstone," Tommy replied, "the greatest statesman that ever lived. I intend to be a statesman, too."

At last he embraced his studies, absorbing information wherever he could find it. After school, he would attend his father's lectures at the seminary, dissecting both the substance and the style of his discourse.

While he remained a plodding reader, he surmounted his dyslexia. In so doing, he fell in love with writing—not just reading the written word but the physical act of writing. He practiced penmanship until it approached calligraphic perfection. Over and over he would write his name—in block print with serifs, in cursive with flourishes. That same fall that he met Brooke, Tommy read the latest issue of *Frank Leslie's Boys' and Girls' Weekly*, which featured a series of articles by Joseph F. Snipes, a stenographic law and news reporter in New York City. One article discussed Andrew J. Graham's *Hand-Book of Standard or American Phonography*, a book about a modern American system of shorthand. He was so stimulated by the concept of speed-writing, he struck up a correspondence with Snipes himself and within months was learning the Graham method. Wilson never lost proficiency in the technique.

The ability at last to read and write with fluency unlocked Tommy's imagination. Moving past the Leatherstocking Tales, he became consumed with knights and pirates and then naval stories, especially those of the British fleet. He clipped pictures of boats from periodicals and studied details of every class of ship, which he could draw with precision. Although he had never seen an ocean, Wilson began imagining that he was an admiral of his own navy, about which he wrote daily reports. Other times he fancied that he commanded his own regiment of Guards, the orders for whom he signed "Thomas W. Wilson, Lieutenant-General, Duke of Eagleton, Commander-in-chief Royal Lance Guards." For several years he continued issuing orders, granting promotions, and "decorating" himself with knighthoods of the Garter and the Star of India, even a seat in Parliament.

At the same time, Joseph Wilson's self-esteem suffered a blow. Much as he enjoyed the vibrant Presbyterian community in Columbia, the church was not satisfied with him. Fortunately, learned and dynamic preachers were always in demand, and the First Presbyterian Church of Wilmington, North Carolina, offered him $4,000 a year to be its pastor. Accepting the position meant leaving a city he liked—all at a moment when his entire family was entering a period of readjustment. The daughters were embarking on their own lives—Marion had just married Anderson Ross Kennedy, a newly ordained Presbyterian minister, and Annie was about to marry the celebrated Reverend George Howe's son, a doctor named George. And, that fall, at age sixteen, Tommy Wilson was starting college.

One hundred twenty-five miles due north of Columbia lay the village of Davidson, North Carolina. In 1837, Presbyterians founded a college in the piedmont. The war had interrupted its growth, but by the 1870s, the mangled single track along the way to Charlotte had been re-laid, and the Atlantic, Tennessee and Ohio was again running trains to Davidson. According to its charter, the school was meant to "educate youth of all classes without any regard to the distinction of religious denominations, and thereby promote the more general diffusion of knowledge and virtue." But there was no mistaking Davidson College's sectarian mission. Students preparing for the ministry and sons of ministers received free tuition; five of the six professors were ministers; and a third of its alumni had become preachers. Clerical members of the faculty preached on the Sabbath, and chapel attendance was compulsory, as were morning and evening prayers. Each week commenced with Bible instruction.

Davidson was still a struggling, rustic village, with little more than one main street. But across the street from the general store and the few other shops that made up the town, a patch of land had been cleared to support the college. Its centerpiece was the Chambers Building, an unadorned three-story brick structure behind a portico supported by four Doric stone columns. It contained dormitory rooms for half the student body, classrooms, laboratories, a library, and meeting halls; its cupola offered a panorama of the entire community and beyond to distant hills. By 1873, the school had 121 students.

By necessity, admission was based more on character than academic standards. Testimonials mattered more than transcripts, though incoming freshmen were examined in English (which included grammar and modern geography), Latin (Caesar, Virgil, and Cicero), Greek (mostly grammar), and mathematics (arithmetic and algebra). Students who did not meet basic requirements could still be admitted on probation, with certain conditions to be met within the first year. All students had to be at least fourteen.

Tommy Wilson would turn seventeen at the end of his first term, roughly the age of most of his forty-one classmates, though he was emotionally younger than his years. He arrived on probation in mathematics and Greek and with conditions in geography and Latin. He moved into the first floor of the north wing with a roommate named John William Leckie, also from Columbia. For $7.15 he was able to furnish his room with a wardrobe (the big-ticket item at $4), a bookcase, a washstand and bowl, two chairs, and two buckets—one old, one new. The college did not provide meals but licensed locals in town to do so. For about twelve dollars a month, Tommy Wilson ate at Mrs. Scofield's boardinghouse. He kept meticulous accounts of every penny he spent, every one of his 103 articles of clothing . . . and, as the semester began, class schedules and books he had borrowed and read, and the number of letters he had sent to and received from each of his family members.

Life at Davidson was Spartan. Students fetched their own water from a central well and cut their own firewood—an absolute necessity in the winter. For all his fragile health, Tommy Wilson engaged as a serious student for the first time in his life. He read rigorously, satisfying his class assignments and his own growing interests, especially in history and politics. His shorthand skills advanced to a level of professional proficiency; and he kept refining his penmanship—writing his name over and over, performing handwriting exercises, producing a signature worthy of great documents. Most of his first-term grades were in the 90s—Logic and Rhetoric, Latin, Composition, and Declamation—with an 87 in Greek; his lowest mark was a 74 in Mathematics. By the second term, the high marks sustained themselves, and his work in Mathematics earned an 88. He found growing satisfaction along with reward in diligence, earning 100 in Deportment.

Two other buildings commanded attention on the Davidson campus, both red-brick Greek Revival temples: the Eumenean and Philanthropic Literary Societies. They had been formed for "the acquirement of literary knowledge, the promotion of virtue, and the cultivation of social harmony and friendship." Tommy joined the former—known as "the Eu"—and became its most zealous member. As newly elected secretary, he kept records and took minutes; he even had a hand in its new constitution—at the very least serving as copyist with his filigreed cursive. Most of all, he discovered a nascent talent for debating. That year, the Eu and the Phi mooted such issues as the superiority of republics to monarchies, the value of the two-party system, and the justifiability of slavery (which the affirmative team won). There in the wilds of North Carolina—among an ardent cohort of similarly motivated teenaged boys and in the absence of his father—Tommy had his first opportunity to find his own voice.

It was the next step in the process of his coming to himself, which he would later describe as a "process of disillusionment." Wilson wrote, "He sees himself soberly, and knows under what conditions his powers must act, as well as what his powers are." Debating the issues of the day also deepened his faith, forcing him to realize how much of his life he had already squandered. "I am now in my seventeenth year and it is sad, when looking over my past life, to see how few of those seventeen years I have spent in the fear of God and how much I have spent in the service of the Devil," Tommy wrote in one of his Davidson notebooks. "If God will give me the grace, I will try to serve Him from this time on." His fellow Eumaneans appointed him to lead them in their devotional exercises. And at that moment, Tommy Wilson's path began to diverge from his father's, as he considered that his powers might be best suited for a life of politics instead of religion.

Never in the best of health, he maintained his classroom attendance; but by the end of the spring term, he had worn himself down and could not keep up with his activities at the Eu. A terrible spring cold overcame him along with an extreme case of the blue devils. With the severity of life at Davidson, he wallowed in feelings of unworthiness and homesickness.

Suffering from headaches of her own, his mother immediately recognized his symptoms and wrote him on May 20, 1874. "You seem depressed," she observed, "—but that is because you are not well. You need not imagine that you are not a favorite. *Everybody* here likes and admires you. I could not begin to tell you the kind and flattering things that are said about you, by everybody that knows you." Having moved from Columbia, she tried to sell him on the virtues of Wilmington, assuring him of "an unusual number of young people about your age there—and of a superior kind—and they are prepared to take an unusual interest in you particularly. Why my darling, nobody could *help* loving you, if they were to try!"

For all his warm feelings for Davidson and some scholastic strides, he stumbled there. The year had been a false start. When Tommy Wilson packed up his room in the spring of 1874, he showed no signs of returning; but with his family uprooted from Columbia, he was not exactly going home again. Boasting a population of fifteen thousand, the North Carolina seaport of Wilmington was the largest town in which the Wilsons had yet resided, and in several ways the most interesting. Situated in the southeast corner of the state, between the Cape Fear River and the

Atlantic, it was a curious mixture. Big-masted brigantines and clipper ships anchored just a few blocks from antebellum mansions. Christians of all sects found a home there, as did a few Jews, who were organizing the first synagogue in the state. Sailors from around the world—Germans, Russians, and Dutchmen—roamed the town. Three blocks from Front Street, with its two- and three-story shops and businesses overlooking the water, was the Presbyterian Church, simple and dramatic with its sharp Gothic spire. The manse sat adjacent to the church, at Fourth and Orange, elm-lined residential streets.

Tommy cocooned himself in his new surroundings—his fifth home in seventeen years—and he was already setting his sights on his sixth. During a Davidson vacation and one of his last days in Columbia, a visitor had entered the Wilsons' lives—the eminent minister and educator Dr. James McCosh, an imposing Scot who was president of the College of New Jersey. President McCosh had given the gawky teenager the once-over, turned to Dr. Wilson, and said with his exaggerated burr, "The boy'll be comin' to Princeton, no doubt."

Tommy had tucked the thought in the back of his mind. He studied with a tutor—especially in brushing up his Greek—and he read ravenously. "When I wanted to find Mr. Tommy in those days," recalled David Bryant, the Wilsons' butler, "I would go to his room, and generally there he would be sitting with his elbows on his knees and his nose in a book. . . . Why sometimes I had to wait a meal; the old Doctor would not let me serve till Mr. Tommy came down. And how proud the old Doctor was of the boy—and the boy of him, too!"

And one day, in one of their regular conversations, Tommy told his father that he had experienced a "Eureka!" moment, that he had "found it" at last. When his father inquired what he had found, Tommy replied, "A mind, sir. I've found I have an intellect and a first-class mind." He explained that he had been reading an abstract book, "and the ease with which he mastered it convinced him that he had a mind."

While Tommy stuck mostly to himself, he did venture into the town. He spent hours at the water's edge, musing about a life at sea. He fantasized once again about what he dubbed "the Royal United Kingdom Yacht Club." He even composed a constitution for his mythical flotilla, an elaborate list of rules and regulations for his make-believe organization, complete with details of officers' duties, times of meetings, fees for entrance, fines for absences, and requirements for bills and resolutions, which demanded the signature of the Commodore—himself.

And he made a friend—John Bellamy, a neighbor and a recent Davidson graduate, two and a half years older, who shared his love of books. Together they went on "reading raids"—sometimes hiking in the pines, other times lying on mounds that had recently covered stashes of Confederate ammunition. They read in silence or, just as often, to each other. Sir Walter Scott was their mutual passion—especially his *Bride of Lammermoor* and *The Pirate*. For Wilson, it was not enough simply to read the books; he insisted that they analyze them. When there was not a book at hand, Bellamy remembered, Tommy launched into discussions of Robert E. Lee and Stonewall Jackson and, of course, Gladstone. Such was the first real friendship Wilson had ever permitted himself with anybody outside his family. "The only trouble with Woodrow Wilson," Bellamy said years later, "is that he was a confirmed and confounded Calvinist." He could not be otherwise. His faith had become his lifeline, just as it had been for his mother—that little girl on the boat, clutching the rope that had been provided to keep her from drowning.

"A man's rootage," Woodrow Wilson would later comment, "means more than his leafage." As he was about to be transplanted in New Jersey soil, his belief in Providence allowed him already to envision his flowerage.

3

EDEN

*Now the LORD had said vnto Abram, Get thee out
of thy countrey, and from thy kinred, and from thy
fathers house, vnto a land that I will shew thee.*

    *And I will make of thee a great nation, and I
will blesse thee, and make thy name great; and thou
shalt bee a blessing.*

—Genesis, XII:1–2

At the end of a spur track of the Pennsylvania Railroad
line, eighteen-year-old freshman Thomas Woodrow
Wilson stepped off the "dinky" train at the little station in
Princeton. In few other places within the thirty-seven reunited states did so much educational, political, and religious history converge as they did in this town of three
thousand people in the middle of New Jersey.

The first seeds of higher education in the United States
had, in fact, been planted elsewhere centuries earlier—only
sixteen years after the Pilgrims disembarked the *Mayflower.*
In 1636, the General Court of the Massachusetts Bay Colony authorized the founding of what became Harvard College. Almost six decades later, a second college—William
and Mary—was founded as an Anglican institution in Virginia; and eight years after that, in 1701, the General Court
of the Colony of Connecticut permitted ten Congregationalist clerics to organize a college to train ministers, naming
it after its primary benefactor, Elihu Yale.

In 1718 the Reverend William Tennent, a Scottish-educated Ulster-man, immigrated to the middle colonies, where he and his sons helped ignite what became known as the Great Awakening, an evangelical move-ment that started in the Congregationalist churches of New England and ran the length of the Appalachians to the Presbyterian churches in the South. On October 22, 1746, Governor John Hamilton issued a charter for the College of New Jersey. While its founders included several of Tennent's disciples who hoped to prepare ministers of the Gospel, they believed equally in educating young men of various religious persuasions for other professions.

One hundred fifty years later, Professor Woodrow Wilson would praise those divines, for they "acted without ecclesiastical authority, as if under obligation to society rather than to the church. They were acting as citi-zens, not as clergymen, and the charter they obtained said never a word about creed or doctrine." They selected the Reverend Jonathan Dickinson to serve as the school's first president in his parsonage in Elizabeth. He died within a year, leaving his student body of ten pupils to his successor, the Reverend Aaron Burr, Sr., who moved the college to his parish in Newark. He established entrance criteria and a curriculum; and, in his tenth year in office, he provided his most enduring contribution.

Burr moved the enterprise to Princeton—then a forty-house village halfway between New York City and Philadelphia. Its position on a low ridge of fertile farmland that close to two of the most thriving cities in the Colonies promised academic seclusion and cultural access. Nathaniel Fitz-Randolph, the son of an original Quaker settler in the area, donated four and a half acres and twenty New Jersey pounds. He passed the hat among his neighbors, while Burr solicited funds from donors who might contrib-ute enough to construct a grand edifice that would serve as the entire col-lege for several years to come. They chose local Stockton sandstone, ochre in color and faintly iridescent. When the building was completed two years later, the trustees wished to name it in honor of the Governor, Jonathan Belcher; but he generously declined—sparing future generations incalculable sophomoric ridicule—and suggested they honor the late King William III, the Prince of Orange, a member of the House of Orange-Nassau.

For years, Nassau Hall reigned as the largest building in the Colonies. Set back from the main street of the town, behind a low iron gate, the building was almost two hundred feet long and fifty feet deep, with a central transept-like projection that added four feet in the front and twelve in the back. A row of windows spanned the length of each of the three floors, with the tops of the basement windows poking their heads just above ground. There were ninety-four of them at the front of the building alone. The exterior walls were more than two feet thick. With its forty-two rooms, Nassau Hall could house a library (mostly Governor Belcher's five hundred books) as well as dormitories and classrooms for as many as 150 students and faculty members and an office for the president; the basement contained the kitchen and refectory. The building's primary feature was the two-story prayer hall that projected from the rear. Not long after the building opened, students discovered the virtues of its long corridors for bowling. Perched atop the hipped roof was a cupola, which housed a large bell that rang at five o'clock in the morning, summoning the students to morning prayers, and throughout the day signaling periods of study, meals, and prayer.

Within a year of taking occupancy, Burr died at forty-one. His wife died less than a year later, orphaning their two young children—including Aaron Burr, Jr., the future Founding Father who turned treasonous. Fortunately, the trustees had been able to impress upon Burr's father-in-law the presidency of the college. And so, in January 1758, Jonathan Edwards, America's foremost theologian—whose sermon "Sinners in the Hands of an Angry God" epitomized the First Great Awakening—moved from Massachusetts to become the new master of Nassau Hall. That March he received an inoculation for smallpox, from which he succumbed. The untimely deaths of his next two successors did not demoralize the college trustees. In fact, they raised their sights and turned to one of Scotland's most eminent scholars and preachers.

Educated at the University of Edinburgh and ordained by the Church of Scotland, John Witherspoon, then in his mid-forties, was an activist evangelical within the Kirk—who had expressed no desire to leave his homeland. Providentially, two persuasive alumni of the College of New Jersey were in Britain that year, and they convinced him and his wife to pack up their five children and venture overseas for a more primitive life and an even more challenging opportunity. To commemorate the night of their arrival in Princeton in 1768, the students lit a candle in each of Nassau Hall's windows.

Witherspoon found a college not living up to its potential—what with an ill-prepared student body and insufficient funds. The preacher in him unabashedly solicited money beyond the confines of the town, and the educator within pushed the curriculum beyond the strictly classical and Christian. He recruited a professor to teach mathematics and natural philosophy and another to teach divinity and moral philosophy. And nobody taught more than Witherspoon himself. "He lectured upon taste and style as well as upon abstract questions of philosophy, and upon politics as a science of government and of public duty as little to be forgotten as religion itself in any well considered plan of life," Wilson would note. Combining his personal library of three hundred books with that of the college, Witherspoon enabled students to sample contemporary politics and literature. He also delighted in the green space surrounding Nassau Hall and its neighboring buildings and contributed to the English language a new word for the college grounds, from the Latin for "field"—"campus."

"It was a piece of providential good fortune that brought such a man to Princeton at such a time," Wilson added. "The blood of John Knox ran in Witherspoon's veins. The great drift and movement of English liberty from Magna Charta down was in all his teachings." He became one of New Jersey's signers of the Declaration of Independence—the only clergyman among the fifty-six delegates.

When the American Revolution began, the college soon had to face the harsh realities of war. On Christmas Night 1776, General George Washington crossed the Delaware River, and a week later Princeton became a battleground. Nassau Hall, which had served as an infirmary until the British converted it into barracks and a jail for suspected rebels, reverted to American hands when Washington delivered a surprise attack and chased the enemy from the building. In time, the college returned to its educational mission, having made activists of many of her sons, including Burr, the poet and pamphleteer Philip Freneau, cavalry officer "Light-Horse" Harry Lee, and—most significant—the young Virginian who became the first Princetonian to return to Princeton for postgraduate study, James Madison. From July to November 1783, the new federal Congress convened in Princeton, turning Nassau Hall into its temporary capitol.

Witherspoon remained president of the college until his death in 1794, getting to witness an astonishing number of his disciples engage in the nation's service. They would include twenty Senators, twenty-three

Representatives, thirteen Governors, three Supreme Court Justices, one Vice President, and a President. "No man," noted Wilson, "had ever better right to rejoice in his pupils."

Like the United States itself, American higher education came of age in the nineteenth century. Building colleges proved an effective way to tame the American wilderness, and religion was no longer their justification. Public schools and libraries also became the tent poles of towns, as essential as churches had once been. With the Morrill Act of 1862, the federal government granted land for the creation of schools that would train students in engineering, agriculture, and even military tactics, establishing colleges in all the states. Still, higher education largely remained the province of the privileged, as few young men could afford time away from their farms or factories to get an education, to say nothing of having to pay for it. For the most privileged, the Eastern college campuses became preserves where sons of the well-to-do could consort with one another and even learn enough to pursue a profession, if necessary. Social clubs, fraternities, and secret societies took root on many campuses, private enclaves where the wealthiest students might enjoy privileges the rest of the student body could not.

After Witherspoon, the adolescent Princeton spent several decades in search of its identity. Under the next few Presbyterian ministers who served as president, Princeton steadily loosened its clerical collar, adding modern languages and current literatures, chemistry, and geography to its curriculum, while a separate theological seminary opened, specifically for the training of church leaders.

The school compensated for its fluctuating enrollment by recruiting heavily in the South. Naturally, debate on campus raged over the issue of slavery. During the Civil War, seventy sons of Princeton gave their lives, half from each side, illustrating its having become the northernmost of the Southern schools and the southernmost of the Northern schools. In December 1864, Princeton conferred an honorary degree upon President Lincoln. Just before the war, a fire had gutted Nassau Hall; so, like the rest of the nation, the college had to reconstruct. In 1868, retirement left a vacancy in its presidency; and, exactly a century after Witherspoon's arrival, Princeton called upon Scotland to send another of her sons on the same mission.

James McCosh was born in Ayrshire—"Bobby Burns" country—and

educated at the University of Glasgow and then Edinburgh. He became a preacher and philosophy professor of international repute at Queen's College, Belfast. Some forty years later, Professor Woodrow Wilson would write of McCosh, "He found Princeton a quiet country college and lifted it to a conspicuous place among the most notable institutions of the country." Nicholas Murray Butler of Columbia University said simply that McCosh shook up "the dry bones of an institution which had been little more than a country high school in New Jersey."

During this period—when Charles William Eliot at Harvard, Andrew White at Cornell, Frederick Augustus Porter Barnard at Columbia, James Burrill Angell at the University of Michigan, and Daniel Coit Gilman, who had just left the presidency of the University of California for the new Johns Hopkins University, blazed new trails in higher education—McCosh expanded the Princeton curriculum and campus. He introduced courses in biology, geology, psychology, art, philosophy, and such social sciences as economics and political science. McCosh encouraged required classes in several disciplines, with some leniency in electives. As the debate over Darwinism raged through the country, the Reverend McCosh asserted, "When a scientific theory is brought before us, our first inquiry is not whether it is consistent with religion, but whether it is true." Rare among ecclesiastics, McCosh argued that Darwin's theory did not diminish the existence of God, but tended to "increase the wonder and mystery of the process of creation." Princeton's student body and faculty doubled in size.

Nothing demonstrated McCosh's intention to elevate Princeton into the ranks of world-class universities more than his building the freestanding Chancellor Green Library—a fanciful work of Victorian Gothic architecture at the right hand of Nassau Hall—to house the college's growing collection of seventy thousand books. McCosh also built the first significant college gymnasium in the country, a Romanesque castle of a building. These and other architectural anomalies, spread among their statelier predecessors across the twenty-acre campus, illustrated Princeton's commitment to innovation as well as tradition.

Tommy Wilson—brown-haired, lanky, and wide-eyed—walked from the station onto a thriving campus that first week of September 1875. On the hill just above the tracks, the most modern college dormitory in America was about to be built—sited to impress arriving passengers, and to be named for Witherspoon. Princeton had abrogated the burden of feeding its 483 students but could not ignore the challenge of housing them— though there was not room for all the incoming freshmen that year, Wilson among them. Fortunately, a number of private homes surrounding the campus were eager for boarders; there was even a hotel at one corner of the campus. Except for his passing acquaintanceship with President McCosh, Tommy knew hardly a soul for hundreds of miles; but no student ever arrived in Princeton more determined to find a place and make a name for himself.

Joseph Wilson had provided his son with an introduction to a local minister and mathematics professor, who put him up for a few nights. Then Tommy found lodging just beyond the new library at the large house of Mr. and Mrs. Josiah Wright. They charged each of seventeen Princeton students ten dollars a week for bed and board. Tommy Wilson's second-floor single room overlooked Nassau Street—a wide, shop-lined dirt road with newly installed gas lamps—which a single rain could turn into a muddy bog.

On Wilson's second morning, all new students assembled in the College Chapel, where McCosh asked them to pledge that so long as they were enrolled at Princeton, they would have "no connection whatever with any secret society"—the school's latest effort to rid itself of at least some of its social divisiveness, especially the ritual of hazing within the already forbidden Greek-letter fraternities. Students were also informed of a compulsory hour-long meeting every Sunday at 2:45 for religious instruction. Furthermore, there would be weekly class meetings with McCosh for recitation on the Bible and his lectures.

Such was the pedagogical model on college campuses, even under the enlightened McCosh. Professors would feed information, and students would routinely regurgitate what they had ingested. Tommy dutifully attended courses in Latin (Livy and Horace), Greek (Demosthenes and Herodotus), Algebra, and an array of English classes, which included the study of Rhetoric, Punctuation and Dictation, Elocution, and Essays. Despite his aversion to rote learning, Wilson satisfactorily performed the stultifying schoolroom exercises.

But he rapidly bloomed outside of class, striking up his first college friendship with a young man from New Jersey who also lived at Mrs. Wright's,

Robert McCarter. "He was quiet and retiring and for a time had few, if any, other friends," McCarter said of Wilson; "we were, therefore, constantly in each other's room . . . chinning together." One memorable conversation, about the Civil War, stretched into an all-nighter. "He was very full of the South and quite a secessionist," said McCarter, ". . . he taking the Southern side and getting quite bitter." Wilson, a son of four Confederate states, had never heard "The Star-Spangled Banner."

At first, most of the students found Tommy Wilson somewhat aloof, until they realized his shyness was a shield. It was the first time he had been exposed to so many people unlike himself, especially a number of sophisticated boys from families of great fortune and privilege. Never impressed or intimidated by social status, he easily attracted companions. Starting with his housemates at Mrs. Wright's, he made one friend at a time.

Within a few weeks, Wilson had found a second home, where he began to assert himself, forging an identity as a thinker and speaker. On September 24, 1875, the American Whig Society—the prestigious literary and debate organization established by Madison—admitted him as one of its 179 members. He took his meals for a while with seventeen Whig men from North Carolina who banded together as the "Tar Heels." A month later, he delivered his first oration before the literary and debating society, a prepared talk entitled "Rome Was Not Built in a Day."

Neither was his scholarly character. He steadily found the primary benefits of a college education lay in its extracurricular offerings, especially in providing autodidactic experiences. Many of Wilson's proclivities had revealed themselves by the time he had arrived at Princeton, and he mindfully spent his hours developing them further. "The rule for every man is, not to depend on the education which other men prepare for him,—not even to consent to it," he realized freshman year; "but to strive to see things as they are, and to be himself as he is. Defeat lies in self-surrender." His first important "victories" occurred during his frequent visits to the new Chancellor Green Library. In Alcoves II through VI, with their carved butternut bookcases, he discovered the histories of the United States and Great Britain. At the head of the south spiral stairs of this brand-new temple of books, he thumbed through bound volumes of *The Gentleman's Magazine* from the preceding year. In the April number, he glommed onto an article called "The Orator," which evaluated the 653 members of the current House of Commons and singled out the chamber's "orator *par excellence*," the one man who could out-talk Prime Minister Disraeli and surpass even Wilson's beloved Gladstone. His name was John Bright.

Representing the Midlands, Bright emerged as the leading spokesman for radicalism in nineteenth-century England. For forty years, the gentleman from Birmingham attacked the aristocracy; he believed the human race had more of a vested interest in the American Constitution than in any other such document. During the Civil War, he voiced solidarity with the Union and rejoiced in its victory. "Slavery has measured itself with Freedom, and Slavery has perished in the struggle," he said. Above all, wrote historian Asa Briggs of Bright's significance, was "that he turned liberalism into a creed, that he made men seek reform because reform was 'right,' and that he refused to separate the spheres of morality and politics." Wilson made such thinking his own.

Wilson also discovered Edmund Burke, a legendary orator and statesman in the House of Commons, an Irish-born Anglican who had supported the American colonists against England's tyranny. Favoring the repeal of the tea duty, Burke had addressed the Americans' having to bear the burdens of monopoly and unfair taxation. "The Englishman in America will feel that this is slavery," he said; "that it is *legal* slavery will be no compensation either to his feelings or to his understanding." Such would mark the beginning of Wilson's own thinking about the need to emancipate people economically.

Years later, in an essay called "Interpreter of English Liberty," Woodrow Wilson would write of another precept he acquired from Burke, one that influenced his own education. Wilson described Burke's four years at Trinity College in Dublin as "years of wide and eager reading, but not years of systematic and disciplinary study. With singular, if not exemplary, self-confidence, he took his education into his own hands." And so, while the Princeton syllabi, which listed Milton, Locke, Hume, Kant, Plato, Aristotle, and Descartes, would consume most of his hours, Wilson too created his own bibliography, his list deeper than it was wide. Once a subject caught his attention, he bored in—almost to the exclusion of everything else—until he could claim expertise.

As with many recovering dyslexics, Tommy Wilson read slowly; and he tended to retain more than most, developing a virtually photographic memory. Upon encountering an unknown word, name, or concept, he would pause to research it to the end. Classmate Hiram Woods, Jr., recalled a discussion with Wilson about *Macbeth*; afterward he found Tommy's nose deep in an encyclopedia learning all he could about Birnam Wood, acquiring a deeper understanding of the play by learning more about the place where Macbeth's soldiers had once encamped. On another occasion with the Woods family in Baltimore, a question about Macaulay's accuracy in his *History of England* arose, and Hiram recalled how Tommy insisted upon consulting two other sources before deciding what the truth was.

Like his father, Wilson was an editor by nature, challenging authors in the margins of their works. He had not completed reading a book until he had transcribed its highlights and then commented upon them. Remembering his father's admonition against a prolix gut, Wilson believed the "man who reads everything is like the man who eats everything: he can digest nothing; and the penalty for cramming one's mind with other men's thoughts is to have no thoughts of one's own." He knew that history offered many examples of great thinkers and leaders who actually "did little reading of books . . . but much reading of men and of their own times."

In Tommy's case, reading begat more reading. Macaulay's *History of England* referred to Samuel Pepys's diary, which made Tommy not only want to read that seventeenth-century journal but also to keep his own. Like Pepys, Wilson wrote his diary in shorthand. But the former kept his diary for a decade, starting at age twenty-seven, during which time he shed light on such events as the Great Plague and the Great Fire of London; the latter was nineteen, chronicling six months of readings and activities with a growing group of friends in a quiet college town. After six months, Tommy discontinued the exercise "for want of time to do it *Justice.*"

He had a longer run emulating John Milton, who famously kept a commonplace book—a *locus communis*—into which he entered thoughts, sayings, proverbs, and prayers. The notion for what Wilson called his "Index Rerum" evidently came from Andrew Graham, whose shorthand method Wilson employed and who had written a recent article on keeping such a compendium. Biographies of writers and statesmen especially grabbed Wilson's attention, reflecting his growing interest in history and even more in politics, especially of the British Empire. Burke—his biography, his style, his views on America—commanded more space than anybody else. Wilson also used the commonplace book to record his expenses—every nickel for an apple, dime for a shave, and dollar for cod liver oil—as well as potential topics for books and essays.

By the end of his freshman year, Wilson proved to be a respectable student—ranking twenty-sixth in a class of 114 students; and his extra-curricular life continued to blossom. He and his boardinghouse boys formed a baseball team and played as often as they could; and he became a zealot of all things Princetonian—which was just then adopting orange and black as its school colors and later the Tiger as its mascot. Before the semester ended, students went to the treasurer's office to draw for a room the next semester; and Wilson had the good fortune to be fifth in the lottery, entitling him to a choice room in Witherspoon Hall. It would not be completed for another semester, but Tommy was assured of prime accommodations for the rest of his stay on campus. And for the first time, he expressed interest in the opposite sex: "A great many pretty girls at the church," he observed in his journal, as he was packing up his room for the summer, "but not nearly as many as we see every day in the sunny south." He was in much better condition than he had been after his year at Davidson, and most of Tommy's diary entries were able to repeat the same phrase, until it became a self-fulfilling mantra: "Thank God for health and strength."

On Monday, June 26, 1876, Tommy Wilson arose early in order to catch the morning train to Baltimore. From there he went to the port and boarded a boat to North Carolina, getting a good night's rest in a stateroom. ("No pretty girls on board," he noted.) The boat arrived in Portsmouth, in the Outer Banks, at dawn, and he spent the entire day riding by coach across dry, dusty roads to Wilmington. He delighted in being "home," despite its unfamiliarity. He found his mother in fragile health but his father as ebullient as ever, having just assumed the editorship of the *North Carolina Presbyterian*, following the Wilson tradition of publishing strong opinions as well as preaching them. Nine-year-old Josie eagerly tagged along with his brother whenever possible, though the college man filled most of the summer reading and writing and spending as much time as possible with his father—often in the basement, where the Reverend Wilson had installed a billiard table.

Having completed Macaulay's *History*, Tommy had moved on to Gibbon's *History of the Decline and Fall of the Roman Empire*. Alongside these major works, he dipped into the *American Cyclopedia*, studying Henry Clay, John C. Calhoun, and anything related to the English form of government. He also dove into a few novels and Shakespeare's plays. With all the surety of a man with a year of college under his belt, Tommy Wilson espoused only bold opinions, sometimes beyond his expertise: he dismissed a review of a book that accused Macaulay of being superficial as "sublimely ridiculous" and *Romeo and Juliet* as one of the Bard's "poorest pieces." On the hundredth anniversary of American independence, he wrote how much happier his nation would be now "if she had England's form of government instead of the miserable delusion of a republic. A republic too founded upon the notion of abstract liberty! I venture to say that this country will never celebrate another centennial as a republic. The English form of government is the only true one."

That summer, Wilson submitted six essays on religion to his father's newsletter. Under the pseudonym "Twiwood," they were published between August and December of that year. They all explored the daily challenges of being a true man of faith. In one essay, "A Christian Statesman," he wrote words that should have come back to haunt him late in life—but did not: "When the statesman has become convinced that he has arrived at the truth, and has before his mind the true view of his subject, he should be tolerant. He should have a becoming sense of his own weakness and liability to err." More and more, even his Scripture-based pieces bore political undertones.

With increasing frequency, Tommy found himself rushing to the First Presbyterian Church that summer, where he climbed to the pulpit to practice his oratory. But any hopes Dr. Wilson might have harbored of his son's becoming a minister were dashed—for Tommy was not rehearsing sermons. In the empty church, he delivered the great speeches of Webster and Gladstone and Burke and Bright.

Tommy and his father ended their summer in Philadelphia at the Centennial Exposition of 1876, the first World's Fair to be held in the United States. It was full of wonders, especially the exhibitions in Machinery Hall and Agricultural Hall—displays of such brand-new marvels as Alexander Graham Bell's telephone, a Remington "Typographic Machine," Heinz ketchup, and Hires root beer. They could visit the right arm and torch of the Statue of Liberty for fifty cents, money earmarked for the assembly of the statue in New York harbor. The Wilsons stopped at Wanamaker's to buy Tommy winter clothes before proceeding to Princeton, where they took a room at the University Hotel for a night before Tommy returned to Mrs. Wright's boardinghouse.

With such friends as McCarter close at hand, he resumed his scholarly routine, though his interest in his classes steadily decreased. Apart from McCosh's course in Psychology—in which Wilson received a final grade of 99.8 percent—Wilson continued to bridle at all the memorization and recitation. Whether the subject was Greek or French or Roman History or Natural History (which, to his surprise, engaged him), the routine led him "to the conclusion that my friends have no doubt come to long ago and that is that my mind is a very ordinary one indeed. I am nothing as far as intellect goes. But I can plod and work." He was already feeling shackled by the rigors of being a "mere student" and yearned for the freedom of the scholar, who "seeks wisdom because he is inspired with a love for it."

Although he was sinking in his class standing, no Princeton student became more visible. "We went to college without an objective," classmate Hiram Woods said of his group of friends, "but Wilson always had a definite purpose." Tommy remained an especially active participant in the Whig Society. He engaged in debates—winning for the affirmative on the propositions "That a liberal education is to be preferred to an exclusively practical one" and "That a protective tariff is now no longer necessary for the protection of our home industries." He also delivered speeches, entitling his most notable effort sophomore year "The Ideal Statesman." It proved to be a blueprint for himself and a book he would later write.

The True Statesman is . . . one who has all the principles of the law carefully arranged in a vigorous mind and to whom all the particulars as well as the broad principles of International law are as familiar as his alphabet. And not only should he have the law of his own country at his fingers' ends, but he should be intimately acquainted with all the more important legislative actions of every country on the globe.

A year later he delivered an oration on Bismarck, his prose noticeably enriched from another year's worth of independent reading, which had taken him into the world of *belles lettres*.

He sat on a number of the Whig Society's committees, and by junior year, T. W. Wilson had been elected Speaker, its highest honor. One fellow member recalled that Thomas Wilson "steadily grew in the estimation of his fellow members until he was recognized as the best debater in the society. . . . He was especially effective in extemporaneous debate." More to the point, another friend would recall a half century after their time in school together, "mere records cannot produce the appealing tones of his voice and the fire in his eyes as he exercised his remarkable skill in debate. He got as much fun out of it as a great many men now achieve in athletics."

But Wilson was not Whig's most victorious debater. He entered two oratorical contests and placed only once; and in just one of four debate competitions did he take the top prize. This was, in part, because the oratorical style of the day was one of considerable artifice, in which gesticulation garnered more points than articulation and vehemence counted more than eloquence. He recognized as much in the brand-new student-run newspaper called the *Princetonian*. "Until we eschew declamation and court oratory," he wrote, "we must expect to be ciphers in the world's struggles for principles and the advancement of causes. Oratory is persuasion, not the declamation of essays." England's House of Commons, Wilson believed, engaged in such modern debate.

With his growing passion for all things British, Wilson decided to establish his own miniature Parliament, what he called the Liberal Debating Club. Naturally, he wrote its constitution. The first of its twenty-three articles defined the society and stipulated that it "shall be founded upon the fundamental principles of *Justice, Morality* and *Friendship*." Toward that end, the club met every Saturday night, at which time the members engaged in debate, speeches, or simply convivial discussion of literature. As in the British system, the presiding officer was a figurehead, while the Secretary of State functioned as a Prime Minister, empowered to execute Article V, which stated, "The questions discussed by this Club shall be political questions of the present century." They included an overhaul of the United States Constitution so that the nation's executive power would be vested in a President who is chosen for one six-year term, and that his Cabinet shall form a Ministry, answerable to the House of Representatives. Before the ten members, Wilson honed his speaking skills, developing a powerful mode of speech that was at once heightened but conversational.

In the middle of his sophomore year, the Class of 1879 voted Wilson one of its two representatives on the newspaper's Board of Editors. When the managing editor stepped aside at the start of Wilson's junior year, Wilson took his place, an office to which he was elected the following semester. "He formulated policies; he was the chief," McCarter would later recall. "He would come around to me and say that he would like me to write on such and such. If he did not like what I wrote, it would not go in. The editors were not a cabinet and seldom if ever met as a group. He was boss and deserved to be."

Wilson became a prolific editorial writer himself. He composed forty opinion pieces over the next two years, alongside reviews of books and even a performance by the great-granddaughter of the legendary actress Sarah Siddons. ("Her chief fault is an exaggeration," the young critic wrote, "which seems to be affectation.") His editorials were almost entirely directed toward enhancing the college experience, usually through greater promotion of extracurricular activities. The rest of his editorials were haughty admonitions to his schoolmates. One was a direct attack on the privileged student who could afford not to succeed—"the habitual loafer." Wilson did not begrudge those who had been given much, but he resented those who took such gifts for granted and failed even to pretend to work.

Never an athlete, Wilson was always conscious of his body, mindful of diet and exercise; and Princeton's sports teams had no more ardent booster. He not only editorialized regularly for greater university support of the athletic programs, but he became active with both the baseball and football teams, getting elected secretary of the Football Association. The game as played in America was rough-and-tumble, with few holds barred—more like rugby than modern-day American football. As with everything else in his life, Wilson's interest in the teams was primarily about merit and achievement. In his new position, Wilson became the moving force behind the sport on the Princeton campus. He organized the team, raised money for its equipment, and, as a coach, even devised plays, insisting on their being followed.

In the spring, Wilson's participation with the baseball team provided one of the most significant experiences of his Princeton career. In a long editorial, he discussed the need to bring a more systematic approach to selecting the University Nine—all of which he said depended on not only a good captain on the field but the selection of the best possible president of the association. "The majority of men in College are sufficiently familiar with the rules of the game to fill the office," he wrote. "The president must, above all things else, be a man of unbiased judgment, energy, determination, intelligence, moral courage, *conscience*." To those who knew Tommy Wilson—which by then included most of his classmates—only one man on campus fit that description.

That very day, Tommy attended a meeting of the Base Ball Association, which had intended to elect his classmate Cornelius C. Cuyler its president. At the start of the meeting, according to a plan Wilson had devised, one of his closest friends moved that they postpone the vote by four weeks, to allow further consideration of Wilson's qualifications. After a debate of the matter, the group voted to delay. "Walked home from the meeting quite elated with our victory," Tommy wrote in his diary that night, "for a victory it was." When the election was held in late October, not only was Wilson made president of the organization but a politician was born.

He soon realized that he was spreading himself too thin. Even Tommy's doting mother urged him to resign the presidency of the baseball club. "It is very pleasant to think that your fellow-students have such confidence in you," she wrote. "But it would be wrong to put aside your more important interests." She added, "You will make a great mistake if you allow anything of the kind to come in the way of your doing your utmost in the direction of your *future* interest."

Humility—drummed into him by both his parents—tempered his ambition. The harder he pushed himself, the more harshly he judged himself. In one self-analysis, he challenged his own literary ability, insisting in the third person that his compositions "go limping about in a cloud of wordy expressions and under a heavy weight of lost nouns and adjectives. Ideas are to his writings what oases are to the deserts, except that his ideas are very seldom distinguishable from the waste which surrounded them."

Shortly after Tommy turned twenty-one, his father wrote:

> You *have* talents—you have *character*—you have a manly bearing. You have self-reliance. You have almost every advantage coupled I trust with genuine love for God. Do not allow yourself, then, to feed on dreams—daydreams though they be. . . . It is genius that usually gets to the highest tops—but, what is the secret heart of genius? the ability to work with painstaking self-denial.

Cautioning his son in the ways of ambition, Dr. Wilson added, "In short, dearest boy, do not allow yourself to dwell upon *yourself*—concentrate your thoughts upon *thoughts* and *things* and *events*. . . . I am not charging egotism upon you. Far from it. I am only warning you against an evil, common to youth."

Since Princeton's inception, every Princetonian has believed he attended the college during its golden age. In retrospect, Wilson's undergraduate years—when McCosh was at the peak of his powers—were a genuine millennium; and the Scotsman pronounced the Class of 1879 "the largest and finest . . . ever to attend me college." A statistical summary of its 124 graduates supported the claim: in addition to future Governor and President Woodrow Wilson, the class would ultimately yield a Justice of the Supreme Court, two Congressmen, a Chancellor of New Jersey, an Attorney General of New Jersey, two Maryland judges, one Princeton dean, thirty lawyers, twenty doctors, and twenty ministers. The men of 1879 would prove to be unparalleled in their generosity, led by a number of wealthy young men, among them Cyrus McCormick, whose father started the McCormick Harvesting Machine Company, Cleveland Dodge, son of a mining industrialist, and such future banking titans as Edward W. Sheldon and Cornelius C. Cuyler.

In February 1877, Witherspoon Hall—a five-story building of blue-gray marble, built upon a dark-stone ground floor—opened its doors. Each floor had its own style of windows; and each face of the building featured its own style of tower, including one conical turret. Its eighty rooms could accommodate 140 students, and its water closet on every floor made Witherspoon the first college dormitory in America with indoor plumbing. Tommy Wilson's suite on the second floor—7 West, with its study, small bedroom, and fireplace—would remain his home for the next two and a half years.

Steadily, Wilson found the most rewarding elements of college came not through the formal academics ("No undergraduate can be made a scholar in four years") but in friendship, that immeasurable influence twenty-year-olds have upon one another before their personalities have hardened. A generation later, he would conclude that "the very best effects of university life are wrought between six and nine o'clock in the evenings, when the professor has gone home, and minds meet minds, and a generating process takes place." For the most part, Tommy Wilson found that communion with seven fellow residents of his dormitory. For the rest of their lives they remained friends, calling themselves "the Witherspoon Gang."

They shared modest backgrounds. Without being part of Princeton's social elite, the Gang provided most of the horsepower for the college's nonathletic extracurricular activities. As with Wilson, oratory and current affairs engaged the other members of the Gang the most, and they joined Whig and Wilson's Liberal Debating Club or worked on his staff at the *Princetonian* or contributed to the *Nassau Literary Magazine*. Most of them prepared for the law, while two hoped to go to medical school. None of Wilson's closest friends was among the twenty-four Seventy-niners who would become ministers. He would remain closest to the Gang member who followed the least traditional postgraduate path: Robert Bridges, an ace debater who pursued a literary life—becoming a newspaper reporter and, eventually, the longtime editor of *Scribner's Magazine*. To their dying days, they remained "Bobby" and "Tommy" to each other.

Of all the members of the Witherspoon Gang, however, Tommy found the greatest kinship with a young man from upstate New York whose career at Princeton most closely mirrored his. Charles Talcott was a fellow debater and a member of the *Princetonian* board who had an eye on a legal and political career. The two of them formally entered into what Wilson called a "solemn covenant" that "we would school all our powers and passions for the work of establishing the principles we held in common; that we would acquire knowledge that we might have power; and that we would drill ourselves in all the arts of persuasion, but especially in oratory . . . that we might have facility in leading others into our ways of thinking and enlisting them in our purposes." Years later, Wilson realized the pact was not just "boyish enthusiasm, though we were blinded by a very boyish assurance with regard to the future and our ability to mould the world as our hands might please." Bobby Bridges would later record that "there was a certain integrity in his ideal from boy to man that gave his friends a peculiar confidence in his ultimate destiny as a leader of men. It was a jest of his in college which ended 'when I meet you in the Senate, I'll argue that out with you.'"

Expanding his social base, Tommy joined an informal "eating club." Although Wilson was poorer than most of the members, he wanted for nothing while at Princeton. One time, though, he did run out of money and could not afford even the postage to write home. Remembering that he had once dropped a penny, he turned his room upside down until he found it, so that he could mail an SOS by penny postcard. Letters from home invariably included a post office money order to tide him over; and Tommy was able to join a dozen men who took their meals in a house on Nassau Street. There were dozens of such establishments around campus— such as the Knights of the Round Table, the Hollow Inn, and the club he joined with Charlie Talcott and Robert McCarter, the Alligators.

"There was not a touch of the pedant or dig about him," wrote Robert Bridges, fifty years after graduation. Tommy exercised with the crew, took the train into New York City to attend the theater (one day he saw Edwin Booth perform twice, alternating between Othello and Iago), and lingered in the Alligator club with Earl Dodge, captain of the football team, scribbling plays on the tablecloth. Said McCarter, "He had clear-cut notions of how the game should be played and insisted on them." By the end of his senior year, nobody had slid more smoothly into more organizations than Tommy Wilson.

Princeton's student body of five hundred men remained homogeneous. Fifty years later, Bridges recalled a crisis in Dr. McCosh's philosophy class when a Negro student from the Theological Seminary entered the classroom. No black man had yet enrolled at the college. Upon his taking a seat in the back row, several Southerners stood and exited. While few schools other than the all-black colleges enrolled more than a handful of African American students, some doors were at least open, albeit but a crack. To the Princeton Class of 1879, however, diversity meant only the presence of Episcopalians, and the odd Methodist.

For all his activity in the classroom and out, Wilson ultimately distinguished himself most as a scholar, through countless hours of independent thought and work. He was bursting with ideas, as every book he read seemed to inspire one he hoped to write. Junior year, he read the newly published *Short History of the English People*, by John Richard Green, which he reviewed in the pages of the *Princetonian* as having the "candor of Carlyle, the concise expression of Gibbon, and the brilliancy of Macaulay." It got Wilson thinking that he might one day chronicle his own country in a similar fashion.

Wilson often contemplated the matter of leadership in America, in part because one of the most exciting elections in American history occurred during his sophomore year. At age twenty, he was too young to vote, but the election of 1876, between Democratic Governor Samuel J. Tilden of New York and Republican Governor Rutherford B. Hayes of Ohio, was the first to engage him. The night before the election, Tommy heard that pools in New York offered its Governor two-to-one odds. Late that night, word reached New Jersey that Tilden had won his home state by seventy-five thousand votes, which seemed to be an electoral prize large enough to give him the Presidency. The next night, Tommy joined the Democrats on campus around a huge bonfire by the Revolutionary War cannon buried muzzle-down on the green. But while the fire blazed, word spread that Hayes had been elected. Tilden had won the popular vote by four percentage points—250,000 votes—but Hayes appeared to have carried the electoral college, with four votes to spare. The final results hung in the balance for days, and then months, as returns were challenged. Cries of fraud and threats of violence erupted, especially in the South, where Reconstruction had left some states with two sets of elected officials; and now Florida, Louisiana, and South Carolina fought over certification of their Presidential electors. Congress created an Electoral Commission composed of five members from the Senate, five from the House, and five from the Supreme Court—all of whom, including the Justices, voted along party lines. Two days before the Constitution called for the inauguration of the new President, the scales tipped in favor of the Republicans. A constitutional crisis had been averted, but evidently at a price: shortly after taking his oath, President Hayes ordered the withdrawal of federal troops from the South. As future historian Woodrow Wilson would write, "The supremacy of the white people was henceforth assured in the administration of the southern States." Reconstruction ended; but the American political system stagnated in a period in which the executive branch was subordinate to the legislative, and the legislative lacked adequate leadership.

This only further enamored Wilson with Britain's parliamentary system, especially after he read a decade-old book called *The English Constitution*, by Walter Bagehot, an English political analyst and journalist. Bagehot (pronounced *badge-it*) defied political labels (considering himself a conservative Liberal) and failed in several stands for election to Parliament; but his dissection of power in the Cabinet-led House of Commons stood unsurpassed. In *The Economist*, which he edited for years, he wrote of both

internal and international socioeconomic issues affecting England. He observed the American Civil War with great interest, sympathizing with the
South but admiring Lincoln. Tommy clung to Bagehot's every word. Not
two weeks after the author's untimely death at fifty-one, Wilson submitted to the Liberal Debating Club a plan for the reformation of America's
federal government, more along the lines of the British Cabinet system, in
which executive and legislative powers would be entrusted to ministers
serving at the pleasure of the majority party.

His senior year, he took classes in history, ethics, and political science,
scoring solidly in the 90s, though chemistry and astronomy brought his
ranking down to thirty-eighth in a class of 167. In January and February
of 1879, he took on yet another task—that of composing a political essay
based on themes he had presented to the Liberal Debating Club. The as-
signment proved so engaging that Wilson relinquished the Base Ball Association presidency.

Although Wilson's essay borrowed heavily from Bagehot's work, he
wrote a prodigious piece—sophisticated beyond his years. In over 8,500
words, the Princeton senior argued that "Congress is a deliberative body in
which there is little real deliberation; a legislature which legislates with no
real discussion of its business. Our Government is practically carried on by
irresponsible committees." He suggested that members of the President's
Cabinet ought to sit in Congress and engage in debate and that the executive and the legislative branches should run the government together, advancing the same agenda. The entire concept was based on faith in the
"display of administrative talents, by evidence of high ability upon the
floor of Congress in the stormy play of debate."

Upon its completion, Tommy sought his father's reaction, only to find
Joseph Wilson's praise mixed and measured. "I will say that your manner
of presentation is worthy of my sincerest commendation," he wrote his son
at the end of February 1879. "I do not think you could improve the composition." And yet—he thought it might "be made to *glow* a little more. It
is to a certain extent, cold." That said, he encouraged Tommy to submit it
to any number of periodicals, adding, "You will find that *practise* is, in this
as in all else, another name for perfection. *You* have only to persevere." In
her mollifying way, Janet Wilson reflexively sent her son a letter assuring
him of her unqualified admiration.

Heeding his father's advice not to tinker with it any longer, Wilson submitted the piece to the prestigious *International Review*. A junior editor there accepted it—one Henry Cabot Lodge, a Boston blue blood six years Wilson's senior who was about to start a long and powerful legislative career with his election to the Massachusetts lower house. The article, entitled "Cabinet Government in the United States," would run in the August issue. It would not be Lodge's last assessment of Wilson's political philosophy, but it would be the most generous.

Spring in Princeton long marked a succession of lazy afternoons until graduation. Wilson's final months defied tradition. He wrote nine editorials in his last six weeks as managing editor of the *Princetonian*, as well as his senior thesis, "Our Kinship with England." Busy as he was, he also discovered a poet whose words he would take to heart for the rest of his life—William Wordsworth.

Unexpectedly, he did forgo one senior activity. The Lynde Debate was one of the featured events at Princeton graduation, for which the participants had to compete in a qualifying match—Whig's top three arguing against the trio from its rival, the Cliosophic Society. Wilson was an obvious contender, and the preliminary topic was of great interest to him: "Resolved that it would be advantageous to the United States to abolish universal suffrage." Upon drawing lots to determine which side he would be arguing, however, Wilson promptly withdrew. On principle alone, he could not bring himself to argue the negative. Dr. Wilson supported his son's decision, saying it would lead to "either a limitation of suffrage or anarchy in twenty-five years or sooner. I do not refer to the Negroes any more than to the ignorant Northern voters." Whether it was because of a white Southern aversion to the Negro having the vote or, like his father's, his attraction to the English belief that only stakeholders—landowners—should be enfranchised, Wilson's feelings remained firm. As he had noted in his diary back in 1876, "Universal suffrage is at the foundation of every evil in this country." Wilson's views on that subject would change over the years; but then, he took comfort in the words of his friend Talcott: "Arguing against settled convictions, in my opinion, injures a man more than it benefits him."

Commencement exercises stretched over four days. They began on Sunday, June 15, 1879, with President McCosh's delivering the baccalaureate address in the Presbyterian Church on Nassau Street. Class Day followed—an informal celebration of the men of 1879—and Wilson was named the class's "model statesman." Beyond that, he was not singled out. While he had once considered himself a candidate for valedictorian, he contented himself by graduating in the top third of the class with a 90.3 percent average. At nine o'clock in the morning of Wednesday the eighteenth, Wilson joined the procession in front of Nassau Hall as it returned to the church for the formal presentation of diplomas. He was listed in the graduation program as one of four winners of a prize from the *Nassau Lit* for his essay on William Pitt, the Earl of Chatham; and, along with forty-one others, he graduated with honors. He was also one of twenty-six seniors invited to deliver an oration in the First Presbyterian Church based on his senior thesis. A few hours later, depression set in, as he found leaving Princeton "harder than I had feared."

Wilson's four years at Princeton had transformed a sheltered and aimless boy from the South into a thoughtful young man with ambition and vision—even an outlook on the world and the place he hoped to hold in it.

A few years later, a relative visited him in Pennsylvania. While she was leafing through one of his college books, a piece of paper fell out: it was a handmade business card, fashioned while he had been a Princeton undergraduate. In his finest penmanship, he had written:

> *Thomas Woodrow Wilson*
> *Senator from Virginia*

4

SINAI

They wandred in the wildernes, in a solitary way:
they found no citie to dwell in.

—Psalmes, CVII:4

Adjustment," Thomas Woodrow Wilson would write years later in *When a Man Comes to Himself*, approaches most men incrementally, a little at each stage of life: "A college man feels the first shock of it at graduation. . . . Of a sudden he is a novice again, as green as in his first school year, studying a thing that seems to have no rules—at sea amid crosswinds, and a bit seasick withal." Upon leaving Princeton, Wilson embarked upon a ten-year odyssey—stopping anxiously at numerous ports but never dropping anchor.

After three weeks in Wilmington, Tommy escaped the summer heat with his family, traveling three hundred miles west—fifteen hours of which were by stagecoach climbing rough roads up the Blue Ridge Mountains. They finally reached a country retreat called Horse Cove, three thousand feet above sea level. Bad weather kept him indoors much of the time, reading Green's *Short History of the English People* and writing a twenty-thousand-word piece called "Self-Government in France." By September's end, he had begun to chart his career course. "The profession I chose was politics," Wilson would explain a few years later;

"the profession I entered was the law. I entered the one because I thought it would lead to the other." He enrolled in the School of Law at the University of Virginia.

Charlottesville sits at the foothills of the Blue Ridge Mountains, equidistant from the capitals of both the nation and the Commonwealth of Virginia. The spirit of Thomas Jefferson infused the town, where the third President had lived most of his adult life at Monticello, the home he had designed. In his final years, he conceived and also designed a second great monument for the community, the University of Virginia, an "academical village" of red-brick buildings trimmed in white, spread across twenty-eight acres.

Inspired by the Pantheon of Rome, the Rotunda commands the campus, rising almost eighty feet to its white dome. A massive portico of Corinthian columns greeted visitors to the college library, offices, and classrooms. Two long rows of connected pavilions, including living quarters, ran south down a terraced slope, embracing a great lawn almost 250 yards in length. The pavilions—with faculty housing evenly spaced among student accommodations—backed onto gardens with serpentine brick walls, which gave way on either side to another row of buildings, the Ranges.

Law schools barely existed in America until the middle of the nineteenth century. Before that, young men "read the law," generally apprenticing to attorneys as they mastered its basic texts. A few colleges offered courses in the subject and, in time, developed curricula. Harvard Law School, founded in 1817, had recently appointed a new dean, Christopher Columbus Langdell, who revolutionized his field by introducing the case method, a dialectic approach to the subject. But by the time "Thos. Woodrow Wilson"—as he enrolled on October 2, 1879—cracked his first law books in Charlottesville, Langdell was the only practitioner of this Socratic method in America.

The School of Law at Virginia, which began in 1826, was more traditional. It had been run since 1845 by an alumnus many considered the outstanding legal scholar of his day, John Barbee Minor. He and another graduate, Stephen O. Southall, taught all the courses to their seventy-nine students. English common law was Professor Minor's religion, Sir William Blackstone's *Commentaries on the Laws of England* his Bible. "He who is not a good lawyer when he comes to the bar," Minor wrote in the course catalogue, "is not a good one afterwards."

In his late sixties and an expert in Scripture and Shakespeare, Minor taught in the standard form of lecture and recitation, drilling his classes with questions about their reading. Students considered his lectures masterpieces. "Thought is requisite as well as reading," Minor wrote in describing the course; "for the purpose of thought, there must be time to *Digest*, as well as the *Industry* to acquire. One cannot expect to gorge himself with law as a Boa Constrictor does with masses of food, and then digest it afterwards." Second only to Wilson's father, the major educational influence in Wilson's life was Minor.

Professor Minor's own four-volume *Institutes of Common and Statute Law* served as the basic text, and Wilson scratched his own shorthand comments in its margins. On the page where Minor justified certain instances of slavery, because its discontinuance would result in "more injury . . . to the body politic" than its maintenance, Wilson wondered, "How about its *gradual* abolition?"—because of the practice's "curse to industry and to morals." In class, one fellow student recalled, "no responses to Mr. Minor's questions were prompter, more precise, or more satisfactory, in every respect, than his." After his first month, Tommy Wilson was still undecided as to how he felt about the University of Virginia. "The course in Law is certainly as fine a one as could be desired," he wrote Bobby Bridges. "Prof. Minor, who is at the head of the 'school,' is a *perfect* teacher. . . . But to *like* an institution one must be attracted by something besides its methods of instruction."

Wilson lived in an uninspiring brick dormitory on the perimeter of the campus—House F in Dawson's Row, which looked out upon open fields and a Confederate cemetery. He missed the Witherspoon Gang and the camaraderie he had enjoyed at Princeton. Since he was an avowed Federalist—an ardent admirer of Alexander Hamilton; a believer in dominant central government; a Southerner without Southern blood who did not embrace states' rights—all the surrounding Jeffersoniana was lost on him.

Having arrived on campus a published writer and accomplished debater, he set about creating new social circles for himself. He ate at a boardinghouse at the end of West Range, where he made his first and most lasting friend in Charlottesville, an undergraduate from Virginia. Richard Heath Dabney was a student of history and an avid reader—four years Wilson's junior but in a three-year program that would award him a master's degree—and he and Tommy took long walks and read to each other. They found a few like-minded students—including one Charles W. Kent, also in a master's program—with whom they liked to roam the hills and discuss their current texts. The three men pledged Phi Kappa Psi together, and Wilson was chosen that semester to represent its chapter at the fraternity's annual convention in Washington; the next year he was elected general president of his chapter. He made even more friends as a member of the chapel choir. After a month on campus, a few of the singers peeled off to form a glee club; and tenors Wilson and Kent sang all the popular tunes of the day. Sunday evenings after chapel services, he repaired to Dr. Minor's house, where several of the men sang hymns long into the night.

Wilson's voice was strongest, however, as a member of the Jefferson Society, one of the university's literary and debating organizations. The "old Jeff" convened every Saturday night in a red-carpeted room in West Range. Within weeks, he was named club secretary; and in signing his first set of minutes, he added a flourish. As though shedding a skin—and suggesting new seriousness—he endorsed the record as T. Woodrow Wilson.

Just days before Christmas 1879, he was asked to present the school's athletic medals at the university field day, and he combined serious comments with some playful doggerel of his own invention. "When all was over," the *University of Virginia Magazine* observed, "Mr. Wilson in that happy manner so preeminently possessed by that gentleman made a perfect little medal delivery speech." Overnight, Wilson became a star on campus, with people awaiting his next public appearance.

The occasion arrived in March, when an overflow crowd that included townspeople came to hear him deliver a serious speech. He selected a predictable subject—John Bright—and his profile of his idol revealed just the sort of statesman Wilson intended to be. "Tolerance is an admirable intellectual gift: but it is of little worth in politics," he said of the great reformer. "Politics is a war of *causes*; a joust of principles. . . . Absolute identity with one's cause is the first and great condition of successful leadership."

Wilson used his remaining moments to take a stand of his own, defending Bright on a controversial matter—his opposition to the Confederacy. Standing in the middle of the Old Dominion, Virginia-born Wilson declaimed, "I yield to no one precedence in love for the South. But *because*

I love the South, I rejoice in the failure of the Confederacy." Taking no moral stand, he explained, "The perpetuation of slavery would, beyond all question, have wrecked our agricultural and commercial interests, at the same time that it supplied a fruitful source of irritation abroad and agitation within. We cannot conceal from ourselves the fact that slavery was enervating our Southern society and exhausting to Southern energies." He concluded his long oration with the words of his subject, who had said, "I see one people, and one language, and one law, and one father over all that wide continent, the home of freedom, and a refuge for the oppressed of every race and of every clime."

Wilson made his local reputation that night. The *Virginia University Magazine* printed the text of his speech in March. In April he delivered an equally deliberative biographical essay on William Gladstone—almost ten thousand words extolling his "poetical sensibility," an intuitive understanding of interests beyond his own. Wilson admired Gladstone's ability to change his views on issues over his long career. As the leading student of politics at the University of Virginia, T. Woodrow Wilson seemed well on his path to the Senate. He was unrivalled at Virginia—except by one man.

William Cabell Bruce shared Woodrow Wilson's political and literary ambitions and seemed to be chasing, if not outpacing, him. Born four years after Wilson in a Virginia town called Staunton Hill, he too demonstrated his literary proclivities and his oratory prowess in the Jefferson Society. When it was announced that these two stars would face off in a debate on the afternoon of Friday, April 2, the contest had to be moved to the Washington Society's larger hall to accommodate the unprecedented crowd. The subject before the two men: "Is the Roman Catholic element in the United States a menace to American institutions?"

A packed house awaited the debaters; and the audience was so enthralled, the faculty judges decided not to render an immediate decision but to publish the results a month later. "Being required to decide between these two gentlemen," they wrote at last in a letter to the school magazine, "our committee is of opinion that the medal intended for the best debater should be awarded to Mr. Bruce."

They voted to bestow a second medal for oratory to Wilson, who considered it a consolation prize and contemplated refusing it. A fellow law student recalled his saying that "he made no pretensions to oratory; that he was a debater or nothing; and that his acceptance of such a trophy would be absurd." Wilson's friends urged him to back down, which he finally did. Decades later, Bruce spoke graciously of his old rival, saying: "I had a more commonplace, conventional mind than his. . . . Extraordinary as his intellect was, he was too abstract, too oracular for a debater." Wilson, he thought, "was much better fitted for the public platform than for a debating assembly." A month later, the university presented a prize for that year's best contribution to the *Virginia University Magazine*. It cited Wilson's excellent work; but it awarded the gold medal to an essay by William Cabell Bruce.

Wilson's earlier sound health gave way to a persistent cold and severe dyspepsia. His father suggested different living accommodations for the next year, though he added that he thought it "queer that, since it came off, you have never referred to your *debate* . . . nor did you send me a copy of yr. magazine article as you promised." It established a pattern that followed Wilson for the rest of his life: the direct correlation between his physical and emotional health. After a few months at Virginia, he tired of studying the law. "I think that it is the want of *variety* . . . that disgusts me," he wrote Charlie Talcott. "Law served with some of the lighter and spicier sauces of literature would no doubt be at all times to us of the profession an exceedingly palatable dish. But when one has nothing but Law, served in all its dryness . . . he tires of this uniformity of diet. This excellent thing, the Law, gets as monotonous as that other immortal article of food, *Hash*, when served with such endless frequency." At twenty-three, the weary student also confronted a new malady—he became lovesick.

After a virtually monastic existence at Davidson and Princeton, Wilson had fantasized about Charlottesville as the setting for his sexual initiation. "I'm still a poor lone laddie with no fair lassie," he had written Bobby Bridges before arriving on campus. "I'm reserving all my powers of charming for the Virginia girls, who are numerously represented around the University, I have heard. Do you think that Law and love will mix well?" Wilson had grown out of his undergraduate gawkiness into a fine-looking man, with strong features and a chivalrous manner. Raised by an adoring mother and two older sisters, he enjoyed not only the company of women but also the pleasure of playing to them. He ached to be in love.

Several of Wilson's cousins attended the Augusta Female Seminary in Staunton, his birthplace, a forty-mile train ride from Charlottesville. The school was run by Mary Baldwin, under whose name the seminary would eventually operate. At Princeton, Tommy had struck up a correspondence with one of those cousins, Harriet Augusta Woodrow—known as Hattie—the daughter of Thomas Woodrow in Chillicothe, the uncle for whom he was probably named. Hattie was no beauty, but she was vivacious and talented and religious. She excelled in French, and she displayed talent for singing and playing piano and organ. Throughout his first year of law school, Wilson took advantage of the proximity and spent holidays in Staunton, where his aunt's spare bedroom was always available. Over the next few months, he took the train into the Shenandoah Valley to spend weekends specifically with Hattie. And before he knew it, Tommy had fallen in love with his first cousin.

It was the first romance for either of them. Hattie kept him at bay, but her resistance only stimulated him further, nearly to the point of desperation. He bought her a beautiful edition of Longfellow, her favorite poet; and he whiled away hours just listening to her sing and play piano, requesting Mendelssohn's "Spring Song" over and over. After Hattie had performed at a concert at Miss Baldwin's, Tommy applauded exuberantly enough to embarrass her. He took to ditching class and missing trains back to school. He made unauthorized trips to Staunton, and he spent hours writing long letters to her. At last, the university reprimanded him. His parents approved of their son's romantic intentions but not at the cost of his education. As always, they defended him—his mother insisting the school's warnings were "wrong and cruel," while his father said, "You were foolish, not criminal. . . . Your head went agog."

Tommy granted himself the summer to loaf. A family party gathered, this time on a farm in Fort Lewis, close to the West Virginia border. He spent most of his time outdoors, rowing on a little stream; when the weather turned too hot, he stayed indoors, revising another piece on Congressional government and reading the speeches of Bright and Webster. In declaring this his last summer of boyhood, he officially bade goodbye to his first name, announcing to friends and family that Tommy was "unsuitable" for a grown man.

Woodrow Wilson returned to Charlottesville happy to be in new quarters for the year. His Spartan room at 31 West Range offered the convenience of being just a garden away from the law school and the novelty of being just up the row from No. 13, where Edgar Allan Poe had roomed as a student. But no sooner had he unpacked than he returned to his own midnights dreary, having "to plod out another long weary session" studying law. He tried to brighten his spirits by writing to Hattie, though his feelings toward her were confused, especially as she planned to move to Cincinnati to further her music studies.

Over the next few months, Woodrow never missed a class. While he had indulged in extensive extracurricular reading his first year—histories, books about oratory, and Shelley's poetry—the only book he checked out from the library his second autumn was on contracts. He tethered himself to the campus, diverting any excess energy into the Jefferson Society, where Providence delivered an unexpected windfall: William Cabell Bruce left Virginia to pursue his studies at the University of Maryland. At the first meeting of the Society that October, the membership unanimously elected Woodrow Wilson its president.

Within weeks, President Wilson introduced his first order of serious business, the "urgent necessity" of revising the Constitution and Bylaws of the Jefferson Society. Under his leadership, the new document was the first reworking of the rules in twenty years. But before his list of reforms could be voted upon, he withdrew from the university due to failing health. He had suffered from respiratory and gastric troubles since the semester began. His parents repeatedly suggested his dropping out, but Woodrow resisted. Just before Christmas, his father wrote at last "that the state of your health *absolutely* requires your return to us"; and, regardless of the college's willingness to refund any tuition, he urged his son simply to "*pack up and leave.*" He was home for the holidays.

"I will not return," Woodrow wrote Robert Bridges from Wilmington on the first day of 1881, "but will prosecute my studies here for the rest of the Winter, when I will settle upon a place to practice and plunge immediately into business. I will be able to study very satisfactorily alone, I am quite sure; for I have had enough guidance from skilled and competent guides to set me fairly in the right track." Mid-January his books arrived from Charlottesville, and he created a study for himself in his parents' home. He kept regular hours reading, writing editorials for the local newspaper, and tutoring his twelve-year-old brother in Latin. In spare moments, he returned to his father's pulpit to recite the great speeches of famous orators. While Wilson maintained a few literary and political correspondences with former schoolmates, he could not shake his cousin

Hattie from his thoughts. He resumed sending her long letters. She reciprocated, without realizing that he was, in fact, suing for her affection.

While suggesting his journey to Ohio that summer was a family visit, Woodrow left for Chillicothe with but one relative in mind. Cousin Hattie had invited him and their cousin Jessie Bones for a round of parties at the end of the social season, which he misinterpreted as a romantic signal. He worked in an uncle's law office, as a cover for his desire to spend time with Hattie, in whose parents' house he was staying. He eagerly agreed to attend the dances and picnics, even though he could not dance and dreaded making small talk. Then, in the middle of the third such event, he could contain himself no longer: he strode onto the dance floor and asked Hattie to leave with him so that they could speak alone. In the words of Hattie's daughter years later, "He told her how much he loved her, that he could not live without her, and pleaded with her to marry him right away."

Practically speechless, Hattie declined. She said it would not be right for them to marry because they were first cousins. Woodrow rebutted that he had already secured the blessing for such a union from both his parents and hers, the bloodlines notwithstanding. At last, Hattie uttered the long unspoken truth—that she simply did not love him the way he wished her to. Woodrow packed his bag and checked into a hotel. Unable to sleep, he dashed off a note on a scrap of yellow paper—imploring Hattie to reconsider the rejection and begging her to "give me the consolation of thinking, while waiting for the morning, that there is still one faint hope left to save me from the terror of despair."

They met again the next day, but Hattie's feelings had not changed. She told him that she "dearly loved him as a cousin and always would," but she had no intention of marrying him. She urged him to return to the house and continue his visit, but he could not bear to. Woodrow asked Hattie's brother to take him to the train station, where they encountered a man just arriving in Chillicothe for one of Hattie's parties. He expressed regret at Wilson's sudden departure; but Woodrow later commented, "If the sentiment was not merely formal, and it probably was, it was not genuine. If he had any feeling at seeing me go away, it was probably a feeling of relief at getting me out of the way." A few years later, Hattie would marry that man.

During a six-hour layover in Ashland, Kentucky, Wilson wrote Harriet—"My darling"—once more. In accepting her desire for him to withdraw, he made one delusional request. He wanted the local photographer to take a formal portrait of her, for which he would pay. Not only that, he specifically requested that she wear her pink dress with its modestly cut neckline and that she appear in profile. Furthermore, he instructed: "Let the picture include your figure to the waist; let your head be slightly bent forward and your eyes slightly downcast"; and he wanted her hair off her face, gently braided and piled high in the back. He insisted that he alone should possess the photograph. It took a week before Wilson reached Wilmington, and, after several nights of "sound and dreamless" sleep, he wrote Hattie again, with the realization that "my love for you has taken such a hold on me as to have become almost a part of myself, which no influences I can imagine can ever destroy or weaken." Hattie sent the photograph, almost exactly as directed; and then she ended her correspondence with her cousin.

He wandered lonely as a cloud. Woodrow visited more relatives in the South; he entertained an offer to teach at a preparatory school; he wrote pseudonymous letters to local newspapers; he deliberated over where to hang his law shingle. After considering several Northern cities, he settled on Atlanta, which he considered "the centre of the new life of the New South." He wrote Charlie Talcott—then launching his own legal career in New York—that Atlanta, "more than almost every other Southern city, offers all the advantages of business activity and enterprise." Since the war, its population had trebled to forty thousand, further strengthening his reasons for remaining in the South. "After standing still, under slavery, for half a century," he added, "she is now becoming roused . . . and waking to a new life." Perhaps he could do the same. At twenty-five, Wilson had never lived in a major city, and, except for the occasional token fee for an article, had never earned a dollar.

Outside forces nudged Wilson into motion. Upon the death of an uncle, his mother received a share of a legally entangled estate, the handling of which she turned over to Woodrow. Just as he was running out of excuses for taking a professional leap, he heard from a Virginia classmate with a business proposition. Edward I. Renick (a distant relative, in fact) wrote from Atlanta that he had recently secured very good office space there and offered to share it and its costs. After perseverating for several more months, Woodrow Wilson accepted the offer.

Atlanta was a boomtown, determined to become a center of industry as its population would double in the next decade. Edward Renick's second-floor corner office at 48 Marietta Street was opposite numerous government buildings; and Wilson's portion of the rent was less than seven dollars. Renick's living accommodations proved just as fortunate—a gracious house at 344 Peach Tree Street, in a fine residential neighborhood, where Mrs. J. Reid Boylston admitted a few boarders for twenty-five dollars a month and was able to take one more. Counting the ten dollars it would cost to supply his office and a forty-five-cent monthly shave and haircut—to trim his new full mustache and muttonchop sideburns (called "paddies")—Woodrow could live quite comfortably on the fifty-dollar allowance his father continued to provide.

Renick supplied most of the companionship he needed. Also the son of a minister, with roots in Virginia and Chillicothe, Renick was a student of the classics as well as the law. The two young attorneys spent hours reading the *Aeneid* to one another when they were not discussing the injustices of the protective tariff against the South. Within weeks, the office mates chose to become partners in business, their strengths complementing one another: Renick preferred the "office work" of the solicitor, while Wilson wished to play the barrister, arguing cases in court. He wrote Robert Bridges that Renick was "a perfect enthusiast in his profession."

Wilson was not. That very week he had told his parents that he was ready to close up shop—even before he had become a member of the Georgia Bar. "*All* beginnings are hard," his father wrote back, "whatever occupation is chosen:—but surely a fair beginning must be made before the real character of the thing begun can be determined. As it is your future is in the land of imagination, and imagination is used to color. Get your feet fully upon the ladder of actual practice—and then, sh'd the ascent prove intolerable, it will not be too late to see what other hill may be attempted. It is hardly like you, my brave boy, to show a white feather before the battle is well joined." Plainly more interested in the subject of the law than in its practice, Wilson never considered it anything more than a stepping stone. Unwilling to solicit business, he procured not a single client. He wrote political articles on the side and waited for clients to come to his door.

That fall a small opportunity knocked when Walter Hines Page dropped in on his friend Renick. Page had done undergraduate work at two Southern colleges before becoming one of the first twenty graduate fellows at Johns Hopkins University. A restless spirit, he dropped his studies to pursue a career in journalism. At twenty-seven, he was reporting for the New York *World*, just then researching a story on the Tariff Commission. Wilson impressed Page with his knowledge of that very subject; and with the Commission's hearing the next day at Atlanta's Kimball House, Page persuaded him to address the group.

While he had yet to appear before the local bar, Wilson had no reservations about standing before the city fathers and a national investigative committee, confident that he was better versed in the subject of tariffs than they. Convinced that the current tariff unfairly taxed the agricultural populations in the South and the West, Wilson scribbled some shorthand notes. He did not believe his comments would "make any impression on the asses of the Commission," but he felt they would at least make their way into the committee's printed report and attract attention.

The next day, the young attorney lectured the officials for half an hour. Walter Page accorded him several praiseworthy column inches, as did *The Atlanta Constitution*. While Page was still in Atlanta, a vitalized Wilson assembled a few like-minded friends in his office for further discussion of the issue. He even organized a discussion group he called the "Georgia House of Commons," for which, of course, he promptly drafted a constitution.

On October 18, 1882, Woodrow Wilson appeared before Judge George Hillyer in the Superior Court of Fulton County for his bar examination. The judge and four lawyers interrogated him for two hours on matters of the law, somewhat more severely than usual because of his recent notoriety. Hillyer would later assert that Wilson's performance was "not short of brilliant"; and when one of the attorneys posed an intentionally tricky question regarding "equity practice," Wilson pled ignorance—only to find the judge himself interceding to say, "Mr. Wilson needn't respond to that question. The Court himself could not answer it." His certificate to practice law in the Georgia state courts was dated October 19; and the following March, he was approved to practice in the federal courts as well. Being licensed did not affect the practice of Renick & Wilson in the least. "The fact of the matter is that the profession here is in a very disorganized state," Wilson wrote Heath Dabney in January 1883, "and young attorneys are unfairly out-bid by unscrupulous elders." He and Renick filed no cases in either the city court or the Superior Court, collecting only a few "minute fees" and "desperate claims."

For months, he had a wealth of time on his hands. He wrote political pieces, including a long-winded tract called "Government by Debate," which was an extension of his prior essays about reconfiguring the federal government. He visited the Georgia Senate gallery and watched what he considered a pitiful display of governance. The dearth of capable public officials made him think he might run for office, but he realized that he was still too new to the region to launch a campaign. Besides, he wrote Bridges on May 13, 1883, "no man can safely *enter* political life nowadays who has not an independent fortune, or at least independent means of support." He considered an offer to lecture at a local college for African American students. ("It may serve to bring you more into notice; and, if any fool object because the pupils are negroes, just let him object," his father counseled.) Wilson's constant dithering continued to affect his intestinal tract. His brother-in-law Dr. George Howe believed he was ailing from "liver torpor." Wilson's father accepted Woodrow's physical condition but suggested the real ailment he had to conquer was his "*mental* liver." He urged his son to choose a path and commit to it.

"What do I wish to become?" Wilson asked himself that May; and he responded: "I want to make myself *an outside force in politics.*" Toward that end, Wilson decided to forsake the law for something he loved. Heath Dabney had left America to study for a doctorate in Berlin, and it filled Wilson with envy. "I can never be happy unless I am enabled to lead an intellectual life," he realized; "and who can lead an intellectual life in ignorant Georgia?" In Atlanta, he said, "the chief end of man is certainly to make money, and money cannot be made except by the most vulgar methods. The studious man is pronounced unpractical and is suspected as a visionary." He applied to become a fellow at Johns Hopkins.

Worst of all, Wilson had made only a handful of casual friends. He showed some interest in his landlady's niece, but his courtship never got beyond the parlor, where he read aloud to her and taught her stenography. He was, as he would later recall, "absolutely *hungry for a sweetheart.*"

Nothing remained for him in Georgia except the final settlement of the William Woodrow estate, which was to be divided between Wilson's mother and her late sister's husband, James W. Bones. More than $35,000 worth of land in Nebraska was at stake. In order to hasten the process and maintain amity between the co-beneficiaries, Wilson chose to deal with his uncle in his hometown of Rome, Georgia, sixty miles away in the northwest corner of the state. Besides the pleasure of leaving the city for a few days, Woodrow would have a chance to visit with his uncle and cousin Jessie Bones—the little girl he had shot from the tree with an arrow in Augusta. She was now living in Rome with her new husband, Abraham T. H. Brower.

Built upon seven hills, Rome was a charming town situated at the confluence of three rivers. While he visited his cousin Jessie that Saturday, one of her neighbors stood on a porch and asked her friend, "Who is that fine-looking man?" The other replied that it was "Tommy Wilson." The next day, the unknowing object of their admiration attended the Presbyterian Church, where he noticed a young woman of luminous innocence. Even though she was wearing a veil, Woodrow could discern her "bright, pretty face," her "splendid, mischievous, laughing eyes." Or perhaps he saw what he wanted to see, for her eyes were somewhat wistful and dark brown. But she possessed, no doubt, an air of gaiety—a kindliness about her round cheeks and delicate mouth. She had burnished copper hair, parted in the middle and combed back almost to her shoulders, with curly bangs. After the service, Woodrow stole another glance in her direction and decided to seek an introduction. She was the minister's daughter, Ellen Louise Axson.

Her grandfather Isaac Stockton Keith Axson had served as a pastor in South Carolina and rural Georgia and as a president of two different Presbyterian female colleges before shepherding the flock who worshipped at the Independent Presbyterian Church in Savannah. Known in church circles as "the Great Axson," he had four children, including Ellen's father, Samuel Edward Axson, who became pastor at the First Presbyterian Church of Rome.

Axson had four children, twenty-one years apart, and his wife, the former Margaret Jane Hoyt, died weeks after her last baby's birth. Thus, at twenty-one, Ellen Louise became a mother to her siblings. Her father had periodically suffered from depression, and the death of his wife put Ellie Lou in the position of his caretaker as well, mistress of the manse. Family lore often spoke of happier days, when the Axsons had once visited the Wilsons in Augusta, and a very young Tommy Wilson had asked if he might hold the infant Ellen Axson in his lap.

It was not startling, then, for Woodrow Wilson to call on the Reverend Axson. "I *had* gone to see him," Wilson would later record, "for I love and respect him and would have gone to see him with alacrity if he had never had a daughter; but I had not gone to see him *alone*." Woodrow was unable to forget the face of the pretty girl in church, and he asked after his daughter's health. Axson summoned Ellen to the parlor, oblivious to the young man's intentions.

"I am quite conscious that young ladies generally find me . . . tiresome, and often vote me a terrible bore—and that I have not the compensating advantage of being well-favoured and fair to look upon," Woodrow would later write the woman standing before him. But in the right company, when he felt comfortable enough to be himself, he was perfectly capable of becoming "highly popular by making a fool of myself, making any and every diversion rather than [being] simply dull." He had pined for female companionship for so long, he had particularized the attributes he sought. As he would later explain, "I had longed to meet some woman of my own age who had acquired a genuine love for intellectual pursuits without becoming bookish, without losing her feminine charm; who had taken to the best literature from a natural, spontaneous taste for it, and not because she needed to make any artificial additions to her attractiveness; whose mind had been cultivated without being stiffened or made masculine . . . and I still thought that 'somewhere in the world must be' at least one woman approaching this ideal, though I had about given up expecting to make her acquaintance."

Woodrow quickly learned that Ellen was a gifted artist, having studied at the Rome Female College and privately with a graduate of New York's National Academy of Design. When she was eighteen, her portfolio won a bronze medal in a competition at the Paris International Exposition, which brought statewide fame and a number of commissions for portraits. Having arranged to take a few walks with her before returning to Atlanta, Wilson also discovered that she was more widely read than he, generally more cultured, and a forthright conversationalist. Woodrow fell in love.

Through May and June, he kept returning to Rome. Settling his uncle's estate was the pretext for all his visits, on which he was accompanied by his other new love—a No. 2 Caligraph from the American Writing Machine Company. Only a decade after typewriters had entered the American market, Wilson purchased this contraption—with its six rows of keys and capable of printing both upper- and lowercase letters—for a whopping

$87. It seemed like a sound investment for a man of letters eager to begin graduate school and a literary career. The machine served a more immediate purpose: once he typed the final Woodrow estate papers, he would be released from his legal occupation and free to return to his preoccupation—which, he revealed to his mother, was winning the hand of Ellen Louise Axson.

His courtship was tender but relentless, as quaint as the times and place. He called on Ellen with offers of buggy rides along the country roads, walks along the Oostanaula River, and boat rides where it met the Etowah and flowed into the Coosa. Jessie Brower planned a large picnic by a spring almost ten miles out of town and arranged to transport a party in a pair of wagons. For the ninety-minute ride down a winding dirt road, Woodrow and Ellen sat together in the back on a pile of wheat straw, their legs dangling side by side. While the others waded in the brook and unpacked the luncheon baskets, Woodrow and Ellen found a meadow of their own, where they looked for four-leaf clovers, blew fluffy dandelion tops, and pulled petals off flowers while chanting, "Loves me, loves me not." When Jessie inquired as to their whereabouts, a youngster among them said he saw Woodrow carving a heart on a beech tree.

Later that day, as they were sitting together in a hammock, Woodrow told Ellie Lou, "You were the only woman I had ever met to whom I felt that I could open all my thoughts." In truth, he meant much more than that, as he explained in a handwritten letter:

> I meant that I had begun to realize that you had an irresistible *claim* upon *all* that I had to give, of the treasures of my heart as well as of the stores of my mind. I had never dreamed before of meeting any woman who should with no effort on her part make herself mistress of all the forces of my natures.

As virginal as he, twenty-three-year-old Ellen could hardly entertain the romantic thoughts Woodrow espoused. To each of the many letters he wrote to "My dear Miss Ellie Lou," she responded reservedly to "Mr. Wilson." After all, she still had younger siblings to care for, to say nothing of her father, who exhibited alarming signs of mental illness.

With his law career completed—"Atlanta is behind me, the boats are

burnt, and all retreat is cut off," he jubilantly wrote Robert Bridges—
Wilson returned to North Carolina to help his family through a rough
patch. Disaffection between Dr. Wilson and his congregation in Wilmington was rising, which was affecting his health; and worse, his wife had
been stricken with typhoid fever. During the weeks before she showed
signs of convalescing, Woodrow spent nights bedside administering his
mother's medication. His only relief came in writing to Ellie Lou.

When his mother was well enough to travel, Woodrow accompanied
her to Columbia, to visit his sister and her family. After a few days, they
all went to Arden in the Great Smoky Mountains, outside Asheville,
North Carolina, where Wilson hoped to enjoy some time before starting
graduate school. In the meantime, Ellen visited friends in nearby Morgan-
ton. The two young lovers wrote to each other consistently, but their letters kept crossing in the mail. The second week of September, Ellen heard
from her father, who had fallen ill and summoned her home. The best
connection she could make required her laying over in Asheville for most
of Friday, September 14; and so she checked into the Eagle Hotel. That
very day Woodrow left his family in Arden to run errands in Asheville.

Roaming the streets, he passed the Eagle Hotel. Looking up to the
second floor, he noticed a young woman in the window and instantly recognized the coil of golden hair. It was Ellen. The flabbergasting improb-
ability of their meeting helped him convince her to remain in Asheville
another two days, as would he.

The next day, Woodrow took Ellen down the road to Arden to meet his
family. His mother was charmed, and she later told Woodrow that "it was
impossible not to love her." On Sunday, just before his departure for school,
he blurted all that he had been bottling inside for five months. He quoted
Bagehot, who had said that a bachelor was "an amateur at life," and that a
man who lived only for himself had not begun to "learn his use . . . in the
world." He asked Ellie Lou Axson to marry him, and she accepted. And for
the first time, they kissed.

Wilson boarded the train to Baltimore, where his father had come to
help him find accommodations. Dr. Wilson immediately discerned a
change in his son; and he said that he was already jealous of Ellen—"for
having so much of [Woodrow's] life, to the ousting of everything else."
Checking into a hotel, the young man composed a letter to Ellen's father,

officially informing him that he had "declared my love to her and been accepted." His only disappointment, as he told him, was that the engagement "must necessarily be prolonged, because my course here will cover two years and our marriage at the end of that period must depend upon my securing a professorship. These facts made me hesitate for some time about declaring my feelings to your daughter, because I felt that I should be selfish to ask her to engage herself to me when my prospects were so indefinite. But our almost providential meeting in Asheville upset my judgment, which is of so little force in such matters." The Reverend Axson sent his blessing. Jessie Wilson expressed her personal happiness, knowing at last that her son's "heart is at rest." Ellen told her brother Stockton she was going to marry "the greatest man in the world."

"What are we aiming at?" asked Daniel Coit Gilman in 1876 at his inauguration as the first president of the Johns Hopkins University. "The encouragement of research . . . and the advancement of individual scholars, who by their excellence will advance the sciences they pursue, and the society where they dwell." That accorded with Wilson's goals as he stated on September 18, 1883, in answering Question VI of the college application. "My purpose in coming to the University is to qualify myself for teaching the studies I wish to pursue, namely History and Political Science." Except to his fiancée, he kept his underlying motives to himself: "A professorship was the only feasible place for me, the only place that would afford leisure for reading and for original work, the only strictly literary berth with an income attached."

Johns Hopkins was a Quaker merchant who had invested in the Baltimore & Ohio Railroad and amassed a $7 million fortune, half of which he left for the establishment of a nonsectarian university in Baltimore. Founding president Gilman accepted his post with the understanding that he might build America's first research university—aiming to advance human knowledge as much as that of its students. It would employ "the German Method," a system of individual scientific investigation in pursuit of the truth. German higher education had long advocated the principle of *Lernfreiheit*, a freedom enjoyed by university students to pursue the subjects they wished to study, as they wished. Under a professor's supervision at a seminar table, they would present their findings to their peers.

Reluctantly Gilman opened the university doors to undergraduates. "There can be no question about this being the best place in America to study, because of its freedom and its almost unrivalled facilities, and because one can from here, better than from anywhere else in the country, command an appointment to a professorship," Wilson wrote Heath Dabney.

The university then consisted of a few remodeled buildings close to Baltimore's business district and the Peabody Institute, six magnificent stories of marble and wrought iron, its bookshelves holding sixty thousand volumes. With no dormitories, the 150 graduate students were left to secure their own lodging, an easy task in a city of 350,000—then the seventh largest in the country.

Wilson settled into a boardinghouse at No. 8 McCulloh Street, where he was surrounded by other university men. Forging no friendships there, he allowed homesickness and self-pity to stoke his work, as, for the first time in his life, he had a "sweetheart" to whom he could unburden himself. "I have never grown altogether reconciled to being away from those I love," he wrote Ellen on October 2, 1883; "and, my darling, my heart is filled to overflowing with gratitude and gladness because of the assurance that it now has a new love to lean upon—a love which will some day be the centre of a new home and the joy of a new home-life!" He poured practically every other waking minute into his scholarly reading and writing. Whether he addressed Ellen as Ellie, Nell, or ultimately Eileen, the torrent of his effusions followed one path: "I shall not begin to lead a complete life, my love, until you are my wife."

Wilson immersed himself in his work at Johns Hopkins. Three days a week, Herbert Baxter Adams, an Amherst graduate and one of America's first German-trained professional historians, taught a course in international relations; Richard Theodore Ely, educated at Columbia before doing graduate work at Heidelberg and becoming one of the founders of the American Economic Association, taught Advanced Political Economy; and once a week Dr. J. Franklin Jameson, also of Amherst and Hopkins itself, taught English constitutional history. Additionally, Adams offered a one-hour course in American colonial history.

The specialty of the department was Professor Adams's Seminary of Historical and Political Science. On Friday nights between eight and ten o'clock, faculty and graduate students gathered in a former biology building, which had become the repository for the archives of Johann Kaspar

Bluntschli, a professor of international law and Adams's mentor from Heidelberg. As the laboratory for the study of political science, the seminar room was also crowded with books and periodicals and maps and busts of such statesmen as Hamilton and Calhoun and Washington and Lincoln and Gladstone. From the end of a massive red table that could seat two dozen, Professor Adams presided over free-form discussions, which included students sharing their writings and ideas for group consideration and correction.

"The main idea here," Adams told his disciples, "is that it is a place where students lecture, and is distinguished from class in that there the instructors lecture." Each of the students was given a drawer in the seminar table; and a generation of significant American historians and economists pulled the first drafts of their works from that table. Periodically important guests speakers led discussions. Wilson briefly befriended a minister's son from North Carolina named Thomas R. Dixon, Jr., who remained only a few months before proceeding to careers in theater, government, the ministry, and literature. His most enduring work—a novel called *The Clansman*—would be based on a childhood memory of a Confederate soldier's widow who claimed a black man had raped her daughter, a crime that would be avenged by the Ku Klux Klan. Although a hotbed of political ideas, the seminar left Wilson strangely cold.

"There's something very rotten in this state of Denmark," he wrote Heath Dabney, who was enjoying an authentic experience in "the German Method" in Heidelberg. Wilson recognized the opportunities within the libraries and "stimulating atmosphere" of Johns Hopkins but questioned the level of instruction. He considered Adams a humbug—"superficial and insincere, no worker and a selfish schemer for self-advertisement and advancement"; Ely seemed "stuffed full of information" but without original thoughts; and Jameson, four years younger than Wilson, did little more than parrot Adams. In short order Wilson realized "that everything of progress comes from one's private reading—not from lectures; that professors can give you always copious bibliographies and sometimes inspiration or suggestion, but never learning."

Wilson created a college of one for himself. He had every intention of playing by the university rules, but after less than a month on campus, he asked his chairman if they might bend them. After tea on October 16, 1883, he told Professor Adams that he had "a hobby which I had been riding for some years with great entertainment and from which I was loath to dismount." Wilson's Constitutional studies were already of such consequence that Adams could see the value for both his student and the school. He released Wilson from much of the "institutional" assignments so that they would not interfere with his independent work. In so doing, Wilson reengaged in his Seminary work with new vitality. He became the keeper of the class minutes and the most powerful orator in the room. He was especially effective in a debate on the Blair bill, which intended to allocate millions of federal dollars to education in rural areas, largely for the purpose of improving Negro schooling. Wilson opposed the bill because such aid would be a deleterious incursion of federal power. Future educational reformer and Pragmatist John Dewey, then a Hopkins student, confronted his colleague's "vigorous attack" on the bill at the red table, but to little avail. He never forgot his table-mate's "eloquence" that day, nor his feeling that Wilson "could go far in politics if he wished."

Wilson did his most impressive work in private. Encamping day after day in a snug alcove of the seminar room or beneath the towering skylight of the Peabody, he read prodigiously and wrote profusely. In the fall of 1883, he delivered his first academic lecture, on the subject of Adam Smith. He invested three weeks of research and composition into this one-hour talk about government control of monopolies.

Wilson's greatest satisfaction came in writing *Congressional Government*, a book that grew out of one of his prior unpublished essays. As he wrote his fiancée, "I want to contribute to our literature what no American has ever contributed, studies in the philosophy of our institutions, not the abstract and occult, but the practical and suggestive, philosophy which is at the core of our governmental methods." In a series of connected essays, Wilson hoped to "treat the American constitution as Mr. Bagehot . . . has treated the English Constitution." Unlike his unpublished tract, this work would avoid advocacy of specific reforms. "I have abandoned the evangelical for the exegetical," he wrote Robert Bridges, which he thought would keep it from being nothing more than a political pamphlet. He worked on the book whenever possible, writing first in longhand and then incorporating his corrections while pecking at his Caligraph.

The book required little new research, as it was largely a collage of other people's ideas. Wilson wrote Heath Dabney that "its mission was to *stir* thought and to carry irresistible practical suggestion." He discussed, especially, a disequilibrium in American government despite the principles of checks and balances. "The President was compelled, as in the case of treaties," he wrote clairvoyantly, "to obtain the sanction of the Senate without being allowed any chance of consultation with it." Tellingly, he added, "He has no real presence in the Senate. His power does not extend beyond the most general suggestion. The Senate always has the last word." For the rest of his life, Wilson would question the efficacy of a government in which power rested in its legislative body while the Chief Executive was the only person elected by all the people. He believed "the prestige of the presidential office has declined with the character of the Presidents. And the character of the Presidents has declined as the perfection of selfish party tactics had advanced."

Wilson slaved from the time he entered Johns Hopkins until the day he left. A doctor friend who saw him feared he was verging on a breakdown. "I am working for big stakes," he wrote Ellen. "I am working for *you*, my darling; and the better my work the sooner you shall be won!" Beyond his long epistles of news, observations, and pining, the only respite Woodrow allowed himself was in joining the newly organized University Glee Club and the Hopkins Literary Society, for which, of course, he wrote a new constitution, rechristening it the Hopkins House of Commons. By the end of October, he had already overtaxed his eyes, which resulted in throbbing headaches. His health steadily worsened, as he remained in Baltimore and worked through the holidays.

It did not improve his mood when he learned that several others in his family were feeling even worse. At a time when his father should have been considering retirement, he began suffering from vertigo and was looking for work beyond Wilmington. At sixty-one he would soon be teaching at South-Western Presbyterian University in Clarksville, Tennessee. His mother continued to languish in malarial fever. "I have, it would seem, been given your love to be my stay and solace," Woodrow wrote Ellen. But she had her own sorrows to deal with, as her father's depression forced him to surrender his parish and move into his father's manse in Savannah. In January 1884, the Reverend Samuel Axson turned violent and was committed to the Georgia State Mental Hospital in Milledgeville.

Ellen joined the rest of her family in Savannah; and, while he could ill afford it, Woodrow scraped together enough money to take the train to Georgia. She spoke of having to break their engagement, but he would hear none of it. After a week together, Ellen realized how deeply in love she was. Woodrow had completely altered her mood, as his presence alone left her "strangely, deeply happy, with a new kind of happiness."

Wilson thought of dropping out of school. At age twenty-seven, he was eager to take responsibility for his life—to marry Ellen and support her younger siblings. His father ascertained that there were few teaching positions available, even fewer without the "signal endorsement" of Johns Hopkins. So Woodrow returned to the grind of graduate studies and his work on *Congressional Government*. Between January and March 1884, he wrote the first half of the book—its introduction and two essays on the House of Representatives. On April 4 he submitted the chapters to Houghton Mifflin in Boston for publication, with a proposition: "If you approve of the parts I send, and would publish the whole as a small volume . . . I shall set out upon the completion of the plan indicated as soon as possible." The publishers would not commit to an incomplete manuscript but wrote back assuring Wilson of their confidence in his ability to "produce an interesting and acceptable book." Wilson read most of the chapters he had finished to the Seminary and submitted them to the administration with his application for one of the university's twenty coveted fellowships.

The Hopkins semester for graduate students ended in late May; in bidding him goodbye, President Gilman informed Wilson that he was going to receive one of the two fellowships in his department—a stipend of $500 along with various academic privileges. He had not even told Ellen that he had applied, for fear of disappointing her had he failed. Now, it seemed, nothing could stop him from completing his book. On the very day that Woodrow reported his joyful news, the Reverend Samuel Edward Axson committed suicide.

For Ellen and Woodrow, the stars remained crossed most of that summer. Again she felt it best to break their engagement, while he thought he should leave school so they might marry at once. A job possibility appeared likely at Arkansas Industrial University in Fayetteville, and she spoke of teaching art in Atlanta. Each talked the other out of any such ideas. Then Woodrow asked if Ellen would visit him in Wilmington, which he could not leave, as his father was away and his mother was ill; Ellen suggested that her grandmother would not hear of such a visit, an unwed girl visiting her fiancé's family. In truth, Ellen had so many things on her mind, she could not focus on marriage. Her seventeen-year-old brother, Stockton, was exhibiting early signs of the mental illness that lay ahead, and her eight-year-old brother, Edward, had begun stuttering. Woodrow slumped into his predictable maladies, virtually unrelieved until news came that Ellen's grandmother had reversed herself about the visit to Wilmington. By summer's end, he had completed *Congressional Government*, having only to run the pages through his Caligraph.

Ellen's fortunes changed dramatically as well. With some money from her father, and her younger siblings in their grandparents' care, she pursued a long-deferred dream—enrolling at the Art Students League in New York City. After a two-week visit with the Wilsons, she and Woodrow cast discretion to the wind and traveled north together, as he insisted upon seeing her settled in Manhattan. They left Wilmington on October 1 and spent that night in separate rooms in a Washington hotel. The next day, they visited the Corcoran Gallery of Art before finding their berths on a sleeping car to New York. Upon arrival, Wilson escorted his bride-to-be to her home for the next year, a boardinghouse at 60 Clinton Place. He hated to leave her there—"in those dreary quarters amidst those horrid people"—but Ellen was too exhilarated by her upcoming year to notice the conditions. She took advantage of both the city's and her school's cultural offerings—visiting museums, theaters, and artists' studios, and taking classes in portraiture, life drawing, perspective, and classical sculpture. She proved herself a highly accomplished fine artist. She and Woodrow corresponded practically every day—long, lyrical letters. "There surely never lived a man with whom love was a more critical matter than it is with me!" he wrote.

Within a week of his return to Baltimore, Wilson mailed his completed manuscript to Houghton Mifflin; and six weeks later they offered him a contract, proposing the standard royalty of 10 percent on the retail price of all copies sold. That same day, Dr. Adams invited Wilson to his office to meet Martha Carey Thomas and James E. Rhoads, who were establishing an all-female college in Bryn Mawr, Pennsylvania. A year younger than Wilson, Miss Thomas was the founding dean of the institution, a daughter of a Johns Hopkins trustee and a formidable scholar in her own right—an alumna of Cornell University, Hopkins, and the University of Zurich, where she studied for her Ph.D. because no American university offered advanced degrees to women. Rhoads had trained as a medical doctor at the University of Pennsylvania but dedicated most of his life to education and philanthropy and was serving as the first president of Bryn Mawr College. Hoping to open in the fall, they were assembling a faculty; and Dr. Rhoads said he was pleased to learn from the interview that Wilson "believed that the hand of Providence was in all history; that the progress of Christianity was as great a factor as the development of philosophy and the sciences; and that wars were to be justified only by necessity."

Girls in the United States had traditionally received education in the home, but by the late eighteenth century, a number of female academies and seminaries had appeared in all corners of the country, evolving into colleges, institutions where women might study the liberal arts and find educational opportunities equal to those afforded men. By the mid-1800s, a number of coeducational colleges had opened—mostly in the Midwest and West: such institutions as Oberlin, the University of Iowa, Carleton, and Stanford. By 1885, there were almost a hundred women's colleges in America, including Mount Holyoke, Vassar, Wellesley, Smith, and Radcliffe. The suggestion that a job at Bryn Mawr would be waiting for Wilson upon the completion of his second year at Hopkins was encouraging, but teaching at an all-female college—one yet to open—required further consideration. Wags were already referring to the new school as "the Johanna Hopkins."

Ellen appreciated the Bryn Mawr offer but could not resist asking, "Do you think there *is* much reputation, to be made in a *girls school* . . . ? Can you be content to serve in that sort of an institution?" Woodrow said, "The question of the higher education of women is certain to be settled in the affirmative, in this country at least, whether my sympathy be enlisted or not." He wrote Heath Dabney that the great advantages to his accepting the position were in "its situation in the midst of the most cultivated portion of the country and the freedom of method, the comparatively limited number of topics to teach, and the comparatively small number of hours per week in teaching them, that will be given each instructor." He assured Ellen that he would much rather teach men, but he thought "good literary work will be much more noticed . . . in the North than in the South." When the school raised its offer from $1,200 per year to $1,500, Wilson accepted a two-year contract. He realized that there simply was no better job available to a graduate student without any teaching experience.

On January 23, 1885, six weeks after receiving his first batch of proofs,

Wilson received two finished copies of his book, *Congressional Government*, a small but impressive blue volume of 333 pages. He immediately mailed one to Ellen, saying, "Everything in the book . . . was written as if to you, with thoughts of what you would think of it." The dedication, however, was to the author's father—"THE PATIENT GUIDE OF HIS YOUTH, THE GRACIOUS COMPANION OF HIS MANHOOD, HIS BEST INSTRUCTOR AND MOST LENIENT CRITIC."

"Never," responded Dr. Wilson, "have I felt such a blow of love. Shall I confess it?—I wept and sobbed in the stir of the glad pain." He read the book more than once, admiring it and gloating over it. From then on, he told his wife, he expected to be referred to as Woodrow Wilson's father. Critical reaction was national and generally favorable, as the book was pronounced "masterly" and "important" and likened to Bagehot's *English Constitution*. His Hopkins classmate Albert Shaw reviewed the book for the *Minneapolis Daily Tribune* and called it "the best critical writing on the American constitution which has appeared since the 'Federalist' papers." The book sold its initial one thousand copies almost immediately, and smaller successive runs were ordered annually over the next fifteen years. New job offers presented themselves, including one from the University of Michigan. His family wondered if he could not get out of the Bryn Mawr contract; but in the end Dr. Wilson advised against it, further suggesting that a year or two at the new college would not be time lost. Woodrow corresponded with Dr. Rhoads about places where he and his new bride might live.

Before starting at Johns Hopkins, Wilson had considered a Ph.D. his meal ticket in academia; now that he had become an overnight sensation in academic circles and had a teaching contract, he questioned the need to cram for countless hours in order to receive a certificate. He also had grave doubts about his ability to master German, as the requirements demanded. He knew that the degree would increase his value in the marketplace, but he knew his mental and physical health would be heavily taxed by "a forced march through fourteen thousand pages of dry reading." Friends challenged his thinking, but Wilson insisted, "I know what I am about."

By the first of June, the betrothed couple left their respective schools for the South, each spending a few weeks among family. "What a sweet preparation we have had for our wedding day!" Woodrow wrote from Columbia on the twenty-first. "How *precious* the experience of these months of our engagement has been! It has brought us to a point where to marry is the only logical, natural, consistent thing we *could* do—hasn't it, darling? To wait longer *now* would be only to torture ourselves." In the common parlance of the day, Woodrow would consistently refer to Ellen as his "little wife," but he intended it more as a term of endearment than diminution, as, ironically, he would most often become the infantilized partner in the relationship, the needy boy seeking a mother's comforting hand. Two days later, the Wilson family arrived in Savannah.

Tacitly, the bride and groom each placed an offering upon the wedding altar. Ellen had decided to abandon serious pursuit of her art. Knowing Woodrow would consider that too great a sacrifice, she assured him that her rather one-track disposition demanded it. "As compared with the privilege of loving and serving you and the blessedness of being loved by you, the praise and admiration of all the world and generations yet unborn would be lighter than vanity. If *now* I held such *greatness* in my hand I should toss it away without a second thought that the hand might be free to clasp in yours."

Woodrow's offering could be found tucked away in a few sentences amid the hundreds of epistles to each other, a private confession only to her. "I do feel a very real regret that I have been shut out from my heart's *first*—primary—ambition and purpose, which was, to take an active, if possible a leading, part in public life, and strike out for myself, if I had the ability, a *statesman's* career. That is my heart's—or, rather, my *mind's*— deepest secret, little lady." His priorities had shifted, and he said he would now content himself interpreting great thoughts to the world. "I should be complete if I could inspire a great movement of opinion," he wrote, "if I could read the experiences of the past into the practical life of the men of to-day and so communicate the thought to the minds of the great mass of the people as to impel them to great political achievement."

Only in that letter to Ellen in 1885, could Woodrow admit that he possessed one thing that he did not have when he first dreamed about a career as a statesman and orator—"that one priceless, inestimable thing," he said, "is *your love*, my Eileen!"

In the evening of Wednesday, June 24, 1885, Woodrow Wilson married Ellen Louise Axson at her grandfather's residence. The large manse, behind the Independent Presbyterian Church, featured a stately parlor with a high ceiling and arched windows and a fireplace, before which Woodrow and

Ellen stood, as the Reverends I. S. K. Axson and Joseph Wilson performed the ceremony before their many relatives. The bride wore a simple white dress, which she had sewn; the groom, a dark suit. All the women cried at the sheer beauty of the ceremony and the couple's obvious joy.

The newlyweds hied to Arden, North Carolina, the hamlet outside Asheville, where they enjoyed a seven-week idyll in a small vine-covered cottage surrounded by a pine forest. "We are out of doors most of the time, walking together and reading, unless I coerce him into singing, for he has a beautiful voice," Ellen wrote her cousin Mary Hoyt. Then they left for New York to see Wilson's parents, who were visiting from Tennessee. By the time Professor and Mrs. Wilson boarded the train for their new lives in Pennsylvania, Ellen was two months pregnant.

In the seventeenth century, William Penn sold much of the land west of Philadelphia to Welsh Quakers; but it was another two hundred years before the extension of the Main Line of the Pennsylvania Railroad encouraged wealthy city dwellers to build estates in the twenty small communities that dotted the countryside west of the Schuylkill River. Bryn Mawr—Welsh for "big hill"—sat in the middle of the Main Line towns, ten miles from the city. The first buildings of its new college were an easy walk from the train depot—Merion Hall, a dormitory, and Taylor Hall, an administration-classroom building, complete with a library, an assembly room, and a campanile. The Victorian Gothic buildings, as yet without landscaping, were massive and stark, looking as though they intended to remain on the campus forever.

The same could not be said of the Wilsons. They arrived in September 1885 with no intention of staying. They moved into one of three frame houses on the periphery of the campus: M. Carey Thomas's was called the "Deanery"; a second wooden house, with its view of the sylvan setting, was called the "Greenery"; and the newlyweds moved into the house in the middle, which was filled with other faculty members and called the "Betweenery." After a season of negotiating, Wilson was able to secure its two best rooms plus board for nineteen dollars a month. The second room was an extravagance, which Woodrow hoped Ellen would consider her study as much as his—for there he "would most need sympathy."

On a stormy September 23, Bryn Mawr College held its inauguration ceremonies in Taylor Hall. The three dozen young women who formed the Class of 1889 and five graduate "fellows" sat in the front rows of the assembly hall; on the platform before them sat President Rhoads and Dean Thomas along with the school's trustees and the faculty, fourteen strong—only a handful, like Wilson, without doctorates. Special guests that day included the presidents of such nearby colleges as Swarthmore and Haverford as well as Dr. Gilman from Johns Hopkins. In fact, this new Quaker institution was still the only place in the United States where a woman could earn a doctorate. Dr. Rhoads told the crowd, "All discussion of the question whether women ought to share equally with men facilities for mental culture in its highest forms is obsolete"—an observation then more wishful than accurate. But nobody questioned the words of the featured speaker that day, poet and diplomat James Russell Lowell, who said, "The object of education is to make men and women of culture."

Economics, politics, and history—departments that would dominate most liberal arts campuses a century later—were seldom found in course catalogues in the 1800s, especially at schools for women. Those disciplines were all combined into one department at Bryn Mawr, under Wilson's direction. He had eight advisees, almost a quarter of the entering class. His only lecture course was in ancient history; but before teaching the early civilizations, Wilson offered the young women four general lectures on the discipline of history. He urged his students not to "learn history" but to "learn *from* history"—by arousing "genuine living interest in the subjects of study." Toward that end, he asked his students to "look into ancient times as if they were our own times, and into our own times as if they were not our own. Suppose that you had yourself wished to thrust Pericles from power, or that Socrates were the grandfather of your collegemate." He urged them to use their imaginations in studying ancient civilizations, as he did in teaching them. From the start, he brought novelty to the traditional curriculum: instead of teaching a semester on the Greeks and then one on the Romans, he bounced between civilizations each week, emphasizing outstanding individuals in Greek society and deathless principles of law in the Roman.

A natural teacher, Wilson forbade his students from taking notes during the first half of the class hour, so that they would not just listen but also consider the general ideas he presented—the broad strokes of that day's story and the players within. Then he would dictate to the class, in perfect outline form, the facts and details that fleshed out the concepts. "He always entered the classroom smiling and animated and always in a good humour," remembered one of his students. "His lectures were fascinating and held me spellbound; each was an almost perfect little essay in itself, well rounded and with a distinct literary style." With his long, silky mustache, he was the most dashing man on campus.

The three women who became Wilson's graduate fellows over the next few years got a closer look at him, and they sensed—for all his Southern gentility—a malcontent. The first student was an abolitionist minister's daughter from Massachusetts, Wilson's age, and already a dean and professor at Northwestern University; she found him patronizing and told a future Wilson biographer that it was a new experience for her "to meet a Southerner who had no special sympathy for Negroes as human beings." Wilson's second "fellow," Lucy Salmon, was even older, a high school teacher with a master's degree; she sat through her tutorials, often listening to him read lectures as though he were auditioning material. He found his third graduate student "exhausting," simply devoid of challenging stimulation that he felt men offered more readily.

"I'm *tired* of carrying female Fellows on my shoulders!" he told Ellen. "When I think of you, my little wife, I love this 'College for Women,' because *you* are a woman; but when I think only of myself, I hate the place very cordially." In short order, the ladies of Bryn Mawr felt as much. The astute Miss Salmon believed these feelings reflected less about where Woodrow Wilson was in his career than where he was not. She was struck by his "extreme personal ambition." More than once she heard him say that "if our system had been like that of England he would have gone into public life."

Wilson decided to publish, to keep from perishing—financially and emotionally. Living on his skimpy salary, with a child on the way, he composed several articles on "administration" and "the art of governing." None would be published as written, but most would reappear in future lectures, books, or speeches. In early spring 1886, he began outlining a textbook in civil government, a work that began as a grammar school text and would mature over the next few years into his most comprehensive volume on government, *The State*.

He never neglected his duties at Bryn Mawr. From the Deanery, Carey Thomas often saw Wilson's light burning through the night, as he

designed a two-year course of study for history and political science majors
and fellows—all of which he was meant to teach—including courses in
American and French history, the Italian Renaissance, and the German
Reformation. Notes for his American history lectures would become the
core of another future book, *Division and Reunion*. For his second-year graduate courses, he composed fifty lectures on "The History, Functions and
Organs of Government." Everything would get recycled.

Throughout this frustrating period, Ellen remained an emotional pil-
lar, despite an uncomfortable pregnancy in the close confines of the Betweenery. She was never above cleaning and mending; but because no
proper Southern lady had been allowed to prepare a meal, she had never
learned how. She now took it upon herself to go into Philadelphia twice a
week to take cooking lessons from Mrs. Sarah Tyson Rorer, one of America's first home economists and dieticians. Seeing that even "domestic science" had become a competitive field, she believed her husband's lack of a
doctorate might hinder him in the future.

At her urging, Woodrow wrote Professor Adams at Johns Hopkins on
April 2, 1886, about completing the requirements for his degree, asking
for some special consideration now that he was no longer a student. Adams
replied that there would be no chance of a degree without examination and
just as little chance that Wilson would fail. Adams would conduct the
three-hour written test in History (covering the fields Wilson was then
teaching), and Ely would read the Political Economy exam, with assurances that the candidate had already qualified. Then the Hopkins professors would subject Wilson to his oral examination, with Adams already
assuring him, *"You will pass that ordeal very easily."* Hopkins agreed to let
Wilson's *Congressional Government* stand as his dissertation, and his lack of
proficiency in German would be ignored. After much discussion, Woodrow and Ellen came to the decision that he would spend the balance of the
spring alone in Bryn Mawr, free to prepare for his examinations, while she
would await the birth of their child in Gainesville, Georgia, attended by
her mother's sister, who lived in a big house with servants and who had
become, in fact, the guardian of Ellen's baby sister.

On April 15, 1886, several weeks before her due date, Wilson escorted
his wife as far as Washington, D.C., where she changed trains at the station, which was then on the National Mall. For the first time, he explored
the city. He visited his former law partner, Edward Renick, then working

at the Treasury Department. In the afternoon, he visited the United States Capitol. With the Senate in Executive Session, he observed the House of Representatives in action. He looked in on the Supreme Court before returning to the station to catch his train back to Philadelphia. Ellen reached Georgia that night and—unexpectedly—gave birth at 11:30 the next morning. Her aunt commented that she did not even groan during her labor, but instead cried only once and insisted the tears came not from the pain "but for Woodrow." The girl would be named Margaret Axson, for Ellen's late mother.

Wilson busied himself every moment he was separated from his wife and child. He finished his teaching for the school year; he studied for his forthcoming examinations at Johns Hopkins; and he visited his publishers in Boston, where he met Abbott Lawrence Lowell, who had criticized Wilson's *Congressional Government* in *The Atlantic Monthly.* Lowell would long remember the appearance in his office of "a tall, lantern-jawed young man, just my age. He greeted me with the words: 'I'm Woodrow Wilson. I've come to heal a quarrel, not to make one.'" With that, a friendship began, one that would mature as Lowell abandoned the law for education, eventually becoming Harvard's president. On May 29, Wilson could write Ellen from Baltimore, "Hurrah—a thousand times hurrah—*I'm through*—the degree is actually secured."

Mid-June, Dr. Woodrow Wilson met his daughter and wife in Georgia. For several joyous weeks, they remained there surrounded by Axsons, including Ellen's brother Stockton, nineteen and suffering from nervous maladies that temporarily kept him from attending college. Strolling leisurely with Wilson along the railway track to a nearby summer resort, the bright young man received his first lessons in Burke and Bagehot. He also saw for the first time the extent to which indigestion and severe headaches afflicted his brother-in-law and how closely related were Wilson's physical and mental indisposition. Stockton was startled to learn of his secret dream, as "Brother Woodrow" revealed that he "would dearly love a seat in the United States Senate but believed that his academic profession had permanently sidetracked him from active politics."

The Wilsons left Gainesville for Clarksville, where baby Margaret met her paternal grandparents. Both were in a state of decline—Woodrow's father professionally, his mother physically. By the time Woodrow and Ellen returned to their cramped quarters in Pennsylvania, Wilson was determined to leave the Betweenery, if not Bryn Mawr itself. In a bold but desperate moment, he even sought a position in Washington, when he saw there was an opening as an Assistant Secretary of State. While his application attracted little attention, such universities as Cornell, Indiana, and Michigan inquired about his availability, as did the Peabody Normal Institute in Nashville, which was then looking for a chancellor and willing almost to double his Bryn Mawr salary.

For many years Wilson would contemplate a magnum opus, a "history of government in all the civilized States in the world," which he was calling *The Philosophy of Politics*. As an étude in preparation for that work, he labored over what he called a "dull fact book," *The State*, which he had contracted with D. C. Heath & Company to write and which would be a comprehensive description of the governments of all nations. The most relevant research material on the subject was, in fact, written in German, which Wilson never mastered. With a dictionary close by, he could translate those texts, but the process was so slow that Ellen took it upon herself to learn the language, so that she could rock the cradle with one hand and write translations with the other. In order to improve his foreign language skills and to get a better sense of *"the modern world"*—away from Bryn Mawr—Wilson thought of taking his wife and child abroad for a year. But just as he was assessing the financial feasibility, Ellen became pregnant again, with the baby due that summer. When his second year of teaching ended, the Wilsons returned to Gainesville, where, on August 28, 1887, their second child was born—another daughter, whom they named after Woodrow's mother.

Back in Bryn Mawr, the family moved into the ramshackle eleven-room Baptist parsonage on Gulph Road, which the local minister did not use. The elder Jessie Wilson had questioned the sense of her son's renting such a large place; but it spawned a new aspect of Woodrow's character—the role of the patriarch. Although he and Ellen would always live modestly, pinching pennies at that, they would never again live by themselves. Woodrow, long dependent on his father's financial support, stepped up at last to the responsibilities of caring for the next generation of Wilsons and Axsons.

The role assumed added significance on April 15, 1888, when Janet "Jessie" Woodrow Wilson died in Clarksville. She had fallen two years prior and never recovered. Transportation and communication being what they were, by the time Woodrow reached Clarksville, his father and brother had left for Columbia, where she was buried in the churchyard. "My mother was a mother to me in the fullest, sweetest sense of the word," he wrote Heath Dabney, "and her loss has left me with a sad, oppressive sense of having somehow suddenly *lost my youth*. I feel old and responsibility-ridden."

The small inheritance from Samuel Axson's estate helped, and so did earnings that trickled in from Woodrow's various writings and lectures. Chief among them was a $500 stipend he earned from an extramural position, lecturing at Johns Hopkins. In the fall of 1886, the president of Cornell had invited Wilson to speak before his Historical and Political Science Association. Recognizing that such appearances served as tryouts for future jobs, he gladly accepted. With a Civil Service system expanding as rapidly as the nation itself, administrative science was becoming a viable branch of political science, a discipline in which Wilson had become expert. He built his paper, "The Study of Administration," around a concept of co-operative government, with local, state, and federal governments remaining independent but working interdependently. Months later, Johns Hopkins invited Wilson to prepare a series of twenty-five lectures over the course of a semester on comparative administrative law. In the spring of 1888, he began to deliver the series, as he would over the next decade.

Meanwhile, Wilson looked for loopholes in his renewed Bryn Mawr contract—which raised his salary to $2,000 per annum for the next three years and stipulated that "he shall have an assistant." Above that clause, Dr. Rhoads had inserted the words "as soon as practicable." After another year had passed and no assistant appeared, Wilson declared that the contract had been breached, for—as he told Bridges—"that was the condition upon which I signed." The Trustees of the College resorted to some unfriendly persuasion, suggesting the law was on their side; but Rhoads informed Dean Thomas that Wilson's attorney felt otherwise. In July 1888, the board acquiesced, and Rhoads gave Wilson the benefit of the doubt as to the reasons for his sudden departure. He expressed his warm personal regards and the "expectation that a most useful career lies before you." Martha Carey Thomas, however, long bore a grudge.

In truth, an attractive contract elsewhere awaited Wilson's signature. He wished it had come from Princeton, but he had recently bungled an opportunity to obtain a position there. Leading alumnus Moses Taylor Pyne had invited Wilson to address the New York Alumni Association's annual dinner at Delmonico's. It was a rah-rah occasion for 250, full of cigar smoke and spirits, college songs, and President McCosh's brief remarks about the school's recent progress. After that, Wilson was to speak for a few minutes about government and education. Desperate to showcase his erudition, Wilson chose as his topic "the scholar in politics." His address was thoughtful and lyrical and completely out of place—twenty minutes that felt like an hour. Many in the audience either ignored him or laughed at him. By the time he finished, he had cleared much of the hall with the worst speech of his life. It kept Princeton from calling for years. Wesleyan University in Connecticut, on the other hand, had recently pursued him, with an offer of $2,500, plus a six-week leave of absence so that he could continue to deliver his lectures at Johns Hopkins. The timing could not have been better. "I have for a long time been hungry," he wrote Bridges in August 1888, "for a class of *men*."

In September 1888, Woodrow and Ellen Wilson moved their family to Middletown, a red-brick New England village on the western bank of the Connecticut River. In 1831 the town had helped several Methodist preachers establish a college there, in the name of their movement's founder, John Wesley. A progressive institution, Wesleyan University reflected many of Methodism's social-minded tenets but always remained nonsectarian, a school for the liberal arts, not theological training. The college encouraged independent study and research and was in the middle of a forty-year "experiment" with coeducation.

The Wilsons unexpectedly found the Wesleyan community a model of Northern hospitality. Their house at 106 High Street—a stone's throw from the campus—had a backyard for the children and a view of the river. After living in five cities in the nine years since he had left Princeton, the young professor had at last found a place where he could light.

Wilson quickly made friends, starting with the Reverend Dr. A. W. Hazen of the Congregational Church. He also found several lively young minds on the faculty, especially Caleb T. Winchester, a Wesleyan alumnus and an English literature scholar. Wilson admired him enough to encourage Ellen's brother Stockton to move to Middletown so that he might study under Winchester. Wilson became addicted to lawn tennis and the two professors played whenever time and weather permitted.

Teaching only upperclassmen, Wilson entitled his primary course

Histories of England and France. It amounted to sixty lectures that traced Western Europe since the fall of Rome. He taught a second course in political economy. For both, he was able to draw upon his Bryn Mawr lectures. He used the notes he had taken for *The State* in his other courses in the history of institutions and the United States Constitution. With his passion for oratory renewed and a wealth of material at hand, Wilson became a first-rate teacher, inspired by his motivated students as much as by his colleagues. "He had a contagious interest—his eyes flashed," one former Wesleyan student recalled. "I can see him now with his hands forward, the tips of his fingers just touching the table, his face earnest and animated, many times illuminating an otherwise dry and tedious subject by his beautiful language and his apt way of putting things."

His mode of pedagogy evolved from a monologue to a Socratic dialogue as the school year progressed. In the beginning of each course, he lectured for the most part, painting the background and affixing a frame. Stockton Axson took two of his brother-in-law's classes and observed firsthand that "he had the great art of quizzing students, of drawing them out by degrees, and of leading them to show what it was they did not understand in the text. He would clarify their own rudimentary notions."

He led his students to understand that the American Constitution, for example, was "not merely a document written down on paper but is a living and organic thing, which, like all living organisms, grows and adapts itself to the circumstances of its environment." He helped a class composed mostly of Northerners understand that only a generation prior, the statesmen of the South had been strict constructionists, looking so microscopically at the Constitution that they failed to realize that the world around it had expanded and changed. "The northern boys began to see that the southern statesmen were absolutely honest in their contention that the Constitution gave them the right to secede, and the very few southern boys . . . began to see that the northern statesmen had a larger vision of a greater United States than had been perceived when the colonies formed themselves into a Union." Wilson would speak frankly as a Southerner about the "War of the Rebellion" and how he believed "in the matter of secession the South was absolutely right from the point of view of a lawyer, though quite wrong from the point of view of a statesman." Watching her husband adapt so readily to Connecticut, Ellen Wilson came to understand his identity. "You are an American citizen—of Southern birth," she told him. "I *do* believe you love the South, darling. . . . I believe you are her *greatest* son in this generation and also the one who will have greatest claim on her gratitude. . . . You *are* free from 'provincialisms' of *any* sort."

The instant contentment Wilson found at Wesleyan quelled his political desires. He would never "stand before the Senate," he would say, suppressing his governmental ambitions; and he began dedicating himself to a new purpose, finding that he "could inspire young men to go into politics and become the kind of leader he would have liked to be." Toward that end, he breathed life into a gasping debating society. And, as in his undergraduate days, Professor Wilson trotted all his college spirit onto the playing field. He got elected to the Advisory Board of the Wesleyan football team and once again coached and provided plays. The home team played a crucial game against Lehigh on Thanksgiving Day 1889, in rain and mud. Once Lehigh scored two touchdowns, Wesleyan seemed too dispirited to compete further . . . until, as one witness remembered, a man rose from the Wesleyan bleachers and stepped in front of the small crowd, wearing heavy rubber boots and a raincoat. He excoriated the Wesleyan fans for abandoning the team and exhorted them to join him in the school yell, beating out the charge with his umbrella and maintaining his cheers until the team had turned the score around. Evidently, this history professor, who now wore a pince-nez, could rally crowds and motivate troops.

As Wilson's presence grew on campus, so too did his extramural reputation. He continued to deliver his lectures at Johns Hopkins—where one of his admiring students was a brilliant young historian named Frederick Jackson Turner, who would soon become the nation's leading interpreter of the frontier in antebellum America. Wilson was regularly invited to speak at other colleges, at historical conventions, and in Middletown on commemorative occasions. And he finished writing *The State: Historical and Practical Politics* in June 1889, with copies in hand by fall—seven hundred pages detailing all forms of government, from the earliest formation of families to Socialism and the modern industrial organization. This volume, he always believed, had sprung from a genuine need—as "no textbook of like scope and purpose has hitherto been attempted."

Wilson dedicated the book to "His Wife, whose affectionate sympathy and appreciative interest have so greatly lightened the labor of preparing" it. While it revealed a prodigious amount of research and some occasional paragraphs of lyrical interpretation, the author himself knew its limitations. "A *fact* book is always a plebeian among books, and it is a fact book," he wrote Heath Dabney, then teaching history at Virginia; "but a great deal has gone out of me into it, none the less, and I hope you will receive it kindly on that account." Frederick Turner, just starting his distinguished career at the University of Wisconsin, wrote his former professor that he was "much pleased" with the book and intended to adopt it in his courses. Harvard did as well, with other colleges following suit. *The Nation* noted, "The work has been very well done. . . . The style is clear, and there is a certain vivacity in the narrative portions of the text that relieves the dryness of the theme." The book would be reprinted many times during Wilson's life.

With a higher salary than he had at Bryn Mawr and several sources of miscellaneous income, Wilson's domestic life flourished on High Street. They continued to stretch their dollars; but, as one of his children would later recall, "Ellen and Woodrow always remembered their two years at Wesleyan as among the happiest in their lives." And then, on October 22, 1889, she gave birth to their third daughter within four years of marriage. The Reverend Joseph Wilson wrote his son outright that he had hoped for a boy, "but the divine Father who has events in His own hand, moulds all things for the best." Woodrow insisted the baby be named after her mother; Ellen suggested a variation. And so, she was named Eleanor, and called Nellie or Nell.

None of Ellen's pregnancies had been easy, and the postpartum months were no better. Depression always hovered, along with memories of her mother's death after her sister's birth. A doctor in New York uncovered possible kidney damage incurred during this last pregnancy. And then, two months after Nellie's birth, Ellen spilled a kettle of boiling lard onto her feet, which forced her to remain in bed for the better part of the next five months. The many relatives assisted with domestic chores, but Woodrow himself waited on his wife, supervised the household, and even bathed his babies. He had never enjoyed such a long stretch of good health.

"The *boyish* feeling that I have so long had and cherished is giving place consciously, to another feeling," Woodrow wrote Ellen that year, "—the feeling that I am no longer young . . . and that I need no longer hesitate . . . to assert myself and my opinions in the presence of and against the selves and opinions of old men, 'my elders.' It may be all imagination, but these are the facts of consciousness at the present moment in one

Woodrow Wilson—always a slow fellow in mental development—long a child, longer a diffident youth, now at last, perhaps, becoming a self-confident (mayhap a self-assertive) man."

With *The State* behind him, Wilson received a tempting offer from Harvard's Albert Bushnell Hart, who was the leader in the budding field of American historiography. He was editing a three-volume series to be called the Epochs of American History, and he hoped Wilson—the Yankee professor from the Confederacy—would write the third volume. It would chronicle the nation from 1829 almost to the present and would be titled *Division and Reunion*. Hart reminded Wilson of the dearth of textbooks in this field and that departments of history were sprouting everywhere. Upon publication of the proposed sixty-five thousand words in the fall of the following year, Wilson would receive $500.

As his wife had suggested, Wilson believed he was uniquely prepared for the job, "the very man who can impartially review the scenes of our American story" during those sixty crucial years. But as attractive as he found the proposition, Wilson declined, citing the strain of overwork: "With my nervous disposition," he feared, "if I were to suspend over myself the whip of a contract . . . my health would, I am afraid . . . desert me at the critical moment." Once told he could have all the time he would need, Wilson signed on to the project. He enlisted the aid of Frederick Turner, hoping to continue the dialogue they had begun in Baltimore about "the growth of the national idea, and of nationality, in our history, and our agreement that the role of the west in this development was a very great, a leading, role."

For all the pleasures of Middletown, Wilson remained as restless as he had been since leaving Princeton on his graduation day in 1879. Realizing his disquiet, several of his friends—chiefly Robert Bridges—had been lobbying members of the Princeton faculty and administration on his behalf. Upon the death of a political economy professor, McCosh's successor, Francis Landey Patton, thought the time had arrived to create a School of Political Science, one that Wilson might head. The two men met to discuss the position, though it was not Patton's to offer. Several old Princeton trustees objected to Wilson—for being Southern and for failing to give enough credit to Christianity and Divine Providence in *The State*. Furthermore, Wilson himself was not sure he could even accept an offer. Wesleyan had been too generous for him to leave the school "in the lurch"; he still had his teaching obligations to Johns Hopkins; and he did not especially want to teach political economy. Patton waited for the dissent to die down; and on the thirteenth of February, 1890, the Princeton trustees elected Woodrow Wilson to the chair of Jurisprudence and Political Economy—at a salary of $3,000, with the promise that within two years, political economy would be separated from the department and Wilson would have to teach only within the field of public law.

After ten years adrift—two graduate schools, a brief law career, teaching on three college campuses, two books, a marriage and three daughters—Woodrow Wilson was right back where he had started, and no closer to his long-hidden desire. But the scholar-gipsy had decided, at last, to settle. His political fever—the Senatorial dream—had broken, though anybody who has ever been so afflicted could have told him that the virus never dies.

Such was the case with William Cabell Bruce, Wilson's debating and literary rival back in Charlottesville, the one whose transfer had allowed Wilson to become president of the Jefferson Society. In Maryland, Bruce followed Wilson's road map to the letter—graduating from the state law school, establishing a practice, serving in the state legislature, and writing on the side. In the end, he won a Pulitzer Prize and Maryland sent him to the United States Senate.

As for Woodrow Wilson—the Princeton offer was lower than he had hoped, especially when Wesleyan said it would raise his salary to $3,500. Williams College even entered the bidding. Then Patton agreed to let Wilson continue lecturing at Johns Hopkins. In March 1890, on his way back to Middletown from his six-week course in Baltimore, Wilson stopped in New Jersey—to look for a house.

5

REFORMATION

*And bee not conformed to this world: but be ye
transformed by the renuing of your minde . . .*

—ROMANS, XII:2

For the second time in his life, Woodrow Wilson would
find himself at Princeton.

The College of New Jersey, as it was still officially
known, had grown in the eleven years since Tommy Wilson's graduation, though more in size than in stature. Enrollment had climbed from 475 to 650 students, and the
faculty had practically doubled to forty. President James
McCosh had long hoped Princeton could be recognized as
a full-fledged university—as Harvard, Yale, Pennsylvania,
and Johns Hopkins had been—with all the status that suggested. "True," he granted upon retiring in 1888, "we have
not medicine or law, but professional schools are not necessary to a university which is a place of learning and not of
the practical arts." In truth, Princeton's own Board of
Trustees held it back, its reactionary members wishing to
preserve the college's parochial nature.

Bermuda-born Francis Landey Patton was a conservative cleric, the twelfth consecutive Presbyterian minister
to lead the college since its founding. His inaugural address tried to appeal to all factions of the Princeton community while offending none. He praised the liberal arts

and academic freedom but expressed the need for more conventional religious values. He discussed "the relation of the university to the problem of
the world's improvement"—suggesting that Princeton might serve beyond
its gates—but he also described it as "an intellectual retreat," an ivory
tower.

For all his intelligence, Patton was lazy and laissez-faire, making him,
in the words of one of his faculty members, "a wonderfully poor administrator." Without a progressive academic agenda—and a leader to advance
it—a college campus slips into narcosis, or worse. Even though a distinguished professoriate offered quality education to aspiring scholars, Princeton in the Gilded Age became a playground for sons of the wealthy.
Princeton's student body came almost exclusively from private preparatory
schools, whose graduates arrived on campus in cliques. The lack of amusements in the isolated country town spawned extravagant extracurricular
activities, and intramural spirit grew fervent. A snobby system of eating
clubs—mansions on Prospect Avenue, just off campus—gained importance among not only undergraduates but also alumni who sought weekend retreats. The architect of a Morgan heir's Princeton manor house, for
example, would design the Ivy Club; wealthy alumni hired McKim, Mead,
and White to erect the University Cottage Club next door, complete with
tennis court. A prodigious undergraduate named Booth Tarkington
started the Triangle Club, which would write and perform original musical plays that would tour the country for the amusement of spirited graduates. Above all, athletics came to dominate campus culture, with sports
news filling half the pages of the *Princetonian*. Football boasted a thirteen-
game schedule, each contest routinely drawing a crowd in the tens of thousands. And President Patton preferred the old policies to the new,
tampering little with the curriculum. He reputedly claimed that he ran
the finest country club in America.

In September 1890, the Wilsons moved into a roomy wood-framed rental
at 48 Steadman Street (soon renamed Library Place), a half mile from
Nassau Hall. It was always a full house. Woodrow's father was spending
more of his time in the North, often keeping company with a widow in
New York City, and gradually extending his visits to Princeton; Ellen's
two brothers and their sister all made the place their home, as did the

family of Wilson's widowed sister, Annie, and his cousin Helen Bones, a student at local Evelyn College, a women's school that lasted ten years without fulfilling its dream of affiliating with Princeton.

Wilson ripped into his new job with undergraduate zeal. He stocked the college catalogue with an astonishing array of eight courses in jurisprudence and political economy, two each semester over the next two years. They were all designed for upperclassmen, and a few were open to graduate students. The courses ranged from public law—"its historical derivation, its practical sanctions, its typical outward forms, its evidence as to the nature of the state and as to the character and scope of political sovereignty"—to studies of political economy and administration. Some courses allowed him to reuse his lectures from his prior teaching, while others required fresh research and composition. All were meant to contribute to his long-imagined *Philosophy of Politics* and to his goal of establishing a school of law at Princeton. By his second year, Wilson was able to shed his classes in economics, teaching only courses that he liked—Mondays and Tuesdays, four hours a week, at eleven and five.

From the start, his students put him to the test. "Back in those days a custom was in vogue among the underclassmen to find out just how 'easy' each 'new prof.' was," recalled one alumnus from the 1890s. One morning, just as Wilson was about to speak, a local drunk rose from one of the seats and created a scene. Wilson asked the man what he was doing there, and the sot replied, "The students invited me in." Grabbing the man by his collar, Wilson said, "I'll invite you out again," as he showed him downstairs, returning to lecture as though the incident had never occurred. From then on, the students were his.

After five years of teaching, he had become a compelling lecturer. He spoke from a rostrum, dictating his major points at the top of the class so that the students could write down the basic precepts. Then he teased out an hour's lecture, weaving anecdotes with opinions, and tying everything together with vivid descriptions of relevant historical events. Periodically, he interjected a stanza of an appropriate poem into the lecture. One former student who would become a colleague said, "I consider Wilson the greatest class-room lecturer I ever have heard. . . . Wilson held his students spell-bound, and at the close of a lecture they would often cheer him, not for the purpose of bootlicking, but because they just could not help it." Where most professors were addressing a score of students at most, Wilson found himself with as many as two hundred students in one class, many of whom dropped in merely to hear him speak. By his second year, the university had to move his lectures to the chapel to accommodate the crowds. As Booth Tarkington observed, "We did not see any rigidity in him. I saw in him only an agreeable, supremely intelligent human being—wise—kind—but a fellow human being. He *looked happy*. His eyes were bright. . . . He seemed to be a person getting what he wanted out of life."

And as he had as an undergraduate, Wilson worked his way to the epicenter of student activities. Barely a month on campus and Wilson was appointed to the Committee on the Senior Class, which defended and acquitted several students on disciplinary matters. He coached undergraduate orators and judged the Lynde Debate. He refereed the Caledonian Games, an interclass competition in track-and-field events; he coached the football team and served on the faculty committee on outdoor sports, urging the formation of new teams wherever possible. A member of the Graduate Advisory Committee of the University Athletic Association, he even sat on a committee to arrange for the restoration of billiard tables. Cap and Gown, one of the new eating clubs, elected him an honorary member. He invited students to drop by his house for informal gatherings; and the undergraduates annually voted Wilson the most popular professor at Princeton. His reach did not end there.

The junior faculty boasted dazzling young scholars in every field, including several contemporaries who were also Princeton alumni—among them Henry B. Fine, Class of 1880, whom colleague Oswald Veblen called the man who put "American mathematics" on the map, and Henry Fairfield Osborn, Class of 1877, a geologist and paleontologist who would soon leave to head the American Museum of Natural History. They concurred with literature scholar Bliss Perry, who discovered upon his arrival that it was "admitted without question then in Princeton that Wilson was the most brilliant man among the younger faculty. He led us inevitably by his wit, his incisive questioning mind, his courage, and his preeminence in faculty debates." Joining every faculty committee offered, Wilson began to influence his senior colleagues and the administration, fixing whatever he thought was broken.

The academic slackness on campus troubled him most, especially the problem of cheating. Students copying off one another's papers had become common practice; and in the waning fashion of the day, men wore

removable celluloid cuffs, on which they could sneak a synthesis of a semester's notes into the examination room. Even more than Woodrow, Ellen Wilson was appalled by such behavior, especially because "there were
so many southern lads who were supposed to have higher notions of honor."
She took it upon herself to raise the subject with a number of the young
men who visited the house, and Woodrow advocated the code he had
known at Virginia for dealing with the problem. Because he believed
heavier surveillance would only encourage greater stealth, Wilson supported an honor system, under which nobody would proctor exams other
than the students themselves, each of whom would pledge his honor as a
gentleman on each test paper itself that he had neither given nor received
aid. Furthermore, the faculty would not sit in judgment of violators; a
student committee would. The plan was ultimately presented at a meeting
of the faculty, which divided largely along generational lines. Bliss Perry
remembered one old-school representative mocking the notion of gentlemanly honor, which Wilson rebutted with enough passion and eloquence
to sway the vote and the direction of the college, as "it was a distinct triumph for the young faculty members who had begun to win an occasional
majority vote in the faculty meetings for the first time."

The pleasures of life in Princeton escalated, especially with the arrival
that year of a fellow alumnus five years Wilson's junior. John Grier Hibben was the son of a Presbyterian minister—of Scottish and Scotch-Irish
descent—who had been the president and valedictorian of the Class of
1882. A dapper Illinoisan with a thick chevron mustache and a pince-nez,
studious and pious, he had pursued graduate work for a year in Berlin
before returning to the Princeton Theological Seminary. Although he was
ordained, a throat condition thwarted a career in the pulpit; and so, in
1891, while pursuing graduate study in philosophy, he became an instructor. Two years later, he received his Ph.D., and two years after that an assistant professorship. Wilson instantly found himself enjoying the most
intense friendship he had ever known.

They saw each other daily, often more than once. "John Grier Hibben
learnt his every thought and ambition," wrote another friend of Wilson's.
"I have talked with Jack Hibben," Wilson would say, "and I am refreshed."
The two men were so happy together, Ellen could but delight in their
closeness. Along with Bliss Perry and their respective wives, the two men
met regularly for tea, often during the week and almost always on

Sundays, during which time Perry found Wilson was "always at his best"—though he displayed a tendency to appear "more interested in what he was saying than in what you were saying; but perhaps this is only like a skillful golfer playing against you who is more intent upon his own shots than upon yours." Ellen said that Hibben became the friend Woodrow "took to his bosom."

Although Wilson also enjoyed playing tennis, riding his bicycle for both its physical and practical benefits, and playing billiards at the Nassau Club, where he was one of the local sharks, nothing fulfilled him more than his family life. He doted upon his daughters, playing silly games with them when they were very young, and reading poems to them as they aged. "Father had a certain spontaneous gaiety, a delicious sense of fun and mischief," Nell later recalled, "and though mother was quiet and took no active part in this, insisting that she was not 'gamesome,' she was the perfect audience for him." A "deep happy peace," said Nell, "permeated the household," with its ever-changing stream of relatives. "So much laughter and teasing and warm friendliness." The children's favorite moments came each evening, after prayers, when the lights had been dimmed and their father would sit in the nursery by the fire and sing lullabies and gentle hymns.

Ellen remained the center of his life. She oversaw the house's redecoration, she tended the garden, and she sewed the children's clothes. She even managed to find a few hours alone, during which she continued to dabble at an easel. She homeschooled the girls in history and literature; and even when they could barely read, they questioned who was greater—Shakespeare or Homer, Milton or Dante? Every Sunday afternoon, Ellen instructed the girls in the Bible, teaching them the Shorter Catechism until they could recite it by heart, for which she rewarded each with her own Bible.

Woodrow considered Ellen an ideal wife, a woman who nurtured without overindulging. In everything he read and wrote, Wilson told a Virginia classmate, "Mrs. Wilson is in all senses my literary partner." In time, he came to consider her even more than that—"simply my critic and mentor" and muse. "I am madly in love with you," he wrote her in February 1895. "I live upon your love,—would die if I could not win and hold your admiration: the homage of your mind as well as your heart." She could argue the large points of philosophy and politics with him one moment and spot a misplaced comma in one of his manuscripts the next.

And after ten years of marriage, their ardor had only intensified. They still corresponded daily whenever they were apart, letters replete with such sentiments as those he expressed in February 1894, when he was delivering his lecture series at Johns Hopkins. "When you get me back you'll smother me, will you, my sweet little lover?" he wrote from his boardinghouse in Baltimore. "And what will I be doing all the while—simply submitting to be smothered? . . . Are you prepared for the storm of love making with which you will be assailed?"

The years of Wilson's professorship at Princeton constituted the most prodigious literary period of his life, as he became a virtual cottage industry. In addition to his classes there and at Hopkins, he agreed to write and deliver a ten-lecture series on constitutional law at the New York Law School, an institution on lower Broadway, which overnight became the second-largest law school in the country. (The school attracted a number of accomplished teachers and attorneys, including Charles Evans Hughes.) On top of that, Wilson published more than two dozen lengthy historical, political, or literary pieces, often in *The Atlantic Monthly,* with dozens of book reviews scattered in other periodicals. Publishers printed several more of his long essays in book form. He also wrote a biography, a five-volume history, and, at last, his historical account of the United States between 1829 and 1889, *Division and Reunion.*

Wilson had signed his contract for *Division and Reunion* in 1889 while at Wesleyan but did not begin the book in earnest until 1891, his first winter at Princeton. It divided that sixty-year period of American history into five parts—thirteen chapters composed of 148 sections, which began with the inauguration of Andrew Jackson as President and concluded with the explosion of unprecedented wealth in the country—"seldom seen since the ancient days of Eastern luxury or Roman plunder." Wilson believed this gave the nation new impetus and identity and suggested that "the century closed with a sense of preparation, a new seriousness, and a new hope."

Division and Reunion remains a model of simplicity and clarity; and though it was intended as a textbook, it lacked neither drama nor original insights, especially in discussing the ramifications of slavery. Among other things, Wilson offered his lucid discussion of the different ways in which the North and South interpreted the Constitution. For the rest of his analysis of this "period of misunderstanding and of passion," Wilson said he could not claim to have "judged rightly in all cases as between parties," but he did claim "impartiality of judgment."

Published in March 1893 in the small format of the rest of the Epochs of American History series—326 pages, with five foldout maps in color, all for $1.25—it was promptly adopted in courses taught at major universities, favorably reviewed, and repeatedly reprinted. Theodore Roosevelt, then a Civil Service Commissioner and author, praised the book in the *Educational Journal*. Historian Frederic Bancroft lauded Wilson's precision of expression, writing, "No one has ever said so much about this epoch in so few words." Frederick Jackson Turner said, "Some of the chapters are destined to live with the classics of our literature and history." Should Wilson embark upon a full-scale study of the nation's past, he believed it would be "*the* American history of our time."

In fact, Wilson had already broken ground on such a project, a massive work that would become *A History of the American People*. It would be almost a decade in the making, as he had to write it piecemeal. By the spring of 1895, he shelved five hundred pages when the editor of *Harper's Magazine* commissioned him to write six biographical essays on George Washington, pieces that would appear serially and then be reprinted in book form. The book contract offered a 15 percent royalty on top of the magazine fee.

During this fecund period, Wilson also delivered scores of speeches, usually on nonpartisan political themes. His reputation as an orator spread along the Eastern Seaboard, and then moved west—to Ohio and Chicago and Colorado Springs, where he delivered a highly regarded series of lectures on political science at Colorado College's summer school. The trip west, especially, had expanded his horizons in ways he had not anticipated, opening his mind to the vastness of the country and its grandeur. The journey across "the most stupendous scenery I ever imagined" also made him realize that he had a deep need to widen his public—"such is your husband," he confessed to Ellen, "—hungry—*too* hungry—for reputation and influence."

Princeton hoped to exploit Wilson's growing renown. In his first five years back on campus, the school recruited him more than a dozen times to address alumni associations. More often than Wilson wished, President Patton would drop out of an engagement, knowing he could dispatch Wilson as his emissary. "He is a rum President, to be sure!" Woodrow wrote

Ellen in January 1894, on one such occasion. "And I, as usual, must make the speech for the college! I am getting very tired of this. It may be an honour; but it looks very much like being made a convenience of." Even worse, it became an inconvenience, as he had a greater need just then for all the honoraria he could collect.

Ever since they had married, Woodrow and Ellen had dreamed of building their own house. In October 1894 they paid $3,000 (with one-third down) for the half acre next door to their rental on Library Place, which was bordered by meadows and surrounded by pines and oaks, with a huge sycamore on one side and a sprawling copper beech in the back. After imagining the house for so long, Woodrow could draw it in detail. Ellen actually sculpted a small clay maquette, which they presented to E. S. Child, a young New York architect.

The Tudor Revival—as designed in the half-timber and half-stucco style that had become popular in town—fell within Wilson's budget of $7,000. With walls two feet thick, it offered seven bedrooms and three bathrooms. Fifty-nine diamond-patterned leaded windows complemented the diagonal timbers of the house's façade. Apart from the capacious living and dining rooms, Wilson's study was the most private chamber in the house. Whenever its connecting door was closed, Nell Wilson recalled, "no one must disturb him and everyone must speak softly." Ellen provided its finishing touches by placing atop the bookcases pictures she had drawn of Gladstone, Bagehot, Burke, Webster, and the Reverend Joseph Wilson.

The house featured two novel elements that especially reflected the owner's wishes. The most unusual was a sleeping porch, purportedly the only one in Princeton—a logical addition from a Southerner who had experienced the torpor of New Jersey summers. The second was a large foyer just beyond the vestibule—a library, in fact, a large wainscoted square room, with bookshelves and stained-glass pocket doors at the rear, which separated it from the dining room. Wilson intended to use this space for occasional seminars, with students sitting around a square table in the center. At the end of February 1896, the Wilsons moved in, the family kneeling together that night, while Woodrow's father prayed for a blessing on the house.

Even as building costs mounted to almost $12,000, the Wilsons stayed the course. Dr. Wilson lent them $2,000; and reckoning Ellen's power of economy alongside Woodrow's industry, they cut few corners—investing

$800 in the best cesspool system available, refusing to delete a ground-floor porch, and paying the extra $74 on the decorative shades to cover their windows. As a result, they got their dream house. But, Ellen said, "All who have any use whatever of tongue or pen are seized upon." Woodrow had supplemented his salary each year at Princeton by earning $1,500 through his outside activities. During the year of construction, he reaped an additional $4,000. The extra income, Ellen noted, carried a heavy tax, as her husband "almost killed himself doing it!"

While writing a letter in 1891, Wilson had complained of difficulty in holding his pen. He thought little of it until late May 1896, when pain shot down his right arm, his hand froze, and some of his fingers became numb. He was alarmed enough to consult a doctor in Philadelphia. The physician, probably not fully apprised of the professional and financial pressures under which Wilson had been toiling, dismissed the condition as "writer's cramp." Looking back on Wilson's medical history with a century of hindsight and knowledge, later experts would presume an occlusion of his left middle cerebral artery. In other words: Woodrow Wilson had evidently suffered a small stroke.

The doctor recommended giving Wilson's hand, if not his entire body, a long recess. As it happened, that very remedy had been in the works. A wealthy and generous neighbor had taken a shine to the Wilsons and had recently asked if they might accept a gift from her—a trip to England at her expense. Woodrow naturally refused; Ellen only partially rejected the idea, insisting that she would not leave the children but that her husband must make the journey. "I am counting so much on the sea voyage, and after that on the mental refreshment, the *rest* without ennui, the complete change from all the trains of thought that have been making such exhausting demands upon you for so long," Ellen told Woodrow. "I simply *can't* have you give it up, darling."

Jack Hibben helped plan the trip and accompanied his friend to New York harbor on May 30, 1896, as Wilson boarded the S.S. *Ethiopia* for Glasgow. The crossing took twelve days and its tedium alone proved tonic. His writing hand rested completely, as his ambidexterity allowed him to take up a pencil with his left. By the time he landed, his arm hardly troubled him. For nine weeks he explored Scotland and England by train and bicycle, transforming the holiday into a pilgrimage. After touring Glasgow and Edinburgh, he wended south, stopping in Alloway to visit

the birthplace of Robert Burns before pedaling on to Carlisle. While sorry
not to find either his grandfather's house or church, simply inhaling the
Caledonian air, he said, was "exhilarating and entertaining." And any disappointments paled the next day when he cycled into Cumbria—the Lake
District. In Grasmere he found Wordsworth's church, grave, and onetime
home, Dove Cottage. Then Wilson rode to Rydal Mount, the poet's primary residence. Because it was not open to the public, he approached a
nearby wall and plucked a tiny flower as a keepsake, which he sent to Ellen. "I don't know how I shall ever describe what I am seeing," he wrote
her. "One who knew nothing of the memories and the poems associated
with these places might well bless the fortune that brought him to a region so complete, so various, so romantic, so irresistable [*sic*] in its beauty,—
where the very houses seem suggested by Nature and built to add to her
charm." His reverie lingered as he journeyed into Shakespeare country,
highlighted by his visit to Anne Hathaway's cottage in Stratford.

The literary stops were but the prelude to his visit in early July to Oxford, which took his "heart by storm." He toured Magdalen College and
looked into several others. In each instance, Wilson marveled at the quadrangles, as he saw the effect a college's architecture could impose upon the
education within. Although Wilson said he had not seen a "prettier dwelling" in England than his in Princeton, he wrote Ellen that if there were a
position for him at Oxford, America "would see me again only to sell the
house and fetch you and the children." Wilson's aches and maladies
subsided.

Except for Walter Bagehot's birthplace and gravesite in Langport, Som-
erset, the rest of Wilson's trip was anticlimactic. London was the greatest
letdown, not for its lack of attractions but because it only reinforced Wilson's aversion to big cities. None of the remaining stops on his itinerary—
Beaconsfield (where he visited Edmund Burke's grave), Tring, High
Wycombe, Chester, Shrewsbury, Dover, Canterbury, Lincoln, Durham,
and the towns of Derbyshire—was as satisfying as his hours spent cycling
alone on the open roads. By August 24, Wilson was back in Scotland,
where he wrote Ellen that his long absence had only drawn him closer to
her, that he was coming to her "like a lover to whom has been revealed the
full beauty and sanctity of love,—with new devotion, new joy, new passion." Three days later, he boarded the S.S. *Anchoria* in Glasgow for
New York.

· · · ·

Wilson returned to the most massive display of school spirit Princeton had ever experienced. For two years, the College of New Jersey had been planning its 150th anniversary celebration—the Sesquicentennial—and the festivities in October 1896 drew scholars and dignitaries from all over the country and Europe. More alumni flocked to Princeton than had ever "gone back" to Nassau Hall at one time.

The three-day celebration began on Tuesday the twentieth with the trustees and professors proceeding from the Marquand Chapel to Alexander Hall, the newest building on campus. It was a rough-stoned but fanciful Romanesque edifice, an ornate assembly hall that was something between a chapel and a castle, with its rose window, elaborate arches, and conical-capped turrets. Its pews could accommodate the 1,500 who were admitted that day for the religious service, welcoming speeches, and concert, which included Brahms's *Academic Festival Overture*.

On Wednesday, the academicians in full regalia convened at the chapel and marched to Alexander Hall. The autumn foliage held its own among all the bunting and banners—orange and black draped alongside red, white, and blue. Months earlier, Professor Andrew Fleming West, the organizer of the Sesquicentennial, had asked Wilson—as both the official spokesman for Whig Hall and the most illustrious speaker on campus— to deliver the academic centerpiece of the jubilee. Fully revived, though not completely recovered, he titled his address "Princeton in the Nation's Service."

Composing the eight-thousand-word speech had been an ordeal. Wilson pounded out as much as he could on his Hammond typewriter with only his left hand. When that proved too onerous, he recruited Ellen and others to take dictation and type. None who heard the speech that day would suspect Wilson had experienced anything but joy in its making.

"We pause to look back upon our past today, not as an old man grown reminiscent," Wilson told the packed crowd, "but as a prudent man still in his youth and lusty prime and at the threshold of new tasks." After summoning the spirit of John Knox, he spent the first half of his address summarizing the early history of both the college and the country, explaining how the earliest presidents of the college had paved the way for Witherspoon, many of whose disciples had helped establish the United

States. That first hour merely prefaced the points Wilson wished to make about the future, how "not all change is progress" and that they were perpetually running the "risk of newness."

In an age of accelerating science, Wilson offered an admonition. "I have no laboratory but the world of books and men in which I live," he said, "but I am much mistaken if the scientific spirit of the age is not doing us a great disservice, working in us a certain great degeneracy. Science has bred in us a spirit of experiment and a contempt for the past. It has made us credulous of quick improvement, hopeful of discovering panaceas, confident of success in every new thing." Wilson sought no suppression of science. Instead, he said, "We must make the humanities human again; must recall what manner of men we are; must turn back once more to the region of practicable ideals." In short, he explained, "I believe that the catholic study of the world's literature as a record of spirit is the right preparation for leadership in the world's affairs, if you undertake it like a man and not like a pedant."

His speech expressed the need for Princeton to participate in public affairs, as he warned against universities becoming detached annexes of research, training scholars only in knowledge of the present. A decade before George Santayana would speak of those who would be doomed to repeat history, Wilson said, "The world's memory must be kept alive, or we shall never see an end of its old mistakes."

While composing the speech, Wilson had felt like a "mountebank," failing to provide a definitive statement of purpose. As he did with all his writing, he had read it to Ellen, who offered praise but also criticism. "It does not end well," she said. "It ends too abruptly. It needs something to lift it and to lift your audience up to the highest plane of vision." She suggested a finale like that of Milton's *Areopagitica*, a few soaring sentences in which the themes of his speech would all rise and meet.

Woodrow knew at once what she meant, and he composed a long final paragraph: "Of course, when all is said, it is not learning but the spirit of service that will give a college place in the public annals of the nation," he said. "It is indispensable, it seems to me, if it is to do its right service, that the air of affairs should be admitted to all its class rooms." He described a place of remove, where Science and Literature each had a place, where "windows open straight upon the street, where many stand and talk intent upon the world of men and business. A place where ideals are kept in heart in an air they can breathe; but no fool's paradise. A place where to hear the truth about the past and hold debate about the affairs of the present, with knowledge and without passion." The impassioned speech closed with a simple question: "Who shall show us the way to this place?"

The audience exploded into applause. Those closest to Wilson embraced him; some wept. Ellen wrote her cousin Mary Hoyt, "It was the most brilliant, *dazzling*, success from first to last. And *such* an ovation as Woodrow received! I never imagined anything like it"—especially as it came from what was being called the most distinguished gathering of minds ever to have assembled in America. Professor Edward Dowden of Dublin's Trinity College said the speech was worthy of Burke.

The rest of the day was given to sport and celebration, with Princeton trouncing the University of Virginia in football—48 to 0. Beneath a full moon that night, undergraduates amassed behind Nassau Hall and then marched for a mile through the town—eight hundred strong, each carrying a torch or lantern emitting orange light. Two thousand alumni, in class sections going back to 1839, fell in behind, each in costume— Professor Wilson among them. "He loved parades," said his daughter Nell, who saw him take part in many. The revelers ended in front of the campus, where Chinese lanterns floated overhead and Nassau Hall glowed from thousands of orange electric lights that outlined the building and its windows all the way up to the crown of the cupola. And there in the reviewing stand, with the university hierarchs, stood the President of the United States himself, Grover Cleveland, just months away from completing his second term. The night ended with fireworks.

The next day, fifty-eight honorary degrees were conferred; President Cleveland delivered an address calling upon educated men to engage in public affairs; and, in the third year of a severe economic depression, President Patton announced that the school had raised $1.35 million for a new dormitory, a library, and several professorships. Finally, he announced that "what heretofore for one hundred fifty years has been known as the College of New Jersey shall in all future time be known as Princeton University."

The school proposed an ambitious agenda of educational expansion— certainly a graduate school and probably a law school. Patton, however, revealed himself incapable of fostering such innovations, which only encouraged others to fill the vacuum in leadership. Professor West, for example, had shown that he could attract talent and produce results. President Cleveland was so entranced by his Princeton experience, he would move to town the following spring. With the assistance of his new friend West, he purchased a colonial mansion, which he even named "Westland." After the campus had quieted, however, only one voice from the Sesquicentennial resonated. *The New York Times* devoted most of an entire column on page 2 to the remarks of Woodrow Wilson.

In charting its fresh course, the new university would adopt his phrase "Princeton in the Nation's Service" as its motto. Over the next few years, however, Wilson would reveal the speech's personal subtext, as it had actually been an exercise in self-exhortation. Only two months shy of forty, the college professor reexamined his own goals. He returned to his former schedule—teaching and writing and lecturing with even more intensity than before. Stockton Axson, whom he had encouraged to become an English professor, observed that Woodrow had become more purposeful, "with less time to sit down for prolonged talks in the old, easy, gossiping way. He was just as companionable as ever, but he was like a man who had things to attend to and could not spend the hours in rambling talk which I had so much enjoyed." He used the time to infuse public lectures on theories of government with personal statements of his current beliefs.

The Presidential election of 1896 was a watershed in American politics, coming after the United States had experienced five controversial elections since 1872. In that period, two men lost the popular vote but won the Presidency; and in the other three elections, third-party candidates kept the victors from achieving majorities. The main issue in 1896 was the depressed economy, and the voters had a clear choice. The most stirring Populist voice of his generation, the "silver-tongued" William Jennings Bryan, argued against retaining the gold standard and became the Democratic nominee for President. "Gold Democrats"—such as Grover Cleveland—formed the National Democratic Party. The Republicans ran Governor William McKinley of Ohio; arguing that "free silver" would create inflation, not jobs, he gained the support of big business, ethnic labor, and urban voters. For the first time in twenty-four years, the American people spoke decisively, handing McKinley an imposing popular and electoral victory. Wilson voted as a Gold Democrat.

The consolidation of businesses into monopolies, the raising of protective tariffs, and the blocking of immigration marked McKinley's first term. So did America's emergence onto the world stage. Invoking the Monroe Doctrine, the new administration argued for Cuba's liberation from Spain and sent the USS *Maine* into Havana harbor in early 1898 to show that America meant business. Upon its sinking—which the yellow journalists of the day attributed to a Spanish attack—the United States found itself in a four-month military conflict against Spain, a battle that would put her colonies up for grabs. Assistant Secretary of the Navy Theodore Roosevelt helped organize a volunteer troop of "Rough Riders" to fight in the Cuban theater. Saber rattling accompanied America's flag-waving, and the United States won what Ambassador John Hay called a "splendid little war," the spoils of which included a small empire—Cuba, Guam, Puerto Rico, and the Philippines.

Delivering a commencement address at the University School of Bridgeport in the middle of the Spanish-American War that spring, Wilson said, "The general mass of men like to be led by men strong in deed, and the literary man influences only a few." Although there was only so much a college professor could do, Wilson began writing political memoranda to himself, items he would incorporate into public lectures. By the middle of that summer, he noted, "We did not enter upon a war of conquest. We had neither dreamed of nor desired victories at the ends of the earth. . . . It was for us a war begun without calculations, upon an impulse of humane indignation and pity." For the first time, Wilson considered the moral imperative involved when a strong country saw a weak neighbor attacked. He wished his nation had not gone to war; but having done so, America assumed responsibilities. Instead of allowing those colonies to be seized by others, he believed, America would act in their best interests by preparing them to care for themselves. "No doubt the war pleases the jingoes," he wrote; "but any war would please them, and this war was undertaken, not just because war is pleasing, but because this particular war was just, and indeed, inevitable; and we have not made ourselves a nation of jingoes by undertaking it."

Having crossed this Rubicon, America had become part of world affairs; and Wilson chose to enter the public discourse. He told his students in 1899 that it was nigh impossible to enter politics without independent means of support or without succumbing to the wishes of a political machine. As though reading the tea leaves of his own future, he admonished any man without wealth who still chose to enter politics to "be careful of his conduct when in office and be ready to sacrifice himself for principle." He warned an audience in Brooklyn in 1900 that America was no longer "a fine provincial nation" and that it behooved the country to "impart liberty" to the new American dependencies—and not just "impossible ideals, but the practical hard headed experience of the race."

In an address at the Taylor Opera House commemorating the 125th anniversary of the Battle of Trenton, Wilson turned what formerly would have been a historical lecture into a statement of public policy. He asked his audience to realize that the newly acquired American colonies needed self-government: "But when will our work there be done, and how shall we know when they are ready?" He noted that not since the first quarter century of the nation had foreign affairs played such a strong part in America's life.

In 1902 he also dissected America's current domestic policy. At "this new turning-point of our life," Wilson told an audience at Vassar College, he had come to see the great "elasticity of American institutions"—the source of which was the Constitution. He felt the great document called for contemporary interpretations and application. In placing few restrictions on the role of the President, for example, the authors had left room for the executive branch to become the most powerful. When it came to gun control, to cite another specific, he was utterly convinced that "the accumulation of arms, and the bearing of concealed weapons, may be forbidden constitutionally," because he believed the Second Amendment was less about private use of guns than the maintenance of a well-regulated militia, as stated in the amendment's often overlooked opening clause.

Increasingly, Wilson was also drawn into university politics, which were as Machiavellian as those of some European principalities. President Patton had suggested great strides during the Sesquicentennial, but the energized campus quickly settled into its old lassitude. Patton dragged his heels in reorganizing the Department of History and did nothing to establish a law school, which Wilson had expected to head. In the spring of 1897, Wilson was embroiled in a more disturbing episode with the administration when he was encouraged to recruit Frederick Jackson Turner for the History Department, only to find Patton, Andrew Fleming West, and several trustees loath to perfect the offer. Wilson finally learned the problem: Turner was a Unitarian; and Patton suggested that conservative Presbyterian trustees would be reluctant to keep supporting the school with such an infidel inside their gates. "They would accept an agnostic," Wilson observed, "but not a Unitarian. Unitarianism is their *bête-noire.*" Wilson felt hung out to dry, having misled an important friend and distinguished scholar. "I am probably at this writing the most chagrined and mortified fellow on this continent!" he wrote Turner, his distress over Patton curdling into distrust. Wilson contemplated leaving, but he could not deny that since his first day on that campus, he had felt possessed by Princeton, a place in which he had by then lived longer than any other.

By the winter of 1898, Wilson's elective course in politics had become the most popular offering on campus, outdrawing classes in the Bible and American literature. And his academic reputation extended beyond New Jersey. In the last few years alone, he had been offered not just professorships (to teach law at Yale or politics at Johns Hopkins) but also presidencies of a half dozen colleges (the University of Illinois at Urbana-Champaign, which offered $6,000, twice his current salary; Nebraska; Alabama; Minnesota; and Washington and Lee). Most tempting was the University of Virginia, which wanted to overhaul its administrative structure and make Wilson its first chief executive. Despite what he considered "sinister influences" at Princeton, he refused them all, believing he was destined to make his mark at his alma mater. In the meantime, he accepted honorary degrees from Tulane and Hopkins and Yale (alongside Theodore Roosevelt, Chief Justice Melville Fuller, and Mark Twain). And he made his restlessness known, stirring things up.

"I am most cordially disposed to do anything in my power to keep Prof. Wilson in Princeton," President Patton wrote Cyrus McCormick, a trustee and Wilson's classmate, "but I confess I do not know what could be done that has not already been done." Patton said he had championed Wilson ever since his arrival as a professor: even against a strong minority in the Board of Trustees, he had nominated him for the chairmanship of his department; he had allowed him to continue lecturing at Johns Hopkins; and he had nominated him as the Sesquicentennial orator. Afraid Patton's inaction would result in Wilson's departure, several alumni who believed that Wilson himself was the key to Princeton's future took a proactive approach.

In late March 1898, Wilson's classmate Cornelius C. Cuyler, the banker Wilson had beaten for the presidency of the Base Ball Association in 1878, declared, "There is no honor too high for you in the future as far as

Princeton is concerned." Aware of "the selfsacrificing [*sic*] work you have rendered Princeton for 10 years past and the small recompense which up to a certain period you have received," he and classmates Cleveland Dodge and McCormick, along with five others, pledged a $2,500 annual supplement to his Princeton salary for the next five years, under the proviso that Wilson would cease delivering lecture courses on other campuses and would commit himself fully to Princeton during that time. Wilson accepted the offer.

Although his concerns over Patton's Princeton ran deeper than finances, this new arrangement afforded him the liberty to write what he pleased and even the luxury of time to travel and think. At Ellen's insistence, he took another vacation, cycling through Cumbria with her brother Stockton. Woodrow retraced much of the itinerary of his first trip abroad, especially in revisiting Wordsworth shrines. Although he enjoyed a brief detour to Ireland—roaming the quads of Trinity College in Dublin in search of Burke's spirit—and shed tears in St. Giles's Church in Edinburgh, where he heard the very hymns his mother had sung to him—there remained "no spot in the world in which I am so completely at rest and peace," he said, "as in the lake country."

Refreshed, and no longer having to moonlight to pay for his house, Wilson found the additional funds spurred him to publish even more—all of which bespoke a growing interest in the politics of the nation. In 1896, Houghton Mifflin had anthologized eight of his essays under the title of the lead piece, "Mere Literature." In a chapter on Bagehot, Wilson seemed to be taking himself to task, writing: "The genuine practical politician . . . reserves his acidest contempt for the literary man who assumes to utter judgments touching public affairs and political institutions. . . . The ordinary literary man, even though he be an eminent historian, is ill enough fitted to be a mentor in affairs of government." Another essay, "A Calendar of Great Americans," examined the national character through several noteworthy lives. Jackson and Lincoln were quintessential Americans in Wilson's eyes. Washington, on the other hand, "hardly seems an American, as most of his biographers depict him," Wilson wrote; and so he spent the next few years trying to right that wrong. His full-length biography *George Washington*, published in 1897 after having been serialized in *Harper's Magazine*, was Wilson's poorest literary effort. Under-researched and overwritten, it adopted a foppish tone that did nothing to Americanize or

even humanize the first President. Even so, with seventy-five dramatic illustrations (most by Howard Pyle, a leading artist of the day), the decorative book added to his fame.

In 1902 Harper and Brothers published Wilson's *History of the American
People*. While not the penetrating story of the nation that he had hoped,
the imposing five-volume set made him one of the best-known historians
in the country. In truth, he never considered himself as much—"I am only
a writer of history . . . a fellow who merely tried to tell the story, and is not
infallible on dates"; but the books became a commercial success, reprinted
in numerous special editions over the years, complete with illustrations
every few pages by the likes of Frederic Remington and Howard Chandler
Christy. While Wilson received $12,000 for the twelve-part magazine se-
rialization alone, money had not been his sole motivation. "I wrote the
history of the United States in order to learn it," he later told an audience
at the University of North Carolina. "That may be an expensive process for
other persons who bought the book, but I lived in the United States and
my interest in learning their history was, not to remember what happened,
but to find which way we were going." With Wilson's growing presence,
one anonymous "Old-Fashioned Democrat" wrote a letter to the editor of
the *Indianapolis News* suggesting that what his party needed just then was
a candidate like Woodrow Wilson—"a man of affairs, a scholar, a patriot,
and a man whose very presence inspires enthusiastic devotion."

As Wilson's personal reputation ascended, Princeton's continued to
slump into mediocrity. Half a decade had passed since Patton had declared
his aspirations for the new university, and he had realized few of them.
Despite strong faculty support, not until December 1900 had a skeletal
"Plan of Organization" for a graduate school, drafted by Andrew West,
been presented; and in April 1902, it was still being refined. A committee
that had been established in 1896 to consider changes in university policy,
administration, curriculum, and faculty had yielded little. The only hope
for the future lay in the recent recomposition of the Board of Trustees,
which was skewing younger and more progressive, and which could now
boast the illustrious addition of Grover Cleveland.

By 1901, the faculty prepared to revolt over slackening academic standards. Wilson's classmate William Magie, a physics professor, called for
a committee to ameliorate matters. When President Patton questioned
its purpose, Magie replied it was to ascertain "what was the cause of the

utterly rotten condition of education in Princeton—and what was the remedy." Stockton Axson, then teaching at Princeton, recalled Patton's attempted explanation: "Gentlemen, whether we like it or not, we shall have to recognize that Princeton is a rich man's college and that rich men frequently do not come to college to study."

The Board of Trustees could endure no more. It averted an outright rebellion by forming an executive committee, which included three faculty members, to assume control of the university, while a group of young trustees, headed by Wilson's classmate Cyrus McCormick, suggested that it was time for Patton to step down. In a backroom deal, they agreed to buy him out—to the tune of six years' salary in cash. They even sweetened the pot with a new position, president of the Theological Seminary. On June 1, 1902, while Wilson lunched at the Princeton Inn, C. C. Cuyler approached him and said, "It looks now, Tommy, as if you were going to have a great deal of responsibility." Wilson did not know exactly what Cuyler meant.

Eight days later, at the June board meeting, Patton stood and announced his resignation and recommended his successor. In an instant, Woodrow Wilson was voted upon. Reported one of those present, S. Bayard Dod, "I never saw so many men of many minds unite so promptly, without debate, without hesitation at the mere mention of a name. When the ballot was taken I thought that there might be one or two blanks." But every man had promptly cast his ballot for Wilson; "when the vote was announced we agreed that it was the act of Providence." Woodrow Wilson had been elected Princeton's thirteenth president, the first who was not an ordained minister.

Patton and the three trustees from the Class of 1879—Cuyler, Dodge, and McCormick—left the meeting for 50 Library Place to inform the president-elect. Despite the prior hints, his selection came as a joyous surprise. Before the delegation could escort him back to campus, Woodrow and Ellen entered his father's room with the news, which got the ailing octogenarian out of bed and excitedly pacing the room. When Woodrow and their guests left, old Joseph Wilson shouted out to his granddaughters, "Never forget what I tell you. Your father is the greatest man I have ever known." Margaret, the eldest at sixteen, assured their grandfather that they knew that already. "You're too young to know," he insisted. "*I* know what I'm talking about. This is only the beginning of a great career."

Wilson made a point of stopping off to share his news with Jack Hibben before going to Nassau Hall. There students and alumni had already gathered to cheer as he mounted the steps to accept the board's offer. At an alumni luncheon the next day, Patton introduced his successor, and Wilson replied, "How can a man who loves this place as I love it realize of a sudden that he now has the liberty to devote every power that is in him to its service?" Ovations greeted him whenever he walked into a room. On June 11, *The New York Times* editorialized, "This new president is a man of distinction. His political writings have made him already well known to the country as a man capable of clear, straightforward thinking upon the problems of government, while his career as an educator testifies to his fitness for the new responsibility. . . . Under his direction a new life, a higher fame, and a greater usefulness to the youth of the nation and to the Nation itself await the university."

Congratulations poured in from Tigers of all stripes—classmates, former students, colleagues, and alumni of every vintage. Nobody doubted that Wilson was the best man for the job, as during his twelve years back on campus he had rendered himself indispensable. Even Theodore Roosevelt—who had recently become President of the United States upon the assassination of McKinley—expressed his pleasure, calling Wilson "a perfect trump." He wrote trustee Grover Cleveland that he had "long regarded Mr. Wilson as one of the men who had constructive scholarship and administrative ability." He planned to attend Wilson's inauguration.

Ellen's pride in her husband was palpable, as was her dismay. Although Princeton was a small private institution, she realized that her husband had suddenly become a public figure, and that "this was the end of the simple, ideal life," the privacy she cherished. She knew in her heart what he had expressed was in his—as he had admitted to Frederick Jackson Turner just months prior—that, "after all, I was born a politician, and must be at the task for which, by means of my historical writing, I have all these years been in training." Wilson would never write another book; but he immediately began to prepare for the next chapter of his life.

"I feel like a new prime minister getting ready to address his constituents," Wilson wrote Ellen, who was vacationing alone with friends in Massachusetts in July 1902, while he remained in Princeton with his father and the children. In devoting himself that summer to "straightening out my ideas" on educational reform, he found some peace of mind. Weeks later, he explained that his recent election had "settled the future for me and given me a sense of *position* and of definite, tangible tasks which takes the *flutter* and restlessness from my spirits." By the time his wife returned, he had drafted his inaugural address, and his dreams of public office had gone dormant. At Ellen's insistence, he spent the final days of his recess in New Hampshire with the Hibbens.

Fifty Library Place sold swiftly, and in September the Wilsons moved into Prospect, the president's house on the southern perimeter of the campus. It was an asymmetrical two-story Italianate villa with a porte cochere, twenty rooms with high ceilings, and a four-story tower. To the rear was a large uninspired garden, though there was a commanding view of New Jersey countryside. The feeble Joseph Wilson had a large back bedroom; the girls liked to use the topmost room of the "medieval" tower for playing Knights and Ladies; and there was even a room over the kitchen for Woodrow's billiard table, a gift from Ellen. So eager were the trustees to ensure the Wilsons' happiness, they provided a $500 redecorating allowance, which Ellen put to prudent use. The president's study, with books from floor to ceiling, faced the campus; its windows looked onto big elms. As Nell was going to bed that first night, she heard her mother crying and her father consoling her. "I should never have brought you here, darling," he said. "We were so happy in our own home." Designing the gardens would become Ellen's most fulfilling project at Prospect, an enduring legacy. Reforming the rest of the university would be Woodrow's task.

Princeton had recently set the bar for academic pageantry, and on October 25, 1902, a perfect autumn morning, the college raised it. Once again, the campus was a spectacle of color, as an unprecedented number of academicians appeared in their hoods and robes—Harvard crimson and Oxford scarlet and Yale blue amid a sea of orange and black. Because of a recent carriage accident, President Roosevelt was unable to attend; and so it fell upon former President Cleveland to lead the procession to Alexander Hall, with Governor Murphy of New Jersey at his side. Woodrow Wilson walked right behind them, followed by representatives from more than a hundred institutions, including the greatest names in higher education, from Maine to California. Four women marched, the presidents of Mount Holyoke, Radcliffe, Wellesley, and Barnard. Booker T. Washington, the head of the Tuskegee Normal and Industrial Institute, a Negro college, walked behind them, his very presence scandalizing many.

Junius S. Morgan marshaled the next division of dignitaries, among them his uncle J. P. Morgan; the former Speaker of the House Thomas B. Reed; several judges and political figures, including former Secretary of War and Presidential son Robert Todd Lincoln; and such literary figures as Mark Twain, William Dean Howells, and publisher Colonel George Harvey. Then came the university trustees, faculty, and alumni, led by the oldest living graduate, a member of the Class of 1832. After the invocation and several introductory speeches, Governor Murphy presented Wilson. Alexander Hall rose to its feet in an ovation that did not abate for almost ten minutes.

Wilson began by referencing his earlier speech, which had been largely retrospective. Calling this one "Princeton for the Nation's Service," he said, "We must now assess our present purposes and powers and sketch the creed by which we shall be willing to live in the days to come." The crux of this address was that in planning for Princeton, "we are planning for the country," that the "service of institutions of learning is not private but public," that the nation "needs efficient and enlightened men," that the "universities of the country must take part in supplying them." Toward that end, Wilson insisted, colleges should not exist as vocational schools, merely to provide "bread-winning [tools]," no matter how honorable and indispensable such education might be.

Wilson spoke of a new approach to liberal studies, one in which the "mind of the modern student must be carried through a wide range of studies in which science shall have a place not less distinguished than that accorded literatures, philosophy or politics." He spoke of the importance of the graduate school, not just as "a body of teachers and students but also a college of residence, where men shall live together in the close and wholesome comradeships of learning," one he intended to build at the very geographic heart of the university. He spoke of escaping "the pedantry and narrowness of the old fixed curriculum" and embracing new ideals, investing in "men who care more for principles than for money, for the right adjustments of life than for the gross accumulations of profit." He wanted Princeton to take charge "not of men's fortunes, but of their spirits." Summoning Witherspoon and Madison, Wilson concluded by suggesting, "We must lead the world." The response was thunderous.

Those who could not fit into Alexander Hall waited at the steps of Nassau Hall, where Wilson summarized his formal remarks. Then he proceeded to the eastern edge of the campus to break ground on a dormitory to be erected in his class's name. A "state luncheon" followed at Prospect.

Upstairs, Joseph Wilson suffered an attack of angina pectoris that night. He was not to leave his bedroom again. Despite all the demands of Woodrow's new office, he sat by his father's side almost every evening, reading aloud or singing Dr. Wilson's favorite hymns. Not three months later—on January 21, 1903—Joseph Wilson died at eighty. Jack Hibben conducted a brief service at Prospect the next day, after which Dr. Wilson's remains were transported to South Carolina. All of Columbia's religious lights appeared for his funeral services in the First Presbyterian Church, where he was buried by his wife in the churchyard. Woodrow was disconsolate for weeks; and, noted daughter Nell, "for weeks it took all of Ellen's love and wisdom" to comfort him.

At his first board meeting as president, Wilson presented a detailed memorandum of his ambitious program for Princeton's future. It was nothing short of "a thorough-going readjustment." He called for a clear definition of each department—with a sequence to its courses—in which each student might concentrate after two years of prescribed courses. Then students should elect some courses that would allow them to specialize further within their majors and some courses from different disciplines, which would round out their educations. This plan of a major with electives and distribution requirements would become the model for most liberal arts curricula across the country for the next century.

The new program, Wilson felt, demanded new methodology. Synthesizing all his classroom experience, as both a student and a professor—and determined to shatter the pedagogical model of lectures and recitation—he boldly recommended a variation on the English tutorial system. He thought each course should offer two lectures a week and a "conference" in which students could meet with a "guide, philosopher, and friend"—to use Alexander Pope's phrase—to discuss books, those that had been assigned and those they had discovered independently. The goal was for students to develop and express thoughts of their own and for teachers to challenge and shape them. In time, the best students would gather in small discussion groups. This would require a change in the faculty: in addition to the current hundred members, Wilson recommended hiring fifty "preceptors," men who would "be employed as tutors, as superintendents and coaches . . . with the task of seeing to it that the reading is done, and is done thoroughly." Moreover, he envisioned these preceptors as being young men who would hold their posts for no more than five years. Where Oxford dons staled during a lifetime of tutoring, Wilson wanted preceptors only so long as they "retained the freshness and enthusiasm of the first years of teaching."

Wilson considered Princeton particularly deficient in three departments—History, Economics, and Biology—and said: "We lack students now only in proportion as we lack reputation." And the university needed to grow. With Princeton's current endowment below $4 million, Wilson told the board that his proposed changes would cost $6 million.

He did not stop there. In order to take its place as a proper university, said Wilson, Princeton must also erect its Graduate School, a School of Jurisprudence, a School of Electrical Engineering, and a Museum of Natural History. Those additions would cost another $6.5 million, and he had not even begun to reckon such other vital needs as new dormitories and dining halls, so that all students would become full-time residents on campus. The numbers boggled the mind; but as a minister's son, Wilson knew no shame in passing the hat. People preferred investing in a large dream rather than small practicalities—to raise dollars to build a new church rather than dimes to patch the old leaky roof.

Wilson appealed to the alumni for the necessary $12.5 million. In late November 1902, he opened his campaign in Chicago, where he addressed one hundred Princeton graduates and spent a few days as the guest of Cyrus McCormick, head of the International Harvester Company. In early December, James Waddel Alexander, the president of the Equitable Life Assurance Society, introduced Wilson to six hundred members of the Princeton Alumni of New York at the Waldorf-Astoria. Alexander Van Rensselaer, founder of the Philadelphia Orchestra Association, presented him to more than one thousand people in Philadelphia. Wherever he went for the rest of his first year in office—Pittsburgh, Albany, Washington, D. C., St. Louis, St. Paul, Cincinnati, and Newark—he encountered cheers as he exuberantly raised awareness and spirits and then funds.

Campus attitudes shifted overnight, adopting a new rigor. "I am not going to propose that we compel the undergraduates to work all the time," Wilson told the New York alumni; "but I am going to propose that we make the undergraduates want to work all the time." He explained that lectures and required reading were meant to be but points of embarkation for students' own intellectual voyages to discover things for themselves. His goal was to "transform thoughtless boys performing tasks into thinking men." To students who could not meet these new standards, he said, "We shall have the pain of parting company with you."

By midterms of his second semester as president, forty-six students were dropped—including "some good athletes," noted the *Princeton Alumni Weekly*. "Draconian," protested many undergraduates. When one student was about to be expelled for cheating, his mother made an appointment with Wilson to plea for clemency. "I am to have an operation," she said, "and I think I shall die if my boy is expelled." Wilson replied quickly, saying, "Madam, we cannot keep in college a boy reported by the student council as cheating; if we did, we should have no standard of honour. You force me to say a hard thing, but, if I had to choose between your life or my life or anybody's life and the good of this college, I should choose the good of the college."

Wilson held his faculty to the same high standards, expecting each professor to be a scholar and teacher of the highest order. He, after all, maintained his teaching load on top of all his duties—and at the first meeting of his constitutional government class, 376 students welcomed him with cheers. By the end of his first year in office, he had purged the academic ranks of anybody who lacked seriousness about teaching. One professor of French who regularly dismissed his classes early and another whose lectures were disorganized ramblings were both let go. The fate of Arthur Frothingham, a professor of art and archaeology whose courses were considered "snaps," was heard in the senior class's "Faculty Song":

Here's to Frothy our latest find,
He's gentle and easy to drive and kind
He had to make his courses hard
Or he couldn't play in Woodrow's yard.

Wilson concluded his first year as president of Princeton by fine-tuning the next year's curriculum, adding courses in music, architectural drawing, eighteenth-century prose, and mineralogy. He not only presided over Princeton's commencement but also delivered addresses at several preparatory schools and Brown University, where he received an honorary degree.

In July, Wilson embarked on a vacation that would last until late September. His children, all in their teens, were sent to relatives in North Carolina so that he could take his wife abroad. To a schoolmaster and his wife, the tour seemed very grand indeed—costing $1,666.88, according to his record of expenses. The trip was affordable, what with his $8,000 annual salary, plus $2,000 for entertainment and the upkeep of Prospect. He and Ellen spent almost two months touring England and Scotland, starting in his beloved Lake District. Woodrow guided Ellen through Wordsworth's haunts, the theaters and galleries of London, Oxford, and Stratford, before they crossed the Channel. It was their first time on the Continent, and they sight-saw for a week in Paris—day-tripping to Versailles, where they visited the Grand Trianon and the Palais. The rest of September, they visited Switzerland and Italy's lakes before sailing home from Cherbourg. The following spring, he sent Ellen back to Europe without him, to fulfill her lifelong dream of seeing Italy's artistic masterpieces.

Only months after her return, Ellen's youngest brother, Edward, who had married after Princeton and moved to Georgia, was involved in a freak accident. He and his pregnant wife and child were about to board a flat ferryboat, when their carriage horses spooked and plunged into the Etowah River. They all drowned. Ellen mourned as though she had lost her own children; but mindful of her family's mental history, she worked her way out of her despair with domestic activity.

Woodrow—who could not think of the boy without welling up— immersed himself in the unremitting task of securing capital. Having visited the major alumni hubs, he turned to an inner core of graduates who would underwrite much of his visionary campaign. He could always rely on the same names—McCormick, Cuyler, Dodge, and Thomas D. Jones, a Chicago businessman—which would be chiseled in stone on new edifices that were doubling the size of the campus. At Wilson's direction, most new construction was in the Tudor Gothic style of Oxford and Cambridge. "We have added a thousand years to the history of Princeton by merely putting those lines in our buildings which point every man's imagination to the historic traditions of learning in the English-speaking race," he told a group of supporters. Over the next few years, the most generous donors would form a Committee of Fifty, which would stimulate not only a steady infusion of funds but also activity among alumni, which Wilson encouraged by having each graduating class become a team of supporters. At its twenty-fifth reunion, in 1904, the Class of 1879 could boast donations of $425,000 to the university since graduation; and within the central vaulted archway of the new red-brick dormitory bearing its name was a private entrance leading to a magnificent room, which Wilson claimed as his aerie. It became the university's development office, as the understaffed president typed out individual appeals for money himself. "I hate above all things to write a begging letter to a generous man like you," he wrote one potential donor, ". . . but in the present circumstances . . . I seem to have no choice in the matter."

No benefactor was more essential to Princeton's revival than Moses Taylor Pyne, Class of 1877. An heir to banking and railroad fortunes, "Momo" Pyne became a university trustee in 1884 at the age of twenty-eight and remained the seminal figure in the life of the college and the town for the rest of his years. He became a one-man alumni council—urging graduates to maintain lifelong ties to their alma mater, establishing alumni clubs across the country, and helping to start the weekly alumni magazine. He chaired the trustees' grounds and buildings committee; and a half dozen buildings on campus were named for him or his family. As head of the committee on finance, he not only supervised the raising of funds but was known to dip into his own pocket whenever a shortfall occurred. His contributions to the school could never be completely accounted for because, it was said, he simply wrote a personal check at each commencement so that the school would not end the year in the red. Although Wilson never kowtowed to his most munificent trustee, he recognized that he would periodically have to stoop.

At his most upright, Wilson approached the richest man in the world. Scottish-born industrialist Andrew Carnegie had just endowed an eponymous institution with $10 million to "encourage investigation, research, and discovery . . . and afford instruction of an advanced character." Wilson spent hours drafting a long appeal, shamelessly bagpiping Princeton's heritage wherever he could. "She has been largely made by Scotsmen," he wrote of Witherspoon and McCosh's college, not failing to speak of himself, being of "pure Scots blood"; and, he added, the school "is thoroughly Scottish in all her history and traditions in matters educational." Seven months later, Wilson's efforts paid dividends, as Carnegie contributed more than $100,000—not for any educational costs but for the conversion of some adjacent swampland into a four-mile lake for the university's crew. Wilson gladly accepted the money but persistently pressed his benefactor for more. When Carnegie said he had already given Princeton a lake, Wilson could but ambiguously reply, "We needed bread and you gave us cake."

Wilson's energetic fortification of the university came at a price—the destruction of his personal health. His right hand flared up again in the summer of 1904, and his chronic gastritis required a treatment that involved siphoning excess acid. At the end of the year, he underwent hernia surgery. The operation went well, but as a result, Wilson suffered from phlebitis in his left leg. That required a long hospital stay and a five-week convalescence in Palm Beach. With Eddie Axson's death, Stockton requiring hospitalization for his recurring mental illness, and daughters Jessie having recently come through a bout of diphtheria and Margaret the measles, Wilson developed a facial tic, which would recur for the rest of his life whenever he was nervous and overtired. Wilson's baccalaureate address in June 1905, not surprisingly, touched upon the subject of well-being—physical, mental, and spiritual. He said that it was God's "saving health, which must be known among all nations before peace will come and life be widened in all its outlooks." The university, he felt, was only growing stronger, as evidenced by its drop in enrollment, a loss only of students who were not serious about their education. In 1905, Wilson and the college proved sound enough to institute his preceptorial system.

"I think that no university in the country has ever, before or since, added to its faculty at one blow so large and so able a new recruitment," wrote Robert K. Root forty years after he had been tapped by President Wilson to become one of the first preceptors at Princeton. Root was a young English instructor at Yale writing a book about Chaucer when he received an unsolicited letter in March 1905 from Wilson himself. Root was "reasonably contented" where he was and had misgivings about "this new-fangled method of teaching." But he could not ignore the handsome offer of $2,000. His interview lasted all of forty minutes, during which time Wilson asked no questions but spoke only of his plans for Princeton. "Before five minutes had passed," Root would recall, "I knew that I was in the presence of a very great man. . . . Had Woodrow Wilson asked me to . . . work under him while he inaugurated a new university in Kamchatka or Senegambia I would have said 'yes' without further question."

Others, such as Edward S. Corwin, a Ph.D. candidate at Pennsylvania, applied for his job; and, like Root, he left his interview believing "that was one of the most memorable moments of my life. Mr. Wilson seemed to me easily the most impressive human being I had ever met." Another of the original squad of preceptors, Luther P. Eisenhart, most remembered Wilson's addressing the first gathering of the fifty chosen young men, and how the "troup was electrified and went forth ready to give their best to an educational adventure." Preceptorials became one of the hallmarks of the Princeton education and a template for American higher education.

Wilson's experiment in education worked from the start. The "severe standards of efficiency and scholarship" governing faculty and students inspired everybody on campus; and every academician in America knew Wilson was the catalyst. "What had been called a high-class country club," said Professor Edwin Grant Conklin, who left Pennsylvania's Zoology Department to teach at Princeton, "began to be a real university."

Princeton rapidly gained national attention. In the autumn of 1905, the Athletic Association asked Wilson if Princeton might host the annual Army-Navy game on its field. He approved. When President Theodore Roosevelt announced that he would be attending the game, Wilson invited him to lunch. He met TR at the Princeton station, and they rode in a carriage up University Place to Nassau Street, the route heavily cordoned with police. A party that included Roosevelt's wife and sister and daughter, military brass, and Secretary of State Elihu Root followed them to Prospect. Afterward, they all went to the field, where the teams played to a 6–6 tie. As had become tradition, the Commander in Chief viewed each half of the game from a different side; and for many, the most memorable sight of the day was that of Roosevelt and Wilson crossing the field together between the halves, TR exuberantly waving his hat to the cheering crowd while the academician followed with modest dignity.

As his and Princeton's fame steadily grew, Wilson received numerous invitations to lecture at schools, churches, businessmen's luncheons, and women's clubs all over the country. Because he considered Princeton's goals tied to those of every college, and the role of higher education bound to the progress of the nation, he tried to accept most of them—three or four a month. He invariably spoke about education and politics, linking his thoughts about universities to those about patriotism, commerce, Americanism, and the "citizenship of the world." His speeches veered into contemporary issues, and he was soon commenting upon Socialism, the Philippines, and William Jennings Bryan.

The Lotos Club of New York—founded in 1870 "to promote social intercourse" among artists and gentlemen amateurs—gathered in a tribute to Woodrow Wilson on February 3, 1906. After several college presidents paid homage, the president of the club introduced the guest of honor, saying, "There are men whom we admire not because they have accumulated great fortunes, but because they have thought great thoughts."

Wilson did not deliver a long speech, nor one that was especially profound. But it combined eloquence with humor, as he moved from generalizations about the national character and the need for knowledge to modern specifics, quoting Tocqueville and Tennyson along the way. While acknowledging that the Republican Party was then a strong majority, he suggested "that it is worth while sometimes to be very impertinent to the majority, and that university men are, if they are worthy of the name, the men especially qualified by their training to entertain independent opinions." Even Supreme Court decisions, he asserted, are not always the final word. They may be wrong and must be challenged. This was why one must always have "the spirit of learning."

Colonel George B. M. Harvey—a journalist who became a businessman in light-rail construction, made a fortune, and then returned to publishing as the owner and editor of *The North American Review*, Harper and Brothers, and *Harper's Weekly*—had a longtime interest in Democratic politics. Because he was considered something of a kingmaker in the reelection of Grover Cleveland, everybody at the Lotos Club paid particular attention when Harvey closed the evening by extolling the virtues of the new Princeton and, particularly, its leader. "It is that type of man that we shall soon, if indeed we do not already, need in public life," Harvey said. Lest he had not made himself clear, he ended by saying, "As one of a considerable number of Democrats who have become tired of voting Republican tickets, it is with a sense almost of rapture that I contemplate even the remotest possibility of casting a ballot for the president of Princeton University to become President of the United States."

Wilson spent the night at the University Club in New York and sent a heartfelt note of thanks to Harvey before going to sleep. "It was most delightful to have such thoughts uttered about me," he wrote, "whether they were deserved or not." Reports of the evening's speeches hit the New York papers the next morning.

Stockton Axson was at Prospect when Wilson returned home, standing at the foot of the staircase just as Ellen was descending. "I see Colonel Harvey has nominated you for the presidency," Stockton said. Woodrow made light of the moment.

"Was he joking?" Ellen asked.

Said Wilson, "He did not seem to be."

6

ADVENT

. . . but God is faithfull, who wil not suffer you to
bee tempted aboue that you are able: but will with
the temptation also make a way to escape, that ye
may bee able to beare it.

—1 Corinthians, X:13

For weeks Wilson modestly insisted he was not seriously considering Colonel Harvey's suggestion. Even so, the *Brooklyn Daily Eagle* dispatched a writer to chase the story, and Wilson's denials of any interest in a Presidential nomination were more convoluted than convincing. His statement that "nothing could be further from my thoughts than the possibility or the desirability of holding high political office" was as false as his modesty.

Before Colonel Harvey focused on him, Wilson had agreed to deliver a speech at the annual Jefferson Day Dinner of the National Democratic Club of New York; and when he addressed the members on April 16, 1906, Wilson made America's third President sound a little like himself. He described Jefferson not as a charismatic public figure but a studious man of letters. Instead of a Renaissance man with European ideas, Wilson described Jefferson as "a typical American," a Virginian who had "lived among . . . the plainest people of his time and drank directly at the sources of Democratic feelings." Wilson added that Jefferson "believed in the right of the individual to opportunity." He was "a poet and a dreamer," able to think at once "in visions and in concrete politics," making him "the great prototype of all true Democracy," to whom "we do not return . . . to borrow policies" but "to renew ideals." Applause repeatedly interrupted the speech, as many in the audience concluded that the party of Jefferson had no greater spokesman.

The administration at Princeton equally valued Wilson's gifts, as he continued to schedule numerous addresses on education, many at regional alumni conferences across the country. Speaking at the annual convention of the Western Association of Princeton Clubs in Cleveland, he illustrated the new "spirit of study" by telling them of an undergraduate who had recently said in a tone of great condemnation that "Princeton was not the place it used to be—that men were actually talking about their studies at the clubs." The preceptorial system, Wilson said, was infusing the student body with "the independent pursuit of certain studies by men old enough to study for themselves." He cautioned against the prevalence of conservatism among college men, those who adhered to the "ideals and tenets" of their fathers. These speaking tours steadily raised Wilson's personal profile, though they left him exhausted.

Back in Princeton for the upcoming graduation exercises, Wilson awakened on May 28 feeling fine until he passed his hands before his face and realized he could see nothing out of his left eye. Ellen accompanied him to Philadelphia, where his ophthalmologist, Dr. George de Schweinitz, diagnosed a blood clot and rupture in his eye. Piecing this with Wilson's symptoms from prior years, he saw a graver medical picture. The sudden blindness combined with the periodic weakness and numbness in his extremities directed the doctor's attention to Wilson's carotid artery—that vessel that begins just below the neck and flows to the brain, supplying blood to its motor and sensory areas as well as the eyes. Wilson had suffered a stroke—probably his second—and the doctor recommended complete rest.

Years later, Nell Wilson recalled her parents' return from Philadelphia. "Father was calm, even gay," she recalled, "but after one look at mother's face we knew that something dreadful had happened." Woodrow's false cheer heightened the children's fears, for it suggested his condition was bad enough to warrant disguise. Nell cried through the night, and only much later did her father admit that he too had become "deeply depressed."

Ellen asked Jack Hibben to meet with Woodrow's doctors in Philadelphia to glean further information. Their prognosis was serious enough to reshape Ellen's role for the rest of her life. "[We] are all making every effort to keep him free from anxiety and worry and above all to keep things quiet for him," Ellen wrote about Woodrow to her cousin Mary Hoyt mid-June. "He is of course *very* nervous—annoyed by the things he usually enjoys,—as for instance the lively chatter of the young people. He is making rather uncomplimentary remarks about the confusion caused by 'seven women in a house.'" He even began asking when his sister and nieces would be leaving. A few weeks later, a Philadelphia internist, Dr. Alfred Stengel, rendered a less grave second opinion—saying that three months' rest should restore him. Indeed, the blood in Wilson's eye was already almost completely absorbed. "Of course 50-year-old arteries do not go back to an earlier condition," Stengel warned the Wilsons; but he expected that Princeton's president could reasonably return to work in the fall. "You have doubtless done too much in the last few years," he said, adding that this warning "simply indicates that excess of work is dangerous."

Over the preceding few years, several Princeton trustees had tried to tell Wilson as much. On one of his visits to Prospect, Moses Taylor Pyne saw Stockton Axson and walked with him on the grounds for the better part of an hour, revealing both his "solicitude and anxiety, saying that the death or disablement of Mr. Wilson would be an extreme catastrophe for the university." In addition, Pyne said Wilson did not exercise sufficiently. Axson agreed, knowing that Wilson's presidential duties had kept him from bicycling, to say nothing of the occasional round of golf, which he had taken up after a previous medical incident; but Axson said that Wilson did at least find time for daily walks. "Walks!" Pyne harrumphed. "He doesn't walk, he only saunters."

Wilson got the message. He canceled all speaking engagements, including any participation in graduation exercises. He worked only at planning an immediate family visit to the English Lake District. At the next meeting of the Board of Trustees, Momo Pyne seconded Grover Cleveland's resolution that "we request, and especially enjoin it upon [President Wilson], that he prolong his vacation to such an extent, as to time and manner of enjoyment as may promise the complete restoration of his health and vigor."

Several friends accompanied the five Wilsons to New York before they set sail on the *Caledonia* at the end of June. On board, one of the friends was meant to hand Wilson a check, a stipend the trustees had voted to bestow upon their president to lessen any financial anxiety. Wilson refused the gift. He later told Ellen, "I cannot afford to let the trustees do this. The relationship between them and myself is now delightful, but none of us can foresee the future. A time may come when I shall have to oppose them on some point of college policy, and I must therefore keep myself a free man. My obligations are to the best interests of the college as I see them, and it would be a mistake to permit any personal favors to stand between me and the discharge of those duties."

On July 10, 1906, the Wilsons arrived in Rydal, and moved into the two-story Loughrigg Cottage, which they sublet from the widow of Henry Curwen Wordsworth, a grandson of Wilson's muse. Outside the bay windows, beyond the gardens, flowed the river Rothay, and the gentle summer rains never kept the family from exploring the emerald meads. "I can only guess that I am improving from the unmistakable increase of energy that comes to me from week to week," Woodrow wrote his sister Annie. He and Ellen visited all the Wordsworth haunts, at which she frequently opened her paint box; with his daughters, he walked the neighboring "fells," clearing his head when he was not losing himself in conversations with local shepherds. He hiked as much as fourteen miles some days. The family spent late afternoons by the fire, indulging in high tea with yellow Devonshire cream and playing whist and euchre.

During one of his solitary walks, crossing the Rothay on Pelter Bridge, Wilson encountered an artist named Fred Yates, who had studied in Paris and exhibited at the Royal Academy in London. "We live near here," said the portraitist. "We're poor, but, thank God, not respectable." Wilson liked him instantly. Yates and his California-born wife had a daughter; and the two families spent many of their evenings together, singing and reading aloud. Yates drew pastel portraits of all the Wilsons and gave painting lessons to Ellen. As Princeton had wanted a picture of its president, Wilson secured the commission for Yates, who rendered his portraits with a muted palette and gentle brushstrokes. The family long agreed that nobody ever captured Woodrow's essence better than Fred Yates.

"No doubt God *could* have made a lovelier country than this Lake District," Wilson wrote Robert Bridges, "but I cannot believe he ever did." Each day revived him a little more; but Ellen had confided to her first cousin Florence Hoyt how difficult it had been watching a man with hardening of the arteries who "lived too tensely." She called it "a dying by inches." In September, Wilson went to Edinburgh to consult with two physicians. The oculist found Wilson's eye "in excellent condition," healed enough for him to resume reading, though he noted a scotoma, a blind spot to which Wilson was already adapting. The Scottish internist was especially encouraging, telling Wilson he could return to work "with perfect safety," that it would be better than leading "an aimless and perhaps anxious year" in Great Britain.

And so, even though the Princeton trustees had given him no timetable, the Wilsons returned home the first week of October 1906. "The summer has brought to maturity the plans for the University which have for years been in the back of my head but which never before got room enough to take their full growth," Wilson wrote Cleveland Dodge. "I feel richer for the summer, not only in health but also in thought and in ability to be of service. A year such as I have planned . . . ought to set all sorts of processes in order, and that without undue strain on me."

The press covered Wilson's return to America, but not for educational reasons. In his final days in Rydal, he had received a telegram from the *New York Evening Post* seeking a comment on the report that his name was being floated as a candidate for the United States Senate from New Jersey. The state legislature would make its choice right after the November election. At the same time, Wilson's most ardent supporter, Colonel Harvey, had mentioned his name to his friend James Smith, Jr., a former Senator and the boss of the Democratic Party from Essex County, where he owned the *Newark Advertiser.* It seemed unlikely that the Democrats would gain the power to elect one of their members to the Senate that year, but Harvey was floating Wilson's name once again as a trial balloon. Faithful to their party boss, all the Democratic candidates of Essex County office pledged that if they were elected, their choice for United States Senator would be Dr. Wilson of Princeton University. He and only he would bring "the purity of purpose and the high intellectual powers which will add honor and prestige not only to New Jersey but to the entire nation." Wilson had told the press two weeks earlier that the mention of his name had come as a great surprise. Furthermore, he declared, "My duty is to Princeton, and I should be reluctant to give up my work there."

Wilson's classmates had raised an additional $6,000 to furnish the large Tower Room over the central arch of Seventy-nine Hall, making it the president's office and the administrative hub of the university. Dramatically situated, with corbelled oriel windows on opposite walls, it offered disparate views of Princeton life. On one side stretched Prospect Avenue, with its growing number of eating clubs—citadels of privilege—and on the other sprawled a vast greensward waiting to be filled with some academic building that might truly transform the college into a university.

In just four years as president of the college, Wilson had reorganized the departments and curricula and restructured the pedagogy with the preceptorial system—which he immodestly considered "the greatest strategic move . . . that has been made in the whole history of American universities." Now he intended to galvanize Princeton with a massive overhaul of campus life. At this time, his notions of education and social life at Princeton began to collide, forming a nucleus of a political outlook. "My own ideals for the University," he would soon articulate, "are those of genuine democracy and serious scholarship. The two, indeed, seem to me to go together. Any organization which introduced elements of social exclusiveness constitutes the worst possible soil for serious intellectual endeavour." Wilson envisioned a new freedom—of education.

The caste system he chose to fight existed on many college campuses—especially the older schools, where fraternities and secret societies reinforced class distinctions. But few if any rivaled Princeton as a bastion of snobbery—a white, Anglo-Saxon Protestant preserve that thrived on exclusivity. Before he could level its social playing field, Wilson felt he had to raze Princeton's upper-class club system, at a time when its private baronial houses continued to rise. There would be more than a dozen clubs, and they were filling to capacity through a selective interview process called "Bicker"; the process still blocked approximately a third of the juniors and seniors from enjoying "the Street." Privileged sophomores, even some freshman, were quietly recruited early. A few of the less advantaged students were admitted each year, allowing them to rub shoulders with their social betters, affording the opportunity to maintain their relationships later in life, often to commercial advantage. The rest were considered outcasts; some of these "muckers" felt stigmatized enough to leave school.

Wilson felt the "slow, almost imperceptible and yet increasingly certain decline of the old democratic spirit of the place and the growth and multiplication of social divisions" was eroding the true Princeton values. These influences, he maintained, not only introduced "a spirit of social

competition which interferes with the natural intercourse and comradeship of the undergraduates, but are also distinctly and very seriously hostile to the spirit of study, incompatible with the principles of a true republic
of letters and of learning." Wilson prepared to wage a holy war for the soul
of the university—a "fight for the restoration of Princeton"—a duel between money and merit, which would determine whether or not the university would be damned or saved.

At the December meeting of the Board of Trustees, Wilson presented
a report that consolidated much of his thinking of the last several years.
He envisioned an intellectual utopia, a community of the mind. "The remedy I suggest is to oblige the undergraduates to live together," he wrote,
"not in clubs but in colleges"—a cluster of quadrangles, each with its own
eating hall, resident masters, and preceptors, all of whom would dine together. He even recommended that the larger clubs convert into colleges,
each one a self-governing unit within the university system, with dormitories attached to the existing structures. In essence, Princeton would become the sort of university where the Witherspoon Gang could have
integrated with the most privileged sons in America.

Even that much integration seemed unlikely at Princeton at the turn of
the century; and the intermingling of any other outsiders remained beyond the pale. The American Negro, for example, was excluded from
Princeton, as he was from most American colleges. Separate campuses for
the education of the black man had appeared—notably Howard University in Washington, D.C., after the Civil War and Alabama's Tuskegee
Institute, where Booker T. Washington had become it's first president.
Elite Northern colleges opened their doors to a few Negroes, mostly at the
graduate level; and in 1896 Harvard had awarded its first Ph.D. to an
African American—W. E. B. Du Bois. But higher education for the African American operated under a traditional policy of de facto segregation
well into the middle of the twentieth century.

With its heavy Southern enrollment, Princeton discouraged Negroes
from even thinking about attending. Even though John Witherspoon had
tutored a handful of freed slaves in the eighteenth century and several
black students from the Princeton Theological Seminary had taken courses
on campus in the nineteenth, when the question arose at Princeton in
1904, Wilson replied that "while there is nothing in the law of the University to prevent a negro's entering, the whole temper and tradition of the

place are such that no negro has ever applied for admission, and it seems extremely unlikely that the question will ever assume a practical form." Just a few years later, Wilson received a brief letter from a student at Virginia Theological Seminary and College, a Baptist institution in Lynchburg, Virginia. "I want so much to come to your School at Princeton," this student wrote. "I am a poor Southern colored man from South Carolina, but I believe I can make my way if I am permitted to come." Wilson replied with regrets—"that it is altogether inadvisable for a colored man to enter Princeton." He recommended starting college in a Southern institution, after which he might attend the Princeton Theological Seminary. If he truly wished to attend a Northern school, Wilson recommended Harvard, Dartmouth, or Brown.

During his academic years, Wilson wrestled with the question of race, without ever divining a solution. He knew all too well the animosity many Southern white men held toward blacks. While his own thinking on this subject may have evolved slightly, the sentiment on his campus had not changed in the least. Unlike Harvard, Yale, Columbia, or the University of Pennsylvania, Princeton was situated in a small rural town, not an urban center. The only person of color whom a student or professor might encounter was somebody who served or cleaned and probably lived in slums students would never even see, only blocks from the college. Some alumni still spoke disdainfully of Wilson's having invited Booker T. Washington to participate in his inauguration as president. Only a decade earlier, the Princeton football team had exited a dining hall when Harvard's team, with its sole black player, entered. Racial integration at Princeton just then surely would have meant confrontation for which neither the college nor its president was ready.

"Time," Wilson believed, "is the only legislator in such a matter." As he wrote on the subject as early as 1897:

The race problem of the South will no doubt work itself out in the slowness of time, as blacks and whites pass from generation to generation, gaining with each remove from the memories of the war a surer self-possession, an easier view of the division of labor and of social function to be arranged between them.

Wilson believed acceptance of others could only come through gradual exposure; but he also knew that the first to cross any barriers of prejudice would incite trouble. No racial advances would be made during Wilson's tenure. Indeed, a Negro would not receive an undergraduate degree from Princeton for another four decades.

Woodrow Wilson treated every person of color, regardless of that person's position, with decency and dignity; but he never failed to consider the color of that person's skin. Beyond any inferred inferiority, he could not deny ethnic differences and social ramifications. He spoke of his household's colored servants as different from the white; and he pronounced President Roosevelt's appointment of a black man as Collector of the Port of Charleston, South Carolina—a position with authority over white merchants—"an unwise piece of bravado," because it was simply "too much" for the whites "to stand." He believed individual Negroes had proved to be "splendid"; but, as a group, he considered them lazy—the only race in Africa that "did not rise"—while the Egyptians, who had endured the same heat, scaled the heights of civilization. He believed interracial marriage would "degrade the white nations."

At the beginning of the twentieth century, Wilson's racial views were fairly centrist in America. Proud bigots served in the United States Congress at that time, uninhibitedly talking in vulgarisms about Theodore Roosevelt's having invited Booker T. Washington to dine at the White House. In a letter to Wilson, Boston-born, Amherst- and Hopkins-educated Professor J. Franklin Jameson thought nothing of referring to "the nigger question." Wilson himself told jokes in Negro dialect—this one to the Pennsylvania Bar Association: "De Lawd told Moses to come fo'th, and he came fif and lost de race"—with no offense intended. In step with his countrymen or not, Wilson's thoughts, words, and actions were, nonetheless, indubitably racist.

Another excluded minority fared better at Princeton, though not by much. "Hebrews," as they were identified, represented a minuscule percentage of the student body, a little lower than Catholics. Most Jews were miserable there—enduring self-loathing if they "passed" as Gentile or social ostracism if they did not. A few felt it was a small price to pay for the quality of the education and the beautiful surroundings. "I was rudely awakened at the end of the first year by discovering all of my class mates landed in clubs," one Leon Levy, Class of 1905, wrote Wilson, "while I wandered hopeless on the outskirts, an Ishmaelite and outcast." Only a few students deigned to consort with him (classmate Norman Thomas, the future political activist and Presidential candidate, among them); and after two years of "cold contempt and icy prejudice," he transferred to the University of Pennsylvania. In 1903, Wilson had hired the first Jew to teach at Princeton, Harvard graduate Horace Meyer Kallen, an instructor in English. His two-year contract was not renewed, leaving him to embark upon a stellar career in philosophy and social reform elsewhere. David McCabe, a Catholic in the Politics Department, was hired shortly thereafter and remained for decades. And at Wilson's urging, in 1906 the university declared its nonsectarian status, avowing that no denominational test would be imposed in its choice of trustees, teachers, or students. Wilson knew that, through incremental change, Princeton could ultimately diversify: indeed, by 1910, Episcopalians outnumbered Presbyterians.

Tangential to his Quad Plan, Wilson believed the second crucial piece to foment social change at Princeton was building a graduate school. He considered the location as important as his timing. This particular quadrangle must be erected "not apart, but as nearly as may be at the very heart, the geographical heart, of the university; and its comradeship shall be for young men and old, for the novice as well as for the graduate." In that way, the graduate students could be part of "harmonizing, invigorating, and elevating the life and thought of the undergraduate students." For the last several years, there had been little action on the subject, but the talk seldom veered far from *The Proposed Graduate College of Princeton University*, by Andrew Fleming West—who had been named its founding dean. His study served as both a manifesto and a sales brochure. Wilson and West shared a vision of a graduate school "of residence, a great quadrangle in which our graduate students will be housed like a household, with their own commons and with their own rooms of conference, under a master, whose residence should stand at a corner of the quadrangle in the midst of them." The great lawn outside 1879 Hall seemed the ideal location.

Recently, however, West's notions had strayed from his original concept. A local widow named Josephine Thomson Swann had recently died and left $250,000 to Princeton for the construction of a graduate college "upon the grounds of said University." Growing impatient with Wilson's spending so much of the board's time and money on other educational reforms, West took it upon himself to raise money to rent and refurbish Merwick, an eleven-acre estate at 83 Bayard Lane, across the street from his own house. It became home to a dozen men, who were only a small corps of Princeton's graduate students. Life at Merwick so delighted West, he took to promoting it as the model for the graduate college—a few dozen select scholars living as country squires, with the dean their Lord of the Manor. Wilson saw Merwick as just another eating club, if not West's own private satrapy.

That fall, the Massachusetts Institute of Technology offered its presidency to Dean West. The choice was completely unexpected. Andrew Fleming West was not versed in the sciences; in fact, he was a man with few academic credentials, a questionable scholar even in his own field. Born in Allegheny, Pennsylvania, he was a son of a troublesome Presbyterian minister and professor of theology. Andrew's education at Princeton was interrupted because of poor health, but he graduated in 1874 and taught Latin in a Cincinnati high school for six years before serving as principal of an academy in Morristown, New Jersey, from which President McCosh plucked him to teach Latin at the college. West wrote a Latin primer and edited a collection of Terence but produced no important works of scholarship.

He distinguished himself, however, with his personality. Affable and authoritative, the portly dean developed a taste for gracious living ("Here's to Andy, Andy West / 63 inches around the vest," noted one verse of the "Faculty Song"), and he mixed easily with the wealthy and powerful. McCosh had bestowed upon him his only advanced degree, an honorary doctorate. Grover Cleveland and Momo Pyne ranked among his closest friends and strongest allies, the latter having bought Merwick, which he leased to the college rent-free.

With both Wilson and West about to cross swords over the future of the graduate school, nothing would have been easier than to allow the dean to leave for Massachusetts. But Wilson recognized that West was as valuable as he was voluble, that Princeton's graduate school had no greater ambassador among prospective donors. When West suggested that Wilson's confidence in him would be reason enough to stay, Wilson himself drafted a gracious resolution on behalf of all the trustees. It said: "The Board would consider his loss quite irreparable. By his scholarship, by his ideals, by his fertility in constructive ideas, he has made himself one of the chief ornaments and one of the indispensable counsellors of the place." West declined MIT's offer.

Before the trustees could debate the revolutionary new agenda, Ellen Wilson insisted her husband stick to his recent vow to take an annual winter vacation. On January 12, 1907, he sailed alone for the Bermuda Islands, which had become a popular destination for wealthy Americans, titled Britons, and such writers as Rudyard Kipling, Frances Hodgson Burnett, and Mark Twain. Almost seven hundred miles east of North Carolina's Outer Banks, the resort offered pink sand beaches and clear blue waters, its tropical warmth thawing some of its English reserve. Upon landing, Wilson checked into the Hotel Hamilton. While the occasional Princeton alumnus on the streets of the town interrupted his solitude, every moment, he wrote Ellen, was bringing "peace and renewal."

Wilson spent most of his time studying and loafing. In the mornings, he composed outlines for the short lecture series on government he had agreed to give at Columbia; in the afternoons, he strolled the waterfront, explored the island on bicycle, or viewed the surrounding sea and reefs in glass-bottom boats. On two Sundays, he delivered sermons in local churches.

On February 5, the Mayor of Hamilton and his wife hosted a small dinner party in Wilson's honor. At the last minute, they invited an American neighbor, who wintered regularly on the island. She had been born Mary Allen in Grand Rapids, Michigan, and grew up in Duluth, Minnesota, where she married a mining engineer named Thomas Hulbert. He died six years later, leaving her with an infant son. The next year, the twenty-eight-year-old married a textile executive from Pittsfield, Massachusetts, a widower named Thomas Dowse Peck. Theirs was a loveless marriage, and the couple steadily grew apart. In Bermuda, Mrs. Peck became a woman of some notoriety—respectably married and traveling with her grown son but living for the most part as an unusually independent woman for her time. She even smoked cigarettes.

A woman of immense charm and no small amount of intrigue, Mrs. Peck was a gifted hostess—a generous conversationalist and an inspired cook, as well as an accomplished pianist. Her salon welcomed every interesting visitor to the island. She had already read about the progressive educator being honored on this particular night. "The face was even more rugged than his pictures showed and seemed plain at first glance," Mrs. Peck would later write of meeting Wilson. "Then came the friendly smile and the voice with its rare clear quality." She and Wilson immediately fell into a conversation filled with the smart banter in which Wilson loved to engage, especially with women. He also spoke devotedly of his wife, and that uxoriousness was a little like catnip.

Mrs. Peck invited Wilson to a dinner party the night before he left Bermuda; but the gentlemen found him so interesting that she and her guest of honor could exchange little more than pleasantries and a few words about Bagehot. Although she missed Wilson's call the next day before he sailed, he left a note saying, "It is not often that I can have the privilege of meeting anyone whom I can so entirely admire and enjoy." Upon his return to the business of Princeton—where the mercury had fallen below zero—he sent her two books, a small volume of his own essays and another of Bagehot's, writing that one "has no right to whet another's appetite for Walter Bagehot without supplying the means of gratifying it." He was sure she would enjoy it "with as much zest as anyone I know." After he was home only a couple of days, the business of his university once again consumed all his time.

In just four years, Wilson had raised the standards of scholarship and more than half the $12.5 million he had proposed when he assumed office. Even more astonishing, he had completely altered Princeton's national reputation. As the *New York Evening Post* put it, "He has ruined what was universally admitted to be the most agreeable and aristocratic country club in America by transforming it into an institution of learning." In 1907—exactly 130 years after General George Washington had led his army to a decisive victory over Britain's royal troops—Wilson commenced the second Battle of Princeton.

On Sunday, June 9, he delivered the baccalaureate address before graduation. With club life on his mind, the Epistle to the Romans inspired him to preach "that non-conformity is not antagonism." He urged each new graduate to become "a man who thinks for himself, a man renewed by fresh contact with the sources and originals of thoughts and inspiration." The purpose of a college education, Wilson said throughout his academic career, was to teach young men to think as differently from their fathers as possible.

The next day, he addressed the Board of Trustees. His message was much the same as his December report, though he tempered its tone. He praised the clubs, faintly—saying they were "not consciously doing anything to the detriment of the University." But, he added, "in spite of their admirable spirit and of every watchful effort they have made to the contrary . . . a system of social life has grown up in the University . . . which divides classes, creates artificial groups for social purposes, and renders a wholesome university spirit impossible." Intellectual and spiritual development, Wilson reminded his board, were "the chief and, indeed, the only legitimate aims of university life." And residential quadrangles addressed that mission. The present system encouraged "disconnection between the life and the work of the University," putting the life of the student and the life of the clubman in competition with one another.

Holding the report of a committee that had studied the problem, Wilson admitted the remedy was "radical" but not out of line with the system it meant to replace. "The associations formed in the quads will be like the associations formed in the clubs," he said, "with the elective principles left out . . . but with all the opportunities for a natural selection of chums and companions that the larger number in residence will afford." Just as Princeton had reformed pedagogy, Wilson now urged the university to reorganize its community structure. "We are making a university," he exhorted, "not devising a method of social pleasure."

For the moment, he called upon each club to vest its property in the hands of a small board of its own choice "who should be charged with administering it for the benefit of the University." The clubs, Wilson said, had been "most honourable and useful," but also transitional, getting Princeton through a period when no social coordination of the university existed. Wilson was so compelling that all but one of the twenty-five trustees present—including Grover Cleveland and Moses Taylor Pyne—voted in favor of his plan, despite its lack of specifics. The *Princeton Alumni Weekly* carried all the statements pertaining to the Quad Plan, allowing all constituencies to study the proposal over the summer.

Alumni reacted within days. Professor and trustee Henry van Dyke of the Class of 1873 wrote of his "profound regret" that Wilson appeared to be proceeding as though his plan had been adopted; van Dyke suggested that Wilson was pulling a fast one on the college, issuing "a change which seems to me full of the gravest perils to the life and unity of Princeton." Andrew West expressed indignation. "I feel bound to say that not only the thing that has been done, but the manner of doing it," he wrote Wilson, "are both wrong—not inexpedient merely—but morally wrong." West praised Wilson's last five years, under which he served "for something more than salary and office"; but now, he contended, "If the spirit of Princeton is to be killed, I have little interest in the details of the funeral."

Most distressing were the words from Jack Hibben. In the days before the two friends parted for their respective summer vacations, Hibben tried alerting Wilson to the mounting opposition to the Quad Plan. Even more than his own reservations, he spoke of the discontent among trustees, faculty, and alumni. As Ellen Wilson could not even imagine her husband enduring this battle without his staunchest ally by his side, she took the liberty of telling Hibben that his words had, in fact, disheartened him for the fight.

"Now, Woodrow it certainly makes my heart exceedingly heavy as I reflect that the poor but well intended offices of friendship have so miscarried," he wrote. "You know that I would never have sought to 'rob you of hope,' as Mrs. Wilson characterized it, unless I had thought that I might at the same time forarm you by forwarning you of the gathering opposition." Hibben hoped Wilson might be willing to reopen the question for further discussion. And he expressed deep regret if his "too blunt & too frank words" had "inflicted wounds which had no healing power."

Wilson delivered an Independence Day speech at the Jamestown Exposition (honoring the tercentenary of the colony's founding) that began as a historical commendation of Thomas Jefferson but ended as a political condemnation of trusts and robber barons. (He shared the podium that day with Governor Charles Evans Hughes of New York, whose trust-busting stands were making him a current favorite for the Republican Presidential nomination in 1908.) Afterward, the Wilsons retreated to upstate New York.

Not unlike England's Lake District, the hamlet of St. Hubert's in the Adirondacks—twenty-five miles from the nearest train station—promised fresh air, breathtaking vistas, and mountain hikes. From his primitive country cottage, Wilson wrote Hibben that his recent comments had not dimmed their friendship because he believed his friend was mistaken about the prevailing sentiment toward his Quad Plan. And before concluding that he might be wrong, Wilson said he must do everything that is honorable "to convince all upon whom I depend for support of the wisdom and necessity of what I propose." Wilson granted there could be negative consequences to his agitation, but wrote, "I should feel a mere contempt for myself should I lose courage or falter: for I never had a clearer sense of duty. . . . To shirk would kill me; to fail need not."

As for what Stockton Axson called Woodrow's "all involving, complete friendship with a man," Wilson wrote that he loved and honored Jack for doing his duty. Woodrow wrote again on July 10: "I shall try to . . . win your love and respect. You would not wish me to do otherwise, and our friendship, by which I have lived . . . is to be as little affected by our difference of opinion as is everything permanent."

Wilson spent much of his summer shaping his argument and shoring up support. "The fight is on," he wrote Cleveland Dodge, "and I regard it, not as a fight for the development, but as a fight for the restoration of Princeton. My heart is in it more than it has been in anything else." In accepting an honorary degree from Harvard at the start of the summer, Wilson had referred to his ancestry, which he trusted would help him through the months ahead. "The beauty about a Scotch-Irishman," he said, "is that he not only thinks he is right, but knows he is right." Wilson wrote two essays that summer, which revealed his bifurcated mind—one called "Education," the other called "Politics." When Ellen's sister Madge discovered a Ouija board up in St. Hubert's, Wilson could not resist conjuring the spirit of James McCosh, seeking support everywhere to his side in the campus arguments. After considerable "conversation" with his model and mentor, Wilson asked, "What do you think of Andrew West, Doctor?" From "the other side," came the reply: "West will burn in hell to the greater glory of God."

"Wilson is not in as good physical or mental condition as I should like to see him," Henry B. Thompson wrote fellow trustee Cleveland Dodge at summer's end. "This subject has taken such a hold on him, he is nervous and excitable, but keeps all this well under restraint in discussion. This, in itself, is exhausting. . . . His holiday has contained too much work and not enough relaxation." On September 19, 1907, Wilson opened the new school year with a reading from the first chapter of the Book of Joshua, in which the Lord spoke upon the death of Moses, urging Joshua to "be strong and courageous, because you will lead these people to inherit the land I swore to their forefathers to give them." He then spoke of the magnificent new classroom building on campus, McCosh Hall.

Nassau Hall had recently been remodeled, its onetime library and chapel transformed into a Faculty Room, largely to Wilson's specifications. The magnificent chamber—seventy-six feet in length—was paneled in English oak; benches flanked each side of a long table, leading to a raised dais from which officers ran the faculty meetings. At four o'clock on Thursday, September 26, over a hundred members of the faculty took their places beneath the portraits of Princeton's former presidents. Two pro-Wilson professors endorsed the trustees' action of the previous June and proposed faculty acceptance in the form of a committee to cooperate with the administration in enacting the Quad Plan. Henry van Dyke objected, offering a counterproposal that suggested the debate was far from over—that the board appoint a joint committee of trustees and faculty to "investigate the present social conditions of the University in conjunction with representatives of the Alumni and students." Its very proposal was a slap in Wilson's face, a suggestion that all his work of the spring was about to unravel. Silence filled the great hall, until another faculty member stood to second the motion.

"Do I understand," Wilson asked in a measured voice that belied his tense expression, "that Professor Hibben seconds the motion?"

"I do, Mr. President," Hibben said calmly. Another faculty member noted, "The air was electric for a few minutes," until the faculty voted to adjourn until the following Monday. Wilson had every reason to believe the faculty remained solidly behind him, which made Hibben's active support of the opposition even harder to bear. After years of grooming his dearest friend for future leadership at the college—favoring him with committee assignments and leaving him in charge during his absences—Wilson had never felt so betrayed. "That is hurting your father dreadfully," Ellen wrote daughter Jessie, then away at school. The wound would fester for the rest of Wilson's life. He would forever thereafter think of Hibben as a "little snob." More than that, he once told Stockton Axson, "Hibben has shaken my faith in friendship."

The faculty reconvened in Nassau Hall on September 30 and listened to spirited support of the tabled van Dyke Resolution. They discussed the need to include alumni in deciding upon the Quad Plan. Well into the two-hour debate, Wilson at last held forth, standing perfectly erect upon the dais. His plea was earnest and emotional. Second-year preceptor William Starr Myers wrote in his diary that it was "one of the most wonderful speeches I have ever heard"; and the votes that day confirmed as much, rejecting van Dyke's measure 80 to 23.

But the battle had just begun. Opposition to the quads raged in what had been renamed the *Daily Princetonian* and in the *Princeton Alumni Weekly*: class and school spirit would diminish, many argued; secret societies would increase; and a social ranking among the quads themselves would develop. Building a defense for the next faculty meeting, on October 7, Wilson prepared unusually extensive notes, with important phrases

written out. And on that day, he spoke as eloquently as he ever had—
holding forth for an hour and a half. An American college, he said in his
central argument, was "not a place for exclusiveness."

"We now have to make our choice of ideal," he told the faculty, "whether
we wish to invite youngsters to a life which they shall form for themselves
or to a life which shall form them." Professor T. W. Hunt, a fixture in the
English Department for almost forty years, wrote Wilson that "it has
never been my privilege to hear a more inspiring address on the subject of
University Education than that which you gave us yesterday." Two of Wilson's statistics reverberated for most of the educators in the room: 9.63
percent of clubmen earned academic honors at Princeton; and for non-
clubmen, that figure was 41.7 percent.

The press picked up the story and created nationwide interest in what
emerged as a class war. Trustees West and Cleveland and van Dyke had
rallied opposition all summer, their ranks growing as they organized a
united front. Not having met a single fellow alumnus who favored Wilson's plan, Adrian Joline, president of the Missouri, Kansas & Texas Railway Company, suggested in the alumni magazine that Wilson was
imposing a plan "without a single redeeming feature." Wealthy alumni
threatened to withdraw support, at a moment when a university could ill
afford antagonizing its donors, what with a major economic recession
looming over the nation: the New York Stock Exchange had lost half its
value in the last year; banks were going bust; unemployment had suddenly
risen from 3 percent to 8 percent. When even Wilson's allies suggested
that he was fighting a losing battle, he only became more obdurate. "We
dearly love Woodrow," said one of them, "but he does drive too fast."

By the time the board gathered in the Trustees' Room in the Chancellor Green Library on the morning of October 17, 1907, all sides of the issue
had been voiced. Wilson proceeded quickly to new business, at which
time Momo Pyne, long a proponent of the new Princeton, now offered
three resolutions that passed, rescinding all of Wilson's recent progress.
Having anticipated such action, Cleveland Dodge promptly offered another resolution, one that would not only allow Wilson to save face but
also protect the university from negative publicity that might arise from
the board having handed its president such a resounding defeat. Dodge
suggested the issue could be reconsidered later. It passed.

Wilson told the New York *Evening Sun* that he did not consider the trustees' vote to be opposition to the quad system on principle so much as an expression of their feeling that the university community was not sufficiently prepared. He said he intended to build support by explaining it to Princetonians across the country. But the board's actions were not lost on him, as a fragment of an unsent letter to the members reveals: "Your rejection," he scratched out in his precise shorthand, ". . . makes it plain to me that you will not feel able to support me any further in the only matter which I feel that I can lead and be of service to you." To his daughter Jessie, he wrote: "It is most humiliating; and I have not yet seen my way to the next step I should take; but God rules in all things, and I am sure that I shall see sooner or later which way my duty lies." He refrained from resigning—"because I saw at last that I did not have the right to place the University in danger of going to pieces; and because I felt that the men who were forcing this surrender upon me had made all that I have accomplished financially possible." Momo Pyne wrote a colleague that he was much surprised to read Wilson's comments in the *Evening Sun*, because the plan had, in fact, been turned down "finally and for good, and the only reason it was not turned down harder was to save the feelings of the President."

Ironically, the defeat enabled Wilson to see the politics of the university with greater clarity. As the fights got more petty, his thoughts got more grand. "The pushing things in this world are ideals, not ideas," he had long held. "We live by poetry, not by prose, and we live only as we see visions." Now he assigned new value to fighting to the death for an ideal. Virtually every Wilson speech thereafter contained a political subtext, often that of attacking the attainment of power through money. His speeches likened a university to the nation, and undergraduates to its citizens.

As had been the case in almost a dozen instances of emotional duress, Wilson's body broke down once again. People attributed the numbness and pain in his right arm and shoulder to neuritis. The constant politicking and the extensive travel had certainly contributed to Wilson's condition; but the person who knew him best believed he was suffering from the "loss of the friend he took to his bosom." Wilson's inability either to explain or to excuse Hibben's behavior gives credence to Ellen's contention. "Mr. Hibben can thank himself for this illness of Woodrow's," Ellen said. "Nothing else has caused it but the fact that his heart is broken."

Wilson sailed on January 18, 1908, for Bermuda, where he put his political losses at Princeton aside for six weeks. But he felt unmoored in other ways as well. For the first time in twenty years, he and Ellen faced an empty nest. Relatives continued to come and go, but the Wilson daughters had grown and moved away from home, each taking after him in a different way. Jessie had become an ethereal beauty and possessed her father's gentle and spiritual temperament; Margaret was a dead ringer for him, inheriting some of his haughty reserve. After they persuaded their mother that higher education would not render them "unfeminine," they both attended the Women's College of Baltimore City, soon renamed Goucher. Having musical ambitions, Margaret remained in the city, where she studied voice at the Peabody Conservatory, a division of Johns Hopkins. The youngest daughter, Nellie, was in her own words "the frivolous one." She looked the least like her father and was—in the words of another family member—"a pretty girl who enjoyed her prettiness." She inherited his private playful side. Unafraid to say she was "bored with Sir Walter Scott and Thackeray and Anthony Trollope," she "loved clothes and dancing and going to football and baseball games with her father or a beau. She said she didn't want to go to college and detected a gleam of sympathy in her mother's eyes." Because Woodrow felt she might become too dependent on the family and Ellen feared she "talked like a Yankee," they sent her to St. Mary's College, an Episcopal boarding school and junior college in Raleigh, North Carolina. With the loss of so many other family members, melancholia frequently overcame Ellen. She sometimes needed to put distance between herself and Woodrow. When he went away, she took to visiting relatives in Georgia.

No sooner had the *Bermudian* docked and Wilson checked into the Hotel Hamilton than he went in search of Mrs. Peck. He found her in Paget, the fashionable area across the harbor from Hamilton. With Mrs. Peck's mother and son and a number of other young people in residence to chaperone, Mrs. Peck invited Wilson to make "Shoreby" his home, to come whenever he liked for tea or simply to lie in the hammock on her verandah above the sea. Her luncheons and dinners provided Wilson with the finest company Bermuda had to offer, including several encounters with Mark Twain. Wilson found himself at Shoreby so often, Mary Peck suggested he place on her mantelpiece one of the pictures of Ellen with which he traveled. Wilson talked constantly of his wife, enough that it suggested his own concerns about Mary Peck's attractiveness. After a few weeks, the two took long walks together, leaving behind the problems at home. "Bermuda is certainly the best place in the world in which to forget Princeton," Woodrow wrote Ellen, "at least Princeton as an organization and a problem." But more than campus politics appeared to be weighing upon him. He asked if Mrs. Peck might give him a whole day to discuss a matter of importance.

The next morning, he arrived at Shoreby's dock, and they walked the South Shore until they came to a bay tree surrounded by roses, oleanders, and cedars. Gazing at the world below—horseback riders, children playing in the sand—Wilson spoke at last. "My friends tell me that if I will enter the contest and can be nominated and elected Governor of New Jersey," he said matter-of-factly, "I stand a very good chance of being the next President of the United States. Shall I, or shall I not, accept the opportunity they offer?"

At first, Mrs. Peck felt like a coin being tossed, until she realized Wilson needed a sounding board. "Why not?" she asked. "Statesmanship has been your natural bent, your real ambition all your life and, God knows, our country needs men like you in her national life!"

Wilson raised the fact that he was not a rich man and that his current position at least provided his family a dignified home and some of the luxury they deserved. "If I know anything of your wife and daughters," Mrs. Peck said, "they would rather *scrub* to earn their bread than have you do less than your best work in life—your full duty." Then Wilson asked if it was fair to desert those who had fought with him in the recent battle at Princeton. Mrs. Peck suggested that perhaps his work there was done. "If your ideas and ideals are right, they will endure." Resigning himself even to the possibility, Wilson added, "The life of the next Democratic President will be hell—and it would probably kill me." And Mrs. Peck suggested he would "rather die in harness, fighting for all the great things for which you stand than live up to less than the best that is within you." After mentioning a few lesser arguments, Wilson said, "Very well, so be it!"

He returned to Princeton on February 27, 1908, his neuritis no better and his future no more certain; but he had the comfort of knowing that he had two years in which to decide. During that time he could pursue two tracks at once, for the choices of education or politics no longer required him to split his personality. Wilson would drive harder than ever to promote his changes for Princeton. The eating clubs had become social trusts—powerful monopolies dictating much of campus life—and like the cartels dominating American business, they needed busting. So, while Wilson's jurisdiction was something less than local, his vision was universal; while the specifics of his speeches differed, his general themes fused into one: his philosophy of equal opportunity over privileged exclusivity remained the same. His Princeton talks and his political talks became virtually one and the same.

Shortly before Wilson's vacation, supporter David B. Jones had written of his distaste for the influence the alumni of wealth were exerting over the university. In urging Wilson to stick to his convictions, even at the expense of paring down the faculty, he wrote, "If Mr. Pyne thinks it best to withdraw his support, I shall be very sorry, but I shall be infinitely more sorry to see the University dominated by the club men of New York, Philadelphia and Pittsburgh." Just as a rising Progressive movement was finding that its primary foe included the same rich men in the East, Wilson found the farther he went from Princeton, the more kindly disposed his audiences were toward his Quad Plan. "The particular threat that seems to me the most alarming to our life at the present moment," he told the alumni of the Princeton Club of Chicago, "is that we are beginning to think in classes, that we are beginning to think in the terms of the capitalistic interest or in terms of the labor interest or in terms of some other . . . interest, like the mining interest or the agricultural interest." He insisted that the order of life which had made America meant that "there must be absolutely a free field and no favor for anybody."

Two days later, Wilson addressed the Commercial Club of Chicago. He spoke not as a college president but as a concerned citizen; but as he had two nights before, he challenged an existing system in which wealth had created unfair advantages in an increasingly predatory corporate world. He addressed the primary issue of the day, which was governmental regulation of immoral business practices. He articulated a position he would carry for the rest of his life—that there were no dishonest corporations or greedy trusts, only dishonest and greedy individuals within those organizations, who must be held accountable. Morality is "never corporate," he said. "Morality is never aggregate. The only way you get honest business is from honest men." The question before the nation was how best to achieve that honesty and fairness. On April 13, 1908, Princeton's president spoke before the National Democratic Club in New York, sharing the stage with two United States Senators and the Governor of Minnesota. "We hear a great deal of candidacies and programmes," he said, "but very little of principles. Parties seem almost to have gone to pieces and to have become indistinguishable." He proposed stronger laws, especially in indicting abusers of the corporate system. "Law, and the government as umpire," he said, "not discretionary power, and the government as master, should be the programme of every man who loves liberty and the established character of the Republic."

By commencement 1908 the Quad Plan was being revisited and Wilson's name increasingly mentioned as a potential candidate. The political undertones to all of Wilson's utterances became more and more apparent to everybody within earshot, even the undergraduates. Among the verses the seniors of "Aughtie-Eight" sang in their "Faculty Song" that year was:

> *Here's to Woodrow, King Divine,*
> *He rules this place along with Fine.*
> *We fear that soon he'll leave this town*
> *To try for Teddy Roosevelt's crown.*

With the Democratic Party about to open its Presidential nominating convention in Denver, word spread that Colonel George Harvey, among others, intended to lobby on Wilson's behalf. The Democratic bench could hardly have been shallower, and Wilson represented the kind of candidate the press corps has always been quick to embrace—a fresh face with an unorthodox background.

As Grover Cleveland's two nonconsecutive terms had been the party's only victories in more than fifty years, the party struggled for an identity as much as a victory. A dozen states in the southeast quadrant of the country guaranteed a solid base of a third of the nation's 483 electoral votes, as they had since 1880; but the Democrats had not been able to field a candidate since Cleveland who could broaden their reach much beyond that. They came closest in 1896 when they embraced Populist values and that party's candidate, William Jennings Bryan, who was able to lasso eleven Western states. But that rural region did not come close to matching the more urban elector-rich Northeast. In 1900, the party hoped familiarity with Bryan might extend his brand; but his second run fared worse than the first. And so, in 1904, the party tried to reach into the Northeast by running Alton B. Parker, a Bourbon Democrat, as conservative members of the party were known. Wilson had supported him, but Parker proved no match for TR.

By the time Wilson was ready to leave for another vacation in the British Isles, it appeared that the delegates would revert to their Western strategy by reenlisting Bryan. But there remained the remote possibility of nominating Wilson for Vice President, as a way of seasoning him for the next election. So real did that undesired possibility seem to Wilson, he left a statement with Stockton Axson, to be published if necessary, refusing to allow his name to be presented at the convention. With Wilson's neuritis so bad that he could hardly hold a pen, Ellen feared her constant anxiety about his condition would only further inflame it, and so she insisted on his spending the summer alone. She would calm her own nerves studying landscape painting in Old Lyme, Connecticut, which had become a thriving artists' colony.

While aboard the S.S. *California*, Wilson forced himself to "turn off his mind" by running for an hour every day on the upper deck, reading only out of his *Oxford Book of English Verse*, and sleeping fourteen hours a day. After docking in Glasgow, Wilson rode his bicycle to Edinburgh. There he remained for several days more, not only to nurse a sore knee but because he wanted to be in a big city during the Democratic Convention, as he was "waiting on the possibility of the impossible happening." Wilson's name was never even raised during the convention. In hopes of carrying a Midwestern state, the convention handed Bryan an Indianan, John Kern, with whom he would suffer his biggest defeat yet, running against TR's handpicked nominee, Secretary of War William Howard Taft.

Wilson got back on his bike, paying homage this year to Thomas Carlyle, the Scot whose thoughts about the "Great Man Theory" ("The history of the world is but the biography of great men") inspired him. He rode through Cumbria—wearing cycling shorts, and a blue shirt and blue tie under a waterproof cape, his pockets packed with a comb and toothbrush, a volume of poetry, and a change of underwear—in search of Carlyle's birthplace. Returning to his familiar Wordsworth country, he renewed his friendship with the Yateses.

That summer Grover Cleveland died. Wilson so admired the former President, he did not begrudge his lack of support in the recent board battles at Princeton. For that he blamed Andrew Fleming West, for manipulating Cleveland into serving as his "dupe and tool." Cleveland's absence would give Wilson some slight advantage in the upcoming board battles; but, recognizing the greater necessity of staying always one step ahead of West, Wilson had already planned an offensive maneuver.

Mid-August, he took a train to the remote Scottish Highlands, where Andrew Carnegie and his wife resided part of each year in Skibo Castle. The castle dated back to the twelfth century and sat upon 120 square miles. The Carnegies had owned the property for a decade and invested £2 million—expanding the living quarters to sixty thousand square feet and adding a lake and a golf course. Wilson's fellow guests included lords and artists and businessmen, all of whom spent their days hunting, fishing, playing tennis and croquet, and swimming in a heated pool. In the evenings, they played whist or billiards or just read and conversed. In his time alone with Carnegie, Wilson managed to plead his case for $3.5 million to underwrite his Quad Plan. He returned to Princeton with his right hand less palsied, but empty.

"It floats!" These two words threatened to sink Woodrow Wilson. Soap had been part of civilization for at least four thousand years, going as far back as the Babylonians, who had discovered a formula for water, alkali, and oils that could dissolve dirt and grease. In the 1830s, a man named Alexander Norris suggested that his two sons-in-law—one of whom made candles, the other soap—merge their companies. William Procter and James Gamble did just that, making a small fortune together as purveyors to the Union army during the Civil War. A decade later, Gamble's son created a phenomenon, combining a strong laundry detergent and a gentle cleaner and whipping in enough air to keep the white cake of soap from sinking. Its two-word advertising campaign helped turn Ivory soap into an American household staple for another century and Procter & Gamble into one of America's leading manufacturers.

At the start of the 1908 school year, William Cooper Procter—one of the cofounders' grandsons—traveled from Ohio to Princeton to see a football game, ostensibly his first visit to the campus since dropping out as a senior in 1883. Recently made president of Procter & Gamble, he was one of the richest men in the Midwest. A few months later, Procter offered Princeton $500,000 for a graduate college, but with strings attached: Princeton would have to match his pledge; and he did not want the Graduate College to be built on the site Wilson had long envisioned, adjacent to Prospect, but on "some other site . . . which shall be satisfactory to me." No one gave Wilson prior knowledge of the gift.

All the negotiations, as became immediately obvious, had been conducted by Dean West, who had been one of Procter's high school teachers in Cincinnati. Stockton Axson immediately recognized the entire transaction as a political plot. Upon leaving Princeton, Procter had become too busy "turning soap fat into millions and attempting to act the dominant part in his community" to give any thought to his alma mater, said Axson.

> But, meanwhile, Princeton become fashionable . . . and association with it meant the sort of pleasing sensation which a snob covets. Procter had money; was arrogant by nature; liked the things which were beginning to be so prominent at Princeton—display and social advantage. So with his money he sought to settle the dispute in a thoroughly characteristic way—by purchase.

Wilson was confounded by an embattlement of riches. The money from the Swann estate, which specifically stipulated that the Graduate College be built on the Princeton campus, had become available; and Wilson, architect Ralph Adams Cram, and the majority of trustees on the Graduate College committee all agreed on its central location. But now Dean West clearly intended to fight with the backing of the Soap King, whose offer was twice the size and stipulated that the one place his money could not be spent was on the very site Wilson had selected. As neither gift was enough to build the graduate school, the funds would have to be pooled. The struggle immediately became about something more than geography and less than educational ideals. In essence, it was about control of the Graduate College; and the personalities of both Wilson and West were overtaking their principles. Procter, obviously prompted by West, said he preferred Merwick as the site but would approve a two-hundred-acre tract of land with golf links that had been donated to the college in 1905.

The Golf Links were the better part of a mile from Nassau Hall, with townspeople living in between. Wilson argued that the Swann bequest could not be applied to either of Procter's preferred sites. For months, trustees and attorneys fought over the legalities of the situation; students and faculty and alumni discussed the practicalities. West argued that the

graduate students should not have to consort with the rowdy undergraduates, whose periodic spring riots, for example, had recently impelled Wilson
to erect a gate around Prospect. He believed Merwick remained the most
congenial spot; and he had long fantasized about all the trappings of a graduate school's great refectory, with oak paneling and Gothic windows and
two or three long tables and professors at the high table. Wilson clung to
his belief that an intellectual community would thrive best when scholars
of all degrees lived among one another and where the Graduate College
would be within sight of the president's house.

By June 1909, Wilson's impatience became apparent in every speech he
delivered, as he became less politic and more political with each breath. At
St. Paul's School in Concord, New Hampshire, that June, he told an audience that included many rich men's sons, "A danger surrounding our modern education is the danger of wealth. . . . The lad who is to inherit money
is foredoomed to obscurity." His dreams for Princeton slipping from his
grasp, he added: "So far as the colleges go, the sideshows have swallowed
up the circus, and we don't know what is going on in the main tent and I
don't know that I want to continue as ringmaster under those conditions. . . . Schools like this one and universities like Princeton must pass
out of existence unless they adapt themselves to modern life." In early July
he told the Harvard chapter of Phi Beta Kappa that he wished for all of
them "that we reorganize our colleges on the lines . . . that a college is not
only a body of studies but a mode of association. . . . It must become a
community of scholars and pupils,—a free community but a very real one,
in which democracy may work its reasonable triumphs of accommodation,
its vital processes of union."

Wilson and his family retreated for the summer to Connecticut, where
Ellen rejoined her community of artists. On the main street of Old Lyme,
a charming town on the eastern bank of the Connecticut River, sat the
home of Florence Griswold, who turned what had been her birthplace into
a boardinghouse for artists only—complete with bedrooms, studio space,
and exhibition rooms. Painter Childe Hassam started coming in 1903, and
promptly attracted scores of colleagues and acolytes, turning the little
town into the epicenter of American Impressionism. Frank DuMond, who
would later mentor Georgia O'Keeffe and Norman Rockwell, taught Ellen; and he was so impressed with her work, he arranged for her to paint
in a private studio. Ellen proved to be no dilettante—her landscapes

revealed expert brushwork, an alluring palette, and even a tendency toward abstraction—and she would soon be exhibiting her work.

Although guests of the artists were not allowed to stay in the house, Miss Florence excepted Wilson. He delighted in Ellen's joy at being at the boardinghouse and adored the town, with no sounds of the rude world beyond the occasional motorcar or train in the distance. He spent his mornings in Old Lyme writing several long pieces on education and his afternoons playing golf on a "sheep pasture course." In the evenings, he read or conversed with his fellow boarders and indulged in an epistolary relationship, one of greater intensity than prior exchanges with a number of women friends. His correspondent was Mrs. Peck.

For more than a century, conjecture has surrounded the relationship between Woodrow Wilson and Mary Allen Hulbert Peck, raising eyebrows—if not serious questions—about their association. This is due in large part to the fact that much of their relationship is enshrouded in mystery—there are omissions in their correspondence, and the alleged commission of acts has been reported secondhand. The surmise of what occurred has become most tantalizing because of the participants themselves—an unconventional woman of dubious respectability and a man of flagrant morality.

Wilson's letters to Mrs. Peck undeniably increased in frequency and frankness between 1908 and 1910; and during that period, Mrs. Peck separated from her husband in Massachusetts and moved into an apartment at 39 East Twenty-seventh Street in New York City with her mother and son. As Wilson had reason to visit the city with some frequency—on matters of both education and politics—he tried as often as possible to include a visit with Mrs. Peck. Sometimes, they were alone. In later years, Wilson himself would admit that there had once been a passage in his life of "folly and gross impertinence" during which he had neglected "standards of honourable behavior." He would later confess to "the contemptible error and madness of a few months," which left him "stained and unworthy," but say that it was a "folly long ago loathed and repented of." Ellen Wilson would once speak of "the 'Peck' affair" as "the only unhappiness" her husband caused her during their married life.

Yet, the letters between Wilson and Mrs. Peck, for all their friendliness, don't reveal, or even suggest, physical intimacy. They do not even imply emotional intimacy. Instead, they merely recount Wilson's actions and thoughts, including the fact that he felt needy. He expressed tenderness toward the unhappy widow and recent divorcée but nothing like the sexual ardor and romantic passion his letters had lavished upon Ellen over many years. His letters to Mary Peck were melodious, but never rhapsodic—at least those letters whose existence is known. If fervent love letters passed between them, especially in those lacunae where no missives now exist, nothing in the letters that would precede or follow such an exchange suggests an affair in the modern meaning. Wilson introduced his wife and family to Mrs. Peck. One might construe that as a clever ruse; but not a single witness ever surfaced who recounted any untoward behavior between them, and there exist few letters from Wilson to Mrs. Peck that do not include happy mentions of or regards from Ellen and the rest of his family—hardly the sentiments a furtive husband might extend to a mistress.

In modern times of looser sexual standards, Wilson's description of his folly too easily appears to be that of a sexual affair. But at the turn of the twentieth century, a man of Wilson's rigid morality held himself to stricter standards. Ellen Wilson had gained weight in recent years, becoming somewhat plump and matronly; but whatever attraction he may have felt for Mrs. Peck, he never expressed even the slightest disapproval of his wife. It seems all but impossible to imagine that he could have subjected Ellen or their children to a woman who was his inamorata.

The Catholic Church refers to the "occasion of sin," external circumstances that might incite moral evil; a future President late in the twentieth century would refer to harboring lust in his heart. In view of Woodrow Wilson's nature, and with no conflicting evidence anywhere else in his life, just being alone with another woman—perhaps touching her hand, even seeking her solace when Ellen was unable to provide the comforting shoulder she had long provided—was probably what Woodrow Wilson considered "folly and gross impertinence." Often omitted in accounts of "the Peck affair" are the rest of Ellen's comments about her husband's indiscretion. She said it was the only such unhappiness in their married life but added that there was nothing "wrong or improper" about it, "for there was not, but just that a brilliant mind and an attractive woman had some-how fascinated—temporarily—Mr. Wilson's mind." Woodrow's love for his wife—and the expression thereof—never wavered. His friendship with Mrs. Peck would continue for several more years, gradually dissipating. Although Woodrow's guilt and Ellen's hurt were real, the "affair" with Mrs. Peck was almost surely not physical.

In September 1909, President Wilson opened the 163rd session of Princeton University, but for the first time felt none of the romance of a new school year. Disenchanted, he wrote Mrs. Peck:

> Sophomores are tiresome young fools, and Freshmen are a great anxiety. . . . Committees meet and discuss the same old cases and questions. . . . There are lectures to deliver, and you are plagued by the same old ignorance: I mean your own, not the students'. Parents flock, with the same old delusion about their sons. Trustees tease you with suggestions and oppositions, alumni criticise, and praise as ignorantly and injudiciously as they criticise.

With the Graduate College fight eroding his spirit, he rallied the energy to confront William Cooper Procter himself. On October 20, 1909, the two met in New York City, the seventh time the benefactor had traveled east in an attempt to get the university to accept his half-million-dollar donation. Wilson's latest argument for an on-campus site, instead of the remote Merwick or the Golf Links, fell on deaf ears. At the trustees' meeting the next morning, Moses Taylor Pyne urged his colleagues, at long last, to accept the "very generous offer" and—by a vote of 14 to 10—they did.

"Suffice it to say that . . . the Trustees adopted a plan of that arch-intriguer West's which I and all my colleagues on the Faculty earnestly opposed,—a plan of deep and lasting consequence to the University and its whole development," Wilson wrote Mrs. Peck three days later. "The money overshadowed all my counsel. They do not trust West any more than I do. They think him a nuisance and would be glad to get rid of him. But they did want the money. . . . Twice, therefore, on two questions as important as can arise in my administration, they have refused to allow my leadership because money talked louder than I did. It is really intolerable." Disgusted and disheartened, Wilson stewed for days, trying to think of a solution.

Where there's a will, there's a way—in this case, Mrs. Swann's. While counsel for all parties examined the codicils for ambiguities, Wilson met again with Procter to present an expedient if not Solomonic solution— the building of two graduate quadrangles: one on campus, using the Swann money, which would satisfy Wilson's needs and meet the strictest

The manse of the Presbyterian Church in Staunton, Virginia—birthplace of Thomas Woodrow Wilson, who later dropped his first name. Born in 1856, he was the third child of the Reverend Joseph Ruggles Wilson and Janet Woodrow Wilson, who was descended from a long line of Scottish ministers.

"Tommy" Wilson, as he was known into his twenties, at age sixteen. Photographed in Columbia, South Carolina, one of four Southern cities in which he was raised.

The College of New Jersey, in Princeton, where Wilson enrolled in 1875.

The Reverend James McCosh came from
Scotland to become the eleventh president of
Princeton (1868–1888).

While Wilson (standing, holding his hat) thrived intellectually at Princeton, he also reveled in
extracurricular activities and joined an eating club—the Alligators.

Thomas W. Wilson, Class of 1879, upon his graduation—with an essay about Congress already accepted for publication and with dreams of becoming a Senator.

→ALWAYS SOMETHING NEW.←

HOTEL ALDINE,

JOHN I. PARRILL,
Proprietor.

Subscriber to SLOAN'S LEGAL AND
FINANCIAL REGISTER and Mem-
ber of the CONTINENTAL
COLLECTION UNION.

Ashland, Ky., _____ 188_

that you seemed to desire it; and another was
that I thought, after what you had said, I
owed it to you to leave matters for the present as they stand — to trust all to you; and
yet I felt that, after the terrible nervous strain
I had gone through, I would not be sure of
having control enough over myself to leave the
subject alone. So, to go away was the kindest
service I could do you; and I did it as such,
notwithstanding the tremendous effort it cost me.

　　We did not have our group picture taken,
did we? Will you do me a great favor — and
do it on my own terms? I am not going to
make any hard request, but one very easily complied with. I want you to go to Simonds' gallery,
wearing your pink dress, or any other dress similarly cut about the neck, — since the photograph
can't reproduce the color — and have a cabinet
taken in profile. Let the picture include your

While studying law at the University of Virginia, Woodrow Wilson fell in love with Harriet "Hattie" Woodrow, his first cousin. After she refused his marriage proposal, he requested at least a photograph of her, posed according to his specifications.

figure to the waist; let your head be slightly bent forward and your eyes slightly downcast. Jessie can arrange the minute particulars of the pose, of course, and the artist must be made to acquiesce. There are two more conditions: there must be only one copy of the photograph, unless you want one for yourself; and I must bear the expense of the work, since it is to be done specially for me. Now, you think me very absurd, don't you? Well, may be I am; but wont you indulge this whim of mine, please, since it is a very innocent one? It wont cost you much trouble and it will give me an immense deal of pleasure. Oh, I forgot something! Don't wear any hat, but let your hair be dressed as it usually is in the mornings. Now you wont refuse me this, will you? however foolish you may think it.

My ride to-day has not tired me very much. I feel quite fresh to-night, though a little sleepy. I am writing in the hotel office, in the midst of all sorts of noises and confusion. Every one of a crowd of men is apparently trying to talk louder than his neighbors, who,

In 1882, Wilson practiced law in Atlanta, though he cared little for the city or the profession.

Before abandoning his career for graduate school in 1883, he did some legal work in Rome, Georgia, where he met Ellen Louise Axson, the daughter of the local Presbyterian minister. Before entering Johns Hopkins University in the fall, he proposed marriage, and she accepted.

While studying for his doctorate in history and political science, Wilson did little else but write hundreds of passionate love letters to his fiancée and sing in the Johns Hopkins Glee Club (top row, second from left).

Even before he had received his degree, Wilson secured a teaching position at a new school for women, Bryn Mawr College—its faculty and students pictured below. (The newlywed Wilson is in the top row, at the far right.)

Yearning to teach "a class of *men*," Wilson (bottom row, third from left) joined the faculty of Wesleyan University in 1889 but remained frustrated for having diverged from a career path into politics.

In 1890, Professor Wilson accepted a teaching position at his alma mater and became the most popular and respected professor on the Princeton campus.

"I am madly in love with you," Woodrow wrote his wife of ten years in 1895. "Are you prepared for the storm of love making with which you will be assailed?" he asked at the close of one long absence.

The three Wilson daughters in 1893:
Jessie, Eleanor (called Nell), and Margaret.

Professor Wilson (photographed in 1893) published dozens of articles, essays, and reviews, several books of political science, a five-volume *History of the American People*, and a biography of George Washington— all within twenty years.

He also became a renowned speaker; and in 1896, the 150-year-old College of New Jersey became Princeton University and named Wilson its Sesquicentennial orator.

In 1902, Woodrow Wilson was elected Princeton's thirteenth president.

Nassau Hall in the late nineteenth century.

In 1906, Princeton conferred an honorary degree upon one of its benefactors, Andrew Carnegie (front, to Wilson's left), then the richest man in the world.

Prospect, the twenty-room residence of the president of Princeton. Ellen transformed the backyard with her formal garden. She would later plant a rose garden at the White House.

Ellen regretted their private lives becoming more public and underwent several crippling personal tragedies.

Ellen and Woodrow on the terrace at Prospect with their daughters—the philosophical Margaret, the soulful Jessie, and the playful Nell.

Suffering from the strains of his new office, Wilson vacationed alone in Bermuda, where he met the twice-married Mary Allen Hulbert Peck. Rumors of an affair between them persisted for the rest of their lives.

In 1906, Wilson traveled with his wife and family to England's Lake District, where he befriended artist Frederic Yates, who drew these portraits of Ellen and Woodrow.

The Faculty Room of Nassau Hall, where meetings of Princeton's Board of Trustees grew increasingly contentious. After Wilson had introduced sweeping innovations that strengthened the character of the university, the trustees blocked his two most controversial plans.

Andrew Fleming West, dean of the Graduate School, was Wilson's leading adversary.

John Grier Hibben was the closest friend Wilson ever had—until he opposed Wilson's views about democratizing the college with residential quadrangles. Wilson neither exchanged another personal word with him nor allowed himself another friendship so intimate.

interpretation of the will; another on the Golf Links, using Procter's money, which would meet his stipulations and the need for their growing graduate student body. Procter said he believed neither in dividing the graduate students nor in their associating with undergraduates. He left unsaid that such a plan would diffuse the power of Dean West, who could not rule from both citadels, especially when one would be situated right between Wilson's house and his office.

After meeting once more with Procter, on December 22, Wilson sat in the Jersey City station and composed a note to Momo Pyne, reporting the benefactor's indifference to a compromise. "The acceptance of this gift has taken the guidance of the University out of my hands entirely," he wrote, "—and I seem to have come to the end." Two days later, Pyne replied that he trusted that Wilson had given the matter further consideration and would withdraw his hastily penciled note.

On Christmas Day, Wilson replied, granting that his note had been written "under deep excitement," but that the "judgment it expressed was not hastily formed." Simply, he explained, "I cannot accede to the acceptance of gifts upon terms which take the educational policy of the University out of the hands of the Trustees and Faculty and permit it to be determined by those who give money." For the sake of his conscience and his self-respect, Wilson put his position on the line, as he asked Pyne and the board to reconsider the Procter gift.

One by one, Wilson's allies unified, outnumbering West's and agreeing to disregard Procter's offer. The next morning, Pyne got delayed in a snowstorm and arrived just minutes before a trustees' meeting at which he presented a letter he had received the night before from Procter. Its contents were stupefying: in order to remain in the game, Procter now consented to Wilson's proposal of separating the two bequests and building two separate graduate quadrangles.

Wilson was gobsmacked, less at the news than the chicanery behind it. With no time for careful consideration, he did not know how he could refuse his own proposition. Wilson could only re-argue that the issue was one "not of geography but of ideals," and he urged the trustees to see that if "the Graduate School is based on proper ideals, our Faculty can make a success of it anywhere in Mercer County." He called upon the trustees to decline the gift. The meeting ended without a decision.

On February 3, 1910, *The New York Times* ran an editorial called

"Princeton." Rather like Wilson's speeches over the last decade, it cast the American campus—Princeton in particular—as a metaphor for the nation. In framing the mission of American colleges—that of "throwing together youths of promise of every kind from every part of the country"—it further suggested that Princeton's current battle was part of a greater political and partisan war. "The Nation is aroused against special privilege," said the *Times*. "Sheltered by a great political party, it has obtained control of our commerce and industries. Now its exclusive and benumbing touch is upon those institutions which should stand pre-eminently for life, earnest endeavor, and broad enlightenment." The newspaper understood that the current struggle was not about a new building for the Graduate College or even the procurement of Procter's funds. It was about whether Princeton—and its peer institutions—were to "direct their energies away from the production of men trained to hard and accurate thought, masters in their professions, men intellectually well rounded, of wide sympathies and unfettered judgment, and to bend and degrade them into fostering mutually exclusive social cliques, stolid groups of wealth and fashion, devoted to non-essentials and the smatterings of culture." The editorial suggested this was essentially the age-old class war between entitlement and merit.

Now that they were under a microscope, trustees on both sides conferred in back rooms, so that their board meeting might proceed with a minimum of controversy. One faculty member reduced the argument to a single question: "Which can Princeton least afford to lose, Professor West & $500,000, or Woodrow Wilson & our honorable rank among American universities?" With trustee sentiment shifting against William Procter and West, the former summarily withdrew his $500,000 offer—a significant victory for Wilson. As his friend Cleveland Dodge wrote him, "Hereafter Princeton University is not to be run by the clamor of an irresponsible body of Alumni."

But Dodge misjudged the situation. All hell broke loose. Many graduates howled that Wilson should not have let so much money slip between his fingers; and many embraced Dean West's view of exclusive higher education. As Wilson's daughter Nell recalled, "Angry protests, vitriolic abuse, demands that the president resign and that Mr. Procter be informed that his terms would be accepted, if he would renew his offer, arrived daily at the president's office." Nell wrote that this was her father's "first experience with unpopularity, and it hurt."

At Ellen's anxious insistence, Woodrow boarded the S.S. *Oceana* for Bermuda on February 12, 1910. He would not see Mrs. Peck, for she was spending that winter in her New York apartment. At the Hamilton Hotel, he wrote an article called "The Country and the Colleges," which linked the "essentially democratic" spirits of learning and American life. ("Learning knows no differences of social caste or privilege. The mind is a radical democrat.") He visited with friends in the evenings, catching up with Mark Twain just two months before his death. Wilson maintained lengthy correspondences with both Mrs. Peck and his wife during his holiday, but his letters to the former were mostly about tea parties. To Ellen, who visited Mary Peck in the city with Nell while Woodrow was away, he expressed his profound love. On February 21, 1910, he wrote, "How sweet it is to think of you, to count on you, to know what you are. We have no compromises to look back on, the record of our consciences is clear in this whole trying business. We can be happy, therefore, no matter what may come of it all." And then he pondered their future. "It would be rather jolly, after all," he wrote, "to start out on life anew together, to make a new career, would it not?"

On a Saturday afternoon in January 1910, Colonel George Harvey had a long lunch at Delmonico's with James Smith, Jr., New Jersey's most powerful Democratic boss—a man Tammany Hall leader Richard Croker called "the greatest one-man-politician in the country." After the state's run of five consecutive Republican Governors, Harvey argued the necessity for a new kind of candidate—specifically, Woodrow Wilson. Smith balked. This former United States Senator who had created his own financial and political fortune through decades of deals under the table expressed serious doubts. He had countless chits to redeem and constituents to consider; and he could not help wondering whether a lifelong academician—whom he called "that Presbyterian priest"—had either the experience or the popular touch necessary to talk to the common folk in his wards. Harvey suggested those very weaknesses were Wilson's strengths: at a time when greedy business interests and corrupt political machines were under attack, nobody could more articulately advocate against special privilege than this politically untarnished moralist.

Smith's backroom boys liked the idea. They believed Wilson's inexperience would require his relying on them to run the government while he

provided an air of Progressivism and propriety. He would be the ideal puppet. The following Saturday, Smith and Harvey reconvened, and the party
boss told him, "I have thought it all over carefully, and I am ready to go
the whole hog." He was prepared to secure the nomination for Wilson once
Harvey could assure him that Wilson would accept. Recognizing that his
own sudden interest in forcing Wilson upon the party could taint the
candidate, Smith said he would declare that if the New Jersey legislature
went Democratic in the election, he would not offer himself to them as a
choice for the United States Senate. Wilson would appear to be his own
man, the nominal head of the Democratic Party in New Jersey.

On March 17, 1910, Harvey and his wife visited Prospect. After dinner
the gentlemen retired to Wilson's library, where Harvey spoke bluntly. "If I
can handle the matter so that the nomination for governor shall be tendered
to you on a silver platter, without you turning a hand to obtain it, and without any requirement or suggestion of any pledge whatsoever," he asked,
"what do you think would be your attitude?" Wilson paced the room, delib-
erating. He finally said that if the nomination came to him in that manner,
"I should regard it as my duty to give the matter very serious consideration."

Over several months, Wilson appeared to be convincing himself as well
as the New Jersey bosses, as he delivered numerous speeches with no educational pretext. A public beyond the Princeton community began paying
attention to this new national voice. "This is what I was meant for, anyhow,
this rough and tumble of the political arena," he confided to Mrs. Peck,
happy to loosen himself from the restraints of his academic position.

One of his first auditions came in early 1910, before the New York State
Bankers' Association at the Waldorf-Astoria. Nearly every financier of importance in the city attended; J. P. Morgan himself sat to Wilson's left.
With the Panic of 1907 still fresh in everybody's mind, Treasury Secretary
Franklin MacVeagh delivered remarks about currency reform. But Wilson
grabbed everybody's attention when he fired round after round into the
crowd of six hundred, accusing New York of being too provincial and its
bankers "too much centred in the affairs of their own institutions" when
they should be serving enterprise everywhere in the nation. "The basis of
banking, like the basis of the rest of life," he preached, "is moral in its
character, not financial." He said there was too much reliance in America
on legal defense of illegal action. Men of commerce no longer even asked if
their decisions put them on a road to profit but, instead, on a road to jail.

He felt the bankers of New York did not trust the country, which is why the country did not trust them. "I beg you gentlemen not to think of my criticism as impertinent," he said, but to consider it "as your own voice calling you to the service of the great country we love." The audience sat in stunned silence, as Wilson's glum dinner partner aggressively puffed his cigar. Then they filled the hall with enthusiastic applause. Morgan actually rose from his chair and publicly and warmly shook Wilson's hand.

Four nights later the Princeton president addressed the Short Ballot Organization, a progressive group committed to simplifying state and local governments. "Nothing is more interesting to me and nothing more discouraging at present than the privacy of public business," he told the crowd at the Hotel Astor. The simplification of government, he said, would yield greater accountability. At the end of the month, he addressed a Democratic Dollar Dinner in Elizabeth, New Jersey, planned in part by the editor of the city's *Evening Times*. One local leader had just returned from Washington, where he found unusual support for Wilson and even convinced Oklahoma's Senator Thomas Pryor Gore to come north to launch a Wilson candidacy. The college president withheld his permission, thinking it all premature; but that did not stop him from delivering more spellbinding speeches.

He continued to hold down his day job, though its satisfactions decreased every week. Anti-Wilson trustees rallied enough support among the alumni to get the Board of Trustees to ask Procter to restore his gift; and when Wilson himself went before alumni groups, especially in the East, he encountered growing hostility. At each alumni gathering, he whipped himself into a frenzy, framing his argument as nothing less than the American Dream. By mid-April, when he faced two hundred alumni in Pittsburgh, he appeared unhinged. He ranted about college having come to serve "the classes, not the masses," and said that it was providing for "certain visible uplifted strata" while ignoring "the men whose need is dire." He rambled about Lincoln, wondering if he "would have been as serviceable to the people of this country had he been a college man." He said American colleges had to be "reconstructed from top to bottom, and I know that America is going to demand it." And then, almost as an afterthought, and sounding irrational, he asked, "Will America tolerate the seclusion of graduate students?"

Wilson's tirade delighted his opposition. "His speech has been universally condemned by every one whom I have seen, whether on his side or against him," Pyne gleefully wrote a fellow trustee, "and I think it can only lead to one result." This condemnation was certainly the case in Pyne's social circle, one member of which published the text and distributed it among Princeton alumni and beyond. Coupled with the press coverage, it caused Wilson's speech to reverberate far beyond Pittsburgh—but not in ways the opposition had anticipated.

"That Pittsburgh Speech" not only gave voice to a lot of dispirited Princetonians but also spoke to average Americans, many of whom considered a college education a privilege of the wealthy. Alumnus and zinc magnate David B. Jones of Chicago suggested that Wilson had suddenly become the conscience of the country, and that to "resign a position second only to the Presidency of the Country as a pulpit, because [Wilson] would not submit to the control of education by money and for money," would attract national interest and might even result in a political nomination. But Wilson still wanted to fight this class war on his home turf. In private conversations and conferences, he continued to argue ideals over practicalities, and he believed he was positioned to defeat West by commencement.

Then, on May 18, 1910, a rich recluse named Isaac Chauncey Wyman died in Massachusetts at the age of eighty-three. His father had fought under George Washington in the Battle of Princeton; and Isaac had graduated from the college there in 1848. He practiced law, went into banking and real estate, and amassed a small fortune. On Sunday the twenty-second, Wilson picked up his Sunday newspaper at breakfast. The front page of *The New York Times* announced: "GIFT OF $10,000,000 LEFT TO PRINCETON. Isaac C. Wyman of Salem, Mass., Bequeaths Bulk of Estate to Graduate School." As Woodrow read the article aloud to Ellen, he broke into laughter, a sound she had not heard from her husband in months. By the time he got to the last sentence of the lead paragraph, he was guffawing. "Almost absolute power in the disposing of the property," it read, ". . . is given to the trustees named in the will, John M. Raymond of Salem and Dean Andrew F. West of the Princeton Graduate School."

Woodrow turned to Ellen and said, "We have beaten the living, but we cannot fight the dead. The game is up."

Later that day, Wilson received a telegram from West and his coexecutor with a more realistic appraisal of the legacy: "Impossible at present to state value of gift for graduate college but it will probably be at least two millions and may be more." The exact number—especially with that many zeroes—no longer even mattered.

"I can hardly believe it. . . . It is all so splendid," a giddy West wrote Momo Pyne from Boston on the drizzling gray day of Wyman's funeral. West had, of course, been privately cultivating the old bachelor for some time. He carried a spray of ivy from Nassau Hall and placed it atop Wyman's casket, and he planted an ivy root from Nassau Hall on his grave.

A perusal of the will convinced Wilson that discretion in administering the Wyman funds had been given to the Board of Trustees, but there was no way to keep West from directing its disbursement. Wilson realized "it would seem small and petulant" if he were to resign in the circumstances, and questioning the legacy in any way would make him seem even pettier. Besides, Wilson could only presume that West would always have another benefactor to pull out of his hat. At the end of May, Wilson invited West to Prospect, where he told his adversary, "You know I have set my face like flint against the site on the Golf Links. But the magnitude of the bequest alters the perspective. You have a great work ahead of you and I shall give you my full support."

Wilson met with several trustees, who assured him that he would "no longer have to suffer the embarrassment of opposition from the Pyne party in the Board." But days later, Wilson attended a meeting of the Committee on Grounds and Buildings, at which several members of the Pyne faction and even Pyne himself continued to nurse their old grudges, displaying what one observer called "a thoroughly nasty" spirit. William Procter visited Princeton in early June, and the university hoped he might reopen his checkbook. A complacent West hosted a luncheon in Procter's honor, to which the Wilsons were not invited. Days later, Procter re-offered his $500,000, almost half of which was earmarked for the construction of the grand dining hall West had long fantasized about. This, on top of the Swann bequest and the Wyman fortune, left Princeton rolling in money, though Wilson no longer controlled the purse strings. (In the end, the Wyman bequest amounted to about $800,000.)

Wilson's baccalaureate address that June sounded valedictory. It was tinged with melancholy, as he visited his own feelings upon the departing seniors. "This is a turning point in your lives," he said, "a day of endings and of beginnings. . . . There is a dull ache at your heart." For the previous classes who crowd the town, he said, "it is a season of reunion, but for you it is a time of parting." Wilson could not help surveying the last two decades, in which Princeton had become "part of the very warp and woof of my life"; but, he said, "it has never in all those years been for a single moment the same Princeton for me that it was in the magical years that ran their cheerful course from the exciting autumn of 1875 to the gracious June of 1879." With each of the many thunderous ovations, tears flowed down his face.

He could not get out of town fast enough. Within a fortnight, Wilson had packed up his office for the summer and prepared to take his family to Florence Griswold's in Old Lyme, on Saturday, June 25. That very moment, "Big Boss" Smith notified Colonel Harvey that he could stall his minions no longer, that if Woodrow Wilson wanted to run for Governor that fall, Smith must have immediate assurance that he would accept the nomination. Harvey had just returned from Europe to the Jersey Shore, and he urgently called Wilson to invite him for dinner on Sunday night at his home in Deal. He wanted him to meet Smith and the powerful editor of the Louisville *Courier-Journal*, Colonel Henry Watterson. With such imposing company gathering, Harvey insinuated that this was a command performance, with national implications. The moment of truth had arrived: either Wilson would appear at the dinner to commit himself to the launch of his new career or Smith would settle upon another candidate. If ever Woodrow Wilson intended to follow his political dreams, this was the moment. He was fifty-three years old, had never run for public office, and would never be handed another plum this ripe.

The Wilsons left for Connecticut as planned, arriving late Saturday. Nell attested that her father "was still reluctant to take the final plunge, reluctant to give up his work at Princeton"; but he said he had every intention of returning to New Jersey for the dinner in Deal. Upon reaching Old Lyme, however, he checked the train schedule, only to learn that the meeting was not meant to be.

"NO SUNDAY TRAIN FROM LYME BEFORE LATE EVENING," he wired Colonel Harvey that night. "EXTREMELY SORRY."

PART TWO

For Governor

Woodrow Wilson

7

PAUL

*And as he iourneyed he came neere Damascus, and
suddenly there shined round about him a light from
heauen.*

—THE ACTES, IX:3

New Jersey, Benjamin Franklin supposedly said, was
like "a barrel tapped at both ends." The fourth smallest of what had become forty-six states lay between the East
Coast's two most populous cities, New York and Philadelphia. With an infusion of immigrants at the turn of the
century, and people settling outside the major metropolitan areas, New Jersey became the most densely populated
state in the nation—2.5 million residents living in but a
few small cities and some 250 incorporated municipalities,
each with its own local administration.

Because government is a conduit of vast amounts of
money, it becomes a breeding ground for graft; and no state
was more infested than New Jersey, which offered financial
incentives to corporations wishing to escape the anti-trust
laws in the major metropolises. Standard Oil of New Jersey, to name but one beneficiary, became the largest organization in the world to produce, transport, refine, and
market oil. Because New Jersey allowed corporations to
own stock in other corporations, Standard Oil readily extended its reach into steel and railroads. The state became

known as the "Mother of Trusts," so corrupt that even Woodrow Wilson conceded that his home of the last twenty years was "one of the backward States of the Union."

Recently, several progressive Republicans in New Jersey had attempted a reform movement called the "New Idea," but they made little headway. Every division of government in the state—from the smallest town to the capital city of Trenton—enjoyed a cozy relationship with some corporation. The Chief Justice of the New Jersey Supreme Court was in the pocket of the Democratic Party's "Big Boss" himself, the former Senator James Smith, Jr.

"Sugar Jim," arguably the most powerful man in the state, came from humble Irish Catholic origins in Newark and had worked his way up in business and politics. When he reached the United States Senate, he manipulated a tariff bill that favored the sugar industry, all the while buying shares in the commodity. His interests expanded to shipbuilding, insurance, newspaper publishing, and banking. At sixty, this blimp of a man conveyed an air of the sunny plutocrat more than the shady autocrat that he was. Woodrow Wilson's missing Colonel Harvey's dinner that Sunday would not only insult Smith but would also indicate his lack of interest in a political future, starting with the governorship.

Fortunately, a young associate of Colonel Harvey named William O. Inglis had a plan. He spent that Saturday night—June 25, 1910—on a train to New London, Connecticut, where he hired a "motor cab" to drive him the fifteen miles to Old Lyme. He arrived at Florence Griswold's just as the Wilson family was heading to church. Inglis was prepared to argue Wilson into returning with him to New Jersey but found that unnecessary. While he did not intend to pursue elected office, neither would Wilson resist it. With no time to spare, they caught an express from New London, which got them to Deal moments before the dinner, which stretched until midnight.

The governorship of New Jersey was on everybody's lips, but they also had larger plans in mind, as evidenced by the presence of Colonel Harvey's third guest—another honorary colonel and a powerful conservative Democrat, Henry "Marse" Watterson, owner and editor of the Louisville *Courier-Journal*. "Whatever one may think of Colonel Watterson," Wilson would later confide to a friend, "there can be no doubt of his immense political influence in his section of the country, and indeed throughout the whole

South." He came specifically to look Wilson over; and before the night had ended, he said that if New Jersey made him Governor, he would "agree to take off his coat and work" for Wilson's Presidential nomination in 1912. The opportunity, Wilson understated, "seems most unusual."

Wilson assured Smith of enough interest that night to buy a little more time, in which he could discuss the matter with two constituencies in particular. The first remained anxiously in Old Lyme. Upon Woodrow's return, the Wilson women all gathered in Ellen's room, where he sat on a small steamer trunk and related that the party leaders had agreed that if he accepted the nomination, he would be left "absolutely free—no pledges of any sort were to be demanded and Smith had further agreed that in no circumstances would he run for the Senate." Then, with a wistful air, Wilson noted, "Colonel Watterson says it will inevitably lead to the Presidency."

Wilson next sought the counsel of his most devout supporters in his reformation efforts at Princeton. He did not want to disappoint them by withdrawing from the school in this crucial hour. "Perhaps it is the fear that this will look to you like a mere case of personal ambition," he wrote David Jones. "To my mind it is a question of which is the larger duty and opportunity." Jones replied that Wilson had brought Princeton to "a position of great distinction"; and even though the political situation in the state and country was "hampered and burdened . . . with incompetency and corruption," he thought "it offers a more important field of service than even the reform of our educational institutions." Recognizing that Wilson was at a crossroads in his life, Cleveland Dodge said, "We should not use any pressure to deter you from a path which your best judgment & conscience indicate to you is a path of duty."

"WALL ST. TO PUT UP W. WILSON FOR PRESIDENT," announced William Randolph Hearst's *New York Journal*, even before Wilson had agreed to anything. The lifelong scholar suddenly realized how quickly the world moved outside the walls of academia. He told a reporter in Connecticut that he was not "seeking" any office at that time. On July 12, 1910, the party powers and the would-be candidate reconvened to consider each other before committing themselves.

Although Boss Smith would not attend, he assembled several of his lieutenants—including a cousin-in-law, James R. Nugent, the Newark boss and state chairman of the party—at the Lawyers' Club on lower

Broadway. Smith called upon his backup choice for the nomination, Judge Robert S. Hudspeth, to examine the president of Princeton. An attorney from Jersey City, a former Speaker of the state's General Assembly, and a member of the Democratic National Committee, Hudspeth began by asking if Wilson was prepared to enter the race. He replied, "I will not accept the nomination unless it comes unanimously. I am not seeking this office."

In order to make that determination, the committee needed to know whether Wilson was a team player, one who would play ball with them. Smith had told Judge Hudspeth that Wilson would be unelectable without the support of the liquor interests in New Jersey, for example; and so Hudspeth asked for his position on the matter of Prohibition. Wilson said, "I believe the question is outside of politics. I believe in home rule, and that the issue should be settled by local option in each community." Hudspeth reminded Wilson that the state party had been opposing local option—the power of small constituencies to vote on such controversial matters—for years. "It is our *bête noire*," he said, a threat to Boss Smith's autonomy. "Well," Wilson said, "that is my attitude and my conviction. I cannot change it."

With Wilson now appearing more recalcitrant than reluctant, Hudspeth posed the most important question, long unspoken. "Doctor Wilson," he said, "there have been some political reformers who, after they have been elected to office as candidates of one party or the other, have shut the doors in the face of the Organization leaders, refusing even to listen to them. Is it your idea that a Governor must refuse to acknowledge his party organization?"

"Not at all," Wilson said. "I have always been a believer in party organizations. If I were elected Governor I should be very glad to consult with the leaders of the Democratic Organization. I should refuse to listen to no man, but I should be especially glad to hear and duly consider the suggestions of the leaders of my party." The answers were not all that the party leaders had hoped, but they were good enough.

Back in Old Lyme, Wilson wrote Cyrus McCormick, "It cost me a great pang, but I felt obliged to say to the New Jersey men that I would accept the nomination for governor, if it came to me unsought, unanimously, and without pledges to anybody about anything. I have all my life been preaching the duty of educated men to undertake just such service as this, and I did not see how I could avoid it." As he had promised the party bosses, Wilson released a statement to the press insisting that he was not a candidate for the gubernatorial nomination but that should it be the wish of the delegates at the state convention, he would accept, deeming it "my duty, as well as an honor and a privilege."

Not even machine support made the Democratic nomination a lead-pipe cinch. Henry Otto Wittpenn, the progressive Mayor of Jersey City, had already announced his gubernatorial candidacy and did not intend to withdraw; progressive State Senator George Silzer of New Brunswick had a large group of followers as well; and the president of the Central Labor Union, along with party leaders in Wilson's own county, announced his endorsement of former Trenton Mayor Frank S. Katzenbach, Jr. The fact that he was an untested college professor with the sudden endorsement of "Sugar Jim" was sure to suggest that a naïve Wilson was simply carrying water for Boss Smith. The would-be candidate knew to lie low until the convention, as making political speeches would only suggest that he was campaigning for the nomination.

Wilson diligently did his homework that summer, toiling over a Democratic state platform. His earliest drafts revealed plans for a thorough administrative reorganization, which would be both economical and efficient; he sought to regulate corporations, particularly in matters of taxes and corrupt practices; he wanted Civil Service reform at the state and local levels; he hoped to give regulatory power to public service commissions and to enact an eight-hour workday. Harvey and Smith urged Wilson to continue his work in private. "The situation is well in hand," Harvey assured him; "there are no breaches in the walls."

Wilson left Old Lyme for Princeton on Wednesday, September 14, 1910, the day before the Democratic delegates in New Jersey were to gather in Trenton to nominate their candidate. The next morning, thousands swarmed around the Taylor Opera House, a few blocks from the state capitol. Only officials and invited guests gained admittance to the hall, which they packed to the rafters. The convention conducted party business in the morning and began its nominating process at 2:30 that afternoon. All the city bosses appeared, none more visible than Jim Smith in the front row, wearing his tall silk hat; and Colonel Harvey sat in a box with easy access to backstage, should the need arise for him to manage any unforeseen disruption in their plot. Wilson's name was in the air—people were clamoring for information about him. He remained twelve miles away, on Princeton's Golf Links.

Because the political system thrived on working one's way up through the ranks, it unsettled even Wilson's "supporters" to have a novice shoved down their throats. They wondered how a genteel professor could hold his own in the jungle of New Jersey politics. "Every progressive Democrat in the Convention was opposed to the nomination of the Princetonian," observed one nondelegate; "and every standpatter and Old Guardsman was in favour of Woodrow Wilson." It simply remained to be seen how the numbers would add up. "Not three men outside of the leading actors in this great political drama had ever seen the Princeton professor, although many had doubtless read his speeches," added the interested observer. "The bosses, with consummate precision, moved to the doing of the job in hand, working their spell of threats and coercion upon a beaten, sullen, spiritless body of delegates."

Regardless of all protest and skepticism that morning, the chairman of the convention announced the tally of the first ballot at 4:55 that afternoon: Woodrow Wilson had received 749 votes, more than twice the number of his nearest rival, Katzenbach. Wilson was the nominee. While delegates re-cast their votes to show party unity, a car rolled up to Prospect to fetch the man of the hour. Wilson answered the door and said, "Gentlemen, I am ready." They whisked him to the Trenton House Hotel, through a side door, and up to Colonel Harvey's room. Clarence Cole, a delegate from Atlantic County who had been drafted to place Wilson's name in nomination, came in to announce that the nomination had been made unanimous.

Despite the suggestion of an undivided party, a great number of delegates were downcast, believing they remained under the yoke of the bosses. Before they could disperse in dissatisfaction, the chairman's voice boomed through the hall: "We have just received word that Mr. Wilson, the candidate for the governorship, *and the next President of the United States*, has received word of his nomination; has left Princeton, and is now on his way to the Convention." Pandemonium raged, and when Wilson entered the hall a few minutes later, even the opposition surged forward to get a good first look at their candidate. He walked to center stage and stood beneath the huge proscenium arch, backed by an energetic cohort of Princeton students.

Looking neither the stern schoolmaster nor the strict minister many had expected, Wilson stood tall and trim, sporting a healthy summer tan and wearing his golfing outfit—a blue sweater beneath his jacket and a soft hat with a narrow brim. The audience felt as at ease as he looked, though upon seeing Wilson's profile for the first time, one man sitting near Stockton Axson could not help commenting, "Gawd, look at his jaw!" Wilson summoned every oratorical experience of his nearly fifty-four years and, in his clear and resounding voice, delivered the first speech of his political life.

"You have conferred upon me a very great honor," he said; ". . . I feel the deep responsibility it imposes upon me. For responsibility is proportioned to opportunity." He promptly reminded his audience that he had not sought the nomination; and so, if elected, he would assume his duties "with absolutely no pledge of any kind to prevent me from serving the people of the State with singleness of purpose."

Upon hearing that last sentence, even the doubting Thomases in the crowd started to believe in him. Among the skeptics was a sprightly Irish American grocer's son from the Fifth Ward of Jersey City, a Roman Catholic whose blue eyes brightened his round pink face. A lawyer and a member of the State Assembly, Joseph Patrick Tumulty was a dejected Silzer man. But Tumulty had never heard an orator quite like Wilson, who allowed simplicity and modesty to punctuate his rhetoric. "Attempting none of the cheap 'plays' of the old campaign orator," Tumulty wrote, "he impressively proceeded with this thrilling speech, carrying his audience with him under the spell of his eloquent words. . . . It was not only what he said, but the simple heart-stirring way in which he said it." Applause came in waves, which kept building.

Wilson concluded with an unexpected message. "The future," he said, "is not for parties 'playing politics,' but for measures conceived in the largest spirit, pushed by parties whose leaders are statesmen, not demagogues, who love not their offices, but their duty and their opportunity for service. . . . With the new age we shall show a new spirit." And then he closed with a question: "Shall we not forget ourselves in making it the instrument of righteousness for the State and for the nation?" The speech had ended, but the people would not let him leave the stage. "Go on, go on," they cried.

He did, extemporizing for several minutes more, saying that he was

absolutely free to serve the people of New Jersey, that the party had a winning platform, that it was "nonsense to declare that the Democratic party
is an enemy of business," and that they must arrive at some common understanding. "For New Jersey," he confessed, "I covet the honor of showing
the other States how corporations can be controlled." Having mesmerized
his entire audience, he turned to the Stars and Stripes hanging over the
speakers' stand. "When I look upon the American flag before me," he said
in unabashedly patriotic language, "I think sometimes that it is made of
parchment and blood. The white in it stands for parchment, the red in it
signifies blood—parchment on which was written the rights of men, and
blood that was spilled to make these rights real. Let us devote the Democratic party to the recovery of these rights." Hardened old politicos wept,
and delegates thanked God that a leader had come to their rescue. Tumulty said they all felt like Crusaders, ready to "dedicate themselves to the
cause of liberating their state from the bondage of special interests." The
crowd mobbed the candidate, requiring the police to rescue him.

Wilson telephoned his wife and children in Old Lyme and cheerfully
reported the evening's events; and in a few days the Wilson women returned to Prospect. "Having, in our innocence, no idea of the ordeal we
were facing," Nell recalled, "we were due for a shock. A college professor
thrust suddenly into active politics made the New Jersey situation more
dramatic than the ordinary gubernatorial campaign." With this new
player in the game, the *New York Evening Post* declared, "It is a great day
for New Jersey and a great day for the nation when a man like Woodrow
Wilson comes forward to help reclaim and vivify our political life." Days
later, the Republicans nominated Mr. Vivian M. Lewis, the genial State
Banking and Insurance Commissioner, who pledged to embrace several
"New Idea" ideas, his only hope of capturing swing votes.

The campaign had a most peculiar beginning, as the Democratic candidate still had a college to run. The day after Lewis's nomination, Woodrow Wilson donned his cap and gown and led Princeton's academic
procession, as he had for the last decade, and conducted opening exercises
in the Marquand Chapel. For the next several weeks, he continued to work
his campaign schedule around his campus obligations, which still included
giving lectures on jurisprudence and politics. While some trustees were
already contriving Wilson's removal from office, many presumed he would
let the election results determine if and when he would resign. But on

October 20, 1910, he opened the board meeting, asked that the regular order of business be suspended, and presented his resignation. With that, trustee Wilson Farrand recorded, he "picked up his hat and coat, and while we all stood in silence, passed from the room and from his connection with Princeton."

The severance was not quite that severe, though Wilson sensed plenty of hostility from his old adversaries. In officially accepting Wilson's resignation, the board generously praised his contribution not only to Princeton but also to higher education in the United States, as they acknowledged his reformation of the curriculum, pedagogy, graduate studies, and the general culture of the campus, instilling his "ideals of character and conduct." But Momo Pyne wanted to know just how long his salary should be paid and how long he should be permitted to stay at Prospect. The trustees decided to support him through the end of the first term of the academic year. Because of Wilson's contributions to scholarship and education, they also bestowed upon him their greatest award, an honorary degree of Doctor of Laws. One hundred eighty students in his Jurisprudence course signed a petition expressing their "sincere desire" that he might still resume his lectures. Wilson gladly accepted the degree; he said he would prefer to remain at Prospect only until the conclusion of the campaign; and he refused any further salary. He wrote the students that with his time "so broken in upon," his teaching from that point on would be too unsatisfactory to be of advantage to them.

"This is really worse than I expected even," Wilson wrote Mrs. Peck ten days after the convention; "there has not been a half hour . . . that I could call my own since the nomination." He was dictating 150 letters a day, which required a pair of stenographers; and there were, he said, "letters by the hundred, newspaper men, photographers, friends, advisers, committees, beggars." The telephone never stopped ringing. Party bosses visited regularly, worried at first that their candidate was what they called "high-browish." The first time Jim Smith walked into Wilson's book-lined study, he held his silk hat in hand and asked in awe, "Do you read all these books, Professor?" Wilson replied, "Not every day"; and their laughter broke the ice. Smith would never fully understand the new politician he had anointed, but one day that September, he unknowingly got a glimmer of Wilson's sincerity about politics. While waiting with Nugent for a meeting at Prospect, Smith soaked up some of the atmosphere of the grand house nestled into the wooded campus, with Ellen Wilson's picturesque garden overlooking the New Jersey countryside. Smith asked, "Can you imagine anyone being damn fool enough to give this up for the heartaches of politics?"

At first, the other politicians treated Wilson like a "schoolboy," but as soon as they began teaching him the rudiments of the state, they instantly found themselves students in his classroom, as Wilson revealed his familiarity with minute nuts-and-bolts local issues as well as large statewide matters. James Kerney, the editor of the *Trenton Evening Times*, sat in on some meetings and delighted in the fact that Wilson already knew every one of the local nabobs by name and his community's concerns.

For all his confidence as an orator, Wilson did not want his family to attend any of his speeches. The rule applied especially to Ellen, whose opinions he valued most. "I don't know what sort of politician I'll make," he told his daughters. "I'm nervous—just plain scared—and if you girls are there, it will be worse." And so, on September 28, 1910, he drafted Stockton Axson to accompany him on the train from Princeton to Jersey City, where he officially opened his campaign. A group of Democrats met him at the station and escorted him to St. Peter's Hall. Armed with his standard set of notes—a single page with a few handwritten sentences, half of them in shorthand—the Democratic nominee for Governor proceeded to deliver a rambling address, full of pauses, clumsy shifts in subject, and several forced attempts at humor. "I never before appeared before an audience and asked for anything," he said, "and now I find myself in the novel position of asking you to vote for me for governor of New Jersey."

Wilson articulated a few themes that would resound throughout his campaign. "I particularly want to confess to one obligation," he said. "If you should vote for me for Governor I shall be under obligations to you, I shall be obedient to the people of this State, to serve them and them only." In addressing the subject of modern corporate law and the need for personal responsibility, he used an analogy that he would long employ—that of an automobile that has been involved in something unlawful: "I say get the man who is running the automobile and teach him to behave and do not take the automobile away," Wilson said; "the automobile is not to blame." But his shying from the limelight made the first part of the speech a dud. Only after a half hour of speaking "ineffectively" did Wilson redeem himself. Just as he was losing his audience, he trusted his instincts and walked to the edge of the platform. "And so I have made my first political appeal. I leave my case in your hands," he said. "I feel that it is a trustworthy jury and with its verdict I shall be content." Wilson acknowledged that he did not think his first campaign speech had been a success, but when he threw himself at the mercy of his audience, in that simple moment of ingenuousness, they responded with a whoop. Observed Axson, "It was the first time he had touched them."

And it was the last time Wilson ever delivered so lackluster a speech. In just the minutes it took to drive him across town to deliver his next, Woodrow Wilson metamorphosed into a political candidate. He realized that in asking people for support—much like a minister passing the collection plate or a college president soliciting funds—he was empowering them, allowing them to share in his ideals, and he in theirs. During his second speech that day, the audience laughed, applauded, and listened intently to his every point.

Over the next six weeks, Wilson delivered more than fifty major speeches across all of New Jersey's twenty-one counties. He spoke only from skeletal notes and straight from his heart. Substantive and conversational, the addresses had a snowball effect—each one, like the campaign itself, steadily gathering momentum, the power of his rhetoric growing as did his commitment to Progressive ideas. Inevitably, he expounded upon topics of national importance, none more far-reaching than the new Payne-Aldrich tariff. It was meant to lower duties on imported products, but the Republican chairman of the Senate Finance Committee, Nelson Aldrich, connived to raise hundreds of other tariffs for the benefit of select industries. Early in his campaign, Joseph P. Tumulty had the opportunity to meet Wilson, who was informed that the young legislator had been present at the Jersey City speech. Wilson beseeched him for an honest opinion of it, saying, "Don't forget that I am an amateur at this game and need advice and guidance." Tumulty urged as much "definiteness" in his speeches as possible.

On the third evening of the campaign, James Smith tested the responsiveness of his "puppet"'s strings. The Boss summoned Judge Hudspeth and said the Newark audience that night would be filled with people interested in the question of Prohibition and that Wilson must take a position against local option. Hudspeth said Wilson had already told the bosses where he stood, and nothing they could say would change his opinion. Smith said Wilson would get heckled off the stage, and Nugent argued that this would rankle his most important supporters. But Wilson held fast, insisting it was a petty matter alongside greater issues of the day. As it turned out, the subject never even arose.

Instead, Wilson stuck to his notes and beliefs and delivered a long and impassioned speech explaining the Democratic platform. He said there was one more plank he would have liked to have seen included, one involving stronger laws of incorporation in New Jersey that would offer "a severe scrutiny." He even took a shot at the Sugar Trust. That night, and throughout the campaign, he spoke with civility about his Republican rival; and he maintained an air of humility about himself, assuring the voters that "no man with any sense of proportion . . . could stand up and pose as the savior of his fellow citizens. . . . But it is perfectly worthy and perfectly dignified to stand up and say: 'Gentlemen, let us all get together and try to understand our common interest.'"

Driving Wilson home that night, Judge Hudspeth reminded him that he owed his nomination to Smith and Nugent and "Little Bob" Davis, the big man in Jersey City. Wilson replied that he had entered the contest without making promises to any bosses. He intended to honor pledges only to the people. His experience at Princeton notwithstanding, Wilson still believed that the only way to reform the party, if not the politics of the state, was by making the strongest appeal possible and by avoiding deals with those who wrote the checks. In an interview with *The Philadelphia Record*, Wilson said the Republican Party had formed "an unholy alliance with the vast moneyed interests of the country," while "Providence in its wisdom directed that the Democratic party should be reserved" for the great task of providing "the salvation of the country."

After only one week on the stump, Wilson was back at the Taylor Opera House, where he unabashedly played to the crowd, releasing the politician he had long repressed. "I am asking you for your votes," he said, "and if you give them to me I will be under bonds to you—not to the gentlemen who were generous enough to nominate me." He called himself "an amateur politician"; and as such, he added, "I shall, not timidly, as standing outside of the ranks of the profession, tackle the profession." Despite the paternal ban, the Wilson girls had secretly entered the hall that night and hidden in one of the boxes. After they told him as much, he never again minded any of his family being in the audience.

Two days later, in Woodbury, Wilson challenged the sincerity of the Republican Party in its talk of progressive reform. He praised some of the party's history and even singled out the insurgent George L. Record, a Congressional candidate whom he admired. Wilson's opponent, Vivian Lewis, had suggested that he intended to be a "constitutional governor" who would not make waves in office. Such would not be the case in a Wilson administration, Wilson himself warned. "I shall not be a constitutional governor, because there is one thing that a man has to obey over and above the State constitution, and that is his own constitution. . . . And although I try to be courteous to the men I differ from, I am always sure they are wrong."

Wilson's crowds increased. On October 12, 2,600 people—including hundreds of Republicans—packed into the Paterson Opera House, with its 1,800 seats. More and more people wanted to sample Wilson's celebrated oratory. On this occasion they were treated to a talk that was part lesson and part sermon, its primary theme "the purification of politics." The next night he filled the Steeplechase Pier in Atlantic City and announced that he was going to dismantle the Republican machine, and that he believed in his heart "that the men who are going to assist with the greatest zest in this matter are Republicans themselves." Wilson seldom failed to deliver at least that one aria of especial eloquence that his audiences had come to expect—a passionate combination of rhetoric and righteousness. In Atlantic City it came toward the end of a long speech, when he said the destiny of the United States was not in its amassing power or wealth but "that she shall do the thinking of the world," and that thinking would be "ruled by our passions. . . . For America . . . is not a piece of the surface of the earth. America is not merely a body of towns. America is an idea, America is an ideal, America is a vision."

Although seldom missing an opportunity to mention his expanding worldview, Wilson never neglected the local issues—waterways, public commissions, the low tax rates railroads were granted. As time passed, he found himself increasingly struggling to save the soul of the state. At Toms River, a Republican village where candidates seldom drew two dozen citizens to hear a political talk, eight hundred people gathered, some arriving on special trains from all over Ocean County. Then, in the Hippodrome in Asbury Park on October 15, he told the throngs, "If you find out that I have ever been or ever intend to be connected with a machine of any kind I hope you will vote against me." On October 21, he covered ninety miles of Warren County, stopping at eight towns and making seven speeches, six of those demanded by locals who had stood waiting for his arrival and insisted upon hearing him.

The Republicans hit Wilson hard, attacking his inexperience, suggesting that the statehouse was not a schoolhouse. To prove his mettle, Wilson challenged any politician in New Jersey to debate any public matter on any public platform. None other than New Idea candidate George Record took up the gauntlet, which came in the form of a nineteen-point questionnaire. Democratic handlers advised against engaging in an exercise that could so easily backfire; but a fortnight before the election, Wilson— the lifelong student of American history—breezed through the exam. In preparation, he jotted shorthand responses right on Record's letter, which he then typed up and emended by hand before submitting his final draft.

Most of the questions required little more than Progressive solutions to statewide injustices; but there were several tricky questions, starting with Record's asking if Wilson thought "the boss system" existed. The candidate replied that it did, and that he would propose to abolish it by "the election to office of men who will refuse to submit to it and bend all their energies to break it up, and by pitiless publicity." Record asked if the leaders of that system included such men as Wilson's benefactors, Smith and Nugent. Wilson said yes. In his next reply he said he would join Record "or any one else in denouncing and fighting any and every one, of either party, who attempts such outrages against the government and public morality."

If Record had intended to expose Wilson as a waffler, if not the conservative Southern Democrat he had been most of his life, he failed miserably. In fact, the exercise allowed Wilson to articulate his positions in the most precise terms. By the time he had answered all the questions, he had completely converted, becoming a veritable New Idea man who had seen the light, an outspoken, unabashed Progressive who believed only a Democrat could lead his state, if not the country, on the path from darkness. Wilson even answered the hardest question of all, one Record had failed to ask. "I am very glad to tell you," he wrote on October 24, 1910.

> If elected, I shall not, either in the matter of appointments to office or assent to legislation, or in shaping any part of the policy of my administration, submit to the dictation of any person or persons, special

interest, or organization. . . . I should deem myself forever disgraced should I in even the slightest degree cooperate in any such system or any such transactions as you describe in your characterization of the "boss" system. I regard myself as pledged to the regeneration of the Democratic party.

Wilson's declaration of his political independence became the talk of New Jersey. Colonel Harvey called it "the most effective political document I ever read." Joseph P. Tumulty, who had by then actively endorsed Wilson, praised the "virility" of the statement. Smith, Nugent, and Davis did not even flinch, since they considered it "a great campaign play."

In the final week of October, Wilson traveled from one end of the "barrel" to the other. He continued to attract Republicans. On Saturday, November 5, he concluded his tour in Newark, where one newspaper reported, "No mortal man ever won the hearts of an awakened people like this man did those in a vast audience in the Krueger Auditorium." Before three thousand enthusiasts, Wilson talked about leadership; and, in so doing, he drew a bead on a distant target—President Taft, who had signed the Payne-Aldrich Tariff Act. "We have begun a fight that it may be will take many a generation to complete," he said, "—the fight against special privilege."

"Letting down the curtain on the first act of the stirring drama of American history, in which he is the new-risen star," *The Philadelphia Record* reported, "Woodrow Wilson to-night was accorded a mark of approval that must ring in his ears and linger in his eyes till the lights go out forever upon his stage of action."

Turnout on the eighth was huge. Wilson was the only person to remain calm at Prospect that Tuesday as early predictions came in. "We stood breathlessly by when he answered the telephone," Nell recalled, "but he would never give the slightest inkling whether the news was favorable or not. . . . Even after he hung up, we had to beg for details."

By ten o'clock that night, the family realized that Wilson had won in a landslide—233,682 votes to Vivian Lewis's 184,626, 54 percent to 43 percent, with a smattering of votes for third-party candidates. He swept fifteen of the state's twenty-one counties. Moreover, Wilson had coattails: New Jersey Democrats gained four seats in the Congress, won four of the seven elections for the State Senate, and walked away with forty-two of the sixty seats in the State Assembly, which meant they could now send a Democrat to the United States Senate. In Washington, the new Congress would reflect the changing sentiment of the nation at large, as the Democrats picked up fifty-eight seats in the House, more than enough to change its leadership. Democrat James Beauchamp "Champ" Clark of Missouri would replace the seemingly omnipotent Old Guard Republican Joseph "Uncle Joe" Cannon, who had pounded the Speaker's gavel for the last seven years.

Wilson received congratulations from all constituencies of his past: the Mayor of Staunton, Southern relatives, the Witherspoon Gang (including his political blood brother, Charles Talcott, who became that very day the first Democratic Congressman elected from his upstate New York district in more than fifty years), Heath Dabney from Virginia, Frederick Jackson Turner ("You are bringing Princeton into the nation's service"), Princeton trustees, and—despite their irreparable separation—a nostalgic Jack Hibben. George Record, who lost his election, offered his political services; and Joseph P. Tumulty praised the victor's courage during the campaign. Wilson sent James Smith a measured note—not to thank him but to say, "I feel very deeply the confidence you have displayed in me, and the deep responsibility to the people which our success has brought with it. I hope with all my heart that I may be able to play my part in such a way as to bring no disappointment to those who have trusted me." Smith replied in equally calculated terms, wiring, "Every well wisher of good government will hail the result as a personal gain."

Wilson had intended to return to Bermuda, but he had no time for a vacation. New Jersey did not provide its Governor with an official residence, compelling the Wilsons to leave Prospect for four rooms in the Princeton Inn until they could find more permanent lodging. The three Wilson daughters were establishing their own adult lives but still depended on their parents. Margaret was adjusting to two rooms in New York City, where she studied music; Jessie did settlement work in Philadelphia, where she lived Monday through Thursday, staying at the Inn on weekends; and Nell commuted weekdays to Philadelphia, where she studied at the Academy of Fine Arts. While they were all packing boxes at Prospect, Jim Smith appeared, with challenging though hardly startling news.

Smith announced to the Governor-elect that he wished to return to the United States Senate. Wilson balked. In September the Democrats had voted in a primary for James E. Martine, a prosperous landowner and developer. "Farmer Jim," as he was known, was the only man who had bothered to list his name in the nonbinding preferential race, and he had received less than a quarter of Wilson's total at that. Even so, Wilson said, for Smith even to present his name for consideration only confirmed all the ugliest suspicions raised during the November election.

Smith utterly dismissed the primary. Although Wilson thought little of Martine, he maintained, "The question who is to enjoy one term in the Senate is of small consequence compared with the question whether the people of New Jersey are to gain the right to choose their own senators forever." The decision rested with the state legislators, most of whom remained beholden to the machine. After making inquiries, Cleveland Dodge informed Wilson that he had heard that all but six of the Democratic Assemblymen were financially obliged enough to Jim Smith "that he owns them absolutely." It fell upon Wilson to decide whether he intended to let the political machinery continue to run or whether to throw a monkey wrench into the works.

"It was a very great victory, and you were one of the most valiant fighters in it," Wilson wrote James Martine on November 14, 1910, in a letter he also released to the press. While even Democrats had suggested to Wilson that "Farmer Jim" was generally incompetent, the Governor-elect believed that was secondary to this opportunity to reform the political system. He began by trying to avoid a confrontation. Wilson asked Dodge if he knew people who might persuade Smith to refrain from running; and he enlisted several newspaper editors to do the same. Then he went to Jersey City, where he explained to "Little Bob" Davis, then in the final stage of a terminal illness, that a failure to support Martine was tantamount to party disloyalty. Davis said he had given his word to Smith and that if Wilson would disengage from this Senatorial election, he would back Wilson's ambitious legislative agenda. "How do I know you will?" Wilson asked. "If you beat me in this the first fight, how do I know you won't be able to beat me in everything?"

"I am very anxious about the question of the senatorship," Wilson wrote Colonel Harvey on November 15, 1910, knowing that if not handled correctly, "it will destroy every fortunate impression of the campaign and open my administration with a split party." In a tone that suggested he thought Harvey would share his letter with the Boss himself, Wilson said he had come to a "very high opinion" of Smith and had little doubt that a second term in the Senate would alter the impressions he left from his first. But he insisted, "His election would be intolerable to the very people who elected me and gave us a majority in the legislature. They would never give it to us again: that I think I can say I know, from what has been said to me in every quarter during the campaign. They count upon me to prevent it." If he did not, Wilson believed, all "their ugliest suspicions, dispelled by my campaign assurances, will be confirmed." Wilson reminded Harvey that their recent victory was due to the "progressives" from both parties who had coalesced into a solid voting bloc. Should Smith become a candidate, he declared, "I would have to fight him; and there is nothing I would more sincerely deplore. It would offend every instinct in me,—except the instinct as to what was right and necessary from the point of view of the public."

Wilson further appealed to Harvey, making a point with national implications. "If the independent Republicans who in this State voted for me are not to be attracted to us," he argued, "they will assuredly turn again, in desperation, to Mr. Roosevelt, and the chance of a generation will be lost to the Democracy." Wilson said all this rested on the shoulders of Jim Smith, who "can make himself the biggest man in the State by a dignified refusal to let his name be considered."

On December 6, Wilson went to Newark, to discuss the situation in the privacy of Smith's home—offering him another two days in which to decide. Wilson said he would interpret silence as an intention to fight for the office. On the morning of the ninth, he issued a long statement to the press, conceding that, legally speaking, it was not the Governor's duty even to advise the legislature in its choice of Senator. "But," he said, "there are other duties besides legal duties. The recent campaign has put me in an unusual position. I offered, if elected, to be the political spokesman and adviser of the people. I even asked those who did not care to make their choice of Governor upon that understanding not to vote for me." It was now his duty to urge every Democratic legislator to vote for James Martine. This meant "war," Wilson wrote Mrs. Peck in Bermuda. "It is hard sledding, but a fellow must fight at every step who means to clean up the dirty politics of this machine-ridden State, and I shall enjoy doing the thing as much like a gentleman as the circumstances permit."

Smith issued his own gentlemanly statement to the press. "Gratitude was not expected of him," he said referring to Dr. Wilson, "but fairness was, and his act denies it." As only one member of the incoming legislature had agreed to be bound by the primary vote, Smith said Wilson "evidently believes that the practises he once condemned of dangling patronage before a hungry constituency may give to his position a support which fairness denies it."

Wilson asked Joe Tumulty, an aggressive fighter in Trenton, to serve officially as his secretary, and even more as his political adviser—"a guide at my elbow in matters of which I know almost nothing." Together they went to Jersey City and Newark, where Wilson exerted pressure by speaking at public meetings. People traveled from other states just to hear him; others read the interviews he freely granted. "Mr. James Smith, Jr., represents not a party but a system—a system of political control which does not belong to either party," Wilson explained to the press. That night, he conferred with New Jersey legislators at the University Club in New York, using unorthodox tactics—reason and inspiration. Smith waged his fight as well, twisting arms.

Trenton, the state capital, was all smiles on the morning of Tuesday, January 17. Ellen Wilson and the girls went downtown to the grand house of a widow, who let them view the inaugural parade from her front room. A big brass band led the way, followed by the State Guard in dress uniform, and then four prancing black horses pulling an open landau in which sat the outgoing Governor, John Franklin Fort, and fifty-four-year-old Woodrow Wilson, in a frock coat and top hat. Crowds cheered and waved flags right up to the Taylor Opera House. Among the thousands of invited dignitaries, only one was conspicuously absent—former Senator James Smith.

The ceremony was simple. The Chief Justice administered the oath of office to the state's thirty-fourth Governor, and Fort handed him the Great Seal of the State. Wilson had worked on his inaugural address over the prior week and a half, limiting himself to a few paragraphs of introduction before reiterating the plans for New Jersey on which he had run. Toward the end of his speech, he added a last-minute thought, one he had jotted in pencil on his speaking copy. "I shall take the liberty from time to time to make detailed recommendations to you on the matters I have dwelt upon," he said, "and on others, sometimes in the form of bills if necessary." The ceremony ended within an hour.

Receptions filled the afternoon, culminating in a ball that night. While Wilson was hardly a fan of such festivities, he suddenly seemed struck by his new position. "All sorts and conditions of people came, men, women, and children," he reported to Mrs. Peck, "and I felt very close to all of them, and very much touched by the thought that I was their representative and spokesman, and in a very real sense their help and hope, after year upon year of selfish machine domination when nothing at all had been done for them that could possibly be withheld." His new responsibilities as a "champion of the common people" filled him with awe. At the evening reception, Nell Wilson could not help noticing two officers at the door, scrutinizing everyone who entered the hall and forbidding anyone from carrying a muff or large handbag. Her heart raced, as she realized for the first time that her father stood in physical danger.

One week later, Woodrow Wilson faced his first gubernatorial test. The county bosses gathered in the capital for the Senate election. Jim Smith held court in his hotel room, an open house that ran through the night as he rallied legislators to vote for him. Wilson and Tumulty lingered in their offices almost until sunrise shoring up votes for Martine. This political match proved to be an eye-opener for the Governor, especially when he learned that one of his trusted advisers—an attorney—was secretly reporting information to the enemy camp. The first ballot gave Martine a decisive lead but not a victory; and the lawmakers adjourned.

The key to a victory rested with the bloc of votes from Hudson County, once controlled by the now deceased "Little Bob" Davis, which had become the bailiwick of a clean-cut young man named James Hennessy. Wilson summoned him, only to learn that that Hennessy had already promised Davis that he would remain loyal to Smith. Wilson had a heart-to-heart conversation with the new county leader, arguing not only that a rejection of Martine would lead to disaster for the party but also that Martine already had the votes. Hennessy caucused his delegation, which decided to back Martine. The balloting at ten o'clock that morning became a formality. Three loyalists stuck by Smith, but the forty-seven other Democrats elected Martine their next Senator. Woodrow Wilson emerged the big winner.

"The whole country is marvelling at it," Wilson boasted to Mrs. Peck, "and I am getting more credit than I deserve." In the end, he pitied Smith, whose strategies had long come right out of Machiavelli's playbook as he preferred to be feared more than loved. "The minute it was seen that he was defeated," Wilson explained further, "his adherents began to desert him like rats leaving a sinking ship. He left Trenton (where his headquarters had at first been crowded) attended, I am told, only by his sons, and looking old and broken. He wept, they say, as he admitted himself utterly beaten. Such is the end of political power—particularly when selfishly obtained and heartlessly used." Smith rapidly descended into financial decline, as he burned through his $5 million fortune. With the Smith forces "routed horse, foot, and dragoons," Wilson believed much of the resistance had dissipated. Even so, he observed, "I know that the work has only just begun."

"My heart aches at the break-up of the old life," Wilson wrote Mary Peck at the end of the month, "interesting and vital as the new life is." He did not realize it, he said, "until it touched our home and sent us into lodging at an inn. I feel like a nomad! The idea of a man of fifty-four (no less!) leaving a definite career and a settled way of life of a sudden and launching out into a vast sea of Ifs and Buts! It sounds like an account of a fool." But in that moment, Woodrow Wilson converted from a political scientist to a politician.

In fact, Wilson had just told the American Political Science Association in St. Louis that "politics is of the very stuff of life. It is very dangerous to reason with regard to it on principles that are fancied to be universal; for it is local." While still in St. Louis, Wilson had also spoken to the City Club, where he handed down a list of moral imperatives as though they had been dictated by God. They formed a declaration of principles by which he intended to live.

> Mind your public business all the year round, not only at election time.
> Force public officials to report often, and watch their eyes to see if they are telling you all they know. . . .
> Concentrate responsibility and hold it accountable.
> You can trust the people, providing you serve them.
> Reveal everything and the people will be just: conceal anything and make them jealous. . . .

Legislators blindly follow leaders. Sometimes the bellwether is trust-
worthy; sometimes he is an old goat.
Cure politics as you would tuberculosis—with open air.
The practical politician should sleep in the open; it will purify him.

Declaring himself an ardent Democrat—"with a big D and a little d," he
liked to say—Wilson pored over the writings of William Simon U'ren, a
fourth-generation blacksmith who became a progressive political leader in
Oregon, where he helped forge such implements for the people as the initiative, the referendum, the recall, and the direct primary. As a professor,
Wilson had opposed these measures; as the most popular figure in New
Jersey, he now considered them "useful tools for an emergency," necessities
in safeguarding the democracy of his state.

The Governor detailed his ambitious new agenda, the most immediate items on which were the regulation of public utilities, a Corrupt
Practices Act, a Direct Primaries Act, and the Employers' Liability Act.
Knowing that the passage of any one of the items would be an ordeal
and the entire package an affront to the Republican opposition and the
Smith Democrats, he asked George Record, the Republican who had
kept Wilson's feet to the fire in the recent election, to prepare the bills
for legislative consideration. Wilson solicited the opposition's support,
meeting with legislators individually and in committee, motivating them
by acting more as a team-mate than a captain. He excluded the bosses
from his conferences. In the case of his election bill—sponsored by one of
his former students, Elmer H. Geran—Wilson recognized that it was
meant to undermine the very system of corruption that still controlled the
legislature.

On February 6, 1911, the Geran bill came before the lawmakers. It was
a sweeping plan by which New Jersey might leapfrog to the vanguard of
election reform in the nation. It included standardized regulations for
voter registration, secret ballots, and direct primaries for all elective offices
and party officials. Boss Nugent took Jim Smith's place working the corridors and the actual floor of the legislature itself, lining up votes in opposition. After a month, enough Democrats in the State Assembly had
their doubts about the bill, which they prepared to defang in caucus.
Learning of this meeting, Wilson asked to be invited. To even his staunchest allies, the Governor seemed to have overstepped the boundary that

separated powers. When Wilson appeared, one legislator flatly asked what constitutional right permitted his presence.

"Since you appeal to the constitution," Wilson replied, "I can satisfy you." He pulled a copy from his pocket and began to read: "The governor shall communicate by message to the legislature at the opening of each session, and at such other times as he may deem necessary, the condition of the state, and recommend such measures as he may deem expedient." For the next three hours, Wilson conducted a preceptorial, which covered material he explored in *The State* and which he intended to apply in his own state. "You can turn aside from the measure if you choose," he said; "you can decline to follow me . . . but you cannot deprive me of power so long as I steadfastly stand for what I believe to be the interests and legitimate demands of the people themselves."

Everybody emerged from the chamber feeling—as one of the legislators reported—"that we had heard the most wonderful speech of our lives. . . . It has been said that debate no longer accomplishes anything in American legislation, that nobody is now persuaded by talk. Here was a case, however, which refutes this idea." The Assembly passed the bill and forwarded it to the Republican-controlled Senate.

Nugent, the chairman of the Democratic State Committee, was so set upon killing the Geran bill there, he began crossing the Senate aisle to court Republicans. At last, Wilson invited him to his office, where he said, "Don't you think, Mr. Nugent, that you are making a grave mistake in opposing the election bill?" Nugent said no and began baiting the Governor. He questioned Wilson as to how he secured the number of votes he already had and said Trenton was buzzing that he got them by patronage. To the man who had prided himself on both campaigning and governing without buying votes with jobs, Nugent had just suggested that Wilson was as corrupt as he. His eyes burning, the Governor quietly rose, bowed, gestured toward the door, and said, "Good afternoon, Mr. Nugent." Expecting a confrontation and frustrated without one, Nugent repeatedly tried to reengage the Governor. But Wilson only repeated himself, adding new emphasis each time he said "Good afternoon, Mr. Nugent." At last, Nugent departed, but not without hurling one final remark at Wilson: "You're no gentleman!" And Wilson snapped right back, "You're no judge!"

Within minutes the story had rung through the halls; and within days, across the country. One editorial cartoon, entitled "Good Afternoon," showed Nugent flying headfirst through a door, propelled by a foot la-beled "Wilson." Waiting on the floor, nursing his bruises, was Boss Smith. Such encounters left Wilson feeling "a bit vulgar," debased to the level of the men he felt obliged to snub. But, he realized, "They commend me to the rank and file, and particularly to the politicians themselves." He did not fully appreciate the greater ramifications, as the quadrennial search for new leadership in the United States was already under way, even though the national election would not be held for almost two years.

Woodrow Wilson's campaign for the Presidency began at the very moment that the groundswell of Progressive thought directed the mainstream of American politics. Without his even announcing that he was running, isolated trickles of support suddenly coalesced, creating a flash flood, the likes of which had seldom been seen in American history. Local media across the country realized it had covered the New Jersey Governor's speeches for years, whenever he had come to town on behalf of Princeton; and now, alumni proved to be an effective army of early organizers, with base camps nationwide. One former student organized a Woodrow Wilson for President Club in Staunton, Virginia, even before Wilson had been elected Governor of New Jersey. Other Princeton alumni—especially such wealthy friends from the Princeton board as Cleveland Dodge, Thomas D. Jones, and Cyrus McCormick—always stood at the ready to underwrite a campaign, with no strings attached. Indeed, Dodge would contribute more than $50,000 of his own money and raise almost as much again from fellow Tigers.

Another group of Democratic kinsmen pledged early support as well—those who recognized the merits of running a transplanted Southerner, one who could deliver the solid bloc of votes from Dixie but could also reach out to the progressive West, the industrial North, and perhaps even the moneyed interests of New York. Chief among the Southerners was Walter Hines Page, who had become a partner in the publishing firm of Double-day, Page & Company and then an editor of the magazine *The World's Work*. Page soon met Walter McCorkle, a Virginian who became a Wall Street lawyer and president of the Southern Society of New York, a social and patriotic organization one thousand members strong. And then reen-tering Wilson's life was William F. McCombs, an Arkansan who had fractured his hip in a childhood accident, which left him permanently lame and reliant on two walking sticks. A brilliant former student of Wilson's, he had graduated from Princeton in 1898 before studying law at Harvard and becoming an attorney. Paying a call on his former professor in the State House in Trenton to discuss the pending Employers' Liability Act, McCombs noticed that Wilson's desk was covered with mail. The Governor explained that it was mostly unanswered requests for him to speak, largely from the Northeast.

Only days after Wilson had booted Jim Nugent from his office, Page, McCorkle, and McCombs invited the Governor to New York for an unexpected conference. These Manhattan Southerners wanted to fund an organization to promote Wilson as the Democratic nominee for President. They intended to raise a few thousand dollars right away to send him on a speaking tour—an exploratory journey without any long-term commitment. They would start planning the itinerary by inspecting the unanswered mail, but they believed the tour should begin by testing Wilson's viability in the West, allowing him to accrue political capital as he worked his way east. It would be arranged largely through the network of Princeton men who were civic leaders, if not elected officials, and it was "not to wear the look of being anything political." Wilson hesitated but consented.

They hired Wilson's secretary, Frank P. Stockbridge, to serve as publicity director. According to him, Wilson delivered instructions that were utterly anomalous, nearly impossible to obey, and counterproductive: "I am not to be put forward as a candidate for the Presidency. . . . You must not ask any one to say a word or print a line in my behalf. Confine your activities to answering requests for information. When such inquiries come, tell them the whole truth; there is nothing to be concealed or glossed over. If you are in doubt as to where I stand on any question of public policy concerning which you are asked, come and see me or telephone."

Upon their acceptance of his ground rules, Wilson agreed to follow this team's game plan. He allowed himself a tryout in Atlanta, where America's top elected officials were gathering for the Southern Commercial Congress. At a breakfast of the Young Men's Democratic League before his major address, Wilson was introduced by Judge George Hillyer, the very Justice who had presided over his examination for admission to the Georgia Bar almost thirty years prior. With Theodore Roosevelt and William Howard Taft also in town, Hillyer said: "Last evening we listened to a man who has been president; this evening we shall hear a man who is president; but we have with us this morning a man who is going to be president."

In case such a pipe dream should ever come true, Wilson clarified what sort of President the nation might expect. At a dinner hosted by Governor Hoke Smith in a hotel banquet hall, he said, "The present is a time of rejoicing for the coming back of the south into national politics." He commented on the power of that cohesive block of Southern Representatives and how it was misperceived as "conservative to the point of being reactionary." For himself, Wilson asserted, "The older I get the more radical I get along certain lines. Radical in the literal sense of the word, and I long more and more to get at the root of the whole matter." With a Jeffersonian belief in the power of the people, he maintained that the current leadership of the United States failed to see the populace as a whole, that most of the country was at the mercy of a "provincial" New York City. "The most serious thing facing us today," he said, "is the concentration of money power in the hands of a few." As soon as he finished speaking to the enthusiastic crowd of eight thousand in the Atlanta Auditorium, he raced home to New Jersey for an even more important meeting, with an audience of one.

Over the course of the twentieth century, history has treated few more unfairly than William Jennings Bryan, often reducing him to little more than a three-time Presidential loser and a Christian fundamentalist buffoon. He did, in fact, head the failed Democratic tickets in 1896, 1900, and 1908; and he died suddenly in 1925 in Dayton, Tennessee, just five days after successfully prosecuting the Scopes "Monkey" Trial, which challenged the teaching of Darwinism. But historical reductions and subsequent theatrical interpretations of Bryan degraded a patriotic American and devout Presbyterian who became the most popular orator of his day, a Presidential candidate at thirty-six years of age, the voice for the silent but angry American. "The Great Commoner," as he was called, invigorated the Democratic Party by urging an activist government with such farsighted notions as enfranchising women, empowering labor unions, and endorsing a graduated income tax. For a decade he edited a hugely popular weekly newspaper, *The Commoner*, much of which he filled with his political preaching. In 1911, Bryan was the party's "elder statesman," though he was only fifty-one—four years younger than Wilson—and while he would probably not head the Presidential ticket in 1912, he could certainly help determine the nominee.

Still living in the Princeton Inn and without a house to keep, Ellen Wilson had become engrossed in the news, reading as many newspapers as possible and clipping any article relevant to Woodrow's unannounced campaign. With their great admiration for the same man, she and Joe Tumulty became "fast friends" and confidants. Remaining in the background, she maintained a clear-sighted perspective on current events. More than once, Tumulty told Wilson, "She's a better politician than you are, Governor"—as she proved the second week of March, when she read that the Princeton Theological Seminary had invited William Jennings Bryan to speak. Ellen promptly invited Bryan to dinner and wired her husband to return from Atlanta as quickly as possible. He arrived in time to join the capacity crowd in Alexander Hall, where Bryan held forth for an hour and a half on "Faith." After the speech, Bryan dined with the Wilsons and two of their daughters at the Inn. The dinner was a revelation for Wilson. "He has extraordinary force of personality, and it seems the force of sincerity and conviction," he reported to Mrs. Peck. "He has himself well in hand at every turn of the thought and talk, too; and his voice is wholly delightful. A truly captivating man, I must admit." The feelings were mutual. After the dinner, Tumulty turned to Ellen and said, "You have nominated your husband, Mrs. Wilson."

At the same time, Tumulty felt compelled to inform Wilson that a good number of lawmakers, especially Republicans, still found him professorial and doctrinaire, that they sensed a cold austerity that "prevented that intimate contact" that was so necessary to push through his legislative program. Eager to display Wilson's good nature, Tumulty arranged a dinner at the Trenton Country Club for Senators from both parties. They gathered in a private dining room, where three black musicians played old Southern favorites. Wilson was at his most charming all night, even when Republican Joseph S. Frelinghuysen walked up to the Governor and challenged him—to a Virginia reel. For the next several minutes, the Governor of New Jersey and the President of the State Senate twirled and do-si-doed around the room to the delight of their legislature. Some days later, Wilson found himself at a fried chicken supper and led another formidable Republican around the floor in a cakewalk. "This is what it costs to be a leader!" Wilson wrote Mrs. Peck, realizing the political gains far exceeded the losses of dignity. "They know me for something else than 'an ambitious dictator.'"

On April 13, 1911, the Republican-controlled New Jersey Senate passed the Geran bill—unanimously. And over the next week, the legislature closed its session by passing Wilson's Corrupt Practices Act, his workmen's compensation act, and another act giving a public commission control over state transportation and utilities. Former rival George Record now proclaimed: "The present legislature ends its session with the most remarkable record of progressive legislation ever known in the political history of this or any State." For that, he credited the Governor, who had delivered on all his major campaign promises and who had effectively put machine politics out of business in the state—all within three remarkable months. "After dealing with college politicians," Wilson explained, "I find that the men with whom I am dealing with now seem like amateurs."

That very night, Woodrow Wilson took the stage at the Murat Temple, an Islamic-themed edifice in downtown Indianapolis, to speak to twelve hundred guests at the Jefferson's birthday banquet of the Democratic League of Clubs. When the committee had invited Wilson to pinch-hit for William Jennings Bryan, who had been called away, nobody in the party leadership quite considered him an actual star. But then the toastmaster read a telegram announcing the results of that day's success in the New Jersey legislature; and in that moment, Woodrow Wilson became a national figure. He reminded his audience that the party of Jefferson—"the patron saint of Democracy"—was "the party of hope."

Wilson had transformed into a true Progressive, and in coming to terms with Jefferson's beliefs, he completed his conversion. In their wisdom, the Founding Fathers had woven elasticity into the fabric of the new nation, and Wilson believed that applied especially to the Jeffersonian principle about the best government being that which governed least. That was said, Wilson now realized, in a day when "the opportunities of America were so obvious to every man," and just as available. But that time had passed, Wilson asserted: "America is now not and cannot in the future be a place for unrestricted individual enterprise."

"I do not find the problems of 1911 solved in the Declaration of Independence," Wilson told the audience in Indianapolis. And over the next year, his thoughts on the subject only intensified. Wilson was "confident" that were Jefferson then alive, he would see the current American trammeled in circumstances that no longer allowed him to pursue happiness because all men were no longer created equal. "Monopoly, private control, the authority of privilege, the concealed mastery of a few men, cunning enough to rule without showing their power," Wilson said, "—he would have at once pronounced the rank weeds which are sure to choke out all wholesome life." To fail to protect the American citizen—"to let him alone"—Wilson believed, "is to leave him helpless as against the obstacles with which he has to contend." Thus, the Governor declared, "law in our day must come to the assistance of the individual." In time, Wilson would declaim, "It is the object of Government to make those adjustments of life which will put every man in a position to claim his normal rights as a living human being." Toward that end, he believed that "government must regulate business, because that is the foundation of every other relationship."

With the $3,000 that Page, McCombs, and McCorkle raised, Frank Stockbridge completed his plans for their noncandidate's tour of the West. Wilson began in Missouri, the home of Champ Clark, the new Speaker of the House, who had Presidential aspirations of his own. Over the next month, Wilson visited a dozen cities, delivering twice as many speeches. Never talking down to his audience, Wilson made the tariff his primary topic, arguing in Kansas City that it had gone from a "system of protection" to one of "patronage." In Denver, twelve thousand people came to hear him deliver a talk about the Bible on the occasion of the tercentenary of its translation into English. He referred to the Scripture as "the people's book of revelation." The Governor spoke several more times in Colorado at the very moment that New York and Denver had just been connected by telephone wire. When the *New York Times* reporter asked a local for news from the Rockies, the Coloradan replied, "The town is wild over Woodrow Wilson and is booming him for president."

For the rest of the Western tour, Wilson's straight talk incited similar enthusiasm. In Los Angeles, he said, "The business of every true Jeffersonian is to translate abstract portions of the Declaration of Independence into the language and the problems of his own day"; and he proudly declared himself a "radical." Before 2,500 people at the City Club in Los Angeles, Wilson explained that he was a Progressive not an insurgent, the former taking the lead in his party while the latter rebelled against the majority of his party. In San Francisco he told four hundred members of the Harvard, Yale, and Princeton clubs that they were the problem with politics in America—for letting government truckle to special interests. In Oregon, Wilson said, "The Presidency of the United States is not an office for which a man can start out and declare he is fitted. On the other hand no man can refuse such a nomination for the office if it be offered him."

"There is a general impression among newspaper men that I dragooned the Legislature of New Jersey into passing a great deal of reform legislation," Wilson told the Press Club of Portland. "I did nothing of the sort." Instead, Wilson explained, the people began to assert themselves against the machines so that legislators could vote their own minds as they had not done in years. Progressive pioneer W. S. U'ren himself introduced the New Jersey Governor of five months at one gathering as "the greatest constructive statesman of the century." By the time Wilson reached the state of Washington, *The Seattle Daily Times* referred to him as "the most logical successor to William Jennings Bryan as the leader of the advanced wing in the Democratic party, and a strong presidential possibility." Wilson persisted in telling the press that the Presidency was not even on his mind. At long last, Ellen told him, "Please, please don't say again that you are not thinking of the presidency. All who know you well know that this is true fundamentally; but superficially, it can't be true and it gives the cynics an opening they seize with glee."

By the time Wilson had returned to New Jersey, the *Newark Evening News* had reported that an informal poll suggested that four out of five Democratic Congressmen were favoring Wilson for their party's nomination the next year. It also indicated that Northerners regarded him as a Northerner or Easterner and that Southerners considered him one of their own. On May 27, 1911, *The New York Times* ran a letter from Thomas Pryor Gore, the blind Senator from Oklahoma. "It is easier to nominate a Democrat who deserves to win than to nominate one who is able to win," he wrote. "We must seek a leader in whom these two qualities are united. I believe that Mr. Wilson answers both requirements." With this statement, Gore became the first major elected official to endorse him for the Presidency.

Wilson took one more trip that spring to Washington, D.C. Led by Page and McCombs, the small team encamped at the Willard Hotel, where Senator Martine ushered in various Representatives from across the country. The visitors included Champ Clark and House Majority Leader Oscar Underwood of Alabama. Neither impressed Wilson as worthy of the nation's highest office. "If I could satisfy myself that Oscar Underwood had a genuine grasp of progressive principles, I should instruct my friends to make no further efforts in my behalf, and work for Underwood," Wilson confided to his inner group. He continued to maintain that he did not want the office himself but acknowledged, "While there is no certainty of my being nominated, on the other hand, if I am nominated, I shall be elected." The campaign committee wanted to expand, but Wilson continued to hesitate, still afraid to suggest that he was running. Frank Stockbridge opened a small New York office at 42 Broadway, and Wilson retreated for his summer vacation.

New Jersey provided its Governor with an ocean-side mansion in Sea Girt, forty-five miles due east of Trenton. It was a big white house whose deep front porch had a long row of rocking chairs. Although it came with a small staff, it did not provide the relaxation any of the Wilsons desired. The National Guard Parade Ground, with public access, lay in front of the house. Locals made themselves at home in the rockers, and sometimes even entered the house. The nearby railroad junction was so close that Wilson often paused midsentence until the latest train had passed. And as Governor, he was expected to review a dress parade of the Guard every Sunday, on horseback. Wilson thought the ceremony an inappropriate use of the Sabbath; even worse, custom dictated that he must perform this weekly duty wearing a frock coat and high silk hat, which made him feel like "a perfect fool." He occasionally managed to escape for a drive in his first automobile—also provided by the state, complete with driver.

Once Wilson realized the futility of finding peace in Sea Girt, he turned the house into a summer camp. He welcomed relatives and even invited Mrs. Peck to visit. The Wilson women found her charming, though she got on his daughters' nerves with her constant suggestions for improving their appearance with chic coiffures and jewelry. Whatever ardor Wilson had once felt had long since transformed into a caring friendship; and the ease of her presence further suggested that an affair in the modern sense of the word had never occurred. Topping the season's guest list were the nation's Governors, who held their annual conference in the seaside town. The rounds of banquets and meetings gave Wilson the opportunity to size up some of his competition. An increasing stream of visitors committed to nominating Wilson also descended on the house. Tumulty practically became a member of the family; and Wilson befriended Dudley Field Malone, an attorney and the son-in-law of New York's newly elected Senator, James Aloysius O'Gorman, whose recent victory had confounded Tammany Hall.

The most significant visitor that summer proved to be a man who immediately gained Wilson's confidence. Seven years his junior, William Gibbs McAdoo was born in Georgia and raised there and in Tennessee, where he entered the state university and read law. He rose quickly in the railroad business—first as an attorney, then as an investor, and soon as president of the Knoxville Street Railway Company, which fell into receivership. McAdoo moved his wife and six children to New York, where he sold railroad bonds. While a frequent commuter on the increasingly crowded ferries between New York and New Jersey, he heard about half-constructed tunnels that lay beneath the Hudson River, abandoned because of tragic accidents and insufficient funding. In 1901, McAdoo took it upon himself to revive the project. At a cost of eight years and $70 million, twin tunnels—known for years as the "McAdoo Tunnels"—connected the two states; and the trains on their new paths under the river were known as "Red McAdoos." They linked to New York's rapid transit system. Because he was president of the Hudson & Manhattan Railroad Company, most assumed he had extracted millions of dollars from the enterprise; but he drew only his salary, $50,000 a year. In the shady world of public utilities, McAdoo was a beacon of progressivism, advocating growth over profits, and even equal pay for women. "The public be pleased" was the motto of this six-foot egret of a man, long-legged and lean with a prominent beak.

A few years earlier, while visiting his son at Princeton, McAdoo had bumped into Wilson on the train platform at the junction. In the time it took Wilson to escort him across the campus, McAdoo became an admirer, finding Wilson's casual talk "somehow inspiring and stimulating." When Wilson entered the gubernatorial race, McAdoo had wanted to help but feared a man in his position would be wrongly suspected of being a tool of big business and Wall Street. Upon meeting Wilson again, he made it clear that the logical remedy for the evils of big business was not to be found in "repressive legislation which attempts to stunt the development of business enterprise," but in letting it grow, surrounded by "adequate supervision and publicity."

Over the years, McAdoo observed a difference between America's two major parties, a division in political thought that defined them historically and for at least another century. "The essential difference," he said, ". . . is that the vital idea of the Democratic Party is *people*, and the vital idea of the Republican Party is *property*." Sensing a kindred spirit, in the spring of 1911, McAdoo committed himself to catapulting Woodrow Wilson to higher office.

McAdoo knew William McCombs, Wilson's self-appointed campaign manager; and despite reservations about him, offered to serve his candidate. The two men met at least once a week, often joined by Walter Hines Page and Oswald Garrison Villard, the liberal editor of the *New York Evening Post* and grandson of abolitionist William Lloyd Garrison. At first, McAdoo admired the job McCombs was doing—the successful Western tour and his having raised an astronomical $200,000 before the convention. But as enthusiasm for Wilson rapidly grew, McAdoo worried that the mentally unstable McCombs lacked the organizational skills to marshal a countrywide campaign. With no national organization beyond a small office at 42 Broadway, it seemed hard to imagine Wilson's competing against Champ Clark, for example, who had coordinated committees advocating his candidacy in every state in the Union.

If the potency of an American political movement can be measured by the anger of its opposition, Wilson's strength first appeared that summer of 1911. In July, Democratic state chairman James Nugent was dining out with a coterie of friends in Avon-by-the-Sea, not five miles up the coast from Sea Girt; officers of the National Guard sat at a nearby table. As the evening wound down, Nugent offered a toast and both parties rose from their seats. "I give you the governor of the state of New Jersey," he said, as everybody raised a glass . . . until he concluded, "—a liar and an ingrate!" Everybody froze in silence. "Do I drink alone?" Nugent asked. All glasses lowered, and several guardsmen threw their wine on the floor. The state organization soon relieved Nugent of his chairmanship.

Wilson's enemies began dredging his past, combing his extensive paper trail in search of embarrassing, if not disqualifying, remarks. In the fifth volume of his *History of the American People*, published in 1902, they found a long paragraph about the demographic shift in immigration to America in the 1880s, in which Professor Wilson had written of certain new arrivals—of "multitudes of men of the lowest class from the south of Italy and men of the meaner sort out of Hungary and Poland, men out of the ranks where there was neither skill nor energy nor any initiative of quick intelligence," as if those countries were "disburdening themselves of the more sordid and hapless elements of their population." Furthermore, Wilson had observed, people on the Pacific coast were enjoying a new federal statute excluding Chinese immigration, even though "the Chinese were more to be desired, as workmen if not as citizens, than most of the coarse crew that came crowding in every year at the eastern ports." At a time when America pigeonholed its population according to national origin, Wilson was trying to explain that the Asians' skill, intelligence, and strong work ethic had forced their exclusion while those "unlikely fellows who came in at the eastern ports were tolerated because they usurped no place but the very lowest in the scale of labor." Now pockets of protesters arose—spokesmen for the three million Polish Americans and the two million Italians who had joined the unskilled labor force in America in the last decade alone. Wilson explained the context of his remarks to those who petitioned him and asked his publishers if he might rewrite one or two passages for future printings of the book. No immigrant movement against him ever took hold.

In 1907, Wilson, then president of Princeton, had written Adrian Joline—an alumnus and president of a railroad company—criticizing William Jennings Bryan's campaign for government ownership of the railroads. "Would that we could do something, at once, dignified and effective, to knock Mr. Bryan, once for all, into a cocked hat," he wrote. Now, almost five years later, Joline released that letter to the New York *Sun*. At least, he figured, it would reveal Wilson's hypocrisy; at most, it would rupture the cordiality between the two prominent Democrats. Wilson made no comment; and when a reporter from the *Sun* asked Bryan what he thought about Wilson's wanting to knock him into a cocked hat, Bryan laughed the comment off, saying, "That's what the *Sun* has been trying to do to me since 1896."

At the same time, some of Wilson's opponents accused him of trying to scam the Carnegie Foundation for the Advancement of Teaching by applying for a pension, even though he did not qualify under new foundation requirements. Like the other "scandals," none of the accusations stuck. Perhaps because of his skimpy political résumé, Wilson proved to be the cleanest candidate for any office in recent memory.

By the start of 1912, he observed, there was "a merry war on" against him, and he was "evidently regarded as the strongest candidate at present, for all the attacks are directed against me, and the other fellows are not bothered." As Democrats flocked to Washington that week for the Jackson Day dinner, rumors spread that another old letter was about to surface, one in which Grover Cleveland cast doubt on Wilson's "intellectual integrity." Wilson continued to ignore the barbs from Princeton or elsewhere. "I believe very profoundly in an over-ruling Providence," he wrote Mary Peck, "and I do not fear that any real plans can be thrown off the track. It may not be intended that I shall be President,—but that would not break my heart—and I am content to await the event,—doing what I honourably can, in the meantime, to discomfit mine enemies!"

On January 8, 1912, seven hundred of the nation's leading Democrats filled the gold-and-white ballroom of the Raleigh Hotel, four blocks from the White House. The head table included the party's past nominees for President and most of those eyeing the future. Everybody watched Bryan's grand entrance, especially to observe his reactions to Clark and Wilson. He greeted the former warmly, and he grasped the latter by the shoulder, lingering in conversation for several minutes. Wilson was the penultimate speaker of the evening, and he laid any tensions to rest. For all the tidal shifts in the party over the last sixteen years, he said, the one fixed point had been "the character and the devotion and the preachings of William Jennings Bryan." He promptly added:

> While we have differed with Mr. Bryan upon this occasion and upon that in regard to the specific things to be done, he has gone serenely on pointing out to a more and more convinced people what it was that was the matter. He has had the steadfast vision all along of what it was that was the matter and he has, not any more than Andrew Jackson did, not based his career upon calculation, but has based it upon principle.

Homage paid, Wilson challenged the Hamiltonian doctrine that those with the biggest asset in the government should serve as the trustees for the rest of the nation, that those who conducted the biggest business transactions should maintain their leadership because the benefits of their prosperity would trickle down. He warned that the great danger to the nation was not the individual combinations in business but the "combination of combinations . . . the same groups of men [controlling] chains of banks, systems of railways, whole manufacturing enterprises, great mining projects, great enterprises for the developing of the natural water power of this country, and that threaded together in the personnel of a series of boards of directors is a community of interest more formidable than any conceivable combination in the United States."

Wilson called upon his brethren to "apologize to each other that we ever suspected or antagonized one another; let us join hands once more all around the great circle of community . . . which will show us at the last to have been indeed the friends of our country and the friends of mankind." With that, he bowed slightly toward the Great Commoner. Bryan later told Judge Hudspeth of New Jersey that Wilson delivered "the greatest speech in American political history." Even allowing for exaggeration and misquotation, Wilson was lionized that night. Bryan's speech had proved anticlimactic, if not abdicative.

Before leaving Washington, Bryan told Wilson not to give another thought to the Joline letter. He knew the gibe had not been personal, simply a disagreement over policy. "All I can say, Mr. Bryan," Wilson told him, "is that you are a great, big man." The Democratic National Committee met, and thirty-two of the fifty-two members declared themselves Wilson supporters.

For years, Colonel Harvey had been carrying the torch for Woodrow Wilson, but now that flame dimmed. Although he was an ardent Democrat, his business interests were strongly tied to Wall Street. With Wilson listing to the left, Harvey and his cohort had second thoughts about the candidate they had tapped. Financial heavyweights—including J. P. Morgan himself, who had not forgotten Wilson's stinging public rebuke of bankers right in front of his nose—leaned on Harvey, assuring him that any amount of money would always be available to fight Wilson.

Wilson, Harvey, and Marse Watterson met in New York to discuss the situation. Exiting the dining room of the Manhattan Club, Harvey linked arms with Wilson and said, "Governor, there is a question I want to ask you, to which I want your very frank answer." It was whether he found the support of his *Harper's Weekly* in any way embarrassing. Wilson said, "I very much wish you would not ask me that question, because the answer to it embarrasses me severely. Some of my friends have told me that the support of *Harper's Weekly* is not doing me any good in the West, but I am very sorry you compel me to tell you this." Harvey said he had feared such a response, and that "we shall have to soft pedal." Watterson said that he would "sing low" himself. And with that, the banner that had long graced the editorial page of *Harper's Weekly*—"For President, Woodrow Wilson"— quietly disappeared.

Fearing his boss might have created a formidable enemy, Tumulty urged Wilson to send a letter to Harvey. Wilson complied, writing: "Every day I am confirmed in the judgment that my mind is a one-track road and can run only one train of thought at a time!" He explained that in responding that night to a simple matter of fact, he had failed to express "a word of sincere gratitude to you for all your generous support, or of my hope that it might be continued." He apologized.

Replying in an equally matter-of-fact tone, Harvey said the only thing possible for him to do "in simple fairness to you, no less than in consideration of my own self-respect, was to release you of your embarrassment so far as it lay within my power to do so, by ceasing to advocate your nomination." He maintained that Wilson's gracious words had compensated for whatever small hurt he may have felt. Wilson realized the damage he had done and hoped a second letter of apology might make amends. He reextended his gratitude for Harvey's generous support and reexpressed his admiration of his "unhesitating courage and individuality." Although the men remained cordial with each other, their relationship never recovered. Harvey publicly shifted his support to Champ Clark.

Stockton Axson considered the Harvey maneuver "as deliberate a frameup as was ever concocted"—politics, plain and simple. Like Boss Smith, Harvey and his friends realized that Wilson was beyond their control, and they did not like the direction in which he was headed. He was not going to serve their interests; and so, after having planted the seed, they wanted to nip this candidacy in the bud. The editorial pages of nonprogressive newspapers across the country became a Greek chorus issuing fatalistic prophecies of what would happen should Wilson's standing improve. Curiously, this new Harvey offensive backfired, as Wilson proved once more that he was beholden to nobody.

A few special benefactors—such as Cleveland Dodge and Edward Filene of Boston, and Henry Morgenthau, a dynamic attorney and real estate investor in New York, where he was a leader in the Reform Jewish community—saw to it that Wilson's campaign was always funded; and as the committee opened offices across the country, it constantly sought new supporters. In October 1911, McCombs had asked McAdoo to accompany him in calling upon a wealthy Texan in Manhattan, a man who could provide a lot more than money.

Edward Mandell House was born in Houston in 1858, the youngest of seven sons. His father, Thomas William House, had emigrated from England and arrived in Texas when he and the territory were young enough for boundless dreams. T. W. House became one of the richest men in the state, amassing more than a quarter-million dollars and almost as many acres of land. Growing up in Houston and Galveston and parked in London while his parents toured the Continent, Edward inherited none of his father's drive to succeed. When T. W. died, Edward benefited instead from a small fortune, which permitted him to drop out of Cornell. He lived as a gentleman for the rest of his life, dabbling in business and in raising cattle and cotton. Untrained for any profession, House indulged in his one passion—politics. He read widely on the subject and got to know all the players in Texas. Between 1892 and 1902, he managed the campaigns of four Texans who became Governors and whom he subsequently advised in office. One of them, James S. Hogg, bestowed upon him the honorary title by which he would be addressed for the rest of his life.

"He has the entire state of Texas in his vest pocket," McCombs told McAdoo on their way to "Colonel" House's apartment at the Hotel Gotham on Fifth Avenue, where he lived much of the year. While his clout had been exaggerated, House did have friends in high places, and he was always looking higher. Ironically, his apparent lack of drive proved to be his greatest asset. As a result, as one longtime friend would say, House's interest in the business of politics was "unselfish."

People called him a kingmaker, but the Colonel's appearance suggested no powerhouse. Short and bald, with a weak chin and gentle blue eyes, House had suffered as a child from a bad fall, severely bruising his head, and from a bout of malaria. Maladies persisted, and hypochondria recurred when they did not. He appeared fragile, and he engaged in no strenuous activity; he had an aversion to the heat, which kept him from Texas for much of the time, especially in the summer; and he avoided the glare of publicity. He had money in his pockets and time on his hands.

House impressed McAdoo and McCombs, though he was not ready to commit to Wilson. A meeting at the Gotham of the two principals on

November 24, 1911, changed that. "The first hour we spent together proved to each of us that there was a sound basis for a fast friendship," House wrote in his diary. Each of their first memories was of life in the South during the Civil War, and they shared a distaste for Reconstruction and the carpet-baggers' mockery of government. "We found ourselves in such complete sympathy, in so many ways," House said, "that we soon learned to know what each was thinking without either having expressed himself."

Shortly after their meeting, House returned to his sprawling Shingle Style home in Austin, where he came down with one of his fevers. While recuperating, he wrote a novella—a peculiar work with fifty-three chapters of one or two pages each—in which he aired many of his economic and political theories. *Philip Dru: Administrator* tells of a futuristic dystopia— the United States of America in the year 1920, when the eponymous hero leads forces from the democratic West against the plutocratic East, resulting in Dru's reforming the nation. "Wealth had grown so strong, that the few were about to strangle the many," it begins. House devoted two of the closing chapters to the constitutions Philip Dru drafted for the states and the nation, devising in great detail a government more like Britain's parliamentary system. Anglophile Woodrow Wilson, who had been writing constitutions since boyhood, had met his alter ego.

Once he was on his feet, Colonel House joined Wilson's ranks, becoming a cohesive element. He linked a strong contingent of Texas supporters, which included state legislator Thomas B. Love, attorney Thomas W. Gregory, and Congressman Albert S. Burleson; he became a mediator between McAdoo and the increasingly volatile McCombs; and having maintained a personal relationship with William Jennings Bryan for more than ten years, he began to insinuate Wilson's name into their conversations. In short order, House and Wilson were exchanging confidences. When House asked him one day if he realized how short a time they had known one another, the latter replied, "My dear friend, we have known one another always." Within a year, Wilson would tell others, "House is my second personality. . . . If anyone thinks he is reflecting my opinion by whatever action he takes, they are welcome to the conclusion."

Although 1912 promised to keep him on the road even more than 1911, Wilson knew the family could no longer call four rooms at the Princeton Inn home. The purchase of a house was beyond their reach, especially with the future so uncertain; and even renting a house was a financial stretch.

When longtime family friends from New Orleans—a pair of spinster sisters—spoke of a long visit north, Nell suggested they all share a rental. She found a charming and affordable furnished house at 25 Cleveland Lane in Princeton, practically around the corner from the Wilsons' former house on Library Place. It had been built by an artist and included a well-lighted large studio in which Ellen could paint and a pleasant garden. The house's only drawback was that it sat next door to his "betrayer," Jack Hibben.

Governor Wilson continued to commute twenty miles each day to his office in Trenton and back; and as the ex officio president of the Princeton Board of Trustees, he appeared for the occasional ceremony on campus, though he steered clear of university business. So it came as something of a shock to him in January 1912 when, as he wrote Mrs. Peck, "the worst has happened at the University: Hibben has been elected President!" The Committee on the Inauguration naturally invited Wilson not only to attend his induction but to make the welcoming address. Wilson declined, falsely claiming a prior commitment. He felt a pang of cowardice for going into New York City the night before his actual obligation, but he explained to Mrs. Peck: "To be present and silent would be deeply hypocritical: to go and speak my real thoughts and judgments would be to break up the meeting and create a national scandal." Wilson sent no congratulations, and the installation proceeded without even the mention of his name. And Princeton settled into an era of quiet conservatism.

Only months after Wilson's first-year legislative victories, the State Assembly changed hands, putting the Republicans in charge of both houses. When Wilson opened the new session of the legislature by asking the lawmakers to consider a number of questions of "efficiency and economy," he realized the legislature had developed a mind of its own. Wilson vetoed more than forty bills in one swoop, which enraged the Republicans. Even so, Wilson was able to enact laws effecting standards for milk and food, creating city planning commissions, reforming child labor practices, establishing free dental clinics, forming a commission on immigration, reorganizing the State Board of Education, and limiting the employment of women to sixty hours a week (which was the first law relating to women wage earners ever passed in New Jersey). He also appointed the first Jew to the state's Supreme Court. Extreme partisanship contributed to more gridlock than Wilson would have liked, but so did Wilson's absenteeism, as he visited more than fifteen states in the first half of the year. Boss Smith tried to fill the vacuum by doing everything possible to undo Wilson's reforms and reassert his own power. His camp hoped to send New Jersey delegates to the national nominating convention with instructions to vote for "Anybody but Wilson."

For the first time, several states would be selecting delegates to the Democratic Convention through primaries. Because Wilson's team of novices would be challenging veteran candidates' political machines, it had to select its battles carefully—a strategy that paid off, at first. Wilson forwent running in Missouri and Alabama, where favorite sons Champ Clark and Oscar Underwood won, respectively, and he found early but limited momentum in the West—Utah, the Dakotas, and Montana. Then the pendulum swung in the opposite direction. Despite enthusiastic receptions wherever he spoke, to say nothing of his and Ellen's strong ties to Georgia, that state went to Underwood. Maryland and Massachusetts turned out for Champ Clark, as did Nebraska and California. Illinois, where Wilson campaigned heavily and Clark did not even appear, went for Clark by a margin of almost 3 to 1. Coffers emptied and spirits sagged; even McCombs told his candidate that the unpredictable tide was turning against them. There was no clear front-runner, and Colonel House felt Wilson's only hope was the party's fear of turning once again to Bryan or worse—Clark, who had the backing of newspaper baron William Randolph Hearst. In the meantime, several states kept Wilson's hopes alive. Pennsylvania supported him, and Ohio split its delegation between him and its Governor, Judson Harmon. Progressive Wisconsin, Kansas, and Senator Gore's Oklahoma all pulled through for Wilson as well. Texas, with its unconventional procedure for determining delegates—combining a primary with caucuses—two-stepped into Wilson's column; and New Jersey, despite Boss Smith's efforts, went for its favorite son. Not since 1860—when slavery divided them, and their delegates deadlocked after fifty-seven ballots—had the Democratic Party been so undecided about its leadership.

Adding to the uncertainty surrounding the upcoming convention in Baltimore was that it still operated under a "two-thirds rule," a device meant to provide the power of unity to the emergent nominee by insisting upon a supermajority—729 votes. Political scientist Woodrow Wilson felt the rule was "a most un-Democratic regulation"; but, ironically, it might just allow him to survive and possibly succeed at a brokered convention. A tally in early June showed Clark leading with 436 pledged delegates to Wilson's 248; Underwood followed with 84, and several other Governors could count on their delegations. Political machines controlled an estimated 224 unpledged delegates across the country, which presumably backed Clark. McCombs urged making peace with Tammany Hall, not only to gain New York's 90 votes but to show the necessary force to attract others. Indeed, it was Tammany Hall's intention to make one of its favorites, Alton B. Parker, the convention's temporary chairman.

Before the gathering of the delegates, Wilson retreated with his family to Sea Girt. As practical as he was self-protective, Wilson distanced himself by looking upon the "political game" as if he were not even a player. "Just between you and me," he wrote Mrs. Peck on June 9, 1912, "I have not the least idea of being nominated, because the make of the convention is such, the balance and confusion of forces, that the outcome is in the hands of the professional, case-hardened politicians who serve only their own interests and who know that I will not serve them except as I might serve the party in general. . . . I have no deep stakes involved in this game."

William Jennings Bryan did. If he was not to be the nominee (a possibility he had not ruled out), he intended to see the party continue down the Progressive path he had blazed, which Parker would obstruct. While attending the Republican Convention in Chicago as a member of the press—and seeing that party torn asunder as it renominated incumbent President Taft instead of responding to the insurgent wing of the party behind ex-President Roosevelt—Bryan wired the Democrats' four leading contenders, asking each to take a stand on the matter of naming a reactionary such as Parker to chair their convention. It was a shrewd political move on Bryan's part, one that would smoke out each man's vision of the party's future. Conservatives Underwood and Harmon supported Parker, and Clark evaded taking a position. McCombs, heading toward a nervous breakdown, pleaded with Wilson to take the middle ground, as Clark had done—to be respectful of Bryan but in a way that would not offend Tammany Hall. Wilson went to his bedroom at Sea Girt and sought the counsel of his wife.

"There must be no hedging," Ellen said; and Woodrow smiled, for he had hoped that would be her response. "YOU ARE QUITE RIGHT," he wired Bryan in response, unequivocally stating that Baltimore was to be "a convention of progressives," and that, like Bryan, his campaign was "in the interest of the people's cause." Upon reading Wilson's response, McCombs wept hysterically. McAdoo was convinced Wilson had made the right move. Bryan lost in his bid to keep the gavel out of Parker's hands, but Wilson succeeded in emerging as the only Progressive in the race. In Sea Girt, tents sprouted on the Governor's lawn, a camp for reporters, photographers, and telegraphers. A special telephone line ran from McCombs's office in the Emerson Hotel in Baltimore to the house—one extension in the master bedroom, the other in a closet under the stairs.

Although few ever know—and even fewer remember—more than a few planks in a political platform, the Democrats of 1912 proposed three dozen issues on which they took stands, all moderately Progressive without appearing radical. Their major issue was a call for the immediate lowering of the "high Republican tariff," which they called "the principal cause of the unequal distribution of wealth." (Every operative of the party could read in his election handbook of how a simple graduation dress made from cloth in the United States cost more to purchase at home than in England, because Republican Senator Henry Lippitt of Rhode Island had insinuated into the current law a heavy tariff for imported cloth, forcing people to buy grossly marked-up American textiles, many of which came from mills owned by Senator Lippitt.) The Democrats pledged further: to toughen anti-trust laws; to support the ratification of two recent constitutional amendments—providing for an income tax and the popular election of Senators; to endorse the recent movement to publicize contributions to Presidential elections; to promote through legislation in each state a primary to select Presidential candidates; to enact a law prohibiting any corporation from contributing to a campaign fund and limiting personal campaign contributions; to reform banking laws to counteract "the present methods of depositing government funds in a few favored banks largely situated in or controlled by Wall Street, in return for political favors"; to renounce "a policy of imperialism and colonial exploitation in the Philippines" and recognize the independence of the island nation; to protect labor, minors, civil servants, and the general public through a commitment to strengthen various governmental agencies relating to food and health. In perhaps the most forgotten item on the list, they advocated a single Presidential term.

By midnight of June 25, 1912, twenty thousand Democrats had gathered in the fetid 5th Maryland Regiment Armory. A little after two o'clock that morning, the state of Delaware yielded to New Jersey so that Judge John W. Wescott, at the candidate's behest, could nominate Woodrow Wilson. Although Wescott had once denounced him, his rousing speech conjured up Wilson's remarks to the Princeton alumni of Pittsburgh, the very words for which he had been lampooned—"The great voice of America does not come from seats of learning. It comes in a murmur from the hills and woods, and the farms and factories and the mills"; the judge cited Wilson further, capturing his essence when he said, " 'No man is great who thinks himself so, and no man is good who does not strive to secure the happiness and comfort of others.' " Sitting in the closet at Sea Girt to hear the news over the telephone, Tumulty learned that the response to the nomination of "the Princeton schoolmaster" lasted more than an hour, longer than anybody else's. Wilson, of course, had long since gone to bed.

State-by-state voting did not begin until dawn; and by the time Wilson had returned from a morning of golf, he had learned from any number of reporters that Clark had taken a decisive lead on the first ballot: 440½ to Wilson's 324; Harmon had fewer than half that number (most of which were from New York), and Underwood had fewer than that. Wilson spoke to McCombs during the day; but for the most part, he carried on nonchalantly, reading aloud from a biography of Gladstone at night. While he slept, his wife and daughters and Tumulty waited through the night for any news. The delegates settled in for what promised to be endless roll calling, waiting for one delegation or another to budge from its position, usually in response to some bartered deal. On the tenth ballot, Boss Murphy of New York announced his state was shifting its support to Clark, effectively knocking Harmon out of the game. Wilson's tally inched upward, but Clark had accrued 556 votes, a simple majority. Saturday morning, McCombs sounded despondent, as he and Wilson discussed Wilson's exit strategy and to whom he should release his delegates. Ellen cried; and Woodrow comforted her, saying, "After all, it is God's will, and I feel that a great load has been lifted from my shoulders." Besides, he added, "now we can see Rydal again."

Later that Saturday, McAdoo confronted McCombs, who was convinced of Clark's impending nomination. McAdoo could not have disagreed more, arguing that Clark had peaked while Wilson had steadily gained. When McAdoo learned that McCombs had a telegram from Wilson authorizing the release of his delegates, McAdoo immediately called the candidate to say, "Your nomination is inevitable, Governor—your delegates will stick, if it takes all summer." Wilson agreed to withhold his withdrawal. On the fourteenth ballot, Bryan announced that as long as New York supported Champ Clark, he would refrain from endorsing him, ostensibly because he wanted to stop the establishment machines from controlling the party. Clark maintained that Bryan's contention was "dishonest" at best, as the Great Commoner really wanted only to deadlock the convention so that the delegates, in desperation, would turn to him a fourth time.

A first-term New York State Senator later claimed credit for the subsequent shift in the convention hall. Thirty-year-old Franklin Delano Roosevelt played his first significant role in a national election that season as he formed a Woodrow Wilson Club and took a delegation to Baltimore, where they were promptly barred from participating in the convention because they lacked proper credentials. Outside the armory, FDR heard that the Mayor, a Clark supporter, had been packing the hall with two hundred Clark men who were required to show nothing more than a specially made Clark button in order to gain admittance. Young Roosevelt happened to know the manufacturer, and he secured three hundred buttons, which he immediately distributed among his fellow Wilson supporters. Once inside, they created an uproar promoting their man.

Wilson steadily chipped away at Clark's lead. Fueling the carnival-like atmosphere, concessionaires were selling peanuts, frankfurters, and beer, the smells of which mingled with the perspiration of the hundreds of delegates in their sixth day inside the overheated hall. On the twenty-seventh ballot, McAdoo challenged the vote of the New York delegation, which meant calling each delegate for his vote; it loosened nine new Wilson supporters. On the thirtieth ballot, Iowa shifted its votes and Wilson pulled ahead, 460 to 455; and the press in Sea Girt insisted upon a statement from the candidate. "You might say," he told them, "that Governor Wilson received the news in a riot of silence." By the forty-second ballot, Indiana had relinquished support for its favorite son, Governor Thomas R. Marshall, in favor of Wilson; and Clark supporters suggested that their man quit the race. On Tuesday, July 2, Illinois, with its 58 votes, jumped on the Wilson bandwagon; and at 3:30 that afternoon, on the forty-sixth ballot, Wilson piled up 990 votes, putting him over the top. Upon receiving the news, the victor searched for his family. Finding Ellen in her room, he said, "Well, dear, I guess we won't go to Mount Rydal this Summer after all."

Joe Tumulty rushed from the house and waved his hands wildly from the porch. From behind a cluster of trees, a brass band emerged blaring "Hail to the Chief." Wilson asked Tumulty if he had instructed them to slink away had he lost. Amid the jubilation, somebody said to the only calm person in the crowd, "Governor, you don't seem a bit excited." A grave Wilson replied, "I can't effervesce in the face of responsibility."

During the post-nomination recess, McAdoo called Wilson, to ascertain his preference for Vice President. Wilson thought the convention should decide. McAdoo said the delegates would want to abide by his choice and, to balance the ticket, suggested Marshall of Indiana, whom he did not know except by reputation as an affable and popular liberal Governor of a Midwestern state. Nobody appeared to have told Wilson that McCombs had, in fact, already horse-traded the position to Marshall in exchange for Indiana's votes. Wilson had earlier mentioned to Albert Burleson of Texas that Marshall was "a small-calibre man," though he conceded that he was a vote-getter. That night, Marshall received the second spot.

Wilson wanted to keep as low a profile as possible until the official start of the campaign in the fall, but that became increasingly impossible as he was suddenly the least-known important figure in American politics. "Our days are not our own any more and are very laborious," he wrote Mrs. Peck, who had just divorced her husband and was thenceforth known as Mary Allen Hulbert. Having to write an acceptance speech for the Democratic Committee on Notification in early August, Wilson gave his secretaries a brief vacation while he "ran away from home." Cleveland Dodge had offered Wilson use of his yacht, a 129-ton schooner, for as long as he wished; and so he, Ellen, Margaret, and his young friend Dudley Malone piled into a car and drove to a dock near Sandy Hook, where they boarded the *Corona*. Over the next six days, they sailed as far north as New London, enjoying the seclusion, for the vessel carried no wireless. Scrawling short-hand into two large notebooks, Wilson composed his speech.

He returned to Sea Girt, where he found thousands of letters of congratulation and advice. Mindful of his campaign's internal politics, Wilson asked an increasingly unpopular McCombs to elevate McAdoo to the position of vice chairman of the National Committee. This transfer of power proved well-timed: within weeks, McCombs suffered a breakdown and had to sit out most of the campaign. William Jennings Bryan offered to assist however Wilson wished; and he suggested that Wilson not count on carrying New York in the election—because of a reactionary Catholic and Wall Street vote. "As I see it," the old warhorse recommended, "your fight must be won in progressive states." A brilliant attorney from Boston named Louis D. Brandeis congratulated Wilson on his announced plan to deal with the existing tariff—which hurt the middle class—by reducing the duties gradually, at the rate of 5 percent per annum. Brandeis said this was not only further evidence of Wilson's commitment to progressivism but also good for business. And Colonel House pointed out that Wilson's election seemed as "certain as anything political ever is, but it can be lost." He offered to see that it would not be.

At five in the afternoon on Saturday, August 3, Wilson left Sea Girt for a strategy session at the University Club in New York. Carrying his own leather satchel, he walked from the house to the little train depot, where he stood absorbed in a magazine; the others on the platform left him alone. The Pullman porter who took his bag did not recognize him, and the railway car was empty except for the reporters who had been encamped on his lawn. When the porter at Pennsylvania Station was slow in getting Wilson's bag, he grabbed it himself and purposefully charged through a bustling crowd, as the press ran to keep up. Once inside the large waiting room, they all expected him to head for the taxicab stand. Instead, they saw him look to the station dining room on his right. It was 7:30, well past Wilson's normal dinner hour; and so the newspapermen were not altogether surprised . . . until he made a sharp left, entering a lunch counter lined with dozens of stools. Perching himself on one of them, the Democratic nominee for President of the United States spread a small paper napkin on his lap and—except for a few reporters—sat unrecognized as he ate his sandwich and washed it down with a glass of buttermilk.

At three o'clock on Wednesday, August 7, 1912, Woodrow Wilson stood on the portico of the mansion in Sea Girt, beside nine Democratic Governors and before thousands of New Jerseyans—many of whom had arrived by farm wagon and automobile. After a few minutes of introduction, he addressed his party's Notification Committee, saying, "I accept the nomination with a deep sense of its unusual significance and of the great honor done me, and also with a very profound sense of my responsibility to the party and to the Nation." As was his practice on momentous occasions, he read his remarks. Establishing both the tone and the substance of the campaign ahead, he said that he intended to "talk politics . . . in words whose meaning no one need doubt, because the times demanded as much. . . . We must speak, not to catch votes, but to satisfy the thought and conscience of a people deeply stirred by the conviction that they have come to a critical turning point in their moral and political development." Plainly, he said, "it is a new age."

Over the next hour, Wilson recapitulated the Democratic platform, voicing the issues and themes that would reverberate until Election Day. He closed his remarks by reminding his audience that a Presidential campaign could "easily degenerate into a mere personal contest and so lose its real dignity and significance." Without his having to mention any names, everybody knew he was speaking of the blustery Theodore Roosevelt, who had recently bolted from the Republican Party and was at that very minute in Chicago, where the first National Convention of the Progressive Party was nominating him as its candidate. To a chortling crowd, Wilson said, "There is no indispensable man. The government will not collapse and go to pieces if any one of the gentlemen who are seeking to be entrusted with its guidance should be left at home." That included TR, who had just claimed to be as tough as a bull moose and had just delivered the rallying cry for the new third party, saying: "We stand at Armageddon, and we battle for the Lord." Wilson found the remark fatuous; and, in private, he could not refrain from impersonating him in a tinny voice, to the delight of his family. "Good old Teddy," Wilson would say, "—what a help he is."

Every Presidential election is a historic watershed; and in 1912, that was especially true. For the first time, a retired President returned to the electoral battlefield, challenging a sitting President from his former party, no less. And for the first time since 1860, there was a serious fourth-party candidate in the race who had no chance of winning but who was a veritable lightning rod. Even Wilson respected the sincerity of the party's followers and its nominee, Eugene V. Debs.

A year older than Wilson, Debs was born in Terre Haute, Indiana, to cultured Alsatian immigrants. In his teens he began working on the railroad; at twenty he became a founding member of the Brotherhood of Locomotive Firemen; and in his thirties he established the American Railway

Union. "He was a tall shamblefooted man," John Dos Passos would lyri-
cize, "had a sort of gusty rhetoric that set on fire the railroad workers in
their pineboarded halls." Flexing all his muscle, Debs escalated a small
wildcat strike against the Pullman Palace Car Company into an event involving hundreds of thousands of laborers; it shut down much of the nation's transportation, necessitated federal troops, and led to several deaths,
a Supreme Court decision, and Debs's imprisonment for conspiracy to interfere with interstate commerce. He read Karl Marx in jail and emerged
a Socialist, soon founding the Socialist Democratic Party of the United
States. In 1905 he helped organize the Industrial Workers of the World—
the "Wobblies"—an organization composed of Socialist comrades and
radical trade unionists. Debs believed in both causes, but he shied from
the labor union's endorsement of anarchy and devoted himself to his party's politics. He was the Presidential candidate of the Social Democratic
Party in 1900 and ran again as the nominee of the Socialist Party of America in 1904 and 1908, winning 400,000 votes (3 percent) in each race.

All media in 1912 was local. The way to ignite an entire nation was by
setting small fires across the country. That meant giving a speech in a
major city and making shorter talks from the back of a train at the smaller
whistle-stops en route to the next city. Regional press would report what
was said, but word of mouth remained the best publicity. Abandoned by
the progressive wing of the Republican Party and considered too liberal by
its conservatives, President Taft waged a spiritless campaign. Finances
limited the fiery Debs; and even his contention that the other parties were
in the hands of the trusts did not keep organized labor from leaning toward the Democrats. The last two months of the campaign really became
an argument between Roosevelt and Wilson. Because the public had experienced TR's bluster before, Wilson became the object of curiosity in the
race. He felt "stumping tours" were "not the most impressive method" of
campaigning, but he understood that he was the newcomer in the eyes of
the electorate and had to make himself known. "The people seemed to
regard me as some remote academic person," he told one newspaper at the
start of the campaign, "but many of them wanted to see what manner of
man I was, what sort of human animal, what freak of nature I might be."

Wilson felt the nation had long since progressed from the Republican
Party's positions and that Taft would come in third. "But just what will
happen, as between Roosevelt and me, with party lines utterly confused

and broken," he wrote Mary Hulbert on August 25, 1912, "is all guess-work." Wilson knew that voters inevitably made visceral decisions, based largely upon how the press had portrayed the candidates. With scholarly detachment, he delineated the differences between the two front-runners:

> He appeals to their imagination; I do not. He is a real vivid person, whom they have seen and shouted themselves hoarse over and voted for, millions strong; I am a vague, conjectural personality, more made up of opinions and academic prepossessions than of human traits and red corpuscles.

On the other hand, Wilson confided, "Roosevelt never works the heart out of himself—I doubt if he *has* a heart for anybody but himself—but I do, and there are some strains (of responsibility *plus* stupid and corrupt resistance and fight) my heart cannot bear for long together." As TR's distant cousin Franklin put it years later, "Theodore Roosevelt lacked Wood-row Wilson's appeal to the fundamental and failed to stir, as Wilson did, the truly profound moral and social convictions."

The Roosevelt campaign was, therefore, eager to make political hay of the rumors of Wilson's alleged affair with Mary Peck. TR's friend Senator Elihu Root insisted that he had evidence linking Wilson to the Peck divorce; and Washington wags referred to Wilson as "Peck's Bad Boy," the name of a popular newspaper series. But Roosevelt did not wish to endow his opposition with more personality than he felt he possessed; and, in truth, there never was any evidence of a relationship. More to the point, Roosevelt felt he had plenty of other political eggs to throw at his opponent, most of which Wilson simply ignored. He viewed the battle ahead as a "splendid adventure"—though he believed that "the next President of the United States would have a task so difficult as to be heartbreaking and that I w'd probably sacrifice my life to it if I were elected."

William Gibbs McAdoo knew nothing of running a national campaign, but given that task, he was an exemplary executive, unafraid of surrounding himself with talented people and delegating responsibility. Homer Cummings, a Connecticut politician, ran the party's speakers' division; Josephus Daniels, a North Carolina newspaper publisher who held a minor position in the Cleveland Administration, oversaw publicity; Abram Elkus, a New York attorney, supervised tasks related to the tariff and foreign affairs; and

Senator T. P. Gore of Oklahoma headed an army of local organizers, some 100,000 precinct committeemen in 2,500 counties across what had just become forty-eight states. Although women would be able to vote for President in only nine states—all in the West—McAdoo appointed Mrs. Jefferson Borden "Daisy" Harriman, a socialite suffragist, to engage women by organizing meetings and mailings. In order to fuel this entire operation, Wilson asked the National Committee to create the position of chairman of the Finance Committee, which he wanted Henry Morgenthau to fill.

"I have long been convinced that financing presidential campaigns by private contributions should be prohibited," McAdoo wrote in 1931. "It is the seed of innumerable evils." He believed the national treasury should fund all Presidential elections, and that contributions by any individual or corporation should be made a criminal offense. As that was not the case, the campaign functioned along guidelines Wilson set for Morgenthau: he would accept no money from anybody who expected a favor in return or from any corporation, even indirectly; he preferred money from small donors; he wished to publicize all gifts to the campaign; and he urged care in the ways in which these dollars were spent. He told Morgenthau the names of three rich Democrats with dubious backgrounds whose money must not infiltrate the campaign. That said, Morgenthau told Wilson to dismiss all thoughts of finance from his mind, which he did. The two men never discussed campaign money again; and under Morgenthau's supervision, ninety thousand citizens contributed $1,110,952.25 to the Wilson campaign.

At the end of August, Wilson sought one contributor in particular, but not for his money. The defining argument between Bull Moosers and Democrats that fall would be over their stands on trusts, and Wilson needed somebody to sharpen his message. Always better on the big picture than on the small particulars, he wanted to discuss the issue with the most incisive mind on the subject. Fortunately, that man had already expressed an interest in his campaign, though when he shuttled from Boston to New York by night boat on August 27, Louis D. Brandeis could not have known that he, as much as anybody, would shape the future of Woodrow Wilson's campaign and career.

One month older than Wilson, Brandeis was born in Louisville, Kentucky, the son of highly cultured Jewish parents from Prague who had fled eastern European anti-Semitism in a moment of political upheaval. His father prospered as a merchant; and an uncle had been a delegate at the

Republican Convention that nominated Lincoln. A brilliant student, Louis graduated from Harvard Law School as class valedictorian, at twenty; and over the next few decades, his practice relentlessly challenged special privilege. He became a public advocate, "the People's Attorney." An ardent Progressive, he helped reform the insurance business in Massachusetts, fought for protective labor laws for women in Oregon, and successfully challenged J. P. Morgan as his New Haven Railroad tried to buy yet another of its competitors.

In Sea Girt, Brandeis gave Wilson a three-hour lesson in trusts. He proved to be "eager to learn," the attorney observed, a serious and deliberate student. Where Theodore Roosevelt announced his plan was to regulate monopolies, Brandeis and Wilson concurred on a more radical approach—one that went to the root of the problem. They wanted to regulate competition before monopolies could form. "Our whole people have revolted at the idea of monopoly and have made monopoly illegal," Brandeis said with absolute clarity, "yet the third party proposes to make legal what is illegal. . . . The party is trying to make evil good, and that is a thing that cannot be done." After meeting with Wilson, he told reporters, "We must undertake to regulate competition instead of monopoly, for our industrial freedom and our civic freedom go hand in hand."

While TR was already selling what he called the New Nationalism, Brandeis and Wilson spoke repeatedly of a legislative program that would move the nation toward industrial freedom—a New Freedom. In a memorandum as politically canny as it was socially caring, Brandeis proposed that the Democratic Party embrace competition, which trusts inhibited. Brandeis positioned the Bull Moosers as a party that embraced big trusts and required big government to control them. Wilson intended to argue that "what this country needs above everything else is a body of laws which will look after the men who are on the make rather than the men who are already made." Wilson would be the Jeffersonian proponent of less government—the friend of big business but the enemy of trusts and unfair business practices.

The 1912 Presidential campaign officially kicked off on Labor Day, September 2, when Wilson delivered a pair of talks in Buffalo, New York. They were the first of five dozen major speeches and a hundred minor public addresses he would deliver before Election Day. For the most part, they were extemporaneous, each appearance requiring a fresh page of notes. A plank or two from the Democratic platform became the spring-board for each speech; and audiences found the addresses both soothing and inspiring, as Wilson spoke in language as poetic as that of any candidate who ever ran for President. He found his steel whenever he steered his talks to the economic oppression of the trusts. Addressing the United Trades and Labor Council of Buffalo in Braun's Park, Wilson said Roosevelt's policies looked to him "like a consummation of the partnership between monopoly and government, because when once the government regulates the monopoly, then monopoly will have to see to it that it regulates the government." At a mass meeting that night, he struck a tone few voters had ever heard from a politician: "If you don't believe the things that I believe, I don't want you to vote for me."

Some tried to belittle Wilson because of his untraditional résumé, but he embraced it. "There is one thing a schoolteacher learns that he never forgets," he said in Buffalo and later elsewhere; "namely, that it is his business to learn all he can and then to communicate it to others." As in his classroom, Wilson believed the role of a leader was not to dictate but to inspire. "You have got to exercise your minds," he told the people. "You have got to discriminate. You have got to set the chess board fully up and see how the game is going to be played." Lest he appear effete, he assured the people that he was "bred in a football college . . . and what wins is team work." The Democratic team, he said, had not just become progressive; it had been so for sixteen years—"and we saw the year 1912 half a generation before it came." Three weeks later he milked his credentials, saying, "It is a fine system where some remote, severe academic schoolmaster may become President of the United States."

Wilson traversed the Midwest through September, becoming more at ease with every speech. He asked the crowd at the Minneapolis Fairgrounds, "Are you going to vote for a government which will regulate your master, or are you going to be your own masters and regulate the government and through the government these men who have tried to regulate you?" In the National Guard Armory in Detroit he said, "The pigmy hasn't any chance in America; only the giant has. And the laws give the giant free leave to trample down the pigmy. What I am interested in is laws that will give the little man a . . . chance to show these fellows that he has brains enough to compete with them and can presently make his local market a national market and his national market a world market."

Wilson reminded the country that under President Roosevelt trusts "grew faster and more numerously than in any other administration we have had."

Wilson challenged his opposition's charges before any had a chance to resonate. He told businessmen in Columbus, Ohio, that one of "the most amazing fictions of our politics" was that the Democratic Party was not interested in the business welfare of the United States. "I am for the regulation . . . of competition," he said; the currency system was antiquated and needed to be more elastic; the tariff had "created the opportunity of monopoly." To the opposition's contention that he offered little more than flowery rhetoric, Wilson announced in Scranton, Pennsylvania, "This is the year in which we must render phrases into reality, when we must change the mist into the bar of iron," and then he reminded audiences of the miraculous turnaround in New Jersey.

Wilson's allure tended to sneak up on people—in sharp contrast to that of his chief opponent. Where TR resorted to histrionics and hyperbole, Wilson quietly converted his followers, building from a political concept to a powerful exhortation. On September 25, 1912, the red meat of his talk to a crowd in Hartford, Connecticut, was the injustice of the Payne-Aldrich tariff; and over the course of an hour, he peppered that talk with allusions to Alice in Wonderland, England's seventeenth-century Petition of Right, the god Baal, Gladstone, Bagehot, Henry Clay, the direct election of Senators, initiative and referendum, the concept of a tabula rasa in politics, and the Latin derivation of the word "radical." Whether one accepted his ideas or not, nobody left one of his speeches unimpressed. His insistence upon raising the populace to his intellectual level made audiences feel better about themselves. More than charm, he had charisma.

On September 26, Taft's and Wilson's campaigns crossed, at the Copley Plaza Hotel in Boston. Taft was a dinner speaker in evening clothes, while Wilson, unrecognized, was checking in for the night, carrying two handbags. Before retiring, Wilson insisted that he would feel uncomfortable sleeping under the same roof as Taft without having greeted him. The two candidates went to a private room for a few minutes, during which they exchanged pleasantries about holding up under the strain of campaigning.

Traveling to the heartland states of Indiana, Nebraska, Kansas, Colorado, Illinois, Missouri, and Ohio, Wilson delved into the core issues of his campaign. In the first week of October, a Congressional committee delivered a stunning report, an accounting of contributions to the Republican National Committee in 1904, when TR had been President. It revealed that three-quarters of its $2 million budget came from corporations or their representatives, a quarter of that from four fortunes—those of J. P. Morgan, John D. Rockefeller, E. H. Harriman, and Henry Clay Frick. Wilson had already accused Roosevelt of being supported by Frick's United States Steel Corporation, which TR denied. But, Wilson explained in a speech in Kansas City, "He was thinking of money. I was thinking of ideas." Wilson said it was a matter of "perfect indifference" to him where Roosevelt got his money; but "it is a matter of a great deal of difference to me where he gets his ideas." Just when this story might have harmed the third party most, a bigger headline came Roosevelt's way.

On October 14, TR was leaving his hotel in Milwaukee to deliver a speech when a maniac shot him in the chest. An eyeglass case and the speech itself, stuffed in his breast pocket, deflected the bullet enough to prevent major harm. In fact, Roosevelt continued on his way that night and delivered his speech—saying, "It takes more than that to kill a Bull Moose." But then he entered a hospital, where doctors opted against removing the bullet. He would need two weeks to recover. So long as Roosevelt could not campaign, Wilson said he would not either. "Teddy will have apoplexy when he hears of this," Wilson told his family. The immediate circle discussed Wilson's getting a bodyguard; but Wilson said, "There is nothing that can be done to guard against such attacks. It seems to me that police and secret service guards are useless if a madman attempts to attack a man in public life." Without discussion, Colonel House wired his friend Bill McDonald, the former captain of the Texas Rangers, to come north to shadow Wilson, leaving him only when he went to bed at night. At the end of October, the candidates returned to the hustings.

A death knell for the Taft campaign sounded—literally—on the thirtieth, when Vice President James S. Sherman died at his home in upstate New York at the age of fifty-seven. He had suffered for years from Bright's disease, a kidney ailment. With only six days until the election, it was impossible for Taft to select a running mate, though the Republican National Committee would later nominate Nicholas Murray Butler, president of Columbia University, to accept any electoral votes in Sherman's name the following February.

That night, Theodore Roosevelt spoke to sixteen thousand fanatical supporters at Madison Square Garden. A forty-five-minute welcome subsided to scattered applause during a speech in which he spoke softly and seemed weak. The next night Woodrow Wilson filled the same arena. Pundits observed that he received twenty minutes of applause more than Roosevelt had; and old-time Democrats said they had never seen an assembly "marked with such spontaneous and whole-souled enthusiasm." Over the next few days, a series of speeches in New Jersey followed, during which Wilson made his closing arguments, warning: "Powers are being built up in this country which, if they are allowed to grow much stronger, may be stronger than the Government of the United States combined."

As Wilson was coming home from a speech in Red Bank, in the dark morning hours the day before the election, his chauffeur did not notice a bump in the road in Hightstown, and Wilson's head struck the roof of the automobile, knocking his pince-nez from his nose and breaking one of its lenses. He felt the top of his head and discovered that it was bleeding profusely. They found a doctor, who shaved his pate and closed the four-inch gash. Wilson felt no ill effects from the accident, but he refused to pose for pictures looking as he did.

The campaign had taken its toll in other ways. Wilson had been suffering for weeks from headaches and indigestion; and he seldom got his desired nine hours of sleep. He gained more than seven pounds. Ellen also suffered; friends and family frequently found her tired and weak. Neither complained—though, with the "pitiless blaze of publicity" engulfing life at Cleveland Lane, she spoke wistfully of their "old lost peace." On Election Eve, Wilson's erstwhile promoter Colonel Harvey congratulated him on the effectiveness of his campaign. "Never before to my knowledge," he said, "has *every* utterance of a candidate added strength."

Wilson's voice was all but gone. He had elaborated upon every topic save one. Although the National Association for the Advancement of Colored People had been incorporated just three years prior, and though a number of black leaders were emerging with the support of several Protestant and Jewish Americans, race remained a marginal issue in the election of 1912. It appeared neither in the platform of any party nor as a priority of any candidate. Theodore Roosevelt had famously invited Booker T. Washington to the White House and appointed a few Negroes to minor positions; but when a dozen men from an African American division of the infantry were accused of going on a shooting rampage in Brownsville, Texas, the then-President Roosevelt authorized their discharges, despite the falsity of the charges against them. Even Eugene Debs made no great efforts to include Negroes, and he was known to make "darkey" jokes in public, a socially acceptable practice.

Such jokes remained part of Wilson's repertoire as well. They were never malicious, though the humor was based on the Negro being slow in body and mind, the stereotype of the day. Nor was it considered inappropriate, even to a Northern audience, when he spoke of an unsuspected item in the Payne-Aldrich tariff as a "nigger" in the woodpile. But increasingly, the African American community bridled at such insensitivity as it grew intolerant of illegalities—starting with the common practice of restricting the black man from the electoral process. Ironically, Wilson—a son of Dixie, heading the Southern-anchored Democratic Party—captivated the colored man more than any other candidate.

Notes from a meeting of the Democratic National Committee revealed its desire to capture this emerging voting bloc. "The negro movement is a very promising factor," said Judge Hudspeth of New Jersey. "It is going to cause a revolution in my judgment, in some states." And he believed Negroes were inclined toward Wilson in high enough numbers to provide a margin of victory. That remained to be seen, as the leading Republican colored newspaper, *The New York Age*, had recently written a scathing editorial against Wilson, questioning how any self-respecting Negro could vote for him. "Both by inheritance and absorption," the journal wrote, "he has most of the prejudices of the narrowest type of Southern white people against the Negro." It reminded readers that Princeton had been the only major college in the North to close its doors to Negroes, that as Governor, Wilson had not included a single Negro in his administration, that his party's platform contained not a word about Negroes, and that he owed his nomination to such proud white supremacist Senators as James K. Vardaman of Mississippi and Benjamin R. Tillman of South Carolina.

Even so, more Negroes saw the election of 1912 as an opportunity for change; and many held that the unlikeliest candidate could open the frankest dialogue between the races. Among them was William Monroe Trotter, a pioneer in the civil rights movement and a founder of the *Boston*

Guardian—an activist newspaper opposed to the accommodating beliefs of Negro icon Booker T. Washington. This articulate Harvard graduate wrote Wilson that "many Colored men" felt he might just be "the democrat to begin the end of democratic aggression against their civil and political rights" and that if elected he would exercise his "personal influence with the Southern democracy in favor of fairer treatment of their Colored neighbors as men." So long as Wilson did not sympathize with racial prejudice, discrimination, disfranchisement, or lynching and did believe in equal rights for all "regardless of race, color or nativity," Trotter said, the colored people of America would support him.

At the start of his campaign, Wilson told a delegation from the United Negro Democracy of New Jersey, "I was born and raised in the South. There is no place where it is easier to cement friendship between the two races than there. . . . You may feel assured of my entire comprehension of the ambitions of the negro race and my willingness and desire to deal with that race fairly and justly." In letters and interviews, he reiterated that commitment throughout the campaign. He told Oswald Garrison Villard, the editor of the *New York Evening Post* and one of the white founders of the NAACP, that he would speak out against lynching—as "every honest man must do so." By November 1912, many Negroes were believing that a leopard could change his spots.

Wilson slept in on Election Morning, Tuesday the fifth. At breakfast he told his family that he had "done what he could" and that the result was "on the knees of the gods." When he arrived at the Princeton fire station to vote, just past ten o'clock, he found reporters and photographers waiting for him. He took his place in line and joked with the officials and press. When his turn came, he gave his name and address and received his ballot. Before walking into the booth, he pointed out to his bodyguard, McDonald, a house where he had taken his meals as a freshman.

That afternoon the tension at 25 Cleveland Lane increased as more and more supporters arrived. With his young friend Dudley Malone and McDonald, Wilson took a long nostalgic stroll through the town, visiting his favorite haunts—fields where Washington had fought and the campus where Madison had studied. Grover Cleveland's telegraph ticker had been set up in the house; and during dinner, results clicked in. The telephone never stopped ringing with breaking news, which Tumulty dutifully reported. Even when Wilson heard unexpectedly good tallies, he muted his feelings, simply saying, "That is encouraging."

After dinner, the family retired to Ellen's studio. Woodrow stood before the hearth, awaiting each bulletin. There were no surprises, just steadily positive updates. The Wilsons amused themselves with conversation for a while; and then, to fill a lull, Wilson grabbed a volume of Robert Browning and read aloud. Nobody paid much attention. Nell kept slipping out of the room, anxious to learn the latest. A little before ten, she was about to return to the reading when she heard the sound of a distant bell. Within a moment, it was clanging wildly; and that unmistakable peal from Nassau Hall drew Ellen to the front door. Tumulty burst from the crowd of newspapermen, calling out, "He's elected, Mrs. Wilson!"

Ellen returned to the studio and found her husband examining the latest tabulations. No words were required. She simply placed her hands on Woodrow's shoulders and raised her face toward his as he leaned forward and kissed her gently. Margaret, Jessie, and Nell approached, and he hugged each of them. And then others entered the room to congratulate him, while a crowd gathered outside. Messenger boys kept arriving with telegrams. "I cordially congratulate you on your election and extend to you my best wishes for a successful administration," read President Taft's from Cincinnati. Theodore Roosevelt had wired from Oyster Bay, New York, "The American people by a great plurality have conferred upon you the highest honor in their gift. I congratulate you thereon."

The final numbers would not be known for days, but that great plurality held through the night. With a four-way race making a majority virtually impossible, Wilson was racking up a decisive victory—50 percent more votes than his closest competitor. In the end, he would win 6,293,454 votes (41.9 percent) to Roosevelt's 4,119,538 (27.4 percent), Taft's 3,484,980 (23.2 percent), and Debs's 900,672 (6 percent). The electoral vote was much more lopsided, as Wilson carried all but eight states: California, Washington, South Dakota, Minnesota, Michigan, and Pennsylvania (88 electoral votes), which went to Roosevelt; and Utah and Vermont (8 electoral votes), which went to Taft. Wilson's 435 electors were more than the nation had ever bestowed upon a single candidate.

Amid the increasing excitement, Nellie Wilson had a chilling moment as she watched all the elation drain from her father's face. In the meantime, the clamor outside demanded his presence. By the time Wilson reached the front door to confront the crowd, his countenance reflected only the gravity of the moment. He was able to suppress his emotions until he looked out and perceived a sea of undergraduates surging into Cleveland Lane, waving flags and singing "Old Nassau." The ancestral wail of a bagpipe pierced the cool night air. At last, the old schoolmaster wept.

For a moment, vanity got the best of him. Mindful of the patch on his head, he wanted to stand above the crowd. Tumulty and Dudley Malone carried a rocking chair to the portal and held it fast, so that Wilson could stand on it. "Gentlemen," he said, "I am sincerely glad to see you. I have no feeling of triumph tonight, but a feeling of solemn responsibility. . . . You men must play a great part. I plead with you again to look constantly forward. I summon you for the rest of your lives to support the men who like myself want to carry the nation forward to its highest destiny and greatness."

After less than two years—only 658 days—of public service, Woodrow Wilson had been elected the twenty-eighth President of the United States. It had all happened so swiftly as to seem predestined, as though millennia of circumstances had paved the way to this moment . . . and all that lay ahead.

PART THREE

8

DISCIPLES

*On the next day . . . they heard that Iesus was com-
ming to Hierusalem . . .*
*   And Iesus, when he had found a yong asse, sate
thereon, as it is written . . .*

—IOHN, XII:12–14

The President-elect slept well.

The revelers on Cleveland Lane had dispersed
around midnight, leaving Woodrow Wilson to turn in by
one. He did not awaken until nine. When he faced the
waiting phalanx of reporters, he revealed, "It has not quite
dawned on me. I had been in an impersonal atmosphere for
the last three months, reading about myself, reading that I
was to be elected, and now I can hardly believe that it is
true."

Before requesting the details of his own historic
election—becoming the first Democrat elected to the
White House in twenty years and the first Southerner since
the Civil War—Wilson inquired about the Congressional
results. In an election with the lowest turnout (58.8 percent) in seventy-six years, he had coattails. Democrats fortified their majority in the House of Representatives by
picking up sixty-one new seats; and while most state legislatures still elected their United States Senators, Democrats
were poised to start the next session of Congress with a

seven-vote majority. The results, Wilson told the press, filled him with "the hope that the thoughtful Progressive forces of the Nation may now at last unite to give the country freedom of enterprise and a Government released from all selfish and private influences, devoted to justice and progress." When somebody pointed out that many in the press had already chosen his departmental secretaries, Wilson replied, "Well, then, you have to forbid me reading the newspapers for they might prejudice me." That afternoon, Wilson and his bodyguard walked to the far perimeter of the Princeton campus—greeting friends along the way and tramping around much of Lake Carnegie.

The next few days brought more than fifteen thousand letters and telegrams and what felt like as many visitors. Overnight, influence peddlers and office seekers pushed the well-wishers aside. Those who restrained themselves least met Wilson's resistance most. As the chairman of his successful campaign committee, William McCombs had every reason to make his way to Cleveland Lane, as he did late Election Night; but his erratic nature, periodic misjudgments, and blatant intentions troubled Wilson. "Before we proceed," the President-elect said upon greeting him, "I wish it clearly understood that I owe you nothing." As McCombs began to recount his contributions, Wilson interrupted to say, "God ordained that I should be the next president of the United States. Neither you nor any other mortal could have prevented that." And though McCombs lingered in Princeton for most of that week, Wilson allowed him no private audience as he confined his few political conversations to telephone calls with Colonel House, whose judgment he already prized above all others', as he would for most of his Presidency.

Colonel House left a remarkable record of his hundreds of encounters with Woodrow Wilson—three thousand typed pages, which he dictated almost daily. They provide telling glimpses of Woodrow Wilson, so long as one never forgets that House is their focal point and that diary can be the falsest art. House presents himself as the man who often suggested Wilson's best ideas and who had cautioned against the worst, an intimate who never overstepped or even misstepped. In truth, Wilson was phlegmatic on few topics. He appreciated new facts and entertained outside opinions; but from those closest to him, he preferred constancy over contention. He generally expected his advisers to react to his thoughts rather than supply him with new ones.

In that capacity, House complemented Wilson perfectly. Stockton Axson wondered how much House actually did see and how much "he, Polonius-like, merely confirmed what the President saw." He seemed "never to say anything rememberable" and was, in fact, "usually silent; and when he spoke, . . . deferentially in agreement with everything W. W. said." Axson granted that most of their serious discussions took place behind closed doors, but he was never aware of House's arguing with Wilson; and he noticed that House "had the tact to refrain from even mentioning public affairs at the luncheon or dinner table unless the President himself should shift the table talk from anecdote and limericks to something serious." No intellectual, House was a rapt listener, a challenging but undemanding conversationalist. He could keep a confidence.

House's greatest talent was in "playing" Wilson—tuning his temperament to Wilson's and seldom striking a discordant note. He was vain but devoid of venality, seeming to want "nothing for himself." That lack of greed kept him, in Wilson's eyes, "clear-sighted"—for he looked at both national and international questions without a personal agenda. Unlike legislators, who had to consider their home districts, and even Cabinet members, who were responsible to their departments, House had a constituency of one. He drew the blueprints of plans Wilson could only sketch; as Axson said, "He relished the personal details involved, which the President disliked." He was not afraid to speak his mind, but was careful never to cross the President. Wilson did not suffer fools; and he enjoyed listening to House—because, in large measure, that meant hearing himself. For his companionship as much as his counsel, House become an indispensable friend.

Over time, House evolved into a figure unique in American history—a full-time unpaid adviser with singular and total access to the President of the United States, and answerable only to him. So long as Woodrow Wilson was pleased, Colonel House operated of his own volition and on his own dime, always behind the scenes. No man in American history ever wielded so much power yet remained so unaccountable. "Take my word for it," said the blind Senator T. P. Gore of Oklahoma, "he can walk on dead leaves and make no more noise than a tiger."

"Clearly," William G. McAdoo wrote of House and Wilson, "he was the friend to whom he could turn and to whom he did turn" when it came to selecting the Cabinet. Moving "outside the periphery of official life," McAdoo noted, House was "better situated than the Governor to look into the merits and capacities of those who were being considered." House began to prepare lists, revealing what one colleague called his "extraordinary political clairvoyance, a subtle feeling for the inwardness of events and the drifts of public opinion."

While House deflected most of the petitioners from the President-elect, the rest of the Wilsons came under siege. The daughters received requests for photographs and autographs and even a few marriage proposals. Dressmakers sent swatches hoping the Wilson women might select from one of their samples for an inaugural gown. Eleanor Wilson indulged in the frivolous exercise more than the others. Because TR's daughter had long since claimed Nellie's favorite color, this new First Daughter opted for a magenta—though "Nell Red," as it would be advertised, never caught on as had "Alice Blue." With the promise of Wilson's new Presidential salary—$75,000 per annum—and plenty of special occasions ahead, the entire family shopped for the first time without considering costs. Ellen suddenly found department store floorwalkers bowing before her and crowds surrounding her. "Oh, Woodrow," she said upon her return from one shopping trip, "we felt like animals in a zoo!" Even Woodrow realized it was time to retire items from his rumpled wardrobe for more elegant suits. He became an understated fashion plate, with immaculate stiff collars and a stickpin just below the knot of his tie, and looked underdressed when he appeared in public without his top hat.

With so many strangers descending upon 25 Cleveland Lane, Wilson stopped taking notice, especially as the Secret Service now stood guard. One evening, he returned from his office in Trenton and met an affable, sandy-haired young man as he rushed out the door, though he did pause to tip his hat. Later Woodrow asked Ellen who he was. "You'd better stop and make his acquaintance the next time," she said. "That's Frank Sayre, and I think you're going to be his father-in-law."

Francis Sayre, valedictorian of his class at Williams and a fresh graduate of Harvard Law School, had taken a job as an assistant in the office of New York City's District Attorney. He had known Jessie for almost two years. Two Sundays before the election, he had rung the Wilsons' bell, only to find the Governor himself at the door. Frank had asked to see Jessie, and her father had said, "Oh, no; she's not at home. She's off teaching her Sunday school class." In that moment, Jessie had appeared on the stairs, and all three of them burst into laughter. Frank proposed marriage later that day, but he and Jessie kept their intentions secret until three days after the election, when she began to wear her ring. "Nothing can separate us now," he wrote his fiancée, "for we know and are sure that God wanted us to join together in our service for him."

In 1913—twenty years before the Twentieth Amendment would shorten a President's "lame duck" period by six weeks—Inauguration Day fell on March 4. With plenty of time to catch their breath, the Woodrow Wilsons checked into the Collingwood Hotel on West Thirty-fifth Street in New York City on November 15. The President-elect spent the next morning with Colonel House at his apartment a few blocks away, discussing the future Cabinet. Shortly after one o'clock, Wilson and his family—except Margaret, who was remaining in New York to pursue her singing career— left for the pier, where they boarded the *Bermudian*. Plans for the departure were kept so quiet, no crowds had gathered. The Wilsons occupied the two choicest suites on the Promenade Deck, their entourage consisting only of his private secretary, Charles Swem, and two Secret Service agents. "I ceased to be a politician when I stepped aboard this ship," Wilson told the press as they set sail for a four-week vacation. "Anybody who comes to see me in Bermuda," he said in parting, "will get the very reverse of what he wants."

Wilson was not to enjoy the anonymity he had known during his prior visits to Bermuda, but he found the quiet civility he had expected. The Mayor of Hamilton, a few local officials, and some applauding citizens greeted them. "As soon as I knew that I had been sentenced to four years hard labour," he told them, "my first thought was to get away to Bermuda and enjoy my liberty while I might." He expressed his hope that "having so received me you will let me go about among you as if I were no one in particular."

Bermuda honored his wishes. The Wilsons moved into Glencove in Paget West, which Woodrow had enjoyed during a prior visit. A high wall surrounded the "cottage" on a secluded point overlooking the sea; a locked gate warded off any visitors, including the Secret Service. From the verandah, Jessie and Nell could dive right into the blue waters. Except for one state dinner and a few small dinner parties, the Wilsons stuck to themselves. Ellen painted; Woodrow picnicked and bicycled with his daughters, golfed, napped, and even indulged in solitaire. He and Nell went several times to the small theater in town, where a stock company performed "excruciatingly bad" productions. ("I shall never grow up," he told her. "I would rather see poor acting than not go to a play when I have a chance.") He devoted part of every morning dictating to Swem, and over the next four weeks, they worked through the stack of vital correspondence, responding to seven hundred letters. Wilson even made time to review the proofs of a book called *The New Freedom*, a compilation of his campaign speeches about to be published. When a newspaper photographer snapped a picture of the President-elect behind the walls at Glencove, Wilson confronted him, declaring, "You're no gentleman, and I'll thrash you if you do that again." The photographer apologized profusely.

Beyond that, Wilson engaged in an activity Presidents seldom allow themselves—contemplation. His experiences as president of Princeton and Governor of New Jersey had taught him that the most opportune moment to institute change was at the beginning of one's tenure—with the wind of optimism at one's back and before the forces of resistance had a chance to gather. And so, Wilson began prioritizing his programs so that he might set them in motion upon his arrival at the White House. He turned directly to those decisions by which the public first judges its Chief Executive, the selection of a Cabinet—ten departmental heads. "In his usual methodical way," Nell observed, "he made a series of charts—a page for each man under consideration, listing the details of their careers, their qualifications, their friends, even the sort of wives they had." And then, in his own form of solitaire, Wilson shuffled the charts, discarding one name each time he considered another. His family grew so exasperated with the secrecy of his process, it began to lose interest. "I don't really care who you choose," Nellie blurted one day, "as long as you make McAdoo Secretary of the Treasury." That delighted her father. "Imagine!" he said to Ellen. "Nell wants me to appoint a man to the Cabinet just because she likes him."

With the President-elect sporting a tropical tan, the Wilsons returned on the *Bermudian* on December 16, 1912. Margaret Wilson and Joseph Tumulty met them at the pier. The four-week sojourn had been "an unmixed blessing," Wilson wrote Mary Hulbert, then Stateside, as those "healing days in Bermuda gave us a great store of peace and vitality upon which to live in the months to come." He would need it, as opposition forces were already plotting to reclaim New Jersey for themselves. Governor

Wilson insisted that he had not finished fighting there—that he had no intention of resigning immediately or even of changing his residence. "It is very important that the people should feel that I am still connected with New Jersey," he said, at least until "the progressive program is complete, even to the dot above the i." Within hours of disembarking, he was on a train to Trenton, where—with the recent Democratic victories—a new generation of would-be state bosses was dispensing patronage, a young Frank Hague of Jersey City among them.

A few weeks later, with his second annual message to the state legislature, Wilson hoped to turn the last year's accomplishments into the drumbeat of the Progressive march onward. For immediate consideration, the Governor raised such matters as the need to alter the state's corporation laws, regulation of investment companies, reform of the criminal justice system, an examination of tax assessment and collection, further empowerment of the Public Utility Commissioners, encouragement of the commission form of government, and conservation of natural resources, including forest preservation. He strongly urged approval of two amendments to the Constitution of the United States that awaited ratification—the Sixteenth, which would empower Congress to levy taxes on incomes, and the Seventeenth, which would establish the direct election of Senators by popular vote. While his ambitious program would face mixed results, Wilson saw the New Jersey legislature address all of it. The State Senate passed a woman suffrage resolution; and legislators agreed to enact a law that would remove jury selection from the hands of sheriffs. Before leaving office, Wilson would sign a set of anti-trust bills—called the "seven sisters"; and shortly thereafter, New Jersey would ratify the constitutional amendments.

Between mid-December and his inauguration, Wilson also delivered a handful of speeches outside the state, reiterating a few basic themes. On his second night after returning from Bermuda, he addressed the New York Southern Society at the Waldorf-Astoria, telling the roomful of transplants from Dixie that America was "not what it was when the Civil War was fought"—that while regional pride was to be appreciated, sectionalism was not, and that the Progressive principles for which he had been fighting in New Jersey should apply across the country. Weeks later, addressing the Commercial Club of Chicago, Wilson said he hoped to bring about an end to "the old feeling that the Southerner was not of the same political breed and purpose as the rest of American citizens" and that he hoped to see the death of "many another prejudice, particularly of these prejudices which are getting such formidable root amongst us as between class and class, as between those who control the resources of the country and those who use the resources of the country."

"The business future of this country," Wilson asserted, "does not depend upon the government of the United States. It depends upon the business men of the United States. . . . only the temper and the thought and the purpose of business men in America is going to determine what the future of business shall be." Wilson indicated several fights he intended to pick—against the protectionist Payne-Aldrich tariff, the banking structure, and the constricting monopolies in America.

Between the New York and Chicago addresses, Wilson visited Virginia. His train stopped at five stations, each crowded with cheering throngs—especially in Charlottesville, where the student body had turned out en masse. In Staunton, most of the town greeted him, including a band playing "Home, Sweet Home." Wilson spent the night in the manse at the top of the hill, in the very bedroom in which he had been born. The next day, December 28, the celebration of his fifty-sixth birthday began with a rhapsodic introduction from his host, a successor to the Reverend Joseph Wilson. "He went out from us as a very little boy, laden with the prayers and benedictions of a small congregation of Christian people," said the Reverend A. M. Fraser of the honoree. "He comes back to us to-day, by the favour of an overruling Providence, a proven leader of men." Wilson visited an old aunt, whom he had not seen since childhood. She had grown extremely deaf and required a long black ear-trumpet, which made conversation no easier. At one point, she said, "Well, Tommy, what are you doing now?" And Wilson said, "I've been elected President, Aunt Janie."

"Well, well," said old Aunt Janie, "president of what?"

Wilson told the citizens of Staunton exactly the sort of President of the United States he intended to be. For a generation, a Protestant-based movement called "the Social Gospel" had infused American thought. With it came improvements in health and housing, and the establishment of salvation armies and Christian associations to help young men from the country adjust to life in the city. The notion that Christian acts might cure social ills was nothing new to Wilson; he approached his new bully pulpit fully aware of his power as evangel in chief. Moral forces were at work,

Wilson told his audience at a birthday banquet at the Staunton Military Academy. In another talk, on the steps of the Mary Baldwin Seminary, he said, "There must be heart in a government; there must be a heart in the policies of government. And men must look to it that they do unto others as they would have others do unto them." Wilson believed such thought strengthened—not softened—him. "This is not a rosewater affair," he said. "This is an office in which a man must put on his war paint. . . . And there must be some good hard fighting, not only in the next four years, but in the next generation, in order that we may achieve the things that we have set out to achieve."

Republican opposition was already insinuating that the Democratic Party was going to institute changes destructive to the economy. Wilson assured his audiences that only those trying to create such panic had reason to fear. To those attempting to game the system, Wilson promised "on behalf of my countrymen, a gibbet as high as Haman."

A member of the press had recently suggested to Wilson that this Christmas must be the happiest of his life. "My young friend," he replied, "evidently you have never been elected President of the United States. Can you see how a man can have a light heart looking forward to the responsibilities of that great office, particularly at this time?"

"The President is not all of the Executive," Professor Woodrow Wilson wrote in *Congressional Government*. "He cannot get along without the men whom he appoints . . . and they are really integral parts of that branch of the government which he titularly contains in his one single person. The characters and training of the Secretaries are of almost as much importance as his own gifts and antecedents." Through the winter of 1912–13, Colonel House discreetly interviewed numerous prospects, arranging with Tumulty for Wilson to meet the most promising contenders in either Trenton or Princeton. With so short a political career of his own, Wilson had few political debts to service; but, reluctantly, he accepted that he headed a century-old party with political machinery in place. With that in mind, Wilson began wading through both enthusiastic and contradictory advice, starting with his first appointment.

"What will be done with Bryan?" was the urgent question. Edith Gittings Reid, an epistolary friend of Wilson's since his days in Baltimore, said, "The East was uneasy and prophesied dire results if Bryan was given a leading position. The West vowed that dire results would

happen—they'd see to it—if he was not given the best that could be had."
Roosevelt called him "a blithering ass"; H. L. Mencken said he was an insincere demagogue, "a poor clod . . . deluded by a childish theology, full of an almost pathological hatred of all learning, all human dignity, all beauty, all fine and noble things." And yet, this unsophisticated icon of the American heartland had been to more places than almost any man alive. Besides his political stumping and countless speeches as the most popular speaker on a rural circuit known as the Chautauqua, he had seen Mexico and Europe; and in 1905, he had taken his family on a yearlong odyssey around the world. He observed Japan at the peak of its empire, China "awakening from the sleep of twenty centuries," and the Philippines as "American ideas [were] spreading." He witnessed imperialism firsthand—the Dutch in Java and the British in India. The Bryans visited Egypt, Syria, and Turkey before the summer heat drove them north to Germany and Austria-Hungary, where he saw royal strongholds unwittingly breed a desire for independence. On an earlier trip to Russia, he had discussed "free speech" with Czar Nicholas II himself ("he seemed quite interested," Bryan observed); and he journeyed to the legendary Yasnaya Polyana, where he spent twelve hours discussing Christian anarchism and pacifism with the landlord, Leo Tolstoy. Wherever Bryan journeyed, he rejoiced in the spreading influence of America. He processed everything through his fundamentalist lens, a fervent belief in the Christian brotherhood of man. Such aspects hardly disqualified him from Cabinet service; but Wilson could not ignore that Bryan had long been a freewheeling leader, with no experience in either statesmanship or having a boss. With such aggressive imperialists as John Hay and Elihu Root having recently run the State Department, it remained to be seen whether a pacifistic Midwestern isolationist could hold his own in a changing world order.

Wilson never doubted that he would offer Bryan a Cabinet position; he struggled only with the question of which one. From the moment he was elected, he began corresponding with Bryan, engaging more with him than with any other politician. "I have thought of you very constantly throughout the campaign and have felt every day strengthened and heartened by your active and generous support," he wrote on November 9. Increasingly, he saw how Bryan might do the same for his Presidency. As William McAdoo suggested, "there was a manifest political advantage in having him in the Cabinet. A very large element of the Democratic Party stood squarely behind the man. His cooperation with the Administration meant the smoothing-out of many diverse views about the currency and the tariff." Indeed, in each of Bryan's Presidential defeats, he had won more popular votes than Wilson had; and he was strongest in the battleground regions beyond the Democratic South, namely the West. Ever since George Washington appointed Thomas Jefferson, the office of Secretary of State has carried the most prestige in the Cabinet. Upon returning from Bermuda, Wilson met Bryan in Trenton and, after four hours, offered him the position. It would be Wilson's one political payoff.

Bryan accepted—and discussed two policies he hoped to instate. The first was a series of treaties between the United States and as many other nations as possible, pre-emptive agreements committing each party to diplomatic resolution of problems before resorting to military means. "The proposed plan provided for the submission of all international disputes of every kind and character to a permanent tribunal for investigation, when not by other treaties submitted for arbitration," Bryan explained. The second proposal was more audacious: Mr. and Mrs. Bryan were dedicated teetotalers; and at diplomatic dinners, Mrs. Bryan said she intended to serve grape juice. Wilson did not object to either—though the juice policy would invite ridicule. He assured Bryan that the Department of State was his to run. Indeed, if Wilson was to master the details of any one department, State seemed the least likely. As he had told a Princeton colleague while preparing for his move to Washington, "It would be the irony of fate if my administration had to deal chiefly with foreign affairs."

Because Wilson intended to focus primarily on the economy, he considered the Secretary of the Treasury the most important Cabinet position. Nobody had proved to be more wise and tenacious during the campaign than William G. McAdoo; and House had since spent more time with him than with any other adviser. While he told McAdoo that he was investigating a number of men and that he wanted the benefit of his judgment, House was vetting McAdoo himself. On the morning of February 1, 1913, McAdoo had just put a fresh blade in his safety razor when a servant summoned him from the bathroom to speak to a Secret Service agent guarding the President-elect.

Wilson and McAdoo had not conversed since the election; but now the future President asked McAdoo to accept this vital position. "He had a delightful way of putting things," McAdoo recalled; "he created the impression that by accepting this great honor I would be doing him a favor." Although House had occasionally suggested that he was being considered for the post, McAdoo regarded himself unfit and told Wilson as much—that he was a man of business, not banking. "I don't want a banker or a financier," Wilson exclaimed. "The Treasury is not a bank. Its activities are varied and extensive. What I need is a man of all-round ability who has had wide business experience." McAdoo also had personal reservations: a widower for less than a year, with six (mostly grown) children, he was not a man of means. The job paid $12,000 a year, which would not go far in meeting the social expenses generally associated with the position. Wilson appealed to McAdoo's sense of duty, explaining that he could not perform the great responsibilities of office alone. "If I can't have the assistance of those in whom I have confidence," he said, "what am I to do?" McAdoo discreetly withdrew from the Hudson & Manhattan Railroad Company.

To serve as the Postmaster General, the largest employer in the United States, Colonel House recommended Albert S. Burleson, an eight-term Congressman from Texas who had become an aggressive Wilson supporter during the Baltimore convention. He struck Wilson as too much of an old-time politician, but House believed his familiarity with the inner workings of Congress and the patronage system would benefit both the department and the President. A letter from Oscar Underwood, the House Majority Leader and chairman of the Ways and Means Committee, with whom Wilson had already taken up the subject of a tariff bill, persuaded the President that Burleson was exactly what this highly political position required, if only because it would please the Speaker of the House. The first Texan ever to serve in a Cabinet and the son of a Confederate officer, Burleson was a known segregationist—which, at that time, was not a political liability. Upon receiving the official offer from the President-elect, Burleson told Wilson, "I will be loyal to your administration and sympathetic with your policies. When I reach the point where I cannot give you my undivided loyalty, I will tender my resignation. When I talk to you, I will always tell you my candid views. I can't know what is in your mind, but I can tell you what is in mine." As the boss of more Negroes in America than any other man, Burleson would prove to have enormous influence on life in Washington and the rest of the nation. For his vow of intense fealty to his administration, Wilson remained equally loyal to him, allowing him to run his department as he saw fit.

Colonel House recommended another Texan he knew well, one whose curriculum vitae closely resembled Wilson's. David F. Houston was born in North Carolina and educated at South Carolina College in Columbia, where he had studied under Wilson's uncle Dr. James Woodrow. After earning a master's degree at Harvard, Houston taught government at the University of Texas, where he became the school's president, a position he would subsequently hold at Texas A&M University before becoming chancellor of Washington University in St. Louis. Many found him cold and incommunicative but also "a man of intellectual force and solid information." Wilson had met him several times over the years and, upon learning of House's confidence in him, offered him the Department of Agriculture. Like most of the men in the Wilson Cabinet, he too wondered how he could relocate and live on the modest salary.

Josephus Daniels was a North Carolinian and, like Wilson, a nonpracticing attorney. This alumnus of the law school at Chapel Hill became active in state and then national Democratic politics, using the press to advance himself and his causes. He ran the Raleigh *News and Observer* and married into the political Worth family. A true Progressive and a friend of William Jennings Bryan, Daniels had helped defuse the "cocked hat" incident and had proved himself valuable as publicity director of the Democratic National Committee. For these reasons—not any maritime experience, for he had none—Wilson chose him to be Secretary of the Navy. His not knowing the ropes bespoke the lack of importance Wilson ascribed to the position. On the heels of the appointment, Wilson remarked to his friend and adviser Walter Page, "You do not seem to think that Daniels is Cabinet timber." Page replied, "He is hardly a splinter." Daniels was also an avowed white supremacist.

Upon receiving the appointment, Daniels immediately found his Assistant Secretary—the ambitious, anti-Tammany Franklin Roosevelt, a genuine lover of the sea. As Daniels noted in his diary, "He had supported Wilson for the nomination, and taken an active part in the campaign, and I found him a singularly attractive and honorable and courageous young Democratic leader." Wilson thought it was a "capital" idea. Although thirty-year-old Roosevelt had served but one term in Albany, he already provoked strong reactions. As soon as his name was floated, New York Senator (and TR's Secretary of State) Elihu Root warned Daniels that "every person named Roosevelt wishes to run everything and would try to be the Secretary." Daniels told him that any man who feared being supplanted by a subordinate was tacitly confessing his own inadequacy for the job. When Wilson heard that story, he was convinced he had both the right Secretary and Assistant. That young FDR was an ardent Democrat and a cousin of TR—and was even married to the former President's niece—gave Wilson and the party some unexpected bragging rights.

A sign of the rising power of the conjoined labor and Progressive movements could be seen in 1913, as a bill arrived on President Taft's desk that would bisect the existing Department of Commerce and Labor. A reluctant Taft signed it on his last day in office, knowing the incoming President would establish the new position if he did not. The first man nominated for Secretary of Labor carried all the credentials Wilson needed to trust him: born in Scotland, the Presbyterian William Beauchop Wilson (no relation to his new boss) had worked in the coal mines of Pennsylvania as a child and then rose in the ranks of the labor movement, becoming an officer of the United Mine Workers of America before getting elected to Congress. McAdoo called him "level-headed, able, and trustworthy."

Wilson had intended his Secretary of Commerce to be one of America's staunchest Progressives, his adviser Louis D. Brandeis. Earliest mentions of his name, however, incited considerable protest. Politicians, businessmen, and attorneys denounced him as a radical—a reckless meddler who would queer any possibilities of investment in a Democratic-led prosperity. Wrote one Boston Brahmin to Cleveland Dodge, knowing he had the President-elect's trust, "I have no hesitation in pronouncing Mr. Brandeis treacherous, and I sometimes doubt if he is sane." Wilson overlooked the specific criticisms and even the unveiled anti-Semitism. But not only did Adamses, Lowells, and Peabodys oppose Brandeis, so too did many Jews themselves, such as Jacob Schiff, the financier and philanthropist—those who had a foot in the establishment door and did not want Brandeis's extremist reputation to spoil opportunities for more accommodating Jews. But plumbing fixture heir and Wilson insider—and latent anti-Semite—Charles R. Crane paid Brandeis nothing but his highest praise, calling him "the only important Jew who is *first* American and then Jew," a tribute that revealed the primary accusation American Jews then faced. Wilson wrote Brandeis supporter Bryan that he felt "the people's lawyer" had been "grossly aspersed," but he simply could not ignore the widespread prejudice against him. Not until a week before the inauguration did he settle on William C.

Redfield of Brooklyn, who had spent his life in business, mining, manufacturing, banking, and insurance before getting elected to Congress, where he earned a reputation as a tariff specialist.

Wilson considered Brandeis a more obvious choice to serve as Attorney General, but giving him that even more sensitive position would have created an even greater outcry. Wilson hoped to enlist Pennsylvania Congressman A. Mitchell Palmer, who had been an ardent supporter at the Baltimore convention. Further study, however, revealed that Palmer had been involved with a few clients with tenuous ties to trusts. And so House lobbied for James C. McReynolds, an attorney who carried Progressive credentials. A Kentucky-born graduate of Vanderbilt University in Tennessee who had studied law in Charlottesville, McReynolds taught and then became an Assistant Attorney General in the Taft Administration. In that capacity, he prosecuted the government's cases against the tobacco and the anthracite coal monopolies. House persisted, and Wilson relented, as both embraced McReynolds's independent spirit. They did not yet realize that his outspokenness included a repugnant personality and name-calling racism.

Still hoping to include Palmer in his Cabinet, Wilson offered him the War Department. Palmer seriously considered the honor up until a week before the inauguration, when he declined. As he explained in a letter to Wilson: "I am a Quaker. Many generations of my people have borne strong testimony against 'war and the preparations for war.' Of course, as a Representative in Congress, I vote for the great supply bills to maintain the military establishment . . . but I do this in response to the sentiment and opinion of a vast majority of the people whom I represent. . . . As a Quaker War Secretary, I should consider myself a living illustration of a horrible incongruity." The very thought of such an appointment revealed how little Wilson considered possible international conflagration. Palmer stood by his conscience and chose not to "sit down in cold blood in an executive position and use such talents as I possess to the work of preparing for such a conflict." With only days remaining before Wilson took office, Tumulty urged him to name somebody from their home state. He suggested Lindley M. Garrison, who had been an attorney in Camden and Jersey City before he became a Vice-Chancellor of New Jersey. Wilson summoned him to Trenton the next day and on the spot offered Garrison the position, which he accepted.

For six decades the Department of the Interior had been the grab bag of the executive branch, looking after Indian affairs, patents, and the District of Columbia jails, among many concerns. Theodore Roosevelt had elevated its stature and deepened its purpose with his drive to protect America's wealth of natural resources, as water, oil, coal, and lumber had become lucrative enterprises. Taft had alienated TR, in fact, when he replaced his friend Gifford Pinchot, who headed the Division of Forestry, with a man more inclined toward private development than public use. There was no question where Wilson stood on the matter: "The raw materials obtainable in this country for every kind of manufacture and industry must be at the disposal of everybody in the United States upon the same terms." Thus, he considered several top Progressives for the Cabinet post, including Franklin K. Lane, a California Democrat who was then chairman of the Interstate Commerce Commission, having been appointed by Roosevelt.

Lane thought himself unworthy of the position; and when Colonel House sounded him out, he recommended another man. Beyond the self-effacement of Lane's letter, Wilson was impressed with his understanding of the job requirements. When his first choice, Mayor Newton D. Baker of Cleveland—a former student of Wilson's at Johns Hopkins and currently a reform Mayor only one year into his position—declined the nomination, Wilson nominated Lane, just four days before the inauguration.

"I must have the best men in the nation," Wilson had written Walter Hines Page at the start of the appointment process, when he had imagined only the most qualified would answer his calls to service. But as McAdoo would later write, "The judging of men is difficult at its best. When it happens to be entangled in a web of extraneous political considerations, it becomes frequently a matter of luck." Page pronounced the Cabinet "distinctly mediocre." In the end, Colonel House said only, "I think, in all the circumstances, we have done well."

Unlike modern Presidential cabinets, which portray as many facets of America as possible, the Wilson Cabinet of 1913 was a ten-way mirror, each panel of which reflected a different aspect of the man at the center. This was mostly a team of Rebels—lawyers from the South who had pursued other professions and never shed their Confederate biases, Anglo-Saxon Protestants all, mostly newcomers to Washington, if not politics altogether. Within the Wilson Cabinet, there would be much discussion but little debate. For the most part, the President would delegate power to his Secretaries (all younger than he) to run their own departments, as he seldom found reason to countermand any of them. Every decision from this administration, noted one close observer, would contain a moral component, inspired by "the breath of God."

For the position of secretary to the President himself—a combination of political adviser and chief of staff—Wilson considered nobody but Tumulty. Although his experience was limited and he had seen little of the world beyond New Jersey, he had ably and loyally served Governor Wilson, keeping the Trenton office running smoothly during the months of transition. Many Democrats challenged Tumulty's understanding of national politics; and hundreds tried to block him from office because of his Catholicism. One letter asked Wilson if he was willing to have "the secrets of the White House relayed to Rome." But Wilson discarded the letter, saying only, "Asinine." In truth, Wilson trusted nobody's understanding of hand-to-hand politics more than Tumulty's. As he always remained behind the scenes, not even Wilson himself knew all that Tumulty did for him in the way of public relations and political maneuvering.

Among these appointments, two men remained conspicuously absent. The first was Colonel House, whom Wilson invited to join his "official family." Beyond the compliment of the offer, House never considered it. "I very much prefer being a free lance, and to advise with him regarding matters in general," House told his diary. He had no inclination to hold office, preferring "to have a roving commission to serve wherever and whenever possible." House created a niche for himself, with as much influence and as little responsibility as he desired. "Had I gone into the Cabinet," he admitted, "I could not have lasted eight weeks." In no time, anyone seeking Woodrow Wilson's attention realized that Colonel House provided the most direct access.

The second missing person was the most covetous of all the office seekers. After months of consideration, campaign manager William McCombs remained on Wilson's mind but never on a list. Wilson praised McCombs's intelligence but felt "he is never satisfied unless he plays the stellar role." Where Lincoln thrived on a gadfly such as William Seward in his Cabinet, Wilson said he feared McCombs could not "work in harness with the other men and that I should never get any real team work from him." More to the point, Wilson simply did not like him and resented even having to spend time with him. After McCombs had accompanied the Wilsons to Staunton, during which time the two men had been alone together for more than an hour, Woodrow told Ellen he felt as if he had been "sucked by a vampire and had been left weak and ill."

When McCombs realized that Wilson favored McAdoo over him for Secretary of the Treasury, he bid to become Attorney General. Wilson's displeasure with the man turned into distaste. He asked McCombs why he suddenly preferred that position, and McCombs said that since he was a lawyer, the appointment would help him enormously when his term of office expired. "What a surprising statement for any man to make!" Wilson exclaimed to his secretary. "Why, Tumulty, many of the scandals of previous administrations have come about in this way, Cabinet officers using their posts to advance their own personal fortunes. It must not be done in our administration. It would constitute a grave scandal to appoint such a man to so high an office."

Many would later denounce Wilson for failing to reward McCombs with any spoils of victory. Unfortunately, he became his own worst enemy. His petty jealousies and grand insecurities became rampant, as did his consumption of alcohol—a bottle of whiskey a day, said Tumulty. And Wilson did remain loyal, offering him the ambassadorship to France. Mc-Combs considered the posting for several months, vacillating daily—even after refusing it. Money was the mitigating factor, as Ambassadors had long been expected to foot the entertainment bills for their embassies, which excluded all but the rich from serving as diplomats in the major capitals. Wilson kept the position open for another year, allowing Mc-Combs to change his mind once more, but he never did.

In his last Annual Message, President George Washington had urged the Congress of 1796 to compensate governmental officers sufficiently, suggesting that "it would be repugnant to the vital principles of our government virtually to exclude from public trusts talents and virtue unless accompanied by wealth." Wilson's overseas appointments reflected the dilemma at hand. He felt uncomfortable turning these positions into political rewards, but because the United States was at peace with the rest of the world and because there were so many envoys to name, he succumbed to repaying several men who were "conspicuous for [their] money." He had hoped to send his friend and former colléague Henry Fine to Germany; but even with the promise of a private stipend from Cleveland Dodge, Fine believed life in the foreign court would strain his financial means. Wilson settled on James W. Gerard, a New York State Justice and onetime Tammany candidate, in part because Gerard had wealth and powerful friends in his influential home state. William Graves Sharp, a Congressman from Ohio whom Wilson sent to France, was a man of more modest means, as was Walter Hines Page, his newspaper friend, whom he named as Ambassador to Great Britain (after two others refused). Another writer, Thomas Nelson Page (no relation), came from an old Virginia family and became famous for his romantic evocations of the antebellum South before Wilson posted him to Rome. Frederic Courtland Penfield, a Wilson supporter with time and money, would spend the next several years in Vienna, the capital of the Austro-Hungarian Empire; Henry van Dyke, from the Princeton faculty, agreed to serve in the Hague; and Henry Morgenthau accepted the ambassadorship to the Ottoman Empire, which then included the Holy Land, where Wilson thought a Jew might provide the necessary balance between the Muslim and Christian populations. While Wilson's diplomatic corps was a diversified group, it lacked the academic heft he had once envisioned; few were expert in their territories, though such proficiency hardly seemed a prerequisite for any of the jobs during that international lull.

While most of Wilson's supplicants pressed for jobs, some pressured for a cause. Samuel Gompers, the president of the American Federation of Labor, went to Trenton expecting a ten-minute conference. Wilson gave the Jewish former cigar maker an hour and a half, during which time Gompers called for more protection of labor in upcoming anti-trust legislation. The appointment of William B. Wilson, a "labor man," pleased him.

Then came advocates of the Negro cause. In the final moments of the campaign, Wilson had sent an open letter to civil rights leader Bishop Alexander Walters of the African Methodist Episcopal Zion Church, assuring "my colored fellow citizens of my earnest wish to see justice done them in every matter, and not mere grudging justice, but justice executed with liberality and cordial good feeling." He said, "They may count upon me for absolute fair dealing and for everything by which I could assist in advancing the interests of their race in the United States." Since the election, rumblings from the South especially suggested that what little progress Negroes had made would be rolled back. Hoping that was not the case, Walters reminded Wilson that the Negro vote numbered 750,000, scattered among several large states; more important were the "moral, re-ligious and industrial uplift of my people." Giles B. Jackson, an African American lawyer who had organized the National Negro Wilson League, hoped Wilson might even refer to the "Negro Question" in his forthcoming inaugural address.

Wilson's pre-inaugural rhetoric suggested that he was grappling with the issue and preparing to stand up to America's sectionalism. At the Mary Baldwin Seminary he had spoken of Jefferson's efforts to "divest his mind of the prejudices of race and locality and speak for those permanent issues of human liberty which are the only things that render human life upon this globe itself immoral." To the businessmen of Chicago, he made an odd argument for fighting monopoly, saying, "We are of the same race, that splendid mixed race into which has been drawn all the riches of a hundred bloods. And now, as a united people we are going to redeem the ancient pledges of America." When Mrs. Oscar Underwood invited the Wilsons to attend the Southern Democratic League ball in early March, Wilson declined, explaining to the Speaker himself, "While I myself am deeply glad to be a Southern man and to have the South feel a sense of possession in me, we shall have to be careful not to make the impression that the South is seeking to keep the front of the stage and take possession of the administration."

New thoughts were bound to collide with old ideas. Wilson's major campaign promises involved reforming the country's financial structure. He was already communicating regularly with Congressman Carter Glass—who represented Staunton, Virginia. Chairman of the House Committee on Banking and Currency, Glass was also a staunch proponent of poll taxes and literacy tests for Negroes. They were also discussing a measure that would divide the country into financial zones, each of which would have a federal bank that issued currency, instead of requiring creditors to borrow from a single central bank. Even with "the full power of the administration," Glass warned, enacting legislation in this area would be difficult. Discussion of increased rights for African Americans could only make it more so. As Wilson drafted his inaugural address, he would refer to equality and justice in America, but as a matter of the economy, not ethnicity.

Among all the radical changes that faced the nation, Wilson had to uproot his family. For almost a quarter of a century, his home had been

Princeton—"where we have enjoyed and suffered so much." Frankly, he admitted to Mary Hulbert, "we dread the change,—not so much the new duties as the novel circumstances in which they must be performed." And yet, for all the anxiety, his neuritis and his headaches had quieted since he left academia for politics. His digestion remained delicate, but he was enjoying his longest stretch of good health in years.

At the start of 1913, Wilson wrote the sitting President about domestic matters at the White House, and Taft took the liberty of replying to Mrs. Wilson. He recommended retaining Mrs. Elizabeth Jaffray, a widow of great efficiency and initiative, in her position as housekeeper in the White House, and Arthur Brooks, the official custodian and valet. Taft called him "the most trustworthy colored man in the District of Columbia" and praised his efficiency in recording every delivery to the Executive Mansion and in preparing for trips and entertainments. Taft wrote Wilson himself that Congress would be willing to spend $5,000 to refurbish a number of bedrooms on the third floor to accommodate guests; and he offered to recommend to the Appropriations Committee a small provision so that the President could have a military aide at his disposal. Beyond that, he informed his successor, "Your laundry is looked after in the White House, both when you are here and when you are away. Altogether, you can calculate that your expenses are only those of furnishing food to a large boarding house of servants and to your family, and your own personal expenses of clothing, etc." With the Presidential salary of $75,000 per annum, and another $25,000 for traveling expenses, the Tafts had been able to save $100,000 during their four years.

To assist further, Ellen Wilson hired a social secretary—a "cave dweller," as the locals referred to the city's permanent residents—named Belle Hagner. Nell Wilson fretted because she was known to be a friend of the Roosevelts; and so Ellen invited their favorite cousin, Helen Bones, to live with them as well, to serve as a personal secretary.

While organizing her move, Ellen disappeared to New York one day on a mysterious errand. That night she handed each of her daughters an "inauguration present"—pearl necklaces for Jessie and Margaret and a bar pin set with small diamonds for Nell. They were the first pieces of jewelry any of them had ever owned. As it had not even occurred to Ellen to get something for herself, Woodrow presented her the next day with a diamond pendant. Ever after the family called it the "crown jewel." Because of all the relocation expenses (on top of this small indulgence) before his new salary kicked in, Wilson secured a $5,000 bank loan, the most he had ever borrowed in his life. "He hated to do it," Nell remarked, "but we could not have made the move to Washington without it."

Bidding New Jersey farewell, the Governor attended a series of meetings and meals with the legislators who had been his allies in reforming the state, what he called the New Jersey "surprise." In an after-dinner talk to the Senators gathered in Atlantic City, he recalled the night he had led them in a cakewalk, which was the first time they had realized "that my long, solemn face was not a real index to my countenance, and that I was . . . a human being." On this occasion Wilson led the twenty-one Senators along the boardwalk for a two-mile midnight stroll in the brisk winter air. He resigned from office on March 1, 1913, and, upon handing the seal of office to his successor, he said, "The rarest thing in public life is courage, and the man who has courage is marked for distinction; the man who has not is marked for extinction, and deserves submersion."

That night the townspeople and students of Princeton said goodbye to Wilson, gathering on Nassau Street and marching with flares to Cleveland Lane, where the band played "Hail to the Chief," "My Country, 'Tis of Thee," and "Auld Lang Syne." The president of the First National Bank presented Wilson with a silver loving cup on behalf of "the Citizens of Princeton." An emotional Wilson addressed the crowd, unable to resist one anecdote of "mortification": he had recently entered a shop to buy an item from a man whose face he had known for years. When Wilson asked if the salesman might send the item to the house, the shopkeeper said, "What is your name, sir?" Now he told his well-wishers that the "real trials of life" were the connections one broke. "I have never been inside of the White House, and I shall feel very strange when I get inside of it," he said. "I shall think of this little house behind me and remember how much more familiar it is to me than that is, and how much more intimate a sense of possession there must be in the one case than in the other." Upon the conclusion of his remarks, the Princetonians in the crowd broke into "Old Nassau."

On Monday the third, Secret Service men, a large crowd, and a line of motorcars waited outside 25 Cleveland Lane. At 10:30, Woodrow and Ellen exited the house, choosing to walk to the train station instead of riding in one of the automobiles. They made a slight detour, strolling down

Library Place, past the house they had built years earlier. Friends and neighbors paid their respects along the way, though most of the townspeople waited for them at the train—a special car followed by a half dozen coaches filled with six hundred rollicksome undergraduates. The family stood on the back platform as the train pulled out of the campus depot at eleven, the First Couple smiling and waving and looking wistful as the spires and towers disappeared from view.

Passing flag-waving crowds all along the route, the train pulled into Washington's Union Station at 3:45. The students hastily detrained, in order to form a double line through which the Wilsons made their way from the Presidential car to the street, where a limousine took them through side streets to the Shoreham Hotel at 15th and H Streets. They completely bypassed the chaotic gathering of woman suffragists who were staging a "pageant" down Pennsylvania Avenue and commanding most of the attention that afternoon—5,000 women demanding their rights as they paraded in front of a crowd of 500,000. One of the guests of honor, the deaf and blind and militant Helen Keller, got waylaid in the congestion and never got to address the crowd; but she had her say in the next day's newspapers, assuring the public and the incoming President that the demonstration symbolized "the coming of the new, not the passing of the old" and that it would "not be long before a president shall ride down these broad avenues elected by the people of America, women and men."

The Wilsons encountered friendlier commotion at the Shoreham. Because the hotel served as headquarters for Princeton alumni, hundreds donned orange and black as they secured badges that would admit them to a number of special events. During one encounter that day, a plump and dapper gentleman approached Wilson to introduce himself: it was Franklin Lane, the new Secretary of the Interior. By late afternoon, the stress of moving caught up to Ellen. The color left her face, and she repaired to her room to rest behind locked doors. After a while, Nell entered, to help her dress for a six-o'clock tea at the White House. Sitting before a mirror, arranging her hair, Ellen put both hands over her face and burst into tears. But she managed to pull herself together before she had to join her husband.

Full of charm, the Tafts explained the White House to the new tenants, and conversation came easily. In the background that afternoon stood a short, handsome, dark-haired lieutenant in the naval medical corps, thirty-five-year-old Cary Travers Grayson. Virginia-born and -educated, Grayson—an Episcopalian—radiated modest confidence. He was quiet and deferential by nature but a lively raconteur when called upon, and Washington hostesses considered him the ideal "extra man." Before the Wilsons departed, Taft jovially drew his successor under his arm and said, "Mr. Wilson, here is an excellent fellow that I hope you will get to know. I regret to say that he is a Democrat and a Virginian, but that's a matter that can't be helped!"

The Wilsons returned to their hotel, where Ellen, exhausted but undaunted, announced, "It's just a bigger Prospect—Sea Girt with no servant problem." A Wilson cousin hosted a dinner at the Shoreham for a few dozen intimates, including Fred Yates, the Wilsons' artist friend visiting from England's Lake District. After dinner the President-elect excused himself to appear at a "smoker"—a dinner of eight hundred Princeton alumni—on the tenth floor of the nearby New Willard Hotel, where he spoke briefly but emotionally about the "comradeship" he felt within the Princeton family, largely because of the university's great role in the nation's service.

Under gray skies, Woodrow Wilson left the hotel the next morning at ten o'clock in a two-horse open victoria. Some one thousand Princeton students—all wearing orange sashes—along with five hundred more from the University of Virginia, served as an honor guard, lining the carriage's route to the White House. Ellen and the girls remained at the hotel, giving themselves ample time to dress. The retinue of undergraduates was permitted to follow the carriage and then gather on the White House lawn, where, once again, they burst into song. A military band announced Wilson's arrival, but he waited on the front porch until the students had finished their medley, concluding, of course, with "Old Nassau"—at the end of which, a hatless Wilson bowed his head. Then he walked between the military aides in full dress uniforms to the Blue Room, where President Taft joined him, followed by the arrival of the new Cabinet and Vice President–elect Thomas R. Marshall. Taft took Wilson by the arm, leading him through the Red Room to the South Portico, where photographers had lined up cameras for official photographs. The incumbent was then tipping the scales at 340 pounds, twice Wilson's weight; and though he was born the year before the incoming President, his girth and big mustache—and, perhaps, his four years in office—made him look considerably older than his successor.

Taft and Wilson entered a large landau drawn by four horses. Great cheers greeted them all along Pennsylvania Avenue. In the meantime, White House chauffeurs drove the Wilson family in automobiles down side streets to the Capitol, where they took seats in the Senate Gallery to witness Marshall's being sworn into office. Senator Miles Poindexter took the floor to deliver a speech that droned on, standing as the only impediment between those inside the chamber and the largest audience that had ever assembled for an inauguration. Three times, as the minute hand of the chamber clock crept toward twelve, an attendant pushed it back. An indignant Nell Wilson wondered how a Senator could be so cavalier. Someone close by provided an explanation, which further described the political climate in Washington: "He's a Republican," said the voice, "—he's doing it on purpose." At last, Marshall took his oath, and everybody moved to seats on the portico of the Capitol. Back at the White House, the flag was lowered and a new one raised.

It was still overcast but a mild fifty-five degrees as the Presidential carriage pulled before the crowd, the incumbent appearing happier than the incoming President. With little pomp, Wilson took his place on the grandstand, which sat slightly above the heads of the 100,000 countrymen who stood there in anticipation. Wilson had asked to be sworn in with his hand on Ellen's small Bible, which Chief Justice Edward Douglass White opened and offered to a Deputy Clerk of the Court to hold. Upon completing the oath of office, Wilson followed the example of George Washington and stooped to kiss the pages of Scripture before him—the 119th Psalm: "So shall I keep thy Law continually: for ever and ever." In that moment, the sun broke through the clouds. The crowd started to push through the barriers to get closer to the platform, so they might better hear their new President. As the police began to force them back, Wilson said, "Let the people come forward."

He proceeded to deliver a stirring inaugural address. Equal parts lesson, sermon, and mission statement, his carefully chosen 1,800 words—composed over the last month—began with a simple proclamation of fact: "There has been a change of government." He described the Democratic takeover of both houses of Congress and the White House in the last two years; and then he asked what that meant. He spent ten paragraphs answering the question.

At first he inspired the audience, describing the bounty of America— "Our life contains every great thing, and contains it in rich abundance."

But he hastened to add that the riches had come at great human cost. He said the government had too often been used for private and selfish purposes, and those who used it had forgotten the people. The change in government, Wilson assured, meant new "vision." He said, "Our duty is to cleanse, to reconsider, to restore, to correct the vile without impairing the good, to purify and humanize every process of our common life without weakening or sentimentalizing it."

For the next few minutes he enumerated the specific Progressive ideas he intended to enact. Not least among them was "safeguarding the health of the nation," as the "first duty of law is to keep sound the society it serves." As he spoke of his ambitious program, many felt they were listening to the most glorious rhetoric from that podium in fifty-two years, when Lincoln summoned "the better angels of our nature" in his first inaugural address. Wilson proclaimed the "high enterprise of the new day: to lift everything that concerns our life as a nation to the light that shines from the hearthfire of every man's conscience and vision of the right. It is inconceivable that we should do this as partisans. . . . The feelings with which we face this new age . . . sweep across our heartstrings like some air out of God's own presence, where justice and mercy are reconciled and the judge and the brother are one."

"This is not a day of triumph," he concluded, "it is a day of dedication." With that in mind, he summoned "all honest men, all patriotic, all forward-looking men, to my side," assuring them that "God helping me, I will not fail them, if they will but counsel and sustain me!" He made no mention of foreign affairs. This speech was about restoring justice to a great but broken nation, a "government too often debauched and made an instrument of evil."

Speaking in his manner of heightened conversation rather than theatrical bombast, Wilson earned wave upon wave of applause at the end. Ellen Wilson quietly left her seat and unobtrusively descended the steps, to stand on a bench directly below her husband. She gazed up at him with a look of rapture.

The President and former President returned to the White House, while the Wilson women were chauffeured separately. Upon their arrival, Ellen and her daughters were taken to their second-floor quarters. Woodrow and Ellen's suite consisted of two bedrooms, a dressing room, and two baths. Bright and airy, with fires burning in the open grates, it overlooked the Ellipse and the Washington Monument. When the girls checked on their mother, they found her at the window, looking down upon Mrs. Taft's formal garden with its graveled paths and geometrical flower beds. "Isn't it lovely, children?" she asked tentatively, already thinking of improvements. "It will be our rose garden with a high hedge around it."

They joined the Cabinet members and their wives and other distinguished guests—two hundred of them—who had gathered in the dining room for a stand-up buffet luncheon. Colonel and Mrs. House were there, though he had chosen not to attend the actual inauguration. "Functions of this sort do not appeal to me and I never go," he wrote in his diary. The former and new Presidents arrived and awkwardly stood together in the vestibule. Wilson invited Taft to remain for the lunch honoring the new administration, never expecting him to accept. But Taft stayed, only to find himself in the unfortunate position of standing alone as the new President received congratulatory handshakes. At last, Wilson returned to Taft, who said in parting, "Mr. President, I hope you'll be happy here." Wilson questioned the sentiment: "Happy?"

"Yes, I know," Taft replied. "I'm glad to be going—this is the loneliest place in the world."

Nellie Wilson overheard the comment and thought the strength of their family would keep that from happening. And then a minor mishap occurred, which, strangely, would ensure that Wilson would never be alone. The President's sister Annie Howe slipped on one of the marble staircases and gashed her scalp and forehead. Several Army and Navy aides were on hand, Dr. Grayson among them. Equipped for medical emergencies, he stitched her wound. This began what would become the most constant and intimate relationship the President had with a man for the rest of his life—a unique affiliation characterized by trust beyond that of any official, as Dr. Grayson would literally have his hand on the President's pulse and, thus, on the well-being of the world. "My official connection with Mr. Wilson was almost accidental," Grayson himself would later explain, "though, as I look back over the long stretch of years, I should like to call it providential."

A little after three, the Presidential party went outside to the reviewing stand in front of the house to watch the longest parade in inaugural history, forty thousand participants over the course of four hours. Young cadets from the service academies marched, including West Point "yearling"

Dwight D. Eisenhower. Woodrow Wilson stood throughout the procession, repeatedly doffing his tall silk hat, while Ellen smiled and waved her lace handkerchief. After the parade, fourteen of the innermost circle dressed for dinner in the State Dining Room. Profusions of roses filled the table, under the soft glow of the great silver candelabra. Everybody stared admiringly at the man sitting quietly at the head of the table. Afterward, a display of fireworks lit up the sky before the various family members set about finding their bedrooms, shrieks of excitement signaling each new discovery. For the first time since Franklin Pierce's inauguration in 1853, there would be no official ball. While other Presidents held to the festive tradition even in times of war and national hardship, Wilson chose to omit the occasion, considering it not just an unnecessary expense but also a source of "graft." Local vendors did not care for this curtailment of their quadrennial windfall, but they got a clear sense of the austerity of their new neighbors. Ellen Wilson appeared too weak to have danced that night anyway.

Wilson dropped into his office, to get a feel of the place and to meet briefly with Colonel House; but he soon rose from his desk to head to the Shoreham Hotel, where he arrived at the tail end of a dinner being held by the Class of 1879. After his strenuous day, the Princetonians had fully expected an announcement that he was too tired to appear; but Wilson beamed as he sat between reelected Congressman Charles Talcott—with whom he had once made a "solemn covenant" to devote themselves to the political arts—and Taft-appointed Justice of the Supreme Court Mahlon Pitney. The "Witherspoon Gang" was there in force.

The President stayed past midnight. Not long after he had returned to the White House and found his bedroom, he began pushing several of the mother-of-pearl buttons set in the wall, hoping to summon an attendant. A doorkeeper hastened to the second-floor residence, only to find Woodrow Wilson standing in his underwear. One of his trunks, which happened to hold his pajamas, never got delivered. It was immediately located at the train station, but it did not arrive at the White House until one o'clock, by which time the President of the United States was sound asleep.

9

BAPTISM

*And Iesus, when hee was baptized, went vp straight-
way out of the water: and loe, the heauens were
opened vnto him, and he saw the Spirit of God descending like a doue, and lighting vpon him.*

—MATTHEW III:16

A rticle I, Section 8, of the Constitution of the United
States ordained the creation of a "District (not exceed-
ing ten Miles square) as may . . . become the Seat of the
Government of the United States." It was christened Columbia, the elegiac term for America, and its "federal city"
was named for the first President. Congress held its first
session in the District of Columbia in 1800, even before the
completion of the Capitol. A National Mall extending from
this great hub to the Potomac River would gradually fill in
with monuments and buildings worthy of the Acropolis.
"Slowly," Henry Adams commented upon the end of the
nineteenth century, "a certain society had built itself up
about the Government; houses had been opened and there
was much dining; much calling; much leaving of cards."
Unlike most world capitals, Washington was neither its nation's chief commercial nor cultural center. Government
was its only industry, powered by the fact that every elected
official held a temporary job with limited time to achieve

his goals. In 1913, Washington, D.C., was a gracious Southern city of 350,000 people.

African Americans accounted for nearly a third of that population, the largest Negro congregation in the country. Most were invisible, unseen or overlooked in their subservient positions. Practically all the black women served as domestics, while the men worked as servants, waiters, and manual laborers. For the most part, Negroes knew their place. The city appeared to have no slums, because the overcrowded ghettos were on its periphery or made up of shacks tucked in the downtown alleys, where thousands subsisted in poverty. With the establishment of the Civil Service, a few Negroes began rising to the middle class, entering through the front doors of the Postal Service and the Treasury Department, where they could hold jobs similar to those of white people. A small upper middle class of blacks had risen in the capital; but, so far as Nell Wilson could tell, the "undisputed leaders of Washington colored society" were the dozens of footmen, doormen, maids, and butlers who staffed the Executive Mansion at 1600 Pennsylvania Avenue. They wore elegant uniforms; and, unlike the masters of the house, they held their jobs for life.

"The White House" became the official name for the sandstone Georgian mansion during TR's stay, referring to both the President's home and his workplace. Because his family had filled so many rooms at a time when the executive branch was expanding, TR had ordered construction of wings off the sides of the house to provide office space. His successor, Taft, created an elliptical room within the West Wing, which became the President's office.

Sunshine filled the White House on March 5, 1913, Woodrow Wilson's first full day at his new job. Arthur Brooks, his personal valet, had laid out his clothes. At precisely 8:30, Wilson sat at the mahogany table in the small family dining room on the north side of the house. Fred Yates joined him and his family, and they rehashed the prior day's events as the President ate his customary breakfast—two unbeaten raw eggs in orange juice, swallowed like oysters, a bowl of porridge, and coffee. The President left at nine for what was then called "the oval room in the Executive offices."

During his first official appointment—with friend and future diplomat Charles Crane—Wilson commented on the days of Washington and Jefferson, when "the President had time to think." His first policy decision revealed his determination to find the hours in which to free his mind. He was going to rid himself of one of the "chief burdens" of his job, the meeting of candidates for appointment to public office. Wilson had telegraphed as much in his constitutional government lectures just a few years earlier, when he predicted that "as the multitude of the President's duties increases," holders of the great office should be "less and less executive officers and more and more . . . men of counsel and of the sort of action that makes for enlightenment."

At ten o'clock Wilson met informally in the Cabinet Room with his ten departmental Secretaries, who were mostly strangers to him and to one another. Thereafter, their semiweekly meetings would usually begin at eleven with Wilson relating an anecdote before presenting issues of immediate concern. Then he would call upon each Secretary in turn, practically simulating a Princeton preceptorial. Shortly after this first meeting, Wilson developed nicknames for all the Cabinet members, which doubled as ciphers during confidential telephone conversations and telegrams between him and Colonel House. Bryan became "Prime"; Secretary of War Garrison was "Mars"; and Secretary of the Navy Daniels became "Neptune." Wilson considered his Cabinet "executive counselors"; and from that day forward, observed Neptune, he gave them "free rein in the management of the affairs of their department. No President refrained so much from hampering them by naming their subordinates. Holding them responsible, he gave them liberty, confidence, and co-operation. More than that: he stood back of them when criticized and held up their hands." The West Wing functioned with a staff of six, including the stenographer Charles Swem, who had accompanied Wilson from New Jersey.

Ceremonial duties consumed most of Wilson's first day in office, as he greeted more than a thousand guests. There was a "Woodrow luncheon" for the two dozen relatives from his mother's side and a "Wilson dinner" for those from his father's. For almost an hour, he received well-wishers in the East Room, the "public audience chamber," which, at almost three thousand square feet and running the width of the house, was the largest in the mansion. Guests arrived by appointment, but many brought guests of their own: one Illinois Congressman arrived with 150 Chicago Democrats; an Atlanta editor ushered in 150 of his newsboys. And then the entire Democratic National Committee appeared. Not until after dinner did Wilson discover the most satisfying moment of the day—when he could address the piles of letters and reports that awaited him next to his old familiar typewriter in the private book-lined study on the second floor.

Although Tumulty had announced that the government would not be conducting Presidential appointments as usual, Wilson immediately faced that disparity between aspiration and accommodation in the thousands of non-Cabinet appointments at his discretion. He believed no President had ever entered the White House so free of political debt, but he quickly learned that he owed more than he had thought. "I am not going to advise with reactionary or standpat senators or representatives in making these appointments," Wilson announced at the start of his administration, as he intended to place capability above party loyalty. "Mr. President," Postmaster Burleson, the savviest political mind in the Cabinet, replied, "if you pursue this policy, it means that your administration is going to be a failure. It means the defeat of the measures of reform that you have next to your heart. These little offices don't amount to anything. They are inconsequential. It doesn't amount to a damn who is postmaster at Paducah, Kentucky. But these little offices mean a great deal to the senators and representatives in Congress."

Burleson put a practical example before him—the nation's fifty-six thousand postmasterships. "The Cardinal," as Burleson was nicknamed, said he hoped he could apply Wilson's standards to all the appointees, but the Congressmen and Senators expected to have their say. "They are mostly good men," Burleson explained. "If they are turned down, they will hate you and will not vote for anything you want. It is human nature. On the other hand, if you work with them, and they recommend unsuitable men for the offices, I will keep on asking for other suggestions, until I get good ones." Wilson remained unconvinced until Burleson addressed the appointment atop a stack of papers—a recommendation from the Congressman in southeastern Tennessee. Wilson had received objections to the appointment and said he could not endorse it. Burleson proceeded to describe the little town near Chattanooga and the Representative's familiarity with the people there. Wilson sat in silence during the long descriptive discourse, finally saying, "Well, Burleson, I will appoint him." Seeing another 55,999 similar instances before him, Wilson relinquished control in the matter, simply asking Burleson where he should sign their commissions. Except for the ability to bring nonpolitical figures (especially academicians) into the government, Wilson found little pleasure in dispensing patronage. Sometimes it actually pained him, as he rejected friends—even family members—who sought judgeships or other appointments.

With ten years between them, Woodrow had always been more of a father figure to Joseph Wilson, Jr., than a brother. While Josie had built his own modest career in the newspaper business in Tennessee, by his late forties, he had reached a dead end and sought a new career. He had been working for the Democratic Party, and McAdoo thought he might make a good candidate for the Senate. Short of that, the current junior Senator from Tennessee, Luke Lea, had another idea.

Since the founding of the Congress, a little-known position called Secretary of the Senate has existed. The Senators themselves elect this officer, who originally had served as their clerk, archivist, and quartermaster. By Wilson's day, the job included overseeing the Senate payroll, its pages, and the public records; it paid $6,500 per annum. After the election of 1912, Senator Lea believed putting Joseph Wilson in that position might give Lea some special access. Josie bought into the idea, and, for a moment, so did his brother—until the Senator from Oklahoma, T. P. Gore, reminded Wilson of, as he put it, "something called the separation of powers."

Even before the Senate elected somebody else, Josie cast his eye on another position, Postmaster of Nashville. Shortly after taking office, the President wrote his brother that it would be "a very serious mistake both for you and for me if I were to appoint you," despite his "struggle against affection and temptation." The brothers' relationship did not change after that—as, after all, they already wrote each other irregularly and saw each other infrequently.

Wilson demonstrated more fraternal feelings toward his advisers, three in particular. "Mr. House is my second personality," the President said, when asked of his silent partner in formulating policy. "He is my independent self," and "his thoughts and mine are one." The two men discussed House's relocating; but, House wrote in his diary, "we both realize that one soon becomes saturated with what might be termed the Washington viewpoint, and that everything is colored by that environment." They concluded it would be best for House to continue living in New York, Massachusetts, and Texas, and shuttling to Washington whenever beckoned, relying on the telephone and on letters in between. House visited the White House ten times that spring alone, as they charted administration policy.

Joseph Tumulty continued as Wilson's political adviser. More than

merely tending to the pesky details of office for which Wilson had no patience, Tumulty's Trenton-tested instincts allowed him to deal with the
press, take the public's pulse, interact with the legislature, and serve as
gatekeeper to the Oval Office—tasks that future Presidents would divide
among a dozen men.

The third crucial member of the Wilson team was Cary T. Grayson,
who was already becoming the most indispensable. After five days as
President—during which he had received nine Justices, dozens of envoys,
and hundreds of commissioners and other governmental functionaries—
Wilson fell ill. He suffered from a severe headache and gastric disorder—
which he referred to as "turmoil in Central America." Dr. Grayson, who
had been monitoring Wilson's sister since her Inauguration Day accident,
found the President in bed. "When you get to know me better," Wilson
explained, "you will find that I am subject to disturbances in the equato-
rial regions." Grayson's first recommendation for Wilson to rest would
become chronic advice.

Grayson did not yet know the extent of his new patient's hypertension,
but he promptly saw that Wilson had been overmedicating his headaches
with coal-tar analgesics—such as the new wonder drug aspirin—which
upset his stomach. His medicine cabinet already held a quart-sized can of
tablets and a stomach pump, which he used regularly in a procedure that
involved inserting a rubber hose from his mouth to his stomach and fun-
neling in enough saline solution to siphon out the gastric acid. Recognizing
a pernicious cycle, Grayson took Wilson off the drugs. The patient accused
the doctor of being a "therapeutic nihilist." Shortly thereafter, the President
invited Dr. Grayson to lunch with Secretary of the Navy Daniels. "There is
one part of the Navy that I want to appropriate," Wilson said. "There have
been a good many applications for the position but Mrs. Wilson and I have
already become acquainted with Doctor Grayson and we have decided that
he is the man we should like to have assigned to the White House." He
became the President's personal physician, and soon a lot more.

As such, he learned all he could about his new patient from various
sources. Long associating Woodrow's prior history of "neuritis" and visual
impairment with the strains of work, Ellen had privately consulted with
Dr. Francis X. Dercum of Philadelphia (who treated her brother Stockton
for his persistent breakdowns), to ask if he thought her husband could
shoulder the Presidency. Dercum knew of Wilson's ruptured blood vessel

years earlier and saw no great danger; but another famous neurologist, Dr. S. Weir Mitchell, disagreed, prophesying that Woodrow Wilson would not live out his first term.

Dr. Grayson reminded Wilson that "he had four hard years ahead of him and that he owed it to himself and the American people to get into as fit condition as possible and to stay there." The regime, Grayson would later recollect, "included plenty of fresh air, a diet suited to his idiosyncrasies as I discovered them by close study, plenty of sleep, daily motor rides, occasional trips on the *Mayflower* [the Presidential yacht], and especially regular games of golf, together with treatment for a persistent case of neuritis from which he had long suffered." As a result of keeping the President engaged in leisure activities every day, Grayson became his regular companion, "drawn into close personal association with him."

Once out of bed, Wilson conscientiously attempted to maintain a balanced schedule. After breakfast, he would dictate correspondence from nine until ten and then receive visitors until one. He would lunch with family members and then work another hour or two. Every afternoon included an automobile ride; and except for some light paperwork, he worked at night only during crises. Sundays he slept in before attending services at the Central Presbyterian Church. He even made time for recreational reading, asking the Librarian of Congress to keep him supplied with detective novels. From the very start of his term, Wilson set his sights on its completion. "The day after I am released from this great job," he wrote, "I shall take a ship for Rydal!" Until then, Wilson had an ambitious legislative program he hoped to bequeath, but every President quickly discovers that he must first untangle the state of affairs he has inherited.

In the centuries since Columbus, Spain, Germany, France, and England had all plundered Central and South America. Mexico became their piñata, which they repeatedly bashed so that more of its treasures would fall at their feet. In the mid-1800s, the United States took some swings as well, annexing Texas and grabbing Mexican land as far north as Oregon. In his *History of the American People*, Wilson characterized the Mexican-American War as "inexcusable aggression and fine fighting." The American presence steadily increased south of the Rio Grande, as Mexico's abundance of oil became more precious than its metals.

Longtime dictator General Porfirio Díaz invited outside investment; and under America's Republican administrations at the start of the twentieth century, "dollar diplomacy"—the belief that the government should exploit all possible business opportunities in foreign countries—earned handsome dividends for Americans. With the rise of this private imperialism, Mexican resentment grew. In 1910 a reform-minded landowner, Francisco Madero, ran against Díaz in a "free election"—only to be imprisoned by his opponent. So began the Mexican Revolution, with Madero marshaling the forces of Emiliano Zapata, Pascual Orozco, and Francisco "Pancho" Villa—all of whom kept turning on one another. In the spring of 1911, Díaz fled the country, and Madero was named President. Not two years later, General Victoriano Huerta had him shot and on February 18, 1913, became President of Mexico.

Two weeks later, President Huerta sent congratulations to the newly inaugurated President Wilson. The gesture was barely reciprocated. Wilson wired a seven-word formal reply—carefully addressed to General—not President—Huerta, to avoid even suggesting diplomatic recognition of what Wilson considered an illegal regime. Days after the inauguration, the New York *World* implicated America's Ambassador, Henry Lane Wilson (no relation), in the overthrow of Madero. Tensions in Latin America were the subject of the first official Cabinet meeting on Friday, March 7; and when they reconvened the following Tuesday, the President read aloud a statement he had written on the subject, taking his first steps into a quagmire not of his creation.

These initial words about Mexico would become the cornerstone of his foreign policy for as long as he held office; and they further signaled his intention to serve largely as his own Secretary of State. "Cooperation is possible only when supported at every turn by the orderly processes of just government based upon law, not upon arbitrary or irregular force," he said. "We hold . . . that just government rests always upon the consent of the governed, and that there can be no freedom without order based upon law and upon the public conscience and approval. . . . We shall lend our influence of every kind to the realization of these principles in fact and practice. . . . We can have no sympathy with those who seek to seize the power of government to advance their own personal interests or ambition. . . . We shall prefer those who act in the interest of peace and honor, who protect private rights and respect the restraints of constitutional provision."

Some other Cabinet members commented that such a statement suggested the new administration was unnecessarily rushing into places where it did not belong. Wilson averred that "something had to be said, that the agitators in certain countries wanted revolutions and were inclined to try it on with the new Administration." As Agriculture Secretary David Houston recalled, "He intimated that he was not going to let them have one if he could prevent it." Secretary Bryan nodded and smiled.

However reluctantly, the United States was taking its first steps along a new path into international affairs, becoming a global overseer. Under Woodrow Wilson, American foreign policy would increasingly find itself clucking its disapproval, if not disdain, for the misbehavior of other nations. The situation in Mexico was just the beginning of a series of conundrums in which Wilson questioned himself as to whether his actions imposed sound public policy or just his own personal morality—all the while questing, of course, to do both.

While the change in Mexico's government had occurred in the prior administration, Taft had postponed taking a position, perhaps out of respect to the incoming President. A quick study of the situation reported that the conditions resulting from American nonrecognition of the Huerta government were already producing "serious inconvenience." Several matters between the two countries hung in abeyance, from water rights along the Colorado River to a border dispute in El Paso; loans from American banks were coming due and would go unpaid. The professor who wrote the report allowed that the circumstances by which Huerta rose to power were deplorable; but, he added, "We cannot become the censors of the morals or conduct of other nations and make our approval or disapproval of their methods the test of our recognition of their governments without intervening in their affairs." Others insisted that standing on the sidelines would threaten American lives, property, and profits.

"I will not recognize a government of butchers," said the President, digging in his heels. "While recognition of Huerta was the *wise* course, as practicality defines wisdom," an ardent supporter later wrote of his decision, "it was not the *right* course." With American land, mineral, and industrial investors pleading for Wilson to change his mind, Wilson told Tumulty, "I have to pause and remind myself that I am President of the United States and not of a small group of Americans with vested interest in Mexico."

Despite suspecting his motives and disapproving his actions, Wilson kept Taft's Ambassador Wilson on the job. If nothing else, he would protect current American business interests in Mexico. But President Wilson also dispatched an emissary of his own to gather intelligence, somebody who could quickly ascertain the Ambassador's role in the coup as well as the legitimacy of Huerta's government. This first secret intelligence agent in the Wilson Administration, William Bayard Hale, had no connection to Mexico and could not even speak Spanish; but, as an Episcopalian priest who had written a campaign biography of Wilson, he could be trusted.

Hale reported a shocking tale of cold-blooded treachery, in which Ambassador Wilson had conspired with Huerta and several other sympathetic foreign ministers to overthrow Madero. Furthermore, Hale noted, "Madero would never have been assassinated had the American Ambassador made it thoroughly understood that the plot must stop short of murder." Hale thought this tale of "treason, perfidy and assassination in an assault on constitutional government" was the most shocking ever to involve an American diplomatic officer. And though it had transpired on President Taft's watch, it was Wilson's problem now. What was worse, Hale concluded, "thousands of Mexicans believe that the Ambassador acted on instructions from Washington and look upon his retention under the new American President as a mark of approval and blame the United States Government for the chaos into which the country has fallen."

Within days, Wilson set in motion the recalling of the "unspeakable" Henry Lane Wilson; and within two months he had been replaced by John Lind, a former Minnesota Congressman and Governor whose knowledge of the territory was negligible. Lind arrived in Mexico with an invitation from Wilson to Huerta—to abandon his office. He suggested that the country hold a general election, in which Huerta would not run. Even Madero's Foreign Relations Secretary Manuel Calero would later write that Wilson's not choosing to recognize Huerta was well within his rights; to destroy him, however, was not. "Huerta was a usurper," Calero granted. "But did it belong to the President of the United States to drive him from the place usurped? This was a matter that concerned exclusively the people of Mexico."

Wilson's initial attempts to push Huerta out of office only strengthened the Mexican leader. As Calero observed, American nonrecognition offered Huerta "the occasion of exhibiting himself as champion of the national dignity, as defender of the sovereignty of Mexico against the intrusion of a foreign government." Resorting to a policy Wilson called "watchful waiting," he and his new diplomatic team in Mexico appraised the alcoholic Huerta's regime one day at a time.

At the Cabinet meeting on March 12, 1913, Secretary Bryan brought up another country going through a revolution. After four thousand years of dynastic rule, Sun Yat-sen had recently declared a Republic of China and was encouraging foreign investment there. The Taft Administration had approved the participation of American banks in an international consortium that might lend $125 million. Wilson had been in office a week when representatives from J. P. Morgan & Company and Kuhn, Loeb & Company called upon Bryan, saying they would not close the deal without express authorization from the government. Wilson was sympathetic to the emerging nation—in part because of almost a century of Presbyterian missionary work in China. In May, the United States recognized China as a republic, one of the first nations to do so. Bryan called it "one of the pleasant duties of this administration." But Wilson strongly disapproved of this so-called Six Power Loan.

The next day, he composed his official response: "The conditions of the loan seem to us to touch very nearly the administrative independence of China itself; and this administration does not feel that it ought, even by implication, to be a party to those conditions." Wilson felt the problem lay in certain demands the loan placed upon the Chinese, who were pledging to secure the loan with burdensome taxes and supervision by foreign agents. His primary objection, however, was that "it gave the monopoly of this nation's interests in China's finances to a small group of American bankers to the exclusion of all other American financiers"—for the present and in the future. That representatives of J. P. Morgan & Company further expected the United States government "to utilize both its military and naval forces to protect the interest of the lenders" in the event of the Chinese defaulting was all Wilson needed to hear. Such responsibilities, he stated, were "obnoxious to the principles upon which the government of our people rests."

Wilson's statement assured the citizens of both the United States and China that he wanted to promote "the most extended and intimate trade relationship between this country and the Chinese republic," and that he

hoped to pursue opportunities through "the open door—a door of friendship and mutual advantage." But, he added, this loan overly entangled
America in the affairs of China. Ever since the Spanish-American War, the
United States had been navigating an imperialistic course, guided most
recently by "dollar diplomacy." With Wilson's quashing the China deal,
he semaphored a change in direction.

That meant immediate reconsideration of agreements the Roosevelt
and Taft administrations had made with a number of other countries
whose governments were in turmoil. Chief among them were the Philippines, an American territory, fought and paid for in 1898—a takeover the
Republican administrations had justified by insisting the Filipinos were
not prepared to govern themselves. Hostilities between the islands and the
United States had existed ever since. Wilson considered whether the Philippines were, in fact, "prepared for independence"; and he decided they
were not. Nor did he believe that the United States had made its best efforts to help them. To the dismay of many Americans, including a few of
his own Cabinet members, Wilson announced that American policy there
was no longer to be "for the advantage of the United States, but for the
benefit of the people of the Philippine Islands." Toward that end, he announced that a majority of seats on the governing Philippine Commission,
which the American President appointed, would be filled by Filipinos.
Tensions dramatically abated, as the Philippines were, at last, on a track
toward independence.

And then there was a political temblor in California that was felt as far
as Tokyo and Washington, D.C., one that also called for moral adjudica-
tion. Americans had for the last decade invested in Asia, and now Asians
wanted to own land in America. There had long been an overt prejudice
against "Orientals" in California, which only intensified as Japanese immigrants especially prospered in agriculture. When enough started to buy
land, the state legislature proposed a bill forbidding foreign ownership.
Japan was deeply insulted. Foreign policy was suddenly conjoined to domestic policy, in a state whose leader, the great Progressive Governor Hiram Johnson, was also a racist. For the next several months, Wilson
attempted to get California to temper the language of the law, but not
only did he wish to avoid trespassing onto states' rights, he also needed all
the Congressional support he could muster for his legislative agenda.

In Washington, he introduced another kind of "open door" policy, one in which the executive branch of government was literally open to the public. By the second week of the Administration, the press and the public were startled to find that anybody was welcome to observe their officials at work. Nobody had ever seen a government so candid and accessible. War Secretary Garrison would swivel in his desk chair and answer questions from strangers who had entered his office; Josephus Daniels said he intended to become the first Secretary of the Navy who would actually visit the Navy yards across the country. Even in the White House, citizens could walk back to the executive offices.

At 12:45 on March 15, 1913, the Wilson Administration made history when it established what would become a convention of the Presidency. That Saturday afternoon, Tumulty ushered 125 members of the press corps into Wilson's office; and for the first time, a President held a White House press conference. Wilson was hardly the first President to talk to a journalist; indeed, Taft met occasionally with newspapermen after hours and granted them a few minutes of questions; and TR cherry-picked members of his "newspaper cabinet," allowing them to transcribe what he chose to dictate. To promote government transparency, Wilson announced that he intended to schedule regular conferences at which any journalist could ask whatever he wanted.

If nothing else, the exercise was a good publicity tool for Wilson. Few could speak off the cuff with such ease, and he sometimes simply chose not to answer a question. Most of his responses—terse and precise—revealed nothing more than necessary, but his witty interplay with the press set the tone for relations between the press and future Presidents. "As he went on talking, the big hit he was making with the crowd became evident," reported *The New York Times* after the first gathering. "There was something so unaffected and honest about his way of talking . . . that it won everybody, despite the fact that many of the men there had come prejudiced against him." Between March and December 1913 alone, Wilson appeared at sixty press conferences.

At the second conference—which moved to the much larger East Room—Wilson took the press into his confidence and asked for its help. "The only way I can succeed is by not having my mind live in Washington," he said. "My body has got to live there, but my mind has got to live in the United States, or else I will fail." Wilson hoped the newspapermen would bring him a sense of the nation beyond the city in which they worked, considering themselves importers as much as exporters. And with that metaphor in mind, Wilson turned to what he believed would be his administration's defining piece of legislation, one that had eluded his predecessors for decades and that required a radical presentation.

In the northwest corner on the second floor of the United States Capitol—just off the Senate chamber—is an anomalous gilt-trimmed salon with a vaulted frescoed ceiling and a brilliantly colored tile floor. It is called the President's Room. George Washington had proposed such a room so that the Chief Executive and Senators might conduct their joint business; but not until the mid-nineteenth century, when the great legislative edifice was expanded and crowned with its iron dome, did it come into existence. In the interim, the Chief Executive almost never came to Capitol Hill. After John Adams left the Presidency in 1801, Presidents virtually discontinued their visits to the two legislative houses. Ostensibly to keep "the President's Annual Message to Congress" from becoming a throne speech—though possibly because he was not a good speaker—Thomas Jefferson messengered his texts to the legislature for a clerk to read, and that practice became standard. Because new Congressional sessions began on the fourth of March every other year, a President might visit his special room but twice a term, to sign any bills passed under the wire on the third. Beyond that, this jewel of a room remained a museum piece.

The Constitution states that the President shall from time to time not only give to the Congress information on the state of the Union but also "recommend to their Consideration such Measures as he shall judge necessary and expedient; he may, on extraordinary Occasions, convene both Houses, or either of them." The morning after his election, Woodrow Wilson had contemplated that clause, thanks to a journalist named Oliver P. Newman. In an off-the-record interview about executive style, Newman had suggested that Wilson might abandon the 112-year-old tradition and deliver important speeches in person. Wilson had stood at the window in his library on Cleveland Lane and stared out, as if into the future. "Newman," he said, "that would set them by the ears."

On second thought, Wilson did not want to antagonize Congress. But the idea kept growing. Thinking it would emphasize the cruciality of all that he wished to propose, Wilson asked the legislature to convene. Reaction from Capitol Hill was swift. Republicans, such as William O. Bradley of Kentucky, cautioned him to remember the separation of powers, saying,

"If Mr. Wilson comes to the Capitol to influence legislation, he will be more foolish than the donkey that swam the river to get a drink of water." Several Democrats, such as John Sharp Williams of Mississippi, denounced the notion as a reversion to royalty. "The practice instituted by Jefferson was more American than the old pomposities and cavalcadings between the White House and the Capitol," Williams said. On April 8, 1913—for the first time since November 22, 1800, when John Adams delivered his fourth annual message—a President of the United States rode the mile and a half from the White House to the Capitol for the purpose of addressing a joint session of Congress.

Wilson staged the appearance with predictable simplicity, arriving by automobile with only a Secret Service guard. He wore a black frock coat and light trousers, his cravat a gray four-in-hand. A small committee of Representatives greeted him, ushering him to Speaker Champ Clark's office for a moment while the Representatives took their places in the House chamber. Then the House doorkeeper stepped into the main aisle and announced, "The Vice President of the United States and members of the United States Senate." They filed in, the Senators sardining themselves on the benches in the first two rows, as Vice President Marshall went to a big armchair on the rostrum facing the crowd, to the Speaker's right. The gallery was packed with visitors who had requested tickets, the President's wife and three daughters, and members of the Cabinet, who were invited to attend informally on their own, so as not to give the appearance of a state occasion. Just before one o'clock, the President appeared in the chamber, escorted by members of each house; and everybody rose and applauded. Wilson shook hands with the Speaker and the Vice President before taking his stand at the Reading Clerk's desk. Speaker Clark formally introduced the President; and everybody applauded again. Wilson bowed.

The President began by stating his primary reason for delivering this message in person, which was his long-held belief in humanizing institutions. He said he wanted them to know that the President of the United States "is a person, not a mere department of the Government hailing Congress from some isolated island of jealous power, sending messages, not speaking naturally and with his own voice—that he is a human being trying to cooperate with other human beings in a common service." The audience applauded.

In a natural voice—stressing history over histrionics—Wilson explained that he had summoned the Congress to emphasize the essential need for tariff reform. This extraordinary session, he said, was a task laid upon him and his party that it had to perform promptly, "in order that the burden carried by the people under existing law may be lightened as soon as possible and in order, also, that the business interests of the country may not be kept too long in suspense as to what the fiscal changes are to be to which they will be required to adjust themselves." While industrial and commercial life had drastically changed in America, the tariff schedules had not; certain manufacturers were benefiting at the expense of consumers. The sooner rates were adjusted, Wilson said, "the sooner our men of business will be free to thrive by the law of nature (the nature of free business) instead of by the law of legislation and artificial arrangement."

"Consciously or unconsciously," Wilson told America's lawmakers, "we have built up a set of privileges and exemptions from competition behind which it was easy . . . to organize monopoly." He said it was necessary to "abolish everything that bears even the semblance of privilege or of any kind of artificial advantage, and put our business men and producers under the stimulation of a constant necessity to be efficient, economical, and enterprising, masters of competitive supremacy, better workers and merchants than any in the world." He insisted this was not only the best thing for American business in an increasingly global economy but also the right thing. His speech lasted nine minutes. Amid the applause, Wilson left the chamber.

In the car with his wife, on the way back to the White House, Wilson kept chuckling under his breath. When, at last, Ellen asked what he was laughing about, he said, "Wouldn't Teddy have been glad to think of that—I put one over on Teddy and am totally happy."

Doubtless, the speech got the better of Teddy Roosevelt, who never shook his contempt for Wilson. At a luncheon in Oyster Bay, during which TR made one snide remark after another about "Professor" Wilson, a New York newspaper editor took the former President to task, suggesting that Wilson also embraced progressive principles. "I am a little hard on Wilson," Roosevelt conceded. "What I object to about him is his mildness of method. I suppose, as a matter of fact," he said, thumping his chest, "Wilson is merely a less virile *me*."

Washington was agog over the precedents Wilson appeared to be breaking every day, and the very next afternoon he returned to the lion's den. With the eleven Democratic members of the Senate Finance Committee, he sat for an hour and a half around the hand-carved table in the middle of the President's Room. In a cloud of cigar smoke, the men strategized passage of the tariff bill, despite political opposition and the power of special interests. Wilson had always been persuasive; now the Senate was realizing that he could also be relentless in getting what he wanted. There had not been a systemic reduction of rates since 1857; and after months of working with Representatives Clark, Underwood, Palmer, and Glass, Wilson was not about to see this bill turn back on itself as the Payne-Aldrich bill had under Taft.

The protective tariff had played an important role in the economy of America, protecting its young industries against foreign competition; but over time, as monopolies evolved, it became, in the words of Treasury Secretary McAdoo, "a general tax on the entire population for the benefit of private industry." If a few vendors of a particular product conspired to fix its price even one cent below the foreign import price, they could continue to monopolize the domestic market and share the wealth among themselves. Wilson believed the reduction, if not the removal, of these tariffs would drive a stake into the heart of the various trusts—whether they controlled the manufacture and sale of steel rails, leather gloves, or sugar. The aim of his administration was to allow high duties on luxury items but to lower those on raw materials and necessities, optimally to no tariff.

Sugar, for example, cost less to produce in Puerto Rico or Cuba than it did in the United States, and the Louisiana planters claimed they would be ruined without tariff protection. The President, the only elected official with a national constituency, had to convince each Representative to look beyond the borders of his district and to consider the nation at large. The "whole art of statesmanship is the art of bringing the several parts of government into effective cooperation for the accomplishment of particular common objects," he had noted back when he was just a political scientist. And in order to turn theory into practice, Wilson had told one Congressman, he intended to play the part of the President as though he were a Prime Minister—"as much concerned with the guidance of legislation as with the just and orderly execution of the law." Wilson's appearance in the Capitol two days in a row expressed not only his belief that the two

branches could more effectively run the government when harnessed together but also that he intended to return to the President's Room often.
Not ten weeks after Wilson had taken his oath, the tariff bill sailed
through the House, where the Democrats enjoyed a 291–134 majority. Of
the five Democrats who opposed the bill, four came from Louisiana.

The Senate would be another matter, what with its fifty-one Democrats to forty-four Republicans (and one Progressive). To secure passage,
Wilson realized he would need sticks and carrots. Furnifold McLendel
Simmons was the ranking Democrat on the Finance Committee, an outspoken white supremacist and the powerful third-term Senator from
North Carolina. He was the presumed chair apparent of the committee—
until President Wilson questioned his ability to push through the Underwood bill that would lower tariffs. Simmons represented the conservative
wing of their party and was long opposed to the Progressive. With his
power threatened, Simmons changed his position, assuring Wilson that he
would support the reforms.

Wilson lured with patronage those Senators who staunchly defended
their state's crops and industries. After he spoke to his new friends in the
press corps of the disturbing power of lobbyists—what he called the "invisible government"—editorials and news reports incited public outcry
across the country. He regularly invited Senators to the White House; and
during one of his visits to the President's Room, he held twenty-three separate conferences. He asked that a special telephone be installed, linking
the Senate and the White House. Because the American Woolen Company
had become the only significant purchaser of wool in the country, he called
upon Attorney General McReynolds to investigate the legality of their
operations, to see that anti-trust laws were not being violated. The "college
professor" had obviously learned the lessons of politics he had taught for so
many years.

Summer descended upon Washington as the Senate tariff debate heated
up, turning into a partisan fight. "The last thing I ever think of doing is
giving up," Wilson wrote Mary Hulbert on June 22, 1913. "But, among
other things, this business means that I am to have no vacation." The
President called upon Congress to remain in session and sweat through
the summer with him. During several months of testimony and debate,
the Underwood-Simmons bill whittled down the basic tariff rates in the
United States from 40 percent to 25 percent. Many items would

get reduced to 0. The 56 percent tariff on woolens would be shrunk to one-third that amount, and the tariff on raw wool would go from 44 percent to 0; the President granted that the sugar tariff should not be immediately eliminated but reduced to 1 percent for a period of three years, after which there would be "free sugar."

In the fiscal year ending on June 30, 1913, the United States Treasury would have received $318 million from customs duties. With the new rates, that would drop to $270 million. The Administration, having to compensate for that shortfall, turned to the recently ratified Sixteenth Amendment to the Constitution, which provided Congress the "power to lay and collect taxes on incomes, from whatever source derived . . ."

The income tax was not new to America. Lincoln first imposed it in order to pay the Union army. It was, in fact, a redistribution of wealth, with the rich paying more than the poor. Congress had repealed it after the Civil War, but the tax reappeared in 1894 to deal with the nation's financial crisis. It provided relief to the agrarian West and South, where incomes lagged behind those in the industrial Northeast, until the Supreme Court declared it unconstitutional because it was not apportioned according to the states' populations. The new amendment overrode that stipulation, thus allowing for a progressive tax structure—with the lowest earners paying no tax while the highest would pay as much as 7 percent. That would affect less than 1 percent of the population but would, in fact, yield $71 million in its first year, more than offsetting losses from the reduced tariffs. The implementation of this new income tax was bundled into the Underwood-Simmons Revenue Act.

So long as the lawmakers were a captive audience that summer, Wilson took advantage of his momentum. On June 23, he returned to address another joint session of Congress—because of what he considered "a clear and imperative duty." Despite the oppressive summer heat, he insisted that "there are occasions of public duty when . . . the work to be done is so pressing and so fraught with big consequence that we know that we are not at liberty to weigh against it any point of personal sacrifice." The need for a new banking and currency system, he said, presented such an occasion. "We must have a currency . . . elastically responsive to sound credit . . . the normal ebb and flow of personal and corporate dealings," he said. "Our banking laws must mobilize reserves; must not permit the concentration anywhere in a few hands of the monetary resources of the country or their use for speculative purposes in such volume as to hinder or impede or stand in the way of other more legitimate, more fruitful uses." Wilson called for a national institution to keep those reserves of money flowing—an archipelago of Federal Reserve Banks.

Because of the inflexibility of the existing banking system, one in which banks across the country were beholden to the trust on Wall Street, the national economy had clogged five times since the Civil War, producing panics. Small rural banks and even the United States Treasury had found themselves at Wall Street's mercy, and a Congressional committee chaired by Representative Arsène Pujo was investigating the power of the bank trust. The Wilson Administration's philosophy was to decentralize the reserves by creating a government-supervised national bank for banks, with twelve branches scattered across the country.

Republicans especially fought this Federal Reserve legislation. As Secretary McAdoo recalled, "They said it was populistic, socialistic, half-baked, destructive, infantile, badly conceived, and unworkable." As the name-callers became educated to the intricacies of the bill, many realized the national economy would be strengthened because there would be more local control of credit and debt. As McAdoo analogized, "The country as a whole was like a town of wooden houses, where the only water for fighting fire was in barrels in back yards, except for one gigantic reservoir many miles away—too far away to be effective." Under the Wilson plan, there would be "twelve large and efficient reservoirs located at strategic points in the community itself," and there would be no need for the "ineffective water barrels in the back yards; the reservoirs are so near, and they are always full." Debate raged about the management of this bucket brigade.

In fact, a similar plan had been devised in 1910 at a secret meeting of the nation's most powerful bankers at the exclusive Jekyll Island Club, a Morgan playground off the coast of Georgia. These members of the trust had proposed a pre-emptive solution to the very problems Wilson now sought to fix—a central bank with regional branches, but one that was privately owned and under their control. John D. Rockefeller's son-in-law, Senator Nelson Aldrich, had presented the bill, and it faced crushing Democratic opposition. Now the President hoped to employ the solid structure of the concept but place it more under the authority of the people, by providing quasi-governmental oversight.

Wilson had discussed the problem for months with Treasury Secretary

McAdoo; Congressman Carter Glass, who was chairman of the House Committee on Banking and Currency; Dr. H. Parker Willis, a University of Chicago economist and adviser to that committee; and longtime advocate of reform Secretary Bryan. During one conversation, McAdoo ironed out a plan regarding interest on the money the government would advance to the Federal Reserve Banks: "What we ought to do," he suggested, "is to give the Federal Reserve Board the power to impose, from time to time, such rates of interest as in its judgment may be wise, or to charge no interest or circulation tax at all. This will make the arrangement flexible and responsive to the needs of the country." Wilson called upon his former Princeton colleague Professor Royal Meeker to poll the nation's leading economists on the state of banking.

After finding a mostly positive consensus, two bones of contention remained—one regarding the backing of the currency issued by the banks, the other regarding the composition of the central board of control. Wilson consulted Louis Brandeis. As he had done in helping forge the basics of the New Freedom, Brandeis articulated what he considered the basic principles of the plan, thus bolstering Wilson's proposals and confidence. First, he said, it was best to enact a "confidence-inspiring" currency bill at an early date, as a watered-down proposal would serve nobody. He said the "power to issue currency should be vested exclusively in Government officials," and that bankers needed government oversight. He told Wilson that whatever bill got passed would have little effect "unless we are able to curb the money trust, and to remove the uneasiness among business men due to its power." Finally, he said the "conflict between the policies of the Administration and the desires of the financiers and of big business, is an irreconcilable one. Concession to the big business interests must in the end prove futile." While the Administration had to consider carefully the recommendations of the banking trust, it was dangerous to heed its advice despite its technical proficiency. This bill was meant to win the public trust, not woo the banking trust. Two days after conferring with Brandeis, Wilson began drafting his speech to Congress, incorporating all the lawyer's ideas.

Brandeis's arguments boiled down to the need for federal supervision. Representative Carter Glass disagreed, believing the banks should have representation; Senator Robert L. Owen of Oklahoma, the chairman of the Committee on Banking and Finance and a longtime Bryan supporter, felt otherwise. McAdoo sought a compromise, but the President had made up his mind. This chronic problem demanded a bold remedy of "public participation and direction"—government control.

When a number of liberal Midwestern bankers protested, their supporter Carter Glass could envision only one unlikely means of turning the President around. He arranged an audience for the financiers to sit directly across from Wilson at his desk. Each banker made his best argument regarding representation on the governing board of the Federal Reserve, after which Wilson turned toward the most vehement of them and quietly asked, "Will one of you gentlemen tell me in what civilized country of the earth there are important government boards of control on which private interests are represented?" The question hung there in silence until Wilson posed a second question: "Which of you gentlemen thinks the railroads should select members of the Interstate Commerce Commission?" The bankers were struck dumb. Carter Glass converted to Wilson's position before they had even exited the office.

One last obstruction threatened passage of the bill, with the Bryan liberals withholding their support unless this condition was met. It involved the Federal Reserve notes—the actual issuance of currency—as being the "obligations of the United States" instead of the regional reserve banks issuing them. Without the United States Treasury standing behind the currency, Bryan felt this bill should not even be presented to Congress, for fear that its omission might antagonize their own party members and even jeopardize the tariff bill. In a meeting with Wilson, the former standard-bearer of the party went even farther. "I called his attention to the fact that our party had been committed by Jefferson and Jackson and by recent platforms to the doctrine that the issue of money is a function of government and should not be surrendered to banks," Bryan recalled. Wilson considered all the opposition—including that of Carter Glass, who felt the government's issuing currency was an unnecessary obligation. The next time Bryan saw Wilson, he learned that "the two difficulties which had seemed insurmountable had been removed."

In the end, Wilson had confected this bill by melding idealism with pragmatism, and nobody questioned that its success or failure should redound upon him. Wilson himself only questioned the timing. "Shall we hasten to change the tariff laws and then be laggards about making it possible and easy for the country to take advantage of the change?" he asked the joint session of Congress. "There can be only one answer to that question. We must act now, at whatever sacrifices to ourselves," he said, landing hard on the word "now" and clenching his jaw. "I should be recreant to my deepest convictions of public obligation did I not press it upon you with solemn and urgent insistence." Opposition sprang: House Minority Leader James Robert Mann criticized Wilson for showing no interest in reaching out for bipartisan support and, just as bad, for addressing the Congress as though he were "a schoolmaster telling fourth-grade school children to be good." A hard fight lay ahead.

After only four months in office, Wilson was already feeling the pressures. With the President's having set such an accelerated pace out of the gate, Colonel House cautioned him to conserve his strength. Wilson would not slacken, and he was already speaking of "the loneliness of his position" in a way that House found "saddening." Having worked behind the scenes on all the President's major initiatives, House deserted Washington for a long vacation. Wilson had no such luxury.

He had intended to spend the summer with his family in Cornish, New Hampshire, a charming village on the Connecticut River, with an active colony of artists for Ellen—chief among them sculptor Augustus Saint-Gaudens, painter Maxfield Parrish, and Impressionist Robert Vonnoh, whose work had greatly influenced hers. Based on little more than photographs, Wilson signed a two-summer lease on Harlakenden, a stately Georgian house that belonged to American writer Winston Churchill. Surrounded by two hundred acres, it offered spacious but simple living and a view of the river and Mount Ascutney. Work in Congress demanded Wilson's presence in Washington—"I can't be cool and comfortable at Cornish while Congress perspires here all summer at my request," he said. He would have to vacation around the legislators' schedule; but he insisted upon his family's leaving him behind—especially his wife, who had been drawn into a maelstrom from the moment she had arrived in Washington.

In addition to the endless succession of afternoon receptions for one hundred and evening banquets for fifty, over which she had to preside, Ellen Wilson imposed additional demands upon herself, the only way she could justify her new role. Unlike many of her predecessors, she had no interest in the frills of being First Lady. A true disciple of the Social Gospel, however, she became the first President's wife to embrace the humanitarian potential of her position, the ability to draw attention to social injustices. "I wonder how anyone who reaches middle age can bear it," she once told a cousin, "if she cannot feel . . . that whatever mistakes she may have made, she has on the whole lived for others and not for herself." And so, Ellen Wilson promptly made it her mission to inspect government buildings, including the Post Office Department and the Government Printing Office, where she found working conditions for women substandard—unsanitary lavatories and insufficient light and fresh air. She also took it upon herself to visit the city's slums, leading members of Congress through squalid alleys right outside their office doors and then urging remedial legislation for the Negroes who lived there.

And Ellen made the White House a home for her husband. She catered to all his needs, still serving as his most discriminating editor and adviser, and encouraging the professorial evenings of old, during which he might study and write and then recite poetry or sing around the piano with his daughters. She maintained Sunday as his day of observance, filled only with family and a restorative ride by automobile or on horseback. In accordance with Dr. Grayson's advice, she kept his meals simple—plain fish and meat courses, a vegetable and potatoes, a salad, and ice cream—served at seven, he in black tie, as was the custom of the house. Never much of a wine drinker, he occasionally allowed himself a "wee dram"—a shot of Scotch whisky. Congress allotted almost $10,000 for the conversion of the third floor of the White House—formerly attic space—for family use, which she spent creating more guest rooms and baths. She took down from the second-floor walls the dark green burlap and animal heads of the Roosevelt era and substituted light pastels and "craft" fabrics. She decorated the master suite in Delft blue and white, its furniture in chintz. The adjoining sitting room housed the Lincoln Bed. Ellen was able to obtain a further appropriation from Congress to remodel the gardens flanking the South Portico. She asked Princeton's landscape architect Beatrix Farrand to design the East Garden—which would feature low hedges and a rectangular lily pond in the center. For the West Garden, she maintained her initial concept of long rows of rosebushes, which not only afforded a pleasant view from her bedroom window but also provided Woodrow with a more becoming "President's walk" from the residence to his office. It became a permanent feature of the White House.

Even though Ellen wanted to spend the summer by her husband's side,

Woodrow insisted his worry over her health in the Washington heat would distract him more than her absence. On the train to New Hampshire, Ellen went to her berth and cried. She was hardly gone before Woodrow wrote the first of that summer's many lachrymose letters to her, explaining his growing understanding of his life in the highest office in the land, where duty superseded all other considerations. "I cannot choose as an individual what I shall do," he wrote on June 29; "I must always choose as President, ready to guard at every turn and in every possible way the success of what I have to do for the people. Apparently the little things count quite as much as the big in this strange business of leading opinion and securing action." Indeed, he found, "The President is a superior kind of slave," and somebody was always watching his every move, analyzing his every gesture, resenting his ever enjoying a holiday.

Wilson at least hoped to have Independence Day off, especially as he had already declined an appearance at Gettysburg; but, he wired Ellen on June 28, "FIND SO LONG AS I AM PRESIDENT, I CAN BE NOTHING ELSE." The next day he wrote to explain that Pennsylvania Congressman A. Mitchell Palmer had informed him that that year's commemoration at the battlefield was to be "no ordinary celebration," as it would mark the semicentenary of the great turning point of the Civil War. "Both blue and grey are to be there," he explained to Ellen. "It is to celebrate the end of . . . all strife between the sections." The President's absence, he noted, would be publicly resented. "It would be suggested that he is a Southerner and out of sympathy with the occasion. In short, it would be more than a passing mistake; it would amount to a serious blunder."

Washington, D.C., became a ghost town, the houses on the best residential streets emptying of all who could escape the summer torpor, the furniture in the great rooms of the White House all covered in white sheets. Feeling "marooned," Wilson prevailed upon Tumulty and Dr. Grayson to move into the Executive Mansion, and he found them good company. The former was married with small children, whom he joined on weekends on the New Jersey Shore; Grayson remained the President's boon companion and constant medical consort. They spent practically all their free time together—dining, theatergoing twice a week, even attending church together. Dr. Grayson prescribed a daily dose of golf.

"An ineffectual attempt to put an elusive ball into an obscure hole with implements ill-adapted to the purpose" is how Wilson delighted in describing the pastime. And perhaps because of the devotion, concentration, difficulty, and even prayer it required, golf became his second religion. He played every day that weather and work permitted. Wilson had supreme powers of concentration, and he loved impossible challenges; but he never became expert at the sport—in part because of his bad eye, which limited his peripheral vision. And so he played a methodical game that compensated for the ocular handicap—short, perfectly straight shots—though once he required twenty-six strokes on a single hole. Seldom did his score rise above 100, because upon reaching three digits, he was inclined to pack up his clubs and quit. One day at the Piping Rock Club in Locust Valley on Long Island, he shot 146, and even admitted as much to a reporter. He liked to play on the less exclusive courses around Washington—especially when they included a relaxing drive across the Potomac to Virginia. He was extremely selective about those in his party, as he forbade any talk of business and never played a second time with anybody who violated the rule. "Each stroke requires your whole attention and seems the most important thing in life," he wrote Edith Reid that summer. "I can by that means get perfect diversion of my thoughts for an hour or so at the same time that I am breathing the pure out-of-doors." His scorecard was not a barometer of his ability—which never changed—but of his mental state, the ease with which he could sink the ball into the hole suggesting how free from his responsibilities he had become. No President before or since played as much golf in the White House as Woodrow Wilson.

The President and his physician found slight relief from the heat on Capitol Hill by cruising down the Potomac and Chesapeake Bay on the Presidential yacht, the *Mayflower*. They spent a sweltering July 3 in Yorktown. Wilson and Grayson eluded the Secret Service agents by saying they were going ashore with the captain of the ship and several sailors. But once the small motor launch had reached the wharf, the two men lost the others and spent the day wandering the sleepy streets of the old town by themselves. They visited the local courthouse and the battlefield and continued up the York River to see the farm that had once been Washington's headquarters—crawling through brambles, shooing away bees, and encountering an angry bull along the way. The locals paid no attention to their visitors until a twelve-year-old girl saw them and said, "Excuse me, sir, but you certainly do remind me of the pictures of President Wilson."

He returned to Washington, only to leave by train early the next morning with Tumulty for Gettysburg, Pennsylvania. There, exactly fifty years prior, Union and Confederate soldiers had fought the costliest battle of the Civil War. The fifty-one thousand casualties (nearly eight thousand deaths) were almost equally divided; but, in retrospect, it proved to be the turning point of the war, as the Confederates steadily retreated over the next two years. In November of 1863, Lincoln delivered his deathless 272-word address, dedicating a portion of the battlefield as a final resting place for those who gave their lives there. In the half century since the battle, Gettysburg came to represent the reuniting of the nation. The symbol was so important that the Congress appropriated more than $2 million to mount a reunion, offering to transport any Civil War veteran from anywhere in the country and to feed and house him during this three-day "Peace Jubilee."

More than fifty thousand veterans flocked to the small town, proudly wearing uniforms and decorations and waving flags. Each man was provided with a cot and bedding in a 280-acre camp of eight-man tents. In the scorching heat, thousands gathered for speeches under a gigantic big top, walked the battlefield, and healed old wounds. The most compelling moment of the reunion came when two small teams of white-whiskered survivors of Pickett's Charge faced each other and shook hands, reaching across the same stone wall each side had once fought to overtake. Goodwill seemed restored, but so little had been resolved: slavery had been abolished, but regionalism and racism in America were as rampant as ever. The survivors looked to Wilson for inspiration.

The world would little note what he said there. The President's entrance into the great tent brought the crowd of ten thousand to its feet. In a black frock coat, he put his top hat down and stood without a podium before the assembly. Holding his text in his left hand, he delivered a peculiarly hollow speech—full of ethereal questions ("Who stands ready to act again and always in the spirit of this day of reunion and hope and patriotic fervor?") while offering few concrete answers. He called upon his countrymen to serve "the people themselves, the great and the small, without class or difference of kind or race or origin." That was as close as he got to the underlying themes of the terrible war that had torn the nation apart. Within a half hour of his arrival, Wilson had returned to his train. He left behind a stillness at Gettysburg—which, in some ways, was his intention.

The nation dedicated to the proposition that all men were created equal was, in fact, built atop an active fault of discrimination. A deep fissure of intolerance remained. State laws, especially in the South, went a long way toward keeping the races apart; but even Northern states were enacting anti-intermarriage statutes. The purportedly color-blind Civil Service had long operated under the "rule of three," by which an employer was able to select from the trio of top applicants, allowing him to bypass Negro candidates. Many in the white majority were unable to accept the concept of all races being on equal footing; and where statutes proved inadequate, some took the law into their own hands. In parts of America, racial violence was so common, Negroes instinctively kept their distance from whites and held their tongues. Lynchings in America occurred weekly. As President, Wilson wished to promote racial progress—equal opportunities and peaceful coexistence—by shocking the social system as little as possible. With both impatient blacks and intolerant whites clamoring for action, there seemed only one solution that might avert upheaval and allow social evolution to take its course.

There were already two Americas. Negro activist James Weldon Johnson wrote of such commonplace practices as the refusal to tip one's hat to a colored woman or to address a Negro as "Mister" as more than trivialities; he added that "they connote the whole system of race prejudice, hatred, and injustice; their roots go to the very core of the whole matter." Such mere trifles, he said, declared that "there is no common ground on which we can stand." At the same time, Agriculture Secretary David Houston, a highly regarded educator and political scientist, was considering the problem of discrimination against the Japanese in California and how they rated more favorably than Negroes—who were as a rule, he would write years later, "of low mental capacity and lazy." So it hardly took anyone aback when Postmaster General Burleson had raised a prickly policy matter at one of the first Cabinet meetings back in the spring: Burleson wanted to segregate white and Negro employees not just in the Postal Service but in all departments of the government.

Many Negroes worked in the railway mail service, he explained, often in the same car with white men. In those instances, he suggested, it was presumed that the white men would outwork the black and resentments would grow. Furthermore, Burleson said, "It is very unpleasant for them to work in a car with negroes where it is almost impossible to have different drinking vessels and different towels, or places to wash."

More than any of Wilson's Cabinet members, Burleson understood the practice of politics; and he had done his due diligence. He had spoken with African American leaders, including organizer Bishop Alexander Walters of the African Methodist Episcopal Zion Church, who, he claimed, endorsed the idea of separating the races. Josephus Daniels wrote in his diary that Burleson said "he had the highest regard for the negro and wished to help him in every way possible, but that he believed segregation was best for the negro and best for the Service." Burleson went even farther that day, asking the President to reconsider even the appointment of Negroes to midlevel clerical offices—including the Register of the Treasury, which a black man had held for years.

Segregation was not new to Washington, having flourished since the Roosevelt Administration. TR may have invited Booker T. Washington to dine in the White House, but he was publicly chastised for it and decades would pass before another African American would find a place at the White House table. Under Taft the dining room for White House employees divided along a color line. So did the Census Bureau. In the few Washington departments that hired Negroes, many worked without question in areas apart from white workers. Some divisions simply became known as "Negro colonies." A Harvard- and Howard-educated attorney named Robert H. Terrell spent a few years in the Treasury Department before Taft appointed him to the Municipal Court of the District of Columbia, making him the nation's first Negro judge; government office lunchrooms refused to serve him or other equally distinguished black men. Negroes who sought equal treatment at lunch counters were only inviting violence.

Legalized segregation—"Jim Crow" laws—seemed a logical way to avoid friction, as it would keep blacks and whites literally from having to rub shoulders. Fifty years after Gettysburg, it seemed unimaginable to most Southerners that white men might have to serve under a black boss. Wilson was still inclined to let each Secretary run his department as he saw fit; and so, on the two racial issues before him, he rendered a split decision: he permitted Burleson and McAdoo to segregate their departments; and he proceeded to appoint a Negro, Adam E. Patterson, as the Treasury Register.

That settled nothing, as each announcement incited intense reaction. Although Wilson believed the purity and fidelity of the white women of the South were its very backbone, he did not subscribe to the primal fear–mongering of many other Confederates. His Johns Hopkins colleague Thomas Dixon, the author of the Ku Klux Klan trilogy, wrote Wilson that he was "heartsick" over the appointment, that unless he withdrew Patterson's name, "the South can never forgive this. . . . The establishment of Negro men over white women employees of the Treasury Dept. has in the minds of many thoughtful men & women long been a serious offense against the cleanness of our social life." Dixon asked Wilson to "purge Washington of this iniquity" and withdraw the appointment.

"I do not think you know what is going on down here," an exasperated Wilson replied, trying to explain the shifting mores in a city where the black population could not be ignored. "We are handling the force of colored people who are now in the departments in just the way in which they ought to be handled." At Treasury, for example, the President was standing by his appointment, as that particular office was being reconfigured into an all-black unit, one of several such divisions there: "I am trying to handle these matters with the best judgment but in the spirit of the whole country," he wrote with some impatience, "though with entire comprehension of the considerations which certainly do not need to be pointed out to me." Wilson considered this plan of putting "certain bureaus and sections of the service in the charge of negroes" a thoughtful means of "rendering them more safe in their possession of office and less likely to be discriminated against."

As Burleson's proposals had portended, Southerners in Congress felt this was their moment to rise again. Senators James Vardaman of Mississippi, Benjamin Tillman of South Carolina, and Hoke Smith of Georgia all announced their refusal to support not only Patterson but any Negro who would be in a position to boss white women. A gracious Patterson requested that Wilson withdraw his name, which he did.

In the meantime, McAdoo and Burleson segregated their departments with all deliberate speed. They supervised the creation of separate but ostensibly equal work, lunch, and lavatory facilities. That summer, Robert N. Wood, president of the United Colored Democracy of the State of New York, wrote Wilson that his people deeply resented the segregation of clerks in the Civil Service throughout the federal government—

> . . . not at all because we are particularly anxious to eat in the same room or use the same soap and towels that white people use, but because we see in the separation . . . of the races in the matter of soup

and soap the beginning of a movement to deprive the colored man entirely of soup and soap, to eliminate him wholly from the Civil Service of the United States. For just as soon as there is a lunch-room or a work-room which the colored man may not enter in a government building, there will be separate tasks assigned the colored men and these will be, as the promoters of segregation have declared, the tasks which white men do not want.

Even Booker T. Washington—"the great accommodator," considered an "Uncle Tom" by uprising black leaders—wrote Oswald Garrison Villard of the NAACP that he had recently spent several days in Washington and that he had "never seen the colored people so discouraged and bitter as they are at the present time."

In a letter signed by Villard, Director of Publicity W. E. B. Du Bois, and President Moorfield Storey, the NAACP vigorously protested the new government policy. "Never before has the Federal Government discriminated against its civilian employees on the ground of color," they wrote. States drafting discriminatory laws were one thing; segregating federal buildings in the District of Columbia was quite another. "It has set the colored people apart as if mere contact with them were contamination," they wrote.

Wilson had not intended such a result, as he did not equate segregation with subjugation. Rather, he considered it a way for Negroes to elevate themselves, getting a foothold in American institutions so that they could start assimilating. He thought the new forces of black workers in the federal government first had to occupy the same buildings as whites before they could share the same rooms. Gradually, he believed, proximity would breed familiarity, and, in time, harmony. Powerful bigots saw segregation as a means to keep the black man down; but Wilson viewed it "with the idea that the friction, or rather the discontent and uneasiness, which had prevailed in many of the departments would thereby be removed. It is as far as possible from being a movement *against* the negroes. I sincerely believe it to be in their interest." While his Cabinet members had put the policy in motion, Wilson stood behind it and owned it. "My own feeling," he told Villard, "is by putting certain bureaus and sections of the service in the charge of negroes we are rendering them more safe in their possession of office and less likely to be discriminated against." Or so he had convinced himself.

"I hope that you will try to see the real situation down here," an exasperated Wilson tried to explain to Oswald Villard. He wished Villard understood the hatred that festered in the hearts of so many Southerners. Wilson suggested that left to his own devices, he would not have instituted these new measures; but finding what he considered a middle ground, he believed a period of tranquillity would open more doors of opportunity for the Negroes. "I believe that by the slow pressure of argument and persuasion the situation may be changed and a great many things done eventually which now seem impossible," Wilson said. "But they can not be done, either now or at any future time, if a bitter agitation is inaugurated and carried to its natural ends." He appealed to Villard and the NAACP to "aid in holding things at a just and cool equipoise until I can discover whether it is possible to work out anything or not." Wilson believed there was so much intolerance in the nation just then that it would take "one hundred years to eradicate this prejudice"; if they could all avoid stirring emotions with incendiary talk and rely on evolution, they might be able to avoid revolution.

For Wilson, segregation remained secondary to the advancement of his New Freedom, though both matters were bound together. "It would be hard to make any one understand the delicacy and difficulty of the situation I find existing here with regard to the colored people," the President of six months wrote Villard. In the matter of appointments, he explained, "I find myself absolutely blocked by the sentiment of Senators; not alone Senators from the South, by any means, but Senators from various parts of the country."

Villard sympathized with Wilson's position, but he did not empathize. "I believe that as with your most immediate predecessors," he wrote, "the time will come when you will find it necessary to go ahead and do what is right without considering their feelings." Villard believed the President was not a bigot, that he supported the advancement of the Negro; and that made it all the more frustrating to see him knuckling under to the Southern Senators. In a subsequent conversation with journalist John Palmer Gavit, Wilson said he had to deal with a Congress dominated by men of such fundamental beliefs; and Gavit understood that the President's opposition to such views "would certainly precipitate a conflict which would put a complete stop to any legislative program." In that moment, then, it seemed the only way to further the New Freedom was on the back of the Negro.

By the end of the year, the Post Office Department and the office of the Auditor for the Post Office were segregated; and soon the District's City Post Office would establish separate windows for Negro patrons as well as the personnel who manned them. At the office of the Auditor of the Navy, screens separated white workers from black, the latter group no longer finding their lavatory on the same floor but in the basement. The Bureau of Engraving and Printing followed suit. Secretary McAdoo proudly removed every white from the Register's Division, not realizing, as Villard wrote Wilson, "that this division will immediately be called the 'nigger division' and that the precedent thus established will be of the utmost danger to the colored people long after the motive has been forgotten and Mr. McAdoo has disappeared from public life." Civil Service positions now required photographs, which tempted some employers simply to overlook the "rule of three." The number of positions available to Negroes, along with the level of those jobs, went in the same direction as their lavatories.

Despite the opposition from the bloc of bigoted Southern Senators, Wilson did repeatedly nominate Negroes to refill positions that they had traditionally held—including the reappointment of Judge Robert H. Terrell to the Municipal Court. In tangling with a Senator or even Speaker Champ Clark, Wilson flatly explained the promise he had made to the black community and that he was honor-bound. He expected equality in all the facilities within the federal buildings.

In the early fall of 1913, the NAACP conducted an investigation of the segregation of colored employees within the government departments. Villard sent the results to Wilson, as he had requested. At the Bureau of Engraving and Printing, the investigator—NAACP Secretary May Childs Nerney—reported that colored women who had dined for nine years with white women had been relegated to a separate table. At the Post Office Department there was an attractive dining room for the white employees but none for the black, which some excused with the argument that there were no restaurants in Washington that would serve blacks and so neither should the government be expected to. Treasury boasted 270 colored employees; but May Nerney found many had been consigned to areas of the building that were poorly lighted and ventilated. Those segregated, she added, were regarded as "a people set apart, almost as lepers. Instead of allaying race prejudice . . . it has simply emphasized it." Because Negroes could now advance only so far, they seemed to have lost their competitive drive. She felt many Negro workers would look for employment elsewhere. Jim Crow, some feared, would next overtake public transportation. Wilson wrote Villard that he intended to right the wrongs within the policy but not to change the policy itself.

As McAdoo asserted in a letter to Villard, "There is no 'segregation issue' in the Treasury Department." He contended that white women had long complained of having to sit at desks with colored men. His personal feelings articulated the current administration's policy: "I shall not be a party to the enforced and unwelcome juxtaposition of white and negro employees when it is unnecessary and avoidable without injustice to anybody, and when such enforcement would serve only to engender race animosities detrimental to the welfare of both races and injurious to the public service." Protesters across the country were already organizing that summer, and an anti-segregation petition with twenty thousand signatures would soon land on the President's desk. In just a few months, Wilson had become entangled in what journalist Gavit would call "the most difficult and embarrassing and dangerous subject" before him—what was merely the culmination of "the crimes and hypocrisies of three centuries."

Wilson managed to find relief in Cornish a few times that summer. The family made time to take long drives together through the New Hampshire countryside; and at night they sat on the terrace, under the stars, as Woodrow regaled them with stories of life in "hectic" Washington. They often entertained neighboring artists; and one night actress Marie Dressler, who summered across the river in Windsor, Vermont, came to perform an evening of songs and stories. But the Wilsons most appreciated their time alone, especially as they announced Jessie's engagement to Frank Sayre that July. Wilson heartily approved of his future son-in-law, especially as he had converted to the Democratic Party and—reminiscent of her father—was giving up the practice of law for a career in academia, starting as an assistant to President Harry Garfield of Williams College.

Harlakenden had an artist's studio, where Ellen painted every day, creating some of her most accomplished canvases to date. Her landscapes had become slightly more Impressionistic, revealing looser brushwork and genuine mastery of composition and color. Robert Vonnoh called Ellen "a real artist" and declared that if she continued, her work would become "really *very* distinguished." In fact, five of her paintings from the summer would be part of an exhibition of the Association of Women Painters and

Sculptors in New York that fall. In reviewing her work, *The New York Times* would say, "Mrs. Wilson is a serious art student and she observed in nature aspects that appeal to the lover of outdoor life." Three of the pictures sold in the $100 range.

As in the earliest days of their courtship—and through thirty years of periodic separations—Woodrow and Ellen still corresponded copiously when they were apart. The duties of office restricted him from writing more than twice a week. Although his letters were largely about his work, his passion still permeated them. He wrote his wife of twenty-eight years that his "dearest indulgence" that summer was in occasionally daydreaming of her beauty and charm. "I adore you! No President but myself ever had *exactly* the right sort of wife! I am certainly the most fortunate man alive!" he declared.

Ellen's feelings ran just as deep, and she sublimated them by immersing herself in family and her artwork. She said she felt like "a soldier's wife," as she suffered through Woodrow's absences. "I *idolize* you," she wrote him, "—I love you till it *hurts*." Ellen passed much of the time without Woodrow by reading his letters from the White House to their three daughters. "And although she still skipped the 'sacred parts,'" remembered Nell, then twenty-three, "we knew by the tender pride in her face that after all the years together they remained the poetic messages of a lover."

Midsummer, Ellen could endure the separation no longer. Accompanied by Nell, she braved the steamy twenty-hour journey to Washington to pay a surprise visit. Woodrow's obvious elation alone made the entire journey worthwhile. He looked tired, strained as he was marshaling votes for his two sweeping economic bills; but he was rejuvenated having Ellen by his side again. They were both amused when Secretary McAdoo called on the President that night and, upon seeing Nell, invited her to play tennis with him the next day. Within a few days of Ellen's arrival, Dr. Grayson encouraged her return to Cornish because of the overwhelming heat and Woodrow's concern about her.

In September, New Jersey Democrats held a primary election, and Wilson took the train to Princeton so that he could vote. Away only six months, he already felt strangely detached from his home of so many years. With a few minutes to kill, he walked through Nassau Hall, only to learn that a crowd was gathering out front. Wishing to avoid a spectacle,

Wilson asked a young man whether a certain back door was unlocked, which would allow for an unobserved exit. Strangely, the man misinterpreted Wilson's inquiry as interest in seeing the president of the college, who was then at home. The fellow raced to inform him, and in a moment, Jack Hibben was on horseback, galloping to Nassau Hall. Flushed with anticipation, he found his former intimate, who had spurned him for years now. "I was told, Mr. President, that you were looking for me," he said. Offering a cold smile but not his hand, Wilson replied, "No, no, you are mistaken." And with that, he turned toward the station, adding, "Good afternoon, Sir." Before boarding the train, Wilson apologized to a member of his small party, explaining, "The man who stopped and spoke to me was my friend. I did more to make him than I did for any other person in the world. I unbosomed my very soul to him. And in the crucial moment of my life, he turned against me. I can never forgive him."

Washington had become Wilson's home now, legislative battles and all. "I of course find a real zest in it all," he wrote Edith Reid. "Hard as it is to nurse Congress along and stand ready to play a part of guidance in anything that turns up, great or small, it is all part of something infinitely great and worth while, and I am content to labour at it to the finish." In the late afternoon of September 9, 1913, the Senate passed his tariff bill, almost entirely along partisan lines. Louisiana's Senators—protecting sugar and cotton—were the only two Democrats to vote against it; and the two most Progressive Republicans (including Robert "Fighting Bob" La Follette of Wisconsin) voted for it. Looking back on the five months in which this bill had been kicked around the floor of the Capitol, opposition Senator Albert B. Cummins of Iowa said that the Congress had surrendered its primacy to "a single will." He told the press that he intended to read the writings of "the man who has more influence in the Congress of the United States than any man ever before had. I refer to Woodrow Wilson."

At nine o'clock on the night of October 3, 1913, fifty guests in evening clothes—including the Congressional leaders and most of the Cabinet—gathered around the President's desk in the Oval Office. A buoyant Wilson entered to applause and took his seat, the tariff measure printed on parchment awaiting his signature. He gilded the ceremony by introducing what would become a Presidential tradition for future historic signings: he autographed the bill with two different gold pens—one for his first name, one for his last—which he presented to Congressman Underwood and Senator Simmons.

"I have had the accomplishment of something like this at heart ever since I was a boy," he told those assembled, "and I know men standing around me who can say the same thing—who have been waiting to see the things done which it was necessary to do in order that there might be justice in the United States." Referencing Shakespeare's *Henry V*, the President said, "If it be a sin to covet honour, then am I the most offending soul alive." He did not choreograph this occasion to pat the men on their backs so much as to push them forward. Their job was only half done. "We are now about to take the second step," he said, ". . . in setting the business of this country free." The House had already passed the currency bill, and now he urged its passage through the Senate.

"How profoundly I thank God for giving you the chance to win such victories," Ellen wrote from Cornish, "—to help the world so greatly;—for letting you work for Him on a *large* stage;—one worthy of the splendid combination of qualities with which He endowed you. . . . It has been the most remarkable life history I ever even *read* about,—and to think *I* have *lived* it with you. I wonder if I am dreaming, and will wake up and find myself married to—a bank clerk,—say!"

Into the fall of 1913, the subject of banks consumed most of Wilson's waking hours. And on September 18, his audacious currency bill—the Federal Reserve legislation, with its restructuring of the nation's banking system—passed the House by a vote of 287 to 85. Forty-eight Republicans supported the President while only three Democrats opposed him. Outside the Capitol, wealthy conservatives quickly weighed in. The president of the National City Bank suggested that Federal Reserve notes would hardly be worth the paper they were printed on; railroad tycoon James J. Hill pronounced the proposal "socialistic"; a Yale economist said American gold would seek investment in Europe and massive inflation would descend; Republican leader James Mann had already denounced the entire plan but now suggested it was a moot point, as none of the 7,500 national banks would even enter the Federal Reserve System.

Seven Democrats and five Republicans sat on the Senate Banking and Currency Committee, and it came as a great surprise when one of the majority, Gilbert M. Hitchcock of Nebraska, announced he had so many objections to the bill that he joined the opposition. A Democratic colleague, James A. Reed of Missouri, followed. That gave the Republicans the edge in keeping the bill from ever leaving their committee. Then Democratic Senator James A. O'Gorman of New York, mindful of his constituents on Wall Street, joined forces. Former Senator Nelson Aldrich trotted out his old plan of a central bank. Thus began, said Vice President Thomas R. Marshall, "the most illuminating and exhaustive discussion of a public question ever held in the Senate of the United States."

Not forgetting the great debates of Clay, Calhoun, and Webster, Marshall said the next five months saw "a practical history of all the banking systems of the world; of all the debts, assets and incomes of all the races of the world; of their armies, their navies, their taxes." Through it all, Wilson maintained his equanimity, though he fumed in private. "Why *should* public men, senators of the United States, have to be led and stimulated to what all the country knows to be their duty!" he rhetorically asked Mary Hulbert. Wilson repeatedly convened with his party's dissenters, separately and together, as well as with Republican members of the committee, winning over one mind at a time. With the able support of Colonel House, McAdoo, and Bryan, he steadily plied his powers of persuasion, arguing that structural change was needed immediately. The off-year elections in early November signaled that Progressivism was still in the air; and one by one, Democrats wandered back into the party fold. Bankers—especially those outside New York—began to embrace the banking bill. Even the final Republican arguments in early December felt stale.

On December 19, 1913, the Senate passed the bill 54 to 34. Every Democrat present, along with six Republicans and one Progressive, voted aye. With a Christmas holiday beckoning, it took only three days of conferences to reconcile the bill with the House version. And on December 23, the President held another signing ceremony in his office, surrounded by his family as well as the officials who had contributed to the bill. For this occasion, he had purchased three gold pens, which he handed to Congressman Glass, Senator Owen, and Secretary McAdoo. He spoke for a few minutes, expressing his belief that, on the heels of the tariff bill, this act "furnishes the machinery for free and elastic and uncontrolled credits, put at the disposal of the merchants and manufacturers of this country for the first time in fifty years." Wilson could not find the words to express his "deep emotions of gratitude" at being part of something so beneficial to the business of America.

It was a profoundly emotional time for Wilson in other ways as well. Only weeks earlier, on Tuesday, November 25, 1913, Jessie Woodrow Wilson had married Francis Bowes Sayre in the East Room of the White House. The bride had hoped for a small and informal wedding; but with the President's soaring popularity in Washington, that became impossible. Four hundred guests—Cabinet members, Senators and Representatives, Supreme Court Justices, and diplomats, along with friends and family of the wedding couple, gathered in the great salon. Just before 4:30, Sayre and his groomsmen (one of whom was Charles Evans Hughes, Jr., son of an Associate Justice) descended the stairway and entered the East Room, where Dr. Sylvester Beach, the Wilsons' pastor in Princeton, and Sayre's brother, a minister, would perform a combined Episcopalian and Presbyterian ceremony.

The procession of attendants entered to the musical accompaniment of the Marine Band, resplendent in scarlet. When all were in place, a bugle heralded the entrance of the President, who was dressed in a dark gray cutaway. Her arm linked through his, the bride wore a white satin dress of her own design, with a long veil and a train three yards in length. To the traditional strains of *Lohengrin*, they walked to the raised platform that had been erected before the great east window. This makeshift chancel was flanked by two large blue vases, filled with gigantic clusters of white lilies. When Dr. Beach asked "who giveth this woman," the President stepped forward and placed his daughter's hand in that of the groom.

The wedding party received guests in the Blue Room, and refreshments were served in the dining room. As there was a $1,000 reward to any journalist who could report on the newlyweds' honeymoon plans, they had prearranged a getaway in Joseph Tumulty's car from the south entrance of the White House. Before they left, Jessie stood halfway up the main staircase and threw her bouquet, right into the hands of her sister Nell. When the festivities had wound down, Woodrow placed his arm across Ellen's shoulders and drew her close as they walked wistfully to the elevator. "I know; it was a wedding, not a funeral," Ellen said to some of the relatives who remained, "but you must forgive us—this is the first break in the family."

And then a second shoe dropped. Over the last few months, Secretary McAdoo, known to his friends as Mac, had become a familiar presence in the White House. The President increasingly relied upon him; and, in time, the young widower frequently appeared during off-hours, calling on Miss Eleanor, as he referred to Nell, to join him for tennis or horseback riding. They enjoyed dancing together at social events; and he soon became a regular visitor in the evenings, hoping they might have a chance to sit alone in the Green Room. Often he would walk with Miss Eleanor to the Washington Monument, where they would sit and watch the sunset. Although she was the most frivolous of the Wilson daughters, McAdoo found her unusually well-informed and opinionated—as she would be, having sat at her father's dinner table for twenty-three years. "It was not long before I discovered that my interest in her was more than platonic," McAdoo later recalled. For a while, he kept his feelings to himself. He was twice her age, and he worked for her father. But the next time they waltzed, he decided to marry her.

At the same time, Dr. Grayson—McAdoo's closest friend and Washington's other most eligible bachelor—grew concerned about his two patients, the President and Mrs. Wilson. He convinced them that they desperately needed a vacation. With Jessie away on her honeymoon in London and Paris, Grayson urged Wilson to spend the Christmas holiday with the rest of his family in the Gulf country. Mississippi Senator John Sharp Williams recommended Pass Christian as an ideal winter resort. One evening just before the Wilsons' departure, knowing that she would be gone for weeks and that he was leaving on a tour of the nation to select sites for the Federal Reserve Banks, Mac revealed his intentions. They agreed to search their souls before committing to each other, or even telling her parents.

Pass Christian was everything Senator Williams had promised— balmy and restful. The Wilsons, Helen Bones, and Dr. Grayson stayed at Beaulieu, an antebellum mansion with tall white columns and garlands of moss hanging from the trees. They celebrated Christmas and Wilson's fifty-seventh birthday; and, inevitably, the President began to chart the next stage of his New Freedom. Returning from a round of golf with Grayson one day, Wilson noticed smoke curling from the roof of a house. They ran to the door to inform the residents, only to have the mistress of the house invite her guests into the parlor to sit down. "I haven't time to sit down," the President said, "—your house is on fire." They were able to get to the roof in time to extinguish it; and afterward, the local firefighters elected Wilson and Grayson members of their department. At that moment, however, the President had much bigger fires to put out—across the Gulf.

Two months earlier, Woodrow Wilson had delivered an address on foreign affairs at a convention of the Southern Commercial Congress in Mobile, Alabama, which several ministers from Latin America attended. The Panama Canal was approaching completion, and the isthmus was about to become the new crossroads of the globe. Before the world rushed in, Wilson wanted to articulate a new policy for his nation. He had every desire to expand the economy but only "upon terms of equality and honor." For Wilson, that meant one principle: "the development of constitutional liberty in the world."

President Wilson hoped to change the course set by his predecessors, as the only American Empire he wished to create was one of ideas. "Human rights, national integrity, and opportunity as against material interest," he said, "is the issue which we now have to face." He seized this occasion to insist "that the United States will never again seek one additional foot of territory by conquest. She will devote herself to showing that she knows how to make honorable and fruitful use of the territory she has; and she must regard it as one of the duties of friendship to see that from no quarter are material interests made superior to human liberty and national opportunity." What distinguished America, he said, were the beliefs on which it was founded. "I would rather belong to a poor nation that was free," he said, "than to a rich nation that had ceased to be in love with liberty." For a century, the Monroe Doctrine had served to keep Europe from securing political control over the nations of the Western Hemisphere; and Wilson believed—as Colonel House realized one day while lunching with him— that it was "just as reprehensible to permit foreign states to secure financial control of these weak and unfortunate republics."

A storm was brewing the January night Wilson went out to a cruiser at sea to confer with John Lind, his special agent in Mexico. Lind reported on Mexico's recent elections, which had prompted General Huerta to nullify the results, dissolve the legislature, and remain as dictator. Regional opposition continued to mount, but the leaders remained too wary of one another to join forces. To defend himself against the insurrections of Venustiano Carranza in the north and Emiliano Zapata in the south,

Huerta mobilized a vast army of federal forces, literally kidnapping men off the streets.

When Wilson had addressed a joint session of Congress months earlier on the subject of Mexico, he had recommended neutrality, forbidding the United States to export munitions there. When this policy did nothing to weaken Huerta, Wilson changed tack, lifting the embargo in order to help arm General Francisco "Pancho" Villa, a popular leader from the north who also held Huerta in great contempt. When that showed little effect, Lind urged an aggressive attack against Huerta. Unfortunately, the Ambassador was neither knowledgeable nor sensitive enough to recognize that the Mexican people preferred Huerta to foreign imposition. Knowing he was not receiving enough reliable information, Wilson returned from his shipboard meeting badly shaken. He felt it was as essential as it was inevitable that the Huerta regime should fall, but he was committed to Mexico's determining its own government—no matter how badly he wanted to intervene.

The Wilsons returned to Washington, where Ellen's ongoing efforts for slum clearance resulted in a bill being introduced in Congress. Although this pleased her, she was always weary and often looked drawn and pale. One night in early March 1914, after shaking hands with three thousand people at a White House reception, she fainted, falling hard on the polished floor of her bedroom. There was no sign of any deep injury, but she was sore for weeks. Ellen insisted she was fine and, referring to her husband, said, "This goose keeps worrying about me for no reason at all!"

Not until April did Ellen show signs of her old self, at which time Woodrow took the entire family—along with Dr. Grayson and a nurse—to the Greenbrier in White Sulphur Springs. The West Virginia resort offered golf, tennis, riding, even a new indoor pool. After a few days, William McAdoo joined them, his engagement to Eleanor having just been announced. In asking for her hand, Mac had suggested to his boss that he would resign to spare the President any embarrassment. "I appreciate your generous and considerate attitude," Wilson said, "but I hope you will dismiss all thought of such a thing. You were appointed Secretary of the Treasury solely on your merit. No one imagined, at that time, that the present situation would arise." He then paused and said with a wink, "But I must admit . . . that, if you had married into my family before I became President, I could not have offered you a position in the Cabinet, no matter how outstanding your record and qualifications might have been." It was a happy Easter for all of them, especially Woodrow and Ellen, who quietly rejoiced in each other's company during long rides in a buckboard, reminiscent of their courtship in Rome, Georgia, thirty years earlier.

On April 9, 1914—the day the Wilsons had left for the Greenbrier—a whaleboat attached to the American war vessel *Dolphin* docked at Tampico—then under Huerta's martial law—and a few sailors disembarked for a routine supply run. These bluejackets did not produce the permits that were required. Mexican soldiers boarded the whaleboat, which flew American flags at the bow and stern, and took the unarmed Paymaster and his crew into custody. When they were but a few blocks into town, an officer of higher authority ordered the Americans' return to the wharf until further instructions arrived. Within ninety minutes, Huerta's forces ordered their release and issued an apology, complete with "an expression of regret" from Huerta himself. The apology did not satisfy Admiral Henry T. Mayo, commander of the naval squadron, who unilaterally demanded a twenty-one-gun salute to the American flag.

The next morning, Secretary of State Bryan wired the President about the incident. Although everything Huerta said or did provoked him, Wilson was annoyed with Mayo, whose demand seemed unnecessary. Colonel House said Mayo should be admonished against making such decisions without authorization, but the Commander in Chief supported his Admiral: "Mayo could not have done otherwise," Wilson wired Bryan back. The Mexican commander in Tampico felt unqualified to order that salute, and the matter escalated to a diplomatic incident. Huerta informed the American Chargé d'Affaires that he would accede to the demand, provided an American ship responded in kind. Wilson agreed, and the confrontation could have ended with forty-two bullets being fired into the air. But then Huerta tried to reopen the negotiation, demanding that a protocol between the two governments be signed. Wilson knew that action could be construed as his recognition of the Huerta government, to which he would not accede. For the first time in his life, Wilson had difficulty sleeping.

Eleven days after the incident, Wilson opened his press conference assuring everybody that there was not about to be a war between the United States and Mexico; but when he took the matter to Congress that afternoon, jingoism filled the air. His welcome before the joint session in the House was disturbingly enthusiastic. "The incident cannot be regarded as a trivial one," he told the legislators—especially as two of the men arrested had been removed from the boat itself, and thus seized from United States territory. Furthermore, the President asserted, this was not an isolated incident. A few days later, an orderly from the USS *Minnesota* was arrested in Veracruz while obtaining his ship's mail. Wilson reaffirmed that he had no intention of going to war, but he asked for Congress's approval to "use the armed forces of the United States in such ways and to such an extent as may be necessary to obtain from General Huerta and his adherents the fullest recognition of the rights and dignity of the United States, even amidst the distressing conditions now unhappily obtaining in Mexico."

Several Republicans saw this as an opportunity for America, once again, to carry a big stick. Alongside Henry Cabot Lodge, the most forthright speaker that day was Senator Elihu Root of New York, who said the insult to Old Glory was the least of the matter: behind that lay "years of violence and anarchy in Mexico" that warranted bold action to reinforce America's position of power in the world. "People seem to want war with Mexico," Wilson told his family after seeing the Congressional reaction, "but they shan't have it if I can prevent it." The Senate authorized the President to employ the armed forces to back his demands "for unequivocal amends for affronts and indignities." Thus empowered, Wilson would have to keep resisting the urge to remove the sword from its scabbard in Haiti and the Dominican Republic as well, nearby nations that had endured years of revolts and coups d'état and which had required American fiscal assistance as well as its occasional military presence to stabilize them and their economies.

Woodrow Wilson had no intention of becoming another TR, an imperialistic warrior who exerted his might because he could; but he did see himself as a Christian soldier, fighting for what was right. Blinded by his desire to remove Huerta, Wilson did not see the irony of demanding a salute from a government he did not even recognize. Between his speech to Congress and the Senate approval, the Administration learned that a ship had left Havana for Veracruz laden with 1,333 boxes of German guns intended for Huerta. Wilson discussed the matter with his Secretaries of State and the Navy. Daniels said, "The munitions should not be permitted to fall into Huerta's hands." The President hesitated to act pre-emptively, but his advisers maintained that if the arms did reach the usurper, it would increase the loss of Mexican lives and the guns might later be turned upon Americans. "There is no alternative but to land," said Wilson. Daniels immediately cabled Admiral Frank F. Fletcher, commander of the Atlantic Fleet, "Seize custom house. Do not permit war supplies to be delivered to Huerta government or to any other party."

On the morning of April 21, 1914, Fletcher's fleet steamed to Veracruz, and eight hundred Marines and Navy bluejackets filled their whaleboats and sailed to the waterfront. By nightfall they had captured the customs house as well as the post and telegraph offices and the railroad station; the next day they overtook the rest of the town. Nineteen Americans lost their lives, and another seventy were wounded; more than a hundred Mexicans died.

On May 11, Wilson went to New York to take part in a memorial for the American sailors killed at Veracruz. Past huge silent crowds, his carriage followed the slow procession of horse-drawn caissons up Broadway from the Battery to City Hall, and then across the Manhattan Bridge to the parade ground of the Brooklyn Navy Yard. Speaking there, he rambled slightly as he attempted to define not only the justification for the action at Veracruz but also the precepts of his nascent foreign policy.

Wilson remained conflicted. Just three weeks earlier, he had told Congress, "The people of Mexico are entitled to settle their own domestic affairs in their own way"; then he resorted to embargoes, invasion, and occupation of Veracruz—punishing Mexico's misbehavior. On this occasion, after a few paragraphs extolling the selfless duty and service of the fallen nineteen, he reached the undefined core of his remarks: "We have gone down to Mexico to serve mankind if we can find out the way. We do not want to fight the Mexicans. We want to serve the Mexicans if we can, because we know how we would like to be free, and . . . a war of service is a thing in which it is a proud thing to die." He would later admit that he could not dismiss the thought of the young men killed in Mexico. "It was right to send them there," he said, "but that does not mitigate the sorrow for their deaths—and *I* am responsible for their being there."

Other news contributed to Wilson's distress that day. The Secret Service had just foiled a plot against his life, and new threats appeared. Officials urged him to review the parade from a stand, which offered some protection. Mayor John P. Mitchel concurred, saying, "The country cannot afford to have its President killed." More important, Wilson replied, "the country cannot afford to have a coward for President."

Just when the Mexican crisis weighed heaviest on Wilson, three men from South America arrived to ease the burden. Ambassadors from Argentina, Brazil, and Chile—the A. B. C. Powers—offered to mediate a settlement between Mexico and the United States. Both parties eagerly accepted, though Wilson made it clear his interest was not in resolving the incident at Tampico but in the "settlement by general pacification of Mexico." Ridding Mexico of its dictator, of course, had been the subtext of Wilson's actions all along, but he hoped this entire matter might establish a policy the United States could pursue going forward. At a time when American mining interests, English oil interests, German commercial interests, and French banking interests were all exploiting Mexico, Wilson told a journalist that he wanted the United States to be more than a good neighbor. The "business, prosperity, and contentment of Mexico mean more, much more, to us than merely an enlarged field for our commerce and enterprise." House's metaphor for the President's foreign policy cheered him: "If a man's house was on fire he should be glad to have his neighbors come in and help put it out, provided they did not take his property, and it should be the same with nations."

William Jennings Bryan had already done a lot of the spadework for America's new foreign policy. As of mid-1914, more than thirty nations—representing four-fifths of the world's population, including most of Europe except Germany—had signed his treaties. These accords provided for the submission of international disputes to a permanent tribunal and the agreement that there would be no hostilities for a year, during which time complaints would be investigated. The notion reminded Wilson of a rule a headmaster at a Southern school had imposed under which any student with a grievance might fight another provided he came first to the headmaster and agreed to fight under his supervision according to the Queensberry rules; it stopped fighting on campus altogether. Wilson decided to put America's new code of ethics to the test.

In 1901, Secretary of State John Hay and British Ambassador Sir Julian Pauncefote had signed an agreement permitting the United States to construct and maintain a canal in Central America; Article III of the Hay-Pauncefote Treaty dictated that the Panama Canal "shall be free and open" to vessels "of all Nations . . . on terms of entire equality." Furthermore, it stipulated, "such conditions and charges of traffic shall be just and equitable." During Taft's last year in office, as the great pathway approached completion, Congress passed an act exempting U.S. vessels engaged in noninternational trade from paying tolls. After all, the lawmakers reasoned, the United States had underwritten the canal's construction, and this exemption applied only to American ships going from coast to coast, not competing against the ships of other nations conducting international commerce. Most Republicans—especially the vocal ex-President Roosevelt—considered the exemption an entitlement; even Democrats endorsed it. Great Britain believed the exemption violated the spirit, if not the letter, of the Treaty.

So did Wilson. The exemption had been on his mind from the start of his term, but he felt he needed a few important legislative notches on his belt before he could persuade even his own party members to defy public sentiment as well as basic accounting. On March 5, 1914, the President returned to Congress with his briefest message ever, urging the repeal of the exemption provision of the Panama Canal Act. He asked the legislators to think beyond themselves. "We ought to reverse our action," he said, ". . . and so once more deserve our reputation for generosity and the redemption of every obligation without quibble or hesitation."

Wilson's position was sound, not only morally but also politically. "When everything else about this administration is forgotten," the President once told his brother-in-law, "its attitude in the Panama Canal Tolls will be remembered as putting the conduct of nations on the same basis as that which prevails among honorable individuals, where a promise is a promise and is kept regardless of personal advantage." He thought the Hay-Pauncefote Treaty was foolish in many ways; but, he said, "We gave Great Britain our word and that word must be respected by us."

As he did whenever he needed to gather legislative support, Wilson dispatched McAdoo and Burleson—his "wet nurses," he called them behind their backs—to the Senate floor, where they threatened and cajoled. The repeal became law by a vote of 50 to 35 in the Senate, and 247 to 162 in the House. Sir Edward Grey, the British Foreign Secretary, thereafter became a great friend of Colonel House and the United States government. The recently retired British Ambassador James Viscount Bryce told friends he considered Wilson's words and deeds in the Panama matter "the finest, most dignified, most courageous thing done in the United States for many years: perhaps, indeed, since Lincoln's second inaugural." Bryce wrote the President himself that his behavior reminded him of the one British statesman "in whom the sense of moral obligation always found expression in the simplest and noblest words"—John Bright. Bryce could have heaped no greater praise.

In his annual message to Congress in December 1913, Wilson had spoken of the need to protect the business communities of America by letting the Sherman Anti-Trust Act of 1890 stand unaltered, even with its large gray areas that allowed some leeway for monopolies. Six weeks later, carried by the strong current of his legislative successes, he returned to Congress to sharpen the definitions—if not the teeth—within that law. Rather than create a new political conflict, he approached the task by encouraging cooperation between two traditionally hostile adversaries. "The Government and businessmen are ready to meet each other half way in a common effort to square business methods with both public opinion and the law," he said. Having turned once again to Louis Brandeis for advice, Wilson proposed several means to correct the nation's unfair business practices.

The core of the problem remained the elite club of tycoons who sat on boards of the nation's major banks and railroads, as well as its industrial, commercial, and public service entities. Those who borrowed and those who lent, those who bought and those who sold, were one and the same— a group with the power to stifle competition. And so Wilson recommended a prohibition of "interlockings of the *personnel* of the directorates of great corporations." Such a prohibition, Wilson contended, "will bring new men, new energies, a new spirit of initiative, new blood, into the management of our great business enterprise," thereby enriching the nation's business activities. Second, he hoped to see the Interstate Commerce Commission superintending the financial operations of the nation's railroads; "the prosperity of the railroads and the prosperity of the country are inseparably connected," he said, and without greater oversight, the interests of the transportation systems were subordinated to their financiers.

Wilson also believed there were enough ambiguities in existing laws to discourage America's entrepreneurs. "Nothing hampers business like uncertainty," Wilson said; and nothing daunted business more than "the risk of falling under the condemnation of the law before it can make sure just what the law is." He believed there should be an interstate trade commission—not another watchdog agency but a bureau that would serve "only as an indispensable instrument of information and publicity, as a clearinghouse for the facts by which both the public mind and the managers of great business undertakings should be guided." As he had asserted when he had run for Governor of New Jersey, Wilson did not believe there were bad corporations, only individuals who did bad things under the corporate guise. "It should be one of the main objects of our legislation to divest such persons of their corporate cloak and deal with them as with those who do not represent their corporation," he said, "but merely by deliberate intention break the law." In other words, malfeasants should be held individually responsible, "and the punishment should fall upon them, not upon the business organization of which they make illegal use." Wilson listed other injustices, insisting that "conscientious businessmen the country over" would be unsatisfied until they had rewritten the "constitution of peace, the peace that is honor and freedom and prosperity."

Congressman Henry D. Clayton of Alabama, who headed the House Judiciary Committee, sponsored a comprehensive anti-trust bill that would bear his name and which contained most of the remedies Wilson had requested and included language that protected labor organizations from being considered illegal combinations themselves in restraint of trade. It passed in both houses with overwhelming majorities. With the cooperation of Senator Francis G. Newlands of Nevada and Commerce Secretary William C. Redfield, Congress also created the Federal Trade Commission just as the nation was entering a period of vast international commerce. The Commission, said Agriculture Secretary Houston, would "give legitimate and honest business advice and guidance and protect it from the unfair competition and practices of dishonest enterprises."

Meanwhile, Wilson did not neglect rural America. Houston estimated that little more than half the country's arable land was under cultivation, and of that, but an eighth was yielding its potential. From the start, the Administration set several programs into motion to stimulate the agricultural economy. More innovative were the plans to unite the scientific and agricultural communities. Houston created an Office of Information to disseminate in readable English the latest discoveries in soil improvement, plant and animal breeding, and the eradication of farm diseases. And then two Southerners—Senator Hoke Smith of Georgia and Congressman A. F. Lever of South Carolina—sponsored a bill that yoked land-grant colleges across the country to farms that would put the latest agricultural methods into practice.

The Smith-Lever Act also promoted greater cooperation between federal and state governments. It hitched most of the nation's three thousand rural counties together to make the United States the world's most productive supplier of food. In 1913, Secretary Houston observed, the rural roads between Richmond, Virginia, and Washington, D.C., were too muddy to allow an automobile to make the journey. Soon the Federal Aid Road Act was put in motion so that the federal and state governments could work together to create highways, linking the modernizing nation's backcountry with its metropolises.

After just a few of Wilson's legislative triumphs, the *New York Evening Post* had asserted that he had "more powerfully shaped more important legislation than any Executive of our time." Wilson maintained his mantra of "cooperation" well into the spring of 1914, transcending the usual political bickering so often that he had produced the greatest spate of legislation the Republic had seen since its founding. Colonel Harvey had recently written that no President, save Lincoln, had been inaugurated with a larger number of perplexing problems before him. And, he added, "no President of the United States has demonstrated greater capacity for true leadership." Reform-minded journalist Ray Stannard Baker wrote in his diary, "The government seems really to have become a popular government. Progress is really being made." The very soul of the District of Columbia seemed revived.

The social event of that season began at six o'clock on May 7, 1914—a Thursday evening—when Eleanor Randolph Wilson married William Gibbs McAdoo in the White House. Largely in deference to Ellen Wilson, whose health remained fragile, the event was as modest as Jessie's wedding had been grand. Beyond McAdoo's fellow Cabinet members and their wives, the attendees were almost entirely old friends and family members. The groom arrived with his six children—half of whom were older than the bride, the youngest of whom served as flower girl. Nell wore a long-trained gown of heavy ivory-colored satin. For the second time in six months, the President walked one of his daughters down the aisle, this time in the Blue Room, which was adorned with lilies and white apple blossoms. The Washington Monument and the blue hills of Virginia stood witness in the background. Once again the Reverend Beach performed the ceremony. The wedding couple stepped into the Red Room, fragrant with American Beauty roses, and received their guests beneath the Gilbert Stuart portrait of Washington. Refreshments followed in the State Dining Room, where Nell cut the wedding cake with one of the military aides' swords. Woodrow and Ellen—she in a creamy lace dress, wearing amethysts he had given her—stood at the front door, holding hands, as their youngest daughter kissed them goodbye. The newlyweds managed to evade the press as they boarded a train for their two-week honeymoon at Harlakenden.

The difference in age between the bride and groom concerned Wilson, though he believed Mac was a "noble man" who would make Nell happy. But selfishly, the marriage left him despondent. Daughter Margaret would never marry and would always remain his favorite intellectual challenger; he and Jessie would be bound forever by their deep faith. But Nell was her father's "chum," the sprite who could release the boyishness that few got to see. "Ah! How desperately my heart aches that she is gone," he wrote Mary Hulbert three days after the wedding. "She was simply part of me, the only delightful part; and I feel the loneliness more than I dare admit even to myself." Nell was torn as well, though she knew her father was not suffering from "the desolate sense of being only half alive" that overwhelmed him whenever he and her mother were separated.

The contraction of the family circle drew Woodrow and Ellen even closer. For months he had been "dreadfully worried" about the health of his wife of twenty-nine years; but at Nell's wedding, Ellen's brother Stockton asked if he was still apprehensive. "No, not now," he said. "She is coming out of the woods. . . ."

10

ECCLESIASTES

*To euery thing there is a season, and a time to euery
purpose vnder the heauen.*

A time to be borne, and a time to die . . .

*A time to weepe, and a time to laugh: a time to
mourne, and a time to dance. . . .*

*A time to loue, and a time to hate: a time of
warre, and a time of peace.*

—ECCLESIASTES, III:1–8

Five hundred people waited on the steps of Blair Arch
that Saturday—June 13, 1914—as the little shuttle
train pulled up to the back door of the Princeton campus.
Two Secret Service men jumped out, followed by Dr. Grayson, Joseph Tumulty, the newlywed McAdoos, and a beaming Wilson. Wearing a snappy blue jacket, white trousers,
white shoes, and a straw boater, he fit right in among his
classmates who were there to welcome him. They mingled
among hundreds of men of all ages in bright-colored baseball uniforms, sailor suits, and kilts; there was even a cohort in Arab garb leading a camel and another group
dressed as buccaneers, with three mules pulling their pirate
ship. The merrymakers were all Princeton alumni, indulging in their annual rite of spring—Reunions, the highlight
of which would be that afternoon's "P-rade," a procession of
all the returning graduates through the campus by class,
from oldest to youngest. A class member offered Wilson a

'79 hatband and an automobile ride to the class headquarters in Seventy-nine Hall, his former office building. The President of the United States said he preferred to walk.

Other than an official handshake with university president Hibben, the only special distinction accorded Wilson that day was the unusually raucous "locomotive" cheers when the men of 1879 "P-raded" before the alumni sections of other years. Later, at dinner, he spoke briefly, saying, in an obvious reference to his successor, "I hope never again to be fool enough to make believe that a man is my friend who I know to be my enemy."

Only those closest to the President knew that pressures in his current position had recently induced nightmares, in which—curiously—his old Princeton enemies recurred. "Those terrible days," Colonel House noted in his diary, "have sunk deep into his soul and he will carry their marks to his grave."

Meanwhile, severe problems mounted at the White House. Even as Argentina, Brazil, and Chile were at Niagara Falls mediating the role America should play in the stabilization of Mexico, revolutionary leaders Carranza, Villa, Pablo González, and Álvaro Obregón were terrorizing each other. And the labor movement in America was reeling from a massacre in the Colorado town of Ludlow, where coal miners had been on strike for more than six months. The Colorado National Guard attacked their tent city of 1,200, killing a score of people—including women and children. The United Mine Workers of America—who counted more than half the nation's colliers among its members—tried to organize the strikers in the region by arming them and exhorting them to take action against the owners and their guards. The ensuing violence resulted in the deaths of dozens more. Not until Wilson dispatched federal troops was order restored. The strike would persist through the end of the year, when the UMWA would run out of money; mine owner John D. Rockefeller, Jr., would ultimately offer acceptable reforms, but Ludlow's mines would be abandoned, becoming a silent monument to the bloodiest struggle in American labor history. During all this time, the nation slogged through a recession that had begun under Taft, waiting for Wilson's bold fiscal reforms to jump-start the economy.

Wilson's most distressing problem, however, was his wife, who continued to weaken. "There is nothing at all the matter with her organically," a distraught Woodrow wrote Mary Hulbert. Mindful of the Axson family's psychological history, he feared the possibility of a nervous breakdown. Characteristically, Ellen kept insisting that Dr. Grayson maintain her husband's regimen of golf, automobile rides, and regular visits to the theater. But for weeks, Woodrow could not help awakening at three o'clock in the morning so that he could sit at Ellen's bedside and monitor her sleep. Nell McAdoo visited daily and observed her father's gait slowing and the lines in his face deepening.

Then, on June 28, 1914, there was a new wrinkle: a teenaged Bosnian Serb shot Archduke Franz Ferdinand in Sarajevo, killing the heir apparent to the Austro-Hungarian Empire. The assassin was a member of a revolutionary group committed to liberating the Slavs from Habsburg rule. Over the next month, his bullet would ricochet around the globe, piquing animosities everywhere. One empire seemed to have been spoiling for just such an international brawl.

After the Franco-Prussian War of 1870–71, dozens of small Germanic states had unified under Chancellor Otto von Bismarck, who spun a web of strategic alliances to assure Germany's domination of Europe without further conquest. Kaiser Wilhelm II, however, had ideas of his own—"to increase this heritage for which one day I shall be called upon to give an account." Every major power was soon poised to tackle age-old enemies.

In July, this bad situation worsened. Diplomatic efforts to avert war came up against unresolved disputes and petulant personalities, especially the crowned heads of Europe. Upon learning from Ambassador Frederic C. Penfield in Vienna of the Archduke's assassination, Wilson sent his shocked condolences to Emperor Franz Joseph. Because the German military felt equipped to take on all its neighbors, a cautious Ambassador James W. Gerard in Berlin wrote Chancellor Theobald von Bethmann Hollweg, asking, "Is there nothing that my country can do . . . towards stopping this dreadful war? I am sure that the President would approve any act of mine looking towards peace." He received no reply.

Upstairs at the White House, Wilson told himself that his wife's strength was returning, until a sudden decline impelled Dr. Grayson to bring in three additional physicians. They concurred that Ellen was suffering from Bright's disease, a fatal inflammation of the kidneys. Dr. Grayson went to the President's office to deliver the dreadful news. Wilson listened in pained silence. "Let's get out of here," he said; and the two men ambled around the South Lawn of the White House, saying little. At last, Wilson exclaimed, "What am I to do!" In a moment, he answered his own question, saying, "We must be brave for Ellen's sake." He rose and marched directly to her room, where he sat by the side of her bed—as he would in the days that followed, whenever the duties of his office permitted. Discussion of her illness was confined to the second floor of the White House.

At a press conference on July 27, a reporter asked the President to comment on America's plans to maintain peace in Europe. Wilson limited his answer, saying only, "The United States has never attempted to interfere in European affairs." The next day—exactly one month after the Archduke's assassination—Austria declared war on Serbia. Lunching with the McAdoos, Wilson merely said, "It's incredible—incredible." Then he added, "Don't tell your mother anything about it." Nell asked her father if the declaration would implicate the rest of the world. Wilson only stared and then covered his eyes with his hand, saying, "I can think of nothing— nothing, when my dear one is suffering."

Nor could he have done anything. By then a war in Europe was inevitable, with more at stake than vengeance for a slain prince. Because of pre-existing treaties, Russia mobilized in defense of Serbia and called upon France to honor the provisions of their Triple Entente with Great Britain. On August 1, Germany declared war on Russia and, two days later, announced war with France, which meant trampling over Belgium, which was neutral. When Germany did not heed a British warning to withdraw from the tiny nation, Great Britain declared war on Germany. Because of an old alliance with Britain, Japan was forced to declare war on Germany as well. In less than a week, seventeen million men were engaged in a fight among at least eight nations.

On August 4, Woodrow sat at Ellen's bedside as she slept. One of his hands held hers while the other wrote a message to the Emperors of Germany and Austria-Hungary, the President of France, the King of England, and the Czar of Russia offering to "act in the interest of European peace, either now or at any other time that might be thought more suitable." At that moment, one of the doctors told the First Family that Ellen was dying. For the first time in their lives, Wilson's daughters saw their father weep.

By Thursday, August 6, Ellen sensed her demise, and she kept asking about the status of her slum clearance bill on Capitol Hill. At the President's urging, Congress instantly passed the Alley Dwelling Act. Learning of the legislation brought a smile to her face. She felt that her business on earth was done—except for making one wish, which she expressed privately to Cary Grayson. She drew him near and whispered, "Please take good care of Woodrow, Doctor."

Grayson summoned the family, and Wilson held her hand as their daughters sat vigil with him. At five o'clock that afternoon, Ellen drew her last breath. She was fifty-four. Tenderly, Woodrow folded her hands across her breast and wandered to the window, where he broke down and cried.

"It is pathetic to see the President," Frank Sayre wrote his mother that weekend; "he hardly knows where to turn." Fortunately, the White House was prepared to make all the arrangements on behalf of a traumatized President. A heavy band of black crepe was hung on the bell-knob at the front door of the White House, and the flag above was lowered to half-mast. A funeral was held at two o'clock on Monday the tenth in the East Room, where America's three assassinated Presidents and President Benjamin Harrison's deceased wife had all lain in state. The service could not have been simpler, with as few people beyond family as protocol required—Cabinet members and their wives, Supreme Court Justices, a Senate delegation headed by Vice President Marshall, and a Representative from each of the forty-eight states. After a few words of Scripture and a prayer, Wilson and his family left the room and then the officials took their leave. An hour later, six policemen who had served in the White House bore the coffin from the East Room to the horse-drawn hearse in front of the mansion. The family, staff, and Secret Service followed in motorcars to Union Station, where the cortege boarded a special train to take Ellen home.

They arrived in Rome, Georgia, at 2:30 the next afternoon, the sleepless President having sat by the casket almost the entire journey. Thousands of people flocked to the station to pay their respects. Every store in town closed that day; and all the church bells tolled as the funeral procession wended through the streets. Eight hundred mourners sat inside the First Presbyterian Church, where Ellen had first heard her father preach; thousands more—including schoolgirls dressed in white, each holding a myrtle branch—stood on the road as the procession moved from the service to the Myrtle Hill Cemetery. A light rain turned torrential as the Wilsons and Axsons stood under a tent for the final prayers before Ellen's coffin was lowered into the ground next to her mother and father. While those around him quietly wept, the President made no effort to conceal his grief. His body shook, and he sobbed openly.

. . . .

"The days . . . that followed were heartbreaking," recalled Dr. Grayson, committed to honoring Ellen Wilson's deathbed wish. This was no simple task, for he knew his patient's history of prostration when under pressure. As Wilson himself had written Mary Hulbert the day after his wife died, "God has stricken me almost beyond what I can bear."

But not beyond. A few weeks later, the President reported, "In God's gracious arrangement of things I have little time or chance to think about myself." With the destruction of his universe, he found strength in the collapse of the world. And like most Americans, he thanked God for the isolation the Atlantic Ocean provided.

Germany activated a modified version of its two-front Schlieffen Plan—which had been sitting in a drawer for a decade—invading France by overwhelming Belgium and Luxembourg and attacking Russia through East Prussia, while Austria-Hungary attacked Serbia. "My own attitude towards the conflict was . . . simple and clear," one young German volunteer would later write in his book *Mein Kampf.* "I believed that it was not a case of Austria fighting to get satisfaction from Serbia but rather a case of Germany fighting for her own existence. . . . And if this struggle should bring us victory our people will again rank foremost among the great nations. Only then could the German Empire assert itself as the mighty champion of peace." He spoke for millions of his countrymen.

The opening salvos had created the gravest international situation in history. During the five-day Battle of Tannenberg on the Eastern Front, the Russians suffered 30,000 casualties; the three-day Battle of Cer in Serbia resulted in 18,500 Austro-Hungarian victims; and in ten days in August, France endured 150,000 casualties—half the numbers of the yearlong Franco-Prussian War. And more than lives were lost. In late August, German troops pulverized the Belgian city of Louvain, for five centuries the intellectual capital of the Low Countries, firebombing its church of St. Pierre, the markets, the university, and its famous library.

The President of the United States had issued a formal proclamation of neutrality on August 4. It forbade any American citizen from accepting and exercising a commission in service of any of the belligerents, and it proclaimed that American waters and ports would not provide a haven for any of the belligerents' ships of war. Two weeks later—while acknowledging hundreds of condolence letters—Wilson reminded the people of the United States that they were "drawn from many nations, and chiefly from the nations now at war." It was, therefore, natural that each American would want to choose sides. But such division within the nation, he cautioned, "might seriously stand in the way of the proper performance of our duty as the one great nation at peace." And then he suggested the seemingly impossible: "We must be impartial in thought as well as in action, must put a curb upon our sentiments as well as upon every transaction that might be construed as a preference of one party to the struggle before another."

Ambassador Page in London adhered to Wilson's policy but could not disguise his own feelings. "A government can be neutral," Page wrote his brother, "but no *man* can be." And Charles W. Eliot, former president of Harvard, confidentially urged Wilson to combine the British Empire, France, Japan, Italy, Russia, and the United States in both "offensive and defensive alliance to rebuke and punish Austria-Hungary and Germany for the outrages they are now committing, by enforcing against those two countries non-intercourse with the rest of the world by land and sea." Even Woodrow Wilson—the man who worshipped Bagehot, Bright, and Wordsworth—was not above personal predilection. While his public statements remained neutral, his private conversation revealed contempt for the German people and their leaders. He said that "German philosophy was essentially selfish and lacking in spirituality." The destruction of Louvain moved him deeply; and he condemned the Kaiser for the rise of militarism. But Wilson sustained his public position, writing Eliot that he favored neither an alliance nor entrance into the war; and, he suggested, public opinion would not support such actions. Even the bellicose Teddy Roosevelt backed the President—for a while. But the Republican leader Henry Cabot Lodge took issue with Wilson from the start, agreeing that American neutrality should be "rigidly honest and fair" but complaining that the demand was "a perfectly unsound as well as utterly impractical position to take."

Sinking into a depression, Wilson tried to maintain the routine of his married life as much as possible. He insisted that his family take advantage of Harlakenden by spending at least the last weeks of summer there, and he would steal as many days in Cornish as he could. But back in the White House, Wilson was wracked by loneliness and guilt. "I sometimes feel that the Presidency has had to be paid for with Ellen's life," he confessed to Dr. Grayson; "that she would be living today if we had continued in the old simple life at Princeton." Stockton Axson did not disagree, but insisted that "she would rather have died when and where she died than have lived at the cost of any diminution of the career in which her husband realized to the fullest his talents and his powers."

"I never understood before what a broken heart meant, and did for a man," Wilson wrote Mary Hulbert in late August. "It just means that he lives by the compulsion of necessity and duty only." Although he was operating on willpower alone, Wilson accepted Dr. Grayson's recommendation that he spend the occasional morning in bed. When Grayson went in to check his condition one day that month, he found the President lying there, tears streaming down his face. "It was a heart-breaking scene," the doctor later recounted to a friend.

At the end of the month, doctor and patient traveled to Cornish, where Harlakenden exuded none of the mirth of previous visits. Colonel House— recently back from an extended European tour, where he had met mostly with diplomats in London and Berlin, and with the Kaiser as well—joined Wilson for two days. One of House's goals had been to discuss disarmament with the Germans, but he encountered mostly contempt and distrust. German Undersecretary for Foreign Affairs Arthur Zimmermann had claimed that the Kaiser's "strong and sincere efforts to conserve peace" had collapsed because Russia had mobilized, destroying any possibility of an understanding.

Wilson hung on House's every word. For the first time he was considering geopolitics tactically, not historically. This war was already challenging the idealistic hopes he had for the future, as he feared a German victory would force the United States into becoming "a military nation." Whoever won, he predicted the war would "throw the world back three or four centuries" and that the future would hold two superpowers—Russia dominating Europe and part of Asia and the United States dominating the Western world. House agreed but added a third superpower: China, he suggested, would dominate Asia.

The two men discussed every policy under the sun, foreign and domestic—including a new vacancy on the Supreme Court. Upon the death of one of Taft's six appointees, Wilson reflexively appointed his Attorney General, James McReynolds, who still carried trust-busting credentials. An unpredictable malcontent who never blended with the rest of the Cabinet, McReynolds quickly revealed himself to be one of the most disagreeable Justices in the Court's history, a cantankerous bigot whose prejudices led him to take archconservative positions utterly at odds with Wilson's belief that constitutions "are not mere legal documents: they are the skeleton frame of a living organism." To take his place in the Cabinet, Wilson promoted Thomas W. Gregory, another Southern Presbyterian, an Austin attorney who had served as a special assistant to McReynolds and was part of House's Texas posse. But however the conversations between Wilson and House began, they always ended by remembering Ellen.

Except for the steady presence of Dr. Grayson and cousin Helen Bones, who served as his hostess when Margaret was not in town, Wilson returned from his brief vacation to a big empty house. His spirits steadily declined that autumn, though he maintained a "steady front" for the world. "My loss has made me humble," Wilson wrote Mary Hulbert in September. "I know that there is nothing *for me* in what I am doing. And I hope that that will make me more serviceable." Into October he performed his required duties but little more, descending into deep lassitude on Sundays—sleeping all morning, and dozing during his motor rides around the city in the afternoon. "I want to run away," he wrote his friend Nancy Saunders Toy, an academician's wife in Boston, that November. "All the elasticity has gone out of me," he added in December. "I have not yet learned how to throw off the incubus of my grief and live as I used to live, in thought and spirit, in spite of it. Even books have grown meaningless to me. I read detective stories to forget, as a man would get drunk!"

With Dr. Grayson enforcing a strict physical regimen, the President at least looked healthy. Tan, clear-eyed, and weighing a lean 176 pounds, Wilson dictated letters to Swem in the house after breakfast, received visitors in the Oval Office from ten until one, allowed a few formal visits after lunch, and then changed into his golfing togs for afternoons on the links. He would find himself with but a few minutes to dress for dinner, after which he might permit a few consultations before secluding himself for the solitary state business of reading and writing. Washington felt like a penitentiary to him. "There is no human intercourse in it," he said, "—at any rate for the President."

One night Wilson restlessly jumped the prison wall, traveling by train with Margaret and Dr. Grayson to New York City. They breakfasted with Colonel House in his apartment at 115 East Fifty-third Street. After a round of golf with the Colonel's son-in-law, Gordon Auchincloss, at Piping

Rock Club, Wilson spent the late afternoon alone with House discussing an American relief effort for Belgium. At nine o'clock they walked from House's apartment just east of Park Avenue to Seventh Avenue, and then down Seventh to Broadway. Periodically they would stop, but once discovered they quickened their pace. By the time they had reached Herald Square, a throng had formed in their wake. They dashed into the Thirty-fourth Street door of the old Waldorf-Astoria, went up in the elevator, crossed to the Thirty-third Street side, and continued their quiet walk down Fifth Avenue to Twenty-sixth Street . . . where they boarded a motor bus back to Fifty-third Street. For the first time in a long time, Wilson seemed to breathe more easily; but when they returned to the apartment, House recalled, the President said "he could not help wishing when we were out tonight that someone would kill him."

The President was not suicidal. But House clearly understood him to say "he had himself so disciplined that he knew perfectly well that unless someone killed him, he would go on to the end doing the best he could." Wilson never doubted his faith. "There are people who *believe* only so far as they *understand*," he said, "—that seems to me presumptuous." The power of religion, he insisted, made *his* life "worth living."

Autumn 1914 brought the first test of the nation's faith in Woodrow Wilson's Presidency—the midterm elections. "The successful leader ought not to keep too far in advance of the mass he is seeking to lead, for he will soon lose contact with them," Wilson had once said by way of dismissing TR as a President who had promised Heaven without delivering it. Because Wilson considered the tariff and the currency at the heart of the movement for enduring reform in America, he thought the Democrats could successfully run more on their program than on their promises. When Frank Doremus, chairman of the Democratic Congressional Campaign Committee, invited the President to take an active role in the campaign, Wilson replied that his administration had been "more fruitful in important legislation of permanent usefulness to the country" than any within memory. With the world in crisis, Wilson felt he could not "turn away from his official work even for a little while" in order to campaign.

Nobody knew how the war abroad would affect the economy at home, but there were already early signs that neutrality would not necessarily protect American commodities. The Governors of the New York Stock Exchange had met just before the war was declared to discuss the possibility of closing the Exchange. Before the meeting, J. P. Morgan himself called Secretary McAdoo for his advice. Whether it was simply a preemptive action to avert a panic or because he did not want to disrupt the establishment of the Federal Reserve System, which was meant to protect banks from such panics, McAdoo recommended shutting down. The Exchange did—for the next four and a half months, the longest closure in the history of the market.

Entering the twentieth month of its recession, the United States confronted a new reality in international commerce: America transported virtually none of the nation's product. Now, with all the major countries of Europe pressing most of their ships into military service, America's stream of maritime commerce dried up. Eight million bales of cotton, to name but one significant export, sat on its wharves and in its warehouses. The excess glutting the market, cotton's price plummeted from 13.5¢ per pound to 6¢, while the cost of shipping what cotton could be stuffed into a cargo ship soared.

The laws of capitalism should have suggested that private enterprise would find a way to profit from the great demand abroad. But, as Treasury Secretary McAdoo observed, "Private initiative becomes extremely timid in times of peril and uncertainty." With a faraway war of indefinite length, American business withdrew from risky investments. McAdoo opposed government ownership of business enterprises—except, he said, "in extraordinary circumstances where the intervention of the government is urgently demanded in the interest of the public welfare."

Lying in bed early one morning, pondering these extraordinary circumstances, McAdoo had an idea. He grabbed a pad and pencil and dashed off a "ship purchase" bill before breakfast—a radical concept of "a shipping corporation of which the American government would own all, or a major part, of the capital stock." Later that day, he presented the idea to Wilson. The President liked it but wanted to sleep on it, as no matter how desperate the need for merchant ships, such a bill was sure to arouse the hostility of every reactionary in the country and the opposition of every powerful business interest. He said they would dismiss the idea as "socialistic."

A short time later, Wilson handed the proposal back to McAdoo and said, "We'll have to fight for it, won't we?" McAdoo said yes. And the

President replied, "Well, then, let's fight." Neither could have predicted the invective of the ensuing partisan battle. "Anyone who did not know the political motives behind our opponent's words would have thought that we had set out deliberately . . . to destroy legitimate commerce, and that our shipping plan was the first step on the road to national ruin." The bill sailed through the House; but the Senate fought against it for almost two years. Much of the resistance came from its fear of Wilson's advancing too far ahead of the public. That September, Congress passed the War Risk Insurance Bill, a measure the Administration backed when the marine insurance companies refused to indemnify against such new perils as mines and torpedoes. That bill seemed just as socialistic but encountered less opposition, McAdoo believed, because businesses calculated that there was no money for them to make in such a venture; it seemed best to allow the government to suffer the loss.

Although the struggle over the ship purchase bill had hardly begun by the time of the midterm elections, the people got the strong sense of the President's passion for it. Republicans used the bill to reunite and challenge the Administration. Even after seven Democratic Senators defected, it appeared that the bill still had enough votes. That prompted the Republicans to resort to one of their most obstructive weapons—the filibuster, the right of one or a series of Senators to hold the floor as long as he could stand and speak. Cots were rolled into the Senate cloakrooms as tag-team speeches—including Ohio's Senator Theodore Burton holding forth for thirteen hours—evolved into the longest continuous session in the history of Congress: fifty-four hours and eleven minutes. It effectively prevented passage of the bill for almost two years, at which point a version of it was voted through. McAdoo reckoned that the Senate delay cost a billion dollars, as the cost of ships rose dramatically while the war persisted. The war risk insurance during that time returned better than a 35 percent profit.

Meanwhile all that cotton sat on the docks as the next crop was being picked. Everybody suspected the war would create a greater need for the bales, though many feared it might be declared contraband, which would reduce further demand. Money in the South—where cotton was the foundation of the financial infrastructure—tightened, threatening an already stressed economy. Once again the Administration stepped in, issuing currency to Southern banks for loans to the farmers, to finance storage of the new crop and to invest for the following year. Once again, the New Freedom was creating elasticity, allowing supply and demand to find their equilibrium. Within weeks, cotton had bounced to 8.5¢ per pound; and Wilson's success at jump-starting a disabled but essential American industry would provide precedent for future Presidents.

The President consulted with J. P. Morgan, Jr., who was concerned that the war and the restrictions imposed by the New Freedom legislation would hurt the American economy. The value of securities was his immediate concern; but Morgan, who was powerful enough to bail out whole countries, was thinking worldwide. The curtailment of international trade, Morgan suggested, should be "a tremendous opportunity for America, but the country is not in a position to take advantage of that opportunity if it does not feel that its own capital invested in its own country is safely and remuneratively placed." In fact, France had just retained the House of Morgan in hopes of securing $100 million.

J. P. Morgan & Company asked the Department of State if there were any objections to such a loan. Robert Lansing, an expert in international law and an adviser to the Department, could offer no legal grounds, but Secretary Bryan suggested several reasons to oppose the transaction—all rooted in the President's stated position. "Money is the worst of all contrabands because it commands everything else," Bryan wrote Wilson on August 10, 1914. "I know of nothing that would do more to prevent war than an international agreement that neutral nations would not loan to belligerents." Bryan contended that a loan to France would sanction future loans to Great Britain or Germany or Russia or Austria, which would tend to factionalize American citizens. Lending institutions would find themselves exerting pressure on the media to support the governments they were financing. All that, Bryan announced, was terribly "inconsistent with the true spirit of neutrality." Wilson agreed, at first.

One of the President's strengths was in remaining as flexible as his nation's currency. Wilson appeared before another joint session of Congress to urge the raising of $100 million in internal taxes to compensate for the loss of revenues from customs. When he saw that the nation's railroads needed financial relief, he expressed as much to the Interstate Commerce Commission. And two months after Bryan spoke against the Morgan loan to France, Wilson reversed himself, as the funding involved was not to be considered loans so much as "credits" for American goods—including guns as well as grains, machinery, meat, and cotton. The nation emerged from its recession.

Without straying from Ellen's rose garden, Wilson limited his midterm campaigning to a few statements, primarily a long letter to House Majority Leader Oscar Underwood—written for publication. In it the President catalogued the Sixty-third Congress's accomplishments and announced the agenda for the Sixty-fourth. (That included a conservation program protecting natural resources and developing water power, in the name of economy as much as ecology.) Without "a Congress in close sympathy with the administration," Wilson wrote, "a whole scheme of peace and honor and disinterested service to the world of which they have approved cannot be brought to its full realization."

The Republican Party remained divided, its Progressive insurgents still unsettled, while the Democrats were uncharacteristically unified. *The New York Times* credited this "reversal of ancient tradition" to the personality of the President himself, saying, "He has inspired the nation with confidence in him as a leader; he has inspired the world with confidence in him as a statesman; it is not strange that he has inspired his party with confidence in him as its chief." In the weeks before the midterm elections, Wilson even extended his hand to Tammany Hall candidates in New York, a machine boss in Illinois, and the old Smith-Nugent machine in New Jersey, where he still voted. In truth, Wilson admitted to Tumulty after two years in office, he had developed new respect for some of the old party warhorses, even a few of the hacks, who loyally stood by his side "without hitching."

Under the newly ratified Seventeenth Amendment, the midterm elections of 1914 marked the first time the people—not the state legislatures—directly elected its Senators. The vote skewed Democratic, with Wilson's party attracting Progressive voters and picking up four seats. The House of Representatives, on the other hand, revealed a growing desire to slow, if not stop, all the radical changes, and the Democrats lost sixty votes there. They maintained a lead of thirty-four votes, but the results distressed the President. He said it did not seem worthwhile to work as hard as he had in the past two years only "to have it scantily appreciated." Colonel House tried to console the President, reminding him that he was not on the ballot; but Wilson said, "People . . . know that to vote against a democratic ticket is to vote indirectly against me." While the Republicans had found votes in the industrial Midwest, Tumulty took heart in the Democrats' successfully planting their flag in the West—where he believed the 1916 election would be won. The President himself took to touting that his party, which had been called "sectional," was becoming "unmistakably national." The biggest loser in the election proved to be the Progressive Party, which ran almost 150 candidates for Congress in 1914 and saw only a handful elected. Insurgents from each of the two major parties drifted back to their respective folds.

After that, Wilson sagged into a diagnosable "acute depression"—the thirteenth such "breakdown" in his adult life. He continued to perform his duties, but he slumped with fatigue at the end of each day. Colonel House shuttled from New York to Washington almost weekly and spent several nights at a time at the White House. His companionship proved to be as valuable as his counsel; when the Colonel could not engage the President after dinner with talk of politics, he would ask him to read aloud. Wordsworth or Thomas Gray's "Elegy Written in a Country Church Yard" always revived him. But Wilson's melancholia persisted. He said that Ellen's death had broken his spirit and that he simply "was not fit to be President because he did not think straight any longer, and had no heart in the things he was doing." On November 12, 1914, his nerves were so frayed that he lost his temper for the first time in the White House.

William Monroe Trotter, a Negro activist and a Wilson supporter in the 1912 election, had already presented the President with a national petition signed by African Americans in thirty-eight states protesting the Administration's segregation of the Departments of Treasury and the Post Office. At that time, Wilson had assured the suppliants that he would personally investigate their complaints. A year later, Trotter appeared in the West Wing of the White House with representatives of the National Independence Equal Rights League to inform Wilson that the conditions for the Negro had only worsened. Negroes felt so betrayed that they had just registered their protest to Wilson's policies at the polls. Discovering their strength as a bloc, they voted against every Democratic candidate except those who opposed segregation.

"In the first place," the President said, bridling at Trotter's remarks, "let's leave politics out of it." Wilson insisted this was "a human problem, not a political problem," and that if "the colored people made a mistake in voting for me, they ought to correct it and vote against me if they think so." As a whole, he said, the American people wished to support the advancement of the Negro race; but Wilson acknowledged that friction still existed and that prejudice in America ran deep. "It takes the world generations to outlive all its prejudices," Wilson said, insisting this was not "a question of intrinsic equality, because we all have human souls." It was a current question of "economic equality—whether the Negro can do the same things with equal efficiency." Once he had proved it, he said, "a lot of things are going to solve themselves."

Trotter had no use for such talk. "Only two years ago you were heralded as perhaps the second Lincoln," he said, "and now the Afro-American leaders who supported you are hounded as false leaders and traitors to the race. What a change segregation has wrought!" Trotter did not stop there. "You said that your 'Colored fellow citizens could depend upon you for everything which would assist in advancing the interest of their race in the United States.'" And then he asked if there was a "new freedom" for white Americans and a "new slavery for your 'Afro-American fellow citizens.'"

That did it. "Your tone, sir," Wilson announced, "offends me." The President said that he had enjoyed the exchange of ideas expressed by this delegation, but Trotter's last personalization had crossed a line. "You are an American citizen, as fully an American citizen as I am, but you are the only American citizen that has ever come into this office who has talked to me with a tone . . . of passion that was evident. Now, I want to say that if this association comes again, it must have another spokesman." Trotter did not back down, insisting he was "from a part of the people" who waited to hear that the President was without prejudice, and then implied that they would defect from the Democratic Party. Trying to dismiss the delegation, Wilson told Trotter, "You have spoiled the whole cause for which you came."

Trotter said he was sorry to hear that, especially—he added, now baiting the President—in an America that professed to be Christian. A fuming Wilson snapped, "I expect those who profess to be Christians to come to me in a Christian spirit." For several more minutes, Trotter held the floor of the Oval Office, expounding upon each of his arguments, insisting that Wilson's policy brought more dangers than advantages. At last, Trotter led his colleagues to the street, where he announced to the press a protest meeting the following Sunday. He intended to take this movement to the churches.

The confrontation galvanized the black community. James Weldon

Johnson—then editing *The New York Age*, the city's oldest African American newspaper—addressed the President in an editorial, saying, "Mr. Wilson, the men who waited upon you did not go to ask any favors; neither did they go . . . to be patted on the head and told to be 'good little niggers and run home.'" No, Johnson said, they were simply citizens asking their "Chief Magistrate" to right a wrong. The President had preached the New Freedom and sent his Army and Navy "in the interest of the landless peons of Mexico," he said, "but not one word has he uttered for fair play to the ten million Negroes in this country." For Johnson, the episode revealed a basic truth about Woodrow Wilson: he "bears the discreditable distinction of being the first President of the United States, since Emancipation, who openly condoned and vindicated prejudice against the Negro."

The white liberal press took Wilson to task as well. Oswald Garrison Villard sent copies of newspaper editorials to the President, lamenting that "an Administration so noble in its feeling for the under-dog . . . cannot do simple justice when it comes to the color line." The *New York Evening Post* suggested that Trotter's "bad manners" aside, the Wilson Administration had drawn a color line where it had not existed. Blacks and whites had worked side by side for half a century, and this administration "went out of its way to create the issue it now deplores."

Wilson regretted the encounter with Trotter, but not for any substantive reason. "Daniels," he later remarked to his Secretary of the Navy, "never raise an incident into an issue. When the negro delegate threatened me, I was damn fool enough to lose my temper and to point them to the door." In retrospect, he believed he should have listened quietly and said he would consider their petition, allowing the matter to pass. "But I lost my temper," Wilson said, "and played the fool." A few months later, Wilson got sucker punched again—but this time from the other side.

In 1914, David Wark Griffith—a former actor from Kentucky who became the predominant filmmaker of his time, transforming motion pictures from a nickel-and-dime novelty into a storytelling art—adapted a bestselling novel called *The Clansman*, by Thomas Dixon, Jr., into a film. Part of a trilogy, the book was inspired by *Uncle Tom's Cabin*. But where Harriet Beecher Stowe's classic novel exposed the evils of slavery, Dixon's rabble-rousing work meant to portray the injustices of Reconstruction. Subtitled *An Historical Romance of the Ku Klux Klan*, it picked the scabs off the nation's Civil War wounds, hoping to incite a reaction to what he considered a growing acceptance of racial equality. A proud white supremacist—who deplored miscegenation and the government in the postwar Confederacy—Dixon depicted Reconstruction from the losing side, suggesting that Negroes had once happily worked in the cotton fields before the war had freed them to run amok. He preyed upon the reader's sentiments by presenting the most blatant racial stereotypes: one character—a former slave—lusts after an innocent white girl; when she plummets to her death from a cliff, to evade his touch, the righteous Klan gallops forth to mete out the ultimate justice, a lynching.

The result was an epic film—the most expensive ($112,000) and the longest (190 minutes) that had ever been produced. Rich in detail and wondrous in scope, *The Clansman* reenacted visceral battle sequences, sentimental love scenes, and even the assassination of Abraham Lincoln. (White actors in blackface assumed the important Negro roles.) Less than a week before its premiere, Dixon arranged a meeting at the White House with the President, his friend and colleague from Johns Hopkins—whose early writings were quoted in the movie's title cards.

A born self-promoter, Dixon could think of no better means of publicizing his work than a Presidential endorsement. He appealed to Wilson, as one historian to another, describing how the camera could record and disseminate history. "Of course," Dixon later wrote Tumulty, "I didn't dare allow the President to know the *real big purpose back of my film—which was to revolutionize Northern sentiments by a presentation of history that would transform every man in my audience into a good Democrat!*" What he did tell the President was "that I would show him the birth of a new art—the launching of the mightiest engine for moulding public opinion in the history of the world." Wilson was still in mourning and said he could not attend a theater, but he was not averse to a small unpublicized viewing.

On February 8, 1915, *The Clansman* premiered at Clune's Auditorium in Los Angeles and became an overnight sensation. Nobody in the new industry had ever witnessed such spectacular storytelling. The Los Angeles chapter of the NAACP sought an injunction against exhibiting the film, claiming it was a threat to public safety because of the violence it would incite. The show went on, but word about the incendiary nature of the film spread. Then, on February 18, Wilson and his daughters and his Cabinet gathered in the East Room for the first running of a motion picture in the White House.

"It is like writing history with lightning. And my only regret is that it is all so terribly true," Woodrow Wilson purportedly said when the lights came up. In fact, Wilson almost certainly never said it. The encomium does not even appear in the unpublished memoirs of the self-serving Thomas Dixon. The only firsthand record of Wilson's feelings about the film appear in a letter three years later, in which he wrote, "I have always felt that this was a very unfortunate production and I wish most sincerely that its production might be avoided, particularly in communities where there are so many colored people." There is no record of his sentiments beyond that, though he surely would have been troubled by the political implications of publicly supporting a movie mired in controversy. Another member of the audience that night reported that the President seemed lost in thought during the film and exited the East Room upon its completion without saying a word to anybody.

The first sentence of the famous "review" definitely captures the voice of a lyrical historian; the second, however, sounds more like Chief Justice Edward White, whom Dixon invited to another screening and who admitted to having shouldered a rifle as a Klansman in New Orleans. Whether the remark was a conflation of the two men's thoughts or a complete fabrication, the comment did not appear in print for more than two decades. In any case, word of a White House screening circulated, and that was tantamount to a Presidential endorsement. By the time the film opened in New York City on March 3, Dixon had urged Griffith to drop the title in favor of the subtitle—*The Birth of a Nation*. Not only did it carry more weight, but it also took the klieg lights off the worst of the controversy.

Before the New York premiere, the NAACP appealed to the courts and the National Board of Censorship to block the film. Its racism disturbed some of the liberal members of the board, but art trumped politics; and the courts followed suit, taking no action. The NAACP picketed the Liberty Theatre, but the protesters went virtually unnoticed by the people in the endless queues. Small riots and protests broke out in Northern cities; William Monroe Trotter led a protest rally in Boston's Faneuil Hall. City councils, editorial pages, and cocktail party guests debated the right to screen the film wherever it played. A former Massachusetts Congressman sought confirmation that the President had viewed the film and had voiced no objection. Wilson turned the controversy over to Tumulty, instructing him to write that the President had seen the film but "was entirely unaware of the character of the play before it was presented and has at no time expressed his approbation of it. Its exhibition at the White House was a courtesy extended to an old acquaintance."

The Birth of a Nation became a national phenomenon. In less than a year, almost a million people saw it at the Liberty Theatre alone. But the stink of racism clung to the movie, and intensified as time rendered society more tolerant. In parts of the South, however, it played like a recruiting film, sparking a revival of the moribund Ku Klux Klan, which now added Catholics, Jews, and immigrants to its list of enemies.

"It seems, indeed," Wilson wrote Mary Hulbert the Sunday before Thanksgiving 1914, "as if my *individual* life . . . consisted only of news upon which action must be taken."

Within a matter of weeks, a man whose worldview hardly extended beyond England's Lake District faced issues on virtually every continent. The Senate was delaying a treaty Bryan had signed with Nicaragua to stabilize the government. Politics forced the President to refuse to grant financial assistance to a desperate Liberia. Exiled in Tokyo, Sun Yat-sen appealed to Wilson to prevent J. P. Morgan & Company from making a loan to Yüan Shih-k'ai, the despotic self-proclaimed Emperor of China. From England, Ambassador Page wrote of how American commerce was tied to Britain's naval operations and how the Germans had carpeted the North Sea with so many mines that at least one ship a day was blown up. Page further declared that he could no longer personally finance his required entertaining in the Embassy. Luckily, one letter from Wilson to Cleveland Dodge elicited the necessary $25,000 to keep him as Ambassador; the money was quietly transferred through Colonel House and Page's son.

On December 1, the conscientious Secretary Bryan presented a memorandum urging American mediation in Europe. It was early enough in the conflict that Bryan felt "these Christian nations" might get past the pride that started the war and kept it from ending. Now, "when all must confess failure to accomplish what they expected," Bryan said, ". . . when new horrors are being added daily, it would seem to be this nation's duty, as the leading exponent of Christianity and as the foremost advocate of worldwide peace," to bring everybody to the table. For all its good intentions, Bryan's memorandum made the President wonder if his Secretary of State was suited to his current office. Foreign policy was no longer a simple matter of signing treaties. It required a more sophisticated view of a world in which every country had become enmeshed with every other and whose political workings had become Byzantine. When Wilson asked Bryan to compose a note to the English government protesting their detention of American ships bound for neutral ports, the President found the draft undiplomatic and unliterary. Wilson rewrote much of it, hoping Bryan would improve upon it further. Three days later he found that Bryan had not changed it at all. The President increasingly turned to Colonel House—whose intellect he respected and whose intuition he trusted. Above all, House enjoyed the diplomatic arts—for which Wilson had limited patience.

Based on his own private conferences, House felt Bryan's plan showed little understanding of the world. House said that the Allies would consider mediation "an unfriendly act" at that moment, that the United States should not be talking peace with Germany until she had reason to change her aggressive military policy, that even though Austria-Hungary had privately indicated a willingness to negotiate, Germany had already declined to do so. The President believed that House could "do more to initiate peace unofficially than anyone could do in an official capacity."

And yet, Wilson did not dismiss Bryan's memorandum out of hand. Its general concepts reinforced his own evolving thoughts, especially the notion of arriving at some enduring international concord without any nation having to achieve victory. For all his lack of experience, Wilson was hardly blind to America's potential role in the world. As early as the second week of August 1914, he had told Stockton Axson that he feared Germany's maritime policies would jeopardize American neutrality.

Wilson began to sketch his own permanent structure for peace. He believed the days of seizing land to build empires had past; great powers had long exploited small states, but even those nations were entitled to democratic ideas and equal opportunities. Private manufacturers of armaments should not be allowed to urge war, for they stood to profit. The world had become a single neighborhood of nations, wherein it would never again be possible for any country to regard a quarrel between two nations as a private quarrel, and "an attack in any quarter was an attack on the equilibrium of the world." Wilson then articulated what he believed were four fundamental principles: there "must never again be a foot of ground acquired by conquest"; it "must be recognized in fact that the small nations are on an equality of rights with the great nations"; ammunition "must be manufactured by governments and not by private individuals"; and there "must be some sort of an association of nations wherein all shall guarantee the territorial integrity of each." Others had considered some of these elements in the past; but nobody had drawn such a bold blueprint.

The holidays proved to be a time to grieve and a time to rejoice. Wilson traveled to Williamstown, Massachusetts, for Thanksgiving with the Sayres, and the family reunited at the White House for Christmas. Wilson's profound loneliness pervaded both occasions. When his friend Nancy Saunders Toy visited in early January, she found the President's sadness at the dining table as palpable as ever. Jessie, eight months pregnant, remained in Washington, while Frank returned to Massachusetts—only to be summoned weeks later, on the seventeenth of January. By the time he arrived, his son had been born—the President's first grandchild and the first baby born in the White House since Grover Cleveland's daughter twenty-one years prior. Wilson was elated but also, as he wrote Mary Hulbert, full of pity "that the sweet, sweet mother could not have been here to share her daughter's joy!" Wilson would not consent to the seven-pound, twelve-ounce boy being named for him; and so, his parents chose Francis Bowes Sayre, Jr., instead.

On December 8, 1914, Wilson appeared before Congress to deliver his Annual Message, the primary topic of which was national defense. To recent outcries that America was not "prepared for war," Wilson granted that the United States was not ready to put a trained military force into the field. What was more, that was how he intended to keep things. "We are at peace with all the world," he said with pride. Toward maintaining that position, he assured the nation, "We never have had, and while we retain our present principles and ideals we never shall have, a large standing army." Wilson hoped to hold America to its tradition of relying upon volunteer soldiers. He supported strengthening the National Guard but also feared the maintenance of a large military machine would only encourage its use.

In January 1915, Wilson began venturing from home, delivering the annual Jackson Day speech at Tomlinson Hall in Indianapolis. Much of his speech was partisan horseplay—calling the Republican Party nothing more than "a refuge for those who . . . want to consult their grandfathers about everything." But he also reiterated his message of neutrality.

Standing before a crowd in Middle America reminded Wilson of an often forgotten truism. The United States is actually an electorate composed of a majority of independent voters sandwiched between two minority parties. "You have got us in the palm of your hand," Wilson told that silent majority. "I do not happen to be one of your number, but I recognize your supremacy because I read the election returns." Wilson believed the way to attract that voter was not by bowing to him but by standing up taller for his beliefs—for he felt his party offered not only "good society" but also "great emotions." Wilson himself admitted to Mary Hulbert that the trip got him out of his rut and that it was "good to get my blood moving in a speech again."

Wilson saw the war in Europe as an opportunity to expand the crusade he had begun in Mexico—liberating "people everywhere from the aggressions of autocratic forces." At a time when TR was attacking him for not assuming a more aggressive posture in the matters of Mexico and Belgium—accusing him of "poltroonery"—the President sent Colonel House back to Europe "to ascertain what our opportunities as neutrals and as disinterested friends of the nations at war are in detail with respect to the assistance that we can render, and how those opportunities can best be made use of." House met with Secretary Bryan to tell him of his mission. "He was distinctly disappointed when he heard I was to go to Europe as the peace emissary," House noted in his journal. "He said he had planned to do this himself."

In a goodbye letter, the President said he hoped the mission might "prove the means of opening a way to peace." He had no delusions regarding its success, and he was unambiguous in defining House's role: "You are to act only as my private friend and spokesman, without official standing or authority. . . . Your conferences will not represent the effort of any government to urge action upon another government." Although Colonel House had never accepted a dime from either a state or the national government for any of his political work, the nature of this trip suggested extraordinary demands at a price beyond his means, and he agreed to a travel and social allowance of $4,000. "Of course you know," the President wired, "my heart goes with you."

On January 30, 1915, Colonel and Mrs. House boarded the largest, fastest, and poshest ship afloat—the Cunard Line's RMS *Lusitania*. The voyage launched a new phase in American foreign policy, that of an unofficial

American diplomat operating with carte blanche. Then, on February 4, while House was still at sea, Germany declared the waters surrounding the British Isles a war zone and warned civilian travelers that they crossed the ocean on belligerent nations' passenger ships at their own risk. The next day, as the *Lusitania* approached the Irish coast, the captain raised the flag of the United States, feigning neutrality.

Upon his arrival in London, House was granted an hour-long audience at Buckingham Palace with King George V, whose contempt for his first cousin the Kaiser prevented any talk of peacemaking. Meetings with British diplomats ensued, including numerous conversations with Sir Edward Grey, an Oxford-educated Liberal Member of Parliament and longtime Foreign Secretary. After a month, House crossed the Channel to France— passing a floating mine along the way—and then proceeded to Berlin, where he met Undersecretary Arthur Zimmermann. All parties showed indifference toward settling the war.

Only months earlier, Ambassador Morgenthau in Constantinople had written that the Ambassadors of England, Russia, and Germany all looked to Wilson to step in as "Peacemaker," that they recognized the folly of this war. But now, each nation was convinced it was winning. Britain's and France's lists of contraband deeply troubled the United States. Britain further declared the North Sea a war zone and began taking into custody ships trading with Germany. This blockade—even of necessities from neutral nations—spurred Germany to expand the war zone to include all waters surrounding the British Isles and to declare that all enemy merchant ships in those waters would be destroyed. On February 10, Bryan notified Germany that he expected assurances that American citizens and vessels would not be in danger even if their ships traversed the war zone; and he said the United States government would hold Germany accountable for inflicting damage upon American citizens or vessels. The British government was warned against deceptive use of the American flag.

In January 1915, Germans destroyed the *William P. Frye*, an American ship transporting wheat from Seattle to England; in March, they torpedoed the British ship *Falaba*, taking the life of an American passenger; in April a German airplane attacked the American steamship *Cushing*; and on May 1, a German submarine torpedoed the American tanker *Gulflight*. Wilson wanted to call the German government to account for its repeated attacks. Bryan felt the President should warn the American people before taking on the Germans, saying that while under international law Americans had a technical right to go where they pleased, there was "a moral duty which they owe to their government to keep out of danger . . . and thereby relieve their government from responsibility for their safety." It was not difficult to depict the Germans as the devils in this struggle, but the British were no angels. Germans wondered why there was so much outrage over the loss of a few innocent American lives when a blockade was starving an entire nation.

"I go to bed every night absolutely exhausted, trying not to think about anything," Wilson wrote Mary Hulbert. He found time to maintain his few correspondences with his women friends; but the President had to resign himself to the fact that there was little hope for a widower of his age to have another stab at romance, especially while he was incarcerated in the White House. There was "a void in his heart," Dr. Grayson recalled. He knew that "however bravely he smiled upon the world he was lonely." As Wilson himself put it in a letter to his daughter Jessie at the end of winter, "My heart has somehow been stricken dumb."

In the spring, Cary Grayson fell in love, and he hoped his feelings might be contagious. He had become smitten with a beautiful young heiress in Washington named Alice Gertrude Gordon, whose friends called her Altrude. Before his death, Altrude's father—a wealthy mining engineer—had prevailed upon a longtime friend, Edith Galt, to "look out for" his motherless teenaged daughter. Mrs. Galt knew her only slightly; but, recently widowed, she agreed to serve as an unofficial guardian. A five-month trip to Europe together bonded the two lonely women; and, as it happened, Mrs. Galt was also friendly with Cary Grayson. One day, while he and the President were motoring through town, they passed her on the street and Grayson bowed in salutation. "Who," the President asked, "is that beautiful woman?"

The question startled Grayson, for it was one of the President's few spontaneous comments in months and his first romantic flutter since Ellen's death. He wondered how he might arrange a meeting. He called upon Mrs. Galt and cleverly asked for her help in dealing with a sick friend—Helen Bones. The President's sometime hostess and longtime houseguest was just then recovering from a serious illness, he said; and, with the

White House still devoid of any social life, Helen Bones desperately needed companionship and exercise. "My dear Doctor," Mrs. Galt said by way of refusing, "as you know I am not a society person. I have never had any contracts with official Washington, and don't desire any. I am, therefore, the last person in the world able to help you."

Trying another approach, Dr. Grayson telephoned Mrs. Galt one morning, asking if he might call upon her. He arrived in a White House car, along with Nell McAdoo and Helen Bones. As it was a beautiful day, Mrs. Galt agreed to join them for a drive. The women delighted in each other's company and arranged to see each other again; and they quickly became friends, exactly as Grayson had hoped. Mrs. Galt—famously the first woman in Washington to drive her own automobile—would take Helen in her electric car out to Rock Creek Park, where they walked along the bridle paths before returning to her house for tea.

She was born Edith Bolling on October 15, 1872, in Wytheville, Virginia—150 miles southwest of Staunton—the seventh of eleven children of William Holcombe Bolling and the former Sallie White. Her ancestors were among the first families of Virginia—predating them, in fact, as she was a direct descendant of the Indian princess Pocahontas. The Bollings lived on a plantation in eastern Virginia until the Civil War destroyed their life of "slaves and abundance." A graduate of the University of Virginia Law School, William Bolling moved to Wytheville, where he established a practice and became a Circuit Court Judge.

His big brick house in the center of town was filled with several generations of the family, plus an old freed slave who had insisted on remaining with them. With so many mouths to feed, they lived modestly. Edith was thirteen before she got past the town limits of Wytheville; and she spent most of her time tending to her father's mother, a sharp-tongued semi-invalid who seldom left the house, her condition the result of a riding accident in her youth. Always dressed in black, Grandmother Bolling taught Edith how to read and write, and then she added French, Bible studies, and all the needle arts. Although tough-skinned, Edith was tender toward those in need. She adored her father, who read the great books aloud at night and the Good Book on Sundays as the lay reader at the Episcopalian Church.

Edith received a boarding school education for a few years, until the limited family funds had to be spent on her younger brothers. By that time, she had shot up to her adult height, a striking five feet nine inches. While hardly well educated, she was a capable young woman—exuberant and domestic. She developed a shapely figure and carried herself with regal bearing.

Edith's oldest sister, Gertrude, had married a man named Alexander Hunter Galt and moved with him to Washington. The winter after her schooling ended, Edith stayed with them for four months and was introduced to a world of culture. Returning one night from a concert to the house on G Street, she found the Galts dining with Alexander's cousin Norman. A decade older than Edith, the lonely bachelor lived with his father in a gloomy brownstone and worked in the family business—"Galt & Bro., Jewellers," established in 1801, the city's leading emporium for silver, timepieces, and fine stationery. Edith Bolling made an immediate impression upon him.

Norman sent her flowers and candy, visited her in Wytheville, and was often at his cousin's house when Edith returned to Washington the following winter. He became so much a part of the family that it never crossed her mind that he would want to marry, especially as she luxuriated in her independence. But at twenty-four, with no plans for a career, she accepted his proposal.

It was a union without passion, but not unhappy. Edith moved into her father-in-law's house until she and Norman could afford a small place of their own. Within a few years, Norman's father, brother, and brother-in-law died, as did Edith's father. In 1903, at age thirty, she gave birth to a son, but complications quickly developed: she would not be able to conceive again; and the infant died after three days. Edith and Norman drifted apart. He became the sole owner of the family business, providing positions for Edith's brothers. Yearning for gaiety, she traveled to New York, attended theater, and shopped for fashionable clothes. In 1908, two years after the couple moved into a larger house at 1308 Twentieth Street NW just off Dupont Circle, Norman died.

"I was left with an active business either to maintain or to liquidate, upon which all my income was dependent," Edith later recounted. She had no business experience, and the estate still owed money to the Galt relatives Norman had bought out. Edith felt further indebted to the employees who had served the firm for decades and to her own three brothers who worked there, supporting their mother and unmarried sister. Edith, at age thirty-five, decided to run the company. She drew the smallest possible salary for herself until her debts were paid. Afterward, she could indulge in an annual grand tour of Europe but always returned to an empty house. By forty, she was settling into a comfortable but lonely widowhood.

Edith had both the time and inclination to enjoy her new friendship with Helen Bones. She delighted in hearing stories about Helen's cousin Woodrow, because they contrasted so sharply with his public image. Edith had previously considered the President "a human machine, devoid of emotion." Now she felt only sympathy for the "lonely man . . . uncomplainingly bearing the burden of a great sorrow and keeping his eye single to the responsibilities of a great task."

One afternoon in March 1915, instead of riding in Edith's electric car, Helen insisted on changing their routine by having a White House limousine take them to the park. After a long walk along muddy paths, Edith suggested returning to her house, where she would have Helen's boots cleaned. "We are not going to your house," Helen said. "I have ordered tea at the White House this afternoon, and you are to go back with me." Edith insisted she could not for fear of being seen with such muddy shoes; but Helen explained that there was nobody home. Cousin Woodrow was playing golf with Dr. Grayson, and they could take the White House elevator directly to the private quarters. "Cousin Woodrow asked me the other day why I never brought my friends back there," she explained. "He really wishes I would have some one in that lonely old house."

But exiting the elevator, Edith was surprised to see the President and his physician, just returned from golf, their shoes as muddy as those of the women. Helen explained that they were about to have tea, and she invited the gentlemen to join them. After the men had changed and everybody's shoes had been cleaned, they gathered for an hour in the oval sitting room on the second floor, where Edith displayed her vivacity and tart sense of humor. Wilson was struck by his guest, with her wide smile and buxom figure. Dr. Grayson had clearly arranged the "chance encounter." Wilson and Helen invited Edith to remain for dinner, but she chose not to overstay her welcome.

The two women continued their walks together, and Edith redeemed her rain check on Tuesday, March 23. The White House sent a car for her, and they picked up Dr. Grayson along the way. Grayson left dinner early

to make a house call at the McAdoos', leaving the President alone to entertain Helen and Edith. He charmed them with stories and, upon Helen's
request, the reading of several poems. Edith reported to her sister-in-law
that night that as a reader, "he is unequalled."

Two weeks later, Helen invited Edith for a drive. The big White House
open touring car picked her up, and returned to get Helen, only to find the
President ready to join them as well. He sat up front with the chauffeur,
while the Secret Service agent took a seat in the back with Helen and
Edith. Wilson and Helen begged Edith to dine with them, explaining
that they would otherwise be alone. After dinner, the three of them sat by
the fire, where the President felt so much at ease that he shared stories of
his youth and of his father. Edith did the same, animatedly talking in her
Virginian accent about the heartache of Reconstruction. The whole evening passed quickly for Edith; and she was touched by Wilson's "warm
personality" and "boylike simplicity."

The following Wednesday, Wilson invited Edith to join his party at
Griffith Stadium, where he tossed out the first ball at the opening game
of the baseball season. They got to watch the Washington Senators shut
out the New York Yankees, 7 to 0. Edith's walks with Helen continued,
and soon Nell and Margaret joined them. With the arrival of warm
weather, Woodrow and Edith and Helen took rides in the afternoon and
the evenings in the comfortable open-air car. Mrs. Galt became a regular
dinner guest at the White House, and the staff began to talk amongst
themselves. "She's a looker," the doorkeeper told Colonel Edmund W. Starling, the newest member of the White House Secret Service detail and
Wilson's personal bodyguard. "He's a goner," confirmed Arthur Brooks,
the President's valet. One evening Edith outshone herself, wearing a
smartly tailored black charmeuse dress designed especially for her by
Worth, the leading Paris designer, and a pair of gold slippers—all meant
to match the corsage of golden roses that had arrived earlier that day with
the President's card. The evening ended early only because the President
was leaving the next morning for his grandson's baptism in Williamstown.

Wilson returned a few days later, on May 3, and invited Mrs. Galt to
dine the next night. Margaret and Helen and Dr. Grayson were there, as
were Wilson's sister Annie Howe and her daughter. It was a prematurely
warm evening; and after dinner, Wilson suggested having coffee on the
South Portico, with its privileged vista of the city. Dr. Grayson left right

after the meal, and suddenly—as if on cue—all the other guests decided to walk around the South Lawn, leaving Edith alone with the President. In that moment, he pulled his chair closer to hers. "I asked Margaret and Helen to give me an opportunity to tell you something tonight that I have already told them," he said. And then, he declared his love for her.

Without thinking, Edith blurted, "Oh, you can't love me, for you don't really know me, and it is less than a year since your wife died."

"Yes," he said, "I know you feel that; but, little girl, in this place time is not measured by weeks, or months, or years, but by deep human experiences; and since her death I have lived a lifetime of loneliness and heartache. I was afraid, knowing you, I would shock you; but I would be less than a gentleman if I continued to make opportunities to see you without telling you what I have told my daughters and Helen: that I want you to be my wife."

Before she could speak again, the President addressed the unique obstacles of his proposal, those even greater than his having known her for only two months. With a spotlight always directed upon the White House, he explained, all who enter were observed; and no matter how hard he worked to protect her, gossip would inevitably begin.

After Woodrow and Edith had talked for more than an hour, she told him if he required an answer that night, it was no. Never having given herself wholly to any man—certainly not to one of Wilson's passions—she had to consider whether she wanted to sacrifice her independence at this stage of her life. She had to ask herself not just how she felt about Woodrow Wilson but also about becoming a wife again—and a public figure at that. At ten o'clock, he and Helen escorted Edith home in silence.

Edith could not sleep that night. She sat in the big chair by her window and stared into the darkness, thinking how he had made her "whole being . . . vibrant!" In the morning hours, she calmed herself by committing her thoughts to paper. Edith considered it "an unspeakable pleasure and privilege" to share the President's "tense, terrible days of responsibility" but felt inadequate, unable to offer any gift so great. "I am a woman," she wrote Woodrow, trying to get used to the very "thought that you have *need* of me."

Hours later, Helen arrived for their walk through Rock Creek Park. She said nothing of the night before until they sat on some stones in the middle of the woods. "Cousin Woodrow looks really ill this morning," she said. Then she burst into tears and added, "Just as I thought some happiness was coming into his life! And now you are breaking his heart." Edith tried to explain how unprepared she had been for the suddenness of Woodrow's announcement—that up until then she had not allowed herself to think of him as anything but the President and a delightful new friend. At the same time, she knew she was right in asking for time to sift through her feelings.

She was in a quandary—"more and more torn by the will to love and help him, and yet unconvinced that I could." Edith handed her late-night letter to Helen, who became the lovers' go-between. She nicknamed her cousin "Tiger"—not, as some have suspected, for his animal desires nor even because of his Princeton connection but because Helen found him "so pathetic caged there in the White House . . . that he reminded her of a splendid Bengal tiger she had once seen—never still, moving, restless, resentful of his bars that shut out the larger life God had made him for."

So began the most ardent chase of Wilson's life. His hundreds of letters to the former Ellen Axson had expressed every romantic sentiment he could conjure, but they were callow sentiments alongside the torrent of words that would now engulf Edith—billets-doux employing every manner of entreaty. There was urgency in the Tiger's pursuit, fueled by the gratitude that he had been granted one final stab at love. The same held true for Edith, except she realized that this was her first.

The last twenty-four hours had left Wilson spent, but Edith's letter replenished him. And that night, he shamelessly stripped his emotions bare. "Here stands your friend, a longing man, in the midst of a world's affairs," he wrote, "—a world that knows nothing of the heart he has shown you . . . but which he cannot face with his full strength or with the full zest of keen endeavor unless you come into this heart and take possession."

Meetings and briefings, of course, came between his morning letters and evening dinners with Edith. He learned of a new conflict between China and Japan and once again offered the protection of the Monroe Doctrine to a new President of Haiti. He was even more troubled by Colonel House's informing him that Allied diplomats were suggesting that the President was pro-German, just as England—with more than two million men in its military ranks—expected to get through the Dardanelles and help Russia, which was already running out of munitions. But until Edith accepted his proposal, Wilson felt as if his world stood still. And then came news that put everything out of mind, not just for America but for most of the world.

On May 7, 1915, the President had just finished lunch and was preparing to play golf when he learned that a submarine had sunk the *Lusitania*. That first bulletin reported no loss of life, but the President canceled his game nonetheless, opting for a drive instead. News dribbled in through the night, giving him time to write Edith, "My happiness absolutely depends upon your giving me your entire love." He feared that she was overthinking the situation, second-guessing what was best for him— "when the only thing that is best for me is your love."

The President was beside himself that night. Possessed, he stepped right past his Secret Service guards and out the front door of the White House onto Pennsylvania Avenue, into a light shower, as though he were headed to Edith's house. Then, instead of veering left toward Dupont Circle, he felt duty pulling him home. By ten o'clock, more details of the day's events were available. It seemed that, without any warning, the German submarine *U-20* had fired two torpedoes into the belly of the *Lusitania*— seven days out of New York and in the Irish Sea. The great liner sank in eighteen minutes, taking 1,198 souls with it—413 crewmembers and 785 passengers, 128 of whom were American citizens.

"The country was horrified, and at that moment the popular feeling was such that if the President, after demanding immediate reparation and apology to be promptly given, had boldly declared that . . . it was our duty to go to war, he would have had behind him the enthusiastic support of the whole American people," recalled Senator Henry Cabot Lodge. Although the sinking of the ship was not a targeted attack on the United States, the *Lusitania* became a battle cry for a growing number of jingoes. Nobody sounded the charge more loudly than Theodore Roosevelt. Even before all the facts were known, he bellowed to the media that the incident was "an act of piracy." He said, "We earn as a nation measureless scorn and contempt if we follow the lead of those who exact peace above righteousness." Roosevelt told his son Archibald, "Every soft creature, every coward and weakling, every man who can't look more than six inches ahead, every man whose god is money, or pleasure, or ease, and every man who has not got in him both the sterner virtues and the power of seeking after an ideal, is enthusiastically in favor of Wilson."

There was, of course, an opposing view, which Secretary Bryan voiced in the Cabinet Room. He felt Americans had to take responsibility for their actions. One week before the *Lusitania*'s crossing, the Imperial German Embassy in Washington had posted admonitory advertisements in fifty American newspapers in a box beneath the Cunard Line's schedule. It reminded travelers that a state of war existed between Germany and her allies and Great Britain and her allies and that travelers sailing in the war zone on British or Allied ships did so at their own risk.

When Bryan heard the news, he immediately wondered if the ship carried "munitions of war." If she did, he said, "it puts a different phase on the whole matter!" Assistant Secretary Lansing reported that an examination of the clearance papers revealed that there had been ammunition on board. International law permitted ships to carry small quantities of ammunition; but upon learning the actual numbers, Bryan said the 4,200 cases of rifle cartridges and 1,250 cases of shrapnel, along with cases of fuses, shell castings, and high explosives meant the United States should rebuke not only Germany for destroying the *Lusitania* but also England for interference in international shipping, particularly for "using our citizens to protect her ammunition." From London, Colonel House cabled that an "immediate demand should be made upon Germany for assurance that this shall not occur again." More than that, the United States must consider the inevitability of going to war. America, he added, "must determine whether she stands for civilized or uncivilized warfare. Think we can no longer remain neutral spectators. Our action in this crisis will determine the part we will play when peace is made, and how far we may influence the settlement for the lasting good of humanity." Ordinary citizens were even more outspoken. One wired the White House, "In the name of God and humanity, declare war on Germany." To that, Wilson took offense, telling his secretary, Charles Swem, "War isn't declared in the name of God; it is a human affair entirely." *The Washington Post* editorialized that it had faith in the "courage, patience and wisdom of President Wilson," and it waited to see how he intended to "uphold the honor and interests of the United States."

In truth, Wilson was not thinking straight—laboring, as he was, over two, even three love letters a day, some requiring more than one draft as

he felt Edith was coming around at last. "You ask why *you* have been chosen to help me! Ah, dear love," he wrote on May 9, "there *is* a mystery
about it . . . but there is no mistake and there is no doubt!"

On May 10, 1915, Woodrow and Edith saw each other in the afternoon
and professed their mutual love. "The most delightful thing in the world,"
he told her, was "that I am permitted to *love you*." With that, the Chief of
State entrained to Philadelphia, where he addressed fifteen thousand people at Convention Hall—including four thousand recently naturalized
citizens. Speaking from his shorthand outline, he spun some romantic ideals before settling down to the issue of American neutrality in the face of
that week's disaster. "The example of America must be a special example,"
he said, ". . . not merely of peace because it will not fight, but of peace
because peace is the healing and elevating influence of the world, and
strife is not." Full of humanity that evening, he blurted, "There is such a
thing as a man being too proud to fight. There is such a thing as a nation
being so right that it does not need to convince others by force that it is
right."

"Too proud to fight," became the next day's headline and an easy target
for the political opposition. "This was probably the most unfortunate
phrase that he ever coined," said Henry Cabot Lodge, the Republican
leader, who always resented Wilson's rhetorical gifts and who intended to
make political hay out of the comment. With 128 Americans at the bottom of the Irish Sea, it struck many as tone-deaf. "It was not the moment
for fine words or false idealism," said Lodge; and this turning the other
cheek gave Wilson's opponents—especially those disavowing neutrality—
the chance to strike again. "The phrase 'too proud to fight,' uttered at such
a moment, shocked me, as it did many others," Lodge said, "and I never
again recovered confidence in Mr. Wilson's ability to deal with the most
perilous situation which had ever confronted the United States in its relations with the other nations of the earth."

The four-word phrase was, in fact, a re-articulation of his attitude
about American neutrality as a badge of "splendid courage of reserve moral
force." But even Wilson himself admitted he was not sure what he had
said in Philadelphia, since Edith remained foremost in his mind. "If I said
what was worth saying to that great audience last night," he wrote her the
next day, "it must have been because love had complete possession of me."

At a press conference the next morning, the President backpedaled, insisting he had not been dictating any policy in Philadelphia, merely speaking for himself. The significance of the *Lusitania* was not lost on him. He told Tumulty that he could not bring himself to ponder the details of the tragedy because, if he did, he was afraid that "when I am called upon to act . . . I could not be just to any one." He vowed not to "indulge my own passionate feelings."

"I could go to Congress to-morrow and advocate war with Germany," Wilson said, "and I feel certain that Congress would support me, but what would the country say when war . . . finally came, and we were witnessing all of its horrors and bloody aftermath." He knew that once the people began poring over the casualty lists, they would wonder why Wilson had not tried to settle the matter with Germany peaceably. "When we move against Germany," he said, suggesting that day would come, "we must be certain that the whole country not only moves with us but is willing to go forward to the end with enthusiasm. I know that we shall be condemned for waiting, but in the last analysis I am the trustee of this nation, and the cost of it all must be considered in the reckoning before we go forward." Wilson insisted he was not afraid to fight; but the deaths of 128 Americans who had been warned against sailing on a belligerent's ship into a war zone did not demand a declaration of war. The next day, the President received unexpected support from his predecessor and former rival: William Howard Taft urged Wilson to stick to his guns. He believed it was the duty of every patriotic citizen to resist the "impulse of deep indignation which the circumstances naturally arouse" and not to second-guess the President.

In the quiet of his study, Wilson typed his nation's response to the loss of American lives at German hands. He reminded the Imperial German government that its current policy was infringing upon the "sacred freedom of the seas." He said its delineation of a war zone touched upon the coasts of many neutral nations (which, in fact, was not true, as the Netherlands was the only neutral country in the war zone) and further infringed upon the rights of noncombatants bound on lawful errands. Submarines, Wilson wrote, "cannot be used against merchantmen without an inevitable violation of many sacred principles of justice and humanity." Wilson called upon the German government to disavow its recent unjust acts, to make reparations, and to take immediate steps to prevent the recurrence of further subversion of the principles of warfare. American citizens were within their rights to travel on the high seas, he insisted, especially as the United States and Germany were bound by "special ties of friendship."

Wilson sent the draft to Bryan for his and Lansing's suggestions—in diction, not direction. Bryan still thought the American government should condemn Allied violations and urge arbitration; Lansing, on the other hand, urged a tougher position. The President followed his instincts and instructed the Secretary of State to transmit his message. Bryan did so, but—he made clear to his boss—"with a heavy heart." Without doubting Wilson's "patriotic purpose," Bryan disagreed with his approach. He believed in "playing the part of a friend to both sides in the role of peace maker," and he feared this note would upset the balance. Bryan did not convey that he felt further compromised by Wilson's increased reliance on Colonel House. Indeed, House was digging back channels, trying to get Britain to lift its embargo if Germany would curb its use of submarines and lethal gases.

At the Cabinet meeting on Tuesday, May 11, the President shared House's latest dispatch from London, which questioned American neutrality. Bryan was hurt that the President had not shared the cable with him before discussing it with the Cabinet as a whole. He became visibly perturbed as the meeting progressed, until he heatedly accused some members of the Cabinet of no longer being neutral. With that, the President turned his steely gaze on the Secretary of State and fixed his jaw. "Mr. Bryan," he said, "you are not warranted in making such an assertion. We all doubtless have our opinions in this matter, but there are none of us who can justly be accused of being unfair." Bryan apologized.

The President and several family members escaped that weekend to the *Mayflower*, which was sailing to New York for the President to review the Atlantic Fleet. "The night was clear and the Potomac River like silver," Edith recalled; and after dinner she and Wilson drifted off alone into the moonlight. He did not speak of romance that night; instead, he leaned on the rail and discussed something she sensed had been troubling him. "I am very much distressed over a letter I had late today from the Secretary of State," he allowed, "saying he cannot go on in the Department as he is a pacifist and cannot follow me in wishing to warn our own country and Germany that we may be forced to take up arms; therefore he feels it is his duty to resign." Edith was no student of politics, but Woodrow was surely testing her instincts. "Good," she said, without a moment of hesitation;

"for I hope you can replace him with someone who . . . would in himself command respect for the office both at home and abroad."

When Wilson said he was thinking of appointing Robert Lansing in his place, she replied, "But he is only a clerk in the State Department, isn't he?" In truth, Lansing was more than that—indeed, a counselor to the Department and a son-in-law of John W. Foster, a former Secretary of State who, Wilson thought, might provide some guidance to the less experienced Lansing. Edith realized she had much to learn if she was to become First Lady; Woodrow realized Edith was full of knee-jerk opinions—all of which would always be what she considered were in his best interests.

At the end of the month, Wilson received a reply from the Germans. They expressed deep regret to the neutral nations that lost lives in the sinking of the *Lusitania* but asked the United States to examine further the details of the event: the *Lusitania* had been constructed with government funds as an auxiliary cruiser in the British navy; and the ship had been transporting ammunition and arms, including guns "which were mounted under decks and masked." In addition, the ship had been known to sail under neutral flags and, in this instance, had been transporting Canadian troops. The German government said it had acted in "just self-defense," that it was protecting the lives of its soldiers by destroying ammunition destined for its enemy. The note suggested that the British had been using Americans as human shields, violating American law, which prohibited the carrying of passengers on ships with explosives on board. Wilson found those paragraphs "wholly unsatisfactory."

But the nation sighed in relief, as the rest of the German note assured the United States of its intentions to renew its instructions to avoid attacking neutral vessels. Wilson and Bryan continued to disagree on the tone with which they should proceed. The President's excruciating headaches returned, but he continued to draft a second note to the Germans. He challenged their assertion that the *Lusitania* was transporting troops and masked guns, and argued that the sinking of a passenger ship involved principles of humanity—"a great steamer, primarily and chiefly a conveyance for passengers . . . was sent to the bottom without so much as a challenge or a warning and that men, women, and children were sent to their death in circumstances unparalleled in modern warfare."

Bryan disapproved. The note omitted any mention of his preference for mediation; there was to be no simultaneous protest sent to England; and it did not bar Americans from traveling on ships carrying ammunition. Worst of all, Bryan felt it offered Germany "no chance to do anything but refuse to discontinue her submarine warfare." Refusing to sign the document, Bryan preferred to resign from office.

After a few sleepless nights, he met with the President for an hour. "Mr. Wilson would not yield a point, nor would Mr. Bryan," recalled Mrs. Bryan. At last her husband said, "Colonel House has been Secretary of State, not I, and I have never had your full confidence." Wilson could not deny the charge. He accepted the Secretary's resignation that night, though they waited a day to make it public. Strangely, after all his doubts about Bryan, the severance hurt Wilson. "It is always painful to feel that any thinking man of disinterested motive, who has been your comrade and confidant, has turned away from you," Wilson told Edith, ". . . and it is hard to be fair and not think that the motive is something sinister. But . . . I have been deserted before. The wound does not heal, with me, but neither does it cripple." In a touching note of valediction that would be published, Wilson wrote Bryan, "Even now we are not separated in the object we seek but only in the method by which we seek it. . . . We shall continue to work for the same causes even when we do not work in the same way."

"Hurrah! old Bryan is out!" Edith wrote Woodrow the morning of June 9. "I know it is going to be the greatest possible relief to you to be rid of him. Your letter is *much* too nice, and I see why *I* was not allowed to see it before publication." Jubilantly she told him "that at last the world will *know* just what he is." William Jennings Bryan had been, in fact, an earnest and principled public servant, making the most of a position in which he was never fully empowered. But Edith called him "that awful Deserter." Wilson realized he would not have to carry grudges so long as he had Edith by his side. "I will be glad when he expires from an overdose of peace or grape juice," she wrote ten days after Bryan's resignation, "and I never hear of him again." With a loving but objective eye, Woodrow wrote Edith, "You are, oh, so *fit* for a strong man! . . . What a dear partisan you are!" He loved her for that—"and how you can *hate*, too. Whew! . . . In my secret heart (which is never secret from you) . . . he *is* a traitor, though I can say so, as yet, only to you."

The second *Lusitania* note went to Germany signed by Robert Lansing, the interim Secretary, who would soon officially assume the post. The German response, sent through Ambassador Gerard in Berlin, showed a willingness to cooperate but asked for the same. Foreign Minister Gottlieb von Jagow said submarine warfare was his nation's only chance of breaking the Allies' blockade. While Germany would not consider the mere presence of Americans on a ship enough to spare it, he did promise protection for American vessels and Americans on neutral vessels—so long as they were not transporting contraband. The seas were calm well into the summer.

Then on August 19, 1915, a German U-boat torpedoed the White Star Liner *Arabic* off the coast of Ireland. Submarines carried orders not to sink passenger ships without warning, but the commander of *U-24* said he interpreted the *Arabic*'s zigzag route as an indication that it was about to ram his boat. Two Americans died. A stern rebuke from Lansing elicited several demotions within the Kaiser's navy and a renewed pledge from the German government not to attack unarmed liners without warning. Less than three months later, *U-38* torpedoed the Italian passenger liner *Ancona* off the coast of Tunisia, taking two hundred lives, nine Americans among them; but in dealing with Germany, America continued to rely on epistolary diplomacy.

Never had so many parts of the world demanded a President's attention. In Mexico, the Carranza forces appeared strong enough to overpower Zapata and Villa and warrant American recognition, vindicating Wilson's policy of "watchful waiting." But Wilson felt obligated to tell the factional leaders that "if they cannot accommodate their differences and unite for this great purpose within a very short time, this Government will be constrained to decide what means should be employed by the United States in order to help Mexico save herself and serve her people." Cotton remained a political football. Great Britain vacillated on its status as contraband, expecting the right to buy American munitions, but then confiscated shipments of America's great export staple intended for even neutral countries. Secretary Garrison continued discussing a regular Army of 300,000 men at the astronomical cost of $1 billion, though Wilson still believed too strong an Army created the compulsion to unleash it. At the same time, delegations of women petitioned the President to support their right to vote; the NAACP pressured the President to demonstrate sympathy for the Negro's cause; while in the Ottoman Empire, the party of "Young Turks" was now helping massacre Armenians; in Denmark, the government negotiated for the American purchase of its territories in the West Indies; and in America, citizens anxiously anticipated the next submarine attack. And through it all, the President wrote Edith Galt, "love has set me free from all real distress." Until May 27.

Woodrow and Edith went for a ride after dinner that night for almost two hours. The driver and Helen Bones sat up front, offering the couple privacy in the back. Only they knew what transpired behind the drawn curtains; but their letters to one another the next morning suggest that Woodrow made advances, which an unready Edith rebuffed. "For God's sake try to find out whether you really love me or not," Woodrow wrote in frustration. "You owe it to yourself and you owe it to the great love I have given you. . . . Remember that I need strength and certainty for the daily task and that I cannot walk upon quicksand." Edith wished she could ease his pain. The young widow was not prudish so much as inexperienced, and in insisting that she loved him, she promised to get past her own barriers. "But *you*," she said, "must conquer!"

The President launched a relentless campaign. "You have invited me to make myself the master of your life and heart," he wrote, coaxing her to trust her instincts. "The rest is now as certain as that God made us . . . and *I shall win*, by a power not my own, a power which has never been defeated, against which no doors can be locked, least of all the doors of the heart." He added, "We will take hands now and walk together without fear withersoever our infallible guide may lead us."

At this ticklish moment in their courtship, an unfortunate guest arrived in Washington—Mary Hulbert. On May 31, Helen Bones was dispatched to meet Mary's early morning train; and Mrs. Jaffray gave her a private tour of the White House. The President made time to take a long drive with her—with Helen Bones chaperoning. It turned out that Mary had not come for romance but for money. Her hard-luck son had suffered a streak of bad health, and he needed cash to close a deal on some land in California's San Fernando Valley, where he intended to grow avocados.

For $7,500 the President assumed the mortgages on two properties the Hulberts held in the Bronx. And he supplemented that by recommending Mary's writing to a few publishers. She left the East Coast for several hapless years in Los Angeles, where neither her literary efforts nor the avocados ripened into sustainable careers. Wilson wrote Mary that he would miss her, but bade her farewell with polite "sympathy and hope," closing that chapter of their lives. From then on, she cobbled together a life of shabby gentility—publishing a cookbook, calling upon the friends she

"Sugar Jim"—New Jersey Democratic Party boss James Smith, Jr., who offered Wilson the opportunity to run for Governor, expecting the academician to serve as his puppet. Instead, Wilson promptly dismantled the party machine.

Governor Wilson in his office in the New Jersey State House in Trenton, 1911.

Wilson proved to be an effective campaigner for his political agenda, executing the most progressive slate of laws in the nation.

After less than a year of public service, Wilson allowed others to promote his candidacy for President. He had no supporters more loyal than newspaperman William Bayard Hale and former state legislator Joseph Patrick Tumulty, who became Wilson's private secretary and political adviser.

After a weeklong convention in Baltimore, the Democrats nominated Wilson as their candidate. On August 7, 1912, at the Governor's summer cottage in Sea Girt, New Jersey, Wilson accepted the nomination.

The election of 1912 pitted Wilson against an incumbent President, William Howard Taft, and a former President, Theodore Roosevelt (seen here), who ran as the candidate for the Bull Moose Party, and Socialist Eugene V. Debs.

On November 5, 1912, Governor Wilson walked to his Princeton polling place and cast his vote. He was elected the twenty-eighth President of the United States in a landslide.

March 3, 1913—the President-elect and Mrs. Wilson walked to the Princeton depot and then departed to Washington, D. C.

"There has been a change of government,"
Wilson proclaimed in his inaugural address on March 4, 1913.

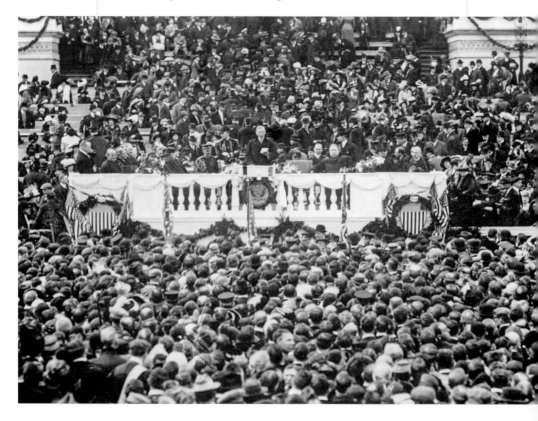

"I'm glad to be going," President William Howard Taft told Wilson upon leaving the White House, "—this is the loneliest place in the world."

The First Lady used her
social position to lobby
for improved housing
in Washington's slums.

Ellen Wilson pouring tea, with her daughters Jessie, Eleanor, and Margaret—as painted by American Impressionist Robert Vonnoh, one of Ellen's teachers when she studied at the Lyme Art Colony in Connecticut.

An accomplished artist, Ellen created a makeshift studio on the third floor of the White House, and exhibited her work in New York and Philadelphia. This oil on canvas—*Winter Landscape*—was painted probably in late 1911 to early 1912.

A team of Rebels: the Wilson Cabinet—mostly Southerners who never shed their Confederate biases. Clockwise from the left: Wilson, W. G. McAdoo, J. C. McReynolds, J. Daniels, D. F. Houston, W. B. Wilson, W. C. Redfield, F. K. Lane, A. S. Burleson, L. M. Garrison, W. J. Bryan.

The President and his Secretary of State, William Jennings Bryan— the longtime standard-bearer of the Democratic Party, who had lent his support to Wilson's nomination. Disagreeing with his handling of the sinking of the *Lusitania* in 1915, Bryan resigned.

Robert Lansing—the son-in-law of one Secretary of State and uncle of another, John Foster Dulles—succeeded Bryan at the State Department.

"My second personality," Wilson called Colonel Edward Mandell House. Unpaid and answerable to nobody but the President, he became Wilson's most trusted roving diplomat and adviser—for a while.

Wilson met Cary Travers Grayson, M.D., a lieutenant in the naval medical corps, at the start of his administration. Over the next eight years, he became Wilson's personal physician and most loyal friend.

Louis D. Brandeis was the leading architect of Wilson's "New Freedom," a program of progressive legislation that included establishing the Federal Reserve System and anti-trust regulation. After a bitter confirmation hearing, he became the first Jew to sit on the Supreme Court.

Wilson was at his most regressive in his civil rights policies, permitting segregation in federal workplaces. He always kept his door open to African American petitioners until activist-journalist William Monroe Trotter arrived with his grievances. "Your tone, sir, offends me," Wilson said, banning him from the White House for the duration of his term in office.

At Dr. Grayson's urging, Wilson sought recreation whenever possible. In the summers, he joined his vacationing family in Cornish, New Hampshire, where he could read a newspaper at his leisure.

Wilson played more golf than any President in White House history—an estimated twelve hundred rounds while in office.

In June 1914, he "P-raded" with his Class of 1879 at their 35th Princeton Reunion.

Tragedy struck in the summer of 1914 when war broke out across Europe and Ellen Wilson unexpectedly died of Bright's disease. Severely depressed, the President relied more than ever on the company of his inner circle— Tumulty, Dr. Grayson, and, as seen here, Colonel House.

In March 1915, Dr. Grayson introduced Wilson to a young Washington widow, Edith Bolling Galt, whom he quietly courted.

That October, they appeared together at a World Series game in Philadelphia; and that December, they married.

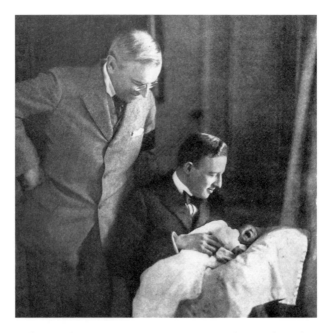

Wilson's other great joy that year was the birth of his first grandchild, seen here in the arms of his father. Francis Bowes Sayre, Jr., the last child to be born in the White House, would become the dean of the National Cathedral.

Wilson received official notification of his re-nomination for President on September 2, 1916, at Shadow Lawn in Long Branch, New Jersey. Standing below him (far left), in a light suit, is Assistant Secretary of the Navy Franklin D. Roosevelt.

Despite a nasty campaign, Wilson was always happy on the hustings. Running against Charles Evans Hughes, a former New York Governor and former Associate Justice of the Supreme Court, Wilson won on the slogan "He kept us out of war."

had once stylishly entertained, even picking up work as an extra in motion pictures—one of which, *The Great Love*, was directed by D. W. Griffith.

The day after seeing Mary Hulbert, Woodrow presented Edith with a ring. It was not an engagement ring, for he knew not to force the issue; but he knew enough to keep pressing. "There is no one else in the world for me now," he wrote her on June 1. Edith was accustomed to removing her rings each night, but this one, she said, would remain, as it gave her "the most exquisite pleasure." In addition to his inundation of love letters—which now spoke of "gentle caresses" and "precious kisses"—Woodrow filled Edith's house with roses and orchids. She became a more frequent visitor to the White House, arriving for tea with Helen but stealing moments with Woodrow. She made herself comfortable in Wilson's study among all his books.

In June, Wilson intensified his campaign by arranging a vacation with Edith in Cornish. Helen Bones and Margaret Wilson invited her to be their guest, and the women left by automobile on the first day of summer, stopping in Princeton, where Helen gave Edith a tour of the campus. As they arrived at Harlakenden, Wilson set out from Washington with Dr. Grayson, stopping in Roslyn, New York, to spend the day with Colonel House.

They spoke of international matters for a while, until Wilson leaned in, saying he had "an intimate personal matter" to discuss. "What would you think of my getting married again?" he asked. Wilson explained that he had met "a delightful woman" and was thinking of asking for her hand. "Do you believe I would lessen my influence with the American people by taking such a step? And when do you think I could do it? I have led such a lonely life that I feel it is necessary for me to have companionship of that sort, and my dear dead wife would be the first to approve." Although House did not let on to the President, Dr. Grayson and Attorney General Gregory had both intimated that such rumors had been swirling within the White House.

House himself approved—if only because the President's health demanded it and because he believed "Woodrow Wilson today is the greatest asset the world has." House confessed to his diary, "If he should die or become incapacitated, it is doubtful whether a right solution of the problems involved in this terrible conflict and its aftermath would be possible." But he cautiously urged postponement until the following spring.

House's advice made sense; but once Woodrow and Edith were reunited in Cornish, all logic went out the window. For the first time, the middle-aged lovers could spend extended periods alone, sometimes even away from the eyes of the Secret Service. "He was like a boy home from school," Edith recalled of those Arcadian days that summer, whenever the President was able to leave Washington. After breakfast they would sit on the terrace together and fish through the pouch of official mail, examining the catch together. When finished, they walked along the banks of the Connecticut River; in the afternoons, they invited the rest of their party to join them on long motor rides through the countryside, after which Dr. Grayson and the family took turns reading aloud from Wilson's *History of the American People*. Edith's favorite time came after a late dinner, when just the two of them sat before a fire in a room where the curtains had been drawn to shut out the cold night air. Together they would read the latest dispatches from around the world. "The President would clarify each problem for me," Edith recalled, "and outline the way he planned to meet it."

"Those days in Cornish had brought the banishment of any doubt of my love for Woodrow Wilson," she later recorded, "but had not overcome my reluctance to marry him while he was in the White House." She was, at heart, a provincial girl unready for a public international life. "I told him if he were defeated for re-election I would marry him, but if not I felt still uncertain." Then on June 29, 1915, she consented, in a note she composed on the West Porch of Harlakenden, while he was close at hand.

Wilson returned to an empty White House on July 19, 1915; and though the walls had been stripped for the summer and the furniture was dressed "in white pajamas," he did not feel lonely. "*You* were not actually here," he wrote Edith, "but your thought and love were here to greet me." For the rest of the summer, he scrawled long letters, sometimes a dozen pages or more, to Edith—interspersing accounts of the day's events with passionate expressions of his preoccupation: "You are everything to me," he wrote the following afternoon.

For the next several months, the President intensified what surely became the most romantic correspondence ever to emanate from the White House—250 letters between them, most of them expressing the desperate fervency of a world leader in crisis. In the middle of the night, precisely one year after Ellen died, he suddenly awakened. He did not know why exactly, but he recounted that in his dream Edith had disappeared and he found himself exclaiming, "Edith, my Darling, *where are you?*" Even though they gave themselves that month away from each other—in part to quell any gossip—Woodrow was revived.

Edith Bolling Galt was engaged in the first full-blown love affair of her life—and a Cinderella story at that. As she explained in a letter to Woodrow, "*I*—an unknown person—one who had lived a sheltered inconspicuous existence, now having all the threads in the tangled fabric of the world's history laid in her hands for a few minutes, while the strong hand, that quicks the shuttle, stops long enough in its work, to press my fingers in token of the great love and trust with which you crown and bless my life." Edith felt new purpose in her life and began training for it with gusto. She boned up on foreign affairs and United States history; she took golf lessons; she adopted Woodrow's quirky use of "okeh"—a Choctaw word meaning "it is so"—which he insisted was the proper form of "O.K." And she offered ferocious support for his decisions and fearless assessments of those who surrounded him, even his innermost circle: Dr. Grayson was above reproach, and the President was already in the process of promoting him; Tumulty she considered "common"; and Colonel House, she dared say, was "not a very strong character." She knew what a "comfort and staff" he was to Wilson, but she considered him "a weak vessel." Woodrow explained that House possessed a strong character and was noble, loyal, devoted, prudent, farseeing, and wise; but, he admitted, "His mind is not of the first class. He is a counsellor, not a statesman." Woodrow suggested that Edith would come to love House—"if only because he loves me and would give, I believe, his life for me." In preparing to become Mrs. Woodrow Wilson, Edith even found herself trying to match his eloquence. "Do you feel my arms 'round your neck and my lips on yours while I whisper—goodnight?" she wrote him mid-August.

When Edith returned to Washington at the start of September, she saw how world events had turned his eyes into "pools of tragic suffering." During their traditional drive, Wilson spoke of the increasing struggle to avoid entrance into the war, to say nothing of all the complications closer to home. "And so, little girl," he said, "I have no right to ask you to help me by sharing this load that is almost breaking my back, for I know your nature and you might do it out of sheer pity." And in that moment—despite the presence of the chauffeur, the Secret Service, and Helen Bones—Edith threw her arms around Woodrow's neck and said, "Well, if you won't ask me, I will volunteer." She agreed to marry him as soon as he was ready. She presumed he would suggest the American public would need a year to get used to the idea of the President taking a second wife.

Wilson divulged his intentions to his daughters, and each responded with enthusiasm. Margaret spoke for her sisters when she wrote Edith late that summer, "I'm so glad that he has your love to help him and support him in these terrible times! . . . I love you dear Edith, and I love to be with you." Edith revealed her secret to her mother and siblings, allowing Woodrow to reach out to them. He made them feel welcome at the White House, and he wrote Edith's mother that he hoped "that you will love me and accept me as your own son." The couple prepared to go public.

But then they encountered the first naysayers—right in the West Wing of the White House. Grayson, the matchmaker, knew how therapeutic it had been for the President to be in love again, but the rest of Wilson's advisers worried about the politics of the situation. Rumors of a love affair would not play as well with the electorate as the suffering of a grieving widower— especially in the quarter of the states (mostly in the Progressive West) that permitted women to vote. With Ellen dead only a year and the Presidential election only twelve months away, the Cabinet decided somebody had to advise the President to wait. They selected the President's son-in-law.

McAdoo—evidently in concert with Colonel House—devised a strangely devilish ploy. Over lunch on September 18, he told the President that he had received an anonymous letter asserting that rumors of his engagement had spread and that the desperate Mrs. Hulbert had been shopping his letters. Whatever her motive, McAdoo suggested, the letters were sure to create a scandal, possibly one that would portray their latest exchange as a $7,500 payoff. Wilson was aghast that Mary Hulbert could ever do such a thing. He knew the innocence of the correspondence, but he could also imagine how desperate Mary had become and how the political opposition in Washington would respond.

Shaken to the core, he dispatched a note to Edith, informing her that there was "something, personal to myself, that I feel I must tell you about at once." He took the liberty of asking if he might defy propriety and call upon her at home. "Of course, you can come to me," a distressed Edith replied, though she asked him to bring Dr. Grayson along, to provide the necessary cover.

Woodrow bared his soul. He told Edith—as he would later record in a letter to her—all about his relationship with "Mrs. Peck" and what he called "a passage of folly and gross impertinence in my life." For that, he was "deeply ashamed and repentant," and also tormented and confused. He could not understand what would possess anybody to publish such letters, knowing the humiliation they would bring. Wilson was contrite—not because Mrs. Peck was unworthy of the sentiments expressed in the letters but because Wilson felt he did not have "the moral right to offer the ardent affection which they express." In fact, the whole cache of mail seems to corroborate that the "affair" with Mrs. Peck did not trespass into the physical. Wilson said his "utter allegiance to my incomparable wife [had not been] in any way by the least jot abated."

None of that lessened either the shame Wilson suffered or the grief "that I should have so erred and forgotten the standards of honorable behavior by which I should have been bound." Now that indiscretion implicated Edith Galt. "Stand by me," he pled. "Don't desert me."

Edith hesitated, and Woodrow left her to sort out her feelings. Each endured a restless night. He lamented the pain he had brought to her. "When it was the deepest, most passionate desire of my heart to bring you happiness," he wrote her the next morning, ". . . I have brought you, instead, mortification and thrown a new shadow about you." After spending the night in her big chair by the window, she wrote Woodrow to apologize for having faltered.

"This is my pledge, Dearest One," she wrote. "I will stand by you—not for duty, not for pity, not for honor—but for love—trusting, protecting, comprehending Love. And no matter whether the wine be bitter or sweet we will share it together and find happiness in the comradeship." Woodrow was overjoyed.

House told the President he did not believe the issue of "the Peck letters" would ever amount to anything. The Colonel never mentioned that he knew that the entire incident had been trumped up. Instead, he graciously accepted the responsibility for planning the impending wedding, which the two men agreed could take place before the end of the year. House conceded that the salutary benefits of Wilson's remarrying far outweighed any political fallout.

A private telephone wire was installed between the White House and Edith's, avoiding any switchboards; letters passed between them several times a day, as did a pouchful of memoranda, with the President's comments and notations, so that Edith could brief herself on his activities. He continued to send flowers every day—orchids if they were dining out or attending the theater, a corsage that she would wear high on her left shoulder. He also changed the routine of his regular automobile ride by making time to stroll with Edith through Rock Creek Park; it was Agent Starling's task to follow them. He wanted to look away, to afford the lovers some privacy, but his job did not permit it. "He was an ardent lover," Starling recalled. "He talked, gesticulated, laughed, boldly held her hand. It was hard to believe he was fifty-eight years old."

The White House announced their engagement on Wednesday, October 6, 1915. In an accompanying statement, the President declared his intention to vote for woman suffrage in New Jersey the following month. He added that he would be voting as neither the leader of the nation nor of his party, only as a citizen of New Jersey. Although there was a strong movement for an equal rights amendment to the Constitution—which his daughter Margaret strongly advocated—Wilson believed this was a matter for each state to settle. The press credited Edith with turning Wilson into a suffragist; but, as Cary Grayson wrote Altrude Gordon, "The joke is that she's against it: but she's too good a diplomat to say anything on the subject these days."

Woodrow and Edith went to New York that Friday, to spend time with Colonel House and his wife. The President bunked at their apartment, while Edith and her mother stayed at the St. Regis Hotel. Before they went to dinner and the theater, Wilson received a jeweler, who arrived at the apartment with thirteen diamond rings, one of which Edith selected. Saturday the couple went to Philadelphia, where Wilson became the first President to attend a World Series game—as the Boston Red Sox beat the Philadelphia Phillies, 2 to 1. Thanksgiving weekend, the President showed off his bride-to-be at the annual Army and Navy football game at the Polo Grounds in New York. They sat in a box on the Army side of the gridiron until halftime, when the Admirals of the Navy came to escort their Commander in Chief across the field to the enthusiastic cheers of the entire stadium. "Every one," Edith observed, "seemed to be our friend." Even though the couple chose to send announcement cards in lieu of wedding invitations, gifts from all over the world began to arrive. Many came from manufacturers, hoping for a White House endorsement, while foreign delegations sent glassware, silverware, jewelry, and furniture. The only gift the President officially accepted was a nugget of California gold, which the state hoped they might hammer into a wedding ring.

Ironically, once the President and Mrs. Galt had made their relationship public, they could spend more time together in private. As they were engaged to be married, there was no need for furtiveness. On Sundays, after attending church, the couple would seclude themselves all day. Almost every night, a Secret Service agent accompanied Wilson to Twentieth Street and sat vigil outside Edith's house, usually until midnight. Often Wilson wanted to walk home along the late-night deserted streets; and Agent Starling could not but notice that the President would unconsciously jig a few steps whenever he had to wait for an occasional milk truck to pass. He also realized that when Wilson got lost in his own thoughts, he often whistled—softly, through his teeth—invariably the same tune, one he undoubtedly had heard in one of his visits to the theater: "Oh, you beautiful doll! You great big beautiful doll! Let me put my arms around you, I could never live without you."

The White House came alive again. The President smiled for most of his photographs. There were frequent small celebrations among intimate friends and family. On November 30, seventy-five members of the Class of 1879 went to the White House for a mini-reunion; the members of the old Witherspoon Gang spent the night in the guest rooms upstairs. "Dinner went off delightfully," Woodrow wired Edith, who had gone to shop in New York. ". . . You were unanimously elected an honorary member of the class amidst loud cheers."

Wilson delivered his State of the Union address on December 7, 1915. While it covered a variety of subjects, they encompassed one overall theme: "national efficiency and security." With war spreading across the globe, Wilson stood confidently behind his firewall, remaining "studiously neutral." While the British push through the Dardanelles had resulted in a bloodbath costing 100,000 lives, Wilson maintained that America's task was domestic—making "a common cause of national independence and of political liberty in America." He said the United States would "aid and befriend Mexico, but we will not coerce her. . . . We seek no political suzerainty or selfish control." He endorsed Pan-Americanism, the notion that the states of the Americas "are not hostile rivals but cooperating friends" and that there was "none of the spirit of empire in it." He expressed his belief in the Second Amendment—"the right of the people to keep and bear arms"—not for the sake of shooting each other but so that its citizens could be "ready and sufficient to take care of themselves and of the governments which they have set up to serve them" with a well-regulated militia.

Wilson called for preparedness—an increase of the regular Army and Navy and the building up of the merchant marine in order to stay competitive. New revenues would be needed. "I, for one, do not believe that the people of this country approve of postponing the payment of their bills," he said. "Borrowing money is short-sighted finance." He recommended a tax on gasoline and on automobiles and internal combustion engines. He urged legislation that would combat new threats of disloyalty and anarchy. He praised the nation for its spirit, which believed in "self-government, industry, justice, liberty and peace," all of which made Americans "heralds and prophets of a new age." Wilson was already contemplating the establishment of a department devoted to homeland security, to deal with "an unavoidable lack of coordination between the different Departments of the Government charged with investigation of . . . the activity of agents of the belligerent Governments in this country." The President wanted to ready the nation for civil defense, not war.

"Wilson is at heart an abject coward," Theodore Roosevelt had recently written his son Kermit; "or else he has a heart so cold and selfish that he is entirely willing to sacrifice the honor and the interest of the country to his own political advancement." Ever since the *Gulflight* was sunk, TR felt the nation should have declared war. He held Wilson "morally responsible" for the loss of American lives on the *Lusitania*; and he vociferously disapproved of Wilson's policy of half-preparedness, of valuing words over action. "There are no bad regiments but there are plenty of bad colonels," the "Hero of San Juan Hill" reminded his son. "The United States would stand like a unit if we had in the Presidency a man of the stamp of Andrew Jackson." In truth, Wilson was a practical centrist: there were ardent pacifists in the country, such as Bryan; and there were even a few dreamers with ideas airier than Wilson's—such as Henry Ford.

On December 4, 1915, the austere automobile manufacturer floated a concept so utopian, it momentarily captured the attention of the world. He sponsored a series of peace conferences in the capitals of neutral European nations, at which he hoped to gather enough representatives to discuss a settlement of the war. Ford believed he could will an armistice into existence. Toward that end, he chartered a Scandinavian ocean liner, the *Oscar II*, and filled it with 166 passengers, including pacifists and activists, journalists, and students. Sailing to Norway, Sweden, Denmark, and Holland, Ford planned to strafe Europe with messages of peace compelling enough to lure the belligerents to the conference table. William Jennings Bryan, Thomas Edison, and three thousand other peace advocates appeared in Hoboken to bid them bon voyage. But the journey attracted little attention from those at war. When this Peace Expedition proved to be futile, Ford himself jumped ship, quietly leaving the tour to sail home on another vessel. The great venture was quickly ridiculed despite its noble ambitions; but it had its defenders. H. G. Wells would write in 1933 that "despite its failure, this effort to stop the war will be remembered when the generals and their battles and senseless slaughter are forgotten." Even Ford conceded, "I didn't get much peace, but I heard in Norway that Russia might well become a huge market for tractors soon."

The President and Colonel House spent most of December 15 together at the White House. Wilson was dissatisfied with American relations with all the participants in the war and wanted House to return to Europe to express America's desire to join the international conversation. After dinner, the two men called upon Edith for a half hour. She expressed regret that House would not be at their wedding; but the Colonel sensitively suggested that his presence would only engender a lot of hurt feelings within the Administration. Indeed, this third Wilson wedding in two years was to be the most exclusive event of his Presidency.

The bride and groom decided not to marry in the White House, eschewing all protocol for something personal. The ceremony and reception would be held in Edith's town house with only their families present. They agreed that both their faiths should be represented—by the pastor of the city's Central Presbyterian Church and an Episcopalian Bishop. Edith invited the latter to be her guest at the Shoreham Hotel in Washington; and because of the strictly familial nature of the occasion, she explained that his wife was not invited. He understood, only to shock Edith on December 16 when he sent her a note from the Shoreham explaining that it would cause his wife "much chagrin to acknowledge to her titled friends that she had not been asked to the marriage of the President where her husband had officiated." As his wife was with him at the hotel, he presumed she would be welcome at the ceremony. Edith read the Bishop's letter twice and handwrote her reply, thanking him for his explanation of the embarrassing situation . . . and then relieving him from his duty of performing the ceremony.

Before sealing her note, she rang the President and read the Bishop's letter and her reply. Woodrow agreed that the Bishop had overstepped but suggested that his position demanded some respect. "No," Edith told Woodrow, "this letter goes to him right now. I will postpone our wedding rather than be bludgeoned into a thing of this kind."

"Yes," replied the President, "I was afraid of that. But, after all, the poor fellow has enough to stand with a wife like that." Edith called upon the rector of her local church to replace the Bishop.

Two days later, on December 18, 1915, White House usher Ike Hoover took charge of Edith's house. He emptied the lower floor of all furniture and moved in a team of decorators and caterers. In the recess of the window in the front room, florists created a semicircular bower filled with maidenhair ferns and a canopy lined in Scotch heather, a tribute to the President's roots. There were many sprays of purple orchids, Edith's favorites, in the room; and the rest of the space was decorated with palms and American Beauty roses. The prie-dieu that had served in several White House weddings was covered in white satin and adorned with more orchids. Back at the White House, the President worked with his stenographer in the morning and hosted the wedding guests for lunch. Late in the afternoon, he and Edith went for a drive, returning to the White House at six. He presented her with a brooch of white diamonds.

With only his Secret Service escort, Wilson arrived at Edith's house at eight o'clock and went upstairs to her sitting room. He waited alone for a half hour, until Hoover tapped on the door. The nearly fifty-nine-year-old groom, in a cutaway coat, white waistcoat, and gray striped trousers, looked upon his forty-three-year-old bride, wearing a black velvet gown and matching hat and her brooch. They descended the stairs together as a small string section from the Marine Band played the wedding march from *Lohengrin*. Downstairs waited their families and a handful of friends, including Tumulty, a few Bolling retainers, Edith's doctor, her "ward" Altrude Gordon, and, of course, Cary Grayson. There were no attendants; and when the minister asked, "Who giveth this woman to be married to this man?" Edith's mother stepped forward and placed her daughter's hand in that of the President of the United States.

A buffet supper followed—oyster patties, boned capon, Virginia ham, chicken salad, caramel ice cream, and a three-tiered wedding cake. While the party was in full swing, Woodrow and Edith slipped upstairs to prepare for their departure. The guests cheered as they left, as did a crowd outside, thrilled to catch a glimpse of the couple as they ducked into the waiting limousine, its Presidential crests covered with pieces of carbon paper. Only the driver and the Secret Service car behind them knew their immediate destination; and they were ultimately able to shake the fleet of newspapermen and the police cars that were in hot pursuit. Several minutes later, they arrived in Alexandria, Virginia. Agent Starling stood at the siding at the edge of the freight yard, where the baggage coach of their special train had already been loaded with luggage and two automobiles, one for the President and one for the Secret Service. As both the White House limousine and the train from Washington pulled up, Starling blinked his flashlight three times and escorted the newlyweds onto their special car virtually unnoticed.

Only then, around midnight, did the engineer receive orders from the officials of the Chesapeake and Ohio directing him to his destination— Hot Springs, Virginia, halfway between Edith's and Woodrow's respective birthplaces. About seven o'clock the next morning, the train pulled into the siding of the station in the small resort town. As it came to a stop, Agent Starling went back to the private car, quietly walking the corridor between the bedrooms. Approaching the sitting room, he heard a familiar tune—as there before him stood a man in a top hat, tailcoat, and morning trousers, his hands in his pockets. He was dancing a jig. Unaware that he was being watched, he suddenly clicked his heels in the air. And then Starling heard the President sing, "Oh, you beautiful doll! You great big beautiful doll. . . ."

11

DELIVERANCE

. . . and the king spake and said to Daniel: O Daniel, seruant of the liuing God, Is thy God whom thou seruest continually, able to deliuer thee from the Lyons?

—DANIEL, VI:20

The Presidential limousine drove the honeymooners to the Homestead, a grand but cozy resort dating back to the 1760s. Intending to stay for three weeks, the First Couple checked into a quiet suite—a large living room with a fireplace, two bedrooms and two baths, a dining room, and their own servants' quarters.

Surrounded by snow-covered mountains, Woodrow and Edith golfed together in the mornings—he shooting around 115, she 200. They took long motor trips in the afternoons. "We do not do anything that needs to be described," he wrote old family friends Lucy and Mary Smith—just "walk and ride and play golf and loaf and spice it all with a little work, not to forget that there *are* duties as well as pleasures in the world." The hotel management trimmed a Christmas tree in their dining room; and three days later, they quietly celebrated Woodrow's fifty-ninth birthday. "We are having a heavenly time here," Wilson rhapsodized. "I shall go back to Washington feeling complete and strong for whatever may betide. I am indeed blessed beyond my (or any other man's) deserts."

On December 30, 1915, a German U-boat fired a torpedo into the British cruiser *Persia* off the coast of Crete. The 500 passengers aboard the merchant ship should have been permitted to disembark; but no warning shot had been fired, and 350 passengers died. Days later came reports of two more vessels torpedoed in the Mediterranean, also without warning. "Personally," Secretary of State Lansing telegraphed the President, "I am very much alarmed over the seriousness of the situation." Woodrow and Edith reluctantly ended their honeymoon.

The President returned to the White House—and the start of an election year, a phenomenon that exaggerates even the pettiest issues. Remaining focused on but one objective—keeping his country from war—Wilson was in for some of the angriest discord ever to come a President's way. Isolationists and pacifists felt he had been too aggressive in response to the German attacks, and the jingoes felt he had been too passive. Even though all the facts regarding the *Persia* were still not known, Tumulty argued for "vigorous action." When he reported that a growing constituency in the country suggested a lack of leadership, Wilson stiffened in his chair. "Tumulty," he said, "you may as well understand my position right now. If my re-election as President depends upon my getting into war, I don't want to be President.

> . . . I have made up my mind that I am more interested in the opinion that the country will have of me ten years from now than the opinion it may be willing to express today. Of course, I understand that the country wants action . . . but I will not be rushed into war, no matter if every damned congressman and senator stands up on his hind legs and proclaims me a coward.

This renewal of German attacks, in clear violation of naval law and international treaties, demanded an escalated response. The United States could not keep sending admonitory notes, protesting one naval incident while coming to terms on another. Severance of diplomatic relations, which Wilson considered the "forerunner" of war, would be the next logical step. Ambassador Page in England wrote Wilson that the British thought the United States was being "hoodwinked" by the Germans and that

America's response was laughable. He said Londoners were referring to Americans as "Too-prouds" and that they hissed when an American image appeared on their moving-picture screens. Colonel House conferred with the new Minister of Munitions, David Lloyd George, and several other Cabinet members, the consensus being that only Wilson's intervention could stop the war. Toward that end, House echoed Lloyd George's feelings that it would enormously strengthen Wilson's hand if he would start building an impressively large Army and Navy.

Such comments meant little to Wilson. He did not work for Great Britain, he reminded Tumulty. "I believe that the sober-minded people of this country will applaud any efforts I may make without the loss of our honor to keep this country out of war." Constantly weighing his military options against the diplomatic, Wilson believed it was time for both—readying America for battle, all the while grasping at solutions to resist it.

After conferring with several leaders on the Continent, House returned to England, where he dined on Valentine's Day 1916, with past, present, and future Prime Ministers Arthur James Balfour, H. H. Asquith, and Lloyd George, along with Foreign Secretary Lord Grey. Although their constituents were far from ready to lay down arms to negotiate, the statesmen all agreed to discuss the matter; and, a week later, House confided in Lord Grey the possible terms for a sweetheart deal, which the latter recorded in what became known as the House-Grey Memorandum. House had said that Wilson was ready to propose a conference that would summon the Allies and the Germans together; and he noted, "Should the Allies accept this proposal and should Germany refuse it, the United States would probably enter the war against Germany." Furthermore, the memorandum said, "if such a Conference were held, it would secure peace on terms not unfavourable to the Allies; and, if it failed to secure peace, the United States would leave the Conference as a belligerent on the side of the Allies, if Germany was unreasonable." Among its terms would be the restoration of Belgium, the transfer of Alsace and Lorraine to France, and the acquisition by Russia of an outlet to the sea in the south.

Wilson approved this peculiar document, which had little value. He did not support secret covenants, and its vagueness suggested that it was little more than an exercise in mediation. House, of course, was not empowered to speak for the United States; and, indeed, the President himself was limited in what he could promise regarding wars and treaties as he was constitutionally restricted by the will of the Senate. Even so, Wilson saw value in keeping diplomatic channels open, and the memo marked the Administration's first official abandonment of isolationism.

Closer to home, on January 10, 1916, a band of Francisco "Pancho" Villa's men held up a train outside Chihuahua City, Mexico, robbing and executing seventeen Americans. The victims were associated with an American-owned company about to reopen a mine, and now many Americans demanded the heads of the murderous Villistas. Wilson restrained himself, reminding Congress and the public that the State Department had warned Americans against traveling in Mexico at that time; and while the President sought justice, the Carranza government retained jurisdiction. As Wilson's cooperation with Carranza had triggered the assault, he hoped this might prove to be an isolated incident, Villa just letting off steam. Wilson continued to commit America to nonintervention—giving the belligerents in Europe and the bandits in Mexico a chance to cool off and come to terms, if not their senses.

The President and Secretary Garrison discussed plans to enlarge the Army and Navy. It meant suggesting war to an isolationist country with no declared enemies and buffered by two oceans. Theodore Roosevelt had been bugling for such action for years—urging a summer training camp for officers that his fellow Rough Rider, General Leonard Wood, had organized in Plattsburgh, New York. There 1,500 volunteers who were not "too proud to fight" could start learning military drills. Members of Wilson's own party, especially in the Congress, opposed expansion of the armed forces. But, as *The New York Times* editorialized, Wilson's "powers of temperate, convincing statement and triumphant suasion are famous." His character now demanded that he "go to the country and inform them of the possibility that we might be drawn into the conflict in Europe, and of the necessity of preparing for it." In two dozen speeches between late January and the end of February 1916, Wilson articulated ideas that would crystallize into the foreign policy that would extend through the next century. He officially kicked off "the President's Preparedness Campaign" at the annual dinner of the Railway Business Association at the Waldorf-Astoria on January 27.

Whether or not the United States would ever enter the war as a combatant, Wilson believed the country could no longer stand as an island.

"America does not constitute the major part of the world," he reminded his audience. "We live in a world which we did not make, which we cannot alter, which we cannot think into a different condition from that which actually exists. It would be a hopeless piece of provincialism to suppose that, because we think differently from the rest of the world, we are at liberty to assume that the rest of the world will permit us to enjoy that thought without disturbance."

Wilson had said in late 1914 that the question of military preparedness was not pressing. "But more than a year has gone by since then," he observed in his long speech, "and I would be ashamed if I had not learned something in fourteen months. The minute I stop changing my mind as President, with the change of all the circumstances in the world, I will be a back number." Indeed, with so much of the world in flux, Wilson relied on flexibility, which struck his opponents as weakness. In truth, Wilson was pursuing a steady—albeit slow—path to war.

At this pivotal moment—when the majority of Americans had migrated from rural areas to urban centers—Wilson began erecting the machinery for the United States to prepare itself for war. He explained that that included not only the creation of a standing army "for the purposes of peace" but also "a great system of industrial and vocational education under federal guidance and with federal aid, in which a very large percentage of the youth of this country will be given training in the skillful use and application of the principles of science in manufacturing and business." Wilson envisioned a society of productive citizens who stood ready to serve as soldiers.

Two nights later, before four thousand people in Pittsburgh, he advanced his argument, explaining the difficulties of reading the constant flow of international dispatches and maintaining the peace. "It amazes me to hear men speak as if America stood alone in the world and could follow her own life as she pleases," he said. The dangers in the world had become "infinite and constant," and he said that he would be negligent if he did not start warning his countrymen that "new circumstances have arisen which make it absolutely necessary that this country should prepare herself, not for war, not for anything that smacks in the least of aggression, but for adequate national defense." A generation later, Wilson's Assistant Secretary of the Navy, Franklin D. Roosevelt, would famously declare, "I hate war"; he no doubt recalled Woodrow Wilson's telling this audience in

1916, "I love peace." And the price for that peace, Wilson said, required "a great plan for national defense of which we will all be proud and which will lead us to forget partisan differences in one great enthusiasm for the United States of America."

Wilson's speech in Cleveland marked a turning point in his campaign for preparedness. David Lawrence, who was part of the touring press corps, discerned a shift in the President's rhetoric—as the long poetic sentences yielded to a punchier delivery. "The President talked," Lawrence observed, ". . . like a man who had really convinced himself." And in so doing, he recovered the unvarnished sincerity that had uplifted people when he first ran for office.

In vast auditoriums and from caboose platforms, Wilson addressed citizens in five Midwestern states, scaffolding the argument that he would later build for America's increasing involvement in the world. In Chicago on January 31, he said it was "a very terrible thing . . . to have the honor of the United States entrusted to your keeping," especially with the great task that had been assigned to his nation—"to assert the principles of law in a world in which the principles of law have broken down." The war, he said, "was brought on by rulers, not by peoples, and I thank God that there is no man in America who has the authority to bring war on without the consent of the people."

Three American Presidents had been assassinated in Wilson's lifetime, as had been a dozen international leaders. Although the incident was kept from the public and even from the President himself, a man tried to take Wilson's life during his preparedness tour. After his speech in Chicago, Wilson had retired to his suite at the Blackstone Hotel for the night. Dr. Grayson went to a supper party, and, upon returning to the Blackstone, discovered the entourage of Secret Service detail in a state of high excitement. "A man had tried to get to the President threatening to kill him," Grayson wrote his fiancée late that night. He turned out to be an unstable "crank," who had written a note saying that he was going to sneak into the President's room and stab him to death with a pair of scissors. The would-be assassin never got closer than a few floors above the Presidential suite before jumping to his death. Wilson slept through the entire incident, until Dr. Grayson entered his room on another pretense, so that he could lock the window, ensuring that everybody else might sleep as soundly as Wilson. Security for the President was subsequently beefed up to prevent any such event from recurring. On February 3, in St. Louis, the President insisted that America was at peace with all the world "because she entertains a friendship for all the nations of the world."

In speech after speech, he turned the argument of national safety into one of "national dignity" and, ultimately, one of forging a new national identity. The trip left Wilson inspired, reminding him of the importance of getting out of Washington, to hear the real voices of America. Upon returning to the White House, however, Wilson found himself listening to just one.

No President and First Lady spent as much of their time together as the Wilsons did, as neither wished to revisit the loneliness each had experienced. Even the possessive Wilson daughters delighted in their stepmother, seeing in her, observed Dr. Grayson, "the deliverer of their father from sadness into joy, and she, in turn, always showed the utmost consideration and affection for them."

The President now took to rising at six o'clock in the morning, at which time he would have a small sandwich and a cup of coffee from a plate and thermos that had been set on a small table outside his bedroom. Then he and Edith (and a Secret Service agent) would go to a course for at least an hour of golf. They would be home in time to breakfast together at eight o'clock sharp and then go to his study together to check "the Drawer," the bin in his desk in which all documents demanding immediate attention had been placed. Edith would sort the papers, placing those requiring his signature before him and blotting each as she set down the next item. Time permitting, he discussed each document with her. By nine o'clock, stenographer Charles Swem would arrive; and Edith would sit close by, listening to Woodrow dictate replies to his mail, marveling at "the lucid answers that came with apparently no effort from a mind so well-stored."

Edith would then leave to tend to housekeeping and social matters along with her own mail, which she dictated to her secretary, Edith Benham. From the big window seat at the end of the west hall, she could see her husband signal to her, as he left the study, to accompany him to the West Wing. If possible, they would stroll through the garden; if not, they would grab the few minutes together walking directly to the Oval Office. Edith tried to schedule her appointments to coincide with his so that they could reconvene for lunch, which they generally reserved for each other.

They did not discuss business over meals. The President spent two afternoons a week in Cabinet meetings; the other days were filled with individual Secretaries or legislators. Whenever possible, Edith and Woodrow would cram in a round of golf or a motor ride before dinner; afterward Wilson tended to his most serious work, assessing problems and addressing them on paper—confidential correspondence, speeches, or policy papers, which he would type himself. Edith would sit up with him, decoding top secret memoranda. They often worked past midnight, until he might say, "You don't know how much easier it makes all this to have you here by me. Are you too tired to hear what I have written?" Beyond their personal bliss, the rest of the world steadily darkened.

Trouble had been mounting within the War Department for months, as its disgruntled Secretary, Lindley M. Garrison, increasingly found himself at odds with his boss. Garrison's views about preparedness and international intervention had long been more aggressive than the President's: Garrison favored a large and permanent conscripted Army, while Wilson preferred a smaller armed force with a large, trained reserve of volunteer citizens at the ready. In truth, the conflict ran deeper than that, as Garrison believed Wilson had "little or no interest in the Army and had rather a disparaging attitude toward it." Within less than a week of Wilson's return from the Midwest, Garrison resigned.

Wilson wasted no time in wiring Newton D. Baker—the former Mayor of Cleveland who had, in fact, refused Wilson's prior offer to serve as Secretary of the Interior. In proffering this post, the President told him, "It would greatly strengthen my hand." The men had met when Baker was an undergraduate at Johns Hopkins and Wilson was lecturing there. He accepted his former professor's offer and appeared in Washington three days later. After Baker—an Episcopalian with pacifistic leanings—had recited a litany of reasons why he should not be named Secretary of War, Wilson asked, "Are you ready to take the oath?" There was good reason for Wilson's urgency.

Wilson realized his Army was so small that he lacked sufficient manpower even to prevent bandits from crossing the long Mexican border. And a few hours before dawn on March 9, 1916—Secretary Baker's first day in office—Pancho Villa and an army of 1,500 descended upon the town of Columbus, New Mexico, three miles across the border. While most of the town slept, the Villistas burned buildings, looted stores, and shot at will, killing seventeen Americans, half of whom were soldiers. Two hundred fifty troopers of the 13th United States Cavalry fought back and chased the marauders five miles into Mexican territory, killing seventy-five.

In fact, the bandits were primitive political operatives, retaliating against Wilson for his recent acceptance of Carranza's de facto government, which Villa hoped to topple by embarrassing both leaders. Until then, such raids as these allowed him to feed and arm his troops, refueling his own dreams of national leadership. Any account of the fearless peasant challenging the Goliath to the north only enhanced his legend. As he fled back to safety, Villa dropped a stash of personal papers, including what appeared to be his final orders just before the Columbus attack, which revealed his true mission: "Kill all the Gringos."

From Fort Sam Houston, Texas, General Frederick Funston wired Secretary Baker that "unless Villa is relentlessly pursued and his forces scattered, he will continue raids." Even before consulting the Carranza government, Wilson authorized a punitive expedition whose sole objective was the capture of Pancho Villa, dead or alive. He ordered Brigadier General John J. Pershing, a Missouri-born graduate of West Point who had distinguished himself in Cuba and the Philippines, to command this force and secure the United States–Mexico border.

Wilson never viewed Pershing's expedition as "an invasion of that Republic nor an infringement of its Sovereignty." Indeed, its whole idea was "to cooperate with the forces of General Carranza in removing a cause of irritation to both Governments and to retire from Mexico so soon as this object is accomplished." In an effort to avoid a war with the United States, Carranza agreed to work with the Americans with mutual permission for American and Mexican forces to cross into each other's territory in pursuit of bandits. While Pershing prepared for his mission, one of Carranza's Colonels declared that should American troops cross the border, he would immediately attack. Caught in a pickle, Wilson told Tumulty and Secretary Baker that should that case arise, he would not send troops into Mexico—because that would amount to waging an interventionist war against Mexico.

Many accused the President of timidity, of failing to seize a political opportunity—nationally and internationally. Tumulty argued that if Wilson did not send troops after Villa, he might "just as well not contemplate running for the Presidency, since he would not get a single electoral vote." When Tumulty found Wilson intractable, he sought out Secretaries

Burleson and Houston; and with their input, Tumulty wrote an urgent letter, restating his case—insisting that biding any more time "would be not only disastrous to our party and humiliating to the country, but would be destructive of our influence in international affairs and make it forever impossible to deal in any effective way with Mexican affairs." Colonel House supported Tumulty, at least in the pages of his diary, saying Wilson's failure to act would destroy his influence in Europe as well.

In the meantime, Villa and his men withdrew deeper into the Mexican wilderness, hiding out in the mountainous country. Even though Carranza now considered Villa his rival, it was awkward allying with American soldiers to pursue a lone Mexican. On March 15, General Pershing led almost five thousand men across the border; Secretary Baker even encouraged the use of Curtiss "Jenny" airplanes based in Texas to conduct aerial reconnaissance. By the end of the month, Pershing was hot on Villa's trail.

Ambivalence filled the Cabinet Room. By early April, Secretaries Baker and Lansing favored withdrawal of the troops from Mexico; the former thought the mission had been accomplished, that the Villistas had been dispersed to the point of ineffectiveness. Secretary Houston argued that if the troops were withdrawn, Villa would rebound into action. After listening to all their arguments, Wilson believed America must remain in Mexico until Carranza could assume the responsibility for bringing Villa to his knees.

That would not be any time soon, as Mexicans were calling Carranza a traitor for consenting to the occupation of his country by a foreign army. Although diplomats from both countries had been negotiating for weeks, he would not commit to an agreement because the United States refused to set a withdrawal date for its troops. And then, on June 20, Pershing's forces encountered resistance in the town of Carrizal—seventy-five miles into Mexico—when a local commandant announced that he would defy the Americans if they sought entry. An hour of battle left nine Americans dead and twenty-five taken prisoner. "The break seems to have come in Mexico," Wilson wrote House; "and all my patience seems to have gone for nothing. I am infinitely sad about it. I fear I should have drawn Pershing and his command northward just after it became evident that Villa had slipped through his fingers; but except for that error of judgment (if it was an error) I cannot, in looking back, see where I could have done differently, holding sacred the convictions I hold in this matter."

Again, Tumulty insisted upon the President's taking stronger action. He told Wilson that he should send a message to Carranza saying, "Release those American soldiers or take the consequences." That, said Tumulty, "would ring around the world." Wilson sent instead for his private secretary, to whom he delivered a long monologue, trying to explain foreign affairs from his chair in the Oval Office.

"Tumulty," he said, "you are Irish, and, therefore, full of fight." And while Wilson appreciated the depth of Tumulty's feelings on the Mexican situation, he—not Tumulty and not the Cabinet—had to bear the responsibility for every action to be taken. "I have to sleep with my conscience in these matters," the President said, "and I shall be held responsible for every drop of blood that may be spent in the enterprise of intervention." He knew declaring war would be politically advantageous, but Wilson insisted, *"There won't be any war with Mexico if I can prevent it*, no matter how loud the gentlemen on the hill yell for it and demand it."

"I came from the South and I know what war is," Wilson reminded Tumulty, "for I have seen its wreckage and terrible ruin." To those who had never seen such devastation, the President suggested, declarations of war came easily. Wilson could only think of a poor farmer's boy or the son of a poor widow in a modest town who would have to fight and die. Some American Presidents have seized the first possible opportunity to pull the trigger; speaking of Mexico, but just as surely meaning anywhere in the world, Wilson said, "I will not resort to war . . . until I have exhausted every means to keep out of this mess."

Wilson's lips quivered as he insisted that he would be just as ashamed to be rash as to be a coward. "Valor," he said, "withholds itself from all small implications and entanglements and waits for the great opportunity when the sword will flash as if it carried the light of heaven upon its blade." Someday, Wilson said, "the people of America will know why I hesitated to intervene."

And then the President revealed an unspoken intricacy of the Mexican situation. Eager for war between Mexico and the United States, Germany had planted propagandists in Mexico to encourage hostilities with its North American neighbor. "She wishes an uninterrupted opportunity to carry on her submarine warfare," said Wilson, "and thus believes that war with Mexico will keep our hands off her and thus give her liberty of action to do as she pleases on the high seas." With war appearing "inevitable," the

President said America could not afford to divide its energies or forces, "for we will need every ounce of reserve we have to lick Germany." Wilson felt he could not yet divulge as much to the American people because they were still at peace with the great power—one, he believed, "whose poisonous propaganda is responsible for the present terrible condition of affairs in Mexico."

General Pershing's troops maintained their search for Pancho Villa, coming closest to their objective when his Lieutenant George S. Patton killed Villa's second-in-command and received notoriety less for the kill than for his driving back to headquarters with the corpse strapped to the hood of his vehicle. In June 1916, Congress approved a National Defense Act, which expanded the National Guard and created a Reserve Officers' Training Corps. Forty-eight states sent over 100,000 men to the border—which they did not cross. Without capturing Villa, Pershing's men served mostly as scarecrows at the border, reservists from all walks of life playing soldier for a few months and enjoying their military excursion. For Mexicans—even those who disapproved of Villa—the eleven-month expedition remained an unforgivable incursion. At the same time, some condemned Wilson for going too far in Mexico and not far enough in Europe.

In dealing with either crisis, Wilson played his cards slowly, hoping each might provide a reasonable opportunity to open some kind of peace negotiations. Mid-February, the German government seemed to do exactly that, issuing a statement that said she had "limited her submarine warfare because of her long-standing friendship with the United States, and because by the sinking of the *Lusitania* which caused the death of citizens of the United States, the German retaliation affected neutrals, which was not the intention, as retaliation should be confined to enemy subjects." Viewing that attitude as a peace offering, several members of Congress offered the strongest plan yet for neutrality—which Wilson fought.

Congressman A. Jefferson McLemore of Texas and Senator T. P. Gore of Oklahoma offered similar resolutions in their respective chambers that would prohibit the issuance of American passports for use on ships of belligerent nations and withdrawing protection of American citizens who persisted in traveling on those ships. Chairman of the Senate Foreign Relations Committee William J. Stone of Missouri and a few colleagues visited the White House to discuss this approach, only to encounter a decided lack of support. "You are right in assuming that I shall do everything in my power to keep the United States out of war," Wilson wrote Stone after their exchange, but just as assuredly he wrote:

> I cannot consent to any abridgement of the rights of American citizens in any respect. The honour and self-respect of the nation is involved. We covet peace, and shall preserve it at any cost but the loss of honour. To forbid our people to exercise their rights for fear we might be called upon to vindicate them would be a deep humiliation indeed.

Senator Gore sought to give his branch the upper hand in this argument by introducing one resolution after another as a way of making the President keep reaffirming his neutrality. In the end, most Congressional Democrats supported Wilson, tabling the Gore-McLemore Resolution, in all its forms.

But Germany continued to provoke. On March 24, 1916, a German submarine torpedoed the French steamer *Sussex* as it was ferrying almost four hundred passengers across the English Channel, from Folkestone to Dieppe. The ship had never been armed, was known for its habitual conveyance of passengers only, and was avoiding routes meant for shipping troops and supplies. Eighty passengers were killed or injured. None was American. It became increasingly difficult for the President to maintain a position of nonintervention with such events continuously occurring. The likes of Theodore Roosevelt never stopped egging Wilson on in the press, criticizing him for neither standing by his demands for "strict accountability" nor adequately preparing the nation for war. American sentiment steadily skewed toward the Allies; but German Americans tended to be anti-English, as did Irish Americans, what with a weeklong rising of Irish republicans against English rule that Easter, an insurrection that would bloom into years of revolution.

Secretary Lansing urged action, specifically a demand for the immediate recall of Count Johann-Heinrich von Bernstorff, the German Ambassador to Washington, and the severance of diplomatic relations with Germany. "I realize that this action is drastic," he wrote the President, "but I believe that to be patient longer would be misconstrued both at home and abroad." Colonel House concurred but feared Wilson would continue to hesitate. "He was afraid," House wrote in his journal on March 30, "if we broke off relations the war would go on indefinitely and there would be no one to lead the way out."

Stronger disagreements raged in Congress, cutting across party lines and creating strange alliances. Leading Republican and interventionist Henry Cabot Lodge sided with Wilson in his stance against Democrats Gore and McLemore; and isolationist Midwestern Republicans, such as Wisconsin's Robert La Follette, allied with powerful Southern Democrats, such as William Stone and Mississippi's James K. Vardaman. On April 19, 1916, the President walked through the political minefield of the Capitol to address a joint session of Congress. Without abandoning his position of peace and neutrality, he delivered a solemn sixteen-minute speech devoid of rhetorical flourishes and moved the nation one step closer to war.

After summarizing the Imperial German government's maritime practices and policies of the prior fourteen months, Wilson insisted his own government had been "very patient." At the same time, Wilson said, it had accepted in good faith Germany's repeated explanations and assurances, despite its continued commitment to "the use of submarines for the destruction of an enemy's commerce." Wilson felt the United States was compelled to issue an official warning: "that unless the Imperial German Government should now immediately declare and effect an abandonment of its present methods of warfare against passenger and freight-carrying vessels this government can have no choice but to sever diplomatic relations with the government of the German Empire altogether."

America realized the seriousness of the situation—*The New York Times* dedicated its entire front page to the speech—and so did Germany. On May 4, 1916, the German government responded at last to the American note in a manner designed to save face for both nations. Germany said it was "prepared to do its utmost to confine the operations of war for the rest of its duration to the fighting forces of the belligerents, thereby also insuring the freedom of the seas." But so long as Great Britain maintained its illegal blockade, Germany said, neutrals could not expect them to restrict the usage of their most formidable weapon. The United States had evidently won this diplomatic battle, as Wilson, once again, averted entry into the war. Colonel House warned Count von Bernstorff that "the least infraction would entail an immediate severance of diplomatic relations," and Bernstorff said he did not believe any further transgressions would occur. In a world of aggressors, Wilson now insisted that "the peace of society is obtained by force." Across America his people began arguing such issues as militarism, compulsory military service, and an armament race.

On the night of May 30, the Wilsons took a small party to Baltimore, where the Friars Club of New York performed an out-of-town "Frolic." Songwriter and performer George M. Cohan was the headliner that night, but a lanky young Oklahoman—part cowboy, part Cherokee—just starting out in vaudeville stole the show by spinning political commentary and a rope at the same time. Will Rogers would later look back on that night as the most nervous performance of his life. With the President right in front of him, he told jokes about the attempted capture of Pancho Villa, saying, "There is some talk of getting a Machine Gun if we can borrow one. The one we have now they are using to train our Army with in Plattsburgh. If we go to war we will just about have to go to the trouble of getting another Gun." Wilson led the entire audience in laughter. After more jokes about Mexico, Rogers turned his attention to Europe, stopping the show when he said, "President Wilson is getting along fine now to what he was a few months ago. Do you realize, People, that at one time in our negotiations with Germany that he was 5 Notes behind?" The President guffawed.

The Presidential election sparked most of the punch lines and rhetoric that year. While Woodrow Wilson still enjoyed the luxury of comfortable Democratic majorities in both houses of Congress, the Republicans were gathering forces to end his progressive program, which had hardly slowed. He encouraged citizens to become as active as his administration. In June 1916, Wilson addressed an open-air convention behind Independence Hall in Philadelphia, to whom he said that Americans needed more than a simple understanding of their ideals. He summoned each citizen to ask not what his country could do for him but "to think first, not of himself or of any interest which he may be called upon to sacrifice, but of the country which we serve." He offered a new motto: "America First."

Not to be confused with a noninterventionist policy that would adopt the same moniker a generation later, "America First" meant "the duty of every American to exalt the national consciousness by purifying his own motives and exhibiting his own devotion." When Wilson said this meant putting the country first in their thoughts—being "ready . . . to vindicate . . . the principles of liberty, of justice, and of humanity"—the crowd cheered. "You cheer the sentiment," Wilson said, looking up from his outline, "but do you realize what it means?" He explained that it carried the responsibility not only of being just "to your fellow men, but that, as a nation, you have got to be just to other nations."

In a "fighting mood," Wilson then said he wanted to take a number of domestic actions, each of which was sure to antagonize large segments of the population, mostly the business community. These issues had all been among his original campaign promises. The President had long favored legislation to prevent the waste or control of the country's natural resources by special interests. While a few of Wilson's predecessors had reserved more than a dozen national parks—comprising millions of acres of natural wonderland—no President had established a proper bureau to preserve that land. Interests clashed: Wilson had signed a bill in 1913 damming the Hetch Hetchy Valley within Yosemite National Park in order to provide more water to San Francisco, and conservationist John Muir went to his death the next year damning the action, which altered the ecology of many square miles of territory. Strict preservationists supported the great parks for the public's benefit, but their interests often conflicted with those of groups promoting tourism—the railroads and land developers who might allow more people to enjoy the parks. Following Taft's example, Wilson approved a third naval oil reserve in the West—Teapot Dome—but his Secretary of the Interior, Franklin Lane, found himself repeatedly blocked in his efforts to get Wilson to sign leases allowing private businesses to tap into those reserves. And so in the summer of 1916, President Wilson signed the National Park Service Act, which not only regulated the existing parkland but allowed for the regulation and expansion of a vast network of hundreds of parks, monuments, and recreation areas. His administration's negotiations with Great Britain (on behalf of Canada) resulted in the Migratory Bird Treaty Act, which protected hundreds of species at a moment when commercial interests threatened to destroy them. In environmental matters, Wilson's guiding principle was to preserve as much as possible while serving as many as possible.

With close to ten million foreigners coming to America in the preceding decade—many from nations with growing hostility toward the United States—xenophobia descended upon this "nation of immigrants" with its 100 million people. After a year of work, Congress passed a bill requiring a literacy test of prospective citizens. Wilson vetoed it. As President, he was loath to exercise this power of one man opposing the majority of two houses of Congress, but he felt this bill violated the spirit of the nation, as it excluded those "to whom the opportunities of elementary education have been denied, without regard to their character, their purposes, or their natural capacity." When the bill appeared before him a second time, he vetoed it again, condemning it as "a penalty for lack of opportunity." But this time the Congress prevailed, planting the first of many hedges against foreign invaders, as the United States inched closer to war.

Wilson had run for President on the proposal of shortening the standard ten-hour workday to eight. At the start of 1916, the railroad workers agitated for that concession from the railway executives. They threatened to strike, which would affect the lives of every American. Henry Ford wired the President that the moment such a strike should occur, the Ford Motor Company—then manufacturing 2,200 cars a day and dependent upon the railroads to transport its product—would shut its factory and all its assembly plants across the country, taking more than forty-nine thousand workers off the payroll. The President reasoned with the railroad brotherhoods to table the rest of their demands while convincing management, in essence, to put America first. Many accused the President of cozying up to labor; but Wilson issued a statement of his own composition stating: "I have recommended the concession of the eight-hour day . . . because I believed the concession right."

Wilson did not leave the capital that summer, so that he could put this legislation—which would become the Adamson Act—on a fast legislative track. After addressing Congress as a whole, he spent the next several days and even nights on the Hill stoking support. The bill's passage averted the strike and marked the beginnings of controversial government intervention into the private enterprise system, bold Presidential action Wilson believed national necessity demanded.

During this time he kept appearing unannounced in the President's Room in the Capitol to lobby Democratic leaders. He also wanted to see the immediate passage of the Keating-Owen child labor bill, which would prohibit the sale in interstate commerce of goods manufactured by children, and the Kern-McGillicuddy bill, a workmen's compensation bill that would protect federal employees in the event of injury or death, thus establishing guidelines for disability insurance. All three pieces of labor legislation quickly passed and received Wilson's signature, establishing guidelines throughout the nation's businesses and industries.

Seldom if ever in American history had a President made good on as many campaign promises as Woodrow Wilson. They were bold pledges, and to help safeguard them, he sent to Congress his most audacious request yet. In January 1916, a vacancy occurred on the Supreme Court when Joseph Rucker Lamar, Wilson's boyhood friend from Georgia, died. A week later, the President asked McAdoo whom he might suggest to take Lamar's place, and without hesitation McAdoo recommended "the people's lawyer," Louis Brandeis. Nobody embodied the principles of the New Freedom more than this essential member of candidate Wilson's first brain trust; and nobody engendered more of Wilson's admiration than this profound liberal thinker, social activist, and spokesman for the voiceless. But Wilson asked McAdoo if he thought Brandeis could be confirmed. "Yes . . . if you appoint him," McAdoo said, "but it will be a stiff fight." Nobody could have known how rigid that opposition would be.

For all his admirers, Brandeis had enemies everywhere. Because he was a trust-buster, Wall Street regarded him as a radical, or worse; because he was "a militant crusader for social justice," as future Justice William O. Douglas would write, the establishment considered him a troublemaker; because he was an attorney who relied on sociological and psychological data, strict constructionists considered him dangerous, a casuist who would use the Court to activate social change. No less an eminence than former President Taft himself (who had long cast a sheep's eye on the high court) privately called the nomination "one of the deepest wounds that I have ever had as an American and a lover of the Constitution and a believer in progressive conservatism."

Largely unspoken, at least in public, was that Brandeis was a Jew—not only the first to be nominated for a position on the Supreme Court, but an active Zionist at that. To Woodrow Wilson—who had appointed the first Jewish professor at Princeton and the first Jewish Justice to the New Jersey Supreme Court—Brandeis's religion meant nothing, except in its controversial correction of a longtime oversight. If nothing else, Brandeis's presence on the Court would neutralize the biggest mistake Wilson felt he had made as President; it would be the only possible antidote to the conservative anti-Semite James C. McReynolds, whom he had named two years prior.

Since George Washington had begun filling the bench, twenty-one nominees had got tangled in the process of Senate confirmation. Some sensed rejection and withdrew, while eight actually failed to obtain the necessary votes. Historically, the process had been a routine vote, aye or nay—generally the same day the nomination was presented. Opposition to

Brandeis was as rabid as it was rapid. Overnight the establishment press proved especially virulent, attacking his character more than his qualifications. Harvard's President A. Lawrence Lowell—who was about to urge a Jewish quota and segregated dormitories on his liberal campus—mustered more than fifty signatories to a petition denouncing the nomination; six former members of the American Bar Association—Taft and Elihu Root among them—formally objected to the appointment. The Senate Committee on the Judiciary announced an investigation of the many charges already leveled against Brandeis; and McAdoo shrewdly urged Brandeis to ask the committee to hold their hearings in public, as he figured most of the objections would fade in the light of day. The nominee stuck to his work and avoided the press, though he did quietly marshal supporters to hold a brief for him in Congress, where he had no intention of appearing.

On February 9, 1916, a Senate subcommittee considering a high court nominee held a public hearing for the first time. Three Democratic and two Republican Senators listened to testimony before a standing-room-only crowd. More than forty witnesses—largely Boston Brahmins or other establishment figures from the losing side of cases that Brandeis had prosecuted—paraded before the tribunal, cloaking their personal criticisms in rhetoric about dishonorable and unprofessional conduct. More compelling advocates countered every charge, while Felix Frankfurter and Walter Lippmann defended Brandeis in the press and former Harvard President Charles W. Eliot sent the committee a ringing endorsement, as did nine of Harvard Law School's eleven law professors. The arguments came down to a partisan vote. To help seal the nomination, chairman Charles Culberson of Texas asked Wilson to expound upon his reasons for nominating Brandeis.

The President happily obliged. As the committee had already put to rest any personal accusations and aspersions, Wilson cited former Chief Justice Melville Fuller, who had called Brandeis "the ablest man who ever appeared before the Supreme Court of the United States." Speaking for himself, Wilson wrote:

I cannot speak too highly of his impartial, impersonal, orderly, and constructive mind, his rare analytical powers, his deep human sympathy, his profound acquaintance with the historical roots of our

institutions and insight into their spirit, or of the many evidences he
has given of being imbued to the very heart with our American ideals
of economic conditions and of the way they bear upon the masses of
the people.

Culberson made the letter public; and Brandeis supporters arranged a few
private social encounters between wavering Senators and the nominee
himself. The four-month confirmation process was as brutal as any the
Court, if not the country, had ever seen—a "low-tech lynching." It opened
the doors for future examination of judicial nominees, who were soon required to defend themselves in person.

After partisan committee votes, the full Senate confirmed Brandeis on
June 1 as the sixty-seventh Supreme Court Justice by a vote of 47 to 22.
One Democrat and three progressive Republicans crossed the aisle. "I
never signed any commission with such satisfaction as I sign his," Wilson
told Henry Morgenthau in concluding another highly successful Congressional inning, with no action more far-reaching than that appointment: if
a Jew could ascend to the country's highest court, there was no stopping
other minorities from shattering other glass ceilings, even though it would
take generations to slough off age-old prejudices. Whenever Brandeis
spoke in judicial conference, for example, Wilson's first appointee, Justice
McReynolds, was known simply to rise and leave the room. He went so far
as to avoid official Court pictures because he did not want to be photographed with a Jew. And when Brandeis retired in 1939—leaving a distinguished legacy of liberal decisions behind him—he received the customary
panegyric letter, signed by his colleagues . . . all except one.

"That summer of 1916 was crowded with every sort of thing," Edith
Wilson would recall. "First on the list was the ever-encroaching menace of
the War in Europe. Then came the Presidential campaign." Nationalism
had become a global epidemic, and it had at last infected the United
States. The First Lady was still trying to process how she had awakened
from her uncomplicated quiet life into a world in which every public
moment was fraught with significance. Woodrow encouraged her to learn
all the verses of "The Star-Spangled Banner," for she would surely need to
know them. Indeed, it had become a season of endless flag-waving, a

coming of age for the nation, its first reunion since the country had divided a half century earlier.

June 14—the day in 1777 on which Congress had adopted the Stars and Stripes as the emblem of the Union—had been sporadically observed ever since the start of the Civil War; but in the spring of 1916, Wilson officially proclaimed it a day for "special patriotic exercises" on which Americans might "rededicate ourselves to the nation, 'one and inseparable,' from which every thought that is not worthy of our fathers' first views of independence, liberty, and right shall be excluded." It had an electrifying effect.

The entire month was filled with one parade after another. The message was the same everywhere: "Americanism" and preparedness. Chicago staged the largest parade in its history, in which more than 130,000 people—each carrying a flag—marched for more than eleven hours. There were neither floats nor costumes, just people from all walks of life—telephone operators, bankers, judges, firemen, Spanish-American War veterans, and druggists—marching to the cheers of one million onlookers. Even militant feminist Alice Paul leading a troop of fifty suffragists down Michigan Avenue, against the flow, drew cheers from the crowd as fellow marchers diverted themselves to the curb so that the ladies might pass. On Long Island, 2,500 "Pilgrims" marched through Oyster Bay to the Roosevelt home at Sagamore Hill—each carrying a flag—to appeal to the Colonel to lead the nation once again. In Hollywood, German-born Carl Laemmle had his Universal Film Manufacturing Company release a forty-reel serial called *Liberty*, and his studio staged a preparedness parade.

Nobody exhibited more patriotism that season than the President himself. At Arlington National Cemetery on Memorial Day, he raised George Washington's time-honored argument against "entangling alliances"; but, by way of national preparation, Wilson suggested, "I would gladly assent to . . . an alliance which would disentangle the peoples of the world from those combinations in which they seek their own separate and private interests and unite the people of the world to preserve the peace of the world upon a basis of common right and justice." On Flag Day, he led a parade of sixty-six thousand down Pennsylvania Avenue, from the Capitol to the White House, and spoke of the flag's importance as it united a people whose citizenship was derived from every nation in the world. "Americanism" became the shibboleth of the day, as Wilson urged citizens to pledge their allegiance to the flag of the United States of America instead of honoring the hyphen that linked every American to the country of his ancestry. Wilson insisted the time had come for "hyphenated" citizenship to end.

That same week, Wilson addressed the graduating class of the United States Military Academy, where he seemed to allude to Teddy Roosevelt as he asserted, "I am an American, but I do not believe that any of us loves a blustering nationality—a nationality with a chip on its shoulder, a nationality with its elbows out and its swagger on. We love that quiet, self-respecting, unconquerable spirit which doesn't strike until it is necessary to strike, and then strikes to conquer." A decade later, Vice President Marshall would reflect on those "long and weary" months of 1916, remembering that Wilson was "busy with the hope of finding some loophole through which he might enter as the great pacifier of the conflict in Europe."

Amid this patriotic fervor, the Republican Party opened its National Convention in the Chicago Coliseum on June 7, 1916. The delegates hoped to select from among a half dozen candidates the one most likely to beat Wilson, but their own house was still in disarray. They had not resolved the differences that had riven the Grand Old Party in 1912 and driven it to defeat. The Republicans remained so divided that the Progressive Party, their offshoot, opened its own convention a mile away, in the Auditorium. The Bull Moosers were eager to rejoin their old herd, should the Republicans be of the same mind. They nominated Theodore Roosevelt, hoping that would incite the Republicans to do the same so they could all join forces.

But the Republicans were not ready to reembrace the man they believed had put personality and even principles before party. As the convention opened, the delegates seemed predisposed to an undeclared candidate who said he would accept the nomination—the former Governor of New York and current Associate Justice of the Supreme Court Charles Evans Hughes. Eager to be drafted, he received as many votes on the first ballot as the next two contenders combined, while former President Roosevelt ran a distant sixth. Hughes obtained the nomination on the third ballot. Running with TR's former Vice President, Charles W. Fairbanks of Indiana, he remained pro-business and eager to enter the war.

As Hughes became the only Supreme Court Justice ever to leave the bench in order to run for President, Wilson promptly elevated the progressive John Hessin Clarke, whom he had appointed as a District Court Judge. Clarke would become a reliable vote within the liberal bloc, though he would remain on the Court only six years. Insiders knew that animosity between him and Justice McReynolds contributed to his early departure; and, indeed, the retirement letter from his brethren—like Brandeis's—would fall one signature short.

Wilson spent the early weeks of June drafting the national Democratic platform. The document expanded upon the programs of the New Freedom; and it made particular mention of extending the franchise to the women of the country, though he maintained that the most effective means of achieving such equality was through state-by-state ratification.

The following week, Democrats gathered at the St. Louis Coliseum for their convention, which was more of a coronation. Although the incumbent did not appear for the ceremonies, he controlled the convention from the White House. The three days of ballyhoo played according to the script, with the exception of one speech. Former New York Governor Martin H. Glynn, at Wilson's behest, delivered the keynote address. Seeing one issue overshadowing all the rest, Glynn provided a brief review of moments in history when Presidents of all parties could have drawn the nation into international hostilities but refrained. As Glynn cited example after example, from Washington to Benjamin Harrison, he recited a simple chorus—"But we didn't go to war." Adams, Jefferson, Van Buren, Pierce, and Grant all "settled our troubles by negotiation just as the President of the United States is trying to do today." The applause at the end of the speech raised the Coliseum's rafters and resonated across the country. While there were plenty of issues on which to run, the Democrats chose to peg their campaign to one irrefutable theme: "He kept us out of war."

The office of the Vice President of the United States was still something between a figurehead and a fool; and in each capacity, Thomas R. Marshall excelled. A few Vice Presidents served as liaisons between the White House and the Senate; but because Wilson made regular Congressional visits, Marshall was redundant even in that role. The President invited him to attend Cabinet meetings but showed so little interest in his opinions, Marshall saw no reason to appear. Like many of his predecessors who served as President of the United States Senate, Marshall considered the Executive Mansion out of bounds. In his four-hundred-page memoirs, Marshall would mention Woodrow Wilson's name only a handful of times.

Even so, he remained a popular figure in Washington. TR's acerbic daughter Alice Roosevelt Longworth especially enjoyed poking fun at him, claiming that his business card read "Vice President of the United States and Toastmaster." Indeed, Marshall was a delightful speaker and always had an amusing quip on the tip of his tongue. During one session when a Senator was holding the floor too long, yammering about all the things "this country needs," Marshall leaned in toward a clerk and said in a stage whisper, "What this country needs is a really good five-cent cigar." The quotation stands as Marshall's most durable legacy, coupled, perhaps, with his anecdote of a mother who had two sons, one of whom became Vice President while the other was lost at sea . . . "and nothing has been heard from either of them since." But while Wilson and Marshall had private policy disagreements, the Vice President never displayed anything but loyalty toward the President. There was no reason to break up a winning ticket. Besides, Indiana—with its admixture of rural and industrial populations—was sure to be a close race in the national election; and the Republican nominee, Charles Fairbanks, had been a popular Hoosier Senator, a political figure once so promising that he even had a town in Alaska named after him.

The railroad crisis and insufferable heat that summer exacerbated Wilson's gastric distress, severe headaches, and extreme fatigue. "I get desperately tired somedays," he wrote his daughter Jessie, "and am glad to get to bed every day." Colonel House was especially mindful of how tired he had looked at Dr. Grayson's recent wedding.

The Wilsons were not able to leave Washington until the first of September for their summer vacation at a large estate called Shadow Lawn, in Long Branch, New Jersey, near Asbury Park. The big white house—complete with a semicircular portico—suggested a seaside version of the Wilsons' home in Washington. Edith said it felt like a hotel and referred to the entry as "the lobby." Woodrow said it reminded him of a gambling hall. But the expansive grounds could accommodate crowds for campaign speeches, and the gates in front provided privacy. Hoping to avoid the scourge of infantile paralysis that plagued the East Coast, the McAdoos, with their two young children, joined the President at the Jersey Shore. The Wilsons and the rest of their extended "family"—which included her brother Randolph, Helen Bones, the Graysons, and Tumulty—quickly settled into Shadow Lawn until the election, in part to reassert Wilson's right to vote in New Jersey. The other reason they abandoned the Executive Mansion for several months, according to Edith, was "my husband declined to use the White House, the Nation's property, for a political purpose."

Because custom prevented Presidential nominees (even sitting Presidents) from attending their nominating conventions, the conventions came to them. On September 2, the Notification Committee of the Democratic Party arrived at Shadow Lawn, with the Vice President, the Cabinet, Congressmen, and party leaders in tow, and twenty thousand partisans in their wake. A speaker's platform had been erected for Wilson. After thanking the party for renewing its trust in him, he catalogued the formidable record the Administration had amassed—from the revision of the tariffs to its most far-reaching piece of legislation, that very week's Revenue Act of 1916. This statute incorporated several items dating back to the Populist movement a quarter century earlier, including a graduated tax rate based on ability to pay. The bill raised the tax from 1 to 2 percent on net annual incomes above $4,000 and included a surtax as high as 13 percent on incomes above $2 million; it also imposed an estate tax as high as 10 percent on $5 million legacies, and, foreseeing a windfall for one particular industry, a steep tax on the manufacture of munitions. Critics gasped at this redistribution of wealth; Wilson considered it "equitable."

His speech—with its recital of 1912 campaign promises delivered—ran justifiably long; but it emphasized America's commitment to the future. "We are to play a leading part in the world drama whether we wish it or not," he said. "We shall lend, not borrow; act for ourselves, not imitate or follow." Far from his 1914 insistence upon neutrality, Wilson now insisted that no nation "can any longer remain neutral as against any wilful disturbance of the peace of the world. The effects of war can no longer be confined to the areas of battle. No nation stands wholly apart in interest when the life and interest of all nations are thrown into confusion and peril. . . . The nations of the world must unite in joint guarantees that whatever is done to disturb the whole world's life must first be tested in the court of the whole world's opinion before it is attempted."

He left New Jersey to make several speeches—including one at Lincoln's birthplace in Kentucky—before bringing his "non-campaign" to a halt when he learned that his sister Annie, ill in New London, Connecticut, had taken a turn for the worse. Woodrow and Edith immediately went north to visit and remained there for several days. Because of the obvious strain on the President, and because nobody could predict how much longer Annie Wilson Howe might live, her physician urged him to return to Shadow Lawn. Two days later, Annie died. They accompanied her coffin to her funeral in South Carolina, where Woodrow walked his wife through his childhood house. He would assume his sister's debts.

Upon returning to New Jersey, the President undertook the double duty of running the country and campaigning for the privilege of continuing to do so. Every Saturday he delivered a political address from the front porch at Shadow Lawn; and any given day brought Cabinet members, Colonel House, Ambassador Page from England, or Vance C. McCormick, a former Mayor of Harrisburg, Pennsylvania, whom Wilson had anointed the new chairman of the Democratic National Committee. Henry Ford, who admired Wilson's strength in maintaining American neutrality and in keeping the trains running, offered nominal (though not monetary) support. He told the President that based on their conferences, he had taken the unusual step of providing pay equality for his women employees. Ignacy Paderewski, the brilliant Polish pianist and political activist, paid a visit, asking the President to remember the Poles caught in the crossfire between Russia and Germany. Edith could not help kneeling on the landing above the two men, watching Paderewski's moving expression as he pled so earnestly for his people.

Wilson did take to the hustings in a few of the many toss-up states. Half the electoral college map was already accounted for: Republican New England plus New York, Pennsylvania, and Michigan would deliver the same number of electors as the solid Democratic South. Thus, the battleground became the Midwest and the less populous but more Populist states of the far West. Except for California, the stakes were so low in each of the farthermost Western states that they hardly merited a nominee's time. Wilson traveled only as far as Ohio, Indiana, Illinois, and Nebraska.

Political campaigns had grown savvier in analyzing demographics; and the Democrats targeted specific constituencies, sending the most appropriate surrogates to address them. In multicultural New York, Jewish, Polish, and Italian leaders mobilized their neighborhoods. William Jennings Bryan campaigned aggressively for Wilson in the West. And, because he was the most consistent vote for peace and progressivism, the National Democratic Speakers' Committee sent the popular blind Senator

T. P. Gore to speak up and down the California coast. Gore disagreed with the President on several issues, but he effectively argued that Wilson had kept America out of war and showed the most promise to continue doing so.

W. E. B. Du Bois wrote the President of his disappointment in his tenure and called upon him to account for the dismissal of colored public officials and for segregation in the Civil Service. As a member of that underclass, he asked what progress Negroes had seen, even when it came to lynching. Wilson replied through Tumulty that he had tried to live up to his original assurances, "though in some cases my endeavors have been defeated." He had, in fact, issued a strong statement condemning lynching—hardly conscience-challenging, one would have thought, though it did mark the first time a President had gone on record doing as much. Although some Negro organizations continued to trust Wilson enough "to do the just thing at the proper time," Du Bois urged his followers to vote Socialist.

Wilson was still the most inspiring orator on the stump. His refusal to talk down to audiences continued to elevate them; and the inevitable patriotic punch line with which he closed every speech went straight from his heart to that of his audience. He was so eloquent the day he addressed the National American Woman Suffrage Association in Atlantic City—maintaining his position of state-by-state enfranchisement—even outgoing NAWSA president Dr. Anna Howard Shaw could not resist him. The very fact that he did not pander for votes by coming out in favor of the federal amendment as so many wanted him to do, she said, "showed such respect for our intelligence" and a "sincerity of purpose when he said he would fight with us."

Wilson could also play rough. An Irish agitator named Jeremiah O'Leary was president of the American Truth Society, an ostensibly nonpartisan—but fanatically anti-English—organization. With their support, O'Leary released an unusually vitriolic letter to Wilson, condemning his "dictatorship over Congress" and his "truckling to the British Empire." Wilson called a press conference, at which he read the wire he had sent in reply: "Your telegram received. I would feel deeply mortified to have you or anybody like you vote for me. Since you have access to many disloyal Americans and I have not, I will ask you to convey this message to them."

And he could be funny. The President instinctively knew how to warm up audiences, invariably opening with a light remark. One of his favorites was about a magazine correspondent researching the life of Mark Twain. The writer had gone to Hannibal, Missouri, where he encountered the only local who actually remembered Samuel Clemens as a child. He was, unfortunately, somewhat feebleminded; and so the interviewer had to keep jogging recollections out of him. He tried prompting the old fellow with the names of famous Twain characters—such as Tom Sawyer and Huckleberry Finn. But upon hearing each name, the old Missourian just blankly scratched his head. In a final attempt, the interviewer asked if he had ever heard of Pudd'nhead Wilson. "Oh, yes," said the old man, looking up and beaming, "I voted for him last year."

Although Wilson appeared younger than his opponent, Charles Evans Hughes—with his sculpted beard and mustache—was, in fact, six years the President's junior. But the two men were in many ways alike. The son of a (Baptist) minister, Hughes was a skilled debater, a lawyer, and a scholar (who had taught Greek and mathematics and, later, law at Cornell); and he too was a compelling orator. But his campaign never expressed either a consistent vision or a positive message. The Republicans' pro-business platform criticized Wilson's positions against tariffs and trusts, but the recession he had inherited had dissipated within two years and citizens felt the Democrats were looking after their interests. Wilson announced to a group of businessmen in Detroit that the United States had just become a creditor nation. It currently held more of the surplus gold in the world than ever before, and "our business hereafter is to . . . lend and to help and to promote the great peaceful enterprises of the world." Finding little traction, the Republicans offered derogatory generalizations or carped over tax tables.

The Republicans denounced Wilson's halting foreign policy, but they had to keep from sounding bloodthirsty. Hughes was nowhere near as vituperative as TR, or even Henry Cabot Lodge, who summarized Wilson's foreign policy after the German sinking of the *Sussex* as little more than "brave words. More notes. More conversation." Because Hughes often restrained his feelings, some Republicans called him "Wilson with whiskers." His tendency to make one set of arguments for pro-German audiences and another for the pro-British earned him the nickname "Charles Evasive Hughes." In the words of Vice President Marshall, the Allies revealed themselves to be the "less corrupter" of the two sides in the Great War; but still, "war was abhorrent to the great mass of Americans, and the campaign of 1916 . . . [was] based largely on the fact that the president had kept us out."

The Republican Party never united behind its candidate. "It had no constructive policy," recalled Secretary McAdoo. "The Republicans carried on a campaign of criticism. Professional critics are seldom elevated to positions where creative talent is the chief quality required." Roosevelt's contempt for Wilson grew satanic—enough for him to set aside his own reservations about Hughes and campaign in a few strategic states for him. "Instead of speaking softly and carrying a big stick," said TR in Louisville, "President Wilson spoke bombastically and carried a dishrag."

TR never stopped attacking the President for reducing the country to an "elocutionary ostrich." Roosevelt derided Wilson's "He kept us out of war" slogan as nothing more than "ignoble shirking of responsibility . . . clothed in an utterly misleading phrase, the phrase of a coward." In reality, Colonel Roosevelt explained, "war has been creeping nearer and nearer, until it stares at us from just beyond our three-mile limit, and we face it without policy, plan, purpose or preparation." Because Roosevelt endorsed Hughes, the Bull Moose Party disbanded. TR hoped to lead his Progressives home to the Republican Party. The more chauvinistic patriots among them followed, but many found greater kinship among the Democrats.

Unlike Wilson, Hughes barnstormed the country. While campaigning in California, he checked into the Virginia Hotel in Long Beach, where Governor Hiram Johnson happened to be staying while running for the Senate. This popular figure rather expected to receive at least a message if not a courtesy call from his party's leader, but none came; and Johnson resumed his campaign running for himself and not his party. Hughes's widely reported snub did nothing to stanch the flow of Progressives to the Democrats, and the Republicans turned even more mean-spirited. Secretary Daniels believed "that no campaign in the history of the country has been quite so marked by viciousness, bitterness and invective. All the elements of hate and misrepresentation were brought into play." As the election neared, Wilson felt his opposition had sunk to unspeakable depths, so low, he told a reporter, that he had "an utter contempt for Mr. Hughes."

Indeed, Hughes shouted for months about the Adamson Act and the intrusion of government into the lives of Americans. He cried that he was not "too proud to fight"; some Republicans whispered about "Mrs. Peck" and the spurious affair while the first Mrs. Wilson was alive, and a party representative offered Mary Hulbert several hundred thousand dollars for Wilson's letters, an offer she refused; other Republicans shrieked that the Revenue Act was nothing less than Socialism. As for the Socialists themselves, their leader, Eugene Debs, forwent a fifth consecutive run for the White House in favor of a more pragmatic path to power. He ran for Congress from his home district in Indiana, railing against the President. "Mr. Wilson, who had all his life been opposed to militarism, has now become the avowed champion of plutocratic preparedness," he argued, "and today he stands before the country pleading in the name of Wall Street and its interests for the largest standing army and the most powerful navy in the world." But after months of campaign cacophony—and with German U-boats cruising the waters off Connecticut and Rhode Island—one phrase continued to resonate: "He kept us out of war."

Social reformers Jane Addams and Lillian D. Wald rallied behind Wilson, as did leftist intellectuals Max Eastman, John Reed, Herbert Croly, a cofounder of *The New Republic*, and one of his first staff members, Walter Lippmann. The latter became Wilson's strongest advocate through articles in his influential magazine of Progressive thought. Where he had once been a strong TR supporter and Wilson critic, Lippmann had now come to appreciate that the President was a man of vision. He argued to his colleagues, "What we're electing is a war President—not the man who kept us out of war. And we've got to make up our minds whether we want to go through the war with Hughes or with Wilson." Lippmann appreciated that truly thoughtful people could—and inevitably should—have the power to change their minds, as he did in the pages of *The New Republic* just before the election. "I shall not vote for the Wilson who has uttered a few too many noble sentiments," he wrote, "but for the Wilson who is evolving under experience and is remaking his philosophy in the light of it."

"If I understand myself," Wilson told Ida Tarbell in an interview in *Collier's* that ran the week before the election, "I am sincere when I say that I have no personal desire for reelection." Indeed, he admitted that he regretted not having been able to read a serious book in years. "It would be an unspeakable relief to be excused, but I am caught in the midst of a process." He reminded the voters that his progressive program was a work in progress; and he asked, "Is it wise that the country should change now, leaving so much at loose ends?" Tarbell could not help thinking of Lincoln in

August 1864, when he felt he might not be reelected and made a secret compact with himself to cooperate as much as possible with the President-elect, to save the Union in the period between the election and the inauguration. For weeks Wilson had been developing a secret compact of his own.

Since 1886, the law had stipulated that in the event of vacancies in the offices of both the President and the Vice President, the line of succession ran through the Cabinet, starting with the Secretary of State. In light of the seriousness of the world situation and the speed with which crises required handling, Wilson devised an exit strategy should Hughes win. He would ask Marshall and Lansing to resign from their positions so that he could appoint Hughes Secretary of State; then Wilson would resign, allowing Hughes to take office immediately instead of having to wait until the following March.

On Sunday, November 5, 1916, the President of the United States sat in his office at Shadow Lawn and typed a strictly confidential letter to the Secretary of State, one unique in Presidential archives. He outlined the plan, not overlooking the "consent and cooperation" of the Vice President and Secretary Lansing himself. Wilson thought his argument compelling enough for both men to accept: "No such critical circumstances in regard to our foreign policy have ever before existed. It would be my duty to step aside so that there would be no doubt in any quarter how that policy was to be directed. . . . I would have no right to risk the peace of the nation by remaining in office after I had lost my authority." He sent the letter and fully intended to act upon it, if necessary—"just as soon as the result of the election was definitely known."

Only that morning, Edith had spoken to her husband about losing the election, which she expected. Such a result was difficult for Wilson to imagine, having just faced tens of thousands in cheering throngs at Madison Square Garden and Cooper Union in New York City. But the candidate's wife had endured sleepless nights, tossing and turning over the opposition to Wilson's Mexican policy, the daily news from Europe, and, most of all, the massive amounts of money the Republicans had spent to smear him. Without knowing of Woodrow's plan, she told him how happy they would be living their own lives. Upon hearing her, Woodrow stood and said, "What a delightful pessimist you are! One must never court defeat. If it comes, accept it like a soldier; but don't anticipate it, for that destroys your fighting spirit." They took a long ride along the Jersey Shore.

Tuesday morning the Wilsons drove to Princeton, arriving a little before nine. Crowds of students and photographers watched the President vote in the firehouse. He spent the rest of the day back at Shadow Lawn working, making lists of states with the number of electors from each. The telegraph company offered to run a special wire into the house so he could receive the election results as they were transmitted, but Wilson said he would rather learn the news by telephone from his campaign directors. Early indications from Colorado and Kansas suggested that Wilson would do better there than he had in 1912. After a quiet dinner, the family passed the time playing Twenty Questions. Then at ten o'clock the telephone rang. A friend of Margaret's in New York was calling with condolences. Margaret could barely speak, spluttering that it was too early to know any results, that the polls were still open in the West. The caller explained that *The New York Times* had announced that it would indicate the winner with a colored light atop its building—white for Wilson, red for Hughes—and there was no mistaking the flash of crimson.

Dr. Grayson arrived from the executive offices in Asbury Park with the news that the New York *World* had also predicted a Hughes victory; and when the President phoned Tumulty, the normally cheery Irishman delivered the same verdict. In spite of that, Tumulty issued a statement that Wilson would win, once the results from the West arrived. Wilson laughed over the phone and said, "Well, Tumulty, it begins to look as if we have been badly licked." Tumulty heard no sadness in his boss's voice and offered more positive signs from the West. "Tumulty, you are an optimist," Wilson replied. "It begins to look as if the defeat might be overwhelming. The only thing I am sorry for, and that cuts me to the quick, is that the people apparently misunderstood us. But I have no regrets. We have tried to do our duty."

Shadow Lawn darkened. At last, Wilson said, "Well, I will not send Mr. Hughes a telegram of congratulation tonight, for things are not settled." And then his face turned grave as he acknowledged the inevitability of Hughes's bringing the country into the war. Hughes himself remained properly silent that night, but Theodore Roosevelt could not help himself from issuing a statement at ten o'clock, saying, "I am doubly thankful as an American for the election of Mr. Hughes. It is a vindication of our national honor." At Shadow Lawn, the butler brought a tray of sandwiches and beverages to the family. At 10:30, Wilson grabbed a glass of milk, said his goodnights, and added, "I might stay longer but you are all so blue."

Edith joined him a few minutes later. "Well, little girl," he said, "you were right in expecting we should lose the election. Frankly I did not, but we can now do some of the things we want to do." She sat on his bed, holding his hand, ready to discuss the future. In an instant he fell into a deep sleep, as though a great burden had been lifted.

Edith was less fortunate. Feeling her husband's pain, she was wide awake at 4 a.m., when someone knocked on her door. Margaret had just spoken to Vance McCormick at Democratic headquarters in New York and learned that the West was reporting unexpectedly favorable results. Margaret asked if they should awaken her father, and Edith said, "Oh no, do let him sleep."

At daybreak, the results remained in doubt. Some newspapers reported the Hughes victory, while the more cautious press only hinted as much— what with New York, Pennsylvania, and Illinois having gone Republican by hundreds of thousands of votes. New Jersey went solidly for Hughes, as did Iowa. But the electoral race remained neck and neck all day. New Hampshire and Delaware were each tipping Republican by only 1,000 votes, and Minnesota by 392 votes. And then Ohio surprisingly swung Democratic. Idaho followed; and so did New Hampshire by 56 votes. A reporter was said to have called Hughes in New York that morning hoping to get his comments on this possible Democratic trend. "The President can't be disturbed," the aide said. "Well," replied the reporter, "when he wakes up tell him he's no longer president."

That comment was premature as well. The race had come down to the one state that had yet to report its results—California, with 13 electoral votes. Poll watchers there guarded every ballot box amid allegations of voter fraud. Each ballot was painstakingly tallied. Into the morning after the election, the race remained a dead heat. A significant reason for the delay was that Sierra County, one hundred miles northeast of Sacramento and high in the Sierra Nevada, had not been heard from. An early snow had fallen upon sixteen rural precincts there. Voters had turned out, but now an entire nation had to wait for horse-drawn wagons carrying the ballot boxes to traverse the snowy crude roads so that the votes of this tiny county could be counted and certified.

Margaret Wilson knocked on her father's bathroom door while he was shaving that morning to tell him that *The New York Times* had printed an "Extra" edition of the paper that day suggesting that the election was still in doubt but leaning Wilson's way. "Tell that to the Marines," Wilson said, running the razor across his face. Incertitude persisted through the day and into the next. On Thursday the ninth, Woodrow and Edith went to Spring Lake to play golf, and while they were at the eighth tee, Dr. Grayson arrived with news from headquarters about California, which was favorable but not definitive. Throughout the ordeal, the President maintained his calm, though Edith discerned his tension. On November 10, California officially went for Wilson by 3,806 votes and the election was over.

Pundits suggested that Hughes's snub of Hiram Johnson cost him the Presidency. A sounder explanation for the traditionally Republican state's turning Democratic that year was that in the final stretch of the campaign, Senator Gore of Oklahoma kept driving the same point to the crowds he drew in the West: "A vote for Hughes is a vote for war. A vote for Wilson is a vote for peace." A decade later, Gore himself concluded, "The women voters in the west elected Wilson on the peace issue." Indeed, twelve states in the Union then allowed women to vote in the Presidential election, eleven of which were in the West, ten of which went for Wilson. Despite their small numbers, women had become an electoral constituency in the United States.

The final electoral vote count was 277 to 254, which fairly reflected the popular vote: 9,126,868 for Wilson and 8,548,728 for Hughes—49.2 percent to 46.1 percent. The Socialist candidate captured 3 percent of the vote, and a few minor candidates less than that. Wilson became the first Democratic President elected to a second consecutive term since Andrew Jackson in 1832. He was also the first man since James K. Polk in 1844 to get elected without carrying his home state. There were other signs of erosion of public support: in Congressional races, the Democrats lost two seats in the Senate, leaving them with a comfortable but decreasing margin of 54 to 42; and they suffered another bad hit in the House of Representatives, dropping to 214 members against 215 Republicans. Because three Progressives chose to caucus with the Democrats, the President's party could cobble together a coalition and maintain control of both houses. The South remained Wilson's igneous base, where he carried some states with more than 90 percent of the vote.

Wilson's dearest friend from Charlottesville, Heath Dabney, pointed out that the President had received more votes than any candidate had ever received for any office on earth—three million votes more than he had received in 1912—and his tallies in the individual states were almost always larger than those of Democratic candidates for Congress or governorships. Woodrow and Edith left directly for Williamstown, Massachusetts, for the baptism of Frank and Jessie Sayre's daughter, named Eleanor Axson; and then the President and his wife returned to the White House, after months away, to begin his second term. Charles Evans Hughes did not concede by telegram until November 22, 1916, claiming he had waited for the official count in California to end. Wilson replied graciously, though he commented to his brother, Josie, that Hughes's wire "was a little moth-eaten when it got here but quite legible."

"My husband . . . was weary and unwell," Edith would recall, "—reaction from the strain of the campaign." Other factors, of course, weighed heavily upon him. Thousands of miles away, the war continued to rage, as the British persisted in blockading and the Germans in torpedoing. The Continent became a charnel house—1916 seeing more slaughter than any year in history, with three of the bloodiest battles ever fought. The months-long Battle of Verdun produced 800,000 casualties; twice that number were wounded or killed in the second half of the year in the Battle of the Somme (where the prescient American poet Alan Seeger had his "rendezvous with Death"); another 1,600,000 people fell that summer in the Brusilov offensive, in which Russia defeated the Central Powers on the Eastern Front; and lesser battles in 1916 saw another 600,000 killed or wounded.

While the seas had remained quiet since the *Sussex* note of the spring had demanded that the Germans stop attacking ships with American passengers, turbulence returned. In less than three weeks, U-boats sank four ships conducting trade between Britain and the United States, taking several American lives. The Germans insisted they were playing by the rules, and notes continued to be exchanged as Germany offered reasonable enough excuses to warrant months of investigation. "Foreseeing an inevitable crisis with Germany over the frequent sinking of our ships," Tumulty recorded, Wilson believed that he could not "draw the whole country with him in aggressive action if before he took the step leading to war he had not tried out every means of peace." His enemies decried his "meekness and apparent subservience to German diplomacy." In truth, the British did not make Wilson's life any easier.

That summer England had imposed a "black list," which forbade Britons from dealing with eighty-five American companies the government perceived as conducting business for the benefit of their enemies. Congress considered retaliation in the form of an embargo on loans and supplies, but the President argued otherwise. He recalled a similar vengeful action in 1807 in which "the states themselves suffered from the act more than the nations whose trade they struck at."

To complicate matters, neither side in Europe was ready to throw in the towel. "Never before in the world's history," observed Wilson, "have two great armies been in effect so equally matched; never before have the losses and the slaughter been so great with as little gain in military advantage. Both sides have grown weary of the apparently hopeless task of bringing the conflict to an end by the force of arms; inevitably they are being forced to the realization that it can only be brought about by the attrition of human suffering, in which the victor suffers hardly less than the vanquished." The brutal fighting had lasted so long, each side was punch-drunk, convinced that the next blow would provide the knockout.

By December, a chink had appeared in the German armor. Wilson received intelligence revealing that "Germany as a whole"—its most militaristic factions aside—appeared "ready to welcome steps toward peace as the food situation, while by no means critical, is becoming more and more difficult and as there is a general weariness of war." Chancellor von Bethmann Hollweg and new Foreign Secretary Arthur Zimmermann showed signs of budging. In London, Colonel House met with a colleague of David Lloyd George's and said that England had become "the only obstacle to peace." Wilson was eager as ever to mediate a settlement, one he felt could include everything England had been fighting for. Even though House had said that the United States had been "quite unneutral in its friendliness to England," both sides complained that America had been partial toward the other. Each wanted commercial advantages from America—in the way of food and munitions—without offering anything in return, not even a willingness to negotiate peace.

On November 25, Wilson sat at his desk and considered the uniqueness of his position. "Perhaps I am the only person in high authority amongst all the peoples of the world who is at liberty to speak and hold nothing back," he wrote. He could speak "as an individual" and "as the responsible head of a great government." As such he felt compelled to speak not only for the people of the United States but "for friends of humanity in every nation." He hoped to produce a series of terms that would deliver "an enduring peace." Unlike prior conflicts, Wilson believed this war—"with its unprecedented human waste and suffering and its drain of material resource"—presented "an unparalleled opportunity for the statesmen of the world to make such a peace possible." Toward that end, Wilson drafted what came to be called a "peace note" to all the powers at war. He told Edith it "may prove the greatest piece of work of my life."

Wilson called upon leaders on both sides to clarify their respective war aims and to consider their progress in the last two years. "The conflict moves very sluggishly," he suggested; and a prolonged war could only lead to "irreparable damage to civilization." Wilson proposed a conference of representatives of the belligerent governments and of the governments whose interests were directly involved. He was not butting in either to mediate or even to propose peace. He was merely calling for "a concrete definition of the guarantees which the belligerents on the one side and the other deem it their duty to demand as a practical satisfaction of the objects they are aiming at in this contest of force." The answers to these questions, he said, would be nonbinding, merely suggestions to help neutral nations determine their future courses of action. "The United States," he said, "feels that it can no longer delay to determine its own."

The next night, Colonel House arrived at the White House, and the President read to him what he had drafted thus far. House thought it was "a wonderfully well written document" but that Wilson's suggestion that "the causes and objects of the war are obscure" would enrage the Allies. House explained that such a remark suggested no understanding of the Allies' viewpoint, which held "that Germany started the war for conquest; that she broke all international obligations and laws of humanity in pursuit of it." The British claimed to be fighting "to make such another war impossible, and to so break Prussian militarism that a permanent peace may be established."

Over the next two weeks, Wilson edited his "peace note." In calling upon the leaders to articulate their objectives, Wilson believed he might get the antagonists to realize that "peace is nearer than we know; that the terms which the belligerents . . . would deem it necessary to insist upon are not so irreconcilable as some have feared." On Friday, December 15, he read his revised version to his Cabinet. McAdoo and Houston strongly opposed sending it, as it "might be regarded as an act of friendship toward Germany and possibly as a threat." After a lengthy discussion, the President said, "I will send this note or nothing." And at 9:30 p.m. on December 18, he sent it. House revealed to his diary, "I find the President has nearly destroyed all the work I have done in Europe. He knows how I feel about this and how the Allies feel about it, and yet the refrain always appears in some form or other." Although he kept his feelings private, he remained angry at the President for weeks—though not as angry as the President became with Secretary Lansing for a highly indiscreet blunder.

Feeling that the "peace note" gave the appearance of complicity with the Germans' recent overtures, the Secretary of State issued his own statement, in which he indicated that the note had sprung from America's increasing involvement with the belligerents. "I mean by that," he added, digging a shallow grave for himself, "that we are drawing nearer the verge of war ourselves, and therefore we are entitled to know exactly what each belligerent seeks, in order that we may regulate our conduct in the future." Wilson was furious. The note not only second-guessed him but provided what he considered an unnecessary addendum, one that would only further cloud the murky waters of diplomacy. Worse, it revealed that Lansing was not in sympathy with Wilson's desire to stay out of this war. The stock market plummeted, as war jitters triggered the most precipitous one-day drop in fifteen years.

The President all but called for Lansing's resignation. Instead, he dictated a follow-up statement for the Secretary to release—which offered both his correction and his contrition. Wall Street bounced back the next day. The "peace note" episode reminded the American foreign policy team that it was essentially a one-man band.

Twenty-two relatives gathered at the White House to celebrate Christmas 1916 and Wilson's sixtieth birthday. "We thank God for all you mean to the World, and trust that your life and strength may be spared for many years," wrote Cleveland Dodge, "to solve the great problems which you, better than anyone else, can solve." Wilson believed as much himself. With the belligerents failing to reply with the terms he had requested, Wilson decided to state his own. He formulated a general resolution to the great conflict and something more—"making the keystone of the settlement arch the future security of the world against wars, and letting territorial adjustments be subordinate to the main purpose." On January 3, 1917, he and Colonel House conferred, laying cornerstones of the foundation. The main tenet was "the right of nations to determine under what government they should continue to live." Beyond that, Wilson thought Poland should be free and independent, Belgium and Serbia should be restored, and the vast Turkish Empire should be dismantled. House urged granting Russia maritime access to the south—"a warm seaport"—without which, he feared, they would surely go to war again. Wilson set to work on a speech that would outline not only an end of the war but also the start of a new age of peace.

For two weeks he toiled, and at one o'clock on January 22, 1917, he appeared before the Senate. While the nation's legislators had grown accustomed to the President's addressing them to explain any number of audacious programs, this visit was singular, for it came with little advance notice and no explanation of its purpose.

Wilson spoke of the duty of the American government in building a new structure of peace in the world. "It is inconceivable that the people of the United States should play no part in that great enterprise," he said. He added that the country owed it to itself and the other nations of the world to "add their authority and their power to the authority and force of other nations to guarantee peace and justice throughout the world." He wanted the American government to originate a "League for Peace." In ending this war, he sought treaties and agreements "which will create a peace that is worth guaranteeing and preserving, a peace that will win the approval of mankind, not merely a peace that will serve the several interests and immediate aims of the nations engaged."

Such a "covenant of cooperative peace," Wilson said, must include the people of the New World if it was meant to "keep the future safe against war." In reassembling a shattered world, Wilson said, there must be "not a balance of power, but a community of power; not organized rivalries, but an organized common peace." That, Wilson said in a statement that would resonate for generations, would require "a peace without victory."

Victory would mean peace forced upon the loser, a victor's terms imposed upon the vanquished. It would be accepted in humiliation, under duress, at an intolerable sacrifice, and would leave a sting, a resentment, a bitter memory upon which terms of peace would rest, not permanently, but only as upon quicksand.

"Only a peace between equals can last," he said.

Wilson was formulating a number of specific points—regarding Poland, armaments, and "freedom of the seas." Above all, he proposed the ideas of "government by the consent of the governed" and that "no right anywhere exists to hand peoples about from sovereignty to sovereignty as if they were property." Wilson concluded by insisting, "These are American principles, American policies. We could stand for no others. And they are also the principles and policies of forward looking men and women everywhere. . . . They are the principles of mankind and must prevail."

Having sat through the speech in rapt silence, the audience in the gallery and the Senators on the floor broke into sharp applause, led by Republican Robert La Follette, who afterward commented, "We have just passed through a very important hour in the life of the world." Senator "Pitchfork Ben" Tillman said it was "the most startling and noblest utterance that has fallen from human lips since the Declaration of Independence." Other members of Congress suggested this expression of a new world vision was the most important pronouncement of an American President since the Monroe Doctrine. (Wilson had even suggested in his text that the rest of the world should adopt Monroe's doctrine—that "no nation should seek to extend its polity over any other nation or people, but that every people should be left free to determine its own polity." *The New York Times* wrote that the speech offered more than a contract for peace; it was "a moral transformation."

But, as expected, Republican critics pounced. Senator Francis E. Warren of Wyoming gibed that "the President thinks he is the President of the world." Others suggested that Wilson was abandoning the Monroe Doctrine, inviting non-Americans to tamper with the workings of the Western Hemisphere. Alice Roosevelt Longworth took wicked delight in the way Wilson had converted the Capitol into his own personal theater and turned each Presidential message into a "show." On this occasion, she thought he had outdone himself. "Peace without victory," she said, "amounted to nothing more than a continuation of cowardly temporizing."

A sanguine Wilson told the press, "I have said what everybody has thought impossible. Now it appears to be possible." He did not expect the

Senate to take specific action as a result of his remarks. This was simply a rare moment in the nation's history in which a President asked the people and its representatives to embrace a philosophy.

Foreign reaction was mixed. Ambassador Page in London said the British admired the idealism of the speech but felt the defeat of Germany was essential for any long-term tranquillity, a peace *with* victory. Privately, some Allied Ambassadors in the United States questioned the President's right to propose terms of a peace to a war in which he was not engaged. The most positive foreign reaction came from the Germans. Ambassador von Bernstorff was still pushing his government to respond to Wilson's earlier request for peace, and he remained in quiet contact with Colonel House.

But on January 31, 1917, Germany announced a new policy, an offensive of unrestricted submarine warfare whereby all ships, belligerent or neutral, in the war zone surrounding Great Britain, France, and Italy, or in the eastern Mediterranean Sea, would be sunk. A specified route would be provided to permit a limited number of well-marked American ships to enter this zone. Bernstorff wrote Colonel House that Berlin had instructed him to inform Wilson that Germany had been prepared to meet virtually all the Allies' peace terms back in December, but no longer. They now believed their new submarine policy would bring the war to its swiftest conclusion. As soon as Tumulty had the German bulletin in hand, he brought it to the President and watched as he read and reread it. Wilson turned gray, his lips tightened, and his jaw locked. Placing the paper back in Tumulty's hand, Wilson quietly said, "This means war. The break that we have tried so hard to prevent now seems inevitable."

Still, Wilson resisted. Despite resenting Germany for misleading him for so many months, he believed "it was for the good of the world for the United States to keep out of the war in the present circumstances." He insisted that he would not allow this turn of events to incite military action "if it could possibly be avoided." He was willing to bear the criticism and contempt that would come from all sides. On February 2, Secretary Lansing, voicing the sentiments of most of the Cabinet, wrote Wilson, "The situation can no longer be tolerated. The time for patience has passed."

The next day, the President returned to Congress. After reviewing Germany's provocative behavior, Wilson announced that he had directed the Secretary of State to inform His Excellency the German Ambassador "that all diplomatic relations between the United States and the German

Empire are severed and that the American Ambassador at Berlin will immediately be withdrawn." Should German naval commanders violate the laws of the sea and humanity, Wilson said, he would "take the liberty of coming again before the Congress, to ask that authority be given me to use any means that may be necessary for the protection of our seamen and our people in the prosecution of their peaceful and legitimate errands on the high seas." Even at this late date, Wilson kept the diplomatic doors open. "We shall not believe that they are hostile to us unless and until we are obliged to believe it."

At two o'clock that afternoon—as Wilson walked before both houses of Congress, an Assistant Solicitor for the State Department appeared at the German Embassy in Washington and handed Count von Bernstorff his passport. "I am not surprised," Bernstorff said, wistfully granting that there was "nothing else left for the United States to do." After eight years in Washington, he told the press that he was finished with politics and expected to retire to his farm to grow potatoes.

Colonel House recorded that Wilson was still of a mind that "it would be a crime for this Government to involve itself in the war to such an extent as to make it impossible to save Europe afterward." The President maintained that his recent declaration was intended to lay "the bases of peace, not war." Wilson spent much of the next week engaged in the same practice that he had as a young boy organizing his baseball team: he drafted a constitution. In this instance it was for that League of Peace to which he had referred, an organization of neutral nations that would be committed to a number of basic precepts—mutual guarantees of political independence, territorial integrity, arms limitation, and a refusal to take part "in any joint economic action by two or more nations which would in effect constitute an effort to throttle the industrial life of any nation or shut it off from fair and equal opportunities of trade." Roosevelt wrote Lodge that he now doubted whether Wilson would go to war under any circumstances. "He is evidently trying his old tactics," he said; "he is endeavoring to sneak out of going to war under any conditions. . . . He is yellow all through in the presence of danger. . . . Of course it costs him nothing, if the insult or injury is to the country, because I don't believe he is capable of understanding what the words 'pride of country' mean. . . ."

On February 28, Wilson granted an audience to a delegation of peace advocates—church leaders, a Socialist labor organizer, a historian, and

Jane Addams among them. Their mission was to impress upon the President his own comments in his "peace without victory" speech and to offer historical examples and moral imperatives for why America should stay out of the war. When Professor William Isaac Hull, one of his former students, urged Wilson to send an appeal to the German people, circumventing the militaristic hierarchy, the President brought the conversation to a close. "Dr. Hull," he said, "if you knew what I know at the present moment, and what you will see reported in tomorrow morning's newspapers, you would not ask me to attempt further peaceful dealings with the Germans."

"GERMANY SEEKS AN ALLIANCE AGAINST US; ASKS JAPAN AND MEXICO TO JOIN HER; FULL TEXT OF HER PROPOSAL MADE PUBLIC," blared the *New York Times* headline the next day. This exposed plot had come in the form of a coded telegram from Foreign Minister Zimmermann to the German Ambassador in Mexico, who was to encourage President Carranza to ally with Germany and to invite Japan to do the same. In return, Mexico would not only receive financial reward but could also reclaim Texas, New Mexico, and Arizona.

In truth, the British had intercepted Zimmermann's note in mid-January but had not relayed it to Wilson, via Ambassador Page, until February 25. The following afternoon, the President appeared before a joint session of Congress. With just days until the arrival of the new legislature, he called upon the Sixty-fourth Congress to take one more bold position. "Since it has unhappily proved impossible to safeguard our neutral rights by diplomatic means," he said, ". . . there may be no recourse but to *armed* neutrality." Without proposing war, Wilson requested certain tools with which to fight German weapons—most especially the authority to supply American merchant ships with defensive arms. That day, a German U-Boat sank the *Laconia*, a former British ocean liner converted to an armed merchant cruiser, as it approached Ireland. Twelve people from among the 75 passengers and crew of 217 died, including a mother and daughter from Chicago.

The House immediately passed an armed ship bill by a vote of 403 to 13, but the Senate balked. Several Senators believed arming merchantmen left the nation only one incident away from war. Midwesterners such as La Follette, along with O'Gorman from New York and Vardaman from Mississippi, decided to dramatize their opposition with a filibuster. In this case, they had only to delay for the two days before the Sixty-fourth Congress would terminate—at noon on March 4. Although seventy-six Senators said they would approve the bill, eleven men held the government hostage.

Because March 4 fell on a Sunday, the formal inauguration of the President was scheduled for the next day. But, as required, Chief Justice White swore Woodrow Wilson in for the second time, in a quiet ceremony. Wilson had been in the President's Room since 10:30 that rainy morning, attending to business and monitoring the filibuster down the hall. The Cabinet gathered over the next hour, along with Tumulty, Colonel House, and Dr. Grayson. No more than thirty people witnessed Wilson take the oath. Edith, the only woman present, stood behind him. Afterward, Wilson kissed the Bible, which was opened to the Forty-sixth Psalm: "God *is* our refuge and strength: a very present help in trouble."

There were no festivities that day, only complaints about the filibuster. With the bill killed, a seething President returned to the White House, where he went to his desk. That night he released a long statement to the press, taking the Senate to task. "In the immediate presence of a crisis fraught with more subtle and far-reaching possibilities of national danger than any other the Government has known within the whole history of its international relations," the President raged, "the Congress has been unable to act either to safeguard the country or to vindicate the elementary rights of its citizens." He felt the United States, especially in times of crisis, could not proceed in this manner. "A little group of willful men, representing no opinion but their own," he said, "have rendered the great Government of the United States helpless and contemptible," making it "the only legislative body in the world which cannot act when its majority is ready for action." The President saw a single remedy—a change in the rules. Within days, Wilson would call upon the newly seated Sixty-fifth Congress to institute an essential of Senatorial procedure—the rule of "cloture," by which a (then) two-thirds majority of the Senate could end a filibuster.

A cold wind blew across the East Portico of the Capitol that Monday, March 5, as the sun tried to burn through the clouds that remained from a recent storm. "The inauguration was not a festival," one onlooker observed; "it was a momentary interlude in a grave business, and it must be got over with as briefly and as simply as possible." Because of new threats against Wilson's life, security was reinforced, with twenty Secret Service agents surrounding him. Only fifty thousand people gathered for the ceremonies; the inaugural parade was half the length of the first; and, again, there would be no Inaugural Ball. For the first time, a First Lady accompanied her husband to and from the Capitol and stood by his side while he delivered a brief speech of 1,500 words.

This address was as unlike his first inaugural as was the spirit infusing the occasion. In 1913 he had spoken not a word about foreign affairs, only of his optimistic domestic agenda. Now he talked almost entirely of the "tragical events of the thirty months of vital turmoil through which we have just passed," which had made "us citizens of the world." There could be no turning back, he said. "The shadows that now lie dark upon our path will soon be dispelled and we shall walk with the light all about us if we be but true to ourselves." Without quite defining the mission, he said, "United alike in the conception of our duty and in the high resolve to perform it in the face of all men, let us dedicate ourselves to the great task to which we must now set our hand."

With that, Woodrow Wilson commenced his second term, delivering the nation to a place it could not even have imagined four years ago. While the United States was far from prepared militarily, its President had conscientiously made it ready mentally and morally to address the inevitable ordeal ahead. To clarify that task, Wilson reminded his countrymen, "We are provincials no longer."

12

ARMAGEDDON

*And the nations were angry, and thy wrath is
come . . .*

—REVELATION, XI:18

With the events of the inauguration behind them,
Woodrow and Edith went home, where the family
had gathered upstairs in the oval sitting room of the White
House to watch the fireworks. Curtained off by themselves
in his study, a weary First Couple invited Colonel House to
sit with them. He found the President holding Edith's hand
and pressing his cheek against hers.

After reviewing the highlights of the day, a revived
President suggested that they take to the streets, where they
could enjoy the new system of lights that illuminated much
of Washington. Wilson had a chauffeur drive them without a Secret Service agent, despite that day's bomb threats.
A car with guards followed closely, as much of Washington
turned out to admire the public buildings along Pennsylvania Avenue, all the way up to the Capitol, with its glow-
ing dome. Within minutes, crowds on the street recognized
the President and cheered. He and his wife retreated to the
White House, where they talked with Colonel House until
eleven.

Two days later, Wilson was suffering from a terrible
cold and exhaustion. Dr. Grayson ordered him to bed,

where he remained for the better part of the next two weeks. Edith had already taken note of the conditions that tended to incite his minor collapses, "when every nerve was tense with anxiety . . . and the burdens resting on his shoulders [were] enough to crush the vitality of a giant."

A slight but discernible change in White House procedure occurred during his convalescence. The filibuster having defeated the armed ship bill, Wilson asked Attorney General Gregory whether he could arm merchant ships without Congressional authorization. When Gregory said yes, the White House asked Secretaries Lansing and Daniels to prepare for the new policy. Curiously, however, communications with the Secretaries passed via Mrs. Wilson. The President was learning that he could use his wife as an operative—"a blind" is how she described herself, blocking unwanted visitors and relaying essential messages in both directions. Edith sat by her husband's bed and read the long memoranda detailing the plans for arming merchant ships. "Mr. Lansing, especially," observed Mrs. Wilson, "saw no hope for peace and urged that we proceed on the theory that we should soon be at war with Germany."

Adding further confusion to a world spun out of control, the people of Russia revolted. After years of steady decimation in the war under an unheeding monarchy, the Imperial Guard mutinied, the Duma formed a provisional government, and—hopelessly fighting his "Cousin Willy," the Kaiser—Czar Nicholas II abdicated his throne, bringing three hundred years of Romanov rule to an end. While the future of that empire remained unclear, the certain death of the dynasty lent greater credence to Wilson's conception of "war against autocracy." It now clearly defined this war as one between Democracy and Absolutism. March 18 brought word of three torpedoed American merchant vessels, with the loss of more than a dozen lives.

Wilson appeared at the 2:30 Cabinet meeting on Tuesday, March 20, his old genial self. Almost immediately he sought advice regarding America's relations with Germany. With the nation in a growing state of agitation, the Cabinet found the President's calmness sobering and reassuring. "Excitement," Robert Lansing noted, "would seem very much out of place at the Cabinet table with Woodrow Wilson presiding." The President gravely posed two questions: Should he summon Congress to meet before April 16, for which he had already issued a call? And what should he say?

McAdoo answered first. He said the war seemed a "certainty," and he could see no reason for delaying American participation. If we did not respond at once, he said, "the American people would compel action and we would be in the position of being pushed forward instead of leading, which would be humiliating and unwise." More than supplying men, which he doubted the country could do at that time, he felt the United States could underwrite the Allies' loans. Houston picked up the ball and said that Germany was already at war with America and that the country should not hesitate to fight back. "The quickest way to hit Germany," he said, "is to help the Allies." Until the United States had amassed a large Army, it could speed up the production of submarines and destroyers, build multitudes of fast ships for freight, and extend liberal credits to Germany's enemies. War Secretary Baker said the current state of affairs demanded drastic action without delay—"that the Germans did not intend to modify in the least degree their policy of inhumanity and lawlessness," and that such acts meant war. He advocated preparing an Army at once. Lansing said it behooved the President to appear before Congress to declare that a state of war already existed between Germany and the United States and to "enact the laws necessary to meet the exigencies of the case." With the Russian Revolution, Lansing added, the time was ideal for entering the war, to fight for a League of Peace with no powerful autocracies among its members. With increasing excitement, he added that public sentiment was strong enough at that moment to sway Congress.

The President asked Lansing to lower his voice. He did not want people in the corridor overhearing their discussion. He remained unsure how to introduce the Russian situation into this American decision. Lansing said those were not causes to go to war; but he believed the character of the autocratic German government—"as manifested by its deeds of inhumanity, by its broken promises, and by its plots and conspiracies against this country"—pertained. Wilson absorbed all of Lansing's words, saying only, "Possibly."

Lansing argued that the sinking of a few American ships, even with the loss of American lives, did not provide a sound enough basis to declare war. The "duty of this and every other democratic nation to suppress an autocratic government like the German . . . because it was a menace to the national safety of this country and of all other countries with liberal systems of government," however, did.

"We have not yet heard from Burleson and Daniels," said the President in a professorial tone. With reluctance, the Postmaster General expressed regrets about having to abandon neutrality but agreed that if the President did not take action, the people would force it. "I do not care for popular demand," Wilson said. "I want to do right, whether popular or not." And so Burleson urged an immediate declaration of war—and, he added, "I want it to be understood that we are in the war to the end, that we will do everything we can to aid the Allies and weaken Germany with money, munitions, ships and men, so that those Prussians will realize that, when they made war on this country they woke up a giant which will surely defeat them." He recommended the issuance of $5 billion in bonds. Wilson turned to the other side of the table and said, "Well, Daniels?"

The eyes of the Secretary of the Navy filled with tears. The most pacifistic of the Cabinet members and a friend of Bryan's, he took his colleagues aback when he announced that he too favored war. "Having tried patience," he said, there was "no course open to us except to protect our rights on the seas." The President's faced dropped.

Once everyone had spoken his piece—all starting from different positions but ending with the same conclusion—the President said, "Well, gentlemen. I think that there is no doubt as to what your advice is. I thank you." As the Secretaries adjourned, Wilson asked Burleson and Lansing to remain, so that he could inquire when he might ask Congress to convene should he decide to do so. Two Mondays hence would be the earliest possible date, they explained. "Thus ended a Cabinet meeting the influence of which may change the course of history," Lansing wrote in a memorandum to himself. "The ten councillors of the President had spoken as one," he said, "and he—well, no one could be sure that he would echo the same opinion and act accordingly." Fifty newsmen waited in the outer executive offices for word about the meeting; but the Secretaries could not say much because they honestly did not know how Wilson would act. They revealed only that he would probably call Congress into extra session within the next two weeks. The President attended the vaudeville show at Keith's Theatre that night.

Over the next several days, the President got outside of the White House as much as possible—not fleeing his responsibilities so much as freeing himself so that he could think. He played golf and took long automobile rides. When he had business to conduct with Cabinet members, he went to their offices—on foot. Wilson was not completely alone, of course: the Secret Service accompanied him. And so did Edith. Observed

Thomas Brahany, the chief clerk of the White House staff, "I think this is the first time in American history that a President's wife has accompanied the President in a purely business call on a Cabinet Officer."

On Friday, March 30, Woodrow Wilson was ready to prepare his remarks to Congress. He knew his next public utterance would alter the world. For this momentous address, he summoned the country's most successful speechwriter, one of its foremost historians, one of its first political scientists, one of its most elegant wordsmiths, a spiritual thinker to provide moral grounding, and, finally, his most trusted stenographer to get it all down on paper. There in the second-story study, Woodrow Wilson sat alone.

Actually, Edith was in the room with him, decoding cipher messages for her husband. They closed the office door with orders that nobody was to disturb him. He started with an outline, graduated to a shorthand draft, which he corrected in shorthand and longhand, and then put his fingers to the keys of his Hammond typewriter. The Wilsons lunched alone, after which Edith took him for an hour's ride in the park. And then it was back to the desk for ten hours over the course of the weekend, finishing after church on Sunday.

Upon the completion of the speech, Edith recalled, Wilson summoned a newspaper friend, Frank I. Cobb, editor of the New York *World*. "I'd never seen him so worn down," the journalist said. "He looked as if he hadn't slept, and he said he hadn't." Indeed, Wilson had wrestled with the situation over several nights. "He tapped some sheets before him," added Cobb, "and said that he had written a message and expected to go before Congress with it as it stood. He said he couldn't see any alternative, that he had tried every way he knew to avoid war." And then the boy who had grown up in the battle-ravaged South added, "I think I know what war means. . . . Is there anything else I can do?" Cobb said Germany had forced his hand.

After breakfast the next morning, Wilson passed to the Public Printer a sealed envelope containing the draft of his self-typed address, and he asked Tumulty to notify Congress that he was prepared to appear as soon as the two houses could organize. He spent the rest of the morning playing golf with Edith. In the afternoon, he walked across the West Executive Avenue from the White House to the State, War, and Navy Building (a grand monstrosity of an edifice, later called the Executive Office Building) to brief Secretaries Lansing and Daniels. Later that day, American Ambassador Sharp further justified the Administration's course of action when he notified Washington that a U-boat had torpedoed the freighter *Aztec*, the first armed American merchantman, taking a dozen lives.

Tension spread. Sensing what lay ahead, seven pacifists from Boston confronted their senior Senator, Henry Cabot Lodge, as he was leaving a committee room. Their spokesman approached Lodge and said his constituents opposed entering the war. Lodge disagreed, replying, "National degeneracy and cowardice are worse than war." The young man said that anyone who wanted to go to war was a coward; and with that, the sixty-seven-year-old Senator called the man a liar and threw a punch, sending him to the floor. Similar arguments broke out across the nation. In the White House, Wilson gave his speech a dry run, reading it to Colonel House. The Colonel admired it immensely, not least of all because he felt it contained concepts he had been urging upon the President since the war began—differentiating between the German government and the German people, demanding the same codes of honor and morals for nations as for individuals, stating that the United States should not join a league of nations of which an autocracy was a member. But the speech, regardless of House's or anyone else's contribution, was pure Woodrow Wilson. Whether or not he was the first to utter them, the ideas and ideals were his. At 6:30, the two joined Wilson's family for a small dinner, during which the war was not discussed.

At 8:10 the household left the Executive Mansion, followed ten minutes later by the President and Mrs. Wilson, accompanied by Tumulty and Dr. Grayson. Despite a light spring rain, cheering crowds lined the streets all the way to the Capitol, where searchlights illuminated the massive flag atop the bright dome. Two troops of United States cavalry in dress uniform with sabers drawn greeted the President at the entrance to the House of Representatives. The members had been in session all day; and now, after an hour's respite, they returned to the great chamber. In a semicircle directly before the Speaker's desk sat the entire Supreme Court—Chief Justice White front and center—without robes. The Cabinet flanked them in the front row to the Speaker's left; the diplomatic corps—including the Ambassador of newly elected President Carranza of Mexico—in evening dress, filled the seats behind. It was the first time the foreign envoys as a cohort had been invited to the great hall. Led by Vice President Marshall, the Senate entered, almost every man carrying or wearing a small American flag. The press and special invited guests packed the gallery, 1,500 people all together. Edith sat with her mother and Margaret Wilson in the front row of the balcony. At 8:32 the Speaker's voice announced the President of the United States. The Justices were the first to rise and cheer, leading a two-minute ovation—the greatest welcome Wilson had received in all his visits to the chamber. The audience settled into silence so deep, Edith said one could hear only the sound of people breathing.

The President appeared nervous at first. He looked pale; his voice quavered, and his fingers trembled. In plain terms, Wilson explained the reason for this extraordinary session: "There are serious, very serious, choices of policy to be made, and made immediately, which it was neither right nor constitutionally permissible that I should assume the responsibility of making." For several minutes, the audience was silent, as Wilson calmly recited a list of recent German atrocities. He pointed out that some of the unarmed ships that had been sunk were carrying relief to stricken Belgians, that there had been not only violations of international law but a disregard for human life, and that property "can be paid for; the lives of peaceful and innocent people cannot be." The "present German submarine warfare against commerce," he insisted, was nothing less than "a war against all nations" and a "challenge to all mankind."

Each nation, Wilson said, must decide for itself how to meet that challenge. "Our motive," he asserted, "will not be revenge or the victorious assertion of the physical might of the nation, but only the vindication of right, of human right, of which we are only a single champion." Armed neutrality, he declared, was no longer an option. "There is one choice we cannot make, we are incapable of making," he said to the utterly still audience: "We will not choose the path of submission—"

The chamber erupted in cheers. Chief Justice White dropped the big soft hat he had been holding so that he could raise his hands in the air and clap. The applause spread from the floor to the galleries. At last the President, having found his voice, continued from the point at which he had been interrupted:

—and suffer the most sacred rights of our nation and our people to be ignored or violated. The wrongs against which we now array ourselves are no common wrongs; they cut to the very roots of human life.

   With a profound sense of the solemn and even tragical character of
the step I am taking and of the grave responsibilities which it involves,
but in unhesitating obedience to what I deem my constitutional duty,
I advise that the Congress declare the recent course of the Imperial
German government to be in fact nothing less than war against the
government and people of the United States; that it formally accept
the status of belligerent which has thus been thrust upon it; and that
it take immediate steps not only to put the country in a more thorough state of defense but also to exert all its power and employ all its
resources to bring the Government of the German Empire to terms
and end the war.

Justice White sprang to his feet, triggering an even greater ovation. He
fought back tears.

   The President was in full command as he cogently articulated how
this had become a war of necessity for America. "Neutrality is no longer
feasible or desirable where the peace of the world is involved and the freedom of its peoples," he said, "and the menace to that peace and freedom lies
in the existence of autocratic government backed by organized force which
is controlled wholly by their will, not by the will of their people."

   "We have no quarrel with the German people," Wilson emphasized,
because this "was a war determined upon as wars used to be determined
upon in the old, unhappy days when people were nowhere consulted by
their rulers and wars were provoked and waged in the interest of dynasties
or of little groups of ambitious men who were accustomed to use their fellow men as pawns and tools." But the actions of the German leadership
demanded a global response, which included an affiliation of democratic
nations. "It must be a league of honour," he said, "a partnership of opinion." Wilson rejoiced at the recent events in Russia and pronounced that
emerging nation a "fit partner" for that league now that it had shaken off
the "autocracy that crowned the summit of her political structure."

   The United States was going to have to pay the price of going to war;
and some of those costs were immediate. They included: extending "the
most liberal financial credits" to those countries already fighting Germany; "the organization and mobilization of all the material resources of
the country to supply the materials of war and serve the incidental needs
of the nation in the most abundant and yet the most economical and

efficient way possible"; the immediate equipping of the existing Navy to deal with the enemy's submarines; and the immediate addition to the armed forces of at least 500,000 men. Toward that end, Wilson believed not in a volunteer Army but the "principle of universal liability to service," along with authorization for additional men as soon as they were needed and could be trained. Wilson said he did not wish to borrow money to pay for all these efforts; he believed it was "our duty . . . to protect our people" through equitable taxation.

In short, Wilson said, Germany had become an international menace, and the United States was "about to accept gauge of battle with this natural foe to liberty and shall, if necessary, spend the whole force of the nation to check and nullify its pretensions and its power." That meant America would fight for nothing less than "the ultimate peace of the world and for the liberation of its people, the German peoples included: for the rights of nations great and small and the privilege of men everywhere to choose their way of life and of obedience." And then Woodrow Wilson justified going to war—with a declaration that would long resonate:

"The world must be made safe for democracy."

The sentence elicited no response at first. Then Senator John Sharp Williams of Mississippi stopped the speech with his applause. Everybody present rapidly comprehended the importance of those eight words, and the acclamation steadily mounted. When it finally subsided, Wilson completed his thought, which was meant to define further America's role in the conflict and to characterize the nation's place in the world for at least the next century. The world's peace, he continued,

> must be planted upon the tested foundations of political liberty. We have no selfish ends to serve. We desire no conquest, no dominion. We seek no indemnities for ourselves, no material compensation for the sacrifices we shall freely make. We are but one of the champions of the rights of mankind. We shall be satisfied when those rights have been made as secure as the faith and the freedom of nations can make them.

With Lincolnesque charity, Wilson reminded his audience that for all of America's arguments with Germany's allies, the Imperial and Royal Government of Austria-Hungary had not actually engaged in warfare

against citizens of the United States. Furthermore, Wilson reminded his
fellow Americans, "We are . . . sincere friends of the German people," including those living amongst them—unless and until they displayed any
disloyalty to the United States.

After thirty-six minutes, Wilson concluded, adapting the words of no
less a reformer than Martin Luther himself. "God helping her," Wilson
said of America's new crusade, "she can do no other."

All members of the three branches of government stood as one. The
Senators waved their small flags wildly, all except Senator La Follette, who
conspicuously stood in silence, chewing gum, with his arms folded. As the
President hastily departed, Senator Lodge strode toward him, extended his
hand, and said, "Mr. President, you have expressed in the loftiest manner
possible, the sentiments of the American people."

Wilson waited for Edith to descend from the gallery, and they rode
with Tumulty back to the White House. Applause accompanied them all
the way home; but inside the car, they remained silent. Before the President joined his family, he and Tumulty sat for a few minutes in the Cabinet Room. "Think of what it was they were applauding," said Wilson,
utterly drained. "My message to-day was a message of death for our young
men. How strange it seems to applaud that."

And then in a startling soul-baring moment, the President told Tumulty that maintaining his impartiality during the last thousand days of
war had been a terrible ordeal. "From the beginning I saw the utter futility
of neutrality, the disappointment and heartaches that would flow from its
announcement," he confessed, "but we had to stand by our traditional
policy of steering clear of European embroilments." While he had appeared indifferent to criticism, Wilson said few had sympathized with his
situation. One person who had recognized those pressures bearing down
on the President was the editor of the *Republican* in Springfield, Massachusetts, who had recently sent an empathic note. Wilson read its few paragraphs to Tumulty, after which he pulled out a handkerchief and mopped
his eyes. And then, Tumulty recalled, the President lay his head on the
Cabinet table and sobbed "as if he had been a child."

Reviews of the speech were reverential, its historical significance lost
on nobody. Walter Lippmann, whose admiration for Wilson had been as-
cending, sent the President a sample of what he had just written for *The
New Republic*: "Any mediocre politician might have gone to war futilely for

rights that in themselves cannot be defended by war," he said. "Only a statesman who will be called great could have made America's intervention mean so much to the generous forces of the world, could have lifted the inevitable horror of war into a deed so full of meaning." From London, Ambassador Page cabled that the pronouncement was "comparable to only two other events in our history—the achievement of our independence and the preservation of the Union." James Gerard, America's recently disinvited Ambassador to Germany, commented that the speech contained "a lofty idealism about it which puts this war on the plane of a crusade. No more momentous document has ever been written in the history of the world." A nearly eighty-year-old director of the United States Chamber of Commerce called the President's office simply to say that he had heard Lincoln speak his immortal words at the Pennsylvania battlefield. "Mr. Wilson's address on Monday," the director said, "will rank with the Gettysburg speech of Lincoln."

The outcome of the ensuing Congressional debate was never in doubt. The Senate began the discussion early on April 4 and voted that night— 82 to 6 in favor of war. The House debate opened the following morning and dragged into the early morning hours of April 6, with some 150 members having their say. Although corralling every vote was hardly a necessity, this particular issue had the rare distinction of seeing virtually every member in his seat. During the first roll call, however, one voice in the back row failed to make itself heard—that of Jeannette Rankin of Montana, the first woman elected to the House of Representatives, in her first month in office. She had endured a long, excruciating day: the National American Woman Suffrage Association had lobbied hard for her to vote for war, to demonstrate that women could be as hawkish as men; and the Congressional Union, representing another faction of suffragists, urged her to show that women were doves. She seemed to vacillate until former Speaker "Uncle Joe" Cannon walked over to the Democratic Representative and said, "Little woman, you cannot afford not to vote. You represent the womanhood of the country in the American Congress. I shall not advise you how to vote, but you should vote one way or the other—as your conscience dictates." When the roll was called for the second time, the Clerk of the House went to Rankin's side to record her choice. "I want to stand by my country," she said, "but I cannot vote for war." It was close to 4 a.m. when all the votes were tallied—373 to 50.

At lunch the next day, Good Friday, the President was informed that a printed copy of the War Resolution—signed by Vice President Marshall and Speaker Clark—was on its way from the Congress. Wilson rushed through his meal and exited the State Dining Room just as the messenger arrived at Ike Hoover's office. The staff discussed moving to the President's study, but Wilson said he would sign it right there, at the usher's desk. "Stand by me, Edith," he said as she handed him a gold pen he had given her. His jaw clenched as he affixed his bold signature to the parchment. He rose from his chair, returned the pen to Edith, and excused himself. Executive clerk Rudolph Forster informed the reporters waiting in the executive offices; and a naval officer in the West Wing went outside and wigwagged to another officer in the window of the Navy Department building that the President had signed the resolution. In an instant, wireless operators were transmitting the news to the world. For only the fourth time, the United States of America had declared war on a foreign nation; and Woodrow Wilson was commanding unprepared forces—just 300,000 men, fewer than 10,000 of whom were officers. The German General Staff ranked the United States militarily "somewhere between Belgium and Portugal."

Weeks later, Wilson drafted his five-sentence last will and testament. The President left all his property to "my beloved wife Edith for her lifetime," with the request that she distribute Ellen's personal articles—such as clothing, jewelry, and art—to his daughters, and an additional stipulation that Margaret Wilson receive $2,500 annually so long as she remained unmarried. Upon Edith's death, the estate was to benefit his children equally.

The day after war was declared, the President wrote a memorandum for himself, a list of measures he hoped Congress would pass in order to "put the country in a thorough state of defense and preparation for action." They included not only fortifying the existing military bills but also amending policies related to shipping, the Federal Reserve, the railroads, and interstate commerce. He believed the nation needed to unify behind a single set of principles, and a single leader. "My mother did not raise her boy to be a War President," Wilson said after a Cabinet meeting, "—but it is a liberal education!"

The naval forces of the United States mobilized immediately, putting every government ship—the commissioned fleet, reserve warships, Coast Guard and Lighthouse Service boats—into active service. In a related action, the United States government seized ninety-one German-owned vessels—twenty-seven in New York harbor, including the *George Washington*. It was a merchant fleet with an estimated value of $100 million and the capacity to transport forty thousand troops—tonnage that would have required a year to manufacture. Most of the ships were not immediately seaworthy. In anticipation of the war declaration, the German crews inflicted wounds on their own vessels, sawing off bolt heads, which would require weeks to replace. By nightfall, more than one thousand Germans—including ship captains and cooks and musicians—were peaceably interned on Ellis Island, where they awaited deportation.

The President issued a proclamation to the American people, which the nation's newspapers carried on their front pages. Because, as he put it, the "entrance of our own beloved country into the grim and terrible war for democracy and human rights" created "so many problems of national life and action," he immediately presented an anxious nation "earnest counsel." This remarkable appeal outlined for the people not only the immediate problems before them but also the many types of "service and self-sacrifice" in which every one of his fellow countrymen could engage.

Besides fighting, the most basic task was to supply food—for Americans at home as well as fighting men abroad, along with the starving people of the nations "with whom we have now made common cause." Once adequately fed, America could consider the rest of the operations of the war—manpower, materiel, machinery, even mules. Wilson said all American industries must be made "more prolific and more efficient than ever," that the industrial forces of the country would become "a great international . . . army . . . engaged in the service of the nation and the world, the efficient friends and saviors of free men everywhere."

In the face of worldwide industrialization, Wilson urged a recultivation of America's agricultural roots. The supreme need of the nation just then was "an abundance of supplies, and especially of foodstuffs." Wilson urged America to "correct her unpardonable fault of wastefulness" and to increase her harvests. Almost overnight, male high school students were released from class, allowed to earn diplomas by manning the family farms. In the cities and suburbs, "Victory Gardens" cropped up almost overnight, as the people began planting vegetables in their backyards and on their rooftops. In Washington, the government offered its unoccupied property to anyone who would farm it; along the Potomac Drive, where cherry blossoms would later bloom, society ladies tended edible gardens. Every housewife was further exhorted to practice strict economy in all her spending, even beyond household purchases, for that would put her "in the ranks of those who serve the nation." Curbing excess, Wilson decreed, was a public duty—"a dictate of patriotism which no one can now expect ever to be excused or forgiven for ignoring."

That applied especially to businesses. Wilson cautioned America's middlemen—whether they were handling foodstuffs or factory goods— that the "eyes of the country will be especially upon you." The country, he said, expected its businessmen to "forego unusual profits, to organize and expedite shipments of supplies of every kind." To the American merchant, he suggested a simple motto: "Small profits and quick services." He begged all editors to publish this appeal; he urged advertising agencies to resound its message; he hoped clergymen would consider these themes worthy of homilies. From his own bully pulpit, Wilson said, "The supreme test of the nation has come. We must all speak, act, and serve together!"

Unity became the driving force behind all Wilson's actions in making the nation ready to fight. The President was determined to centralize as many of the agencies and industries as possible under a single command. That meant training a nation of rugged individuals to come together as one, in working for their common cause. He appointed men of all political persuasions to scores of new positions, based solely on ability, regardless of their political histories. An air of nonpartisanship in the capital would allow the Congress to enact two dozen major pieces of legislation in the next year—each of which helped put the nation on war footing, changing the very character of the country.

Loyalty was the standard by which Wilson measured every one of his countrymen, starting with those in his administration. Despite Edith's dislike for Tumulty's commonness, Wilson could not deny his decade of unimpeachable devotion. Although Colonel House scarcely veiled his pretensions to power, he had never refused the President, and he possessed expertise in foreign affairs that nobody else in the Administration did. And though Dr. Grayson had made an "indelicate and objectionable" request for an admiralship, Wilson promoted him over many who had served longer, largely because he could never dismiss his personal allegiance to the man who had introduced him to his wife. Edith confidentially divulged her dislike for the President's son-in-law—finding him ambitious and "thoroughly selfish"; but Secretary McAdoo had consistently proved himself the ablest member of the Cabinet, proactive and persuasive. Now Wilson called upon him to serve as the controller of European war loans and as Chairman of the Federal Farm Loan Bureau, General Manager of the Liberty Loans, and Chairman of the War Finance Corporation.

Transportation provides the lifeblood of a nation, and as 1917 wore on, Wilson came to grips with the fact that the United States simply had no continental railway system. It also lacked a sufficient number of railcars and the capital to build more. The Anti-Trust Act of 1890 prohibited the major companies from merging competing lines or making rate agreements among themselves. "Federal control of the railroads was, in fact, inevitable," McAdoo later wrote of the situation; but neither Wilson nor anybody else in the Administration wanted to put his hand on the throttle. By year's end Wilson felt compelled to say "that it is our duty as the representatives of the nation to do everything that is necessary to do to secure the complete mobilization of the whole resources of America by as rapid and effective means as possible." He seized the railroads with nothing more than a proclamation.

The Army Appropriations Act of the prior year had not only earmarked money to augment America's fighting force but had also authorized the President to exercise federal control whenever emergency war measures were required. Opposition immediately voiced the fear that this marked the first step of government ownership of the railroads. The Administration readily pointed out that in England, where private corporations owned the railways, the government had taken control the day His Majesty had declared war on the Kaiser; France, Italy, and Germany also exerted the same control. Wilson explained to the nation, "Only under government administration can an absolutely unrestricted and unembarrassed common use be made of all tracks, terminals, terminal facilities and equipment of every kind."

Based on his earlier experience building the Manhattan tunnels, McAdoo recommended several railroad executives, any of whom might run this new Railroad Administration. After discussing the list, Wilson asked McAdoo himself to direct the operation. "I don't want to urge it," Wilson said. "I am merely asking if you think you could undertake it?" Upon reflection, McAdoo said that he could, and that the problems were more than questions of transportation. "It is a matter of finance as well as of operation," he said. With one hand running the trains and the other holding the Treasury's money, McAdoo was inclined to think it would be less of a burden for him to be in charge himself than working with somebody else. Two million railroad workers were suddenly in his employ, as McAdoo became the first man to consider the nation's 240,000 miles of railway lines as a whole. By consolidating services, McAdoo eliminated a superfluous one-sixth of the nation's passenger-train miles, enhancing efficiency and saving more than $100 million; the railway-car shortage of 1917 would become a surplus a year later; a coal famine was averted through greater efficiency; and McAdoo increased the pay for practically every railroad worker to a "decent living wage." Nobody objected until the war was over, when the railroads were returned to private hands and political opponents accused him of throwing money around so that the workers would elect him President of the United States.

The Army Appropriations Act had also established the Council of National Defense, a committee of a half dozen Cabinet Secretaries (War, Interior, Navy, Commerce, Agriculture, and Labor) who worked in concert with a seven-member commission, boasting the likes of labor leader Samuel Gompers and a half dozen business tycoons, including Julius Rosenwald, the president of Sears, Roebuck and Co. The committee's most significant personage from the private sector was an almost mythical figure named Bernard Baruch, who was identified in a press release as a banker.

"I am not a banker, and never have been," Baruch himself would later state; ". . . I regarded myself as a speculator." The son of a German Jewish doctor and a mother whose Sephardic ancestors settled in colonial New York, Baruch grew up in South Carolina and then New York, where he graduated from its City College. A self-made millionaire by thirty, mostly through shrewd investing, he continued to amass a fortune, along with a reputation for being a scrupulous financial wizard. As the war approached, Baruch had been so concerned that the nation was not prepared for all eventualities that he had written friends within the Administration. The President invited him to the White House for an exchange of ideas, and— shortly after that—to join the Council of National Defense. "Next to my father," Baruch would recall, "Wilson had the greatest influence on my life. He took me out of Wall Street and gave me my first opportunity for public service."

The Advisory Commission of the Council of National Defense was created to advance "the coordination of industries and resources for the national security and welfare." That meant managing the logistics as well as the economics of mustering, lodging, training, equipping, and transporting millions of men. As his Cabinet showed, Wilson believed in tapping leaders from outside the government to serve inside his administration. Baruch admired how each of his colleagues naturally assumed the lead in his field of expertise. The president of the Baltimore and Ohio Railroad headed the committee on transportation, the director general of the American College of Surgeons oversaw medicine and sanitation, Rosenwald supervised dry goods, clothing, and supplies, and Baruch looked after raw materials and minerals. "From the time the problem of industrial mobilization first gripped my interest," Baruch recalled, ". . . I had recognized that victory in modern war depended upon the speed and efficiency with which the nation could convert its economy from peace and employ its resources for war."

He created a template for all the major industries in America by enlisting national leaders in each industry—from aluminum to zinc. When a demand for copper, for example, suddenly surged along with its price, Baruch called on Daniel Guggenheim and other magnates and reasoned with them to meet the government's needs at a fair price. Not only did this price-fixing save the government $9 million but it led industry to put patriotism before profits, enabling cooperation between people instead of corporations. When French Ambassador Jean-Jules Jusserand complained that gasoline shipments to France were being stalled, Baruch got to the heart of the problem with one telephone call to a colleague on the oil committee. Through these powerful appointments and cooperative committees, Wilson was able to cut through endless red tape.

Baruch urged the President to create "a centralized purchasing agency with authority over prices and the closing of defense contracts." Wilson could not go that far, but he did establish a War Industries Board, in which military leaders sat with industrial bosses and could at least coordinate the purchase of war supplies. Products were simplified and standardized, allowing for mass production, which was more efficient and economical. The WIB's power was minimal; but once Baruch was named its chairman, he realized he could regulate where he could not negotiate. His committee assumed influence by becoming the nation's "priority machine"—directing, restraining, and stimulating war production as situations demanded, allocating materials where required, and ending unhealthy competition. Practicalities often determined policies. Should a locomotive, for example, be sent overseas to transport soldiers to the front or sent to South America to haul nitrates for bullets? Taking the stays out of women's corsets supplied enough metal for two warships.

Like Wilson, Baruch found it abhorrent that they should have to discuss prices and profits when "blood will flow so freely and suffering will become so great"; but the American entrance into the war was about to create the greatest burst of production in the nation's history. With it would come torrents of money. From the start of his work, Baruch sought to "reduce prices to the point we believe proper, yet keep wages up, preserve our financial strength, keep production of these absolutely vital materials at full blast and increase our resolution and determination to conduct the war to a successful conclusion." Instead of fixing prices, Baruch preferred flexibility; and he thought a strong centralized purchasing power could do much to control the economy, through the contracts it dispensed and "moral suasion."

President Wilson created an alphabet soup of boards and agencies to supervise the various aspects of the war effort, all of which he coordinated. While the President never saw the value in a "coalition cabinet" that consciously teamed rivals, he observed a policy of inclusion. His administration benefited from literally dozens of Republicans, many from the worlds of banking and business: three Republican Assistant Secretaries of War served Newton Baker, alongside Morgan banker E. R. Stettinius, who was put in charge of supplies; five of the eight members of the War Trade Board were prominent Republicans, as was the Red Cross chief, H. P. Davison, another Morgan banker; Republicans Frank Vanderlip of National City Bank ran the War Savings Stamps Campaign, and Russell C. Leffingwell (later a Morgan partner) became an Assistant Secretary of the Treasury. Former President Taft headed the National War Labor Board; and Harvard Law Professor Felix Frankfurter, a former Bull Mooser, left Cambridge to become an assistant to Secretary Baker, to act as Judge Advocate General and to chair the War Labor Policies Board, on which Navy Undersecretary Franklin Roosevelt would serve. Wilson also created a special

War Cabinet—which met on Wednesdays in his study. Its core included: the Secretaries of the Treasury, War, and Navy Departments as well as Baruch; Williams College President (and son of a Republican President) Harry Garfield, whom Wilson named to oversee the Federal Fuel Administration; Edward N. Hurley, a tool industry tycoon who had chaired the Federal Trade Commission and was reassigned to the United States Shipping Board; Democratic Party chairman Vance McCormick, head of the War Trade Board; and the man who distinguished himself more in the war years than any other Wilson appointee, a mild-mannered Quaker named Herbert Clark Hoover.

Orphaned at nine, Hoover was raised by an uncle in Oregon before entering the inaugural class at Stanford University, from which he graduated with a degree in geology. Starting his career as a mining engineer, he traveled to Australia and China, where he devised a process for extracting zinc. He became both a respected scholar in his field and a wealthy consultant. By the time the war began, Hoover had become a financier living in London. With over 100,000 Americans—mostly tourists—desperate to get home, he organized a committee to engineer their return. So effective was he, Ambassador Page called upon him to consider applying that same sort of American know-how to the feeding of Belgians in need. Hoover excelled at the task, performing feats of diplomatic and commercial magic in getting millions of tons of food distributed to ten million starving men and women. Shuttling across Europe, Hoover saw German deprivation as well, the result of the British food blockade. At Wilson's behest, he returned to Washington, where the President asked him to organize American food activities. He agreed, so long as he could continue to head the Belgian relief as well. He imposed one other condition: that he would receive no payment for his services and that the whole of the force under him, exclusive of clerical assistance, would do the same.

Unsentimental and brusque, Hoover expressed alarm and pessimism after assessing the current food situation, and with good reason. America's prior year's production of cereals—including wheat, corn, oats, barley, rice, and rye—was four-fifths of the six billion bushels it had been the year before; and adverse weather already assured that the coming year would yield even less. To make matters worse, adequate national rail service was not yet up and running to accommodate the crops on hand.

At age forty-two, he embarked upon what one scholar called "the greatest experiment in economic organization the world had seen"—a nationwide exercise in extra production and economy. The President strong-armed Congress into passing a Food and Fuel Control Bill that granted power to the Administration to fix prices and exert other controls over the production and distribution of living essentials. The Lever Act—named for its South Carolinian sponsor—became an omnibus bill overloaded with excess baggage, riders from Representatives who bartered for inclusion of their pet causes in exchange for their votes. In this instance, the growing movement of Prohibitionists had their say, attaching a rider that banned the production of distilled spirits from any produce that might be used for food.

The entire nation rolled up its sleeves and tightened its belt so that as much food could be sent to Europe as possible. The Administration called upon the nation to go "meatless" at least one meal a day and one day a week, commonly Monday; it sent a similar request to go "wheatless," at least once a day and all day Monday and Wednesday. In time, at least one "sweetless" day of the week was encouraged, usually Saturday. Billboards and newspapers featured appeals to save food. Housewives enrolled as "members of the Food Administration"; their numbers included Edith Wilson, who signed a pledge endorsing "food conservation," for which she received a red, white, and blue card featuring spears of wheat, which she displayed in a White House window, like an ordinary housewife. Herbert Hoover's moon face became the symbol of economizing, if not deprivation, as mothers withheld spoonfuls of sugar from their children's cereal in his name; and the verb "Hooverize" entered the lexicon—"to be sparing or economical."

Hoover delivered phenomenal results. At the start of the war, the United States could pledge to export 20 million bushels of wheat; it sent 141 million. In just one quarter of a year, the country restricted its consumption of sweets enough to send 500,000 tons of sugar abroad. In addition to beef, the nation increased its pork production by a million tons. American restaurants reported having saved thousands of tons of meat, flour, and sugar in a single two-month period. Dumps nationwide noticed discernible decreases in garbage. Its first year in the war, America sent Europe twice as much food as it had the year before.

Americans conserved fuel as well. Because the industrial and military need for coal and oil became insatiable, management rewarded workers with wages and the basic standard of living increases that unions had been demanding for years; union membership soared. Energy czar Garfield closely monitored the national fuel supply; and when shortages appeared, he ordered non–war related factories to shut down for days at a time or one day a week. Citizens and businesses protested the clumsy manner in which the Administration dropped such actions upon them; and, in fact, the government never adequately explained that the closures were more about allowing a day for the transportation system to meet war demands. Political opponents grumbled persistently about the Administration's lack of readiness, harshly criticizing Wilson's inadequacy as a leader; but all good citizens bundled up nonetheless as they endured "heatless" Mondays. Even the Wilsons observed "gasless Sundays," substituting a ride in a horse-drawn carriage for their weekend limousine drives. The switch was thrown on electric advertisements, streetlights dimmed, and "lightless" nights were eventually ordered, twice a week, even on Broadway. Wilson introduced Daylight Saving Time to America, which created an extra hour of farm work every day and which saved an hour of artificial light, reducing the use of electric and coal power.

Within weeks of America's entry into the war, Edith Wilson was tending eight sheep her husband had brought to graze on the White House lawn. The flock trimmed the grass, thus saving manpower; and at shearing time, they provided ninety-eight pounds of "White House Wool"— two pounds of which were sent to each state and the Philippines—which raised at auction close to $100,000 for the Red Cross. Edith also pulled out her old sewing machine and sat for hours, making pajamas for the sick and injured. (Whenever their fingers were free, all the Wilson women observed the Red Cross motto of "Knit Your Bit," by producing socks and sweaters. Margaret contributed to the war effort by embarking on two long concert tours, which earned some $10,000 for the cause.) Whenever the President saw a Food Administration or Red Cross card in somebody's window, his eyes filled. "I wish I could stop and know the people who live here," he would say, "for it is from them that I draw inspiration and strength."

The President hoped the rest of the country might share his feelings. Toward that end—and to carry the "Gospel of Americanism" to every corner of the globe—the President established the most controversial board of all, the Committee on Public Information. While other government boards dealt primarily with the nuts and bolts of winning the war, the CPI dealt with the ephemeral business of public perception—what Secretary Baker called "mobilizing the mind of the world so far as American participation in the war was concerned." Where the knee-jerk reaction for most countries going to war, he said, was to impose strict censorship, the CPI intended to expose information. Or so it would have people believe.

Because the United States had entered the Great War for neither territory nor treasure but for intangible ideals, the President felt the need to capture the public's hearts and minds. He hired a journalist named George Creel—a muckraker out of Denver who had been a Wilson loyalist in the last two elections—to head the CPI. The Great War differed most essentially from previous conflicts in its recognition of public opinion as a major force, Creel wrote in his memoir *How We Advertised America*. "The trial of strength was not only between massed bodies of armed men, but between opposed ideals, and moral verdicts took on all the value of military decision."

Ever since the incursions in Mexico, there had been a delicate balance between the White House and the newspapers regarding coverage of military operations. Although the number of press conferences had sharply declined from weekly events to only two in all of 1916, Wilson's administration still offered plenty of access and transparency. "Starting with the initial conviction that the war was not the war of an administration, but the war of one hundred million people," Creel would write, "we opened up the activities of government to the inspection of the citizenship. A voluntary censorship agreement safeguarded military information of obvious value to the enemy, but in all else the rights of the press were recognized and furthered." But "information" was a product manufactured by people's minds; and as such, it could not be measured like wheat, meat, and sugar. And though the CPI maintained that no other belligerent nation allowed "such absolute frankness with respect to every detail of the national war endeavor," the fine line between fact and opinion—between morale-building and manipulation—all but disappeared. With $100 million to spend at its own discretion, the CPI would issue all the war news it considered fit to print. The department did not overtly censor information, but it covertly shaped it.

Secretary Baker said the war "was to be won by the pen as well as by the sword." Tellingly, Creel enlisted teams of not just historians but also publicists to write pamphlets outlining "America's reasons for entering the war, the meaning of America, the nature of our free institutions, our war aims" and stacking them alongside the "misrepresentations and barbarities" of the German government. A few dozen of these booklets went into production, each extolling a different aspect of the American vision. An army of volunteers blanketed the country with seventy-five million copies; millions more were spread around the world. Another team issued an official daily newspaper, reporting on the activities of each government department. And Creel conscripted some of the most respected writers in America—including Owen Wister, Booth Tarkington, William Dean Howells, and Edna Ferber as well as journalists Ida Tarbell, Ray Stannard Baker, and William Allen White—to write about the American way of life in "letters," which were translated and delivered to any foreign press that would publish them.

To help fight years of German propaganda and to recraft what the Administration considered an unfair image of the United States, Creel hired several bright young men, including one who would not only distinguish himself immediately but would also emerge later as one of the most important propagandists of the century, a pioneer in the field of public relations. Edward Bernays, a nephew of Sigmund Freud, headed the CPI's export service. Born in Vienna and raised in New York, where he became a press agent shortly after graduating from Cornell, Bernays appreciated his uncle's work in exploring unconscious desires; and, perhaps better than anybody else at the CPI, he recognized the importance of tapping less into what the masses thought than into what they felt.

The CPI created a speakers division, which organized meetings across the country—forty-five "war conferences," providing information about America's evolving status in all the battles. It oversaw an organization called the Four Minute Men—seventy-five thousand speakers who volunteered in more than five thousand communities, where they generally appeared in motion picture theaters during the four minutes it took for the projectionists to change the reels. More than 750,000 speeches, on topics ranging from food conservation to "Maintaining Morals and Morale," were delivered to an estimated eleven million audience members—every one, Creel said, "having the carry of shrapnel."

Another division of the CPI produced motion pictures, which were initially documentary in nature. As the war continued, the film industry produced feature films centering on the war that grew increasingly brutal in their portrayal of the enemy. Lon Chaney starred in *The Kaiser, the Beast of Berlin*. In *The Heart of Humanity*, Erich von Stroheim played a brutal "Hun" who attempts to rape a nurse before throwing a baby out a window. D. W. Griffith himself produced another wartime epic, about young lovers in France torn apart by the war and reunited by killing a sadistic German rapist. If that were not enough to rouse any American, the CPI distributed posters and window cards—based on almost 1,500 original drawings contributed by the artists themselves. At the beginning of the war, the artwork represented mostly romantic evocations of the glories of the great cause. Howard Chandler Christy and James Montgomery Flagg painted flag-clad beauties urging Americans to "Sow the Seeds of Victory" by considering "every garden a munitions plant." Flagg would also create one of the most enduring American images, a recruiting poster showing a white-haired Uncle Sam wearing a star-spangled top hat and declaring, "I WANT *YOU* FOR U.S. ARMY." A year later, the American posters turned ugly, depicting Germans as slobbering apes carrying off Lady Liberty. War exhibits traveled the state-fair circuit, not only spreading the American message but also generating income in the millions of dollars.

Beyond America, the CPI spread its word to the Allies, the neutral nations, and the enemy. Creating a daily news service to publicize stories by both wire and the wireless, America opened small offices in all the major capitals of the world, except those of the Central Powers. Stories about American education, finance, labor, medicine, and agriculture were sent everywhere, as were the speeches of Woodrow Wilson, marking the first time in history that the speeches of a head of state received universal distribution. "Every conceivable means was used to reach the foreign mind with America's message," Creel said; that included the novel idea of inviting leading foreign correspondents—particularly those from neutral nations—to come to America. Upon America's entrance into the war, the CPI had received $5.6 million from the President's discretionary fund and a Congressional appropriation of $1.25 million; in the end, it earned some $3 million from its films and expositions, thus costing the government less than $5 million. Creel called this a bargain for waging a "world-fight for the verdict of mankind." But there were hidden costs in trying to win that verdict.

On June 15, 1917, the Sixty-fifth Congress passed the Espionage Act—

one of the most provocative pieces of legislation in American history. It represented the greatest possible expression of patriotism and the suppression of free speech. In 1798, when the young nation had almost gone to war with France, President Adams had propounded the Sedition Act, which made the publication of "false, scandalous, and malicious writing" against the government or its representatives a crime. Adams's opposition—chiefly Jefferson and Madison—considered the act a violation of the First Amendment. Sixty-five years later, when the states were at war with one another, Lincoln suspended the writ of habeas corpus on several occasions and imposed martial law based on the Constitution's allowance whenever rebellion or invasion threatened "the public Safety." Furthermore, he stifled free speech in punishing critics of his policies.

At least as far back as the sinking of the *Lusitania*, Wilson had been concerned about Germany's covert activities. He had addressed the subject head-on in his 1915 State of the Union Address when he spoke of naturalized United States citizens "who have poured the poison of disloyalty into the very arteries of our national life." The President had asked Congress for legislation to help combat this problem. "Such creatures of passion, disloyalty, and anarchy must be crushed out," he said. On April 2, 1917, the President appealed for the authority Adams and Lincoln had been given, with enough power to make good on his vow to deal with any disloyalty in the nation "with a firm hand of stern repression."

Congress had introduced several new bills, including one from Representative Edwin Webb of North Carolina and Senator Charles Culberson of Texas targeting espionage and treason. They included all the powers the President might need, including a provision to monitor information of, from, and about the government—essentially making it illegal for a person to publish information that the President declared "useful to the enemy" in time of war. It amounted to nothing less than censorship.

While the bulk of the bill dealt with spies and saboteurs, a few sections wandered into gray areas, particularly in empowering the executive branch. One section, for example, declared it illegal even to "attempt to cause disaffection in the military," while another allowed the Postmaster General to determine which writings were of a "treasonable or anarchistic" nature and, as such, subject to the ban.

Democratic liberals, to say nothing of the journalists Wilson had courted for four years, could hardly believe that he could condone such legislation. Progressive Republicans, such as Senators William E. Borah and Hiram Johnson, and the predictable chorus of right-wing Republicans, such as Henry Cabot Lodge, opposed him as well. Hearst editor Arthur Brisbane called upon the President to comment on the importance of "the absolute freedom of the press." Wilson replied that he could "imagine no greater disservice to the country than to establish a system of censorship that would deny to the people of a free republic . . . their indisputable right to criticize their own public officials." He insisted that he would regret the loss of "patriotic and intelligent criticism" during the trying times and said, "So far as I am personally concerned, I shall not expect or permit any part of this law to apply to me or any of my official acts, or in any way to be used as a shield against criticism."

Even with that assurance, the bill struck at the very heart of a free society. It asserted that the chosen leaders of a nation should have the right in times of war to suspend the normal freedom of the press. Opponents contended there was never good reason to withhold or doctor information, while supporters maintained that absolute transparency in a time of war might threaten national security.

Congressman Webb opened the House debate by condemning the press for conveying the impression that his bill trampled upon the First Amendment. At a time when men were offering their lives to win the war, he thought newspapers should be willing to sacrifice the right to publish stories the President thought injurious. The nation had given Wilson its trust to command its Army; so too should he be entitled to control its information. Representative Dick Thompson Morgan of Oklahoma, a Republican, said: "In time of great national peril, it is necessary sometimes that individual citizens shall be willing to surrender some of the privileges which they have for the sake of the greater good."

Morgan's own Senator could not have disagreed more. "I am opposed to any censorship of the press at this time," said Democrat T. P. Gore, "because censorship goes hand in hand with despotism." A strong disciple of the freedom of speech, he said that censorship strikes at the very foundation of a free democracy. Hiram Johnson called the amendment "vicious" and "un-American." Lucien Price, an astute political pundit, editorialized in *The Boston Daily Globe* that May, "The American people could not long endure the necessary war-time conscription of men and property, if the truth were also conscripted." He called his fellow citizens "the greatest reading public in the world," one that could not tolerate "a shutdown of news just as they enter the war themselves."

Tumulty sent Wilson an excerpt from a biography of John Adams, which claimed that the greatest blunders of the Federalist Party were the infamous Alien and Sedition Acts and that "no one has ever been able heartily or successfully to defend these foolish outbursts of ill-considered legislation which have to be abandoned, by tacit general consent, to condemnation."

When a canvass of votes in the House suggested that censorship as included in the Webb bill would not prevail, the President stepped up to reaffirm his position that censorship was "absolutely necessary to the public safety." He sent Representative Webb a letter—to be released to *The New York Times*—expressing his confidence that the great majority of the American press would observe "a patriotic reticence about everything whose publication could be of injury"; but he still insisted that there were in every country "some persons . . . whose interests or desires will lead to actions on their part highly dangerous to the nation in the midst of a war."

The censorship section was cut from the bill, and that compromise allowed the overwhelming nonpartisan passage of the Espionage Act. What remained left a watchdog government with enough authority to intimidate. Much of what had been excised was inserted in a later piece of legislation, the Sedition Act of 1918, which prohibited "disloyal, profane, scurrilous, or abusive language about the form of government of the United States," or its military or naval forces or the uniforms or the flag thereof; and it prohibited any language intended to cast upon them "contempt, scorn, contumely, or disrepute."

For all his experience raking muck, Creel proved himself remarkably adept at sanitizing. While the recent debate had raged, he composed a detailed memorandum to help organize the CPI. Topic number one was "censorship," a word, he said, that was "to be avoided." Creel suggested nothing nefarious; indeed, he insisted the entire spirit of his agency must be "one of absolute co-operation. It must go upon the assumption that the press is eager and willing to do the handsome thing, and its attitude must be one of frankness, friendship and entire openness." He and the President were on the same page; and, for the most part, the White House and the press remained mutually respectful throughout the war.

Wilson seldom abused the arsenal of powers the Congress had granted him. "From the war's beginning," David Lawrence observed, "Mr. Wilson made frequent visits . . . to the different war bureaus. He developed the habit of dropping in when least expected." Lawrence suggested these visits were part of his exercise and relaxation regimen—a chance to stretch his legs—but he was also exerting the common touch, keeping the rapidly expanding government bureaucracy a place where even the President might drop in on any given day.

With Wilson's "ability to delegate work, his loyalties to subordinates, and his speed in evaluating problems," Herbert Hoover would recollect forty years later, "he proved a great administrator." Hoover added that Wilson's "religious and moral upbringing expressed itself in a zeal for financial integrity which characterized the conduct of a war practically without corruption."

To the stirring drumbeat of the CPI, the people of the nation compensated for their deprivations with a spirit that had not united them since the country's founding. Everybody pitched in. Just as the British Royal Family shook all German nomenclature from its family tree—Battenbergs becoming Mountbattens, and the House of Saxe-Coburg and Gotha adopting the family name Windsor—so too did Americans expunge all things Teutonic. Across the country, hamburgers were rechristened "liberty steaks," and sauerkraut became "liberty cabbage." German shepherds were called Alsatians; Berlin, Iowa, turned into Lincoln, Iowa; and Brooklyn's Hamburg Avenue was renamed after Wilson. Some school boards discontinued teaching the German language. Otto Kahn, a German-born partner in the New York banking firm of Kuhn, Loeb & Company as well as the chairman of the Metropolitan Opera Company, wrote the President to ask whether he felt opera in German sung by German artists should continue in his opera house. Wilson hated to see the loss of German opera, but he left the decision to Kahn and his board—which chose to bar German works. With all the changes, German Americans unavoidably became victims of hysteria, discrimination, and, in one instance, lynching. Aware of the bigotry, Wilson urged tolerance, speaking repeatedly and reassuringly of his "confidence in the entire integrity and loyalty of the great body of our fellow-citizens of German blood." Considering the general spirit of the nation, he would later reflect "that America was never so beautiful as in the spring, summer and autumn of 1917 when people were stirred by a passion in common, forgot themselves and political differences in an urge to put all they had, all they were, to use in a great purpose."

Despite Woodrow Wilson's having no military experience, he proved to be a highly effective Commander in Chief—decisive and delegative. His battle plan had two fundamentals: first, that the nation would submit to a national draft; second, that the United States would not send those fighting men abroad as "replacement troops" for the Allies but as United States soldiers fighting under the American flag.

Among Congress's first pieces of business after its declaration of war was a Selective Service bill. Recognizing the inadequacy of mustering a volunteer Army (only thirty thousand men had signed up by the end of April 1917), Congress debated the need for conscription, America's first mandated military service since the Civil War. While such an act struck many as the very sort of autocracy the soldiers would be sent to fight against, Wilson asserted that the heart of the selective draft was the idea that "there is a universal obligation to serve and that a public authority should choose those upon whom the obligation of military service shall rest." It provided for a system that was both fair and functional, giving control to local draft boards in their creation of a national Army, determining not only who but how each man in the pool might serve. A local board might determine that a fellow volunteering to fight in France could better serve by remaining in his wheat field or coal mine. Wilson believed such a bill would create the greatest impression of "universal service in the Army and out of it, and if properly administered will be a great source of stimulation." A section of the Selective Service bill stated that, unlike in the Civil War draft, nobody could purchase or otherwise furnish a substitute for himself.

One fifty-eight-year-old Rough Rider could hardly contain himself. Itching to be back in uniform and in the spotlight, Theodore Roosevelt had quietly assembled his own division, communicating for months with men all over the country who wanted to serve with him. Only three days after the declaration of war, he went to Washington, determined to see Wilson. He had no formal appointment; but he told those around him, "I'll take chances on his trying to snub me. He can't do it! I'd like to see him try it!"

Late the next morning, Tumulty telephoned to say that the President would see the former President at noon. They met in the Green Room and promptly got past the awkwardness of their previous vicious rivalry. In truth, Wilson had invited TR to the White House three years earlier for a delightful half hour of nonpolitical conversation over glasses of lemonade; but on this spring day, the Colonel came on a very specific mission. He commended Wilson on his war message and on his bill for selective conscription and then proposed the division he hoped to lead. Roosevelt found Wilson slightly awkward, sounding defensive about his policy of the last three years over which they had crossed swords. "Mr. President," Roosevelt interjected, "what I have said and thought, and what others have said and thought, is all dust in a windy street, if now we can make your message good. Of course, it amounts to nothing, if we cannot make it good. But, if we can translate it into fact, then it will rank as a great state paper, with the great state papers of Washington and Lincoln. Now, all that I ask is that I be allowed to . . . help get the nation to act, so as to justify and live up to the speech, and the declaration of war that followed." After half an hour, the two men were bantering and laughing together.

Before leaving the White House, TR asked if he might call upon Tumulty in the executive office. Wilson summoned his secretary to the Red Room, where there were handshakes and backslaps. Roosevelt heartily greeted several of his former household staff and said to Tumulty, "You get me across and I will put you on my staff, and you may tell Mrs. Tumulty that I will not allow them to place you at any point of danger." Back on the street, he told the crowd of newsmen, "The President received me with the utmost courtesy and consideration," and said that the President would rule on his request "in his own good time." Wilson asked Tumulty what he thought of the Colonel, and he replied that the man's enthusiasm was overwhelming. "Yes," said Wilson, "he is a great big boy. I was, as formerly, charmed by his personality. There is a sweetness about him that is very compelling. You can't resist the man. I can easily understand why his followers are so fond of him." Not aware that TR still felt little more than contempt for Wilson, the President seriously considered the Colonel's proposition.

Roosevelt lingered in the capital, where he granted audiences and courted old friends from Congress, hoping they might include a provision in the Selective Service bill that would allow volunteer forces to go directly to the front while America trained her conscripted Army. "We owe this to humanity," he wrote the Democratic chairman of the Senate Committee on Military Affairs. The Selective Service Act passed on May 18, 1917, and included this Roosevelt exception, to be executed at the President's discretion. Wilson announced that day that he would not avail himself of any volunteer divisions, that to do so "would seriously interfere with . . . the prompt creation and early use of an effective army." He determined that such divisions would contribute little to the effective strength of the armies currently engaged against Germany.

No matter what good theater it might make to send TR to the Western Front, Wilson could see no strategic reason to do so. He wired Roosevelt that his conclusions were based "entirely upon imperative considerations of public policy and not upon personal or private choice," but the Roosevelt camp had its doubts. "It seemed to us that the President's refusal was undoubtedly influenced by political considerations," wrote TR's daughter Alice Roosevelt Longworth, who suggested that there simply was not room for another star on the world stage—one President behind a desk, another leading a charge. Said Alice, "It was the bitterest sort of blow for Father."

Ten million American men between the ages of twenty-one and thirty, on the other hand, registered for the draft on June 5, 1917. Although there had been threats of resistance, the day passed without incident. Over the next year and a half, almost five thousand local boards would register nearly twenty-five million men, assigning each a number between 1 and 10,500. Then, a little before ten o'clock in the morning of July 20, 1917, in a room in the Senate Office Building, Secretary of War Baker stood before a crowd of government officials. Wearing a blindfold, he dipped his hand into a large glass jar and fished out a capsule, inside of which was the number 258. It was announced and written on a chalkboard, and newsreel cameras recorded the event. Over the next sixteen and a half hours, other officials and eventually local college students pulled the 10,499 remaining capsules, thus completing the first and largest such lottery in history. Shortly thereafter, more than 10 percent of those registered would be called up and then selected according to five categories of eligibility—factoring marital, medical, and occupational status along with the number of dependents one supported. Not everybody answered the call: 350,000 men—including a discernible number of German Americans, Socialists, and pacifists—simply resisted. Over the course of America's involvement in the war, the age limits would stretch to include all men between eighteen and forty-five. Over 150,000 lads under military age joined the Students' Army Training Corps, getting a jump on their preparation for service, usually on a college campus; and 80,000 men—mostly young businessmen—earned commissions after three months of twelve-hour days at officers' training camp. A Presbyterian minister wondered whether he could serve his country best by going to the front or staying in his parish; Wilson said that "it is the duty of these gentlemen to stand by their flocks, unless it is very evident that they can be dispensed with."

Suddenly the United States government was responsible for feeding, housing, clothing, and training millions of men. In just three months, thirty-two encampments requiring hospitals, power stations, sewage systems, theaters, libraries, and, often, railroad tracks and stations were built, a marvel of administration and construction. At a cost of roughly $10 million each, half these "cantonments" provided wooden barracks for the national Army; the other half provided tent camps, with wooden floors, for the National Guard. Stretching from Camp Devens in Massachusetts to Camp Kearney in California—all named for military heroes and most clustered in the South—each cantonment accommodated 40,000 soldiers. According to Secretary Daniels's final reckoning, 4,272,521 men served in the wartime Army.

Manpower proved easier to supply than firepower. By the time enlisted men appeared in camp, only a small fraction of the standard-issue Springfield rifles were on hand. By the end of the war, Springfield could supply only half the American Expeditionary Force's needs, forcing the government to purchase weapons from other companies. Because time was of the essence, Secretary Baker could not afford to gather competitive bids on every item the government needed. The War Department placed orders at once with Colt, Lewis, and Vickers for machine guns, anything to get weapons into soldiers' hands as quickly as possible. For months, American soldiers used European equipment. Indeed, not until late in the war would an American squadron fly American planes. As Charles G. Dawes—a Midwestern banker who became a Brigadier General in charge of supply procurement—quickly learned, it was essential to acquire any weaponry on hand and pay the going rate. The result was a fighting force that was never completely standardized but one that could improvise when necessary.

The Commander in Chief encouraged as much in what Josephus Daniels called the "most remarkable address of the war." It seemed to Wilson that the greatest obstacle in this "unprecedented war" was the German submarine, which the legendary British Admiralty had been unable to overcome—largely because of its timorous approach to the problem. (They repeatedly rejected America's idea of including convoys to accompany their ships across the Channel, for example.) On Saturday, August 11, 1917—as the core of the United States Navy was preparing to transport men and materiel overseas—the Wilsons cruised down the Potomac on the *May-flower* for their regular summer weekend jaunt. Then, without any public announcement, they sailed into the York River, where the massive dreadnoughts that constituted the Atlantic Fleet were at anchor. Unceremoniously, Wilson boarded the flagship *Pennsylvania*, where he found all the officers of the fleet gathered on the quarterdeck. With no press even aware of his presence, Wilson addressed the men "in confidence," delivering a personal inspirational message.

Wilson asked the sailors before him—from Ensigns to Admirals—to strategize beyond the lessons in their manuals, to

> please leave out of your vocabulary altogether the word "prudent." . . .
> Do the thing that is audacious to the utmost point of risk and daring,
> because that is exactly the thing that the other side does not understand. And you will win by the audacity of method when you cannot
> win by circumspection and prudence.

Wilson believed "the most extraordinary circumstance of modern history is the way in which the German people have been subordinated to the German system of authority, and how they have accepted their thinking." The purpose of this war, he told those about to fight, was "to see to it that no other people suffers a like limitation and subordination. . . . We are in some peculiar sense the trustees of liberty." Edith saw that her husband had inspired the men profoundly. He shook hands with every officer.

Thus began the most colossal conveyance of fighting men the world had ever known. The United States Navy swelled from 65,000 to 500,000; and, by the end of 1917, it had transported 145,918 men across the Atlantic Ocean. The next year it carried two million more. In all the months of mass passage, only 768 American soldiers and sailors were lost at sea.

In truth, Wilson had not anticipated building so sizeable a war machine. He read every night from a khaki-covered pocket edition of the

Bible that a soldier had sent him, and he prayed for the hostilities to end. The threat of the American invasion might encourage the Germans to withdraw to the peace table; and there was always the hope that the Allies might just win the war on their own before the Yanks arrived.

In August 1917, Pope Benedict XV appealed to the leaders of all the belligerent governments, asking them to stop turning the civilized world into "a field of death" and forcing Europe to take "a hand in its own suicide." He insisted that there should be a simultaneous and reciprocal reduction of armaments and that arbitration should begin right away. Secretary Lansing presumed this appeal emanated from Austria-Hungary— with its heavily Catholic population and strong support of the Vatican. He questioned the Pope's motives and suggested that he had become an unwitting "agent of Germany," eager to restore peace to Catholic Belgium and Poland but making no mention of Slavic Serbia and Montenegro. Wilson felt the Pontiff offered nothing more than a return to the status quo before the war, without removing any of the elements that provided the pretext for the war. "It is none of our business how the German people got under the control of such a government or were kept under the domination of its power and its purposes," he wrote in shorthand in preparing his reply, "but it is our business to see to it that the history of the world is no longer left to their handling." Wilson expressed doubt that such a peace could be based upon a restitution of the German government's power or upon "any word of honor it could pledge in a treaty of settlement and accommodation." He would not take the word of the present German rulers as "a guarantee of anything that is to endure, unless explicitly supported by such conclusive evidence of the will and purpose of the German people themselves as the other peoples of the world would be justified in accepting." The President looked forward to the possibility of a "covenanted peace."

On December 4, 1917, the President delivered his State of the Union Address and spoke almost entirely about the war, clarifying America's objectives. "We shall regard the war as won only when the German people say to us . . . that they are ready to agree to a settlement based upon justice and the reparation of the wrongs their rulers have done," he said. Observing that Austria-Hungary had become nothing more than "the vassal of the German Government," he now recommended a declaration of war against that empire. Three days later, Congress complied—by a unanimous vote in the Senate (La Follette was absent) and by all but one vote in the House.

The declaration cemented the bond between the United States and the Allies, signaling that all Germany's friends were now America's enemies. That only induced new talk that Austria-Hungary wished to arrive at a separate peace and extract itself from the war, which would, in turn, weaken Germany. In fact, Britain would soon enter secret talks with Austria on that very subject, as it desperately waited for the Americans to train and unleash the full force of their Army. When Vice Admiral William Sowden Sims—who was appointed Commander, United States Naval Forces Operating in European Waters—arrived in London, he learned a shocking truth that the British government had withheld from its people and the rest of the world. It was underreporting the tonnage of ships it had been losing each month. It was in the millions.

Some bumptious Englishmen—including Winston Churchill—would later claim that "America should have minded her own business and stayed out of the World War," that the Allies were on the verge of making peace with Germany in the spring of 1917. But few of Churchill's countrymen agreed. Most were undyingly grateful for American participation. Admiral John Jellicoe, head of the Royal Navy, privately told Admiral Sims upon his arrival, "They will win, unless we can stop these losses—and stop them soon." King George summoned Ambassador Page to Windsor Castle to tell him how much his nation appreciated the help of the Americans and to confess how badly they needed it. In September 1917, new Prime Minister David Lloyd George sent Wilson some hard facts, specifically that "in spite of the efforts of the Allies to raise and equip armies and to manufacture munitions, in spite of their superiority in men and material and the perfection to which they have brought their offensive arrangements, the Germans . . . find themselves in possession of more and not less Allied territory." As the American convoy plan met immediate and long-term success, the hopes of the King, like those of every citizen of the Allied nations, rested on American leadership.

General Frederick Funston was the presumptive leader of the American forces until his sudden death just weeks before the declaration of war. Many supposed that General Leonard Wood, leading spokesman for America's Preparedness Movement, might fill his boots, though his close relationship to TR did not endear him to Wilson. Ironically, Wilson had distrusted Wood since a meeting in early 1913, at which the General had done nothing but badmouth Roosevelt, in an obvious attempt to curry favor with Wilson. That only made the President doubt Wood's discretion and loyalty. And so, Secretary Baker and Wilson turned to General John J. Pershing, then fifty-seven years old. Tall, stiff-backed, and square-jawed, with a manicured mustache and a commanding voice that he used as little as possible, Pershing consistently had displayed leadership as he had risen through the ranks: with the 6th Cavalry, fighting Apaches and Sioux; commanding the 10th Cavalry—a regiment of the African American "buffalo soldiers," which earned him the nickname "Black Jack"; teaching at West Point; fighting in Cuba and the Philippines; and serving in diplomatic postings in Japan and the Balkans before leading the 8th Calvary in the punitive expedition along the Mexican border. He had said little during the preparedness quarrels.

After one meeting at the White House on May 24, Wilson immediately sent Pershing to Europe, with several thousand troops, to establish his command and demonstrate support for the Allies. Those Americans fortified morale more than they did the front lines. Despite constant pressure to fill in with "doughboys" wherever the French "poilus" and British "Tommies" had suffered great losses, Wilson reiterated that "we will leave to General Pershing the disposition of our troops, but it must be an American Army, officered and directed by Americans, ready to throw their strength where it will tell most." Like Wilson's Cabinet officers, Pershing was given virtually free rein of his personnel, creating a centralization of his forces and avoiding internecine warfare by having the absolute approval and obedience of his Generals. Pershing did not want his troops to lose their national identity by becoming absorbed in the Allied armies. Wilson felt the same about all his country's war efforts: when he saw a poster from the Food Administration referring to "Our Allies," he asked Herbert Hoover to substitute the words "Our Associates in the War," explaining, "I have been very careful about this myself because we have no allies and I think I am right in believing that the people of the country are very jealous of any intimation that there are formal alliances."

Pushing the United States into the international arena, Wilson relied heavily on Colonel House's secret intelligence-gathering project—"the Inquiry"—which Secretary Lansing helped define in a memorandum he wrote in optimistic preparation for the peace talks. Because it would be impossible to find any negotiators who possessed full knowledge of the myriad of issues involved, Lansing had recommended assembling a team of experts whose knowledge cut across different countries and different disciplines, each of whom would prepare a pamphlet that could assist in deciding the United States' role in the determination of boundaries and the redistribution of colonial possessions. He had further recommended that House supervise the entire effort.

Working out of unimposing offices, the Inquiry quietly went about its work, as House assigned Sidney Edward Mezes to administer this think tank. Mezes happened to be Mrs. House's brother-in-law; and House insisted that he was not only trustworthy but also supremely qualified. A lifelong academician and philosopher, Dr. Mezes was then president of the City College of New York and was "well grounded in both political and economic history," had a progressive outlook, and was conversant in French, German, Italian, and Spanish. To serve as his secretary, House recommended Walter Lippmann, whose abilities were so impressive, the anti-Semitic House surmounted his objections—because "unlike other Jews he is a silent one." The mission of the Inquiry was not simply to gather information but also to apply it in rebuilding the world after the current apocalypse.

At the end of 1917, its secret work grew complicated when a newspaper revealed its existence. Then a series of secret agreements among the Allies, predetermining how the Central empires would be dismantled and divided after the war, came to light. Great Britain, France, Russia, Japan, and—perhaps most problematic—Italy (which had joined the Allies) had all privately agreed to new covenants, creating a system of alliances as labyrinthine as those that had kindled the war. They imagined whole new countries drawn from territory between Germany and the Middle East. Affixing such territorial purposes to the war contradicted Wilson's ideals. One cannot determine precisely what the President knew and when he knew it, because he proceeded to act as though these pacts did not exist. He believed he would be able to bring everybody around to his way of thinking—regardless of secret treaties—in due time. As the President wrote Colonel House: "When the war is over we can force them to our way of thinking, because by that time they will, among other things, be financially in our hands." By year's end, however, it looked as though the Allies might not have a chance at any spoils.

During the first four weeks of autumn, the Austro-Hungarian and German armies overwhelmed the Italians at Caporetto. Starting with a surprise attack, from which the Italians never recovered, the battle effectively knocked its army out of commission; the retreat felt like a turning point in the war, as in addition to some 30,000 Italian casualties, 250,000 of their men were taken prisoner. Morale sank, and soldiers deserted. The retreat broke more than the back of the Italian armed forces; it fractured the spirit of the entire Allied cause. One young Red Cross ambulance driver from Oak Park, Illinois—Ernest Hemingway—would later capture that moment, saying, "Abstract words such as glory, honor, courage, or hallow were obscene." In the meantime, in Russia the Bolshevik government was hoping to draft a separate peace with the Germans. Such a treaty would hurt the Allies, allowing the Germans to remove their armies from the Eastern Front so they could fight on the Western. And in the far reaches of the Ottoman Empire, one small plot of sand proved to have far-reaching implications.

Commander of Britain's Egyptian Expeditionary Force since June 1917, British General E. H. H. "Bloody Bull" Allenby had steadily pushed his campaign east across the Sinai desert. How Palestine might figure into an Allied victory in the war had not been determined; Zionists had long prayed it might become a permanent homeland for the millions of Jews dispersed around the world. On November 2, 1917, after consideration by the British War Cabinet, Foreign Minister Balfour wrote Lionel, the 2d Baron Rothschild, a representative of the Zionists, a short letter, the core of which read:

> His Majesty's Government view with favour the establishment in Palestine of a national home for the Jewish people, and will use their best endeavours to facilitate the achievement of this object, it being clearly understood that nothing shall be done which may prejudice the civil and religious rights of existing non-Jewish communities in Palestine, or the rights and political status enjoyed by Jews in any other country.

By December 9, Allenby's troops had captured Jerusalem; and at noon on the eleventh, the Bloody Bull and his officers dismounted so that they could enter the Holy City on foot. They were the first Christian army to seize the city from the Turks since 1099. The Balfour Declaration was not a legal document, merely a statement of intention; but it became the groundwork for the Jewish state that would remain a bone of contention over the next century. Secretary Lansing suggested to the President that he refrain from taking any position on Zionism—as the United States was not at war with Turkey, the Jews were far from united in their own feelings about a Jewish state, and there were many Christians who would "undoubtedly resent turning the Holy Land over to the absolute control of the race credited with the death of Christ." But Wilson told Lansing that he had already assented to the Balfour Declaration, recognition that would prove to be fundamental to the region.

The President dispatched House to Europe, to sit at the Inter-Allied War Council meeting in Paris, where they discussed means of coordinating all their war efforts. With the Allies stumbling on the European fronts, Wilson saw the opportunity for his man to "take the whip hand" in directing the global agenda, for the United States not only to "accede to the plan for a unified conduct of the war but insist upon it." General Pershing apprised Baker that he hoped to have America's fighting forces in active service by the summer of 1918. "Winning the war is vital to our future," he said, "and if humanly possible it ought to be done in 1918. There is no telling what might happen if we defer our utmost exertion until 1919."

"A supreme moment of history has come," Wilson said in concluding his State of the Union Address that December. "The eyes of the people have been opened and they see. The hand of God is laid upon the nations. He will show them favour, I devoutly believe, only if they rise to the clear heights of His own justice and mercy." To assist in this ascent, the President asked Colonel House for a memorandum from the Inquiry that would pose the different questions a peace conference must consider and propose achievable answers. Mezes, attorney David Hunter Miller, and Walter Lippmann generated a comprehensive but highly readable document—*The Present Situation: The War Aims and Peace Terms It Suggests*. It delineated America's political and military objectives from Berlin to Baghdad—paying particular attention to the Poles, Czechs, South Slavs, and Bulgarians. It enumerated America's assets, laying out especially how money, if skillfully handled, could be wielded like a weapon, used both to threaten enemies and to lure friends; and it assessed its liabilities—the military impotence of Russia, the "strategic impossibility" of any military operation that could cut to the heart of Middle Europe, the "costs and dangers" of a war of attrition on the Western Front, the possibility that the Germans might agree to a settlement over Alsace-Lorraine without changing the basic balance of power in Western Europe, and the instability of Italy, where social revolution loomed. The proposal offered a program for a "diplomatic offensive," the best possible scenarios for each of the players in the world drama—including ways of creating discord between Austria-Hungary and Germany and harmony among the Allies. Finally, and most incisive, the Inquiry memorandum offered a statement of peace terms—ten items, territory by territory.

Colonel House delivered the report on December 23. It evidently went unread through the holidays, during which time representatives of the newly established Bolshevik regime under Vladimir Lenin officially opened talks with the Central Powers in Brest-Litovsk (which would become Brest, Belarus) to discuss a settlement.

At the first plenary session of the Brest-Litovsk Peace Conference, Russia presented a manifesto—six principles that centered on a theme of liberation. They included banning "forceable annexation of territory seized during the war," restoring independence where it had been seized, protecting minorities in multinational territories with "special laws," safeguarding weaker nations against such bullying tactics as boycotts and blockades, and, most important, allowing national groups to determine their own political futures through referendums. British Ambassador Cecil Spring-Rice had a private audience with Wilson shortly after those terms were made public; and from Washington, he promptly confided to Foreign Minister Balfour, "Situation here is such that the President must in self-defence make some answer to the Bolshevists' appeal."

That very day—Friday, January 4, 1918—Colonel House handed the President an expanded version of the Inquiry's statement of peace terms. Over the next twenty-four hours, Wilson could not help incorporating at least the sentiments of Lenin's principles, if not a few specifics, into his own thinking, especially where Russia was concerned. At half past ten on Saturday morning, he and his right-hand man outlined general provisos and then proceeded to specific territorial adjustments. Working directly from the Inquiry's memorandum, they considered each proposition from both the Allied and Central Powers vantage points. House generally served as the anvil against which Wilson hammered his ideas. The President defined most of the basic stipulations in shorthand and then refined them at his typewriter. Two hours later—having "finished remaking the map of the world," as House put it—Wilson asked the Colonel to number his short typed statement. They agreed upon the sequence, with one exception—the creation of a peace association, which Wilson thought should come at the very end, as a way of rounding out the message. That became his fourteenth point.

Also that day, Prime Minister Lloyd George delivered a long speech to the Trade Union Conference in London in which he articulated his nation's position. The basis of any territorial settlement in the war, he said, was the principle of "government by consent of the governed"—what he now called "self-determination." When the text reached Washington, Wilson's spirits sank; he thought the address made many of his very same points. House argued that Lloyd George's remarks simply laid a foundation for Wilson's speech and that Wilson "would once more become the spokesman for the Entente, and, indeed, the spokesman for the liberals of the world."

On Sunday, Wilson secluded himself in his study and incorporated his fourteen points into a speech. He toiled until day's end, at which time he read his address to Colonel House. A single theme ran through the text— what Wilson would describe as "the principle of justice to all peoples and nationalities, and their right to live on equal terms of liberty and safety with one another, whether they be strong or weak." House called the address "a declaration of human liberty and a declaration of the terms which should be written into the peace conference." More than that, he diarized, "I felt that it was the most important document that he had ever penned." The next day Wilson read the speech to Secretary Lansing.

Two days later, the President appeared before both houses of Congress at noon and got right down to business. "We entered this war," he said, "because violations of right had occurred which touched us to the quick and made the life of our own people impossible unless they were corrected and the world secured once for all against their recurrence. What we demand . . . is that the world be made fit and safe to live in." All the peoples of the world, Wilson added, were partners in this interest; and with that, he stood before the Congress and the world to present his Mosaic "programme of the world's peace . . . the only possible programme."

Wilson's first five points were edicts for all the nations to obey: "open covenants of peace, openly arrived at" (thus, no secret treaties); "absolute freedom of navigation upon the seas"; "the removal, so far as possible, of all economic barriers" and an equality of trade conditions among all the nations consenting to the peace; a reduction of national armaments "to the lowest point consistent with domestic safety"; and "a free, open-minded, and absolutely impartial adjustment of all colonial claims."

The next eight points eradicated the old imperial borders of specific territories and entreated the rest of the world to honor the new boundaries. Several of the stipulations carried their own Wilsonian homilies. Point VI called for the German evacuation of all Russian territory and the allowance for "the independent determination of her own political development and national policy," so that she might join the community of free nations under institutions of her own choosing; more than that, Wilson said, the "treatment accorded Russia by her sister nations in the months to come will be the acid test of their good will, of their comprehension of her needs as distinguished from their own interests, and of their intelligent and unselfish sympathy." Point VII insisted upon the evacuation and restoration of Belgium—as no other single act would so much serve "to restore confidence among the nations in the laws which they have themselves set and determined for the government of their relations with one another. Without this healing act the whole structure and validity of international law is forever impaired." Point VIII demanded the release of all French territory and the restoration of its invaded portions—particularly "the wrong done to France by Prussia in 1871 in the matter of Alsace-Lorraine, which has unsettled the peace of the world for nearly fifty years." Point IX sought a readjustment of Italy's frontiers "along clearly recognizable lines of nationality." Point X said the peoples of Austria-Hungary "should be accorded the freest opportunity of autonomous development." Point XI addressed the Balkan states, granting "political and economic independence and territorial integrity," especially in according Serbia "free and secure access to the sea." Point XII disassembled the Ottoman Empire, assuring the Turkish portion a secure sovereignty and the other nationalities the right to develop autonomously, and mandating that the Dardanelles should be permanently opened as a free passage to ships of all nations. And Point XIII urged the creation of an independent Polish state, complete with free and secure access to the sea.

Three and a half years earlier, when the fighting in Europe broke out, H. G. Wells published a series of articles that were compiled into a book entitled *The War That Will End War.* As the fighting persisted, so did that phrase, which modulated into "the war to end all wars." As Woodrow Wilson became the principal voice of the era—and because that sentiment encapsulated his outlook—the slogan was attributed to him. And nothing addressed that concept—thus permanently affixing it in the public's mind—more than his Fourteenth Point: "A general association of nations must be formed under specific covenants for the purpose of affording mutual guarantees of political independence and territorial integrity to great and small states alike."

President Wilson said the United States would fight until those fourteen "arrangements and covenants" were achieved. As he had suggested in the past, America carried no vendetta against Germany, no jealousy of German greatness, no desire to block her legitimate influence or power. "We wish her only to accept a place of equality among the peoples of the world—the new world in which we now live,—instead of a place of mastery," he said. "The moral climax of this the culminating and final war for human liberty has come," he concluded on behalf of the people of the United States, "and they are ready to put their own strength, their own highest purpose, their own integrity and devotion to the test."

"God was satisfied with Ten Commandments. Wilson gives us fourteen," France's Premier Georges Clemenceau would gibe; the British wondered how Point II might affect their ruling the waves; and the German press took Wilson to task for employing "all his demagogic artifices . . . to prevent Russia from closing a separate peace with the Central Powers." But most of the rest of the world heartily embraced Wilson's speech. The "extreme radicals, even the socialists, approve it," House triumphantly noted in his diary, "and so do the conservatives and reactionaries." Paderewski of Poland sent grateful salutations; speaking in Edinburgh, Balfour referred to the speech as a "magnificent pronouncement"; muckraker Lincoln Steffens and peace activist Jane Addams both conferred their praise; and the French press, cabled General Pershing, offered "unqualified approval." Even Colonel Roosevelt told *The New York Times* that he was "much pleased" with it. Thanks to George Creel, when the Germans advanced into Russia in early

1918, they found the walls of the towns placarded with the Fourteen Points—not just in Russian but also translated into German; 300,000 handbills were distributed in five days in Petrograd alone. The CPI printed and disseminated more than four million copies of Wilson's speech.

The Germans were just as eager as the Allies to end the war, but Chancellor Georg von Hertling showed no signs of embracing the Fourteen Points. Factions within the Reichstag were prepared to compromise but— as the ongoing talks at Brest-Litovsk indicated—only on their terms and to their advantage. Strikes broke out in Berlin and Vienna, and revolution was in the air. House delighted at the schisms the Fourteen Points had created among the German politicians; and Wilson capitalized on the divisiveness by returning to Congress on February 11 to reaffirm his points, offering four principles for their enactment.

Each part of the final settlement must "be based upon the essential justice of that particular case," especially in its striving for a permanent peace; the peoples and provinces were not to be bartered "as if they were mere chattels and pawns in a game, even the great game, now forever discredited, of the balance of power"; every territorial settlement must be in the interest of the populations concerned and not as a part of an adjustment against rival states; and all "well defined national aspirations" must be considered in light of their effect on "perpetuating old elements" that might break the peace of Europe and beyond. Wilson said he offered no threats, insisting that the power of the United States "will never be used in aggression or for the aggrandizement of any selfish interest of our own"—only to serve freedom. The subtext of Wilson's speech was clear: he welcomed peace efforts but intended to fight until Germany forsook its militaristic ways.

"What is at stake now is the peace of the world," Wilson continued. "What we are striving for is a new international order based upon broad and universal principles of right and justice,—no mere peace of shreds and patches." The President explained that in raising his Fourteen Points he had meant only "that those problems each and all affect the whole world" and that "unless they are dealt with in a spirit of unselfish and unbiased justice, with a view to the wishes, the natural connections, the racial aspirations, the security, and the peace of mind of the peoples involved, no permanent peace will have been attained." When Germany suggested it would determine the futures of Russian territory and a place for an independent Poland, Wilson became even more outspoken. "People are not to be handed about from one sovereignty to another by an international conference of an understanding between rivals and antagonists," he said. "National aspirations must be respected; peoples may now be dominated and governed only by their own consent." And then he added, " 'Self-determination' is not a mere phrase. It is an imperative principle of action, which statesmen will henceforth ignore at their peril." Two weeks later— after losing two million soldiers—Russia would surrender a third of its population and farmland and half its industrial centers.

Germany realized it had only a few months before American troops would arrive in Europe. And so, beginning on March 21, it committed all possible resources to a spring offensive. This involved four major attacks, the goals of which were to break through the Allied lines, outflank the British forces, which extended to the English Channel, and close in on the French. Under the direction of Generalquartiermeister Erich Ludendorff, the Germans forced the British 5th Army to retreat thirty miles and lose 100,000 men. They continued to inflict serious damage to the French as they drove them back, coming within striking distance of Paris. Severely compromised, the Allies closed ranks behind a single leader, naming Marshal Ferdinand Foch Supreme Commander of the Allied Armies. While the Germans gained significant ground and suffered fewer losses than the Allied armies, Foch was able to keep the enemy from inflicting the coup de grâce. After four years of horrific warfare, victory on neither side was in sight: German casualties in the spring offensive practically equaled those of the British and French combined. There were more than 1.5 million casualties all together.

That was the same number of doughboys who reached France by June 1918—all fresh and inspired by one of Wilson's most stirring speeches. Before fifteen thousand people at a rally in Baltimore on April 6—the anniversary of "our acceptance of Germany's challenge to fight for our right to live and be free, and for the sacred rights of free men everywhere"— Wilson had delivered not just a call to arms but an announcement of America's new military strength. With all the passion of one of his heroes, Shakespeare's Henry V, Wilson cried, "Force, Force to the utmost, Force without stint or limit, the righteous and triumphant Force which shall make Right the law of the world, and cast every selfish dominion down in the dust." America's former prince of peace had become a full-fledged warrior king, dispatching millions of young men unto the breach of the greatest carnage the modern world had ever seen.

"In Flanders fields the poppies grow," began the most popular poem of the era, an elegy that laced propaganda with pastoral imagery. But the casualties on those fields mounted so high they opiated the mind, keeping people from processing all the horror. With its profusion of noble sentiments and heartwarming songs, the Great War still presented itself as a romantic conflict; but it would be for the last time, as new technology mechanized war, turning from conventional weaponry to more diabolic tools of devastation. Sophisticated automatic rifles and machine guns took more lives in more efficient and gruesome new ways. In the century since shrapnel was introduced, it had developed to the point that each cylinder shot into the air could now release dozens of exploding lead marbles, damaging their human targets not only immediately but also later through the infections the lead balls induced. The Germans developed a highly effective flamethrower. And by 1915, both sides in the war employed poison gas—starting with tear gas and chlorine and progressing to mustard gas. The latter had the ability to corrode the skin and erode the lungs, leading to blindness if not death. Submarines, tanks, and airplanes contributed to the ever-increasing slaughter as armies spent months at a time living and fighting in trenches, behind barbed wire, sometimes losing hundreds of thousands of lives while gaining only a few feet of muddy ground.

With sanitation facilities crude at best, the soldiers were subjected to every imaginable disease, from nephritis to pneumonia along with trench fever (a form of rickets) and trench foot (similar to frostbite). Rats were rampant, dangerous for the parasites and diseases they carried; lice bred beyond control. "Shell shock" became a familiar auditory and psychological affliction; and corpses tangled in barbed wire became a common sight. Poetry now reflected a discernible shift in tone, as much of the early idealism succumbed to grotesque reality.

And then appeared the Fourth Horseman of the Apocalypse—Pestilence. During the unusually cold winter of 1918, a lethal influenza spread, evidently from Camp Funston, Kansas. With some fifty thousand men in close quarters, most of them shipping out overseas and scattering across Europe, only to share crowded unsanitary foxholes, the war created a global Petri dish for a pandemic. Within a year, the Spanish flu—as it came to be called because Spain's King Alfonso XIII became its most publicized survivor—would be responsible for half the deaths of American soldiers. Lasting four centuries, the Black Death had killed 75 million people. This outbreak of influenza would infect a billion people, killing 100 million of them.

War inflates peacetime numbers, particularly economic statistics. A military workforce in the millions, supported by thousands of new bureaucracies—from draft boards to the National Screw Thread Commission—had to be funded. "I now had to face the prodigious problem of war financing," recalled Treasury Secretary McAdoo. "With each fresh calculation the sum had grown larger, and the figures were appalling. There were so many uncertain factors in the problem that a definite conclusion was not possible." But McAdoo realized that he had to generate several billion dollars within a few months. His predecessor during the Civil War, Salmon P. Chase, had been afraid to appeal to the people for money, and so he relied heavily on private bankers and agents to sell bonds; McAdoo considered this a fundamental error. "Any great war must necessarily be a popular movement," he believed. "It is a kind of crusade; and, like all crusades, it sweeps along on a powerful stream of romanticism."

The day after the war was declared, McAdoo went to Congress to confer with members of the House Ways and Means Committee and the Senate Finance Committee. He submitted a draft of a bill seeking authorization to issue $7 billion worth of bonds. "The request for such an enormous amount of money startled Congress and the country," McAdoo recalled. But he explained that he did not intend to offer the entire batch of bonds at once. He also detailed the importance of sending $3 billion as loans to the Allies—"substitutes for American soldiers" until they had actually arrived. North Carolinian Claude Kitchin, Majority Leader and chairman of the House committee, noted that the bill contained "the largest authorization of bond issues ever contained in any bill presented to any legislative body in the history of the world." With near unanimous support, it passed both houses of Congress within two weeks.

Selling bonds became one of the great morale builders during the war. Business was good enough that anybody with money could earn a higher rate of interest from other financial instruments; but the Administration literally capitalized, as McAdoo said, on "the profound impulse called patriotism." They took the campaign to the people—farmers and factory workers and millionaires alike—giving every citizen an opportunity to serve the country by investing in it. After consulting with several business titans, particularly two of the nation's leading financiers—J. P. Morgan and Paul M. Warburg—McAdoo settled on $2 billion at a 3.5 percent rate of interest, high enough to maximize widespread participation but low enough to minimize the government's burden. Calling them "Liberty Loans," he embarked on a four-week speaking tour to drum up subscribers. With the support of the major banks, the Four Minute Men, women's clubs, and politicians of all persuasions (with the notable exception of Ohio's Republican Senator Warren G. Harding), and with newspapers and billboard owners and advertising agencies offering free services, the First Liberty Loan drive ended after one month, oversubscribed by more than $1 billion. Four million citizens had invested, 99 percent of them paying from $50 to $10,000. On May 31, 1917, the President invested $10,000. In order to give the Treasury greater flexibility by not requiring approval each time it needed to float a bond—and to empower Congress with control over the amount of moneys the nation could borrow—in September 1917, Congress created a limit it called a "debt ceiling," this first one set at $11.5 billion.

Three more drives followed over the next fifteen months. McAdoo had been so unsure about the first bond issue that Congress had exempted the income the bonds produced from all but inheritance taxes. Now he returned to Congress to suggest that surtaxes be applied in certain instances. To ensure the success of these subsequent campaigns, Washington called upon the nation's most powerful new sales force—movie stars. In the last five years, a Los Angeles community of orange groves and pepper trees had blossomed into Hollywood, the home of one of the most lucrative industries in the nation; and its famous players did whatever they could to boost the war effort—appearing at benefits, drawing publicity, and raising spirits as well as money. After Wilson received Charlie Chaplin, Mary Pickford, and Douglas Fairbanks at the White House, they accompanied McAdoo on his bond tours and turned throngs of fans into subscribers wherever they went. Sometimes the crowds grew too vast to hear the stars talk, and the actors resorted to their pantomime skills in encouraging the public to invest in the nation. On one tour, stone-faced cowboy William S. Hart crammed rallies in nineteen cities into ten days and sold $2 million worth of bonds. The four Liberty Loan campaigns raised $17 billion. By then the Victory Liberty Bond Act had raised the debt limit to $43 billion, far above the $25.5 billion in total federal debt.

McAdoo had never intended for bonds to finance the entire war; he believed the "soundness and stability" of America's financial structure depended on raising not less than one-third of its expenditures through taxation. The Revenue Act of 1916 sought to raise $200 million, more than half derived from the income tax; the basic rate inched from 1 percent to 2 on annual incomes over $3,000, and there was a surtax of 6 percent on incomes over $500,000 that slid upward to 13 percent on incomes over $2 million. The next year, the United States experienced the sharpest spike in its tax history. A 2 percent tax was imposed on incomes of $1,000, with graduated surtaxes amounting to as much as 67 percent in the cases of multimillion-dollar incomes; this not only generated more revenue but enrolled more taxpayers. Congress introduced excess-profits taxes—8 percent on businesses and individuals earning more than $6,000 annually. In the years just before the war, hundreds of employees of the Bureau of Internal Revenue had collected $280 million annually. After America entered the war, ten thousand workers collected $2.8 billion.

On May 23, 1918, McAdoo urged a higher tax on profits generated by war industries, an increase in the income tax on unearned incomes, and a heavy tax on luxuries. The only reasons to challenge the legislation, said McAdoo, were political. Congressional elections were less than half a year away, and he noted that many members had told him they were worried that such taxation would result in the Republicans seizing the House of Representatives. McAdoo said he felt the fear was "ill-founded." He believed the electorate would have more respect for those representatives who were willing to announce their positions than those who dodged the issue. Either way, he asked the President, "how can we allow any political consideration to stand in the way of our doing the things which are manifestly demanded to save the life of the Nation?" The question launched what would become a perennial debate between people who insisted that businesses—the very people who invested in the growth of America— were being treated unfairly and those who contended that the redistribution of wealth was not only equitable but stimulative to the economy. Between 1917 and 1918, the nation's gross domestic product grew from $60 billion to $75 billion; and the federal deficit—that is, the amount by which government expenditures exceeded revenues—shot from $1.1 billion to $9 billion.

On May 27, Wilson appeared briefly before another joint session of Congress and presented the facts as McAdoo had laid them out. Winning the war was paramount; hundreds of thousands of America's men—"carrying our hearts with them and our fortunes"—were hastening to Europe; there could be "no pause or intermission" in their crusade; and that required raising additional moneys. "Only fair, equitably distributed taxation . . . drawing chiefly from the sources which would be likely to demoralize credit by their very abundance," he said, "can prevent inflation and keep our industrial system free of speculation and waste."

"No new taxes" would later become an evergreen American political slogan; but Wilson proposed the exact opposite. He insisted it was the government's duty in that moment to introduce new taxes and raise the old ones. While no elected official ever wanted to take such a position, the President exhorted Congress to embrace the challenge. That required a major concession on all their parts, which he audaciously presented in a slogan of his own: "Politics is adjourned."

Both houses of the Sixty-fifth Congress had cooperated with the executive branch in enacting Wilson's vigorous wartime agenda, and so he reluctantly asked them to extend themselves further by abrogating the very essence of their existence—the playing of politics. So long as they were waging war, the President of the United States blandished, "the elections will go to those . . . who go to the constituencies without explanations or excuses, with a plain record of duty faithfully and disinterestedly performed." Whether one agreed with the President or not, his rousing speech offered a profile in courage.

Debate extended for several months, though it would prove nearly impossible to resist a Commander in Chief who spoke with such unabashed patriotism. "Have you not felt the spirit of the nation rise and its thought become a single and common thought since these eventful days came in which we have been sending our boys to the other side?" he asked that May. He believed Americans were so united in their resoluteness to win the war, they would undergo any sacrifice toward that end. "We need not be afraid to tax them," Wilson added, "if we lay taxes justly."

The great variable in the equation, of course, was in the definition of the word "justly." McAdoo favored taxing "war profits," as the chemical and the steel industries, for example, were benefiting hugely from the conflict. He pointed out that the Allies borrowed about $9.5 billion from America during the war years, but they spent close to $12 billion there in that period. Most of that money went to munitions-makers, who were notorious profiteers. McAdoo estimated that gains from war profiteering amounted to close to $3 billion. In the meantime, progressive Representative Kitchin targeted "excess profits." He noted that that such companies as Ford, Standard Oil, and American Tobacco had been earning excessive profits before and during the war and deserved to be taxed accordingly after the war. Henry Cabot Lodge cautioned that so much taxation would curb future investment, thus generating less in income taxes and keeping average Americans from buying Liberty Bonds. Such debates would last months as well, but Wilson still had no compunction asking for these new revenues. After all, he said in his speech on May 27, 1918, "Just as I was leaving the White House I was told that the expected drive on the western front had apparently begun."

From the moment he landed in London, it had been General Pershing's plan to hang fire until he had mustered a substantial enough force to win the war. Before late May 1918, American troops had barely muddied their boots, obtaining only occasional battle experience. Because of the exigencies of the spring offensive, Pershing temporarily allowed Marshal Foch to intersperse some of his troops among the combined British and French forces. Then, on May 28, 1918, some 3,500 soldiers of the 28th Infantry Regiment of the U.S. 1st Division took offensive action in a small battle at Cantigny, seventy-five miles north of Paris. Assisted by French airplanes above and tanks on the ground, the Americans overtook the town and advanced into German-held territory in a matter of hours. Beyond the military victory was the psychological boost. This small band proved that Americans knew how to fight, and it offered a preview of what millions of robust doughboys could do. The Battle of Belleau Wood lasted almost the entire month of June and ended in an American victory. The Yanks won again in July at Château-Thierry. By August, Foch decided to take advantage of the shift in momentum and commence his own offensive, one that would last the next hundred days. The Allied armies fought in the Battle of Amiens (the first day of which Ludendorff called "the Black Day of the German Army," as a massive arrival of British tanks allowed the soldiers to emerge from the trenches to fight), the Battles of the Somme, the Battle of the Argonne Forest, and at St. Mihiel, where the Americans won another decisive battle.

Even Winston Churchill, chary in praising outsiders, could not help acknowledging the vitality the Americans brought to the bloody battlefields. He would later cite a Frenchman's account of country roads suddenly filled with that "inexhaustible flood of gleaming youth in its first maturity of health and vigour." Backhanded though the compliment may have been, he added, "Half trained, half organized with only their courage and their numbers and their magnificent youth behind their weapons, they were to buy their experience at a bitter price. But this they were quite ready to do." According to one military historian, the American Expeditionary Force "seized 485,000 square miles of enemy-held territory and captured 63,000 prisoners, 1,300 artillery pieces, and 10,000 mortars and machine guns."

In the words of Woodrow Wilson, "Our men went in force into the line of battle just at the critical moment when the whole fate of the world seemed to hang in the balance and threw their fresh strength into the ranks of freedom in time to turn the whole tide . . . so that henceforth it was back, back, back, for their enemies, always back, never again forward!" In short order, "the commanders of the Central Empires knew themselves beaten." But Churchill was right about the bitter cost. While the decisive streak of American military victories was not exactly Pyrrhic, it was pricey. In 150 days of combat, the AEF suffered the loss of 116,516 soldiers and sailors, almost half of whom died in combat, while most of the rest succumbed to influenza; another 204,002 were wounded; and 3,350 men were reported missing.

Half those losses came in the first six weeks of the fall of 1918 in the Argonne Forest, a dense wood next to the Meuse River, where the United States fought the largest battle in its history, before or since, with 1.2 million soldiers. It would result in the deaths of 26,277 Americans, more than had ever died in a single battle. There Alvin York, a sergeant born in a log cabin in Tennessee, led an attack on a machine gun nest, which resulted in the killing of 28 Germans and the capture of 132 more, rendering him a symbol of American heroism. Captain Harry Truman of Independence, Missouri, led a battery that supported the tank brigade of George S. Patton, without losing a single man. He would return Stateside and become a haberdasher. And overhead, an Indianapolis 500 racecar driver from Ohio named Edward Rickenbacker was becoming one of the war's flying aces. American, French, and German casualties totaled 300,000 in the Meuse-Argonne offensive.

The war fomented great social change, as it imbued the nation with moral force and generated economic growth. On foreign battlefields, soldiers with roots in more than fifty different nations came together, as bankers shared foxholes with bums. Historian and future Yale President Charles Seymour observed that "the youthful plutocrat saw life from a new angle, the wild mountaineer learned to read, the alien immigrant to speak English." Materially speaking, the gross domestic product of the United States had doubled since 1914—to $75.8 billion—with half that rise coming since America's entrance into the war; and the gross public debt had almost trebled, to $14.6 billion. More than the steel and explosives industries benefited. Gillette, to name but one company, signed a deal with the government to produce 3.5 million razors, to be shipped to all enlisted men. With the muscle of the American workforce—its young males—largely in uniform, unemployment reached record lows, halving to 3 percent in 1918, some months dipping below 2. More women worked outside the home than ever before. Typewriters and telephones created a demand for clerical workers and operators, jobs deemed appropriate for them. The need for workers in the industrial North—notably Chicago, Cleveland, and Detroit—caused a migration of African Americans from sharecropping farms in the South. Even "colored girls" were able to find nondomestic work. But racial hatred and segregation persisted.

Less than a week after Congress had declared war, the President heard from the black pastor of Shiloh Baptist Church in Washington, D.C. He reminded Wilson that "the Colored people" accounted for one-tenth of the American population and that the time had come for their President to assure them that he and his administration desired their "hearty, united and enthusiastic support in carrying on the War" and that "no discrimination or injustice will be practiced by the Government." Days later, Wilson received a more stringent document from the Boston branch of the National Equal Rights League, signed by William Monroe Trotter, his former adversary, who suggested that the war allowed for some progressive social reordering. "There is need no longer of subjection of Americans to the race prejudices of fellow Americans," insisted the long proclamation.

"In the presence of a common danger and a common obligation, with a war devastating Europe caused by racial clannishness and racial hatred . . . let the United States of America and the people thereof give up race proscription and persecution at home." In short, they entreated Wilson to give the same encouragement for volunteering or enlisting to all Americans "by vouchsafing the same free chance to enlist, to rise by merit, and on return home, the same right to civil service, and to civil rights without bar or segregation."

Wilson saw no signs that the country was ready for that. Localized racial violence had become commonplace in the South, and now disturbances moved north, as blacks were taking jobs held formerly by whites. The old bugaboos of black men preying upon white women and black women seducing white men played into people's fears. Such had been the talk for months in East St. Louis, Illinois. After a few isolated incidents of brutality, the city conflagrated into what came to be called a "race riot." In truth, it was a pogrom.

On July 2, 1917, a phalanx of whites marched down a thoroughfare of the city and waited at a main intersection. As black people appeared, the mob attacked, pointlessly and relentlessly shooting, clubbing, stoning, and stomping people to death; they set fire to two hundred homes in the African American neighborhood; they dumped bodies into the Cahokia Creek. State troopers and the Illinois National Guard came to quell the melee, but witnesses saw men in uniform turn on the black victims as well. During two days of chaos, thousands of blacks took flight; and though officials tallied thirty-nine deaths, anti-lynching activist and journalist Ida B. Wells figured 150 people died. Governor Arthur Capper of Kansas wrote President Wilson not only to convey his outrage at the savagery but also to condemn the "damning effects of liquor," which had evidently fueled the massacre.

William English Walling—a wealthy, Harvard-educated grandson of Kentucky slave-owners, who cofounded the NAACP—wrote the White House, declaring the "unchecked savagery" in East St. Louis the worst since the Civil War. "There is no oversupply of labor anywhere in America today," Walling wired, "massacre clearly due to effort of the anti-Negro element of the South to check exodus of colored labor which promised to force south to suspend the reign of terror which has ruled there for half a century and to give negroes better pay and to treat them like human beings." Walling added, "There should be an immediate Presidential proclamation that in the present military exigency the full military power of the nation will be used in defense of the lives and liberty of our colored fellow citizens."

Wilson called upon Attorney General Gregory to get to the bottom of "these disgraceful outrages." But, as Wilson soon wrote the Republican Congressman in St. Louis, Missouri, the federal attorneys and agents investigating the case required violations of federal statutes in order to act. "Up to this time," he admitted sadly, "I am bound in candor to say that no facts have been presented to us which would justify federal action." The President seemed as surprised as he was appalled that such a "tragical matter" should have been possible. As protesters across the country took to the streets and petitions seeking action arrived at the White House, Wilson offered little more than assurances that this local matter was being investigated. Of greater concern was the global war and the national conscription of an Army which he believed was clearly not ready for integration.

Secretary of War Baker wrote the President in August "that this is not the time to raise the race issue," for it was now his intention "to preserve the custom of the Army, which has been to organize colored people into separate organizations." Necessity would dictate that some colored men would train in Southern camps with white soldiers. Racist South Carolina Governor Coleman Livingston Blease insisted that he did not wish Negro troops to be stationed in his state; Congressman Lever feared the worst should such integration be forced upon his district—as did the President. Late that July, the 3rd Battalion of the 24th Infantry Regiment—654 black enlisted men serving under eight white officers—was sent to Houston; from the moment of their arrival, the black soldiers had clashed with white civilians. On August 23, some black troops mutinied, breaking into the arsenal and procuring guns, which they used indiscriminately as they rampaged through town. Fifteen people were killed and twelve others assaulted. Congressman Joe Eagle telegraphed the President to say that this behavior "conclusively proves tragic blunder committed in ordering negro troops to Southern camps. Besides this tragedy the presence of negro troops here has largely demoralized local negro feeling and conduct. Unless all these negro troops are sent away quickly my opinion that last night's tragedy is but a prelude to a tragedy upon enormous scale." Race riots flared from Philadelphia to Chicago. In Estill Springs, Tennessee, a Negro charged with murder was tortured with red-hot irons, then doused in oil and burned to death before a crowd of men, women, and children. Lynchings across the South became epidemic, and the sight of black bodies swinging from trees was common.

In February 1918, civil rights activist James Weldon Johnson led a small delegation of ministers from the New York branch of the NAACP to the White House for an audience with the President. It was one of the few important congregations of black leaders to visit the White House since Wilson's dismissal of William Monroe Trotter in 1914. Johnson's mission on this day was specific, though it carried a broad message. In the immediate aftermath of the Houston race riot, a court-martial had sentenced thirteen men to death; and the condemned were hanged in pre-dawn darkness, without review. A subsequent court-martial sentenced another sixteen soldiers to death, but that verdict came just days after a new policy from the War Department declared a suspension of military death sentences without Presidential review. And so the NAACP delegation arrived with a petition with 1,200 signatures requesting clemency for those Negro soldiers facing the gallows. Johnson stood as he read the document, which spoke, he claimed, for the "great mass of the Negro population of the United States," the twelve million patriotic Negroes, many of whom wanted nothing more than to express their loyalty through military service. It detailed the "long series of humiliating and harassing incidents" that had sparked the riots, all part of an ingrained anti-Negro culture that was becoming increasingly institutionalized inside the American military as it had long been in Southern communities.

The presentation moved Wilson deeply. He asked for more facts about the immolation at Estill Springs—about which he had heard nothing—and he expressed dismay "that such a thing could have taken place in the United States." The delegation pressed him to offer a public utterance against mob violence and lynching, but Wilson said that he did not think word from him would have any "special effect." When the gentlemen from Harlem disagreed—stressing that "his word would have greater effect than the word of any other man in the world"—Wilson promised to "seek an opportunity" to say something.

For more than half an hour, the President sat with the delegation. Johnson had seen Wilson before from a distance and found him an austere figure. Now, sitting only a few feet away, the President struck him as "very human. His head, no longer inclined forward, rested back easily, and the sternness of his face relaxed and, occasionally in a smile, became com-pletely lost." He asked questions about the Negro in America and even offered a few reminiscences of his boyhood in the South. After the meet-ing, Johnson confessed that he could not rid himself of "the conviction that at bottom there was something hypocritical about him." But, he noted, "I came out . . . with my hostility toward Mr. Wilson greatly shaken."

The President made good on his word on July 26, 1918, when he found his "opportunity" and released a thoughtful statement, which he tied to the war effort. "I allude to the mob spirit," he said, without pointing to a particular individual or region. "There have been many lynchings," he added, "and every one of them has been a blow at the heart of ordered law and humane justice." He declared such actions nothing less than un-Amer-ican. "We are at this very moment fighting lawless passion," Wilson stated, and lynchers only emulated Germany's disgraceful example by disregard-ing the sacred obligations of the law. He said, unequivocally, "Every American who takes part in the action of a mob or gives it any sort of countenance is no true son of this great Democracy, but its betrayer, and does more to discredit her by that single disloyalty to her standards of law and of right than the words of her statesmen or the sacrifices of her heroic boys in the trenches can do to make suffering peoples believe her to be their savior." He implored every Governor, law officer, and citizen to cooperate, "not passively merely, but actively and watchfully—to make an end of this disgraceful evil."

One month later, Wilson issued another race-related statement, this one based upon his review of the Houston riot cases, particularly those of the sixteen men facing the death penalty. He upheld six of the sentences—"because the persons involved were found guilty by plain evi-dence of having deliberately, under circumstances of shocking brutality, murdered designated and peaceably disposed civilians." The rest he com-muted to life imprisonment because the men were not shown to have caused any deaths, despite their engagement in riotous and mutinous be-havior. Wilson did not stop there. He said, "I desire the clemency here ordered to be a recognition of the splendid loyalty of the race to which these soldiers belong and an inspiration to the people of that race to fur-ther zeal and service to the country of which they are citizens and for the liberties of which so many of them are now bravely bearing arms at the very front of great fields of battle."

Not even James Weldon Johnson had made a case for the innocence of the six men who would be hanged. He acknowledged that President Wilson maintained his policy of reviewing death sentences from the courts-martial, and he praised his anti-lynching statement. In the autobiography he wrote fifteen years later, Johnson granted that his earlier "estimate of Mr. Wilson was actually colored and twisted by prejudice."

Four hundred thousand black American soldiers served during the war—in segregated units. Some camps were integrated, but the black soldiers trained separately. Most of the black regiments sent overseas were service units, digging trenches and burying bodies—the "nasty side of army life"; but forty thousand engaged in actual combat. To ease racial tensions, the War Department created a Negro officer training camp, so that black soldiers could take orders from men their own color. Whenever Negro soldiers stepped beyond the boundaries of segregation, they faced indignities; but the numbers in which they enlisted suggested that they were eager to prove their worthiness as first-class citizens. As the Texas Grand Master of the separate-but-equal Prince Hall Freemasonry said, "We believe that our second emancipation will be the outcome of this war. If the world is to be made 'safe for democracy,' that will mean us also." Even at a death rate more than twice that of the white American dough-boy, the black soldier was willing to stake his life on the promise that noble service would free him from segregation and mob violence.

Each pace forward incited efforts to push the Negro back. The war created enough circumstances in which the two races proved that they could coexist. But as 1918 drew the races into their closest contact ever, it also created the greatest repulsion. More lynchings than the nation had seen in a decade and a revitalized nationwide Ku Klux Klan lay just ahead. In addressing delegates from the National Race Congress at the White House on October 1, 1918, Wilson reminded the Negroes, "We all have to be patient with one another. Human nature doesn't make giant strides in a single generation. . . . I have a very modest estimate of my own power to hasten the process, but you may be sure that everything that I can do will be accomplished."

It both encouraged and disheartened African Americans to see the President's power at work when it came to challenging discrimination for another group—women, whose movement for suffrage began back in 1848 at a convention in Seneca Falls, New York. Even in the front lines of this surge for equality, division existed between those who supported the evolution of their cause by working within the system and the revolutionaries, who sought immediate change and were prepared to defy the law if it would help achieve it. Arguments over class and race within each division had impeded progress for two generations. For a few decades, the National American Woman Suffrage Association, headed by medical doctor Anna Howard Shaw and a former teacher, Carrie Chapman Catt, had made considerable headway. It was not enough for Alice Paul, a highly educated activist from Pennsylvania with legal training, who joined the more militant Congressional Union for Woman Suffrage, which she transformed into the National Woman's Party in 1916. Decades younger than the NAWSA leadership, she felt it was time to revolt.

For years Wilson had endorsed women's suffrage and received its proponents in the White House, even when they disagreed with his approach. He admired Dr. Shaw and Mrs. Catt, but as this inveterate drafter of constitutions told a delegation seeking his support for an equal suffrage amendment in January 1915, "I . . . am tied to a conviction, which I have had all my life, that changes of this sort ought to be brought about state by state."

To many, Wilson was hiding behind states' rights. A year later, he tried convincing another suffrage delegation otherwise, as he remained committed to pushing New Jersey to adopt a state amendment. "It may move like a glacier," Wilson told two hundred members of the Congressional Union at the Waldorf-Astoria, "but when it does move, its effects are permanent." After Wilson had spoken, an emboldened Mary Ritter Beard, wife of Columbia University historian Charles A. Beard, asked the President whether the Clayton Anti-Trust Act had been enacted state by state. "I do not care to discuss that," an annoyed President said, and the meeting came to an end, with visible disappointment. Even his unmarried daughter, Margaret, who could always appeal to his sense of reason, steadily urged him to back a federal amendment, and she pressured Colonel House as well.

The battle lines in the matter of women's suffrage were drawn more between generations than genders, as the issue was not yet of imperative concern to the American public. Not even Progressives and, more important, women themselves were of one mind on the subject. The issue was not just about voting, or even keeping women in their place; many enlightened people considered it the beginning of a breakdown in traditional family values. Theodore Roosevelt wrote, "Women do not really need the suffrage," though he did not think "they would do any harm with it." His two sisters opposed it; his younger wife supported it, mildly. Wilson was still unable to envisage a world in which women might play a strong political role. "Suffrage for women," he said one morning when his old friend Nancy Saunders Toy was staying at the White House, "will make absolutely no change in politics—it is the home that will be disastrously affected. Somebody has to make the home and who is going to do it if the women don't?" But, valuing people of intelligence exercising their democratic rights, Wilson strongly favored their enfranchisement; and, as he had promised, he applied personal and party pressure on each state legislature as it considered this question.

Growing numbers of disgruntled women continued to coerce the White House. For several months before Wilson's second inauguration, Alice Paul's National Woman's Party protested outside the Executive Mansion—several hundred "silent sentinels" every day, standing at the north gates, carrying banners. "Mr. President, how long must women wait for liberty?" was a favorite slogan; "Kaiser Wilson" was another. They reported at ten o'clock and remained until 4:30. Sometimes they chained themselves to the White House fence. Believing the angry protesters would thrive on opposition, the Administration instructed the police to take no action against them, thus limiting their press coverage.

On the first extremely cold day of their protests, the President sent Ike Hoover outside with a message for the dissidents. Just as they expected to be shooed from the vicinity, Hoover invited them all inside to the lower corridor of the White House, where the President specifically asked that they be served hot tea or coffee. "Excuse me, Mr. President," Hoover reported a moment later, "but they indignantly refused." Wilson asked that a servant carry hot bricks to the White House gates to provide warmth, a courtesy they accepted through the winter.

Although the passion of the suffragists moved him, in May 1917, Wilson wrote Mrs. Catt that he felt the time was inopportune for women to press their claim, as the Congress was consumed with the conduct of the war. The President continued his own efforts—lobbying state legislatures and urging the formation of a House committee to promote a Nineteenth Amendment to the Constitution, which had been defeated in that chamber three years earlier. When a mission of Russian diplomats arrived at the

White House in June, a boldly stenciled ten-foot-wide banner greeted them, declaring: "We, the women of America, tell you that America is not a democracy. Twenty million American women are denied the right to vote. President Wilson is the chief opponent of their national enfranchisement." Many women in the crowd expressed outrage that the protesters unfairly chose to speak for them; some cried "Treason!" Several men ripped the banner to pieces. Upon the President's orders, neither the police nor the Secret Service took any action other than maintaining order. Dr. Shaw of NAWSA said this sort of agitation only injured the suffrage cause; even sympathizers in Congress condemned the action. Alice Paul announced to the press, "We have ordered another banner with the same wording, and we intend to show it in the same place." The President wrote of the fracas to his daughter Jessie, "They certainly seem bent upon making their cause as obnoxious as possible."

On Bastille Day, Alice Paul's National Woman's Party took a different approach. It assembled sixteen socially prominent women—including the daughters and wives of distinguished Americans—to march quietly to the front gates of the White House. Carrying banners exclaiming "LIBERTY, EQUALITY, FRATERNITY," they refused to move on and waited to be arrested. It was an entirely peaceful demonstration, as courteous as a cotillion. An officer approached each woman, removed his hat, bowed, and advised her of the law she was breaking, before placing each of them under arrest. Even the crowd of thousands who turned out regularly to menace the protesters, watched in silence except for their quiet applause. Three days later a judge found the suffragists guilty of unlawful assembly and sentenced each to a twenty-five-dollar fine or sixty days in the District of Columbia workhouse in Occoquan, Virginia. They chose Occoquan.

No sooner were they incarcerated than the President summoned the District Commissioner in charge of the police. "Mr. Wilson was highly indignant," recalled Commissioner Louis Brownlow. "He told me that we had made a fearful blunder, that we never ought to have indulged these women in their desire for arrest and martyrdom, and that he had pardoned them and wanted that to end it." Brownlow then had the painful duty of informing the President that the women had refused his pardon. In the meantime, the incident provoked exactly what Wilson had feared— unwanted publicity. Newspapers ran accounts of the daughter of a former Secretary of State and the sister-in-law of a former Secretary of War being required to rise at 6:30, wear loose gray dresses, and eat hominy, cabbage, and vegetable soup. Most "unnecessarily humiliating" of all, reported *The New York Times*, was that the suffragists had been quartered with Negro women.

Wilson was further humiliated when Dudley Field Malone, the Collector of the Port of New York, decided to represent the women. The President met with his old friend for more than half an hour. Malone insisted that Wilson could enact national suffrage almost immediately if he sincerely believed in it. At that point, with the nation mounting its war effort, Wilson said he did not feel he could go to Congress with such a demand. Malone asked why Wilson considered it right to demand of Congress all the important legislation he had pushed through and not this measure.

"I know of nothing that has gone more to the quick with me or that has seemed to me more tragical than Dudley's conduct," Wilson wrote Colonel House, "—which came upon me like a bolt out of the blue. I was stricken by it as I have been by few things in my life." Rather than accept that he had inadequately justified his position, he dismissed Malone's new role in the women's rights movement as an overreaction. "Here is one more item of tragedy added to this time of madness. We must not let the madness touch us," he wrote House, replaying in his mind what Kipling had said about keeping his head when all about were losing theirs.

During the 1916 election, Malone had campaigned hard for Wilson, notably in the woman suffrage states; California, of course, had delivered the President his cliffhanging victory. Malone had promised the women there that if they reelected Wilson, he would devote himself to the passage of the federal suffrage amendment. Now Malone felt hypocritical working for an administration that would not allow him to honor that commitment. As England and Russia in the midst of the Great War had promised women national enfranchisement, he could not reconcile the President's position. Unless the government took a step in that direction, Malone asked, how could it "ask millions of American women in our homes, or toiling for economic independence in every line of industry, to give up by conscription their men and happiness to a war for Democracy in Europe, while these women citizens are denied the right to vote on the policies of the Government which demands of them such sacrifice?" He told the President, "It is high time that men in this generation . . . stood up to battle for the national enfranchisement of American women." On September 7, 1917, he tendered his resignation, which the President reluctantly accepted.

Wilson steadily continued his work on behalf of the movement at the state level. In the November 1917 elections, another five states embraced woman suffrage—most notably New York. Wilson had advanced the cause there by addressing a large delegation of its Woman Suffrage Party at the White House shortly before the election and then releasing his remarks to the press. Women had played a significant role in the war effort—not least of all the women of NAWSA, who sold a million dollars' worth of bonds. Praising their "ardor and efficiency," Wilson had insisted then that "this is the time for the states of this Union to take this action." In a post-election White House meeting, the woman leaders praised the President for his support; but even Mrs. Catt said "the time had come to grant the Federal amendment." This time, Wilson agreed.

Until she saw some actions to back the President's words, Alice Paul and her followers escalated their war for equality. They continued to write quotations on their banners that they thought would embarrass the President, such as the one that read "WE SHALL FIGHT FOR THE THINGS WHICH WE HAVE ALWAYS HELD NEAREST OUR HEARTS—FOR DEMOCRACY, FOR THE RIGHT OF THOSE WHO SUBMIT TO AUTHORITY TO HAVE A VOICE IN THEIR OWN GOVERNMENTS." They were, of course, quoting Wilson himself and were consequently immune from charges of sedition. When Alice Paul was hauled into court for obstructing traffic, she claimed she was exempt from the court's jurisdiction on the grounds that she and her sisterhood had no part in making the laws that brought her there. Paul was released, only to find herself back in court a few weeks later, at which time she was sentenced to Occoquan. There she demanded to be considered a "political prisoner" and began a hunger strike.

Wilson called for both a physician and a Commissioner of the District of Columbia to examine the prisoner's conditions. On November 9, 1917, Commissioner W. Gwynn Gardiner filed a detailed report, with the surprising observation that Miss Paul had volunteered that "she recognized the fact that President Wilson was a friend to the suffragists, but that they had determined upon picketing as a means of bringing the cause before the people of the country and keeping it before them." She stated further that she had decided upon this hunger strike as a means of "compelling those in authority to accede to her demands." Because she was physically frail and refused to eat, the workhouse insisted on force-feeding her through a tube that would be inserted down her throat. Gardiner consulted with Dr. William Alanson White, a renowned psychiatrist and superintendent of St. Elizabeth's Hospital, the government hospital for the insane. White explained that this was "an every-day occurrence" at his institution, that for twenty years he had been feeding patients in this manner with no ill effect, and he recommended it for Miss Paul. Her room, Gardiner reported, was "well-lighted, well-ventilated, and perfectly clean." On the night of November 14, however, Occoquan became Bedlam. After Paul had undergone her forced feeding, many of her fellow soldiers protested what they considered inappropriate indignities—including the wearing of prison stripes. Their obstinacy ignited what became known as the "Night of Terror," complete with threats and physical abuse.

By the first week of 1918, another vote on the women's suffrage amendment was advancing in the House of Representatives. Elizabeth Bass, who headed the Women's Bureau of the Democratic National Committee, sent the President a short letter wondering "if you know how a word or two from you today . . . would enthrone you forever in the hearts of the women of the United States as the second Great Emancipator." Of greater significance was Bass's observation that they were living in fast-changing times—"when all foundations are shifting," and even the most extreme advocates of states' rights had just abandoned their position and passed a Prohibition amendment, of which Wilson did not approve. On January 9, Wilson advised the Democratic members of the House Suffrage Committee to vote for the federal amendment "as an act of right and justice to the women of the country and of the world." The next day the House voted 274 to 136 in favor of the Nineteenth Amendment to the Constitution, without a single vote to spare in attaining the requisite two-thirds majority. Republicans supported the measure four to one, while Democrats, mostly from the South, split down the middle. A far more difficult fight lay ahead in the upper house.

All that year Wilson and the suffragist leaders lobbied Senators. The vote was set for September 30, and according to every straw poll, the amendment would be two votes shy of passage. On the twenty-eighth, women from NAWSA called on Secretary McAdoo to discuss eleventh-hour strategy. They handed him a list of Senators they believed might still be talked into voting for their cause. McAdoo looked it over and said he had already talked himself hoarse pleading the case. But the next morning, Sunday, he had an idea. The only possible means of winning was to have the President address the Senate. There were, unfortunately, two significant obstacles: Wilson did not discuss public questions on the Sabbath; and there was no precedent for a Chief Executive to address a chamber of Congress in order to influence a vote on pending legislation.

McAdoo called his father-in-law at ten o'clock that morning and stated his case. He said he did not believe anything at this point would change two votes; but, knowing how to appeal to the President's penchant for lost causes, he said, "I felt that since no President of the United States had ever spoken in favor of woman's suffrage, and that since we were fighting a war for democracy, it seemed to me that we could not consistently persist in refusing to admit women to the benefits of democracy on an equality with men." McAdoo argued that even if the speech fell on deaf ears within the legislature, the public, just weeks away from electing a new Congress, would hear his message. Wilson said that not only was there no precedent for such a speech but it would provoke resentment. At five o'clock that afternoon, Edith called McAdoo on the telephone to say that her husband was writing his speech.

At one o'clock the next day, Wilson appeared at the Capitol. The chamber quickly filled with Senators, their umbrage apparent. Through the "frigid atmosphere," he spoke for fifteen minutes, hoping that the "unusual circumstances of a world war in which we stand" justified his presence. He said, "I regard the concurrence of the Senate in the constitutional amendment proposing the extension of the suffrage to women as vitally essential to the successful prosecution of the great war of humanity in which we are engaged."

Wilson reminded his audience that the entire world was looking "to the great, powerful, famous Democracy of the West to lead them to the new day . . . and they think, in their logical simplicity, that democracy means that women shall play their part in affairs alongside men and upon an equal footing with them." In the past, some anti-suffragists had maintained that men's defense of the nation with bullets entitled them to ballots; for the first time, a Commander in Chief argued that the nation had made partners of the women in this war: "Shall we admit them only to partnership of suffering and sacrifice and toil," he asked, "and not to a partnership of privilege and right? This war could not have been fought, either by the other nations engaged or by America, if it had not been for the services of the women." He went further, saying, "This measure which I urged upon you is vital to the winning of the war." Just as women had helped in the war effort, so too would they help in drafting the peace: "We shall need their moral sense to preserve what is right and fine and worthy in our system of life as well as to discover just what it is that ought to be purified and reformed. Without their counsellings we shall be only half wise." The President asked the Senate to lighten his task by placing in his hands the "spiritual instruments" he needed to close the war.

He swung no votes that day. With victory still out of reach, the two factions of the suffrage movement joined forces, each side having learned from the other. Alice Paul softened her approach to President Wilson while Carrie Chapman Catt got tougher. Moving their armies to the Capitol, the two suffrage leaders privately assured Southern legislators that giving women the vote was not meant to diminish states' rights or augment Negroes' powers; it was simply about lifting the "sex restriction." Publicly, they targeted anti-suffrage legislators from both houses in the upcoming elections. A number of longtime Senators saw reason to worry. "The women have earned it," Wilson told Stockton Axson. "I am sorry it had to come in this way"—through the agitations of war—"but they must have what they have justly won."

With the young men of the American Expeditionary Force at last in the line of fire, Wilson considered virtually every act of Congress a measure of patriotism. That meant not only giving full voting rights to women but also seizing certain rights from other Americans. To ensure that the soldiers had the complete support of the Americans at home, Congress passed the Sedition Act on May 16, 1918. With the strong encouragement of Attorney General Gregory, this amendment to the Espionage Act of 1917 conferred certain policing powers upon the Postmaster General and further curbed citizens in expressing political opinions. Protest against this new law was vehement, but it found little backing in any branch of government.

When still teaching at Princeton, Wilson had written that the Sedition Act of 1798 had "cut perilously near the root of freedom of speech and of the press. There was no telling where such exercises of power would stop. Their only limitations and safeguards lay in the temper and good sense of the President and the Attorney General." Now as President, with Americans dying for their country, Wilson would brook no speech that even suggested sedition. He left the actual pursuit of violations to his hard-line Postmaster General and Attorney General. Both men were leery of the Socialist Party and the Industrial Workers of the World because both organizations had opposed American entry into the war, which they considered a capitalist struggle at the expense of the workers. Questions arose as to whether vocal opposition to the war qualified as seditious.

Paranoia permeated the nation. Local watchdog organizations formed to ferret out enemies within America's borders. The largest and best-organized group of this nature banded under the Justice Department's Bureau of Investigation. Calling itself the American Protective League, by 1918 it claimed over six hundred branches with 250,000 card-carrying members whose only real power was intimidation. Gregory boasted to McAdoo that after almost a year of operation, there had been only three instances of "objectionable" APL conduct.

The American Union Against Militarism—which became the American Civil Liberties Union—begged to differ. In August 1917, this left-leaning pacifist organization sent the President a list of recent cases they thought would convince him that civil liberty in America was being "seriously threatened under pressure of the war." The authors of the letter—including Lillian D. Wald and Roger Baldwin—provided evidence that constitutional rights were being overlooked. They cited unlawful arrests of people exercising their rights of free speech and peaceable assembly—meetings and parades that had been disrupted by the military, orders from overzealous District Attorneys, and arbitrary actions by Post Office officials who declared certain publications "unnmailable" because of their content. Wilson assigned the Attorney General to investigate the charges because he personally esteemed the people who had signed the letter. When the Postmaster General clamped down on eighteen periodicals, the President immediately received a letter from Max Eastman, Amos Pinchot, and John Reed, who asked, "Can it be necessary, even in war time, for the majority of a republic to throttle the voice of a sincere minority?" Again, Wilson intervened, writing Albert Burleson, "These are very sincere men and I should like to please them." The Postmaster General insisted that their opposition to the war, especially the conscription law, went so far as to "obstruct the Government in its conduct of the war." The matter quickly moved through the courts, until the Supreme Court ruled in favor of the government.

On June 16, 1918, Eugene Debs campaigned for the Socialist Party in Canton, Ohio, where he had just visited three comrades who were serving time in a workhouse for having encouraged young men to refuse induction into the Army. Debs kidded with his audience about the care he had to take in selecting his words, and then he proceeded to inform his 1,200 listeners that the government had been trying to suppress the Socialist message, that the master class had always taught and trained the workers "to believe it to be your patriotic duty to go to war to have yourselves slaughtered at their command." He urged his listeners "to know that you are fit for something better than slavery and cannon fodder," and he harangued the government for prosecuting those who resisted what the ruling class called "patriotic duty." Two weeks later, Debs was arrested and charged with ten counts of sedition.

At his trial in September, Debs's attorneys presented no witnesses, only the defendant himself, who spoke for two hours. The court found him guilty. Upon receiving a ten-year prison sentence, he spoke once more, telling the judge: "Your Honor, years ago I recognized my kinship with all living beings, and I made up my mind that I was not one bit better than the meanest on earth. I said then, and I say now, that while there is a lower class, I am in it, and while there is a criminal element I am of it, and while there is a soul in prison, I am not free." The words would echo for decades; but Woodrow Wilson still considered Debs a traitor.

Within months his case came before the Supreme Court. The Espionage Act of 1917 criminalized the conveyance of "information with intent to interfere with the operation or success of the armed forces of the United States or to promote the success of its enemies"; and, for all of Debs's elocutionary caution, the Justices considered his Canton speech an obstruction of military recruitment. In considering whether the defendant's conviction violated his First Amendment right to the freedom of speech, the Justices referred to a nearly identical case decided the preceding week, *Schenck v. United States*. The Court had ruled that an individual distributing leaflets urging opposition to the draft was not safeguarded. Justice Oliver Wendell Holmes, Jr., had written the unanimous opinion for the Court, which famously asserted that "the character of every act" depended upon its context.

The most stringent protection of free speech would not protect a man in falsely shouting fire in a theatre and causing a panic. . . .

The question in every case is whether the words used are used in such circumstances and are of such a nature as to create clear and present danger that they will bring about the substantive evils that Congress has a right to prevent. . . . When a nation is at war many things that might be said in time of peace are such a hindrance to its effort that their utterance will not be endured so long as men fight and that no Court could regard them as protected by any constitutional right.

Holmes wrote the opinion in the Debs case as well, which was also unanimous.

Woodrow Wilson felt Debs had violated every tenet of unity and loyalty that he held dear. The President was quick to note that Debs had every right to exercise his freedom of speech before the war. But, Wilson maintained, "once the Congress of the United States declared war, silence on his part would have been the proper course to pursue." It galled Wilson that while "the flower of American youth was pouring out its blood to vindicate the cause of civilization, this man, Debs, stood behind the lines, sniping, attacking, and denouncing them."

America entered a period of repression as egregious as any in American history. Members of the Cabinet manipulated the offensive laws, but Woodrow Wilson's fingerprints were all over them. "The new espionage act," wrote H. L. Mencken, "gives the Postmaster General almost absolute power to censor American magazines. He may deny the mails to any one that he doesn't like, for any reason or no reason. No crime is defined; no hearing is allowed; no notice is necessary; there is no appeal." Wilson periodically asked Postmaster Burleson to show leniency toward some potential scofflaws, especially left-wingers he knew to be intellectually sincere; but the government arrested 1,500 citizens in 1918 for little more than criticizing it; and close to 2,500 "enemy aliens" were interned during the war.

Worse than the actual suppression of written material was the atmosphere of suspicion the Administration created, one so noxious that it coerced most "law-abiding" citizens into censoring themselves, inhibiting one of the very freedoms for which America was fighting overseas. Only later did Mencken write, "Between Wilson and his brigades of informers, spies, volunteer detectives, perjurers and complaisant judges, and the Prohibitionists and their messianic delusion, the liberty of the citizen has pretty well vanished in America. In two or three years, if the thing goes on, every third American will be a spy upon his fellow citizens."

Wilson was not blind to the injustices his administration had imposed. But at a moment when many American soldiers were marching off to their deaths, he considered temporary restraints on civil liberties minor infringements. He conceded his own uncertainty about finding the right balance in his policies but not about erring on the side of precaution. As he wrote liberal activist Max Eastman: "I think that a time of war must be regarded as wholly exceptional and that it is legitimate to regard things which would in ordinary circumstances be innocent as very dangerous to the public welfare, but the line is manifestly exceedingly hard to draw and I cannot say that I have any confidence that I know how to draw it. I can only say that a line must be drawn and that we are trying, it may be clumsily but genuinely, to draw it without fear or favor or prejudice."

In the beastly hot summer of 1918, Wilson could no longer avoid another problem that had long troubled him. "I have been sweating blood over the question what it is right and feasible (*possible*) to do in Russia," he wrote Colonel House on July 8, months after that empire had collapsed and surrendered, leaving its problems for the Allies to solve. France and Britain abhorred the thought of Bolshevism spreading to their countries; and they realized that the German armies at the Eastern Front would now be reassigned to the Western Front, increasing their threat. Allied supplies were stockpiled in the northwesternmost cities of Murmansk and Archangel, which Russia could no longer defend. For months, the Allies relentlessly pressured the United States to join them in an invasion.

Wilson wanted no part of the plans. His recent forays into Mexico (where he had been ensnared his entire first term) and the Dominican Republic and Haiti (where American troops would remain mired until 1924 and 1934, respectively) had proved certain limitations of foreign policy: not even boundless military might offered a guarantee of stabilizing a foreign government. Although averse to Bolshevism, Wilson was not adverse. He believed armed resistance could easily backfire and that trying to stop a revolutionary movement with ordinary armies was "like using a broom to sweep back a great sea." Wilson continued to resist the Allies' pleas.

Lord Reading—a justice rendering temporary ambassadorial service in Washington—gathered that the President feared that once American troops were in Russia, some action by the French or British would interfere with Russian domestic affairs and suck America in even deeper. Reading reported to Prime Minister David Lloyd George that "the President is apprehensive lest any intervention should be converted into an anti-Soviet movement and an interference with the right of Russians to choose their own form of government." In their efforts to enlist American support, the French went so far as to send Henri Bergson to Washington, but the renowned philosopher failed in his efforts. Wilson had just read a report from an explorer named George Kennan—well versed in Russia (and a cousin of a teenager of the same name, who would later become an influential diplomat in the same region). He wrote the Administration of the need to eschew the Bolshevik government—as they were "usurpers," criminals, and enemies of the Allies, with nothing to offer them, not even the ability to restore order across Russia's vast geography. A massive Siberian intervention—involving as many as a million men—was then being staged to help White Russian forces overtake the Reds.

In the extreme opposite corner of Russia, seventy thousand interned Czech freedom fighters found themselves stranded in Vladivostok. They had been plotting to return to the front by journeying across the Pacific, where they would go by ship to America and on to France; but the Bolsheviks detained them. The Allies could only benefit from the addition to their ranks; and the Czechs' freedom-loving spirit appealed greatly to America. Philosopher and politician Tomáš Masaryk met with Wilson in Washington, and the President proved susceptible to the cause. On August 5, 1918, he agreed to commit military aid in the Siberian expedition—five thousand American troops to help protect the Allied stockpiles in the northwest and seven thousand more to help the Czech legions in the southeast. If nothing else, an American presence in Russia could keep a closer eye on imperialistic Japan, which saw an opportunity to harpoon Russian territory for itself. Masaryk thanked Wilson for his action. "Your name," he wrote him, ". . . is openly cheered in the streets of Prague,—our nation will forever be grateful to you and to the people of the United States."

Unfortunately, by the time American and Allied troops reached the northern military stores, winter had put any defensive operations on ice, and the war on the Eastern Front had shut down. The United States asked Japan to match its troops, but they sent twelve thousand men instead.

Within months, seventy thousand Japanese troops had arrived, with more on the way; and they had seized the Chinese Eastern Railway. "The presence of our troops in Siberia is being used by the Japanese as a cloak for their own presence and operations there," Secretary Baker wrote the President, "and the Czecho-Slovak people are quite lost sight of in any of the operations now taking place." Baker suggested that the longer America stayed, the more Japanese would arrive; but it seemed just as dangerous to leave the Japanese unchecked as they increased their presence. The United States would remain for several more years, seeing once again that military interventions—like the memories of invaded nations—are never short. While the American Expeditionary Force Siberia was not the actual start of the subsequent Cold War, it planted the seeds of distrust that Russians would recall decades later.

As the war in Europe expanded, the President's life contracted. He continued to delegate the running of specific operations to his Generals, Cabinet Secretaries, and Commissioners, leaving him to focus on the panoramic vision of the war's aims. While others sorted out details, he treasured his time alone with Edith, and socialized with few people beyond his family. He obeyed Dr. Grayson's advice to the letter, allowing for as much daily exercise and leisure as possible. He played golf every morning—at least nine holes, knowing he could play eighteen on weekends. In the winter, the White House staff painted his golf balls red, so that he could spot them more easily on the snow-covered links. Nothing eased his worries more than visits to the theater. He especially enjoyed the vaudeville offerings at B. F. Keith's Theatre just across Fifteenth Street from the White House grounds. He tended to enjoy these shows more than dramatic plays, because even a bad variety act was sure to be followed by something amusing. The family delighted in hearing him laugh.

Beyond the diversion, an evening at Keith's offered the President a microcosm of America, a mixture of ethnicities presenting all-American entertainment. Any given night featured a variety of animal acts, circus acrobatics, classical and popular music, and comedy. A Hungarian-born Jew named Erik Weisz performed feats of magic and "escapology" as Harry Houdini; and English-born Vernon Castle and his wife, Irene, introduced American audiences to the tango and fox-trot. Countless Italian-, Irish-, and Jewish-American comedians became headliners, as lacing their monologues with hearty ethnic humor, and laughing at themselves before others could, proved an effective means of integrating their people into white, Protestant America. Negro storytelling was a popular feature as well—usually mocking the colored man's laziness or ignorance. The sketches were good-natured, no more derogatory in content than those of any other ethnicity; the only difference, of course, was that white people in black makeup delivered the anecdotes. These "darkey stories" and minstrel songs carried Wilson back to his childhood in Dixie. He was a devoted fan of George Primrose, a tap-dancing fireball in blackface; and in the privacy of the Oval Room upstairs at the White House, Woodrow would frequently slip a record on the Victrola and break into a spirited jig solely for Edith's entertainment. She marveled at how light on his feet he was, and he often said he envied Primrose and "wished he could exchange jobs" with him.

Nobody dominated the current stage more than George M. Cohan, who came from a family of Irish Catholic vaudevillians and wrote dozens of plays and revues and hundreds of songs. During the war they turned unusually patriotic, and his song "Over There" became America's wartime anthem. It was a rousing call to arms whose lyrics announced that "the Yanks are coming." Wilson could not get the number out of his head; and at a time when he anguished over dead and wounded soldiers, he often sang it to himself. Stockton Axson noticed that his voice invariably broke whenever he reached the last line—"And we won't come back till it's over over there."

Remarkable for someone whose health had been so fragile all his life, the President maintained his strength through the war. Apart from the occasional cold that kept him in bed, he did suffer two medical incidents, neither neurological. On April 19, 1918, while taking part in a campaign to promote Liberty Bonds, Wilson dismounted from a British tank and set his left hand down upon a red-hot exhaust pipe. He suffered serious burns, which required dressing his hand for months. "Now I am going about like a hotel waiter with a white glove over the bandages," Wilson wrote his daughter Jessie, ". . . feeling as if I ought to be handing something to somebody!" (The President's insurance company refused to pay indemnity on the grounds that he was ambidextrous and, therefore, not incapacitated.) And in the early fall, Wilson's nasal passages became so congested that he went weeks without breathing properly or sleeping well. Dr.

Grayson discovered polyps and determined that they should be removed. Wilson agreed to a polypectomy but insisted the procedure be kept secret. Without telling anybody but their respective wives, Wilson and Grayson sneaked out of the White House on September 7 and went to a local doctor, who removed the growths. The operation proved to be more complicated than anybody had anticipated, but neither the press nor the public ever had an inkling their President had been ill. It would not be the last time Dr. Grayson and the Wilsons would keep a medical matter from not only the public but even the innermost circles of the White House. For the moment, Grayson believed the President could live another ten years, even endure a third term—"if nothing untoward happened."

From the moment America entered the war, Woodrow Wilson proved to be a formidable Commander in Chief, directing the conversion of a peacetime nation into the globe's mightiest military-industrial complex, one in which every citizen played a role. He ruled mostly with his rhetoric, which remained as sharp as a bayonet. On September 27, he kicked off the Fourth Liberty Loan drive saying, "The common will of mankind has been substituted for the particular purposes of individual states." While the doughboys continued to lead the Allies to one victory after another, the nations of Europe—the Allied and Central Powers alike—could already envision the future. "Individual statesmen may have started the conflict," Wilson said that night, "but neither they nor their opponents can stop it as they please. It has become a peoples' war, and peoples of all sorts and races, of every degree of power and variety of fortune, are involved in its sweeping processes of change and settlement."

Wilson presented truths he now considered axiomatic: a nation's military power should not determine the fortunes of its people; strong nations should not be free to wrong weak nations; people should be ruled by their own will and choice, not by arbitrary and irresponsible force; there should be certain common standards of right and privilege; and the assertion of right should not be haphazard but the result of "common concert to oblige the observance of common rights." The audience stood and cheered, and the government raised $7 billion with this bond.

Two days later, Bulgaria became the first of the Central Powers to surrender; and independence spread across the region. Within eight days, Poland declared itself an independent state; the following week a provisional government of Czechoslovakia formed; and eleven days later a council established itself in Budapest preparing to create a Hungarian nation separate from Austria. The Germans, recognizing the inevitable, realized that their best hope for rational terms of surrender was with the opponent they had fought for the shortest time. On October 6, 1918, Prince Max von Baden, the German Imperial Chancellor, formally requested the President of the United States "to take steps for the restoration of peace, to notify all belligerents of this request, and to invite them to delegate Plenipotentiaries for the purpose of taking up negotiations." Prince Max accepted as a basis of those negotiations Wilson's Fourteen Points and his pronouncements in his address of September 27.

Wilson requested explication. He presumed Max's letter meant that Germany accepted his terms, that further discussion was warranted only to sort out the practical details, and that German withdrawal of all her armies to German territory was implicit in this acceptance. Another volley of notes discussed the American demand that the process of evacuation and the conditions of an armistice all be matters left to the judgment of the American and Allied governments and that no arrangement could be accepted by the United States "which does not provide absolutely satisfactory safeguards and guarantees of the maintenance of the present military supremacy of the armies of the United States and of the Allies in the field." On October 12, the Germans accepted Wilson's demands, but their army kept fighting. Days later, Germany agreed to cease submarine warfare; and by the end of the month, the Allied commanders met to discuss means of rendering Germany militarily impotent. While the Kaiser went into seclusion in Belgium, refusing to abdicate, Sultan Mehmed VI of the Ottoman Empire requested terms of capitulation, as did the Emperor of Austria. At the end of the first week of November, Prince Max sent a delegation of diplomats to France to negotiate specifics of his nation's surrender and then announced his resignation.

Before Wilson could claim victory in the Great War, he had to engage in one last battle—the midterm Congressional elections of 1918. Although politicians had to some degree abided since January by Wilson's decree of adjourning politics, each party longed to blame the other for the nation's woes and to claim its successes. The Republicans were powerless so long as they remained mute, as the successful culmination of the war put the Democrats at an advantage. By the end of that summer, the Republicans realized they could bite their tongues no longer. Republican National

Committee chairman Will Hays toured the country repudiating the Administration's policies; in August, Senator Lodge spoke out against the Fourteen Points; in September, Republican Congressmen urged the election of a Republican Congress; on October 24, Colonel Roosevelt wired three influential Republican Senators, encouraging them to reject the Fourteen Points. While Germany had already consented to those terms, Roosevelt said, "such a peace would represent not the unconditional surrender of Germany but the conditional surrender of the United States."

Wilson intended to refrain from campaigning, and he instructed his Cabinet not to embark on political tours. Roosevelt's comments, however, warranted a Presidential response. In stressing the critical nature of the times, he boiled his argument down to a peculiarly political point:

> If you have approved of my leadership and wish me to continue to be your unembarrassed spokesman in affairs at home and abroad, I earnestly beg that you will express yourself unmistakably to that effect by returning a Democratic majority to both the Senate and the House of Representatives. I am your servant and will accept your judgment without cavil, but my power to administer the great trust assigned me by the Constitution would be seriously impaired should your judgment be adverse, and I must frankly tell you so because so many critical issues depend upon your verdict.

He emphasized the need for "unified leadership" in the nation, which a Republican Congress would divide. Adding to this strangely inappropriate statement, Wilson said, "The return of a Republican majority to either House of the Congress would, moreover, certainly be interpreted on the other side of the water as a repudiation of my leadership." In ordinary times, he said, he would not feel at liberty to make such a public appeal. "But these are not ordinary times."

"Criticism and ridicule," to use Tumulty's terms, were hurled at Wilson, justifiably. In politicizing the war, he had committed a serious gaffe. He had not only "lowered himself," as Secretary Lane noted privately, but he had also diminished his constituents. Outside the capital, Republicans had joined the war effort as much as Democrats; and the President's message seemed to ignore their contributions, to say nothing of the Republican support he had received within the Capitol. Democrats offered numerous examples of Presidents from Washington to TR who had made similar electoral appeals. Even Lincoln midwar had campaigned by cautioning the electorate against "swapping horses in midstream." By Election Day, however, some simply made Wilson the whipping boy for the staggering confusion in the world.

Western Civilization lay prostrate from the most convulsive four years it had ever known. Four dynasties that had long dominated much of the world had fallen; and the combat itself produced stunning statistics: 885,000 British soldiers died, as had 1,400,000 French (more than 4 percent of their population) and 1,811,000 Russians; the Central Powers lost over 4,000,000 soldiers. All together, close to 10,000,000 soldiers died in the Great War, and more than 21,000,000 were wounded; counting civilian deaths, as the result of disease, famine, massacres, and collateral damage, somewhere between 16,500,000 and 65,000,000 people died—1.75 percent of the population of the participating nations. Wilson could already sense that the men in the trenches on both sides were undergoing an emotional change, that they would "return to their homes with a new view and an impatience of all mere political phrases, and will demand real thinking and sincere action." With American soldiers still in harm's way, Wilson resented that the Republicans—especially Roosevelt and Lodge—used the final weeks of the campaign to clamor for "the undesirable and impossible," namely "a vengeful peace." Wilson would not engage in that argument. "So far as my being destroyed is concerned," he wrote Senator Henry F. Ashurst, "I am willing if I can serve the country to go into a cellar and read poetry the remainder of my life. I am thinking now only of putting the US into a position of strength and justice. I am now playing for 100 years hence."

The United States had undergone profound changes of its own, arguably more in the last two years than at any other time in its history. Such paroxysms offered voters countless reasons to ignore Wilson's appeal for a Democratic Congress. Conscription and governmental restrictions—especially of gasoline and coal—persisted; tax rates remained at unprecedented highs; race relations dipped to historic lows; and hatred of foreigners and contention over labor prevailed.

Despite the impending victory in Europe, America was suffering. Naïveté and idealism had soured into skepticism and disillusionment; and influenza spiked in the United States that fall, killing in a single week almost five thousand people in Philadelphia, to name but one city. The disease sent more than a quarter of the nation to bed, killing more than a half million Americans. Many public events and venues—including political rallies and even Keith's Theatre in Washington—shut down. Many voters were either too ill or too afraid of getting ill to go to the polls. Those who took their chances found many of their fellow citizens wearing face masks.

While Republican candidates vociferously challenged the President's request for political support, Wilson fell silent, right up to Election Day. On November 5, turnout was light, but the message was emphatic. Republicans took control of both chambers of Congress. In the House, they picked up twenty-five seats, which marked more than a one-hundred-seat gain since Wilson had entered the White House, giving them the majority and the speakership that went with it. In the Senate, Republicans gained seven seats—reclaiming, at last, their pre-Wilson majority. Despite his joy that the war was ending, Wilson privately revealed that he was "of course disturbed by the result of Tuesday's elections, because they create obstacles to the settlement of the many difficult questions which throng so on every side."

No longer the peacetime nation that long disavowed foreign entanglements, America had become a mighty fortress, the first industrial superpower of the twentieth century. The country boasted a towering infrastructure for a massive system of defense, replete with the machinery for further expansion. Its heavy industries had demonstrated their ability to work in concert with the government and one another, becoming proficient if not expert in mass production. Because of its vast natural resources, the United States could feed not only itself but the rest of the world as well.

America had become an extroverted nation, a force of morality for all humanity. It was prepared to unleash its power whenever necessary—to protect its citizens and their globalizing interests and to stand vigil over the rest of mankind. Colonel House believed the war had given Wilson "a commanding opportunity for unselfish service." He told the President that the great figures in history—from Alexander to Napoleon—"had used their power for personal and national aggrandizement"; but Wilson now had the rare opportunity to "use it for the general good of mankind."

While it was Woodrow Wilson's intention to lead his nation into a millennium, he now faced a hostile incoming Congress. Notwithstanding, he remained confident that "by one means or another the great thing we have to do will work itself out." After all, he reminded one junior member of the Administration, "I have an implicit faith in Divine providence. . . ."

PART FOUR

13

ISAIAH

*The Spirit of the Lord God is vpon me, because the
Lord hath anointed me, to preach good tidings vnto
the meek, hee hath sent me to binde vp the broken
hearted, to proclaime libertie to the captiues . . .*

—ISAIAH, LXI:1

At noon on Thursday, November 7, 1918, the United
Press Association's office in Paris cabled its headquarters in New York that Germany and the Allies had signed
the Armistice. Within three minutes, the national censors
had approved its dissemination; and within half an hour,
word had spread nationwide.

By one o'clock, all of New York City's bells and sirens
had sounded, and similar demonstrations across the country followed. People in Manhattan poured into the streets—
in what *The New York Times* called "a delirious carnival of
joy which was beyond comparison with anything ever seen
in the history of New York." Factories in Boston closed,
and parades spontaneously erupted through the town. Chicago's stores, offices, munitions plants, and City Hall shut
down, while its opera company interrupted rehearsal and
broke into "The Star-Spangled Banner." In Columbus,
Ohio, the massive crowds surrounding the State House demanded remarks from Governor James M. Cox. And in
Washington, D.C., people gravitated to the South Lawn of

the White House, where the euphoric crowd, dancing and tossing their hats in the air, waited for the President to appear. Nell McAdoo was leaving the Treasury Building, only to have a total stranger throw his arms around her and kiss her. Edith Wilson bustled to her husband's study, urging him to the portico, where he might address the gathering below, but he refused. He was one of the few men in the world who knew for a fact that this national hysteria was based on a false report.

Correspondents in Europe soon got their stories straight, and the next day the New York *Globe* characterized the misinformation as "the greatest and most cruel hoax in the history of journalism." The source of the falsehood was never discovered, but many suspected a German agent had perpetrated the deception "to create popular desire and demand among the Allied people for the German-sought armistice." Wrote Arthur Hornblow, Jr., a young intelligence officer, "From a psychological point of view the best possible way of making the public *want* an armistice would be to tell them that there *was* an armistice, and let them taste of the joy that would naturally await upon the news." That very day, in fact, German delegates were on their way to surrender at a secret site.

Marshal Foch spent the night on the outskirts of the village of Rethondes in the forest of Compiègne. At dawn, a train carried him, his staff, and British officers to an obscured railroad siding. Around seven, another train—including a carriage still marked with Napoleon III's coat of arms—shuttled the German plenipotentiaries to another siding in the woods. At nine, the German representatives walked the heavily guarded hundred yards that separated the trains and entered the Wagon Lits Company car 2419D. After formal salutations, the teams sat across from each other at a long wooden table. Foch told his interpreter to ask the Germans what they wanted. Matthias Erzberger, the civilian head of the German delegation, said, "We have come to receive the Allied Powers' proposals for an armistice." An offended Foch interrupted to say, "Tell these gentlemen that I have no proposals to make to them." The Frenchman made motions to leave, when another member of the German team interceded, asking Foch to put semantics aside. Count Alfred von Oberndorff said they had come—after receiving a note from President Wilson—to accept Foch's terms.

The parley proceeded, but not without hiccups. For more than a week, Germany had been in the middle of a revolution. Sailors had mutinied; Bolsheviks were seizing power across the country; and Kaiser Wilhelm clung to his throne. And so, while Foch had given his enemies seventy-two hours in which to sign the terms of surrender, Erzberger questioned his legal ability to do so. The Kaiser did not abdicate until November 9— when he retreated to Holland, where he would spend the rest of his days in what he considered temporary exile. As the clock was running out, a second team of German diplomats arrived, announcing that a Republic had been proclaimed under a Socialist Chancellor. Several hours later, they received the requisite authorization.

Wilson spent the morning of Sunday the tenth with Edith at services in the Presbyterian Church. They lunched alone and took a long drive in the afternoon. Several Bollings joined them for an anxious dinner, after which Edith's mother said to her son-in-law, "I do wish you would go right to bed; you look so tired." Woodrow said he wished he could—"but I fear The Drawer; it always circumvents me; wait just a moment until I look." He returned with four or five long encrypted cables, which he handed to Edith. Her brother Randolph stayed until one o'clock, helping her decode the important messages, though none contained the news the world awaited. Back in the train car outside Rethondes, the delegates ironed out minor wrinkles; and shortly after five o'clock in the morning Paris time, they signed the documents. It was agreed that the Armistice would officially begin on the eleventh hour of that eleventh day of the eleventh month. Around three o'clock Washington time, word reached the White House in a series of telegrams from Colonel House, who was in France. Together Edith and Woodrow decoded his cable: "Autocracy is dead. [Long live] democracy and its immortal leader. In this great hour my heart goes out to you in pride, admiration and love." Edith would later recount that stunning moment in which they simply stood mute, "unable to grasp the full significance of the words."

The President caught a few hours of sleep before he issued a simple announcement that the Armistice had been signed and that work was suspended that day for all government employees. "A supreme moment of history has come," he handwrote. "The hand of God is laid upon the nations. He will show them favour, I devoutly believe, only if they rise to the clear heights of His own justice and mercy." Pandemonium broke out once again across the country and in the major capitals of the world. Wilson spent the rest of the morning in his study writing the speech he would deliver at one o'clock that afternoon.

Wearing a black tailcoat and light gray pants, he strode before the Congress. A standing ovation welcomed him, the audience's cheers extending to the gallery as the presiding officers permitted the spectators to join in the demonstration. Wilson quieted the chamber and launched into defining the terms to which the Germans had agreed in "these anxious times of rapid and stupendous change." Eleven military clauses pertained to the Western Front, from the cessation of operations to the immediate evacuation of invaded countries; five clauses dictated Germany's actions on the eastern frontier, including its abandonment of territory that had belonged to Russia, Romania, or Turkey before August 1, 1914. Germany had one month in which to capitulate unconditionally in East Africa; and similar terms applied to all hostilities at sea, including the surrender of submarines and surface warships, as well as the Allied freedom of access to and from the Baltic and Black Seas and the evacuation of seized Russian war vessels. The existing Allied blockade would continue. Repatriation of all civilians from the Allied or Associated nations must occur within a month. Applause interrupted several of these points, its intensity commensurate with the severity of the terms against the Germans. The mention of the return of Alsace-Lorraine to France, for example, brought the spectators to their feet. Any suggestions of leniency toward the enemy met silence. After modestly reciting all thirty-five terms of the Armistice, the President of the United States declaimed one last sentence. "The war," he said, "thus comes to an end."

America had won a decisive victory. Even Senator La Follette, who had sat silent until then, broke into applause. Arizona Senator Henry F. Ashurst dined with French Ambassador Jusserand in the Senate restaurant, only to see the diplomat burst into tears of joy. Cheering throngs lined the streets as Wilson returned to the White House, and for weeks praise was heaped upon him wherever he went. King George V sent a "message of congratulation and deep thanks in my own name and that of the people of this empire." The next day, *The New York Times* lauded the nation and, even more, Woodrow Wilson, whose "clear vision of the moral objects for which the nations took up arms against Germany . . . won for him very early acknowledged pre-eminence as the spokesman of the allied cause." As most of the world agreed, "He has been a great leader."

Washington celebrated all day, sweeping even Wilson into the festivities. November 11 happened to be the birthday of the King of Italy, and the Italian Ambassador was celebrating the occasion that night with a ball. A little before eleven o'clock, the President proposed to Edith that they crash the party. The Ambassador was only too happy to welcome a giddy Wilson, who toasted the King and lingered for another hour. Back at the White House, Woodrow and Edith sat on a couch by her bedroom fireplace, where he read a chapter from the Bible before retiring.

The next morning the President felt the first undertow of politics amid the waves of congratulation. The mere possibility that Wilson himself would attend the Peace Conference caused considerable controversy, at home and abroad, as its location and leadership could alter the outcome. Two neutral nations, Switzerland and the Netherlands, offered to host the meeting, which meant Wilson might preside; but the great blood-soaked battleground, France, felt entitled to hold the event. Colonel House reported from Paris that the French thought Wilson should not even appear for the negotiations. A ceremonial visit would be welcome, but even Americans in France, he said, "are practically unanimous in the belief that it would be unwise for you to sit in," for fear "that it would involve a loss of dignity and your commanding position." It would certainly overshadow House's own presumed position there. Premier Clemenceau got word to Wilson that "he hoped you will not sit in the Congress because no head of a State should sit there. The same feeling prevails in England."

Wilson understood the situation but considered his presence nonnegotiable. He maintained that he played the same role in the United States that Prime Ministers played in their countries. "The fact that I am head of the state," he wrote House, "is of no practical consequence." As journalist David Lawrence observed, "To have stayed in America and sent a member of his Cabinet as head of the delegation would have permitted the Prime Minister of Great Britain and the Premiers of the other countries to outrank the chairman of the American delegation." The President would never accept such an arrangement, as it would belittle both the role of the United States in the peace talks and the influence America had exerted in defining the aims of the war. Wilson already inferred that the French and English leaders wished to exclude him for fear he might lead the weaker nations against them. Beyond that, the more Wilson saw of the Allies' postwar posturing, the more convinced he became that they would insist upon "a peace of force and vengeance." The President, on the other hand, contended that only on "a peace of justice could a stabilized Europe be rebuilt."

More than ever, Wilson believed his League of Nations was essential to the new world order. An organization in which every sovereign member state had pledged to discuss disputes before going to war, he insisted, was the only way to prevent future local disagreements from turning global. Wilson also believed this league had to be an integral part of the Peace Treaty, not an afterthought. "Such was his faith," observed Dr. Grayson, "and he was fully aware that he himself must be the chief apostle of that faith . . . in the face of many who called themselves 'realists' and would demand that the business of the day be dealt with rather than future contingencies." Wilson's decision to head the American Peace Commission was less a matter of convention than of conscience. In the words of Cary Grayson, "He *must* go."

Not everybody shared Wilson's vision, of either America or the world. Less than two weeks after the Armistice, Theodore Roosevelt was building opposition to Wilson's plans and support for his own possible Presidential run in 1920. In a letter to fellow imperialist Rudyard Kipling, he called the League of Nations a "product of men who want everyone to float to heaven on a sloppy sea of universal mush." Even though he had recently been bedridden with lumbago, arthritis, and the symptoms of what would prove to be an embolism of the lung, TR continued to write world leaders and dictate newspaper editorials denouncing Wilson and his Fourteen Points. Meanwhile, Wilson quickly assembled his team of four Peace Commissioners.

The President sought associates less to help craft his peace plan than to execute it. He presumed Colonel House's participation, though a few of House's recent comments had made him look twice at the man he had once called his "second personality." He found Secretary of State Lansing unimaginative but dutiful, and his absence would have presented an overt diplomatic breach. He thought Secretary McAdoo, who had literally made the American trains run on time during the war, while also heading the Treasury Department and overseeing domestic and international war loans, would be enormously useful applying his expertise to prostrated Europe; but, after years of public service, McAdoo was exhausted and so were his financial assets. Three days after the Armistice, he tendered his resignation to his father-in-law. He and Nell would leave for a three-month holiday in Santa Barbara before settling in New York, where he would launch a lucrative law practice and contemplate a run for the Presidency. It would be an ambition Wilson would never fully support. He believed McAdoo was a man of action and that the next President would inherit a world that required a man of reflection. Wilson replaced his son-in-law at the Treasury with Congressman Carter Glass.

Although Secretary Baker was inexpert in military matters, his proficiency during the war would have made him a worthy counselor at the talks. But with Lansing absent, McAdoo departing, and the sudden announcement by Attorney General Gregory that he would be tendering his resignation for "pecuniary" reasons, everybody thought it best to keep Baker in the Cabinet Room, where he could keep a steady hand on the rudder. He recommended General Tasker Bliss, who had served as the Army's chief of staff and on the Supreme War Council in France.

The final chair became somewhat controversial, as Wilson hoped to provide at least the suggestion of nonpartisanship. Because the Senate had to approve all treaties, several prominent Republicans in the upper house were mentioned, Henry Cabot Lodge chief among them. He was not only the leading Republican Senator, but he also chaired the Senate Foreign Relations Committee. His well-known enmity toward the President kept anybody from seriously considering the idea, though pundits ever since have suggested that if chosen, he would have ensured passage of the Treaty.

Recognizing that he would have enough foreign adversaries to contend with at the conference table, Wilson chose not to borrow trouble by commissioning his bitterest foe. Beyond that, he believed the Constitution prohibited appointing Lodge, or any other legislator, because of the stipulation that "no Senator or Representative shall, during the time for which he was elected, be appointed to any civil office under the authority of the United States, which shall have been created."

Wilson's opponents would further question the President's right even to negotiate a treaty, but as he had stated as a college professor, a President "may guide every step of diplomacy and to guide diplomacy is to determine what treaties must be made." The Senate possessed the power to disapprove of a treaty, but the executive branch of the American government could dictate its terms.

Tumulty recommended Elihu Root—TR's Secretary of State, a former United States Senator, and a Nobel Peace Prize laureate. But Wilson worried about Root's conservatism and his aggressive opposition to the Administration's early policy of neutrality. William Howard Taft was also considered, but the idea of a former President serving as an aide to a sitting President seemed awkward for both parties.

Eventually, Wilson settled on a seasoned diplomat, Henry White—who had served in Roosevelt's administration as the First Secretary in London under Ambassador Hay and subsequently as TR's Ambassador to Italy and then to France. Roosevelt called him the "most useful man in the entire diplomatic service." Republicans—Lodge among them—immediately denounced the appointment as cosmetic, dismissing White as a Republican in name only. With the delegation filled, Woodrow Wilson prepared for Paris. A page from one of his own books reminded him that "the initiative in foreign affairs, which the President possesses without any restriction whatever, is virtually the power to control them absolutely." The Senate—even Democrats—already felt Wilson was freezing them out.

In the course of a long conversation about postwar hopes, Wilson received advice from Stockton Axson, who recommended that he gather at the White House all the leaders in the American war effort, Democrats and Republicans alike. He hoped Wilson might imbue them with a sense of his personal gratitude and then say "that the worst and hardest was yet to come . . . in the readjustment of the world," and "that their cooperation, their loyalty to the country, and to the great cause, will be even more needed then, than it was during the war." Edith looked up from her knitting and concurred. Axson insisted that Wilson could have the leaders from both sides of the aisle eating out of his hand. Wilson acknowledged the wisdom of the notion but said there was no place large enough to hold that many people. Axson recommended the East Room. The President nodded and even conceded that it "would be a step that would help to suppress party opposition." But he never acted upon the idea, and antagonism festered.

By the time Wilson tried to rally the Congress behind him in his sixth Annual Message on the State of the Union, the lawmakers felt marginalized. He entered the overflowing chamber on December 2, 1918, to what one onlooker called an "ominous silence." Even delivering a patriotic speech did little to thaw his audience. Starting with an evaluation of the nation's war effort, Wilson attributed most of its success to "the mettle and quality of the officers and men we sent over and of the sailors who kept the seas, and the spirit of the nation that stood behind them." He singled out various bureaus and constituencies that had contributed to the nation's success—especially America's women. He spoke of the specific challenges ahead as the country returned to a peacetime economy. Still, little received applause, even when his supporters tried to incite an ovation. Secretary Daniels found the Congressional reserve nothing short of "churlish." But one diplomat's wife, who viewed the proceedings through her opera glasses, wrote in her diary that "the President's *complete* disregard of the Senate following on top of his very tactless appeal to the country to return a Democratic Congress, has made him just about as thoroughly and completely unpopular in his own country as any president has been or could be."

Wilson concluded his speech by announcing his intention to leave for Paris. He reminded the Congress that the Central empires had accepted the bases of peace that he had outlined to the Congress the prior January and that they were ideals for which American soldiers had fought. Now, he explained, "I owe it to them to see to it, so far as in me lies, that no false or mistaken interpretation is put upon them, and no possible effort omitted to realize them." Wilson said it was his duty to "play my full part in making good what they offered their life's blood to obtain."

Toward that end, Wilson said in parting, "May I not hope . . . that in the delicate tasks I shall have to perform on the other side of the sea . . . I may have the encouragement and the added strength of your united support?" Emphasizing the magnitude of his undertaking, he assured the lawmakers, "I am the servant of the nation. I can have no private thought or purpose of my own in performing such an errand." He said he would make his absence as brief as possible, hoping to return having translated into action "the great ideals for which America has striven."

Even before Wilson had exited the Capitol, it was clear that both the House and Senate were divided. His valedictory wishes felt labored, and the response was the "ice bath" the Republicans had promised. One Washington Brahmin, Caroline Astor Drayton Phillips, kept her eye on Edith Wilson as she departed, and it was the first time the woman had seen the First Lady look "pale and stern and terribly sad." The next day, Republicans in both houses did what they could to constrain the President. Senator Knox of Pennsylvania offered a resolution that would limit America's role at the Peace Conference to those matters germane to America's entry into the war, which would postpone discussions involving laws of the sea and a League of Nations. Senator Sherman of Illinois denounced the

President for leaving the country and asked his colleagues to declare his absence "an inability to discharge the powers and duties" of his office. More than that, he accused Wilson of "an act of legislative and executive sabotage against the government" so long as Congress was in session and domestic conditions were unstable.

Amid such hostility, the President still possessed the ability to exude what some considered a spiritual glow. No fan of Wilson, Mrs. Phillips, for one, had felt "a sensation of light and warmth" when the President had spoken. "My heart and mind became filled with confidence in the President, with faith in his ideals," she wrote in her diary. As Woodrow Wilson boarded his midnight train for Hoboken, Mrs. Phillips foresaw for him a "hard and bitter fight at the Peace Congress." She felt "that he was sacrificing all personal ambition to obtain what he believes to be a paramount necessity for the world." She believed "that he will reveal the . . . subconscious ideal, which lies in the souls of men all over the world, for something far better than we have ever known."

And so the *George Washington* set sail on December 4 and landed in France on the thirteenth. Woodrow Wilson had jettisoned any doubts the dissidents might have instilled about the world's readiness for his ideals. The unprecedented sendoff in New York harbor made him feel that failure to achieve his goals was not an option. He proceeded to the historic receptions in Brest and Paris and London, which only boosted his confidence. On New Year's Eve, the President and First Lady rode the Royal Train to Dover and crossed the Channel; and then the President of France's train took them from Calais to Paris. The next morning he played his first game of golf on French soil at St. Cloud; and in the afternoon he called a conference of the members of the American Mission at the Hôtel de Crillon, where they were quartered. With a few weeks before the official meetings got under way, Wilson consented to one more state visit.

Italy hoped to show its appreciation of the United States and, in so doing, curry favor with the man who would soon determine many of its new borders. At the government's insistence, the Wilsons rode from Paris in the King of Italy's train—with its china and glassware bearing Italian arms and its servants in royal scarlet livery. Crowds lined the tracks across Italy; and when it stopped at one small town, the Mayor compared the President's visit to "the second coming of Christ."

The Royal Train reached the Eternal City at 9:30 on the morning of

January 3, 1919. "The reception in Rome," recalled Secret Service agent Edmund Starling, "exceeded anything I have ever seen in all my years of witnessing public demonstrations. The people literally hailed the President as a god—'The God of Peace.'" The people of Rome filled the cobblestone streets with flowers, and a blizzard of white roses fell from the windows above as Wilson rode through hysterical mobs who were shouting, singing, and weeping. Wilson addressed the Italian Parliament, the nation's press, King Victor Emmanuel III and Queen Elena, and their guests at a state dinner at the Quirinal Palace. The Mayor of Rome honored Wilson with citizenship of his city. Ike Hoover had witnessed the French and English receptions for the President; but the Italians, he observed, seemed "to consider him as another Savior come to earth."

The next day, Wilson and his entourage faced more hysteria at the only venue that then seemed worthy of his presence—the Vatican. The majordomo escorted him through dozens of chambers, past colorfully costumed Swiss Guards and courtiers, until he arrived at a small throne room. At the tinkling of a bell, the diminutive Pontiff, dressed all in white except for his red sandals, entered. Accompanied only by a pair of interpreters, Benedict XV took the President by the hand into the Papal study for a brief private conversation—the first meeting between an American President and a Pope. Strangely, by the time the President had left the Vatican, the crowd had vanished. The officials later told Wilson that the police had dispersed the multitudes because of a potential threat of a riot. But later, Wilson explained to Edith that the government had broken up the demonstration for fear that the President might try to enlist the people's support for his Fourteen Points—to which Italy had agreed as the basis of the Armistice but to which it did not necessarily intend to adhere.

The First Couple left Rome the next morning, stopping in Genoa and Turin (where a thousand mayors from Piedmont gathered to greet the President) and Milan (where the Wilsons attended a performance of *Aida* at La Scala). Of all the places they had visited, Milan provided the apotheosis. Beyond the overwhelming crowds, observed Grayson, "there was a reverence everywhere that touched the President deeply." People lit votive candles before his picture. "There is bound to be a reaction to this sort of thing," Wilson told his doctor. "I am now at the apex of my glory in the hearts of these people, but they are thinking of me only as one who has come to save Italy, and I have got to pool the interests of Italy with the interests of all the world, and when I do that I am afraid they are going to be disappointed and turn about and hiss me."

Wilson recognized that once the international conference began, it would be every world leader for himself, advancing his own country's agenda. Upon his arrival in Paris, Wilson returned to his supreme priority. He pulled out his draft of a Covenant for the League of Nations, to which he now added finishing touches.

Theodore Roosevelt—who that very week had complained to a newspaper editor about Wilson's being a "silly doctrinaire at times and an utterly selfish and cold-blooded politician always"—would have had plenty to say in the impending debate. But on January 6, 1919, he fell silent, dying in his sleep. The State Department drafted a proclamation for the President to sign, but Wilson felt it was inadequate. He enhanced the tribute to his longtime rival, praising the Colonel's war record and his awakening the nation "to the dangers of private control which lurked in our financial and industrial systems." The President ordered suitable military honors at his funeral and the display of flags at half-staff at the White House and departmental buildings. In addition to the Vice President's temporary new duties of running the Cabinet meetings, Wilson asked Marshall to represent him at both TR's private and state memorial services.

The absence of Wilson's most persistent critic did not lessen opposition to the President's policies. In fact, Henry Cabot Lodge doubled his own efforts. Two weeks before Roosevelt died, Lodge had sat with him, discussing the proposed league. Neither man subscribed to such a global plan. Opposed to Wilson's direction, Roosevelt had said just before his death, "Let each nation reserve to itself and for its own decision, and . . . make it perfectly clear that we do not intend to take a position of an international Meddlesome Mattie. The American people do not wish to go into an overseas war unless for a very great cause, and where the issue is absolutely plain."

To anybody abroad, such talk seemed petty. The Armistice was in effect, but the devastation was part of every European's life. The great victory for Democracy had left millions of lives in disarray, with many of its cities wanting reconstruction amid the rubble of the fallen autocratic empires. Parts of two continents would have to be built from scratch: revolutions had created seventeen new constitutional republics; and ten new nations had declared their independence and were struggling to find their footing in constitutional governments. People rejoiced at being rid of their dictators, but they yearned for stability. Communists said they could offer as much to the Russians, and the Germans continued to consider that alternative for themselves.

Since his arrival in Europe, Woodrow Wilson had delivered seven formal speeches, each full of high-minded ideals and inspiration. When adviser Herbert Hoover suggested that Wilson must not ignore "the shapes of evil inherent in the Old World system," the President replied that a new spirit infused all of humanity. Hoover agreed. He did not hyperbolize when he stated, "Woodrow Wilson had reached the zenith of intellectual and spiritual leadership of the whole world, never hitherto known in history."

Across the Seine from the Place de la Concorde stood a two-story edifice of the Second Empire, the Ministry of Foreign Affairs, known simply by its location—the Quai d'Orsay. Its ground floor contained a succession of heavily gilded reception rooms with high ceilings and tall windows, each salon more splendid than the last. This would become the theater for the great diplomatic drama about to unfold.

While more than two dozen nations would make up the Peace Conference, the principals realized the need for a smaller leadership group if they were to accomplish anything. The heads of government and the foreign ministers of France, Great Britain, Italy, the United States, and Japan formed the Council of Ten. On Sunday, January 12, 1919, the leading players engaged in two full dress rehearsals at the Quai d'Orsay: at 2:30 the Supreme War Council met to discuss an extension of the Armistice; and at 4 p.m. the Council of Ten convened to discuss the ground rules for the upcoming plenary sessions, at which all the invited nations would be seated. The afternoon allowed everybody to get a feel for the room and one another. It was quickly recognized that the crucial arguments concerned a quartet of nations and that their leaders could best resolve those matters in private conversations, in an aptly named Council of Four.

The most towering personality in this foursome belonged to the diminutive Georges Clemenceau. Seventy-seven and sporting a bristling white walrus mustache, the French Prime Minister was a lifelong Radical Republican who had become a physician, a writer-publisher, and a political prisoner all before turning twenty-four. To evade further harassment, he

had sailed for America, where he learned English, started a medical practice in New York City, sent articles to Paris newspapers, and taught French
and horseback riding at a girls' school in Stamford, Connecticut, only to
marry one of his students. He returned to Paris and politics, as both a
public official and a newspaper publisher, who was derided and later redeemed for printing "J'Accuse," Émile Zola's historic defense of the falsely
persecuted Captain Alfred Dreyfus. In 1906, he became the seventy-
second Prime Minister of France for three years and was reinstated as the
eighty-fifth eight years later. Because of a skin condition, he almost always
wore gloves. John Maynard Keynes, then a young economist advising the
British delegation, later noted that Clemenceau—a friend of Claude
Monet—"felt about France what Pericles felt of Athens—unique value in
her, nothing else mattering." He maintained that Clemenceau was "a foremost believer in the view of German psychology which thinks that the
German understands and can understand nothing but intimidation, that
he is without generosity or remorse in negotiation"—that one must never
conciliate, only dictate to a German. The Gallic leader sought security and
revenge; and for his longtime ferocity as his nation's advocate, France nicknamed him "the Tiger."

An even more cunning political animal was David Lloyd George, at
fifty-six the youngest of the Big Four. Born in 1863, and losing his father
the following year, he put himself on a fast track of law and politics and
never deviated, becoming a Member of Parliament at twenty-seven and
rising steadily in the government. In 1916 he became the first and only
Welsh Prime Minister of England. With an outsider's eagerness to
please, he proved unusually adroit in speaking and writing his second
language, English; and few men could read a room as insightfully as Lloyd
George. He held the unfortunate position of head of a coalition government, forced to juggle the wishes of all sides in matters of colonies and
concessions. In a sketch he wrote but withheld for years, Keynes said,
"Lloyd George is rooted in nothing; he is void and without content." And
yet, he granted, the Prime Minister had highly sensitive political instincts.
"To see the British Prime Minister watching the company, with six or
seven senses not available to ordinary men, judging character, motive, and
subconscious impulse, perceiving what each was thinking and even what
each was going to say next, and compounding with telepathic instinct the
argument or appeal best suited to the vanity, weakness, or self-interest of

his immediate auditor," he wrote, "was to realize that the poor President would be playing blind man's buff in that party." Lloyd George traveled to Paris with a personal secretary, who was also his mistress and whom he addressed in their private correspondence as "My dear Pussy." Dr. Grayson thought Lloyd George was "as slippery as an eel."

The commedia dell'arte featured a favorite stock character—the Capitano—a braggart and coward who carried a sword he never used and who burst into emotional fits when challenged. Vittorio Orlando—who was Italy's third Prime Minister during its four years of war—filled that role whenever he appeared. Clemenceau would soon call this stumpy Sicilian-born lawyer with Mafia ties "the Weeper." Italy wanted a place at the table, like the other victors of the war, and expected its spoils as spelled out in a secret pact, the Treaty of London.

Then there was the President of the United States—tall, trim, with fine-cut features—hailed not only as a victor but also a prophet. "In addition to this moral influence the realities of power were in his hands," young Keynes perceived.

> The American armies were at the height of their numbers, discipline, and equipment. Europe was in complete dependence on the food supplies of the United States; and financially she was even more absolutely at their mercy. Europe not only already owed the United States more than she could pay; but only a large measure of further assistance could save her from starvation and bankruptcy. Never had a philosopher held such weapons wherewith to bind the princes of this world.

These four men and their associates gathered on the garden side of the Quai d'Orsay, in the Bureau du Ministre, the office of Stéphen Pichon. It was a large salon lined with eighteenth-century Gobelins tapestries and high bow windows and double-doors that opened onto a magnificent rose garden. Clemenceau sat before its great fireplace, facing all the others, who sat classroom style in chairs before him.

They began by considering the many matters of representation, providing a small sample of the conundrums that lay ahead. Montenegro, for example, was in the process of formation; the United States recognized the government of its king, and Wilson urged its accreditation. There were questions about the British Empire—whether Australia, for example, deserved greater representation than, say, New Zealand. While Wilson's "heart bled" for Belgium and Serbia, he wanted to limit their participation because neither had "made a voluntary sacrifice" in the war. Japan had been invited to bring five delegates to the Conference, even though, Clemenceau said, she "had not done very much in the War, and what she had done had been mainly in her own interests." Russia, in the midst of its civil war, would not be represented at all. Then, just as the leaders were making genuine headway, uniformed servants appeared to serve afternoon tea. Wilson had to restrain himself from voicing his surprise that with the weighty affairs of the world's future under discussion, the Conference should be interrupted by such triviality. But he honored the custom, even as he realized it was a political ploy, a way for the host to stage-manage every detail of the proceedings.

When these preliminary talks resumed, Grayson opened one of the windows, and Lloyd George remarked that it was the room's first breath of fresh air since the reign of Louis XIV. Clemenceau and his team immediately waved their hands in disapproval. They were embroiled in a heated argument with Italy's Foreign Minister, Sidney Sonnino, and Grayson had hoped the breeze might cool their tempers. But complaints from the French resulted in their closing the window. The repeated French objections to the open window, it appeared, were less about ventilation than about controlling the atmospherics of the peace talks. At the end of that first session, Wilson realized the Conference would be operating at a pace considerably slower than he had anticipated. That evening, he commented to his wife's social secretary, Edith Benham, that the first day reminded him "of an old ladies' tea party."

At the Council of Ten meeting on January 13, the leaders began to prepare the agenda for the Conference by proposing the topics they would consider. They included: new states; frontiers and territorial changes; and colonies—most especially the outposts of the German Empire, over which Japan, Great Britain, and Italy were already slavering. Because Wilson believed the dispensation of those colonies should fall under the jurisdiction of the League of Nations, he urged the establishment of that body as their primary order of business.

Every group encounter revealed more of each nation's desires. At the same day's meeting of the Supreme War Council, British Foreign Minister Balfour expressed his wish to seize Germany's navy; he suggested telling the vanquished, "If you want food you must hand over your ships." French Minister of Industrial Reconstruction Louis Loucheur announced that the French had no interest in Germany's reparations being paid in kind, and they expected the return of all stolen goods. Wilson consistently argued that "so long as hunger continued to gnaw, the foundations of government would continue to crumble," and that food, therefore, should be distributed promptly to friends and enemies, if only to ward off Bolshevism. On January 15, the great powers debated which should be the official language of the Conference. The hosts naturally argued for their native tongue; Lloyd George thought French and English should be considered equally official, and Wilson concurred. Without denying the precision of French in diplomatic matters, he argued that English was the diplomatic language of the Pacific and was comprehended by more people—including Clemenceau—than any other language represented at the Conference. Orlando indicated that he spoke no English. It was late afternoon before they agreed that the Conference would be trilingual. It promised to be a very long conference.

Five days before the commencement of the full summit, Wilson raised the problem he believed would be the ultimate fly in the ointment—Italy. While mindful of treating Orlando as an equal in the Council of Ten (if not as one of the Big Four), the President pre-emptively pointed out that the secret "Treaty of London"—under which Italy was to receive territory for joining the Allies—could not be considered binding. Wilson said the anticipated boundaries in that agreement had been laid down to protect Italy from the Austro-Hungarian Empire, and that empire no longer existed. Furthermore, the empire had been broken up into a number of states no one of which would be strong enough to menace Italy. Thus, both the basis and the purpose of that treaty no longer existed. Before facing the Conference at large, Wilson wanted to assure Orlando that Italy's frontiers with its new neighbors would be fair, and he invited Orlando to step up as the representative of a great power in the new world order by sacrificing petty national interests for greater global principles. In this reasonable and direct manner, Wilson steadily asserted his authority. Herbert Bayard Swope, ace reporter for the New York *World*, suggested that the Conference was beginning with Wilson as "the central figure in the room, the others paying him marked deference." Those who had thought him cold at first now "thawed under his influence."

Hundreds of petitioners who had come to Paris in hopes of a moment on the world stage had requests for the President. The provisional government of Lithuania, to name one, sent Wilson a plea—not for a seat at the table but only for "standing room back against the wall—where we have stood so long—waiting to be heard when the question of our fate is to be determined." Zionist leader Chaim Weizmann wrote Wilson that the "Jewries of nearly every country" had assembled just across the Channel and were "united in favour of a Jewish Commonwealth in Palestine and that a large majority of them have already definitely pronounced themselves in favour of a British Trusteeship of Palestine." And Wilson was asked to address a congress of women workers at the Trocadéro Palace—which made Clemenceau object to any further demonstrations honoring him. That included any events that might glorify America's part in the war or endorse the League of Nations.

That did not stop anyone from trying to capture Wilson's attention. W. E. B. Du Bois had organized a Pan-African Congress with fifty-seven "representatives of the Negro race" and hoped to be heard. Samuel Gompers met with the President to discuss the international labor situation, particularly "to what extent it would be possible for the League of Nations to devise and control a labor plan that would prevent worldwide economic unrest and trade disturbances." Wilson informed the head of a delegation from Armenia that it was difficult to "assign representatives to political units which have not yet been received into the family of nations." And Nguyen Tat Thanh, a twenty-nine-year-old from Indochina, who eked out a living cooking, teaching Chinese, and colorizing photographs when he was not converting to Marxism, received no response to his asking Wilson to recognize his homeland. He would soon adopt the pseudonym Ho Chi Minh—which meant "He Who Enlightens"—and then spend the rest of his life seeking proper acknowledgment of Vietnam. "Paris is now filling up with all sorts of people from all the little corners of the earth, leaders of ambitious new nations, awaiting the coming peace conference," Ray Stannard Baker jotted in his notebook. "About every second man of this type one meets, fishes out of his pocket a copy of a cablegram that he or his committee has just sent to President Wilson. It is marvellous indeed how all the world is turning to the President! The people believe he means what he says, and that he is a just man, set upon securing a sound peace."

The opening weekend of the Conference began with torrential rains, and the President awakened that Saturday morning—January 18, 1919— with a cold that kept him in bed until noon. At 2:30, limousines began to arrive at the Quai d'Orsay, bearing small flags of their nations on their hoods or bunting in Allied colors across the tops of their windshields. Two thousand people lining the Quai cheered as Wilson's car pulled up at 2:50, its passenger sufficiently reenergized. Ten minutes later the ruffle of drums and blare of trumpets announced the arrival of President Poincaré, who joined the plenary session. The signature element in the small palace's gorgeous white and gold hall—with frescoed cupids dancing on high—was an imposing fireplace and its mantelpiece. A beautiful round clock set within the mantel gave the room its official name, the Salon de l'Horloge. Above the clock, in a large niche, stood a marble statue of France holding the torch of civilization. Four magnificent chandeliers, reflected in large mirrors, illuminated the chamber. Although the French renamed the grand hall the Salle de la Paix for the duration of the talks, Clemenceau had seen to it that they officially began on the forty-eighth anniversary of Bismarck's achieving national unification, which had set Franco-Prussian relations on the path to war.

The lesser powers believed they would be treated the same as the mighty but promptly realized that the table in the Salle de la Paix was not round. Each of the delegates found his designated crimson leather–covered chair at a great three-sided arrangement—a head table with two long arms, all covered in green baize. Seating indicated a country's standing. Clemenceau sat at top center, Lloyd George and his delegation and the other Commonwealth nations on his left, Wilson and the Americans on his right. Around that bend, as far from the center of power as Czechoslovakia and Serbia but not as far down as Belgium or Brazil, sat Premier Orlando, one of seventy representatives from thirty countries. Secretariats lined the four walls. Everyone rose for Poincaré and remained standing for his brief welcoming remarks, in French—which were translated—after which he withdrew.

Clemenceau asked for nominations of a permanent chairman of the Conference, and Wilson proposed Clemenceau. The President generously offered that this was no mere tribute to their host nation but was because "we have learnt to admire him and those of us who have been associated with him have acquired a genuine affection for him." Lloyd George and

Sonnino seconded the motion, which was adopted unanimously. Although this small ceremony was the only business of the day, Clemenceau used his acceptance speech as an opportunity to stake some ground.

"President Wilson has special authority for saying that this is the first occasion on which a delegation of all civilised peoples of the world has been seen assembled," he said. And then he laid his objectives on the table:

> The greater the bloody catastrophe which has devastated and ruined one of the richest parts of France, the ampler and more complete should be the reparation . . . so that the peoples may be able at last to escape from this fatal embrace, which, piling up ruin and grief, terrorises populations, and prevents them from devoting themselves freely to their work for fear of enemies who may arise against them at any moment.

While baring his hatred for the enemy, Clemenceau spoke repeatedly of the amicable relationships among those assembled, suggesting that "success is only possible if we all remain firmly united." He said, "We have come here as friends; we must leave this room as brothers." Toward that end, he did not let this first session close without an offering to Wilson.

"Everything must yield to the necessity of a closer and closer union among the peoples who have taken part in this great war," Clemenceau said. "The League of Nations is here. It is in yourselves; it is for you to make it live; and for that it must be in our hearts. As I have said to President Wilson, there must be no sacrifice which we are not ready to accept." After his remarks, Clemenceau invited the delegates to submit memoranda detailing the crimes and punishments to be assigned to "the authors of the war."

Every posture of these talks would be fraught with the politics of leadership, every gesture a play for power. In observing just a few perfunctory motions, young British diplomat Harold Nicolson already sensed Clemenceau's high-handedness, especially with the smaller powers. Whenever asking if there were any objections, he merely said with machine-gun rapidity, "Non? . . . Adopté." Two days later, Nicolson dined with Balfour, who told him that Clemenceau had worn a bowler to the opening session.

Balfour apologized to the "old Tiger" for his own top hat, saying, "I was told . . . that it was obligatory to wear one." Replied Clemenceau, "So was I."

From the moment of Wilson's arrival in Paris, Poincaré and Clemenceau and almost every other Frenchman urged the President to visit the war sites so that he could see the devastation the enemy had inflicted. It was a bald attempt to win his sympathies and influence his judgments as to the compensation France deserved. In truth, the repeated suggestion offended him, just as his refusals perturbed his hosts. One night after weeks of the entreaties, an American friend having nothing to do with the Conference casually asked the President when he intended to visit the devastated regions. "Et tu, Brute?" he said, only half joking. "I don't want to see the de*vast*ated regions," he replied, using a quirky archaic pronunciation of the word and offering an explanation:

> As a boy, I saw the country through which Sherman marched to the sea. The pathway lay right through my people's properties. I know what happened, and I know the bitterness and hatreds which were engendered. I don't want to get mad over here because I think there ought to be *one* person at that peace table who isn't mad. I'm afraid if I visited the de*vast*ated areas I would get mad, too, and I'm not going to permit myself to do so.

Steadily, the French convinced themselves that Wilson had grown unsympathetic to their cause; and, noted Edith Wilson's private secretary, Edith Benham, "they are fearful he may give too good terms to Germany if he doesn't see the horror of the war and is prejudiced in their favor." Dr. Grayson, who virtually shadowed the President, could see that the French simply did not understand Wilson's equanimity. "They did not realize that he as much as any of them hated Germany and all her ways," he observed, "but that he was holding himself in hand because he knew that peace terms drawn up in furious rage would defeat their own ends, that to destroy Germany economically would make just reparations impossible." Wilson continued to draw a distinction between the former German Imperial government and the German people. The people had done evil, but it was done under wrong leadership. He felt that "to keep cool" was the first essential to the making of "a peace of justice," that whipping himself into "a passion of rage" would render him unfit for the present task. Germany must be punished, he asserted, "but in justice, not in frenzy."

"As a matter of fact," Wilson said, "if I had my way I'd adjourn the Peace Conference for one year, and let all these people go home and get the bile out of their systems." But he knew, of course, that a world of starvation and instability demanded immediate attention. Bolshevism fed off such conditions, and there was no time to lose. That very week, police in Lausanne arrested several German and Russian Bolsheviks carrying false passports on their way to Paris, where they had plotted to assassinate Clemenceau, Lloyd George, and Wilson. Rumors implicated the People's Commissar of War, Leon Trotsky, in this criminal cell. Communism was becoming not just a contagious sociopolitical movement with which democratic leaders disagreed; it was turning into an international terrorist threat.

At the next meeting of the Council of Ten, on January 21, Wilson read a proclamation he had prepared in an effort at least to acknowledge the Conference's greatest deficiency—namely, the absence of Russia. "The Associated Powers are now engaged in the solemn and responsible work of establishing the peace of Europe and of the world," he said, "and they are keenly alive to the fact that Europe and the world cannot be at peace if Russia is not." Recognizing the "absolute right of the Russian people to direct their own affairs without dictation or direction of any kind from outside" and not wishing to exploit the country in any way, Wilson proposed that all the political factions in Russia declare a truce and send delegates to a conference on the Princes Island—Prinkipo—in the Turkish Sea of Marmara, where representatives of the Associated Powers would help them sort out their differences enough to seat them at the table in Paris.

It was not a well-laid scheme, and it quickly went awry. Anti-Bolshevik forces refused to attend, and there was dissension among the Bolsheviks themselves. Furthermore, the invitation spurred Latvians, Letts, and Estonians to request audiences, in order to establish their own states, separate from whatever government might end up ruling Russia. In the meantime, the Allied Powers themselves disagreed on the merits of such a conference. British troops were still fighting alongside the White armies of Russia, and Lloyd George could not ignore the vociferous anti-Bolshevik rhetoric at home. "A poisoned Russia, an infected Russia, a plague-bearing

Russia; a Russia of armed hordes . . . preceded by swarms of typhus-bearing vermin which slew the bodies of men, and political doctrines which destroyed the health and even the souls of nations," was how Bolshevik Russia had recently been described by the new War Secretary, Winston Churchill. In a few weeks Churchill would add, "Of all tyrannies in history the Bolshevist tyranny is the worst, the most destructive, and the most degrading. It is sheer humbug to pretend that it is not far worse than German militarism." French diplomat Paul Cambon thought the idea of summoning a horde of Russian dissidents to an island in the Sea of Marmara was little more than the "idealistic promptings of President Wilson's mind."

At their second plenary session, on January 25, 1919, the delegates considered the creation of a League of Nations. Wilson took the floor. "We have assembled for two purposes," he explained, "—to make the present settlements which have been rendered necessary by this war, and also to secure the peace of the world." The League of Nations, he said, "seems to me to be necessary for both of these purposes." With his longtime penchant for humanizing institutions, Wilson asked his audience to remember that "we are not representatives of government, but representatives of peoples." He reminded the others present that the United States had not engaged in the war out of fear of enemy attack or with thoughts of "intervening in the politics . . . of any part of the world" and that the maintenance of future harmony required "the continuous superintendence of the peace of the world by the associated nations of the world." The League of Nations must be established not as some occasional organization "called into life to meet an exigency" but as one "always functioning in watchful attendance . . . that it should be the eye of the nations to keep watch upon the common interest, an eye that does not slumber, an eye that is everywhere watchful and attentive." Without that League, he said, "no arrangement that you can make would either set up or steady the peace of the world."

Ever since that day in Paris, many have considered Woodrow Wilson's idée fixe an idealistic pipe dream. For him, it was anything but. He did not consider the League part of a peace settlement so much as its very foundation—the chassis on which the framework of the peace could sit and the future of international cooperation could advance. To act otherwise meant perpetuating the ancient feuds over the same patches of territory.

Wilson still sought no gains for his country—other than the desire not to return to war. That, he said, required the creation of a League of Nations, for he regarded it "as the keystone of the whole programme which expressed our purpose and our ideal in this war and which the Associated Nations have accepted as the basis of the settlement." He insisted it was the mandate of his people, the reason for America's soldiers having shed blood; and his return to the United States without having made every effort to realize that program would only invite "the merited scorn of our fellow-citizens." Wilson spoke of the American doughboys he saw every day on the streets of Paris. "Those men came into the war after we had uttered our purposes," he said. "They came as crusaders, not merely to win the war, but to win a cause; and I am responsible to them, for it fell to me to formulate the purposes for which I asked them to fight." Wilson's oration played well. Colonel House said it was "the very best speech" the President had ever delivered. The delegates voted for the Commission to frame the League's constitution.

The rest of the plenary session was devoted to forming committees dealing with "the personal guilt and responsibility of the authors of the war," the internationalization of waterways, and reparation and damages, as well as one on the League of Nations. Wilson had no way of knowing that, just two days prior, England's Lord Curzon had written Lord Derby that the League of Nations held no more interest to him than writing rules about the freedom of the seas—that the League had "nothing whatever to do either with the war or with the immediate task of concluding peace." French diplomat Paul Cambon granted that Wilson possessed certain rhetorical gifts but said privately that he was "out of touch with the world, giving his confidence to no one, unversed in European politics, and devoted to the pursuit of theories which had little relation to the emergencies of the hour." The longer-serving combatants in the war held a shorter view of the world than Wilson's. "The business of the Peace Conference," said Cambon, is "to bring to a close the war with Germany, to settle the frontiers of Germany, to decide upon the terms which should be exacted from her, and as soon as possible to conclude a just peace."

Feeling one step closer to his goal, Wilson awakened early the next morning to visit some of the "devastated" areas between Paris and Rheims. It was not meant to be an in-depth tour, just a chance to add a dimension to names that had already become part of military history. A caravan of

eight motorcars stopped fifty miles northeast of Paris on the highway overlooking Belleau Wood. As a military aide explained the battle there, the
President exited his car, climbed the hill, and visited a trench that Marines
had occupied before advancing on the enemy. To the right, Wilson saw his
first American graveyard since his arrival in France. He uncovered his head
and gazed upon the lines of crosses. Then they proceeded to Château-
Thierry. As it began to snow, Wilson and his party stopped for lunch in a
special train that had followed them. Afterward, the party drove through
one destroyed town after another. They stopped at Rheims, which the
Germans had systematically bombarded, block by block, until its population of 250,000 had scattered, leaving just 3,000 people burrowing in
cellars. Snow blanketing the city, the Presidential party boarded the train
back to Paris at five o'clock. When asked, the President uttered, "No one
can put into words the impressions received amid such scenes of desolation
and ruin." Speaking later to a delegation from the Federation of Protestant
Churches of France, he said, "Happily, I believe in God's providence. Simple human intelligence is incapable of taking in all the immense problems
before it at one time throughout the whole world. At such a juncture if I
did not believe in God I should *feel utterly at a loss.*"

The leaders of the Conference realized that President Wilson had to
return to America in time for the closing of Congress on March 4 and that
he would need something to show his people. After his stirring performance on January 25, they recognized the value in pacifying him with his
League just so they might proceed to their own territorial wish lists. In
allocating pieces of the German and Ottoman Empires, the only arrangement Wilson could countenance was the concept of "mandates," which
South African General Jan Smuts had suggested. Under this arrangement,
pieces of the fallen Central empires would be placed in the trust of the
entire family of nations, the League. Wilson was most concerned that
these mandates not be treated as colonies. In explaining to one journalist
America's natural aversion to acquiring "outlying" new territory, he referenced the Philippines and how "impatient" the United States was until
"we could give them autonomy." By the end of January, the Council of
Ten had delineated three classes of mandates: those of countries whose
populations were civilized but not yet organized, such as Arabia; distant
tropical colonies, such as New Guinea, that were not an integral part of
any mandatory country; and countries that formed "almost a part of the

organization of an adjoining power." One after the other, each country lodged its complaints and staked its ground.

Baron Makino of Japan reminded the Council that at the outbreak of the war, the German military and naval base at Kiaochow in China constituted a serious threat to international trade and shipping, to say nothing of the peace in that corner of the world. The Japanese government, in concert with the British, had given notice to the Germans to surrender that territory to China, and when it failed to reply, Japan had fought with the British and succeeded in taking hold of the region as well as its significant railway lines. He now justified his government's claims to the unconditional cession of territory in Shantung Province (including its railways) as well as all the German-owned islands in the North Pacific.

China saw things differently. Wellington Koo, the Columbia University–educated Chinese Minister to the United States, delivered an impassioned speech, insisting that Japanese domination of the railroad lines would give them "absolute control over all of China's natural resources." He demanded that they be returned to China with compensation. On most issues of "dividing the swag," Wilson found himself in the minority, insisting that captured colonies should be controlled by the League of Nations and administered under the mandatory system, whereby the nations best fitted to do so would control the territories, which could, in turn, always appeal directly to the League to remedy any injustice. The Japanese had already grabbed some of China's "most sacred soil," including the Tomb of Confucius. Wilson sided with the Chinese.

The principles of the League of Nations aside, Lloyd George questioned whether Wilson had thought through its practicalities. Developing colonies, he said, was less about dividing spoils than multiplying debt. "Great Britain had no Colony from which a contribution towards the national expenditure was obtained," he said; and he thought the same situation would apply to Mesopotamia, Syria, and other parts of the Ottoman Empire should the mandatory system be applied there. "Whoever took Mesopotamia would have to spend enormous sums of money for works which would only be of profit to future generations," he said; and he wondered who was to bear the costs in the present. "Was the League of Nations to pay?" he asked. "How would it be possible to raise sufficient money to carry out all the necessary works for the development of these countries from which no returns could be expected for many decades?" He asked if the League would be levied to make good on the annual deficit of any nations under a mandate. Wilson granted that certain expenses—such as defense—would be borne by the League.

Sensing the sentiments in the room, Wilson added that the world would not accept many of the actions being discussed—such as "the parcelling out among the Great Powers of the helpless countries conquered from Germany." Such actions, he said, would make the League of Nations "a laughing stock." Orlando asked if Wilson intended all questions relating to the disposal of conquered territories to be referred to the League. If so, he suggested the world would think "that this Conference had done nothing, and a confession of impotence would be even more serious than disagreement amongst the delegates."

By the end of the month, the Allies were turning on one another. Premier William Morris Hughes of Australia "bitterly opposed" any agreement that did not transfer New Guinea to his nation—a position that galled Wilson, for Hughes appeared to hold the world hostage for his country's personal gain. "Australia and New Zealand with 6,000,000 people between them," he said, "could not hold up a conference in which, including China, some twelve hundred million people were represented." And that was just one dispute that had to be settled. On January 30, 1919, alone, the Council of Ten also heard positions regarding the disposition of Samoa, Smyrna, Adalia, the north of Anatolia, Armenia, Syria, Mesopotamia, Palestine, Arabia, Uganda, Nigeria, Algeria, Morocco, Kurdistan, the Caucasus, Baku, Lebanon, Odessa, Persia, the Czechoslovak Republic, the Congo, the Cameroons, Romania, and Serbia. Delegates began to realize the necessity of abandoning singular national desires in favor of a worldview.

Through patient and eloquent reasoning, Wilson was able to sway Lloyd George and then Japan and Italy to his side, resulting in the approval of the mandatory system for African and Pacific territories. He granted that many of these mandates were more duty than privilege; and while he was disinclined to see the United States reap any advantage from the war, he was equally against letting his nation shirk any duty. But any demand for America to share in that burden, he said, would require a postponement until he could explain the matter to his people, most particularly the Senate. Charles Seymour of the American Peace Commission found it discouraging to see the Council of Ten wasting so much time on details of technical disputes that should be left to subordinates; and with Wilson's departure impending, Colonel House thought the President should devote his time to the League. "I urged him," House wrote in his diary on January 31, 1919, "to . . . make it his main effort during the Conference. I thought he had a great opportunity to make himself the champion of peace and to change the order of things throughout the world."

On the afternoon of February 3, Wilson opened the first meeting of the Commission on the League of Nations at the Hôtel de Crillon. Although he was the first world leader to support such an organization, Wilson readily acknowledged it was the work of many heads and many hands. A few academicians and Liberal politicians in England had actually devised just such an international society in the middle of the war; and a few American associations—including the League to Enforce Peace, which former President Taft had led—organized simultaneously. Wilson had authorized David Hunter Miller, a law partner of House's son-in-law, Gordon Auchincloss, to work with British adviser Cecil Hurst in putting together a draft of a constitution that would incorporate suggestions from General Smuts and Great Britain's Lord Robert Cecil. Being the last and foremost proponent of the document, Wilson would forever be acknowledged as its "author," despite his earnest efforts to correct the record.

From February 3 to 13, the Commission—representing fourteen nations—met ten times, parsing every word of the document and perfecting its fine points. At almost every turn, the French attempted to interject their need to scold Germany. The Covenant had thirteen articles of governance and organization and ten Supplementary Agreements, which defined the structure of mandates, called for "humane conditions of labor," promised "to accord to all racial or national minorities . . . exactly the same treatment and security" accorded the majorities, and insisted upon "no law prohibiting or interfering with the free exercise of religion." The document contained several more utopian elements: Article IV, for example, required "the reduction of national armaments to the lowest point consistent with domestic safety"; Article V maintained that disputes among the "Contracting Powers" would be subjected to arbitration before armed force would be considered.

The backbone of the League Covenant came in Article X with its establishment of collective security. It asserted that hostile actions by a non-signatory party against any of the League members would result in a united effort of members to blockade the infractor—"closing the frontiers of that Power to all commerce or intercourse with any part of the world, and to employ jointly any force which may be agreed upon to accomplish that object." The member nations would agree to unite in coming to the aid of their colleagues "against which hostile action has been taken, and to combine their armed forces in its behalf."

The French were paranoid about a rearmed Germany; and at the February 11 meeting of the Commission, they questioned whether they should enter into the League if it lacked an international army. Wilson explained that the only method by which the organization could achieve its ends was through a "cordial agreement" and goodwill. "All that we can promise, and we do promise it," he said, "is to maintain our military forces in such a condition that the world will feel itself in safety. When danger comes, we too will come, and we will help you, but you must trust us. We must all depend on our mutual faith." After the meeting, Lord Cecil privately warned one of the French diplomats that the League of Nations was "their only means of getting the assistance of America and England, and if they destroyed it they would be left without an ally in the world." At another formal gathering of diplomats, Cecil had spoken to the French off the record, saying that "America had nothing to gain from the League of Nations"—that she could ignore European affairs and look after her own—and that "the offer . . . for support was practically a present to France." The Commission spent the entire next day reading each of what had become twenty-seven Articles of the Covenant as reported back from the Drafting Committee.

With his departure drawing near, Wilson conferred with Colonel House about his role during this absence. House said he had four objectives— reducing Germany's military forces to their peacetime footing, delineating Germany's boundaries, reckoning Germany's reparation bill, and determining how Germany should be treated economically. He told the President he thought he could "button up everything" during the four weeks the President would be away. Wilson looked startled, even alarmed, knowing how long drafting the Covenant had taken—and those talks had begun with a general consensus. Wilson now perceived a change within House, an increasing sense of empowerment over the last few weeks, one that seemed to grow as Wilson's embarkation approached. House hastily added that he did not intend to settle all these matters, merely to "have them ready" for Wilson's return. House asked the President to bear in mind that "it was sometimes necessary to compromise in order to get things through. Not a compromise of principle, but a compromise of detail." He reminded Wilson of his own compromises since their meetings began. "I did not wish him to leave expecting the impossible in all things," House wrote in his diary. In fact, Wilson never expected House to broker any deals in his absence, nor did he desire it.

Turning to domestic politics, House suggested that the President sail not to New York or even Virginia, as planned, but to Boston. He thought it would prove beneficial if the Europeans could see Wilson receive an enthusiastic homecoming after his two months away and that he could expect that from New England, which he had seldom visited. With legislators already preparing for battle, it would also allow him to plant his flag in the home state of his archrival, Senator Henry Cabot Lodge. House further proposed a dinner at the White House for the Senate and House Foreign Relations Committees as soon as was practicable. Wilson thought an address to Congress would provide an adequate platform from which to describe his peace efforts. But House convinced him that it would deprive the essential legislators of a chance for "discussion, consultation, or explanation." Wilson agreed.

As this meeting in Paris was the biggest story of the century, the press questioned its access to the proceedings, always expecting more from the man who demanded open covenants of peace, openly arrived at. Wilson believed in the transparency of their business, but he also understood the fragility of the situation—dozens of nations, often with conflicting desires. The fate of the League of Nations was too delicate to leave to journalists to misrepresent. More than impractical, allowing newspapermen to sit in on intimate discussions among the Council of Ten or the Big Four seemed impertinent. Befriending the press might have helped his cause, especially in having to proselytize to a skeptical Senate and an agnostic public; but Wilson never believed journalistic access could guarantee greater support. He wanted to offer the public a fully realized plan rather than some half-baked ideas. He fretted over leaks in the press and European portrayals of him as a dreamer with little practical sense.

Within days of Wilson's arrival in Paris, George Creel had recommended a daily press conference, a concept to which Wilson subscribed. Immediate demands, however, made it clear that the President would rarely have time for such an exercise, and the constantly changing situation would make it impossible to talk "with any degree of certainty" until things were in writing and approved. And so, even before formal talks had begun, Wilson had invited Ray Stannard Baker to join the Peace Commission as its press representative, an intermediary between the Commission and the other journalists. Ironically, this lack of direct access to the President forced the newspapermen to rely on less reliable outsiders— representatives of smaller countries or low-level diplomats who did not know the entire picture. Major players realized they could control stories through the very leaks Wilson feared.

"It is highly important that the right news be given out," Wilson had said, at a time when the volatility of the talks fueled rumors on a daily basis. He had asked Baker to visit him every night at seven o'clock, at which time he would recap that day's events, suggesting that any completed business be furnished to the press but that pending matters be omitted. Edith Wilson said that she could set her watch to the nightly arrival of Baker, who never missed an appointment, though he sometimes had to wait more than an hour if the President was detained. She sat in on the briefings so that she could be fully apprised of the work of the Conference without her husband's having to repeat himself.

On February 14, 1919, the President awakened to what would be the most momentous day of the Conference thus far. As he would be leaving for home that night, he made a point of providing an hour-long interview with almost twenty American correspondents, his first press conference since arriving in Europe. As House observed, he addressed them "in the pleasantest and frankest way." He expressed his regret that he had not been able to converse with them daily, adding, with a laugh, that "every one else had had his ear." And though his own schedule in the last few weeks had been filled with League activity, he gravely emphasized that "the most tremendous issue in the world to-day concerns the economic situation." Everything else, he said, could wait until the wheels of industry were again in motion. "You can't talk government with a hungry people," held the President. That said, he diplomatically added that all the participating nations wanted to reassure France that "what she has just gone through never will occur again." While the weeks of talks had been full of tension, Wilson confessed that he learned how to take advantage of long speeches by stealing catnaps, knowing he could awaken in time to hear the translations. Colonel House marveled at Wilson's performance before the press. "It is to be remembered that he did not want to see them," House told his diary, "and yet when he got to talking, he was so enthused with what he had to say that it looked as if he would never stop."

As much as anybody, Edith Wilson knew that Colonel House had been of "inestimable help" to her husband, and she liked him personally; but she could not help voicing a long-held suspicion that spoke to the root of his character: House almost never disagreed with her husband. "It seems to me that it is impossible for two persons *always* to think alike," she told Woodrow. "I find him absolutely colourless and a 'yes, yes' man." As in the past, Wilson defended him; but it was not the first time Edith had cast a baleful eye on her husband's most trusted adviser.

Even though she knew the meetings in Paris permitted participants only, Edith had set her heart on attending that Valentine's Day session of the Conference at which her husband was to submit the report of the League of Nations Commission. It was nothing less than the Covenant for the League, for which he had garnered the unanimous approval of the fourteen nations on his committee. Knowing that her husband reflexively resisted asking for favors, Edith disclosed her desire to Dr. Grayson, who hoped to attend the session as well. He thought of approaching Clemenceau, who, he believed, would permit their attendance. Edith presented this plan to Woodrow, who said, "In the circumstances it is hardly a request, it is more a command, for he could not very well refuse you." That suited Edith. "Wilful woman," he said, "your sins be on your own head if the Tiger shows his claws." And Edith replied, "Oh, he can't, you know; they are always done up in grey cotton."

Clemenceau did consent to Edith's eavesdropping on the session—with conditions. At the far end of the grand salon, opposite the great clock, heavy red brocade curtains concealed a narrow alcove, which had space for two chairs. If she and Grayson agreed to remain concealed—so that the wives of other delegates would not pester him in the future—they could take their places before the diplomats arrived and remain until the last of them had exited. By peeking through the curtains, they could witness this moment of history.

At 3:30 that afternoon, Edith and Dr. Grayson were in their places, able to see President Wilson open the third plenary session. "I had arranged most of the program," House wrote in his diary; but Woodrow

Wilson had prepared all his life for this day. With only a few expository detours, Wilson read out loud the Covenant for a new world order, while delegates followed along with their reading copies. The most eye-popping article remained the defensive alliance to which the United States and all the other signatories would be committed. This article allowed that certain cases might require the Executive Council "to recommend what effective military or naval force the members of the League shall severally contribute to the armed forces to be used to protect the covenants of the League." The members would further pledge to "support one another in the financial and economic measures which are taken under this Article." He insisted that this armed force would be used only as a last resort, "because this is intended as a constitution of peace, not as a league of war."

"Your speech was as great as the occasion. I am very happy," Colonel House jotted on a slip of paper, which he passed to the President. "Bless your heart," Wilson replied. "Thank you from the bottom of my heart." House would note the exchange in his journal entry for the day, writing that the President was unfailingly interesting when he spoke. But the Colonel, about to exercise his new authority with the delegation, could not help himself from adding, "The President . . . talks entirely too much."

A number of speeches in approval of the Covenant filled the rest of the plenary session, after which Wilson ducked into a second press conference. The Covenant presentation behind him, Wilson relaxed and turned anecdotal. He told of one private conversation between him and Clemenceau, in which the old Tiger accused the President of having "a heart of steel." Wilson disagreed, saying, "I have not the heart to steal." Wilson prophesied that the difficult portion of the Conference lay ahead—upon his return from America—when they would approach the great territorial questions, many of which were snarled by secret treaties. For now, Wilson rejoiced that the concept of the League that had been adopted at the plenary session of January 25 had on this day received near unanimous approbation. The first phase of the Peace Conference had produced the tangible results the President had sought. Observed one junior member of the American Commission in his diary, "It seems impossible now that what Wilson has started out to do will not be done. . . . Today will be perhaps the greatest date in the history of the world. The birth of the brotherhood of man."

Wilson attended one more conference on February 14, at the Quai d'Orsay. Under Lloyd George's aegis, Britain's new War Secretary, Winston Churchill, hoped to address the leaders on the subject of Russia before the President sailed for home. Clemenceau said the subject seemed too important for such a brief and unexpected meeting; but Wilson politely allowed that Churchill had made the effort to anticipate his departure, and so they should at least hear his concerns. Wilson insisted that they were all in need of more intelligence on the subject, which was why he had hoped the conference at Prinkipo might have come to fruition. "What we were seeking was not a *rapprochement* with the Bolsheviks," Wilson said, "but clear information." And if the Bolsheviks would not come to Prinkipo, Wilson was now thinking that emissaries should go to them.

In fact, he and House had discussed just such a plan raised by William Bullitt, a brilliant Yale-educated Philadelphian. Only twenty-eight years old, this member of the American delegation proposed his own mission to Moscow to meet with the Lenin government—not to negotiate but to investigate. As Wilson strongly felt "there should be no interference with internal affairs of Russia, but that the Allies would do everything possible . . . to help the Russian people from the outside," he approved the plan. At best it might buy some time in which some of the diverse Russian factions might consolidate; at worst it could yield facts about the cryptic Lenin government. Accompanied by legendary muckraker Lincoln Steffens, who had turned Marxist, Bullitt left on this sub rosa operation.

Fearing that the Allies might cozy up to Lenin, Churchill had crossed the Channel to warn the Supreme War Council that a complete withdrawal of Allied troops from Russia would mean the destruction of all non-Bolshevik armies there. Without further military resistance to the Red Army, he insisted, an "interminable vista of violence and misery was all that remained for the whole of Russia." Wilson said the existing forces of the Allies were not enough to stop the Bolsheviks, and the United States, for one, was not prepared to reinforce its troops. It was "certainly a cruel dilemma," he added. The removal of Allied soldiers would result in Russian deaths; but, Wilson said, "they could not be maintained there forever and the consequence to the Russians would only be deferred." With the *George Washington* awaiting his arrival in Brest, Wilson cast his lot with the group's decision. With no intention of acceding to Churchill's suggestions, Wilson did not understand why Lloyd George had even allowed him to appear in the first place.

That long day over at last, Edith Wilson blended into the crowd of diplomats and well-wishers among the fleet of motorcars, each with a flag flapping in the cool night breeze. She found her husband in the blue limousine with the Presidential seal. As she entered the car, he removed his top hat and leaned back. "Are you so weary?" she asked.

"Yes, I suppose I am," he said, "but how little one man means when such vital things are at stake." He elaborated, articulating the very essence of his mission. "This is our first real step forward, for I now realize, more than ever before, that once established the League can arbitrate and correct mistakes which are inevitable in the Treaty we are trying to make at this time," he said. "The resentments and injustices caused by the War are still too poignant, and the wounds too fresh. They must have time to heal, and when they have done so, one by one the mistakes can be brought to the League for readjustment, and the League will act as a permanent clearing-house where every nation can come, the small as well as the great." He smiled at his wife and added, "It will be sweet to go home, even for a few days, with the feeling that I have kept the faith with the people, particularly with these boys, God bless them." Edith let Woodrow savor the moment in silence the rest of the way to their residence, where soldiers stood at salute as they entered.

Colonel House accompanied them to the train station. Despite a heavy rain, a long crimson carpet lined with palms extended from the curb to where President Poincaré, Clemenceau and his entire cabinet, and numerous diplomats were waiting. Wilson bade House adieu, placing an arm around his shoulders and all his faith in House's hands. In Wilson's absence, Lansing would be the titular head of the American Commission, but House was entrusted to speak on the President's behalf. Wilson knew that France, especially, would be eager to exploit his absence by rushing into place certain terms about the geographical boundaries of Germany and the inclusion of war costs in the reparations demands. Wilson said he was unwilling to allow anything beyond mechanical basics to be determined while he was gone. With so many matters involving "the fortunes and interests of many other people," he said, "we should not be hurried into a solution arrived at solely from the French point of view." As he plainly expressed to House, "I beg that you will hold things steady with regard to everything but the strictly naval and military terms until I return."

At 10:30 the next morning, the Presidential train pulled up to the pier in Brest, where American soldiers and local French officials awaited. Wilson thanked the people of France and their government for treating him as a friend. At 11:15 the ship set sail, carrying a number of hitchhikers, including Assistant Secretary of the Navy Franklin D. Roosevelt and his wife, Eleanor. The majority of the passengers were sick and wounded soldiers. The President himself was visibly fatigued from his two-month ordeal in Europe. Still, he brimmed with optimism, his spirits soaring as high as the dove bringing the olive leaf to Noah.

Stateside, Joseph Tumulty had kept the White House functioning and the President fully briefed. He also planned Wilson's arrival in Boston and his Foreign Relations Committee dinner at the White House, as the nation and its legislators were already taking sides. "Plain people throughout America for you," he radiogrammed the President. "You have but to ask their support and all opposition will melt away." Despite the rough crossing and another cold, the President used much of the voyage for rest and recreation—exercise in the sun by day and movies after dinner. While aboard ship, he received joyous word from his son-in-law Frank Sayre, whose message simply said: "Woodrow Wilson Sayre and Jessie send love." The namesake was the President's fourth grandchild.

On the morning of February 19, while Wilson was mid-Atlantic, a French anarchist shot five times at Clemenceau while he was en route to the Quai d'Orsay. One of the five bullets passed through his neck, miraculously missing any major arteries, and lodged in his shoulder. By day's end, the old Tiger had returned to his residence and was making light of the matter. But it served as a grim reminder that this was still an age of anarchy. Three days later, Clemenceau summoned House and urged a speedy settlement with Germany.

The Wilsons threw a small shipboard luncheon in honor of Washington's birthday on the twenty-second. They invited the Franklin Roosevelts, whom they found charming company. Conversation turned naturally to the League, which Ambassador to Russia David R. Francis said he believed the people of the United States would support. "The failure of the United States to back it," Wilson said, "would break the heart of the world, for the world considers the United States as the only nation represented in this great conference whose motives are entirely unselfish."

The *George Washington* arrived in Boston Harbor in a fog, but Woodrow Wilson had never been so clear. Even though he had been absent from his desk longer than any President in history, he knew the political realities that awaited. He asked Tumulty to explain to the local authorities that his immediate duty was "to get to Washington and take hold of my work there." He had hoped to minimize all formalities and, if possible, even eliminate having to speak, for fear of giving his visit a political taint. Tumulty trimmed the schedule to a reception at the pier, a private luncheon, and a short public address; to do any less, he suggested, would not only embarrass the local officials but would also disappoint the many thousands who would assemble to greet Wilson. "Your arrival awaited in Boston with splendid and entirely non-partisan enthusiasm," he explained.

Boston declared Monday the twenty-fourth a local holiday in honor of the President's return. An estimated 200,000 Bostonians cheered him and the fifty-car procession along most of the three-mile route from the pier to the Copley Plaza Hotel. For security reasons, some of the streets were roped off and emptied, with a sharpshooter standing atop every block of buildings along the way. After lunch, Wilson went to Mechanics Hall, not having imagined the throngs that were waiting. By the time Republican Governor Calvin Coolidge had introduced him to the crowd of seven thousand, with a surprising pledge to support the President in his plans if it meant an end to war, Wilson's adrenaline was pumping.

He delivered an especially deft speech, masking its politics in patriotism and addressing any concerns about his long absence. "I have been very lonely . . . without your comradeship and counsel," he told the enthusiastic crowd. He said the proudest fact he could report was "that this great country of ours is trusted throughout the world"; and he said the Conference was moving slowly due to "the complexity of the task which is undertaken." The Europe he left was full of hope, he said, "because they believe that we are at the eve of a new age of the world, when nations will understand one another. . . . If America were at this juncture to fail the world, what would come of it?"

Anticipating the donnybrook ahead, Wilson explained that he had not gone to Europe merely to spout idealism. "We set this nation up to make men free," he said, "and we did not confine our conception and purpose to America, and now we will make men free. If we did not do that, all the fame of America would be gone, and all her power would be dissipated." Throwing off the gloves, he said, "I have fighting blood in me, and it is sometimes a delight to let it have scope."

To sustained applause, Wilson exited the hall for South Station. After brief whistle-stop speeches in Providence, Rhode Island, and New London and New Haven, Connecticut, Wilson went to sleep, awakening in Washington. He went directly to the White House, where he signed the large number of documents that had piled up in his absence. That afternoon, he presided over a Cabinet meeting, at which he detailed the chicanery with which he had to deal in Paris. Although his detractors suggested that the Europeans were duping him at the Peace Conference, Wilson was, in fact, wise to their subterfuge from the start. He knew that the French were constantly trying to weaken his position by coercing the press to emphasize the power of Republican opinion in the United States or by exaggerating fears of a renewed German offensive. At the same time, he was parrying not only the Allies' insistence upon extensive German reparations but also their entreaties to forgive their own respective debts. And though the spreading threat of Bolshevism had been enough for him to authorize the Bullitt mission, Wilson felt that much of the reported chaos in Russia was exaggerated.

On February 26, his second night back in the White House, Wilson hosted the dinner Colonel House had recommended, that of members of Congress on their respective foreign affairs committees. For the first time in two years, the White House was illuminated as though for a state dinner. But the lights did little to brighten the mood of half the guests. Promptly at eight, thirty-four legislators were directed to the State Dining Room. After the meal, Henry Cabot Lodge escorted Edith Wilson, the only woman present, to the East Room, where chairs were set up in an elongated circle. As the President took his place at the top of the oval, his wife took her leave. He opened the discussion with an informal statement, explaining that the other world leaders had "agreed upon the need and the importance of forming a League of Nations, of doing something practical to bind the nations together"—to prevent any flare-ups of the past war and the ignition of any future wars. With that, he said, "Ask anything you want to know, gentlemen, and ask it as freely as you wish." They did—until midnight.

Wilson fielded questions about disarmament, the Monroe Doctrine, and what some considered a surrender of American sovereignty. Wilson explained that the Executive Council of the proposed League could issue no order without unanimity and that any such orders must be submitted to each of the governments represented on the council. With every country overseeing every other, any arms race would be limited and transparent. He suggested that the sanctity of the Monroe Doctrine must be maintained, that the century-old policy was the bedrock of the Covenant. Wilson asserted that any attempts to eliminate war would require some sacrifice, each nation yielding something for the greater good of the whole world. And while he showed great respect for the power of the Senate Foreign Relations Committee to withhold its approval of a treaty, he expressed the hope that the present draft of the Covenant would not face radical changes from the committee, as it had been framed to mutual satisfaction by fourteen nations. Wilson imposed no limits on what his guests might say to the press. But everyone in the East Room recognized the political importance of this issue. While winning the war may have occurred on the Democrats' watch, the Republicans were not about to let them co-opt the peace.

Republican Senator Frank Brandegee of Connecticut assured reporters that nothing Wilson said that night changed his opinion about the League of Nations. "I am against it," he told *The New York Times*, "as I was before." An indifferent Henry Cabot Lodge thought the dinner was perfectly pleasant; but, he noted in his diary, "We went away as wise as we came." And while Lodge had chosen not to confront Wilson in his own house, he noted that "the President's performance under Brandegee's very keen and able cross-examination was anything but good."

Two days later, Lodge delivered a long speech in the Senate, shredding the Covenant article by article. "My effort," Lodge later recounted, ". . . was to try, by showing the objections to the League proposed, to make it apparent that the thing to do was to make peace and deal with the League later when we could take our time in doing so, and thereby to demonstrate the League should not be yoked with the treaty of peace and thus create the risk of dragging them both down together." Lodge asked his colleagues, "What is it that delays the peace with Germany?" And then he answered his own question: "Discussions over the League of Nations; nothing else. Let us have peace now, in this year of grace 1919. That is the first step to the future peace of the world. The next step will be to make sure if we can that the world shall have peace in the year 1950 or 2000."

While the President was still in residence and the Sixty-fifth Congress still in session, Lodge took aggressive action. With no time to launch a full-scale resolution against the League, he circulated among Republican Senators and Senators-elect (not yet eligible to vote) a round-robin letter pledging opposition to the League. He gathered thirty-seven signatures. While not a binding document, it publicly demonstrated that the President faced serious opposition. Adding insult to that injury, the Republicans invoked a filibuster in the Congress's final hours, allowing certain appropriations simply to wither without approval. The only reason Wilson had even sailed home from France was to sign eleventh-hour bills. Bringing the body to a screeching halt served only to humiliate him. The Republicans signified that Wilson's resumed absence from Washington would only rile an even unfriendlier Sixty-sixth Congress. More irritated than chagrined, Wilson left the Capitol and proclaimed: "A group of men in the Senate have deliberately chosen to embarrass the administration of the Government. . . . It is plainly my present duty to attend the Peace Conference in Paris. It is also my duty to be in close contact with the public business during a session of the Congress. I must make my choice between these two duties, and I confidently hope that the people of the country will think that I am making the right choice."

In his time home, Wilson had been able to complete just one significant piece of business—the appointment of a new Attorney General. From the moment Thomas Gregory had announced his intention to step down from the office, Tumulty had recommended former Congressman A. Mitchell Palmer, a strong supporter of the Administration—a man of intelligence and integrity. For over a year, he had acted as the nation's Alien Property Custodian, seizing and sometimes selling "enemy property." Gregory advised against appointing him Attorney General, as had House, who found the glad-handing Palmer overbearing. In this politically challenging moment, Wilson listened more to his two savviest Cabinet members, Burleson and Daniels, as well as party chairman Vance McCormick, all of whom strongly endorsed Palmer as progressive, fearless, and "effective on the stump." This Swarthmore-educated Pennsylvania Quaker, who used "thee" and "thou," seemed a welcome addition to a heavily Southern Cabinet. He was also levelheaded, especially when it came to the incendiary issues of sedition. While he had been aggressive in his seizure of German-owned property during the war, he also sought to release ten thousand German aliens in government custody; and he had opposed the local raids of the American Protective League as America was entering the war, publicly pronouncing the organization "a grave menace." Within days of his return to the White House, Wilson had announced his selection of Palmer, but in its session-end filibuster, the Senate took one more dig at the President by failing to approve him.

The Department of Justice required particularly strong leadership in that moment. With the war over, the Administration faced a number of vital issues, including the matter of clemency toward America's "political prisoners." In his final days in office, the hard-nosed Gregory had received a number of communications referring to the Espionage Act. He maintained that not one person had been convicted for *mere expression of opinion* but that all had been convicted at trials by jury of willful violations of the law whose aim was to prevent "deliberate obstruction to the prosecution of the war." Since the end of the war, Gregory had reconsidered all those convicted and found several no longer deserved their sentences. He asked Wilson to review individual cases, if not the entire policy; and the President hoped to put a new Attorney General immediately in place to do the same. Wilson recommended to Postmaster General Burleson that it was also time to reconsider their position in combating sedition. "I cannot believe that it would be wise to do any more suppressing."

Congress closed on March 4, and Wilson boarded a train at Union Station that day at two o'clock, returning to the *George Washington* in Hoboken. He made two stops along the way. The first was in Philadelphia, where he went to Jefferson Hospital to visit his daughter Jessie and his newborn grandson. The President delighted in the plump infant, who was yawning as his eyes remained closed. "With his mouth open and his eyes shut," Wilson said, "I predict that he will make a Senator when he grows up." The Presidential entourage continued its journey, reaching New York City, where he addressed a capacity crowd at the Metropolitan Opera House, sharing the great stage with none other than former President Taft, who spoke in favor of the League. When it was Wilson's turn to speak, a band struck up George M. Cohan's signature tune, and Wilson told the enthusiastic crowd, "I will not come back 'till it's over, over there.'"

He explained how the last war could have been avoided if Germany had stopped to consider that Great Britain would ally with France and Russia. He said that the League of Nations was meant to serve as a sign-post, "as a notice to all outlaw nations that not only Great Britain, but the United States and the rest of the world, will go in to stop enterprises of that sort."

After the speech, the Wilsons were ferried across the river to the Hoboken wharves, where they boarded their ship. The President was ex-hausted from having driven himself harder in the last three months than at any other time in his life. But he remained awake until past mid-night, at which time he derived great satisfaction in commissioning A. Mitchell Palmer as his Attorney General through the power of a recess appointment.

Somebody observed that it had been exactly thirteen weeks since Wil-son had first boarded the *George Washington*, a good omen that was not lost on Dr. Grayson. Except for another shipboard cold and fever during the eight-day crossing, Wilson had remained remarkably healthy in all that time. After examining him that week, Grayson found all his vital signs "unusually good" for a man of sixty-two. Even Ray Stannard Baker marveled not only at Wilson's strength—especially upon learning of the gastric and neurological conditions that had plagued him for years—but also his ability to disconnect from strife. Some days the President watched five hours of moving pictures. Confining himself to his cabin, where he slept or played a variation of solitaire called canfield, the President self-diagnosed his current bouts of neuralgia and an attack on his "equato-rial zone" as nothing more than "a retention of gases generated by the Republican Senators," which he said were "enough to poison any man." Ray Baker further observed that Wilson was "a good hater—& how he does hate those obstructive Senators." He realized the President was now inclined to "stand by the Covenant word for word as drawn, accept-ing no amendment, so that the 37 of the round-robin will be utterly vanquished."

Wilson faced an even greater threat to his blood pressure. Colonel House's communiqués from Paris had become worrisome, to say the least. In one report, House had suggested that the issue of the League was still in play; in another he wrote of Clemenceau's requesting certain restraints against the republics on the west bank of the Rhine. Another noted that everything in Wilson's absence had "been speeded up." All together, the wireless dispatches from the Continent suggested that House had over-stepped in his role just as the French had overreached. Wilson urged with-holding even provisional consent to policy decisions until his arrival.

The *George Washington* could not deliver him to France fast enough. For several more days, Wilson remained at sea, anxiously playing solitaire.

14

GETHSEMANE

Then commeth Iesus with them vnto a place called
Gethsemane . . .

—MATTHEW, XXVI:36

And being in an agonie, he prayed more earnestly,
and his sweat was as it were great drops of blood
falling downe to the ground.

—LUKE, XXII:44

The *George Washington* reached Brest at 7:45 in the evening of March 13, 1919. For reasons of security—and the French government's desire to withhold any further accolades for the American President—the reception was reduced to a diplomatic minimum. The welcoming committee included only a few dignitaries, including Colonel House. With little fanfare, the Wilsons boarded the special train and were on their way to Paris by 10:30. Wilson and House huddled privately in his stateroom while Edith retired to hers. The President listened to his most trusted adviser report the latest French attempts to detach the League Covenant from the Peace Treaty and to create a Rhenish Republic, a buffer state between France and Germany. Before his return to America, Wilson had told House he would not tolerate the latter, which would

"absolutely denude Germany of everything she had and allow Bolshevism
to spread throughout that country."

A little after midnight, Edith heard the Colonel leave. She opened the
connecting door to Woodrow's compartment. "The change in his appearance shocked me," she recalled later. "He seemed to have aged ten years, and
his jaw was set in that way it had when he was making superhuman effort
to control himself." Without saying a word, he held out his hand, which she
grasped. "What is the matter?" she asked. "What has happened?"

"House," he said, smiling sardonically, "has given away everything I
had won before we left Paris. He has compromised on every side, and so I
have to start all over again and this time it will be harder, as he has given
the impression that my delegates are not in sympathy with me." In Wilson's absence, the Colonel had apparently had his first taste of power.
House explained that upon learning the American press opposed linking
the League to the Treaty, he had made executive decisions relinquishing
certain points, for fear that the Conference would withdraw its approval.
"So," Woodrow told Edith, "he has yielded until there is nothing left."

She stood there, holding her husband's hand, dumbfounded—if only
because she believed the majority of the American press supported the
League. At last, Woodrow threw back his head, and Edith saw a steely
glint in his eyes. "Well," he said, "thank God I can still fight, and I'll win
them back or never look these boys I sent over there in the face again. They
lost battles—but won the War, bless them. So don't be too dismayed." The
Wilsons sat and talked for several hours, as the train rushed through
the night toward Paris.

Wilson conferred again with House in the morning. Although the
Colonel's diary reflects little of the President's displeasure, Wilson was
clearly distraught. "Your dinner to the Senate Foreign Relations Committee was a failure as far as getting together was concerned," he told House.
He spoke with "considerable bitterness" of his treatment that night at the
hands of Senator Lodge, who had refused to ask any questions or even "to
act in the spirit in which the dinner was given." House maintained that
the dinner had at least spiked criticism that Wilson was acting unilaterally, failing to consult the Senate about foreign affairs. House expressed no
culpability in his diary, only that "the President comes back very militant
and determined to put the League of Nations into the Peace Treaty."

Dr. Grayson immediately felt the chill in the air and realized that the

President was relying on him for more than medical advice. Grayson and Tumulty had periodically used each other to relay information to the President; and just that week Grayson intuitively asked Tumulty to "communicate freely with me, giving me any pointers and suggestions that you may see fit." The doctor monitored the President's every move and watched Clemenceau and Poincaré as they welcomed Wilson's train at the Gare des Invalides. The President told the old Tiger that he hoped he was not feeling any ill effects from the recent shooting. "On the contrary," said Clemenceau, "I think it did me good."

The Wilsons settled into a new "White House" at 11 Place des États-Unis, on a quiet block between the Étoile and the Seine. Although it came lavishly furnished—with pictures by Rembrandt, Delacroix, and Goya—it felt "more homey" than the Murat Palace. Its only drawback was that the bedrooms were on the ground floor. The President's, in the back, along with a study, faced a garden, while Edith's was streetside, facing a park with a Bartholdi statue of Lafayette and George Washington. As if to compensate for its exposure to the street, it came with a gold-fixtured bathroom so lavish it made her giddy. A grand hall and staircase led to a second floor of public salons; the third floor had five bedrooms and plenty of secretarial space; and quarters on the fourth floor could accommodate twelve servants. The President would have preferred to pay for his lodging, but Clemenceau insisted upon the Republic's hosting its distinguished guests. "This house," Edith recalled, "was suddenly transformed into a workshop as the President, without an hour's delay, laid about him to win back what had been surrendered by Colonel House."

Wilson assessed the damage, first by spending an hour with his neighbor Lloyd George, who spoke not only of the daily trials at the conference table but also the tribulations he faced at home—railway workers were threatening to paralyze all of England, while miners were urging government seizure of their industry. After lunch, Wilson visited the American Commissioners, who were bivouacked at the Hôtel de Crillon, and dressed them down for failing to protect the League and the Germans' basic territorial rights. The French had already announced the creation of a Rhenish Republic, which Wilson described as nothing less than a personal "embarrassment." From three to five in the afternoon, he met with Clemenceau and Lloyd George in Colonel House's room. And after dinner at his residence, Wilson conferred with Premier Orlando, who described his private war with his cabinet ministers, many of whom were insisting on claims along the Adriatic coast, where Jugoslavs were already agitating.

The next morning, Wilson met again with Clemenceau and Lloyd George and asserted that any thought of a preliminary treaty without inclusion of the League was simply unacceptable. It contradicted the initial plenary session, at which the delegates agreed that the League was integral to the peace settlement—indeed, "the initial compelling paragraph of any peace treaty." Wilson insisted that "there were so many collateral questions which must be referred to the League of Nations . . . that its creation must be the first object, and that no treaty could be agreed upon that would deal only with military, naval and financial matters." The Premiers got the message. By day's end, Ray Baker had disseminated a statement denying all reports of a separate treaty with Germany that excluded the League. "It will cause a fluttering in the dove-cotes," Baker wrote in his diary, noting further: "Here is a man who *acts*: and has *audacity*."

Colonel House rendered a different picture of Wilson. Having occupied the seat of power for several weeks, he resented being put back in his place. His quiet petulance slowly surfaced. The next day, House and Lord Cecil met with Wilson to discuss how the Covenant might be amended, clarifications the Colonel thought would "make the Covenant a better instrument" and remove the Senate's objections. "The President, with his usual stubbornness in such matters, desires to leave it as it is, saying that any change will be hailed in the United States as yielding to the Senate," House wrote, "and he believes it will lessen rather than increase the chances of ratification." Again, House assured Cecil that the President would make "considerable concessions." Still inebriated with power, House wrote, "My main drive now is for peace with Germany . . . and I am determined that it shall come soon if it is within my power to force action." Days later, he soberly lamented, "I have no authority to decide questions on my own initiative as I did while the President was away."

"All to do over again," Woodrow grumbled to Edith. Through the month of March, six days a week, Wilson sat in one meeting after another, caroming from the Quai d'Orsay, where the Supreme War Council, the Council of Ten, and the League of Nations Commission met, to the Hôtel de Crillon, and then back to his private study, where the Council of Four convened, often twice a day. There, answers to all questions were always close at hand from experts who could run down the stairs from the great ballroom, which had been converted into a vast office. Typewriters clattered day and night.

On the surface, the conferees in Paris were united in their initial task of reindustrializing and revitalizing the world. Toward that end, the United States had sent an American Commission that included more than one hundred of the nation's most distinguished men, current and future leaders among them: Samuel Gompers advised the labor panel; Bernard Baruch worked on economics and commerce; Herbert Hoover oversaw food and provisions, Thomas Lamont of J. P. Morgan & Company and Secretary of State Lansing's nephew John Foster Dulles assisted the banking and finance committee. The latter's brother, Allen, served as a technical adviser. Among the younger men were Ulysses S. Grant's grandson, Colonel House's son-in-law, Gordon Auchincloss, and Christian Herter. The specialists who had been part of the initial Inquiry—historians, geographers, and experts on Western Europe, the Orient, Italy, the Balkans, Russia, and Poland— continued to report to House's brother-in-law, Sidney Mezes. The delegations from other nations were just as prodigious—what with John Maynard Keynes advising the British delegation and Jean Monnet the French. A thirty-year-old protégé of French Minister of Commerce Étienne Clémentel, Monnet was already espousing an expansion of inter-Allied economic councils with which he had worked, creating the nucleus of what he called "the Economic Union of Free Peoples." The other participants were dealing with too many immediate problems to consider such an enormous proposal, but Monnet believed the notion of a European Economic Community would have its day. Wilson's constant challenge remained getting his peers to put long-term global needs ahead of immediate national interests.

His conscience was his guide, especially when it came to reparations. But there were countless factors to debate, mostly the Allies' unconscionable demands. The British wanted to bill the Germans for damage to civilian life and property and also wanted compensation for "improper treatment of interned civilians." The French sought compensation for the loot of food, raw materials, livestock, machinery household effects, and timber. In addition, they wanted compensation to French nationals who had been deported and forced into labor camps. Panels had to determine to what extent Germany's co-belligerents—Austria-Hungary, Bulgaria, and Turkey—were liable. Then all those bills had to be stacked alongside the Central Powers' ability to pay.

A Sub-Committee of the Commission on Reparation of Damage was created to crunch the numbers. During the spring of 1919, this panel met thirty-two times, analyzing scores of reports on the assets of two continents—determining how much of the enemies' money was in cash, securities, or receivables in foreign countries and deciding how much might be paid in raw materials "of which each of the Allied States had most need and which the enemy might be required to deliver in part payment." The degree of detail approached ridiculousness. The fourth meeting of this subcommittee, for example, was devoted to the resources of Bulgaria. Investigators counted its grains in hundreds of millions of tons and its livestock and poultry into the billions—all 9.5 billion chickens, 405 million geese, 210 million turkeys, and 162 million ducks. The statisticians determined how many hectares were owned by peasants, schools, monasteries, and farmers' banks. Because rose-growing was a specialty of Eastern Roumelia—the flowers' extract being a valuable commodity—the subcommittee counted the number of petals that particular Bulgarian province yielded. The ninth meeting of the subcommittee examined the foreign securities owned by Germany. Copious tables listing the number of canal boats sunk during the war, the Portuguese worker's daily consumption of "albuminous substances," and the appraisal of artworks were all summarized in dizzying specifics, though sometimes the assessors pulled numbers from the sky. The subcommittee noted that enemy vessels destroyed 2,479 British mercantile vessels, the replacement costs of which could be figured at $150 per gross ton; but when it came to evaluating the loss of cargoes, Keynes said, it was "almost entirely a matter of guesswork." Adding the costs of soldiers' pensions and allowances, the total assessment against Germany came in around $40 billion, though the French claimed it was really twice that much and that Germany could afford $100 billion, if not twice that sum.

With so many vying interests at the Peace Conference, no problem had a perfect solution. Every financial formula contained an X factor of human complications. Much of Germany's wealth, for example, lay in its natural resources—particularly in coal, the mines of which sat in territories that could not simply be annexed to other countries. The Saar Valley, on the west bank of the Rhine, was German in every trait; but the French wanted its coal for their iron fields in Lorraine. Upper Silesia had a mixed population of Germans, Czechoslovakians, and Poles, all of whom also wanted its coal and iron ore. Keynes noted, however, that economically it was "intensely German," and that those resources fired the industries of eastern Germany. Their loss would flatten the economic structure of the German state, inhibiting Germany's ability to pay the very restitution the Allies sought. Where prior peace congresses allowed victors to grab their spoils, Wilson pled with the Big Four to settle their differences rationally, considering the historical, geographic, ethnological, and economic implications.

While restitution was an essential component of the peace talks, reconstitution of the fallen empires held equal importance. On March 20, 1919, the Council of Four (minus Orlando) met in Lloyd George's flat, where they opened the century's biggest can of worms—the Arab portions of the old Ottoman Empire that stretched from the Mediterranean and the Red Sea to the Persian Gulf. The region held the resource that would fuel the next century—oil. The opening discussion about the area just coming to be called "the Middle East" had two primary goals: creating an Arab Confederation of States detached from Turkey; and arbitrating the claims of Great Britain and France to that territory. Both issues were complicated by an early agreement the Arabs had struck with the British, parts of which conflicted with yet another of those well-kept secret treaties.

During the war, French diplomat François Georges-Picot and English adviser Sir Mark Sykes had sought to strengthen the bond between their two nations by anticipating victory and dividing the Ottoman Empire among themselves and Russia (before that nation's surrender) into spheres of influence. Essentially, the French would control Syria and Lebanon and the northern regions of modern Iraq; Great Britain would control Mesopotamia and Palestine, including what would become Jordan; and the Russians would obtain Armenia and Kurdistan. The remaining desert would be surrendered to the Arab empire as zones under British or French influence. The agreement was signed in May 1916. All but ignored in the agreement, of course, were the Arabs themselves, who had recently found a dynamic champion in a diminutive British army officer named Thomas Edward Lawrence. Transfixed by the region, Lawrence hoped to transform it, as he helped organize the Arab armies behind Faisal—a charismatic son of the Grand Sharif of Mecca—in their revolt against the Ottomans. At the same time, he led a diplomatic charge against his own country in promoting Arab independence. Even though England, France, and the Arabs had been joined in opposing the Turks, the Sykes-Picot Agreement, which Lawrence learned about only after it was signed, was an affront to the Arabs. And the following year, the Balfour Declaration complicated matters further by acknowledging Britain's support for establishing an independent Jewish state.

The concerned parties descended upon Paris in 1919, with "Lawrence of Arabia" escorting Faisal, in full desert garb, into the salons of the Allied diplomats. Lawrence himself often appeared similarly robed, drawing attention to his cause. Wilson joked that Sykes-Picot sounded like a blend of tea, but the problems it created were no laughing matter. Lloyd George told the Council of Four that if Damascus, for example, fell under French administration, the British would have "broken faith with the Arabs." General Allenby topped that, suggesting that French imposition upon an unwilling Syria would surely lead to war. Wilson argued that France and Great Britain's positions were moot since they had accepted his Fourteen Points, which superseded all prior agreements.

In a further complication, shortly before the peace talks, Faisal had signed an agreement with Dr. Chaim Weizmann, president of the World Zionist Organization. It honored the Balfour Declaration and encouraged development of a Jewish homeland in Palestine. It suggested both parties— scions of the same Semitic family tree—felt like outsiders and needed each other in order to sustain harmony in their mutual quest for independence. Wilson had long believed compromise could prevail when even ancient enemies sat together at the same table. He hoped to establish Faisal's place in the Conference and argued further that because one of the parties to the Sykes-Picot Agreement—Russia—was no longer a participant, that agreement was nullified. Believing in "the consent of the governed," the President said establishing Middle East mandates would depend on the Syrians accepting French oversight and the Mesopotamians accepting that of Great Britain. Similar conundrums appeared daily, and the revelation of one secret treaty after another only contributed to what Harold Nicolson called "an atmosphere of discord and disorder."

"An undeniable tone of pessimism prevails here," Ray Baker wrote in his diary the day that Syria was first discussed. And the problems in the Middle East were the least of it. He worried about the instability in Germany and the industrial situation in England, to say nothing of the mounting attacks on Wilson and the League at home. But the problem in Paris was more fundamental than all that.

Each day, Wilson realized to a greater degree that he and the other world leaders approached the world with differing visions. Taking a macro viewpoint, Wilson looked at the entire forest; his fellow peacemakers examined the micro situations for their own countries, seeing only the trees. The President believed in doing everything possible to see that self-determination might prevail in the new nations but increasingly saw that he would have to keep placating the great powers in order to protect the lesser ones. It was a delicate balance, for at any given moment a world leader could simply walk out on the entire proceedings. And France increasingly revealed less interest in self-determination than in the simple castration of Germany.

The American Commission remained especially mindful of Poland, which it considered a keystone to a reconstructed Europe. Its land had been seized and partitioned for years; its people were struggling to establish themselves as a democratic state; and it provided a crucial buffer between Germany and Russia, a firewall between Communism and Western Europe. Secretary Lansing and his colleagues advised Wilson to appoint an Ambassador to the wobbly republic as soon as possible, which he did. In the meantime, Hungary underwent a series of revolutions, one of them organized by Communist Béla Kun. He promptly declared himself dictator, launching a Red Terror, confiscating property, and murdering thousands of his own people. Communism also seeped into the Baltic states of Latvia, Lithuania, and Estonia. In Riga, a Latvian Soviet Republic took hold, releasing thousands of prisoners who, with the Communists, looted stores, homes, and banks. They used machine guns to mow down innocent citizens, those deaths matched by starvation and disease. American food supplies seemed the best antidote to the raging ills and instability.

Twelve days after Wilson returned to Paris, William Bullitt came back from his Russian expedition. He had met Lenin himself, who charmed the young diplomat. "The Soviet government is firmly established, and the Communist Party is strong politically and morally," Bullitt reported. His fellow traveler Lincoln Steffens would later remark to Bernard Baruch, "I have seen the future, and it works!" Bullitt promptly submitted a white paper urging recognition of the Red regime. On March 28, the altruistic but pragmatic Herbert Hoover, while acknowledging the massive number of deaths due to hunger in Russia, insisted, "We cannot even remotely recognize this murderous tyranny without stimulating actionist radicalism in every country in Europe and without transgressing on every National ideal of our own." Furthermore, he asserted, "I feel strongly the time has arrived for you again to reassert your spiritual leadership of democracy in the world as opposed to tyrannies of all kinds." He suggested an examination of Bolshevism from its political, economic, humane, and criminal points of view. Having more sway with the President than Bullitt, he urged Wilson to understand the movement's "utter foolishness as a basis of economic development." Hoover had no doubt that real democracy was the straighter road to "social betterment."

Increasingly, Wilson realized the Conference was becoming less about such humanitarian issues as feeding hungry peoples than it was about politics. That was mostly because of the French, with their endless political ploys. Clemenceau, who constantly reverted to positions he had already surrendered, became Wilson's bête noire. Repeatedly the President explained that much of the world's sympathy toward France was the result of their believing she had been wronged by Germany. "Now if the policies are to be carried out which you are advocating, and which wrong the German people," he tried reasoning with the French Premier, "the world must naturally turn against you and France, and through sympathy alone it may be likely to forget Germany's crimes." In talking about the Rhenish buffer state the French sought, Wilson finally convinced Clemenceau. But, as he confided to Lord Cecil after dinner on March 18, talking to the French was like pressing a finger into an India rubber ball: "You tried to make an impression," Wilson said, "but as soon as you moved your finger the ball was as round as ever." Wilson said that he would never consent to dividing the country on the west bank of the Rhine from Germany, but he was prepared to agree to something "in the nature of an alliance between England and America and France to protect her against sudden aggression, in addition to the protection which she would already have by the League of Nations." That appealed to the European leaders in the abstract, but one could never overestimate Clemenceau's insatiable desire for security and revenge.

Stalling had become Georges Clemenceau's greatest stratagem. He had the luxury of time, while the other world leaders had nations awaiting their returns. Wilson, especially, had fierce opposition mounting in his absence. And each day of dithering in Paris meant further starvation and destabilization in the world. By the end of his first week back at the conference table, Wilson was reaching the end of his tether. That Saturday, after hours filled with discussion of Polish borders, thirty-seven amendments to the League Covenant, and a plea from the Japanese about racial equality, an exhausted President blurted to his wife and physician, "It is hard to keep one's temper when the world is on fire and we find delegates, such as those of the French, blocking all of the proceedings in a most stubborn manner simply by talking and without producing a single constructive idea designed to help remedy the serious situation existing." He complained that the French now considered the League just another hedge against Germany. "They talk and talk and talk and desire constantly to reiterate points that have been already thoroughly thrashed out and completely disposed of. . . . They simply talk."

The next morning at eight—accompanied only by Dr. Grayson and Miss Benham and as few guards as the Secret Service would permit—the Wilsons inspected some battle sites. Without French supervision, they revisited Rheims and Vaux and Château-Thierry before proceeding to Noyon, Lassigny, and Montdidier. The Germans had left the legendary medieval château in Coucy in ruins, prompting Wilson to shake his head and decry, "What a pity that a place like this should be destroyed when there was no military or other advantage to be gained—only wantonness." In Soissons he saw the remains of a town that had endured almost daily bombardment, forcing its inhabitants to live in cellars for months at a time. Townspeople swarmed around the local inn, where Wilson and his party took their lunch. There a French officer passed a message along that "the soldiers wanted the President to know that they were back of him and his plans of peace, and they did not want him to allow France to get a kind of peace that Clemenceau . . . [was] desirous of having made." Upon his return to Paris that night at eight, Wilson said that the day had been instructive but "exceedingly painful." He allowed that it had enabled him "to have a fuller conception than ever of the extraordinary sufferings and hardships of the people of France in the baptism of cruel fire through which they have passed."

At the Council of Four the next day, Wilson spoke of his trip, though he did not dwell on the horrors of the past. "At this moment," he said, "there is a veritable race between peace and anarchy, and the public is beginning to show its impatience." He told of a woman who had approached him amid the rubble of Soissons, asking, "When will you give us peace?" Seeking an answer, Wilson said they had to address the most urgent questions—reparations, the protection of France against aggression, and the Italian frontier along the Adriatic coast—without delay. He told visiting Secretary Daniels, "The only exercise I get is to my vocabulary." Clemenceau muttered that Wilson "thought himself another Jesus Christ come upon the earth to reform men."

Because there was little time for recreation, Dr. Grayson urged the President to make his rounds from the "new White House" on foot, whenever possible. Wilson asked his wife to buy a map of Paris, so that he could chart different routes for himself; but within days, it fell into disuse. Grayson repeatedly implored him at least to slow the pace of his workday, but the President said, "We are running a race with Bolshevism and the world is on fire. Let us wind up this work here and then we will go home and find time for a little rest and play and take up our health routine again." Wilson's left cheek twitched. He was in a constant state of fatigue, his patience wearing thin.

Wilson harped on the same refrain, that crushing Germany would only result in another war. Prefacing his remarks with sympathy from having just seen the devastation of the countryside, Wilson argued that it was his duty to bring about permanent peace conditions that would benefit the entire world. "Don't you see," he asked Clemenceau on March 25, 1919, "that the very program that you propose to impose, carrying with it an excessive burden of taxation for generations, would be the greatest encouragement that could be held out to the German people to go over to Bolshevism?" On March 26, he added, "We owe it to the peace of the world" to present a treaty "founded on justice." On the twenty-seventh he said, "Our greatest error would be to give [Germany] powerful reasons for one day wishing to take revenge. Excessive demands would most certainly sow the seeds of war." At the end of that morning's session, Dr. Grayson asked Wilson how he was feeling. "I feel terribly disappointed," he said. "After arguing with Clemenceau for two hours . . . he practically agreed to everything, and just as he was leaving he swung back to where we had begun." Wilson, Lloyd George, and Orlando considered drawing up their own peace terms and departing, leaving Clemenceau's government to live with the consequences.

After a week of no progress in discussing reparations, the Council of Four turned again to the Saar Valley. Clemenceau insisted that its cession to France and the control of its mines had been among his country's primary war aims and that he would not sign the Treaty without it. Wilson said that stipulation had never been disclosed. Tensions between the two leaders escalated until the Tiger growled that Wilson had become "the friend of Germany." To the man who had mobilized a nation and sent two million men to fight by France's side, at the cost of 100,000 American lives, this was more than Wilson could bear. His jaw tightening and his eyes burning, Wilson accused the Frenchman of deliberately stating untruths. In light of Clemenceau's persistent refusal to cooperate, Wilson asked, "In that event, do you wish me to return home?" Looking just as furious, Clemenceau humphed that he did not wish the President to leave . . . that he would instead. With that, he turned on his heel and exited.

The afternoon session resumed as though the morning exchange had never occurred. "Knowing the President as I do," however, Robert Lansing wrote, "I am sure that he will not forgive, much less forget, this affair. From now on he will look upon Clemenceau as an antagonist. He will suspect his every suggestion and doubt his honesty. The President is a wonderful hater." Clemenceau, who coughed profoundly throughout the proceedings, showed contrition only in saying that he would never forget "that our American friends . . . came here to assist us in a moment of supreme danger." But he expressed his conviction that Wilson was naïve in seeking justice for the Germans. "Do not believe that they will ever forgive us," he said; "they only seek the opportunity for revenge. Nothing will destroy the rage of those who wanted to establish their domination over the world and who believed themselves so close to succeeding."

The exchange that day summed up the peace talks in a nutshell. Where Wilson had idealistically maintained that "there is throughout the entire world a passion for justice," Clemenceau argued the realpolitik of the world based on experience. "The history of the United States is a glorious history," he said, "but short. A century for you is a very long period; for us it is a little thing. I have known men who saw Napoleon with their own eyes." The discussion turned to the historic tug-of-war over Alsace, which, Lloyd George reminded, dated as far back as 1648. Upon hearing that, Orlando spoke up at last, insisting they must exclude such historical arguments; "otherwise," he said, "Italy could, if she wished, claim all the former territories of the Roman Empire." Wilson laughed; Clemenceau did not.

On Monday the Big Four returned to the coal mines. They discussed a promising proposal of France's owning the mines and administering the territory under a League mandate with a plebiscite in fifteen years to determine the nationality of the region. And then they agreed upon some Polish borders. But soon Clemenceau had backslid to his "interminable arguments." Dr. Grayson watched Wilson as he attempted to keep the conversation on point, but it was "very plain that the constant strain of trying to make men work, who had no desire to work, along the lines necessary was having its effect on the President." He was turning peevish. "I think the President is becoming unreasonable, which does not make for solutions," Colonel House imparted to his diary.

After another day bogged down in verbiage, Wilson spoke to House on the telephone for close to an hour, complaining about Clemenceau's stubbornness. House sensed that Wilson was feeling isolated, that having given him his League of Nations, everyone was prepared to hang him out to dry. In passing, the President said that he did not think Paul Mantoux, the recording secretary and interpreter, liked him; and then in a completely unguarded moment, he said, "Indeed, I am not sure that anybody does."

On Thursday, April 3, 1919—after an early afternoon visit from King Albert of Belgium—the President excused himself from the Council of Four meeting and staggered to his room. His doctor found him suffering from intense pains in his back and head, severe coughing spells, considerable upset in his "equatorial zone," and a fever of 103 degrees. Because he did not want anybody to interpret his absence as a sign of quitting, Wilson advised Grayson to announce that he had taken to his bed. At first, Grayson announced only that the President was suffering from a severe cold. Although he would subsequently diagnose this baffling illness as the onset of influenza, doctors have studied Wilson's symptoms over the decades and come to various conclusions. Some suggest that the President suffered from some other viral infection, as there had been no cases of Spanish influenza reported in Paris that spring, and most of his symptoms subsided within days. On the other hand, several doctors noted that influenza viruses attack not only pulmonary organs but also the heart and brain; and, along with his difficulty breathing, Wilson also endured an infection of the prostate and bladder. Strangely, despite a lethargy that lingered for weeks, he displayed a contradictory impulse to carry on without a "care in the world"—signs of anosognosia, a mental condition in which the disabled is unaware of his disability. That led some doctors to consider a case of encephalitis, which was known to cause changes in personality and periodic spurts of heightened energy. Wilson's history of cerebral vascular disease also suggests a small stroke. One other possible label has been assigned to Wilson's condition, one as mysterious as it is unsettling.

Dementia is seldom diagnosed in its earliest stages because its manifestations are almost imperceptible at the onset. In retrospect, however, one can often trace its development. Early signs of the condition include apathy toward former enthusiasms, increased impatience, self-absorption to the point of insensitivity toward others, and a creeping sense of compulsive as well as suspicious behavior. Most of those symptoms were, in fact, chronic attributes of Woodrow Wilson, and the rest could be credited to a man with little leisure time, a President anxious to return to the Oval Office, from which he had been absent for close to half a year. But Wilson's current and future symptoms justify its consideration.

Theories have abounded for a century—none of which can be certified, though this much can be asserted: Woodrow Wilson had suffered for more than twenty years from hypertension and progressive cerebral vascular disease, which had resulted in small strokes; he had increasingly become aware of his own absentmindedness—enough to ask that memoranda of important conversations be written—a state he referred to as his "leaky" brain. And that metaphor might just have pinpointed the true nature of his neurological condition, that he had long been suffering from "lacunar infarctions"—a trickling of blood in the brain from lesser blood vessels— rather than an occlusion of a major vein or artery. Whatever the case, in April 1919, at a moment of physical and nervous exhaustion, Woodrow Wilson was struck by a viral infection that had neurological ramifications.

The President had long been a hero to his valet, and his sudden display of behavioral changes troubled Ike Hoover. Generally predictable in his actions, Wilson began blurting unexpected orders, often reversing his own household policies. Because his secretaries and innermost staff worked unusually long hours, Wilson had placed use of the automobiles at their disposal, urging them to see Paris whenever possible; suddenly, after that first weekend in bed, he issued orders that the cars were thereafter off-limits except for official use. Ike Hoover said Wilson also became "obsessed with the idea that every French employee about the place was a spy for the French Government." He sometimes stopped speaking when the help was present because he had convinced himself that all the domestics understood English and were reporting his conversations to Clemenceau, even though the Secret Service found only one servant who spoke any English. Twice he created a scene over pieces of furniture that had suddenly disappeared, which nobody else in the household had observed. He began to require a Secret Service agent to guard his office when he was not present; and he now placed papers from his desk into a strongbox. Recalling the President's puzzling behavior, Ike Hoover said, "We could but surmise that something queer was happening in his mind" and that "he was never the same after this little spell of sickness."

Seeing no reason for the Conference to recess, Wilson designated House to take his place, even though the Colonel no longer held his complete confidence. With the meetings held downstairs from his bedroom, Wilson could not imagine House's allowing the conversations to drift too far from his principles. But the next day, Wilson insisted the meeting be moved upstairs to the sitting room off his bedroom, in and out of which House would pop like a character in a French farce. The Colonel boasted more than once that he could move the proceedings along with much greater dispatch than the President himself, and Ray Baker saw why: "The Colonel sides with the group which desires a swift peace on any terms," while "the President struggles almost alone to secure some constructive & idealistic result out of the general ruin."

With Wilson temporarily out of commission, Clemenceau and Lloyd George tried to chip away at his position on reparations. The British Prime Minister turned House's head with flattery, suggesting that it was better for him to conclude this particular round of the peace talks than the President. Sensing after three days that the talks were straying from his righteous path, Wilson asked that the Conference be held right in his bedroom. "To lie in bed and think of problems that you cannot pitch into and dispose of naturally make the mind more active and prevents sleeping," the convalescent explained to his doctor. "When you can handle them in person it is easy enough to dismiss them after you go to bed. To know that I am responsible for them and cannot take part in the proceedings makes me restless." He claimed that a little overexertion made him feel better. Having a number of issues he wanted to sort out, he asked Grayson to summon Bernard Baruch. And to make the arrangements for gathering his advisers one afternoon, he turned to his wife. "Can't I tell Colonel House to do it?" Edith asked. And Woodrow emphatically replied, "No."

Practically everything about House now irritated the President. By Monday, April 7, Wilson's temperature was normal, and with a clear head, he asked Grayson, "Do you see any change in House[?] . . . He does not show the same free and easy spirit; he seems to act distant with me as if he has something on his conscience." Grayson was loath to agree, but he did not hesitate to speak his mind regarding House's son-in-law, Gordon Auchincloss, who had come to be considered something of a joke because of his exalted opinion of himself. Even the President had heard that Auchincloss made constant digs behind his back and had commented that "little Woody's" fortunes at the bargaining table were because of his father-in-law. Wilson told Edith and Dr. Grayson that he no longer wished Auchincloss to conduct any business in his name.

The problem had deeper implications. Not only was Auchincloss feeding stories to the press that exaggerated Colonel House's importance at the peace talks, but House began to believe them. One afternoon Edith Wilson read an article in an American paper that described House as "the brains of the Commission." At that moment, the Colonel arrived for a conference with the President, who was not available. After some friendly conversation, Edith asked House if he had been aware of any of the "awful attacks on Woodrow," such as the one before her. After she read several paragraphs aloud, House blushed and asked if her husband had seen the article. When Edith said he had not, the Colonel suddenly said that he had to leave, taking the newspaper with him. Later she related the story to Dr. Grayson, who suggested not only that Auchincloss was stirring up the stories but also that House himself was feeding self-serving tips to the press. "I don't believe it, Dr. Grayson," said Edith, who had always questioned House's loyalty, "for if it were true Colonel House would be a traitor." Grayson told her that he had caught House talking to a journalist and posing on the roof of the Crillon for a photographer. The moment House saw Grayson, he hastily departed. Edith told Woodrow about her encounter with the Colonel, omitting the information Grayson had given her. "Oh, if Colonel House had only stood firm while you were away none of this would have to be done over," she lamented. "I think he is a perfect jellyfish." Wilson replied, "Well, God made jellyfish, so, as Shakespeare said about a man, therefore let him pass, and don't be too hard on House. It takes a pretty stiff spinal column to stand against the elements centred here."

That defense aside, the President began considering House in the same terms Ray Baker had written in his diary:

> More & more he impresses me as the dilettante—the lover of the game—the eager secretary without profound responsibility. He stands in the midst of great events, to lose nothing. He gains experiences to put in his diary . . .

Meanwhile, Wilson trusted House less and less. The Colonel, without explanation, stopped visiting the Wilsons' residence except for business meetings. He now peppered his diary with criticism of the President's actions; and he liked one negative quip enough to preserve it in his journal: "Wilson talks like Jesus Christ and acts like Lloyd George." Before the spring was over, House wrote in his diary, "I seldom or never have a chance to talk with him seriously and, for the moment, he is practically out from under my influence."

Although still febrile, Wilson experienced a surge of emotional energy. Husbanding his strength, he showed an intolerance for wasted time and an inclination toward snap decisions, some in impetuous variance to positions he had long held. If definitive progress was not to be made in a timely manner, Wilson told Grayson, he would simply go home. On Sunday, April 6, Wilson asked him to ascertain the location of the *George Washington* and to order its immediate retrieval to Brest. "When I decide, doctor . . . to carry this thing through," he told Grayson, "I do not want to say that I am going as soon as I can get a boat; I want the boat to be here."

News of deploying the ship from dry dock in America was, according to Ray Baker, "the greatest sensation of the entire Peace Conference." Tumulty—minding the store in Washington—informed the President through Admiral Grayson that the action seemed politically ill-advised, that Washington viewed it "as an act of impatience and petulance on the President's part," if not an act of "desertion." And then Clemenceau and his Finance Minister, Louis Lucien Klotz, "talked away another day," producing nothing more than what Wilson called a "mass of tergiversations." After the meeting he complained to Grayson of having "Klotz on the brain." He knew he had made the right decision in beckoning his ship.

The American advisers in Paris considered Wilson's action a turning point in the talks. Henry White thought the time had come for an end to private proceedings—that the Councils of Ten and Four were being used to discredit the President, that he should announce that all future decisions would be arrived at during plenary sessions, and that "not one American soldier, dollar or pound of supplies for military purposes will be furnished until Peace is made." Herbert Hoover was of a similar mind, believing the Allies were bound in the end to accept the League for fear of losing American financial support. "It grows upon me daily that the United States is the one great moral reserve in the world today," he wrote the President, and that "if the Allies cannot be brought to adopt peace on the basis of the Fourteen Points, we should retire from Europe lock, stock and barrel." Unfortunately, the Allies had the United States over a barrel, one the President had rolled out himself. Knowing Wilson's deathless adherence to the League, the other leaders believed he would yield ground on thirteen of the points in order to preserve his precious fourteenth, and they held it hostage.

Whether it was his stubbornness about the League or some euphoric manifestation of one of his medical conditions, Wilson emerged from his sickbed the second week of April in what one doctor later characterized as a "hypomanic state." The Big Four quickly came, at last, to several agreements, in which the President conceded points that differed from his prior positions. He agreed, for example, to a clause (written by John Foster Dulles of the Commission on Responsibilities) assigning Allies' damage to German aggression. Having once renounced such a policy, he now accepted a British proposal to try the Kaiser (living in exile in Holland) for war crimes. He relented on the matter of the Rhenish Republic, allowing French occupation with a future plebiscite. While many within his own delegation questioned his judgment, none of these positions, in truth, was vital enough for him to kill the peace process, especially as the French were showing a willingness to budge from some of their original positions. Wilson characterized all these agreements as diplomatic victories, and in one fundamental way, they were: they allowed him to preserve the League as part of the Treaty.

His recent behavior suggested a susceptibility to suppliants of all sorts and the possibility of further concessions. At a meeting of the League of Nations Committee on April 10, Wilson received a delegation representing the International Council of Women and the Suffragist Conference of the Allied countries and the United States, which petitioned for universal suffrage and against sexual and slave trafficking in women and children. The next day, before his round of Council meetings, he received two Galician goatherds—who arrived in native mountain costume and reeking of goat—representing two small colonies that hoped the new Poland would include them. Only hours later, the President was hosting a lunch for the most glamorous visitor to Paris that season, Marie, the Queen of Romania, whom he had met the day before and who promptly invited herself to his residence. The scandalous blonde—who had boasted of a "love child"— did not endear herself to the President by arriving twenty minutes late and with extra guests. She obviously hoped to lobby for a favorable drawing of Romania's borders, though secretary Edith Benham could see from the tightening of Wilson's jaw that a sliver of Romania was being sliced off for each minute she was tardy. The President suggested starting the meal without her, but his wife persuaded him not to breach the rules of etiquette merely because she had.

Once she had arrived, the Queen proved to be a sparkling conversationalist, intelligent and fast-talking and outspoken, especially in hailing the virtues of monarchies for being "less liable to breed Bolshevism than were democracies." But her charms were utterly wasted on the President, who politely evaded all her blunt questions about the personalities at the Conference. He brought the luncheon to a close so that he could appear on time at the Quai d'Orsay for the three o'clock plenary session devoted solely to a presentation by the Commission on International Labor Legislation. The delegates adopted clauses establishing a forty-eight-hour workweek, banning child labor under the age of fourteen, and ensuring equal pay for women and men "for work of equal value in quantity and quality."

The following Thursday, Wilson endured his busiest day yet—eighteen appointments, mostly with spokesmen for minor nations and principalities. It began with a committee of Irish American politicians hoping to engage the President in influencing the establishment of an Irish Republic, a political hot potato for Great Britain. Since it struck Wilson as both imprudent and inappropriate to engage in Britain's internal politics, he kept future contact on an unofficial basis. The day's procession also included representatives from China, an Assyrian-Chaldean delegation seeking representation in what would become Iraq, and a Dalmatian delegation wishing to be free of Italy, Albania, Romania, Armenia, and Serbia as well as the Orthodox Eastern Churches. "After all this ocean of talk has rolled over me," he told War Secretary Baker, who was visiting, "I feel that I would like to return to America and go back into some great forest, amid the silence, and not hear any argument or speeches for a month." But the most strident discussions had yet to begin.

After months of holding back—as Wilson knew he would—Vittorio Orlando held forth. In return for joining the Triple Entente, Italy cited the secret Treaty of London and claimed the South Tyrol up to the Brenner Pass. Rumors suggested the massive display of Italian affection for Wilson during his New Year's visit accounted for his inexplicably allowing close to a quarter of a million German-speaking Tyrolese to fall under Italian rule. Wilson himself would later admit that he conceded the territory based on "insufficient study" and that he came to regret this "ignorant" decision. The Treaty of London also guaranteed Italy portions of Dalmatia along the Adriatic, and some of the islands therein. Wilson was prepared to challenge these claims, but he knew that Britain and France would stand by the Treaty. Then came Italy's biggest challenge.

Nestled in an inlet of the Adriatic Sea—not forty miles from Trieste, where the coastline turned from Italy to Croatia—sat Fiume, a port that had long served Austria-Hungary. In the generation preceding the war, Fiume saw great economic growth, in large measure because Hungary (with its own Catholic persuasion) had encouraged Italian immigration there. Within the last decade, the population of the city itself had become home to more Italians than Croatians, though counting all the suburbs gave Fiume a Croatian majority. In signing the Treaty of London, Italy had not included the city among its demands. Now it did. On April 17, 1919, Ambassador Page in Rome wrote Colonel House that Italians had come to feel as passionate about Fiume as the French did about Alsace and Lorraine. Despite the recent spike in the Italian population there, Wilson insisted that Fiume—historically, culturally, geographically, and economically—was a Croatian port, one that properly belonged to the Jugoslavian nation that was taking form, whose people called it Rijeka.

Wilson believed he had conceded enough to Italy, and he considered the Dalmatian coast essentially Slavic. On April 18, he met privately with Lloyd George and Clemenceau, in hopes of creating a united front in blocking Orlando, who was hinting that he would walk out of the Conference if his demands were not met. Wilson asked Ray Baker if he thought Orlando was bluffing, and Baker thought not. The other members of the Big Four had received enough bounty to present to their constituents—including an acknowledgment of the Monroe Doctrine, which Wilson could show naysayers back home. And now Orlando wanted his trophy.

On the morning of the nineteenth, Orlando presented his claims to the Council of Four, and Wilson flatly refused him. He disliked having to disappoint the Italian Premier, for whom he had developed a fondness, but he said it was impossible to accept conditions that so contradicted the very principles that Italy had accepted at the time of the Armistice. Wilson acknowledged Orlando's strongest argument—that natural borders must be strongly considered. "The slope of the mountains not only threw the rivers in a certain direction but tended to throw the life of the people in the same direction," Wilson observed; and that largely accounted for his assenting to the claims in the Tyrol, even in Trieste and most of the Istrian Peninsula. "Outside of these, however," recorded Sir Maurice Hankey, who kept the minutes of the meeting that morning, "further to the South all the arguments seemed to him to lead the other way. A different watershed was reached. Different racial units were encountered. There were natural associations between the peoples." Wilson maintained that something more than mountains and the flow of streams defined a nation. Despite Orlando's arguments that Jugoslavia had ports beyond the Italian-populated Fiume on which to rely, Wilson said the essential point was that "Fiume served the commerce of Czecho-Slovakia, Hungary, Roumania as well as Jugo-Slavia." Hence, it was necessary to establish its free use as an international port.

The inconstant Lloyd George announced that Great Britain would stand by the Treaty. Wilson argued that such a solution would draw the United States into an unfair, even impossible, situation. His country had entered the war in the name of certain principles that were at cross-purposes with the Treaty of London. Italy's Baron Sonnino unexpectedly reminded the President that in May of 1918, he had spoken publicly of America's interest in "the present and future security of Italy." Wilson insisted that "Dalmatia was not essential to the security of Italy." The foursome agreed to table the matter until the next day. That night Wilson attended the theater for the first time in a month—a divertissement that worried members of the President's party as some of the girls onstage began to remove some of their garments. The President did not look away.

The next day—Easter Sunday—Wilson resurrected the question of Fiume. Orlando argued that a failure to grant the port to his people would result in a "reaction of protest and of hatred." When Wilson had heard enough, he read two of the Fourteen Points that applied to the frontiers of Italy and Serbia's right to access to the sea, and then he read Orlando the riot act. He reminded his fellow leaders that "the material and financial assistance of the United States of America had been essential to the successful conclusion of the War" and that the United States had declared its principles upon entry into that war, principles acclaimed by those present that morning. Wilson said it was "incredible" to him that Italy was turning its current position into an ultimatum, but he was clear that the United States would not sign a treaty that surrendered all that Italy demanded, even if that meant Orlando's walking out before signing. After the President's remarks, Orlando rose from his chair, walked to the window, and burst into tears. He did not appear at the meeting of the Council of Four the next day or the day after that.

"You will surely admit," Wilson said to Clemenceau and Lloyd George, "that it is I who caused America to enter the war, who instructed and formed American opinion little by little. I did it while standing by principles which you know. Baron Sonnino led the Italian people into war to conquer territories. I did it while involving a principle of justice; I believe my claim takes precedence over his." Wilson instructed financial adviser Norman Davis to sit on a $50 million loan Italy had requested—"until the air clears—if it does."

With Orlando showing no signs of rejoining the group, Wilson resorted to a tactic that had served him well ever since his days as an embattled college president. He would take his case to the people—in this instance by publishing a friendly and levelheaded statement outlining his position regarding Italy's territorial claims. It did not play well. Orlando responded with his own long statement to the press, in which he took the President to task. "The practice of addressing nations directly constitutes surely an innovation in international relations," he said sarcastically. "I do not wish to complain, but I wish to record it as a precedent, so that at my own time I may follow it, inasmuch as this new custom doubtless constitutes the granting to nations of larger participation in international questions." Protesters marched in Rome; the crowds that had beatified Wilson months prior now burned him in effigy. The Italian press derided "Wilsonian peace," and Orlando announced that he was withdrawing from the Peace Conference.

On the heels of this Italian retreat from signing the Treaty or joining the League, the President faced an even more crucial ordeal. In late April, after sitting in silence, the Japanese wished to be heard. In fact, Japan had spoken up in February when it suggested amending the clause providing for "religious equality" by adding racial equality as well. Equating the yellow race with the white would not play well across the British Empire—nor in the United States, where anti-Asian laws persisted. The further implication that the black man might stand alongside the white man there was also still anathema. Harold Nicolson knew "no American Senate would ever dream of ratifying any Covenant which enshrined so dangerous a principle."

Nor would Woodrow Wilson. Only recently, the President had read an article on the strikes in Germany, and it rekindled his fear of Bolshevism. He had serious concerns about Communism creeping into America. The most likely vessel for that occurrence, he confided to Dr. Grayson, was "the American negro returning from abroad." He related an anecdote of a lady friend who wanted to employ a black laundress and offered to pay the standard wage, but she demanded that she be given more because that money "is as much mine as it is yours." In the millions of pages documenting Wilson's administration, the President rarely expressed a belief in inequality among the races; even his discussions of segregation expressed a policy meant for the good of both peoples. But on this incautious occasion, he revealed his true unreconstituted nature, what could only be perceived as genteel racism. He pointed out to Grayson that during the war, the French had placed their Negro soldiers shoulder to shoulder with the whites. That concept, Wilson said, "has gone to their heads." For all his talk of evenhandedness, Wilson did not consider the races fundamentally equal, and he had no intention of equalizing them under the law.

The topic of racial equality had been tabled in Paris for several months, but the Japanese now raised it once again, though they were prepared to sacrifice it in order to leverage a greater reward: Shantung Province—in the middle of China's east coast, on the Yellow Sea—the birthplace of

Confucius, a sacred region for Taoists and Buddhists, and a center of the Boxer Rebellion. Since the final days of the nineteenth century, much of the province had fallen under the German sphere of influence. In 1917, Great Britain, needing ships, appealed to Japan, which secretly agreed to supply them in return for all the Pacific islands that Germany held north of the equator plus the Chinese province of Shantung, including its prosperous ports, especially Kiaochow. Britain would receive the German islands south of the equator. This was practically the first Wilson had heard of this secret treaty. Now Baron Makino informed a plenary session that he would not press the "racial equality" clause he had sought earlier, but when it came to Shantung, his delegation was prepared to walk if it did not get its way. Losing two members of the Big Five would render the Conference a debacle.

According to every Wilsonian standard, Shantung should remain Chinese, but Japan's strategic advantage of already occupying Kiaochow bolstered her treaty-guaranteed right to the rest of the province. After dinner on April 25, Wilson tried to unknot this latest secret entanglement by talking to Dr. Grayson, rather the way he used to converse with Colonel House. "England's secret treaty with Japan would mean that when it came to a showdown England would side with Japan," he reasoned. That meant not only that Japan might not stand by the Fourteen Points and would withdraw from the Conference but that England might follow as well. "If I only had men of principle to stand by me," he lamented. By adhering to his principles without compromise, Wilson figured Japan, Italy, and England would not sign the Peace Treaty—and he would have to "shoulder the blame for obstructing the peace of the world." He wished the Japanese might see some way of saving face but yield in their demands and that the League of Nations might settle the matter later. Most of Wilson's experts advised his standing by the principles that had brought them this far. House admitted that his sympathies were "about evenly divided, with a feeling that it would be a mistake to take such action against Japan as might lead to her withdrawal from the Conference." Tumulty cabled from Washington that "the selfish designs of Japan are as indefensible as are those of Italy." But, Wilson noted, "they do not seem to realize what the results might be at this crucial time in the world's history."

He wrestled with what would become of the League of Nations if Italy refused to return and Japan departed. Having watched the President sweat blood, Ray Baker wrote in his diary that night: "He is at Gethsemane."

Secretary of State Lansing wrote himself a memorandum, calling this submission to the Japanese a "surrender of the principle of self-determination, a transfer of millions of Chinese from one foreign master to another." He thought it better to exclude Japan from the League than to abandon China. Speaking on behalf of Henry White, Herbert Hoover, and himself, General Tasker Bliss went further, sending the President a long letter in which he concluded: "If it be right for Japan to annex the territory of an Ally [China], then it cannot be wrong for Italy to retain Fiume taken from the enemy." If the United States abandoned the democracy of China to the domination of the "Prussianized militarism of Japan," he said, "we shall be sowing dragons' teeth"—a reference to a mythical prince who planted such teeth, from which sprang armed warriors.

For one of the few times in his life, Wilson suffered from insomnia; and after lunch on April 30, Dr. Grayson urged the haggard President to ride with his wife through the Bois de Boulogne before that afternoon's meeting. Wilson consented, knowing that he was sure to fall asleep once inside the car. "My mind was so full of the Japanese-Chinese controversy," he told Grayson. "But it was settled this morning, and while it is not to me a satisfactory settlement, I suppose it could be called an 'even break.' It is the best that could be accomplished out of a 'dirty past'"—one that got even grimier when he learned that France had also signed a secret treaty with Japan.

The next morning, Wilson bowed to the Japanese demands, leaving the American delegation "mortified and angry." His loyal supporters tended to blame Colonel House, who was, in fact, the only supporter of the deal. Charles Seymour thought the decision revealed that Wilson was "more the practical politician than has sometimes been supposed." Instead of risking the dissolution of the Conference and the destruction of the Covenant, he based his decision not on the future conditional or the past imperfect but on the present indicative.

The Japanese promised to restore Chinese sovereignty to Shantung, though they intended to retain all the economic rights that formerly belonged to the Germans—specifically railways and the mines associated with them. Wilson maintained that had he not fallen on this sword, the Japanese would have departed from the Conference, which, he believed, would have led to an old-fashioned military alliance with Russia and

Germany, a perpetuation of the same thinking that had led to this war. With the acceptance of these terms, the Treaty was virtually settled—with the League of Nations still intact.

That same afternoon, May Day, had started quietly enough but ended with a number of bloody confrontations in the streets between labor and the cavalry. For Wilson, it seemed one stress more than he could bear. In addition to surrendering to the Japanese terms, he officially approved of arraigning the Kaiser and possibly trying him for war crimes. And then, after several more hours of intense discussion, he suddenly announced to Edith and Dr. Grayson after lunch, "I don't like the way the colors of this furniture fight each other.

> The greens and the reds are all mixed up here and there is no harmony. Here is a big purple, high-backed covered chair, which is like the Purple Cow, strayed off to itself, and it is placed where the light shines on it too brightly. If you will give me a lift, we will move this next to the wall where the light from the window will give it a subdued effect. And here are two chairs, one green and the other red. This will never do. Let's put the greens all together and the reds together.

Wilson's bizarre comments did not end there. He described the Council of Four meetings, how each delegation walked like schoolchildren each day to its respective corner. Now, with the furniture regrouped, he said each country would sit according to color—with the reds in the American corner, the greens in the British corner, and the rest in the center for the French.

Sensing it was a manifestation of stress, Grayson made little of the aberrant behavior, prescribing only an automobile ride. "Mr. President," he said lightheartedly, "I think if you ever want a job after leaving the Presidency you would make a great success as an interior decorator." Wilson smiled and said, "I don't mean to throw bouquets at myself but I do think that I have made a success of the arrangement of this furniture."

In retrospect, Wilson's behavior that day might have been "ludic"—activity somewhere between playful and delusional, and which sometimes accompanies improvement after brain injuries. Or perhaps it was nothing more than an attempt to impose order on circumstances beyond his control.

His thoughts about moving the furniture quickly passed, but Wilson's rearrangement in Asia did not. News of the settlement reached Peking on May 3, 1919, churning up a tsunami of shame and outrage. Students in Shanghai proclaimed that they had turned to Woodrow Wilson looking for the deliverance he had prophesied; "but no sun rose for China," they wrote. "Even the cradle of the nation was stolen." The next day, three thousand of them protested at Tiananmen Square before pouring into the streets, leaving angry petitions at the embassies of the Big Four and burning the house of one of China's envoys. This "May Fourth Incident" provided the tinderbox for pro-national and anti-imperialist sentiment, which ignited a political and cultural awakening, starting with a massive boycott of all things Japanese. For many it signaled the closing of the door the West had opened twenty years earlier. In Hunan it turned a young college graduate, Mao Tse-tung, into a radical newspaper publisher. "We are awakened!" read one of his editorials that summer. "The world is ours, the state is ours, society is ours!"

Centuries earlier Confucius had said, "To go beyond is as wrong as to fall short." That philosophy dominated Wilson's actions as the German delegation was about to arrive in Paris to receive the Peace Treaty. Wilson had heard that Germany still believed he was the one man who would see that "she would get justice at his hands." But he predicted to Grayson that he would become the object of their animosity once they got their hands on the document. "The terms of the treaty are particularly severe," Wilson granted, "but I have striven my level best to make them fair, and at the same time compel Germany to pay a just penalty. However, I fully realize that I will be the one on whom the blame will be placed. In their hearts the Germans dislike me because if I had kept America from entering the war Germany would have defeated the Allies. So I know that they blame me for their defeat."

The Allied leaders had grown contemptuous as well. Down to crafting the final paragraphs of the Treaty with Germany, they stopped at nothing in achieving their individual goals, each still thinking nationalistically. England and now even France forgot how they had beseeched the United States to join in their fight. Their lack of loyalty to President Wilson matched their growing lack of gratitude. Wilson complained about the

French, who had recently shown only "a lack of appreciation" as they assumed the attitude that "France did it all." The British behavior was even worse. Winston Churchill was already speechifying that the war had "proved the soundness of the British race at every point" and that "in every country, it is to the British way of doing things that they are looking now." It was only a matter of time before he would tell a New York newspaper editor that "America should have minded her own business and stayed out of the World War.

> If you hadn't entered the war the Allies would have made peace with Germany in the Spring of 1917. Had we made peace then there would have been no collapse in Russia followed by Communism, no breakdown in Italy followed by Fascism, and Germany would not have . . . enthroned Nazism.

Wilson—once "the prophet of the world"—found himself rolling in the political mud, preserving as much of his grand plan as possible. Said Ray Baker: "He must bargain and bluff, give way here, stand firm there. Miserable business—but *wise*."

And after four months of talks, the time had arrived to see how the Fourteen Points had translated into the Treaty of Versailles. While the printer was setting it in type, a member of the American Commission and Sir Maurice Hankey arrived at the temporary White House to point out two insertions that Clemenceau had made in the Treaty, unilaterally, presumably expecting them to slip by unnoticed. One was a liberty he had taken, which House called "a perversion of the entire mandatory system." Wilson simply ordered their excision. Over the next several days, John Foster Dulles combed the eighty-five-thousand-word text and discovered even more tampering. Bernard Baruch did the same. "The French seem to be always up to some skullduggery," Wilson commented; "the word 'honorable' doesn't seem to mean anything to them."

On the morning of Wednesday, May 7, 1919, while the Big Three were tying up a few loose ends before that day's official presentation of the documents to the German delegates, Premier Orlando entered the room and took his chair, as if he had never walked out. He did not want to miss that afternoon's pageant, which would be short on ceremony, though long on symbolism.

King Louis XIV had built the magnificent Château de Versailles, ten
miles west of Paris, to stand as his monument "to all the glories of France";
and when Bismarck had dictated his harsh peace in 1871, he had added
ignominy to the French defeat by selecting Versailles for the occasion.
Now, on the perimeter of the château gardens, resplendent with lilacs and
chestnut blossoms, world leaders gathered once again at the Trianon Palace Hotel, this time allowing the French to reclaim not only their land but
also some of their glory. Tables and chairs were configured in the hotel
dining room to replicate the Salle de la Paix at the Quai d'Orsay; and by
three o'clock, all the Allied plenipotentiaries were seated (except for the
habitually late Paderewski, who was evidently used to audiences being in
their seats before he walked onto the stages of concert halls). In fact, the
German delegation of six had been waiting in Versailles for a week—some
of them believing the talks had slowed intentionally in order for this day
to coincide with the fourth anniversary of the sinking of the *Lusitania*.

As soon as everybody was seated, Clemenceau, wearing yellow gloves,
stood and announced that this was neither the time nor the place for "superfluous" words. "The time has come when we must settle our accounts,"
he said. "You have asked for peace. We are ready to give you peace." He
offered to explain any terms the Germans might require, but he said there
would be no oral discussion—only observations submitted in writing
within the next fifteen days. With copies of the 413-page books (in French
on the left-hand pages, English on the right, and illustrated with large
folding maps) before them, Clemenceau added that "this Second Treaty of
Versailles has cost us too much not to take on our side all the necessary
precautions and guarantees that that peace shall be a lasting one."

Ulrich, Count von Brockdorff-Rantzau, the German Foreign Minister,
did not stand, which delegates interpreted as insolence. "We cherish no
illusions as to the extent of our defeat—the degree of our impotence," he
said without repentance, ". . . and we have heard the passionate demand
that the victors should both make us pay as vanquished and punish us as
guilty." But he said they were required to admit that they alone were "war-
guilty" and that "such an admission on my lips would be a lie." While he
did not seek to exonerate Germany from all responsibility, he refuted the
idea that Germany—"whose people were convinced that they were waging
a defensive war"—should solely be "laden with the guilt," as the last half
century of imperialism of all European states had "chronically poisoned

the international situation." He reminded the Conference that the block-ade against Germany persisted to that day, taking the lives of hundreds of thousands of noncombatants since the Armistice. He made no attempt to delay the restoration of territory in Belgium and northern France that Germany had occupied. In order to do that, he said, they needed the technical and financial participation of the victors. "It must be the desire of impoverished Europe that reconstruction should be carried out as successfully and economically as possible," he said. Before even reading the Treaty, he endorsed the League of Nations. And he reminded the victors, "A Peace which cannot be defended in the name of justice before the whole world would continually call forth fresh resistance." Several people had observed that the Count was trembling violently when he entered the room, had fumbled with his chair in trying to sit down, and could not suppress the shaking of his hands and knees—all of which probably explained why he had not stood in the first place. Wilson dismissed the speech as "stupid," finding it "not frank & peculiarly Prussian!"

The Treaty of Versailles contained 440 articles, divided into fifteen sections. The first was the League Covenant. The second and third sections redrew Germany's borders, and much of the rest of Europe's. Germany would cede 5,600 square miles of Alsace-Lorraine to France, 382 square miles to Luxembourg and Holland, and almost 22,000 square miles, including West Prussia, to Poland. Dantzig would become a "free city," an internationalized zone under the guarantee of the League of Nations; and a separated East Prussia would hold a plebiscite to determine its nationality. Furthermore, Germany was to recognize the total independence of German Austria and Czechoslovakia, and to respect the independence of all territories that had been part of the former Russian Empire. Section IV itemized the German renunciation of all her overseas possessions—from Liberia, Morocco, and Egypt to Siam and Shantung, including whatever claims she had in Turkey and Bulgaria.

The next few sections were more onerous, as they compelled Germany to dismantle its military infrastructure. Its massive army of millions would be reduced to 100,000 soldiers, the once ominous navy to no more than 15,000 sailors manning three dozen vessels of war, including six small battleships and no submarines. Conscription was to be abolished, as were the manufacture, storage, and design of arms and munitions of war; no dirigibles could be kept, and only a limited number of unarmed seaplanes; and the manufacture of aircraft was forbidden for six months. While the reckoning for reparations was far from completed, the Treaty required a down payment of £1 billion within two years, in either gold, goods, ships, or other specific forms of compensation. In the meantime, the Inter-Allied Reparation Commission would continue to tabulate the cost of war loss and damage, including injuries caused to civilians by acts of war, directly or indirectly, air bombardments, damage to property other than naval or military materials, all Allied war loans to Belgium, and—of great importance—pensions for Allied soldiers. Much of the rest of the document curtailed Germany's control of rivers and railways and nullified many of her pre-war contracts, treaties, and property rights. Lest the vanquished nation even consider mounting a military comeback, the Council of Three released an appendix to the Treaty, the pledge from President Wilson and Prime Minister Lloyd George to propose to their respective legislatures to "come immediately to the assistance of France in the case of an unprovoked attack by Germany." With that, cabled Canada's representative, Prime Minister Robert Borden, to his Minister of Finance, "the curtain rang down upon the first scene of the last Act of the terrible drama which has occupied the world's stage for nearly five years."

For Woodrow Wilson, the rest of his time abroad was a vexatious denouement, as the Peace Commission carved free and independent countries out of the fallen Austro-Hungarian and Ottoman Empires. As if he were the hero in a Greek tragedy, Wilson's "flaws" seemed to dictate a series of reversals in his actions. In retrospect, considerable evidence suggests that as early as April 28, the President had experienced another "cerebrovascular accident." The first indications of his having suffered a small stroke appeared during a plenary session regarding the Covenant, in which he read his remarks with some difficulty, omitting passages that were written out for him and relying on Baron Makino to make certain points because he was simply unable to. Then, for the first time in decades, his elegant cursive turned crabbed, forcing him to switch to writing with his left hand. Days later, in giving an informal after-dinner speech, he meandered into eloquent but pointless blather. And the following week he had another impulse to rearrange his sitting room, suddenly finding that the purple furniture clashed with the green.

Dr. Grayson did everything he could to inject more leisure into the

President's schedule—even arranging a day at the Longchamps Race Course. The "elasticity" of his patient's physical and mental makeup—he sprung back to his old self with the least amount of refreshment— continued to impress Grayson. But the pressure of the Council of Four meetings did not relent. The leaders continued to convene at least once a day, as they braced themselves for the German reaction to the Treaty.

"The German Peace Delegation has finished the first perusal of the Peace Conditions which have been handed over to them," wrote Brockdorff-Rantzau on May 10, 1919, in the first of several notes he would send the Council of Four. He said the draft of the Treaty contained "demands which no nation could endure, moreover, our experts hold that many of them could not possibly be carried out." Marshal Foch had a battle plan prepared should the Germans not agree to the terms in a timely manner, but most of the "peacemakers" verged on bankruptcy themselves. And so France, Great Britain, Italy, and even the United States could ill afford to re-stoke the engines of war and proceed to occupy Germany. When the Germans submitted their 119-page counterproposal on May 28, the only common ground was the League of Nations; and when it came to that, the Germans argued with the terms under which they might sit at the table with the rest of the family of civilized nations. The Germans would artfully use the Fourteen Points to wangle more time and fewer constraints. This peace that was meant to be dictated and signed within two weeks would be dickered for almost two months. Wilson was indignant at the German response, saying the terms comported with the principles of the Armistice.

But even some of the Treaty's authors entertained second thoughts. Jan Smuts of South Africa, whom Wilson held in highest regard, said the more he studied the terms, the more he disliked them. He felt the territorial and reparation clauses were so crippling that Germany would never be able to make good on all the provisions, to say nothing of regaining its footing again. "Under this Treaty," he wrote Wilson a week after the terms had been published, "Europe will know no peace." And with America's promise to defend France against aggression, he said, neither would the United States. "I pray you will use your unrivalled power and influence to make the final Treaty a more moderate and reasonable document." Wilson agreed that consideration should be given to all the German objections; but, he wrote back, "inevitably my thought goes back to the very great offense against civilization which the German State committed, and the necessity for making it evident once for all that such things can lead only to the most severe punishment."

Over the next several weeks, the Council of Four pored over every territorial dispute. Tempers wore thin, reducing their efforts to playground politics that often required a referee. One morning session collapsed into an argument over Asia Minor, as Clemenceau accused Lloyd George of misrepresenting the terms of the secret treaties. The Welshman resented being called a liar and insisted upon an apology. The Frenchman said, "That's not my style of doing business." Wilson stepped in, and at the end of the meeting said, "You have been two bad boys, and so it would be well for you to shake hands and make up." They moved toward each other, but several seconds passed before Lloyd George held out his hand, which Clemenceau grasped. Turning toward a smiling Wilson, they both burst into laughter. The same day the Italians announced their intention to seize several Greek islands (under the pretense that they had been ceded by the Treaty of London), Wilson learned that Italy had just changed the name of a road from Via Wilson to Via Fiume. The President laughed at the news and called them "a big lot of babies." In one candid moment, Orlando unwittingly admitted that Fiume was only of sentimental value to Italy, but he had behaved so mulishly about it because his people made him. The Big Four often worked from a map in the President's room, one too large for any table to accommodate. Whenever it was needed, they spread it on the floor. One morning Dr. Grayson entered the salon, only to find the four most powerful men in the world on their hands and knees, studying the chart. "It had every appearance," noted Grayson, "of four boys playing some kind of a game."

In the spring of 1919, that quadrumvirate on the floor erased more boundaries and created more new nations than had ever been drawn at a single time. And whenever Clemenceau and Lloyd George fell into another argument, scrapping over patches of Asia Minor, Wilson reminded them that they were engaged in the "bargaining away of peoples." He vigilantly protected the Jews, wherever they settled, from Poland to Palestine. More than once did Wilson recall having reassured Rabbi Stephen Wise and the American Jewish Congress that he and the Allied nations fully agreed "that in Palestine shall be laid the foundations of a Jewish commonwealth."

While the United States had no direct interest in most of the territorial settlements, Wilson continued to involve himself as the others tore at the

Habsburg Empire. Austria and Hungary (then in the midst of a series of revolutions) would be divided into two separate landlocked countries, neither of which would ever be powerful enough to rise to any significant stature. The Treaty sanctioned a union of Czechs and Slovaks into a sovereign independent state. Similarly, the Independent Kingdoms of Serbia and Montenegro joined with the State of Slovenes, Croats, and Serbs as well as much of Dalmatia, and Bosnia and Herzegovina to form Yugoslavia. Parts of the Habsburg Empire—Bessarabia, Bukovina, and Transylvania—joined the Kingdom of Romania.

The Ottoman Empire offered a map with more blank space on which to draw. Out of the secret treaties and mandates and assurances to Arab leaders, new nations would be built in the sand. They proved problematic because they too bundled diversified populations, often with ancient ethnic and religious differences. Tensions naturally rose in the area as each of these disparate peoples sought self-government and independence while they were in conflict among themselves as well as with their mandatories. Adding to the friction was the steadily increasing demand for the oil beneath their feet. They agreed that the Allies would occupy for several years the nucleus of the empire—Constantinople, which bridged two continents—before the Republic of Turkey would be formed. To the south as far as Acre and to the east as far as the Tigris River, France collected on its claims from the Sykes-Picot Agreement, exercising its "tutelage" over the mandates of Syria and Lebanon. Great Britain assumed responsibility for Palestine, which divided in order to create Jordan on the East Bank of the eponymous river, and then beyond to Mesopotamia. In the end, this modern state of Iraq seemed destined to remain a delicate imbalance of incompatible, even warring, factions—Shi'ites, Sunnis, and Kurds— bound together by man-made borders when they might more naturally have divided into three separate countries.

The most unsettled and unsettling problem at the Peace Conference remained Russia, which had left more bodies on the battlefield than any of the belligerents. With neither a vote nor a voice at the Conference, it was consigned to watching the Allies grab all the bounty. Much of the problem was Russia itself, then more consumed with the revolution inside its borders than the political evolution on the outside. Ray Baker suggested that "Wilson's mind was never quite clear on the question of dealing with Bolshevist Russia." He seemed unable to comprehend the idea of building a nation around an economic precept; and most of what he understood of the country's state of affairs, said Baker, "was repugnant to him."

William Bullitt tried to convince Wilson otherwise, as he advocated American recognition of the Bolshevik regime. He returned from his meeting with Lenin with an understanding that the Communist leader was prepared not only to make an armistice on all fronts but also recognize anti-Communist governments throughout most of the former Russian Empire—including what would become Baltic nations. Soviet expert George Kennan would later assert that the terms Bullitt conveyed did offer an opportunity for the Western powers to extract themselves from "the profitless involvements of the military intervention in Russia" and might have allowed for the "creation of an acceptable relationship to the Soviet regime." But Wilson put no faith in them because he believed the Bolsheviks were "the most consummate sneaks in the world." Kennan also suggested the unseasoned and "impatient" Bullitt was not the most effective advocate for his pro-Bolshevik position. And Bullitt did not realize that he had submitted his report the very moment that the President had become ill, which explained why the junior diplomat got no reply to his request for even a fifteen-minute meeting. He took further umbrage at Lloyd George's speaking dismissively in the House of Commons of "some American" who had investigated the proposal of recognizing the Bolshevik government in Moscow but who had evidently not turned up enough to warrant it. The Wilson Administration left him in the cold, claiming no interest in the mission. And Bullitt quit.

Further upset by the decisions Wilson made regarding Shantung, the Tyrol, Dantzig, and the Saar Valley, Bullitt fired off a scathing letter to the President of the United States explaining his resignation. Bullitt said he was one of the millions who had believed in Wilson's promises of "unselfish and unbiased justice," but "our government has consented now to deliver the suffering peoples of the world to new oppressions, subjections and dismemberments—a new century of war." In a final flurry of bitter disappointment, Bullitt added, "I am sorry that you did not fight our fight to the finish and that you had so little faith in the millions of men, like myself, in every nation who had faith in you." Lansing accepted Bullitt's resignation without comment. Wilson found it "insulting." He continued to believe, as he had told the Democratic National Committee when he had been Stateside in February, that the Conference might end before the vast Russian territories had been recomposed, "but if we go home with a League of Nations, there will be some power to solve this most perplexing problem."

Lansing—who had been relegated to the role of errand boy for months—also thought the Treaty was "bad," insufficient to uphold the League; but he continued to perform his job, no matter how menial it became. Herbert Hoover believed the economic terms would ruin Germany and wreak Bolshevism there; but he continued in his unceasing efforts to supervise the feeding of Europe, where the ongoing blockade continued to starve masses of people. Wilson, of course, knew that opposition was building at home and granted that it was "a terrible compromise"; but he believed it would pass in the Senate—League and all—not because it was just, noted Baker, "but because the American people don't know, don't care, and are still dominated by the desire to 'punish the Hun.'" Several other members of the American Commission—including historian Samuel Eliot Morison and future FDR "brain-truster" Adolf Berle—left their posts before the Treaty was done. "The consequences of Wilson's refusal to turn his mind to the question of Russia were considerable," wrote Bullitt, presumably referring to the next several decades, in which relations between the Soviets and the Western powers would freeze over. "It is not impossible that Wilson's refusal to burden his 'one track mind' with Russia may well, in the end, turn out to be the most important single decision that he made in Paris."

Bullitt's animus toward Wilson swelled over the next several years, until he unburdened himself to his psychotherapist and subsequent friend, Sigmund Freud. Harboring his own resentment of the pious American president, the Austrian doctor agreed to analyze Woodrow Wilson in absentia, through the details of his life as Bullitt presented them. The result was a spiteful book that scorned practically everything about Wilson, with repeated references to his oversized ears and much more about what was between them—what Freud characterized as a Christ complex. The leitmotiv of the coauthored study was the subject's abnormal adoration of his father, the Reverend Wilson, and his lifelong wavering between self-identification with the Son of God and his need to assert himself as nothing less than God. "Tommy"'s repressed rage toward the Reverend Wilson, said Freud and Bullitt, manifested itself in a life of hypocrisy and self-contradiction. When *Thomas Woodrow Wilson: A Psychological Study* was published in the 1960s, critics suggested the book debunked Freud more than Wilson.

Valid or not, the analysis did capture some of the flaws of its subject, and Bullitt was not the only man in Paris to perceive them. "The President, it must be remembered, was the descendant of Covenanters, the inheritor of a more immediate presbyterian tradition," wrote Harold Nicolson. "That spiritual arrogance which seems inseparable from the harder form of religion had eaten deep into his soul." Like Bullitt and Freud, Nicolson also wrote of Wilson's "one-track mind," saying,

> This intellectual disability rendered him blindly impervious, not merely
> to human character, but also shades of difference. He possessed no gift
> for differentiation, no capacity for adjustment to circumstances. It was
> his spiritual and mental rigidity which proved his undoing. It rendered
> him as incapable of withstanding criticism as of absorbing advice. It
> rendered him blind to all realities which did not accord with his precon-
> ceived theory, even to the realities of his own decisions.

He was like a brave knight-errant, John Maynard Keynes observed. "But this blind and deaf Don Quixote was entering a cavern where the swift and glittering blade was in the hands of the adversary."

Whether the European leaders had outfoxed Wilson or not, Keynes thought the problems with the Treaty were not the fault of one man. He found the Big Four themselves guilty of dwelling on the subject of reparation at the expense of rehabilitation. For all the redrawing of Europe, he felt nobody had thought enough to rebuild the defeated Central empires or to reclaim Russia or restore the "disordered finances" of France and Italy, or even to stabilize the new nations. "It is an extraordinary fact that the fundamental economic problems of a Europe starving and disintegrating before their eyes, was the one question in which it was impossible to arouse the interest of the Four. Reparation was their main excursion into the economic fields," Keynes wrote of Wilson, Clemenceau, Lloyd George, and Orlando, "and they settled it as a problem of theology, of politics, of electoral chicane, from every point of view except that of the economic futures of the States whose destiny they were handling." Like Bullitt, Nicolson and Keynes exited the Conference as disgruntled underlings, confident that they had more facts than their leaders, certainly more than Wilson. But political leaders view the world through different prisms from those of junior diplomats and with different perspectives. With his League in place, Wilson considered the Treaty a victory for mankind.

After the morning session of the Big Four on May 30, 1919, the Wilsons and Dr. Grayson rode to Suresnes, four miles west of Paris. There, on a gentle slope surrounded by acacia groves, the French government had offered a few acres to recognize the ultimate sacrifice of many Americans. The President was dedicating the cemetery that hot, sunny Decoration Day, consecrating a final resting place for 1,500 doughboys who were buried in a precisely measured grid, row after row of white crosses. Local women had decorated each grave with a wreath and a small American flag, a gesture that brought a lump to Wilson's throat as he entered the ground he was meant to hallow. Thousands of veterans in khaki filled the hillside, boys all looking older than their years, many with visible scars and empty sleeves.

Wilson stood on a small platform in the middle of the burial ground and removed his top hat. Edith could not help observing that in just the last few months, her husband's hair had turned white. Extemporizing from notes, he delivered one of the most poignant speeches of his life. The notes proved to be an essential crutch, for the pathos of the occasion almost broke the President's self-control. "No one with a heart in his breast, no American, no lover of humanity," he began, "can stand in the presence of these graves without the most profound emotion. These men who lie here are men of unique breed. Their like has not been seen since the far days of the Crusades. Never before have men crossed the seas to a foreign land to fight for a cause which they did not pretend was peculiarly their own, but knew was the cause of humanity and of mankind."

His mind filled with details of the final push to complete the Peace Treaty, Wilson extolled the spirit of the American soldiers as he reminded the world that "these men did not come across the sea merely to defeat Germany and her associated powers in the war. They came to defeat forever the things for which the Central Powers stood, the sort of power they meant to assert in the world, the arrogant, selfish dominance which they meant to establish; and they came, moreover, to see to it that there should never be a war like this again." It was left to civilians, such as himself, the President said, to "use our proper weapons of counsel and agreement to see to it that there never is such a war again." Of all the matters that had been thrashed out in the last six months, he said, only the concept of the League had met "unity of counsel" and unanimity of acceptance.

"I beg you to realize the compulsion that I myself feel that I am under," Wilson said in closing, striking a startling personal note. "By the Constitution of our great country I was the Commander in Chief of these men. I advised the Congress to declare that a state of war had existed." And then, owning all that had befallen his troops, Wilson squarely confronted the most grievous task of any head of state. "I sent these lads over here to die," he said. "Shall I—can I—ever speak a word of counsel which is inconsistent with the assurances I gave them when they came over?" Wilson paused for a moment before saying that there was "something better . . . that a man can give than his life, and that is his living spirit to a service that is not easy, to resist counsels that are hard to resist, to stand against purposes that are difficult to stand against." And in that moment, he appeared to take a vow before the crowd, giving his countrymen at home and all the world a preview of what was to come: "Here stand I," he said, "consecrated in spirit to the men who were once my comrades and who are now gone, and who have left me under eternal bonds of fidelity."

Few bothered to fight back their tears. After renditions of Chopin's "Funeral March," the American and French national anthems, and a lone bugler sounding "Taps," the crowd was undone. The Wilsons drove back into town in silence, except for the President's own torrent of emotion.

"As lonely as God—a slave he is!" noted Ray Baker. "Yet he is the only great, serious responsible statesman here: when all is said, a great man: a Titan struggling with forces too great even for him."

But at home a drumbeat of anti-Wilson rhetoric continued. His critics kept hammering that Wilson's mission to France was purely political—that this entire expedition had been personal exploitation, building his base for a third term. Just as Wilson made it clear to his supporters that they must pour all their energies into the adoption of the League, the Republicans decided to channel all their powers into its defeat. If they could win that one issue, they might reclaim their authority in American politics.

Obviously, Wilson could not return in time to open the Republican-controlled Sixty-sixth Congress, but he sent a long message explaining why he had assembled the legislators and why he would not be present. Washington had to approve certain appropriations in order to keep the government running; and Paris was in the middle of negotiations. While the President hesitated to press any legislative suggestions in his absence, he sent close to three thousand words of recommendations. He revisited his early Progressive themes as he hoped the country would return to a

On April 2, 1917, less than a month after his second inauguration, President Wilson stood before Congress and delivered a war message, insisting, "The world must be made safe for democracy."

The Great War had been ravaging Europe since 1914, but the United States did not declare war until April 1917. The isolationist country, with an Army of a few hundred thousand, mobilized—shipping two million men to the front. At home, citizens poured all their resources into the war effort—including the Wilsons, who kept a flock of sheep at the White House, to trim the lawn and to grow wool for the Red Cross.

Wilson had long supported women's suffrage, but only through state-by-state adoption; with American women contributing to the war effort, he became the most persuasive advocate for the Nineteenth Amendment.

The Wartime Cabinet

The war fought and won, President Wilson sailed to France on the *George Washington* in December 1918 to settle the peace. He would spend the next six months in Europe.

Paris welcomes its hero; on the right with French President Raymond Poincaré.

Wilson received further acclaim in England.
After his arrival in Dover, he was the guest of King George V.

In the courtyard of Buckingham Palace, the President met American soldiers released from German prison camps.

The American Peace Commissioners: Colonel House, Secretary Lansing, the President, Ambassador Henry White, General Tasker H. Bliss.

France's Premier Georges Clemenceau—
"the Tiger"—who sought revenge against
the Germans at every turn.

Great Britain's Prime Minister David
Lloyd George, whom one American
adviser said was "slippery as an eel."

Italy's Prime Minister Vittorio Emanuele
Orlando, whom Clemenceau dubbed
"the Weeper," because he burst into tears
whenever his demands were not met.

January 18, 1919—the opening of the Paris Peace Conference
in the Salle de la Paix in the Quai d'Orsay.

Representatives of nearly every population in the world flocked to Paris in the
first six months of 1919. Among them were Emir Faisal (center), who would
become the King of Greater Syria and the King of Iraq, and an Englishman
named T. E. Lawrence (third from right), known as "Lawrence of Arabia."

Wilson inspected the ruins of the library of Belgium's University of Louvain.

Official war painter Sir William Orpen captured the world-weariness of President Wilson in Paris, where he fought for an equitable peace based on his Fourteen Points.

Orpen's rendition of the Council of Ten, which reshaped the world, at the Quai d'Orsay.

The Hall of Mirrors at the Palace of Versailles during the signing of the Treaty, the centerpiece of which was Wilson's League of Nations.

Clemenceau, Wilson, and Lloyd George (far right) exit the Palace of Versailles on June 28, 1919, after the signing. Their faces reveal exhaustion more than joy.

The United States Senate had to approve the Treaty, and Republicans had planned its obstruction even before the terms had been agreed upon. Wilson's nemesis was the senior Senator from Massachusetts, Henry Cabot Lodge.

When Wilson found Senate resistance too great, he took his cause to the people. Despite excruciating headaches, he embarked upon a cross-country tour in September 1919. In St. Paul, Minnesota, at the Tacoma Stadium (upper right), and at the Greek Theatre at Berkeley (bottom) —Wilson rallied audiences in favor of the Treaty and the League of Nations.

After a speech in Pueblo, Colorado, Wilson broke down and returned to Washington, looking like a ghost of the man he had been three weeks prior. Days later, he suffered a stroke, which was kept from the public for the rest of his Presidency.

Wilson did not lose his powers to think or speak, but his left side was immobilized. For the next eighteen months, a conspiracy of Edith Wilson, Dr. Grayson, and Tumulty essentially ran the country. Some consider this "woman behind the man" (in a touched-up photograph) America's first female President.

For more than six months, the President held no Cabinet meetings. By the time he was able to conduct minimal government business, he faced several new Secretaries (clockwise, after Wilson on the far left): D. F. Houston; A. Mitchell Palmer (who had authorized notorious raids during the President's illness, in hopes of ridding the country of seditious terrorists); Josephus Daniels, E. T. Meredith; W. B. Wilson; J. W. Alexander; J. B. Payne; A. S. Burleson; N. D. Baker; and Bainbridge Colby, who replaced a disgruntled Robert Lansing as Secretary of State.

March 4, 1921. After the Senate did not pass the Treaty of Versailles, Wilson faced further humiliation: his successor, Warren G. Harding, reversed as many of Wilson's policies as possible.

The Wilsons remained in Washington, retiring to an elegant house at 2340 S Street NW.

For years, Colonel House had enjoyed the honored position as Wilson's most trusted confidant. But during the Peace Conference in Paris, the President felt his adviser had overstepped. Upon his return to America, Wilson never spoke to him again. Only Dr. Grayson remained in Wilson's good graces to the end.

As Wilson's health declined, his post-Presidential popularity rose. Crowds greeted him whenever he appeared in public, as on Armistice Day 1921.

On Wilson's sixty-fifth birthday, servant Isaac Scott helped the hemiplegic ex-President.

On special occasions, Wilson offered a few words from his doorstep—greeting women from the Pan-American Conference in April 1922; and again (with Edith at his side) on Armistice Day, seven months later.

At age sixty-seven, on
December 28, 1923.

"I am a broken piece of machinery," Wilson uttered shortly before dying on February 3, 1924.
His casket was taken from S Street to the National Cathedral, where he remains buried.

peacetime economy. He called for improvement in workers' conditions through "the genuine democratization of industry"; he addressed inequities in the tax system—calling for a reduction in sales taxes but an increase in excess profits taxes and estate taxes. With the demobilization of the military forces, he thought it safe to remove the wartime ban upon the manufacture and sale of wine and beer. And he asked Congress to endorse the cause he had been urging upon reluctant Senators that spring: suffrage for women. In a few weeks, the House would overwhelmingly pass the suffrage amendment; and two weeks after that, the Senate would deliver the two-thirds majority by two votes. The amendment moved to the states, where three-quarters of their legislatures were required for ratification. Alice Paul predicted that women would be voting for the next President.

With the opening of this Republican Congress, Wilson knew that passing any of his legislation would be an uphill battle. Ignoring the abuse already being hurled, Wilson hoped to continue leading the United States from its inherent provincialism to a more worldly vision. Off the record, he had derided his rivals for having "horizons that do not go beyond their parish" and said they were "going to have the most conspicuously contemptible names in history." He found himself thinking of March 5, 1921, for on that day he intended to return to a private scholarly life, and of having "the privilege of writing about these gentlemen without any restraints of propriety." Until then, however, he had to face not only the American Congress and the warring Allies as they completed the Treaty but also the one adversary that could reduce the last six months of work to naught.

"Will the Germans sign?" were the words on everybody's lips in Paris. Although the Armistice had been accepted, Allied armies prepared to resume battle and prolong the blockade. Germany was technically boxed into accepting the peace terms as handed to them. But the enemy stuck to its initial response that the "exactions of this Treaty are more than the German people can bear." The loss of treasury and the territory that might replenish it, and rendering Germany unable to assert itself in a modern world, all but ensured that this peace treaty would become a declaration of the next war. The Social Democratic government of Chancellor Philipp Scheidemann in Germany was against his country's signing.

So, strangely enough, were many leaders in Great Britain. In addition to fears of revenge, Liberal and Labour factions there questioned the efficacy of creating a fiscal vacuum in the middle of Europe, one certain to suck the financial systems of the Continent down the drain with it. When Lloyd George returned to Paris from London in early June, he spoke of moderating the terms of the Treaty. At the Council of Four meeting on June 2, 1919, he discussed reducing reparations, redrawing borders, reexamining the need for more plebiscites, and removing multitudes of "pinpricks" whose cumulative effect was lacerating. Later, at a meeting of the American delegation, Wilson announced, "I have no desire to soften the treaty, but I have a very sincere desire to alter those portions of it that are shown to be unjust, or which are shown to be contrary to the principles which we ourselves have laid down." Clemenceau, of course, remained "absolutely rigid" about leaving all the terms as agreed upon.

In a moment of growing desperation, Lloyd George asked Bernard Baruch if he might arrange a private meeting between him and the President. In doing the Prime Minister's bidding, Baruch suggested that Lloyd George had been struggling between his campaign promises of toughness toward the Germans and "the dictates of his conscience." But his dilemma was greater than that. Once he and Wilson came face-to-face, Lloyd George told him that unless they altered the terms of the Treaty, neither the British army nor fleet would compel Germany to sign. The President sat in silence, his jaw clenched, while the Prime Minister reiterated the changes in the Treaty that he required. At last, Wilson had heard quite enough. "Mr. Prime Minister," he said, "you make me sick! For months we have been struggling to make the terms of the Treaty exactly along the lines you now speak of, and never got the support of the English. Now, after we have finally come to agreement, and when we have to face the Germans and we need unanimity, you want to rewrite the Treaty."

For months Colonel House had said Lloyd George "changes his mind like a weather-vane," and Wilson knew the political winds had not stopped blowing. While he maintained that the current terms were strict but fair, he said he would agree to the British proposals—if the French agreed. But in every delegation there were rivalries within rivalries, and even though Wilson knew that Marshal Foch, among others, feared Clemenceau's harsh insistences as well, he knew nobody in France was strong enough to defy him. Wilson could offer little more than his allowing the Prime Ministers to duke out their differences, telling them that he "did not desire a lenient treaty, but a just one." In the meantime, the Scheidemann government in Weimar stood firm, as the peacemaking appeared to be doomed.

While Lloyd George and Clemenceau found enough modifications between them to save face, the Wilsons accepted an invitation from the King and Queen of the Belgians to visit their country. For two days they toured by motorcar and train, sandwiching royal receptions between visits to Belgium's important sites. Beginning in the northwest corner of the country, between Nieuport and Ypres, they sometimes drove as fast as fifty miles per hour over dusty roads through territory where armies had fought and leveled whole towns. Skeletons of dead horses littered the woods, and clusters of graves dotted the landscape. Except for part of a tower, the old cathedral in Ypres was a heap of bricks; the once magnificent Cloth Hall, from the thirteenth century, was in ruins. As he walked the entire length of its seawall, Wilson listened to the wartime history of Zeebrugge, from which Germany had launched the terror of its submarine attacks. In Louvain, the university conferred a degree upon the President in its historic library, which had been reduced to a roofless shell with charred walls. Wilson delivered heartfelt talks throughout his visit and a proper address to the Belgian Parliament, in which he spoke with new understanding of this "valley of suffering." Now, more than any country in the world, it illustrated the need for a League. Minor adjustments were being made to the Treaty, but it still appeared that only divine intervention could impose German approval.

And then, the very day the Wilsons returned to Paris, the Scheidemann government collapsed under the strain of his refusal to ratify the Treaty. With the selection of a new coalition under Chancellor Gustav Bauer came the announcement from Weimar that the government of the German Republic was prepared to sign the Treaty of Versailles. The acceptance included a last-ditch effort to remove the "war-guilt clause," but the victors would yield no more.

The citizens of Paris danced in the streets. In Rome, Premier Orlando finally had something serious to cry about, as his government was overthrown. And before the Allies could appropriate the Kaiser's seventy-five ships that were interned in Scapa Flow, a bay in the Orkney Islands, the German navy ordered their immediate destruction. While burning French flags, the Germans scuttled most of their vessels. The action made Wilson think they were "savage enough to start war again." In Washington,

Republican leaders discussed how best to detach the League component from the Treaty and defeat it. They went so far as to consider a proposal to have Congress unconditionally declare a state of peace between Germany and the United States—for no better reason than to invalidate the last six months of Wilson's work. Official war painter Sir William Orpen put the finishing touches on his portrait of Wilson, showing a world-weary President with the creases and jowls and heavy lids over sunken eyes that the last six months had produced.

After the Council of Three session on Tuesday, June 24, Wilson, Clemenceau, and Balfour adjourned to Versailles to inspect the arrangements for the signing. Their host had selected the centerpiece of the palace—the Galerie des Glaces, the Hall of Mirrors—for the occasion, not only because it was one of the most spectacular rooms ever constructed but also because there the Germans had concluded the last war on a note of humiliation. This *grande galerie* was 240 feet long and 35 feet wide. Opposite its signature feature—a series of seventeen arches, each composed of twenty-one mirrors—matching windows opened onto extensive gardens. Upon seeing the space available to them, Wilson said he would like to include his wife and daughter at the proceedings. Clemenceau agreed that a few ladies should be present. Back at the Paris White House that night, the family circle found champagne glasses on the table. Miss Benham attempted to toast the President's health, but Wilson pre-empted her by raising his glass: "To the Peace, an enduring Peace, a Peace under the League of Nations."

The final settlement was not what Wilson had envisioned upon his arrival in Paris, as his critics never forgot. Maynard Keynes repeatedly called it a "Carthaginian peace," one so brutal that it would pulverize Germany into a wasteland. And Harold Nicolson enumerated his many grievances: the covenants of peace were not openly arrived at, as much of the Conference's work had been conducted in private; the freedom of the seas was not secured; the German colonies were distributed in a manner that was "neither free, nor open-minded, nor impartial"; several frontiers were drawn in contradiction to the nationalities as well as the desires of their populations.

On the other hand, the Treaty embodied the essence of the Fourteen Points and more. Belgium was restored; Alsace-Lorraine was returned; Poland was recognized; and Austria-Hungary was redrawn as a collection of smaller, more discrete free and independent states. When public forums had proved unworkable for the volume of questions that required negotiation, discussions had gone private; but the final covenants were "open," with no secret treaties. Reductions of armaments and the removal of economic barriers were addressed in a global forum and seriously considered by experts of many countries. Wilson had indubitably tempered the revenge Clemenceau had sought; and he believed the League of Nations could correct what mistakes existed in the Treaty. For the first time, mankind had a blueprint for peace that was practicable, universal, and, theoretically, permanent. President Woodrow Wilson had left his country for more than six months, solely to promote the concepts of global responsibility, self-determination, collective security, and moral imperatives, establishing them as fundamentals of United States foreign policy.

Over the next several months, experts did the basic arithmetic, tallying the final costs of the war and how much Germany should pay. Even without reckoning such future expenditures as pensions and such losses as loans that would never be repaid, Lloyd George told Wilson that the war had cost the United Kingdom £8.5 billion. The sums from all the belligerents totaled $125 billion, a fifth of which the United States had run up. It would be another two years before the final bill for reparations would be sent to the Germans—£6.6 billion ($33 billion). Even at that figure, numerous concessions were made so as not to break the German bank. Over the next decade, the Germans would make good on £1.1 billion. On the eve of the Treaty signing, Lloyd George wrote Wilson that he hoped the United States would consider finding "some way of really assisting the financial needs of the world" by stepping up as its leading creditor.

After an early breakfast on Saturday, June 28, 1919, Wilson crossed the street to Lloyd George's flat, where Clemenceau also awaited. The German delegation had arrived in Paris early that morning, and now the Council of Three examined the credentials of Dr. Hermann Müller, the new Foreign Minister, and Herr Johannes Bell, the Minister of Communications. Finding everything in order, they sent word that the signing would occur at Versailles at three o'clock that afternoon.

At two o'clock the President and Mrs. Wilson and Dr. Grayson drove to the Élysée Palace, where they bade adieu to President and Madame Poincaré and then proceeded under cloudy skies to Versailles, the road to which was lined with guards. As they approached the palace, the sun broke through.

The Hall of Mirrors shimmered. Again, the placement at the three-sided table approximated that at the Quai d'Orsay, with Clemenceau in the center, Wilson and the American delegation on his right, Lloyd George and his colleagues on his left. The remaining delegates assumed their familiar positions. Distinguished guests—such as Edith and Margaret Wilson—filled one end of the room, while the international press corps filled the other. Because the French had distributed more tickets to the event than there were seats and benches, several minutes of commotion ensued, as people scrambled to find standing room in the hall. It was five years to the day since a teenaged Bosnian Serb had shot Archduke Franz Ferdinand in Sarajevo.

At 3:10, Premier Clemenceau called the session to order. A small table had been set up directly before him on which sat the Treaty and several accompanying documents. To expedite the formalities, each of the signers had pre-impressed his personal seal. Wilson had used his signet wedding ring, which had been fashioned from the chunk of gold the State of California had presented him upon his marriage and which bore his name in stenographic ciphers. Once the Allies and Associated delegates were seated, a marshal ushered the German delegation into the room. Wilson had suggested that they be the first to sign the great document, so as not to give them any time to change their minds. Without flourishes and within three minutes, Ministers Müller and Bell approached the small table and affixed their signatures.

A beaming Wilson was next to sign the Japanese vellum document, rendering an unusually cramped signature. Lansing, White, House, and Bliss followed. Back at their seats, the President whispered to Lansing, "I did not know I was excited until I found my hand trembling when I wrote my name." The rest of the delegations quietly proceeded to the table—including the Italians, without the recently deposed Orlando. By 3:50, Clemenceau closed the proceedings with four words: *"La séance est levée."*

Only two incidents marred the occasion. When its request to sign the Treaty with a reservation regarding the Shantung settlement was denied, the Chinese delegation chose not to appear. And though he signed the Treaty because it meant ending the war, General Smuts filed a document declaring the peace unsatisfactory. For everybody else, it seemed a day of glory—a historic moment marked, ironically, by a barrage of cannonfire from a battery in the southern part of the majestic gardens.

Afterward, Wilson, Clemenceau, and Lloyd George descended to the terrace at the rear of the palace, where thousands stood and cheered and, ultimately, pushed past the security so that they might get closer to the three leaders. The President's guards closed in to protect him; but as Dr. Grayson observed, "Women cried out that they just wanted to touch him." Planes circled overhead, and guns were fired into the air. After the Big Three and Barons Sonnino and Makino toasted the peace over glasses of wine, the Wilsons returned to Paris. The route was crowded with people waving flags and shouting, *"Vive Wilson."*

While Paris rejoiced, the Wilsons enjoyed a quiet last supper in France. Lloyd George stopped in to say goodbye and to explain that he was simply too fatigued to be part of the impending farewell ceremonies at the train station. Although they had quarreled often during the last six months, Lloyd George said, "You have done more than any one man to bring about further cordial and friendly relations between England and the United States. You have brought the two countries closer together than any other individual in history." The Wilsons left for the Gare des Invalides, where gendarmes held back a massive crowd. Inside, the principals of the Conference stood on the platform, along with practically every member of the French government and the American delegation. Clemenceau said he felt as though he were "saying good-bye to my best friend."

The man who had until recently claimed the distinction of being Wilson's best friend faced a decidedly different parting. After weeks of decreasing contact with the President, Colonel Edward Mandell House was little more than a face in the crowd on the train platform that night. His last conversation with Wilson, in fact, had left House unsettled. The Colonel had urged Wilson to return to the Senate in a conciliatory spirit, one of "consideration" instead of confrontation. "House," the President replied, "I have found one can never get anything in this life that is worthwhile without fighting for it." House disagreed, extolling the virtues of compromise and contending "that a fight was the last thing to be brought about, and then only when it could not be avoided." Those would be the last sentences the two would ever exchange in person, as the President chose never to see him again.

At 9:45 that night, the train left the station for Brest. Woodrow and Edith stood pensively at the window, relieved that they were, at last, on their way home. As the City of Light receded into the darkness, he broke the silence. "Well, little girl, it is finished, and, as no one is satisfied, it makes me hope we have made a just peace," he said, looking into her eyes; "but it is all on the lap of the gods."

15

PASSION

*And they spit vpon him, and tooke the reed, and
smote him on the head.
    And after that they had mocked him, they tooke
the robe off from him, and put his owne raiment on
him, and led him away to crucifie him.*

—MATTHEW, XXVII:30–31

For more than six months, Dr. Grayson had prescribed as much rest as possible, but not until the *George Washington* transported the President away from the unceasing pressures did a weary and homesick Woodrow Wilson comply. With more than a week of fair skies and calm seas, he slept regularly into the late morning, walked and sunbathed on deck in the afternoon, and dined with guests, watched movies, and joined the sing-alongs at night. He could not abandon himself completely, however, for he knew of the turbulence ahead.

Article II, Section 2, of the Constitution defined the President's predicament: "He shall have Power, by and with the Advice and Consent of the Senate, to make Treaties, provided two thirds of the Senators present concur." Wilson spent hours on the Atlantic trying to compose the speech with which he would present the Treaty of Versailles to Congress. Anxious to measure the opposition that would greet him, he asked Tumulty for a list of Senators inclined to fight the Treaty and of any "particularly virulent" powers in the media. Tumulty named conservative publishing magnates William Randolph Hearst and Colonel Robert McCormick in Chicago, as well as liberals Oswald Villard of *The Nation*, former member of the Inquiry and Wilson supporter Walter Lippmann of *The New Republic*, and Wilson's earliest patron, George Harvey. Sailing into such formidable resistance from the press—and apparently two votes short of the sixty-four he would need in the Senate—Wilson had difficulty finding the right words.

For the first time since Grayson had met him, the President expressed complete dissatisfaction with his work on a speech. He blamed the "false start" on his disdain for his awaiting audience, insisting that if he had greater respect for Congress and its ability to reason, he could do a better job. Grayson wondered if that was all that ailed him. Wilson could collect his thoughts but had trouble organizing them; and his right hand was cramping so badly again that he had to write with his left.

On Tuesday, July 8, 1919, the ship docked in New Jersey. The Presidential party crossed the river to Manhattan. The largest crowd that had ever greeted Wilson in the city filled the sidewalks from the Twenty-third Street ferry to Carnegie Hall. There he delivered a brief address to an enthusiastic crowd—"a few words from the heart."

"Why, Jerseyman though I am," he said, "this is the first time I ever thought that Hoboken was beautiful." Speaking of America's new stature, Wilson said, "It is a wonderful thing for this nation, hitherto isolated from the large affairs of the world, to win not only the universal confidence of the people of the world, but their universal affection." He referred to the fight ahead only obliquely, talking about America's having done "the large thing and the right thing" in spreading freedom around the world. "I am afraid some people," he added, ". . . do not understand that vision. They do not see it. . . . [But] I have never had a moment's doubt as to where the heart and purpose of this people lay."

The Wilsons boarded their train at Pennsylvania Station. Although he had anticipated his return for months, he knew that Washington was about to engage in its most bitter debate since the Civil War. When his train pulled in at midnight, he was happily surprised to discover more than ten thousand people had gathered at Union Station to welcome him home. "It is very touching," he told Edith and Dr. Grayson. Thousands more waited for him outside the Executive Mansion, including one former resident and ill-wisher—Alice Roosevelt Longworth, who stood in the crowd, crossing her fingers in the sign of the "evil eye" and crying, "A murrain on him!" Even though Wilson had come to regard his current home more as a prison than a palace, he heard only cheers that night. "This house," he said, "never looked so beautiful."

By morning, Wilson had made plain his desire to put the Treaty on a fast legislative track. He wanted to keep it as simple as possible—an up or down vote on the Treaty itself, without any Senate tinkering. He intended to make himself immediately available to the Foreign Relations Committee and to postpone presenting the side agreement to defend France. He held in reserve a plan to campaign for the League across the country should the Treaty's passage ever appear to be in jeopardy. At a press conference that morning, he insisted that Article X of the League Covenant—about collective security—was its very spine; if deleted, the League was "only a debating society."

The Republicans were in no rush. They believed every delay would contribute to the Treaty's derailment, which would allow them to fix the peace. They intended to deconstruct every clause of the President's handiwork, dissecting each word. While the Foreign Relations Committee indicated that it would honor a Presidential request to appear before it, the Republicans chose to postpone his testimony until a time that would serve them better. They suggested that the President had completed his duties in regard to the Treaty in Paris. One Kansas Congressman introduced a bill that day that would make it unlawful for a President to absent himself from the territorial jurisdiction of the United States during his term of office or to perform his duties beyond the District of Columbia. Tumulty's intelligence notwithstanding, anti-League forces were claiming forty-nine votes in the Senate, which included a few Democrats.

Although Woodrow Wilson's trips down Pennsylvania Avenue had become routine during the last six and a half years, his visits to the Capitol continued to make history. Not even torrential rains could keep crowds away that Thursday, July 10, 1919. The Senate chamber began filling two hours before he was expected. The President arrived minutes before noon and walked the familiar path to the President's Room on the second floor. A welcoming committee—which included Vice President Marshall and Henry Cabot Lodge, then the nation's most senior Senator—escorted him to the chamber. "Mr. President," Lodge asked, seeing the twenty-by-fourteen-by-six-inch package under Wilson's arm, "can I carry the Treaty for you?" Wilson smiled and replied, "Not on your life." Democratic Senator John Sharp Williams from Mississippi said, "Don't trust him with it, Mr. President." And everybody laughed about the document . . . for the very last time.

The first President of the United States ever to enter the Senate and physically deliver a treaty, Wilson received a standing ovation, and even a few Rebel yells. But the Republicans withheld their applause. When the room had quieted, the President proceeded to discuss the Treaty, which he said constituted "nothing less than a world settlement." Reading from typewritten cards, he delivered an unexpectedly lackluster speech, largely an insipid lesson in history and politics, occasionally enlivened by rhetorical flourishes. Wilson explained that it was impossible to accommodate the varied interests of so many nations without what he called "many minor compromises." As such, he said, the Treaty "is not exactly what we would have written. It is probably not what any one of the national delegations would have written. But results were worked out which on the whole bear test." He refrained from detailing the compromises, letting the final document speak for itself.

Wilson had never liked reading from prepared texts and did so only when the solemnity of the occasion demanded. In the course of his nearly forty minutes that afternoon, he stumbled several times, going back to reread the sentences he had misread. Steadily he improved, especially as he approached the apex of his speech: "That there should be a league of nations to steady the counsels and maintain the peaceful understanding of the world," he explained, ". . . had been one of the agreements accepted from the first as the basis of peace with the central powers." It had "become the first substantive part of the treaty to be worked out and agreed upon." Now, twenty-one years after the Spanish-American War had thrust the United States into the world arena, the nation had "reached her majority as a world power." As such, he said, "a new role and a new responsibility have come to this great nation that we honour and which we would all wish to lift to yet higher levels of service and achievement." Wilson gathered his strength as he spoke of the "united power of free nations" that "must put a stop to aggression." The only hope for such peace, he insisted, was the League. "Shall we or any other free people hesitate to accept this great duty?" he asked the Senate in Wilsonian fashion. "Dare we reject it and break the heart of the world?"

Only in these final seconds did the speech take flight. At last, the President looked up from his manuscript and faced the unresponsive bloc of Republicans and spoke from the heart:

> The stage is set, the destiny disclosed. It has come about by no plan of our conceiving, but by the hand of God, who led us into this way. We cannot turn back. We can only go forward, with lifted eyes and freshened spirit, to follow the vision. It was of this that we dreamed at our birth. America shall in truth show the way. The light streams upon the path ahead, and nowhere else.

Arizona Democrat Henry Ashurst wrote in his diary that day, "I was petrified with surprise."

Everybody on either side of the aisle had expected a masterpiece, an "accounting of the most momentous cause ever entrusted to an individual." If nothing else, the Senate would have liked to have been part of the treaty-making, if not as it was happening then at least in hearing about it now. But, the gentleman from Arizona noted, "his audience wanted raw meat, he fed them cold turnips." Republicans winked at one another. With that, Wilson set the bulky Treaty upon the Vice President's rostrum and left the chamber, unaware of his failure to deliver.

Ashurst, on the other hand, proved to be unusually observant that day. He seemed to be the only one to have noticed a pronounced "contraction" of the back of the President's neck during the speech. And—as if prompted by Wilson's speaking of a war in which masses had been "bled white"—he also detected a strange blanching of his ears. Ashurst lamented that his findings suggested "a man whose vitality is gone." But in fact, something more serious had apparently transpired, as the tightening in Wilson's neck surely suggested pain and the pallor an insufficiency of blood flowing to the head. Both, indeed, may very well have been harbingers of a cerebral episode, if not a minor incident itself.

In the President's Room, Wilson received thirty visitors, all Democrats but one. He issued talking points to get them over the Treaty's imperfections. He opposed reservations to the Treaty because they would only delay if not destroy the fragile peace. The Monroe Doctrine, which was nothing more than a declaration of a nineteenth-century President, never had any legal standing, but the peacemakers in Paris had agreed to protect its position. Wilson had felt that the Treaty could take no action in the matter of Irish independence because the document disposed of territory taken from the enemy, not possessed by the Allies.

Republicans dismissed the speech as a string of glittering generalities. "Soap bubbles of oratory and souffle of praises," mocked Brandegee of Connecticut. Senator Borah of Idaho observed that the President had returned from six months in search of peace with little of substance beyond a sidecar arrangement with France that defined a new alliance for war. At a Sinn Féin rally of seventeen thousand Irish Americans at Madison Square Garden that night, the mention of Wilson's name prompted three minutes of booing.

Wilson continued to believe that popular sentiment supported the League; but he failed to realize that for six months, the most dynamic force within the Democratic Party had been an ocean away, allowing public opinion to drift. Secretary of Agriculture Houston, who was traveling in the West when the President returned, had grown increasingly aware of opposition efforts to denigrate the Treaty, especially the League Covenant. "I had the impression," he wrote, "that certain Republican leaders were determined, not so much to bring about the rejection of the Treaty, as to destroy the President's prestige, to pull him down, and to make such modifications of the Treaty, whether necessary or not, as would enable them to say that the final outcome was their accomplishment, and that they had saved the nation from the ills which the Treaty would have brought upon it." Houston urged Wilson to simplify his rhetoric. But Wilson did not see fit to listen, and in that moment, he began to lose his grip on the national argument.

Houston ascribed Wilson's hesitancy to overconfidence—less in himself than in his constituents. Wilson, he said, "is a firm believer in the doctrine that truth is mighty and will prevail. Seeing an issue very clearly himself, he trusts the masses of the people too implicitly also to see it clearly and to see it as he does, in the short run as well as in the long run." But Wilson did not realize that along with isolationist reactionaries, he lacked the support of many disenchanted liberals, several of whom had been with him in Paris. John Maynard Keynes was completing *The Economic Consequences of the Peace*, a devastating book that upbraided each of the Big Four, not least of all Wilson. Its three-part serialization in

The New Republic that year—at the urging of its New York editor, Walter Lippmann—would make an international name for the young economist as well as big problems for Wilson.

But neither Houston nor almost anybody else in Washington knew the full extent of the opposition Wilson was up against. The President himself did not know that the Republicans had been plotting the demise of his treaty for months before it even existed. Only years later did Franklin D. Roosevelt divulge a secret he had kept to himself about Henry Cabot Lodge and a small coven of Republicans, which included party chairman Will Hays. In late January 1919, as the Peace Conference was opening, this handful of Republicans held a clandestine meeting in Washington to discuss means of dismantling whatever accord Wilson brought home. As Roosevelt later imparted only as an unnamed source, "Hays, Lodge and others made up their mind before they knew anything about the Treaty or the League of Nations that they were going to wreck it whether their consciences demanded it or not."

Having been gone from home for so long, Wilson could not appreciate the tectonic shifts across the national landscape. Just as ramping up for war had rocked the nation, so too did demobilization. While Germany was the epicenter of massive economic inflation, prices in America had practically doubled between 1913 and 1919; in July 1919 alone, they spiked by 4 percent. The press referred so often to this inflation as the "high cost of living," it earned its own acronym. By the end of the month, the railroad brotherhood unions advised the President that unless they saw some severe action toward reducing the HCL, two million railroad workers would demand wage increases, which would amount to close to a billion dollars. Management, of course, attributed the inflation to such increases and linked these demands to the unions, many of which had foreign-born leaders, some of whom chanted the same slogans that were shouted in Bolshevik Russia.

James Weldon Johnson, field secretary for the NAACP, dubbed those hot months of 1919 the "Red Summer"—though for a different reason that had even graver consequences. Three dozen race riots erupted in America that season, half of them in July, producing the bloodiest rash of interracial violence in American history. Hundreds were killed, and tens of thousands were left homeless. At least five dozen black men died at the end of a rope. Many Negroes—especially those who had fought in the war—had viewed 1919 as the year in which they might advance in the mainstream of American society. The very thought of such gains only threatened whites who wished to restrain them, and not just in the South. No less an authority than Mississippi's Governor Theodore Bilbo asserted that very month, "This is a white man's country, with a white man's civilization, and any dream on the part of the Negro race to share social and political equality will be shattered in the end."

Between Bisbee, Arizona, on July 3 and Syracuse, New York, on the thirty-first, whites ignited racial tensions in black communities, which spontaneously combusted into arson, looting, and gunfire in several Northern cities, including Philadelphia and Baltimore. The mayhem in Chicago lasted a week. After several days in which the local police could not quell the murderous riots in Washington, D.C., Secretary of War Baker called in two thousand federal troops, including three hundred Marines. But the fighting force that distinguished the bloodbath in the national capital was the Negro community itself, choosing, as Johnson wrote, "not to run, but to fight—fight in defense of their lives and their homes." Lamentable though these riots were, Johnson believed the Red Summer, especially those pogroms in Washington and Chicago, marked "the turning point in the psychology of the whole nation regarding the Negro problem," informing the white population as it empowered the black. The President expressed concern over the conflagrations, but considered them local problems at a time when he was concentrating almost exclusively on global issues.

Nationally, the most pressing domestic problem lay in the readjustment of the labor force, as American doughboys flooded the job market. Unemployment at the end of the war was less than 2 percent; two years later, it would be greater than 5 percent; a year after that, it would reach 12 percent. Not all the changes were as easily measured. Millions of Americans yearned for the peaceful normality of old, when the United States had flourished in wholesome isolation; millions more presumed the psyches of America's returning soldiers must have altered. The catchiest song of the day asked, "How ya gonna keep 'em down on the farm, after they've seen Paree?" The steady migration from rural communities to urban centers increased, marking the first moment that a majority of Americans lived in cities. The war had ended just before Second Lieutenant F. Scott Fitzgerald was supposed to ship overseas. In July 1919, he went home to Minnesota to rewrite his first novel, in which he proclaimed, "Here was a new generation . . . dedicated more than the last to the fear of poverty and the worship of success; grown up to find all Gods dead, all wars fought, all faiths in man shaken."

A postwar recession accompanied the postwar disillusionment, and the Dow Jones industrial average instilled fears of continued stagnation at best—closing at the end of the year a little over 100, barely five points higher than when the decade began. But through the third and fourth quarters of 1919, the economy remained healthy enough for Wilson to focus almost exclusively on what he considered his legacy—the passage of the Treaty, complete with its Covenant. Unfortunately, that meant his having to face his most formidable enemy, an "HCL" of another sort.

Henry Cabot Lodge was the only son of a Bostonian widow whose ancestors had arrived in Massachusetts in 1700. Subsequent generations of Cabots amassed a fortune, mostly in shipping. "Boston incarnate," wrote Henry Adams, referring not only to Lodge's pedigree but also to his education, which revolved completely around Harvard College. He earned a bachelor's degree, a law degree, and the school's first doctorate in political science before teaching there for several years. As patronizing as he was patrician, Lodge suffered from what Adams called "Bostonitis," symptoms of which included "chronic irritability" and the quality of "thinking too much of himself." At the same time, Adams described his Harvard protégé as an "excellent talker, a voracious reader, a ready wit, an accomplished orator, with a clear mind and a powerful memory." About to launch his political career in the state legislature in 1879, Lodge also served as a junior editor of a New England journal called the *International Review*. In that capacity, he had accepted and published that first major literary effort of Princeton senior Thomas W. Wilson, six years his junior.

Barely in his twenties, Wilson had been strangely prescient. His treatise had challenged the very structure of American government, questioning a President's ability to lead in a system in which the legislature outweighed the executive branch and conducted most of its business in closed-door committee rooms. While young Wilson had not recommended demolishing the Congress in favor of a Parliament, in which its leader spoke for the majority; he had boldly recommended a cabinet that could sit among the representatives as a link between the two branches. Over the years, especially during TR's administration, Wilson saw how a vibrant personality could galvanize a Presidency. But the basic system still troubled him, as it fostered antagonism between the branches, especially if different parties controlled them. Strong personalities on either side all but guaranteed hostile stalemates.

Lodge, the Republican leader in the Congress, considered Woodrow Wilson able, ambitious, and "by no means a commonplace man." He went so far as to praise him as a "master of the rhetorical use of idealism." In his posthumously published account of the League, he went to great lengths to insist that he never harbored any "personal hostility to Mr. Wilson"—a point he made five times on page 23 alone. But after six years of disagreeing with the President on practically every major position—and perhaps because Wilson had dethroned him as the nation's "scholar in politics"—Lodge's enmity toward Wilson had steadily escalated.

This petty academic rivalry in Lodge's mind should not be underestimated. His account of the League fight reminded his readers that, despite what newspapers said about Woodrow Wilson, "he was not a scholar in the true sense at all." Even his vaunted speeches, Lodge added, were practically devoid of classical allusion or literary quotation; and for all his education, Lodge said, he was "not a widely-read man." One Senator commented, "If only President Wilson had not been a college prof and didn't know how to write so well this issue would come out all right." Wilson tacitly bore his own grudge, one reminiscent of the fight over the graduate school at Princeton, when he battled the privileged, who had been handed everything for which he had to work. Before the end of the President's first term, Lodge had imparted to his dearest friend, TR, "I never expected to hate anyone in politics with the hatred I feel toward Wilson."

Seldom has the American body politic been so fractious as it was in 1919. Despite two victories at the polls, the President had not won either of his elections with a majority; and his strong, unyielding views further polarized his constituents. The Republicans held a majority in both houses, though only narrowly in the Senate. Each of the parties was further fractured by strong opposing factions within, especially when it came to the Treaty. Wilson was counting on all forty-six Democratic Senators, though two had already expressed their disapproval of the Treaty.

The Republicans were more divided. Lodge counted fifteen Republican Senators completely unwilling to vote for the Treaty under any circumstances. They became known as the "Irreconcilables." Thirty-four of his party members were "Reservationists," torn between insisting upon major revisions or "mild" ones. The latter group could be swayed to the

Wilson camp should he offer some concessions. Lodge had also identified three Democratic Irreconcilables, whose votes meant the most to him, for their small margin could allow him to maintain that Wilson's own party defeated the Treaty. In seeking the necessary two-thirds majority, the President and Lodge would vie for the independent thinkers within the Senate: Wilson hoped to build momentum through the weight of his office and the force of his oratory; Lodge intended to throw into his path every legislative obstacle at his disposal, if not defeating the Treaty altogether then at least transforming it into something Republican. A painstaking probe of the Treaty, he figured, would only expose its flaws.

At the start of this contest, momentum seemed to be in the President's favor. "I don't see how we are ever going to defeat this proposition," said freshman Republican Senator James Watson of Indiana to Lodge. The Senate elder sighed. "Ah, my dear James," he said placatingly, "I do not propose to try to beat it by direct frontal attack, but by the indirect method of reservations." Watson would accept the strategy for a while, but in a later encounter he said, "Suppose the President accepts the treaty with your reservations. Then we are in the League." Lodge offered a paternal grin and a personal insight, explaining how much Wilson hated him. "Never under any set of circumstances in this world," he said calmly, "could he be induced to accept a treaty with Lodge reservations appended to it." Unconvinced, Watson said that was a "slender thread on which to hang so great a cause."

"A slender thread!" Lodge scoffed. "Why, it is as strong as any cable with its strands wired and twisted together."

No sooner had President Wilson delivered the Treaty than was Senator Lodge on his feet moving that it be sent to the Foreign Relations Committee, which he chaired and had packed with Irreconcilables. Thus, the document was now under his jurisdiction, and on his schedule. Within minutes it was dispatched to the Public Printer; and five hours later, *The New York Times* reported, it had been set in type, ready for distribution. But strangely, as Lodge himself noted in his memoirs, three days passed before his committee members received the text. And then, Lodge announced that he would conduct extensive public hearings—for at least a month, if not longer.

Not home even a week, Wilson already looked weary and his writing hand had stiffened yet again. He still considered touring the country to explain the Treaty to the people. More immediately, he announced visiting hours, during which Senators might appear at the White House unannounced. When his own party leaders informed him that it would be impossible to pass the Treaty without some reservations, Wilson realized the need to develop a more aggressive strategy. In the sudden absence of Democratic leader Thomas S. Martin of Virginia, who had become terminally ill, Wilson turned to Gilbert Hitchcock of Nebraska. Although the Senator had quarreled with the President over the Federal Reserve Board, Hitchcock had become a trusty proponent of the League. He was Wilson's strongest advocate in the Senate and a worthy Minority Leader, though a somewhat dubious challenger to his Republican counterpart.

Henry Cabot Lodge closely monitored each of his committee's members as the President reminded them that this was not a partisan issue—that it was "their duty to vote for the treaty just as he had presented it to the Senate." With each step forward, Lodge introduced a new set of stalling tactics. He issued one request after another for information and documentation. And then he decided that he owed it to the country to read the entire Treaty aloud, all 264 pages, word by word, in a committee room—insisting a charter of such importance demanded as much. Committee members sometimes wandered in and out for the recitation; more often, Lodge found himself speaking to four marble walls and a scribe. His performance would kill two weeks.

At first, Wilson's private sessions proved effective—as he advanced a positive message while providing explanations for each of the Treaty's stipulations. On Friday, July 18, British liaison Sir William Wiseman found the President confident that he was winning over his opposition—including a number of those Senators who had pledged themselves to defeat the League even before they had read the Covenant. Wilson regretted that Taft was knuckling under party pressure and now leaned toward reservations. Confiding to Wiseman that he was considering some cosmetic concessions in the Treaty's language, he said yet again that he would embark on a nationwide tour only upon finding insufficient Republican support. That pleased Edith, who worried that her husband could not withstand such an ordeal, especially during the torrid summer.

Dr. Grayson shared Edith's concerns. He took to encouraging any recreation for the President whenever possible. Despite storm warnings and Wilson's experiencing an apparent case of indigestion, Grayson even endorsed a weekend cruise to Chesapeake Bay on the *Mayflower*, just to keep him from working. Unfortunately, electrical storms struck, and so too did Wilson's gastric disorder, turning into what Grayson diagnosed as acute dysentery. At least that was what he told the press. The intense heat and strain since his return from Europe logically explained his condition; but subsequent reconsideration of the prior days' symptoms—the headaches, pallor, cramped hand, and difficulty reading and speaking— suggest a minor stroke. Whatever the case, this "transient incapacity" was likely related to some progressive cerebrovascular condition.

Back in the White House, Wilson took to his bed and canceled the next day's schedule. That did not stop Senator Lodge, who tightened the reins on his team and encouraged any disruptions to Wilson's plans. Opposition leaders leaked to the press that they were prepared to provide the President with a list of the thirty-five Senators pledged to reject the Treaty in its present form—two more than were required. Their reasons ranged from the general burdens of collective security to a specific distrust of the Japanese ever to make good on their promise to yield Shantung. Some radical Republicans simply avowed to kill the entire Treaty if their demands were not met. By Tuesday the twenty-second, the President had resumed meeting with Senators, while Lodge compiled a list of witnesses for his hearings, encouraged discussion of every sort of amendment to the Treaty, and maintained his steady demand for more documents.

Edith Wilson watched her husband achieve diminishing returns as he lobbied Senators—arguing that neither he nor they had "the moral right further to modify any Article unless every other country should be granted the same privilege." To do so would negate a half year of work and emasculate the pact. On July 28, Lodge completed his word-by-word reading of the Treaty.

After letting another three days pass, he called the first of sixty witnesses. Lodge's account of the diligence with which he and his committee had studied the Treaty masked the fact that their primary task was less to understand it than to undermine it. His goal was to ensure the Senate's dissent. The early witnesses included members of the Administration, such as Secretary of Labor William B. Wilson, who were friendly to the President but had little to offer by way of enlightenment. In thirteen days of actual testimony—stretched across the next six weeks—many of the witnesses who paraded before the panel in Room 310 of the Senate Office

Building shared one common trait—an ability to embarrass the President. The committee properly called Secretary of State Lansing to testify, and the questions targeted his dissatisfaction with the Treaty and his descriptions of having been marginalized during the Peace Conference. His circumspect hesitations spoke louder than any criticisms he could have directed toward his boss. Irish American witnesses bemoaned their cause being ignored in the Treaty. And then, allowing a plea for racial equality, the committee invited a Negro delegation, its spokesman none other than William Monroe Trotter, the only man Wilson had ever banished from the White House. Halfway through the hearings, Lodge decided his committee could make its best case by cross-examining the defendant himself. The President welcomed the opportunity, though he should have been more careful what he wished for.

Wilson was, in fact, experiencing a mental decline, which was discernible to others. On several occasions in late July and early August, he responded to queries about the Treaty with incorrect information—instances of recent actions and events that he could not recall. His once photographic memory began to blur. On August 8, 1919, he delivered to a joint session of Congress a dull address full of run-on sentences about the high cost of living.

The rest of his activities that month further reflected scattered thought and divided attention. The issues of race riots, soaring food prices, and impending railroad strikes would have challenged any President in the best of health. In his current condition, the sixty-two-year-old Wilson could only offer short shrift to every situation but the Treaty, thus salving problems without solving them. Recognizing its historical significance, Wilson performed one incidental duty to notable effect, when Secretary Newton Baker informed him that any number of official documents and communications required a name for the war they had just won. The Navy had informally adopted "the War Against Teutonic Aggression," while the commanders of the Allied armies called it "the Great War for Civilization." Great Britain chose "the War of 1914–1918." From a sampler Baker sent, Wilson selected "the World War."

As it joined the ranks of the American Revolution, the Mexican War, the Civil War, and the Spanish-American War, Upton Sinclair and Clarence Darrow urged Woodrow Wilson to consider that the World War was over and that he ought to reconsider the motives of men—most particu-

larly Eugene Debs—who had spoken their consciences and whose imprisonment for disagreeing was no longer "self-defense but a punishment
undeserved." Wilson took the case to heart and wrote Socialist John Spargo
that he would "deal with the matter as early and in as liberal a spirit as
possible." But matters of the peace process kept intervening amid bouts of
forgetfulness and fits of temper.

Senators argued the Treaty all summer—mostly Republicans expressing their distaste while Democrats proposed the least amount of compromise to make it palatable. The only fresh thought that season came from
Henry Cabot Lodge himself, who reminded people that the Treaty's adherents did not have a monopoly on idealism. He tried to rival Wilson in
eloquence, but he could make his case with little more than platitudes and
a negation of Wilson's plan. So tired had the Treaty "debate" become, the
press curtailed its coverage.

That was not the case, however, on Tuesday, August 19, 1919, when the
Administration set another precedent by inviting the Foreign Relations
Committee to 1600 Pennsylvania Avenue. Although the separation of
powers kept the legislative branch from requiring a Chief Executive to appear before it, Woodrow Wilson embraced this opportunity. At ten o'clock,
all but one of the seventeen Senators arrived and found a ring of chairs in
the East Room. Wilson sat in the farthest corner, with Senator Lodge on
his right and Virginia's Senator Claude A. Swanson on his left. The rest of
the Senators completed the circle, which was broken by a few tables for
stenographers Charles Swem from the White House pool and five others
from the Senate. Neither photographers nor journalists were admitted,
though much of the basement floor of the White House had been converted into a makeshift pressroom. Reporters and typists filled its main
corridor and oval room, which had been rigged with tables and typewriters
so the stenographers could run with the news as it broke.

After the President read a long statement expressing the need to expedite consideration of the Treaty, the Senators grilled him for the next three
hours. Although not always accurate, Wilson parried any opposition, even
the incisive questions from Irreconcilables Hiram Johnson and William
Borah, whom Walter Lippmann had prepared with insider information.
Only once did Wilson seem agitated—when first-term Ohio Senator
Warren G. Harding raised a series of questions about America's
moral obligations as opposed to the legal, which suggested he had not

listened to the answer Wilson had just provided. He struck the President as having "a disturbingly dull mind, and . . . it seemed impossible to get any explanation to lodge in it." Close to 1:30, Senator Lodge—who had let others speak for him—brought the proceedings to a close. The President asked his guests to remain for luncheon—a spread of melon, spring lamb, cold Virginia ham, salad, vegetables, and ices that awaited in the State Dining Room. "It will be very delightful," the courtly Wilson told his adversaries. And for the next hour, everybody tucked into what one Senator told the press was surely a five-dollar-a-plate meal. The conversation was apolitical and pleasant.

"He was nervous, but he certainly handled himself magnificently," Dr. Grayson said, calling the day "a triumph" for the President. Given that Wilson had recently suffered a cerebral incident, that was true. But objective observers judged the day a failure. The semipublic display had been more about presentation than information, and it changed nobody's heart or mind. "To those of us who just looked on and listened," noted Ike Hoover, "the President was not at his best. . . . In fact, all through this period he manifested an over-anxiety toward his guests." The transcript of the proceedings revealed as much. Talk of "national good conscience" and moral responsibilities overshadowed the specifics of the Treaty. Worst of all, perusal of the record exposed more than a dozen errors in the President's testimony—incorrect dates, erroneous assertions regarding the uncertainty of the Treaty's fate, and forgotten elements of the pact and its evolution, especially when it came to the secret treaties. As they were all apparent mental lapses, the President emerged that day as a man as compromised—physically and mentally—as his treaty.

Bernard Baruch, who saw the President regularly, knew he was not opposed to making concessions so long as the Covenant remained intact. Believing he would accept any number of Senate corollary resolutions interpreting the Treaty, Baruch discussed the matter with him, Attorney General Palmer, and War Secretary Baker. Two days after the Foreign Relations Committee met at the White House, one of Wilson's key allies, Senator Key Pittman of Nevada, introduced several "interpretative" reservations in language that suggested not only the President's blessing but even his dictation. Earlier in the week, Wilson had stood behind the clarity of the Treaty's points, but now he was granting the need for further elucidation. To some, he was sounding more like a seasoned politico than a principled statesman.

By the end of August, Wilson realized that he was winning no converts in Washington. As opposition intensified, several Democrats urged him to play his trump card and take his case directly to the people. Wilson knew where to find the nation's most independent thinkers. Reigniting the same voters who had delivered his reelection meant going west—where greater acceptance of new ideas came with the territory. The White House's chief telegrapher, Edward Smithers, charted a four-week itinerary, which covered ten thousand miles with stops in twenty-nine cities. The President would speak in all but four of the states west of the Mississippi, half of which were represented by Irreconcilables. It would be Wilson's last opportunity to rally public opinion. Failure to wrest control of the argument would mean he had returned from Europe with nothing more than victory without peace.

While Tumulty generally considered Wilson's political fortunes paramount, in this instance, he made an exception. In a quiet moment alone with the President, he raised the subject of his health. "I know that I am at the end of my tether," Wilson said, "but my friends on the Hill say that the trip is necessary to save the Treaty, and I am willing to make whatever personal sacrifice is required, for if the Treaty should be defeated, God only knows what would happen to the world as a result of it." He acknowledged that such a trip might mean "the giving up of my life." But, he said, "I will gladly make the sacrifice to save the Treaty." Tumulty looked at the "old man" before him—grim in his determination to fight to the end, like some "old warrior." In fact, it was the young soldiers who impelled Wilson to make the trip. "If the Treaty is not ratified by the Senate," he told Edith, "the War will have been fought in vain, and the world will be thrown into chaos. I promised our soldiers, when I asked them to take up arms, that it was a war to end wars; and if I do not do all in my power to put the Treaty in effect, I will be a slacker and never able to look those boys in the eye. I must go."

A few days before his scheduled departure, Bernard Baruch called on a gaunt and pale Wilson to cancel his trip. Short of that, he asked the President to consider a brief respite during which he could compose his speeches. The President insisted he lacked the time. "Mr. President,"

Baruch asked, making his best argument, "if anything happens to you, what will we do?" Wilson replied with an unanswerable question: "What is one life in a great cause?" He had determined this was his cross to bear.

Dr. Grayson made the final appeal. Having already argued that the rigorous schedule, the inability to exercise, the constant strain of speech-making and handshaking, the discomfort of living on a train for a month—especially in the summer, when the steel cars would become ovens—could all be lethal, he visited the President in his study. Before Grayson could speak, Wilson looked up from his writing and said, "I know what you have come for. I do not want to do anything foolhardy but the League of Nations is now in its crisis, and if it fails, I hate to think what will happen to the world. You must remember that I, as Commander in Chief, was responsible for sending our soldiers to Europe. In the crucial test in the trenches they did not turn back—and I cannot turn back now. I cannot put my personal safety, my health, in the balance against my duty—I must go." Still holding his pen, Wilson rose from his desk and walked to the window, silently gazing upon the Washington Monument. Looking as though he had just signed a death warrant, he turned to his physician, who saw tears in his eyes. Grayson realized there was nothing for him to do except pack his own bags and provide the best medical attention that he could.

An unexpectedly jaunty Woodrow Wilson—in his straw boater, blue blazer, white trousers, and white shoes—strode through Washington's Union Station that Wednesday evening, September 3, 1919. The Presidential car—like the yacht, called the *Mayflower*—was attached to the rear of a Pennsylvania Railroad train and came configured with a sitting room, which doubled as a dining area, and then a bedroom for the First Lady, which connected to that of her husband; each had a single bed and a dressing table. Beyond that was an "office," with a table on which the President's typewriter sat. Finally, there was a compartment for Edith's maid and another for Dr. Grayson. Brooks, the valet, would sleep on the leather couch in the sitting room. Ahead of the *Mayflower* was a string of baggage cars, a diner, and Pullman cars to accommodate Wilson's four stenographers, seven Secret Service agents, and the largest press corps ever to make a Presidential tour. Because radio was still in its infancy, Wilson would rely upon those two dozen representatives of the media—journalists, still photographers, newsreel photographers, and an official from the Western Union Telegraph Company—to capture him as he attempted to regain the support of the people. The train pulled away from the station a little after seven.

No President had ever gone to such lengths for a cause. Candidates in the past had campaigned for their own political fortunes; sixty-two-year-old Wilson was sallying forth across America purely for an ideal. He came prepared, having filled eight pages with thoughts and themes he intended to draw upon. The next twenty-seven days would showcase the quintessential Woodrow Wilson, who believed oratory suffused with reason, emotion, and depth of character could convert a nation.

The quest began inauspiciously the next morning at eleven, when the *Mayflower* arrived under gray skies in Columbus, Ohio. A local streetcar strike kept many away, and the morning rain doused the spirits of some who ventured downtown, but Wilson found a capacity crowd of more than four thousand waiting for him at Memorial Hall, where close to two thousand people had been turned away. Despite a headache, he touched upon most of the salient aspects of the Treaty and reminded his audience of the reason they had gone to war. This treaty, he said, sought "to punish one of the greatest wrongs ever done in history." He called the terms "severe" but "not unjust." By one o'clock the *Mayflower* was heading west.

Big crowds gathered at the small stations along the way, and Wilson stood on the rear platform to shake hands. In Richmond, Indiana, he delivered a short speech about the Treaty:

> The chief thing to notice about it . . . is that it is the first treaty ever made by great powers that was not made in their own favor. It is made for the protection of the weak peoples of the world and not for the aggrandizement of the strong. . . . The extraordinary achievement of this treaty is that it gives a free choice to people who never could have won it for themselves. It is for the first time in the history of international transactions an act of systematic justice and not an act of grabbing and seizing.

He asked his fellow citizens what difference a political party label made "when mankind is involved."

The train arrived in Indianapolis at six, and after a quick dinner, the Wilsons greeted a nonpartisan reception committee, which included the

Republican Governor, James Putnam Goodrich. An automobile parade, complete with a band, led the President to the Fair Grounds, where an audience of close to twenty thousand awaited in the Coliseum. In a slightly husky voice, Wilson attempted to reach everybody in the hall, but a few hundred people at the perimeter left in frustration. Within five minutes, Wilson had captivated those who had remained.

Nobody seemed to care that he mistakenly spoke at the outset of the assassination of the Archduke Franz Ferdinand in Sarajevo, Serbia, when he meant Bosnia. This crowd, like the others that would follow, seemed less interested in small details of the past than in Wilson's larger vision for the future. He stuck to the manner that had served him for the last decade, that of never speaking down to his audience. In so doing, he lifted their spirits and raised their aspirations. He called upon the commonsense Hoosiers to ignore the misinformation his opponents were spreading about Article X of the League Covenant and consider for themselves that "there is no compulsion upon us to take [the advice of the Council of the League] except the compulsion of our good consciences and judgment. . . . There is in that Covenant not one note of surrender of the independent judgment of the government of the United States, but an expression of it." By 10 p.m., the President was on his way to Missouri.

The *Mayflower* reached St. Louis before dawn, though the President rested on board until nine. Civic ceremonies filled the morning, and 1,500 people paid two dollars each for lunch and the privilege of hearing Wilson address the Chamber of Commerce. The Republican Mayor, Henry William Kiel, announced that most of the host committee was, in fact, Republican—opponents of the Treaty at that, as seemed to be the case with the majority of Wilson's audiences that day. He said that he was glad to hear his own phrase repeated by his adversaries—that "politics was adjourned." The President's headache persisting, Dr. Grayson was able to take him for a brisk walk in a local park, providing some exercise before his speech that night to twelve thousand people in Convention Hall. In this city with its large German American population, Wilson spoke of the need to rebuild Germany, if only so that she could pay her reparations bill. He further stated that America "went into this war to see it through to the end," but that the end had not yet come. "This is the beginning, not of the war," said Wilson, "but of the processes which are going to render a war like this impossible." At eleven o'clock the Presidential train started across the state, arriving the next morning, Saturday, in Kansas City.

Thousands of schoolchildren, each waving an American flag, lined a five-mile parade route, as the President rode to Convention Hall. Recharged by an overflow crowd of close to twenty thousand cheering citizens, Wilson walked from the back of the hall to the stage to deliver one of the most ebullient and bare-knuckled speeches of his life. "I came back from Paris bringing one of the greatest documents of human history," he said, before spending the better part of the next hour proving as much. He clarified that the Treaty was "in spirit and essence . . . an American document," since American principles had penetrated to the hearts of the peoples of Europe and their representatives. Most significant of all, he said, was the Covenant of the League of Nations, which substituted consultation and arbitration for "the brutal processes of war." That methodology, he reminded his listeners, was the central principle of the Bryan treaties, instituted in the earliest days of Wilson's presidency. He spoke of the new power grab in Russia, where the Bolshevik government was proving itself more cruel than the Czar or even the Kaiser had been in "controlling the destinies of that great people." He warned, "If you don't want little groups of selfish men to plot the future of Europe, we must not allow little groups of selfish men to plot the future of America."

"I have come out to fight for a cause," Wilson said, leading with his chin. "That cause is greater than the Senate. It is greater than the government. It is as great as the cause of mankind, and I intend, in office or out, to fight that battle as long as I live." He explained that his ancestors were "troublesome Scotchmen," among whom were some of that nation's most stubborn and strong, the Covenanters. Upon taking his leave of the stage, Wilson said, "Here is the Covenant of the League of Nations. I am a Covenanter!"

By nightfall he was three hundred miles to the north, in Des Moines, Iowa. As in the preceding cities, the elected officials who greeted him were for the most part Republicans, which fueled Wilson's argument that the nation was looking for a unified, nonpartisan response to the Treaty. He observed that the "isolation of the United States is at an end, not because we chose to go into the politics of the world, but because . . . we have become a determining factor in the history of mankind."

On Sunday the President rested in a hotel in Des Moines. He had garnered banner headlines in the nation's newspapers his first five days on the
road. Articles initially spoke of Lodge as having taken the lead in the early
innings of this great debate, but now that Wilson was swinging for the
fences, the shift in the country's mood was palpable. An overnight Republican survey in Missouri revealed that the President had flipped the state
from anti- to pro-League. Because Wilson could dip into a $25,000 travel
fund allotted the President, one Republican Congressman from Missouri
proposed a resolution providing $15,000 to defray the expenses of any
Senators who sought equal time on the road opposing the Treaty. Edith
Wilson noticed that the waves of approval helped calm her husband's nervous energy and headaches. With friendly crowds gathering at every junction, Tumulty wanted the President to address them from the rear
platform. Here Dr. Grayson put his foot down, as he anxiously knew that
each appearance and each bad night's sleep depleted his patient's reserves.

At 5 a.m. on September 8, the *Mayflower* rolled into Omaha, Nebraska;
and over the next week, it would zigzag north before heading west. The
itinerary required as many as four speeches some days, and Wilson alone
composed his material. Before retiring each night, he jotted notes for the
program the next day, as he tailored each speech with an unexpected twist
or inspiring phrase. He walked onto the stage of the Auditorium in Omaha
with a prop—a copy of the Treaty, so that all could see it was a lot more
than the few clauses that had been debated endlessly in the press. "Why,
my fellow citizens," Wilson said, "this is one of the great charters of human liberty, and the man who picks flaws in it—or, rather, picks out the
flaws that are in it, for there are flaws in it—forgets the magnitude of the
thing, forgets the majesty of the thing, forgets that the counsels of more
than twenty nations combined . . . were . . . unanimous in the adoption
of this great instrument." Wilson readily conceded that this treaty created
only a "presumption" that there would not be another war—because "there
is no absolute guarantee against human passion." But he predicted with
absolute certainty that "within another generation, there will be another
world war if the nations of the world—if the League of Nations—does not
prevent it by concerted action."

"Sometimes people call me an idealist," he told an audience at the Armory that night in Sioux Falls, South Dakota. "Well, that is the way I

know I am an American." Wilson's talk was not always so elevated. He said America could stay out of a society composed of the governments of the world, but that would cast suspicion on their nation. He hoped the American farmer would appreciate that "you can make more money out of men who trust you than out of men who fear you." He posited that friendship made American wheat taste better than that of Australia or Argentina, that it made American cotton better than that of India. During the night, the *Mayflower* coupled onto the Chicago & Northwestern Railroad line to Minnesota.

Wilson encountered his first political slap the next morning as his train car waited for the reception committee to arrive at the St. Paul station. Knowing the President was scheduled to address a special session of the state legislature, Governor Joseph. A. A. Burnquist—chairman of the committee and a bitter Republican opponent of the Treaty—intentionally detained the group at the Capitol for half an hour, arriving at the station with neither explanation nor apology. The President of the United States turned the other cheek. Without mentioning a single name, Wilson concluded his address with a word about the reception committees he had encountered on his tour. Most, he said, had been made up of Republicans, which gave him great pleasure—"because I should be ashamed of myself if I permitted any partisan thought to enter into this great matter. . . . Everybody knows that we are all Americans. Scratch a Democrat or a Republican, and underneath it is the same stuff."

After lunch, the President faced an enthusiastic reception on the streets of Minneapolis and then delivered a speech in the Armory. By the time he had returned to St. Paul for another speech that night, the city was abuzz over Governor Burnquist's insult that morning. Fifteen thousand Minnesotans jammed into the Auditorium and heard the President pay tribute to the soldiers who had fought in the Civil War to preserve the Union. Although he had been born and bred in the South, he said saving the Union was "the greatest thing that men had conceived up to that time." Now, Wilson said, "we come to . . . the union of great nations in conference upon the interests of peace." So rousing was Wilson, the Mayor of St. Paul leapt to the stage upon the conclusion of the address. "All those in favor of the ratification of the Treaty without a single change will vote Aye," he shouted to the crowd. And fifteen thousand shook the hall in agreement.

Each of the next five nights saw the President traveling west on the Northern Pacific Railway. And just as Wilson approached their home states, Senators Borah and Johnson launched their own nationwide opposition tour of the nation, leaving the Foreign Relations Committee with forty-five proposed amendments and four reservations to the Treaty. Because Wilson had no new themes to convey, he had to rely heavily on performance to persuade. The press removed coverage from the front pages and some days did not publicize his tour at all. Through North Dakota, Montana, Idaho, and Washington, Wilson maintained his breakneck pace nonetheless. Pounding headaches and asthma attacked him regularly, and Dr. Grayson could provide little treatment beyond propping up the President with pillows. After several nights, Wilson chose not even to bother the doctor. He simply grabbed his pillows and chair and caught what few winks of sleep he could before the next day's events.

In the meantime, four million American workers struck their jobs that year in nearly four thousand clashes between management and labor. The Amalgamated Association of Iron, Steel, and Tin Workers had attempted to organize the steel industry for decades, demanding union recognition; and in September, a national strike shut down half the industry. The violence between unionists on one hand and scabs and police on the other became so great in Gary, Indiana, the United States Army had to declare martial law. Boston faced a more difficult labor situation when much of its police force struck, prompting several nights of looting that required Governor Calvin Coolidge to unleash his State Guard. That action—calling the strikers "traitors"—transformed the Governor into a national figure representing law and order. Wilson called the strike "a crime against civilization," for the obligation of a policeman was "as sacred as the obligation of a soldier. He is a public servant, not a private employee, and . . . has no right to prefer any private advantage to the public safety." The racial violence of the Red Summer was no longer in flames but still flickering; September remained quiet until the end of the month, when disturbances broke out in Omaha and a few days later in a small town in Arkansas. Wilson expressed his "shame as an American citizen at the race riots . . . where men have forgot humanity and justice and orderly society and have run amuck." And the nation was just confronting one of the most peculiar legislative ideas ever to infringe upon American life— Prohibition, which had been ratified as the Eighteenth Amendment to the Constitution at the start of the year. To implement that amendment, the House originated the Volstead Act that summer, and by September, Congress was preparing to send the law to the President's desk for his signature.

Elsewhere on the Hill, Senator Hitchcock submitted his minority report to the Foreign Relations Committee, urging ratification of the Treaty without amendments or reservations. Neither side found any give in this tug-of-war. Senator Lodge's hearings on the Treaty droned on, crescendoing with the appearance of William Bullitt, whose disgruntlement after his resignation from the American Peace Commission still festered. For hours—facing Lodge and five Republican colleagues—Bullitt made no effort to disguise his contempt for the Treaty of Versailles. His comments did little damage, for he was an obviously spurned minor player in the talks. But at the end of his interrogation, enjoying his moment in the sun as he cast a shadow over Wilson, he spoke about the senior members of the American diplomatic team, and how Lansing, Bliss, and White had "objected very vigorously to the numerous provisions of the treaty." Lodge commented that their objections to the Shantung provision were already known and asked if there was anything else to which they had objected. As though choreographed, Bullitt said, "I do not think that Secretary Lansing is at all enthusiastic about the League of Nations as it stands at present." With that, he produced a memorandum of a conversation he had with the Secretary on May 19. Bullitt quoted Lansing as having said, "I consider that the league of nations at present is entirely useless. The great powers have simply gone ahead and arranged the world to suit themselves. England and France in particular have gotten out of the treaty everything that they wanted, and the league of nations can do nothing to alter any of the unjust clauses of the treaty." Upon learning of Bullitt's testimony, Lansing—about to embark on a fishing trip on Lake Ontario—offered the press no comment.

The President—who heard the news from the press corps aboard the *Mayflower*—did the same, though Tumulty saw that Wilson was "incensed and distressed beyond measure." Four days later, Lansing telegraphed the President his version of what he had said to Bullitt, a feeble explanation concluding with his wish to do everything he could to promote ratification of the Treaty. He said he regretted that he ever had any conversation with "the disloyal young man who is seeking notoriety at the expense of the respect of all honorable men." Wilson summoned Tumulty to his compartment. "Read that," he said, handing him the wire, "and tell me what you think of a man who was my associate on the other side and who confidentially expressed himself to an outsider in such a fashion?" For months in Paris, suspicions about Lansing had nagged the President. "But here in his own statement," Wilson said, "is a verification at last of everything I have suspected. Think of it! This from a man whom I raised from the level of a subordinate to the great office of Secretary of State of the United States. My God! I did not think it was possible for Lansing to act in this way." No task more pressing awaited the President's return to the White House than demanding Lansing's resignation.

The same morning that Wilson read Lansing's telegram, Dr. Grayson observed small drops of saliva at the corners of the President's mouth. His lips quivered slightly, and more spittle appeared. His face turned white. Grayson examined the rest of the itinerary, hoping to edit it.

Tumulty disagreed. He knew that the Treaty's great broker was also its most convincing speaker, and Wilson had another five thousand miles of territory to cover in which he could rally support. By the time he had reached Spokane on September 12, his voice had weakened and, the *Seattle Post-Intelligencer* reported, "there was a suggestion of a man very much fatigued in his delivery." He instinctively pumped his speeches with more emotion and vivid imagery. He spoke of the unconquerable nature of truth, even if you "blind its eyes with blood."

Before almost seven thousand in the Portland Auditorium, he brought the house down when he insisted that "peace can only be maintained by putting behind it the force of united nations determined to uphold it and prevent war." And then he revealed that he had just read them a quotation from Henry Cabot Lodge in 1915. He earned a second round of laughter and applause when he said, "I entirely concur in Senator Lodge's conclusion, and I hope I shall have his cooperation in bringing about the desired result."

Grayson insisted the President walk for half an hour before the train departed, but the staff squeezed an interview into those few minutes instead. A local reporter asked if the tremendous enthusiasm for the President was not lopsided, with the "adventurous" West leaning more favorably in his direction than the East. Wilson said the West was more demonstrative but that he believed approval of the League was just as strong everywhere. "I am confident," he said before boarding the *Mayflower*, "that I shall not appeal in vain to the conscience of the American people."

The next leg of the trip was the longest—772 miles on the Southern Pacific Railroad to San Francisco. It allowed the President to rest his voice and enjoy the magnificent scenery, which included loyal supporters all along the route. It troubled Dr. Grayson to learn the next morning in Oakland that Wilson's head was pounding. For Tumulty, California was all-important, as the forward-thinking state of rival Hiram Johnson had scheduled more speeches than any other.

Wilson soldiered through two full days in the Bay Area. On Thursday the eighteenth, he addressed 1,500 members of the Associated Business Men's Clubs of San Francisco, 10,000 people at the outdoor Greek Theatre at the University of California, Berkeley, and more than 12,000 in the Oakland Municipal Auditorium. "I believe in divine Providence," Wilson had said at breakfast. "If I did not, I would go crazy. If I thought the direction of the disordered affairs of this world depended upon our finite endeavor, I should not know how to reason my way to sanity. But I do not believe there is any body of men, how ever they concert their power or their influence, that can defeat this great enterprise." His day finished with a six-hundred-mile ride south.

Under the California sun, support for Wilson and his treaty kept growing. Thirty thousand people awaited him in the San Diego Stadium, where he experimented with a new electrical device that Grayson called a "voice phone." On the speaker's platform at one end of the bowl stood three sides of a twenty-square-foot glass room; the "fourth wall" featured a table with megaphones, from which electrical wires carried the voice to "resonators" at various points in the stadium. Boxed in and dependent upon a mechanical contrivance, Wilson said it was the most difficult speech he ever delivered. But, except for one badly wired spot, all thirty thousand attendees could hear his seventy-minute presentation, a favorite part of which was not only the old Lodge quotation supporting a league but one from TR supporting such an organization as well. It was tempting to think that orators could thenceforth address entire coliseums at once. If only the time had come when a President could use the radio to deliver fireside chats right into people's homes, Wilson could have conducted an even more effective campaign without any of the physical duress.

After dinner that night, former President McKinley's Secretary of the

Treasury, Lyman J. Gage, a dyed-in-the-wool Republican, introduced Wilson to a much smaller assembly, assuring everybody in the room that if McKinley were still alive, he would not only endorse the President's actions but he would also say, "God bless you, Woodrow Wilson."

Two hundred thousand people greeted Wilson on the streets of Los Angeles (population: 503,812) the next day—one of the most enthusiastic demonstrations in the city's history. A capacity crowd filled the Shrine Auditorium to hear him that Saturday night, and the local press was almost unanimously supportive. Veteran newspaperman Charles H. Grasty wrote in *The New York Times*, "This is Woodrow Wilson country now, as Senator Johnson will find out when he returns." Even Harry Chandler, the fiercely Republican publisher of the *Los Angeles Times*, admitted that the majority of Southern California was pro-League, by as much as 6 to 1. More compelling, Chandler said, was that "we have come to a point where it is a question of partisanship or patriotism," and the League "is not our politics now but our religion." General consensus among the press was not just that Los Angeles had been the climax of the tour but that the President had swung the national debate in his favor.

In anticipation of the punishing itinerary home, Edith Wilson had hoped for a quiet Sunday entirely to themselves. But Woodrow had planned a nostalgic reunion. From the Presidential Suite of the Alexandria Hotel, he typed a luncheon invitation to Mary Allen Hulbert. She was living in a little house in Hollywood in reduced circumstances. Scintillating dinner parties in Bermuda, hosting the likes of Mark Twain and a Princeton president contemplating a run for public office, had become distant memories. She rode a streetcar downtown for her 1:30 engagement, and the First Lady waited at the door of the suite to greet her. "Because of the work scandalmongers had done to make an intrigue of that friendship," Edith later recorded, "I was glad to receive her, and show my disdain for such slander." In an instant Wilson and Dr. Grayson joined them, and the four withdrew for lunch and stilted small talk.

The two women sized each other up, offering faint praise for each other in their respective memoirs. Mrs. Hulbert would devote ten pages to the encounter, Mrs. Wilson fifteen lines, in which she referred to her guest as Mrs. Peck. Edith described "a faded, sweet-looking woman who was absorbed in an only son." Mary saw somebody unlike her photographs in the newspaper—"much more junoesque, but handsome, with a charming smile that revealed her strong, white teeth." After lunch the President insisted upon hearing the details of Mary's life during the last four years. The story of her decline consumed much of the afternoon. She spoke of the President's enemies and how they had slandered her and offered exorbitant amounts of money for his letters. As both of them had survived the ordeal, they laughed; but Wilson brought the story to a close saying, "God, to think that you should have suffered because of me!"

When the President had to leave the room for a quick conference, Edith thought Mary might take that as a cue to depart, but she seemed oblivious to the preciousness of the President's time. "Poor woman," Edith recalled, "weighed down with her own problems, of course she did not understand. Darkness had fallen when she finally rose to go." Before leaving, Mary asked her old friend why he was the recipient of so much "venomous personal animosity."

"That's just it," Wilson said, with a flick of his hand. "If *I* had nothing to do with the League of Nations, it would go through like that." He said that Lloyd George, Clemenceau, and Orlando had all failed him. And in that moment, Mary Hulbert noted later, her personal troubles faded as she found herself looking into the face of "tragedy." Placing his hand on that of his wife, the President asked if there was anything he could do for Mary. Nothing for her, she said nobly, but he might consider helping her son. Edith walked their guest to the elevator, which the latter said "quickly dropped me out of the life of my friend Woodrow Wilson—forever." A wistful "Mrs. Peck" boarded a streetcar back to her bungalow.

A few hours later, Woodrow Wilson began his journey back to the White House, via Sacramento, across the Sierra Nevada, from one station to the next. While he was suffering from asthma and headaches, the six hundred miles of tracks that day cut through forest fires and burrowed through tunnels in which smoke mingled with train exhaust. At the other end, changes in pressure further attacked Wilson's respiratory system. By day's end, his head throbbed and his face twitched. In Reno, Nevada, he spoke for well over an hour, his remarks funneled to several remote venues through telephone receivers placed near megaphones. Then it was back onto the train for another 576 miles, stopping in Ogden, Utah, the next day for a few remarks before proceeding to Salt Lake City.

By then, Dr. Grayson considered his patient's fatigue a serious condition, which recurring headaches and coughing spells exacerbated. Throat irritation interfered with what little sleep he was getting, and the latest news from Washington was sure to ruin the rest. Senator Lodge had invited his Republican colleague Porter J. McCumber, a Mild Reservationist from North Dakota, to lunch at his house. By the time the meal ended, McCumber had agreed on a significant reservation to Article X of the Covenant, one that several Democrats came to support as well. The President fumed.

Hours before his speech that warm night in Salt Lake City, more than fifteen thousand people packed the Mormon Tabernacle, while thousands more gathered around the temple. Inside the unventilated hall, the air turned so thick that Edith Wilson took a whiff of lavender salts to keep from fainting and doused a handkerchief in the potion for her husband to take with him to the rostrum. He railed against that day's reservation, inaccurately explaining that it would mean reopening negotiations with all the nations that had been present at Versailles, including Germany. This reservation, he contended, was nothing less than taking a knife to the Treaty and cutting out "the heart of this Covenant." For ninety minutes he sermonized feverishly, and Edith saw that perspiration had soaked through his coat. Back at their hotel, Wilson changed clothes, only to saturate the fresh garment in a matter of minutes. Back on the train, Grayson spoke of a "nervous condition."

The next afternoon in Cheyenne, Wyoming, the President conceded that he was ill, but he delivered his longest speech yet, often wandering from subject to subject, sounding as tired as he looked. He reboarded the *Mayflower* to go to the next station. In their room at the Brown Palace Hotel after their late-night arrival in Denver, Edith suggested a break in the schedule for a few days of rest. "No," Woodrow replied, "I have caught the imagination of the people. They are eager to hear what the League stands for; and I should fail in my duty if I disappointed them." So obvious was Edith's dismay, he assured her, "This will soon be over, and when we get back to Washington I promise you I will take a holiday." Dr. Grayson was counting the days.

The next morning, the President delivered a rousing speech to twelve thousand people; and before lunch, the Atchison, Topeka & Santa Fe Railway was transporting him to Pueblo, a city of fifty thousand, for a two-hour visit. As they approached the city, the President relaxed on the rear platform and asked to review that afternoon's arrangements. An aide told him he would visit the Fair Grounds, where he would greet the crowd before proceeding to the auditorium. "Who authorized such an idiotic idea?" he asked. When the aide said the visit had always been part of the day's plans, he demanded to see Tumulty and the original program. Tumulty appeared with the document, signed with Wilson's trademark "Okeh, W. W." The President snickered and said, "Any damn fool who was stupid enough to approve such a program has no business in the White House." He sent word that he would not appear at the Fair Grounds but changed his mind upon reaching Pueblo, when the reception committee informed him that ten thousand people had already assembled there. He agreed to ride around the racetrack of the fair and wave his hand. He disappointed many, especially those who had traveled from outlying towns hoping to hear him speak, but Wilson felt he had to conserve his strength for the main address in the city's new Memorial Hall.

"It seemed like we would suffocate in there," recalled one former seventh-grader who had been among the three thousand people packed into the brick building. Agent Starling accompanied the President from the car to the auditorium, and Wilson stumbled on the single step at the entrance. Starling caught him and kept his hand on his arm as he all but lifted him up a few more steps to the speaker's platform. Wilson did not object—which surprised Starling, as the President had always refused even the suggestion of physical assistance. "This will have to be a short speech," Wilson indicated to the gang of newspapermen who were about to hear variations on his themes for the fortieth time. "Aren't you fellows getting pretty sick of this?"

The big horseshoe balcony with its shiny brass rail embraced the President as he rose to speak. After a raucous welcome, he delivered a heartfelt speech, remarkable in many ways. The intimacy of the hall allowed for a more personal address, something almost conversational; and in delivering it, Wilson touched upon all the main points he had refined over the past three weeks. His weariness showed, especially in the weakness of his voice, but his frailties only enhanced the emotion of his message. For the first time, the reporters heard him falter on a line, having to restart it more than once; and unexpected pauses suggested both mental confusion as well as physical exhaustion. Starling was so concerned, he remained poised to catch the President should he collapse. He recalled Wilson's passion on this occasion, his working himself to tears.

The effect was overpowering, as toward the end of his speech, the President struck several deeply emotional chords. He spoke of the responsibility he felt as the advocate for a special class of citizens. "My clients," he explained, "are the children; my clients are the next generation. They do not know what promises and bonds I undertook when I ordered the armies of the United States to the soil of France, but I know. And I intend to redeem my pledges to the children; they shall not be sent upon a similar errand." When the President spoke of Decoration Day at the cemetery in Suresnes, there was hope, not anger, he said, that "some men in public life who are now opposing the settlement for which these men died could visit such a spot as that. . . . I wish that they could feel the moral obligation that rests upon us not to go back on those boys, but to see the thing through." In dissociating America from the others who fought in the war, Wilson said, "There seems to me to stand between us and the rejection or qualification of this treaty the serried ranks of those boys in khaki—not only those boys who came home, but those dear ghosts that still deploy upon the fields of France." In those moments of Wilson's speech, Tumulty would later recount, "a great wave of emotion, such as I have never witnessed at a public meeting, swept through the whole amphitheatre." Not only were Edith and most of the women in tears, but he also saw several men, including the hard-boiled press corps, sneaking handkerchiefs from their pockets.

Instead of pulling out all the stops as he reached his conclusion, Wilson soft-pedaled his delivery, letting his words alone carry the message. "There is one thing that the American people always rise to and extend their hand to," he said, "and that is the truth of justice and of liberty and of peace. We have accepted that truth, and we are going to be led by it, and it is going to lead us, and, through us, the world, out into pastures of quietness and peace such as the world never dreamed of before."

Back at the train, Wilson complained again that his head ached. The pain had not stopped all day, sometimes blinding him. Dr. Grayson thought a walk might offer relief; and so, twenty miles out of Pueblo, the train stopped on the tracks, letting the Wilsons and Grayson off to stretch their legs on a country road for almost an hour. Agent Starling trailed behind. An elderly farmer happened by and, recognizing the President, presented him with a head of cabbage and some apples, hoping they might become part of his dinner that night. Walking toward the train, Wilson saw a soldier in a private's uniform, evidently ill, sitting on the porch of a house set back from the road. The President climbed over the fence to talk to him, and the boy's parents and brothers soon joined them, visibly moved to see the President of the United States ministering to the sick soldier.

The walk did him a world of good. The pain subsided, his appetite returned, and after dinner with Grayson and Tumulty, the Wilsons prepared for bed. When the President heard that crowds were forming at each station in Colorado, he remained awake, finding five thousand people at Rocky Ford. Grayson extended Wilson's apologies to the crowd for not being able to appear, but just before the train pulled away, Wilson emerged to grasp the hands of those closest to him. He waved goodbye and then retired for the night.

Edith repaired to her room, where her maid brushed her hair and gave her a massage. At 11:30, by which time she thought her husband had fallen asleep, he knocked on their connecting door and asked to see her. She found him sitting on the side of his bed, his head pressed against the back of a chair set in front of him. The pain had grown so unbearable, he asked her to summon Grayson. The doctor arrived and found a man in the middle of a breakdown. He was nauseated; his face twitched; he gasped for air in the worst asthmatic attack of the trip. Wilson complained that the walls of the tiny compartment were closing in on him. He dressed, and they moved to the roomier "office," where nobody could offer any remedy beyond bolstering him with pillows. Duty now demanded that Grayson recommend canceling the rest of the tour, which Wilson begged him not to suggest. In the hostile political climate, he knew that his enemies would pounce upon his cessation as a sign of weakness. He told Grayson that he would be better by Wichita and that any further discussion of aborting the trip would only keep him awake the rest of the night. Sometime around 4:30, while sitting upright in his seat, Wilson fell asleep. Edith shooed Grayson off to bed, saying she would maintain the vigil.

Dr. Grayson promptly awakened Tumulty, to apprise him that continuing the trip could have fatal consequences. The two advisers conferred with

Mrs. Wilson, who had just endured what she called "the longest and most heartbreaking" night of her life. As they were all of the same mind, Grayson waited for the President to awaken, at which time he would explain their decision. But when he entered the President's compartment, he found Wilson shaving, with no intention of abandoning the schedule. Edith and Tumulty expressed their opinions, but the President would not listen. "Don't you see that if you cancel this trip," he explained, "Senator Lodge and his friends will say that I am a quitter and that the Western trip was a failure, and the Treaty will be lost." Tumulty assured him that nobody would ever consider him a quitter. Gradually, Wilson faced the truth.

"My dear boy," the President said, crumbling, "this has never happened to me before. I felt it coming on yesterday. I do not know what to do." His left arm and leg had numbed. Looking at Tumulty, he begged for a twenty-four-hour reprieve, a postponement: "I want to show them that I can still fight and that I am not afraid." Privately, Grayson argued, at last, that Wilson owed it to the country as well as to Mrs. Wilson and his children to "stop now before very serious developments should occur." He maintained that Wilson was unable to deliver another speech. Now, too exhausted even to fight back, the unhappy warrior allowed, "If you feel that way about it, I will surrender." And then, he quietly added, "This is the greatest disappointment of my life."

Grayson beckoned Tumulty back into the room. "I don't seem to realize it," Wilson told him, "but I seem to have gone to pieces. The Doctor is right. I am not in condition to go on." Unable to face anyone, he looked out the window at the flat countryside instead, as tears rolled from his eyes. "He accepted the decree of Fate as gallantly as he had fought the fight," Edith recollected; "but only he and his God knew the crucifixion that began that moment—to stretch into interminable years, during which the seal he put on his lips, never to . . . voice a syllable of self-pity or regret, remained unbroken."

Edith made her own private compact as well, one that would assume public ramifications. First light had revealed how drawn and lined her husband's face had become, suggesting interior distress even more severe. Life as she knew it "would never be the same." And from that hour forward, she decided, "I would have to wear a mask—not only to the public but to the one I loved best in the world; for he must never know how ill he was, and I must carry on."

Tumulty sprang into action, calling for a stenographer and composing a statement for the press. It said that Dr. Grayson had insisted upon the cancellation of the rest of the tour—Wichita, Oklahoma City, Little Rock, Memphis, and Louisville—despite the President's "earnest desire to complete his engagements." From the rail yard sidings in north Wichita, the newspaper correspondents raced to find telephones so that they might break the news to the world. By telegram, Wilson informed each of his daughters—Margaret visiting in New London, Jessie Sayre in Cambridge, Massachusetts, and Nell McAdoo about to arrive in Los Angeles—that he was returning to Washington and that there was nothing to be alarmed about. The reception committee in Wichita sent an emissary to the train to inform the President that 25,000 Kansans had hoped to see him; and a telegram from the committee in Oklahoma City expressed sorrow, as they had expected 100,000 people—more than inhabited the city—to welcome him. After making most of the arrangements for the direct departure back to Washington, chief clerk Thomas Brahany went to the President's compartment. He found Wilson sitting alone, slouched over, "with his head hanging and with one side of his face drooping and with saliva running out from the corner of his mouth."

Wilson remained indisposed in his stateroom and in pain. Although most of the press dealt with the news in a fair and balanced manner, several opposition newspapers—such as the New York *Sun*—suggested that the whole matter was a ruse, that the President was not really sick. Within hours, however, word had reached most of the nation; and, as Grayson wrote in his journal that day, "there was deep sorrow for the most part among those who had watched the hard fight that the President had made in carrying his side of the Treaty controversy to the people themselves." Whether one agreed with Woodrow Wilson or not, nobody disputed his dedication to his cause. More to the point, the tour was influencing Senators, as two who had been wavering had come back in line against all amendments. It looked as though the President might be able to craft a few "mild reservations or interpretations" and have his treaty approved.

At eleven o'clock that morning, the *Mayflower* pulled out from Wichita. Along the tracks, from one station to the next, crowds gathered to watch the train pass—offering no cheers, only silent respect. Railroad officials charted the fastest route home—which retraced much of the outbound trip. Sympathetic messages arrived: a batch of telegrams awaited the President in St. Louis very early Saturday morning; cablegrams forwarded from Washington were brought on board several hours later in Indianapolis, including well-wishes from King George and Premier Clemenceau. Nothing could lift the President's spirits or ease his pain. And though time was of the essence, Grayson asked that the train slow down because the *Mayflower*, being the rearmost car, rocked wildly from side to side, which kept Wilson from sleeping. The engineers periodically sped up, but in Harrisburg, Pennsylvania, Grayson insisted the train was not to exceed twenty-five miles per hour for the rest of the trip. They lowered the shades to block onlookers, creating the air of a funeral cortege. When Wilson was not trying to rest in his bed, he sat mute in the office compartment, where Edith kept him company, knitting and attempting to divert him with small talk. But, she observed, "the air was so heavy with unspoken agony that all seemed a travesty."

The President was up and dressed at eleven o'clock that Sunday when the train finally reached Washington—exactly forty-eight hours since Wichita. Although he looked like a ghost of the man who had left Union Station twenty-five days earlier, he summoned his strength and walked unassisted and perfectly erect from the *Mayflower*. Margaret Wilson ran through the train shed to greet him and waited as he bade farewell to the railroad personnel and newspapermen. She joined Edith, Grayson, and the Secret Service as they advanced toward the motorcars waiting outside. More than a thousand people in the station cheered. With a smile and a nod, he especially acknowledged the applause of a group of wounded soldiers on a bench in the Red Cross canteen.

Within minutes the President was back in the White House. He wanted to attend church, but Grayson ordered him to bed at once. Too restless to nap and in too much pain to work, he wandered the long hall of the second floor, back and forth between his study and Edith's room. As it was a sunny early autumn day, with the first smack of cool air he had felt in months, he and Edith and Grayson took a two-hour drive through the city parks. The President dozed most of the time.

Upon their return, Admiral Grayson (as he was officially known) pulled rank. He believed Wilson needed a complete rest cure, and he imposed strict conditions. From that moment forward, he said, the President "should not be bothered with any matters of official character," especially questions of a controversial nature. He banned conferences with Cabinet members and any other officials. "It was to be a complete rest, not partial rest," Grayson underscored, "and nothing was to be allowed to interfere with the President's restoration to health if possible."

The next day Edith invited ten of the journalists from the Western tour to tea. She hosted them alone, and they learned that the interdiction against official conferences was in effect indefinitely. The day after that, an urgent message from Sir William Wiseman of the British government arrived, requesting an audience with Wilson. Edith asked him to appear at eleven, at which time she said the President was too ill to receive him but if Wiseman would transmit the information, she would have a reply for him at two o'clock. In that interval, she mentioned the visit to her husband, who waved it off as nonessential. Grayson arranged for Wilson's ophthalmologist and a leading neurologist to examine him at the end of the week.

A shroud of secrecy descended upon the White House, which only raised suspicions. As Secretary of State Lansing saw things, the President's advocacy of the Covenant had become nothing less than "a veritable obsession," which had caused an abnormal mental state, a monomania that "excluded everything else from his thoughts." Only complete rest, he suspected, would allow him to "regain normality."

By October 1, his third day home, Wilson displayed small signs of improvement. He catnapped at night and during his daily drives, and his appetite was returning. He expressed renewed interest in his work, though Edith arranged to run motion pictures at night in the East Room to divert him. That night he felt chipper enough to play billiards for a few minutes. Later, he insisted on reading Scripture to Edith, as he had done every night during the war, and she delighted in hearing some vitality back in his voice. After his reading, Wilson wound his watch, and they talked a while before he went to his room. Minutes later, Edith noticed that Woodrow had left his timepiece on her table. When she returned it, he grumbled about losing his memory. She said that was nonsense, that she forgot such things all the time. Afterward, she felt leaving the watch behind had not worried him that much; it was simply that "he did not want to relax the tight hold he was keeping on himself."

Edith had been having troubles of her own getting through the night, as she awakened frequently in order to monitor her husband's rest. At dawn on October 2, she found him sleeping soundly, but then around

8:30, he was sitting on the side of his bed, reaching for a water bottle. As she handed it to him, she noticed his left hand had gone limp. "I have no feeling in that hand," he said. He asked her to rub it. But first, he wanted help in getting to the bathroom. She supported him as he staggered those few yards, but it required a huge effort on his part. More terrifying to her were his spasms of pain with every step. Edith asked if she could leave him alone long enough for her to telephone Dr. Grayson. He said yes; and in that split second, Edith made a curious decision.

Instead of going to the nearby bedroom phone, which connected to operators at the White House switchboard, she hastened down the hall to a private phone wired directly to the desk in the Usher's Room. Ike Hoover answered the call, and Mrs. Wilson said, "Please get Doctor Grayson, the President is very sick."

While still on the phone, Edith heard a noise from the President's apartment. Rushing back, she found her husband lying on the bathroom floor, unconscious.

16

PIETÀ

*Then tooke they the body of Iesus, & wound it in
linnen clothes, with the spices, as the maner of the
Iewes is to burie . . .*

—JOHN, XIX:40

E dith pulled a blanket from the Lincoln Bed and draped
it over her husband's inanimate body. At last he stirred
and requested a drink of water. In fetching it, Edith also
grabbed a pillow, returning to elevate his head as she cra-
dled him.

Minutes later, a White House car delivered Dr. Grayson. He hastened upstairs and rapped gently on the locked
bedroom door. Ike Hoover waited in the hall as Grayson
and Mrs. Wilson lifted the President into his bed. The left
side of his body was immobile. After examining his patient, Dr. Grayson returned to the hall. "My God, the President is paralyzed!" he said to Hoover, whom he immediately
ordered to summon both Admiral E. R. Stitt of the Naval
Medical Corps and the nurse who had attended Ellen Wilson in her final illness. Within hours, an array of doctors
joined them, starting with a pioneer in neurology, Francis
X. Dercum, professor of nervous and mental diseases at
Philadelphia's Jefferson Medical College. Edith's family
physician, Sterling Ruffin, Wilson's classmate Edward P.
Davis, and eye specialist George de Schweinitz followed.

Dercum examined Wilson in bed. He found his left leg

and arm in a condition of "complete flaccid paralysis," with the lower half of the left side of the face drooping. The President was conscious but somnolent. His temperature, pulse, and respiration were all normal, but in addition to his left side having lost all feeling, his left eye responded feebly to light. He had suffered a thrombosis—an ischemic stroke—a clot in an artery of the brain. Nothing had ruptured. Wilson's abilities to think and speak escaped unimpaired. An air of quiet exigency filled the President's bedroom as the medical team decided how to convert the White House into a convalescent home. The three Wilson daughters made their way to Washington.

Outside the bedroom, the domestic staff remained completely in the dark. At day's end, when the furniture needed rearranging to accommodate incoming medical apparatus, Grayson allowed only Ike Hoover to help him and the nurse move the various pieces. Hoover could not keep his eyes off the President stretched out in the large Lincoln Bed. "He looked as if he were dead," Hoover observed. As Edith Wilson would impart years later, "For days life hung in the balance."

Nobody divulged as much to the public. "No details, no explanations" were the orders of the day, recalled Ike Hoover. Outside the White House, people knew only that the President was suffering from nervous exhaustion and that such attendant conditions as his intestinal troubles were manifestations of the assault on his central nervous system. Only the few within earshot of the Lincoln Bed even uttered the word "stroke." Grayson told the press that he was confident Wilson's "reserve stamina . . . will carry him through the crisis."

Within days, the President had emerged from danger but had entered a twilight zone—a state of physical exhaustion, emotional turbulence, and mental unrest. The "burning question," Edith Wilson would later explain in her memoirs, became "how Mr. Wilson might best serve the country, preserve his own life and if possible recover." That did not necessarily reflect the order of her priorities, as she asked the doctors for their candor. They all asserted that Wilson's brain was "as clear as ever" and that the immediate upturn in his condition suggested something close to a full recovery lay ahead. But, they insisted, recovery was unattainable "unless the President were released from every disturbing problem during these days of Nature's effort to repair the damage done."

Edith asked how that was possible when a Chief Executive only deals with problems. Dr. Dercum—with his bald head and walrus mustache—leaned toward her with an unexpected nostrum. "Madam," he said, "it is a grave situation, but I think you can solve it. Have everything come to you; weigh the importance of each matter, and see if it is possible by consultation with the respective heads of the Departments to solve them without the guidance of your husband. In this way you can save him a great deal." Dercum reminded her that the President's nerves were "crying out for rest" and that "every time you take him a new anxiety or problem to excite him, you are turning a knife in an open wound."

Edith suggested allowing Vice President Marshall to succeed, as the Constitution stipulated, thus granting the President the vital rest he required. Dercum disagreed. "For Mr. Wilson to resign," he explained, "would have a bad effect on the country, and a serious effect on our patient." In terms more political than medical, he noted that the President had staked his life on ratification of the Treaty. If he resigned, Dercum said, "the greatest incentive to recovery is gone." As the President's mind remained "clear as crystal," Dercum said Woodrow Wilson "can still do more with even a maimed body than any one else." Grayson had told Dercum of the President's having discussed all public affairs of the last four years privately with Edith. Knowing that, Dercum deputized her, insisting, "He has the utmost confidence in you."

"So began my stewardship," Edith would admit two decades later. In that capacity, she would determine not only what matters should come before the President but also when. More than a mere sentry, the second Mrs. Wilson took it upon herself to filter and analyze every issue that required Presidential action, executing those duties to the best of her ability. As she explained: "I studied every paper, sent from the different Secretaries or Senators, and tried to digest and present in tabloid form the things that, despite my vigilance, had to go to the President." In insisting that she never "made a single decision regarding the disposition of public affairs," Mrs. Wilson failed to acknowledge the commanding nature of her role, that in determining the daily agenda and formulating arguments thereon, she executed the physical and most of the mental duties of the office.

Edith Bolling Wilson did not become, as some have asserted, "the first female President of the United States." But she came close. She considered herself more of a lady-in-waiting to her husband than an executive; but she was in a position to act, while he could only react. Unschooled in politics—and unskilled—she held not the least desire for any power, other than the power to heal her husband. She just wanted Woodrow to get better.

And so began the greatest conspiracy that had ever engulfed the White House. With only virtuous intent, the plot unfolded—one that was hardly a scrupulous interpretation of the Constitution, which provided for "the Case of Removal, Death, Resignation or Inability" of the President with the ascension of the Vice President "until the Disability be removed, or a President shall be elected." The devoted wife, the dedicated physician, and—soon—the devout secretary debated among themselves how to proceed, even though the legal issue ought not have been theirs to decide. But the Constitution provided neither means nor measures to determine Presidential disability, so they took the law of the land into their own hands, concluding what best served Woodrow Wilson best served the country. Their behavior tacitly acknowledged that this was a power grab, as they enshrouded the Presidency in as much secrecy as possible.

With the White House ominously dark and silent, Lansing, the most discontented Cabinet member, wanted answers. Without realizing that Wilson's illness was all that had kept him from being discharged, the Secretary of State requested a private audience with Tumulty. The Secretary came to the Cabinet Room at 11:30 on Friday, October 3, to propose that Vice President Marshall serve in a Presidential capacity. Lansing carried a volume known as Jefferson's *Manual*—parliamentary procedure for use in the Senate—from which he read aloud the Constitutional clause describing the circumstances under which the duties shall devolve upon the Vice President. Tumulty grew indignant. "Mr. Lansing," he said brusquely, "the Constitution is not a dead letter with the White House. I have read the Constitution and do not find myself in need of any tutoring at your hands." He asked Lansing just who should declare the President's disability, and Lansing said that should fall upon either Dr. Grayson or Tumulty himself.

"You may rest assured that while Woodrow Wilson is lying in the White House on the broad of his back I will not be a party to ousting him," said his first and most faithful political aide. "He has been too kind, too loyal, and too wonderful to me to receive such treatment at my hands." At that moment, Dr. Grayson appeared. Tumulty turned to him and said, "And I am sure that Doctor Grayson will never certify to this disability.

Will you, Grayson?" The doctor assured Lansing that the President's mind was "clear and acute" and that he would not be party to suggesting his incapacity. With neither willing to sign such a statement, any further suggestions of removing the President would be futile, if not faintly seditious.

Lansing believed nonetheless that the President's state was "dangerous," as was that of the government of the United States. At first he thought the Vice President should convene an emergency session of the Cabinet that weekend, but after his meeting with Tumulty he realized that it would "unduly alarm the nation." In the absence of leadership and the evident decision of the White House to bypass Marshall, Lansing felt somebody had to be in control of the executive branch. He and Tumulty agreed that he would call a meeting for the following Monday. In yielding nothing more than that to the Secretary of State, however, Tumulty officially became Mrs. Wilson's accomplice, interpreting the health of the President and that of the nation as one and the same.

Within days, newspapers reported rumors that Wilson had suffered a cerebral lesion or hemorrhage, to which Dr. Grayson issued only nondenial denials. He and the other attending physicians had agreed on a policy of not answering any questions, and that vagueness only fueled more gossip.

Cabinet members chewed on any morsel of information they could find. When David Houston ran into Newton Baker at the Shoreham Hotel on Friday, the Navy Secretary said the silence from the White House had him "scared literally to death." Two days later, again at the Shoreham, Houston happened to see the Vice President and Mrs. Marshall lunching. The Agriculture Secretary paid his respects and found Marshall deeply disturbed—not at any news that he had heard but at all that he had not heard. He felt he should be briefed, officially and immediately. Then, revealing what a ridiculous position the Vice Presidency had become, he also said that "it would be a tragedy for him to assume the duties of President, at best; and that it would be equally a tragedy for the people; that he knew many men who knew more about the affairs of the government than he did; and that it would be especially trying for him if he had to assume the duties without warnings." The first Vice President to serve two terms since 1825, he pled for any "real facts."

After a few days in which Wilson's condition was still touch and go, the co-conspirators felt obliged to prepare Thomas Marshall for the worst.

To keep from drawing attention to any possible succession, Edith agreed to a briefing through a third party. Although it meant divulging the nation's darkest secret to another person, they decided to entrust a middleman—J. Fred Essary, Washington correspondent for the Baltimore *Sun*. Upon receiving a few facts, he went to Marshall's office and, sitting next to him at his desk, privately explained the reason for his visit. As Essary reported the situation, Marshall sat speechless, staring at his clasped hands. Essary awaited some reaction but received none. He rose, approached the door, and looked back at the amiable little man from a small town in Indiana, still gazing at his hands. Not until Marshall saw Essary years later in Indiana did he apologize for his behavior that day. "I did not even have the courtesy to thank you for coming over and telling me," Marshall explained. "It was the first great shock of my life." Alice Roosevelt Longworth would later cackle over what had become Washington lore for years—that upon learning the direness of the President's situation, the Vice President had fainted.

The President's health showed incremental signs of improvement. Within days of his stroke, he was sleeping much of his days and nights. His appetite slowly returned, as did his sense of humor. Wilson had difficulty in swallowing and had to be coaxed into eating. After Mrs. Wilson was able to feed him several mouthfuls by spoon, he signaled for Grayson to draw close enough to hear something he had to say. "Doctor," he whispered,

> A *wonderful bird is the pelican*
> *His bill will hold more than his bellican.*
> *He can take in his beak*
> *Enough food for a week*
> *I wonder how in the hell-he-can.*

When Dr. Grayson focused a light on his eyes and explained he was examining his pupils, Wilson replied, "You have a large order, as I have had a great many in my day." By that weekend, Wilson asked that a stenographer be called, so he could dictate some letters. Grayson talked him out of even thinking of work by reminding him that, as a good Presbyterian, he should honor the Sabbath.

On Monday, October 6, the Cabinet convened for close to two hours.

Lansing announced that the President would not be returning to the public business for some time and that they should consider a new modus
operandi. He thought the Vice President should be prevailed upon; and he
asked his colleagues to consider what constituted Presidential "inability"
and who was to decide it. Secretary Houston reminded the others at the
table that after President James A. Garfield had been shot, he lingered in
bed for two months without a declaration of inability, while the Attorney
General ran the government. At Lansing's beckoning, Grayson appeared.
He briefed the Secretaries to the effect that the President's mind was "not
only clear but very active." He then added, with an inscrutable gaze, "The
President asked me what the Cabinet wanted with me and by what authority it was meeting while he was in Washington without a call from him."
He said the President was more than a little perturbed when he heard that
the meeting was taking place. Lansing was taken aback. Secretary Baker
suggested that Grayson tell the President that they only met "as a mark of
affection," and he asked the doctor to convey their unanimous sympathy
with their assurance that they were all looking out for his interests.

In a moment alone, Daniels suggested to Grayson that an honest acknowledgment of the President's condition might elicit sympathy and even
greater support instead of the current "uncertainty and criticism." Grayson
agreed but was clearly under orders from Mrs. Wilson, who knew her husband's desires. In truth, it seems unfathomable that either of them would
have breathed a word about the Cabinet meeting to the convalescent.

The press and the public began to discuss the issue of "disability." In
the cases of prior Presidents' deaths, the various departments functioned
autonomously. Now some wondered what would happen if Wilson's Cabinet members disagreed about his ability to serve, whether a decision required unanimity or just a majority vote. Others were concerned about the
extraordinary war powers that had been granted to the Chief Executive
and whether a Cabinet member might seize the opportunity to advance his
own agenda.

With any number of people assuming duties the President had once
performed himself, the White House put a new mode of operation to the
test on October 7. While he should not have had such matters on his
mind, Wilson wanted to communicate with Josephus Daniels regarding
the Navy forces in the Adriatic Sea. He called Edith to his side and dictated
his message to her, which she handed to a White House stenographer.

While he transcribed the message and delivered it to the Secretary's office, she called Daniels herself to announce its impending arrival. The reply reversed the same route. Wilson had hoped to greet the participants at the opening of an industrial conference in Washington that week. In his stead, Tumulty wrote the brief welcome and asked Labor Secretary Wilson to deliver it; Samuel Gompers read a second, longer message at the conference, which Interior Secretary Lane had written. So adamant was Dr. Grayson about Wilson's adhering to his "absolute rest cure," he prohibited the President's signing anything but the most essential documents and even ordered the removal of newspapers from his bedroom, for they would only agitate him. When Colonel House returned to the United States, he solicitously wrote Edith, but she chose not even to tell her husband that he was back.

At the end of October, H.R. 6801, the Volstead Act—"to prohibit intoxicating beverages"—arrived at the White House for the President's signature. In vetoing and returning it to Congress, he enclosed his customary message of explanation for his action; but on this occasion, Tumulty wrote the justification and Secretary Houston vetted it. The House overrode the veto 175 to 55 that same day; the Senate overrode 64 to 20 the next. Within three months, the United States was under the influence of Prohibition—the first constitutional amendment ever to abridge rights of the people.

The next week Lansing submitted a Thanksgiving Proclamation for Wilson's approval, and its return the next day troubled him. Practically every other document he had ever submitted to the President came back with corrections in the schoolmaster's hand. This was unmarked, except for a disturbingly illegible signature, in pencil. Lansing could not see how Wilson could possibly "conduct the government for months to come." He told House that the President was already displeased with his having called one or two Cabinet meetings but that he intended to continue doing so, because he thought it "the proper thing to do." To the public, the mystery prevailed as to whether the President had suffered a stroke.

The charade continued. Dr. Grayson never strayed from the party line: "His body was broken," he said of the President, "but his intellect was unimpaired and his lion spirit untamed. His collapse brought no weakening of his purpose." That was not the whole truth. Ike Hoover, one of a handful of people permitted into the sickroom, saw that the President lay there most of the time "helpless." Hoover saw improvement, but he said what most refused to admit: "There was never a moment during all that time when he was more than a shadow of his former self. He had changed from a giant to a pygmy in every wise. He was physically almost incapacitated; he could articulate but indistinctly and think but feebly." So pathetic was the sight, Hoover said the few who served him turned away from his gaze. Not Edith. So long as the government continued to function and Wilson's judgment determined its policy, she saw no reason to alter the practice of sequestering her husband and issuing documents in his name, even if it required a certain amount of extrapolation on her part. "I carried out the directions of the doctors," she would later write. "Woodrow Wilson was first my beloved husband whose life I was trying to save, fighting with my back to the wall—after that he was the President of the United States."

A month passed during which no government official, not even a secretary, saw the President of the United States. Nobody even shaved him. Once a day, somebody would hoist him from his bed and set him in a comfortable chair. After several days, Wilson tried an invalid rolling chair, but that proved ineffective because he could not sit upright in it. At last, Hoover suggested a rolling chair such as those on the boardwalk in Atlantic City. The White House rented one from a New Jersey dealer for five dollars a week, and in time, bought it outright. For months, Wilson used the chair whenever he left his bed.

Just as Wilson seemed to be improving, he suffered another setback. A troubling prostatic condition worsened, creating a urinary obstruction. One of Wilson's doctors urged the high-risk operation of an abdominal incision and the insertion of a catheter into the patient's bladder. Grayson balked, calling upon Doctor Hugh Hampton Young of the Johns Hopkins Medical School, the country's authority on the prostate gland, to join the private White House team. He believed the dangers of the operation outweighed those of waiting. Overloaded with information, Edith sided with those who would allow nature to take its course. It did, but not without sapping much of the President's strength. While it forced him to submit to more rest, it allowed him, at last, to turn a corner for the better. For a month, Woodrow Wilson had been able to perform only the most basic duties of office.

By the end of October, the White House troika of Edith, Grayson, and

Tumulty believed that Wilson was far enough out of the woods to expose the President in a few carefully managed visits. At four in the afternoon on the thirtieth, Attorney General Palmer became the first Cabinet member to see the President since his stroke. They conferred for twenty minutes about an impending coal strike, one that the Administration was challenging on grounds that it violated the Lever Act, one of those war measures that still lingered, endowing the executive branch with extraordinary powers. Palmer reported to the press that the President was alert, attentive, and had offered "suggestions of his own." He also wired the Ambassador to Japan, "Alarming rumors concerning president's condition quite unfounded. Physically weak but in every other respect in splendid shape. Doctors report him rapidly improving. He transacts public business daily."

Little more than an hour later, Wilson engaged in a more publicized private meeting. For months, King Albert and Queen Elisabeth of Belgium, and their son Prince Leopold, had planned a trip to the United States, where they were meant to be guests at the White House. They were mid-ocean when Wilson suffered his stroke. As a result, they downscaled their itinerary and turned their ceremonial visit into a less formal tour of the States, traveling largely incognito. While visiting Washington, they stayed in the private residence of an Administration diplomat, and the Thomas Marshalls entertained them.

Beyond his genuine admiration of the King and Queen, these noble survivors of German aggression making a state visit would have served Wilson well in his fight for the League. Recognizing the publicity value in the President's receiving visitors and knowing what a boost it would be for Wilson to greet them, the White House arranged an informal meeting. Edith, Jessie Sayre, and Margaret Wilson received them in the Red Room. After tea, Edith asked if she might take His Majesty to see the President. Before doing so, the Royal Couple presented Edith with a beautiful wooden box, which contained eighteen plates, each with a hand-painted representation of a historic place in Belgium, some of which had since been destroyed. Queen Elisabeth presented Edith a fan of Belgian lace, adorned with diamonds and sapphires.

Upstairs, King Albert demonstrated only "sympathy and solicitude" as he beheld the frail creature in his dressing gown and with a mustache and long white beard. While Dr. Grayson stood by, they spoke for a few minutes, after which Albert presented the china dishes and discussed each of the scenes depicted thereon. The President, in turn, offered the King a specially bound set of his *History of the American People*, the first volume of which he had autographed. After they said their goodbyes, Edith gave the Royal Couple a tour of the White House. Just when she thought they were leaving, the Queen said she wished to see the President. Edith saw no graceful way of denying her, and by the time they had returned to the bedroom, Wilson had removed his robe and returned to bed with a favorite gray woolen sweater that he had bought years earlier in Scotland draped over his shoulders. The Queen was delighted to have come upon him studying his new plates with a large magnifying glass. When the President asked after the young prince, the Queen said he was downstairs. Grayson permitted his entry as well. Present for all three of the bedside visitations, he provided the details to the press, including the King's having told the President, "I hope that your ideas and ideals will be carried out. My feeling is that they will be."

Two weeks later, the Wilsons received the Prince of Wales, the man who would become King Edward VIII. Conversation between the President and the British media darling remained light, of little more substance than Wilson's misinforming him that his grandfather Edward VII had slept in the very bed before him when he had visited President James Buchanan in 1860.

Court intrigue accompanied the Prince of Wales's visit, as the British Ambassador, Lord Grey, had been requesting a Presidential audience for weeks, and he was deliberately not asked to accompany Edward. That was evidently the result of Grey's having invited an adjutant from England, Major Charles Kennedy Craufurd-Stuart, to be part of his delegation in America. Craufurd-Stuart, unfortunately, had a penchant for gossip, dining out on outrageous remarks. One such jape making the rounds of Washington's finest tables was his comment that when Wilson had proposed to Edith, "she was so surprised that she nearly fell out of bed."

The bedside visit between the twenty-five-year-old Prince and the sixty-two-year-old President created a lot of cheery coverage, a welcome relief from the gloomy reports emanating from the White House. It suggested Wilson's continuing recovery. Later that day, the press also reported his being wheeled to the rear porch of the White House, where he enjoyed the open air. On November 12, he called for a mirror and took a long look, turning his head from side to side. "Doctor," he called out, before reciting one of his favorite limericks:

> *For beauty I am not a star,*
> *There are others more handsome by far,*
> *But my face I don't mind it*
> *For I am behind it,*
> *It's the folks in front that I jar.*

He received his first shave in six weeks.

In all that time, the Senate had maintained its distance from the White House, less out of respect than for political advantage. Democrats did not want to draw attention to their leader's helplessness, while Republicans happily exploited it. Lodge's intention had never been to dispose of the League altogether, merely to disguise it as a Republican plan, thereby damaging the opposition party and Wilson's reputation. Now, with the President sidelined longer than anybody had ever imagined, Lodge realized he could actually kill the entire Treaty, League and all. Lodge said he merely wanted "to Americanize the Treaty and the Covenant"—which Secretary David Houston translated as: "he would show the people that the Republicans had sufficiently rewritten the Treaty to save the situation." With the Irreconcilables in his pocket, Lodge attempted to appeal to the Mild Reservationists by appearing reasonable, knowing that the minute he suggested anything directed toward Article X, the President would be intractable.

Between the day of the President's stroke and November 6, the Senate had approved in committee a list of fifty-two modifications to the Treaty— some minor administrative paper cuts, others substantive amputations. Senator Albert B. Fall alone introduced three dozen petty proposals—such as America's sitting on commissions related to governance of the Saar Basin or sending troops to Upper Silesia or drawing the new Belgian border. Senator Lawrence Sherman of Illinois wanted to insert a phrase invoking "the gracious favor of Almighty God"; Senator Gore proposed adding an "advisory vote of the people" on top of any League decisions regarding nations resorting to war; La Follette wanted to excise the labor articles from the Treaty; Lodge wanted to strike the Shantung provisions. Under Hitchcock's leadership, all the President's men in the Senate had successfully defeated the amendments, prompting Lodge to spring right back with a list of what Hitchcock called "destructive reservations." These items substantively reduced Lodge's objections to fifteen points. In polishing them for presentation on November 6, the Republican forces designated the first as a "preamble," so that Lodge could offer his own fourteen counterpoints. The opposition had effectively gridlocked the Treaty—to the point that anybody who had Wilson's ear over the next two weeks offered but one solution: compromise.

Gilbert Hitchcock was the first such visitor, sandwiched between the royal visits. Edith had allowed the President's initial business conference because his advocate in the Senate sought guidance in attracting his undecided colleagues. Granted a half hour, he had encountered an "intellectually alert" but cadaverous Wilson, still with his wispy white beard. Propped up in bed, he buried his limp arm under the bedclothes. Wilson said he would accept "any compromise the friends of the treaty thought necessary to save the treaty, so long as it did not destroy the terms of the pact itself." And he made it plain that Lodge's reservations would "kill the treaty." Hitchcock insisted that without some changes, American entrance into the League would be impossible. Wilson asked how many Senators would vote for the Treaty without reservations, and Hitchcock told him "not forty-five out of ninety-six." Wilson groaned: "Is it possible, is it possible?"

Hitchcock proved to be a dogged spokesman; but, as Senator Tom Connally of Texas observed, he was simply "no match for the snarling growls and the biting fangs of Lodge, Borah, Johnson and Reed." As always, Lodge kept zeroing in on Article X of the Treaty, the guarantee against external aggression through collective security. Hitchcock insisted repeatedly that any such action demanded unanimity from the League Council and Congressional approval before America could commit to engaging in League actions. Lodge paid no attention, knowing that, in politics, constant repetition can harden even obvious falsities into facts. He just kept saying, "The article bypassed Congress."

While Edith had feared too much politics might weaken her husband, she knew that it was his lifeblood. Still, she filtered the information that reached him, limiting incoming opinions on the Treaty to those from friends in court. Tumulty reported that his inbox was filled with messages urging compromise. Bernard Baruch implored Wilson to accept that "half a loaf is better than no bread." Herbert Hoover wrote that, considering the reservations as a whole, "they do not seem . . . to imperil the great principle of the League of Nations to prevent war" and should be accepted at once. Even the banished Colonel House—bedridden himself, with gallstones—got involved in an intricate back-channel effort that might not only rescue the Treaty but also put him back in Wilson's good graces.

House urged Stephen Bonsal, his worldly attaché from Paris, to meet with his friend Henry Cabot Lodge. In the course of their conversation on October 28 at Lodge's house near Dupont Circle, Bonsal got the impression that the Senator was not as confident of "hamstringing" the Covenant as he appeared in public and that he was even prepared to compromise. Over two more conversations during the week, Bonsal induced Lodge to pencil right on a copy of the Treaty fifty words of "inserts," which included a few phrases that underscored Congressional authority. Bonsal persuaded Lodge to agree that those conditions were implicit within the original document, but the old Senator maintained that he had improved the Treaty, the language of which he had found unworthy. "It might get by at Princeton," he said, "but certainly not at Harvard."

Bonsal sent the Lodge-edited Treaty—which would surely have met Senate approval, if not unanimity—to House, who claimed to have forwarded it to Tumulty. Nobody knows if it ever got past his desk or if Mrs. Wilson simply dismissed it because it came from Colonel House or because she or the President saw Lodge's rewrite of Article X, which Wilson would have automatically rejected. In all likelihood, nobody ever saw it—certainly not Senator Hitchcock.

At first he thought that Lodge "merely wished to weave into the Covenant some of his great thoughts, so that this world charter would not, in the future, be regarded as a party document." Now Hitchcock realized that Lodge's "hatred of Wilson is very deep and his talking point is that, as the President did not permit any real Republicans to participate in the drafting of the Treaty," the Republicans now had "a perfectly free hand in the matter of ratification," a greater responsibility than would have been theirs had they been included during the initial drafting process. For his part, Hitchcock—like most of his Democratic colleagues—favored a ratified Treaty in almost any form, if only to "end the present disastrous anarchy that prevails in world relations." But he was obligated to honor the

President's commands. Even when the White House handed them down indirectly, the message remained clear. "I am merely told 'the President will not budge an inch,'" Hitchcock told Bonsal. "His honor is at stake. He feels he would be dishonored if he failed to live up to the pledges made to his fellow delegates in Paris."

And then, as the Senate vote approached, not even Edith Wilson could hold back any longer. "In my anxiety for the one I love best in the world," she confessed years later, "the long-drawn-out fight was eating into my very soul, and I felt nothing mattered but to get the Treaty ratified, even with those reservations." While sitting at her husband's bedside, she said, "For my sake . . . won't you accept these reservations and get this awful thing settled?"

Woodrow turned his head on the pillow and reached out to take Edith's hand. "Little girl," he said, "don't you desert me; that I cannot stand. Can't you see that I have no moral right to accept any change in a paper I have signed without giving to every other signatory, even the Germans, the right to do the same thing? It is not *I* that will not accept; it is the Nation's honour that is at stake." Almost immediately, Edith felt ashamed for having joined his "betrayers," even momentarily. "Better a thousand times to go down fighting," he said, "than to dip your colours to dishonourable compromise."

On November 17, Senator Hitchcock returned to the White House for another meeting with the President. The Senator found a different man—clean-shaven and sitting up taller—in the Lincoln Bed. Hitchcock raised the subject of the Lodge Resolution, which he had sent in advance and which Dr. Grayson had read to the President. Wilson wasted no time in expressing himself: "I consider it a nullification of the Treaty and utterly impossible," he said. Wilson maintained that the Lodge reservations cut "the very heart" out of the Treaty. "I could not stand for those changes for a moment because it would humiliate the United States before all of the allied countries," he said. Hitchcock asked the President to explain just what effect a defeat of the Treaty would have.

"The United States would suffer the contempt of the world," he said. "We will be playing into Germany's hands. Think of the humiliation we would suffer in having to ask Germany whether she would accept such and such reservation!" The President experienced a surge of energy such as he had not felt since taking to his bed. He unleashed a furious tirade over the political situation as well as his physical inability to combat it. "If the Republicans are bent on defeating this Treaty," he said, "I want the vote of each, Republican and Democrat, recorded, because they will have to answer to the country in the future for their acts. They must answer to the people." And then, making threats an invalid could not really back, Wilson said, "I am going to debate this issue with these gentlemen in their respective states whenever they come up for re-election. . . . I shall do this even if I have to give my life to it." His spleen vented, Wilson said he held no hostility toward the Senators in opposition—only "an utter contempt." With the exception of interpretations, Wilson insisted he was as unwilling as ever to compromise on anything that would require "a recommitment to council with other nations."

Wilson spent almost another hour asking Hitchcock to walk him through the last six weeks of legislative knavery that had led to the impending vote. "I have been lying on my back and have been very weak," he said. He knew that he had been "kept in the dark" except for what Edith and Grayson had told him; and, he imparted that "they have purposely kept a good deal from me." Upon leaving, the Senator said, "Mr. President, I hope I have not weakened you by this long discussion." Wilson smiled and said, "No, Senator, you have strengthened me against the opponents." In the hall, Hitchcock said to Grayson, "I would give anything if the Democrats, in fact, all the Senate, could see the attitude that man took this morning. Think how effective it would be if they could see the picture as you and I saw it this morning!"

For the first time since his stroke, attendants rolled Wilson in his wheelchair onto the South Lawn, where his flock of Red Cross sheep continued to graze. Hitchcock returned to the Senate to make his best efforts to convince his colleagues. He drafted a letter—which he sent to Mrs. Wilson—for the President to send back, which stated his position on the upcoming vote. It urged friends and supporters of the Treaty to vote against the Lodge Resolution—"for in my opinion the resolution in that form does not provide for ratification, but rather for defeat of the treaty." Later that day, Edith read the letter to her husband, who dictated some minor changes, the most consequential of which was changing the word "defeat" to "the nullification."

At Hitchcock's direction, those Democrats who favored the Treaty caucused on the morning of November 19, 1919, to discuss the Lodge

Resolution. Senator Underwood of Alabama moved that they unite against it; and then Hitchcock drew "Wilson"'s letter from his breast pocket and read those same instructions to his most loyal supporters. Senator Ashurst asked to examine the letter and could not help noticing that the President's signature had been rubber-stamped in purple ink. At noon the Senate convened for a final debate of the Treaty. It played out as Hitchcock had predicted: the Lodge Resolution of ratification met defeat, with thirty-nine ayes against fifty-five nays—a combination of forty-two Democrats and thirteen Republicans, the Irreconcilables among them. Oscar Underwood introduced the unencumbered Treaty, exactly as Wilson had delivered it from France, and it faced an almost identical result, thirty-eight ayes to fifty-three nays. Incredulously, Henry Ashurst recorded in his diary that night that the Treaty of Versailles—a six-month labor of the world's leaders, ratified by the principal Allied and Associated Powers and even signed by the enemy—could muster the votes of only thirty-eight United States Senators. With the Senate adjourning, Lodge would declare he had done all the compromising he intended to do. Underwood and Hitchcock concurred that the Treaty was deadlocked, but not dead. Partisan politics was that day's only victor, the Treaty its victim. There would be a few months before everybody would revisit the document, during which time the President could allow the Senate to redraw the Treaty. One man held the power to break the stalemate, but he remained stuck in bed and in his unwillingness to compromise.

Fearing the effect "the fatal news" from Capitol Hill would have on her husband, Edith broke it to him gently. Silence filled the room for a moment, until Woodrow said, "All the more reason I must get well and try again to bring this country to a sense of its great opportunity and greater responsibility."

Such wishful thinking did not seem out of place in the current White House, which was awash in denial. In order to maintain strict silence, Edith had banned the public from the White House and its grounds. In the private quarters and the empty public rooms, staff members tiptoed, unaware of just how sick the patient upstairs was. Those few in the know kept up appearances, pretending everything was all right and covering for the President wherever possible. Opacity bred suspicion, and the longer this masquerade continued without the President's appearing in public, the worse the rumors became. Some said Wilson had lost his mind. His reciting limericks was twisted into talk of his babbling nursery rhymes. Enemies whispered that bars had to be placed over the White House windows—as, in fact, people suddenly became aware of such metalwork, failing to realize that President Roosevelt had installed it years earlier to protect the glass from his rambunctious children. In truth, the President's health slowly and steadily improved; but as Ike Hoover later revealed, "If there was ever a man in bad shape, he was. He could not talk plainly, mumbled more than he articulated, was helpless and looked like a man fatally ill. Everybody tried to help him, realizing he was so dependent for everything."

Vice President Marshall showed up at the White House one day, hoping to see the President, but he could not get past Mrs. Wilson. She said she would convey news of his visit, but Marshall was never to hear from the President again. In addition to presiding over the Senate, he continued to make speeches on the after-dinner circuit. He privately believed Wilson should accept mild reservations, but he publicly stood behind the President.

While Marshall was in the middle of a speech on November 23, 1919, under the auspices of the Loyal Order of Moose of Atlanta, a prominent local stepped to his side and delivered the news that President Wilson had died. Marshall bowed his head, as did everyone else who had heard. After a moment, he faced the crowd and said, "I cannot bear the great burdens of our beloved chieftain unless I receive the assistance of everybody in this country." As men in the auditorium bowed their heads and women cried, the organist in the hall played "Nearer, My God, to Thee." Marshall hastily left the stage to telephone the Associated Press, only to learn the entire story was a hoax. Marshall would later confess to Josephus Daniels that he had been stunned, first by grief and then by "the awful responsibility that would fall upon me. I was resolved to do my duty but I can truly say that I dreaded the great task."

The incident encouraged nobody at the White House to alter the current protocol. The inner circle closed ranks. Tumulty kept the gate of the West Wing, while Edith controlled access to the bedroom and Grayson constantly observed the President. Because the public would expect a Presidential statement on the first anniversary of the Armistice, Tumulty composed it. While the three paragraphs lacked the President's eloquence, they spoke of the need to seek peace in international councils. With the Congress set to reconvene on December 2, he also began drafting the Annual Message in the President's name. Wilson's inability to deliver (to say nothing of write) the speech himself would be a particular disappointment to the President who had reintroduced the tradition of appearing in person before the Congress. Eventually, relying on contributions of the Cabinet officers and sentences and sentiments from Wilson's Western tour, Tumulty was able to prepare a draft of Presidential stature. Wilson had the speech read to him, and he offered corrections, which his wife transcribed.

The State of the Union message—generic and bland—touched upon such issues as the need for the executive branch to submit a budget, to simplify the tax code, to achieve a better understanding between capital and labor, and to temper "the widespread condition of political restlessness in our body politic." Reaction from Congress followed party lines. Democrats praised its call to action, while Republicans issued baiting criticism. George Moses of New Hampshire said it was "a very poor piece of literary mechanics, considering its putative authorship." Fall of New Mexico said, "The President's message doesn't mean anything. I wonder when he wrote it."

The White House—presumably Tumulty—dealt with the latter issue by talking to *The New York Times*. The paper ran a page-one item detailing the marked improvement in Wilson's handwriting, even in the "extremely clear and unwavering" nature of his shorthand notes—when, in truth, the President was still incapable of writing such notes and none existed. Two months after Wilson had disappeared from public view, Congressmen were asserting that "whatever the state of his health it is time that Congress and the country should know the facts."

"The question as to whether the President is actually and generally performing his official duties and whether he is mentally and physically capable of doing so is growing more and more insistent," Robert Lansing wrote in a memorandum for his own files. He particularly questioned the authorship of the Annual Message, and was correct in assessing that "the loose stones are there but the cement is not." Seasoned politico Albert Burleson considered Tumulty's fabrication of the speech both "a fine piece of political work" and a "deception." Lansing said, "If it ever gets out it will make a fine scandal." Short of that, Republicans believed they had found a great potential embarrassment for the President. A chorus of Senators declared that Wilson was constitutionally unable to discharge his duties. Without any substantiation, George Moses announced that Wilson had suffered a brain lesion and was unable to "transact business."

Two thousand miles away and almost ten years into Mexico's violent revolution, the Carranza government arrested an American consular official named William O. Jenkins, accusing him of staging his own kidnapping in order to discredit the current regime. The crusty and corrupt Senator from New Mexico, Albert Fall, had been complaining for weeks that the United States had no President. "We have petticoat government," he said, pounding on a table. "Wilson is not acting. Mrs. Wilson is president." And now the Senator seized the opportunity to summon Wilson not only to respond with aggressive military action but also to receive a committee, one consisting of Hitchcock and himself. At last, the Republicans would unmask the President. When Dr. Grayson presented the proposition to his patient, Wilson said he was happy to oblige.

Grayson milked the acceptance, telling Fall that the President was "undergoing a rest cure" and that he personally preferred Wilson's avoiding controversial matters . . . but that he saw no reason why the President could not "transact any business" and meet the Senate's demands. Fall called the doctor's bluff and asked when they might visit. Grayson said at 2:30 that very afternoon, a Friday. When Fall suggested the matter could wait until Monday, by which time he could consult his caucus, Grayson insisted there was no reason to delay this visit—which Wilson called "a smelling committee," one meant to ascertain whether his corpse had begun to rot.

When the two-man delegation arrived at the Executive Mansion, Senator Fall asked Grayson how long they could stay. The doctor dealt the prickly Republican Senator a "staggering blow" when he imposed no time constraints. The three men ascended to the second floor, where the Wilsons awaited in the carefully staged bedroom at the end of the hall.

The President had directed all the lights in his room turned on, to create a bright atmosphere. He remained in bed, his head only slightly elevated, his left arm buried under the covers, while papers were placed on the nightstand to his right—props with which he might demonstrate dexterity. Edith greeted the visitors, a pencil in one hand and a pad in the other—"so I would not have to shake hands with him," she later wrote of

Fall. She sat quietly through the entire meeting, taking notes in her flow-ery schoolgirl penmanship. "I hope you will consider me sincere," said the gentleman from New Mexico, by way of opening the meeting. "I have been praying for you, Sir."

"Which way, Senator?" the President replied, according to Edith, who also recounted Fall's laughing at the quip. And with that, for all intents and purposes, the meeting was over—as the President revealed that his wit and his wits remained intact. But the visit lasted another forty-five minutes, during which time Wilson displayed a thorough grasp of the Mexican situation, including knowledge of Fall's investments south of the border. Called to the telephone during the meeting, Grayson learned that Jenkins in Mexico, in fact, had been released the previous night. The doctor interrupted the conference to impart this information, which ren-dered further discussion pointless. Wilson spoke of getting on his feet again soon, so that he could visit the Capitol "and take up personally prob-lems affecting the Government." He asked Fall to convey that sentiment to his colleague from New Hampshire, hoping Senator Moses would be "reassured." When Fall descended in the elevator, Secret Service agent Starling asked how he had found the President. "If there is something wrong with his mind," said Senator Fall, "I would like to get the same ail-ment." Wilson had delivered a consummate performance, conveying a vi-tality beyond his actual capacity.

That did not, however, put the issue of Presidential inability to rest. The public was willing to overlook Wilson's condition so long as its limi-tations remained abstract; but some in the Administration were less san-guine, especially the Secretary of State. While Wilson was mentally competent, Lansing wondered how long a physically incapacitated Presi-dent could run the country. Fall had left the White House having failed to ascertain the extent of Wilson's paralysis, his nerves, and his overall strength. "I feel that the secrecy which has prevailed should come to an end," Lansing wrote in a memorandum intended for history's eyes only. And though he had no intention of exposing his boss, he succinctly stated what he considered a constitutional crisis, one nobody had chosen to ad-dress: "It is not Woodrow Wilson but the President of the United States who is ill. His family and his physicians have no right to shroud the whole affair in mystery as they have done."

. . .

"Things fall apart," William Butler Yeats wrote that year; "the centre cannot hold; / Mere anarchy is loosed upon the world." While he was pondering the dissolution of one era with dark visions of the next, he might just as well have been describing the Wilson White House. Although Wilson's physical condition continued to improve, his mind often raced ahead of his body's limitations. Post-stroke depression clouded many of his thoughts, some of which were faintly delusional. Frequently petulant because he was stuck in the world of his own mind most of the time, with few stimuli and little information beyond that which his wife and physician spoon-fed, many of Woodrow Wilson's actions after October 2, 1919, were highly questionable. Unfortunately, nobody but Edith could challenge him; and in her efforts to ensure his health, she had abdicated that responsibility. The country, like its leader, drifted.

After eleven weeks in which Edith had allowed the President to perform the absolute minimum that his job required, the logjam of untended business brought the White House to a virtual standstill. Tumulty wrote Mrs. Wilson on December 18, 1919, listing more than a dozen items that demanded the President's attention. They were necessary not only to maintain the steady flow of government business but also because failure to address them would highlight the President's negligence.

Washington has always relied on temporary appointees to administer the nation's bureaucracies. And at the end of 1919, the Civil Service, Federal Trade, Interstate Commerce, and United States Tariff Commissions all needed positions filled; the Waterways Commission had seven vacancies. Often the bureaucracies themselves, not just the people running them, had term limits, which required Presidential attention.

The Railway Control Act of 1918, for example, had authorized the government to operate America's railroads for the duration of the war and a "reasonable time" thereafter. Railroad czar McAdoo and his successor, Walker Hines, had run the trains more effectively than private ownership. But now, a year after the Armistice, the future of the system could be delayed no longer. Because of an inevitable drop-off in traffic as the nation retreated to a peacetime economy, a period of losses and liquidation ensued. Many companies made claims against the government for damage to their property. Hines wrote Wilson that "widespread uncertainty" might easily become "the basis of unfair manipulation of the prices of railroad securities," employees were pressing for increases in wages, and somebody had to take responsibility for maintaining the property currently in the hands of the Railroad Administration. Over the course of a week, the necessary paperwork—which should have required a few hours—passed through a dozen hands, always reverting to Edith and barely averting a crisis.

Equally troublesome, American foreign policy had been rudderless for months. Despite Secretary Lansing's repeated insistence, Britain's Ambassador ended his brief posting in Washington without any communication from the President. The snub was not enough to kick off an international incident, but it was an insulting misstep. In the meantime, the diplomatic corps simply floated, with at least eight countries—China, Italy, and the Netherlands among them—without an American Ambassador. In some cases, envoys had been selected but awaited final authorization from the President. One country desperately needed not only an Ambassador but the recognition that might assure its democratic future. Having deposed a military dictator, Costa Rica teetered on the brink of financial ruin and feared the return of the despot as it waited seven months for the United States to recognize its government.

As 1919 saw more changes in the world order than any year in centuries, the White House infrastructure begin to collapse. Upon the death of Virginia Senator Martin in November, Carter Glass surrendered his secretaryship to fill the seat, leaving a vacancy at the Treasury Department. The fourth Sunday into the New Year, David Houston awoke with the grippe, only to receive a call from the White House informing him that Mrs. Wilson wished to see him that afternoon. "Of course, you know that I did not ask you to take the trouble to come merely to drink tea," she said. While the President upstairs was reluctant to move Houston from the Agriculture Department, she said, "he now needs you more in the Treasury." After she delivered all her husband's arguments for his assuming the new position, Houston said, "I am in the harness until March 4, 1921, if he wishes it, and as long as I am with him, I will dig stumps, or act as Secretary of the Treasury, or assume any other task he assigns me." Edith smiled and said, "That is just what the President said you would say."

Wilson's severe mental and physical limitations forced a hurried selection of inferior appointments to his recomposed Cabinet. In discussing

Houston's replacement at Agriculture, for example, Mrs. Wilson said the President had been considering Edwin T. Meredith—a Populist Iowan with a history of newspaper and agricultural publishing and unsuccessful runs for the Senate and the governorship. Houston acknowledged that he had the right background but questioned his intellectual ability and "whether he was Cabinet size or not." Meredith received the appointment a week later, as the President simply lacked the energy to conduct a thorough search. (Meredith would leave no mark on government that could match his significant legacy in magazine publishing, especially when he changed the name of his periodical from *Fruit, Garden and Home* to *Better Homes and Gardens*.)

Interior Secretary Lane had talked of resigning for months, taking issue with the President even before the League fight, over leasing certain oil properties. The deals appeared to be legal, but Wilson—who had maintained a scandal-free administration—told Lane he wanted to study them before releasing government property to private capital. After Wilson fell ill, many such leases came to the President's desk for signature. Edith studied each such matter, put the papers in neat stacks, and carried them to the Lincoln Bed, where he signed as many documents as possible before tiring. The first time she presented one of these oil leases, however, he said, "That will not be signed, and, please, until I am able to study that situation do not bring me any more of them. It is better to let things wait than do a thing that to my uninformed judgment seems most unwise." Lane pressured Mrs. Wilson, saying the President's inaction reflected poorly on his running the Interior Department.

Even before Lane served notice, the President had sought his replacement. Mrs. Wilson told Houston that her husband preferred somebody not from the far West because most of the Department's problems stemmed from that region and "it was difficult to find a Western man who would take a sufficiently detached or national view." Within weeks, the White House had announced the appointment of Judge John B. Payne, a powerful attorney and party politician from Chicago who was also a member of the Shipping Board.

Prior to the President's stroke, Commerce Secretary Redfield had spoken of resigning, and on November 1 he returned to the private sector. Six-term Democratic Congressman Joshua W. Alexander of Missouri—a second choice, but the first in the alphabetical listing on the roster of a

Congressional Committee on Commerce—replaced him. Houston thought him "totally unfit."

And then the Cabinet almost lost Labor Secretary W. B. Wilson as a result of the first serious rupture between two department heads. Management and labor had called a ceasefire during the war, but after the Armistice, each side sought to reclaim its ground. The major struggle was between the colliers and mine operators, which sparked a dispute between Secretary Wilson and the President's old friend Harry Garfield, the acting Fuel Administrator and consumers' advocate. Miners threatened to strike if they did not receive a pay raise, and Garfield enlisted the help of Attorney General Palmer, who announced that the Cabinet unanimously supported his decision to enjoin the miners, which he said the Lever Act empowered him to do. W. B. Wilson was incensed because he had been negotiating with the miners and because the President had promised Samuel Gompers that the Lever Act would never be used to secure an injunction against labor. Only a hastily assembled bucket brigade of memos between the Cabinet Room and the Lincoln Bed could douse the ire of the Labor Secretary, as the President sided with him. More important, Josephus Daniels convinced the Labor Secretary that in those troubled times, it was "his duty to stick." He did, and Garfield resigned. "A well Wilson," Daniels later noted, "would have nipped the injunction in the bud."

A larger problem blossomed in the State Department when it became the Secretary's duty to leave. "Mr. Lansing should have retired long before," Edith would note. Like his predecessor, William Jennings Bryan, Robert Lansing realized that Wilson dictated his own foreign policy, which reduced the Secretary to little more than a facilitator. Even more humiliating, during the most challenging months in the Department's history, Wilson had always positioned Lansing behind Colonel House, often ignoring him. For his part, the President found Lansing devoid of imagination, a man of some insight but no vision. His evident displeasure with the final Treaty had demoralized Wilson at a time when he was "expending the last ounces of his strength" on its behalf. Once Wilson was confined to his bed, Lansing worked quietly but steadily to get the President to step down. As Wilson's health returned, he began to engage, at last, with the Secretary of State, but not in the way Lansing had expected.

In his series of memoranda to himself, Lansing steadily built a case against Wilson's continuance in office, and ultimately against his own. "I

don't know how I am going to stand the present state of affairs much longer," he wrote on December 10, 1919. "It has become almost intolerable."
Lansing believed Wilson was well enough to choose a successor at State
and to invalidate anything Lansing did in the interim; but he felt beholden
enough to the office not to resign until the President offered strong cause
to do so. He was correct in assuming that the President distrusted and
disliked him. "I don't care a rap about his good will," Lansing told himself,
"but I do care about his preventing me from properly conducting our foreign affairs."

Lansing never realized that his continued disappointments without
confrontation were among the reasons for Wilson's misgivings about him.
"I must continue," he recorded, ". . . though the irrascibility [sic] and tyranny of the President, whose worst qualities have come to the surface during his sickness, cannot be borne much longer." Lansing believed nobody
dared cross Wilson for fear of triggering another stroke. In the meantime,
he noted, "his violent passions and exaggerated ego have free rein." Unable
even to schedule an audience with him, Lansing went to the White House
at the turn of the new year to meet with Mrs. Wilson to stress the importance of taking action on several matters that he had already brought to
the President's attention. "The President," Edith snapped, "does not like
being told a thing twice." On January 7, 1920, Lansing told himself, "It is
only a question as to when I should send in my letter of resignation. I cannot wait much longer." He did not have to.

One month later—amid a volley of correspondence regarding Japanese
interests in Siberia and the conversion of Fiume into a free city under the
League's protection—Wilson sent Lansing a startling letter. "Is it true, as
I have been told," the President asked, "that during my illness you have
frequently called the heads of the executive departments of the Government into conference?" If that were the case, Wilson said, he felt it his
duty to remind the Secretary that under constitutional law and practice,
only the President had the right to summon the heads of the executive
departments into conference, and only he and the Congress had the right
to ask their views on public questions. The letter was the first that Lansing
had seen in months that bore the President's signature.

He felt the President's irritability had progressed to irrationality, which
he charitably assigned to his medical condition. He considered the brief
missive "brutal and offensive," especially as he considered the question

"entirely superfluous." He had no doubt that the President had known for months that he had called regular Cabinet meetings—unless, indeed, the President had become mentally imbalanced and completely forgetful. He replied that he had frequently assembled the Cabinet "to meet for informal conference," the result of the Secretaries' need to confer on interdepartmental matters. He insisted he never intended to overstep any constitutional boundaries, but if the President believed that Lansing had failed in his loyalty, he was prepared to resign. In fact, Lansing looked forward to the reprieve. "Woodrow Wilson is a tyrant," he wrote on February 9, "who even goes so far as to demand that all men shall *think* as he does or else be branded as traitors or ingrates. . . . Thank God I shall soon be a free man!"

The President's memory had not failed him. To the contrary, Wilson recalled every one of Lansing's infractions. He resented the Secretary's lack of enthusiasm for the Treaty and, even more, his expressing his opinion both privately and publicly—which had enabled Bullitt to quote Lansing before the Senate committee. These petty betrayals formed just the tip of the iceberg, as Wilson gradually realized that he had selected the wrong man for the position in the first place, a man who did not share his worldview. As Daniels observed, "Lansing was a Big Stick diplomat who believed in Dollar Diplomacy and in Force and had no part in Wilson's idealism and faith in real democracy." The last straw for Wilson came with Lansing's handling of the Jenkins affair, in which he seemed to encourage war with Mexico. Wilson's questioning Lansing about the Cabinet meetings was merely the pretext he offered for four years of untrustworthiness and attempts to steer foreign affairs from the President's path.

When Tumulty learned of the President's intention to discharge Lansing, he sat with him on the South Portico and argued that public opinion would say "it was the wrong time to do the right thing." Although still physically weak, Wilson in his "invalid chair" grabbed hold of his adviser's phrase and said, "Tumulty, it is never the wrong time to spike disloyalty. When Lansing sought to oust me, I was upon my back. I am on my feet now and I will not have disloyalty about me."

Edith implored her husband to state that his reasons for accepting the resignation went beyond the calling of meetings, that there had been "an accumulation of disloyalty." To cite only Lansing's last and most minor offense, she said, looked petty. Woodrow laughed. "Well, if I'm as big as you think me," he said, "I can well afford to do a generous thing. If not I must take the blame." On February 11, 1920, Wilson wrote Lansing that he wished to take advantage of his "kind suggestion" to relinquish his office.

"Thank God," the Secretary of State wrote in his desk diary that day, "an intolerable situation is ended." For Lansing, perhaps; but he did not intend to let the President's letter go unanswered. The next day, instead of a one-line resignation, he sent a long letter justifying all his behavior in the last year—starting in Paris, where he had found his advice unwelcome, and proceeding to the calling of Cabinet meetings, which he believed were in the best interests of the Administration and the Republic. He insisted he had never sought to "usurp" Presidential authority. On Friday the thirteenth, Wilson accepted the resignation, effective immediately. Lansing's last act of business at the State Department was to mimeograph the final correspondence between him and the President, which he disseminated at 7:30 that evening.

"The President delivered himself into my hands and of course I took advantage of his stupidity," Lansing noted in his latest private memorandum, "for it surely was nothing less than stupidity on his part." So manifest were Wilson's "irritation and jealousy" in his letters and "so peevish" his tone, Lansing believed the President was not in his right mind. "I imagine that a pretty good-sized bomb has been exploded, which will cause a tremendous racket in this country and find an echo abroad." Lansing was right. Every newspaper in the country questioned the White House's decision.

Making matters worse was that just a few days earlier, urologist Hugh H. Young of Johns Hopkins—who was part of Wilson's medical team— had divulged details of his cerebral thrombosis. Although the doctor was quick to state that neither the vigor nor the lucidity of the President's mental processes was affected, these first details of his condition to reach the press cast suspicion over the White House. Coupled with Lansing's dismissal, the story assumed a life of its own. Appearing to be covering up, the White House had to produce other doctors to control the damage. Tumulty met with the President on Sunday, where he found the valet cutting his hair in the bathroom. "Well, Tumulty," Wilson said with a twinkle, "have I any friends left?" And Tumulty replied, "Very few." Wilson said that in a few days "what the country considers an indiscretion on my part in getting rid of Lansing will be forgotten, but when the sober, second thought of the country begins to assert itself, what will stand out will be the disloyalty of Lansing to me."

Wilson was partially correct. The Lansing dismissal was quickly forgotten, but only because it ignited a more incendiary discussion about the President's overall competence. Newspapers invited physicians to offer their professional opinions. Dr. Arthur Dean Bevan, ex-president of the American Medical Association, took the White House to task for suggesting that the President had suffered from exhaustion when, in fact, he had suffered a paralyzing stroke. "He is evidently slowly recovering from the paralysis of his arm and leg and may recover fairly well, although never completely, the use of his limbs," said Bevan. "But the diseased arteries, which were responsible for the stroke and the damaged brain, remain and will not be recovered from." That being the case, he added, "A patient who is suffering as the President is . . . should under no circumstances be permitted to resume the work of such a strenuous position as that of President of the United States." Technically, Bevan reminded the press, the United States was still at war; and if Wilson as Commander in Chief of the Army and Navy were called before a nonpartisan medical board, "he would be at once retired as physically incapacitated to perform the duties of the position." Lansing heard that word on Capitol Hill was that the "President is crazy."

And then, in a Cabinet not known for grandstanding, one department head took advantage of the President's absence in a most aggressive, if not egregious, manner. Forty-eight-year-old Attorney General A. Mitchell Palmer was not only the youngest member of the Cabinet but also the most ambitious. With a national election less than a year away, he had his eye on the Oval Office and his hands on the issue on which he could run for election—national security.

The country had been rife with protests and growing hysteria all year. In early February 1919, the Mayor of Seattle had called for federal troops to prevent a massive workers' shutdown from becoming a subversive uprising. Later that month, while the President had been Stateside between sessions of the Peace Conference, the Secret Service had thwarted the attempts of a band of Spanish anarchists to assassinate him. In April a mail bomb arrived at the Atlanta home of Georgia's junior Senator, Thomas Hardwick, which maimed a housemaid. Identically wrapped packages, each containing a similar bomb, had been addressed to another five Senators, four Cabinet members, captains of capitalism John D. Rockefeller and J. P.

Morgan, and Supreme Court Justice Oliver Wendell Holmes, who had just ruled in the back-to-back cases that resulted in a definition of "clear and present danger" and the start of Eugene Debs's ten-year prison sentence. May Day 1919 saw protests from coast to coast that turned violent. Seeing the political havoc in Russia, some Americans became paranoid. Because there appeared to be outside agitators everywhere, xenophobia grew and "true Americans" sought to secure their borders. Anarchists, Communists, Socialists, striking union members, recent immigrants, people of color or with accents were all tarred with the same brush.

On the night of June 2, 1919—while his wife and daughter slept— Attorney General Palmer heard a car stop outside his townhouse on R Street. Carrying a suitcase, a man sprang from the car but tripped in the garden, and his bag exploded. Neighbor Franklin Roosevelt rushed across the street and learned that physical harm had come to nobody except the perpetrator, who died. At the same hour that same night, bombs at the homes of eight anti-radical judges and legislators—in Boston, New York, Pittsburgh, and Cleveland—also detonated. In all but one of those bombings, lives were spared. But back on R Street, one life got changed.

In his first days as Attorney General that spring, Palmer had been quick to recommend commutations of sentences for political prisoners, and he secured the release of five thousand enemy aliens on parole. Now he intended to vanquish "the Red Menace"—an international cabal of terrorists without borders that threatened to overthrow the American government. This war on terror was not just a political issue for the ambitious Quaker; it had become a personal vendetta.

In August 1919, Palmer enlisted a recent law graduate, J. Edgar Hoover, who was exactly half his age, to head the General Intelligence Division of the Justice Department's Bureau of Investigation. His orders were to collect enough information about radical aliens to deport them. Taking advantage of wartime sedition laws, Palmer authorized a series of pre-emptive attacks on a virtually invisible—and possibly imagined—enemy.

On November 6, 1919—the second anniversary of the Bolshevik revolution—he and the zealous Hoover unleashed an army of agents and local police forces into action in several cities. They busted into homes and meetinghouses with warrants for the arrest of more than six hundred suspected radicals. They found no bombs, but they did seize several tons of political literature. Before the end of the year, the Labor Department deported 249 anarchists back to Russia, Emma Goldman among them. The raids were so well organized, most civilians had to admire the thoroughness of Palmer and Hoover's work. The nation's press—in which the raids were not even the lead story—generally applauded the restoration of law and order, and encouraged more such vigilance.

On January 2, 1920, Palmer delivered just that. Federal and local agents raided "centers of Red activities" in more than forty cities and towns, from Nashua, New Hampshire, to Los Angeles. For the most part, Palmer had warrants for the arrests of the suspects, largely immigrants who had sworn allegiance to the United States but then seemed bent upon overthrowing its government. He issued instructions for the conduct of the agents during the raids, which included that "violence to those apprehended should be scrupulously avoided" and that any citizen arrested as a Communist must be present while officers searched his home. Because so many different police departments were involved in the raids, it was impossible to supervise every arresting officer's behavior; and one cannot measure how much illegal behavior the federal agents overlooked as they trampled across the civil rights of many American citizens. It did become immediately apparent, however, that the local constabularies were far more severe in their arrest procedures than instructed. When Palmer tried to stop Illinois's chief law officer from conducting his own raids, the State's Attorney refused, accusing Palmer of "pussyfoot politics." Palmer and Hoover's plan had inflamed the Red Scare immeasurably, essentially encouraging fanaticism and fearmongering.

Only when the exhilaration surrounding the raids had died down did people realize the great Communist plot to usurp the United States was not as evolved as the Justice Department had suggested. The Communist Party had no great arsenal of guns and explosives; most of those arrested were not seditious, merely discontent; and their literature was not as dangerous as feared. The people realized that Palmer had ignored at least three constitutional rights—the freedom of speech, the right of the people to be secure against unreasonable searches and seizures, and citizen protection against being deprived of life, liberty, or property without due process of law. An absence of leadership created this blatant abrogation of civil rights, surely the nadir of the Wilson Administration.

A few hundred more citizens were deported. And just as the segregation of Washington had given license to other states to maintain Jim Crow laws, so did the Palmer raids empower states and cities to impose their own standards of good citizenship, complete with loyalty oaths and witch hunts. Legionnaires and Klansmen became local vigilantes. And while the raids themselves ceased, their effects would linger through the century. Palmer, once known as a Progressive Congressman who supported labor and women's suffrage, would forever be remembered for the three months in which he abused the power of his office to an unprecedented extent. He geared up his Presidential campaign, running on a theme of "Americanism."

No evidence exists that the President had any prior knowledge of the raids, as Edith and Dr. Grayson continued to shield him from news outside the White House. Grayson said, "He is perfectly calm about everything that comes up *except* the treaty. That stirs him: makes him restless." In mid-December 1919, Wilson took his first halting steps since his collapse. A treeless Christmas and the President's sixty-third birthday passed quietly. "It has been the hardest year of your life and one that will live in history," the ever-faithful Tumulty wrote Wilson on December 28. "It may take time but you will be vindicated." Alas, Wilson strove not for vindication, but for victory.

Obsessed with the Treaty, he continued to dream up strategies to enable its passage. That month he concocted a harebrained scheme, which he asked Tumulty to draft into an open letter to the nation. He had long asserted that an overwhelming majority of the people desired its ratification, as he believed his seventeen-state tour had confirmed. Thus, with the Senate standing in the way of the people's will, the President wanted a national referendum. The Constitution providing no machinery for such a vote, he devised one. He intended to challenge more than half the nation's Senators to resign their seats and "take immediate steps to seek re-election . . . on the issue of their several records with regard to the ratification of the Treaty." If a majority of those gentlemen was reelected, Wilson promised to resign from office, as would the Vice President. Wilson had Edith ask the Attorney General to provide the legal ramifications of these mass resignations. Palmer's reply suggested the impossibility of such a phenomenon, to say nothing of the implausibility of any such mass compliance.

Kicking off the election year, the Democratic National Committee had hoped to receive a message from the President at its Jackson Day dinner.

Senator Ashurst warned Dr. Grayson that many members no longer wished to hear a demand for ratification of the Treaty without reservations, as it would further split an already divided Senate. Wilson would, of course be unable to attend the dinner, but he asked Tumulty to compose a letter to be read aloud, one that would incorporate his idea of a referendum. Tumulty obeyed, though he wondered if the President was not shooting himself in the foot. He asked Secretary Houston to vet the remarks, and he too pronounced the statement "unwise." He altered the letters in ways Wilson accepted, and the President even added a sentence of his own, stressing a moral point.

The party faithful roundly cheered the President's remarks that night, but one of the evening's guests of honor, William Jennings Bryan, neutralized their effect when he spoke of the need to come to an immediate agreement within the Senate to keep the Treaty "out of politics," for fear that it was not a winning issue for them in November. Instead, he argued for ratification of the Treaty without delay, even if that meant compromise.

The President still would not hear of it. With debate on the Treaty about to begin anew, Wilson had taken nothing from the Republican arguments except the need to dig his heels in deeper. He had released a statement that he had "no compromise or concession of any kind in mind," but intended that "the Republican leaders of the Senate shall continue to bear the undivided responsibility for the fate of the treaty and the present condition of the world in consequence of that fate." When Senator Hitchcock pressed Wilson to make peace with their chief adversary, the President snapped, "Let Lodge hold out the olive branch!"

In exasperation, several Senators from both sides of the aisle formed a bipartisan committee to produce a compromise of its own. Before they reached a final agreement, Tumulty wrote Mrs. Wilson that it behooved the White House to offer its own such document, for fear that a successful Senatorial compromise would preclude the President from having any say at all. He wrote a draft of a letter for Wilson to send to Hitchcock stating his "irreducible minimum" terms. Two days later, he wrote her again to announce that the "psychological moment" was approaching, providing the President "his great opportunity," perhaps his last. Before the bipartisan conference reached an agreement, the Republican Majority Leader threatened to strip Lodge of his leadership unless he blocked the super-committee. Lodge told those negotiating that he would not consider further changes to his reservations.

Just when Wilson seemed as vital as he had been in months, an influenza epidemic descended upon Washington, and the President appeared to be among its victims. Dr. Grayson informed nobody other than Edith and Margaret Wilson of his condition, for fear of what the press and the President's enemies would do. That proved to be sound thinking, as within two days his flu-like virus had passed. But as had occurred in Paris after he had been similarly stricken, he suffered curious repercussions: frequent mood swings in which he experienced random moments of euphoria and depression, defiance and defeatism. But compromise remained unthinkable.

Ray Baker—who had just published a book about Wilson in Paris and had become the family's "court" historian—lunched with Edith Wilson that week. She trusted him as much as anybody outside the innermost circle. And even Baker—a true believer in the Wilsonian cause—used the opportunity to nudge her toward compromise by telling her what people outside the White House were feeling. He spoke of their wholehearted support of the spirit of the Treaty and their hope for a League, but he added that they were "profoundly disturbed" to see it bogged down in politics and semantics. For that, he suggested, people were just as inclined to blame Mr. Wilson as Mr. Lodge. "They think him stubborn," Edith declared. Baker simply reminded her how much depended on this issue, including the very existence of her husband's beloved League. "I know," she said, "but the President still has in mind the reception he got in the west, and he believes the people are with him."

Presidents traditionally speak of the isolation of the White House, but none had been as removed as Woodrow Wilson—confined for months to a bed, seeing almost nobody and hearing no direct news. "This sick man, with such enormous power, closed in from the world," Baker noted in his diary, "& yet acting so influentially upon events!" Edith seemed to be in full accord with Baker's desire for the President to offer "some great gesture" that would clear the bottleneck and allow passage of the Treaty. "Yet he hardens at any such suggestion," Baker observed: "yielding anything to the Senate seems to drive him into stubborn immovability."

"Was there ever such a situation in our history!" Baker mused on January 23, 1920. "Everything must come through one overstrained woman!" He found himself conjuring images of "this lonely sick man, attacked from all sides" and contrasting them with the same man he had seen just the year before as he was hailed along the great boulevards of Europe. Tumulty wrote Wilson "that our forces are rapidly disintegrating." A long meeting with supportive Senators Joseph T. Robinson of Arkansas and Carter Glass convinced him that the public was demanding "immediate action," even if it meant accepting the Lodge reservations.

The next Sunday night—February 29, 1920—Tumulty joined fifteen members of the Democratic Party's power elite—Hitchcock and Glass from the Senate, Texan John Nance Garner from the House, a few governmental board chairmen, and more than half the Cabinet: resolute Wilsonians all—for dinner at the Chevy Chase Club. Party chairman Homer Cummings presided over an agenda the first item of which was how to deal with the Treaty situation. He read a letter from Frank I. Cobb, Wilson's most ardent defender in the press, who advocated acceptance of the reservations. Hitchcock seconded the opinion, expressing a willingness to prolong the fight but a preference to accept its futility.

"Well, I think we are all of one opinion, which is that the President should accept the reservations and be advised that this is our recommendation," said Carter Glass at last. "But—"; and, with that, he paused for dramatic effect. "I would like, to know," he proceeded, "in the present condition of the President's mind and his state of health, who among us will be willing to go to him and tell him that he should accept the reservations." Each man sat in silence, waiting for one of the other fifteen to speak.

Ray Baker was willing to bell the cat, and he arranged an audience with the President during his now daily outing to the South Portico. The issue arose and just as quickly fell with "sad finality," as Wilson had convinced himself that the opposition was composed of "evil men" hell-bent on destroying the League.

Carter Glass informed the President that a rewording of Article X endorsed by President Taft had proven acceptable to Lodge, the Mild Reservationists, and a host of "uncompromising friends of the Administration." Edith Wilson replied that the President felt Taft's proposed reservation was "not drawn in good faith" and that her husband believed "absolute inaction on our part is better than a mistaken initiative." When Wilson's son-in-law discussed the partisan gamesmanship in play, Wilson said,

"Mac, I am willing to compromise on anything but the Ten Commandments"—which meant that "there could be no compromise where the moral law or high principle was involved."

Spring arrived early, and the President left the White House grounds on March 3 for the first time in five months. From the rear entrance of the White House, he walked with a cane to a waiting motorcar, into which attendants assisted him. For more than an hour, he and Edith and Dr. Grayson rode along the Potomac to Capitol Hill. They passed Senator Borah, who smiled and waved. The drive proved therapeutic enough to become part of Wilson's regimen once again. He would wear a cape instead of an overcoat, because of the difficulty threading his left arm through the sleeve, and the staff would place him in the contoured front seat, where he could not slide or topple over as he did in the back. Timed with his return, Agent Starling would organize a group to stand and cheer as the car pulled through the White House gate. When the Secret Service men lifted Wilson from the car after the first of these staged welcomes, the President had tears in his eyes. "You see," he said to Edith, "they still love me!"

Realizing that the Senate was in the homestretch of its marathon debate, the President dictated one last letter to Hitchcock about the League—1,400 words full of his familiar phraseology, more fixed in his argument than ever. Over the next few days, he tinkered with the text, and his pencil markings in both shorthand and longhand revealed penmanship only slightly less readable than before his stroke and editorial skills as precise as ever. "Either we should enter the League fearlessly," he wrote, "accepting the responsibility and not fearing the role of leadership which we now enjoy, contributing our efforts towards establishing a just and permanent peace, or we should retire as gracefully as possible from the great concert of powers by which the world was saved." The White House sent the letter to Senator Hitchcock on March 8, releasing copies to the major newspapers for publication the next day.

The impending vote on the Lodge reservations would probably be the last opportunity to accept some form of the Treaty, yet Wilson was encouraging even his supporters as well as the Treaty's detractors to kill it. And the public wanted to hear no more discussion of the subject because everything had already been said. As *The New York Times* indicated, "The gulf between the President and Senator Lodge is unbridgeable"; *The Washington Post* branded the President an "affirmative irreconcilable." Even the pro-Wilson New York *World* chastised him for not realizing that "these reservations at their worst are merely an expression of opinion on the part of a temporary majority of the Senate" and that what "a reactionary Senate under the leadership of Henry Cabot Lodge does a progressive Senate under enlightened leadership can undo." Remarked Brandegee of Connecticut, "The President has strangled his own child."

Lodge offered a minor rewrite of Article X, which afforded the President one final opportunity to compromise. Hitchcock wrote that he assumed Wilson would not accept it, and the President replied, "You are quite right." After the Senate vote, the next opportunity to consider a Treaty, if indirectly, would be in the upcoming Presidential election, in which the Republicans could run as a party of reconciliation.

Although Edith and Dr. Grayson continued to shield the President from pessimistic news, they permitted Tumulty to maintain daily visits with him on the South Portico, because sitting alone and sidelined only heightened his anxiety. A few days after the March 8 letter to Hitchcock, Tumulty found him "deeply depressed," for the inevitability of the Treaty's defeat was sinking in. After reading aloud his daily report on the situation, Tumulty stepped back from Wilson's wheeled chair and said, "Governor, you are looking very well to-day." A doleful Wilson shook his head and said, "I am very well for a man who awaits disaster." And then he lowered his gaze and wept.

On March 15 the Senate adopted Lodge's final language, but Woodrow Wilson's "ides of March" came four days later. The day dragged on with speeches until six o'clock, when a quorum call drew the Senators to the floor for an immediate vote. Forty-nine favored the Lodge version of the Treaty, while thirty-five opposed—with twelve absent Senators pairing their votes, grouped in a two-to-one ratio because of the two-thirds requirement to pass. For want of seven votes, the Treaty did not pass. Almost as many Democrats voted for ratification as those who remained loyal to the President. Wilson's dream, commented Senator Lodge with glee, was as "dead as Marley's ghost." The United States would neither ratify the Treaty Wilson had carried from Paris nor join the League of Nations. It fell upon Tumulty to break the news to his chief, who received it stoically, saying only, "They have shamed us in the eyes of the world."

In an attempt to buoy the President's spirits, Tumulty reminded him that only the Senate had defeated him and that "the People" would vindicate his course. "Ah," said Wilson, "but our enemies have poisoned the wells of public opinion. They have made the people believe that the League of Nations is a great Juggernaut, the object of which is to bring war and not peace to the world. If I only could have remained well long enough to have convinced the people that the League of Nations was their real hope, their last chance, perhaps to save civilization!"

Grayson said the President had never truly believed the Treaty would be rejected, and it induced a depression. When Grayson encountered his patient after receiving the news, Wilson said, "I feel like going to bed and staying there." But he could not sleep, and Grayson bunked in the White House that night, stopping in the President's bedroom several times. At three o'clock in the morning, Wilson turned to him and said, "Doctor, the devil is a busy man." Moments later he asked Grayson to pick up his Bible and read from 2 Corinthians, Chapter 4, Verses 8 and 9, which he did:

> We are troubled on every side, yet not distressed; we are perplexed, but not
>   in despair;
> Persecuted, but not forsaken; cast down, but not destroyed . . .

"If I were not a Christian," Wilson said, "I think I should go mad, but my faith in God holds me to the belief that He is in some way working out His own plans through human perversities and mistakes."

Wilson stewed over this situation for the rest of his life. He believed the League of Nations represented "the birth of the spirit of the times," and its foes would be "gibbeted and occupy an unenviable position in history along with Benedict Arnold." Edith took the news just as hard, bearing her own grudge against the man bent on destroying her husband. Years later she declared her conviction that "Mr. Lodge put the world back fifty years, and that at his door lies the wreckage of human hopes and the peril to human lives that afflict mankind today." One morning in March 1920, Grayson commented on the balminess of the day. Wilson replied, "I don't know whether it is warm or cold. I feel so weak and useless. I feel that I would like to go back to bed and stay there until I either get well or die. I cannot make a move to do my work except by making a definite resolve to do so."

With another year to his term, Woodrow Wilson became the lamest duck ever to inhabit the White House, residing more than presiding for the rest of his days there. As spring arrived, he adopted the comfortable routine of a retiree. At nine o'clock every morning he exerted the greatest effort of his day, laboriously walking from his bedroom to his study, only steps away. At his desk he caught up with paperwork for an hour before an attendant wheeled him to the elevator and outside to the gardens. Around noon, he was wheeled to the East Room for his favorite indulgence—a motion picture. Douglas Fairbanks—the swashbuckling star of the silent screen and a successful film producer, who had actively participated in the Liberty Bond rallies—had sent Wilson in late 1918 a "projecting machine," hoping it might provide him some amusement. Wilson especially enjoyed Westerns starring William S. Hart.

At one o'clock, the President would lunch for an hour and then rest in bed for at least an hour. Gradually, a few afternoon appointments were permitted; but he derived the most good from a motor ride, an hour or two into Virginia or Maryland over roads that became so familiar, he and Edith made several friends along the way: two little brothers who would raise the flag when the President passed; a curly-haired tot who saluted and said, "Hi, Wilson!"; an elderly woman who knitted an afghan for the President to place over his knees. During the day's activities, Edith almost never left his side, especially toward sunset, when she would read to him, if he was not already engrossed in a detective story. Now that he was eating proper meals again, Wilson's digestion normalized, and he gained twenty pounds. After dinner, he and Edith pulled out decks of cards and played separate hands of canfield. The President was able, at last, to sleep through the night.

While Wilson evaded slipping into a "second childishness," much of his newfound happiness could be attributed to the arrival of a new friend, a daily visitor who proved to be the President's greatest diversion—his physician's two-year-old son. A precocious little boy, Gordon Grayson became the President's playmate. Taking a glass of milk in the late morning sun, Wilson would give the accompanying biscuit to his young friend; and if the toddler arrived late, the Wilsons would wait for Gordon to ask for his "tookie." During the noontime screenings, Gordon would sit on the footrest of the President's chair and provide his own commentary. Before leaving on afternoon drives, Wilson would call for his "little partner," and Gordon became a regular passenger, as the President delighted in pointing out places of interest along the way. "His conversation with the little fellow," Dr. Grayson noted, "seems to please him and cheer him and brighten his spirits." When the Ringling Bros. and Barnum & Bailey Circus came to the capital that spring, Wilson requested that its arrival parade alter its route, detouring from Pennsylvania Avenue to Executive Avenue, behind the White House. As the animals and performers marched by, the President of the United States sat on the roof of the East Wing, with young Gordon at his side holding a yellow balloon.

Such small pleasures lifted Wilson's spirits, but the demise of the Treaty would forever weigh him down. At two o'clock in the morning of Tuesday, April 13, 1920, Wilson summoned Dr. Grayson to his bedroom. He needed to talk, which he did for the next two hours. "When I get out of office and my health has recovered," he said, "I want to devote a good deal of time to showing what a disorganization the United States Senate is." He spoke of his having "asked our boys to go overseas and to fight in the trenches for a principle," for which many gave their lives, and how the Senate rendered that fight meaningless. Henry Cabot Lodge haunted him but not as much as those lives lost in vain. "Could any self-respecting man ask our boys to go into another war? Could you expect them to make such a sacrifice," Wilson asked Grayson, "and then have a crowd in the Senate like this throw away what they had fought for?"

Wilson's health finally improved enough for him to evaluate his physical condition and consider his obligations. "My personal pride must not be allowed to stand in the way of my duty to the country," he said. "When I am well, I feel eager for work. I judge my condition because now I do not have much desire for work." Grayson suggested that Wilson call a Cabinet meeting, so that he might talk to his advisers and determine exactly how much leadership he was exerting. "If you will do this," said Grayson, "I am confident that you will find that you are doing more than you realize. You are running your office by correspondence and this naturally makes you feel greatly out of touch with things. Moreover, it gives you the impression that you are inefficient."

A little before ten o'clock the following morning, April 14, a perfectly groomed President sat at his desk in his study, awaiting the arrival of the

Cabinet for his first meeting with them since September 2. To many of the new members, Wilson did not appear sickly. His face looked full—thick and jowly even—and he exuded cheer. But each of the returning members shuddered. In a break from tradition, Ike Hoover announced each of the entrances, which bewildered them, and Wilson's failure to rise from his chair troubled them. David Houston, newly installed at Treasury, was aghast. "The President looked old, worn, and haggard," he recalled. "It was enough to make one weep to look at him.

> One of his arms was useless. In repose, his face looked very much as usual, but, when he tried to speak, there were marked evidences of his trouble. His jaw tended to drop on one side, or seemed to do so. His voice was very weak and strained.

True to form, Wilson opened the meeting with jovial banter, but Houston found it little more than a "brave front." Silence descended, and the department heads realized the President could barely initiate serious conversation.

The ranking Cabinet officer might logically have spoken up in that moment, but the Secretary of State had the least experience of anybody in the room—only three weeks on the job. Most people in the Administration had presumed Robert Lansing's Undersecretary, Frank L. Polk—who possessed the writing skills and foreign affairs experience the President sought—would have been the natural successor. Instead, Wilson had chosen a fifty-year-old New York attorney named Bainbridge Colby. Because he had little experience with international matters, the selection surprised the nominee as much as diplomatic Washington—which allowed Senate Republicans to re-question the President's capability. But Colby was hardly a man without merits. His résumé included a term in the New York State Assembly and two unsuccessful runs as a Progressive candidate for the United States Senate, anti-trust work as a special assistant to the United States Attorney General, and membership on the Shipping Board, which resulted in his participating in the 1917 Inter-Allied Conference in Paris. In his efforts to strengthen the merchant marine, Wilson had found Colby in command of his information. Above all, from the moment Colby had left the Progressive Party in 1916 to support the Democrats, Wilson had valued his loyalty. With Colby by his side, he believed he would never have to wonder if somebody had his back.

With legal issues dominating the news, the Attorney General stepped in to direct much of the discussion that morning. Strikes had broken out across the country—involving elevator operators, truckers, and railroad workers—much of which Mitchell Palmer attributed to the Bolsheviks and the IWW. Labor Secretary Wilson blamed the unrest on economic conditions and the HCL. The two argued, largely over Assistant Secretary of Labor Louis F. Post, who had summarily dismissed most of the cases that stemmed from the Palmer raids simply because he did not believe membership in the Communist Party should mandate deportation. Palmer claimed that Post had released "alien anarchists" and ought to be relieved of his office, that his removal would be enough of a threat to end the strikes. Secretary Wilson said such action would aggravate the situation. "The President seemed at first to have some difficulty in fixing his mind on what we were discussing" and said little, David Houston observed. Indeed, this was apparently the first the President had heard of Palmer's fanatical operations with J. Edgar Hoover.

After an hour, Dr. Grayson poked his head into the study, a signal prearranged with the President to bring the meeting to a close. Wilson shook his head, indicating that he did not wish to be interrupted. Fifteen minutes later, Grayson returned, only to be dismissed a second time. At 11:30, the doctor entered with Mrs. Wilson, who said, "This is an experiment, you know." And the President adjourned the meeting. Grayson deemed the experiment a success, but one White House visitor reported that Wilson remained "a very sick man"—with a drooping jaw, vacant eyes, and a fixed scowl.

Based on the information they gathered for their psychological autopsy, William Bullitt and Sigmund Freud would later present an even bleaker picture. They pinpointed the breakdown outside Pueblo, Colorado, as the virtual death of Thomas Woodrow Wilson, because from that moment forward, he was "no longer an independent human being but a carefully coddled invalid." He was at the mercy of unpredictable, often illogical synapses, a neurological system gone haywire. "The Woodrow Wilson who lived on," they determined, "was a pathetic invalid, a querulous old man full of rage and tears, hatred and self-pity."

The President's worst moments came at night, when he was alone with his thoughts. One evening, he again summoned Dr. Grayson and asked the nurse to leave them alone. "I have been thinking over this matter of resigning and letting the Vice-President take my place," he divulged. "It is clear that I should do this if I have not the strength to fill the office." He said that he would quit the moment he realized that his sickness was causing the country any ill effects. The declaration, of course, begged the larger question of whether a man in his mental state was in any position to judge. Even more revealing was the bathetic manner in which the rest of Wilson's scenario unspooled:

> I shall summon Congress in special session and have you arrange to get me wheeled in my chair into the House of Representatives. I shall have my address of resignation prepared and shall try to read it myself, but if my voice is not strong enough I shall ask the Speaker of the House to read it, and at its conclusion I shall be wheeled out of the room.

Wilson developed his own routine for dissolving his night frights. He kept a small flashlight on a stand by his bed, and whenever he was too distressed to sleep, he shone it upon Fred Yates's pastel portrait of Ellen. Night after night, he would stare into his late wife's eyes until he calmed down. He made plans for the following spring to visit the Lake District.

In the meantime, much of Washington continued to buzz about the second Mrs. Wilson. The cantankerous Justice McReynolds, for one, had remained friendly with Vice President Marshall, Colonel House, and Dr. Grayson, and he thought Marshall should have demanded a medical opinion under oath from the President's physicians as to his true condition and then presented that opinion to Congress, which could have declared the President disabled and spared the country several "disastrous months." Grayson also wished to let Marshall serve and said as much to McReynolds and others. But Mrs. Wilson objected. He had told the First Lady that the President had raised the subject and would have stepped aside; but Edith, more concerned with her husband's constitution than the nation's, refused to listen. "If he had resigned, the entire current of recent history might have been changed," House mused in his diary in the late spring of 1920. And even if he did not, he would have saved his treaty—"had he not been so stubborn."

Wilson never raised the subject of resignation again. He believed what Grayson considered true, "that he had the strength to administer the office capably." Reading newspapers once again, Wilson noted talk of the Senate's declaring peace on its own and wondering if he would veto such a resolution. Wilson told Grayson he would take no executive action, other than writing an excoriating message, one so distasteful that he had no doubt the Senate would try to impeach him for it. "If I were well and on my feet and they pursued such a course," he told Grayson, "I would gladly accept the challenge, because I could put them in such a light before the country that I believe the people would impeach them." Wilson the historian said the Senate had never been as unpopular as it was in that moment; and with the approach of the national conventions, he daydreamed of taking a referendum for his treaty to the people. In idle moments he drafted a series of questions for the electorate—did they wish to make use of his services as President, did they approve of the way in which the Administration conducted the war, did they wish the Treaty of Versailles ratified? Tumulty recommended to the First Lady that the President declare publicly that he would not run for a third term. He believed it would depoliticize the future of the Treaty. Wilson saw nothing to be gained from such a gesture. It would only hand the leadership of the party to William Jennings Bryan; and he felt it presumptuous to decline something that had not been offered.

There was one other factor. No President of the United States had ever defied George Washington's tradition of leaving office after two terms. But along with other talk that sounded slightly deranged, Wilson told his physician that he was considering it. Even though he said, "Everyone seems to be opposed to my running," Wilson had conjured a plot in which the Democratic Convention would find itself in a "hopeless tie-up," and, with the world in so much turmoil, the Peace Treaty with its League of Nations would become the dominant issue. Then, Wilson said, "there may be practically a universal demand for the selection of someone to lead them out of the wilderness." The only person he could envision, of course, was himself. He roughed out a new Cabinet.

Grayson was glad the President did not ask for his opinion, medical or otherwise, because he did not want to tell him the depressing truth—"that it would be impossible for him to take part in such a campaign." Nor did Grayson wish to delude him, because he feared the inevitable letdown would affect the President physically as well as psychologically. Wilson believed that the man elected that fall would determine "whether the United States will be the leader of the world or back among the stragglers." He had no intention of backing any Democrat for the nomination. Like a broken-down fire horse, he waited for the sound of the bell.

While a hostile Congress, an inexperienced Cabinet, and his own compromised health prevented any real progress, Wilson gave the appearance of being back in action. With strikes and runaway inflation commanding most of the headlines, Wilson once again issued statements and performed the ceremonial duties of his office. Regular Cabinet meetings resumed, the President chairing his second meeting two weeks after the first. Foreign diplomats who had been queuing for months finally got to parade through the White House to present their credentials, and the President begin filling his long vacant ambassadorships. In the summer of 1920, Secretary Colby articulated America's position on Russia, reminding the world that the United States was the first government to acknowledge the validity of the revolution and recognize Russia's provisional government. Since that time, however, the rulers had ceased to govern by the will or the consent of the people.

Many in the Administration resented Colby, not only for being ill prepared but also for toadying to the President. Admiring the way he thought and wrote, Wilson made him the teacher's pet. At the President's direction, Colby wrote a note on the Polish situation that became the American doctrine toward Russia well into the next decade. He declared, "It is not possible for the Government of the United States to recognize the present rulers of Russia as a government with which the relations common to friendly government can be maintained. This conviction has nothing to do with any particular political or social structure which the Russian people themselves may see fit to embrace." In short, Colby concluded, "We cannot recognize, hold official relations with, or give friendly reception to the agent of, a government which is determined and bound to conspire against our institutions; whose diplomats will be the agitators of dangerous revolt; whose spokesmen say that they sign agreements with no intention of keeping them." An "iron curtain" was already being drawn between Russia and the non-Bolshevik world. Wilson found Colby's white paper "excellent and sufficient."

In one of the few interviews he granted a journalist that year, Wilson said, "I do not fear Bolshevism, but it must be resisted. . . . If left alone, it will destroy itself. It cannot survive because it is wrong." In fact, he had suggested as much at his first meeting with the new Cabinet, when he buttonholed Mitchell Palmer and told him "not to let the country see red." As that was an apparent call for extra vigilance more than further violence, the Attorney General's infamous raids came to an end.

Meanwhile, an undaunted Louis Post at the Labor Department persisted in undoing the results of Palmer's recklessness, dismissing cases left and right. As a result, he became the target of a witch hunt himself—secretly investigated by Hoover at the Bureau of Investigation and publicly attacked by the House Committee on Immigration and Naturalization. Several Congressmen as well as the American Legion called for his dismissal. Strongly anti-Communist though the President was, he supported his Secretary of Labor, who backed his subordinate on constitutional grounds, praising him for resisting what would prove to be one of the most egregious miscarriages of justice in American history. "We will not deport anyone simply because he has been accused or because he is suspected of being a Red," the White House asserted. "We have no authority to do so under the law. . . . Mr. Post . . . I am satisfied ranks among the ablest and best administrative officers in the Government service."

One agitator, however, would receive no mercy from the President. Eugene V. Debs had been a thorn in Wilson's side for years now. Having served over a year in prison and with his health failing, he had more petitioners than ever pleading for lenience—not only liberal intellectuals but also labor leaders, including Samuel Gompers and Secretary Wilson. At one meeting of the Cabinet, Payne and Daniels and even Mitchell Palmer himself all advocated clemency. Tumulty agreed to meet with a committee of Socialists presenting a petition for Debs's pardon, only to read before their meeting that the National Convention of Socialists included several radical speeches favoring the Soviet form of government and attacking Wilson. At last, the President put the matter to rest. "I will never consent to the pardon of this man," he told Tumulty.

I know that in certain quarters of the country there is a popular demand for the pardon of Debs, but it shall never be accomplished with my consent. . . . While the flower of American youth was pouring out its blood to vindicate the cause of civilization, this man, Debs, stood behind the lines, sniping, attacking, and denouncing them. Before the war he had a perfect right to exercise his freedom of speech and to express his own opinion, but once the Congress of the United States declared war, silence on his part would have been the proper course to pursue.

Wilson knew his refusal to pardon Debs would be denounced. "They will say I am cold-blooded and indifferent," he recognized, "but it will make no impression on me. This man was a traitor to his country and he will never be pardoned during my administration."

Although many of his recent decisions seemed sclerotic in nature, Wilson had not become completely hard-hearted. That year alone, he granted stays and pardons for crimes far more serious than political dissent. Elizabeth Stroud had written Edith Wilson, pleading for the President to consider the plight of her son, Robert, a convicted murderer whose case had undergone a tortured journey through the courts. Wilson commuted his death sentence to life imprisonment in solitary confinement—first at Leavenworth and then at Alcatraz, where he became a renowned ornithologist.

Wilson also continued to demonstrate his sensitivity toward women, as the war had catalyzed a reconsideration of their role in society. That spring, he nominated Helen Hamilton Gardener—longtime activist in NAWSA—to fill a vacancy on the Civil Service Commission. Upon Senate approval, she became the first female to hold such a high federal position. Women realized that the government's glass ceilings could be shattered. In the fourteen months since the proposal to amend the Constitution and enfranchise women had passed in both houses of the Congress, Wilson had steadily lobbied state legislatures to ratify. The tally got stuck at thirty-five approvals, one short of the three-quarters necessary. Then, on August 18, 1920, the Tennessee House of Representatives came around, thereby enacting the Nineteenth Amendment. For the first time, any American over the age of twenty-one—regardless of gender or race—qualified to vote.

The election of 1920 promised to be historic in other ways as well. With Vice President Marshall having shied away from higher office, the upcoming campaign was the first since 1896 in which both the Democratic and Republican Parties would presumably nominate party leaders who had never run on a national ticket. President Wilson, however, continued to fool himself into believing he would run for a third term, and some surrounding him nursed the delusion. So began the most surreal few weeks in the Wilson Presidency, a moment when nobody could bring himself to tell the emperor that he was not wearing any clothes.

"I saw the President the other day and found him a very old-looking tired man," the new British Ambassador, Sir Auckland Geddes, reported to Lloyd George. "He is not really able to see people and ought to be freed from all cares of office." And yet, even with a side of his body rendered useless, he was not ready to let go. Both Dr. Grayson and Edith believed another run for office would kill him, but each knew even suggesting as much reflected a disloyalty the President could not tolerate. She anxiously placated him while the doctor worked behind the scenes doing everything he could to keep the possibility of a nomination from even arising.

Mid-June—as Democrats prepared to leave for their convention in San Francisco, the first such event in the West—Carter Glass stopped by the executive offices. Dr. Grayson confided to him the President's latest scheme—that he would run for office solely to continue his fight for the Covenant and would resign upon its adoption. Grayson begged Glass "to do all possible to guard against such an untoward development." He told Grayson bluntly that he did not think the convention could be induced to nominate a man in the President's disabled condition, and that even if he were in robust health, the Democrats, to say nothing of the nation, did not seem prepared to overcome their antipathy to a third term.

Three days later, Glass met the Wilsons for tea on the South Portico of the White House. The Senator expressed regret that the President was "not in physical form to lead a great fight for the League of Nations," for the people might very well suppress their third-term aversion if things were otherwise. Neither of the Wilsons responded. Glass reengaged them when he said that he would "rather follow the President's corpse through a campaign than the live bodies of some of the men mentioned for the nomination." Wilson liked that, and they discussed the current contenders. The President dismissed every possibility with a backhanded compliment at best—most especially a run by Ohio's able and affable Governor, James M. Cox, whose candidacy, he said, would be "a fake."

"There is no man who can devise plans with more inspiration, or put them into operation with more vigor, than can Mac," Wilson had said of his son-in-law, for whom he always felt that twinge of distrust that any boss feels for a man who marries his daughter; "but I never caught Mac reflecting." The President admitted he might be wrong, but he thought that very quality "to be essential to a successful and wise administration in the near future." McAdoo had announced just the day before that he "would not seek the nomination for the Presidency," but as Wilson and Glass realized, McAdoo had never said he would not accept it.

Grayson accompanied Glass to the train, telling him as he parted for the convention, "If anything comes up, save the life and fame of this great man from the juggling of false friends." The doctor explained that he had served three Presidents and not one had been ready to relinquish the office. To a second party operative, Robert W. Woolley, Grayson detailed Wilson's physical condition, reiterating that he must not be nominated. "No matter what others may tell you," he insisted, "no matter what you may read about the President being on the road to recovery, I tell you that he is permanently ill physically, is gradually weakening mentally and can't recover. He couldn't possibly survive the campaign." Wilson had indeed enjoyed weeklong periods of improvement, during which he transacted business with Tumulty, but setbacks ensued, usually depressions. "Cary," Woolley said, "the name of the President will receive many an ovation, his desire as to the platform will prevail, in other ways will he be honored, but his ambition to succeed himself is definitely hopeless." Said Grayson, "We must not take any chances."

Ten thousand Democrats—men and women—filled San Francisco's Civic Auditorium on June 28, 1920. Even before the speeches—when the keynoter would be paying homage to the President and his principles—the convention got off to a boisterous start. An enormous flag rose above the rostrum, and the appearance of a gigantic likeness of the President whipped the crowd into a frenzy. When a spotlight illuminated this portrait, the delegates paraded through the aisles and around the arena. All hell broke loose—except within one large area. After seven years of Wilson's Presidency, Tammany Hall and Wall Street still had not embraced him, and the New York delegation sat silent and still during this storm of adulation. Some among them expressed the fear that the parade would incite a stampede for a third term. After a few minutes, a few pro-Wilson New Yorkers could sit on their hands no longer. A fistfight broke out, and the thirty-eight-year-old Assistant Secretary of the Navy—six-foot-two-inch

Franklin Roosevelt—grabbed the state's standard from the hands of a Tammany man and joined in the parade, taking a few delegates from the Empire State along.

The convention had no decided frontrunner, though Wilson's son-in-law felt like an emotional favorite. In Washington, the President appeared indifferent, but as one ballot followed another with no candidate emerging, Wilson took increasing interest in the press reports that came over the in-house telegraph wire. He began to suffer from insomnia, asthma, and anxiety. By July 3, Governor Cox had a measurable lead over McAdoo, with Palmer a distant third. After sixteen ballots, the convention deadlocked. Grayson went to his patient's room at three o'clock that morning to deliver the latest tallies. Wilson said nothing, except that he believed Cox was "the weakest of the lot." Almost simultaneously, Bainbridge Colby, in a spur-of-the-moment gesture of loyalty to the President, sent him a telegram from San Francisco explaining that amid all the competition, the "outstanding characteristic of the convention is the unanimity and fervor of feeling for you." After monitoring the situation closely, he said an opportunity had arrived in which to move for a suspension of the rules and nominate the President by acclamation. To Colby's surprise, Wilson assented.

Colby was caught in a political riptide. The party insiders closed ranks to sink the President's plans—all feeling it would result in defeat, some knowing it might mean his death. They forced a chagrined Colby to send another telegram to the President, this time rescinding his plan—explaining that Democratic leaders did not command votes sufficient either to set aside the convention rules or to nominate him and that such a public display would only injure the party's chances in the upcoming election—as well as any hope left for the League. Wilson accepted the decision, though he suspected misconduct, especially when he heard that Burleson was supporting McAdoo and that there was serious talk among the California and New York delegations of running Bainbridge Colby.

Between the thirtieth and thirty-eighth ballots, McAdoo and Cox ran neck and neck, the former leading by a nose; but on the next roll call, Palmer, a distant third, released his delegates, and Cox pulled ahead. On the forty-third ballot he received a majority of the votes, and on the next vote the rest of the delegates jumped on the bandwagon. In November, the genial Governor of Ohio would run against his junior Senator, Warren G.

Harding, whom the Republicans had nominated weeks earlier. Harding's running mate would be the Massachusetts Governor who had shut down Boston's police strike, Calvin Coolidge. Cox would run with the fervent New Yorker who had grabbed the state standard during the opening parade—Franklin D. Roosevelt. Wilson sent congratulatory telegrams to each of the men on the Democratic ticket with "cordial" best wishes. Back in the White House, devoted stenographer Swem watched the President's moods all week. He believed Wilson had preferred Cox over McAdoo—"solely out of jealousy toward McAdoo." Either way, there was no doubt in Swem's mind the President was "a bitter man" over the Cox nomination—"not that he disliked Cox but because he didn't get it himself."

Upon the Cabinet's return to Washington, Ike Hoover observed that "they met with a cold reception from the President." A few of them earned their way back into his good graces, but he showed only the most obligatory interest in the campaign, or much else. One late morning, while Wilson was eating his crackers and milk on the South Portico, a breathless Tumulty ran up the steps waving a piece of paper. Once the butler had taken his leave, he blurted, "Governor, we've got 'em beat! Here is a paper which . . . is absolutely true, showing that Harding has negro blood in him. This country will never stand for that!" While Tumulty raved, Wilson quietly sipped his milk. "Even if that is so," the President said, "it will never be used with my consent. We cannot go into a man's genealogy; we must base our campaign on principles, not on backstairs gossip. That is not only right but good politics. So I insist you kill any such proposal."

At 10:30 on July 18, 1920, a warm Sunday morning, Cox and Roosevelt arrived at the White House for the President's blessing. They had to wait until the President had been wheeled to the South Portico. After fifteen minutes, the guests were shown outside; and, as they approached the man in the wheelchair—his left shoulder covered with a shawl to conceal his paralyzed arm—Cox murmured, "He is a very sick man."

Cox warmly greeted the President, who, in a low and weak voice, thanked the two men for coming. His frailty brought tears to Cox's eyes. But Wilson revived when he spoke of the campaign ahead, as he briefed the two hopefuls with substantial details and humorous anecdotes. He referred the nominees to the information about Harding's ancestry and was pleased to see they concurred with his decision to squelch it. When the conversation turned to the main topic, Cox assured his host, "Mr.

President, we are going to be a million percent with you, and your Administration, and that means the League of Nations." Wilson looked up and said in a barely audible voice, "I am very grateful. I am very grateful."

After close to an hour, the aspirants left the President for the executive offices to prepare statements for the press. As Roosevelt recalled, Cox just sat down at a table, asked Tumulty for paper and pencil, summoned his skills as a former newspaperman, and wrote a release committing the ticket to making the League "the paramount issue of the campaign." Franklin Roosevelt said, "It was one of the most impressive scenes I have ever witnessed."

The men returned to the President for lunch, where Mrs. Wilson, Dr. Grayson, Tumulty, and Carter Glass joined them. Wilson quickly realized that he had misjudged the quality of Cox's character, and he commented that he thought Cox would find the White House a comfortable home. The guests left by way of the White House's basement, where stenographer Swem handed them the President's statement, which assured Cox of "an absolutely united party and . . . an absolutely united nation." Confident that he would be serving alongside the next Commander in Chief, Roosevelt announced his resignation from the Navy Department. On his way out, Cox told Tumulty that "no experience of his life had ever touched him so deeply" as meeting the President. "No man could talk to President Wilson about the League of Nations and not become a crusader on its behalf," he said.

Cox and Roosevelt waged an aggressive three-month campaign. There was little the President could do beyond offering a public statement or two, which he did. On September 16, political terrorists bombed Wall Street, killing thirty-eight people and injuring four hundred, making it the deadliest act of terrorism the nation had witnessed. Wilson privately opined that a Republican victory would result in "the most terrible industrial situation in this country," which would create a breeding ground for Bolshevism. In launching his campaign, Harding attacked Wilson's earlier position on the Panama Canal, which had exempted the United States from certain tolls. Off the record, Wilson referred to Harding as shallow and voluble, dismissing him as "nothing."

On October 3, the President stated that the election had become a national referendum on the League. He asked his fellow Americans why they should "be afraid of responsibilities which we are qualified to sustain

and which the whole of our history has constituted a promise to the world
we would sustain." Wilson said every nation awaited the November verdict. He was completely confident of the outcome.

The President had spent part of Election Day engaged in physical
therapy—struggling with a cane to mount a few low steps. When he
paused for news, he learned that Cox was trailing badly. There would be
no late-night wait for results. The earliest returns foretold a landslide. Before dawn it was plain that the entire country had gone Republican, except
the South—which, for the first time since Reconstruction, was not "solid."
A fugitive Tennessee gave Harding thirty-seven states to Cox's eleven, an
electoral count of 404 to 127. The popular vote of 16.1 million to 9.1 million (60.3 percent to 34.1 percent) marked the widest popular-vote margin
in a century. Even Democratic stronghold New York City went for Harding. More than 900,000 people voted defiantly for the Socialist candidate,
Eugene V. Debs, who ran from the Atlanta Federal Penitentiary. The Congressional results slapped Wilson in the face as well, yielding a Senate with
fifty-nine Republicans and thirty-seven Democrats and an even more lopsided House, with its majority of 302 to 131. The victors were only too
happy to embrace Wilson's premise that the election had been a referendum on his League.

Wilson admitted his disappointment to Tumulty, predicting a period
of isolation that would translate into a loss of business, ultimately producing a depression.

When Tumulty suggested the Democratic loss might prove a blessing
in the long run, Wilson rebuked him. "I am not thinking of the partisan
side of this thing," he said. "It is the country and its future that I am thinking about. We had a chance to gain the leadership of the world. We have
lost it, and soon we will be witnessing the tragedy of it all." Of Harding's
victory, he could only wonder, "How can he lead when he does not know
where he is going?" The day after the election, the Wilsons took their automobile ride through Washington, as though nothing had happened. In
fact, Stockton Axson found his brother-in-law as serene that day as in the
moments of his prior victories. "I have not lost faith in the American people," Wilson said. "They have merely been temporarily deceived. They will
realize their error in a little while."

Secret Service agent Starling, who had tracked Wilson since 1914, observed that the election had, strangely, made the President more cheerful.

He could enjoy his own new freedom, as the Congress would virtually shut down until Inauguration Day, leaving Wilson only a few ceremonial duties.

An unsettling sense of purposelessness quickly replaced joy, and Wilson's feelings darkened with the approach of winter. "I hobble from one part of the house to the other and go through the motions of working every morning," he wrote daughter Jessie, "though I am afraid it is work that doesn't count very much." Foreign affairs always demanded attention, but the President followed a policy of noninterference as much as possible. He feared the new party in power might take the United States into the League but "in such a niggardly fashion" as to proceed "from prejudice and self-interest and a desire to play a lone hand and think first and only of the United States," thereby robbing the nation of dignity and influence. Dr. Grayson confirmed that Wilson's physical health improved after the election, but his nerves were on edge. "He takes it less easily, does not make light of it or joke as he did," Grayson said. "He more easily loses control of himself & when he talks is likely to break down & weep." Wilson's temper shortened. He barked at nurses, threatening to throw them all out; and he periodically did the same to Grayson, whom he summoned regularly in the middle of the night, whether something was wrong or not. He was in a near-constant state of irritation.

Nothing soothed him more than movies, and the daily matinees became essential to his well-being. One of Edith's brothers regularly brought the President copies of the latest photoplay magazines, which he studied intently, looking for films he wished to order for the coming weeks. At the end of November, they had viewed all the available Westerns, melodramas, and love stories, and they requested the Signal Corps documentary footage of his trip to Europe.

Ray Baker was there that day, and he watched the White House ushers lift the heavy red rug of the main hall and lay it aside as the sixty-three-year-old President lumbered toward him, his left arm hanging, his left leg dragging. His eyes reflected the liveliness of his mind, but Baker shook hands with a broken man—stooped, gray-faced, and white-haired. Together they walked into the East Room. The President, Mrs. Wilson, Dr. Grayson, and Baker sat quietly in the dark as the projector from Douglas Fairbanks threw flickering images onto the screen of that extraordinary week less than two years ago, when Woodrow Wilson—tall and hale and waving his hat to the enraptured throngs—was known as "the Savior of the World." There he was sailing into the harbor at Brest . . . arriving in Paris . . . leaving Buckingham Palace . . . and everywhere flags waved and hundreds of thousands of people tossed roses and exuded so much adulation, one could almost hear their cheers emanate from the silent screen. Periodically, Wilson would comment on the scene before them, in a lifeless voice. When these glorious pictures came to an end, the audience found itself in a dim cavern of stark reality. Several attendants went to the chair of the President, who sat hunched and silent. One placed a foot against his, to brace him as he stood. Without saying another word, Wilson shuffled out of the room, to the rhythm of his cane tapping against the marble floor.

With limited energy, Wilson worked on one important document during this period, his last State of the Union message. He surely would have wished to make a final appearance before Congress, to solidify the tradition he had reestablished; but volatile as his emotions were, it was best that he did not deliver the address in person, as his appearance would surely have provoked an ovation from which he might not have recomposed himself. On Monday, December 6, 1920, the Congressional leadership came to the White House to notify the President formally that Congress had reconvened. The two Senators and three Representatives waited in the Blue Room; and as the President entered, aided by his cane, he immediately noticed Henry Cabot Lodge and said, "Gentlemen, I hope you will excuse me from going through the formality of shaking hands with you individually, but, as you see, I cannot yet dispense with my third leg." Wilson stood close enough to Senate Minority Leader Underwood to whisper, "I used the excuse of this 'third leg,' as I did not want to shake hands with Lodge." The two Democrats chuckled, and then Wilson announced that he would transmit his message to the Congress the next day. When the legislators had left, Wilson could not resist saying to Grayson, "Can you imagine what kind of a hide Lodge has got, coming up here in these circumstances and wanting to appear familiar and talk with me?"

A far cry from 1913, when Woodrow Wilson made his first dramatic appearances before joint sessions of Congress, a clerk in each chamber read the annual message as Senators and Representatives followed along reading printed copies. Except for a sentence of Abraham Lincoln's—"Let us have faith that right makes might, and in that faith let us dare to do our duty as we understand it"—and a few Wilsonian phrases, the text lacked luster. It perfunctorily urged revision of tax laws, care for the economy, and increased veterans' benefits; and he further recommended a loan to Armenia and the independence of the Philippines. It made no mention of the Treaty, but it did ask the lawmakers to remember the purity and spiritual power of democracy: "It is surely the manifest destiny of the United States," he said, "to lead in the attempt to make this spirit prevail."

The Wilson Administration wound down, the hours growing longer and quieter. Solicitous letters from friends arrived along with occasional testimonials. One particularly generous encomium from 105 women whose names could be found in the *New York Social Register*—Eleanor Roosevelt among them—simply wanted to express the belief that "the name of Woodrow Wilson will be added to those of Washington and Lincoln as the men of vision in American history." On November 15, bells pealed in Geneva, inaugurating the League of Nations—"the first time in the history of mankind," as Edwin L. James phrased it in *The New York Times*, that "forty-one nations of the world sat together in common council." The League opened by sending a message of thanks to President Wilson with the desire that the United States would soon "take her rightful place in the League." And on December 4, 1920, Albert G. Schmedeman, the United States Ambassador to Norway, informed Wilson in a "strictly confidential" telegram that the Nobel Committee of the Norwegian Parliament intended to honor "his crucial role in establishing the League" with its prize for Peace. Woodrow Wilson became the third American to win the honor—following Theodore Roosevelt and Elihu Root, each of whom had criticized Wilson for dragging his feet before declaring war.

The better the news abroad, it seemed, the more bitter he became—ill-tempered, angry, even mean. "The President these days is much given to gratifying whatever petty prejudices he has," noted Charles Swem. He based his approvals of his final appointments upon the Senators in support of the nominees and blackballed everyone on his enemies list. Final bills went signed or unsigned because of similar prejudices. During his daily drives, he grew so intolerant of those who passed his car, he ordered the Secret Service to apprehend them for questioning; he even wrote the Attorney General to ask if the President did not also have the powers of a magistrate, as he wished to fine the speeders a thousand dollars. When an admirer of the President had sent him a particularly bad portrait and later asked if it had been received, Wilson replied that "unfortunately" it had been "received in good shape." He managed to get one letter off to his old companion Jack Hibben, but with no friendly intent; rather, he wished the Princeton president would send him the big table in the study at Prospect, which he had purchased years earlier with his own money. His bitterest reply came when several classmates asked him to subscribe to the Princeton Endowment Fund and he refused—"because I do not believe at all in the present administration." He came to accept that part of his problem at Princeton had been in trying "to change old institutions too fast"; he muttered that the place "was bought once with Ivory Soap money."

In late January 1921, the red-baiting Attorney General himself presented Wilson with an application for pardon from Eugene V. Debs, complete with legal arguments as well as moral imperatives. "Debs is now approaching 65 years of age," Palmer wrote. "If not adequately, he has surely been severely punished." The form required only the President's signature. Wilson examined the document, grabbed his pen, and then wrote the word "Denied."

For almost two years, the Wilsons had mused about where they might live upon leaving the White House. Woodrow began rating their top five cities in terms of climate, friends, opportunities, freedom, amusements, and libraries. New York ranked highest, followed by Baltimore, Boston, and Richmond. Washington ran a distant fifth, but that was the city they chose. Although they counted few friends there and it offered "zero" freedom, other factors tipped the scales: the Library of Congress promised the best facilities for researching the book about government that Wilson proposed to write; and the city had long been Edith's home. In late 1920, she went out each morning at eight—while a valet helped Woodrow prepare for the day—to house hunt.

By mid-December she had inspected a half dozen places that interested her, including one on S Street, just off Massachusetts Avenue's Embassy Row, not far from Dupont Circle. After hearing the enthusiasm in his wife's voice as she described it, Wilson privately called upon her brother

Wilmer Bolling to work with the agent in ascertaining the price and searching the title. The day they worked out the details, as Edith recalled, he insisted that she attend a concert, a luxury she had forsaken since his stroke. When she returned to the White House, she found Woodrow sitting by a fire in the Oval Room upstairs, where he handed her the paperwork. He was purchasing the $150,000 house as a gift for her.

The sum represented more than half the money from his life savings, most of it squirreled away from his generous Presidential salary. Fortunately, the $40,000 honorarium that accompanied the Nobel Prize had just arrived. On top of that came an unexpected $100,000 windfall, when Grayson rallied ten of Wilson's dearest friends—including Cleveland Dodge, Cyrus McCormick, Jr., and Bernard Baruch—to contribute toward the house's purchase. The Wilsons would take ownership on January 31, 1921.

Since 1912, Congress had considered granting annual pensions to retired Chief Executives, but it would not enact the Former Presidents Act until 1958. Wilson felt he still had to earn a living, to say nothing of spending his time constructively. Colleagues urged him to write a history of his eight years in the White House, but he refused, thinking there was little to add to what he considered a transparent administration. Publishers invited him to write everything from an elementary history of the United States to a biography of Jesus. To the demand for his memoirs, Wilson emphatically said, "There ain't going to be none." One day Edith found Woodrow alone in his study, at his typewriter. She was thrilled to see him in his familiar place, even more so when he announced that he had written the dedication to his book on government, which he now had the leisure to compose. With that, he pulled from the machine a slip of paper. The paragraph-long dedication to "E. B. W." explained that this was a book "in which I have tried to interpret life, the life of a nation, and she has shown me the full meaning of life." The rest of the page expressed his love for her in clauses rhapsodic enough to suggest writing the dedication meant more to him than writing the book. That proved to be the case, as that was the only page he would complete.

Toward the end of February 1921, Cabinet members visited the President individually to pay their final respects. Bainbridge Colby—who had performed admirably in his position, notably during a recent trip to Latin America—spoke graciously of the honor Wilson had bestowed upon him.

Pleased with their association, the President said, "Well, Colby, what are you going to do?" The Secretary of State said that he would probably return to New York and "open a musty law office again." After his current experience, that sounded dreary, he admitted, "but I must make a living."

"Well, I, too, must make a living," Wilson said. "As I was once a lawyer, why not open an office together here in Washington?" Colby asked if he really meant that. Wilson said yes—"I can't face a life of idleness; besides, I must so something to add to my income." The next day, Edith had occasion to see Colby, who asked about the seriousness of the President's offer. She said that he had blurted it impulsively. When he asked what she thought of the prospect, she said that she was ambivalent—"that his mind must have something to feed on" but that she did not see how he could actively participate in a practice. Intrigued, Colby said he could arrange the business in such a way as to obviate any objections.

On Tuesday, March 1, 1921, the Cabinet returned to the executive offices of the West Wing for its last official meeting. David Houston had arrived early and saw the President approach, walking with great difficulty across the White House grounds. It was a "brave" endeavor, he recalled, one so tragic that he looked away and waited in a nearby room in order for Wilson to situate himself without embarrassment. The President spent the bulk of the meeting reviewing the Administration's accomplishments. After tying up loose ends, the Cabinet members asked about his prospects for the future. "I am going to try to teach ex-presidents how to behave," he said. He could not help himself from adding, "There will be one very difficult thing for me, however, to stand, and that is Mr. Harding's English."

Their business behind them, Secretary Colby expressed on behalf of his colleagues the great distinction they all felt serving him "in the most interesting and fateful times of modern history." They promised to watch his progress toward better health and pray for his complete recovery. As David Houston, one of the three Cabinet members to last the entire Administration, prepared to speak, he noticed the President struggling with emotion. His lips trembled, and in his attempts to talk, tears rolled down his cheeks. "Gentlemen," he said after a pause, "it is one of the handicaps of my physical condition that I cannot control myself as I have been accustomed to do. God bless you all." They all rose, and each shook hands with him, saying a quiet goodbye. As a parting gift, the Cabinet members chipped in to purchase the President's chair from the government. It would join his furniture that was being pulled from storage and moved to S Street.

On March 3, the Wilsons invited the Hardings to tea. They met in the Red Room, where the President-elect sat with one of his legs slung over the arm of his chair.

The Wilsons rose early on the fourth, and by nine o'clock the Congressional leadership, Cabinet officers, and numerous aides had gathered for the arrival of the Hardings and the Coolidges. As they approached, Edith went upstairs to offer her husband any last-minute help, only to find him completely dressed in his morning coat and gray trousers. Brooks, the valet, held his top hat and gloves and handed him his cane. They took the elevator down and went to the Blue Room, arriving just as the Hardings entered. They proceeded to the porte cochere, where several cars waited—marking the first time that automobiles and not horse-drawn carriages would convey a President-elect to his inauguration. Still and motion-picture photographers captured the event.

Wilson had fully intended to observe the great traditions of the day, especially that most symbolic moment of orderly transition—accompanying his successor to the platform on the East Portico of the Capitol and watching him take the oath of office. But prior to Inauguration Day, Dr. Grayson had inspected the structure and discovered that reaching the platform would demand the President's climbing long, steep stairways, which he could not do.

Wilson and Harding drove together to the Capitol, behind a squadron of cavalry at a brisk trot, as all of Washington seemed to line the route. Wilson looked straight ahead, never acknowledging the crowds, for he insisted they had shown up to salute the new leader. The Presidential car arrived at the main entrance of the great domed building, where the fifty-five-year-old man of the hour sprang up the steps, leaving President Wilson to proceed alone to a small, private lower door around the corner—often used as a freight entrance—where an attendant with a wheelchair would take him inside. Edith, in a car right behind them, fumed over Harding's thoughtlessness. As Alice Roosevelt Longworth would later comment: "Mr. Harding was not a bad man. He was just a slob."

Dr. Grayson and Edith accompanied Wilson to an elevator that brought them to the second floor of the Senate, where he entered the President's Room for the last time. He had more than a half hour in which he signed a few bills and received the many dignitaries who had come to pay their respects, General Pershing and the Cabinet among them. Harding arrived with Coolidge and asked if Wilson wished to enter the Senate chamber for Coolidge's swearing in, but he declined, as his continued presence would only impede the day's program.

Shortly before noon, Senator Lodge entered, and Wilson's smile dissolved. "Mr. President," he said, "as Chairman of the Joint Committee I beg to inform you that the two houses of Congress have no further business to transact and are prepared to receive any further communications you may care to make."

"Tell them I have no further communication to make. I thank you for your courtesy," he replied in his most formal tone. "Good morning, Sir."

With that, it was time to inaugurate the twenty-ninth President of the United States. Harding and Coolidge approached Wilson, the former asking in a whisper if he would remain for the swearing in. "I'm sorry, Mr. President," Wilson said, "it cannot be done." The steps still daunted him. Turning to Senator Knox, he said, "Well, the Senate threw me down before, and I don't want to fall down myself now." The dignitaries all moved toward their places for the ceremonies, and the outgoing President and his wife and doctor slipped away.

The Marine Band played "Hail to the Chief," and the eyes of the world turned to the convivial Midwesterner on the East Portico of the Capitol raising his right hand. Few saw the hobbled figure struggling into the White House limousine, which then pulled away through the dead-quiet city streets. *The New York Times* could not refrain from characterizing Wilson's unheralded exit from the public stage as "tragic." Following two policemen on motorcycles, the car sped past 1600 Pennsylvania Avenue and then veered toward Massachusetts Avenue. There was silence in the limousine until Edith, resentful of Harding's discourtesy in leaving her husband to enter the Capitol on his own, could restrain herself no longer. She criticized him with all her fury.

And as the car turned onto tranquil S Street, Woodrow Wilson laughed.

17

RESURRECTION

*. . . and loe, I am with you alway, euen vnto the end
of the world . . .*

—MATTHEW, XXVIII:20

At 12:15 the White House limousine reached 2340 S
Street NW.

Only the most faithful had come to pay homage—too
few onlookers to warrant extra police to patrol that section
of town known as Kalorama. The secluded suburban en-
clave of large gracious houses—perched above much of the
city—stood in stately silence. For the first time since his
days as a college professor, Woodrow Wilson came home to
a house that he actually owned.

Waddy Butler Wood, a popular Washington architect,
had designed the Georgian Revival house in 1915 for a
Boston businessman and lobbyist who resided there during
Congressional sessions. Edith had immediately recognized
that it "fitted to the needs of a gentleman's home"—
offering dignity without pretension and comfort without
extravagance. The red-brick edifice, trimmed in limestone,
sat back from the road and stood four stories high. A trip-
tych of huge Palladian windows on the second floor dominated the façade of the house, while a modest two-pillared
portico, crowned with a wrought-iron railing, encased the
front door. Before moving in, Edith had commissioned

Wood to modify the house to accommodate its new tenants. He added a gated automobile entrance and a side door from the driveway to provide wheelchair access. Inside, the Otis Elevator Company installed an electric elevator.

The ex-President's car pulled into the new entrance, and Secret Service agent Starling assisted him from the vehicle to his chair, which he rolled into the elevator. Wilson thanked Starling for his years of loyal service. Edith shook his hand and offered her gratitude. The chauffeur drove Starling back to the Capitol, where he immediately began serving his next President, as he would three more after that. But as the limousine pulled away, Starling would later note, "Our hearts were behind us, where we had left a great man and a great woman."

Wilson ascended to the second floor, where a new team of servants—the late Mr. Galt's family retainers, Isaac and Mary Scott, whom Edith called "the best of the old-time coloured Virginia stock"—served luncheon in the dining room. The moment the meal had ended, Grayson suggested his patient excuse himself and rest. "Mr. President—," he said, only to be interrupted by the man himself, who corrected him: "Just Woodrow Wilson."

Although Edith fretted over all the abrupt changes Woodrow had to face, her immediate concerns faded the moment he left the elevator on the third floor and stood leaning on his cane at the threshold of his bedroom. Every personal article from his room at the White House had been placed in the same relative position on S Street. Edith had ordered a bed to match the dimensions of the Lincoln Bed—eight feet six inches by six feet two inches; footrests and easy chairs and pillows and tables and lamps were all situated exactly where Wilson would expect to find them. A favorite war-time banner and a Red Cross poster adorned the walls, and the brass shell from the first American bullet fired in the World War sat on the mantel. His familiar wooden shaving stand—complete with bowl, mirror, razor, and strop—stood near the south window. Edith was especially glad to see Ruth Powderly, the Navy nurse who had been attending him in the White House. Technically no longer attached to the former Commander in Chief, she had insisted on staying with him at least until he got settled. Touched though he was by her devotion and eager to retain her, he insisted that she keep her stay brief, as the government employed her, not he.

Wilson did allow himself one government perquisite. Upon Warren Harding's becoming President, Dr. Grayson's White House detail officially ended, subjecting him to reassignment. In an act of unexpected generosity, Harding had issued an unrequested order that Dr. Grayson be assigned to Washington, where "his services would be available to Mr. Wilson and that in no circumstances was he to be ordered elsewhere without the President's consent."

By the time Wilson had risen from his nap, Warren Gamaliel Harding's inauguration had ended. Seldom in the nation's history had the change in government swung so far in the opposite direction, as evidenced by the new President's stiff address. Twice the length of either of Wilson's inaugural addresses—and larded with "gamalielese," as H. L. Mencken referred to his pompous circumlocutions—Harding's speech exhorted Americans to "strive for normalcy" and to shun military, economic, or political commitments to any authority other than their own. The address set European ministers on edge. The venal arrogance and anti-intellectual tone appeared even starker alongside the hearty praise of Wilson that flooded the press that week. Jan Smuts of South Africa spoke for many foreign leaders in an article that ran in the *New York Evening Post* and was syndicated widely. Wilson had not failed in Paris, Smuts asserted, but humanity itself had let the world down. He maintained that the Covenant that Wilson had protected was "one of the great creative documents of human history" and that one day all nations would march behind its banner. Despite his legislative failure, Wilson had already "achieved the most enviable and enduring immortality," and future Americans "will yet proudly and gratefully rank him with Washington and Lincoln, and his fame will have a more universal significance than theirs." Smuts added that hundreds of years hence, "Wilson's name will be one of the greatest in history."

Frank I. Cobb seconded that opinion in a long panegyric in the New York *World.* "No other American has made so much world history as Woodrow Wilson," he observed. In drawing a sharp contrast to President Harding, Cobb reminded his readers that Wilson dealt almost exclusively with ideas. He cared little for party politics, and patronage bored him, as did the actual administration of government. He pronounced Wilson the most profound student of government among all the Presidents—with the exception of Madison, "the Father of the Constitution." Wilson's foreign policies had obscured the rest of his administration, he said, but his domestic policies alone guaranteed him an elevated position in American history. Cobb called Wilson's control over Congress for six years "the most impressive triumph of mind over matter known to American politics." Wilson's words led the nation not simply into a war but into a crusade, one in which "international relations have undergone their first far-reaching moral revolution."

A little after three that afternoon, Wilson appeared at one of his third-floor windows and discovered five hundred people outside cheering. For the rest of the afternoon, a steady stream of automobiles and primitive tour buses—"rubberneck" cars, they were called, horseless wagons that could carry twenty passengers—rode into S Street. Friends and former colleagues dropped by to pay their respects, including former Attorney General Palmer and former Secretary Daniels, various Democratic Senators and Representatives, and Joe Tumulty, whose future was uncertain now that Wilson had no further need for a chief of staff.

Guests entered a generous foyer, with a floor of black marble with white inset squares. To the immediate left was what became Wilson's front office, an ample room with a fireplace. John Randolph Bolling—an inhibited, slightly hunchbacked, younger brother of Edith's—moved there to serve as Wilson's secretary and chief usher. As the actual secretarial work would require a steadily decreasing number of hours, he devoted much of his time to assembling scrapbooks, producing a detailed timeline of his brother-in-law's life. He referred to his office as his "dugout," which his sister visited each day in order to tend to some of the mail. The room also became a temporary workspace for Ray Baker, who had earlier expressed his desire to write a book about the Paris Peace Conference and in time had received carte blanche to Wilson's papers. During this transitional period, Baker became Wilson's in-house biographer, and Edith especially appreciated having somebody they both trusted on hand to spend constructive time with her husband.

Beyond the dugout was a gentlemen's cloakroom, a trunk room for storage, and, after some remodeling of servants' quarters, a billiard room. The other side of the entrance hall had a ladies' coatroom, as well as the kitchen—with its zinc sink and early General Electric refrigerator—and the servants' dining room. A mezzanine hall, which served in part as an annex for Wilson's books, was up three marble steps from the entrance, and a wide stairway carried visitors to the second-floor drawing room. It was almost six hundred square feet, furnished with a combination of

French and English pieces that Edith and Woodrow brought from their prior marriages. Because the Wilsons would seldom entertain on a grand scale, this parlor became something of a museum, housing many of the artifacts from his Presidency: a mosaic of St. Peter, a gift from Pope Benedict XV; silver-framed photographs of King George and Queen Mary; and the hand-painted plates from the King and Queen of Belgium. A black Steinway D concert grand piano sat before a huge Gobelins tapestry depicting *The Marriage of Psyche*, a gift Ambassador Jusserand had presented to Edith in 1918 on behalf of the people of France.

In the opposite corner of the second floor was a large dining room, furnished with a graceful, narrow-legged Sheraton dining set. A portrait of Edith hung over the mantelpiece. The room connected to a solarium, its glass doors opening onto a terrace that faced south, overlooking a long, brick-walled garden with several large evergreens. The sunroom and its porch connected on its eastern side to the room where the Wilsons found themselves spending most of their time—a serene wood-paneled library. Before they had moved in, Edith had requested the installation of two bookcases to accommodate much of Wilson's eight-thousand-volume library. Furnished with his Cabinet chair from the White House and the great table from Prospect (which Hibben had shipped at the university's expense), the room became the Wilsons' inner sanctum.

The first day in his new house, Wilson could not resist glancing out the window. The crowd steadily swelled into the thousands. Each glimpse of him prompted applause, which he acknowledged with a wave. When a procession of League advocates marched down S Street and stopped in front of the house, he granted an audience to a few of its leaders. Wilson received them in the drawing room, where they presented him with a huge white wicker basket filled with roses and tulips and lilacs. He shook hands, saying, "It makes me very happy to see you on this occasion. I am proud of you all." When the delegation left, a man in the crowd outside called for three cheers for Wilson, which were loud enough to bring him to an open window. He smiled, bowed, and waved a white handkerchief. The crowd quieted, as it appeared that Wilson might speak. But instead, he raised his right hand to his throat, suggesting soreness, though Edith knew he simply feared that his voice would break. He smiled and bowed a few times and then fell from sight. He spent the rest of the day in his bedroom, and stayed there for the next several weeks.

In late March, Ray Baker went upstairs to talk with his subject. He found the sixty-four-year-old propped up in bed, "looking inconceivably old, gray, worn, tired"—his hair thin, his skin parchment yellow, his face an aquiline caricature of its former looks. Only the eyes still burned, suggesting the activity of his mind. Dr. Grayson had revealed that Wilson was suffering a recurrence of trouble with his prostate, but as Baker noted in his diary, the former President was suffering from more than physical ills.

> He has been lost. . . . He seems lonelier, more cut-off than ever before. His mind still works with power, but with nothing to work upon! Only memories & regrets. He feels himself bitterly misunderstood & unjustly attacked; and being broken in health, cannot rally under it.

Homer Cummings, the former chairman of the Democratic National Committee, paid a bedside visit one month later, and found Wilson "more depressed than I had ever known him to be." In discussing foreign affairs, Wilson proved as uncompromising as ever. He had a new antagonist to curse, Harding's Secretary of State, Charles Evans Hughes. Wilson spoke of the "deplorable consequences" of America's failure to ratify the Treaty and of America's "helpless attitude" at a time when Europe was attempting to rebuild itself. He feared the military leaders occupying the Ruhr District were sowing the seeds of future discontent. He claimed that the United States had abandoned "a fruitful leadership for a barren isolation." Most chilling, Wilson told Cummings that the course of events was "leading inevitably to another world war."

Cummings assured Wilson of his own faith in the League and that he relied on all the "philosophy" he could summon to endure the humiliation he felt as an American in seeing its defeat. "If I had nothing but philosophy to comfort me," Wilson said, "I should go mad." When Cummings asked him to expound, the old man could not find the words. His voice quavered and he broke down. Cummings caught only his suggestion that they were all but small instruments in a greater divine plan.

No President had left the White House feeling so utterly depleted as Woodrow Wilson. By mid-May, he was still lying in bed most days—"too much," thought Grayson, who urged him "to get at some work that will engage, even to exhaustion, his self-consuming mind." But Wilson lacked the spirit. He whiled away hours reading with his one good eye, mostly potboilers. He tried to remain indifferent to the news, but he could not always suppress his acrimony. Upon becoming the new Ambassador to Great Britain, Colonel George Harvey—Wilson's first important benefactor—delivered a speech that ridiculed the former President and the League. When Grayson referred to Harvey as a skunk, Wilson retorted without batting an eye, "No, no, Grayson, you are wrong: a skunk has a white streak."

Knowing her husband always responded to the call of duty, Edith fashioned an activity to get him out of bed in the morning. Stacks of mail arrived every day, and she told him that many warranted a reply. Randolph Bolling sorted them; and after Woodrow and Edith breakfasted together in the solarium—if she could get him that far—they would descend to the dugout. Wilson dictated a great number of short replies, leaving his brother-in-law to respond to those letters that did not require a personal touch. Wilson would then take his daily walk—back and forth across the vestibule. When he tired, he returned to his bedroom, where Isaac Scott had prepared his shaving stand. The one-armed exercise remained the most arduous of the day, but one he insisted upon performing himself. For the most part, Wilson remained in his dressing gown and slippers. Only the occasional guest could get him to the dining room for a formal meal. After lunch he rested for a solid hour. Bolling ushered those few with appointments to the library, where they would find Wilson in an armchair by the fire. Even when he remained in his bedroom, Wilson rigorously performed basic calisthenics to strengthen his muscles and received regular massages. So while his hair had turned white and he often replaced his trademark pince-nez with framed spectacles, Wilson's physique stayed relatively trim.

Nothing refreshed Wilson more than his motor trips around the city. He had especially liked one car in the Presidential fleet, the big black Vestibule Suburban car the government leased from Pierce-Arrow in Buffalo, New York. The six-cylinder, forty-eight-horsepower vehicle with its steering wheel on the right represented the height of luxury—eight feet high with running boards, silver-plated door handles and bud vases, German silver carriage lights, and whitewall tires—then selling for $9,250. Upon entering civilian life, he purchased the big black "used car" for

$3,000, personalizing it by having the Presidential seal on either side painted over and putting his initials in their place. He jazzed up the car with a few thin orange stripes on its body and orange accents on the spokes of the wheels. In further homage to Princeton, he replaced the Presidential hood ornament of an eagle with that of a tiger. Wherever the Wilsons drove each afternoon, the reception along the way lifted his spirits, as he invariably received cheers from the people he passed.

They always returned home by seven, so that Woodrow could change back into his dressing gown and eat dinner at a small table in the library. By the light of the fire and a dim lamp, Edith read to him until he was ready for sleep, usually around nine o'clock. While he prepared for bed, Edith and her brother would dine. Then she would visit her husband in his bedroom and read to him again until he drifted off. At that moment, he would reach for the Bible on his nightstand and read a few verses before falling asleep. The routine seldom varied, except when a local theater owner sent reels of the newest films to S Street so that Wilson could watch them in his library, employing the Douglas Fairbanks projector and a portable screen. A pianist would sometimes visit, playing the score on an upright instrument tucked in a corner of the room.

Starting in late April 1921, his favorite diversion came on Saturday nights, when the Wilsons and a few guests ritually went to Keith's Theatre on Fifteenth Street. The manager reserved seats in the last row of the theater, which not only allowed for easy access from its side door but also for Wilson to slip in without creating much of a scene. In no time his appearances had become so predictable, the public considered his presence a featured act. As Wilson entered in evening clothes, the entire audience would offer a standing ovation and the performers would present him with flowers. By the time the show ended, as many as a thousand people would swarm to the G Street entrance, where Wilson's Pierce-Arrow waited. Some of the entertainers would rush outside without taking time to remove their greasepaint. By summer, Wilson could enter the big car on his own, cheerfully doffing his hat. Sandwiches and ginger ale awaited at home, where he and Edith would stay up and review that night's songs and routines. The house was well stocked with a collection of records to which Wilson could listen on the Victrola: the latest recordings from Harry Lauder, John Philip Sousa, Nellie Melba, and Alma Gluck; Enrico Caruso's rendition of "Over There"; and the blackface comedy routines of Moran and Mack. By fall, Wilson often propped himself up in bed with a writing board, making notes in shorthand. He even took to sitting at a desk in order to type personal letters on his Underwood with one hand.

For all the optimistic signs of his activity, Wilson's physical health had not improved much. His regimen masked the fact that his left arm and leg were still paralyzed, and his digestive tract remained as problematic as ever. Those surrounding him believed his only real salvation lay in some "systematic mental occupation," at least an hour each day. Stockton Axson, for one, hoped something might spring from the conversation Wilson had started with Bainbridge Colby about a law partnership.

Colby had not only pursued the idea but also took it upon himself to open a few doors so that Wilson would be readily admitted to the New York State Bar and that of the District of Columbia. Just before noon on June 25, the former President arrived at the District's Supreme Court, where all the justices gathered to witness Wilson taking the oath.

The following week, Colby drafted the announcement of the new partnership Wilson & Colby, "Attorneys and Counsellors at Law," with offices at 1315 F Street (in the American National Bank Building) in Washington and at 32 Nassau Street in Manhattan. Colby would man the New York office and come to Washington once a week to consult with his partner in the capital, who intended to spend an hour in the office every day. Colby proposed mailing two thousand engraved notices, but after compiling his list of contacts, Wilson suggested five thousand. On August 16, Wilson rode to F Street, where he entered the building through the rear and walked to the elevator without assistance. He met Colby in their suite, where the bookshelves remained empty and the walls bare, but the large desks and richly upholstered chairs suggested a law firm that intended to remain in business for years to come.

But, for the second time in his life, Wilson displayed his inherent lack of interest in practicing law. As with the launch of his first practice, Wilson faced a dearth of clients—though this time for different reasons. The firm faced an ethics problem—as Wilson refused to accept any case in which he felt his former official position might influence the decision in his clients' favor. He presumed his partner would follow suit. In February 1922, for example, Costa Rica approached the new firm about a border dispute with Panama. In light of America's most recent dealings with the former during Wilson's last days in office, he deemed the clients inappropriate. A few months later, American banks hoped the firm might smooth over a deal pending with Ecuador. Wilson feared it would contribute to new monopolies in the South American nation and felt uncomfortable associating his name with the transaction. Again, he asked Colby to "comprehend my feelings and indulge my scruple."

The most intriguing potential clients who hoped to engage Wilson & Colby were officers of the Sinclair Consolidated Oil Corporation, who sought representation in two investigations about to take place before the United States Senate. One case dealt with the fluctuating price of gasoline; the other concerned Sinclair's recent acquisition of property in Wyoming known as Teapot Dome. Through some sleight of hand endorsed by Harding, the land had come under the jurisdiction of Interior Secretary Albert B. Fall, who had, in turn, leased the vast oil field to Sinclair. Colby wrote Wilson that this promised to be "a very substantial and important employment"—a high-profile hearing with compensation in six figures. Colby also looked forward to working with ex-Senator George Sutherland of Utah as co-counsel. "Do you see any objection to accepting this employment?" he asked his partner.

Wilson did. A private oil company seeking representation from a former President whose conservation policies opposed such leases seemed highly suspect. Wilson only knew what he had read in the newspapers, which gave the impression "that some ugly business is going on in respect to the Teapot Dome," but he knew that "the oil companies are constantly attempting to invade that Reserve with or without right." Worse, Wilson considered Senator Sutherland "one of the most thick headed and impenetrable of the Senate partisans." Again, Colby deferred to Wilson's judgment. After yet another instance in which Colby had to refuse a $500,000 retainer for a case he felt sure would not compromise Wilson's integrity, he spoke to Edith. "Of course I want to go on as long as we can hold out," he said, "but day after day I sit in my office and see a procession walk through—thousands and thousands of dollars—and not one to put in our pockets. It is a sublime position on the part of your husband, and I am honoured to share it as long as we can afford it."

The Wilsons appreciated Colby's steadfastness, but Edith urged her husband to end the partnership, freeing Colby to earn a living. Wilson regretted only that he had hindered Colby more than helped him, especially as Colby had been so solicitous in his attempts to engage Wilson in a new occupation when he clearly had little interest. Tellingly, after his first visit to the offices, Wilson never set foot in them again. His only residual from the enterprise was a distribution of $5,000, to which he felt so unentitled, he blew the money on a Rauch & Lang electric car for Edith, a newer model of the vehicle she had famously driven around Washington before their marriage.

Colby would announce the termination of the partnership in December 1922, saying that Wilson wished to redirect his energies to politics. The midterm elections that year reflected the unpopularity of the Harding Administration—halving the Republican lead in the Senate, and putting the Democrats within striking distance of recapturing the House, what with a gain of more than seventy-five Representatives. Wilson said the people regretted the verdict they had delivered in 1920, "and are preparing to render one in favor of the policies they then unwisely condemned." The party was coming back, Colby asserted, "on a tide of revived Wilsonism." Wilson himself, Colby suggested, wanted to "direct the flowing of this tide." And Colby was one of the few who knew that the former President was, in fact, considering another run for the White House.

Madness did not fuel this pipe dream so much as anger. Within Harding's first months in office, Congress introduced the highest tariffs in American history. The all-Republican government—with its protectionism and allegiance to big business—would make every attempt it could to erase Wilson's record.

On August 25, 1921, the United States signed the Treaty of Berlin, which officially ended the war with Germany. This neutered version of Wilson's Treaty of Versailles incorporated the Lodge reservations. That week, the nation also signed treaties with Austria and Hungary. The Revenue Act of 1921 dramatically reduced taxes for the very rich, which Treasury Secretary Andrew Mellon argued was necessary in order to stimulate economic growth. During his first Christmas in office, Harding commuted the sentence of Eugene V. Debs.

More than politics, White House ethics had changed. The capital buzzed with stories of the President's liquor consumption, poker games, extramarital affairs, and cronies in high places, not the least of whom were Secretary Fall and Attorney General Harry M. Daugherty, a renowned Ohio political fixer. The louche President set the tone for the rest of the nation, encouraging licentiousness. In the words of the country's new literary sensation, F. Scott Fitzgerald, "America was going on the greatest, gaudiest spree in history"—as a lost generation ran wild in what Fitzgerald christened "the Jazz Age." To many across the nation, the priggish Woodrow Wilson had never looked more attractive.

"Never," observed Ray Baker from his desk in the dugout, "was there such a swift change of public regard for a man than for Mr. Wilson since he left the White House." This wave of admiration manifested itself in scores of ways, beyond the appreciation expressed in the press and the batches of mail. The house at 2340 S Street became a highlight of the rubberneck wagon tours of Washington, and every afternoon at three o'clock, people gathered to watch the Wilsons as they departed for their daily drive. In May, the Reverend Sylvester Beach of Princeton reported from the General Assembly of the Presbyterian Church in Indiana that the entire convocation rose to its feet and cheered for five minutes upon a Czech minister's mention of Woodrow Wilson and the League of Nations. President Alderman of the University of Virginia wrote Wilson that many of the school's students, acting upon "an independent impulse," raised money to place a bronze tablet on his former room at 31 West Range. When the boys asked Alderman for an appropriate inscription, he suggested five words from Horace—"*Justum ac tenacem propositi virum*" ("A just man who sticks to his principles"). Plaques, bridges, and streets in Wilson's name popped up around the world, from Montevideo to Bordeaux, including an avenue in Paris and a drive in Los Angeles. More than fifty Woodrow Wilson clubs sprouted on college campuses in appreciation of his "generous service to humanity." Many of the younger generation felt called to service by his "inspired leadership to establish justice and peace as the basis for a new international conception of freedom."

In the meantime, several prominent women banded to promulgate Wilson's principles. They took their idea to Cleveland Dodge; and soon more Wilson supporters, including the members of the Woodrow Wilson clubs, joined this movement to establish "a nation-wide tribute to Woodrow Wilson in appreciation of his great service for world peace." At a meeting at New York's Biltmore Hotel, several admirers developed a plan to raise $500,000 for the cause, and formed a steering committee that included Henry Morgenthau, Adolph Ochs, Bernard Baruch, Daisy Harriman, and Franklin D. Roosevelt, who served as chairman. Their initial impulse was to give several substantial prizes each year to the college students who wrote the best papers on "international subjects related to the development of the League of Nations." This endowment became the cornerstone for the Woodrow Wilson Foundation and paved the way for future institutions that would link policy and scholarship in his name, most notably the Woodrow Wilson International Center for Scholars. Roosevelt maintained an active interest in the organization despite being struck ill in August 1921, at his summer home on Campobello Island. It left him paralyzed below the waist. By September, the Roosevelts announced that he had poliomyelitis but that it was a mild case that would have temporary effects. His unabating work on the Foundation helped conceal the actual seriousness of his condition.

On October 4, 1921, President Harding wrote Wilson of an "unusual assemblage" to take place at Arlington National Cemetery—the burial of an unknown soldier from the World War. Great Britain and France had each established a similar monument the year prior on Armistice Day; and an act of Congress in Wilson's final minutes as President authorized the exhumation of an unnamed American soldier from one of the cemeteries in France for entombment in a new marble sarcophagus at Arlington. "Undoubtedly it will be the part of the President to have a presidential party of a considerable number on that day," Harding wrote, "and I have thought it would be fine if you could find it agreeable for you and Mrs. Wilson to accept an invitation to become members thereof."

Although his disability would prevent him from visiting the grave, Wilson was determined to pay his respects to the fallen by riding in the procession that would transport the Unknown Soldier's casket from the Capitol to the cemetery. He requested an open carriage instead of a motorcar. After a series of slights on the part of the Harding White House, the Wilsons arrived at the appointed minute in their victoria, their servant Isaac Scott sitting with the coachman. No guard appeared to escort them, and when a police sergeant led them to the forming parade, they discovered that their place had already been filled. As the procession began to move down Pennsylvania Avenue, behind the flag-draped caisson, the Wilsons had to wait and then wedge themselves unceremoniously into the first available space, far behind the officials and between two phalanxes of marching veterans. Thousands lined the great boulevard, observing the passing of the Unknown Soldier in solemn stillness.

Then, as the two-horse carriage bearing the Wilsons appeared—the former President in a dark suit and overcoat and high silk hat, and wearing a small red poppy in his lapel—whispers spread through the crowd. Slowly a ripple of applause broke out. When all the observers realized that it was Wilson himself, there was a steady wave of approbation that lasted the entire way to the White House. There Wilson detached from the procession, as he had been instructed, and retreated to S Street. He told a newspaperman that the ovation had embarrassed him "because it was given in a funeral procession."

Later that day, many found themselves drawn to S Street, spontaneously paying homage to the man some were calling "the Known Soldier." Not until Wilson appeared at his front door at three o'clock did he discover twenty thousand people had amassed in front of the house. For ten minutes they roared, offering three cheers for the League of Nations, another three cheers for Woodrow Wilson, and three more for "the greatest soldier of them all!" Leaning hard on his cane, the former President walked down the five front steps of his house in order to greet three disabled veterans in a car in his driveway. Then he went back inside, where he and Edith appeared at a window on the second floor. The crowd, not ready to disperse, again demanded his presence.

He returned to the front door, where several committees of Wilson societies had gathered. Hundreds of children waited as well, one of whom handed him a letter, which said, "Young as we are we have learned to admire you and the great principles for which you stand. . . . We, as future citizens of the United States, will do our best to perpetuate these ideals you have fought for so bravely." A member of the League of Nations Association spoke of the burial at Arlington, saying, "We haven't forgot the ideals for which we went to war and for which this soldier died." He assured Wilson that his work "shall not die."

"I wish that I had the voice to reply and to thank you for the wonderful tribute that you have paid me," Wilson told the crowd. "I can only say God bless you." Silence followed, until one man boomed, "Long live the best man in the world!" The crowd cheered once again, and tears streamed from Wilson's eyes. Trembling, he reached for Edith's hand. Like most of the crowd, she cried as well. The throng spontaneously broke into "My Country, 'Tis of Thee," and the Wilsons held on to each other as he said goodbye and kissed his wife's hand. They entered the house, but the people remained for another hour, silent and still.

The spiritual nature of the afternoon was lost on none of its witnesses. Even Senator John Sharp Williams of Mississippi, who had served in Congress since 1893, had been drawn to S Street. He found himself as inspired as all the others, who wanted nothing "political or actual to be accomplished," he wrote Wilson, "except to show good will to you for the present, faith in you for the future, and an endorsement of you in the past." The tide had definitely turned, he said, in its feelings not only toward Wilson but also his beliefs.

No less a figure than muckraker and teacher Ida Tarbell, who had been lecturing across the country, discovered that Americans were awakening to the responsibilities of foreign affairs and Wilson's approach to them. After the political denunciation he had received the year prior, she wrote an article for *Collier's* called "The Man They Cannot Forget," in which she asked why people from so many walks of life revered him. Her rhetorical answer lay in his having inspired their greatest moments through the example of his deeds as well as the power of his words. She believed the essence of Wilson's mission on earth was to elevate mankind. He made overused American catchphrases and high-minded political rhetoric real—personal and deep, "the working basis on which men may strive to liberty of soul and peaceful achievement." Above all, she wrote:

> He made them literally things to die for, lifting all of our plain, humble thousands who never knew applause or wealth or the honor of office into the ranks of those who are willing to die for an ideal—the highest plane that humans reach.

Although Wilson had never worn a military uniform, soldiers and their families held him in special regard. They felt he had sacrificed as much as they had, and they said as much in the letters that poured into S Street. An especially moving display occurred one Saturday night at Keith's Theatre, when an elderly actor came before the footlights and addressed the audience. "My only boy was killed in the war," he said, "and not in words can I express how much I miss him." He described a recent visit to Walter Reed Army Hospital, where he encountered what he called "pieces of still living men." He candidly admitted that he found comfort knowing his boy "was sleeping peacefully in France" and not among the shattered victims he had visited. "But one of the greatest casualties this war has produced," he said, on a note of pride, "is the distinguished man who is in this audience tonight." Audience members wept openly as they rose to their feet and cheered, some leaping onto their seats and waving handkerchiefs. A girl stepped down from the stage and walked to seat U-21 to hand Woodrow Wilson a bunch of flowers.

There was a Wilson revival in the making, and his most devout follower of the last decade had to scurry to find his place in it. Not even on S Street—where Bolling performed secretarial duties, Baker advised, and Colby, Baruch, Norman Davis, and Louis Brandeis appeared for political conversation—was there a specific role for Tumulty. In November 1921, he published *Woodrow Wilson As I Know Him*, a hagiographic memoir, meant to show not only Wilson's great intellect but also his "great heart." At least one critic found the book an "incredibly vulgar, oleographic caricature," with the author basking in reflected glory. While Wilson never displayed any interest in it, the volume was just one of many that quickly appeared.

With access both to Wilson and his papers, which had no strings attached, Ray Baker published a three-volume work entitled *Woodrow Wilson and World Settlement*. It contributed enormously to Wilson's growing popularity. He allowed that Wilson's mission to Paris had failed to actualize his dreams, but he gave the public a sense of Wilson's own estimation of his work there. He had told Baker one afternoon while lying in bed, "I am not an impractical idealist, nor did I, at Paris, want everything torn up by the roots and made over according to some ideal plan." With Professor William E. Dodd of the University of Chicago—already the author of a short Wilson biography, and a future Ambassador to Germany—Baker produced six volumes of Wilson's public papers. With a healthy monthly stipend from Bernard Baruch, Baker spent another fourteen years writing an eight-volume biography to honor the former President.

Marginalized, Tumulty frantically sought ways to reenter Wilson's life. On April 5, 1922, he wrote the "Governor," as he continued to call him, that the National Democratic Club of New York City was holding its annual Jefferson banquet that week and that it would "hearten and inspire" the audience to receive a message from him. Even an expression of regret at not being able to attend would suffice, Tumulty said, as it would also extend Tumulty's credibility as an insider to the former President. Wilson refused. He felt it would be "quite meaningless" unless he offered a serious expression of his view about the current national situation, and he did not consider this an appropriate occasion for breaking his silence.

The next morning, Tumulty called Mrs. Wilson and asked if she could not get her husband to send a letter to the dinner. Edith asked if Tumulty had not received his reply. Although he had, he fretfully stressed the importance of Wilson's writing something and beseeched her to persuade him. "No, Mr. Tumulty," Edith said, "you know him well enough to know that when he has thought a thing out and decided it there is no use to continue arguments." Then Tumulty said he had an important personal matter he needed to discuss with Wilson, and he asked if she could at least arrange for a meeting that afternoon. She respected the wish and set the meeting for three o'clock, just before the Wilsons' daily drive. An anxious Tumulty arrived early and sat in the dugout with Randolph Bolling, asking him if Mrs. Wilson had gotten Wilson to compose a message for the dinner. Bolling thought not; and because Wilson was feeling low that day, he recommended that Tumulty not even raise the matter.

Because of the "personal" nature of Tumulty's mission, Edith left the two men alone. By the time she returned from an errand, he had gone. She said to Woodrow that she hoped Tumulty had not bothered him about that message for the dinner. He said, "No, I am glad to say he had the good taste not to mention it." When she asked what he had come to discuss, it turned out to be a vague conversation about American ideals, clearly a hasty substitute for what he had hoped to talk about. Days later, the morning newspapers wrote up the speech Governor Cox had made at the Jefferson banquet . . . along with the message "from Woodrow Wilson": "Say to the Democrats of New York that I am ready to support any man who stands for the salvation of America, and the salvation of America is justice to all classes." Because Cox had addressed those very points, the audience logically interpreted the banquet as the unofficial launch of his campaign—with Wilson's endorsement. "My husband," Edith recalled a decade later, "was thunderstruck."

Wilson summoned Edith's brother and asked him to dispatch a letter to Louis Wiley of *The New York Times* expressing the former President's dismay—not only because he had never sent any message but also because of his suggested support for Cox to head the ticket again. He valued Cox as a loyal friend of the League but believed defeated teams required new captains to turn them around. Later that morning, while shaving, he told

Edith it had just occurred to him that Tumulty had been at the banquet and that perhaps he could shed light on what had occurred. Dictating to her, he said, "It is obviously my duty as well as my privilege to probe the incident to the bottom."

A chagrined Tumulty hastened from New York, and after many desperate hours attempting to see Wilson in person, he sheepishly owned up to having composed the message himself. He realized the embarrassment he had caused his former boss and the need to rectify what he maintained was a misunderstanding on his part. He offered a contorted explanation to *The New York Times*. While he assumed responsibility for the delivery of the fabricated message, he wrote Wilson, "I think you will hold me blameless for the unjust interpretations put upon it."

Tumulty knew he had not adequately apologized, and so the next day he sent Wilson a more detailed explanation, which only dug a deeper hole for himself. He realized he had betrayed the Governor's trust, but he presumed Wilson would take into account that since the earliest days of their association, as he said, "I have had but one thought, but one ambition, and that was to serve you and the great purposes which I know lay close to your heart." Now he prostrated himself, affirming, "You will find me as a mere private in the ranks, deferring to your unselfish leadership and defending your policies at every turn of the long road which lies ahead of us." If Wilson found it necessary to rebuke him, Tumulty said, he would not complain, nor would he "wince under the blow nor . . . grow in the least faint-hearted or dispirited." In all his protestations, Tumulty never simply acknowledged that Wilson had explicitly stated he never wished to send a message in the first place. He was shown the same door as Hibben and House before him.

Several days later, Dr. Grayson asked Wilson whether he had had a good night, and he said no. "I am not worrying about the Tumulty incident," he told his doctor. "If Tumulty had been my son and had acted as he did, I would have done the same thing." But it clearly weighed on his mind, heavily enough for Edith to suggest that Wilson air their full correspondence in the press. "No," he said, "let the unpleasant affair fade out. Tumulty will sulk for a few days, then come like a spanked child to say that he is sorry and wants to be forgiven." Days later, Grayson expressed regret that Wilson had severed relations with Tumulty. Wilson snapped that the doctor did not know what he was talking about and that it was none of his business. During a house call a few days later, Wilson asked his wife and attendant to leave the room, so that he could discuss a private matter with Grayson. "I want to apologize for the way in which I spoke to you the other day," he said. Thereupon he showed Grayson the correspondence detailing the entire affair, which had culminated in Tumulty's evasive apology. For his part, the doctor never thought ill of his patient, always understanding his frustration. As Grayson explained one day to Axson, "He has to hate *somebody*."

Despite his mixed feelings for Tumulty, Wilson never questioned his loyalty nor forgot his service. He would even encourage New Jersey leaders to back him for the Senate because of his extensive political training. But Joseph Tumulty all but retired from politics, devoting the rest of his career to a successful law practice. Woodrow Wilson never saw him again.

In truth, more had contributed to this severance than had met the eye. Once he had moved to Kalorama, Wilson's political itch had flared up, and Tumulty's actions had encouraged it further. As was known to but a handful of people, Wilson had been preparing a white paper for months, a refreshening of progressive principles for the new decade. In June 1921, he approached the chief architect of the New Freedom, Louis Brandeis, and found him willing to collaborate on this manifesto, despite its blatantly political nature. Either out of gratitude that Wilson had elevated him to the Supreme Court or perhaps because his contributions were meant to be unofficial, he actively participated, certainly eager to advance his own progressive ideas. Wilson did not mention that he planned to offer this statement as a platform for the Democratic Presidential nominee in 1924, but as he called upon such members of his administration as Colby, Houston, Baruch, and Norman Davis, and party supporters Thomas Chadbourne and Frank I. Cobb, to help him shape a casual collection of opinions into a systematic set of issues, one could hardly imagine any other purpose for their work.

"The Document," as the collaborators called it, contained nineteen points. They included the necessity to reconstruct the progressive countries of the world and the belief that a broad-minded, liberal agenda could best provide reform. Furthermore, the policy statement demanded the immediate resumption of America's international obligations as established in the Treaty of Versailles, and it condemned the group of men who catalyzed the current "evil results as the most partisan, prejudiced, ignorant and unpatriotic group that ever misled the Senate of the United States."

Despite Republican control of the government, the Document pointed out that the Republican Party had not enacted a single piece of ameliorative legislation in the last three years. It also demanded a revision of the tax laws that would impose less upon the lower and middle classes; and it advocated a new Cabinet member, a Secretary of Transportation, who could untangle the complex skein of local and national laws to improve the flow of people and goods. "The world has been made safe for democracy," the Document read, "but democracy has not yet made the world safe against irrational revolution."

Over the next two and a half years, Wilson reworked the Document. With his longtime belief in the co-operation of government between the branches, he added a paragraph that the President and the members of his Cabinet should be accorded a place on the Congressional floor whenever the legislature was discussing affairs entrusted to the executive branch. The President should take part and be held accountable. With such matters occupying his thoughts, Wilson did nothing to suggest that he supported Cox for the 1924 nomination, because he had set his sights on his own nominee—once again, the only man who could reassert those programs that were "the best assurance for the promotion of social welfare, of justice, and of individuals and of national prosperity."

Support for his own candidacy presented itself almost every day, as the house on S Street became a mecca for liberals. In April 1922, for example, the League of Women Voters held an international conference in Baltimore to discuss world peace and social reform, gathering delegates from twenty-two nations of the Western Hemisphere. On the twenty-eighth, a thousand of them descended upon Wilson's house, merely to pay tribute to a man who had championed both peace and women's rights. Dressed in a frock coat and silk hat, he greeted them at his front door, looking especially frail that day and explaining that he was unable to make an address. He favored them instead with a limerick. The women responded with a chorus of "America," "Onward, Christian Soldiers," and a lusty cheer for the League of Nations. Throughout the spring, Wilson maintained a substantive correspondence with Cordell Hull, chairman of the Democratic National Committee, who sought his advice about mobilizing the party during the upcoming midterm elections. Even Vice President Coolidge paid homage to the League of Nations that June in a commencement address, praising its "noble aspiration for world association and understanding," its imperfections notwithstanding.

By summer, Wilson believed the Democrats would return to power, finding themselves with "the greatest opportunity for service that has ever been accorded it." He believed the Harding Administration, with its attempt to "reestablish all the injustices of the past," had disenchanted the electorate, resisting "progress" with its chatter of getting back to normalcy. When the Council of the League of Nations confirmed the British mandate of Palestine in July, Zionist organizations remembered with gratitude Wilson's "distinguished and unselfish cooperation" on their behalf. When Supreme Court Justice John Hessin Clarke announced his retirement that September, he told Wilson that with his remaining strength, he intended to do all he could to promote American entrance into the League. "To me," he said, "it is the indispensable as well as the noblest political conception of our time and, very certainly, to have launched it as you did makes secure for you one of the highest places in history." And when Emily Newell Blair, a former suffragist and founder of the League of Women Voters, realized that women were not voting as a reliable bloc, she took it upon herself to organize them as Democrats. She did this, she wrote Wilson in October, "because of the debt the American women owe you, not only for the suffrage but for the fight you made for ideals." By autumn a Democratic sweep in the midterm elections was in the air, and with it even the growing possibility that the senior Senator from Massachusetts would be unseated.

Henry Cabot Lodge won his sixth term, eking out a victory by a few thousand votes. Wilson wrote his daughter Jessie that he hoped the election results at least "gave him a jolt which may make even him comprehend the new temper of the voters." The Democrats did not recapture either chamber, but they did enjoy considerable success—gaining five seats in the Senate and seventy-six seats in the House, putting legislative control within their reach. Members of the Farmer-Labor Party found greater kinship among Democrats, as the agrarian Midwest and the members of the American Federation of Labor no longer saw the Republican Party sensitive to their needs. Immigrants in the big cities became firmly Democratic. Two years earlier, New Yorkers had swept Governor Alfred E. Smith out of office. Now they apologized by awarding him a landslide victory over his replacement. Across the country, Democratic victories rebuked two years of

Harding and his policies—especially the tariff—and he was already being talked about as a one-term President. On the midterm Election Night, tens of thousands of people milled outside newspaper offices in Washington, and when one paper projected a picture of Woodrow Wilson on a screen, the crowd cheered lustily. Daniel C. Roper, Wilson's manager from the 1916 campaign, sent congratulations to his former candidate; and without divulging any private plans, an encouraged Wilson wired back, "Twenty four will complete the result which twenty two had begun."

Four days later, five thousand admirers flocked to S Street for what had come to be called "the annual Armistice Day pilgrimage." Wilson totemized the World War's hopes for a peaceful future, and this year such luminaries as former Ambassador Morgenthau, University of Virginia President Alderman, and former Secretary of Agriculture Meredith joined the exuberant throngs. Streetcar lines added extra cars to transport the worshipful to Kalorama. Wilson appeared, with a big malacca cane in one hand and looking healthier than he had in years. Festivities began outside his front door with a medley of Southern songs. Then Morgenthau spoke, referring to the election results as a rejection of "materialism and selfishness." A few heard Wilson exclaim, "Hear, hear!"

Hooking his cane in the upper pocket of his coat, Wilson stood on his own two feet. He spoke for several minutes, delivering his longest address since Pueblo. With all his old passion, he spoke of that "group in the United States Senate who preferred personal partisan motives to the honor of their country and the peace of the world." He reminded the crowd, "Puny persons who are now standing in the way will presently find that their weakness is no match for the strength of a moving Providence." Wilson retreated inside the house, only to reappear in a second-story window, with Edith at his side. For ten minutes the fans cheered. And then the sea of people parted, forming two long lines on either side of S Street, so that the Wilsons could ride through for their daily outing. Block after block, he acknowledged the roaring crowd, smiling and raising his hat.

Upon turning sixty-six, Wilson received two unexpected tributes. On December 27, 1922, Franklin Roosevelt informed him that in little more than a year, the organizers of the Woodrow Wilson Foundation had raised $1 million. The fund's income would be used, Roosevelt said, to prompt public welfare, democracy, and peace through justice. The next day, Wilson's birthday, he welcomed four of the Foundation's board members and learned that most of their funding had come not from wealthy benefactors (such as Henry Ford, who had contributed $10,000) but from thousands of ordinary citizens, each of whom supported his vision with a dollar. The delegation left Wilson virtually speechless. "I wish I could have controlled my voice so I could really have expressed what I felt," he told Edith afterward; "but I could not trust myself lest I break down and cry." Despite a cold downpour that day, more than a hundred people waited in the rain, hoping for a glimpse of Wilson.

The second extraordinary gesture came from the United States Senate, an expression of "pleasure and joy" upon hearing of the former President's continued recovery to good health. "When all of us are forgotten," said Senator William J. Harris of Georgia in introducing the resolution, "the name of Woodrow Wilson will be remembered as the greatest of the century." While many of the Republicans appeared to be busy during the actual vote, there was no debate and the resolution passed with a hearty chorus of "ayes." Vice President Coolidge appended his own personal greeting in a letter that accompanied the message that was sent to S Street. Wilson told Dr. Grayson, "Think of them passing it and not meaning it. Of course, I do not mean to say that all who voted for it were not sincere, for I know many were sincere, but I feel sure some of them were not. I would much rather have had three Senators get together and draw up a resolution and have it passed with sincerity than the one that was passed today."

Wilson thought of reentering the public arena as he had entered years ago—through the written word. He conceived an ambitious book, which he was calling *The Destiny of the Republic*. It would "set forth . . . the ideals and principles which have governed my life, and which have also . . . governed the life of the nation." He tried typing with his one good hand, and when that proved too awkward, he dictated passages to Edith.

The opening lines of his text articulated the basis of what his successors would call "Wilsonianism":

Unlike the government of every other great state, ancient or modern, the government of the United States was set up for the benefit of mankind as well as for the benefit of its own people,—a most ambitious enterprise, no doubt, but undertaken with high purpose, with clear vision, and without thoughtful and deliberate unselfishness, and undertaken by men who were no amateurs but acquainted with the world

they lived in, practiced in the conduct of affairs, who set the new government up with an ordiliness [*sic*] and self-possession which marked
them as men who were proud to serve liberty with the dignity and restraint of true devotees of a great ideal.

Wilson never wrote much more than a few paragraphs of the book. As
with his prior attempts, his lavish dedication to Edith was its most realized passage.

A year passed before he could tease any of his thoughts into even a
short essay, which he did in "The Road Away from Revolution." Wilson
pecked out a thousand words on his typewriter with his right hand, arguing that the Russian Revolution had been an attack against capitalism, a
system that was not above reproach. Sometimes he worked late at night,
insisting he could not sleep until he had committed his thoughts to paper.
He said civilization could not survive materially unless it were redeemed
spiritually, that it could be saved "only by becoming permeated with the
spirit of Christ and being made free and happy by the practices which
spring out of that spirit."

Former propaganda chief George Creel had once volunteered to act as
his representative in placing any of his writing. In April 1923, Wilson
asked him to consider handling this essay. But upon reading the piece,
Creel felt the best he could do for Wilson was to suppress it. In gentle but
frank terms, he wrote Edith that its publication—what would be Wilson's
first public document since his collapse—would not live up to the people's
expectations. While strongly advising against printing it for the public, he
realized such advice would crush Wilson's confidence and might push him
back into depression.

The Wilsons could have used the money that newspaper syndication of
the article would pay, but Creel put his client's psychological needs before
the financial. He spoke to an editor friend who offered $2,000 for the
rights to publish it in *Collier's*, where it could appear with dignity and without exaggerating its importance by turning this trifle into a media event.
Creel wrote up a second letter for Edith to show her husband, a recommendation to accept the less lucrative deal because syndication would entail "a huckstering campaign that will undoubtedly have many disagreeable
reactions." Edith considered how best to approach Woodrow.

Days later, in the Pierce-Arrow, with Stockton Axson there for moral support, she screwed up enough courage to say that somebody had read the piece and did not think it did justice to him. His temper flared—not with Edith necessarily, but with all the people who had been urging him for months to write something. "They kept after me to do this thing," he said in irritation, "and I did it." Edith tried to mollify him, telling him not to get on his "high horse about this." She simply wanted to forward the suggestion that he expand the piece by amplifying his argument. He read between the lines. "I have done all I can, and all I am going to do," Wilson insisted. "I don't want those people bothering me any more." When they returned home, Wilson went upstairs to his bedroom, and Axson sat in the dugout. After a few minutes, Axson heard a peculiar sound—Edith, in the hallway, was sobbing. He went to console her in this, one of the few times anybody ever saw her break down. "All I want to do is just to help in any way I can," she insisted. "I am not urging him to do things he doesn't want to do. I just want to help and I just don't know how to help."

Axson examined the article and suggested cutting, not lengthening—thus lessening it from a significant treatise to a simple pronouncement. Edith asked if he would present his findings to her husband, which he did. "Why, you see exactly the point," Wilson said. "Fix it." After Axson had excised a few paragraphs and retyped the article, Wilson submitted it himself to *The Atlantic Monthly*, which had published his essays in the past. Editor Ellery Sedgwick gratefully accepted the piece for $300. It reached a fraction of the audience it might have, and the author abandoned all further literary efforts.

Wilson recognized the silent strain under which Edith had functioned over the last five years. For a while he inquired about the cottages at the Grove Park Inn, a popular resort in Asheville, North Carolina, where he imagined they might spend a few months. As he never proceeded in his negotiations with the hotel proprietor, the junket met the same fate as the renewal of his law practice, the writing of his book on political theory, and his third run for the Presidency—though he did go so far as to make notes for his acceptance speech and his third inaugural address. Then, thinking his real contribution to society had been in education, not politics, Wilson contacted a former student, then at the Rockefeller Foundation, to investigate the possibility of his becoming a university president once again—only this time at a new school, one willing to accept his innovative teaching concepts. All these gauzy visions allowed him to maintain that fine line between illusion and delusion—to imagine such exploits without having to confront the hard facts that they were beyond his capability. Indeed, for all the liveliness of Wilson's dreams, he remained prone to exhaustion and mood swings, a stroke victim with advancing arteriosclerosis who was unable to navigate a flight of stairs, a handicap then considered a fatal political liability.

Presidential incapacity became a national story once again—in the summer of 1923, when Warren Harding embarked upon a cross-country tour to the Pacific Coast. For months it had been whispered that the robust fifty-five-year-old President-elect who had bounded up the Capitol steps to his inauguration only twenty-nine months earlier had grown exceedingly tired in office as the result of heart disease. Harding showed symptoms of food poisoning in Vancouver, Canada, rushed through a speech in Seattle, and had to cancel another in Portland. On August 2, he suffered a fatal heart attack in his hotel suite in San Francisco.

The news shocked Wilson. Despite the great differences in their politics and personalities—and the fact that Wilson thought him a "fool," except for the fact that there was "nothing in his conduct that the country can laugh at with the slightest degree of enjoyment"—the two Presidents had maintained a cordial relationship. Wilson sent prompt and "profound sympathy" to Harding's widow.

By the light of a kerosene lamp at their house in rural Plymouth Notch, Vermont, Vice President Calvin Coolidge took the oath of office from his father, a notary public. The following day, Coolidge invited Wilson to participate in Harding's funeral services on Wednesday, the eighth. Wilson appreciated the honor of joining the procession, in which he hoped to include his wife and Dr. Grayson, but his lame leg, he said, made it impracticable for him to attend the exercises at the Capitol, where Harding's body was to lie in state. On the day of the services, Wilson waited in his open car outside the White House for more than an hour until the flag-covered casket was carried from the East Room to the artillery caisson. While Marines in full-dress uniforms wilted under the hot August sun, Wilson remained collected—until one dazed Colonel rushed up, wondering if he might ask a question. "Certainly," said Wilson. "Could you tell me whether Senator Lodge has arrived or not?" Wilson uttered that he could not. Then he turned to Grayson and asked "what asylum that Colonel had escaped from." For the next few minutes, the *New York Times* reporter noticed that Wilson was visibly moved, his eyes fixed upon the coffin of his successor, nine years his junior. As Wilson's car rode down Pennsylvania Avenue, following Coolidge and the new Chief Justice, William Howard Taft—recently appointed upon the death of Edward Douglass White—hundreds of people along the sidewalks paid homage to Wilson by removing their hats. Upon reaching the Capitol, Woodrow and Edith veered back to S Street.

The ovation Wilson received at Keith's Theatre that Saturday night surpassed any he had received before. The headliner, a French soprano named Mademoiselle Diane, closed the show with a special mention of the distinguished guests. When they reached their car in the stage door alley, a double quartet surrounded his car, singing "Just a Song at Twilight." By the time the song ended, five hundred people had gathered, including that evening's entire cast. Wilson was so captivated by the reception, he asked the chanteuse to sing the "Marseillaise," and she obliged. The crowd cheered, Wilson raised his hat, and the car drove off. A man in the crowd shouted, "There's the man you can't forget."

Wilson's popularity continued to climb, especially as the Harding Administration underwent immediate and unfortunate postmortems. His controversial Interior Secretary, Albert Fall, had resigned earlier that year as the Senate began to investigate his oil leases, specifically Teapot Dome. Fall was found guilty of conspiracy and bribery and sentenced to a year in prison, becoming the first United States Cabinet member to serve time as a result of malfeasance in office. Other scandals followed, including those involving a number of mistresses Harding had entertained during his White House residency. One of them, Nan Britton, claimed he was the father of her illegitimate daughter. Because Florence Harding had not allowed an autopsy of her husband, further suspicions clung to his reputation, as people questioned whether the President had died of a heart attack, a stroke, suicide, or even poison at his wife's hand. The taciturn Calvin Coolidge proved to have a steadying influence on the nation. Despite his conservative policies, Wilson looked upon him favorably as a courteous and decent man.

Many marveled at Wilson's endurance during that especially torpid summer, though few said the same of Edith. A long profile in *The New York Times* commented on his rehabilitation and even suggested his possible reentry into politics. The journalist attributed much of his restoration to the constant devotion of his wife, who had not left him for more than a day and a half since he had been stricken in Pueblo. After years of priding herself on her own good health, Edith recognized that she was simply worn out. Friends in the shore town of Mattapoisett, Massachusetts—Charles Sumner Hamlin, the first chairman of the Federal Reserve Board, and his wife—invited Edith to visit. Woodrow encouraged her to accept, especially after Dr. Grayson said if she did not, she would "break down completely." The doctor volunteered to stay at S Street in her absence.

Woodrow missed Edith terribly, but her week away made him realize, as he typed in one of his daily notes to her, "how completely my life is intertwined with yours." She returned in September considerably revived but could not say the same for Woodrow. For the first time, she noticed how much he had aged, not in just the last week but in the last few years. His progressive arteriosclerosis, lack of exercise, and age itself contributed to his physical malaise and mental depression. Then his good eye began to fail, the result of small retinal hemorrhages. He maintained his regimen, but he could no longer recognize people on the street, and reading became a chore. His world darkened.

Wilson's outings to Keith's and his enjoyment of moving pictures tapered off. His reading was reduced to leafing through illustrated magazines—*Country Life*, *National Geographic*, *Photoplay*, *Screenland*, *Theatre Magazine*, and *Vanity Fair*—sometimes using a magnifying glass and flashlight to study details. Edith continued to read to him, mostly old favorites—Bagehot and Sir Walter Scott. And he played thousands of hands of canfield.

For the most part, he received only those visitors whose presence guaranteed a few minutes of easy conversation. Clemenceau visited the United States for the first time in more than fifty years, and he and Wilson enjoyed what the former called an "affectionate" reunion. "We didn't discuss the future," the old Tiger later reported, "—only the occasional good moments of the old days." He said, "[We] fully forgave each other for our bitter quarrels at Versailles. That was all in the past; and both of us had lost." In October 1923, the Wilsons entertained Mr. and Mrs. David Lloyd George, and both men laid aside their past differences, as the conversation degenerated into reciting limericks. Colonel House called one afternoon and left his cards for both Mr. and Mrs. Wilson. Surely he knew he would not find Wilson at home during the hour of his ritual drive; and just as surely Wilson could have reached House while he was in Washington—if Edith ever even mentioned the calling cards to Woodrow. Later, a number of mutual friends tried to reconnect the two old friends, but Edith never saw fit to relay their entreaties.

Visitors winnowed down to family members—Stockton Axson, Edith's mother and siblings, and, of course, Wilson's daughters. Her singing career as thin as her voice, Margaret spent years finding herself. While she was questioning her faith and searching for answers, she periodically turned up at S Street. The McAdoos visited from Los Angeles, where they were raising their two young daughters and where Mac had become general counsel to a new producing partnership of Hollywood's most important stars— Chaplin, Pickford, and Fairbanks. With his 20 percent ownership in the company, United Artists provided him an opportunity to earn some significant money and make influential contacts. McAdoo continued to plot a course to the White House, which Wilson never embraced, but Nell's sprightly appearance never failed to cheer him. And that year Jessie announced that the government of Siam had invited her husband, Frank Sayre, to take a leave from teaching law at Harvard to advise the progressive Asian nation as it opened doors to Western political thought. Wilson's heart sank at the thought of his serene daughter going so far away for so long, but he urged his son-in-law to accept what seemed to be a most interesting offer. During their farewell visit to Washington in early September, Wilson took one of his afternoon drives with his grandson Francis Junior, then eight years old. As they were driving up Massachusetts Avenue, a bystander recognized the car and shouted out, "I'm for the League!" The somewhat startled boy yelled back, "I'm for the League!" And with that, he recalled a lifetime later, "Grandfather didn't say a word. He just dissolved into tears for reasons I didn't understand, pulled me into his arm, and kissed me on the forehead."

Among Wilson's guests that autumn was Bernard Baruch's eldest daughter, Belle. She and a friend staunchly supported the League of Nations through a group they helped finance called the Nonpartisan League. They hoped to boost both their leagues by getting Wilson to speak over the radio on "The Significance of Armistice Day." Although new to broadcasting, he agreed to an Armistice Eve address. Edith noticed her husband's trepidation. Where he formerly could speak off the cuff for hours, his crippled body, his failing eyesight, and his fear of speaking into a microphone constrained him terribly. For two weeks he fretted, as he labored over eight paragraph-long sentences. Without ever mentioning the League by name, he wrote of his country's great wrong in not bearing a responsible part in the administration of the peace after sending her soldiers to fight the war. Edith repeatedly suggested that he abandon the speech, but he insisted doing so would make him feel "like the most arrant coward."

Radio technicians arrived in the morning of November 10, 1923, and worked for hours running wires through the house to the library. Wilson spent the day in bed, suffering from a nervous headache. Just before 8:30 p.m., however, he descended in his dressing gown. He had asked to deliver the address standing because he had always spoken on his feet. Because his throbbing headache worsened his poor vision, Edith sat behind him, holding a carbon copy of the text should he need her prompting. Stations in Washington, New York, and Providence carried the speech, which reached across most of the nation. Some towns installed speakers in their civic auditoriums to simulate the collective experience of a live address. Tentative at first but finding his stride, Wilson delivered his remarks without incident—other than his discouragement over his performance. His self-criticism was harsh but understandable, for this new medium—radio—required more than a little artificiality, the demand of orating to an invisible audience. Public reaction the next day was full of praise.

Crowds, complete with banners and brass bands, began forming on S Street early that Armistice Day. Flowers, telegrams, and letters poured in. Because a short formal ceremony was planned, with Carter Glass introducing the guest of honor, Wilson decked himself out in a morning coat, gray trousers, and a silk hat. When he appeared at the front door of his house at 2:30 that afternoon, twenty thousand supporters filled the five blocks between Massachusetts and Connecticut Avenues. Journalist Raymond Clapper recalled the crowd was predominantly female, no doubt many of them mothers mourning a lost son. Many had been on their knees, praying in the street. Wilson spoke only two minutes, and the crowd interrupted him three times with overwhelming applause, moving him to tears. He asked them to transfer their homage to the men who had made the Armistice possible, especially General Pershing. Wilson said he was proud to have commanded "the most ideal army that was ever thrown together." Before leaving his admirers, he added one last thought: "I am not one of those that have the least anxiety about the triumph of the principles I have stood for. I have seen fools resist Providence before and I have seen the destruction, as will come upon these again—utter destruction and contempt. That we shall prevail is as sure as that God reigns."

Wilson met the holidays with good cheer—enjoying family and intimate friends and a stirring Christmas Eve at Keith's, where the entire cast (including the zany comedy team of Olsen and Johnson) as well as the audience stood and sang "Auld Lang Syne." But his spirits soon plunged. Margaret, his most contemplative daughter, often sat with him in silence, at which time she felt his soul stirring. During one such "conversation" in December, he startled her by saying, "I think it was best after all that the United States did not join the League of Nations." Margaret asked why. "Because our entrance into the League at the time I returned from Europe might have been only a personal victory," he said. "Now, when the American people join the League it will be because they are convinced it is the right thing to do, and then will be the *only right* time for them to do it." With a faint smile, he added, "Perhaps God knew better than I did after all."

On December 28, 1923, Woodrow Wilson turned sixty-seven. The highlight of the celebration came at three o'clock, when the Wilsons went to the side entrance of the house for their daily excursion. In lieu of the Pierce-Arrow, a brand new Rolls-Royce Silver Ghost touring car waited in the driveway. It was a black six-passenger limousine with a narrow stripe and Wilson's initials monogrammed in Princeton orange. Other modifications included a high top and wider doors so that he could enter the car without stooping. Four friends—Cleveland Dodge and Tom Jones from his Princeton days, Bernard Baruch and Jesse H. Jones, businessmen he had engaged in government work—had privately shared the $12,782.75 cost.

Dodge and Jesse Jones also created a trust for Wilson that would provide an income of $10,000 a year for the rest of his life. With characteristic grace, Dodge wrote the former President that while they were prompted by their love and admiration for him, "the trust is in fact intended as a slight material reward for your great service to the world, and while being fully cognizant that in taking this privilege of friendship we are honoring ourselves, we are nevertheless unwilling that you deny it to us, because it is indeed a very great privilege and pleasure." On a less personal note,

Dodge and Jones drafted a memorandum explaining that they were simply providing what they thought Congress should for all retiring presidents, especially those who had lived unselfish lives and had no opportunity to lay aside sufficient savings for their retirement. Both men considered the transaction completely above board because neither had ever sought or received a single political favor from Wilson. This annuity, Wilson said, "lifted Mrs. Wilson and me out of the mists of pecuniary anxiety and placed us on firm ground of ease and confidence." He wrote Dodge, "Surely no other man was ever blessed with so true, so unselfish, so thoughtful, so helpful a friend as you are and always have been to me!"

The icing on the cake that day came from Franklin Roosevelt, who announced that the Woodrow Wilson Foundation was officially accepting nominations for its first annual prize of $25,000, to be awarded "to the individual who has rendered within the year the most unselfish public service of enduring value." Then, at its annual year-end meeting, the American Historical Association unanimously elected Wilson its president. He accepted the honor but wrote in reply, "I cannot be sure that I shall be fit for the duties that fall to the occupant of that office."

That was not false modesty. Recently asked about his health, the former President quoted one of his predecessors: "John Quincy Adams is all right, but the house he lives in is dilapidated, and it looks as if he would soon have to move out." Whenever conversation turned to the League, Wilson's eyes still shone, and he would insist, "The world is *run* by its ideals." When former student and public servant Raymond Fosdick ended a visit in January 1924, the last image he took with him from S Street was of Wilson's "tear-stained face, a set, indomitable jaw, and a faint voice whispering, 'God bless you.' With his white hair and gray, lined face, he seemed like a reincarnated Isaiah, crying to his country: 'Awake, awake, put on thy strength, O Zion; put on thy beautiful garments, O Jerusalem!'"

On the sixteenth, the Democratic National Committee concluded its meeting by adopting a resolution endorsing the Administration of Woodrow Wilson, assuring him that they were preparing for that year's Presidential campaign inspired by his administration's achievements and his high ideals. When he learned that two hundred committee members wanted to make a pilgrimage to what they called the "shrine of peace" on S Street, he agreed to receive them in his library.

On Saturday, January 26, Dr. Grayson prepared for a sorely needed week's vacation, a shooting holiday at Bernard Baruch's Hobcaw Barony plantation in South Carolina. Before departing, he called on the Wilsons, especially Edith, just out of bed after a week with the grippe. She expressed anxiety at his leaving. Letters her husband had dictated were piling up on his table unsigned, which indicated to her that his energy was waning. Grayson said he did not share her fears. When he left, she went to Woodrow's room and found him despondent. She asked if he "felt badly," and he said, "I always feel badly now, little girl, and somehow I hate to have Grayson leave." Edith said she could still catch him, but he said, "No, that would be a selfish thing on my part. He is not well himself and needs the change." And then, very deliberately, he said the unspeakable: "It won't be very much longer, and I had hoped he would not desert me; but that I should not say, even to you."

Over the next few days, the stacks of unsigned letters rose. Edith went out to dinner on Tuesday, and her brother Randolph Bolling checked on Wilson at ten o'clock that night. The nurse asked him if Dr. Grayson was in town, because she thought the patient had become "a very sick man." When Bolling said Grayson was in South Carolina, she replied, "Oh, I wish he were here." After midnight, Edith awakened Randolph, telling him to summon the doctor home. Grayson did not receive the message until the following noon. He boarded the next train to Washington. Based on the symptoms Edith described and Wilson's medical history, he suggested it was an indigestive attack.

Examining his patient on Thursday, the thirty-first, Grayson remained unalarmed. But Edith wanted a second opinion. She called Dr. Sterling Ruffin, her internist, who concurred with the night nurse. "He is a very sick man," he told Edith, and he advised Grayson's spending the night in the house. The next morning at eight, Edith came downstairs to tell Randolph that she believed Woodrow was dying and that they should notify his children. While they were talking, Grayson entered and said that Wilson had taken a sudden turn for the worse in the early morning hours. His systems were shutting down.

Bolling telephoned Margaret in New York, telegraphed Nell in California, and cabled Jessie through the Siamese Embassy, advising them all of their father's condition. Margaret arrived that afternoon. Despite everybody's discretion, the press caught wind of the story. Grayson invited Dr. Harry A. Fowler to consult, and when he informed Wilson that he had his two colleagues outside the sickroom ready to examine him, Wilson attempted a smile and said, "Be careful. Too many cooks spoil the broth." The next day Altrude Grayson drove over with two of their sons; the younger remained in the car with his mother while six-year-old Gordon, the President's young companion after his stroke, was invited upstairs, briefly, to look in on his old friend. Faintly, Wilson smiled.

With repeated visits from physicians and the convergence of family members upon S Street, reporters gathered outside the house for what they realized was a death vigil. They erected a small shack to shelter themselves from the winter weather. They saw Margaret arrive alone, followed by Wilson's younger brother, Josie, who was so much a stranger to Washington that few even recognized him. That night, Grayson released a statement saying that Wilson had not been allowed out of bed all day.

The next morning's headlines warned that Wilson was dying. The news, President Coolidge wrote Mrs. Wilson, had disquieted the nation. "I join in the universal prayer that there may very soon be a change for the better." Dr. Grayson telephoned the White House to inform the President that both Wilsons wanted him to know how much they had appreciated his letter. Grayson added that the former President was too weak to talk but upon having the letter read to him managed to say, "He is a fine man."

Wilson steadily declined. He ingested only a few sips of broth. With his kidneys failing came uremic poisoning. The doctors administered oxygen and morphine to ease any pain. Dr. Grayson chose his patient's final moments of lucidity, when he was fully conscious, to pronounce that his death was imminent, and Wilson did not recoil. "I am ready," he said. "I am a broken piece of machinery. When the machinery is broken——." His voice trailing off, he never completed the thought, but he recovered enough to whisper, "I am ready."

While they were not Woodrow Wilson's last words, they proved to be striking enough to resonate as such. In truth, he revived for a moment and rested his hand on Grayson's arm. "You have been good to me," he said. "You have done everything you could." Grayson turned away in tears and left the room. After composing a brief statement, he faced the hundreds standing outside in the cold, the press among them. "He knows his condition," Grayson said, choking on his words. "He is the gamest man I ever knew." And as he read in a tremulous voice from his bulletin, several in the crowd rushed up to him, grabbing at the paper in his hand—as if stopping the announcement might prevent the inevitable.

After almost a two-year absence, Tumulty stopped by the house several times that day but did not gain admittance. He returned that night and asked for Grayson, insisting that his decade of loyal service had earned him the right to one final encounter. The doctor agreed, though he said the patient was sleeping. Edith hardly left her husband's side, and Grayson knew, of course, that she had no interest in Tumulty. By midnight, most of the crowd had dispersed, though the press corps remained. At midnight, a window on the second floor opened, and Isaac Scott poked his head out to say, "Mrs. Wilson asks you to please go away. She is trying to sleep." The house darkened, except for a faint light from her room.

By then, Wilson had slipped into unconsciousness. "Profoundly prostrated," one bulletin had reported. Grayson fought back tears with each discouraging update. All that Saturday, people dropped by—Herbert Hoover, Cordell Hull, Carter Glass; diplomats and well-wishers left their cards on the butler's silver tray; the crowd on S Street swelled; Tumulty returned. But only Wilson's wife and daughter and physician, and a few nurses, could enter the dying man's bedroom. At one point during the day, at a moment when his wife had left his side, he whispered a single word: "Edith." He hovered in a twilight state for the rest of the night.

Dawn broke on a raw Sunday, February 3, 1924. Grayson's 9 a.m. bulletin announced that Wilson remained unconscious and weak but alive. Church bells rang, producing a strange occurrence. At first dozens, and then hundreds of worshippers entered S Street and knelt before No. 2340. One could see people's lips moving in silent prayer, producing a profound stillness.

Inside the house, inexplicably, Wilson's eyes opened. Edith leaned in and held his right hand, while Margaret grasped his left. Two nurses stood at the foot of the bed. Dr. Grayson took hold of his wrist to monitor his pulse. Wilson's wife and daughter gently called to him, but he did not respond. After ten minutes, his eyes closed. At 11:15 the machinery gave out, as his pulse ebbed and then stopped.

Grayson appeared at the front door at 11:20. Reading very slowly and in a subdued voice, he announced the death, saying, "The heart muscle was so fatigued that it refused to act any longer. The end came peacefully." As he detailed the medical causes of the death—the arteriosclerosis and hemiplegia with which Wilson had lived for years and the "digestive disturbance" that had signaled this fatal siege—he did not even attempt to keep from crying. Those in the street too far away to hear Grayson's words had only to watch him blotting his face with a handkerchief to know the end had come.

Within minutes the rest of the world knew. In Bangkok, a telegram notified Frank Sayre, who left his office that morning to break the news to Jessie, who was "heartbroken." They could do no more than attend the next day's memorial services in the local English church. Nellie McAdoo and her husband were on the California Limited, halfway across the country, with another few days before they would reach Washington. Radio programs everywhere interrupted their Sunday morning sermons to announce Wilson's death. Within minutes of hearing the news at Washington's First Congregational Church, the Coolidges left the service and drove directly to S Street. The President told Joseph Wilson and Randolph Bolling that the government awaited instructions from the family as to how it might assist with the funeral, whether it be an official state occasion or a simple private ceremony.

For his immediate part, Coolidge issued a proclamation announcing Wilson's death and directing that the flags of the White House and of the departmental buildings be displayed at half-staff for thirty days. He also ordered suitable military and naval honors for his funeral. The next day the President wrote Admiral Grayson that while he had no jurisdiction over the Capitol, he would certainly use his good offices to have Wilson's body lie in state if the family desired; and he offered Arlington National Cemetery for his interment. He placed the Departments of State, War, and Navy at the family's disposal.

Edith Wilson took charge, starting with the question of a burial place. Mindful of her husband's position in the world but in keeping with his character, she wanted to maintain as much dignity and modesty as possible. Wilson had repeatedly said that he did not wish to be buried in Arlington. Staunton, Augusta, Columbia, and Wilmington all laid legitimate claims, but Wilson had hardly returned to any of them; he had kin buried only in South Carolina, and the family plot in the churchyard was full. Princeton, where he had spent most of his life—and where Witherspoon, Jonathan Edwards, and Grover Cleveland rested in its historic cemetery— seemed appropriate were it not for the unpleasantness of his departure.

Rome, Georgia—alongside his wife of almost thirty years—was never even considered. The solution lay practically around the corner.

A mile and a half up Massachusetts Avenue, the Cathedral Church of St. Peter and St. Paul—known as the Washington National Cathedral—sat atop Mount St. Alban. It had been under construction since 1907, and would remain unfinished until 1990; but the neo-Gothic edifice—the second-largest cathedral in the United States—was operational, and its Gloria in Excelsis Tower, which would crown the structure, was destined to become the highest point in the capital. As it rose in fits and starts, its hierarchy was desperate to establish it as the Westminster Abbey of the nation, a center for spiritual ceremony and commemoration, complete with an American version of Poets' Corner. In fact, the Episcopal Bishop of Washington, James Edward Freeman, had actively solicited celebrated Americans for their burial rights. Freeman now offered Mrs. Wilson the Bethlehem Chapel of the National Cathedral, a modest but impressive sanctuary with a high vaulted ceiling and stained-glass windows, for both her husband's service and burial. The chapel could accommodate only three hundred mourners, which pleased the widow, as it provided an excuse to forgo a state funeral.

Edith decided to hold a short service at the house, followed by another at the cathedral on Wednesday, February 6. The former would be more personal, the latter adhering to Washington protocol. By handwritten note, she invited the Coolidges to both ceremonies. Upon reading in the newspapers that the Senate was suspending its business for three days and that a delegation had been assigned to attend the cathedral rites, she immediately composed a brief personal letter. "As the funeral is private and not official," she wrote Henry Cabot Lodge, "and realizing that your presence would be embarrassing to you and unwelcome to me, I write to request that you do *not* attend."

Lodge replied promptly and courteously. He explained that when the Senate committee had been appointed, he had no idea that its members were expected to attend a private service in the house or that the church service was anything but public. "You may rest assured," he wrote by hand, "that nothing could be more distasteful to me than to do anything which by any possibility could be embarrassing to you." The press would announce that Lodge withdrew from the proceedings because of a respiratory condition.

Tensions on S Street still ran high, as the circumstances elicited the worst of Edith's behavior. The McAdoos reached Washington on Monday at a particularly troubling moment in his career. Just as he was seeing a clear path to the White House, investigations of the Teapot Dome scandal revealed that one of the co-conspirators, Californian Edward L. Doheny, had paid extravagant fees to McAdoo. The association alone was enough to sully his reputation. After arriving at S Street and paying his respects, McAdoo withdrew to his father-in-law's library with a number of his supporters to discuss damage control. Finding Nellie teetering on hysteria, Edith lashed out at her for caring more about getting her husband elected President than she did about the death of her father. Margaret, who had been dabbling in Christian Science, flitted about the house, wearing a beatific smile, insisting there was no reason to lament because death was merely an illusion. Edith felt she could obtain no support from her stepdaughters, then or in the future. And the feeling was mutual.

Wednesday was cold and gray, with a passing storm periodically delivering heavy rain mixed with snow. Thunder sounded all morning, but it was, in fact, gunfire—salvos to the former President from the nearby military bases. Other salutes spread across the country. Every town and city acknowledged Wilson's death, usually with the ringing of bells or by observing moments of silence. Edith had Army trucks deliver to nearby hospitals the hundreds of flower arrangements sent in sympathy. She received in all eight thousand messages of condolence. "The names of kings and the great of the earth were on these tributes," noted Josephus Daniels, "and the names of loyal, humble friends and comrades."

At two-fifty, the President and Mrs. Coolidge arrived at 2340 S Street. Two hundred others gathered inside as well—Wilson's former Cabinet members and advisers, including Tumulty and his wife, who had not been invited until McAdoo arranged for their entry. Ike Hoover was present along with Starling from the Secret Service, a small contingent of Princetonians, and a few Woodrows, Wilsons, Axsons, and Bollings. Before the fireplace in the library sat Wilson's open black steel casket—covered with a spray of Edith's beloved orchids.

At exactly three o'clock, the Reverend James Taylor of the Central Presbyterian Church raised his voice to recite the Twenty-third Psalm— "The Lord is my shepherd." Edith stood on the landing above, her sobs threatening to drown out the preacher. The Reverend Sylvester Beach,

Wilson's pastor from Princeton, spoke next, a few sentences about Wilson's "zeal in behalf of the Parliament of Man, in which the mighty nations should be restrained and the rights of the weak maintained." Then Bishop Freeman of the National Cathedral read a few lines from Wilson's own Bible. As the clock on the landing chimed the quarter hour, eight servicemen entered the room and carried the coffin down the stairs, out the front door, and through a double line of guardsmen to the waiting hearse.

After eight years of maintaining her composure to help sustain her husband, Edith—in black and a heavy veil—wept without compunction as her brother Randolph took her arm and escorted her down to the waiting car. McAdoo followed, attending Nellie and Margaret. The Coolidges were right behind. Then the rest made their way to their cars and up Massachusetts Avenue for Wilson's final procession. Eight men in uniform accompanied the hearse, four on either side, with files of eight flanking them and with soldiers and Marines positioned along the entire route, holding back the solemn crowds on both sides of the road. Fifty thousand more waited outside the church, their umbrellas accentuating the somberness of the day. The great church bells tolled, and as the funeral caravan turned right onto the Way of Peace up to the Bethlehem Chapel, the carillon sent forth a slow rendition of "Nearer, My God, to Thee," which resounded for blocks.

Once the pallbearers had placed the casket before the altar, the three clergymen conducted the Episcopal ritual for the Burial of the Dead, beginning with the words of John: "I am the Resurrection and the life." The service, which was broadcast on radio and to the mourners outside, included readings of Psalms and the singing of one of Wilson's favorite hymns, which began: "Day is dying in the west. / Heaven is touching earth with rest." The Lord's Prayer and the Apostles' Creed followed. The Bishop closed the ceremony with his benediction, and the organ played the recessional hymn, "The Strife Is O'er, the Battle Done."

The chapel emptied, except for the family and a few intimates, and the eight servicemen guarding the casket. Workmen approached the center of the chapel and removed a marble slab and then a concrete slab, revealing the vault below. As the men lowered the heavy black casement down beams to its catacomb, a bugler from the 3rd United States Cavalry stood outside playing "Taps." That very moment, across the Potomac at Arlington National Cemetery, another bugler echoed the call.

All but one of this last group of mourners accompanied the widow back to S Street, where she would live out the rest of her days. Cary Grayson, who had promised Ellen Wilson on her deathbed that he would look after her husband, complied to the very end, remaining until the servicemen had replaced the great stone slab.

The Bethlehem Chapel did not remain Woodrow Wilson's final resting place. As construction of the cathedral proceeded, his survivors favored a more accessible shrine. In 1956—the centennial of Wilson's birth—he was re-entombed in a new limestone sarcophagus in its own bay on the south side of the nave. Its top is carved only with his name, dates, and a cross fashioned after a Crusader's sword. Eighty-five-year-old Edith Wilson had largely withdrawn from the public eye, except for occasions that honored her late husband. Naturally, she attended the reconsecration ceremonies, over which Wilson's grandson the Very Reverend Francis B. Sayre, Jr.—the boy who once exclaimed that he was "for the League!"—presided in his role as dean of Washington National Cathedral.

A little more than four years later—on January 20, 1961—Chief Justice Earl Warren administered the Presidential Oath to John F. Kennedy on the East Portico of the Capitol. Few recognized the small elderly woman in the third row on the President's Platform, or would even have believed that Mrs. Woodrow Wilson was still alive. Later that cold day, Edith rode in the inaugural parade, sharing the backseat of a convertible car with another former First Lady, Eleanor Roosevelt. On December 28, 1961—what would have been her husband's 105th birthday—Edith Wilson was meant to dedicate a new bridge across the Potomac that was being named in his honor. But, suffering from heart and lung ailments, she died in her bed on S Street that night at eighty-nine. She was interred beside her husband's tomb.

"Cathedrals do not belong to a single generation," Dean Sayre once said. "They are churches of history. They gather up the faith of a whole people and proclaim the goodly Providence which has welded that people together as they have hoped and suffered and believed across the centuries." Few, if any, figures in modern history held loftier dreams and endured greater pain and maintained deeper faith than Sayre's grandfather, especially in promoting the "ideals of public service, liberal thought, the extension of democracy, and peace through justice," as Franklin D. Roosevelt defined his idol's vision.

And as the sun sets each day, the crepuscular light curiously illuminates a little more of the past, as the passage of each year further defines its epoch. In one decade after another, one sees that the silhouette of history that spreads across the capital city of the United States of America is not just that of its national cathedral but increasingly that of the President who is buried therein. It is the lengthening shadow of Wilson.

ACKNOWLEDGMENTS

BIBLIOGRAPHY

NOTES AND SOURCES

INDEX

ACKNOWLEDGMENTS

In 1965, when I was in the eleventh grade, my mother handed me a copy of Gene Smith's *When the Cheering Stopped*, which examined Woodrow Wilson's last years and Edith Wilson's role in the White House after her husband's stroke. I have been reading about Wilson ever since, but I kept feeling that I had never read a book that captured the essence of his character. From such feelings spring new biographies.

By the time I began writing this book, my subject had been dead more than seventy-five years, and there were few people alive who had known him. In 2001, however, I was fortunate enough to spend a beautiful day on Martha's Vineyard with his grandson the Very Reverend Francis B. Sayre, Jr., former Dean of the National Cathedral and, at that time, the only living person to have been born in the White House. Then in his mid-eighties, he remained a dynamic and articulate presence, who readily offered stories and observations of his mother and her sisters and their father. After Dean Sayre's death in 2008, the family discovered a mother lode of papers—hundreds of theretofore undisclosed personal letters—which Dean Sayre's son Thomas allowed me to mine for this book. Utmost thanks to Thomas H. Sayre for his trust and instant friendship.

I was also privileged to meet on several occasions with the late Cary T. Grayson, Jr., son of President Wilson's physician and as elegant a gentleman as I have ever known. He too shared not only his reminiscences and some of his family's lore but also an unexamined trove of Grayson family archives, which—like the Sayre Papers—brought countless personal details to my portrait of Wilson. I am sorry he did not live to see the book to which he contributed so generously. I am grateful as well to Cary Grayson, Jr.'s wife, Priscilla, for her gracious spirit.

In 1973 I had the good fortune to be invited to tea—"or something more important"—at the Washington, D.C., home of Alice Roosevelt Longworth, whom I was then interviewing for my biography of Maxwell Perkins. During the course of our conversation, I had expressed my interest in Woodrow Wilson; and her detestation of the man was still great enough for her to extend a standing invitation to tea whenever I was in town—primarily, I believe, so that she could ridicule Wilson (and me) to the delight of the other guests I encountered during my three subsequent visits. Although writing a book about Woodrow Wilson had not yet entered my thoughts, I knew enough to preserve her comments.

Because the research for this book was mostly archival, I depended on the expertise of many librarians and assistants at several institutions. Peter F. deVaux was the first to tell me of an ardent group of citizens then in the process of establishing a Presidential library in Staunton, Virginia—at Wilson's birthplace; and as the Woodrow Wilson Presidential Library took shape, I came to work with a highly dedicated corps of people there. I am extremely grateful to Founding Executive Director Eric Vettel and Heidi Hackford, who helped me break ground on my research, and to the library and museum's current president, Don W. Wilson. Other faithful friends of this book in Staunton include Peggy Dillard, William R. Browning, Joel Hodson, Pamela Dixon, and Linda McNeil, who gave me my first tour of the Wilson birthplace.

Davidson College alumnus A. Alex Porter paved the way for my 2006 visit to his alma mater. My thanks to him and the school's former president Robert "Bobby" Vagt, who graciously walked me through the campus and its history. Jan Blodgett provided great assistance at the Davidson College Library; and David McClintock, Mark Grotjohn, and J. Gill Holland further enhanced my visit there.

My thanks to John M. Sherrer III at the Historic Columbia Foundation in South Carolina and Erick Montgomery, Executive Director of Historic Augusta, Inc. I am grateful to Steve Oney for introducing me to the late Edwin J. Cashin, a scholar and lifelong student of Georgia history, who proudly guided me from one end of Augusta to the other, leaving no artifact unturned.

The spirit of Woodrow Wilson has never left his house at 2340 S Street in Washington, in large measure because of the dedicated people who keep the flame burning there. Especially helpful in my research over the last decade were former director Frank J. Aucella, John Powell, Claudia

Bismark, and Carter Cunningham. Recently, Sarah Andrews and the House's new director, Robert A. Enholm, have already assisted me beyond measure.

I am grateful to the staffs of the Newark Public Library, the Library of the University of Virginia, and the Library of Congress for their friendliness and efficiency. Special thanks to Donald A. Ritchie, Historian of the United States Senate, who provided a fascinating tour of the President's Room and much of the rest of the Capitol.

Princeton University is the heart of all Wilson research, and I am grateful to University Librarian Karin Trainer, Associate University Librarian Ben Primer, and Curator of Manuscripts Donald Skemer for always welcoming me back to their reading rooms. My friend Daniel J. Linke, the University Archivist and Curator of Public Policy Papers, made my days in the Seeley G. Mudd Manuscript Library as pleasant as they were productive. Great thanks to him and the team at Mudd, especially Tad Bennicoff, John DeLooper, Christine Kitto, Amanda Pike, and Marlis Hinckley, Class of 2016.

While researching and teaching at Princeton during the 2007–8 school year, I was surrounded by an extraordinary community of scholars and staff. For countless kindnesses, thanks to my friends in the Joseph Henry House—Cass Garner, Lin DeTitta, and Christine Hollendonner. Several others made my time in Princeton pass all too quickly—most especially Diane and H. Kirk Unruh, Jr., Carol and François Rigolot, Susan and Toby Levy, the late Charles Ryskamp, and Wilson expert Robert Cullinane. Jeff Nunokawa proved to be a terrible landlord and a boon companion. I have been further privileged to count as friends two of Wilson's most inspiring successors in Nassau Hall, Presidents Harold T. Shapiro and Shirley M. Tilghman.

All Wilson studies in the last half century stand on the foundation of work produced by Arthur S. Link, who collected, edited, and annotated *The Papers of Woodrow Wilson*. These volumes are a monument not only to Wilson but to historical research. Other Wilson scholars whose works provided particularly valuable information and insights include James Axtell, Ray Stannard Baker, John Morton Blum, Kendrick A. Clements, John Milton Cooper, Jr., Thomas J. Knock, and W. Barksdale Maynard.

Over the course of this long project, my agent, Lynn Nesbit, has sorted out any number of issues, always with grace and aplomb. I value her friendship as much as her representation.

A number of other friends have provided great emotional support during the thirteen years it took to complete this book. Their constant vigilance, even when I was off in another century, sustained me more than they know. My heartfelt thanks to Greg Berlanti, Tony Bill, Gary Cohen, Kevin Lake, Eric Lax, Nancy Olson Livingston, John Logan, Bryan Lourd, Elsie and McKinley C. McAdoo, and Douglas Stumpf. I am sorry two friends who spurred me on for so many years departed before they could see the results: Casey Ribicoff, who never failed to ask provocative questions; and Gore Vidal, who never failed to give provocative answers, challenging almost everything Wilson had said or done. Fellow biographer David T. Michaelis has been my ideal reader for the last few decades; and his steadfast faith in this book has been a continual source of inspiration. He has long proved himself the very best of friends.

In my experience, the greatest scholars are also the most generous. That is certainly the case with Alan Brinkley, to whom many of us have turned for counsel since our undergraduate days. I am beholden to him for his critical reading of this manuscript, as he once again demonstrated that he is both a friend and historian of the highest order.

My deepest regret is that my father, Richard Berg, did not live to see this book. He was no great fan of history; but, as a motion-picture writer and producer, he loved good drama. He watched over every scene herein. My brothers—Jeffrey, Tony, and Rick—all augmented their traditional support, compensating for his absence.

In an age of great transition in the publishing industry, I continued to work with a team of people at G. P. Putnam's Sons who remain extremely dedicated to books, whatever form they take. Carole Baron, Marilyn Ducksworth, Mih-Ho Cha, and the late Dan Harvey nurtured this book at the beginning; and in recent years, I have been fortunate enough to work with Susan Petersen Kennedy, who allowed the book to progress according to its own calendar. Ivan Held has taken a deep personal interest in the work of not only the author but of all who have had a hand in the making of this book. I have had the good fortune to work once again with the same superb editorial team that I encountered fifteen years ago, with a few new additions. My greatest thanks to Neil S. Nyren for his sharp insights and his gentle humor. Thanks also to Sara Minnich, Claire Winecoff for her meticulous care, and, most especially, Scott Auerbach. Catharine Lynch and Meredith Dros have overseen this volume's production, making the most of the very talented Claire Vaccaro's design. Kate Stark, Alexis Welby, and Kelly Welsh have cheerfully ushered the author into the twenty-first century. My friend Ian Chapman has monitored every detail of this book's British publication.

This book is dedicated with boundless love and gratitude to three people. Kevin McCormick has been my partner through four books now, but I have never relied on his devotion more than during "the Wilson administration." He has consistently offered support of every kind before I needed to ask for it; and he helped hammer out most of the thoughts in this book.

While my father got me interested in writing, my mother, Barbara Berg, got me interested in reading—especially nonfiction, specifically about the early part of the twentieth century and Woodrow Wilson. Her unceasing curiosity and indomitable energy never cease to amaze and inspire.

Phyllis Grann is the most gifted editor I know. She has perfect pitch and the rare ability to focus on details without losing sight of the big picture. Although she has left Putnam, she was the first person there with whom I discussed the idea of writing about Wilson, and she has faithfully remained this book's editor and godmother.

The moment after I had first mentioned Woodrow Wilson to her, Phyllis asked how I ever got interested in him in the first place. I told her about that book my mother had pressed into my hands when I had been in high school. Phyllis went silent for a moment . . . and then told me that in 1964, when she was a secretary at William Morrow & Company, her boss, Lawrence Hughes, had said, "Phyllis, you say you want to be an editor. Let's see what you can do with this." He set down on her desk the manuscript of *When the Cheering Stopped*.

I think Wilson would have called that Providence.

—A.S.B.
Los Angeles
April 2013

BIBLIOGRAPHY

Ackerman, Kenneth D. *Young J. Edgar: Hoover, the Red Scare, and the Assault on Civil Liberties.* New York: Carroll & Graf, 2007.

Adams, Henry. *The Education of Henry Adams.* New York: Modern Library, 1931.

Alderman, Edwin Anderson. *Woodrow Wilson: Memorial Address.* Washington, DC: Government Printing Office, 1925.

Annin, Robert Edwards. *Woodrow Wilson: A Character Study.* New York: Dodd, Mead, 1924.

Arnett, Alex Mathews. *Claude Kitchen and the Wilson War Policies.* Boston: Little, Brown, 1937.

Aucella, Frank J., and Patricia A. P. Hobbs with Frances Wright Saunders. *Ellen Axson Wilson: First Lady—Artist.* Washington, DC: Woodrow Wilson Birthplace Foundation, 1993.

Axson, Stockton. *Brother Woodrow: A Memoir of Woodrow Wilson.* Princeton, NJ: Princeton University Press, 1993.

Axtell, James. *The Making of Princeton University: From Woodrow Wilson to the Present.* Princeton, NJ: Princeton University Press, 2006.

Bagehot, Walter. *The English Constitution.* 1867. Reprint, Ithaca, NY: Cornell University Press, 1966.

———. *Physics and Politics.* New York: Cosimo Classics, 2007.

Bailey, Anne J. *War and Ruin: William T. Sherman and the Savannah Campaign.* Lanham, MD: Rowman & Littlefield, 2002.

Baker, Ray Stannard. *American Chronicle: The Autobiography of Ray Stannard Baker.* New York: Charles Scribner's Sons, 1945.

———. *Woodrow Wilson: Life and Letters,* Potomac Edition. 8 vols. New York: Charles Scribner's Sons, 1946.

Balio, Tino. *United Artists: The Company Built by the Stars.* Madison, WI: University of Wisconsin Press, 1976.

Barry, John M. *The Great Influenza: The Epic Story of the Deadliest Plague in History.* New York: Viking, 2004.

Baruch, Bernard. *Baruch: The Public Years.* New York: Holt, Rinehart and Winston, 1960.

Battey, George Magruder. *History of Rome and Floyd County.* Atlanta: Webb and Vary, 1922.

Beaty, Mary D. *A History of Davidson College.* Davidson, NC: Briarpatch, 1988.

Berkin, Carol, X. Miller, R. Cherney, and J. L. Gormly. *Making America.* Boston: Wadsworth, 2011.

Billington, Monroe Lee. *Thomas P. Gore: The Blind Senator from Oklahoma.* Lawrence, KS: University of Kansas Press, 1967.

Blight, David W. *Race and Reunion: The Civil War in American Memory.* Cambridge, MA: Belknap Press of Harvard University Press, 2001.

Blum, John Morton. *Joe Tumulty and the Wilson Era.* Boston: Houghton Mifflin, 1951.

Bonsal, Stephen. *Unfinished Business.* New York: Doubleday, Doran, 1944.

Boos, Dr. I. *Diseases of the Stomach.* Philadelphia: F. A. Davis, 1907.

Bragdon, Henry Wilkinson. *Woodrow Wilson: The Academic Years.* Cambridge, MA: Belknap Press of Harvard University Press, 1967.

Briggs, Asa. *Victorian People: A Reassessment of Persons and Themes, 1851–67*. New York: Harper
      Colophon Books, 1963.

Brinkley, Alan. *The Unfinished Nation: A Concise History of the American People*. New York: Alfred A.
      Knopf, 1993.

Brown, David J., ed. *Staunton, Virginia: A Pictorial History*. Staunton, VA: Historic Staunton
      Foundation, 1985.

Brown, K. L., ed. *Woodrow Wilson's Pierce-Arrow*. Staunton, VA: Woodrow Wilson Birthplace
      Foundation, 1990.

Brownell, Will, and Richard N. Billings. *So Close to Greatness: A Biography of William C. Bullitt*.
      New York: Macmillan, 1987.

Brownlow, Kevin. *Hollywood: The Pioneers*. New York: Alfred A. Knopf, 1979.

———. *The War, the West, and the Wilderness*. New York: Alfred A. Knopf, 1979.

Brownlow, Louis. *A Passion for Anonymity: The Autobiography of Louis Brownlow, Second Half*. Chicago:
      University of Chicago Press, 1958.

Bruce, William Cabell. *Recollections*. Baltimore: King Brothers, 1936.

Bryan, William Jennings. *The Memoirs of William Jennings Bryan*. Edited by Mary Bryan. Philadelphia:
      John C. Winston, 1925.

Bullock, Edna D., ed. *Short Ballot*. White Plains, NY: H. W. Wilson, 1915.

Burleigh, J. H. S. *A Church History of Scotland*. London: Oxford University Press, 1960.

Calero, Manuel. *The Mexican Policy of President Woodrow Wilson As It Appears to a Mexican*. New York:
      Smith & Thomson, 1916.

Calvin, John. *Institutes of the Christian Religion*. Translated by Ford Lewis Battles. Philadelphia: West-
      minster, 1960.

Carroll, James Robert. *The Real Woodrow Wilson: An Interview with Arthur S. Link, Editor of the Wilson
      Papers*. Bennington, VT: Images from the Past, 2001.

Cashin, Edward J. *General Sherman's Girl Friend and More Stories About Augusta*. Columbia, SC:
      Woodstone, 1992.

Chernow, Ron. *The House of Morgan: An American Banking Dynasty and the Rise of Modern Finance*.
      New York: Atlantic Monthly Press, 1990.

Churchill, Winston. *The World Crisis: 1911–1918*. London and New York: Thornton Butterworth and
      Charles Scribner's Sons, 1923.

Clapper, Raymond. *Watching the World*. New York: Whittlesey House, 1944.

Clark, Champ. *My Quarter Century of American Politics*. 2 vols. New York: Harper & Brothers, 1920.

Clements, Kendrick A. *The Presidency of Woodrow Wilson*. Lawrence, KS: University Press of Kansas, 1992.

Coben, Stanley. *A. Mitchell Palmer, Politician*. New York: Da Capo, 1972.

Coffman, Edward M. *The War to End All Wars: The American Military Experience in World War I*.
      New York: Oxford University Press, 1968.

Connally, Tom. *My Name Is Tom Connally*. New York: Thomas Y. Crowell, 1954.

Cooper, John Milton, Jr. *Breaking the Heart of the World: Woodrow Wilson and the Fight for the League of
      Nations*. Cambridge: Cambridge University Press, 2001.

Cox, James M. *Journey Through My Years*. New York: Simon & Schuster, 1946.

Creel, George. *How We Advertised America: The First Telling of the Amazing Story of the Committee on Public
      Information That Carried the Gospel of Americanism to Every Corner of the Globe*. New York: Harper &
      Brothers, 1920.

———. *Wilson and the Issues*. New York: Century, 1916.

Daniels, Josephus. *The Life of Woodrow Wilson, 1856–1924*. Philadelphia: John C. Winston, 1924.

———. *The Wilson Era*. 2 vol. Chapel Hill, NC: University of North Carolina Press, 1944.

Day, Donald, ed. *The Autobiography of Will Rogers*. Boston: Houghton Mifflin, 1949.

———. *Woodrow Wilson's Own Story*. Boston: Little, Brown, 1952.

Dos Passos, John. *U. S. A.: Nineteen Nineteen*. 1932. Boston: Houghton Mifflin, Sentry Edition, 1963.

Duiker, William. *Ho Chi Minh*. New York: Hyperion, 2003.

Eksteins, Modris. *Rites of Spring: The Great War and the Birth of the Modern Age*. Boston: Houghton
      Mifflin, 1989.

Elliot, Margaret Randolph Axson. *My Aunt Louisa and Woodrow Wilson.* Chapel Hill, NC: University of North Carolina Press, 1944.

Ellis, John. *Eye-Deep in Hell: Trench Warfare in World War I.* Baltimore: Johns Hopkins University Press, 1976.

Esher, Viscount. *The Journals and Letters of Reginald Viscount Esher.* Edited by Maurice V. Brett. London: Nicholson and Watson, 1938.

Farber, Daniel, ed. *Security v. Liberty: Conflicts Between Civil Liberties and National Security in American History.* New York: Russell Sage Foundation, 2008.

Farwell, Byron. *Over There: The United States in the Great War, 1917–1918.* New York: W. W. Norton, 1999.

Finch, Edith. *Carey Thomas of Bryn Mawr.* New York: Harper, 1947.

Fitzgerald, F. Scott. *This Side of Paradise.* New York: Charles Scribner's Sons, 1920.

Foner, Eric. *Reconstruction: America's Unfinished Revolution—1863–1877.* New York: Harper & Row, 1988.

Freud, Sigmund, and William C. Bullitt. *Thomas Woodrow Wilson: A Psychological Study.* Boston: Houghton Mifflin, 1967.

Fussell, Paul. *The Great War and Modern Memory.* New York: Oxford University Press, 1975.

Gay, Peter. *Freud: A Life for Our Time.* New York: W. W. Norton, 1988.

Giddings, Paula J. *Ida: A Sword Among Lions.* New York: Amistad, 2008.

Glass, Carter. *An Adventure in Constructive Finance.* New York: Doubleday, Page, 1927.

Grayson, Cary T. *Woodrow Wilson: An Intimate Memoir.* Washington, DC: Potomac Books, 1977.

Grayson, David. *The Autobiography of Ray Stannard Baker.* New York: Charles Scribner's Sons, 1945.

Hagedorn, Ann. *Savage Peace: Hope and Fear in America, 1919.* New York: Simon & Schuster, 2008.

Hale, William Bayard. *Woodrow Wilson: The Story of His Life.* Garden City: Doubleday, Page, 1912.

Hanioğlu, M. Şükrü. *A Brief History of the Late Ottoman Empire.* Princeton, NJ: Princeton University Press, 2008.

Hatfield, Mark O., with the Senate Historical Office. *Vice Presidents of the United States, 1789–1993.* Washington, DC: United States Government Printing Office, 1997.

Heaton, John L. *Cobb of the World: A Leader in Liberalism.* New York: E. P. Dutton, 1924.

Hemingway, Ernest. *A Farewell to Arms.* New York: Charles Scribner's Sons, 1929.

Herman, Arthur. *How the Scots Invented the Modern World: The True Story of How Western Europe's Poorest Nation Created Our World and Everything in It.* New York: Crown, 2001.

Hitler, Adolf. *Mein Kampf.* Translated by James Murphy. North Charleston, SC: CreateSpace Independent Publishing Platform, 2011.

Hodgson, Godfrey. *Woodrow Wilson's Right Hand: The Life of Colonel Edward M. House.* New Haven, CT: Yale University Press, 2006.

Hoeveler, J. David, Jr. *James McCosh and the Scottish Intellectual Tradition: From Glasgow to Princeton.* Princeton, NJ: Princeton University Press, 1981.

Hoffman, Donald. *Mark Twain in Paradise: His Voyages to Bermuda.* Columbia, MO: University of Missouri Press, 2006.

Hoover, Herbert. *The Ordeal of Woodrow Wilson.* New York: McGraw-Hill, 1958.

Hoover, Irwin Hood (Ike). *Forty-Two Years in the White House.* Boston: Houghton Mifflin, 1934.

Hosford, Hester E. *The Forerunners of Woodrow Wilson.* East Orange, NJ: East Orange Record Print, 1914.

House, Edward M. *The Intimate Papers of Colonel House, Arranged as a Narrative by Charles Seymour.* 4 vols. Boston: Houghton Mifflin, 1926.

———. *Philip Dru: Administrator.* 1912. Middlesex, England: Echo Library, 2006.

Houston, David F. *Eight Years with Wilson's Cabinet, 1913–1921.* 2 vols. Garden City: Doubleday, Page, 1926.

Hulbert, Mary Allen. *The Story of Mrs. Peck: An Autobiography.* New York: Minton, Balch, 1933.

Hurley, Edward N. *The Bridge to France.* Philadelphia: J. B. Lippincott, 1927.

Jaffray, Elizabeth. *Secrets of the White House.* New York: Cosmopolitan Book Corporation, 1927.

Johnson, James Weldon. *Writings.* New York: Library of America, 2004.

Kandell, Jonathan. *La Capital: The Biography of Mexico City.* New York: Random House, 1988.

Karabel, Jerome. *The Chosen: The Hidden History of Admission and Exclusion at Harvard, Yale, and Princeton.* New York: Houghton Mifflin Harcourt, 2005.

Kazin, Michael. *A Godly Hero: The Life of William Jennings Bryan.* New York: Alfred A. Knopf, 2006.

Kennan, George F. *Memoirs: 1925–1950.* Boston: Little, Brown, 1967.

Keynes, John Maynard. *The Economic Consequences of the Peace.* 1919. Reprint, New York: Penguin Books, 1995.

Keyssar, Alexander. *The Right to Vote: The Contested History of Democracy in the United States.* New York: Basic Books, 2000.

Kissinger, Henry. *Diplomacy.* New York: Simon & Schuster, 1994.

Knox, John. *Letter to the Commonalty of Scotland.* Dallas: Presbyterian Heritage Publications, 1995.

Kohlsaat, H. H. *From McKinley to Harding.* New York: Charles Scribner's Sons, 1923.

Konvitz, Milton R., ed. *The Legacy of Horace M. Kallen.* Cranbury, NJ: Associated University Presses, 1987.

Lane, A. W., and L. H. Wall, eds. *Letters of Franklin K. Lane.* Boston: Houghton Mifflin, 1922.

Lansing, Robert. *War Memoirs.* Indianapolis: Bobbs-Merrill, 1935.

Lash, Joseph P. *Helen and Teacher: The Story of Helen Keller and Anne Sullivan Macy.* New York: Delacorte, 1980.

Lawrence, David. *The True Story of Woodrow Wilson.* New York: George H. Doran, 1924.

Leitch, Alexander. *A Princeton Companion.* Princeton, NJ: Princeton University Press, 1978.

Levin, Phyllis Lee. *Edith and Woodrow: The Wilson White House.* New York: Charles Scribner's Sons, 2001.

Link, Arthur S., ed. *The Papers of Woodrow Wilson.* 69 vols. Princeton, NJ: Princeton University Press, 1966–1994.

———. *The First Presbyterian Church of Princeton.* Princeton, NJ: First Presbyterian Church, 1967.

Livermore, Seward W. *Politics Is Adjourned: Woodrow Wilson and the War Congress, 1916–1918.* Middletown, CT: Wesleyan University Press, 1966.

Lodge, Henry Cabot. *The Senate and the League of Nations.* New York: Charles Scribner's Sons, 1925.

Longworth, Alice Roosevelt. *Crowded Hours.* New York: Charles Scribner's Sons, 1933.

Lucas, Marion B. *Sherman and the Burning of Columbia.* Columbia, SC: University of South Carolina Press, 2000.

MacMaster, K. Richard. *Augusta County History: 1865–1950.* Staunton, VA: Augusta County Historical Society, 1988.

MacMillan, Margaret. *Paris 1919: Six Months That Changed the World.* New York: Random House, 2001.

Marsden, George M. *The Soul of the American University: From Protestant Establishment to Established Nonbelief.* New York: Oxford University Press, 1994.

Marshall, Thomas R. *Recollections of Thomas R. Marshall: A Hoosier Salad.* Indianapolis, IN: Bobbs-Merrill, 1925.

Mayer, Arno J. *Wilson vs. Lenin: Political Origins of the New Diplomacy 1917–1918.* Cleveland and New York: Meridian Books, 1969.

McAdoo, Eleanor Wilson, ed. *The Priceless Gift: The Love Letters of Woodrow Wilson and Ellen Axson Wilson.* New York: McGraw-Hill Books, 1962.

———. *The Woodrow Wilsons.* New York: Macmillan, 1937.

McAdoo, William G. *Crowded Years.* Boston: Houghton Mifflin, 1931.

McCombs, William F. *Making Woodrow Wilson President.* New York: Fairview, 1921.

McCosh, James. *Twenty Years of Princeton College.* New York: Charles Scribner's Sons, 1888.

McWhirter, Cameron. *Red Summer: The Summer of 1919 and the Awakening of Black America.* New York: Henry Holt, 2011.

Mead, Walter Russell. *Special Providence: American Foreign Policy and How It Changed the World.* New York: Alfred A. Knopf, 2001.

Meigs, Cornelia. *What Makes a College? A History of Bryn Mawr.* New York: Macmillan, 1956.

Mencken, H. L. "Five Men at Random." In *Prejudices: Third Series.* New York: Alfred A. Knopf, 1922. First appeared in *Smart Set,* May 1920.

———. *My Life As Author and Editor.* New York: Alfred A. Knopf, 1993.

Moggridge, D. E. *Maynard Keynes: An Economist's Biography*. London and New York: Routledge, 1995.

Monnet, Jean. *Memoirs*. Translated by Richard Mayne. Garden City, NY: Doubleday, 1978.

Montgomery, Erick. *Thomas Woodrow Wilson: Family Ties and Southern Perspectives*. Augusta, GA: Historic Augusta, 2006.

Moore, John Hammond. *Columbia and Richland County: A South Carolina Community, 1740–1990*. Columbia, SC: University of South Carolina Press, 1993.

Morgenthau, Henry. *All in a Lifetime*. Garden City: Doubleday, Page, 1923.

Morris, Edmund. *Colonel Roosevelt*. New York: Random House, 2010.

Mulder, John M. "Joseph R. Wilson: Southern Presbyterian Patriarch." *Journal of Presbyterian History* 52 (1974).

Muraskin, William A. *Middle-Class Blacks in a White Society: Prince Hall Freemasonry in America*. Berkeley, CA: University of California Press, 1975.

Myers, William Starr, ed. *Woodrow Wilson: Some Princeton Memories*. Princeton, NJ: Princeton University Press, 1946.

Nasaw, David. *Andrew Carnegie*. New York: Penguin, 2006.

Nicolson, Harold. *King George the Fifth: His Life and Reign*. Garden City, NY: Doubleday, 1953.

———. *Peacemaking, 1919*. Boston: Houghton Mifflin, 1933.

Northen, William J. *Men of Mark in Georgia: A Complete and Elaborate History of the State from Its Settlement to the Present Time*. Atlanta: A. B. Caldwell, 1907–1912.

Oberdorfer, Don. *Princeton University: The First 250 Years*. Princeton, NJ: Trustees of Princeton University, 1995.

Ozment, Steven. *Protestants: The Birth of a Revolution*. New York: Doubleday, 1992.

Patton, Francis Landey. *The Inauguration of the Rev. Francis Landey Patton*. New York: Gray Bros., 1888.

Perry, Lewis. *Intellectual Life in America: A History*. New York: Franklin Watts, 1984.

Pershing, John J. *My Experiences in the World War*. New York: Frederick A. Stokes, 1931.

Pollock, Edwin T., and Paul F. Bloomhardt, compilers. *The Hatchet of the United States Ship "George Washington."* New York: J. J. Little & Ives, 1919.

Post, Louis F. *The Deportations Delirium of 1920: A Personal Narrative of an Historic Official Experience*. Chicago: C. H. Kerr, 1923.

Poucher, William A. *Perfumes, Cosmetics & Soaps, with Especial Reference to Synthetics*. New York: D. Van Nostrand, 1927.

Preston, Diana. *Lusitania: An Epic Tragedy*. New York: Walker, 2002.

Prior, James. *Life of the Right Honourable Edmund Burke*. London: Henry G. Bohn, 1854.

Reid, Edith Gittings. *Woodrow Wilson: The Caricature, the Myth, and the Man*. New York: Oxford University Press, 1934.

Rhinehart, Raymond P. *Princeton University*. New York: Princeton Architectural Press, 1999.

Roosevelt, Theodore. *Letters and Speeches*. New York: Library of America, 2004.

———. *Newer Roosevelt Messages*. Edited by William Griffith. New York: Current Literature, 1919.

Sayre, Francis Bowes. *Glad Adventure*. New York: Macmillan, 1957.

Schickel, Richard. *D. W. Griffith: An American Life*. New York: Simon and Schuster, 1984.

Schneer, Jonathan. *The Balfour Declaration: The Origins of the Arab-Israeli Conflict*. New York: Random House, 2010.

Seale, William. *The President's House: A History*. Washington, DC: White House Historical Association, 1986.

———. *The White House: The History of an American Idea*. Washington, DC: American Institute of Architects Press, 1992.

Selden, William K. *Club Life at Princeton*. Princeton, NJ: Princeton Prospect Foundation, n.d.

Seymour, Charles. *Woodrow Wilson and the World War: A Chronicle of Our Own Times*. New Haven, CT: Yale University Press, 1921.

Short, Philip. *Mao: A Life*. New York: Henry Holt, 2000.

Smith, Gene. *When the Cheering Stopped: The Last Years of Woodrow Wilson*. New York: William Morrow, 1964.

Sragow, Michael. *Victor Fleming: An American Movie Master*. New York: Pantheon Books, 2008.

Stalker, James. *John Knox: His Ideas and Ideals.* New York: A. C. Armstrong & Son, 1905.

Starling, Edmund W., and Thomas Sugrue. *Starling of the White House: The Story of the Man Whose Secret Service Detail Guarded Five Presidents from Woodrow Wilson to Franklin D. Roosevelt.* New York: Simon & Schuster, 1946.

Startt, James D. *Woodrow Wilson and the Press: Prelude to the Presidency.* New York: Palgrave Macmillan, 2004.

Steel, Ronald. *Walter Lippmann and the American Century.* Boston: Little, Brown, 1980.

Stoddard, Henry L. *As I Knew Them: Presidents and Politics from Grant to Coolidge.* New York: Harper & Brothers, 1922.

Stone, Geoffrey R. *Perilous Times: Free Speech in Wartime, from the Sedition Act of 1798 to the War on Terrorism.* New York: W. W. Norton, 2004.

Teachout, Terry. *The Skeptic: A Life of H. L. Mencken.* New York: HarperCollins, 2002.

Thomas, Charles M. *Thomas Riley Marshall, Hoosier Statesman.* Oxford, OH: Mississippi Valley Press, 1939.

Thorp, Willard, Minor Myers, Jr., and Jeremiah Stanton Finch. *The Princeton Graduate School: A History.* Princeton, NJ: Association of Princeton Graduate Alumni, 2000.

Trask, David F. *Captains and Cabinets: Anglo-American Naval Relations, 1917–1918.* Columbia, MO: University of Missouri Press, 1973.

Tribble, Edwin, ed. *A President in Love: The Courtship Letters of Woodrow Wilson and Edith Bolling Galt.* Boston: Houghton Mifflin, 1981.

Truman, Margaret, ed. *Where the Buck Stops: The Personal and Private Writings of Harry S. Truman.* New York: Warner Books, 1989.

Tuchman, Barbara. *The Guns of August.* New York: Macmillan, 1962.

———. *The Zimmermann Telegram.* New York: Macmillan, 1958.

Tumulty, Joseph P. *Woodrow Wilson As I Know Him.* Garden City, NY: Doubleday, Page, 1921.

Urofsky, Melvin I. *Louis D. Brandeis: A Life.* New York: Pantheon Books, 2009.

Vansittart, Peter, ed. *Voices from the Great War.* London: Pimlico, 1998.

Waddell, Joseph Addison. *Annals of Augusta County, Virginia.* Richmond, VA: William Ellis Jones, 1886.

Watkins, Mel, ed. *African American Humor: The Best Black Comedy from Slavery to Today.* Chicago: Lawrence Hill Books, 2002.

Watson, James E. *As I Knew Them.* Indianapolis: Bobbs-Merrill, 1936.

Weinstein, Edwin A. *Woodrow Wilson: A Medical and Psychological Biography.* Princeton, NJ: Princeton University Press, 1981.

Weisman, Steven R. *The Great Tax Wars: Lincoln to Wilson, the Fierce Battles over Money and Power That Transformed the Nation.* New York: Simon & Schuster, 2002.

Wheeler, W. Reginald, ed. *A Book of Verse of the Great War.* New Haven, CT: Yale University Press, 1917.

Whitcomb, John, and Claire Whitcomb. *Real Life at the White House: Two Hundred Years of Daily Life at America's Most Famous Residence.* New York: Routledge, 2000.

White, William Allen. *Woodrow Wilson: The Man, His Times, and His Task.* Boston: Houghton Mifflin, 1924.

Williams, Wythe W. *The Tiger of France: Conversations with Clemenceau.* New York: Duell, Sloan & Pearce, 1949.

Wilson, Andrew. *A President's Love Affair with the Lake District: Woodrow Wilson's "Second Home."* Windermere, Cumbria: Lakeland Press Agency, 1966.

Wilson, Edith Bolling. *My Memoir.* Indianapolis: Bobbs-Merrill, 1938.

Wilson, Woodrow. *Congressional Government: A Study in American Politics.* Boston: Houghton Mifflin, 1885.

———. *Division and Reunion: 1829–1899.* New York: Longmans, Green, 1902.

———. *George Washington.* New York: Harper & Brothers, 1897.

———. *A History of the American People.* 5 vols. New York: Harper & Brothers, 1902.

———. *Mere Literature and Other Essays.* Boston: Houghton Mifflin, 1896.

———. *An Old Master and Other Political Essays.* New York: Charles Scribner's Sons, 1893.

———. *The State: Elements of Historical and Practical Politics.* Boston: D. C. Heath, 1889.

———. *When a Man Comes to Himself.* New York: Harper & Brothers, 1901.

NOTES
AND SOURCES

Most of the documents cited below appear in *The Papers of Woodrow Wilson*, sixty-nine volumes edited and annotated by Arthur S. Link and a team of scholars. The books were published between 1966 and 1994. Those documents that appear in this "comprehensive edition of the documentary record of the life and thought of the twenty-eighth President of the United States" are referenced at the end of each notation with Arabic numerals indicating the volume and page number in which they appear.

Wilson's archives are housed primarily in either the Library of Congress or the Seeley G. Mudd Manuscript Library of the Princeton University Library; and many documents—including those from heretofore unseen collections recently made public by the families of Dr. Cary T. Grayson and Jessie Wilson Sayre—reside in the Woodrow Wilson Presidential Library in Staunton, Virginia.

In a few instances, information was obtained through interviews; those citations are designated with (I). Stray documents and newspaper clippings are identified as much as possible, though sometimes they are without sources (n.s.) or dates (n.d.) or page numbers (n.p.). Publishing data for references listed only by an author's name or initials followed by page numbers can be found in the Bibliography.

ABBREVIATIONS

(A)	Address
ASB	A. Scott Berg
ASL	Arthur S. Link
CD	Cleveland Dodge
CG	*Congressional Government* (by WW)
CTG	Dr. Cary Travers Grayson
(D)	Diary
EAW	Ellen Axson Wilson (WW's first wife)
EBW	Edith Bolling Galt Wilson (WW's second wife)
EMH	Edward Mandell House

EWM	Eleanor ("Nell" or "Nellie") Wilson McAdoo (WW's daughter)
FDR	Franklin Delano Roosevelt
HCL	Henry Cabot Lodge
JD	Josephus Daniels
JPT	Joseph Patrick Tumulty
JRW	Joseph Ruggles Wilson (WW's father)
JWS	Jessie Woodrow Wilson Sayre (WW's daughter)
JWW	Janet "Jeanie" Woodrow Wilson (WW's mother)
(M)	Memorandum
MAH	Mary Allen Hulbert (Peck)
(N)	Notes
NYT	New York Times
PUL	Princeton University Library
(R)	Remarks
RL	Robert Lansing
RSB	Ray Stannard Baker
(S)	Speech
SA	Stockton Axson
(T)	Telegram
TR	Theodore Roosevelt
(U)	Unpublished
WGM	William Gibbs McAdoo
WJB	William Jennings Bryan
WW	Woodrow Wilson (W alone signifies Wilson)
WWPL	Woodrow Wilson Presidential Library

1 ASCENSION

DECEMBER 4, 1918—WW LEAVING HOBOKEN: CTG (D), Dec. 4, 1918, 53: 313–6; "President Starts Abroad," NYT, Dec. 5, 1918, 1–2; Pollock, 221–9; EBW, 172–3; Starling, 117–21.

WW CHARACTERIZATIONS: Cecil Harmsworth to Colonel David Flynn, Mar. 18, 1927, n.s.; Lawrence, 13, 360; Freud, 129; Evalyn Walsh McLean (U-N, privately held), n.d.; Tribble, xvii; Carroll, 41; R. B. Fosdick (D), Dec. 11, 1918, 53: 366; EAW, "Personal" (description of WW), July 28, 1912, 24: 573; EMH (D), June 10, 1919, 60: 373; George F. Kennan, "The Legacy of Woodrow Wilson," Princeton Alumni Weekly, Oct. 1, 1974, 11; Alderman, 19, 32; WW (A), "Importance of Bible Study," (privately published); Francis B. Sayre, Jr., to ASB (I), Sep. 30, 2001; Nancy Toy (D), Jan. 3, 1915, 32: 8; Frank I. Cobb, "WW: An Interpretation," Mar. 4, 1921, 64: 216–29; RSB, IV: 55; CTG (press conference), Dec. 19, 1918, 53: 447; Ida Tarbell (I), c. Oct. 3, 1916, 38: 325; Walter Lippmann, "The 14 Points and the League of Nations," Cambridge, MA (Harvard

University): League of Free Nations Association, 1919 (digitized 2008); WW to Samuel Thompson, Jr., Dec. 31, 1923, 68: 515; Keynes, 38; Nicolson, Peacemaking, 79; CTG (D), May 2, 1919, 58: 332; Kissinger, 52; Clements, ix; Truman, 16; WW to D. R. Stuart, Jan. 30, 1921, 67: 105; RSB (D), Mar. 21, 1919, 56: 128.

THE CROSSING: "With the Country's Good Wishes," NYT, Dec. 5, 1918, 12; R. B. Fosdick (D), cited in Hodgson, 194; W. C. Bullitt (D), Dec. 9 [10], 11, 1918, 53: 350–53n2, 367; EBW, 172–3, 174–5; CTG (D), Dec. 7, 8; R. B. Fosdick (D), Dec. 8, 12, 1918, 53: 340, 371, 384–5; "President Spends Sunday Evening in Old Navy Fashion," The Hatchet, Pollock, 213; Clive Day to Elizabeth Day, Dec. 10, 1918, 53: 349; Isaiah Bowman (M), Dec. 10, 1918, 53: 353–6; Sragow, 65–74; EBW to family, Dec. 15, 1918, 53: 397.

RECEPTIONS IN BREST AND PARIS: CTG (D), Dec. 13, 14, 15, 19, 21, 22, 24, 25, 1918, 53: 378–9, 382–4, 391, 439, 458–9, 467, 488–9, 502–5; EBW, 175–83, 185–8; I. Hoover, 77; "Meester Veelson," as quoted in Dos Passos, 208–214; RSB, article draft, Nov. 29, 1920, 66: 439;

EMH (D), Dec. 14, 15, 19, 21, 1918, 53: 390, 400–1, 448, 466; H. Hoover, 68–9; T. N. Page to WW, Dec. 24, 1918, 53: 494–6; E. Benham (D), Dec. 10, 21, 1918, 53: 357–8, 459–61; News report of WW (I), Dec. 18, 1918, 53: 422–30; R. B. Fosdick (D), Dec. 14, 1918, 53: 384; WW (S), Dec. 21, 1918, 53: 461–3; EBW to family, Dec. 24, 1918, 53: 499–501; WW (R), Dec. 25, 1918, 53: 505–7.

RECEPTIONS IN LONDON AND CARLISLE: CTG (D), Dec. 26, 27, 29, 1918, 53: 508–12, 519–22, 537–41; EBW, 191–206; EBW to family, Jan. 2, 1919, 53: 591–5; "Buckingham Palace Banquet," program, Dec. 27, 1918; WW (two S), Dec. 28 and 29, 1918, 53: 531–3, 541; Kennan, "The Legacy of Woodrow Wilson," *Princeton Alumni Weekly*, Oct. 1, 1974, 11; H. Hoover, 68.

2 PROVIDENCE

WW ANCESTRY AND BIRTH: W family Bible (at WWPL), 1: 3; Ozment, ix; Calvin, 926; Knox, quoted in Burleigh, 154; Stalker, 243; Herman, quoting Sir Walter Scott on p. viii; Hale, 16–20; "W Visits Grandfather's Church," *NYT*, Dec. 30, 1918, 2; Thomas Woodrow to Robert Williamson, Feb. 23, 1836 [Boyhood Home of President WW, Augusta, GA]; *Minutes of the Synod of South Carolina*, Spartanburg, SC: Band & White, 1907, 69–78; RSB, I: 6–14; WW, "After-dinner Remarks," Mar. 17, 1909, 19: 103; D. J. Brown, 9–15, 24, 34; MacMaster, 22; WW to C. A. Talcott (referring to "the uncle after whom I am named"), Sep. 22, 1881, 2: 81.

STAUNTON; AUGUSTA: Waddell, 275–80; JWW to Thomas Woodrow, Apr. 27, 1857, [PUL: WW Papers, Project Records, Folder 7]; Montgomery, 19–82; WW (S), Feb. 12, 1909, 19: 33; WW, *DR*, 208–9, 212; JRW, "Mutual Relations of Masters and Slaves As Taught in the Bible" (Augusta, GA: Steam Press of Chronicle & Sentinel, 1861)," Jan. 6, 1861; Henry Ward Beecher, "Peace, Be Still," Jan. 4, 1861 (*American Sermons: The Pilgrims to Martin Luther King, Jr.*, New York: Library of America, 1999, 645–64); R. L. Dabney, *Discussions Evangelical and Theological* (Harrisonburg, VA: Sprinkle Publications, 1962, IV: 180; Henry Louis Gates, Jr., and John Stauffer, "A Pragmatic Precedent," *NYT*, Jan. 19, 2009, A25; RSB, I: 30, 31, 33, 36, 38–9, 42–7, 51–2; Jefferson Davis recalled in JD (D), Apr. 30, 1917, 42: 168; Bailey, 80; ASL, "W's Imaginary World," 1: 20–2; WW to L. I. M. Wylie (re: Uncle Remus), Dec. 15, 1916, 40: 169; Weinstein, 15–9;

WW (S), Oct. 24, 1914, 31: 222; CTG (D), May 27, 1919, 59: 528; Helen Bones to RSB, July 2, 1915 [RSB Papers: PUL]; Jessie Bones Brower to RSB, May 9, 1926 [RSB Papers: PUL]; Samuel G. Blythe, "A Talk with the President," *Saturday Evening Post*, Jan. 9, 1915 [Dec. 5, 1914], 31: 395–6; WW, Talk to Washington Y. M. C. A., Jan. 26, 1915, 32: 126; WW (R), Apr. 21, 1915, 33: 49–50; WW to EAW, Apr. 19, 1888, 5: 719; WW to W. J. Hampton, Sep. 15, 1917, 44: 199; Freud, 10, 12, 66; WW (S, re: Robert E. Lee), Jan. 19, 1909, 18: 631–5; Northen, 354; WW (A), Dec. 10, 1915, 35: 329–36.

COLUMBIA: Lucas, 83–94; Moore, 203–4, 224; WW, *DR*, 252, 268, 278; WW, *History*, V: 46–9; Foner, xix–xxii, 461–9; Mencken, 171–6; Brinkley, 413–6; n.a., *WW Family Home Interpretation Supplement*, Historic Columbia Foundation, June 6, 2005, 1–9; RSB, I: 59–60, 64, 66–7, 71; WW, *When a Man*, 1, 2, 37; Jessie W. Bones, cited in RSB, I: 57; parsing Webster: CTG (D), May 27, 1919, 59: 528; ASL (N), 1: 20–2; Mulder, 255.

DAVIDSON: *Davidson College Catalogue: 1874–1875*; WW (N), c. Sep. 29, 1873, 1: 30–31; Minutes of Eumenean Society, November 7 and 21, 1873, Jan. 3, Mar. 27, 1874, 1: 35 and 36–7, 39–40, 42; WW, *When a Man*, 2–3; Beaty, 86–7, 128–37, 233–4; "in the service of the Devil," cited in Henry W. Bragdon, "The WW Collection," *Princeton University Library Chronicle*, Nov. 1945 (VII: 1), 8; Walter L. Lingle, "WW at Davidson College," *Davidson College Bulletin*, Dec. 15, 1933, n.p.; JWW to WW, May 20, 1874, 1: 50.

WILMINGTON: JWS and EWM to RSB (re: McCosh), cited in RSB, I: 84; White, 58–67; WW, "Rules and Regulations," ca. July 1, 1874, 1: 54–56; John Bellamy to RSB, cited in RSB, I: 79; David Bryant to RSB, cited in RSB I: 78; RSB, I: 23.

3 EDEN

PRINCETON HISTORY: Perry, 134–8; WW, "Princeton Sesquicentennial," *NY Tribune*, 10: 9–10; "Princeton in the Nation's Service" (S), Oct. 21, 1896, 10: 11–31; Link, 8; Oberdorfer, 22–35, 43, 58; Rhinehart, 4–7, 35–7; Leitch, 301–4, 425; WW, "The Personal Factor in Education," Sep. 12, 1907, 17: 325–33; Bragdon, 19; Hoeveler, 233–43; RSB, 1: 83.

WW'S ARRIVAL AT PRINCETON; FIRST YEAR: Hoeveler, 29, 263; *Catalogue of the College of New Jersey for the Academical Year 1875–'76*, 18–22; WW to Hiram Woods, Jr., Aug. 10,

1876, 1: 175n1; Robert McCarter, quoted in Bragdon, 21–2; RSB, I: 82, 86–8; WW, *ML*, 68, 113; Briggs, 197–202; Edmund Burke, quoted in Prior, 142–3; WW, "Notebooks," c. Jan. 1, 1876, 1: 76; WW to EAW, Apr. 22, 1884, 3: 144; WW, "My Journal" (shorthand D), June 3, 1876, 1: 130–2, 134, 140, 142, 145–9, 153, 166, 221; WW, "Index Rerum," 1: 87–127.

SUMMER, 1876; THRIVING AT PRINCETON: WW, "A Christian Statesman," Sep. 1, 1876, 1: 188–9; WW, "My Journal," 1: 157, 190–1, 193, 217, 400–1; ASL (N), 1: 441n1; WW, "The Ideal Statesman," 1: 241–5; WW, "Bismarck," 1: 325–8; RSB, I: 94; WW, articles in *The Princetonian*, 1: 336–7, 402–405, 460, 461–3, 467; WW's voice described by Robert Bridges, "A Personal Tribute," *Fifty Years of the Class of 1879*, Princeton, NJ: (privately printed) Princeton University Press, 1931, 1; WW, "Constitution of the Liberal Debating Club," 1: 245–9; C. A. Talcott, Minutes of Liberal Debating Club, Mar. 31, 1877, 1: 255; Leitch, 380; Bragdon, 35–41 (McCarter, quoted on page 35); JWW to WW, Nov. 20, 1878, 1: 435; WW to JRW, May 23, 1877, 1: 265–6; JRW to WW, Jan. 14, 1878, 1: 340–1; JWW to WW, Jan. 22, 1878, 1: 342; JRW to WW, Jan. 25, 1878, 1: 345–6.

PRINCETON—"WITHERSPOON GANG" AND UPPERCLASS YEARS: JWW to WW, Feb. 16, 1877, 1: 250; Rhinehart, 25–6; WW, quoted in "Function of Universities," *Boston Evening Transcript,* Jan. 3, 1903, n.p.; WW to EAW, Oct. 30, 1883, 1: 499–505; Bridges, *op. cit.,* 3, 6; JRW to WW, Dec. 10, 1878, 1: 441; Leitch, 146; McCarter, quoted in Bragdon, 40; WW, "Review of Green's 'A History of the English People,'" May 2, 1878, 1: 373–5; RSB, I: 196; WW, "My Journal," Nov. 6, 1876, 1: 221; WW, *DR*, 283–7; C. A. Talcott, Minutes of Liberal Debating Club, Apr. 5, 1877, 1: 255–7; ASL (N), "Cabinet Government in the United States," 1: 492–3; WW's grades recorded in WW (N), 1: 444n1; WW to W. M. Sloane (draft of letter), c. Dec. 5, 1883, 2: 566–9; WW, "Cabinet Government in the United States," *International Review,* VI (Aug. 1879), 1: 493–510; JRW to WW, Feb. 25 and Mar. 11, 1879, 1: 459–60 and 464; WW (N), "Wordsworth," May 14, 1879, 1: 481–4; WW, editorials, 1: 467–71.

COMMENCEMENT: ASL (N) re: Lynde Debate, 1: 145; JRW to WW, Mar. 20 and Apr. 17, 1879, 1: 466 and 477; WW, Notebook, June 19, 1876, 1: 143; C. A. Talcott to WW, May 21, 1879, 1: 484; JWW to WW, May 13, 1879, 1: 479–80;

WW to C. A. Talcott, July 7, 1879, 1: 487–8; "business card" described by Mary Hoyt, quoted in RSB, I: 104.

4 SINAI

WILMINGTON; CHARLOTTESVILLE: WW, *When a Man,* 7–9; WW to Robert Bridges, July 30, Sep. 4, and Nov. 7, 1879, 1: 489–90, 539–42, and 580–3; WW, "Self-Government in France," Sep. 11, 1879, 1: 515–39; WW to EAW, Oct. 30, 1883, 2: 500; WW (N), Marginalia, re: Minor on slavery, c. Nov. 10, 1879, 1: 583; Hiram Woods, Jr., to WW, Oct. 28, 1879, 1: 580; "Collegiana," *Virginia University Magazine, XIX* (Dec. 1879), 190–5, 1: 588; RSB I: 112–3, 119; Minutes of Jefferson Society, Mar. 6, 1880, 1: 608; WW, "John Bright," *Virginia University Magazine* (Mar. 1880), 354–70, 1: 608–21; WW, "Mr. Gladstone, A Character Sketch," *Virginia University Magazine* (Apr. 1880), 401–26, 1: 624–42; "Collegiana," *ibid.,* 643–6; J. W. Mallet to J. F. B. Beckwith, May 3, 1880, 1: 651; Bruce, 80; ASL (N), "W's Debate with William Cabell Bruce," 1: 652; JRW to WW, May 6, June 5 and 7, Oct. 5, 1880, 1: 654, 658 and 659–60, 682; WW to C. A. Talcott, Dec. 13, 1879, and May 20, 1880, 1: 591–3 and 1: 655–8; WW to Robert Bridges, Sep. 4, 1879, Aug. 22, and Sep. 18, 1880, 1: 539–42, 671–4, and 675–8; WW to Harriet Woodrow, c. Apr. 14 and Oct. 5, 1880, 1: 647–50 and 678–82; JWW to WW, June 5 and Aug. 23, 1880, 1: 659 and 674; Marion Bones to WW, June 14, 1880, 1: 660; WW, "Constitution and By-Laws of the Jefferson Society," Dec. 4, 1880, 1: 688–99; JWW and JRW to WW, Dec. 14, 1880, 1: 701; ASL (N), "W's Withdrawal from the University of Virginia," 1: 704.

RETURN TO WILMINGTON; PROPOSES TO HARRIET WOODROW: WW to Robert Bridges, Jan. 1, 1881, 2: 9–11; WW to Harriet Woodrow, Jan. 15–19, Sep. 25, and 26, 1881, 2: 12–7, 83, and 84–9; WW to R. H. Dabney, Feb. 1, 1881, 2: 17–9; RSB I: 130; Helen Welles Thackwell, "WW and My Mother," *Princeton University Library Chronicle* (Autumn 1950), v. 12, 6–18.

ATLANTA: WW to Robert Bridges, Aug. 22, 1881, and Mar. 15, Aug. 25, Oct. 28, 1882, and Jan. 4 and May 13, 1883, 2: 75–9 and 106–10, 136–8, 147–8 and 280–1 and 354–9; WW to C. A. Talcott, Sep. 22–Oct. 1, 1881, 2: 80–3; James Bones to WW, Mar. 21, 1882, 2: 111–3; E. I. Renick to WW, Jan. 15, 1882, 2: 96–7; WW, "Account of Personal Expenditures," May–June,

1882, 2: 129–30; SA, 35; JRW to WW, Aug. 20, 1882, and Feb. 13, 1883, 2: 135–6 and 303–4; WW to R. H. Dabney, Jan. 11 and May 11, 1883, 2: 284–7 and 350–4; WW (N), "Opposing the Protective Tariff," c. Sep. 23, 1882, 2: 139; WW, "Testimony," Sep. 23, 1882, 2: 140–3; WW, "Draft of a Constitution for Georgia House of Commons," c. Jan. 11, 1883, 2: 288–91; ASL (N), "W's Practice of Law," 2: 144–5; RSB I: 148; Thomas W. Thrash, "Apprenticeship at the Bar: The Atlanta Law Practice of WW," *Georgia State Bar Journal*, v. 28, no. 3 (Feb. 1992), 149; ASL (N), "Government by Debate," 2: 152–7; WW, "Government by Debate," c. Dec. 4, 1882, 2: 159–275; WW to Hiram Woods, Jr., Apr. 25, 1883, 2: 340–2; WW, "Culture and Education at the South," Mar. 29, 1883, 2: 326–32; RSB, I: 150; George C. Osborn, "WW As a Young Lawyer," *Georgia Historical Quarterly 41* (June 1957), 126–42; George Howe, Jr., to WW, May 31, 1882, 2: 131–2.

COURTING EAW: WW to EAW, July 16, 30, Sep. 18, 27, 29, Oct. 11, 18, 30, 1883, 2: 387–90, 395–9, 427–8, 442–5, 445–7, 465–9, 480–3, 499–505; RSB I: 161; EWM, *PG*, 3–4; Aucella, et al., 5–6; WW to Robert Bridges, July 26, 1883, 2: 393–4; ASL (N), "W and His Caligraph," 2: 366–8; Jessie Bones Brower to WW, July 15, 1883, 2: 386–7; JWW to WW, June 7 and 12, 1883, 2: 365 and 368–9; Battey, 36, 292; George C. Osborn, "Romance of WW and Ellen Axson," *North Carolina Historical Review 39* (Winter 1962), 32–57; ASL (N), "The Engagement," 2: 426–7; WW, *When a Man*, 10; WW to S. E. Axson, Sep. 19 and 24, 1883, 2: 430–1 and 436; SA, 91.

BALTIMORE AND JOHNS HOPKINS: D. C. Gilman, "Inaugural Address," Feb. 22, 1876; WW, "Application," Johns Hopkins University, Sep. 18, 1883, 2: 429–30; WW to EAW, Sep. 29, Oct. 2, 16, 30, Nov. 11, 13, 20, 27, 1883, Jan. 1, 4, 16, 31, Apr. 20, June 3, 5, 25, 29, July 1, 3, 13, Oct. 7, Nov. 27, 30, Dec. 6, 7, 15, 18, 1884, Jan. 29, 1885, 2: 435–7, 445–8, 449–50, 478–80, 499–505, 523–5, 527–30, 550–3, 641–4, 644–8, 657–60, 667–8, 3: 137–9, 203–5, 208–9, 215–6, 221–3, 225, 228–30, 243–4, 337, 489–92, 498–500, 517–8, 521–25, 541–4, 552–3, 4: 196–7; WW to R. H. Dabney, May 11, 1883, and Feb. 17, 1884, Feb. 14, Oct. 28, 1885, 2: 350–4 and 3: 25–8, 4: 247–50, 5: 37–8; Bragdon, 104–5; Minutes of the Seminary of Historical and Political Science, May 8, 1884, 3: 172; WW to Robert Bridges, Dec. 15, 1883, Nov. 19, 1884, Feb. 27, 1886, 2: 585–6, 3: 464–6, 5: 26–7; John Dewey to H. W.

Bragdon, July 14, 1940, quoted in Bragdon, *op.cit.*, 111; WW, "Adam Smith" (lecture draft), c. Nov. 20, 1883, 2: 542–4, 541; WW, *CG*, Dedication page, and text: 5: 34–5, 132–3, 174, 179; JRW to WW, Sep. 25, 1883, Oct. 4, Nov. 6, 1883, 2: 441–2, 454–5, 519–20; EAW to WW, Jan. 28, 1884, Apr. 7, Nov. 28, 1884, 2: 664–6, 3: 115–8, 494–5; JWW to WW, Dec. 4, 1883, 2: 563–4; WW to Houghton Mifflin & Co., Apr. 4, 1884, 3: 111–2; Houghton Mifflin & Co. to WW, Apr. 28 and Nov. 26, 1884, 3: 149 and 486; SA, 91, 103; M. W. Kennedy to WW, Apr. 15, 1884, 3: 130–1; ASL (N), "Ellen's Visit to Wilmington and Her Trip with Woodrow to Washington and New York," 3: 329–30; WW to Albert Shaw, Feb. 21, 1885, 4: 274–6.

CONGRESSIONAL GOVERNMENT; JOB OFFERS: WW to EAW, Apr. 27, Nov. 8, Dec. 10, 1884, Jan. 24, Feb. 20, June 16, 1885, 3: 414–5, 529–30, 4: 3–5, 271–2, 532, 719; WW, *CG*, Dedication page; JRW to WW, Jan. 30, Mar. 17, 1885, 4: 208, 377; JWW to WW, Mar. 17, 1885, 4: 376; Bragdon, 135–7; Albert Shaw, "CG," *Minneapolis Daily Tribune*, Feb. 15, 1885, 4: 284–6; RSB, I: 236.

WW-EAW WEDDING AND HONEYMOON: WW to EAW (confessing "my heart's . . . deepest secret"), Feb. 24, 1885, and June 21, 1885, 4: 286–8 and 733–5; EAW to WW, Mar. 28, 1885, 4: 424–6; EWM, *PG*, 147; Margaret Godley, "Cousins Recall Wedding of WW and 'Miss Ellie Lou' Here," *Savannah Evening Press*, Sep. 4, 194, n.p.; JRW to WW, July 27, 1885, 5: 7; RSB, I: 239.

BRYN MAWR, SETTLING IN: Addie C. Wildgoss to WW, July 30, 1885, 5: 9–10; WW to EAW, May 9, 1885, May 30, June 7, 1886, Oct. 8, 1887, 4: 574–6, 5: 269–70, 294–5, 612–3; Finch, 164–5; J. E. Rhoads to WW, Feb. 11, 1885, 4: 236; Meigs, 42–7; James E. Rhoades, "Address at the Inauguration of Bryn Mawr College," Philadelphia: Sherman and Co., 1886; WW (N), c. Sep. 24, Oct. 1, c. Oct. 15–c. Dec. 1, 1885, 5: 18–23, 23–25, 27–35; RSB, I: 260–4, 290; Bragdon, 148–53; WW to J. B. Angell, Nov. 7, 1887, 5: 625–7; WW, "Copy of Bryn Mawr Catalogue," c. Feb. 1, 1888, 5: 659–63; ASL (N), "W's Desire for a Literary Life," 5: 474–5; EWM, *PG*, 148, 159–60; WW to H. B. Adams, Apr. 2, 1886, 5: 150–1; H. B. Adams to WW, Apr. 7, 1886, 5: 154–5; JRW to WW, Apr. 5, 1886, 5: 152.

EAW GIVES BIRTH; WW'S PH.D.: WW to EAW, Apr. 1, 16, 24, May 29, 1886, 5: 156–7,

157–8, 169–70, 267; L. C. H. Brown to WW, Apr. 16, 1886, 5: 158–9; WW to Robert Bridges, Apr. 19, 1886, 5: 163–4; A. L. Lowell, "Ministerial Responsibility and the Constitution," *Atlantic Monthly, LVII,* Feb. 1886, 180–93; WW, "Responsible Government under the Constitution," c. Feb. 10, 1886, 5: 107–24; H. W. Bragdon, "WW and Lawrence Lowell," *Harvard Alumni Bulletin, XLV* (May 22, 1943), 595; SA, 35–6; Robert Ewing to WW, May 28, 1887, 5: 508; EWM, *PG,* 159–60; Thomas Dixon, Jr., to WW, June 7, 1887, 5: 515–6; JRW to WW, June 11, 1877, 5: 517; RSB, I: 275; WW to R. H. Dabney, Nov. 7, 1887, 5: 500–1.

RETURNING TO BRYN MAWR, AND DEPARTING: JRW to WW, Apr. 30, 1887, 5: 500–1; WW to EAW, Apr. 17, 18, 19, 20, 1888, 5: 718–20; WW to R. H. Dabney, May 16, 1888, 5: 726; SA, 58; C. K. Adams to WW, Mar. 12, 1885, Oct. 13 and 22, 1886; 4: 357–8, 5: 351 and 357; WW, "The Study of Administration," c. Nov. 1, 1886; 5: 359–80; Johns Hopkins University Trustees Minutes, Jan. 17, 1887, 5: 431; H. B. Adams to WW, Jan. 21 and 25, 1887, 5: 431–2 and 435–6; Bragdon, 188; "Agreement Between Trustees of Bryn Mawr College and WW, Ph. D.," Mar. 14, 1887, 5: 468–9; WW to Robert Bridges, Nov. 30, 1887, and Aug. 26, 1888 ("hungry . . . for a class of *men*"), 5: 632–3 and 763–5; WW to president and trustees of Bryn Mawr College, June 29, 1888, 5: 743–7; J. E. Rhoads to M. C. Thomas, June 30 and July 6, 1888, 5: 748, 749; ASL (N), "W's First Failure at Public Speaking," 5:134–7; ASL (N), "W's Lectures on Administration at the Johns Hopkins, 1892," 7: 381; Robert Bridges to WW, Nov. 5, 1889, 6: 410–1.

WESLEYAN: "Wesleyan's Gift," *Hartford Evening Post,* Dec. 17, 1889, 6: 453–4; WW to Robert Bridges, Nov. 27, 1888, 6: 25; SA, 37–8, 60–4, 65, 259–60n24; WW, "History and Political Economy," *Wesleyan Catalogue: 1888–1889,* 6: 26–7; RSB, I: 299–301, 315–7; EAW to WW, May 22, 1886, 5: 249–51; EWM, *PG,* 164, 171; WW, "Constitution for Wesleyan House of Commons," c. Jan. 5, 1889, 6: 39–45; "Wesleyan House of Commons," *Wesleyan Argus,* Jan. 18, 1889, 6: 45–7; Carl Price, (Wesleyan) *Alumnus,* Mar. 1924, cited in RSB, I: 305; F. J. Turner to Caroline Mae Sherwood, Jan. 21, 1889, 6: 58; WW, *TS,* xxxiv, 29, 660; WW to R. H. Dabney, Oct. 31, 1889, 6: 408–9; R. H. Dabney to WW, Mar. 1, 1890, 6: 536–7; F. J. Turner to WW, Jan. 23, 1890, 6: 478–9; D. M. Means, "W's 'The

State,' " *The Nation,* Dec. 26, 1889, 6: 458–62; WW to W. W. Thompson, June 28, 1915, cited in RSB, I: 324; JRW to WW, May 9 and Oct. 30, 1889, 6: 217–8 and 408; WW to EAW, Mar. 9, 1889, 6: 139–40; M. W. Kennedy to WW, Oct. 12, 1889, 6: 402; A. B. Hart to WW, Apr. 23 and May 10, 1889, 6: 174–5 and 218–9; WW to A. B. Hart, May 13, 1889, 6: 240; WW to F. J. Turner, Aug. 23, 1889, 6: 368–71.

PRINCETON OPPORTUNITY: WW to Robert Bridges, July 23, Aug. 9, 1889, and Jan. 27, 1890, 6: 356–7, 363–4, and 480–1; Robert Bridges to WW, July 15 and 30, 1889, 6: 330 and 359–61; RSB, II: 5; F. L. Patton to WW, Feb. 18, 1890, 6: 526–8; WW (D), Feb. 13, 1890, 6: 523; Horace Elisha Scudder to WW, Dec. 20, 1889, 6: 424–5.

5 REFORMATION

RETURN TO PRINCETON: McCosh, 61–8; Thorp, 46–8; Bragdon, 203–6, 209, 213, 272; Hoeveler, 335–7; Rhinehart, 26–7; "The Favor of a University," *NYT,* Feb. 11, 1887, 3; Patton, 17–9, 24, 42–3; Axtell, 42, 65; SA, 222; WW to A. W. Howe, Apr. 21, 1895, 9: 247; ASL, "W's Teaching at Princeton," 7: 5–7; WW, anecdote of the town drunk, related in *Princeton Alumni Weekly, IV* (Apr. 23, 1904), 466–7, 15: 272–3; WW, lecture (N), July 2–10, 1894, 8: 597–608; Raymond Fosdick to RSB, n.d., RSB, II: 10, 12; Myers, 38; WW to R. H. Dabney, July 1, 1891, 7: 233; Princeton Faculty Minutes, Oct. 24, 1890, Apr. 24 and Nov. 6, 1891, Jan. 18, 1893, 7: 51, 195, 322, 8: 79; "Caledonian Games," *The Princetonian, XVI,* June 6, 1891, 7: 219; WW to *The Princetonian* editors, Jan. 8, 1892, 7: 374; C. B. Newton to WW, Nov. 9, 1891, 7: 342; Leitch, 488–9; Bliss Perry to RSB, quoted in RSB, II: 16–7; Mark Bernstein, "Shirt Cuff and Other Artifacts of Student Life," *Princeton Alumni Weekly,* Oct. 7, 2009, n.p.

PERSONAL LIFE—HIBBEN AND FAMILY: Reid, 63; Freud, 103, 130; Bliss Perry to RSB, n.d., in RSB, II: 53; SA, 28–9; EWM, *TWW,* 13–5; EAW to WW, Feb. 16, 1895, 9: 202; WW to C. W. Kent, June 29, 1893, 8: 273; WW to EAW, Feb. 6, 1894, Feb. 18, 1895, 8: 460, 9: 206.

WW LITERARY LIFE: ASL (N), "W's *Division and Reunion,* 8: 147; WW, *DR,* x, 299; Frederic Bancroft, review of *DR, Political Science Quarterly, VIII* (Sep. 1893), 533–5, 8: 345; F. J. Turner to WW, July 16, 1893, and Dec. 24, 1894, 8: 279 and 9: 118; ASL (N), "W's *Short History of the*

United States," 8: 279–81; Harper & Bros. to WW, May 5, 1896, 9: 500; WW to Harper & Bros., May 16, 1890, 9: 504–5; WW to EAW, Jan. 29 and 30, July 29 and 30, 1894, 8: 442, 632 and 634.

LIBRARY PLACE: EMW, *TWW*, 18; E. S. Child to WW, Jan. 14, 16, May 7, 1895; 9: 121–2, 123, 252; WW to Child & de Goll, Architects, Jan. 19, 1895, 9: 123; EWM, *PG*, 201; E. S. Child to EAW, Feb. 18, 1895, 9: 207; WW to EAW, Jan. 25, 1895, 9: 126; EAW to F. J. Turner, Dec. 15, 1896, 10: 80.

CEREBRAL INCIDENT; TRIP TO BRITAIN: WW to A. B. Hart, Aug. 21, 1891, 7: 274; EWM, *PG*, 201–2; Weinstein, 141; Bragdon, 220; WW to EAW, June 28 and 29, July 9, Aug. 24, 1896, 9: 528, 529, 537–8, 575; Andrew Wilson, 6–7.

SESQUICENTENNIAL ("Princeton in the Nation's Service"): Theodore J. Ziolkowski, "Princeton in *Whose* Service?," Jan. 23, 1991, appears in J. I. Merritt (ed.), *The Best of PAW* (Princeton, NJ: Princeton Alumni Weekly, 2000), 53–8; Oberdorfer, 98; Leitch, 438–40, RSB, II: 33–6; *NY Tribune*, Oct. 22, 1896, 10: 9–11; WW, "Princeton in the Nation's Service," Oct. 21, 1896, 10: 11–31; ASL (N), 10: 11–12n1; "Oration by Professor Wilson," *NYT*, Oct. 22, 1896, 2; SA, 42–3, 97; EAW to Mary Hoyt, Oct. 27, 1896, 10: 37–8; EWM, *PG*, 207.

WW'S POLITICS AND PUBLIC ADDRESSES: SA, 42–3, 73, 264; "University School," *Bridgeport* (CT) *Evening Post*, May 25, 1898, 10: 534; WW, "What Ought We to Do," c. Aug. 1, 1898, 10: 574–6; "Our Obligations," *Waterbury* (CT) *American*, Dec. 14, 1899, 11: 297–300; "Philadelphian Society," *Daily Princetonian*, May 19, 1899, 11: 119; "Liberty and Its Uses," *Brooklyn Daily Eagle*, Jan. 14, 1900, 11: 374–5; WW, "Ideals of America" (S), Dec. 26, 1901, appeared in *Atlantic Monthly, XC* (Dec. 1902), 721–34, 12: 208–27; WW, "Leaderless Government" (S), Aug. 5, 1897, 10: 288–304; WW, "American Constitutional Law," Mar. 2, 1894, 8: 563; "Address by WW," *Poughkeepsie Daily Eagle*, May 3, 1902, 12: 362.

PRINCETON POLITICS AND WW'S ASCENT: C. E. Green to WW, Mar. 27 and 28, 1897, 10: 195 and 197; WW to F. L. Patton, Mar. 28, 1897, 10: 196; SA, 262; WW (D), Jan. 21, 1897, 10: 120; WW to EAW, Feb. 27, 1896, Jan. 29 and Feb. 16, 1897, 9: 457, 10: 123 and 164; F. L. Patton to C. H. McCormick, Apr. 4, 1898, 10: 497–9; WW to F. J. Turner, Mar. 31, 1897, 10: 201; News item, *Princeton Press*, Feb. 19, 1898, and

Nov. 24, 1900, 10: 402 and 12: 35; WW to Jenny Hibben, June 26, 1899, 11: 136; Bragdon, 225; JRW to WW, Jan. 3, 1897, 10: 95; G. W. Miles to WW, Apr. 7, 1898, 10: 501–2; H. M. Alden to WW, Jan. 8, 1901, 12: 69; D. C. Gilman to WW, Mar. 16, 1901, 12: 108; J. E. Webb to WW, Mar. 11, 1901, 12: 106; W. P. Johnston to WW, June 16, 1898, 10: 557; *Princeton Alumni Weekly, II* (Oct. 26, 1901), 67–8; "Pres. Remsen Is Inaugurated," Baltimore *Sun*, Feb. 23, 1902, 12: 282; F. L Patton to C. H. McCormick, Apr. 4, 1898, 10: 496–9; C. C. Cuyler to WW, Mar. 28, May 16, Dec. 23, 1898, 10: 485, 529–30, 11: 91.

WW RETURNS TO BRITAIN; LITERARY SURGE: Andrew Wilson, 8; WW to EAW, July 2, 7, and Aug. 20, 1899, 11: 142–3, 155, and 234–6; SA, 84–9; WW, *ML*, 73–4, 197, 201; "Old-Fashioned Democrat" to Editor of *Indianapolis News*, May 1, 1902, 12: 356–8; WW to R. W. Gilder, Jan. 28, 1901, 12: 84; WW, "Robert E. Lee" (S), Jan. 19, 1909, 18: 639.

WW BECOMES PRESIDENT OF PRINCETON: M. T. Pyne to A. F. West, Oct. 16, Nov. 27, Dec. 14, 1900, cited in Thorp, 67–8; ASL (N), "The Crisis in Presidential Leadership," 12: 292; SA, 117–8, 271; C. C. Cuyler to C. H. McCormick, July 2, 1902, 12: 473–4; WW to EAW, June 1, 1902, 12: 390–1; S. B. Dod to WW, June 25, 1902, 12: 457; EWM, *PG*, 225; J. G. Hibben to RSB, cited in RSB II: 131; *Princeton Alumni Weekly, II* (June 14, 1902), 133–4, 12: 421–2; "WW," *NYT*, June 11, 1902, quoted in RSB II: 131; M. T. Pyne to WW, June 19, 1902, and TR to Grover Cleveland, June 17, 1902, both cited 12: 441; WW to F. J. Turner, Jan. 21, 1902, 12: 240.

WW'S INSTALLATION; DEATH OF JRW: WW to EAW, July 19, 1902, 14: 27; EWM, *TWW*, 61–5, 68; EAW to WW, July 24, 1902, 14:43; "WW Installed at Princeton," *NYT*, Oct., 26, 1902, 1; "WW Inauguration," *Princeton Alumni Weekly, III* (Nov. 1, 1902), 83–6, 14: 191–5; WW, "Princeton for the Nation's Service" (S), Oct. 25, 1902, 14: 170–85; EWM, *PG*, 230; RSB, II: 142; "Rev. Joseph R. Wilson, D. D.," *Princeton Press*, Jan. 24, 1903, 14: 330; "Funeral Services of the Late JRW" and "JRW," Columbia (SC) *State*, Jan. 24, 1903, 14: 331 and 331–3.

WW'S INNOVATIONS: E. G. Reid, 98; WW to Board of Trustees, Oct. 21, 1902, and Dec. 10, 1903, 14: 150–61 and 15: 69–75; Neil Rudenstine, "WW: Ideas and Goals for United States Higher Education," *WW at Princeton: Perspectives from University Presidents*, Princeton, NJ:

WW School, 2006, 28; WW (M), "Departmental Organization," c. Nov. 20, 1903, 15: 55–6; WW, "College and Methods of Instruction" (S), 15: 79–98; WW, "Report to Faculty," Apr. 16, 1904, 15: 252–63; ASL (N), "The New Princeton Course of Study," 15: 277–92; E. S. Corwin, "Departmental Colleague," in Myers, 22; WW (S) to Princeton Alumni of NY, Dec. 9, 1902, 14: 273; News items, *Princeton Alumni Weekly, III* (Nov. 8, 1902, and Mar. 7, 1903), 116 and 355, 14: 203 and 383; Mary Hoyt to RSB, quoted in RSB, II: 152; Axtell, 55; EAW to WW, May, 1903, 14: 440–1; "Faculty Song," 1903 Campus Songs, n.d., 14: 441; Finance Committee Report, Oct. 14, 1902, 14: 144.

WW AND EAW TO EUROPE; DEATH OF EDWARD AXSON: WW, "Record of a European Trip," July 10–Sep. 22, 1903, 14: 521–43; EAW to WW, May 25, 1904, 15: 348; WW to Robert Bridges, Apr. 28, 1905, 16: 86; EWM, *PG*, 240.

PRINCETON'S EXPANSION: Weinstein, 162, 163; WW (S), to Princeton Alumni of NY, Dec. 9, 1902, 14: 269; Minutes of Princeton Board, Dec. 8, 1904, 15: 569–70; News item, *Princeton Alumni Weekly, IV* (June 18, 1904), 600–1 and (Jan. 7, 1905), 213, 15: 390 and 577; WW to J. H. Reed, c. Jan. 13, 1904, 15: 124–6; M. T. Pyne to WW, July 30, 1904, 15: 424–6; C. W. McAlpin to WW, Jan. 13, 1906, 16: 282; Nasaw, 612; WW to Andrew Carnegie, Apr. 17, 1903, 14: 411–5; "Princeton Lake," *Princeton Press*, Dec. 5, 1903, 15: 66–7; "Pres. W Convalescing," *Daily Princetonian*, Jan. 7, 1905, 15: 577; WW to W. B. Pritchard, July 5, 1990, 11: 553–4; WW, "Baccalaureate Address," June 11, 1905, 16: 125; RSB II: 153; WW, "Report to Board of Trustees," Dec. 13, 1906, 16: 516; John DeWitt to WW, Oct. 29, 1904, 15: 531; R. K. Root, "Wilson and the Preceptors," Edward S. Corwin, "Departmental Colleague," Luther P. Eisenhart, "The Far-Seeing Wilson," E. G. Conklin, "As a Scientist Saw Him," J. Duncan Spaeth, "As I Knew Him and View Him Now," all in Myers, 13–16, 19 and 28, 64, 55–6 and 59, 87; "Army and Navy Crowd," *Daily Princetonian*, Dec. 4, 1905, 16: 242–3; WW (N), Oct. 28, 1905, 16: 208; "Two College Presidents Spoke," *Providence Journal*, Feb. 10, 1906, 16: 309–12.

LOTOS CLUB SPEECH: F. R. Lawrence, quoted in *NYT*, Feb. 4, 1906, 16: 293; WW (S) at Lotos Club, Feb. 3, 1906, 16: 292–9; G. B. M. Harvey (S), Feb. 3, 1906, 16: 299–301; WW to G. B. M. Harvey, Feb. 3, 1906, 16: 301; SA, 151.

6 ADVENT

FIRST POLITICAL FLIRTATION: WW to St. Clair McKelway, Mar. 11, 1906, 16: 330; WW, "Address on Thomas Jefferson," Apr. 16, 1906, 16: 362–9; "The Jefferson Celebration," *Brooklyn Daily Eagle*, Apr. 17, 1906, 16: 373n3; "Head of Princeton Defines Education," *Cleveland Leader*, May 19, 1906, 16: 396–7; James Mathers, "Annual Convention of the Western Association of Princeton Clubs," *Princeton Alumni Weekly, VI* (May 26 and June 2, 1906), 632, 651–5, 16: 405–11.

SUDDEN ILLNESS; RECUPERATION IN ENGLAND: EAW to Mary Hoyt, June 12, 1906, 16: 423; Weinstein, 149, 165–6; SA, 44–6; EWM, *TWW*, 93, 94–6; ASL (N), 16: 412n1; WW to N. M. Butler, June 1, 1906, 16: 413; WW to C. W. McAlpin, July 19, 1906, 16: 431; Minutes, Princeton Board of Trustees, June 11, 1906, 16: 422; WW to Annie W. Howe, Aug. 2, 1906; 16: 432; WW to EAW, Aug. 27 and Sep. 2, 1906, 16: 441 and 445–6; Andrew Wilson, 19; EWM, *PG*, 241–2; WW to Robert Bridges, Sep. 6, 1906, 16: 451; EAW to Florence Hoyt, June 27, 1906, 16: 429–30.

PLANS FOR PRINCETON'S SOCIAL REFORM: WW to CD, Sep. 16, 1906, 16: 453–4; "WW's Stand," NY *Evening Post*, Oct. 2, 1906, 16: 454–5; "WW's Position," *NY Evening Post*, Oct. 15, 1906, 16: 456–7; n.t., *Princeton Alumni Weekly, VI* (June 9, 1906), 673–4, 16: 419; WW, "Report on Social Coordination of the University," *Princeton Alumni Weekly, VI* (June 12, 1907), 606–15, cited in Day, 80; WW to H. B. Brougham, Feb. 1, 1910, 20: 70; WW, "Supplementary Report to Board of Trustees," c. Dec. 13, 1906, 16: 519–25.

MINORITIES AT PRINCETON: WW to J. R. Williams, Sep. 2, 1904; 15: 462n; G. M. Sullivan to WW, Nov. 20, 1909, 19: 529; WW to G. M. Sullivan (draft), c. Dec. 3, 1909, 19: 550; C. W. McAlpin to G. W. Sullivan, Dec. 6, 1909, 19: 558; J. C. Hemphill to WW, Jan. 22, 1906, 16: 286; "The Conservatism of the South," Charleston (SC) *News and Courier*, Jan. 22, 1906, 16: 286–8; WW to J. C. Hemphill, Jan. 26, 1906, 16: 288; J. F. Jameson to WW, Nov. 18, 1889, 6: 427; WW (N), June 30, 1904, 15: 400; WW, "The Making of the Nation," *Atlantic Monthly, LXXX* (July 1897), 1–14, 10: 230; ASL (N), 19: 462n2; WW

(N), Feb. 26, 1909, 19: 69; Mary Yates (D), July 31, 1908, 18: 386–7; Karabel, 71; L. M. Levy to WW, c. June 25, 1907, 17: 223; J. R. Wright to WW, Sep. 16, 1904, 15: 471; Konvitz, 17.

ANDREW FLEMING WEST AND GRADUATE COLLEGE: Andrew Fleming West, *Proposed Graduate College of Princeton University,* (Princeton: 1903), cited in 16: 414n2; Thorp, 77, 107; W. M. Sloane, et al., to Board of Trustees of Princeton University, Oct. 15, 1906, 16: 458; S. H. Thompson, Jr., to WW, Feb. 7, 1910, 20: 84–5; SA, "Princeton Controversy" (M), Feb. 1925, RSB Papers, cited in Bragdon, 468n10; WW, "A Resolution," c. Oct. 20, 1906, 16: 467; Thorp, 109.

WW TO BERMUDA: EWM, *PG,* 243; WW to EAW, Jan. 14–16, 22, 30, 1907, 17: 3–7, 10–12, 25–7; WW to MAH, Feb. 6 and 20, 1907, 17: 29 and 48; ASL (N), 17: 29–30; Hulbert, 158–63; Bragdon, 220; EAW, quoted in Florence Hoyt to RSB, RSB Papers, cited in Weinstein, 188.

QUAD FIGHT: NY *Evening Post,* quoted in EAW to Anne Harris, Feb. 12, 1907, 17: 35; WW to CD, Feb. 20 and July 1, 1907, 17: 47–8 and 240–1; CD to WW, Dec. 19, 1906, July 2 and Aug. 6, 1907, 16: 534–5, 17: 243 and 341; D. B. Jones to WW, May 15, 1907, 17: 147–8, Franklin Murphy, Jr., to WW, June 7 and 18, 1907, 17: 187 and 216; WW, "Baccalaureate," June 9, 1907, 17: 187–96; WW, "Address to Trustees," June 10, 1907, 17: 199–206; RSB, II: 231; WW (N), June 11, 1907, 17: 209; Henry van Dyke to WW, July 5, 1907, 17: 260; Henry van Dyke to W. A. White, May 17, 1924, quoted in 17: 260n1; A. F. West to WW, July 10, 1907, 17: 270–1; John Grier Hibben to WW, July 8, 1907, 17: 262–4; WW, "The Author and Signers of the Declaration of Independence," July 4, 1907, 17: 248–59; WW to J. G. Hibben, July 10, 1907, 17: 268–9; SA, 204–206; WW, "The Personal Factor in Education," c. Aug. 1, 1907, 17: 325–33; WW, "Politics," c. July 31, 1917, 17: 309–25; WW, "Address at Harvard," June 26, 1907, 17: 226; Elliot, 230; H. B. Thompson to CD, Sep. 10, 1907, 17: 379–81; "Opening Exercises," *Daily Princetonian,* Sep. 20, 1907, 17: 394–5; Minutes, Princeton Board meeting, quoted in RSB, II: 256–7; Minutes of Faculty, Sep. 26, 1907, 17: 402; EAW to JWS, Sep. 27, 1907 [PUL: JWS Papers, MC 216, Box 2]; W. S. Myers (D), Sep. 30 and Oct. 7, 1907, 17: 408–9 and 424; "The 'Quad' System," *Daily Princetonian,* Oct. 2, 1907, 17: 411–13; P. van Dyke to Editor of *Princeton Alumni Weekly, Princeton Alumni Weekly, VIII* (Oct.

2, 1907), 20–1, 17: 413–4; WW (N), Oct. 7, 1907, 17: 420–1; T. W. Hunt to WW, Oct. 7, 1907, 17: 424–5; WW to D. B. Jones, Sep. 27, 1907, 17: 401; A. H. Joline to editor of *Princeton Alumni Weekly, VIII* (Oct. 9, 1907), 36–8, 17: 428–31; H. B. Thompson to CD, Oct. 15, 1907, 17: 434–5; H. B. Fine to SA, quoted in RSB, II: 245; Minutes, Board of Trustees of Princeton University, Oct. 17, 1907, 17: 441–3; "Princeton's Quad," NY *Evening Sun,* Oct. 18, 1907, 17: 444–5; WW to Board of Trustees, Oct. 17, 1907 (unsent), 17: 443–4; WW to M. W. Jacobus, Oct. 23, 1907, 17: 450–1; M. T. Pyne to A. C. Imbrie, Oct. 23, 1907, 17: 453–4; WW (N), Oct. 24, 1907, 17: 454; WW to JWS, Oct. 21, 1907 [PUL: JWS Papers, MC216, Box 2].

WW'S HEALTH; RECUPERATION IN BERMUDA: ASL (N), 17: 550n1; Freud, 130; James Kerney (N), Oct. 29, 1923 [PUL: MC169]; SA, 205–6; Minutes, Princeton Board of Trustees, Jan. 9, 1908, 17: 594; EWM, *PG,* 256; WW to EAW, Feb. 4, 1908, 17: 611–3; Hulbert, 163–72; Hoffman, 96.

POLITICS—PRINCETON AND THE NATION: D. B. Jones to WW, Nov. 12, 1907, 17: 496; WW (A) to Princeton Club of Chicago, Mar. 12, 1908, 18: 18–34; WW, "Report and Recommendations Respecting Undergraduate Social Conditions at Princeton University," Apr. 8, 1908, 18: 238; WW, "The Government and Business" (A), Mar. 14, 1908, 18: 35–51; WW, "Law or Personal Power" (A), Apr. 13, 1908, 18: 263–8; WW, "Baccalaureate Address," June 7, 1908, 18: 323–33; "Faculty Song," as appears in *Carmina Princetoniana: The Songbook of Princeton University* (New York: G. Schirmer, 1968), 35; SA, 153–4; EWM, *PG,* 246.

WW RETURNS TO BRITISH ISLES: WW to EAW, June 26, 27, 29, July 1, 6, 13, Aug. 16, 1908, 18: 343–4, 345–7, 349, 351–3, 361–4, 399–401; RSB, II: 284.

W. C. PROCTER AND GRADUATE COLLEGE: Poucher, 3–99; Thorp, 113, 120–3; W. C. Procter to A. F. West, May 8, 1909, 19: 189–9; SA, 136; W. C. Procter to WW, June 7, 1909, 19: 237–8; A. F. West, "The Proposed Graduate College of Princeton University," quoted in RSB II: 292; "St. Paul's Anniversary," Concord (NH) *Evening Monitor,* June 3, 1909, 19: 226–8; WW (A), June 7, 1909, as printed in *Union College Bulletin, II* (Aug. 1909), 32–43, 19: 231–7; WW, "Baccalaureate Address," June 13, 1909, 19: 242–51; WW,

"The Spirit of Learning" (A), July 1, 1909, *Harvard Graduates' Magazine, XVIII* (Sep. 1909), 1–14, 19: 277–89.

EAW IN OLD LYME: WW to MAH, July 11 and 18, Sep. 5, 1909, 19: 307–10 and 311–14, 357–9; Aucella, et al., 5–6, 13–4; EWM, *TWW*, 104–7; RSB, II: 302.

THE PECK "AFFAIR": WW to EBW, Sep. 19 and 21, 1915, 34: 491–2 and 500; CTG, quoted in Breckinridge Long (D), Jan. 11, 1924, 68: 527; WW to EAW, June 26, 1908, 18: 372; WW to MAH, Sep. 5 and 26, 1909, 19: 357–9 and 392–4; Freud, 92, 154, 132.

GRADUATE SCHOOL BATTLE: WW to MAH, Sep. 26, Oct. 24, 1909, and Feb. 14, 1910, 19: 392, 442–4, and 20: 126; W. C. Procter to M. T. Pyne, Oct. 20, 1909, 19: 424; Minutes, Princeton Board of Trustees, Oct. 21, 1909, 19: 435–9; RSB, II: 313–4, 322–3; WW to M. T. Pyne, Dec. 22 and 25, 1909, 19: 620 and 628–31; M. T. Pyne to WW, Dec. 24, 1909, 19: 627; Wilson Farrand (N), n.d. [Selected Papers of Wilson Farrand, PUL: #CO155]; WW to H. B. Thompson, Jan. 17, 1910, quoted in RSB, II: 322; WW to Hiram Woods, Mar. 23, 1910, 20: 285–7; "Princeton," *NYT*, Feb. 3, 1910, 20: 74–6; WW to H. B. Brougham, Feb. 1, 1910, 20: 69–71; H. B. Brougham to RSB, Aug. 21, 1924, quoted in RSB, II: 328n3; G. M. Harper to Wilson Farrand, Feb. 3, 1910; CD to WW, Feb. 6, 1910, 20: 82; EWM, *PG*, 255; EAW to WW, Feb. 21, 1910, 20: 152–3; WW to EAW, Feb. 14 and 21, 1910, 20: 125–6 and 145–6; WW, "The Country and Colleges," c. Feb. 24, 1910, 20: 157–72; EWM, *TWW*, 106–7.

NJ BOSSES APPROACH WW: "James Smith, Jr. Fails in Business," *NYT*, Nov. 21, 1915, 1, 6; EWM, *PG*, 260; RSB, III: 45, 48–9; ASL (N), "Colonel Harvey's Plan for Wilson's Entry into Politics," 20: 146–8; William O. Inglis, *Collier's*, Oct. 1916, cited in RSB, III: 46–8; WW to MAH, Sep. 5, 1909, 19: 358; "Statesmanship in Banking," *NY Evening Post*, Jan. 18, 1910, n.p.; "Bankers Warned Their Narrowness Harms Country," NY *World*, Jan. 18, 1910, n.p.; "Panics Needless MacVeagh Asserts," *NYT*, Jan. 18, 1910, 3; "Wilson to Bankers," *NY Tribune*, Jan. 18, 1910, 20: 23–7; Bullock, 99; WW (A) to Short Ballot Organization, Jan. 21, 1910, 20: 32–43; WW (A) on Grover Cleveland, National Democratic Club, 20: 257–62; WW (A) to Democratic Dollar Dinner, Mar. 29, 1910, 20: 297–303.

GRADUATE SCHOOL DEFEAT: WW, "Abstract of Address to Western Association of Princeton Clubs," Mar. 26, 1910, *Princeton Alumni Weekly, X* (Mar. 30, 1910), 412–5, 20: 291–6; WW (A) to Princeton Club of NY, Apr. 7, 1910, *Princeton Alumni Weekly, X* (Apr. 13, 1910), 447–53, 20: 337–48; H. B. Thompson to CD, Apr. 15, 1910, 20: 361–2; "Disaster Forecast by Wilson," Apr. 17, 1910, *Pittsburgh Dispatch*, Apr. 17, 1910, 20: 363–5; WW, "Pittsburgh Speech," *Princeton Alumni Weekly, X* (Apr. 20, 1910), 467–71, 20: 373–6; M. T. Pyne to Bayard Henry, Apr. 20, 1910, 20: 377–8; D. B. Jones to WW, May 19, 1910, 20: 459–60; WW to E. W. Sheldon, May 16, 1910, 20: 456–7; "Gift of $10,000,000 Left to Princeton," *NYT*, May 22, 1910, 1; SA to RSB, quoted in RSB II: 346; SA, 142; J. M. Raymond and A. F. West to WW (T), May 22, 1910, 20: 464; A. F. West to M. T. Pyne, May 22, 1910, 20: 465–6; WW to Hiram Woods, May 28, 1910, 20: 482–3; WW to T. D. Jones, May 30, 1910, 20: 483–4; EWM, *TWW*, 101, 106–7; A. F. West, "Narrative of the Graduate College" [U typescript, PUL: Graduate School Records], 75–109; H. B. Thompson to E. W. Sheldon, May 31, 1910 (two letters), May 31, 1910, 20: 488–9 and 489–90; WW to MAH, June 5, 1910, 20: 500–1; WW, "Baccalaureate Sermon," June 12, 1910, 20: 520–8; ASL (N), 20: 451–2; Lawrence, 32; RSB, II: 351.

WW LEAVES FOR CONNECTICUT: EWM, *TWW*, 107; WW to G. B. Harvey (T), Jun. 25, 1910, 20: 541.

7 PAUL

WW ENTERS NEW JERSEY POLITICS: Hosford, 13–20, 31–2, 37, 49–61; EWM, *PG*, 265; WW (S), Oct. 17, 1912, 25: 428; Morgenthau, 132–3; RSB, III: 55–6; WW to D. B. Jones, June 27, 1910, 20: 544–5; EWM, *TWW*, 108–9; "Wall St. to Put Up W. Wilson for President," *NY Journal*, June 18, 1910, cited in RSB, III: 61; G. B. M. Harvey to WW, July 7 and Aug. 12 and Sep. 9, 10, 1910, 20: 563 and 21: 52 and 87–8, 88–9; ASL (N), "Lawyers' Club Conference," July 8, 1910, 20: 565–6; Hudspeth, cited in RSB, III: 63–4; WW to G. B. M. Harvey, July 14 and Aug. 3, 8, 1910, 20: 576–7 and 21: 35, 41n1; WW (S), to Princeton University Board, Oct. 20, 1910, 21: 362; WW, quoted in *Newark Evening News*, July 15, 1910, 20: 581; H. E. Alexander to WW, July 23, 1910, 21: 23; WW to James Kerney, Aug. 2, 1910, 21: 34; WW, "Proposed Democratic State Platform," Aug. 9, 1910, 21: 43–6; RSB, III: 70; WW to Edgar Williamson, Aug. 23, 1910, 21: 59–61; WW

(S), "The Lawyer and the Community," Aug. 31, 1910, 21: 64–81.

WW NOMINATED FOR GOVERNOR: Tumulty, 16–8, 19–23, 26; RSB, III: 77–9; SA, 159; WW, "Acceptance Speech," Sep. 15, 1910, 21: 91–4; EWM, *TWW*, 110–1, 120; *NY Evening Post*, Sep. 16, 1910, cited in RSB, III: 81; "Jersey Republicans Name Vivian Lewis," *NYT*, Sep. 21, 1910, 3.

RESIGNATION FROM PRINCETON: "Princeton's 164th Year," Trenton *True American*, Sep. 23, 1910, 21: 151–2; EWM, *TWW*, 111; Princeton University Board, Resolution, c. Oct. 19, 1910, 21: 353; M. T. Pyne to WW, Oct. 19, 1910, 21: 353; WW to Princeton University Board, Oct. 20, 1910, 21: 362; Wilson Farrand (M), n.d., 21: 363; WW to L. C. Woods, Oct. 27, 1910, 21: 444; C. W. McAlpin to WW, Nov. 3, 1910, 21: 536–9; WW to D. P. Foster, Oct. 29, 1910, 21: 470–1; M. T. Pyne to W. C. Procter, Oct. 25, 1910, 21: 434; "Students Give Parade for Wilson," Trenton *True American*, Oct. 11, 1915, 21: 289.

GUBERNATORIAL CAMPAIGN: WW to MAH, Sep. 25, 1910, 21: 163–4; Tumulty, 27, 28–30, 42; EWM, *PG*, 263; J. Smith, quoted in RSB, III: 83; Kerney, 62; EWM, *TWW*, 110–2, 114; SA to RSB, RSB III: 87, 93–4, 96; "Crime of Trusts," NY *World*, Sep. 18, 1910, 21: 134–6; SA, 159–61; WW (S), Sep. 28, 29, 30, and Oct. 1, 3, 5, 13, 15, 21, 25, and Nov. 2, 5, 1910, 21: 181–91, 193–8, 202–12, and 213–8, 229–38, 245–59, 310–20, 328–34, 423–33, and 508–18, 564–76; "Who WW Is," *Philadelphia Record*, Oct. 2, 1910, 21: 220–5; "W Talks Pure Politics," *Newark Evening News*, Oct. 12, 1910, 21: 301–6; "W Gets Great Reception," Trenton *True American*, Oct. 15, 1910, 21: 325–7; "W Reads a New Lesson," *Philadelphia Record*, Oct. 22, 1910, 21: 382–5; G. L. Record to WW, Oct. 17, 1910, 21: 338–47; WW to G. L. Record, Oct. 24, 1910, 21: 406–11; G. B. M. Harvey to WW, Oct. 25, 1910, 21: 433; JPT to WW (T), Oct. 25, 1910, 21: 433; "W Free of Alliances," *Philadelphia Record*, Oct. 25, 1910, 21: 413–21; "W's Last Call Greatest," *Philadelphia Record*, Nov. 5, 1910, 21: 561–4; W. H. Page to WW, Nov. 5, 1910, 21: 576.

WW ELECTED GOVERNOR OF NEW JERSEY: EWM, *TWW*, 115; RSB III: 106–7; "W Speech for Students," *Newark Evening News*, Nov. 10, 1910, 22: 3–4; T. R. Marshall to WW (T), Nov. 9, 1910, 21: 603; G. L. Record to WW, Nov. 9, 1910, 21: 596; JPT to WW (T),

Nov. 8–9, 1910, 21: 589; WW to J. Smith, Jr., Nov. 9, 1910, 21: 590.

WW AS GOVERNOR-ELECT: WW to MAH, Jan. 13, 1911, 22: 329–30; RSB, III: 108, cites Trenton *True American*, Dec. 24, 1910; CD to WW, Nov. 18, 1910, 23: 72–3; WW to J. E. Martine, Nov. 14, 1910; 22: 36–7; RSB, III: 111, 124, 132–5; M. C. Ely to WW, Nov, 23, 1910, 22: 85–6; W. W. St. John to WW, Nov. 22, 1910: 22: 81–2n1; Tumulty, 57–8, 60–2; WW to G. B. M. Harvey, Nov. 15, 1910, 22: 46–8; WW to MAH, Dec. 7 and 16, 1910, 22: 141–2n1 and 204–5; WW, "Statement," Trenton *True American*, Dec. 9, 1910, 22: 153–4; James Smith, "Statement," *Newark Evening News*, Dec. 9, 1910, 22: 166–7; WW to O. G. Villard, Jan. 2, 1911, 22: 288–9; EWM, *TWW*, 118–9.

WW INAUGURATION AND FIRST GUBERNATORIAL TEST: "Governor W Takes Office in Jersey," *NYT*, Jan. 18, 1911, 3; WW (S), Jan. 17, 1911, 22: 345–54; WW to MAH, Jan. 22 and 29, 1911, 22: 362–4 and 391–3; Tumulty, 67–71; WW, "Statement," *Newark Evening News*, Jan. 24, 1911, 22: 365; "James Smith, Jr. Fails in Business," *NYT*, Nov. 21, 1915, 1.

NEW JERSEY POLITICS: WW to MAH, Jan. 13, 15, and Mar. 26, 1911, 22: 329–30, 333–4, and 517–9; WW, "The Law and the Facts" (S), Dec. 27, 1910, 22: 264–72; WW to W. S. U'ren, Dec. 14, 1910, 22: 197; RSB, III: 131, 139–44; Tumulty, 73.

WW "ENTERS" PRESIDENTIAL CAMPAIGN: McAdoo, 114–20; Startt, 113–5; McCombs, 5–6, 32; 34–9; F. P. Stockbridge, "How WW Won His Nomination," *Current History, XX* (July 1924), 561–4; WW to MAH, Mar. 5, 13, and Apr. 2, 16, 1911, 22: 477–80, 500–1, and 531–4, 570–2; "WW Finds Opens Arms of Welcome Here," *Atlanta Journal*, Mar. 10, 1911, 22: 487–91; WW (S), Mar. 10, 1911, 22: 491–8; RSB, III: 114, 209–11, 212–3, 225, 230–2; EWM, *TWW*, 120–4; EWM, *PG*, 265–6; WJB, quoted in *Newark Evening News*, Apr. 6, 1911, quoted in James Chace, *1912: Wilson, Roosevelt, Taft & Debs—The Election That Changed the Country* (New York: Simon & Schuster, 2004), 130; Tumulty, 74–7; "An Astonishing Legislature," *Jersey Journal*, Apr. 22, 1911, quoted in August Heckscher, *Woodrow Wilson* (NY: Charles Scribner's Sons, 1981), 694n43; "W Glad to Be a Radical," *St. Paul Dispatch*, May 25, 1911, 23: 93–5.

PROGRESSIVISM; WW COMING TO TERMS WITH JEFFERSON: "People Look to

Man, Not to Party," *Indianapolis News*, Apr. 13, 1911, 23: 554–6; WW (S), Apr. 13, 1911, 22: 557–68; "Tariff Reform the Keynote at Jefferson Dinner," NY *World*, Apr. 14, 1912, 24: 330–2; WW (S), Sep. 25, 1912, 25: 250; Arthur Schlesinger, Jr. (S), "A Question of Power," Oct. 5–6, 2000 (published in *American Prospect*, Apr. 23, 2001).

WW WESTERN TOUR: "W Trusts the Public," *Kansas City Star*, May 5, 1911, 23: 3–5; WW (S), May 7, 1911, 23: 12–20; EAW to WW, May 11 and June 2, 1911, 23: 30–1 and 127–8; WW (S), May 12, 1911, 23: 32–40; "People of U.S. Should Name Senators," *Los Angeles Examiner*, May 14, 1911, 23: 50–1; "W Hailed As Political Prophet," *San Francisco Examiner*, May 16, 1911, 23: 55–8; U'Ren First Gains Gov. Wilson's Ear," *Portland Morning Oregonian*, May 18, 1911, 23: 60–3; "Press Club Is Host," *ibid.*, May 19, 1911, 23: 68–9; "W Opposes Judge's Recall," May 20, 1911, *ibid.*, 23: 73–6; "WW Welcomed on His Visit to Seattle," *Seattle Daily Times*, May 20, 1911, 23: 76–8; "Outlines His Views," Lincoln (NE) *State Journal*, May 27, 1911, 23: 96–102; T. P. Gore to H. S. Breckinridge, May 25, 1911, quoted in *NYT*, May 27, 1911, 23: 113n3.

SUMMER 1911; ENTRANCE OF WGM: RSB, III: 231, 237, 238; EWM, *TWW*, 132–3; WW to MAH, July 30, 1911, 23: 239–40; McAdoo, 109–120.

PRIMARY CAMPAIGN: Fred Williams to R. F. Pettigrew, published in *NYT*, Feb. 2, 1912, 24: 270; "Who Sought a Pension," NY *Sun*, Dec. 5, 1911, 23: 564–5; WW to *Newark Evening News*, Dec. 6, 1911, 23: 565–6; WW to H. S. Pritchett, Nov. 11, 1910, 22: 23–4n1; Lane, 84–5; WW, *History*, V: 212–4; Nicholas Pietrowski to WW, Mar. 11, 1912, 24: 241–2; WW to Nicholas Pietrowski, Mar. 13, 1912, 24: 242–3; WW to Harper & Brothers, Mar. 4, 1912, 24: 223; WW to A. H. Joline, Apr. 29, 1907, 17: 124; WW (U letter), Jan. 8, 1912, 24: 8–9; RSB, III: 247–8, 257–67; WW to MAH, Jan. 7, 14, 1912, 24: 5–6, 43–4; WW (S), Jan. 8, 1912, 24: 9–16; Morgenthau, 139–44; Tumulty, 83–8, 97; SA, 172–3; WW to G. B. M. Harvey, Dec. 21 and Jan. 11, 1911, 23: 603 and 24: 31; G. B. M. Harvey to WW, Jan. 4, 1912, 23: 652.

EMH: RSB, III: 294–309; Houston, 21–2; McAdoo, 127–8; House, 5, 107–11; Freud, 144–5; WW to MAH, Feb. 12, 1911, 22: 424–7; Hodgson, 7; SA, 207.

FINAL DAYS AS GOVERNOR; PRIMARIES: WW to MAH, Oct. 8, 1911, and Jan. 14,

May 11, June 9, 1912, 23: 424–5 and 24: 43–4, 391–2, 466–7; EWM, *TWW*, 127–8; EAW to J. G. Hibben, Feb. 10, 1912, 24: 149–50; H. D. Thompson to WW, Apr. 1, 1912, 24: 274–5; WW to H. D. Thompson, Apr. 3, 1912, 24: 284; WW (S), Jan. 9, 1912, 24: 18–25; WW to House of Assembly, Apr. 2, 1912, 24: 276–84; "Forty Vetoes Start Fight," Trenton *True American*, Apr. 12, 1912, 24: 324–8; "WW to Citizens of New Jersey," Trenton *True American*, May 24, 1912, 24: 429–34; RSB, III: 309–11, 356; McAdoo, 129–30, 156–9; WW to EMH, Oct. 24, 1911, 23: 480; Tumulty, 106–16; EWM, *PG*, 271–74; McAdoo, 137–42; *Democratic Text-Book: 1912* (New York: Isaac Goldman, 1912), 2, 115, 32; EWM, *TWW*, 158, 162, 164–5.

BALTIMORE CONVENTION, 1912; RECEIVES NOMINATION: Chace, *op. cit.*, 151; Tumulty, 120–1, 124; EAW, quoted in Baltimore *Sun*, July 3, 1912, RSB, III: 350; EWM, *PG*, 273; EWM, *TWW*, 162, 164–5; RSB, III: 356, 362; McAdoo, 156–9; "Gov. W Not Elated by Victory," *NYT*, July 2, 1912, 24: 522–8; WW to MAH, July 14, 28, 1912, 24: 550–2, 572; "W in Hiding to Write Speech," *NYT*, July 23, 1912, 24: 562–3; Luke Lea to WW, July 13, 1912, 24: 545–8; WGM to WW, July 25, 1912, 24: 570; WJB to WW, c. July 22, 1912, 24: 565; L. D. Brandeis to WW, Aug. 1, 1912, 24: 580; "W Here; Dines at a Lunch Counter," *NYT*, Aug. 4, 1912, 24: 585–9.

PRESIDENTIAL CAMPAIGN, 1912: WW (S), Aug. 7, 1912, 25: 3–18; EWM, *TWW*, 149, 154, 173–4; Dos Passos, 25–7; WW, quoted in Baltimore *Sun*, Oct. 7, 1912, cited in RSB, III: 375, 398–400; WW to MAH, Aug. 25 and Sep. 1, 29, 1912, 25: 55–6 and 66–7, 284–5; McAdoo, 163–5; M. F. Lyons to Charles Seymour, c. Oct. 29, 1947, M. F. Lyons (M), "Record of Monies That McCombs Was Personally Instrumental in Obtaining, Oct. 2, 1947," and M. F. Lyons, Minutes of Democratic National Campaign Committee, Aug. 11, 1912 [Maurice F. Lyons Collection: PUL]; Morgenthau, 150–3; Urofsky, 342–7; "Gov. W Agrees with Mr. Brandeis," *NYT*, Aug. 29, 1912, 25: 56–9; WW (two S), Sep. 2, 1912, 25: 69–79 and 80–92; WW to R. H. Dabney, Jan. 11, 1912, 24: 29; WW (speeches:, Sep. 4, 16, 17, 1912, 25: 98–109, 148, 148–56; WW (three S), Sep. 18, 1912, 25: 164–9, 169–72, 172–84; Sep. 19, 1912, 25: 186–98; Sep. 20, 1912 (2 S), 25: 198–203 and 203–12; Sep. 23, 1912, 25: 221–31; Sep. 25, 1912, 25: 234–45; Oct. 4, 8, 1912, 25: 332–8, 385–90; "Taft Meets W for Pleasant Chat," *NYT*, Sep. 26,

1912, 25: 269–71; "Gov W in Princeton Today," *Princeton Press*, Sep. 28, 1912, 25: 273; WW, "Platform of the New Jersey Democratic Party," Oct. 1, 1912, 25: 305–10; "W Sends Sympathy," *NYT*, Oct. 16, 1912, 25: 418–9; Hatfield, 325–32; "Roosevelt Stills Garden Tumult," *NYT*, Oct. 31, 1912, 1; "Garden Crowd Wild for Wilson," *NYT*, Nov. 1, 1912, 1; "Gov. W Hurt but Will Speak Despite Injury," *Trenton Evening True American*, Nov. 4, 1912, 25: 508–10; "W Laughs Over Bald Spot," *Newark Evening News*, Nov. 4, 1912, 25: 510–11; EWM, *PG*, 274; G. B. M. Harvey to WW, Nov. 4, 1912, 25: 512–3.

THE NEGRO VOTE: WW (S), Oct. 3 and 5, 1910, 21: 236 and 255; M. F. Lyons, Minutes, *op. cit.*, Aug. 11, 1912; W. M. Trotter to WW, July 18, 1912, 24: 558–9; "W and the Negro," *NY Age*, July 11, 1912, 24: 558–90; WW, quoted in *Trenton Evening News*, July 31, 1912, 24: 574; WW to Alexander Walters, Oct. 16, 1912, quoted in RSB, III: 388; WW to Alexander Walters, Oct. 21, 1912, 25: 448–9; O. G. Villard (D), Aug. 14, 1912.

ELECTION DAY, 1912: EWM, *TWW*, 180–1; EWM, *PG*, 274–5; "Mr. W Jokes While Voting," *Trenton Evening True American*, Nov. 5, 1912, 25: 517–8; "Kiss from Wife Tells W He's President-Elect," *NY World*, Nov. 6, 1912, 25: 519–20; SA, 174–5; W. H. Taft to WW (T), Nov. 5, 1912, 25: 521; TR to WW (T), Nov. 5, 1912, 25: 521; Election results, Brinkley, A–34; WW (S), Nov. 5, 1912, 25: 520–1.

8 DISCIPLES

POST-ELECTION; EMERGENCE OF EMH: EWM, *TWW*, 182, 183–5; "W Ends Talk: Takes Time to Think," *NYT*, Nov. 6, 1912, 1, 25: 523–6. McCombs, 209; Annin, 126; EMH (D), Nov. 16, 1912, 25: 550; SA (N, commenting on RSB ms, Collection #440: PUL), 197–205; Freud, 146; House, I: 93; McAdoo, 179; EAW, "Description: Personal," printed in *St. Louis Post-Dispatch*, July 28, 1912, 24: 573; Sayre, 41–2; F. B. Sayre to Jessie Wilson (U), Oct. 30, Nov. 3, 7, 13, 16, 1912 [WWPL].

FAMILY TO BERMUDA: "W Sails on Bermudian," *NYT*, Nov. 16, 1912, 5; "Gov W Enjoys His First Day at Sea," *NYT*, Nov. 17, 1912, 1; WW (R), Nov. 18, 1912, 25: 551; EWM, *TWW*, 185–8; "Tanned by Sun, W Returns in Fine Health," *Trenton Evening Times*, Dec. 16, 1912, 25: 589–90; WW to WGM, Nov. 20, 1912, 25: 552;

"W Says He Will Use Fists on Photo Man," *Trenton Evening News*, Nov. 22, 1912, 25: 556; EWM, *PG*, 276; WW to MAH, Dec. 22, 1912, 25: 615–6; "W Means to Keep Fight Up in Jersey," *Trenton Evening News*, Dec. 17, 1912, 25: 591–2.

VICTORY LAPS—NEW YORK, CHICAGO, AND VIRGINIA; FINAL BUSINESS IN NEW JERSEY: WW (A) to NY Southern Society, Dec. 17, 1912, 25: 593–603; WW (S) to Commercial Club of Chicago, June 11, 1912, Jan. 11, 1912, 27: 29–39; Rev. A. M. Fraser, quoted in RSB, III: 428; "W in the Room Where He Was Born," *NYT*, Dec. 28, 1912, 1; "W Tells Plans at Birthday Fetes," *NYT*, Dec. 29, 1912, 3; EWM *TWW*, 195; WW (A) at Mary Baldwin Seminary, Dec. 28, 1912, 25: 626–32; WW (A) to New Jersey legislature, Jan. 14, 1913, 27: 46–54; WW (S) on signing "Seven Sisters," Feb. 20, 1913, 27: 120–2; " 'Seven Sisters' Bills Signed by W," *NYT*, Feb. 20, 1913, 20.

CABINET APPOINTMENTS: WW, *CG*, 257; House, I: 84, 99; Reid, 137–9; H. L. Mencken, "Bryan," Baltimore *Evening Sun*, July 27, 1925; Bryan, 188, 312–3, 318–20, 384–6; Kazin, 130; WW to WJB, Nov. 9, 1912, 25: 532–3; McAdoo, 177–8, 180–6; Annin, 162–3; EMH (D), Dec. 19, 1912, 25: 614; EMH, I: 90–2, 97, 106–7, 113; RSB, III: 45, 452–4, 447, and IV: 55; O. W. Underwood to WW, Jan. 13, 1913, 27: 44–5; WW to O. W. Underwood, Dec. 17, 1912, 25: 593; EMH (D), Jan. 8, 1913, 27: 20; JD (D), Mar. 6 and Apr. 11, 1913, 27: 157 and 290–2; JD (D), Mar. 6, 1913, 27: 157; H. L. Higginson to CD, Nov. 21, 1912 [PUL]; C. R. Crane to WW, Feb. 10, 1913, 27: 107–8; WW to WJB, Feb. 27, 1913, 27: 138; EMH (D), Feb. 14–6, 1913, 27: 112–6; A. M. Palmer to WW, Feb. 24, 1913, 27: 132; Tumulty, 138; WW (A), Jan. 11, 1913, 27: 31; W. H. Page, quoted in RSB, IV: 23; EMH (D), Feb. 21, 1913, 27: 126.

STAFF APPOINTMENTS AND AMBASSADORS: EWM, *TWW*, 196–7; Lawrence, 89–90; RSB, III: 448, 458–9, and IV: 34; EMH, I: 89, 99, 100; WW to JPT, Nov. 25, 1912, 25: 561; Freud, 147; Tumulty, 127–37; EMH (D), Jan. 15, Feb. 13, Mar. 20, 1913, 27: 57, 110, 200; McAdoo, 174; Lawrence, 35; Houston, 15; WW (M), quoted in McCombs, 228; "Pick Rich Men for Foreign Positions," *The Toronto World*, Mar. 24, 1913, 3; "The Homes of Ambassadors," *NYT*, Apr. 11, 1913, 8; EMH (D), Feb. 13, 1913, 27: 110–111; H. B. Fine to WW, Mar. 12, 1913, 27: 173–4; EMH (D), Jan. 17, 1913, 27: 63.

SAMUEL GOMPERS; NEGRO ADVO-CATES: Samuel Gompers to Executive Council of AFL, Dec. 21, 1912, 25: 614–5; WW to Alexander Walters, Oct. 21, 1912, 25: 448–9; Alexander Walters to WW, Dec. 17, 1912, 25: 606–8; Giles B. Jackson to WW, Dec. 23, 1912, 25: 619–21; WW (A) at Mary Baldwin Seminary, Dec. 28, 1912, 25: 632; WW (A) to Commercial Club of Chicago, Jan. 11, 1913, 27: 39; WW to O. W. Underwood, Jan. 21, 1913, 27: 66–7; Carter Glass to WW, Jan. 27, 1913, 27: 79–80; EMH (D), Jan. 8, 1913, 27: 21.

WHITE HOUSE DOMESTIC STAFF; LEAVING NEW JERSEY: WW to MAH, Feb. 16 and Mar. 2, 1913, 27: 116–7 and 146; WW to W. H. Taft, Jan. 2, 1913, 27: 5; W. H. Taft to EAW, Jan. 3, 1913, 27: 12; W. H. Taft to WW, Jan. 6, 1913, 27: 16–8; EAW to W. H. Taft, Jan. 10, 1913, 27: 28–9; EWM, *TWW*, 198–9; WW (A) in Staunton, Dec. 28, 1912, 25: 635; WW (A) to NJ Senators, Jan. 28, 1913, 27: 85–90; "W Neighbors' Farewell," *NYT*, Mar. 2, 1913, 1, 2, 27: 141–2; WW (A) to neighbors in Princeton, Mar. 1, 1913, 27: 142–4; EWM, *PG*, 276.

WW ARRIVAL IN D.C.; PRE-INAUGURAL ACTIVITY: Lash, 389–91; McAdoo, 181–2; EWM, *TWW*, 200, 304–6; "W Evades Vast Crowd," *NYT*, Mar. 1, 1913, 2; RSB, IV: 16; EWM, *PG*, 277; F. Yates to family, Mar. 5, 1913, 27: 155–6; WW (A), "Princeton Smoker," Mar. 3, 1913, 27: 147–8; James W. Kisling (D), Mar. 2–5, 1913 [WWPL]; I. Hoover, 49–59.

INAUGURATION DAY AND NIGHT: WW, "Inaugural Address," Mar. 4, 1913, 27: 148–52; EWM, *TWW*, 205, 207–8, 210; EWM, *PG*, 277; EMH (D), Mar. 4, 1913, 27: 152–3; I. Hoover, 55–9; Grayson, ix, 1; RSB, IV: 16; "W Opposes Inaugural Ball," *Trenton Evening Times*, Jan. 17, 1913, 27: 59–60; SA (N) [PUL: 440], 324; A. W. Halsey to WW, Mar. 5, 1913, 27: 154; WW to A. W. Halsey, 27: 156–7.

⁹ BAPTISM

WASHINGTON, D.C.—HISTORY AND DEMOGRAPHICS: Adams, 260–3; *Thirteenth Census of the United States: 1910*, v. 4: 285–96; EWM, *TWW*, 223; Grayson, 275.

WW'S FIRST DAYS IN THE WHITE HOUSE: EWM, *TWW*, 223, 244; F. Yates to E. C. M. Yates, Mar. 5, 1913, 27: 155; C. R. Crane, quoted in RSB, IV: 13–4, 17–8; WW, "Constitutional Government," Mar. 24, 1908, 18: 23; EMH (D), Feb. 14 and Mar. 8, 1913, 27: 113–4 and

163–4; Houston, I: 37; Daniels, *Life*, 139–40; WW, "Warning to Office-Seekers," Mar. 5, 1919, 27: 153; WW to P. C. Knox, Mar. 5, 1913, cited in RSB, IV: 14; Alex B. Lacy, Jr., "The White House Staff Bureaucracy," *Society* (vol. 6, no. 3), Jan. 1969, 50; A. S. Burleson to RSB, cited in RSB, IV: 43–7, 50–2; Freud, 67–9; J. R. Wilson, Jr., to WW, Jan. 27, 1913, 27: 82–3; T. P. Gore quoted by Gore Vidal to ASB (I), Jan. 28, 2004; WW to J. R. Wilson, Jr., Apr. 22, 1913, 27: 346.

HOUSE, TUMULTY, AND GRAYSON: EMH, I: 114, 116; EMH (D), Mar. 8, 1913, 27: 164; Blum, 67; Lawrence, 89; CTG to RSB, quoted in RSB, IV: 22; CTG, 1–4, 14–5, 80–1; Freud, 149; Boos, 344–6; Weinstein, 20, 250–3; WW to MAH, Aug. 10, 1913; 28: 135; WW to Herbert Putnam, May 22, 1913, 27: 464; WW to F. Yates, May 26, 1913, 27: 475.

MEXICO: WW, *History*, IV: 122; Kandell, 391, 397; Creel, *W and Issues*, 5, 7; V. Huerta to WW (T), Mar. 4, 1913, 27: 152; WW to V. Huerta (T), Mar. 7, 1913, 27: 158; Mark E. Benbow, "All the Brains I Can Borrow," *Studies in Intelligence* (v. 51, no. 4), Dec. 2007, 3; RSB, IV: 239; Houston, I: 43–4; WW (S), "Relations with Latin America," Mar. 12, 1913, 27: 172–3; J. B. Moore to WW, May 15, 1913, 27: 437–40; RSB, IV 245; JD (D), Apr. 18, 1913, 27: 331; EWM, *PG*, 278; C. W. Thompson to R. A. Bull, May 22, 1913, 27: 465; CTG, 30; JPT, 146–7; JD, *Life*, 176; W. B. Hale, "Report," June 18 and July 9, 1913, 27: 550–2 and 28: 31; WW comments regarding H. L. Wilson written on (T) from W. B. Hale to WW, c. June 25, 1913, 28: 7; WW to WJB, July 1 and 3, 1913, 28: 17 and 22; WJB to WW, July 8, 1913, 27: 26–7; WW to EAW, July 27, 1913, 27: 85; Calero, 13–7.

CHINA; PHILIPPINES; JAPAN: "W Upsets China Loan Plan," *NYT*, Mar. 19, 1913, 13; WJB to WW, Jan. 5, 1913, 27: 14; WW (S) on Chinese Pending Loan, Mar. 18, 1913, 27: 192–4; WJB, 361–2; Louis C. Fraina, "Imperialism in Action" (reprinted from *The Class Struggle*, Sep.–Oct. 1918), 4–5; JD (D), Mar. 12, 1913, 27: 174–5; RSB, IV: 62, 454–7; WW to J. S. Williams, July 15, 1913, quoted in RSB, IV: 455; Thomas A. Bailey, "California, Japan, and the Alien Land Legislation of 1913," *Pacific Historical Review 1* (Mar. 1932), 36–59; "Cabinet's Open Door Amazes Old-Timers," *NYT*, Mar. 16, 1913, 2.

PRESS CONFERENCES: "W Wins Newspapermen," *NYT*, Mar. 16, 1913, 2; ASL (N), "Introduction," 50: xiv.

TARIFF AND INCOME TAX: Lawrence, 81–4; "W Innovations Excite Washington," *NYT*, Feb. 28, 1913, 1; "President's Visit Nettles Senators," *NYT*, Apr. 8, 1913, 1, 3; "Congress Cheers Greet W," *NYT*, Apr. 9, 1913; JD (D), Apr. 8, 1913, 27: 268–9; WW (S), "Tariff Reform," Apr. 8, 1913, 27: 269–72; JD, *Life*, 158–60; WW to MAH, Apr. 8 and June 22, 1913, 27: 273 and 556; WGM, 196, 203; RSB, IV: 98–100, 112, 120–3, 170; WW, "Constitutional Government," 18: 105; Clements, 36; WW to J. C. McReynolds, Apr. 17, 1913; 27: 321; Weisman, 272; Houston, I: 50.

BANKING AND CURRENCY REFORM: WW (S), "On Banking and Currency Reform," June 23, 1913, 27: 570–3; WGM, 204–14, 229, 234; WJB, 370–3; WW to F. K. Lane, June 12, 1913, 27: 511–2; L. D. Brandeis to WW, June 14, 1913, 27: 520–1; RSB, IV: 165–9; Glass, 115–6; "Money Reform Now Is W's Demand," *NYT*, June 24, 1913, 1–2.

EAW AS FIRST LADY; PLANS FOR SUMMER 1913: EMH (D), May 11 and 25, 1913, 27: 413–4 and 227; EWM, *TWW*, 229–30, 236, 238, 250; Seale, 774–8, 784; Whitcomb, 251–2; WW to EAW (T), June 28 and Aug. 10, 1913, 28: 11 and 132–4; WW to EAW, June 29, 1911, 28: 11–2; WW to MAH, June 29 and July 27, 1913, 28: 12–4 and 86–7. WW's golfing is discussed in: CTG, 40–4, 46; Samuel G. Blythe, "A Talk with the President," Dec. 5, 1914, 31: 392; WW to Edith Reid, Aug. 15, 1913, 28: 161; Whitcomb, 258; the Dwight D. Eisenhower Memorial Commission estimated the number of holes W played: www.eisenhowermemorial.org/stories/Ike-Golf. htm; "W a Stranger in Old Yorktown," *NYT*, July 4, 1913, 1, 3.

WW AT GETTYSBURG; SEGREGATING WASHINGTON, D.C.: WW (A), July 4, 1913, 28: 23–6; "Gettysburg Cold to W's Speech," *NYT*, July 5, 1913, 1; Johnson, 462; Houston, I: 51; JD (D), Apr. 11, 1913, 27: 290–2; August Meier and Elliott Rudwick, "The Rise of Segregation in the Federal Bureaucracy, 1900–1930," *Phylon* (v. 28, no. 2), 178–84; WW, "To the Women of the South," c. Jan. 1, 1910, 27: 574; Thomas Dixon, Jr., to WW, July 27, 1913, 28: 88–9; WW to Thomas Dixon, Jr., July 29, 1913, 28: 94; WW to O. G. Villard, July 23, Aug. 21 and 29, Sep. 22, Oct. 3 and 17, 1913, 28: 65, 202 and 245–6, 316, 352 and 413; ASL (N) re: A. E. Patterson to WW, July 30, 1913, 28: 98n; Moorfield Storey and others to WW, Aug. 15, 1913, 28: 163–5; Robert N. Wood to WW, Aug. 5, 1913, 28: 115–8; Booker T.

Washington to O. G. Villard, Aug. 10, 1913, 28: 186–7; O. G. Villard to WW, Aug. 27, Sep. 29, and Oct. 14, 1913, 28: 239–40, 342–4, and 401–2; J. P. Gavit to O. G. Villard, Oct. 1, 1913, 28: 348–50; WGM to O. G. Villard, Oct. 27, 1913, 28: 453–5; Nancy Weiss, "The Negro and the New Freedom," *Political Science Quarterly*, Mar. 1969 (v. 84, no. 1), 61–79; Kathleen L. Wolgemuth, "WW and Federal Segregation," *Journal of Negro History* (v. 44, no. 2), Apr. 1959, 158–73; Henry Blumenthal, "WW and the Race Question," *Journal of Negro History*, v. 48, no. 1 (Jan. 1963), 1–21; RSB, IV: 224–5; M. C. Nerney to O. G. Villard, Sep. 30, 1913, 28: 402–10; J. S. Williams to WW, Mar. 31, 1913, 29: 387–8; WW to J. S. Williams, Apr. 2, 1914, 29: 394; WW to Champ Clark, May 4, 1914, 29: 543; W. M. Trotter to WW, Nov. 6, 1913, 28: 491–5.

WW IN CORNISH: EAW to WW, July 29, Aug. 6, and Sep. 9, 1913, 28: 96, 127, and 269; "President's Wife Shows Landscapes," *NYT*, Nov. 15, 1913, 11; "Mrs. W Earns by Art," *NYT*, Nov. 22, 1913, 1; EWM, *TWW*, 251, 253–4, 259; Sayre, 36; WW to EAW, July 27, Aug. 12, and Sep. 17, 1913, 28: 85, 145, and 279; WW to E. G. Reid, Aug. 15, 1913, 28: 160–2.

TARIFF AND BANKING BILLS: "Senate Passes Tariff," *NYT*, Sep. 10, 1913, 1–2; EWM, *TWW*, 259, 267; "W Signs New Tariff Law," *NYT*, Oct. 4, 1913, 1; WW (S), Signing Tariff Bill, Oct. 3, 1913, 28: 351–2; EAW to WW, Oct. 5, 1913, 28: 363–4; WGM, 248–9; Marshall, 242–3; WW to MAH, Sep. 28 and Oct. 12, 1913, 28: 336–8 and 395; WW to B. F. Shively, Oct. 20, 1913, 28: 418; WW to Annie Wilson Howe, Oct. 12, 1913, 28: 396–8; WW (R), re: Federal Reserve Bill, Dec. 23, 1913, 29: 63–6.

JWS MARRIED; EWM ENGAGED: EWM, *TWW*, 259–64, 271–3; Sayre, 45–8; "Miss W Bride of Francis B. Sayre," *NYT*, Nov. 26, 1913, 1, 3; WGM, 272–4; CTG, 28–9, 31; WW to JPT, Dec. 27, 1913, 29: 77n.

MEXICAN CRISIS ERUPTS: WW (A), Latin American Policy (Mobile, AL), Oct. 27, 1913, 28: 448–53; EMH (D), Oct. 30, 1913, 28: 476–7; "W Meets Lind on Ship," *NYT*, Jan. 3, 1914, 2; Kandell, 422; WW (A), Aug. 27, 1913, 28: 227–31; EWM, *TWW*, 271, 275–7; Calero, 18; Creel, *W and Issues*, 8.

EAW'S HEALTH; WGM AS FUTURE SON-IN-LAW: EWM, *PG*, 314; WW to MAH, Mar. 15, 1914, 29: 346; EWM, *TWW*, 275; WGM, 274–5; RSB, IV: 474.

TROUBLE IN VERACRUZ: Calero, 16–20, 23; JD, *Life*, 180–5; WJB to WW (T), Apr. 10, 1914, 29: 420–1; EWM, *TWW*, 277–9; EMH (D), Apr. 15, 1914, 29: 448; WW to WJB (T), Apr. 10 and 19, 1914, 29: 421 and 466; Creel, *W and Issues*, 9–11; WJB to Nelson O'Shaughnessy (T), Apr. 19, 1914, 29: 464–5; "President Before Congress," *NYT*, Apr. 21, 1914, 2; WW (A), "Mexican Crisis," Apr. 20, 1914, 29: 471–4; RSB, IV: 328; Elihu Root, *Congressional Record, 63rd Congress, 2nd Session*, v. 51, 6986–7; WW, "Memorial Address," May 11, 1914, 30: 13–5; SA (N) [PUL: 440], 303; CTG, 45; HCL, 19; Edward G. Lowry, "What the President Is Trying to Do for Mexico," *World's Work, XXVII* (Jan. 1914), 29: 94.

FORGING FOREIGN POLICY; HAY-PAUNCEFOTE TREATY: EMH (D), Apr. 15, 1914, 29: 448; WW, "Annual Message to Congress," Dec. 2, 1913, 29: 4; WJB, 386–7; JD (D), Apr. 8, 1913, 27: 267–8; JD, *Life*, 195–7; JPT, 162–8; WW (A), "Panama Canal Tolls," Mar. 5, 1914, 29: 312–3; EMH, I: 192–206, which includes W. H. Page to EMH, Aug. 28, 1914 [203–4], SA (N) [PUL: 440], 298; EWM, *TWW*, 282–3; Marshall, 420; James Viscount Bryce to WW, Mar. 6, 1914, 29: 320; Lawrence Godkin to JPT, Mar. 26, 1914, 29: 380–1.

OTHER FIRST-YEAR LEGISLATION: WW (A), "Trust Legislation," Jan. 20, 1914, 29: 153–8; L. D. Brandeis, "The Solution of the Trust Problem," *Harper's Weekly, LVIII* (Nov. 8, 1913), 18–9; F. G. Newlands to WW, Feb. 6, 1914, 29: 227; W. C. Redfield to WW, May 5, 1914, 29: 544–5; Houston, I: 195–6, 199–208; WW (S), "Rural Credits," Aug. 13, 1913, 28: 146–8; George Harvey, quoted in RSB, IV: 195; RSB, IV: 208.

EWM-WGM WEDDING: EWM, *TWW*, 285–7; WGM, 276–7; EMH (D), May 7, 1914, 30: 6–7; "Eleanor W Weds W. G. McAdoo," *NYT*, May 8, 1914, 1, 13; SA, 219, 283; WW to MAH, May 10, 1914, 30: 12–3; EWM, *PG*, 315, SA (N) [PUL: 440], 303; RSB, IV: 452.

10 ECCLESIASTES

PRINCETON REUNIONS, JUNE 1914: "President Is Just 'Tommy,'" *NYT*, June 14, 1914, 9; J. G. Hibben to WW, June 6, 1914, 30: 156; WW to J. G. Hibben, June 9, 1914, 30: 163; EMH (D), Dec. 12, 1913, 29: 33–4; WW (S), June 13, 1914, 30: 176–80.

POLITICAL TRAVAILS; EAW'S HEALTH: WW to CD, July 19, 1914, 30: 288; B. B. Lindsey

to JPT, May 16, 1914, 30: 38–9; J. P. White to WW (T), May 18, 1914, 30: 46; WW to MAH, June 7 and 21, 1914, 30: 158 and 196; CTG, 33; EWM, *TWW*, 296–7.

WAR BEGINS IN EUROPE; EAW DECLINES: Vansittart, 12–15 (Ambassador Gerard quoted, 14–5); WW to Franz Joseph I (T), June 28, 1914, 30: 222; WW to MAH, July 12, 1914, 30: 227; WW to E. P. Davis, July 28, 1914, 30: 312; SA, 283; CTG, 34–5; WW (R), at press conference, July 27, 1914, 30: 307; W. H. Page to WW, Aug. 9, 1914, 30: 366–71; press release re: WW to Heads of State, Aug. 4, 1914, 30: 342; EWM, *PG*, 315; "Mrs. W Dies in White House" and "Wife Inspired President," *NYT*, Aug. 7, 1914, 1; F. B. Sayre to Mrs. R. Sayre, Aug, 1914 [WWPL]; SA (N) [PUL: 440], 326; "Service at Capitol for Mrs. W, *NYT*, Aug. 8, 1914, 7; "Prayer at Tribute to President's Wife," *NYT*, Aug. 11, 1914, 9; "Mrs. W Buried Beside Her Parents," *NYT*, Aug. 12, 1914, 9.

WW SUFFERS THROUGH OPENING SALVOS OF WAR: CTG, 35–6; WW to MAH, Aug. 7 and 23, Sep. 6 and 20, 1914: 30: 357 and 437, 31: 3–4 and 59–60; WW to EMH, Aug. 17, 1914, 30: 390; W. H. Page to WW, July 29, 1914, 30: 316; Hitler, 135–6; RSB, IV: 161; Jacques Davignon to Emmanuel Havenith, Aug. 28, 1914, 30: 458; "President W Proclaims Our Strict Neutrality," *NYT*, Aug. 5, 1914, 7; RSB, IV: 52; WW, "Appeal to American People," Aug. 18, 1914, 30: 393–4; W. H. Page, quoted in RSB, IV: 67; C. W. Eliot to WW, Aug. 6 and 20, 1914, 30: 353–5 and 418–20; EMH (D), Aug. 30, 1914, 30: 462; WW to C. W. Eliot, Aug. 19, 1914, 30: 403; TR, quoted in JD, *Life*, 245; HCL, 26, 30; EMH to WW, Aug. 7, 1914, 30: 359; SA, 226; WW to Florence Hoyt, Oct. 2, 1914, 31: 119; CTG to EBW, Aug. 25, 1914, 31: 564.

WW IN CORNISH; CARRIES ON IN WHITE HOUSE: EMH (D), Aug. 30, Nov. 6 and 14, 1914, 30: 461–7, 31: 274 and 317–20; WW, *DR*, 211; RSB, V: 113; WW to MAH, Sep. 20, Oct. 11, Nov. 8, 1914, 31: 60, 141–2, 280–1; WW to Nancy Toy, Nov. 9 and Dec. 12, 1914, 31: 289 and 455; S. G. Blythe, "A Talk with the President," *Saturday Evening Post*, Jan. 9, 1915, 3–4, 37–8, 31: 390–403; WW to Mahlon Pitney, Sep. 10, 1914, 31: 19; Nancy Toy (D), Jan. 3, 1915, 32:9.

MIDTERM ELECTION, 1914; EARLY WARTIME FINANCIAL POLICY: JPT, 101, 126, 183; WW to F. E. Doremus, Sep. 4, 1914, 30: 475–8; WGM, 290–8, 300, 304, 309; WW (U statement), c. Mar. 4, 1915, 32: 313–6; WW (S), Dec. 7, 1914, and Dec. 8, 1915, 31:416 and 35: 301; RSB, V: 88–91, 105; "Plan Big Loan Fund for Wool Growers," *NYT*, June 13, 1920, 99; J. P. Morgan, Jr., to WW, Sep. 4, 1914, 30: 485; WJB to WW, Aug. 10, 1914, 30: 372–3; Colville Barclay to Sir Edward Grey, Aug. 16, 1914, 30: 386; WW to J. P. Morgan, Jr., Sep. 17, 1914, 31: 39; WGM, 305; WW (S), Sep. 4, 1914, 30: 473–5; WW to W. M. Daniels, Oct. 29, 1914, 31: 247; WW to H. L Higginson, Oct. 29, 1914, 31: 247; "American Bankers May Make Loans," NY *World*, Oct. 16, 1914, 31: 153; Chernow, 186; WW to O. W. Underwood, Oct. 17, 1914, 31: 168–74; "The Democratic Peacemaker," *NYT*, Oct. 6, 1914, 10; WW to MAH, Sep. 20, 1914, 31: 59; EMH (D), Nov. 4 and 6, 1914, 31: 263–5 and 274–5; WW to Hugo Munsterberg, Nov. 7, 1914, 31: 276–8; WW to Nancy Toy, Nov. 9, 1914, 31: 289–91; Freud, 80, 156, 214.

RACE—W. M. TROTTER; *BIRTH OF A NATION*: W. M. Trotter (A) to WW, Nov. 12, 1914, 31: 298–301; WW, remarks and dialogue with W. M. Trotter, Nov. 12, 1914, 31: 301–8; "President Resents Negro's Criticism," *NYT*, Nov. 12, 1914, 1 Johnson, 608–11; O. G. Villard to JPT, Nov. 17, 1914 (with excerpts from NY *World* and NY *Evening Post* editorials of Nov. 13, 1914, 31: 328–9; WGM to WW, Nov. 28, 1914, 31: 360–1; WGM to F. I. Cobb, Nov. 26, 1914, 31: 361–3; JD to FDR, June 10, 1933, 31: 309n; Thomas Dixon, Jr., to JPT, Jan. 27, 1915, 32: 142, and May 1, 1915, cited in 32: 142n; WW to JPT, Apr. 28, 1915, and c. Apr. 22, 1918, 33:86 and 47: 388n3; Mark Calney, "D. W. Griffith and the Birth of a Monster," *American Almanac*, Jan. 11, 1993, n.p.; WW (R), on race, Dec. 15, 1914, 31: 464–5; D. W. Griffith to WW, Mar. 2, 1915, 32: 310–1; WW to D. W. Griffith, Mar. 5, 1915, 32: 325.

FOREIGN AFFAIRS—LOSING FAITH IN WJB; VENTURING BEYOND WASHINGTON: WJB to WW, Sep. 30 and Dec. 1, 1914, 31: 102 and 378–9; WW to WJB, Oct. 1, 1914, 31: 114; Sun Yat-sen to WW (T), 31: 372–3; W. H. Page to WW, Nov. 4 and 30, 1914, 31: 262 and 370–2; WW to CD, July 12, 1914, 30: 277; EMH (D), Oct. 2, Dec. 3, 1914, and Jan. 24, 1915, 31: 122, 385, and 32: 117; Nancy Toy (D), Jan. 2 and 3, 1915, 32: 8 and 9–10; Reid, 168; WW to EMH, Dec. 2, 1914, 31: 379; SA, 193–6; CTG, 49; WW to Nancy Toy, Dec. 12, 1914, 31: 456; WW to MAH, Nov. 22, 1914, Jan. 10 and 17, 1915, 31: 344, 32: 43 and 83; WW (S), Oct. 20 and Dec. 8,

1914, 31: 184–6 and 414–24; WW (S) in Indianapolis, Jan. 8, 1915, 32: 29–41; Reid, 174; F. K. Lane to WW, Jan. 9, 1915, 32: 43; EMH to WW, Jan. 9, 1915, 32: 43; RSB, V: 164.

EMH TO EUROPE; SUBMARINE WARFARE AND BLOCKADES: EMH (D), Jan. 12, 1915, 32: 61; WW, cited in Hodgson, 105; WW to EMH, Jan. 18 and 29, 1915, 32: 84–5 and 157–8; WW to EMH (T), Jan. 29, 1915, 32: 159; EMH (D), I: 352–3, 359–61, 403; RSB, V: 164, 165, 265, 275; W. H. Page to WW, Feb. 10, 1915, 32: 211–5; H. Morgenthau to WW, Nov. 10, 1914, 31: 428n; JD, *Life*, 280–1; W. H. Page to WJB, Mar. 15, 1915, 32: 378–82; WJB, 420; WGM, 322; CTG, 49; WW to MAH, Feb. 14, 1915, 23: 233; WW to JWS, Mar. 14, 1915 [WWPL].

EBW ENTERS: EBW, 1–13, 17–23, 51–4, 56–67; CTG, 50; Freud, 157; "W Hurls First Ball at Washington," *NYT*, Apr. 15, 1915, 10; WW to EBW, Apr. 30, May 4–5, 5, 6, 7 (two letters), 1915, 33: 90, 110–1, 111–2, 117–9, 124–6 and 126–7; Starling, 44; EBW to WW, May 5, 1915, 33: 108–10; WJB to WW (with enclosures), May 6, 1915, 33: 113–5; WJB to Paul Fuller, Jr., May 6, 1915, 33: 116–7; EMH to WW, May 7, 1915, 33: 121–3.

LUSITANIA SINKS; WW COURTS EBW; WJB RESIGNS: EBW to WW, May 7, 1915, 33: 127–8; ASL (N), 33: 128n1 and 129n1; "Lusitania Sunk by Submarine . . . Shocks the President," *NYT*, May 8, 1915, 1–2; HCL, 32–3; "Roosevelt Calls It an Act of Piracy," *NYT*, May 8, 1915, 1; TR, "Murder on the High Seas," statement, cited in John Whiteclay Chambers II, *The Eagle and the Dove* (Syracuse, NY: Syracuse University Press, 1991), 60–1; WJB, 420–4; Preston, 391; TR, press release, May 9, 1915, quoted in TR, *NRM*, 847–52; Herman Ridder, "Vale Lusitania," *NYT*, May 8, 1915, quoted in 33: 135n4; WJB to WW, May 9, 12 (three letters), and 13, June 9, 1915, 33: 134–5, 165–7 and 167–8 and 173, 180, 375–6; EMH to WW (T), May 9, 1914, 33: 134; Charles Swem (D), May 10, 1915, 33: 138; *Washington Post* editorial, quoted in 33: 135n1; WW to EBW, May 9, 10, 11 (two letters), June 9, 10, Aug. 13, 1915, 33: 136, 146–7, 160–1 and 162, 377–8, 381, 34: 192; EBW to WW, May 10, June 9 and 18, 1915, 33: 146, 378 and 421; WW (S—"too proud to fight"), May 10, 1915, 33: 147–50; Janet W. Wilson to WW, Nov. 15, 1876, 1: 228; JPT, 236–7; WW (S), Apr. 20, 1915, 33: 37–41; WW, press conference, May 11, 1915, 33: 153; JPT, 232–34; W. H. Taft to WW, May 10, 1915, 33: 150–1;

WW to W. H. Taft, May 13, 1915, 33: 184; WW to WJB (draft), May 11, 1915, 33: 155–8; Weinstein, 285; EMH (D), June 20 and 24, 1915, 33: 425 and 449; EBW, 62–4; "Official Translation of the German Note," *NYT*, June 1, 1915, 2; JD, *Life*, 253–4; WW, "First Draft of Second Lusitania Note," June 3, 1915, 33: 328–31.

WW EAGER TO MARRY AMID INTERNATIONAL TURMOIL: J. W. Gerard to RL, July 8, 1915, quoted in WW to RL, July 13, 1915, 33: 500n1; JD, *Life*, 255; WW to EBW, May 28 and 29, June 1, 3, 17, 18, and Sep. 11, 1915, 33: 278 and 284–5, 301–2, 334, 417, 421, and 34: 453; EMH to WW (including Lincoln Steffens to EMH, Aug. 7, 1915), Aug. 9 and Oct. 1, 1915, 34: 146–8 and 35: 3–4; RL to WW, Aug. 14, 21, and Nov. 20, 1915, 34: 196–7, 34: 280, and 35: 227–8; WW to WJB, June 2, 1915, 33: 304; Morris Sheppard to WW, July 22, 1915, 34: 13; WW to L. M. Garrison, July 21, 1915, 34: 4; L. M Garrison to WW, Sep. 17, 1915, 34: 482–5; L. M. Garrison to JPT, Nov. 1, 1915, 35: 149–50; Louis Wiley to WW, Sep. 30, 1915, 34: 452; O. G. Villard to WW, Oct. 28, 1915, 35: 120; EBW to WW, May 28, June 3, 17, 21, 29, 1915, 33: 278–9, 335, 418, 434, 458; Helen Bones to WW, May 29, 1915, 33: 285; Helen Bones to MAH (T), May 29, 1915, 33: 286; Hulbert, 244–8, 257–8; WW to MAH, May 6 and July 7, 1915, 33: 120 and 482; MAH to WW, c. June 10, 16, and 20, 1915, 33: 382, 412, 424; EMH (D), June 24, 1915, 33: 448–53; EBW, 70–4.

WW-EBW SECRET ENGAGEMENT: WW to EBW, July 20 (two letters), Aug. 6, 24, 25, 27, 28, Sep. 10 (two letters), 11, 18, 19 (7:20 a.m. and 9:10 a.m.), 1915, 33: 537–9 and 539–42, 34: 102, 301, 327–8, 346–7, 352–3, 440 and 441, 453, 489, 491–2 and 492; EBW to WW, Aug. 13, 15, 25, 26, 27, 28, Sep. 3, 18, 19, 20 (7:45 p.m.), 1915, 34: 194–5, 213, 327–8, 338, 347–9, 357, 415, 489–90, 495–6; WW to JD, July 2, 1915, 33: 465; EBW, 75–6; Margaret W. Wilson to EBW, Aug. 16, 1915, 34: 268–9; WW to Sallie White Bolling, Aug. 29, 1915, 34: 363; WW to Bertha Bolling, c. Aug. 29, 1915, 34: 364; JD, *Wilson Era*, 454; Weinstein, 290; EMH (D), Sep. 22, Dec. 15, 1915, 34: 506–8, 35: 357–60; WW to Samuel Gompers, Sep. 24, 1915, 34: 512; SA, 246–7; SA, draft of announcement, c. Oct. 2, 1915, 35: 16–7; Freud, 157–8; I. Hoover, 66–7, 70; Starling, 51–2.

WW-EBW ENGAGEMENT ANNOUNCED; INTERNATIONAL PRESSURE MOUNTS: WW, statement on suffrage, Oct. 6,

1915, 35: 28; EMH (D), Dec. 15, 1915, 35: 355–61; "W Watches Red Sox Win," *NYT*, Oct. 10, 1915, 18; EBW, 81–3; CTG to A. G. Gordon, c. Oct. 19, 1915 [WWPL]; WW to MAH, Oct. 4, 1915, 35: 23–4; MAH to WW, c. Oct. 11, 1915, 35: 53; Starling, 55–7; EBW to WW, Nov. 28, 1915, 35: 262–3n; WW to EBW (T), Dec. 1, 1915, 35: 281; W. H. Page to WW, Oct. 16, 1915, 35: 74–9; EMH to WW (enclosed: Sir Edward Grey letter, Sep. 22, 1915), Nov. 10, Dec. 1 and 16 (with Enclosure II), 1915, 35: 186–7, 279n1 and 363; WW to Haigazoun H. Topakyan, Oct. 28, 1915, 35: 119; RL to WW, Nov. 20, 1915, 35: 227–30; WW (S), Dec. 7, 1915, 35: 293–310; TR to Archibald Roosevelt, May 19, 1915, and TR to Kermit Roosevelt, Aug. 28, 1915, TR, *Letters*, 695–8; "Ford Abdicates; Sails for Home" and "Mr. Ford's Family Amazed," *NYT*, Dec. 25, 1915, 1–2; Ford, quoted in Vansittart, 87. For more on the Peace Ship, see: Burnet Hershey, *The Odyssey of Henry Ford and the Great Peace Ship* (New York: Taplinger, 1967).

WW-EBW WEDDING: EBW, 84–6; I. Hoover, 70–5; WW to EBW, Dec. 18, 1915, 35: 370; "President W Weds Mrs. Galt," Dec. 19, 1915, 1–2; Starling, 61–2.

11 DELIVERANCE

HONEYMOON: EBW, 86–8; Starling, 66; WW to L. M. Smith and M. R. Smith, Dec. 27, 1915, 35: 399; RL to WW (T), Jan. 3, 1916, 35: 422.

SUBMARINE ATTACKS; PANCHO VILLA; PREPAREDNESS POLICY: JPT, 249–50; JPT (M), Jan. 4, 1916, 35: 424; W. H. Page to WW, Jan. 15, 1916, 35: 435; EMH to WW, Jan. 15, 1916, 35: 484–6; RL to WW, Jan. 27, 1916, 35: 531; B. R. Tillman to WW, Feb. 14, 1916, 36: 173; EMH to WW, Aug. 8, 1915, and Feb. 15, 1916, 34: 133–4n and 36: 180n1–2; EMH to Edward Grey, Mar. 10, 1916, EMH, II: 220; EMH (D), Mar. 6, 1916, 36: 212; CD to WW, Jan. 14, 1916, 35: 478n1; L. M. Garrison to RSB, Nov. 12, 1928 [RSB Papers: PUL]; EBW, 93; RSB, VI: 13.

PREPAREDNESS TOUR: WW, (two S) Jan. 27, (two S) 29, 31, (two S) Feb. 3, 1916, 36: 5 and 7–16, 26–7 and 35–41, 63–73, 114–21 and 110–4; "Table 1—Urban and Rural Population: 1900 to 1990" (U.S. Census Bureau, Oct. 1995—www.census.gov/population/censusdata/urpop0090.txt) accessed Oct. 13, 2010; Lawrence, 158–61;

assassination attempt, in G. A. Gordon to CTG, Jan. 31, 1916 [WWPL].

WW-EBW DOMESTIC ROUTINE: CTG, 52; Jaffray, cited in RSB VI: 176; EBW, 89–92.

GARRISON RESIGNATION; MEXICAN EXPEDITION: Reid, 185; L. M. Garrison to RSB, Nov. 12 and 18, 1928 [RSB Papers: PUL]; L. M. Garrison to WW, Feb. 10, 1916, 36: 164; WW to L. M. Garrison, Feb. 10, 1916, 36: 164; WW to N. D. Baker (T), Mar. 5, 6, 1916, 36: 251, 259; N. D. Baker to WW (T), Mar. 6 and 31 (with enclosure J. J. Pershing to N. D. Baker, Mar. 31), 1916, 36: 259 and 397; RSB, VI: 38; WW (S), Feb. 2, 1916, 26: 104; "Night Attack on Border," NYT, Mar. 10, 1916, 1–2; F. Funston to N. D. Baker, Mar. 10, 1916, 36: 283; EMH (D), Mar. 17 and Apr. 6, 1916, 36: 335–6n1 and 424–5; N. D. Baker to Chief of Staff (M), Mar. 10, 1916, 36: 285; H. L. Scott to Adjutant General, Mar. 19, 1916, 36: 285–6; N. D. Baker to WW (M), Mar. 10 and 15 (with enclosure), 1916, 36: 286–7 and 313–4n1; WW, press release, Mar. 10, 1916, 36: 287; F. L. Polk to Associated Press (T), Mar. 17, 1916, 36: 332; D. Lawrence to WW, Mar. 14 and June 2, 1916, 36: 309n1 and 152–5; JPT to WW, Mar. 15 and June 24, 1916, 36: 317n1 and 37: 291–2; WW to RL, Mar. 30 and June 21, 1916, 36: 382n2 and 37: 277–8n; F. L. Polk to WW, Mar. 20, 1916, 36: 342–3n1; F. K. Lane to RSB, Apr. 13, 1916, cited in RSB, VI: 72; WW to EMH, June 22, 1916, 37: 281; JPT, 157–9; WW, draft of (A), June 26, 1916, 37: 302; "Cardenas's Family Saw Him Die at Bay," NYT, May 23, 1916, 5.

ARGUING INTERVENTION: German statement in WGM, 366; Billington, 70; W. J. Stone to WW, Feb. 24, 1916, 36: 209–11; WW to W. J. Stone, Feb. 24, 1916, 36: 213–4; WW to E. W. Pou, Feb. 29, 1916, 36: 231–2; WW, draft of (N), Apr. 10, 1916, 36: 452–6; H. A. Garfield to WW, Apr. 24, 1916, 36: 545n1; TR to Archibald Roosevelt, May 19, 1915, TR, Letters, 696; RL to WW, Mar. 27, 1916, 36: 372–3; EMH (D), Mar. 30, 1916, 36: 388; WW (A), Apr. 19, 1916, 36: 509–10; WW to EMH (T), Apr. 21, 1916, 36: 520; EMH to WW, Apr. 25 and May 6, 1916, EMH, II: 239 and 36: 628–9; G. v. Jagow to J. W. Gerard, May 4, 1916, 36: 621–6; WW, in a colloquy, May 8, 1916, 36: 645; American Union Against Militarism to WW (M), c. May 8, 1916, 36: 632–3.

WILL ROGERS: Day, Will Rogers, 40–3; "W at Friars' Frolic," NYT, May 31, 1916, 11.

1916 PRESIDENTIAL CAMPAIGN BEGINS: WW (S), June 29, 1916, 37: 324–8;

Democratic Text-Book: 1912, 3–43; Greg Sarris, "After the Fall," Outdoors, Los Angeles Times, Apr. 5, 2005, 5; WW to F. K. Lane, May 26, 1916, 37: 111; RSB, VI: 104, 106; Brian E. Gray, "National Park Service Act" (eNotes.com, 2010); United States Census, 1910 and 1920; WW to House of Representatives, Jan. 26, 1915, 32: 142–4; Henry Ford to WW (T), Sep. 1, 1916, 38: 125; W. S. Stone, et al., to WW, Aug. 18, 1916, 38: 48–9; WW, statement, Aug. 19, 1916, 38: 49–50; RSB, VI: 110; WW to JD, July 18, 1916, 37: 431n1.

BRANDEIS TO SUPREME COURT: WGM, 342–6; Urofsky, 438 (quotes W. H. Taft to Gus Karger, Jan. 31, 1916), 450, 749; WW to C. A. Culberson, May 5, 1916, 36: 609–11; WW to H. Morgenthau, June 5, 1916, 37: 163.

"AMERICANISM" SUMMER OF 1916: EBW, 100–2; WW, proclamation, May 30, 1916, 37: 122–3; "Hosts in Chicago on Defense Parade," NYT, June 5, 1916, 1, 14; Rotogravure section, NYT, June, 4, 1916; WW (A), May 27, 30, June 2, 13, and 14, 1916, 37: 115, 126, 147–8, 217, and 221–5; JD, Life, 268; Marshall, 336–7.

NOMINATING CONVENTIONS: WW, draft of National Democratic Platform, c. June 10, 1916, 37: 190–201; A. M. Palmer to WW, June 14, 1916, 37: 227; WW to H. S. Cummings, June 15, 1916, 37: 229; WW to Carter Glass (T), June 15, 1916, 37: 229; Carter Glass to WW (T), June 15, 1916, 37: 231; Martin H. Glynn, quoted in RSB, VI: 250–2; A. R. Longworth to ASB (I), June 5, 1973.

POST-CONVENTION, PRE-CAMPAIGN, 1916: "President Sees Dr. Grayson Wed," NYT, May 25, 1916, 13; EMH (D), May 24, 1916, 37: 106; RSB (I) with WW, May 12, 1916 [RSB Papers: PUL]; Weinstein, 305–6; Freud, 183–4; WW to JWS, Mar. 21, 1916 [WWPL]; WW (R), June 30, 1916, 37: 332–5; WW (A), July 4, 1916, 37: 353–8; H. S. Cummings (M), Aug. 7, 1916, 38: 7–8; EBW, 103–4; WW to Obadiah Gardner, Aug. 19, 1916, 38: 50–1n1; WW (S), Sep. 2, 1916, 38: 126–39.

WW CAMPAIGN OF 1916: WW (A), Sep. 4 and 8, 1916, 38: 142–5 and 161–4; EBW, 105–6, 113; Annie W. H. Cothran to WW, Mar. 23, 1917, 41: 457–8; WW to Henry Ford, Sep. 20, 1916, 38: 187n1–2; H. C. Wallace to EMH, Aug. 31, 1916, 38: 139–41; EMH (D), Nov. 26, 1916, 40: 85–6; Billington, 80–1; W. E. B. Du Bois to WW, Oct. 10, 1916, 38: 459–60; WW to JPT, Aug. 11, 1916, 38: 24n2; WW to Giles B. Jackson, Sep. 7, 1916, 38: 157n1; W. E. B. Du Bois to JPT, Oct. 24,

1916, 38: 522n1; RSB (M), May 12, 1916, 37: 37; Anna Shaw, quoted in Norman Hapgood to WW, Sep. 16, 1916, 38: 178–9; J. A. O'Leary to WW, Sep. 29, 1916, 38: 285–6; JPT, 214, JD, *Life*, 238.

REPUBLICAN CAMPAIGN OF 1916: WW (A), July 10 and Oct. 7, 1916, 37: 384 and 364; HCL, 73–4; Marshall, 336; McAdoo, 363–5; TR to Kermit Roosevelt, Aug. 28, 1915, TR, *Letters*, 698; "Roosevelt Blames W for Raids," *NYT*, Oct. 11, 1916, 6; TR (S—speaking "bombastically and carrying a big dishrag"), Oct. 19, 1916, in TR, *NRM*, 1073; JD, *Life*, 274–5; WW (I) with H. N. Hall, Oct. 31, 1916, 38: 565.

FINAL ARGUMENTS IN 1916 ELECTION: EBW to MAH (unsent D), c. Nov. 1, 1916, 38: 589; Emanuel Julius, "Eugene V. Debs, Interviewed for *Appeal*," *Appeal to Reason*, July 1, 1916, 6; Hulbert, 264; RSB VI: 290; Marshall, 336; Steel, 100, 106, and 608n11, citing Walter Lippmann, "The Case for Wilson," *The New Republic*, Oct. 14, 1916; Ida Tarbell, "A Talk with the President of the United States," *Collier's* (Oct. 28, 1916), 38: 323–34; W's resignation plan in EMH (D), Oct. 19 and Nov. 19, 1916, 38: 617–8 and 678–9, and WW to RL, Nov. 5, 1916, 38: 617–8; EBW, 113–8.

ELECTION DAY 1916 AND AWAITING RESULTS: RSB VI: 297; JPT, 216–24; TR, cited in RSB VI: 296; Reid, 186; EBW, 116; JD, *Life*, 276; Mark Grossi, "Sierra Area Had Pivotal Role in 1916," *Fresno Bee*, Nov. 10, 2000, n.p.; "W Ahead in California by Over 3,100," *NYT*, Nov. 10, 1916, 1, 2; William Hard (I) with T. P. Gore, Aug. 18, 1926 [Hard Papers—145: 2/7: PUL]; R. H. Dabney to WW, Nov. 23, 1916, 40: 61–2; C. E. Hughes to WW (T), Nov. 22, 1916, 40: 38; WW to J. R. Wilson, Jr. (T), Nov. 27, 1916, 40: 90.

WAR ABROAD AND AMERICAN DIPLOMACY: EBW, 120–1; JPT, 253; RSB, VI: 328, 374; WW, *History*, III: 192–4; WW (U), "Prolegomenon to Peace Note," c. Nov. 25, 1916, 40: 67–70; J. C. Grew to EMH, Dec. 1, 1916, 40: 160–1; EMH (D), Nov. 20 and 26, Dec. 20, 1916, Jan. 11, 1917, 40: 4–6n and 84, 304–5, 445; WW (R), Nov. 14, 1916, 38: 637–40; WW to W. J. Harris (draft), Feb. 7, 1917, 41: 146–8; WW, Peace Note (draft), c. Nov. 25, 1916, 40: 70–4; WW, "Annual Message," Dec. 5, 1916, 40: 155–9; WW, "Appeal for Statement of War Aims," Dec. 18, 1916, 40: 273–6n; Houston, I: 219; RL (S), Dec. 21, 1916, 40: 306; WW to RL, Dec. 21, 1916, 40: 307n–311; "Peace and War Talk Hit Stocks," *NYT*, Dec. 22, 1916, 1, 2; "Wall Street Relieved

by a Wave of Buying," *NYT*, Dec. 23, 1916, 1, 3; "Financial Markets," *NYT*, Dec. 23, 1916, 12.

CHRISTMAS, 1916; W FORMULATES PEACE TERMS: WW to L. M. Smith and M. R. Smith, Dec. 27, 1916, 40: 336; CD to WW, Dec. 27, 1916, 40: 338; EMH (D), Jan. 3, 1917, 40: 403–7; WW (A—"peace without victory"), Jan. 22, 1917, 40: 533–9; "W's Terms for League of Peace," *NYT*, Jan. 23, 1917, 1, 2; "President's Own Comment," *NYT*, Jan. 23, 1917, 1; "Scene in the Senate," *NYT*, Jan. 23, 1917, 2; Longworth, 242; CD to WW, Jan. 24, 1917, 41: 7; W. H. Page, (M) #5514, Jan. 20, 1917, 40: 532; EMH (D), Dec. 27, 1916, II: 423–4.

GERMANY ESCALATES SUBMARINE WARFARE; W RESPONDS: WGM, 367; JPT, 254–5; RSB, VI: 448–9; EMH (D), Feb. 1, 1917, 41: 87–8; RL to WW, Feb. 1, 1917, 41: 99; WW (A), Feb. 3, 1917, 41: 108–12; "Bernstorff Was Not Surprised," *NYT*, Feb. 4, 1917, 1, 5; WW (A—draft), Feb. 3, 1917, 41: 112n1; WW, "Bases of Peace" draft, quoted in RSB, VI: 465–6; TR to HCL, Feb. 20, 1917, TR, *Letters*, 718–9; "A Visit to the President," *Friends' Intelligencer*, Mar. 10, 1917, 41: 302–4n2.

ZIMMERMANN NOTE AND REPERCUSSIONS: "Germany Seeks an Alliance," *NYT*, Mar. 1, 1917, 1; WW (A), Feb. 26, 1917, 41: 283–7.

SECOND INAUGURATION: EBW, 130; EMH (D), Mar. 3, 1917, 41: 317–8n; WW, statement, Mar. 4, 1917, 41: 318–20; "President Inaugurated," *NYT*, Mar. 6, 1917, 1; WW, "Second Inaugural Address," Mar. 5, 1917, 41: 332–5.

12 ARMAGEDDON

POST-INAUGURAL EXHILARATION AND EXHAUSTION: "President Reviews a Parade," *NYT*, Mar. 6, 1917, 3; EMH (D), Mar. 5, 1917, 41: 340–1; EBW, 130, 116; "Take Motor Ride at Night," *NYT*, Mar. 6, 1917, 3.

WW AND CABINET RESPOND TO GERMANY: JD (D), Mar. 8 and 20, 1917, 41: 364 and 444–5; EBW, 131–2; RL (M), 41: 436–44; Houston, I: 241–4; T. W. Brahany (D), Mar. 20 and 26, 1917, 41: 445 and 473–5; EMH (D), Apr. 29, 1917, 42: 162; Heaton, 268; RSB, VI: 506.

APRIL 2, 1917—"SAFE FOR DEMOCRACY" SPEECH: T. W. Brahany (D), Apr. 2, 1917, 41: 531; EMH (D), Apr. 2, 1917, 41: 528–30; "President Holds War Conferences," *NYT*, Apr. 3, 1917, 3; RSB, VI: 508; Lansing, 238–9; "Armed

American Steamship Sunk," *NYT*, Apr. 3, 1917; "Lodge Knocks Down Pacific Assailant," *NYT*, Apr. 3, 1917, 5; "President at Golf During the Forenoon," *NYT*, Apr. 3, 1917, 10; "Must Exert All Our Power," *NYT*, Apr. 3, 1917, 1; Starling, 87; Houston, I: 253–6; EBW, 132–3; Lawrence, 208–9; WW (A), Apr. 2, 1917, 41: 519–27; "Lodge Congratulates the President," *NYT*, Apr. 3, 1917, 2; JPT, 256–9.

RESPONSE TO SPEECH; DECLARATION OF WAR: W. Lippmann to WW, Apr. 3, 1917, 41: 537; W. H. Page to WW (T), Apr. 3, 1917; Gerard, quoted in T. W. Brahany (D), Apr. 6, 1917, 41: 558; WGM to WW, Apr. 3, 1917, 41: 541; Lawrence, 210–2; "Seek to Explain Miss Rankin's 'No,'" *NYT*, Apr. 7, 1917, 4; Starling, 89; EBW, 133; Seymour, 117; WW, Last Will and Testament, May 31, 1917, 42: 426.

MOBILIZATION; BARUCH; HOOVER: "Government Acts Swiftly" and "27 Ships Taken Here," *NYT*, Apr. 7, 1917, 1–2; WW (M), Apr. 7, 1917, 42: 3; JD (D), Nov. 26, 1917, 45: 128; Samuel Gompers to WW, Aug. 2, 1917, 43: 352–4; W. G. Sharp to RL, Aug. 2, 1917, 43: 355; WW, "Appeal to American People," Apr. 15, 1917, 42: 71–5; EBW, 135–6, 160–1; Seymour, 118–29, 160, 162–70; WGM, 454–9, 464, 483–91; JPT to WW, Nov. 18, 1916, 38: 674; EMH (D), Jan. 3 and 12, Mar. 3, 1917, 40: 402 and 463, 41: 318; WW (A), Jan. 4, 1918, 45: 449; Baruch, 17, 23–5, 38–40, 55, 232; N. D. Baker to WW (includes Baruch M), May 28, 1917, 42: 411–7; JPT, 268–70; H. Hoover, 1–5, 8; WW (S), May 19, 1917, 42: 344–5; Houston, I: 256–9; "Hooverize" is defined in *Oxford English Dictionary*, VII: 374; RSB, VII: 409.

CONTROL OF IDEAS: PROPAGANDA; SEDITION: Creel, *How We Advertised*, xiii, xvii–xviii, 3, 6, 7, 10, 13, 84–7, 261–6; Stone, 113–7, 147–8, 586n32, 587n39; WW, "Annual Message," Dec. 7, 1915, 35: 306–7; WW (A), Apr. 2, 1917, 41: 526; Geoffrey Stone, "On Secrecy and Transparency" (which cites H. R. 291, tit. I § 4, 65th Congress, 1st Session, in 55 Congressional Record H1590-1 and 1695, Apr. 30 and May 2, 1917), *American Constitution Society for Law and Policy*, June, 2008, 4; A. Brisbane to WW, Apr. 20, 1917, 42: 107–8; WW to A. Brisbane, Apr. 25, 1917, 42: 129; "Canvass Forecasts Doom of Censorship," *NYT*, May 28, 1917, 4; JPT to WW, May 8, 1917, 42: 245–6; WW to E. Y. Webb, May 22, 1917, 42: 369–70; ASL (N), 42: 247; G. Creel (M), enclosed in JD to WW, Apr. 11, 1917, 42: 39–41; WW to JD, Apr. 12, 1917, 42: 43; Lawrence, 228;

H. Hoover, 13; F. C. Barnes to WW, c. Oct. 12, 1917, 44: 364; O. H. Kahn to WW, Apr. 6, 1917, 42: 7; WW to JPT, c. Apr. 7, 1917, 42: 8–9; SA (N) [PUL: 440], 314; JD, 281–2; WW to L. C. Dyer, Aug. 1, 1917, 43: 336; Brinkley, 618.

BUILDING AN ARMY; TR VOLUNTEERS: E. W. Pou to JPT, Apr. 11, 1917, 42: 42; WW to G. T. Helvering, Apr. 19, 1917, 42: 97–8; Longworth, 245–6; Morris, 486–8; JPT, 285–9; TR to WW, May 18, 1917, 42: 324; WW (S), May 18, 1917, 42: 324–6; T. W. Brahany (D), Apr. 10, 1917, 42: 31–2; EMH to WW, Apr. 10, 1917, 42: 29–30n1; JD, 284; "Drawing for Nation's Draft Army," *NYT*, July 21, 1917, 1, 6–8; Coffman, 29–31; Clements, 145–8; Seymour, 125, 129–31, 143–6, 137–40; R. H. Morris to JPT, Aug. 29, 1918, 49: 420; WW to JPT, Sep. 2, 1918, 49: 419; JD, *Life*, 285; Pershing, I: 26–8; JPT, 295–6; Lawrence, 220–2; WW (A), Aug. 11, 1917, 43: 427–31; EBW, 139–40; WW (A), Dec. 2, 1918, 53: 275.

PAPAL APPEAL; EUROPEAN ASSESSMENT OF THE WAR; WW DISPATCHES PERSHING: Pope Benedict XV's appeal, enclosed with RL to WW, Aug. 13 and 21 (enclosed with "Comments on the Pope's Peace Appeal"), 1917, 43: 438–9 and 18–22; W. H. Page to RL, Aug. 15, 1917, 43: 482–5; WW (N), "Reply to Benedict XV," c. Aug. 16, 1917, 43: 487–8; N. D. Baker to WW, Aug. 20, 1917, with W. Lippmann (M), "Reply to the Pope's Proposal," 43: 532–4; RL to W. H. Page, Aug. 27, 1917, 44: 57–9; WW, "State of the Union Address," Dec. 4, 1917, 45: 194–202; R. H. Campbell to EMH, Jan. 2, 1918, 45: 430–1; Trask, 94–5; *Congressional Record*, Oct. 21, 1939, vol. 84, 686; Churchill, 692; Coffman, 94–5; W. H. Page to WW (T), Apr. 17, 1917, 42: 82; Nicolson, *King George*, 55; D. Lloyd George to WW, Sep. 3, 1917, 44: 125–30; Seymour, 147–8; JD, *Life*, 282; G. Creel to WW, Dec. 8, 1917, 45: 246; WW to G. Creel, Dec. 10, 1917, 45: 257; W. G. Sharp to N. D. Baker, Jan. 31, 1918, attached to WW to N. D. Baker, Feb. 4, 1918, 46: 237; "W Sees End of War Only When Germany Is Beaten," *NYT*, Oct. 8, 1917, 44: 325–7; EMH (D), Oct. 24, 1917, 44: 437–9.

"THE INQUIRY"; PALESTINE: WW to EMH, July 21 and Sep. 19, 1917, 43: 238 and 44: 216–7, enclosing RL (M), 44: 217–9; EMH to WW, Sep. 20, 1917, 44: 226; H. B. Brougham to WW, Sep. 28, 1917, 44: 275–6n; A. J. Balfour to WW, Jan. 31, 1918, 46: 180–1; Lord Reading to A. J. Balfour (T), Mar. 18, 1918, 47: 63–4; Hemingway, 196; A. J. Balfour to Sir William

Wiseman, Oct. 16, 1917, 44: 323–4; W. H. Page to RL, Nov. 23, 1917, 45: 148–9n2, which contains the official Declaration of Balfour to L. W. Rothschild, Nov. 2, 1917; RL to WW, Dec. 13, 1917, 45: 286, with 286n1 recording WW's response; WW (M), ca. Nov. 20, 1917, 45: 86; Pershing, I: 237–8.

DEVELOPMENT OF FOURTEEN POINTS: WW, "State of the Union Address," Dec. 4, 1917, 45: 202; EMH (D), Dec. 18 and 30, 1917, Jan. 9, 1918, 45: 323–4 and 399, 45: 550–8; S. E. Mezes, D. H. Miller, W. Lippmann, "The Present Situation," c. Jan. 4, 1918, 45: 459–74; Mayer, 296–7 and 329–67, discusses the effect of Lenin's manifesto at Brest-Litovsk Conference; C. A. Spring Rice to A. J. Balfour, Jan. 4, 1918, 45: 454–7 and (T) on same date marked "Personal & Most Secret," 45: 458; Count O. Czernin, comments, Dec. 25, 1917, 45: 386n2; "Lloyd George Restates Britain's War Aims," *NYT*, Jan. 6, 1918, 1, 2; RSB, VII, 453–4; WW (A), Jan. 8, 1918, 45: 534–9; EMH, III: 342; Esher, IV: 215; RSB, VII, 456n2; "Roosevelt Pleased by Wilson Message," *NYT*, Jan. 9, 1917, 2; WW to I. J. Paderewski, Jan. 11, 1918, 45: 569; "Balfour Pronounces Speech 'Magnificent,'" *NYT*, Jan. 11, 1918, 2; WW to Lincoln Steffens, Jan. 15, 1918, 45: 593; WW to Jane Addams, Jan. 15, 1918, 45: 593; N. D. Baker to WW, Jan. 15, 1918, enclosing J. J. Pershing to Chief of Staff, Jan. 14, 1918, 45: 594–5; G. Creel to WW, Jan. 15, 1918, 45: 596–7, enclosing E. G. Sisson to G. Creel, c. Jan. 13, 1918; Creel, 288–9; L. R. Colcord to WW, Jan. 27, 1918, 46: 113–4n2; EMH (D), Jan. 29, 1918, 46: 167–8; G. Auchincloss to WW, Jan. 31, 1918, enclosing W. C. Bullitt to EMH (M), Jan. 31, 1918, 46: 183–93; WW (A), Feb. 11, 1918, 46: 318–24; Cathy Porter (re: Russia's plight), quoted in Vansittart, 225.

DOUGHBOYS ARRIVE IN FRANCE: Vansittart, 237; WW (A), Apr. 6, 1918, 47: 267–70; Churchill, III: 454; "In Flanders Fields," by John McCrae, first published Dec. 8, 1915, in *Punch*; Houston, 296–7; Barry, 169–72.

FINANCING THE WAR; WGM, 372–8, 383–91, 410–12; RSB, VII: 93n1; WW to Mary Pickford, Apr. 9, 1918, 47: 301–2n2; Brownlow, *War, West, Wilderness*, 108; Balio, 24; WGM to WW, May 23, 1918, 48: 121–7; WW (A), May 27, 1918, 48: 162–5; WGM, 423; Weisman, 304, 329, 333–4.

AMERICANS IN COMBAT: Clements, 150–1; Farwell, 19–20; WW (A), Dec. 2, 1918, 53: 276; Seymour, 134.

AFRICAN AMERICANS' ROLE: usgovernmentspending.com/us_20th_century-chart.html; J. M. Waldron to WW, Apr. 12, 1917, 42: 49–51; E. T. Morris, W. M. Trotter, et al., to WW, Apr. 20, 1917, 42: 113–6; Giddings, 560–2; Arthur Capper to WW (T), July 6, 1917, 43: 112; WW to JPT, c. July 5 [enclosing W. E. Walling (T), July 3, 1917] and 9 [enclosing Forum of Los Angeles to WW (M), July 8], 1917, 43: 103–4 and 128–30; WW to T. W. Gregory, July 7, 1917, 43: 116; WW to L. C. Dyer, July 28, 1917, 43: 299–300; N. D. Baker to WW, Aug. 17, 1917, and Aug. 22, 1918, 43: 506–7 and 49: 324–8; WW to N. D. Baker, c. Aug. 21, 1917, enclosing A. F. Lever to D. F. Houston, Aug. 20–1 and 24, enclosing J. H. Eagle to WW, 1917, 44: 10 and 62–4; J. W. Johnson, petition, Feb. 19, 1918, 46: 383–5; Johnson, 492–3; WW, statement, July 26, 1918, 49: 97–8; WW, statement, Aug. 31, 1918, 49: 400–2; R. B. Fosdick to WW, Sep. 27, 1918, enclosing "Status of Negro Problem at Newport News," 51: 136–8; Texas Grand Master, quoted in Maraskin, 220; WW (R), Oct. 1, 1918, 51: 168.

WOMEN'S SUFFRAGE: Keyssar, 199, 216, 217; WW (R), Jan. 6, 1915, and Jan. 27, 1916, 32: 23 and 36: 3–4; "Women Force W to Say No to Suffrage," *NYT*, Jan. 28, 1916, 2–3; EMH (D), Dec. 15, 1915, and July 26, 1917, 35: 360 and 43: 290–1; TR to Harriet Taylor Upton, Nov. 10, 1908, and to M. E. L. Swift, Mar. 7, 1911, TR, *Letters*, 599–600 and 640; Nancy Toy (D), Jan. 5, 1915, 32: 21; WW to W. R. Crabtree, Feb. 28, 1917, 41: 299; WW (R), Dec. 9, 1916, 40: 195–6; T. W. Brahany to WW, Jan. 6, 1917, 40: 420–1; WW to L. J. Frazier, Jan. 23, 1917, 40: 549; "Suffragists Will Picket White House," *NYT*, Jan. 9, 1917, 1; EBW, 125; T. W. Brahany (D), Mar. 4, 1917, 41: 329–30; WW to C. C. Catt, May 8, 1917, 42: 241; WW to E. W. Pou, May 14, 1917, 42: 293; WW to J. T. Heflin, June 13, 1917, 42: 497; J. T. Heflin to WW, June 28, 1917, 43: 36; "Crowd Destroys Suffrage Banner at White House," *NYT*, June 21, 1917, 1–2; WW to JWS, June 22, 1917, 42: 560; Gilson Gardner (M), c. July 17, 1917, 43: 201–2n; "Suffrage Arrests Disappoint Crowd," *NYT*, July 15, 1917, 18; Louis Brownlow, 78–9; "Suffragists Take 60-Day Sentence," *NYT*, June 18, 1917, 1, 6; "W Shocked at Jailing Militants," *NYT*, July 19, 1917, 1–2; WW to EMH, July 29, 1917, 43: 314; Dudley Field Malone to WW, Sep. 7, 1917, 44: 167–9; WW to JPT, c. Nov. 10, 1917, enclosing W. G. Gardiner to WW, Nov. 9, 1917, 44: 559–62; "Accuse Jailers of Suffragists," *NYT*,

Nov. 17, 1917, 1, 4; "Sees Suffragists All Turning Anti," *NYT*, Nov. 16, 1917, 1, 6; V. B. Whitehouse to WW (A), Oct. 25, 1917, 44: 440–1 and WW reply, Oct. 25, 1917, 44: 441–2; White House Staff to WW (M), Nov. 6, 1917, 44: 523n1; E. M. Bass to WW, Jan. 8, 1918, 45: 542; WW to E. M. Bass, Jan. 9, 1918, 45: 545; WW (S), Jan. 9, 1918, 45: 545n1 and appears in "Wilson Backs Amendment," *NYT*, Jan. 10, 1918, 1; SA (N) [PU: 440], 214; C. C. Catt to WW, Sep. 29, 1918, 51: 155–7; WGM, 496–8; WW (A), Sep. 30, 1918, 51: 158–61; Creel, *How We Advertised*, 212–21; WW to A. H. Shaw, May 22, 1918, 48: 117.

WARTIME SEDITION; DEBS: WW, *History*, III: 153; T. W. Gregory to WGM, June 12, 1917, and Feb. 1918, 42: 510–8 and 518n5–519; L. D. Wald, Roger Baldwin, et al., to WW, Aug. 10, 1917, enclosing (M) "Invasion of Civil Rights," 43: 420–4; WW to T. W. Gregory, Aug. 17, 1917, 43: 503; Max Eastman, et al., to WW, July 12, 1917, 43: 165–6n2; WW to A. S. Burleson, July 13, 1917, 43: 164; www.marxists.org/archive/debs/works/1918/canton.htm, accessed Sep. 10, 2011; JPT, 505; WW (A), Dec. 4, 1917, 45: 195; Teachout, 144–5; Stone, 588; Mencken, 120; WW to A. S. Burleson, July 13, 1917, enclosed with Max Eastman, Amos Pinchot, and John Reed to WW, July 12, 1917, 43: 164–6n; WW to Max Eastman, Sep. 18, 1917, 44: 210–1; U. Sinclair to WW, Oct. 22, 1917, 44: 467–72; Alan Brinkley, "World War I and the Crisis of Democracy," appears in Farber, 27–41; Brinkley, 618.

BOLSHEVISM AND RUSSIA: WW to EMH, July 8, 1918, 48: 550; Council of Four (N), Mar. 27, 1919, 56: 328; Lord Reading to A. J. Balfour, July 19, 1918, 49: 36; Lord Reading to D. Lloyd George, July 12, 1918, 48: 603; Henri Bergson (D), July 25, 1918, 49: 94–6; George Kennan to RL, May 28, 1918, 48: 183–8; T. G. Masaryk to WW, Aug. 5, 1918, 49: 185; N. D. Baker to WW, Nov. 27, 1918, 53: 327–9.

WW'S DOMESTIC LIFE AND HEALTH DURING WAR: E. T. Brown to M. C. M. Brown, Dec. 7, 1917, 45: 236–7; EBW, 145, 158; JWS to F. B. Sayre, Jan. 2, 1918 [WWPL]; "Call for War Stirs the City," *NYT*, Apr. 3, 1917, 5; SA (N) [PU: 440], 303; Freud, 81, 171, 197; WW to H. B. Fine, Apr. 20, 1918, 47: 383n1; WW to JWS, May 3, 1918, 47: 502; CTG to A. G. Grayson, Sep. 8 and 17, 1918 [WWPL]; EMH (D), Aug. 18, 1918, 49: 286; WGM, 409–10.

WW AS COMMANDER IN CHIEF; ALLIES WINNING THE WAR: Freud, 171; WGM,

409–10; WW (A), Sep. 27, 1918, 51: 127–33; Max, Prince of Baden, to WW, Oct. 6, 1918, 51: 253; WW to German government, draft of (N), Oct. 7 and 14, 1918, 51: 255–7 and 333–4.

MIDTERM ELECTIONS, 1918: N. D. Baker to WW, Oct. 26, 1918, 51: 455; TR to HCL (T), Oct. 24, 1918, 51: 455n1–456; Lawrence, 236; JPT, draft of appeal, c. Oct. 11, 1918, 51: 304–6; N. D. Baker to WW, Oct. 26, 1918, 51: 455; WW, appeal, Oct. 19, 1918, 51: 381–2; JPT, 322–30.

HUMAN COSTS OF WAR: WW to Toastmaster, Mar. 20, 1918, 47: 83–4; EMH (D), Oct. 15, 1918, 51: 340–1; H. F. Ashurst (D), Oct. 14, 1918, 51: 339; Barry, 329, 332; WW to T. F. Logan (expressing "faith in Divine providence"), Nov. 8, 1918, 51: 640; WW to RL (two letters), Apr. 18, 1918, 47: 357 and 358; EMH (D), Oct. 24, 1917, 44: 437; JD (D), July 9, 1918, 48: 578.

13 ISAIAH

FALSE ARMISTICE: "United Press Men Sent False Cable," "City Goes Wild with Joy," "Middle West Goes Wild," "Crowds Parade in Boston," *NYT*, Nov. 8, 1918, 1, 3; EBW, 169; Arthur Hornblow, Jr., "The Amazing Armistice," *The Century Magazine*, Nov. 1921 (privately reprinted), 1, 15.

ARMISTICE: Foch, Erzberger, and Oberndorff quoted in RSB, VIII: 570–2, 578, 580; EBW, 170; EMH to WW (T), Nov. 11, 1918, 53: 34; WW, statement, c. Nov. 11, 1918, 53: 34; "Truce Electrifies Congress," *NYT*, Nov. 12, 1918, 1–2; WW (A), Nov. 11, 1918, 53: 35–43; H. F. Ashurst (D), Nov. 11, 1918, 53: 35; King George V to WW (T), printed in *NYT*, Nov. 14, 1918, 53: 53; "President W," *NYT*, Nov. 12, 1918, 14; EBW, 170–1.

PEACE CONFERENCE CHOICES: "W at Peace Table, Rumor Says," *NYT*, Nov. 13, 1918, 1, 3; WW to EMH (T), Nov. 13 and 16, 1918, 53: 66 and 96–7; EMH to WW (T), Nov. 14 and 15, 1918, 53: 71–2 and 84–5; CTG, 57–8; 85; TR to Rudyard Kipling, quoted in Vansittart, 259; Morris, 550, 553; WGM, 498–505; WW re: WGM, quoted in RSB, VIII: 241–2; T. W. Gregory resignation recorded in JPT to WW (T), Jan. 9, 1919, 53: 705; JPT, 337–8; Lawrence, 316–9; TR on H. White, TR, *Letters*, 614; WW, "Constitutional Government in the United States," 18: 120.

WW'S PRE-DEPARTURE DISCUSSIONS; CONGRESSIONAL APPEARANCE: SA, quoted in RSB, VIII: 242–3; Caroline Astor Drayton

Phillips (D), Dec. 5, 1918 [FDR Library: Joseph P. Lash Papers, C44: 46]; WW, "State of the Union Address," Dec. 2, 1918, 53: 274–86; JD (D), Dec. 2, 1918, 53: 301; H. F. Ashurst (D), Dec. 2, 1918, 53: 305; WW to J. R. Mann, Dec. 3, 1918, and ASL (N), 53: 308; "Senators Clash over Trip," *NYT*, Dec. 4, 1918.

WW SAILS TO EUROPE; FRANCE, ENGLAND, AND ITALY: EBW, 211–2; CTG (D), Jan. 1, 2, and 4, 1919, 53: 577–8, 589, and 605–7; Starling, 124; WW (A), Jan. 3, 1919, 53: 602–3; I. Hoover, 79; CTG, 66; WW, drafts of "Covenant," 53: 655–86; RL (M), Jan. 11, 1919, 54: 3.

DEATH OF TR: TR, quoted in J. M. Blum and A. D. Chandler (eds.), *Letters of TR* (Cambridge, MA: Harvard University Press, 1954), VIII: 1420–1; WW, proclamation, Jan. 7, 1919, 53: 635; JPT to WW (T), Jan. 6, 1919, 53: 624; N. D. Baker to WW, Jan. 1, 1919, 53: 624 and n6; WW to T. R. Marshall (T), Jan. 7, 1919, 53: 636; HCL, 134–5.

CURTAIN RISING ON PEACE TALKS: H. Hoover, 69–70; F. L. Polk to American Commissioners (M), Jan. 17, 1919, 54: 126; RSB, VIII: 577; Keynes, 4, 32–44; EBW, 233; JD, *Life*, 307; Keynes re: D. Lloyd George, quoted in Moggridge, 329; CTG to A. G. Grayson, Apr. 23–5, 1919 [WWPL]; Maurice Hankey (N: Council of Ten), Jan. 12 and 13, 1919, 54: 23–6 and 47–8; CTG (D), Jan. 12, 1919, 54: 5; Edith Benham (D), Jan. 12, 1919, 54: 34; Lord Derby to A. J. Balfour, Dec. 22, 1918, 53: 470–2; Maurice Hankey (N: Supreme War Council), Jan. 13, 1919, 54: 37–42; WW to V. E. Orlando, Jan. 13, 1919, 54: 50–1; JPT to CTG, Jan. 16, 1919, 54: 106–7n1; H. B. Swope, "Personal Cordiality Wins Colleagues to President," NY *World*, Jan. 15, 1919, n.p.; Creel, *How We Advertised*, 401.

CONFERENCE BEGINS: CTG (D), Jan. 18, 1919, 54: 126–8; "Brilliant Opening Scene" and "Bugles Greet Delegates," *NYT*, Jan. 19, 1919, 1; Protocol of Plenary Session, Jan. 18, 1919, 54: 128–32; Nicolson, *Peacemaking*, 242, 245; Lawrence, 258–9; E. Benham (D), Jan. 20, 1919, 54: 175; CTG, 70–1; "Arrest Bolsheviki Reported on the Way to Attack W," *NYT*, Jan. 19, 1919, 1; "Red Plot Reported to Assassinate W, Clemenceau and Lloyd George," *NY Tribune*, Jan. 20, 1919, 1.

NONPARTICIPANTS AND PETITIONERS: Maurice Hankey (N: C10), Jan. 21 and 22, 1919, 54: 187 and 204–6; CTG (D), Jan. 22, 1919, 54: 199; Churchill, V: 263 and "Bolshevist

Atrocities" (S), Apr. 11, 1919, quoted in W. S. Churchill (ed.), *Never Give In!* (New York: Hyperion, 2003), 77; Paul Cambon, quoted in Lord Curzon to Lord Derby, Jan. 23, 1919, 54: 235–6; Lithuanian delegation to WW, Jan. 23, 1919, attached to RSB to WW, Jan. 24, 1919 [RSB Papers: PUL]; Chaim Weizmann to WW, Jan. 24, 1919, 54: 258; E. Benham (D), Jan. 27, 1919, 54: 307; CTG (D), Jan. 28, 1919, 54: 309; WW to Boghos Nubar, Jan. 23, 1919, 54: 226; Duiker, 59–60.

SECOND PLENARY SESSION: ESTABLISHING LEAGUE OF NATIONS; WW VISITS WAR SITES: Protocol of Plenary Session, Jan. 25, 1919, 54: 265–8; CTG (D), Jan. 25 and 26 (war sites), 1919, 54: 262–3 and 278–81; EMH to WW, Jan. 25, 1919, 54: 271; Lord Curzon to Lord Derby, Jan. 23, 1919, 54: 235–6; WW (R) to French Protestants, Jan. 27, 1919, 54: 282–3; EBW to J. R. Bolling, Jan. 27, 1919, 54: 305.

MANDATES; COMMISSION ON LEAGUE OF NATIONS: WW (R), Feb. 28, 1919, 55: 321; E. Benham (D), Jan. 18 and 21, 1919, 54: 149 and 197; Maurice Hankey (N: C10), Jan. 21, 24, 27, 28, and 30, 1919, 54: 188–9, 250–1, 291–2 and 300–1, 325–7, and 350–1 and 371; CTG (D), Jan. 28 and 30, Feb. 13, 1919, 54: 308–9 and 348, 55: 120; D. H. Miller (D), Jan. 30 and Feb. 12, 1919, 54: 379 and 55: 118; C. Seymour to his family, Jan. 30, 1919, 54: 385; EMH (D), Jan. 31, 1919, 54: 407; Minutes of Commission on the League of Nations, Feb. 10, 11, and 13, 1919, 55: 41–51, 79–80, and 121 and 136; "Covenant" of League of Nations, Feb. 3, 1919, 54: 449–58; Lord Cecil (D), Feb. 4, 1919, 55: 80.

WW PRESENTS COVENANT: EMH (D), Feb. 14, 1919, 55: 193–6; Maurice Hankey (N: C10), Jan. 30, 1919, 54: 351; Creel, *How We Advertised*, 413–4; EBW, 226–7, 236–40; Truman Talley, "Feed World and Then Talk Peace," *NY Herald*, Feb. 15, 1919, 55: 161–3; WW (A), Feb. 14, 1919, 55: 164–78; EMH to WW, Feb. 14, 1919, 55: 178; CTG (D), Jan. 22 and Feb. 14, 1919, 54: 199 and 55: 160; the junior member of the American Commission was Arthur Hornblow, Jr. (D), Feb. 14, 1919 (private collection); Maurice Hankey (N: Supreme War Council), Feb. 14, 1919, 55: 180–3.

WW LEAVES PARIS: WW to EMH (T), c. Feb. 23, 1919, 55: 230; WW to RL (T), Feb. 23, 1919, 55: 231; WW (S), Feb. 15, 1919, 55: 197; "Last Message to France," *NYT*, Feb. 16, 1919, 1, 2; EBW, 236, 240.

WW RETURNS TO U.S.: T. Talley, *op. cit.,* 55: 161–3; EBW, 233, 240–1; EMH to WW (T), c. Feb. 21, 23, 1919, 55: 223, 233; JPT to WW (T), Feb. 15 and 22, 1919, 55: 197–8, 226; CTG (D), Feb. 19, 20, 22, 24, 1919, 55: 207, 217, 224, 235–8; F. B. Sayre to WW (T), Feb. 23, 1919, 55: 234. [WW's grandchildren: After their firstborn, Francis Sayre, Jr., and before the birth of Woodrow Wilson Sayre, Francis and Jessie Wilson Sayre also had a daughter, Eleanor Axson Sayre, born Mar. 26, 1916; W. G. and Eleanor Wilson McAdoo had a daughter Ellen, born May 21, 1915; and they would have a second daughter, Mary Faith McAdoo, born Apr. 6, 1920.] RL to WW (T), Feb. 19, 1919, 55: 209; WW to JPT (T), Feb. 22 (10:41 a.m. and 4:55 p.m.), 1919, 55: 225 and 226; WW (A), Feb. 24, 1919, 55: 238–45; "Challenge to His Critics," *NYT,* Feb. 25, 1919, 1.

WW IN WHITE HOUSE; MEETS CONGRESSIONAL DELEGATION: CTG (D), Feb. 25 and Mar. 4, 1919, 55: 254 and 409–12; W. E. Rappard to Hans Sulzer, Feb. 13, 1919, 55: 151–4; JD (D), Feb. 25, 1919, 55: 266; "President Expounds League of Nations," *NYT,* Feb. 26, 1919, 55: 268–76; HCL, 100, 117, 260; WW, U statement, c. Mar. 4, 1919, 55: 408; WW (S—"A group of men . . . have . . . chosen to embarrass the administration"), Mar. 4, 1919, 55: 408–9.

REPLACING A.G. GREGORY WITH PALMER: JPT to WW (T), Jan. 12 and Feb. 1, 4, 1919, 54: 31–2 and 429, 485; WW to T. W. Gregory, Feb. 26, 1919, 55: 276; T. W. Gregory to WW, Jan. 17 and Mar. 1, 1919, 54: 125, 346–7; WW to JPT (T), Jan. 31, 1919, 54: 410; Hagedorn, 226; Coben, 200; CTG (D), Feb. 27, 1919, 55: 294; WW to A. M. Palmer, Mar. 12, 1919, 55: 482–3; WW to A. S. Burleson, Feb. 28, 1919, 55: 327.

WW RETURNS TO *GEORGE WASHINGTON,* VIA PHILA. AND NYC: WW (A), Mar. 4, 1919, 55: 413–21; CTG (D), Mar. 9–10, 11 and 12, 1919, 55: 471, 473–4, 480–1; RSB (D), Mar. 8, 1919, 55: 465–6; EMH to WW (T), Mar. 4 and 7, 1919, 55: 423 and 458–9; WW to EMH (radiogram), Mar. 10, 1919, 55: 472.

14 GETHSEMANE

FRANCE—BREST TO PARIS: CTG (D), Mar. 13 and 14, 1919, 55: 487–9 and 496–7; EBW, 245–6; EMH (D), Mar. 14, 1919, 55: 499–500; Freud, 233–4.

WW BEGINS WORK ANEW: RSB (D), Mar. 15 and 27, 1919, 55: 531 and 56: 337; EBW,

247–8; EMH to WW (T), c. Feb. 21 and 25, 1919, 55: 223 and 256–7; CTG (D), Mar. 14 and 15, 1919, 55: 497–8 and 529–31; EMH (D), Mar. 16 and 22, 1919, 55: 538 and 56: 180; Lord Cecil (D), Mar. 16, 1919, 55: 539.

SECOND ACT OF PEACE TALKS BEGINS: MIDDLE EAST; EASTERN EUROPE; RUSSIA: CTG (D), Mar. 18, 19, and 22, 1919, 56: 62, 88, and 163–5; Lord Cecil (D), Mar. 18, 1919, 56: 81; Maurice Hankey (N: C10), Jan. 27 and Mar. 20, 1919, 54: 284 and 56: 104n1, 113; Monnet, 78–81; Keynes, 83–5, 116–8, 131–2, 135, 141, 152, 161, 204; "Financial Capacity of Enemy States, Annex II, 4th Meeting," Feb. 19, 1919 [RSB Papers: Box 15, Folder 31, 5—PUL]; "Middle East" defined in *OED,* IX: 743; Nicolson, *Peacemaking,* 136, 140–3; RSB (D), Mar. 20, 1919, 56: 103; RL to WW, Mar. 20, 1919, 56: 123; H. Hoover, 133–5; Brownell, 86–9; H. Hoover to WW, Mar. 28, 1919, 56: 375–8; Ellery Sedgwick to JPT, Mar. 21, 1919, 56: 162–3.

WW REVISITS BATTLEFIELDS; CONFLICTS WITH CLEMENCEAU OVER REPARATIONS: CTG, 71–2, 85; CTG (D), Mar. 23, 25, 26, and 27, 1919, 56: 194–200, 246–9, 283–6, and 312; P. Mantoux (N: Council of Four), Mar. 24, 26, and 27, 1919, 56: 208–9, 290, and 316; EMH (D), Apr. 1, 1919, 56: 517–8; RSB (D), Apr. 1, 1919, 56: 518; WW to JPT (T), Mar. 22 and 26, 1919, 56: 191 and 310; JPT to WW (T), Apr. 4, 1919, 56: 618; "Bryan Supports League," *NYT,* Mar. 12, 1919, attached to JD to WW, Mar. 27, 1919, 56: 346n1; JD (D), Mar. 27, 1919, 56: 338; Nicolson, *Peacemaking,* 196.

SAAR VALLEY DISCUSSION: EMH (D), Mar. 28, 1919, 56: 349–50; RL (M), Mar. 28, 1919, 56: 351–2; RSB (D), Apr. 3, 1919, 56: 578; P. Mantoux (N: C4), Mar. 28 and Apr. 1, 1919, 56: 366–70 and 508; CTG (D), Mar. 28, 29, 30, Apr. 1, 1919, 56: 347, 408, 429, 490; G. L. Beer (D), Mar. 30 and Apr. 1, 1919, 56: 434 and 490; C. H. Haskins to WW (with enclosure), Apr. 1, 1919, 56: 514; EMH (D), Apr. 1 and 2, 1919, 56: 518 and 540; Freud, 245–6.

WW'S HEALTH; LOSING FAITH IN EMH: CTG (D), Apr. 3 (with ASL N), 4, 5, 6, 7, and 8, 1919; 56: 556–7 (557n2), 584, 57: 3–4, 50–2, 62–7, and 99; H. Hoover, 198–9; Weinstein, 338–9; Bert E. Park, "The Impact of W's Neurological Disease During the Paris Peace Conference," 58: 611–30; Edwin A. Weinstein, "WW's Neuropsychological Impairment and the Paris Peace Conference," 58: 630–5; James F. O'Toole,

"Some Observations on W's Neurological Illness," 58: 635–8; ASL, "Editors' Commentary," 58: 638–9; I. Hoover, 98–9; Weinstein, 340–1; RSB (D), Apr. 4 and 19, 1919, 56: 588–9 and 57: 508–9; EMH (D), Apr. 5 and May 30, 1919, 57: 34–5 and 59: 624; EBW, 248–52; Freud, 226–7; CTG to A. G. Grayson, Apr. 23–5, 1919 [WWPL]; RSB (D), Apr. 3, 1919, 56: 577–8.

SUMMONING *GEORGE WASHINGTON*: CTG (D), Apr. 6, 7 (with ASL N), and 15, 1919, 57: 50–1, 62–67 (63n1), and 351; EBW, 249; RSB, *American Chronicle*, 402; H. Hoover, 199, 202; JPT to CTG (T), Apr. 9, 1919, 57: 177; RSB (D), Apr. 7, 1919, 57: 68–70; H. White to WW, Apr. 12, 1919, 57: 301–2; H. Hoover to WW, Apr. 11, 1919, 67: 273–4.

WW LEAVES SICKBED; MARIE OF RO-MANIA: Weinstein, 339; P. Mantoux (N: C4), Apr. 5, 1919, 57: 22; P. Mantoux, cited in Weinstein, 343n; Clements, 182; Park, *op. cit.*, 58: 623; RSB (D), Apr. 8, 1919, 57: 140; Minutes, League of Nations Commission, Apr. 10, 1919, 57: 218–9; EBW, 257–60; CTG (D), Apr. 10, 11, and 17, 1919, 57: 190–3, 238–9, and 426–30; E. Benham (D), Apr. 11, 1919, 57: 241–2; "Clauses Proposed for Insertion in the Treaty of Peace," attached to H. M. Robinson to WW, Mar. 24, 1919, 56: 236–8 and cf.: ASL (N), 57: 240n5; WW to P. G. Gerry, Apr. 17, 1919, 57: 446; F. P. Walsh and F. F. Dunne to WW, May 31, 1919, 59: 643; EMH (D), May 31, 1919, 59: 645; RSB (D), Apr. 11 and May 31, 1919, 57: 240–1 and 59: 646; CTG to WGM, Apr. 12, 1919, 57: 304.

ITALIAN DEMANDS: Nicolson, *Peacemaking*, 169–71; RSB (D), Apr. 18, 20, 22, and May 28, 1919, 57: 467–8, 527, 585, and 59: 575; T. N. Page to EMH, Apr. 17, 1919, 57: 434–7; CTG (D), Apr. 19, 20, and 23, 1919, 57: 477–8, 512–3, and 58: 3; Maurice Hankey (N: C4), Apr. 19, 20, and 22, 1919, 57: 482–94, 514–7, and 614; EMH (D), Apr. 20, 1919, 57: 527; N. H. Davis to WW, Apr. 18, 1919, 57: 470; WW to N. H. Davis, Apr. 19, 1919, 57: 445; H. Hoover, 206; EBW, 254–6; T. N. Page to American Mission (T: #260), Apr. 24, 1919, 58: 91–2; "Orlando Makes Protest," *NYT*, Apr. 25, 1919, 58: 97–101.

JAPANESE DEMANDS: Nicolson, *Peacemaking*, 145–7; CTG (D), Mar. 10, Apr. 25 and 30, May 1, 1919, 55: 471, 58: 110–13 and 244–5, 274–7; H. Hoover, 79, 208; Lawrence, 261; RL (M), Apr. 28, 1919, 58: 185; Seymour, 314–7; EMH, IV: 449–52; JPT to WW, Apr. 24, 1919, 58: 105; RSB (D), Apr. 25, 1919, 58: 143; RL (M), Apr. 28,

1919, 58: 185; Tasker Bliss to WW, Apr. 29, 1919, 58: 234; Tasker Bliss to E. A. Bliss, May 1, 1919, 58: 320; EMH (D), Apr. 28, 1919, 58: 185–7; RSB (D), Apr. 30, 1919, 58: 270–1n; EMH to Baron Makino, Apr. 28, 1919, EMH, IV: 453–5, including 453n2; Maurice Hankey and P. Mantoux (N: C4), May 1, 1919, 58: 277–8; Weinstein, 342n50 (N.B.: the term "ludic" was first used by Jean Piaget); Freud, 262–3; Short, 90–4.

PRESENTING THE TREATY: Confucius, *The Analects*," XI: 16; Seymour, 317–8; CTG (D), May 2, 4, 5, 7, and 8, 1919, 58: 332, 422, 430–1, 499–504, and 535–6; Churchill, "The War Is Won," Dec. 16, 1918, quoted in W. S. Churchill (ed.), *op. cit.*, 75–7; Churchill to William Griffen (editor of *NY Enquirer*), Aug. 1936, quoted in Vansittart, 162; RSB, *American Chronicle*, 416; Freud, 264; EMH (D), May 5, 7, 1919, 58: 443, 520–1; B. Baruch to WW, May 8, 1919, 58: 548–9; RSB (D), May 7, 1919, 58: 529–30; "Rantzau Proclaims Germany Unrepentant," "Treaty of Peace Is Solemnly Presented," "1871–1919," "Germans at Versailles," "Clemenceau's Speech," May 8, 1919, *American Daily Mail*, 1; Brockdorff-Rantzau (R), May 7, 1919, 58: 514–7; WW, statement, May 6, 1919, 58: 489–90; Sir R. Borden to Sir T. White (T), May 7, 1919, 58: 517–20.

WW'S HEALTH; POSSIBLE STROKE: ASL (N), 58: viii; WW (M), May 8, 1919, 58: 559; WW (R), May 9, 1919, 58: 598–600; RSB (D), May 17, 1919, 59: 245; CTG (D), May 8 and 10, 1919, 58: 536 and 59:3.

GERMANS CONSIDER TREATY: Brockdorff-Rantzau to Clemenceau, May 9, 1919, 59: 13n5; WW to Brockdorff-Rantzau, May 10, 1919, 59: 28n3; Maurice Hankey and P. Mantoux (N: C4), May 10, 1919, 59: 709; J. Smuts to WW, May 14, 1919, 59: 149–50; WW to J. Smuts, May 16, 1919, 59: 187; CTG (D), May 11, 21, and 23, 1919, 59: 39–40, 321–2, and 419–20; D. H. Miller (D), May 13, 1919, 59: 82–3.

REDRAWING MAP OF THE WORLD: E. Benham (D), May 23, 1919, 59: 420; Maurice Hankey (N: C4), June 23, 1919, 61: 88–93; F. Frankfurter to WW, May 8, 1919, 58: 555–6; H. Hoover, 224–6.

RUSSIA AND BULLITT MISSION: RSB, "Russia," n.d. [RSB Papers, 18/1, 20: PUL]; Francis P. Sempa, "William C. Bullitt: Diplomat and Prophet," *American Diplomacy* (Chapel Hill, NC: Americandiplomacy.org, 2003); Kennan, 79–80; WW (R), Feb. 28, 1919, 55: 320; Brownell, 93; W. C. Bullitt to WW, May 17, 1919, 59: 232–3;

RL to WW, May 20, 1919, 59: 314; RSB (D), May 19 and 23, 1919, 59: 287 and 447–8; Freud, 253–4; Gay, 559.

ASSESSMENTS OF TREATY: Nicolson, *Peacemaking*, 198; Keynes, 41, 226–7.

WW AT SURESNES: EBW, 260; CTG (D), May 30, 1919, 59: 605–6; WW (R), May 30, 1919, 59: 606–10; EMH to WW, May 30, 1919, 59: 610; RSB (D), May 30, 1919, 59: 621–2.

REACTION TO TREATY—IN U.S., FRANCE, ENGLAND, AND GERMANY: RSB (D), Apr. 3, May 19, 28, 31, and June 13, 1919, 56: 578, 59: 286, 574, 647, and 60: 532–3; C. Seymour to family, May 31, 1919, 59: 648; JPT, 364–5; "W, the Third Term and the Treaty," *Springfield Republican*, May 17, 1919, enclosed with WW to JPT, June 2 and 6 (T), 1919, 60: 41–2 and 247; WW, "Special Message to Congress," May 20, 1919, 59: 289–97; WW to JPT (T), May 13, 1919, 59: 120; "Suffrage Wins in Senate," *NYT*, June 5, 1919, 1; WW (R), Feb. 28, 1919, 55: 309–23; CTG (D), May 22, 29, June 2, and 15, 1919, 59: 370–2, 577, 60: 18–9, and 570; Maurice Hankey (N: C4), June 13, 1919, 60: 498; Brockdorff-Rantzau to G. Clemenceau, May 29, 1919, 59: 579–84; ASL (N), 61: 35n; Maurice Hankey and P. Mantoux (N: C4), June 2, 1919, 60: 27; WW, discussion with American delegation, June 3, 1919, 60: 67; Baruch (reporting WW telling D. Lloyd George: "You make me sick!"), 120–1; G. L. Beer (D), June 1, 1919, 60: 17; V. C. McCormick (D), June 3, 1919, 60: 72; "German Envoys Tell the Cabinet to Reject Allied Peace Treaty," *NYT*, June 19, 1919, 1–2; EBW, 26.

WILSONS VISIT BELGIUM: EBW, 261–7; CTG (D), June 18, 1919, 61: 3–8; WW (A), June 19, 1919, 61: 16–20; WW (R), June 19, 1919, 61: 21.

GERMANS READY TO SIGN TREATY; PREPARATIONS: RSB (D), June 20 and 26, 1919, 61: 34–5n1 and 231; G. A. Bauer to G. Clemenceau, June 21, 1919, 61: 72–6; CTG (D), June 23 and 24, 1919, 61: 78–9 and 118–9; RL (M), June 28, 1919, 61: 327; Tasker Bliss to E. A. Bliss, June 24, 1919, 61: 135; JPT to WW (T), June 21, 1919, 61: 66; "Knox Resolution Cannot Be Passed," *NYT*, June 21, 1919, 1; WW to T. W. Lamont, June 27, 1919, 61: 290; "Conference Officials Prepare for Signing," *NYT*, June 22, 1919, 2; EMH (D), June 21 and 23, 1919, 61: 45 and 112–5; E. Benham (D), June 24 and 26, 1919, 61: 135 and 188–9; WW to J.-J. Jusserand, June 25, 1919, 61: 173; WW (R), June 26, 1919, 61: 238.

ANALYSIS OF TREATY: Keynes, 35, 36, 56, 151; Nicolson, *Peacemaking*, 43–4; Seymour, 323–5; JD, *Life*, 312; D. Lloyd George to WW, June 26, 1919, 61: 223–5; financial costs recorded in MacMillan, 480.

SIGNING OF TREATY: CTG (D), June 28, 1919, 61: 302–6; RL (M), June 28, 1919, 61: 321–8; W. L. Westermann, June 28, 1919, 61: 328–32; EMH (D), June 28, 1919, 61: 332–3.

WILSONS LEAVE FRANCE: EMH (D), June 29, 1919, 61: 354–5; EBW, 271.

15 PASSION

VOYAGE HOME: WW (A), July 4, 1919, 61: 378; CTG (D), July 1, 2, 3, 4, 5, and 6, 1919, 61: 360–3, 369–70, 374–6, 377–8, 385, and 396; V. C. McCormick (D), July 4 and 5, 1919, 61: 383 and 385–6; JPT to CTG, July 2, 1919, 61: 372–3; WW to JPT (T—handwritten), July 3, 1919, and ASL (N), 61: 376n.

WW ARRIVES IN NJ; RETURNS TO WHITE HOUSE: CTG (D), July 8, 1919, 61: 400–1; WW (A), July 8, 1919, 61: 401–4; Longworth, 285–6; CTG (D), July 8, 1919, 61: 401; "Capital Greets W Warmly," *NYT*, July 9, 1919, 3.

POLITICAL BATTLE FOR TREATY BEGINS: WW, Report of Press Conference, July 10, 1919, 61: 417–24; "W Revises Speech on Treaty for Senate Today," *NYT*, July 10, 1919, 1, 3; "Offers Bill to Keep Presidents Home," *NYT*, July 10, 1919, 3; "Insist Majority Can Amend Treaty," *NYT*, July 11, 1919, 1–2; CTG (D), July 10, 1919, 61: 416–7; "Ovation to the President," *NYT*, July 11, 1919, 1–2; WW (A), July 10, 1919, 61: 426–36; H. F. Ashurst (D), July 11, 1919, 61: 445–6; ASL (N), 61: 446n; "W Greets Callers," *NYT*, July 11, 1919, 1–2; "Comments Divide on Party Line," *NYT*, July 11, 1919, 1, 3; "17,000 Boo and Hiss President W at Sinn Fein Rally," *NYT*, July 11, 1919, 1, 7; Houston, II: 5–6; FDR to RSB, Feb. 20, 1922 [RSB Papers: PUL]; Berkin, 581–2; E. J. Howenstone, Jr., "The High-Cost-of-Living Problem after World War I," *Southern Economic Journal*, v. 10, no. 3 (Jan. 1944), 222; "Foods Drop As Everybody Aims Smash at H. C. L.," *Chicago Daily Tribune*, Aug. 16, 1919.

"RED SUMMER" OF 1919—STATE OF THE NATION: "Negroes Again Riot in Washington," *NYT*, July 23, 1919, 1–2; "Gov. Bilbo Blames French Reception and Negro Press," *Jones County* (MS) *News*, July 8, 1919, 1, cited in McWhirter, 71; Johnson, 658–9; "Urban and Rural

Population: 1900–1990" (Washington, D.C.: United States Census Bureau, 1995); Fitzgerald, 304; "U. S. Business Cycle Expansions and Contractions" (Cambridge, MA: National Bureau of Economic Research, Aug. 10, 2011).

HCL: Adams, 419–20; HCL, 2–3, 23, 160, 163–5, 224–6; WW, "Cabinet Government," 1: 505, 509; HCL to TR, Mar. 1, 1915, cited in John A. Garrity, *Henry Cabot Lodge* (New York: Alfred A. Knopf, 1968), 312; WW, "Constitutional Government," 18: 60; "Insist Majority Can Amend Treaty," *NYT*, July 11, 1919, 1–2.

WW COURTS SENATORS; MEDICAL ISSUES: Sir William Wiseman to A. J. Balfour, July 18, 1919, 61: 541–3; WW to T. W. Lamont, July 19, 1919, 61: 544n; HCL, 56–60; "W Invites Senators," *NYT*, July 15, 1919, 1–2; "Committee Finds Treaty Readings," *NYT*, July 29, 1919, 1, 3; "W to Consult Congress Members," *NYT*, July 14, 1919, 2; "W Frankness Getting Results," *NYT*, July 19, 1919, 2; "Wilsons on Cruise Despite the Storm," *Washington Post*, July 20, 1919, 61: 562–3; "President W Returns Ill," *NYT*, July 21, 1919, 61: 569–70; "W Stays in Bed," *Washington Post*, July 22, 1919, 61: 578–9; Park, *op. cit.*, 62: 629; "35 to Block League," *Washington Post*, July 20, 1919, 61: 563–5; "W Says He Decided Shantung," *NYT*, July 22, 1919, 61: 593–5; "Deny W Power," *Washington Post*, July 23, 1919, 61: 596–8; WW to HCL, July 25 and Aug. 14 (draft), 15, 1919, 61: 623 and 62: 278–81, 310; I. Hoover, "Memoir," 63: 632; EBW, 273; N. H. Davis to WW, July 26, 1919, 62: 7; CTG to A. G. Grayson, July 29 and 30, 1919 [WWPL]; WW (M), Sep. 3, 1919, 62: 621; JPT to WW, Aug. 15, 1919, 62: 309; HCL to WW, Aug. 14, 1919, 62: 275; ASL, "Introduction," 62: viii; WW (A), Aug. 8, 1919, 62: 209–19 (especially 209n1).

NAMING THE WAR; RECONSIDERATION OF DEBS: N. D. Baker to WW, July 23, 1919, 61: 611; WW to N. D. Baker, July 31, 1919, 62: 69; C. S. Darrow to WW, July 29, 1919, 62: 58–9; WW to John Spargo, Aug. 29, 1919, 62: 559.

LEAGUE FIGHT: HCL HEARINGS; FOREIGN RELATIONS COMMITTEE AT WHITE HOUSE: Cooper, 136–7; *Congressional Record, 66th Congress, 1st Session*, Aug. 12, 1919, 3778–84; "Jovial Luncheon After Conference," *NYT*, Aug. 20, 1919, 1–2; JPT, 422–5, 435; Steel, 163; "President Defends Treaty to Senators," *NYT*, Aug. 19, 1919, 62: 535–6; Houston, II: 14–7; CTG to A. G. Grayson, Aug. 19 and 22, 1919 [WWPL]; I. Hoover,

"Memoir," 63: 632; WW, "Conference with Foreign Relations Committee" (transcript), Aug. 19, 1919, 62: 339–411; "Offer a Compromise," *Washington Post*, Aug. 21, 1919, 62: 429–32n3; Baruch, 135–6; "Itinerary—Tour of the President to the Pacific Coast" (private collection), Sep. 3–30, 191; EBW, 274; CTG, 95–6.

WESTERN TOUR—FIRST PHASE: EBW, 274–5; "W Begins Tour for Treaty," *NYT*, Sep. 4, 1919, 1–2; ASL (N), "W's Speeches on His Western Tour," 63: 5–6; "W Defends Treaty and League As Tour Begins," *NYT*, Sep. 5, 1919, 1–2; WW (A—Columbus), Sep. 4, 1919, 63: 7–18; WW (R), Sep. 4, 1919, 63: 18–9; CTG (D), Sep. 4, 5, 6, 8, 9, 1919, 63: 3–5, 31–3, 63–6, 93–6, 122–4; WW (A—Indianapolis), 63: 19–29; WW (two A—St. Louis), Sep. 5, 1919, 63: 33–42 and 43–51; WW (A—Kansas City), Sep. 6, 1919, 63: 66–75; "W Likens Treaty Obstructionists to Bolsheviks," *NYT*, Sep. 7, 1919, 1–2; WW (A—Des Moines), 63: 76–88; "W Gaining Support," *NYT*, Sep. 7, 1919, 1, 2; "Wants Senate Trailers Paid," *NYT*, Sep. 4, 1919, 2; WW (A—Omaha), 63: 97–107; WW (A—Sioux Falls), Sep. 8, 1919, 63: 107–17; WW (A—St. Paul), Sep. 9, 1919, 63: 125–31; WW (A—Minneapolis), Sep. 9, 1919, 63: 131–8; WW (A—St. Paul), Sep. 9, 1919, 63: 138–48.

REACHING THE NORTHWEST; NATIONAL CONCERNS; BULLITT TESTIMONY; RL DISLOYALTY: CTG (D), Sep. 25, 1919, 63: 489; Samuel Gompers, et al., to WW (T), Sep. 4, 1919, 63: 30n1; WW (A—Helena), Sep. 11, 1919, 63: 196; W. J. H. Cochran to JPT, Sep. 11, 1919, 63: 198–200n; RL to WW, Sep. 17, 1919, 63: 337–340n; Brownell, 97–8; "Bullitt Asserts Lansing Expected Treaty to Fail," *NYT*, Sep. 13, 1919, 1, 2; JPT, 441–3.

MEDICAL CONCERNS AS TOUR CONTINUES: Breckinridge Long, "Memoir" (U), 1924, quoted in 63: 339n4; CTG (D), Sep. 12, 18, 19, 20, 21, 1919, 63: 210–11 (211n5 cites *Seattle Post-Intelligencer*, Sep. 13, 1919), 340–1n, 369–70, 396–7, 423–4; WW (A—Helena), Sep. 11, 1919, 63: 195; WW (A—Portland), Sep. 15, 1919, 63: 281; WW (A—Portland Auditorium), Sep. 15, 1919, 63: 284–5; WW, quoted in (I) for *Oregon Daily Journal*, Sep. 16, 1919, quoted in 63: 277n7; WW to B. Baruch, Sep. 17, 1919, 63: 336; "Labor Conferees Chosen," *NYT*, Sep. 18, 1919, 1–2; "Says W Has Socialization Idea," *NYT*, Sep. 18, 1919, 1; WW (A—Berkeley), Sep. 18, 1919, 63: 350; CTG, 7–9; WW (A—San Diego), Sep. 19, 1919, 63: 376; "Find W Shy Only in Private,"

NYT, Sep. 22, 1919, 1, 3; Elliot, 299; WW to MAH, Sep. 20, 1919, 63: 419; Hulbert, 267–77, EBW, 281.

WESTERN TOUR, TURNING EASTWARD: CTG, Jr., to ASB (I), Oct. 14, 2006; CTG (D), Sep. 22, 23, 24, 25, 1919, 63: 426, 446, 467, 487–90; HCL, 183–5; Guy Mason to JPT (T), Sep. 22, 1919, 63: 445; WW (A—Salt Lake City), Sep. 23, 1919, 63: 449–63; EBW, 281–3; CTG to A. G. Grayson, Sep. 25, 1919 [WWPL].

PUEBLO AND RETURN TO WASHINGTON: Starling, 151–3; Peter Roper, "Remembering W in Pueblo," *Pueblo Chieftain*, Sep. 25, 1994, n.p.; WW (A—Pueblo), Sep. 25, 1919, 63: 500–13; EBW, 284–5; JPT, 446–8; CTG (D), Sep. 26, 27, 28, 1919, 63: 518–21, 526–7, 532–3; WW (A—in Los Angeles Shrine Auditorium), Sep. 20, 1919, 63: 413; WW to JWS (T), Sep. 26, 1919; T. W. Brahany (I), Aug. 19, 1926 [Hard Archives, VIII: PUL]; A. S. Burleson to WW, Sep. 29, 1919, 63: 534–5; "W Returns to Washington Worn and Shaken," *NYT*, Sep. 29, 1919, 1, 3.

WHITE HOUSE RECUPERATION AND COLLAPSE: EBW, 286–7; "W Sleeping Better and Improving," *NYT*, Sep. 30, 1919, 63: 536–7; CTG to H. A. Garfield, Oct. 1, 1919, 63: 538–9; RL to F. L. Polk, Oct. 1, 1919, 63: 539–40; "President Is Again Jaded After Another Restless Night," *NYT*, Oct. 2, 1919, 1; CTG 100; I. Hoover, 100–1.

16 PIETÀ

WW'S INVALIDISM: EBW, 288–9; CTG, 100, 109; " 'Very Sick Man,' Says Grayson," *Washington Post*, Oct. 3, 1919, 63: 543–5; F. X. Dercum to CTG, "Dr. Dercum's Memoranda," Oct. 20, 1919, 64: 500–7; I. Hoover, 100–3; JD, *Life*, 339.

GOVERNMENT DURING WW'S ABSENCE: *Constitution of the United States*, Article 2, Section 1; JPT, 442–5; Houston, II: 36–40; RL (D), Oct. 3, 1919, 63: 547n; "Rumor Busy about W," *NYT*, Oct. 13, 1919, 63: 564–7; Thomas, 204, 225–7, 236; "More Encouraging Day," *NYT*, Oct. 5, 1919, 63: 550–1; CTG, 108; JD (D), Oct. 5, 6, 7, 1919, 63: 552, 555, 557; "W Has a Good Day," *Washington Post*, Oct. 6, 1919, 63: 552–3; Breckinridge Long (D), Oct. 7, 1919, 63: 558–9; CTG (M), Oct. 6, 1919, 64: 496; JD, *Wilson Era*, II: 511–3; Weinstein, 360; "President Needs Long Rest," *NYT*, Oct. 12, 1919, 63: 561; "Reports W Suffered Shock," *NYT*, Oct. 11, 1919, 63: 561–4; "W Still Gains," *Washington Post*, Oct. 7, 1919, 63: 555–6;

EBW to JD (M), Oct. 7, 1919, 63: 556–7; JD to EBW, Oct. 7, 1919, 63: 557; JPT to W. B. Wilson, Oct. 6, 1919, 63: 554; F. K. Lane to WW, Oct. 19, 1919, 63: 582–3; "WW," statement to industrial conference, Oct. 20, 1919, 63: 584–5; EMH to EBW, Oct. 22, 1919, 63: 587–8; "WW," veto message, Oct. 27, 1919, 63: 601–2; RL (M), Nov. 5, 1919, 63: 618–9; I. Hoover, 103–4; CTG 101, EBW, 290–2; "Spent Restless Day," *Washington Post*, Oct. 15, 1919, 63: 572–3; "President Improves after a Setback," *NYT*, Oct. 18, 1919, 63: 577–9; B. E. Park, "WW's Stroke of Oct. 2, 1919," 63: 644–6; RSB (D), Nov. 5, 1919, 63: 622; Freud, 291.

EBW, CTG, JPT PERMIT VISITS, INCLUDING TWO ROYAL PARTIES: ASL (N) to JD (D), Nov. 4, 1919, 63: 613n; A. M. Palmer to R. S. Morris, Nov. 3, 1919, 63: 608n; EBW, 292–6; CTG, misc. (N), n.d., 64: 489; "Belgian Royalties See the President," *NYT*, Oct. 30, 1919, 63: 602–6; [N.B.: The Belgian Royals stayed at the home of Breckinridge Long]; EMH (D), Dec. 22, 1919, 64: 217; Levin, 399–401; Smith, 116–7; "President on the Porch in a Wheeled Chair," *NYT*, Nov. 15, 1919, 1, 64: 32–3; "Prince Sees Wilson," *Washington Post*, Nov. 14, 1919, 64: 31–2.

WW CONDUCTS BUSINESS; HITCHCOCK VISITS, TRIES TO RALLY SENATE SUPPORT: Cooper, 661n17; "Lodge Forces Win Opening Skirmish," *NYT*, Nov. 8, 1919, 1–2; CTG (M), Nov. 17, 1919, 64: 43–5; G. M. Hitchcock, "W's Place in History," 64: 45n1; William Hard, "Amendments" [PUL: Hard, 145, 3/15, x.3]; Connally, 101; G. M. Hitchcock to EBW, Nov. 15, 1919, 64: 37–8; EBW, 296–7; H. Hoover, 282–3; Bonsal, 274–80, CTG (M), Nov. 17, 1919, 64: 43–5; "President Will Pocket Treaty" and "President Out on the Lawn," *NYT*, Nov. 18, 1919, 64: 45–50; "President Outdoors Again," *NYT*, Nov. 19, 1919, 64: 57; G. M. Hitchcock to EBW, Nov. 17, 1919, enclosing Hitchcock's draft of letter for "WW to G. M. Hitchcock," Nov. 17, 1919, 64: 51.

NOVEMBER 19, 1919, SENATE VOTE; STRANGENESS WITHIN WHITE HOUSE; T. R. MARSHALL: H. F. Ashurst (D), Nov. 19, 1919, 64: 62–4; "Lodge Resolution Beaten," *NYT*, Nov. 20, 1919, 1–2; "Lodge Declares for Political Fight on Peace Treaty," *NYT*, Nov. 22, 1919, 2; O. W. Underwood to WW, Nov. 21, 1919, 64: 69–70; EBW, 297–8, 300; Smith, 111; I. Hoover, 104–5; Thomas, 211–2, 227–8; "False Telephone Report of President's Death," *NYT*, Nov. 24, 1919, 1.

WW'S ABSENCE AROUSES SUSPICIONS; "SMELLING COMMITTEE": JPT to EBW, Nov. 17, 1919, 64: 42; "WW," statement, Nov. 11, 1919, 64: 7; WW, "State of the Union Address," Dec. 2, 1919, 64: 106–16n; "Congress Comment Divides," NYT, Dec. 3, 1919, 2; "President's Health Shows Steady Improvement," NYT, Dec. 3, 1919, 1; RL (M), Dec. 4, 1919, 64: 123–5; "President Jests on Moses Story," Dec. 5, 1919, 64: 132–3; CTG (M), Dec. 5, 1919, 64: 135–9; JD, Wilson Era, II: 513; Houston, II: 140–1; "W to See Senators," NYT, Dec. 5, 1919, 1; EBW, 298–9; Smith, 133; Starling, 155; RL (M), Dec. 5, 1919, 64: 139–40.

GOVERNMENT IN DISARRAY: William Butler Yeats, "The Second Coming"; JPT to EBW, Dec. 18, 1919, and c. Feb. 3, 1920, 64: 204–5 and 355, including ASL (N), 356–7; Clements, 210–1; McAdoo, 505–9; W. D. Hines to WW, Dec. 15, 1919, 64: 188–9; A. M. Palmer to WW, Dec. 23, 1919 (with enclosures: W. D. Hines to WW, Dec. 23, 1919, and WW proclamation, Dec. 24, 1919), 64: 222–7; JPT, statement, Dec. 24, 1919, 64: 228; RL to JPT, Nov. 26 and Dec. 15, 1919, 64: 95 and 187–8; F. L. Polk to JPT, Dec. 26, 1919, 64: 229–30; RL (D), Dec. 29, 1919, 64: 235; L. S. Rowe to JPT, Jan. 3, 1920, 64: 245; B. F. Chase to N. H. Davis, July 8, 1920, 65: 505–6; B. Colby to WW, July 31, 1920, 65: 571; Houston, II: 60–2; EBW, 301–2; Rudolph Forster to JPT (T), Sep. 5, 1919, 63: 52n4; EMH (D), Dec. 12, 1919, and Mar. 2, 1920, 64: 185 and 65: 41; JD, Wilson Era, 546–8; JD (D), Dec. 5 and 9, 1919, 64: 141 and 166; "President Makes Proposal to Coal Miners," NYT, Dec. 7, 1919, 64: 142–5; WW to Harry Garfield, Dec. 13, 1919, 64: 185; Harry Garfield to WW, Dec. 13, 1919, 64: 186.

RL DEPARTURE: RL (M), Dec. 4, 5, 10, 1919, Jan. 7, Feb. 9, 13, 1920, 64: 123–5, 139–40, 179, 255–6, 385–6, 415–9; RSB (D), Jan. 23, 1920, 64: 320; EMH (D), Jan. 3, 1920, 64: 243; N. D. Baker to WW, Feb. 7, 1920, 64: 389–90; RL to WW, Feb. 9 (two letters), 12, 1920, 64: 388–9 and 390–1, 408–10; WW to RL, Feb. 7 and 11, 1920, 64: 383 and 404; JD, Wilson Era, II: 519, 521–3; JPT, 445; EBW, 301; RL (D), Feb. 11 and 14, 1920, 64: 405 and 428; Bert E. Park, "The Aftermath of W's Stroke," 64: 527; "Sees President Near Recovery," NYT, Feb. 11, 1920, 64: 394–6; "President Will Never Recover" and "Doctor Dercum Declares Mind of President W Is Keen," Philadelphia Press, Feb. 15, 1920, 64: 432–4.

SEDITION; RED SCARE; PALMER RAIDS: WW to A. M. Palmer, Mar. 12, 1919, 55: 482–3; WW to A. S. Burleson, Feb. 28, 1919, 55: 327; Ackerman, 20, CTG (D), June 4, 1919, 60: 114–5; "200 Caught in New York," NYT, Nov. 8, 1919, 1, 2; Stone, 223; "Raid from Coast to Coast," NYT, Jan. 3, 1920, 1, 2; "Raiders Ordered to Make Cleanup Thorough," NYT, Jan. 3, 1920, 1; "Raids on 13 Centres Here," NYT, Jan. 3, 1920, 1, 2; "Reds Plotted Country-Wide Strike," NYT, Jan. 4, 1920, 1, 2; RSB (D), June 23, 1920, 64: 320; "W Walks," Washington Post, Dec. 14, 1919, 64: 187; "W Reported Much Better," NYT, Dec. 21, 1919, 64: 211; JPT to WW, Dec. 28, 1919, 64: 233.

WW PLOTS NEW STRATEGY FOR TREATY PASSAGE: WW, to "My Fellow Countrymen," c. Dec. 17, 1919, 64: 199–202; A. M. Palmer to WW, Dec. 22, 1919, 64: 214–5; WW, redraft of Jackson Day message, Jan. 7, 1920, 64: 252–5; Houston, II: 47–9; JPT, draft of Jackson Day message, Jan. 6, 1920, 64: 247–250; D. Houston (N), Jan. 7, 1920, 64: 250–2; "Clash at Jackson Dinner," NYT, Jan. 9, 1920, 1; "W Will Make No Offer," NYT, Dec. 15, 1919, 1, 2; JPT to EBW, Jan. 15 and 17, 1920, 64: 276–7n and 287; Cooper, 302–10; RSB (D), Jan. 23, 1920, 64: 320–1; CTG to SA, Jan. 24, 1920, 64: 324–6; JPT to WW, Feb. 27, 1920, 64: 479; JPT, 429; H. S. Cummings (D), Feb. 29, 1920, 65: 24; Hurley, 243–5; RSB, American Chronicle, 474; B. Long to JPT, Sep. 22, 1919, 63: 444; EBW to Carter Glass (draft), Feb. 11, 1920, 64: 405; Carter Glass to WW, Feb. 9 and 12, 1920, 64: 387 and 410–1; WGM, 514–5.

WW'S RENEWED STRENGTH; FINAL ATTEMPT AT TREATY PASSAGE: "W Has a Ride," NYT, Mar. 4, 1920, 65: 42; I. Hoover, 106; Starling, 156–7; WW to G. M. Hitchcock, Mar. 5 and 8, 1920; 65: 54 and 67–71; newspapers citing gulf between WW and HCL, quoted in ASL (N), 65: 71–2; Watson, 198; G. M. Hitchcock to WW, c. Mar. 11, 1920, 65: 80; Louis Seibold, "Visit to White House," June 17, 1920, 65: 403; JPT, 455–6; "Senate Adopts Curb by Lodge on Article X," NYT, Mar. 16, 1920, 1, 3; "Lack 7 Votes to Ratify," NYT, Mar. 20, 1920, 1–2; JD, Wilson Era, 464; EBW, 303, CTG (D), Mar. 31, 1920, 65: 149.

WW AS "LAMEST DUCK": H. S. Cummings (D), May 31, 1920, 65: 348; L. Seibold, op. cit., 65: 401–15; WW to JPT, Oct. 29, 1918, 51: 485; WW to Douglas Fairbanks, Jan. 13, 1919, 54: 53; CTG to CD, May 29, 1920, 65: 341–3; EBW, 304–5; Smith, 157; CTG (M), c. Mar. 22, 1920, 65: 111; "W Hails Colors in a Circus Parade," NYT, May 18, 1920, 65: 290–1; CTG (M), Apr. 13, 1920, 65: 179–80.

WW RESUMES CABINET MEETINGS; COLBY: CTG, 112–4; Houston, II: 68–70; JD, *Wilson Era*, II: 527–8; Smith, 147–8; CTG (M), Apr. 14, 1920, 65: 186; JD (D), Apr. 14, 1920, 65: 186–8; RL (D), Apr. 14 and May 29, 1920, 65: 188 and 343; Freud, 292; CTG, 114; CTG (N), n.d., 64: 490; WW to Joe Cowperthwaite, Sep. 3, 1920, 66: 92.

WW CONSIDERS RESIGNATION: EMH (D), Jun. 10, 1920, 65: 384; RSB (D), Feb. 4, 1920, 64: 362–3n1; WW (N), c. June 10, 1920, 65: 382; JPT to EBW (asking WW to declare he would not run for third term), Mar. 23, 1920, 65: 117–9; CTG, 116–7; JD, *Wilson Era*, 557; Marc Peter to Giuseppe Motta, May 28, 1920, 65: 338–40 (N. B.: 338n2); B. Colby to WW, Aug. 9, 1920 (with enclosed N), 66: 19–25; W. W. Hawkins (UI), Sep. 27, 1920, 66: 153–8; JD, *Wilson Era*, II: 545–6; H. Hoover, 150; Post, 275–7; Norman Hapgood to WW, Nov. 9, 1920, 66: 343; Samuel Gompers, to WW Dec. 15, 1920, 66: 515–6; W. B. Wilson to WW, Dec. 18, 1920, 66: 533; JPT to WW, May 12, 1920, 65: 276; JPT, 505; John Roberts to WW, Sep. 21, 1920, 66: 132; Helen H. Gardener, Mar. 22, 1920, 65: 115–6.

WW CONSIDERS THIRD TERM; 1920 DEMOCRATIC CONVENTION: Sir Auckland Geddes to D. Lloyd George, June 4, 1920, 65: 369–72; Carter Glass (M), June 16 and 19, 1920, 65: 400 and 435–6; SA, 197; JD, *Wilson Era*, II: 553, 555–7; Smith, 161–2; "Opening Session Spirited," *NYT*, June 29, 1920, 1, 2; H. S. Cummings to WW (T), June 28 and July 3, 1920, 65: 470–1n and 492–3; CTG (D), July 2 and 3, 1920, 65: 488 and 491; JPT to EAW, July 4, 1920, 65: 493–5; WW to H. S. Cummings, July 2, 1920 65: 489; B. Colby to WW, July 2 and 4, 1920, 65: 490 and 496; Charles Swem (D), c. July 6, 1920, 65: 498–9; WW to J. M. Cox (T), July 6, 1920, and ASL (N), 65: 499n1; Starling 157.

ELECTION OF 1920; COX AND FDR VISIT WW: I. Hoover, 106–7; EBW, 305–7; Cox, 241–4; CTG, 119; JPT, 499–502. W. W. Hawkins (UI), Sep. 27, 1920, 66: 156–7; WW to J. Cox, Oct. 29, 1920; JPT to WW, Sep. 24 and Oct. 10, 1920, 66: 141n and 214–6; WW, statement, Oct. 3, 1920, 66: 181–3; SA, 198–9; RSB, draft of article, Nov. 29, 1920, 66: 440; Charles Swem (D), Nov. 3, 1920, 66: 306–7; RSB 485; SA to JWS, Nov. 4, 1920, 66: 319–20; Starling, 612.

WW'S FINAL DAYS IN WHITE HOUSE: WW to JWS, Oct. 25, 1920, 66: 266–7; WW to L. C. Woods, Dec. 1, 1920, 66: 447; RSB (D),

Nov. 28 and Dec. 1, 1920, 66: 435–6 and 451; RSB, draft of article, Nov. 29, 1920, 66: 438–52; CTG (M), Dec. 6, 1920, 66: 479; WW, "State of the Union Address," Dec. 7, 1920, 66: 484–90; "W Urges Nation to Lead Democracy," *NYT*, Dec. 8, 1920, 1, 2; Eleanor Roosevelt, et al., to WW, c. Feb. 14, 1921; 67: 135–6; "League Assembly Opens, Hails W," *NYT*, Nov. 16, 1920, 1, 2; A. G. Schmedeman to WW (re: Nobel Prize) (T), Dec. 4, 1920, 66: 477–8.

PARTING SHOTS: N. H. Davis to WW, Dec. 8, 1920, 66: 492–3; RSB (D), Jan. 22, 1921, 67: 82; Charles Swem (D), Sep. 9, 1920, Jan. 15, 30, and Feb. 17, 1921, 66: 103, 67: 67–8, 103–4, and 143; Starling, 157; WW to R. B. Fosdick, Oct. 22 and Nov. 28, 1923, 68: 451n2 and 493–4; R. B. Fosdick to RSB, June 23, 1916 [RSB Papers, Box 108: PUL]; WW to J. G. Hibben, Dec. 22, 1919, 64: 213; WW to W. R. Wilder, May 3, 1920, 65: 246; A. M. Palmer to WW (re: Debs pardon), June, 29, 1921, 67: 98–102.

POST–WHITE HOUSE PLANS: EBW, 307–12, 314–8, 326–7; WW to C. Z. Klauder, Dec. 16, 1920, 66: 518–9n; CD to CTG, Feb. 14, 1921, 67: 136–7n; G. Creel to EBW, Feb. 15, 1921, 67: 141–2; Houston, II: 147–9; WW to C. E. Bacon, Oct. 18, 1920, 66: 242; WW to Curtis Brown, Sep. 17, 1920, 66: 121; J. R. Bolling to Macmillan Co., Apr. 15, 1921, 67: 259n.

INAUGURATION DAY 1921: CTG, 121; Longworth, 325; EBW, 317–9; "W's Exit Is Tragic," *NYT*, Mar. 5, 1921, 67: 205–14.

17 RESURRECTION

MOVING INTO 2340 S STREET: "W's Exit Is Tragic," *NYT*, Mar. 5, 1921, 5; "WW House—Reduced Copies of Measured Drawings,"lcweb2.loc.gov/pnp/habshaer/dc/dc0100/dc0104/data/dc0104data.pdf, accessed Feb. 19, 2013; Starling, 163–4; EBW, 320–2; WW to CTG, Mar. 2, 1921, 67: 185; "Harding Kept Grayson Within Wilson's Call," *NYT*, Aug. 3, 1923, 68: 398–9; "W Kills 4 Bills in Last Day in Office," *NYT*, Mar. 5, 1921, 8; W. B. Wilson to WW, Mar. 1, 1921, 67: 178–80; WW, veto message, Mar. 3, 1921; 67: 191–4; J. Smuts, "WW's Place in History," syndicated article, Mar. 3–4, 1921, 67: 27n; F. I. Cobb to WW, with "WW—An Interpretation," Mar. 4, 1921, 67: 216–9; EBW, 322–5; ASL (N) appending RSB (D), Mar. 20, 1921, 67: 236n; J. G. Hibben to WW, Jan. 6, 1920, 64: 246.

WW'S NEW ROUTINE: RSB (D), Mar. 22, May 25, 1921, 67: 237–8, 288–9; H. S. Cummings (M), Apr. 25, 1921, 67: 268–70; EBW, 324–6; L. C. Probert, "W Stricken 2 Years Ago, Now Puts in Healthy Day," *NY Tribune*, Sep. 26, 1921, 67: 395–8; "WW's Pierce-Arrow," K. L. Brown (ed.) (Staunton, VA: WW Birthplace Foundation, 1990); "W Attends the Theatre," *NYT*, Apr. 23, 1921, 67: 268; Smith, 218, "W Is Cheered by Theatre Crowd," *NYT*, Aug. 27, 1921, 67: 380–2; WW to E. G. Reid, Oct. 16, 1921, 67: 423; WW to B. Colby, Oct. 24, 1921, 67: 430.

WILSON & COLBY: SA to J. G. Hibben, June 11, 1921, 67: 310; EBW, 327–9; B. Colby to WW, Mar. 29, Apr. 18, 1921, 67: 248, 261; "W Goes to Court to Be Admitted to Bar," *NYT*, June 26, 1921, 67: 328–9; J. R. Bolling to B. Colby, July 4, 1921, 67: 343–4; RSB (D), July 29, 1921, 67: 361; B. Colby to J. R. Bolling, July 1, 1921, 67: 337–8; "W at His Law Office for First Time," *NYT*, Aug. 17, 1921, 1; WW to B. Colby, Feb. 17, May 19, June 10, Aug. 22, and 23 (unsent), 1922, 67: 548, 68: 56–7, 74, 119–20, and 120–1; B. Colby to WW, Dec. 5, 1921, 67: 472–3; J. R. Bolling to B. Colby, Dec. 6, 1921, 67: 475; "W Concentrates on Politics," *Washington Evening Star*, Dec. 13, 1922, 68: 235n.

HARDING ADMINISTRATION: W. B. Wilson to WW, Mar. 1, 1921, 67: 178–80; WW, veto message, Mar. 3, 1921, 67: 191–4; Day, *Rogers*, 117, 121; F. Scott Fitzgerald, "Early Success," *The Crack-Up* (New York: New Directions, 1945), 87.

INCREASED ADMIRATION FOR WW: RSB (D), Mar. 20 and May 27, 1921, 67: 237 and 295; S. W. Beach to WW (T), May 21, 1921, 67: 287; E. A. Alderman to WW, Dec. 29, 1921, 67: 498–9; J. H. Westcott to WW, Dec. 11, 1921, 67: 482; R. C. Stuart, Jr., to WW (T), Apr. 7 and 28, 1921, 67: 253 and 273–4; ASL (N), [re: WW Foundation], appended to R. C. Stuart, Jr., to J. R. Bolling, Apr. 27, 1921, 67: 272–3; WW to FDR, July 4, 1921, Jan. 5, and Apr. 30, 1922, 67: 341–2, 504, and 68: 39; J. R. Bolling to FDR, Sep. 3, 1921, 67: 386 and ASL (n2—re: FDR's polio); WW to E. Roosevelt, Nov. 9, 1921, 67: 448–9.

BURIAL OF UNKNOWN SOLDIER AND REACTION: W. G. Harding to WW, Oct. 4 and Nov. 8, 1921, 67: 400–1 and 445–6; J. R. Bolling to W. Lassiter, Oct. 25, 1921, 67: 432; WW to W. G. Harding, Nov. 8, 1921, 67: 444–5; WW to Louis Seibold, Nov. 12, 1921, 67: 453–4n; "W in Tears As 20,000 Acclaim Him World's Hero," *NY World*, Nov. 12, 1921, 67: 449–53;

"Ovation for W in Line and at Home," *NYT*, Nov. 12, 1921, 1, 2; EBW, 331; JD, *Life*, 17; J. S. Williams to WW, Nov. 12, 1921, 67: 454–5; WW to Ida Tarbell, Feb. 26, 1922, 67: 557–8n, includes excerpt of Tarbell, "The Man They Cannot Forget," *Collier's, LXIX* (Feb. 18, 1922), 14; CTG (M), c. Dec. 28, 1922, 68: 251; R. V. Oulahan, "W, Stronger Physically, Turning Again to Politics," *NYT*, June 10, 1923, 68: 382.

JPT, MARGINALIZED: JPT, xii; "Tumulty and W," *NYT*, Mar. 16, 1922, 4; RSB, *American Chronicle*, 495–8, 503, 515; JPT to WW, Apr. 5, 12, and 13, 1922; 67: 602, 68: 14–5, and 20–23; WW to JPT, Apr. 6 and 10, 1922, 67: 602 and 68: 10; B. Colby to WW, Apr. 6, 1922, 67: 602–3; J. R. Bolling to B. Colby, Apr. 7, 1922, 67: 604; EBW, 333–40; J. R. Bolling to Louis Wiley, Apr. 10, 1922, 68: 11; "Doubt Is Cast on W 'Message' to the Cox Dinner," *NYT*, Apr. 11, 1922, 68: 11–12; WW to editor of *NYT*, Apr. 12, 1922, 68: 14; Blum, 264; "Tumulty Regrets the Misunderstanding," *NYT*, Apr. 14, 1922, 3; CTG (M), May 22, 1922, 68: 60; SA (N) [PUL: 440], 316, 443; WW to James Kerney, Oct. 30, 1923, 68: 592.

"THE DOCUMENT": WW to L. D. Brandeis, June 20, 1921, and Apr. 9, 1922 (with enclosed "Confidential Document"), 67: 319–20n and 68: 4–5 (68: 5–9); WW to N. D. Baker, June 20, 1924, 68: 534–5; WW, addition to the Document, Aug. 7, 1922, 68: 105–6.

MORE TRIBUTES: "1,000 Women Cheer at Wilson's Home," *NYT*, Apr. 29, 1922, 68: 36–9; Cordell Hull to WW, May 27, 1922, 68: 70–1; WW to Calvin Coolidge, June 14, 1922, 68: 76n [quotes Coolidge (R) at American University, June 8, 1922]; WW to Cordell Hull, June 27, 1922, 68: 86; H. S. Cummings (M), June 28, 1922, 68: 90; L. Lipsky to WW (T), July 24, 1922, 68: 100n2; J. H. Clarke to WW, Sep. 9, 1922, 68: 131–2; E. J. N. Blair to WW, Oct. 17, 1922, 68: 156; WW to JWS, Nov. 9, 1922, 68: 180; ASL (N), 68: 180n1, appended to D. C. Roper to WW (T), Nov. 8, 1922, 68: 179; "Gloom at Capital," *NYT*, Nov. 8, 1922, 1, 5; WW to D. C. Roper, Nov. 8, 1922, 68: 180; "W Sees Nation Moving Forward," *NYT*, Nov. 12, 1922, 68: 185–8; FDR to WW (T), Dec. 27, (10 p.m. and 11:13 p.m.), and 28, 1922 (T), 12:54 a.m., 68: 245–6; RSB (D), Apr. 4, 1922, 67: 585; Family of F. M. Thompson to JD (copy of T), Jan. 14, 1922, 68: 266; EBW, 341–2; "Senate Felicitates W on Birthday," *NYT*, Dec. 29, 1922, 68: 247–8.

WW'S LITERARY EFFORTS: CTG, 131, WW to editor of *Washington Post*, c. Apr. 15, 1922,

68: 24; RSB (D), Apr. 4, 1922, 67: 585; WW, "Plans and Notes for Books," c. May 1, 1922, 68: 138–42; WW to J. F. Jameson, May 11, 1922, 68: 52; EBW, 347–8; WW, "The Road Away from Revolution" (draft), c. Apr. 8, 1923, 68: 322–4, final version, c. July 27, 1923, *Atlantic Monthly*, CXXXII (Aug. 1923), 145–6, 68: 393–5; WW to G. Creel, Apr. 9, 1923, 68: 325–6; G. Creel to EBW, Apr. 19 and 24, May 1, 1923, 68: 342–4 and 347–9n, 353–4; EBW to G. Creel, Apr. 20, 1923, 68: 344–5; WW to Ellery Sedgwick, May 2, 1923, 68: 354; CTG (M), May 22, 1922, 68: 58–9n.

DEATH OF HARDING: CTG, 136; WW to CD, Aug. 15, 1922, 68: 113; WW to Florence Harding (T), Aug. 3, 1923, 68: 398; Calvin Coolidge to WW, Aug. 4, 1923, 68: 399; "Ordeal for W to Attend Funeral," *NYT*, Aug. 9, 1923, 68: 402–3; "Washington Crowd Gives W Ovation," *NYT*, Aug. 12, 1923, 68: 404; White House Staff to Calvin Coolidge (M), Feb. 2, 1924, 68: 553.

EBW HOLIDAY; WW'S DIMINUTION: R. V. Oulahan, *op. cit.*, June 10, 1923, 68: 375–83; EBW, 351–2; WW to EBW, Aug. 29, 1923, 68: 412; EBW to WW, Aug. 31, 1923, 68: 415; CTG, 138–9; WW (N) for third inaugural address, c. Jan. 21, 1924, 68: 542; WW to R. B. Fosdick, Oct. 22 and Nov. 28, 1923, 68: 451n2 and 493–4; R. B. Fosdick to WW, Nov. 27, 1923, 68: 492–3; RSB (D), Jan. 22, 1921, 67: 82; R. B. Fosdick to RSB, June 23, 1926 [PUL: RSB Papers, box 108].

WW'S LIFE QUIETS: WW to Moore-Cottrell Subscription Agencies, Oct. 13, 1923, 68: 449–50; EBW, 346–7; "Tiger and W Recall Old Times in Cordial Reunion," *NYT*, Dec. 7, 1922, 68: 226–8; Williams, 234; "Col. House Calls, W Not at Home," *NYT*, Oct. 14, 1921, 67: 419; C. H. McCormick, Jr., to EBW, Jan. 13, 1924, 68: 528–9; EBW to C. H. McCormick, Jr., Jan. 13, 1924, 68: 529–30; SA (N) [PUL: 440], 316; JWS to WW, Apr. 18, 1923, 68: 338; WW to JWS, Apr. 28, 1923, 68: 351–2, Francis B. Sayre, Jr., to ASB (I), Sep. 30, 2001.

ARMISTICE DAY ADDRESS, 1923: EBW, 352–5; WW, radio address, Nov. 10, 1923, 68: 466–7; Clapper, 312–3; "W Overcome Greeting Pilgrims, Predicts Triumph," *NYT*, Nov. 12, 1923, 467–71.

HOLIDAYS AND BIRTHDAY, 1923; HONORS: Smith, 232–3; Reid, 236; EBW, 357; CD and J. H. Jones to WW, Oct. 1, 1923, 68: 441; CD to WW, Oct. 2, 1923, 68: 441–2; CD to EBW, Oct. 2, 1923 (two letters), 68: 442–3 and 444; WW to CD, Oct. 4 and Dec. 30, 1923, 68: 445 and 513; WW to CD, et al., Jan. 20, 1924, 68: 534; "W Is Honored on 67th Birthday: Friends Give Auto," *NYT*, Dec. 29, 1923, 68: 509–10; J. S. Bassett to WW, Dec. 30, 1923, 68: 514; WW to J. S. Bassett, Jan. 2, 1924, 68: 516; Smith, 234–5; "W Receives Party Committee," *NYT*, Jan. 17, 1924, 68: 531–2; WW (N) for third inaugural, c. Jan. 21, 1924, 68: 543; J. R. Bolling to J. W. Gerard, Jan. 31, 1924, 68: 551.

CTG LEAVES FOR HOLIDAY; WW FATALLY ILL: EBW, 358–60; J. R. Bolling (M), n. d., 68: 548–50; CTG, 110, 139; "Ex-President WW Dying," *NYT*, Feb. 2, 1924; 68: 553–60; CTG, Jr., to ASB (I), Oct. 14, 2006; Calvin Coolidge to EBW, Feb. 1, 1924, 68: 552; White House Staff to Calvin Coolidge, Feb. 2, 1924, 68: 553; Smith, 240; "WW's Life Slowly Ebbs As Night Passes," *NYT*, Feb. 3, 1924, 68: 561–6; "Throng in Prayer at W Home," Feb. 4, 1924, 68: 570–3; "WW Passes Away in Sleep," *NYT*, Feb. 4, 1924, 68: 566–70.

OBSEQUIES: Sayre, 95; Calvin Coolidge, proclamation, Feb. 3, 1924, appears in Alderman, iii; Calvin Coolidge to CTG, Feb. 4, 1924, 68: 573; Margaret Wilson to JWS, Feb. 8, 1924 [WWPL]; EBW to Calvin Coolidge, Feb. 4, 1924, 68: 574; EBW to HCL, Feb. 4, 1924, 68: 574 and 574n; HCL to EBW, n.d., quoted in Smith, 250; Robert Cullinane to ASB (I), Dec. 6, 2007; Smith, 250–1, 253–7; JD, *Life*, 363–9; "Simplicity Marks Service in the Home," Feb. 6, 1924, 68: 575–9; "W Buried in Cathedral Crypt with Simple Rites As Nation Mourns," *NYT*, Feb. 7, 1924, 68: 579–84.

POSTSCRIPT: "Artisans at Work on W's Tomb," *NYT*, June 4, 1956, 31; "Diagram of Seating on President's Platform," Jan. 20, 1961 [JFK Library]; Photograph AR6280–1M [JFK Library]; Dean F. B. Sayre, Jr., Washington National Cathedral, "Cathedral Staff," http://www.nationalcathedral.org/staff/francisSayre.shtml, accessed May 30, 2010; FDR, CD, and Hamilton Holt to WW (T), Apr. 6, 1922, 67: 603.

INDEX